SAMBUCUS – EPISTULAE

EUROPA HUMANISTICA

Collection fondée par l'Institut de recherche et d'histoire des textes,
Paris et dirigée par le Centre d'études supérieures de la Renaissance, Tours
24

Johannes Sambucus (1531–1584)
(*Emblemata,* Antwerp, Plantin, 1566, f. A1ᵛ)

JOHANNES SAMBUCUS

Epistulae

Edited by Gábor Almási and Lav Šubarić

BREPOLS

© 2024, Brepols Publishers n.v., Turnhout, Belgium.

All rights reserved. No part of this publication may be reproduced, stored in a retrieval system, or transmitted, in any form or by any means, electronic, mechanical, photocopying, recording, or otherwise without the prior permission of the publisher.

D/2024/0095/85
ISBN 978-2-503-61098-6
ISSN 2565-8859

Printed in the EU on acid-free paper.

CONTENTS

Preface		15
Acknowledgements		25
Letters		27
1549		
1.	Veit Amerbach to Sambucus, 17 February	27
2.	[Sambucus to Philipp and Theodor Apianus, 25 March]*1*	30
1550		
3.	[Sambucus to Timotheus Apianus, 13 August]	30
1551		
4.	[Sambucus to Wolfgang and Georg Kremer]	31
1552		
5.	[Sambucus to the sons of Ferenc Révay]	31
6.	Sambucus to Archduke Maximilian, Elected King of Bohemia, 1 February	31
1553		
7.	Sambucus to Georg von Pappenheim, 1 January	35
8.	Sambucus to Archduke Maximilian, Elected King of Bohemia, [spring]	37
9.	Sambucus to István Dobó, 13 September	38
1555		
10.	Sambucus to Georgius Bona and Nicolaus Istvánffy, 1 February	38
11.	[Sambucus to Nicolaus Olahus, 1 August]	40
12.	[Caspar Nidbruck] to Sambucus, 7 September	40
1556		
13.	Sambucus to Heinrich Stiebar, 1 April	42
14.	Paolo Manuzio to Sambucus, 30 June	43
15.	[Sambucus to Johann Friedrich and Ferdinand Hoffmann, 30 June]	45
1558		
16.	[Sambucus to Archduke Maximilian, Elected King of Bohemia, 15 March]	45
17.	Sambucus to Archduke Maximilian, Elected King of Bohemia, [May–June]	45
18.	Sambucus to Archduke Maximilian, Elected King of Bohemia, [May–June]	46
19.	[Sambucus to Georgius Draskovich, 24 November]	47
1559		
20.	[Sambucus to Marian Leżeński, 1 January]	47
21.	Sambucus to Miklós Oláhcsászár, 1 October	48
22.	Sambucus to Jakob Fugger, 22 October	48

* Letters indicated with rectangular brackets are included in *Humanistes du bassin des Carpates II. Johannes Sambucus.*

	23.	Giovanni Faseolo to Sambucus, 28 October	50
	24.	Piero Vettori to Sambucus, 3 November	51
	25.	Francesco Robortello to Sambucus, 3 December	52
1560			
	26.	Sambucus to Conrad Gesner, 18 January	53
	27.	Sambucus to Theodor Zwinger, 1 March	55
	28.	Paolo Manuzio to Sambucus, [May]	57
	29.	Paolo Manuzio to Sambucus, [summer]	59
	30.	Sambucus to Hieronymus Wolf, 12 December	60
1561			
	31.	Sambucus to Henri de Mesmes	62
	32.	Sambucus to Henri de Mesmes	63
	33.	Sambucus to Henri de Mesmes	64
	34.	Sambucus to Henri de Mesmes	65
	35.	Sambucus to Daniel Rechnitz, 11 August	66
1562			
	36.	Sambucus to Conrad Gesner, 13 February	67
	37.	Sambucus to Paolo Manuzio, 19 June	68
	38.	Sambucus to Aldo Manuzio Jr., 30 December	70
1563			
	39.	Sambucus to Archduke Maximilian, King of Bohemia, 18 January	71
	40.	Sambucus to Emperor Ferdinand I, [first half of September]	72
	41.	Sambucus to Abraham Ortelius, 22 September	75
	42.	Sambucus to Emperor Ferdinand I, 28 September	77
	43.	Hadrianus Junius to Sambucus, [c. November–December]	78
	44.	Hadrianus Junius to Sambucus, [December]	82
1564			
	45.	Sambucus to Jean Grolier, 3 January	83
	46.	Hadrianus Junius to Sambucus, [January]	84
	47.	Sambucus to Abraham Ortelius, 19 January	85
	48.	Hadrianus Junius to Sambucus, 20 January	87
	49.	Sambucus to Hadrianus Junius, 10 February	87
	50.	Hadrianus Junius to Sambucus, [February]	88
	51.	Hadrianus Junius to Sambucus, 1 March	89
	52.	Sambucus to Fulvio Orsini, 13 April	91
	53.	Sambucus to Jean Matal, 6 May	92
	54.	Hadrianus Junius to Sambucus, 24 May	94
	55.	Georg Cassander to Sambucus, [July]	95
	56.	Hadrianus Junius to Sambucus, 23 August	96
	57.	Sambucus to Karl II, Archduke of Austria, 1 September	99
	58.	Sambucus to the Mayor and the Council of Trnava, 10 September	100
	59.	Hadrianus Junius to Sambucus, [November–December]	101
	60.	[Sambucus to Johannes Listhius, 11 November]	103
	61.	Sambucus to Jean Matal, 11 November	103

1565

62.	[Hubertus Giphanius to Sambucus]	105
63.	Hadrianus Junius to Sambucus, [January–February]	105
64.	Hadrianus Junius to Sambucus, 10 March	106
65.	Guglielmo Sirleto to Sambucus, [c. April]	107
66.	Sambucus to the Imperial Chamber, 26 April	108
67.	[Sambucus to Philipp von Winneberg, 13 July]	110
68.	[Sambucus to Karl II, Archduke of Austria, 11 August]	110
69.	[Sambucus to Christophe Plantin, 23 August]	110
70.	Hadrianus Junius to Sambucus, 2 September	111
71.	Hadrianus Junius to Sambucus, [autumn?]	112
72.	Georg Cassander to Sambucus, [c. 28 October]	113
73.	Sambucus to Emperor Maximilian II, 22 November	116

1566

74.	Christophe Plantin to Sambucus, 12 January	117
75.	Sambucus to Paolo Manuzio, 1 February	120
76.	Sambucus to Guglielmo Sirleto, 20 February	121
77.	Sambucus to Johannes Crato, 23 March	123
78.	Sambucus to Johann Andrea of Schwanbach, 31 March	124
79.	Sambucus to Johannes Crato, 1 April	130
80.	Sambucus to the Mayor and the Council of Trnava, 15 April	131
81.	Sambucus to Imre Kalmár, Mayor of Trnava, 12 November	132
82.	Sambucus to Johannes Crato, [1566?]	134

1567

83.	Sambucus to the Mayor and the Council of Trnava, 1 January	135
84.	Sambucus to Pompilio Amaseo, 13 January	136
85.	Joachim Camerarius Sr. to Sambucus, 21 January	138
86.	[Sambucus to Ferenc Forgách, 1 February]	139
87.	[Sambucus to Koloman Egerer Jr.], 13 February	140
88.	Sambucus to Theodor Zwinger, 23 March	140
89.	Sambucus to Joachim Camerarius Jr., 25 March	141
90.	Sambucus to Johannes Sturm, 1 April	142
91.	Joachim Camerarius Sr. to Sambucus, 24 April	143
92.	Sambucus to Joachim Camerarius Sr., 1 June	144
93.	[Sambucus to Emperor Maximilian II., 24 June]	145
94.	Sambucus to István Nyilas, 27 June	145
95.	Sambucus to the Mayor and the Council of Trnava, 3 July	146
96.	Sambucus to Johann Sommer, Mayor of Trnava, 4 July	147
97.	Sambucus to the Mayor and the Council of Trnava, 10 July	148
98.	Sambucus to Johann Sommer, Mayor of Trnava, 10 July	149
99.	Sambucus to Emperor Maximilian II, 27 July	150
100.	[Laurentius Sifanus to Sambucus, 13 August]	151
101.	Sambucus to Emperor Maximilian II, 1 September	151
102.	Sambucus to the Hungarian Chamber, 11 September	152

103. Sambucus to the Mayor and the Council of Trnava, 2 November   153
104. Sambucus to the Mayor and the Council of Trnava, 2 December   154

1568
105. Hadrianus Junius to Sambucus, [beginning of 1568?]   155
106. Sambucus to Johannes Oporinus, 8 February   156
107. Sambucus to Emperor Maximilian II, 21 February   158
108. Johannes Oporinus to Sambucus, 31 March   159
109. Sambucus to the Mayor and the Council of Trnava, 3 April   161
110. [Sambucus to Archdukes Matthias, Maximilian, Albrecht and Wenzeslaus, 5 April]   161
111. Joachim Camerarius Sr. to Sambucus, 5 April   162
112. Antonius Verantius to Sambucus, 12 May   162
113. Johannes Oporinus to Sambucus, 20 May   163
114. Sambucus to Conradus Hubertus, 12 June   165
115. Sambucus to Theodor Zwinger, 8 July   166
116. Piero Vettori to Sambucus, 14 August   167
117. Sambucus to Johannes Crato, 25 August   168
118. Sambucus to Piero Vettori, 1 September   169
119. Sambucus to Theodor Zwinger, 23 September   172
120. Joachim Camerarius Sr. to Sambucus, [late September]   173
121. Sambucus to Joachim Camerarius Sr., [late September]   175
122. Sambucus to Piero Vettori, 11 November   176
123. Sambucus to Piero Vettori, 26 November   176

1569
124. Joachim Camerarius Sr. to Sambucus, 4 January   177
125. Sambucus to Eusebius Episcopius, 20 January   178
126. Gerartus Falkenburgius to Sambucus, 22 February   179
127. [Sambucus to Joachim Camerarius Sr., 6 March]   180
128. [Sambucus to Johannes Listhius, 15 March]   181
129. Sambucus to Piero Vettori, 6 April   181
130. The Council of Trnava to Sambucus, 14 April   184
131. Sambucus to István Nyilas, Mayor of Trnava, 14 May   184
132. Sambucus to Michael Otrer, 15 May   185
133. Sambucus to István Nyilas, Mayor of Trnava, 16 May   188
134. Sambucus to Theodor Zwinger, 31 May   189
135. Sambucus to the Mayor and citizens of Trnava, 30 August   190
136. Simone Galignani to Sambucus, 1 September   191
137. Sambucus to István Nyilas, Mayor of Trnava, 6 September   193
138. Sambucus to István Nyilas, Mayor of Trnava, 15 September   194
139. Sambucus to Michael Otrer, 1 October   195
140. Sambucus to Piero Vettori, 13 November   196
141. Sambucus to István Nyilas, Mayor of Trnava, 26 December   197

1570
142. Joachim Camerarius Sr. to Sambucus, 22 January   198
143. Sambucus to the Council of Trnava, 27 February   200
144. Sambucus to Piero Vettori, 30 April   200

145. Benito Arias Montano to Sambucus, [early May]	202
146. Benito Arias Montano to Sambucus, 6 May	204
147. Sambucus to Joachim Camerarius Sr., 7 May	205
148. Sambucus to Johannes Crato, 9 May	210
149. Sambucus to Theodor Zwinger, 17 May	211
150. Piero Vettori to Sambucus, 20 May	213
151. Johannes Crato to Sambucus, 26 May	213
152. Sambucus to Benito Arias Montano, 1 June	217
153. Sambucus to Piero Vettori, 31 August	218
154. Sambucus to Johannes Crato, 1 September	219
155. Sambucus to Piero Vettori, 12 September	220
156. Sambucus to Johannes Crato, 31 October	222
157. Carolus Utenhovius to Sambucus, 1 November	223
158. Sambucus to Johannes Crato, 20 November	225
159. Sambucus to Theodor Zwinger, 20 November	227
160. Sambucus to Johannes Crato, [1570?]	228

1571

161. [Claude Aubery to Sambucus]	229
162. Sambucus to Hugo Blotius, 27 April	229
163. Sambucus to Theodor Zwinger, 7 June	231
164. Sambucus to Emperor Maximilian II, 1 July	233
165. Sambucus to Emperor Maximilian II, 5 August	235
166. Sambucus to Karl II, Archduke of Austria, 1 September	235
167. Antonius Verantius to Sambucus, 19 October	236
168. Marco Mantova Benavides, to Sambucus, [late October–early November]	236
169. Sambucus to Don John of Austria, 1 November	238
170. Sambucus to Hugo Blotius, 1 November	238
171. Sambucus to Paolo Manuzio, 1 December	239
172. Sambucus to Piero Vettori, 1 December	241
173. Conrad Dasypodius to Sambucus, 2 December	242
174. Sambucus to Theodor Zwinger, 8 December	244
175. Sambucus to Johannes Crato, 10 December	245
176. Antonius Verantius to Sambucus, 13 December	246
177. Sambucus to Hugo Blotius, 21 December	248
178. Sambucus to Johannes Crato, [1571–1572]	249

1572

179. [Sambucus to Augerius Busbequius]	250
180. Justus Lipsius to Sambucus	250
181. [Sambucus to Antonius Verantius, 5 February]	252
182. [Johannes Löwenklau to Sambucus, 8 March]	252
183. Sambucus to Hugo Blotius, 16 April	252
184. Sambucus to Hugo Blotius, 25 June	254
185. Sambucus to Marcus Antonius Muretus, 15 July	255
186. Sambucus to Piero Vettori, 15 July	255
187. Sambucus to King Rudolf, 1 October	256

188. Sambucus to Hugo Blotius, 8 October	259
189. Sambucus to Abraham Ortelius, 25 October	260
190. Sambucus to Piero Vettori, 8 November	261
191. Sambucus to Johann Sommer, 13 December	263

1573

192. Sambucus to Piero Vettori, 1 January	264
193. Sambucus to Samuel Grynaeus, 5 January	265
194. Sambucus to Johann Baptist Weber, 8 January	266
195. Sambucus to Emperor Maximilian II, [8 January]	267
196. Sambucus to Emperor Maximilian II, [January]	269
197. Sambucus to Hugo Blotius, 12 January	269
198. Sambucus to Theodor Zwinger, 6 February	271
199. Sambucus to Guglielmo Sirleto, 9 February	272
200. Sambucus to Theodor Zwinger, 10 February	273
201. Antonius Verantius to Sambucus, 25 February	275
202. Sambucus to Hugo Blotius, 6 March	276
203. Sambucus to Nicasius Ellebodius, 26 March	277
204. Antonius Verantius to Sambucus, 20 April	279
205. Sambucus to Theodor Zwinger, 1 July	281
206. Sambucus to Johann Sommer, Mayor of Trnava, 2 July	282
207. Sambucus to the Mayor and councillors of Trnava, 22 July	283
208. Abraham Ortelius to Sambucus, 1 August	284
209. Sambucus to the Mayor and the Council of Trnava, 21 August	285
210. Sambucus to Abraham Ortelius, 2 September	286
211. Sambucus to Johann Sommer, 6 September	287
212. Sambucus to Johann Sommer, 8 September	288
213. Sambucus to Piero Vettori, 26 October	288
214. Sambucus to Hubertus Goltzius, 13 November	289
215. Sambucus to Johannes Crato, 20 November	291
216. Sambucus to Stephanus Pighius, [December]	292
217. Sambucus to Johannes Crato, 3 December	293
218. Sambucus to Johann Sommer Mayor of Trnava and István Nyilas, 18 December	294
219. Sambucus to Nicolaus Reusner, 1 March, [1573–1574?]	295

1574

220. Sambucus to Johann Heinrich Herwart, 1 January	295
221. Sambucus to Joachim Camerarius Sr., 1 February	296
222. Sambucus to Theodor Zwinger, 7 February	298
223. Joachim Camerarius Sr. to Sambucus, 19 February	300
224. Sambucus to Aldo Manuzio, 5 March	301
225. Sambucus to Johann Sommer, Mayor of Trnava, 19 March	302
226. Sambucus to Theodor Zwinger, 20 March	303
227. Sambucus to Johannes Crato, 19 April	304
228. Sambucus to Aldo Manuzio, 1 May	305
229. Justus Lipsius to Sambucus, July	306
230. Sambucus to Stephanus Pighius, 30 August	307

231. Stephanus Pighius to Sambucus, September	308
232. Sambucus to Stephanus Pighius, 16 October	308
233. Sambucus to Theodor Zwinger, 18 November	309
234. Sambucus to Johannes Crato, 20 November	311
235. Sambucus to Piero Vettori, 17 December	312

1575

236. Sambucus to Johannes Crato, 23 January	313
237. Sambucus to Nicolaus Reusner, 13 February	314
238. Sambucus to Johannes Crato, [January–February]	315
239. Sambucus to Johannes Crato, [February]	316
240. Sambucus to Johannes Crato, [late February]	317
241. Sambucus to Joachim Camerarius Jr., 4 April	318
242. Sambucus to Johannes Crato, 4 March	319
243. Sambucus to Johannes Crato, 9 March	320
244. Sambucus to Johannes Crato, [spring]	322
245. Sambucus to Johannes Crato, 6 April	323
246. Sambucus to Hugo Blotius, 23 April	324
247. Sambucus to Joachim Camerarius Jr., 26 April	326
248. [Gulielmus Canterus to Sambucus [May]]	327
249. Sambucus to Joachim Camerarius Jr. 17 June	327
250. Sambucus to Hugo Blotius, 30 August	328
251. Sambucus to Hugo Blotius, 10 September	329
252. Sambucus to Johannes Crato, 12 September	330
253. Sambucus to Fulvio Orsini, 16 September	332
254. Sambucus to Hugo Blotius, 3 November	333
255. Sambucus to Joachim Camerarius Jr., 9 November	334
256. Sambucus to Johannes Crato, 30 November	335
257. Sambucus to Fulvio Orsini, 8 December	335
258. Sambucus to Johannes Crato, [1575?]	337

1576

259. [Johannes Löwenklau to Sambucus, [January–February]]	337
260. Sambucus to Johannes Crato, 3 January	338
261. Sambucus to Theodor Zwinger, 1 March	339
262. Sambucus to Theodor Zwinger, 12 March	340
263. Sambucus to Aldo Manuzio, 21 March	342
264. Sambucus to István Radéczy, 7 April	343
265. Sambucus to István Radéczy and the Hungarian Chamber, 8 May	344
266. Sambucus to Theodor Zwinger, 14 May	346
267. Sambucus to Joachim Camerarius Jr., 14 June	347
268. Sambucus to Theodor Zwinger, 9 July	348
269. Sambucus to István Radéczy, 13 August	349
270. Sambucus to Johannes Crato, 15 September	350
271. Sambucus to Theodor Zwinger, 13 October	351
272. Johannes Crato to Sambucus, 20 October	353
273. Sambucus to Hilfreich Guett, 20 October	359

274. Sambucus to King Rudolf, 21 October	360
275. Sambucus to Johannes Crato, 17 November	361
276. Sambucus to Johannes Crato, 10 December	363
277. Sambucus to Johannes Crato, 31 December	365

1577

278. Henri Estienne to Sambucus	366
279. Sambucus to Johannes Crato, 16 January	368
280. Sambucus to Johannes Crato, 1 February	369
281. Sambucus to Johannes Crato, 8 March	370
282. Sambucus to Johannes Crato, 13 April	371
283. Sambucus to Theodor Zwinger, 14 April	373
284. Sambucus to Johannes Crato, 22 April	373
285. Sambucus to Johannes Crato, 19 May	374
286. Sambucus to Johannes Crato, 25 May	376
287. Joachim Camerarius Jr. to Sambucus, 1 June	377
288. Sambucus to Johannes Crato, 13 June	378
289. Sambucus to Joachim Camerarius Jr., 7 July	379
290. Sambucus to Johannes Crato, 18 July	381
291. Sambucus to Guglielmo Sirleto, 29 July	382
292. Sambucus to Piero Vettori, 22 August	383
293. Sambucus to Piero Vettori, 13 September	384
294. Sambucus to Joachim Camerarius Jr., 17 September	386
295. Sambucus to Theodor Zwinger, 12 November	387
296. Sambucus to Piero Vettori, 20 November	388
297. Sambucus to Johannes Crato, 4 December	389

1578

298. Sambucus to Theodor Zwinger, 8 January	390
299. Sambucus to Joachim Camerarius Jr., 31 January	391
300. Conrad Dasypodius to Sambucus, 1 February	392
301. Sambucus to Joachim Camerarius Jr., 7 March	394
302. Jean-Antoine Sarasin to Sambucus, [spring–early summer]	395
303. Sambucus to Piero Vettori, 22 April	397
304. Sambucus to Piero Vettori, 19 May	397
305. Sambucus to Johannes Crato, 20 May	398
306. Sambucus to Piero Vettori, 23 May	400
307. Sambucus to Joachim Camerarius Jr. 12 June	401
308. Sambucus to Adam von Dietrichstein, 28 July	402
309. Sambucus to Johannes Crato, 29 July	403
310. Sambucus to Emperor Rudolf II, 2 August	404
311. Sambucus to Fulvio Orsini, 6 August	405
312. Sambucus to Henri Estienne, 15 August	407
313. Sambucus to Nicolaus Reusner, 23 August	408
314. Sambucus to the Imperial Chamber, 30 August	409
315. Sambucus to Johannes Crato, 31 August	411
316. Sambucus to Hartmann II von Liechtenstein, 17 September	412

317.	Sambucus to Theodor Zwinger, 18 October	412
318.	Sambucus to Archduke Ernst, 16 November	413
319.	Sambucus to Johannes Crato, 19 December	414
320.	Sambucus to Joachim Camerarius Jr., 22 December	415

1579

321.	Piero Vettori to Sambucus, 28 January	416
322.	Sambucus to Joachim Camerarius Jr., 31 January	417
323.	Sambucus to Johannes Crato, 31 January	418
324.	Sambucus to Johannes Crato, 25 April	419
325.	Sambucus to Theodor Zwinger, 14 May	420
326.	Sambucus to Theodor Zwinger, 16 August	421
327.	Sambucus to Theodor Zwinger, 1 September	422
328.	Sambucus to Hilfreich Guett, [shortly before 29 September]	423
329.	Jan Meller Palmier to Sambucus [second half of 1579]	424

1580

330.	Sambucus to Joachim Camerarius Jr., 7 September	425
331.	Sambucus to Joachim Camerarius Jr. [December]	426

1581

332.	Sambucus to Ruprecht von Stotzingen, 1 January	427
333.	Sambucus to Joachim Camerarius Jr., 8 January	429
334.	Sambucus to the Hungarian Chamber, 8 February	430
335.	Sambucus to Hilfreich Guett, 9 February	431
336.	Sambucus to Joachim Camerarius Jr., 10 February	431
337.	Sambucus to Nicolaus Reusner, 26 March	433
338.	Christophe Plantin to Sambucus, 22 April	434
339.	Sambucus to Henri Estienne, 29 April	434
340.	Bonaventura Vulcanius to Sambucus, 15 June	436
341.	Andreas Dudith to Sambucus, 22 June	437
342.	Sambucus to Joachim Camerarius Jr., 1 July	439
343.	Sambucus to the Mayor and the Council of Trnava, 18 July	440
344.	Martin Crusius to Sambucus, 4 August	440
345.	Sambucus to Christophe Plantin, 26 August	442
346.	Piero Vettori to Sambucus, 1 September	443
347.	Sambucus to Piero Vettori, 21 October	444

1582

348.	Sambucus to the Hungarian Chamber, 24 January	445
349.	Justus Lipsius to Sambucus, 15 March	445
350.	Sambucus to Theodor Zwinger, 31 March	446
351.	Sambucus to Justus Lipsius, 1 May	447
352.	Sambucus to Fulvio Orsini, 1 August	449
353.	Reinerus Reineccius to Sambucus, 31 August	451
354.	Sambucus to Boldizsár Batthyány, 10 September	452
355.	Sambucus to Boldizsár Batthyány, 25 September	455
356.	Sambucus to Reinerus Reineccius, 26 October	456
357.	Sambucus to Jacobus Monavius, 31 October	457

358. Sambucus to Eusebius Episcopius, 1 November	458
359. Sambucus to Theodor Zwinger, 9 November	459
360. Sambucus to Piero Vettori, 22 November	460
361. Sambucus to Joachim Camerarius Jr., 25 December	461

1583

362. Sambucus to Henricus Porsius	463
363. Sambucus to Johannes Crato, 4 February	454
364. Sambucus to Emperor Rudolf II, 20 February	465
365. Sambucus to Joachim Camerarius Jr., 3 March	466
366. Theodor Zwinger to Sambucus, 12 March	467
367. Franciscus Modius to Sambucus, [March 1583]	468
368. Christophe Plantin to Sambucus, 18 May	469
369. Sambucus to Giovanni Michiel / Baccio Valori, 1 July	471
370. Carlo Sigonio to Sambucus, 28 September	473
371. Sambucus to Michael Neander, 1 November	474
372. Sambucus to Theodor Zwinger, 7 November	475
373. Sambucus to Fulvio Orsini, 15 November	476

1584

374. Sambucus to Joachim Camerarius Jr., 8 April, [1584?]	478
375. Sambucus to Nicodemus Frischlin, 18 April	479
376. Sambucus to Theodor Zwinger, [21 June?]	480
377. Franciscus Modius to Sambucus, [1581–1584]	482

Abbreviations	484
Bibliography	485
Index	493

PREFACE

Johannes Sambucus (1531–1584) was a significant and characteristic figure of late Renaissance humanism and the Habsburg court. As the epitaphs written by his friends and colleagues underlined, he was a philologist, book collector, imperial historian, councillor and doctor. While his collection of books and manuscripts and his related publishing activity have always been acknowledged as Sambucus's greatest merits, more recently, his emblems collected in the *Emblemata* of 1564 and 1566 made him a particularly appealing figure for historical research.[1] Less attention has been given to the rest of the c. 90 publications that were the result of Sambucus's activity as a humanist and antiquarian. Among them, the most precious group were the more than twenty Greek and Latin publications "*ex bibliotheca Sambuci*," based on his own codices and edited by Europe's best philologists, many of which were first editions.[2]

Sambucus's manuscript collection comprised more than 750 codices; in 1578 he sold 530 of them to Rudolf II. It was one of the greatest private collections in Northern Europe, especially with regard to the number of precious Greek autographs. Sambucus's printed books numbered 3,501 after his death, to which one can add 103 music sheets.[3] Considering that Sambucus came from a middle class family (his father was a patrician in the city of Trnava by its Slovak name, Nagyszombat by its Hungarian name and Tyrnau by its German name), the creation of this collection was a remarkable accomplishment on its own. Even more remarkable were the 22 years of his academic touring all over Europe, the fame he won as an man of erudition and the contacts he established with the greatest names in the Republic of Letters.

---

[1] On Sambucus, see most recently Gábor Almási's bio-bibliographical article in *Companion to Central and Eastern European Humanism* and the excellent studies in *Iohannes Sambucus / János Zsámboki* (edited by Christian Gastgeber and Elisabeth Klecker). For monographs, see Gerstinger, "Johannes Sambucus als Handschriftensammler"; Anton Vantuch, *Ján Sambucus. Život a dielo renesančneho učenca* [Life and work of a Renaissance savant] (Bratislava: Slovenská Akadémia, 1975); Visser, *Joannes Sambucus*; Almási, *The Uses of Humanism*; and the recent text edition *Humanistes du bassin des Carpates II. Johannes Sambucus*, which also provides a bibliography of Sambucus's editions (pp. 239-244). Useful studies on Sambucus go back as far as to the end of the eighteenth century. See Karl G. Windisch, "Biographie. Lebensbeschreibung des Johann Sambucus," *Allergnädigist-privilegierte Anzeiger* 6 (1776), 174-176, 183-184, 191-192, 205-208; idem, "Beitrag zur Lebensgeschichte des Johannes Sambucus," *Ungarisches Magazin* 4 (1781), 414-423 and 10 (1787), 498-499; Illésy, "Sámboky János történetíróról"; István Bálint-Nagy, "Der weltberühmte Historicus Johannes Sambucus (1531–1584) als Arzt," *Südhoffs Archiv für Geschichte der Medizin* 24 (1931), 150-174; Bach, *Un humaniste hongrois*; Várady, "Relazioni di Giovanni Zsámboky"; Gulyás, *Sámboky János könyvtára*, 7-118; Téglásy, *A nyelv- és irodalomelmélet*; Viskolcz, "The fate of Johannes Sambucus's library"; Gábor Almási and Gábor Farkas Kiss, "In search of Sambucus. His philology, publications and friends', in *Iohannes Sambucus / János Zsámboki*, 35-126 (which is an English version of the French introduction to *Humanistes du bassin des Carpates II. Johannes Sambucus*); Gábor Almási, "The Familiar Style: The Letters of Johannes Sambucus (1531–1584)," *Acta Comeniana* 33 (2019) [2020], 9-26.

[2] See the bibliographic article by Almási (as in note 1).

[3] The most precise study is Viskolcz, "The fate of Johannes Sambucus's library." On the printed volumes see Gulyás, *Sámboky János könyvtára*, 31. Gulyás's book was newly edited by Varga András, Monok István and Ötvös Péter, eds., *A Zsámboky-könyvtár katalógusa* (Szeged: Scriptum, 1992), available at http://real-eod.mtak.hu/1458/ (accessed on 22 May 2023).

The primary objective of Sambucus's correspondence was to enhance his activity as an editor and publisher of Classical and Byzantine works. Most of his correspondents were philologically minded humanists of his kind, and the central themes of the letters were the publications in process. Although Sambucus focused in his correspondence for the most part on matters of scholarship and touched only rarely on contemporary events (politics, wars, epidemics, etc.), his letters add considerably to our knowledge of both humanist learning and philological activity and also contemporary everyday life, the prevailing religious climate, political thought, patronage systems, court careers and intellectual relationships.

A short biography of Sambucus
Johannes Sambucus was born to a wealthy family in Trnava, which was connected through parental relationships to the leading families of the city.[4] In his early letters, he proudly referred to himself "Pannonicus Tirnavienses," that is, the Pannonian of Trnava. His family belonged to the upper class of the free royal cities of Hungary. This elite group experienced considerable mobility between the fifteenth and sixteenth centuries though that movement was essentially urban and rarely meant integration into the country's nobility and land-owning high society. Sambucus's family was among the exceptions. His Hungarian father, Péter Zsámboky Szabó, who served twice as mayor and was the owner of three houses, was ennobled in recognition of his political services in 1549, when Sambucus was 18. His mother's origins are unclear; she may have come from the nationally mixed or Slovak family of Ivan Horváth Petranský. Sambucus had four sisters (Katalin, Anna, Magdolna, and a fourth whose name is not found in the sources). They all married into good families and allegedly died before the death of their father Péter in 1565.[5]

Sambucus's father invested heavily in his only son's education. In 1542, at the age of 11, Sambucus enrolled in the University of Vienna, where he studied an array of subjects, including Greek with the geographer Georg Rithaymer. He probably remained in Vienna until 1545, when he enrolled in the University of Wittenberg, though he apparently missed Melanchthon's lectures, in part because the Schmalkaldic War forced students to leave the city in late 1546. Sambucus returned to Vienna only to continue his studies at the University of Ingolstadt in 1548, where he studied with Veit Amerbach and Peter Apian. On 29 August 1549 he left Ingolstadt. He probably visited the University of Tübingen before travelling to Strasburg, where he met Johannes Sturm and other members of his academy and also worked for the local publisher. Here, he published his first book, Lucian's dialogues, in an edition meant for students. This was followed by many other publications, several of which presented Sambucus as a Latin and Greek poet. Passing through Basel and Dole he finally arrived in Paris in late 1550. In 1552, he obtained the degree of master of philosophy. Crossing Dole again, he left France on 6 of March, probably stopping in Basel and Strasbourg and staying in Ingolstadt until January of the following year. In early 1553, in the age of 22, Sambucus finally returned home via Augsburg to seek a new source of financing. Although he managed to catch the attention of Emperor Ferdinand and obtain a minor commission, it was eventually Archbishop Nicolaus Olahus who employed him as a tutor for his nephew Georgius Bona. Sambucus arrived in Padua in October 1553, and Bona (who was already in Italy) was joined

---

[4] This biography is based on Almási's recent bio-bibliographical article (as in note 1) and his monograph *The Uses of Humanism*.
[5] See Vantuch, *Ján Sambucus* (as in note 1), 28-44; Bakonyi, *Magyar nyelvű írásbeliség*, 68-69. On the sisters, see letters 79-81.

by Nicolaus Istvánffy as his student. For "practical reasons," Sambucus took up the study of medicine, but he remained dedicated to Greek and Latin literature after 1555, when he became a licentiate (he never obtained a doctoral degree or practiced medicine seriously). In the following two years, he continued working as a tutor, touring also neighbouring Venice, Bologna and Florence and probably venturing as far as Rome.[6] In late 1557 he returned with Bona to Vienna, met Emperor Ferdinand in Prague and became a member of the imperial court as *aulae familiaris*, with a yearly salary of 100 florins, thanks also to the support of Archduke Maximilian. Sambucus used this vaguely defined position as a means of continuing his study tour and enlarging his growing collection of books and manuscripts, a collection which he had first begun to build in Paris in 1551. From Vienna, he returned to Padua at the end of 1558, and soon he started tutoring Jakob Fugger. In the spring of 1560 he travelled to Paris for a second time (probably still with the young Fugger), passing through Zurich in Whitsun and then very probably Basel. In Paris, he published his *Dialogues on Ciceronian imitation*,[7] and entered into the highest circles of antiquarians and philologists. In the summer of 1561 we find him in Melun, while the itinerary of the following year is less clear. He arrived from Paris to Genova in mid-1562, searched the libraries of the peninsula systematically and travelled as far as Apulia.[8] Finally, after a short stop at home (attending Maximilian's coronation as king of Hungary in Pressburg), Sambucus arrived in Ghent and Antwerp in September 1563, where the first edition of his famous *Emblemata*, a masterly document of his erudition, scholarly network, innovative mind and aesthetic sense, was published by Christophe Plantin in 1564. By 1564 Sambucus was ready to occupy a central position in the erudite circles of the imperial capital and start rising above his fellow citizens. His major capital was not his noble title or family background but the erudition and socio-intellectual network he obtained during the 22 years of his academic touring. All of this was thanks to his vast curiosity and resolute investment in learning.

Eventually, Sambucus settled in Vienna in May 1564 as the owner of a large private collection of manuscripts and books, the author and editor of several publications appearing with first-rate publishers and a respected member of the Republic of Letters. Thanks to his talents and successful networking, Sambucus's career rose rapidly in Vienna. In 1566 he was given the office of imperial historian, and a year later he married Cristinna Egerer, the daughter of a wealthy Viennese merchant, who would become the mother of two daughters and a son (probably a third daughter was born after Sambucus's death). In 1567 he also obtained the titles of *medicus aulicus* and *comes palatinus*, to which the title of *consiliarius aulae* was added two years later, neither of which had much practical significance. From 1568 in addition to his yearly 200-florin lifelong pension (paid by the Hungarian Chamber), he also received 100 talers yearly for his services as imperial historian (paid by the Imperial Chamber), which was gradually raised to 300 by 1573. Sambucus invested his salary and the money lent to him by his wife and relatives in the purchase of two prestigious Viennese houses and a manor in Mannersdorf, close to the Hungarian border, to which he retired several times to avoid the plague. After a rapid rise, stagnatation came relatively early in his career, due as much to the death of several of his former patrons as to the increasing pressure of rival humanists and

---

[6] Gerstinger, "Johannes Sambucus als Handschriftensammler," 271; Várady, "Relazioni di Giovanni Zsámboky," 11.
[7] Sambucus, *De imitatione Ciceroniana* (see letter 22).
[8] Várady, "Relazioni di Giovanni Zsámboky" 17-20. If he ever visited Greece, this must have happened at this time. Cf. with letter 344.

the financial difficulties of the court. Either Sambucus invested in a manner disproportionate with his salary, which from the mid-1570s started to go unpaid by the court, or he needed money for new investments, by 1573 he had decided to sell his exceptionally large collection of manuscripts. Although Emperor Maximilian II was positive about the purchase, it was only in 1578 that Rudolf II ordered Archduke Ernst to complete the transaction. For the 530 manuscripts (most of them Greek) sold to the Imperial Library and for his unpaid salary, Sambucus received an invoice of 6,200 guldens, 3,500 of which still had not been paid in 1582. The fate of Sambucus's remaining c. 200 mss. and c. 3,500 books, catalogued in 1587, is less well known; they certainly did not make their way en bloc into the imperial library, as was thought earlier.[9]

As an imperial historian, Sambucus left contemporaries and posterity disappointed. Most of his historical work consisted of shorter battle descriptions, which he published as appendices to his two editions of Bonfini's *Rerum Ungaricarum decades* (1568 and 1581), his major historical publication. Likewise, despite his title as titular doctor of the court and his licence to treat courtiers (in spite of his lack of a medical degree), Sambucus hardly did more than give occasional advice to some aristocratic patients. His work as a poet was clearly more consistent than his work as a historian (or physician). He was not only a prolific Latin (and Greek) poet himself but also showed good taste in collecting and publishing the poetry of Janus Pannonius (his interest in the golden age of Matthias Corvinus also had patriotic and political roots). Sambucus also contributed to contemporary aesthetical theories in both his dialogue on Ciceronianism and his paraphrase and commentary to Horace's *Ars poetica*.[10] Most significantly, however, his interests lay in collecting, collating, editing and publishing precious old manuscripts of writings by Greek (and Latin) authors from his private collection.[11] As a young scholar, Sambucus typically published texts with a focus on pedagogical or religious questions, using in part his own translations or paraphrases. Several of these books were prepared as gifts for his patrons. According to his 1583 one-sheet printed bibliography (*Catalogus librorum*…), his first work was a certain 'Tabellae dialecticae in usum Hefflmari' (either unpublished or lost), which was probably some teaching material that Sambucus had prepared for a private student at the age of 16. Only a year later, he translated two speeches by Xenophon into Latin in Ingolstadt. From the age of 19, his books started being published by the best humanist publishers of Europe. The most famous editions came out in the years that followed his settlement in Vienna: editions of Petronius, Lucretius, Aristaenetus, Diogenes Laertius, Pannonius, Bonfini, Theophylactus, Gregorius Nyssenus, Theodorus Ducas Lascaris, Eunapius, Joannes Stobaeus, etc. In many of these works, Sambucus's most important contribution was the provision of one or more manuscripts and the organisational work for the publication, relying on the work of humanist colleagues (e.g. Hadrianus Junius, Obertus Giphanius, Laurentius Sifanus, Gerhard Falkenburg, Willem Canter, Claude Aubery, Johannes Löwenklau, etc) in collating, editing and translating the manuscripts.

In the late 1570s, the pace of Sambucus's book production began to slow down, and he failed to complete several of his dearest projects, such as a new Greek edition of Dioscorides's *Materia medica*. Sambucus often complained about the avarice of printers, but the real problem was his own physical distance from the best European publishing centres and the decreasing number of extraordinary manuscripts in his library or available in Vienna. Despite lower

---

9 Viskolcz, "The fate of Johannes Sambucus's library."
10 Sambucus, *Ars poetica Horatii*.
11 An analysis of this activity is given in *Humanistes du bassin des Carpates II. Johannes Sambucus*, i-lxxiv.

production, Sambucus remained a dynamic figure, and he managed to keep his good position both at court and in the Republic of Letters, which is amply proven by the correspondence he maintained during the last years of his life. Despite his financial troubles, he died relatively rich and left a respectable library behind. Although many of his maunscripts found their way into the imperial library, the letters he received, except for a few, were not preserved.

On the correspondence
Compared to the archives of first-rank sixteenth-century humanists, the corpus of Sambucus's surviving correspondence is medium-sized, containing now 377 letters.[12] The primary objective of this correspondence was to enhance Sambucus's activities as an editor and publisher of classical and Byzantine works, the majority of which came from his own impressive manuscript collection. As an imperial historian, Sambucus also felt it his duty to publish books related to Hungary's history and to make his country's best humanist authors, including figures like Janus Pannonius, known to the world. His correspondence, however, hardly reflected such minor interests in history. Sambucus considered himself to be first and foremost a collector and publisher and second of all a courtier. Most of his correspondents were philologically-minded men of the same kind, and the central themes of their letters were publication projects, philological enterprises and bibliophilic or antiquarian activities. Apart from his fellow courtier Johannes Crato, who was also one of his closest friends, those with whom he maintained his most lasting friendships lived far away. They included Piero Vettori in Florence, Theodor Zwinger in Basel and Joachim Camerarius Sr. and Joachim Camerarius Jr. in Leipzig and Nuremberg respectively.

If some of his contemporaries were better models of Ciceronian elegance than Sambucus, he did not lack the skills. Certainly, he was well-trained in the theory of letter-writing: he was only 20 when he started to prepare an anthology on the art.[13] Overall, Sambucus translated and published three of the four key ancient Greek theoretical texts on letter-writing: works by (Pseudo-)Libanius and (Pseudo-)Demetrius of Phaleron appeared in 1552 and a short but significant extract on letter-writing from Demetrius's *On Style* was released in 1567.[14] Sambucus's 1552 anthology on epistolography also contained appendices comprising earlier tracts on letter-writing, including works by Erasmus, Vives and Celtis.

If Sambucus's letters do not always present him as a great master of style, this has less to do with the state of his talents than with his distaste for verbosity and his self-fashioning as a busy scholar for whom correspondence was primarily a research tool. For Sambucus, outside of matters of scholarship, hardly anything was serious enough to warrant discussion. His letters were intended to advance his work as a collector and editor, which should, in turn, serve the public interest. Nonetheless, if most of his epistolary output sought to realise his scholarly ambitions and was meant for professional humanist insiders who could appreciate their load of complex constructions and unusual or rare words, other aspects reflected the spontaneity and directness of the familiar style. The majority of these scholarly letters are short, dense and filled with all sorts of information and allusions. From sentence to sentence, Sambucus often jumped from one topic to another. Starting often *in medias res*, as is fitting for a familiar letter, his letters were often written hurriedly (*raptim*) in short and not always grammatical sentences. Sambucus liked to use the phrase *et cetera*, suggesting that while he could expand

---

[12] In this section we have relied on Almási, "The Familiar Style" (as in note 1).
[13] See letters 4 and 5.
[14] See letter 87.

on the subject, there was no point in doing so since the addressee knew all too well what he was talking about (which was hardly always the case).

As an example of Sambucus's usual scholarly correspondence, we may consider a letter he sent to Johannes Crato, the imperial physician, who had accompanied the emperor on his travels to Prague. In this case, Sambucus's chief goal was to promote the sale of his library:

> "Greetings. I hear [the court] is publicly preparing for its departure. Before this happens, I would greatly desire [*discupio*] to get some inkling [*subintelligere*] of what the emperor has in mind regarding [my] little library [*bibliothecula*]. I don't really care [ἐλαχίστου ποιήσω] whether he [the emperor] takes it or not so long as I don't have to worry about offending the emperor if the library gets another owner [although] I don't think [that he would take offence] as he has stopped caring about such things. I ask in the name of the beauty of learning and your most humane and prompt readiness to help any one of your friends that you seize a good opportunity to bring up [my business] again. [...] [Postscript:] That ungrateful Italian [Girolamo Mercuriale] to whom I entrusted Palladius's commentary of *Epidemics* [Ἐπιδημιῶν] 6 [by Hippocrates] and [George of] Trebizond's [translation of] Aristotle's *History* [of Animals], including parts of my own translation etc., together with [a book by Paulus] Aegineta, has neither published them nor sent them back to me. I hear he copied out the most important things and got someone in Venice to have the books sent back to me. Such refined company! [*Das sein feine Gesellen!*] But these people should go to hell [εἰς κόρακας]; we are Germans [*germani*]."[15]

If Sambucus's plain style may at times seem dry (and this is one of his more colourful letters), we should remember that his use of rarefied terms like *discupio* or *subintelligere* and his word play served not only to show off and elevate his writing in the world of pedantic sophistry but also to entertain. This was also the function of the letter's self-ironising ending, with its play on *germanus*, which also means "brotherly", "true" and "sincere" and, thus, contrasted with the duplicity of the Italian Mercuriale. Although the insertion of Greek words or, as in the current case, a German sentence might make for a juicier letter, the unusual and extravagant idioms that took the place of Ciceronian classicism did not make for easy reading. The loss of an easily accessible language was compensated for with a sketchy, semi-colloquial sentence structure and grammatical incompleteness.

Sambucus's epistolary flair was more impressive in his letters to his social superiors, but even when writing to men of greater social prestige and higher rank, he continued to use the familiar style, which allowed him to disguise the social difference between himself and the recipient of the letter. These letters can often be read as attempts to establish contact with peers. Sambucus clearly disliked highlighting his social inferiority through the use of flowery language. When addressing the emperor and other powerful patrons, he used a style that remained direct and to the point, and his handwriting was only moderately tidier: it still suggested a degree of casualness and immediacy. Sambucus preferred to use Tua/Tuae in his letters, even when communicating with emperors. After the death of Maximilian, when Sambucus first addressed Rudolf II, he originally used the formal V. (Vestrae), only to replace it with T. (Tuae) in the final version.[16]

---

[15] See letter 240.
[16] See letter 274.

No vernacular language had the same measure of status-neutrality as Latin. In this sense, the Latin familiar letter had a special social function and Sambucus's correspondence offers a perfect example for it. It was the use of the Latin familiar style that enabled him to join (and at the same time create) a "community of learning" that connected learned men of any social rank, including social upstarts like Sambucus and powerful patrons like the emperors.

On the edition

The present effort to publish Sambucus's correspondence has an important precedent. In 1968 Hans Gerstinger (1885–1971) published a collection of Sambucus's letters in the annual journal of the Austrian Academy of Sciences.[17] Gerstinger was a remarkable philologist, Byzantinist and palaeographer. Since 1923, he led the papyrus department, and in 1931–1936 he directed the papyrus and manuscript departments of the Austrian National Library. From 1940 he was professor at the University of Graz, where he also served as dean and rector. Sambucus's Greek and Byzantine interests first caught the attention of the Byzantinist Gerstinger at an early stage of his career. By 1926 he had published a monograph on Sambucus's work as a collector, providing a list of the Greek and Latin codices that remained in the holdings of the National Library and had once belonged to Sambucus. This was only the beginning of his study of the Hungarian humanist, whose letters he started collecting already before World War II (fortunately, since most of the 48 letters addressed to the imperial physician Johannes Crato were destroyed during the war).[18] In 1948 and 1965 he published Sambucus's diary, which was a considerable achievement in palaeography.[19] In 1965, when the talented Hungarian researcher Ágnes Ritoók-Szalai (1931–2022) visited the 80-year-old Gerstinger, the great Austrian philologist was already working on his edition. He was transcribing one letter per day and dictating it to his secretary, whether the letter consisted of only a few lines or ran to several pages.[20] Eventually, Gerstinger concluded his study of Sambucus with the publication of 165 letters in 1968.[21] Contemporaneously, in the same journal, a Slovak colleague, Anton Vantuch (1921–2001), published 28 letters held by the State Archives of Trnava.[22] (Some letters, of course, had been published in different editions before Gerstinger's work, most importantly by István Várady.[23]) Significantly, the edition in Gerstinger and Vantuch contained only the letters written by the Hungarian humanist (1556–1584) and did not include those addressed to him or the printed prefaces and dedicatory epistles written by or addressed to him. Gerstinger was aware of the fact that his collection was not complete. As he claimed in the introduction, he published those

---

[17] Gerstinger, "Die Briefe."
[18] The original letters had been lost long before the war. Gerstinger only had access to the copies made by Samuel Benjamin Klose (1730–1798) held in the archives of the University of Wrocław.
[19] Hans Gerstinger, "Aus dem 'Tagebuche' des kaiserlichen Hofhistoriographen Johannes Sambucus (1531 bis 1584)," in *Die Österreichische Nationalbibliothek*, ed. Josef Stummvoll (Vienna: Bauer, 1948), 373-383; idem, "Aus dem Tagebuch des kaiserlichen Hofhistoriographen Johannes Sambucus (1531–1584)," *Österreichische Akademie der Wissenschaften. Philologische-Historische Klasse. Sitzungsberichte*, 248 (1965), 1-53.
[20] Ágnes Ritoók-Szalai, "Juhász László és a *Bibliotheca*," in idem, *Kutak: tanulmányok a XV-XVI. századi magyarországi művelődés köréből* (Budapest: Balassi, 2012), 350-359, at 358.
[21] Gerstinger, "Die Briefe." He transcribed a few letters addressed to Sambucus in the notes of the edition or in independent journal articles. See, for example, the letter by Martin Crusius, published in 1929 (see letter 344).
[22] Vantuch, "Die Sambucusbriefe."
[23] Várady, "Relazioni di Giovanni Zsámboky col'umanesimo italiano."

letters of which he had "learned from the relevant manuscript catalogues or from the inquiry addressed to the responsible archives."[24]

Preparations for a fuller edition of Sambucus's correspondence were launched in 2006 by Gábor Almási and with the backing of a three-year Bolyai János fellowship, which was supervised by István Monok, who was at the time director of the National Library of Budapest. It was thanks to Professor Monok that this project was later narrowed down in the context of the book series *Europa Humanistica* to the publication of the paratexts (including the prefaces and dedications) of all the books initiated, managed, edited by, or addressed to Sambucus, which concerned the transmission of pre-1500 texts (including most of the publications "*ex bibliotheca Sambuci*"). This project was realised in collaboration by Gábor Almási and Farkas Gábor Kiss and with the assistance and support of Jean-Françoise Maillard and Jean-Marie Flamand of the Institut de recherche et d'histoire des textes of the CNRS. The resulting French volume was published by Brepols in 2014 (*Humanistes du bassin des Carpates II. Johannes Sambucus*).

The present volume is the continuation of this earlier work, undertaken first with the support of the five-year "Lendület fellowship" programme of the Academy of Sciences of Budapest, directed by Farkas Gábor Kiss in 2015-2019 and then through collaboration with Lav Šubarić in the Ludwig Boltzmann Institute for Neo-Latin Studies in Innsbruck since 2019. In comparison with the edition in Gerstinger (and Vantuch), this edition contains 377 letters, although 32 of the letters listed in this edition and already published in 2014 have not been reproduced here. Our aim was to check all possible manuscripts and compare them to earlier editions if there were any. Unlike Gerstinger, we also included published dedicatory epistles and 78 letters *received* by Sambucus. Next to these letters, we have also found a considerable number of additional letters written by Sambucus and preserved in different archives of Europe and in rare publications.[25]

Despite the fact that the known body of Sambucus's correspondence has significantly grown, this publication will not fundamentally modify our knowledge of his life. Nevertheless, it does provide a much fuller, a great deal more nuanced and in many places also more correct image of Sambucus and his environment. The c. 575 names included in the index show that the volume offers a rather broad view on the intellectual (and religious) culture of contemporary Central Europe and the imperial court in particular.

In transcribing the texts included in this multi-lingual collection, we have applied different principles to different type of material. For letters in vernacular (fourteen in German, eight in Hungarian, four in Italian, and one in French), we have provided documentary transcripts. We tried to preserve all spelling variants and idiosyncrasies found in the original sources, in line with demands that national philologies place on the editions of texts from the early modern period. When editing Latin letters (348 in total), we followed the usual practice observed in Neo-Latin editions. Our primary goal was to provide an easily readable text tailored to classically trained readers, which however still retains some Neo-Latin characteristics. To this

---

[24] Gerstinger, "Die Briefe," 5.
[25] During the years, we have pursued work in numerous archives, and also reached others through exchanging letters and the help of our colleagues. In 2019 Gábor Almási and Farkas Gábor Kiss also visited the Staatsbibliothek in Munich in order to transcribe Piero Vettori's drafts of letters addressed to Sambucus in Clm 791. Gerstinger was not interested in these letters (which were sent to Sambucus) and probably did not even know about them. Várady knew of the letters but published only the one that had a legible transcription (letter 118). However, elderly and apparently sick Vettori's handwriting is so difficult to read that we were unable to include all his drafts into this edition.

end we have spelled out all abbreviations (with exception of some single letter abbreviations, such as "D." for "Dominus" or "Doctor," "S." for "Salutem" or "S. D." for "Salutem dicit"). We have moderately standardized the orthography, normalizing the use of "u" and "v" according to their role as a vocal or a consonant, transcribing "j" as "i," and removing diacritical marks (such as accents on adverbs, e.g. "longé"), while retaining spelling variations commonly employed during Sambucus's time (such as "caussa," "comuniter," "literaria," "Thurca," and the few instances in which the diphthong "ae" was spelled as "e"). Capitalisation, much loved by sixteenth-century contemporaries, has been adjusted to conform to modern English spelling rules. We have restricted it to personal, geographical, and national names as well as book titles, months and days (days of the week, Kalends, Nones and Ides). Honorary appellatives such as "Sacratissima Maiestas," "Dominatio Vestra" or "Reverendus" and titles like "Rex," "Consiliarius," and "Episcopus" were left capitalised when used in the vocative case. Regarding the consequent modernization of punctuation, our aim has been to enhance the understanding of the text through clear indication of syntactical structures. We have replaced most of the colons and semicolons by commas and full stops. When possible, we have divided excessively long sentences into shorter ones. If the correspondents refer to quotations, quotation marks have been used. The two Greek letters and interspersed Greek passages have been edited along similar lines as the Latin ones, with us occasionally adding or correcting accents and spiritus and normalizing the capitalization and punctuation to make the texts more accessible to readers familiar with Ancient Greek.

Similar to Gerstinger's publication, this is also not a critical edition. In most cases, there exists only one textual witness for each letter, whether it be a draft, the original letter itself, a later copy, a contemporary print, or a later edition. In the few instances where textual variants exist and might influence the interpretation, we have included them in the notes. We have transcribed all available letters from the earliest witnesses (242 from manuscripts, 94 from early modern prints, and 41, when no other source was available, from modern editions). Consequently, we have not explicitly indicated every instance where our transcription differs from those of earlier editors. In places where transcription proved to be especially difficult, we have indicated the difficulties in the text, and at times also provided the reading of the earlier editors and transcribers in the notes. In those cases where no original letters or their drafts have survived, we have silently corrected the typographic errors made by printers and later editors. Our own conjectures have been included in the text and identified in the notes, which in these cases also feature the readings provided by earlier scholars. Similarly, we have selectively utilized the notes of Gerstinger and Vantuch, referring to their contributions in many but not all cases.

In the notes we have given English translations of all Greek words, phrases and quotes. Longer biographical notes on the people mentioned in the main text are given upon their first mention, and readers can refer to the index in order to find them. While we have made efforts to include cross-references to the letters in the notes, we also strongly encourage our readers to utilize the index. Hungarian letters are summarised in detail, the Greek letters (of which there are two) are translated.

ACKNOWLEDGEMENTS

In the long process of collecting, transcribing and editing Sambucus's letters, we have received the support and help from many institutions and individuals. We are immensely grateful to all of them. The major part of our work was financed by the Ludwig Boltzmann Institute for Neo-Latin Studies in Innsbruck (2019–2023), the "Lendület" programme "Humanism in East Central Europe" (2014–2019) and, earlier, by a Bolyai János fellowship (2006–2009). The latter two grants are managed by the Hungarian Academy of Sciences. Special thanks goes to the mentor of the project, István Monok, former director of the Széchenyi National Library and currently director of the Library of the Hungarian Academy of Sciences, who promoted our work in innumerable ways and also took charge of the process of typesetting. A few of the letters had already been transcribed by Csilla Bíró, researcher at the Széchenyi National Library working in collaboration with Monok; we would like to thank Bíró for her contribution. We are very grateful to our colleague Ivan Lábaj, assistant professor in the Department of Classical and Semitic Philology at Comenius University in Bratislava, who povided invaluable help in the preparation of the index. Lábaj, an enthusiastic scholar of Sambucus who at present is working on an edition of Sambucus's poems, also discovered a few letters in rare prints. In transcribing several of the letters, we have relied on the expertise of our colleague Farkas Gábor Kiss, associate professor and head of department at the Institute of Hungarian Literature and Cultural Studies at Eötvös Loránd University of Budapest, who has been one of the most stalwart supporters of the project since the outset and who kindly included it into his "Lendület" programme, mentioned above. We also owe a debt of thanks to Borbála Lovas, assistant professor at the same institute, who has generously corrected our transcription of the Hungarian letters. We are obliged to Dávid Molnár, senior researcher at the Department of Cultural Heritage at the University of Tokaj-Hegyalja, and Miklós Janzsó, researcher at the Széchenyi National Library, who helped us in proofing the Greek and Latin transcriptions. We are particularly grateful for the enthusiastic research by Kees Teszelszky (former curator in the National Library of the Netherlands), who found some letters preserved in European archives. We are also very grateful to the former and the present Hungarian delegates of the Austrian State Archives, István Fazekas and András Oross, who were both extremely supportive and contributed significantly to our search for letters. Some colleagues working in more distant archives were also particularly helpful, including Jakub Roháč at the State Archives in Trnava, who sent us copies of Sambucus's letters preserved in his home city, and William Stoneman at the Houghton Library in Cambridge (Mass.). We are likewise grateful to friends and colleagues who helped us at different stages of the project by checking individual letters, addressing questions that arose in problematic passages, copying archival material or in other ways: William Barton, Christian Gastgeber, Paola Molino, Áron Orbán, Simon Smets, Arnoud Visser and Grigory Vorobyev. Finally, we would also like to thank Thomas Cooper for his invaluable work in copyediting and Viktória Vas for her careful typesetting. Paduae, a. d. X Kalendas Iunii MMXXIII.

LETTERS

1.
Veit Amerbach to Sambucus
17 February, 1549, Ingolstadt

Dedication in *Viti Amerpachii Enarratio ad M. T. Ciceronis orationem pro Milone, nunc primum in lucem edita, eiusdem annotationes quaedam breves ad Topica Ciceronis* (Basel: Ioannes Oporinus, 1550), f. a2^r-a4^v.[1]

Sambucus's many and significant virtues are the cause of Amerbach's great affection towards him. When Sambucus arrived in Ingolstadt, upon their first meeting he already displayed his zeal for learning and revealed his erudition, drawn not only from Latin but also from Greek authors. Since then he never ceased to advocate (philological) scholarship, caring equally for the language and the contents. In addition, his sincerity and his affection for Amerbach are quite unlike the behaviour of many other friends and students, who pretend to be friendly but act the contrary way. Therefore, Amerbach's affection for Sambucus grew in short time so strongly that he now counts him among his best friends and would do anything for him, just as Sambucus would do the same for him, and he believes their friendship will be eternal and also his children will inherit it. He cherishes their interaction even more, because friendships are today based on self-interest and hatred of the truth, and virtue, if there is still a place for it at all, hangs only by a thread. As soon as truth causes offense, it is completely banished. No wonder, as even among the leading churchmen one finds those who would rather use flattery in order to be loved than risk giving offense by speaking the truth and be hated, and they do so under the pretext of trying to be modest, peaceful and law-abiding. Although only few church laws are being followed, those concerning moderation in criticism are observed too zealously and propagated by people ignorant of true honesty and piety. Christians live by the rule that flattery creates friends, while the truth causes hatred. They do not listen to the prophet's command to speak the truth to each other. The truth is more important than peace, if it were not, we would have to consider Christ, the apostles, the prophets, and wise men who castigate the vice of men as disruptors of peace, as they had indeed been judged. One cannot teach philosophy and propagate virtues without attacking vices. This would be like asking for peace from cruel enemies. Just as one must fight wars to secure peace, so one must fight vices to achieve virtues. If someone thinks that only vices themselves, but not people committing them should be criticized, he is either crazy or stupid. However, Amerbach approves of St. Augustine's opinion that one should hate vices and not the people. If considered correctly, this is no contradiction. With regards to the publication of this commentary, considering Sambucus's attitude, he could not but dedicate it to Sambucus; not in order to bestow honour on him but to strengthen the bond between them and to keep Sambucus on course. Sambucus may need no incitement but people can always change, and Amerbach wanted to preform this service

---

[1] We thank Ivan Lábaj for finding this letter.

of a friend and a teacher not only for Sambucus's sake, but also for his own. Sambucus only needs to accept Amerbach's acknowledgement and never let himself be led away from truth and from other virtues, honest arts, efforts and actions. This way, Amerbach will not regret any favour and Sambucus will be helped and defended by God and gain merit for the Church.

Vitus Amerpachius[2] Ioanni Sambuco Tirnavensi Pannonio S. D. P.

Tuum ingenium et tuae virtutes nec paucae, nec parvae in hac aetate faciunt, Ioannes, ut non leviter aut parum te amem. Postquam enim huc venisti ac es collocutus mecum semel, statim et ingens tuum optimarum literarum studium et non exiguam earum doctrinam, perceptam non tantum ex Latinis, verumetiam Graecis auctoribus ac iis optimis quibusque non obscure mihi declaravisti nec ab eo tempore desiisti constanter hoc institutum urgere, sic tamen, ut cum linguarum ac sermonis cura (quae hoc tempore ut rara est, ita maxime ad solidam eruditionis laudem necessaria) semper solicitudinem rerum, aut certe parem curam coniungeres. Accesserunt huc synceritas et modestia cum non plebeia significatione magni cuiusdam erga me amoris ac studii propemodum singularis. In quo perstitisti hactenus fortiter ac longe aliter, quam facit vulgus amicorum et discipulorum, qui, dum verbis et gestibus humani sunt, aut potius blandiuntur ac faciunt contrarium, vere altera manu panem ostendunt, altera ferunt lapidem, quod aiunt, cum per se ἅπας λόγος, ἂν ἀπῇ τὰ πράγματα, μάταιόν τι καὶ κενὸν[3] sit, ut graviter ait Demosthenes. Quare meus vicissim in te amor et studium paulatim (etsi magna haec initio quoque fuerunt) hoc non longo tempore creverunt ita, ut hic te nunc inter praecipuos meos amicos habeam nec ullam operam, ullum officium grave mihi putaverim aut magnum etiam, quod in te vel tu voluisti, vel ego debere sensi a me conferri, sicut nec tu quicquam intermisisti, quod mihi gratum esse aut honorificum putares, ut in magnam spem venerim amicitiam et inter nos fore perpetuam et a me velut partem aliquam haereditatis ad meos liberos perventuram esse. Fuit mihi tua consuetudo ac adhuc est hoc etiam iucundior, quod in amicitiis nunc fere nihil est, nisi (ut sunt mores hominum) et odium veritatis et captatio commodi alicuius aut suavitatis minime liberalis et virtus omnis procul tanquam exulat. Quod si et haec locum habet, nequaquam tenet primum, ut debebat, sed ultimum, et hic etiam persaepe vix haeret velut serico filo aut bombycino aut gossipino, ut cum nostris loquar. Non raro certe ad primam veritatis offensam avellitur ac ita profligatur, ut vix ullum eius maneat vestigium. Nec est hoc mirum, cum etiam inter eos qui sedent ad gubernacula naviculae divi Petri non raro inveniantur, qui malint obsequio tuti esse ac amari, quam dicendo verum periclitari et haberi odio, non tamen sine praetextu modestiae, pacis et tranquilitatis, adeoque studii non violandarum legum, ut inanem laborem in faciendo altero taceam. Huc res iam deducta est, ut, cum aliae paucae leges et canones observentur, praesertim

---

[2] Veit Amerbach (1503–1557) was a humanist, theologian and scholar. As a young man, he embraced the Reformation and became a teacher at the University of Wittenberg, where he also taught physics. After theological disagreements (over the "sola fide" doctrine) and philosophical controversy over the soul with Philip Melanchthon, Amerbach, influenced by Aristotelianism, moved to the University of Ingolstadt, where he continued lecturing on rhetoric and philosophy. He taught several of Sambucus's later patrons in Vienna, such as Georg Sigismund Seld and Johann Ulrich Zasius (Almási, *The Uses of Humanism*, 133). The letter shows Amerbach as someone in need of partners in his fight for (religious and philosophical) truth, which pays no respect to confessional divides or other (institutional) expectations of conformism. See Günther Frank, "Veit Amerbach (1503–1557). Von Wittenberg nach Ingolstadt," in *Melanchthon in seinen Schülern*, ed. Heinz Schilling (Wiesbaden: Harrasowitz, 1997), 103-128 (further bibliography on p. 103).

[3] Every word [is] vain and idle, if action is missing. Demosthenes 2.12.

quae ad solidas virtutes, mores, magnas opes et dignitates pertinent, ac non valde, ut fiat hoc, urgeatur, hae unae de servando modo in reprehensionibus et insectationibus fere nimium aut observentur faciendo aut extendantur exponendo a semidoctis et veram honestatem ac pietatem non aut satis intelligentibus, aut suo quasi pede metientibus. Ac ita hoc obsequium amicos, veritas odium parit, magis vivendi sit regula Christianorum, quam illud *Credidi, propter quod locutus sum*,[4] aut simile quidpiam, ac id quidem ob hoc in psalmo sequens, *Ego autem humiliatus sum nimis*.[5] Hoc si non est τὸν κώνωπα διαλύζειν, τὸν κάμηλον καταπίνειν,[6] certe nihilo est melius, aut etiam deterius est. Repellimus enim a nobis dedita opera spiritum paracletum, qui debebat nos docere omnem veritatem, ac minime audimus prophetam praecipientem, *Loquimini veritatem unusquisque cum proximo suo*.[7] Nec obstat, quod ibi additur, *Veritatem tantum et pacem diligite*,[8] cum veritas paci praeponatur, nec aliud scandalum sit prohibitum, quam datum, ut vocant, nisi Christum, apostolos, prophetas et sapientes alios propterea peccavisse, maledicos fuisse, conviciatores aut malevolos dicendum est, quod a plurimis iudicati sunt hominum flagitia reprehendentes perturbatores tranquillitatis et seditiosi. Aut philosophiam quis doceri posse aut debere putat, laudari et inculcari virtutes hominibus ita, ut non vituperentur et evellantur ex animis illorum vitia. Quod sane aliud nihil esset, quam aut pacem docere sine belli collatione, aut eam expectare, quaerere, petere ab armatis et saevis hostibus, nullas conditiones admittentibus, desidendo, nihil repugnando ac tantum corpora concedendo illis ad caedem, servitutem et alias contumelias, possesiones ad luxum ac turpitudinem. Sicut enim bellum gerendum est, quando geritur, ut pax habeatur, ita pugnandum est cum vitiis tanquam hostibus nostris publicis et privatis, ut virtutes, quasi quaedam pax animorum, ac tranquillitas aut recuperetur, aut conservetur, quae firmissimum etiam est vinculum societatis et pacis inter se hominum procul dubio. Nunc si quis tantum vitia putaret insectanda, quae per se, ut res brutae ac pendentes aliunde, nihil commerentur, non homines etiam, aut posse hoc fieri, si non esset insanus, tamen a stulto nihil admodum hic differet. Ac propterea nunquam hoc dictum nescio cuius, qui odit vitia, homines odit,[9] probavi, praesertim in vero sensu et non sophistico, sed illud sancti Augustini potius, de viciis habendis odio, non hominibus.[10] Tametsi autem hoc videtur cum nostra sententia pugnare, non tamen pugnat, si quis recte, non perverse, ut nunc solent homines facere, accipiat. Sed haec alias.

Ad propositum redeo. Cum essem has annotationes ad *Milonianam* cum iis, quas nuper Ciceronis *Topicis* relegens hoc opusculum adscripsi obiter, editurus et cogitarem, qualis tuus esset erga me animus, facere non potui, quin eas tibi dedicarem, non tam ut aliquid ex ea re tibi honoris accederet, quam ut confirmarem ita nostram coniunctionem ac te retinerem in coepto studiorum cursu. Quanquam enim sperabam te facturum hoc, etiamsi non esses incitatus, ac velut accensus his facibus, tamen, quia sumus homines et saepe nonnihil mutamur praeter omnium opinionem, in hac re monitoris, amici, hominis, praeceptoris quoque, si pateris, officium facere volui non tua modo, sed et mea caussa. Tui vicissim est officii, meum studium et hanc animi testificationem boni consulere ac nunquam admittere, ut

---

[4] Ps. 115:1.
[5] Ps. 115:1.
[6] To strain out a gnat and swallow a camel. Cf. Matth. 23:24.
[7] Zc. 8:16.
[8] Zc. 8:19.
[9] Plinius, *Epistulae* 8.22.
[10] Cf. Augustinus, *Epistulae* 153.1.3.

quicquam a cultura veritatis (quae aut est ipse Deus, aut expressum eius quoddam vestgium) sociarumque virutum aliarum ac artium honestissimarum adeoque studiorum et actionum, quae decent praestantiam nostrae naturae, omnium, te abducere patiaris. Hoc si facies, nullius meae benevolentiae me, nullius me conatus, nullius operae me poenitebit, ac Deum tu semper adiutorem habebis, defensorem et amicum, optimeque mereberis de vera illa et viva sponsa Christi salvatoris nostri, matre nostra ecclesia. Vale. Datum Ingelstadii, XIII. Calendas Martias anno post salutem 1549.

2.
Sambucus to Philipp and Theodor Apianus[11]
25 March 1549, Ingolstadt

Dedication in Sambucus, Δημηγορίαι, 3-5. Published in *Humanistes du bassin des Carpates II. Johannes Sambucus*, 13-15.

3.
Sambucus to Timotheus Apianus[12]
13 August 1550, Strasbourg

Dedication in Λουκιανοῦ Σαμοσατέως Διάλογοι οὐράνιοι, ἐνάλιοι καὶ νεκρικοί. *Luciani Samosatensis Dialogi coelestes, marini et inferni, cum vulgata versione, quibus propter singularem elegantiam adiecti sunt eiusdem Menippus et Timon. His addita sunt argumenta una cum quorundam dialogorum* μυθολογία *latinis versibus tractata per Ioannem Sambucum Tirnaviensem Pannonium* (Strasbourg: Wolfgang Köpfel, 1550), f. ii^r-iii^v. Published in *Humanistes du bassin des Carpates II. Johannes Sambucus*, 9-11.

---

[11] Little is known about Petrus Apianus's son Theodorus, who died between 1608 and 1613. His brother Philipp Apianus (1531–1589) inherited the professorship of his father in Ingolstadt but was later forced to leave the university because of his Protestant sentiments. He studied in Italy, became doctor of medicine in 1568 and moved to Tübingen, where he became professor of mathematics and a famous topographer. On 28 August 1549, Philipp left Ingolstadt for Strasbourg in Sambucus's company (who had enrolled at the University of Ingolstadt a year before on 17 July 1548), where they studied under Johannes Sturm until the autumn of 1550, when they continued their tour towards Paris (Philipp left Strasbourg a bit earlier, probably in the company of Petrus Lotichius Secundus, Sambucus joined them at the university town of Dole in Burgundy). The next year, Sambucus and Philipp made another excursion to Dole (without Lotichius), and presumably they stayed there together until 1552, when they apparently returned together to Ingolstadt at the news of the agony of Philipp's father. On the way back they stopped, again in Dole, leaving France on 6 March 1552. In January 1553, Sambucus was still in the Apianus's house in Ingolstadt (see letter 7). See Zon, *Petrus Lotichius*, 299-300; Almási, *The Uses of Humanism*, 211-213; *Humanistes du bassin des Carpates II. Johannes Sambucus*, 13; the article on Philipp Apianus by Siegmund Günther in *ADB* 46 (1902), 23-25; *Philipp Apian und die Kartographie der Renaissance [Ausstellungskataloge]*, ed. Hans Wolff (Weissenhorn Bayern: A.H. Konrad, 1989), and letter 52, note 303.

[12] Timotheus Apianus (?–1562), one of the younger sons of the astronomer Petrus Apianus, was a land surveyor. He appears to have still been living in Ingolstadt at the time of the publication. See *Peter Apian: Astronomie, Kosmographie und Mathematik am Beginn der Neuzeit; mit Ausstellungskatalog*, ed. Karl Röttel (Eichstätt: Polygon-Verl. Buxheim, 1995), 336.

4.
Sambucus to Wolfgang and Georg Kremer[13]
1551, Paris

Dedication in *Epistolarum conscribendarum methodus una cum exemplis incerti autoris, Graece et Latine, in utriusque linguae studiosorum gratiam nunc multo quam antea et emendatior, et locupletior edita. Ioanni Sambuco Pannone Tirnaviensi interprete. Item Ἐπιστολικοὶ τύποι, hoc est Epistolarum formae quasi figuris designatae. Libellus plane aureus, nunc primum ab eodem Ioanni Sambuco de Graeco Latinus factus. Adiecimus et aliorum de scribendis epistolis libellos* (Basel: Johannes Oporinus, 1552), 3-8. Published in *Humanistes du bassin des Carpates II. Johannes Sambucus*, 17-20.

5.
Sambucus to the sons of Ferenc Révay[14]
1552, Paris

Dedication in *Epistolarum conscribendarum methodus* (as in the previous letter), 28-29. Published in *Humanistes du bassin des Carpates II. Johannes Sambucus*, 20-21.

6.
Sambucus to Archduke Maximilian, Elected King of Bohemia
1 February 1552, Dole

Dedication in Johannes Huttichius, *Romanorum principum effigies: cum historiarum annotatione, olim ab Io. Hutichio confecta: nunc vero alicubi aucta et longe castigatiora opera Ioanni Sambuci Tirnaviensis Pannonii. Quae tertiae, huic editioni accesserint versa pagina indicat. Cum gratia et privilegio caesareo* (Strasbourg: Wolfgang Köpfel, 1552), f. 2ʳ-5ᵛ.

---

[13] The Kremers were a Viennese patrician merchant family. Wolfgang and Georg were brothers, the sons of Wolfgang Sr., who worked as an agent of the Herwart family of Augsburg. The brothers matriculated at Wittenberg (1545), Padua (1552) and Vienna (1556). In 1559 Gabriel and Georg Kremer bought a coat of arms in Orléans. See Otto Titan von Hefner, *Bürgerliches Wappenbuch, Bürgerliche* (Nürnberg, Bauer et Ruspe, 1857), t. 5: *Die Wappen bürgerlicher Geschlechter Deutschlands und der Schweiz*, 1ˢᵗ part, p. 10, table 7; Matschinegg, *Österreicher als Universitätsbesucher in Italien*, 265, 267; Attila Tózsa-Rigó, "Bécsi kereskedők keleti irányú kapcsolatrendszere és pozsonyi partnerei a 16. században" [The eastern network and Pressburg partners of Viennese merchants in the sixteenth century], in *A történettudomány szolgálatában. Tanulmányok a 70 éves Gecsényi Lajos tiszteletére*, eds. Magdolna Baráth and Antal Molnár (Budapest–Győr: MOL, 2012), 325-345.

[14] The dedicatees were János Révay (Réwai) (c. 1530–c. 1571) and Lőrinc Révay (Réwai) (c. 1532–?). Their father Ferenc Révay (Réwai) (1489–1553) had a high political office in Hungary: he was deputy palatine (1542–1553). He had all his sons educated in Padua (1546–1553). Their tutor was Sigismundus Torda Gelous, who possibly already knew Sambucus at the time. It is curious that Sambucus dedicated this preface to the Révay sons, if they were in far-away Padua; the dedication suggests that they were in Paris in 1552. See Vilmos Frankl (Fraknói), "Réwai Ferencz nádori helytartó fiainak hazai és külföldi iskoláztatása," *Értekezések a történeti tudományok köréből* 2 (1872–73), part 6. On the political career of the Révays see Géza Pálffy, "Különleges úton a Magyar Királyság arisztokráciájába: a Révay család a 16. században" [A special path into the aristocracy of Hungary: the Révay family in the 16th c.], *Történelmi Szemle* 51,1 (2009), 1-20.

As a prince, Maximilian should reflect on the example of Scipio and other forerunners, who learned a great deal from history. Relying on prudence and the knowledge of former examples, he should know how to anticipate or deflect misfortune. He should especially reflect on the living examples of his uncle Charles V and his father Ferdinand. While reading Homer, Alexander the Great did the same (according to Demetrius Phalereus), but there are also the examples of Scipio (as told by Diodorus Siculus), Antonius Severus, Proxenus (who took Xenophon's advice), who diligently consulted historical works, and Sambucus adds several other examples. Even the emperors are much poorer without the knowledge of historical examples, which they can best gather from old books. However, since they do not have time to read sufficiently, it is praiseworthy if others prepare short summaries of historical learning for them. A great master of this art was Johannes Huttichius, who eagerly studied antiquity and diligently grasped the images of Roman emperors, from Julius Caesar to Ferdinand. Sambucus sends Huttich's work to Maximilian in a corrected version, as he wanted the third edition of the book to come out in his honour so that Maximilian could understand his eagerness and the hope Sambucus has put in him. The Hungarian estates also cherish great hopes with regards to Maximilian's future military activity against the Turks, especially since he himself actively requested to take over the political leadership in the country. He can achieve more when consulting these kinds of texts and learning from the virtues and vices of others. Succouring Hungary and liberating its occupied parts is a great responsibility for Maximilian. Sambucus finally asks Maximilian to accept his family among his clients. They are threatened by Turkish attacks. He promises works of greater value, but Maximilian should also make sure to have more stories to be remembered about him. Maximilian should fear God as if he were Ajax.

Maximiliano regi Bohemiae, archiducique Austriae,[15] Iohannes Sambucus Tirnaviensis Pannonius salutem.

Quod Scipionem fecisse legimus, Maximiliane Rex, bonique omnes faciunt, omnino idem tibi faciendum cogitato. Is enim quoties praeclaris animi dotibus celebritateque illa virtutum aliquid posterorum comendatione dignum moliebatur, intueri in veterum imagines solebat, praesertim eorum, qui nomen insequenti excipiendum memoria sibi constituissent. Nempe ea vestigia persequenda, Princeps, quibus cum laude conatus fortium assequaris atque etiam fortunae vim iniquam prudentia exemplorumque perspicientia vel antevertere possis, vel declinare. Est profecto vis quaedam tacita exemplorum iam antegressorum, qua commoveri debeant principes viri. Et est, Maximiliane Illustrissime, cur hanc tu prae caeteris voluntatem in historias modo susceptam constantem habeas atque comprobes, et usque eo, ut, si vel hanc minimam cohortationem admittas, navasse iam te operam valde tibi persuasum esse velim.

Etenim res maiorum tuorum gestae memoriam tibi commovere debent, imprimis, qui nondum vitam edidere, patrui Caroli Quinti et parentis Ferdinandi.[16] Qui ipsi hactenus per omnem vitam a rebus gestis invictos se praestiterunt, opibus et gloria floruerunt. Quorum quidem ego nihil neque de clementia, neque singulari fortunae afflatu hoc tempore dicam, quod et praesentes adhuc intueris, et in memoriam cunctorum, quae ab illis gloriose aut

---

[15] Sambucus's decision to dedicate a book to Archduke Maximilian (1527–1576), the eldest son of Ferdinand I King of Hungary and Bohemia (1503–1564), was a most timely gesture, since Maximilian (accompanied by the famous elephant Soliman) was on his way back to Vienna from Spain, where he had spent some years pursuing study, and he was eager to take part in politics. On the early years of his life see Holtzmann, *Kaiser Maximilian*.

[16] Emperor Charles V (1500–1558) and his brother Ferdinand I, King of Hungary and Bohemia (1503–1564).

incaepta sunt, aut confecta, utilem ac iucundam venire potes. Tantum dico, te videre et quidem unum omnium optime animadvertere, vel quam sint illi polyhistores, vel quantopere secum illos complectantur, qui memoriter egregie facta apud eos commemorant. Factitabat idem Alexander, Homerum legendo, adeoque consuetudine D. Phaleraei.[17] Sed neque secus Scipio, quomodo Diodorus in scriptis reliquit,[18] quotidiana cognitione doctior fiebat. Itemque Antonius Severus,[19] qui antequam quicquam aggrederetur, historicos, velut oracula, consulebat, ut memoria vetera repetendo, quid ex re futurum esset, quid non, illi prenunciarent. Nunc etiam Proxenus memoriter legebat, usu et consuetudine aliis antecedebat, qui Xenophontem in intimis colere συμβούλονque[20] numero habere non dubitavit.[21] Et certe cum consilium per se amplum quiddam est ac sanctum, ut recte ait in Theage Socrates,[22] tum vero illud summum etiam, quod de institutione alicuius vitaeque informatione petitur, sine quo ne Jupiter quidem ipse, si credimus, potest carere. Hinc Achates tribuitur Aeneae[23], habuit enim Achilles Pallada, cuius commoderationi impetus animi submittebat, Socrates suum illum ementitum daemona.[24] Numa suam Aegeriam atque alii aliud numen συμβουλευτικόν[25] habuisse finguntur.[26] Ex quo significatur absque consilio exemplisque adeo bonorum vitam, praesertim qui cum honoribus essent ac summo magistratu, indigam existere ac inopem. Quod ipsum quoniam expeditius est, quam ut egeat demonstratione, sine exemplorum cognitione imperatorum animos fieri minores atque angustiores. Unde, quaeso, haec melius condidiceris ac in usum sevocaveris tuum, quam de veterum libris, res gestas qui literis accurate consignarunt?

Quia vero tibi tuique similibus otium legendi quorumvis annotationes arduis negotiis subtrahitur, vehementer probanda est eorum opera operosa et otium non otiosum, qui ex omni acervo historiarum, quae antiquiora sunt ac potiora, nec ita remota a nostris temporibus, in brevem comprehensionem, velut quasdam tabellas, coniecerunt, ad quas vel principes, gravioribus distenti, oculos tamen atque animum afferre possint. Huius generis vero scriptores συλληπτικοὶ καὶ ἀπομνημονευματικοί,[27] cum multi exstiterunt etiam ab aetate nostra recentes, haud tamen a quoquam id melius praestitum, quam a Ioanne quodam Hutichio, viro, me hercle, diligenti et variae lectionis atque omnis antiquitatis perstudioso. Hic enim principum Romanorum, quod fieri potuit, effigies ab artificibus expressas figuris diligenter curavit atque totius monarchiae huius postremae casus a Iulio Caesare ad patruum usque tuum atque parentem breviter summaque cum arte detexuit.

---

[17] Athenean statesman Demetrius Phalereus (c. 350–c. 280 BC) was also a celebrated philosopher and scholar.
[18] Diodorus Siculus claims that Scipio, while weeping over the destruction of Carthage, quoted Homer. *Bibliotheca historica* 339iii, 23 (fragments).
[19] Antonius Severus, commonly called Caracalla (188–217), was one of the cruellest emperors and a great admirer of Alexander the Great.
[20] advisor
[21] Proxenus of Thebes was an educated soldier, a contemporary and a friend of Xenophon.
[22] The message of Plato's *Theages* is very different and much more ambiguous than Sambucus's interpretation here.
[23] Achates was a close friend of Aeneas, accompanying him throughout his adventures, but we hardly know much about his character.
[24] The embarrassing association between Socrates and Achilles, two greatly different characters, was already made by Plato (*Apologia* 28b-d).
[25] advising
[26] Aegeria is a Latin Goddess of healing, springs, sacred knowledge and inspiration. She was said to have inspired her lover King Numa to reform important religious practices.
[27] of compendia and records

Cuius ego librum, optime Princeps, nunc ad te mitto, non meum quidem illum, sed tamen auctum iam alicubi ac longe castigatiorem a morte autoris. Qua mei studii annotatione tamen diminutum de illius opera nihil volo, nam id quidem per mihi esset iniquum. Sed volui repetitum nunc tertio sub praelum, tua commendatione tuaeque virtutis indicatione divulgari, quo de mea voluntate inter Pannonas reliquos minus gratioso, fortasse infimo quoque tecum constituere possis et quam spem de tuo animo simus ingressi, nec non amabili fortitudinis indole, iam nunc intelligas.[28] Non ita pridem proceribus Ungariae probatissimus populoque gratissimus imperator dictus es, et id adversus hostem Dei atque hominum Thurcam, qui prorupta quadam tyrannide et conscelerato erga pietatem animo est, ingratus de procreatore illo mundi ac religione cultusque in Deum. Quam tu quidem provinciam quando animo alacri propemodum depoposcisti, ingens laetitia et spes omnibus data est, libertatis ab hoste vindicandae.[29] Quod ipsum tu felicius σὺν θεῷ[30] ut perficias, omnino omnis labor huiusmodi scriptis cognoscendis, maioribus etiam delibandis, te poenitere minime debebit, siquidem fortiter factorum atque etiam divinitus institutorum memoria multum profeceris. Laudatione videlicet virtutum excitamur, deformatione viciosorum peneque monstrorum quorundam facile ad emendationem nostrorum comparamur. Ex te autem scire potes vel quantum onus iam tibi incumbat, vel quantum in eam rem conferre debeas, quo inclinatis temporibus Ungariae succurras, labefactatas eius peneque depositas partes praesens subleves ac sustentes. Haec tibi esse studio tametsi non ignorem, verum ut testis et amplificator tuae voluntatis viderer, horum te paucis admonere libuit, nosti enim illud Nasonis:

> Qui monet ut facias, quod iam facis, ille monendo
> laudat et hortatu comprobat acta suo.[31]

Iam vero ego te postremo per eum, qui nos in gratiam reconciliavit sanctissimam Cristum Iesum, per hanc spem nostram de te conceptam, per omnem fortunam oro et obsecro, parentes meos, qui Tirnaviae degunt, meque una in clientelam ut recipias aliquam.[32] Sumus enim expositi quibusvis Thurcarum excursionibus. Ac simul hunc libellum, in quo

---

[28] Sambucus (or Köpfel) attached various other writings to Huttich's work: *De historia Romanorum* by Sextus Rufus, poems on emperors by Jacobus Micyllus, Ursinus Velius, Decimus Magnus Ausonius and Georgius Sabinus (f. 142-206). Earlier editions: J. Huttichius, *Imperatorum Romanorum Libellus. Una cum imaginibus, ad vivam effigiem expressis* (Argentorati: Köpfel, 1526); idem, *Ioannis Huttichii Imperatorum et Caesarum vitae: cum imaginibus ad vivam effigiem expressis* (Argentorati: Köpfel, 1534). Sambucus's decision to edit a corrected version of Johann Huttich's (1480?–1544) numismatic collection reflects his good sense for fashion and his interest in illustrated antiquarian studies. Indeed, the 1550s was the great decade of numismatic publications. Cf. Christian E. Dekesel, "The 'Boom' of Numismatic Publications between 1550 and 1559," in *Wissenschaftsgeschichte der Numismatik*, ed. Rainer Albert (Speyer: Numismatische Ges., 1995), 210-223. Presenting Roman coins with images of emperors with short summaries of their lives was conceived to match the princely habit of keeping numismatic collections and at the same time function as a light, entertaining history.

[29] The Hungarian estates initially put a great deal of trust in Maximilian, and they demanded that he should at least move to the country, learn their language and represent Ferdinand. As soon as Maximilian returned from Spain, he received from his father operational command in Hungary, but 1552 was a year of major military disasters for Hungary. In 1556, Maximilian became responsible for Habsburg military administration in Hungary but that did not mean that he actually came to Hungary.

[30] with God

[31] Ovidius, *Tristia* 5.14.45-46.

[32] This is Sambucus's first attempt to obtain some form of patronage from the Habsburgs. Cf. with letter 8. Seeing that as a 21-year-old student he had accomplished very little and done no particular service to the dynasty, this appeal may seem somewhat odd. Cf. Almási, *The Uses of Humanism*, 147-148.

constantiae, fortitudinis, aequitatis reperies exempla, clementer excipito interim, dum aliquid ipse elucubrem tuae maiestatis dignum, quodque cum tuis laudibus atque gloria coniunctum sit ac etiam cumulate tuum animum gaudio adficiat.

Interea tu macte animo elabora, ut indies de te plura narrari atque in literas mitti possint, quae ad posterorum cognitionem transmittantur. Ἄλκιμος inquam ἔσσ', ἵνα τίς σε καὶ ὀψιγόνων εὖ εἴπῃ[33] verum est enim Μικροῦ δ' ἀγῶνος, οὐ μεγ' ἔρχεται κλέος.[34] Ac perpetuo memineris illius Aristotelis: Δεῖ τοὺς νοῦν ἔχοντας τῶν δυναστευόντων μὴ διὰ τὰς ἀρχὰς, ἀλλὰ διὰ τὰς ἀρετὰς θαυμάζεσθαι, ἵνα τῆς τύχης μεταπεσούσης τῶν αὐτῶν ἀξιῶνται.[35] Vale sisque commendatus omnipotenti Deo, quem nisi secus, quam Aiax ille metueris, nisique omnem spem in eum contuleris, habere adiutorem non poteris. Dolae Burgundionum, Calendis Februarii 1552.

7.
Sambucus to Georg von Pappenheim
1 January 1553, Ingolstadt

Dedication in Johannes Sambucus, *In Christi natalem oratio Ioannis Sambuci Pannonii, habita Ingolstadii tertio et quinquagesimo anno ineunte. Eiusdem sententiae aliquot hymni eodem autore* (Augsburg: Philippus Ulhardus, 1553), f. Ai^r-Aii^v.

Bishop Pappenheim should understand that this dedication expresses Sambucus's high opinion of men who are animated by religious zeal. Sambucus had already heard about this zeal for religious amendment some years before from a fellow citizen called Delicasius, and he highly praises it and promises to come up with more serious works in honour of Pappenheim. Sambucus encourages Pappenheim to stay loyal to his office and not to follow those who lead people astray, which, he knows, will not happen in his bishopric. The bishop should receive his immature oration on Christ's birth and the attached poems as sign of his love of and respect for his virtues and office. Sambucus promises to dedicate more serious writings to the bishop in the future.

Amplissimo religiosissimoque principi, domino Georgio a Papenhaim,[36] Ratisponensi antistiti, Ioannes Sambucus S. D.

Mitto tibi, quam nuper pro celebri scholae huius conventu habui, orationem meam, ut, quid de eorum amore sentiam, qui religionis, virtutumque amore non solum tenentur, sed exolendos etiam se his praecipue dederunt, cum animo tuo cogites, quaeque adeo passim de te dicantur, iam intelligas. Neque vero, Amplissime Pontifex, eo hanc lucubrationem apparere in tuo nomine volui, quia putarim huiusmodi esse, quae gratiam mihi tuam adiungere posset, verum ad patrocinium niti me tuum singularis humanitatis omnisque vitae tuae commendatione,

---

[33] Be brave, so that even someone of those born later may praise you. *Odyssea* 1.302.
[34] Minor works are not followed by great splendour. Sophocles, frg. 938.
[35] Those among the rulers who have wisdom should be admired not because of the rule, but because of the virtues, so that when their fate undergoes a change they are deemed worthy [of praise]. Sambucus leaves out the word ἐγκωμίων (of praise). The sentence is ascribed to Aristotle by Strabo, *Florilegium* 45.18.
[36] Georg Marschalk von Pappenheim, Bishop of Regensburg (1548–1563) was a zealous Catholic, whose rule met with resistance in the city. Josef Staber, *Kirchengeschichte des Bistums Regensburg* (Regensburg: Habbel, 1966), 119-123.

velim tibi persuadeas. Cum enim ante annos aliquot, ex doctore Delicasio,[37] cive propemodum meo, de constantia tui animi deque religionis ipsius emendatione cogitationes atque omnis disciplinae Christianae intellexerim, tum vero cotidie audio, quam vehementer doleas διὰ τὴν νῦν ἐπιπολάζουσαν κακοπραγμοσύνην καὶ τὸ κακομηχανεῖν περὶ πάντα,[38] teque in primis in coniunctionem attrahi moeroris, satis animadverto. Οὐδὲν γὰρ ἴχνος λείπεται παρ' ἡμῖν τῆς ἀρχαίας πιστότητος,[39] ut ait Polybius. Quam voluntatem tuam, utinam, omnes qui ad hos dignitatis gradus evocati sunt, prompte susciperent vellentque eandem rebus communibus navare benevolentiam, dolorem extinctae pietati praestare. Non dubitarem sane religionis vulnera moresque vitiosos brevi sanari posse. Quo de tenebris emersa veritas, se ad frugem, ut aiunt, pristinam tandem reciperet. Atqui de his pluribus tecum ut agam, neque tempus, neque ipsa occasio permittit. Quando enim ipsum munus per est exiguum, si copiose animi mei significationem verbis testarer, tuarumque laudum praedicationem instituerem: in vitio poneretur, ac parum a me cogitato factum id nonnullis posset videri. Cum praesertim alias hoc sim facturus, cum lautius aliquid cum nominis tui commemoratione, in vulgus proficiscetur. Etenim constitutum habeo aliquid ornatius edere, cum annotatione tui officii, ut amore tibi atque observantia mea utcumque satis fiat.

Tu vero sanctissimo tuo ne desis officio, etiam atque etiam te vehementer oro et obtestor: nec eorum vestigia persequitor, quibus non solum non excubat cogitatio sibi creditorum, sed etiam venatorum more, ut psalmographus ait, retia explicant, suos ut excipiant, atque adeo ob suam voluptuariam vitam, comprehensos in aeternum interitum coniiciunt. Quod ipsum in tua gubernatione, Praesul, ne accideret, egregie hactenus abs te procuratum est. Atque de his rebus, D. Delicasius, vir, ut, quod sentio, dicam, et morum commoderatione amabilis atque idem iuris elegantiorisque litteraturae doctissimus, mecum communicavit.

Quem ego hominem, quia scribendi genus non barbarum, sed purum, sed prudens complexus est, ita charum habeo, ut amore, cui concessurus sim, ex omnibus habiturus sit ille neminem. Hanc vero tu praeclaram episcopatus commendationem ut retineas, tuaeque severae vocationis ut semper commemineris, per Deum, provideto. Postremo illud est, quod te rogem, ut partim virtutibus atque tuae functioni, a qua argumentum hoc non est alienum, partim amori erga te meo, tribuas, quod tibi offerram cognoscendam in Christi natalem orationem meam hanc puerilem. Cui etiam odas aliquot a me confectas, ut adiungi patiare, plane te rogo. Si meum hoc studium probari tibi videro, dabo operam, et fortassis diligentia consequar, ut plura tibi dedicata facile et grate ferre possis. Vale, optime Antistes, et Sambucum una cum oratione, non quidem illa eleganti, accommodata tamen ad religionis sapientiam, in clientelam suscipito. Ingolstadii ex aedibus Apianis.[40] Ipsis Calendis Ianuarii. Anno 1553.

---

[37] Sambucus refers here to a certain Hungarian Johannes Delicasius, hardly mentioned in literary histories. He may be the same Delicasius, "utriusque iuris doctor," who worked as vicar-general in the bishopric of Regensburg. Cf. *Die Urkunden-Regesten des Kollegiatstiftes U. L. Frau zur Alten Kapelle in Regensburg*, ed. Joseph Schmid (Regensburg: J. Habbel, 1912), 2:103 and 137.

[38] (You grieve) about the present prevalence of treachery and mischief in everything. Cf. Polybius, *Historiae* 13.3.1-2.

[39] because there is no trace of the ancient honesty among us

[40] Interrupting his journey from France back to Hungary, Sambucus spent Christmas and probably much of 1552 in the Apianus' house, where he earlier had studied. See letter 2, note 11; letter 3; and letter 52, note .

8.
Sambucus to Archduke Maximilian, Elected King of Bohemia
[Spring 1553], [Vienna]

The original is preserved in Hugo Blotius's collection of letters in Vienna, ÖNB, Cod. 9737^{z14-18}, V, f. 324^{r-v}.

With reference to his needs, Maximilian's benevolence towards learned men, the book on emperors that he dedicated to the archduke, the coloured manuscript on Aristotle's ethics that he gave him as a gift, Sambucus asks for patronage in the form of a life-pension of an annual sum of 50 Hungarian golden florins and membership in the group of aulae familiares. This would allow him to continue with his engaged search for old manuscripts and Hungarian histories and would serve the good fame of Maximilian through the works he would publish.

Serenissime Rex Maximiliane, domine, domine mihi semper clementissime.

Cum necessitas ipsa, tum vero humanitas ista regia et clemens erga doctos voluntas et antiquitatis studiosos fecit, ut vestram serenitatem supplex pro subsidio meorumque conatuum accederem tutela. Quo sim in antiquis codicibus colligendis et patriae chronistis conquirendis animo, in libro de imperatoribus vestrae serenitati dedicato et nuper Ethicorum illo picto volumine oblato ex parte significavi.[41] Quare ne rebus necessariis ad vitam procurandis in hoc libero fervore et ociolo abducar, supplico vestrae serenitati, dignetur liberalitate atque clementia laboribus meis gratiose succurrere, adeoque durante vita quotannis 50 aureis Ungaricis providere.[42] Quam ego iam dudum celebrem apud omnes clementiam vestram perpetua praedicatione et publica semper scriptorum meorum digna memoria tuebor. Itemque ut me suis aulicis et familiaribus domesticis anumerari faciat, supplico. Gratiosissimum responsum a vestra serenitate expecto meque totum commendo etc. Vestrae serenitatis infimus cliens, Ioannes Sambucus Tirnaviensis.

Verso (Sambucus's hand): Humilima supplicatio Ioannis Sambuci Tirnaviensis Pannonii. Supplicat vestrae serenitati is, qui librum *De imperatoribus vestrae* serenitati dedicaverat et nuper volumen illud *Ethicorum* pictum obtulit, ut, quoniam antiquis libris conquirendis et patriae chronicis edendis incumbit, dignetur, quo omnia melius fiant, sibi providere vestra serenitas in vita quotannis 50 aureis Ungaricis, deinde ut inter aulicos vestrae serenitatis recipiatur.

---

[41] The gift volume in question is most probably *Ethica ad Nicomachum* by Aristotle (Vienna, ÖNB, Cod. Phil. gr. 4), which contains ten miniatures and which Sambucus must have given to Maximilian upon his arrival in Vienna (*nuper*). For the dedicated book (Huttichius's *Romanorum principum effigies*), see letter 6. As it appears from letter 17, Sambucus was later convinced that the book, dedicated to Maximilian still in Dole, was not presented to Maximilian by the friends to whom he had entrusted it. If this is true, Maximilian could not really have had any idea what Sambucus was talking about in this letter. Still, the fact that this letter was preserved among Blotius's manuscripts (which means it ended up in Maximilian's library) might suggest that Maximilian read the letter and connected it with Sambucus's activity as a publisher and book collector (and perhaps even with Huttichius's volume).

[42] This letter (like the analogous letters 17 and 18) was unknown to previous research on Sambucus's court career (cf. Almási, *The Uses of Humanism*, 147-151). Curiously, in late 1557, Sambucus received exactly what he requested in this letter.

9.
Sambucus to István Dobó
13 September 1553, Vienna

Dedication in Johannes Sambucus, *De rebus ad Agriam gestis, Anno M. D. LII. narratio*, which first appeared as an attachment to Petrus Ransanus, *Epitome rerum Ungaricarum*, f. a^v.

Tinódi Sebestyén presented this story (of the battle of Eger) in Hungarian verses to King Ferdinand. The king wanted to read it in Latin and commissioned Sambucus to translate it. Partly trimming it, partly changing and restructuring it, Sambucus finished the job in a few days and dedicated it to Dobó, as the triumph over the enemy forces was his merit, the memory of which will survive through this narration.

Magnifico heroi, domino Stephano Dobo de Ruzka, Transylvanorum vayvodae etc.[43] Ioannes Sambucus S. D.

Historiam hanc Ferdinando regi et aliis cum Sebastianus Thinodii[44] Ungaricis descriptam rythmis exhibuisset, eamque rex commendari vidisset, Latinam cognoscere voluit.[45] Quod negocium mihi datum, quibusdaqm partim resectis ac immutatis, partim commodius dispositis, ut veritas et locus monebant, intra paucos dies, ut potui, totum absolvi. Ac quoniam res tua potissimum industria et virtute administrata est, libellum tibi dicavi, ut, cuius fortitudine ac felicitate cuncta prospere successerunt, eiusdem laus et memoria cum ipsa narratione semper extaret. Tu hanc operam boni consule, atque Transylvaniam satis mobilem et quae longe ampliorem aliquando scribendi materiam suppeditabit, feliciter gubernes. Vale. Viennae Idibus Septembris. MDLIII.

10.
Sambucus to Georgius Bona and Nicolaus Istvánffy
1 February 1555, Padua

Dedication in Sambucus, *Poemata*, 2-3.

---

[43] The heroic defence of the castle of Eger against the Ottomans in 1552 was immortalised by the famous historical novel *Eclipse of the Crescent Moon* by Géza Gárdonyi. The captain of the castle, István Dobó (1502–1572), was richly rewarded for his resolute command by Ferdinand I, but later his son Maximilian II accused Dobó of conspiracy and had him imprisoned.

[44] Sebestyén Tinódi Lantos (c. 1510–1556) is the most famous popular lyricist and minstrel of sixteenth-century Hungary, who commemorated several battles of his time. On Tinódi see Béla Varjas, "Tinódi politikai pártállása" [The political stance of Tinódi], in *Irodalom és ideológia a 16–17. században*, ed. Béla Varjas (Budapest: Akadémia, 1987), 91-112; Péter Király, *A lantjáték Magyarországon a XV. századtól a XVII. század közepéig* [Lute playing in Hungary in 15-17th centuries] (Budapest: Balassi, 1995); *Tinódi Sebestyén és a régi magyar verses epika* [Sebestyén Tinódi and old Hungarian epic poetry], ed. István Csörsz Rumen (Kolozsvár: Kriterion, 2008); Pál Ács, "Tinódi Sebestyén és Bornemissza Gergely," *Hadtörténelmi közlemények* 122,2 (2009), 477-486; and see the article by Dávid Molnár in *Companion*.

[45] Tinódi must have presented the work to King Ferdinand on the occasion of his ennoblement on 25 August 1553. Apparently, Sambucus received the commission (either directly or indirectly) from Ferdinand pretty quickly. By 13 September he was ready with the Latin prose rendering of Tinódi's poem. On later variations made by Tinódi see the study by Gyöngyi Domokos in *Tinódi Sebestyén* (as in the preceding note 44), 55-77.

Sambucus could not say no to the enthusiasm of Georgius Bona and Nicolaus Istvánffy, who also helped him put together this volume of poetry, adding also some of their poems. Although he has never thought to publish his poetry, it may be useful for them and may encourage them to pursue similar efforts, as they have already started offering their poems to Sambucus. The book will be a testimony to Sambucus's benevolence towards them, to which they always have loyally responded. Nicolaus Olahus should make sure that they keep dedicating themselves to studies and discipline. Sambucus promises the publication of other works: a volume of Greek epithets, considerations about Ciceronian imitation, and translations of Plato.

Ingeniosis et natura modestis Georgio Bona[46] et Nicolao Istvanfy,[47] nobilissimis adolescentibus Sambucus S. D.

Habetis vulgo, vestris quod studiis negare minime potui. Quos enim dissolutos versus proposui vosque magna ex parte coniunxistis, eos cum aliis notatione publica communicamus adeoque etiam vestros aliquot adiunximus.[48] Et quamvis nihil minus fore unquam putavi, quam ista aliquando lectione omnium posse cognosci, quia tamen id a me spe impetrandi contendistis, morem gessi mihi quidem non difficilem, vobis certe quidem etiam utilem. Cum enim cognita omni syllabarum varietate atque versuum adeo generibus de vestro mihi iam quiddam offerre coeperitis, hac voluntate vobis accommodata, in hoc ipso cursu retinendos esse vos censui, et me hercule, excitandos. Idque hoc adeo, ut, quemadmodum conamini propediem simile quiddam elucubrare, sic memoriam vestrorum lusuum gratam hoc modo praeberem. Nec vero minus incredibilis erga vos benevolentiae testes has fore pagellas arbitror, qui amori diligentiaeque vobis navatae, constanter adhuc quidem respondistis. Quod ipsum ut perpetuo extet, dum aetas hisce collocanda studiis fuerit, reverendissimus archiepiscopus Strigoniensis D. Nicolaus Olahus vos commovere debet.[49] Qui, ne quicquam optimarum

---

[46] György (Georgius) Bona (1539–1559) was the talented nephew of the erudite archbishop Nicolaus Olahus (see the next letter). As Sambucus's pupil, Bona stayed in Italy until 1558. He returned to Hungary with Sambucus, but soon died, though he was still a young man. Upon his death Sambucus wrote the following words on Bona: "Georgio Bona Civiensi, Transylvano, pietate constantissima, religione non aliena, conscientia sana, incredibili ut ingenii, sensu erga omnes probo, mirifica prudentia, moribus egregiis, famae celebritate vel absentibus noto, maximi afflicti regni suorumque spei adolescenti, qui Italia, Germania Boemiaque perlustratis, celeriter se in gratiam Ferdinandi caesaris, labenti ut patriae, omnibus bonis prodesset, contulerat suosque illustraret." J. Sambucus, *Oratio in obitum ... Georgii Bona* (Patavii: G. Perchacinus, 1560), f. B2ʳ. See the article by Gábor Almási in *Companion*. Cf. letter 22, note 77.

[47] Nicolaus (Miklós) Istvánffy (1538–1615) came from a learned noble family. After his studies in Italy, where he was tutored by Sambucus until 1556, he served briefly as secretary to Olahus. He was then employed by the Hungarian Chamber. He became royal councillor and vice-palatine, which was among the highest positions in Hungary. He was a prolific Latin poet, famous for having written the history of his century in elegant Latin prose (Isthvanfius, *Historiarum de rebus Ungaricis libri XXXIV*), which remained for centuries the most widely read history of the epoch. On Istvánffy see Gábor Nagy, "'Tu patriae, illa tuis vivet in historiis.' Előkészület egy új Isthvánffi Miklós életrajzhoz" [Contributions to a new biography of Miklós Istvánffy], *Századok* 142 (2008), 1209-1248; Zoltán Csehy, "Vita pubblica e vita privata negli epitaffi di Miklós Istvánffy," in *Vita pubblica e vita privata nel Rinascimento*, ed. Luisa Secchi Tarugi (Florence: Franco Cesati Editore, 2010), 285-293; idem, "Militiae Martisque decus. Adalékok Istvánffy Miklós történelmi tárgyú epitáfiumainak szövegmintázataihoz" [On the textuality of Miklós Istvánffy's epitaphs on military subjects], in *Humanista történetírás*, 57-65; *"A magyar történet folytatója"* and the article by Gábor Nagy in *Companion*.

[48] Sambucus inserted poems by Istvánffy and Bona on f. 9-10. The volume is introduced by Lotichius Secundus's poem to Sambucus, and the first poem by Sambucus is addressed to Nicolaus Olahus.

[49] Nicolaus Olahus (1491–1568) was an outstanding learned man and probably the most significant patron of sixteenth-century humanists in Hungary. As a member of the clergy, he had an exceptional career in the service of the Habsburg dynasty. Born in Transylvania to a distinguished Romanian father and a Hungarian mother, he

artium studiis constituendis morataeque disciplinae in vobis desit, amabili sua gratia perficit. Cui quidem vestra ut diligentia itemque mihi, ex altera quasi parte, respondeat, providete, quaeso. Atque his contenti nunc sitis, donec operosum illud Graecorum epithetorum volumen, item de imitatione Ciceroniana cogitationes atque etiam sermones aliquot Platonis mea interpretatione factos Romanos publice conspiciatis.[50] Idque ipsum vos brevi habituros minime omnium ignoratis. Valete. Patavii Kalendis Februarii. 1555.

11.
Sambucus to Nicolaus Olahus
1 August 1555, Padua

Dedication in Nilus [Cabasilas], *Nili patris sancti et archiepiscopi Constantinopolitani illius misericordis Oratio ad Deum contra barbarorum incursiones, bella intestina, pestem, famem ac mortis vim praesentem*. Ioanne Sambuco Pannonio Tirnaviensi interprete (Patavii: [Gratiosus Perchacinus], 1555), [Ai^v] Published in *Humanistes du bassin des Carpates II. Johannes Sambucus*, 23-25.

12.
[Caspar Nidbruck[51]] to Sambucus
7 September 1555, Augsburg

A copy of the letter is kept in Vienna, ÖNB, Cod. 9386, f. 5.

---

was educated in episcopal courts and remained in the service of Queen Mary of Hungary after the tragic Battle of Mohács (1526). He followed Mary to Brussels as her secretary and returned to Hungary only in c. 1540, when his career began to take off at a rapid pace. By the end of his life, he was the most powerful politician in the country. As a humanist, Olahus put together a manuscript volume of poems and produced a famous chorography of Hungary and a history of Attila. In Flanders, he entered into regular correspondence with Erasmus. As the uncle of Georgius Bona, he was Sambucus's most important patron in 1553–1558. See Birnbaum, *Humanists in a Shattered World*, 125-167; Cristina Neagu, *Servant of the Renaissance: The Poetry and Prose of Nicolaus Olahus* (Bern–Oxford: Peter Lang, 2003); István Fazekas, "Miklós Oláh, Secretary to Queen Mary of Hungary, 1526–1539," in Orsolya Réthelyi et al., eds., *Mary of Hungary, the Queen and Her Court 1521–1531* (Budapest: Budapest History Museum, 2005), 41-48; Emőke Rita Szilágyi, "Epistolae familiares – baráti (?) levelek. Oláh Miklós barátai levelezése tükrében" [Epistolae familiares – friendly (?) letters in the correspondence of Nicolaus Olahus], in *MONOKgrahia. Tanulmányok Monok István 60. születésnapjára*, eds. Judit Nyerges et al. (Budapest: Kossuth, 2016), 668-672; Nicolaus Olahus, *Epistulae. Pars I: 1523–1533* and *Pars II: 1534–1553* ed. Emőke Rita Szilágyi (Budapest: Reciti, 2018, 2022); and the article by Áron Orbán in *Companion*.

50   Sambucus's work on Greek epithets was apparently never completed (cf. with letters 92, 111 and 241 and see the index). In his *De imitatione ciceroniana dialogi tres* (see letter 22), one of the speakers was actually the young Bona. For his translations of Plato see letter 19.

51   This manuscript codex of Hugo Blotius (ÖNB, Cod. 9386) contains letters by various authors; this one (although lacking any indication concerning its author) has been rightly catalogued as written by Nidbruck. The item in Blotius's codex preceding this letter is also by the same author. Caspar Nidbruck (Kaspar von Ni(e)dbruck, 1525–1557) was an erudite, committed Protestant councillor to both Archduke Maximilian and King Ferdinand. He studied in Orleans, Strasbourg (with Calvin) and Wittenberg (with Melanchthon) and ultimately earned a Doctor of Law degree in Italy. During the five years when he served the Austrian Habsburgs, he took part in numerous highly important diplomatic missions (in preparation to the Imperial Diets), and he established contacts with many of the most significant Protestant learned men.

From a letter of Georg Tanner Nidbruck has understood that Sambucus was a lover of antiquity. He is asking Sambucus with reference to the duties of friendship (although they do not know each other, even if Nidbruck seems to remember to have seen Sambucus in Vienna) to convey his letters addressed to Tanner, including the present one. Nidbruck wants to have a frequent correspondent with Sambucus, and keep up friendly relations with him through the letters. During the diets of Pressburg and Sopron he made some Hungarian friends, like Sigismundus Torda. He now asks Sambucus to enter into correspondence with him on classical authors (i.e. manuscripts) that Sambucus may find in Italy, and replace Tanner in this role when he will not be there any longer. He offers to be a contact person at court.

Salutem plurimam.

Ex literis domini Georgii Tanneri[52] amici mei charissimi intellexi te antiquitatis secum perstudiosum esse, et si quid in posterum ad ipsum velim, id tibi transmitterem. Quapropter te rogatum volo, ut hasce ad ipsum non gravatim cures perferri. Impono tibi hoc amici officium, licet ignotus, in tui gratiam non minus facturus. Nam docti et pii viri mihi sunt prae caeteris omnibus longe charissimi. In horum numerum te quoque ex commendatione Tanneri adscribam, et si recte memini, Viennae te vidi. Utcunque neuter memor sit, in posterum tamen crebra literarum transmissione amicitiam colemus. Cum domino Sigismundo Geloo,[53]

During his travels, he searched through plentiful libraries, made significant discoveries, encouraged the bibliophile activity of men like Augerius Busbequius and Sambucus and vigorously supported the publication project of the Magdeburg Centuries. He also left behind some legal commentaries and indices for the study of Greek. His correspondence is well preserved in ÖNB, Cod. 9737i–k and 10364. On Nidbruck see Robert Holtzmann's article in *ADB* 52 (1906), 621-629; Luka Ilić, "Calvin, Flaccius, Nidbruck, and Lutheran Historiography," in *Calvinus Pastor Ecclesiae: Papers of the Eleventh International Congress on Calvin Research*, eds. Herman J. Selderhuis and Arnold Huijgen (Göttingen: Vandenhoeck & Ruprecht, 2016), 319-332.

[52] Nidbruck contacted Tanner through a mutual friend named Bonifacius Amerbach. Georg Tanner (1518–1583?) was a humanist scholar, jurist and later professor of Greek at the University of Vienna. He studied in Padua from 1552 and pursued archival research, mainly in Venice. He probably remained a life-long friend of Sambucus's (they also lived in the same street in Vienna), but the sources offer few indications of their relationship. At the end of 1551 or the beginning of 1552, Tanner (and maybe also Sambucus) was still in Strasbourg, from where Tanner, at the encouragement of the young Sambucus, sent some manuscripts to Oporinus in Basel. In 1551, Sambucus dedicated his *Epistolarum conscribendarum methodus* to Tanner's private students, the Viennese Wolfgang and Georg Kremer (see letter 4). See also Tanner's letter of 22 January 1566 to Basil Amerbach in *Briefe an Bonifacius und Basilius Amerbach 1554–67*, ed. Roderich v. Stintzing (Bonn: Adolf Marcus, 1879), 64. On Tanner see Franz Gall, "Georg Tanner. Ein Waldviertler Gelehrter des 16. Jahrhunderts," in *Festschrift Franz Loidl zum 65. Geburtstag*, ed. Viktor Flieder (Vienna: Hollinek, 1970), 2:118-131; Viktor Bibl, "Nidbruck und Tanner," *Archiv für österreichische Geschichte* 85 (1898), 379-423. Sambucus dedicated emblem no. 189 in *Emblemata* (1564) to him.

[53] Sigismundus Torda Gelous (Zsigmond Torda Gyalui) (1510?–1567) was born in Transylvania and studied in Krakow, Wittenberg and Padua. In 1546–1551, he served as the tutor to János and Lőrinc Révay in Padua (and a third brother named Mihály), who are the dedicatees of letter 5, the sons of deputy palatine Ferenc Révay. Torda was an outstanding humanist who published some significant editions and also the first Latin translation of Euripides's *Orestes*. Torda finally found employment in the Chambers of Hungary, but he stayed in touch with Melanchthon and Joachim Camerarius. His relationship with Sambucus must have been ambiguous. Some of Sambucus's publishing projects were probably conceived originally by Torda (see *Humanistes du bassin des Carpates II. Johannes Sambucus*, 110-111; Almási, *The Uses of Humanism*, 173-176). When Torda died, Sambucus asked Maximilian II to allow him to inherit some of Torda's possessions, though this request was eventually denied, as Torda had heirs (see letter 265). On Torda's life, see the biography by Ágnes Póka, in *Gyalui Thorda Zsigmond naplója (1558–1568)* [The diary of Gy. T. Zs.], ed. Ágnes Póka (Budapest: Történettudományi Intézet, 2021), 8-40, and the article by Ágnes Póka in *Companion*. See also Miloslav Okál, "La vie et l'ouvre Sigismond Gélous Torda," *Zborník filozofickej fakulty univerzity Komenského*, 6 (1974), 105-155; Tibor Szabó, "Szegedi Kőrös Gáspár a padovai egyetemen" [Gáspár Kőrös at the Univ. of Padua],

item cum aliquot aliis bonis viris in Hungaria intercedit mihi familiaritas. Utpote quae in aula sacrae regiae maiestatis et serenissimi Regis Maximiliani, praeterea in conventibus superioribus Posoniensi anno 52 et Semproniensi 53[54] cum ipsis contracta sit. Tu quoque dignaberis de antiquis autoribus et aliis quae repperies in Italia me certiorem reddere, et rogo ut absente domino Tannero vices eius suppleas crebra literarum scriptione iisque de negotio literario refertissimis. Si vicissim tibi in aula vel etiam amico ob tuam commendationem commodare queam, senties me paratum. Ex inclusa scheda intelliges quo tuas in posterum mittere possis, ut certo reddantur. Vale in domino. Datae Augustae Vindelicorum. 7. Septembris anno 1555.

Address: Ad Ioannem Sambucum Pannonicum de dato 7. Septembris 1559.[55]

13.
Sambucus to Heinrich Stiebar
1 April 1556, Bologna

A copy of the letter is kept in Hamburg, Staats- und Universitätsbibliothek, Sup. ep. (4⁰) 19, f. 5ʳ-6ʳ. Published in Petrus Lotichius Secundus, *Carminum libellus*, ed. Johannes Sambucus (Bologna: Anselmus Giaccaellus, 1556), f. Aiiʳ⁻ᵛ; and Gerstinger, "Die Briefe", 47-48.

Sambucus dedicates the book of poems by Petrus Lotichius Secundus, written in the memory of Daniel Stiebar, to the French knight Heinrich Stiebar von Buttenheim, whom he met in France, and who appreciates the poetical talents of Lotichius. Sambucus confesses to be a lifelong friend and study-partner of Lotichius, who, being feeble and troubled by things in Bologna, could not prepare anything more serious than this book. Sambucus also consoles Heinrich Stiebar over the death of his uncle.

Ioannes Sambucus Tirnaviensis Henrico Stibaro Equiti Franco.[56]

Amicitia iam in Gallia constituta facit, ut non solum te mecum tacitus amem, verum etiam publice compellem huncque libellum tibi commendem.[57] Ac tametsi non ignoro vel quanti tu ingenium poetae cum aliis merito semper feceris, vel quantum ille te diligat, quia tamen

---
    in *Orvostörténeti Közlemények* 141-144 (1993), 53-62. A letter between Nidbruck and Torda is preserved in ÖNB, Cod. 10364.
[54] Nidbruck refers here to the diets in Pressburg and Sopron.
[55] The address is written by another hand.
[56] Little is known about Heinrich Stiebar von Buttenheim. He may have been the son of Paulus Stiebar von Buttenheim, canon of Würzburg. See *Proben des hohen Teütschen Reichs Adels*, ed. Johann Octavier Salver (Wirzburg: Buthor, 1775), 429. It appears from the letter that Heinrich Stiebar had been tutored by Petrus Lotichius Secundus in France (where he first met Sambucus) and was a nephew of Daniel Stiebar, who died the summer before, and whose death appears to have occasioned the publication of Petrus Lotichius Secundus's *Carminum libellus*. The nobleman Daniel Stiebar (1503–1555) was an erudite patron and friend of humanists (particularly of Joachim Camerarius, but also of Erasmus and others) and lived a politically active life as a canon of Würzburg. In 1549 he became an important maecenas of Petrus Lotichius Secundus, who was also friend of Joachim Camerarius. See Adam, *Vitae Germanorum iureconsultorum*, 105-110; Zon, *Petrus Lotichius Secundus*, 159-161, 255-260.
[57] Next to the elegies on Daniel Stiebar's death (also one by Sambucus) Lotichius Secundus's *Carminum libellus* contained poems addressed to Sambucus, Johannes Sturm, Guillaume Rondelet, Georgius Sabinus, Hilarius Cantiuncula and others. It is a monument of the strong friendship between Lotichius and Sambucus.

luctus et doloris publici non modo ille testis esse cupit, sed etiam amplificator atque adeo tutor memoriae in aeterna laude versantis, idcirco cum tuo nomine divulgandas has elegias arbitratus sum, non equidem ut te in lachrymas deducamus, quas recentes et acerbissimas tibi accidisse omnibusque bonis intellego, sed ut exordium testatae et gratiosae voluntatis erga defunctum esse cogitares.[58] Fatetur Lotichius[59] se longo amplius liberalitati et cineribus Danielis Stibari iure debere.[60] Sed cum aliis rebus impeditus, languore et molestia de coelo spirituque Bononiensi contracta nunc praestare maius, quodque mente informarat, non potuit.[61] Cuius rei testem me addo, quem et contubernii pene societas et studiorum omnisque vitae necessitudo illi coniunxit. Itaque patiamini, quaeso, hanc qualemcumque significationem moeroris concedi mortuo, qui ad sempiternam domum discessit. Neque putetis ita satisfactum dolori privato, sed in aliud tempus reservari, quantum quisquam in hanc societatem luctus allaturus unquam est. Vale ereptique patrui mortem aequo animo feras, cuius salus hoc certior est, quod ipsius preces apud eum, qui ultro viam salutis munivit ac ostendit, faciliores semper fuisse credimus. Bononiae Calendis Aprilis, Anno MDLVI. Ioannes Sambucus.

14.

Paolo Manuzio[62] to Sambucus
30 June 1556, Venice

---

[58] Reference is made to the death of Daniel Stibarus, cf. note 56 above.

[59] Petrus Lotichius Secundus (1528–1560) is among the most appreciated Neo-Latin poets. He was born in the Würzburg Diocese, studied with Camerarius in Leipzig and with Melanchthon in Wittenberg and travelled to Paris with Daniel Stiebar in c. 1550. He started studying medicine in Montpellier and continued in Padua and Bologna. For a bibliography see Zon, *Petrus Lotichius Secundus*; *Humanistische Lyrik des sechzehnten Jahrhundert: lateinisch-deutsch*, eds. Wilhelm Kühlmann, Robert Seidel and Hermann Wiegand (Frankfurt: Deutscher Klassiker Verlag, 1997), 113-145. On his relationship to Sambucus see Stephen Zon, *Petrus Lotichius Secundus*, 146-147, 298-304; Almási, *The Uses of Humanism*, 211-212. Lotichius addressed several poems to Sambucus. See *Carm.* I, 19; *Eleg.* II, 5 and III, 9, in Petrus Lotichius Secundus, *Poemata omnia*, ed. Peter Burman (Amstelaedami: Schouten, 1754), 3:109-116; 228. Manuscript poems between the two friends can be found in Vienna, ÖNB, Cod. 9977, f. 18ʳ-19ᵛ; Cod. 9737i, f. 3. Also see Sambucus's epitaphium on Lotichius's death, which he included into his *Emblemata* (1564): no. 194. They met each other first most probably in Wittenberg in 1546. In 1550 they met again in Paris and probably stayed more or less together until November 1551, when Lotichius (only a month later than Carolus Clusius) enrolled at the University of Montpellier to study medicine. Unlike Sambucus, Lotichius obtained a degree in medicine the next month (probably still in Bologna, where it was cheaper), and his example may have motivated Sambucus to take a similar path from 1555.

[60] Cf. note 56 above.

[61] Lotichius was presumably poisoned in Bologna. His health deteriorated and he never fully recovered. Sambucus was apparently the person closest to him at the time. Lotichius addressed a beautiful poem to Sambucus bidding him farewell and declaring his intention to leave his possessions to Sambucus (*Eleg.* III, 9).

[62] Paolo Manuzio (1512–1574), the third son of Aldo Manuzio, took over the Aldine press in the 1530s. Paolo's son Aldo Manuzio Jr. (1547–1597) was to some degree a child prodigy. He was sent to Padua to study with a private tutor in 1556 at the age of nine, where he met Sambucus. On Paolo Manuzio and his family see Emmanuele Antonio Cigogna, *Delle Inscrizioni Veneziane*, vol. 3 (Venezia: G. Orlandelli, 1830), 49-71; Anne Jacobson Schutte, "The Lettere Volgari and the Crisis of Evangelism in Italy," *Renaissance Quarterly* 28 (1975) 639-677; Barberi, *Paolo Manuzio*; Paul F. Grendler, "The Adages of Paolo Manuzio. Erasmus and the Roman Censors," in *In laudem Caroli. Renaissance and Reformation Studies for Charles G. Nauert*, ed. James V. Mehl (Kirksville: Thomas Jefferson University Press, 1998), 1-21; H. George Fletcher, "Paulus Manutius in aedibus populi romani. The campaigne for Rome," in *Aldus Manutius and Renaissance Culture. Essays in memory of Franklin D. Murphy*, ed. David S. Zeidberg (Florence: Olschki, 1998), 287-321; Tiziana Sterza, "Paolo Manuzio," in *DBI* 69 (2007), 250-254. On Aldo Manuzio Jr. see the article by Emilio Russo, in *DBI* 69 (2007), 245-250. On their correspondence see Pastorello, *L'epistolario Manuziano*, 11-20.

Published in Paulus Manutius, *Pauli Manutii epistolarum libri quatuor, eiusdem quae praefationes appellantur* (Venice: Manuzio, 1560), f. 152ʳ-153ʳ.[63]

Paolo Manuzio responds to a letter by Sambucus, in which he praised the talents (i.e. Latin learning) of Manuzio's nine-year-old son Aldo and may also have suggested publishing Aldo's works. Manuzio confirms that he also highly appreciates Sambucus and friendship in general. This can also be testified by Andreas Dudith, who cannot be sufficiently praised. Manuzio alludes to some kind of offer or initiative by Sambucus, of which Andreas Dudith spoke to him three days after Manuzio's visit in Padua.

Sambuco suo, Patavium.

Non mediocre amoris argumentum, quod de filiolo gratularis et sperare te significas, ut patri etiam orationis Latinae facultate antecellat. Quid? Ergo ille tibi magnum videbitur praestare, si opinione et fama nos anteierit eloquentiae? Ego illi, qua primum hora editum in lucem vidi, bonam mentem precatus a Deo sum. Hoc nobis debet esse antiquissimum, et hoc ei si contigerit, reliqua iure contemnet, aut si voluerit, facile consequetur. Mea vero studia si imitabitur, quae certe, quod fateri sine arrogantia possum, ad honestum referuntur. Aditus ad laudem difficiles non habebit, quo mihi studiose contendenti fortuna semper, nescio, quo meo fato, viam interclusit. Verumtamen, mi Sambuce, cum tua tuique similium fruar benevolentia, quid desiderem? Quid potest esse amicitia iucundius? Quid etiam fructuosius? Cum et amant inter se boni viri, et est inter eos quasi certamen amoris et officii. Equidem, de te quid sentiam, si ad te ipsum scribam, certe scio, qui tuus pudor est, legeres invitus. Testem tibi do iudicii mei gravem adolescentem (et adde, si quid vis: nihil enim tribues immerenti) Andream Duditium,[64] quem cognovi tuis laudibus me narrante etiam atque etiam laetari. Quod si tenerem artem eloquentiae, sicuti tu in epistola tua, amore potius in me, quam iudicio effusus existimas, sane coloribus egregiis imaginem tuarum virtutum exprimerem, voluntatem vero illam et praeclaros conatus ad augendas fortunas nostras, de quibus postridie, quam a vobis discessi, quiddam in sermone Duditius significavit, mehercule sic ornarem, ut nihil esse posset illustrius.[65] De quo quia tam amanter cogitasti gratias agerem, et, ut perpetuo cogitares atque ageres cohortarer; si hoc humanitas tua, illud amicitia nostra pateretur. Ut ut autem res ceciderit (a te enim principia sunt, exitum praestare non potes) partes meae non requirentur: prosequar enim vel beneficium laude, vel animum certe tuum memoria sempiterna. Vale. Venetiis.

---

[63] For later editions see Pastorello, *L'epistolario manuziano*, 60.
[64] Andreas Dudith (1533–1589) was one of Hungary's most famous humanists in the sixteenth century. On Dudith, see Pierre Costil, *André Dudith humaniste Hongrois (1533–1589). Sa vie, son oeuvre et ses manuscrits grecs* (Paris: Les Belles-Lettres, 1935); Almási, *The Uses of Humanism* (also on his relationship with Sambucus). Sambucus dedicated an emblem in the *Emblemata* to him (1564), 38. Andreas Dudith's name was signalled with an asterisk in later editions of Manuzio's letters.
[65] Sambucus may have offered his help in publishing Aldo's writings.

15.
Sambucus to Johann Friedrich and Ferdinand Hoffmann[66]
30 June 1556, Padua

Dedication in Hippolytus Thebanus, *Ex opere ipsius chronico de ortu, et cognatione Virginis Mariae libellus*. *Nunc primum et conversus, et in lucem datus per Ioannem Sambucum Tirnaviensem Pannonium* (Patavii: Gratiosus Perchacinus, 1556), f. Aii^{r-v}. Published in *Humanistes du bassin des Carpates II. Johannes Sambucus*, 26-27.

16.
Sambucus to Archduke Maximilian, Elected king of Boemia
15 March 1558, Vienna

Dedication in Ransanus, *Epitome rerum Ungaricarum*, f. A2^r-A3^r. Published in *Humanistes du bassin des Carpates II. Johannes Sambucus*, 27-31.

17.
Sambucus to Archduke Maximilian, Elected king of Boemia
[May–June 1558], [Vienna]

The original is preserved in Hugo Blotius's collection of letters in Vienna, ÖNB, Cod. 9737^{z14-18}, V, f. 326^r-327^v.

Sambucus presents Maximilian a copy of the book (Ransanus's Epitome rerum Ungaricarum*) he edited and enlarged as a sign of his deference (i.e. status as a client). He is very sorry that the book on emperors (Huttichius's* Romanorum principum effigies*), which he had dedicated to Maximilian six years earlier and entrusted to friends (as he had been away from Vienna), was not presented to the king, but he promises shortly to get hold of a copy and give it to him. He informs Maximilian about his return to Italy within ten days, although he will not leave without Maximilian's mandate: if the king wants to use him to purchase codices, he should not forget to give a written statement to that effect. Since the weather is getting hotter, it would be better to leave still in the current month. He places his old books in the power and under the authority of Maximilian.*

Serenissime Rex Maximiliane, domine, domine, mihi semper clementissime etc.

Offero serenitati vestrae hunc librum, opera mea nonnihil auctum et editum, ut obedientiae perpetuae atque studii erga serenitatem vestram debiti significationem.[67] Quem supplico

---

[66] Johann Friedrich (1535–1590) and Ferdinand (1540–1607) Hoffmann zum Grünbühel were Austrian noblemen from Styria studying law at Padua. Both of them followed their father and pursued careers at the imperial court. See Matschinegg, *Österreicher als Universitätsbesucher in Italien*, 428-429; Klaus Eckart Ehrlicher, "Die Hoffmann, Freiherren zu Grünbühel und Strechau," in *Burg Strechau – Glaube und Macht*, ed. Gernot Axmann (Lassing: Gemeinde Lassing, 1992), 79-86. They were also the patrons of Hilarius Cantiuncula's *Hendecasyllaborum liber* (Venetiis: [n.d.], 1555).

[67] See the preceding letter.

clementer a suo cliente accipere dignetur, donec longe maiora serenitati vestrae, si Deus vitam mihi produxerit, exhibeam. Dedicaram serenitati vestrae ante annos sex librum de imperatoribus, sed absente me illum serenitati vestrae non fuisse ab amicis meis exhibitum valde doleo, sed propediem sum exemplaria habiturus ac serenitati vestrae subiectissime daturus.[68] Caeterum serenitas vestra sciat me in Italiam intra decem dies profecturum, quo quia sine mandatis vestris non sum abiturus; sed, se eadem serenitas vestra opera mea in conquirendis manuscriptis codicibus uti dignabitur, religiosa et constanti fide sum eam daturus. Supplico, ut instructionis oblatae quamprimum meminerit.[69] Aestus enim crescent indies molestiae. Satius igitur est, ut hoc mense iter ingrediar. Cui me unice tanquam domino clementissimo fidem meam commendo, Deus eandem serenitatem vestram conservet. Vestrae sacratissimae maiestatis cliens, Ioannes Sambucus.

Meos etiam vetustos libros in potestate ac imperio serenitatis vestrae humilime pono.

Verso (Sambucus's hand): Humilima supplicatio Ioannis Sambuci.

18.
Sambucus to Archduke Maximilian, Elected king of Boemia
[May–June 1558], [Vienna]

The original is preserved in Hugo Blotius's collection of letters in Vienna, ÖNB, Cod. 9737[z14-18], V, f. 323[r-v].

Sambucus recently let Maximilian know that he was going to leave before the summer heat got worse. Now he wants to tell the king again that he is leaving for Italy in a few days. If Maximilian thinks Sambucus's work of purchasing books will be worthy of him, he should promptly order Peter Haller to settle the issue via instructions presented by Sambucus. He pledges to serve with diligence. However, if Maximilian changes his mind or wishes to postpone the business, he should likewise let Sambucus know about it. He has gone through the books held in the library of the college and has taken some notes and given them to Haller.

Serenissime Rex Maximiliane, domine, domine mihi semper clementissime etc.

Nuper etiam serenissimae maiestati vestrae humilime significavi me, ante quam calores sint molestiores, iter ingressurum. Idem nunc etiam serenissimae maiestati vestrae subiectissime perscribendum duxi, intra paucos dies in Italiam profecturum. Quare, si serenissimae maiestati vestrae mea opera in conquirendis libris digna et sufficiens videbitur, quam primum Petro Hallero imperare dignetur, ut secundum instructionem meam exhibitam negocium procuret.[70] Sentiet serenissima maiestas vestra meam debitam et fidelissimam diligentiam,

---

[68] See letter 6 and letter 8, note 41.
[69] Maximilian does not seem to have given Sambucus any written instructions and Sambucus probably remained idle in Vienna until the end of the year. Cf. letters 18-19.
[70] Peter Haller (1490?–1569) was a merchant and entrepreneur from Sibiu (Hermannstadt, Szeben) who had an amazing career both as a businessman and a public servant in a great number of prestigious positions. In 1557, he became the Saxon count, and held this highest position in the Transylvanian German "nation"

nulla ex parte defuturam. Quod si vero sacratissima maiestas vestra vel sententiam mutarit vel hoc negocium differendum existimet, clementissime significare velit. Cui me totum humilime commendo et responsum gratiosum expecto, sacratissimae maiestatis vestrae humilimus servitor, Ioannes Sambucus.

Libros bibliothecae in collegio omnes evolvi et quosdam annotavi, quos Hallerus penes se habebit.[71]

Address: Serenissimo ac illustrissimo principi ac domino, domino Maximiliano, regi Boemiae, archiduci Austriae ducique Burgundiae etc., domino suo semper clementissimo. Sambucus.

19.
Sambucus to Georgius Draskovich[72]
24 November 1558, Vienna

Dedication in Plato, *Dialogi duo Platonis, Alcibiades secundus et Axiochus. Interprete Ioanne Sambuco Pannonio Tirnaviense*, ed. and trans. Johannes Sambucus (Vienna: Michael Zimermann, 1558), f. Aii[r-v]. Published in *Humanistes du bassin des Carpates II. Johannes Sambucus*, 33-34.

20.
Sambucus to Marian Leżeński[73]
1 January 1559, Padua

Dedication in Ianus Pannonius, *Iani Pannonii deinde episcopi Quinqueecclesiensis facti, ilius cum omni antiquitate vatis comparandi, lusus quidam et epigrammata, nunc primum inventa et excusa, opera Ioannis Sambuci Tirnaviensis Pannonii*, ed. Iohannes Sambucus (Padua: n.d., 1559), f. A2[r]-A4[v]. Published in *Humanistes du bassin des Carpates II. Johannes Sambucus*, 36-39.

---

for years. His first contacts with the imperial court were established in 1543 and 1547, when he was sent to Ferdinand I as a representative of the Transylvanian estates. At the time at which the letter was written, he was "Pfennigmeister," and he apparently was also responsible for Maximilian's Chancellery. Gusztáv Gündisch, "Peter Haller, Bürgermeister von Hermannstadt und Sachsengraf (1490?–1569)," *Deutsche Forschung im Südosten* 3 (1944), 43-102; idem, "Haller Péter gazdasági vállalkozásai. Adalékok a XVI. századi erdélyi polgári életforma történetéhez" [The businesses of P. Haller. Contributions to the history of the middle class in sixteenth-century Transylvania], *Erdélyi Múzeum* 52 (1947), 18-29; Almási, *The Uses of Humanism*, 151.

[71] There is a report by Peter Haller of this work, see Almási, idem.
[72] Georgius Draskovich (György Draskovics or Draskovits, Juraj Drašković, 1515–1587) was an Italian educated, learned Catholic churchman of Croatian origin. Ferdinand made him a bishop just two days before this dedication was written. He was soon sent to the Council of Trent as Ferdinand's legate. Later, he became bishop of Zagreb, bishop of Győr and Croatian ban, and he was eventually made a cardinal. See Josephus Koller, *Historia episcopatus Quinqueecclesiarum*, vol. 6 (Posonii: Landerer, 1806), 1-191; István Fazekas, "Vita a pozsonyi prépostság méltóság betöltéséről 1555-ben. Adalék Draskovich György pályakezdéséhez" [Debate on the appointment of the provost of Pressburg in 1555. On the beginning of György Draskovich's career], in *Memoriae trader*, eds. Ádám Füzes and László Legeza (Budapest: Mikes, 2006), 115-124; and the article by Dávid Molnár in *Companion*.
[73] Marian Leżeński (Lezentius) (1530–1559) was a Polish canon studying in Padua together with Sambucus. See Jan Ślaski, "Marian Leżeński, un polacco a Padova (1556–1559)," *Quaderni per la storia dell'Università di Padova* 38 (2005), 171-196.

21.
Sambucus to Miklós Oláhcsászár
1 October 1559, Padua

Dedication in Johannes Sambucus, *Oratio in obitum... Georgii Bona*, A1ʳ. Republished in Sambucus, *Orationes duae funebres*, f. [Ai]ᵛ.

Sambucus encourages Oláhcsászár, saying that Oláhcsászár should not sadden his soul when he reads this farwell to his brother Georgius Bona, but should proceed on the path of glory. [74]

Magnifico domino Nicolao Olahczasar etc. Sambucus S. D.[75]

Oratiunculam de obitu fratris hanc meam accipies ut amoris erga utrunque et memoriae semper futurae testem, ita vero leges, ut in maximarum laudum ingressu progrediaris nec ullo aut luctu, aut molestiis animum contrahas, quin egregiam patriae voluntatem, aperte, ut coepisti, suppedites atque tueare. Nihil tu fratri amantissimo gratius, nihil amplitudine ista tua et spe omnium dignius praestiteris. Vale. Patavio Calendis Octobris 1559.

22.
Sambucus to Jakob Fugger
22 October 1559, Padua

Dedication in Iohannes Sambucus, *De imitatione ciceroniana dialogi tres*, 1561, f. 1ᵛ-2ᵛ.

At the request of Jacob Fugger, Sambucus wrote down his former conversations with the late Georgius Bona concerning the question of imitation, conversations which they had held on the beautiful hills of Padua. Although he hardly adds anything new to this erudite disputation, he does not want to obscure the value of his work either. Whereas Fugger must have heard better things from his teachers, Sambucus wanted to link this work to his name. If Fugger finds it useful, Sambucus will think he has achieved a lot and will not fear criticism. He will attempt to produce something better in the future, although he has tried to express his ideas simply and briefly. It is unworthy to praise Jacob and his family in this place, and it would go beyond his talents. Greetings to Johannes Tonner and Michael Geizkofler.

Illustri adolescenti Iacobo Fuggero, domino in Kirchperg et Weissnhorn comiti, D. Antonii filio.[76] Sambucus S. D.

---

[74] In this first edition of the oration, the attached Greek and Latin epitaphs were written by Sambucus, Joachim Camerarius, Michele Sofianos, Andreas Dudith and Nicolaus (Miklós) Istvánffy. As an attachment there were also two letters of consolation by Giovanni Faseolo and Francesco Robortello addressed to Sambucus (see letters 23 and 25). A new edition also included letters by Piero Vettori and Paolo Manuzio (see letters 24 and 29) and a long poem by Adrien Turnèbe in memory of Bona, as well as a new epitaph by a certain Jacobus Maniquet. See also the next letter.

[75] Miklós Oláhcsászár (d. 1568?) was Bona's half-brother, captain and owner of Lánzsér and other properties; his wife was Anna Frangepán. See his correspondence with Archbishop Nicolaus Olahus in Budapest, MOL, OL, P 184, Mf. 34764, 1.1 and 2.1-4 (in 2.3 there is a letter by Bona to Oláhcsászár sent from Padua).

[76] Jakob Fugger (1542–1598), youngest son of the famous banker, art patron and the founder of the

Quem de imitatione ad colles amoenos et salubres istos Patavinos cum Georgio Bona, tempore alienissimo patriae summoque luctu meo adolescente nuper extincto sermonem habueram, eum te requirente per intervalla hisce chartulis mandavi atque tripartite retuli.[77] Quo in tam controversa eruditorum disputatione, dissidentibus iudiciis in hac veteris eloquentiae perturbatione etsi nihil fere novi, quodque prae aliis cuiquam satisfecerit, dixisse me animadvertam, aliquid tamen dixi, nec mihi foetus meos ita displicere ipse sino, ut quid cogitarim aut etiam conatus sim, obscurare probantibus aliter amicis aut prorsus alios nescire aliquando velim. Ac tu quidem a praeceptoribus longe his meliora sine dubitatione audivisti, verumtamen parere volui atque efflagitata vulgo tuo etiam nomine legi. Unde si ad exemplum tibi propositum et stili utilitatem aliquid decerpseris, multum me praestitisse opinabor, nec iudicia corrupta extimescam, sin in quo alios reprehendo, ipse offendi, quod humanum est, sed ignovisse longe humanissimum. Dabo operam, ut posthac meliora efficiam atque edam. Certe facili et plana dictione, ut meam sententiam breviter (nam multa possent addi ac illustrari) nunc explicarem nihilque in hoc scriptionis genere affectatum inepte relinquerem, adnisus sum.

De ingenio autem, Iacobe, moribus tuis elegantissimis, de magnifici parentis erga me honorifica et copiosa voluntate omnique omnino istius familiae splendore, in qua tantopere laudes florent tuque eas cupidissime persequeris, nihil repeto, quod nec dignitas opusculi tanta praeconia mereatur nec ingenium illa meum capere aut stilus informare posset et in disiunctissimis quibusque terris eorum memoria disseminata omnibus ita viget, meo ut testimonio relictum nihil inveniam. Ceterum exempla et quemadmodum exercitatio singulorum capiunda sit, cum aliquo maiorum vigiliarum opere paulo post accipies. Vale, et Ioannem Tonner iuris utriusque consultissimum et Michaelem Gayzcofflerum a me salutabis.[78] Undecimo Kalendas Novembris MDLVIIII. Patavii.

Fuggerbibliothek Anton Fugger (1493–1560) was Sambucus's private student at the end of the 1550s. See Pölnitz and Kellenbenz, *Anton Fugger*, 3.2:228-229; Diana Egermann-Krebs, *Jacob Fugger-Babenhausen (1542–1598): Güterpolitik und Herrschaftspraxis* (Augsburg: Wissner, 2015). See Sambucus's signature in letter 26.

[77] Sambucus republished the funerary oration that he wrote upon the death of Georgius Bona (published already in 1560, see the previous letter) as an attachment to his Ciceronian dialogues together with the oration on the death of Jacob Stubenberg (which he had published separately in 1559). Moreover, Bona, who was Sambucus's interlocutor in the dialogues, was honoured now with extra letters of condolence addressed to Sambucus (see letter 21, note 74). On Sambucus's dialogue, see Daniel Škoviera, "Latein und Nationalsprachen im ersten Gespräch von Johannes Sambucus, *De imitatione Ciceroniana*," in *Iohannes Sambucus / János Zsámboki*, 291-314; Ivan Lábaj, "Sambucus on Ciceronianism. An overview focussing on the second dialogue of *De imitatione a Cicerone petenda*," in idem, 315-331; Téglásy, *A nyelv- és irodalomelmélet*; idem, "János Zsámboky (Sambucus) and his Theory of Language," *Hungarian Studies* 10 (1995), 234-252.

[78] Sambucus dedicated two emblems to the legal expert Johannes Tonner in *Emblemata* (1566), 113, 248. Johannes Tonner worked as a tutor to the Fugger brothers Marx and Hans and accompanied them to Spain in 1552. In 1564–1571, he was preceptor to Maximilian's sons Rudolf and Ernst in Spain, and he later became Rudolf II's imperial councillor. Michael Geizkofler/Geitzkofler (1527–1614) was the Fuggers' bursary officer responsible for loans. See Pölnitz and Kellenbenz, *Anton Fugger*, 3.2:228-229; Gábor Almási, "Educating the Christian prince for learning and peace: the cases of Archdukes Rudolf and Ernst in Spain (1564–1571)," *Central European Cultures* 1 (2021), 2-43.

23.
Giovanni Faseolo to Sambucus
28 October 1559, Venice

Published in Sambucus, *Oratio in obitum ... Georgii Bona*, f. D4^{r-v}. Republished in Sambucus, *Orationes duae funebres*, f. Ciiii^v-Ciiiii^r.

Faseolo heard of Georgius Bona's death in Hungary from Sambucus's letter. He loved the character of Bona and found it apt for any praiseworthy activity. He was astounded by Bona's zeal in studying Greek with Sambucus. Bona (who had attended Faseolo's public lectures) had said that he did not think true nobility meant some series of obscure ideas; it was about the imitation of great ancestors. Bona had talked about the old noble blood from his father's part and about his mother's family's splendid deeds, but most importantly he had striven to imitate Archbishop Nicolaus Olahus, who was his uncle on his mother's side.

Ioannes Faseolus[79] Ioanni Sambuco suo S. P. D.

Georgium tuum, atque adeo nostrum, non solum summa nobilitate, sed etiam omnibus animi corporisque dotibus ornatissimum adolescentem superioribus diebus in Pannonia diem suum obiisse ex tuis literis cognovi. Quod mihi certe acerbissimum fuit. Amabam enim rarissimi iuvenis ingenium, indolem, mores eumque non solum ad praeclaram omnem cognitionem, sed ad laudabilem etiam quamcunque actionem maxime aptum iudicabam. Sed quid agas optime Sambuce? Censorii certe Catonis sententia, quam oraculi potius vim obtinere Plinius eruditissimus vir existimavit, verissima est, senilem namque iuventam praematurae mortis signum saepissime esse videmus.[80] Dii boni, quae nostri huius adolescentis gravitas? Quae probitas? Qui pudor? Quae modestia? Quod in bonas artes studium? Obstupesco sane, cum quo ardore et qua pene perpetuitate Graecis literis, quas te duce atque auctore complexus erat, operam navaret, mecum ipse considero.

Non solent profecto, qui tam sublimi in nobilitatis rerumque omnium gradu a fortuna aut Deo potius optimo maximo constituti sunt, tales esse. At is semper fuit huius adolescentis sensus, ut veram nobilitatem non in inani quadam fumosarum imaginum serie, ut ipse aliquando dicere solitus erat, sed in praeclara suorum maiorum imitatione collocatam putaret. Neque mirum, si aut ita sentiret, aut loqueretur, qui illud Aristotelis γενναῖον[81] te, ut opinor, ostendente iam novisset. Incitabantque eum quamplurima maiorum facta mihique persaepe permultorum suorum tum paterni avitique sanguinis, tum materni praeclarissimas actiones enarrare solebat. Quem vero in primis propositum haberet, quem unum praesertim imitari cuperet, ad cuiusque exemplum se totum suamque omnem vitam fingeret atque formaret, is Nicolaus Olahus avunculus erat. Hunc enim Strigoniensem archiepiscopum Ferdinando caesari, regi vestro, iucundissimum, summae auctoritatis in tota ea regione virum, egregia probitate eximiisque omnibus virtutibus praeditum in ore semper habebat. Doleo equidem mea, doleo tua, sed doleo imprimis de immatura Georgii morte illustrissimi huius viri caussa. Nobis namque charissimus fuit, quia tibi privatim,

---

[79] Very little is known about Giovanni Faseolo (†1572), who began teaching on the writings of Greek and Latin authors and probably also on Aristotle at the University of Padua in 1545. See the conference paper "The 'studia humanitatis' and Renaissance Thomism at the University of Padua" by Matthew Gaetano at academia.edu.
[80] Plinius, *Naturalis historia* 7.51.
[81] noble

mihi autem publice fuerit auditor, huic vero ex sorore nepos, qui ex insigni quodam erga eum amore potius iam filius dicendus esset. Permulta attamen sunt, quae virum amplissimum atque sapientissimum consolari poterunt, quae tibi quoque, quae tua est doctrina atque humanarum rerum usus, notissima sunt. Haud enim iam longior futurus sum, optime Sambuce, quippe cum et ex huius adolescentis desiderio vehementer angar et ad eum hominem me nunc scribere intelligam, a quo potius propter eius peritiam, quae ad animi motiones sedandas valent, petenda sint, quam ut aliorum ope egere videatur. Vale igitur meque quamprimum ad vos domumque rediturum expecta, hanc autem communem omnium hominum conditionem aequo animo feras senectamque, ut ille ait,[82] in poenam vivacem esse in memoria habeto. Venetiis V. Calendas Novembris MDLIX.

24.
Piero Vettori to Sambucus
3 November 1559, Florence

Published in Sambucus, *Orationes duae funebres*, f. Cii^v-Ciii^r.

Vettori was so greatly disturbed by the news of Bona's death (both because of the mutual love between Sambucus and Bona and the case of Hungary) that he was hardly able to do anything that day and on the following ones. It is from Sambucus's writing that Vettori understood the great intellectual virtues of Bona, which matched those of his glorious forerunners (in particular those of Nicolaus Olahus) and promised even to supersede them. Vettori praises Sambucus's philosophical consolation, to which there is little to add. Finally, he encourages him to continue enlarging his library full of old manuscripts and make it famous through his own works.

Petrus Victor[83] Ioanni Sambuco.

Interitu Georgii Bona, et qui te inaudito eoque mutuo amore prosequebatur, ita omnino tua patriaeque vestrae causa perturbatus sum, quid ut eo die et aliquot sequentibus egerim, vix faciam, ita mihi ipse velut ereptus fueram. Augebat dolorem hunc ingenii mirifici et, quas tu testatas eleganter commemoras, virtutum recordatio, susceptus universae Ungariae squalor et ob tantam spem decusque amissum vulgo luctus ostensus, quae me legentem gravissime

---

[82] Cf. Plinius, *Naturalis historia* 7.167.
[83] Piero Vettori (1499–1585) was among the best Latin philologists of sixteenth-century Italy. He became Sambucus's correspondent and exchanged letters with him for the rest of his life. Sambucus may have already met him on his first tour to Rome in the summer of 1557. On Vettori see Angelus Maria Bandini, *Petri Victori senatoris Florentini vita* and *Index operum Petri Victorii*, in *Clarissimorum Italorum et Germanorum epistolae ad Petrum Victorium Florentinum*, vol. 1 (Florentiae: [n.d.], 1758), IX-CIV; Lucia Cesarini Martinelli, "Pier Vettori e gli umanisti tedeschi," in *Firenze e la Toscana dei Medici nell'Europa del '500. Vol. 2: Musica e spettacolo; Scienze dell'uomo e della natura*, ed. Giancarlo Garfagnini (Florence: Olschki, 1983), 707-726; Salvatore Lo Re, "Piero Vettori e la natione todesca a Siena: irenismo e inquisizione al tempo di Francesco de' Medici," *Bollettino della Societa di studi valdesi* 123 (2006), 52-92; idem, "Tra filologia e politica: una medaglione di Piero Vettori (1532–1543)," *Rinascimento* 45 (2006), 247-305. Antonietta Porro, " Pier Vettori: editore di testi greci. La 'Poetica' di Aristotele," *Italia medioevale e umanistica* 26 (1983), 307-358; Raphaële Mouren, "Un professeur de grec et ses élèves: Piero Vettori (1499–1585)," *Lettere italiane* 59 (2007), 473-506. Vettori's letters are held in the British Library. See Cecil Roth, "I carteggi volgari di Piero Vettori nel British Museum," *Rivista storica degli archivi toscani* 1 (1929), 7, fasc. 3, 1-34.

commoverunt. Audieram ornatissimum adolescentem, illustri natum loco, liberali et indice bonitatis vultu suppetere illi domesticas laudes, quibus a multis seculis maiores eius affluxerint, et imprimis hoc tempore extet avunculus archiepiscopus Strigoniensis, exemplum honestatis et humanitatis antiquae, pietatem et mentem ad aethernum Deum incredibilem, sed et gloriae studium ita ipsum quoque naturae vi incitatum fuisse, ita omnem liberalem doctrinam complexum, ut veteres suorum imagines non solum expressurus, sed longe superaturus erat, ubi intellexi, itaque in medio spatio interceptum, id vero ad luctum me vehementius accibat. Sed non secus, mi Sambuce, qui tuo nuncio dolore me convulneraras, ac ille medicinam, qua moerorem diluerem, idem attulisti. Quid enim est, quod sancte simul et philosophice ad consolationem tui deinde avertendas ab animo meo graviores cogitationes apteque ea epistola non adduxisti? Ut si vicissim id coner, nimis libero esse animo et ocio tibi abundare videri possim. Proinde ne tuis literis prorsus a dolore abductus, neve ingenio tuo ac studiis, quae tibi copiose in hanc rem cuncta suppeditant, diffidere videar, utemur pariter tuis argumentis et non singularem, sed universum communemque hominum, quem in morte spectare solumus, casum lenius feramus. Quod te et velle et posse hocque ipso, quo tantopere affligeris, acerbissimo exemplo declaraturum prosus confido. Vale, mi Sambuce, et Georgium sua sede domicilioque Dei acceptum perfrui amaenissimis illis voluptatibus facile feras, tuamque nobilem bibliothecam, quam ita ἐπιπόνως καὶ σπουδαίως,[84] vetustissimis manu scriptis codicibus locupletas, exornare tuisque lucubrationibus notam facere ne desistas. Tertio Novembris 1559.

25.
Francesco Robortello to Sambucus
3 December 1559, Bologna

Published in Sambucus, *Oratio in obitum*, f. D3[r-v]; idem, *Orationes duae funebres*, f. Ciii[v]-Ciiii[r].

As much as Sambucus's letters usually make Robortello glad, this recent one was very distressing. Robortello loved Bona, a student of his public lectures, who made such progress in Greek that he was superior to students older than he. Sambucus is right to say that this trauma concerns all of Hungary, which can recover from its present ills only through the will of men of outstanding virtue. His talents and noble blood were appreciated in his country, and he was loved by King Ferdinand himself, who immediately placed great hopes in him when he was presented by his uncle Nicolaus Olahus. Finally, Robortello excuses himself for not having sent some poems as well, but his daily obligation to interpret texts does not leave him time even for writing or commenting. He nevertheless promises to send Sambucus something.

Franciscus Robortellus[85] Sambuco suo S. D.

---

[84] laboriously and earnestly
[85] Francesco Robortello (1516–1567) was an excellent philologist who taught in Pisa, Venice, Bologna and Padua (from 1561 until his death). He was a professor to many East Central European students studying in Italy. His letter to Sambucus demonstrates that Sambucus spent a longer period of time in Bologna with his pupils, who apparently enrolled at the university. On Robortello see Gian Giuseppe Liruti, *Notizie delle Vite ed Opere scritte da Letterati del Friuli*, 4 volumes (Venice: Modesto Fenzo, 1762, reprinted in Bologna: Forni Editore, 1971); Antonio Carlini, "L'attività filologica di Francesco Robortello," *Atti dell'Academia di Udine* 7 (1966–1969), 6-36; MacCuaig, *Carlo Sigonio*, 25-28, 43-50; Matteo Venier, "Francesco Robortello, Discorso sull'arte ovvero sul metodo di correggere gli autori antichi," *Ecdotica* 9 (2012), 183-218; and Matteo Venier's voice in *DBI* 87 (2016), 827-831.

Magnam laetitiam quae mihi ante affere solebant literae tuae, eas enim libenter lego, tum quia perpolitae sunt, tum quia te mei amantissimum esse scio, magnum proximis diebus attulerunt dolorem. Quibus mihi significabas de tam praestantis adolescentis, a quo nihil non erat expectandum, morte tam subita. Amabam ego illum, mi Sambuce, mirum in modum, plurimique faciebam tum propter singularem modestiam et virtutem in omni genere, tum quia Patavii, dum meus esset auditor, summum in eo ingenium et maximum ardorem in literis Graecis perdiscendis perspexeram, in quibus tam magnos fecerat progressus, ut omnes suos non modo aequales, sed etiam qui provectiore essent aetate, superaret. Magnum certe, ut et tu scribis, non modo familiae ipsius vulnus illatum, sed et universae Pannoniae censeo. Si enim ab iis, qui eximia sunt virtute praediti non sublevetur aliquando, qui finis sit vestrorum malorum futurus, non video. Valebat ille ingenio et propter nobilitatem magna fuisset apud suos gratia et regi ipsi vestro iam erat carissimus. Quidni? Neminem enim pluris facit quam Strigoniensem archiepiscopum, adolescentis avunculum, cuius consilio et opera tam multis annis in maximis rebus agendis usus est, et summus est ingenii et virtutis extimator. Saepe multi mihi retulerunt, subito cum ad regem fuisset ab avunculo adductus, delectatum ea indole et virtute, quae in ipso etiam vultu et oculis elucescebat, magnam de eo spem concepisse. Sed quis nostris proficimus querelis? Mortuus est, nec revocari ad vitam potest. Moderate ut feramus, est necesse, et illius memoriam pie colamus. Ac sane cum his literis versus aliquot ad te misissem, sed tamen multis hoc tempore sum districtus occupationibus, ut nihil mihi sit ocii reliquum ad commentandum et scribendum aliquid, praeter ea, quae publice quotidie interpretari soleo. Verum propediem ad te aliquid mittam. Cupio enim meam erga illum benevolentiam quacunque ratione possum apud omnes testatam relinquere. Vale, et me, ut facis, ama. Bononia III. Nonas Decembreis. MDLIX.

26.
Sambucus to Conrad Gesner
18 January, 1560, Padova

The original is kept in Zürich, Zentralbibliothek, Sammlung Hottinger, Ms. F. 61.98[r-v]. Published (inadequately) in Téglásy, "Conrad Gesner és magyar barátai," 202-205.

Sambucus omitted a few titles from the list of his selected books, which he had included in the previous letter to Gesner. Now he asks him also to send these works to the compilers of Gesner's Bibliotheca. Having listed the books (which he collected with much money for common use), Sambucus mentions that Archduke Maximilian ("our king") was so greatly interested in collecting rare books (partly because of Sambucus's exhortation) that the learned Hungarian ambassador in Constantinople has already collected c. 1,000 old codices. This met with resentment among the Greeks in Venice, who wanted to have this practice banned by the patriarch of Constantinople because the Latins profit from Greek books more than from anything else. But they have nothing of value there anyway, except for some theological works.

S. D.

Optime ac doctissime Gesnere,[86] in proximis literis, quibus indicem meorum quorundam librorum incluseram, festinatione praepropria factum, ut hos sequentes omitterem.[87] Itaque te pro tua fide et humanitate, pro voluntate, quae literis coniungi solet, oro, hos etiam ad compendiorum tuorum confectores[88] καὶ καταλογοποιητάς[89] mittas, qua re benevolentiam in te eorum augebis, et me necessitudine sanctissima devinxeris, a qua dissentire fuerit impium, discedere inofficiosum, permanere vero longe utilissimum et maxime delectabile. Vale, Patavio, 18 Ianuarii 1560.[90]

Ioannes Sambucus, Iacobi Fuggeri praeceptor.

Divi Gregorii ad Petrum dialogi 22 religione pleni.[91]
Chronicorum synopsis rythmica [!] Constantini Manassae.[92]
Matthaei κοιέστορος[93] et Angeli Panareti contra Latinos in quibus ab iisdem dissident.[94]
Planudis *Chronicorum* ad Copronimum usque ἐκλογὴ.[95]

---

[86] Conrad Gesner (1516–1565), the famous natural historian, doctor and philologist, founder of modern bibliography. His "Bibliotheca universalis seu catalogus omnium scriptorum locupletissimus in tribus linguis, graeca, latina et hebraica exstantium," which was the first universal bibliography of all books, first appeared in 1545. See Matthias Freudenberg, "Ges(s)ner, Konrad," in *BBKL* 15 (1999), 635-650; Urs B. Leu, *Conrad Gessner (1516–1565), Universalgelehrter und Naturforscher der Renaissance* (Zurich: NZZ Libro, 2016). Still in the spring of 1560 Zwinger and Sambucus met in Paris at Pentacost, as indicated in Gesner's *album amicorum*. In France, Sambucus selflessly wrote out his emendations on a poem by Quintus Serennus Sammonicus for Gesner, and he kept in touch with him until Gesner's death (even sending him a Greek botanical manuscript). He may also have sent him a dedicated copy of the *Emblemata*, which was in Gesner's library. Téglásy, "Conrad Gesner és magyar barátai," 207-209.

[87] On Sambucus's collection of codices see Gerstinger, "Johannes Sambucus als Handschriftensammler."

[88] Sambucus must have known that the project of the bibliography had been handed over to Gesner's younger colleague Josias Simler. See the title of the second edition of the *Bibliotheca* in 1555: *Epitome Bibliothecae Conradi Gesneri, conscripta primum a Conrado Lycosthene Rubeaquensi: nunc denuo recognita et plus quam bis mille authorum accessione (qui omnes asterisco signati sunt) locupletata per Josiam Simlerum Tigurinum* (Tiguri: apud Christophorum Froschoverum, 1555).

[89] catalogue-makers

[90] Gesner's note in the margin: "Accepi 23 febr."

[91] A selection from Pope Gregory I, *Dialogi*.

[92] Constantine Manasses (c. 1130–c. 1187) was a Byzantine chronicler and poet, author of a chronicle or historical synopsis which comes to an end in 1081. Sambucus's two copies are held in Vienna, ÖNB, Cod. Hist. gr. 72 and 77. For the use of these copies in the edition cf. letters 27, 108, 113, 115, 119, 134, 159, 174 and 376. The resulting edition was *Annales Constantini Manassis: nunc primum in lucem prolati, et de Graecis Latini facti, per Ioannem Lewenclaium. Ex Ioanni Sambuci V. C. bibliotheca* (Basileae: Episcopius, 1573).

[93] quaestor

[94] Matthew Angelos Panaretos (fourteenth century) was a Byzantine theologian who wrote over twenty polemic treatises against the errors of the Catholic church. Sambucus mistakenly supposed that two separate authors were at work here. Sambucus's copies of Panaretos are held in Vienna, ÖNB, Cod. Theol. gr. 103 and 109.

[95] Maximus Planudes was a thirteenth-century byzantine monk and polyhistor, best known for compiling the poems of the *Greek Anthology*. Nothing is known of the historical excerpts mentioned here. As they are supposed to cover the time until the rule of Constantine V Copronymus (741–775) this cannot refer to the so-called *Excerpta Planudea*, which only include excerpts concerning Roman republican and imperial history. It could however refer to patriarch Nicephorus's *Breviarium historicum*, first edited in 1616 by Dionysius Petavius (*S. Nicephori Patriarchae Constantinopolitani breviarium historicum, de rebus gestis ab obitu Mauricii ad Constantinum usque Copronymum* [Parisiis: Chapelet 1616]), or an epitome of it.

Michaelis Apostoli contra Gazae defensionem de ente Aristotelis pro Planude[96] responsio ad Bessarionem.[97]
Nicephori philosophi et rhetoris epitaphius λόγος de Antonio.[98]
Gregorii Nisseni *De vita Theodori Martyris*.[99]
Theodori Smyrnaei de physica doctrina, et principiis ἐπιτομὴ ἐκτεθεῖσα τμήμασι τέταρσι[100]
Alexandri Sophistae libellus τὰς τῶν ἱερῶν βοτανῶν περιέχουσα κράσεις[101]

Hi praeterea apud me sunt, quos maximis sumptibus et non sine ingenio ac industria coëgi ad communem utilitatem.

Illud te non nescire volo, Maximilianum nostrum regem[102] ita vetustate omni, inprimis librorum, incensum cupiditate, partim mea commemoratione, partim exemplo privatorum, ut nunc Constantinopoli qui legatus est nostras Ungarus,[103] vir doctissimus, precio et pecunia congesserit codices antiquos ad mille. Quam rem Graeci quidam primarii Venetiis indigne ferentes, de communi consensu Constantinopolin scripsere, ut prohiberet patriarcha eas nondinas periculosas et sibi infames, cum nulla ex re Latini quaestum et honorem maiorem, quam ex Graecis libris adipiscantur. Sed mi Gesnere, quid illi amplius, praeter theologos quosdam habent? Sed de hac re proxime ad te. Ego nec labori, nec sumptui parcam, pergo. Vale. Ioannes.

In the margin (Gesner's hand): Maximilianus magno pretio multos ex Graecia libros avertit. Graeci patriacham monent, ut id prohibeat: eum magnum inde questum ad [...] futurum.
Address: Doctissimo atque humanissimo domino Conrado Gesnero, medico etc., patrono et amico observandissimo. Tiguri Helvetiorum.

27.
Sambucus to Theodor Zwinger[104]
1 March 1560, Padua

The original is kept in Basel, Universitätsbibliothek, Handschriften, Frey Mscr II 26, no. 208. Published in Gerstinger, "Die Briefe," 48-50.

---

[96] *Planude* is a lapsus. Actually, the work defends Plethon, not Planudes.
[97] Michael Apostolius was a Byzantine scholar who came under the protection of Cardinal Bessarion and worked as teacher, copyist and author in Crete and Italy. Sambucus's copy is held in Vienna, ÖNB, Cod. Phil. Gr. 85.
[98] Nicephorus Philosophus lived in the ninth century. His encomion for Patriarch Antonius Cauleas is transmitted in the Vienna manuscript ÖNB, Cod. Hist. Gr. 3 (f. 109ᵛ-121ᵛ) from Sambucus's library.
[99] It is contained in the same manuscript, ÖNB, Cod. Hist. Gr. 3 (160ᵛ-166ʳ).
[100] Epitome presented in four sections. Theodore of Smyrna, a quaestor in Bizantium at the turn of eleventh and the twelfth centuries, wrote several philosophical and theological works. Sambucus's specimen of his *Epitome* is preserved in Vienna, ÖNB, Cod. Theol. gr. 134 (f. 238ʳ-262ᵛ).
[101] Containing mixtures of the holy herbs. This manuscript seems to be lost. The only known copy is held in Oxford, Bodleian library, Baroccian. 150, f. 67ʳ-76ᵛ.
[102] Maximilian was crowned king of Hungary only in 1563.
[103] It is not clear who the person in question was. To our present knowledge, "Hungarian" members of Ferdinand's delegation (the legates Antonius Verantius and Ferenc Zay and the men who accompanied them, Johannes Belsius and Hans Dernschwam) were not present in 1560. The greatest book collector among them was Dernschwam, but it is more likely that Sambucus was referring here to Zay. Certainly, none of them collected 1,000 old codices.
[104] Theodor Zwinger (1533–1588) was an extraordinarily learned humanist and medical scholar of Basel. He studied in Basel, Lyon, Paris, and Padua, where he obtained a medical degree and where he became friends with Sambucus. Zwinger's uncle was the printer Johannes Oporinus. After Oporinus's death he collaborated most closely with the printer Pietro Perna, especially on the editions of Paracelsus. See Gilly, "Zwischen Erfahrung und Spekulation."

Sambucus has understood from the letters of Zwinger and Oporinus that Zwinger was a conscientious friend and Oporinus a reliable correspondent. He is working on Theophylact hard, in a manner that will not betray the name he has already made in learning. He can easily make an accord with Oporinus, if he promises to print the unpublished part of Zonaras's history, even if Anton Fugger fails to agree. He would send Zwinger the Chronicle of Manasses and Doxopatres's Commentary on Hermogenes had Zwinger not reduced his hopes about German interest in Greek literature and were he not afraid of their delayed publication. Zwinger should write him about the position he has taken in Oporinus's firm. Zwinger should send back to Sambucus his badly compiled notes via the Brechters to Johannes Tonner in Augsburg, who is in a close relationship with Anton Fugger, who will return everything to him. Zwinger should make sure that Oporinus does not lose anything he has received from Sambucus but is not going to publish. Zwinger knows that in spending money for books and being almost prodigal his goal is not to possess but to collect and preserve. Zwinger should tell Oporinus what he wrote and excuse Sambucus for not having written to him. Jacob Fugger is returning Zwinger's greetings.

S. D.

Accepi tuas itemque Oporini,[105] quibus, quod vehementer cupiebam, intellexi te in officio amicum, in respondendo Oporinum esse memorem. De hoc tibi gratiam habeo, atque si non par, mutuum tamen studium, cum voles, cognosces. De Theophylacto velim scias me operam convertendi ita suscepisse, ut, si quid mihi adhuc a bonis et eruditis tributum fuit, non obscurem ad eamque rem has occupationes conditionis, quas nosti, non aeque commode inservire. Pergo tamen et urgeo me ipse.[106] In Zonarae, quod editum non fuit, *historia* mihi facile cum Oporino meo conveniet, si vel nolente Antonio Fuggero, vel dissimulante, se editurum promiserit, ut in meis ad ipsum significavi.[107] *Chronica* Manassae ad vos mitterem[108] (mea enim *Chronica Pannonica* Viennae sunt excusa[109]) atque etiam Doxopatrem in ideas Hermogenis doctissimas, nisi mihi exiguam spem de Graecarum literarum studio per Germaniam fecisetis, et vererer, ne diutius laterent.[110] Scribetis tamen et tu, quod caepisti amici negocium atque munus apud Oporinum. Praefatas *Epitheses*[111] meas turbate et modice

---

[105] Johannes Oporinus (1507–1568) was among Basel's most learned humanist publishers. In his early years he worked as a scribe for Paracelsus. He taught Latin in the local grammar school and Greek at the university, but as of 1542 he dedicated himself exclusively to publishing. See Andreas Jociscus, *Oratio de ortu, vita, et obitu Ioannis Oporini Basiliensis* (Strasburg: Rihelius, 1569); Martin Steinmann, *Johannes Oporinus. Ein Basler Buchdrucker um die Mitte des 16. Jahrhunderts* (Basel: Helbing & Lichtenhahn, 1967); Martin Steinmann, "Aus dem Briefwechsel des Basler Druckers Johannes Oporinus," *Basler Zeitschrift für Geschichte und Altertumskunde* 69 (1969), 104-203; *En Basileia polei tēs Germanias: Griechischer Geist aus Basler Pressen*, ed. Frank Hieronymus (Basel : Universitätsbibliothek, 1992), digitalised at https://ub.unibas.ch/cmsdata/spezialkataloge/gg/inhalt.html (accessed on 12 March 2024); and Carlos Gilly, *Die Manuskripte in der Bibliothek des Johannes Oporinus* (Basel: Schwabe, 2001).

[106] See Theophylactus, *Explicationes in acta Apostolorum*. The manuscript in question is in Vienna, ÖNB, Cod. Theol. gr. 150 (Gerstinger, "Sambucus als Handschriftssammler," p. 355, no. 66).

[107] Financed by Anton Fugger and edited by Hieronymus Wolf, Zonaras's history appeared in a beautiful bilingual edition: *Ioannis Zonarae Monachi ... Compendium historiarum in tres tomos distinctum* (Basel: Oporinus, 1557). Sambucus owned a codex of Zonaras's *Annales* (Vienna, ÖNB, Cod. Hist. Gr. 43). See Gerstinger, "Sambucus als Handschriftssammler," 340 and 379.

[108] Manasses, *Annales*.

[109] Ransanus, *Epitome rerum Ungaricarum*. See letter 16.

[110] The codex in question is in Vienna, ÖNB, Cod. Phil. gr. 145. See Gerstinger, "Sambucus als Handschriftssammler," 370, no. 248. Cf. with letter 298.

[111] The reference may concern Sambucus's notes in Hieronymus Wolf's Zonaras-edition (see note 107).

congestas remittetis Augustam per Brechteros ad Ioannem Tonner doctorem Augustam, qui est intimus et iocundus domino Antonio Fuggero, qui omnia simul ad me transmittet. Reliqua etiam, quaeso, vel non excusurus Oporinus, quae a me habuit, ne perdat. Scis enim, quam in conquirendis etiam minimis, et comparandis, multo magis conservandis his rebus sim solicitus, sumptuosus et pene prodigus. Vale, et haec Oporino nostro non moleste illius commoditate referes, quo interpretaberis meam illi opinionem et simul, cur minus ad ipsum scripserim, excusabis. Patavio Calendis Martii 1560. Fuggerus te resalutat.[112] Tuus Sambucus.

Address: Excellentissimo medico et philosopho, Theodoro Zwingio [!], amico suo carissimo. Basileae apud Oporinum.

28.
Paolo Manuzio to Sambucus
[May 1560],[113] Venice

Published in Manutius, *Pauli Manutii epistolarum libri quatuor*, f. 153^r–154^v.

When Manuzio heard about the news of the death of his son, he felt so confused that he hardly knew if he was a man and forgot completely that his son had entered this life–like in a guesthouse–under the condition that he would also leave it when summoned by God. He was stirred by Sambucus's remarkable argument on reducing sorrow. With all the misfortunes behind him, he has learned to despise fate. Fortune can take away everything but not his mind and faith. Manuzio compares the fate of his son, free of anxiety in heaven, with what we call life. Wise men desire virtuous life, not longevity. Manuzio could easily satisfy Sambucus and others who encourage him to write, but in their leisure they have no idea about how greatly family life confines his free time. It would be inhuman to neglect the family, while dedication to the family's sustenance means to neglect one's studies, which need one to be free of worries. Sambucus would respond like others that his studies would bring him profit, but this is something that contradicts his times. That old patronage of great men has already dried up. They follow shadows, they spend on festivities and wars. Some of them want a little glory by their generosity but lack most the virtue that they pretend to have. Sambucus knows the recent example of this behaviour by a person, considered very noble, who promised everything, enjoyed Manuzio's generous help, but did nothing. Many suffer the same kind of sickness, the less dignity they have, the more they do so. Manuzio has heard that there are people, especially one, who support Archduke Maximilian, who, as a learned person, wants to be a patron of liberal arts. He asks Sambucus to find out how Maximilian would receive his book and to recommend him to the archduke.

Iohanni Sambuco. Patavium.

Ego vero, accepto nuncio de obitu filioli mei, ita sum perturbatus, ut me tamen hominem esse meminerim et illum in hanc vitam, tamquam in hospitium, ita esse ingressum, ut accitu

---

[112] Jakob Fugger, Sambucus's private student.
[113] The dating of the letter is based on the calculation of the time of the death of Ottavio Manuzio, Paolo's ten-month-old son. See Dudithius, *Epistulae*, 1:79.

summi Dei aeternum illud caeleste domicilium petiturus aliquando discederet.[114] Quod si me casus iste nec opinatus ita perculisset, ut omnino iacerem, excitarer tamen prudentia litterarum tuarum, in quibus de luctu minuendo disputas egregie, tuamque declaras tum homine Christiano dignam bonitatem, tum erga me benevolentiam singularem. Verum ego, optime Sambuce, multis iam infortuniis hoc sum assecutus, ut fortunam ipsam didicerim contemnere. Quae mihi, ut eripiat reliqua, numquam adimet ea, quae nec ipsa dedit, nec dare cuiquam potest, rectam mentem, optima studia, pietatem in Deum. Praeclare actum opinor cum filio meo. Fruitur conspectu et consuetudine caelestium animorum, non angitur curis, non spe ducitur, nihil timet adversum. At nos, qui dicimur vivere, quibus hac falsae lucis usura nihil est carius, quam multa exercent? Quid laboramus, quid cupimus, quod etiam si contingat, animus acquiescat? Itaque vere sapientes homines, non ut diu, sed ut recte et cum virtute viverent, optare soliti sunt. Quod equidem conor et, ut spero, consequar. Nihil enim magis cogito, nihil specto, quam ut serviam studiis meis et ita vivam, ut vitae rationem Deo simul et hominibus aliquando possim reddere. Quare, cum me vocas ad scribendum, confirmantur consilia mea iudicio tuo. Ac tu quidem in hoc officio cohortandi facis idem, quod multi, quibus facile possem satisfacere, si per domestica negotia liceret. Sed, obsecro, nolite ex otio vestro meum spectare. Vobis enim certa et expedita sunt omnia, mihi unicum est vectigal industria mea, qua liberos alere, tueri familiam cogor. Et, si negligam, deseretur humanitas, sin, ut debeo, diligenter curem, iacere studia necesse est, quae solutum curis omnibus animum postulant. At inquies: ipsa tibi studia fructum ferent. Cane aliis cantilenam istam, mores ac tempora ignorantibus, mihi non persuadebis experto. Vetus illa principum virorum benignitas exaruit. Inania plerique sequuntur, nihil solidum amant, nihil magnificum, nihil illustre. Vides alios, quasi perdendis tantum frugibus nati sint, immanibus epularum sumptibus opes exhaurire; alios, quasi etiam homines ipsos, non modo fruges, perdere pulchrum sit, thesauros effundere, collectos acerbissime in ea bella, quae vastitatem agris, urbibus incendia, humano generi, aliena stultitia miserrimo, cladem et exitium important. Musae interim ubique locorum algent, neglectae ab iis, qui fovere eas ut maxime poterant, ita maxime debebant. Etiam illud indignum, quod existunt, qui specie liberalitatis gloriolam aucupentur, et eam virtutem, a qua longissime absunt, quasi familiarem suam, sic in ore habeant, ut amare videantur.[115] Exemplum recens in manibus est, hominis, ut a multis accepi, nobilissimi, qui mihi et obsignata charta, quid ultro promiserit, et postea, cultus a me diligenter omni genere officii, qualem exitu se praebuerit, non ignoras. Hoc fere morbo laborant multi, eoque gravius, quo minus eorum dignitas et amplitudo fert. Unum aut alterum, sed unum in primis animo excellere, et personam principis egregie sustinere audio, summi filium imperatoris, ipsum orbis terrae imperio dignissimum, Maximilianum regem. Quem de ornandis liberalibus disciplinis cogitare, cum eas optime calleat, minime miror. Itaque factum a me non insipienter puto, qui de mittendo ad eum libro nostro, te quidem approbante, nec mediocriter adhortante, consilium ceperim. Quod ille si cognoverit et si me apud eum testimonio tuarum litterarum in aliqua gratia posueris, magnopere laetabor, idque si a te impetro, et debere me tua causa plurimum arbitrabor, et, ubi res exigat, studiosissime praestabo. Vale. Venetiis.

---

[114] In less than a year Manuzio lost two of his sons, Ottavio and Girolamo. On the bitterness that he felt see some of his other letters listed in Pastorello, *L'epistolario Manuziano*, 287-297. Cf. Gábor Almási, "Értelmiségi apák a 16. században" [Intellectual fathers in the 16th c.], in "*...Nem egyetlen történelem létezik*". *Ünnepi tanulmányok Péter Katalin 80. születésnapja alkalmából*, eds. Zita Horváth, Noémi Viskolcz et al. (Miskolc, 2017) = *Publicationes Universitatis Miskolcinensis, Sectio Philosophica* 21 (2017), 27-61.

[115] Certain editions do not contain the following part of the letter.

29.
Paolo Manuzio to Sambucus
[Summer of 1560], Venice

Published in Manutius, *Pauli Manutii epistolarum libri quatuor*, f. 164ʳ-165ʳ; Sambucus, *Orationes duae funebres*, f. Cʳ-Cii[v].[116]

Manuzio warns against excessive sorrow: it is human to feel pain but one should control it. He has experience in these matters. Fortune often crosses one's path, but Sambucus can take infinite examples from Greek and Latin authors. Humans, unlike animals, are given a rational mind, and it is disgraceful to abandon nature's path. Is dying disgraceful? Only when someone lived in a hollow way, which is not the case of Bona. Sambucus should learn moderation from the books he is studying. Having given consolation to him over the death of his son, Sambucus will certainly be able to offer the same with regards to Bona's death and make the fuits of his studies thus appear. Nicolaus Olahus will anyway find consolation in his life experience and natural prudence.

Paulus Manutius Sambuco suo.

Quod fratrem tuum Georgium, florenti adhuc aetate extinctum, immoderate luges, ignosco moerori tuo, nec tamen laudem tribuo.[117] Dolere enim tanquam fratris interitu, et eius fratris, quo nemo amabilior, nemo fuerit virtute praestantior, hominis est; modum autem dolori nullum constituere, nunquam lachrimis abstinere, nunquam ex animo moestitiam pellere, Sambuci non est. Periit frater, iure commoveris. Aegre enim divellimur quasi a natura coniuncti, quod ego quoque sum expertus. Periit is, qui familiam suam, qui patriam, qui provinciam universam ornare vehementer suis laudibus et illustrare poterat. Hoc quidem ab eius virtute expectandum fuit, sed magnam habet fortuna vim: ea saepe nobis ad eximiam laudem contendentibus transversa incurrit, saepe nostra studia debilitat, saepe moratur industriam. Quo de genere quid ego te doceam, doctissimum virum, cui prope infinitam exemplorum vim vel Graeca monimenta, vel etiam Latina suppeditant? Florem igitur virtutis amemus. Erepto ante maturitatem fructu, quando hoc singulare non est, sed commune cum multis, modice feramus. Quid, si ne dolendum quidem est? Omitto enim historias, ad philosophiam te voco. Quid igitur illa praecipit? Si quid casus afferat, leniter accipiendum, nec enim ut aliter accidat, in nobis est. Si quid culpa contractum, angi aequum esse. Certe enim qui ad praeclare agendum nati simus, ideoque mente et ratione praeter caeteras animantes instructi, tantis bonis abuti et quasi a natura desciscere turpissimum est. An tu igitur mori, quasi aliquid turpe, reprehendes? Quod si non turpe, nec dolendum, nisi si quis ita vixerit, ut nihil umquam homine dignum praestiterit, quod abest longissime a fratre tuo, qui probitate, ingenio, studiis artium optimarum, prudentia etiam adolescens ita excelluit, ut eum Pannonia paene cuncta viventem unice dilexerit, mortuum laudibus et memoria prosequatur. Quae cum tibi veniunt in mentem, iniquus profecto nimis in te ipsum es, nisi luctum minuis et ex animo dolorem penitus evellis. Quin te decuit maxime, qui totos dies ponas in iis libris, unde vitae moderatio, unde animi tranquillitas petitur, ad propinquos, ad amicos in Pannoniam eiusmodi litteras mittere, in quibus illi sitam esse non minimam sui doloris medicinam intelligerent. Nam vir

---

[116] For later editions see Pastorello, *L'epistolario manuziano*, 60.
[117] Cf. letters 21-25.

eximius, Nicolaus Olahus, archiepiscopus Strigoniensis, qui Georgium Bona et quia sorore sua natus erat, et quod in eo summa virtus enituit, in oculis gestabat, non dubito, quin tanti vulneris remedia sumat a se ipso, quem non modo aetas et usus maximarum rerum erudierit, verum etiam prudentia quaedam naturalis, quae plane vincit omnem artem, numquam a constantia discedere patiatur. Nec tamen vereor, ut qui mihi paucis ante mensibus in filioli mei obitu consolationem adhibueris,[118] idem tibi in tuo casu mederi aliqando non facile possis. Quod si facies, fructus apparebit studiorum et Georgii fratrem agnoscemus, cuius ingenium ac mirificam prudentiam oratio illa, loculenter imprimis a te scripta, declarat. Vale, Venetiis.

30.
Sambucus to Hieronymus Wolf
12 December 1560, Paris

The original is kept in Vienna, ÖNB, Cod. 9736, f. 1^{r-v}.[119] Published in Gerstinger, "Die Briefe," 51-54.

In this polite letter, Sambucus recommends Carolus Utenhovius to Hieronymus Wolf. Wolf's example of virtue and integrity inspires others. Sambucus always knew Wolf as someone open to true friendships, and his recommendation of Utenhovius will certainly be appreciated by Wolf. As they talked about Wolf recently at Jean Dorat's place, Utenhovius started strongly desiring to become his friend and get access to his "museum." Wolf can reckon how greatly Sambucus was boasting of their friendship. As for Utenhovius's talents, it is sufficient to look at his translation of Nonnus's Dionysiaca. Nevertheless, Nonnus's text is very difficult to interpret, and it is hardly possible to do so without textual comparisons, for which Sambucus and Utenhovius are asking Wolf's help. If he has access to another copy in the library of the Fuggers, he should either give it to Sambucus and Utenhovius or edit the text himself by comparing the problematic places. This Herculean labour would make erudite men very grateful. Finally, Sambucus excuses his long letter with reference to Utenhovius's eagerness and solicitude. He has not received the funerary epigrams yet, otherwise he already would have returned them to Wolf with the inclusion of other poems.

Domino Hieronymo Volfio.[120] Sambucus S. D.

Ea est humanarum literarum et omnis philosophiae, quod tu minime ignoras, Volffi, natura, ut qui eas tractant, nunquam deserere humanitatem possint atque cupidos virtutum et honestatis

---
[118] See the preceding letter.
[119] The survival of this letter among Sambucus's manuscripts suggests that it was not sent to Wolf in this form or it is a copy Sambucus prepared for some reason (which he usually never did).
[120] Hieronymus Wolf (1516–1580) was a remarkable German Graecist and philologist, a librarian in Augsburg's public library and a collector and publisher of Byzantine sources. In 1551, he was made secretary and librarian of the Fugger library. Sambucus dedicated a poem to him in the *Poemata* and apparently also asked him for a poem upon Bona's death (see the end of the letter). Their relationship was probably more indirect (through the Fuggers) than direct. For Sambucus's emblem to Wolf see *Emblemata* (1564), 26. On Wolf see Gadi Algazi, "Food for Thought: Hieronymus Wolf grapples with the Scholarly Habitus," in *Egodocuments in History: Autobiographical Writing in its Social Context since the Middle Ages*, ed. Rudolf Dekker (Hilversum: Verloren, 2002), 21-44. On Wolf's relationship to the Fuggers and Oporinus see Fritz Husner, "Die *Editio Princeps* des Corpus Historiae Byzantinae. Johannes Oporinus, Hieronymus Wolf und die Fugger," in *Festschrift für Karl Schwarber* (Basel: Schwabe, 1949), 143-162.

ament, in eorum progressibus maxime capiant. Quod ipsum, si quisquam alius, tu profecto ita multis exemplis declarasti, ut μίμησιν παρέχης[121] et ad simile officium alios iuste incitaris. Cognovi ego te semper facilem, ad amicitiam non fictam comparatum. Ea re fit, ut praeter eruditionem, quae amplissima et varia est, mores quoque tuos ac vitam omnes praedicent, liberaliter tuam necessitudinem familiares aliis deferant. In quibus et ipsum me si antea observasti, nunc, liquide velim, confirmes, qui tibi Carolum Uthenhovium,[122] praeter aetatem πολύγλωσσον[123] et nobilissimum iuvenem commendo, quo officio iam nunc praemium quoddam percipere mihi videor. Is enim cum alias saepe, tum nuper apud Ioannem Auratum[124] de te amanter et honorifice locutum me cum audivisset ac de tot monumentis nomen cognitum, ita secum complecteretur, ut nisi tuam illi voluntatem simul et benevolentiam adiungerem, minime sibi satisfacturus esset, facile morem gessi et hisce meis, qui aliter optabilis erat, ad amicitiam tuam et museum illud locuples eruditumque pectus patefacere aditum volui et innuere. Vide, quantum apud alios nostra familiaritate glorier, quantum mihi concedam et pro omnibus loqui prolixe ausim. Sed nisi ego sensus, Hieronyme, tuos minus deprehendi, hunc tu iuvenem accipies, ut commeatu literarum et aliquando ipso congressu tibi carissimum habeas. Itaque non te rogabo, nec pluribus eius laudes commemoro, quem vel ex Nonni *Dionysiacis* convertendis, quid possit ac velit, non secus ac de unguibus leonem possis agnoscere.[125] Quod ille suum institutum ita urget, ne moram

---

[121] you can present imitation

[122] Carolus Utenhovius (1536–1600) was a Dutch humanist who was educated in Paris and had literary connections all over Europe. On his connection with Sambucus see letter 113 and 157, Sambucus's emblem (*Emblemata*, 1566, 65) and Utenhovius's poem published in Gerstinger, "Die Briefe," 53-54. Gerstinger suggests that this poem may have been written in 1561 in Melun, where Sambucus stayed in August (see the next letter). On Utenhovius see Leonard Forster, "Charles Utenhove and Germany," *Daphnis* 6 (1977), no. 4, 81-100; Philip Ford, "Carolus Utenhovius: A Tale of Two Cities," in *Between Scylla and Charybdis*, 149-160.

[123] many-tongued, i.e. multilingual

[124] Jean Dorat (1508–1588) was one of the central figures of literary life in Paris and the French language movement and a leader of the poetic circle *La Pléiade*, which was made up mostly of his pupils, including Pierre Ronsard. He was immensely prolific in Greek and Latin poetry and had the honorary title of *poeta regius*. Sambucus dedicated a poem on friendship to him in Δημηγορίαι, 130. For Sambucus's emblem to Dorat see *Emblemata* (1564), 87. See Geneviève Demerson, *Dorat en son temps: culture classique et présence au monde* (Clermont-Ferrand: Adosa, 1983); Henri Demay, *Jean Dorat: (1508–1588), "l'Homère du Limousin", âme de la Pléiade, et poète des rois* (Paris: L'Harmattan, 1996); Jean Dorat, *Mythologicum, ou interprétation allegorique de l'Odyssée, X-XII et de L'hymne a Aphrodite*, ed. Philip Ford (Geneva: Droz, 2000); *Jean Dorat, poète humaniste de la Renaissance*, eds. Christine de Buzon and Jean-Eudes Girot (Geneva: Droz, 2007).

[125] If Sambucus's letter may have sounded to Wolf a little pompous and presumptuous, the references to Jean Dorat and Nonnus's *Dionysiaca* served to function as counterpoints. Sambucus was apparently already in possession of at least one of his *Dionysiaca* manuscripts (presently in the ÖNB, Cod. Phil. gr. 45 and 51), which conserved a rich, important, still unpublished poem on the story of Bacchus by the late-antique poet Nonnus, which must have been a real sensation in the circle of Jean Dorat. In 1571, on occasion of the wedding of Charles IX and Elisabeth of Austria, Dorat was one of the masters of ceremony, ordering a cycle of 24 paintings from Niccolo d'Abbate and Camillo, his son, to be placed in the great hall of the Palais Episcopal. The paintings were to tell the story of Bacchus on the basis of the poem by Nonnus, which fit well into the irenic world of mid-century humanism (but not so well during the French Wars of Religion). As Frances Yates commented, "this newly discovered poem might also have seemed suitable as an allegory of the new hopes of religious harmony". Frances Yates, *Astraea: the Imperial Theme in the 16ᵗʰ Century* (London: Routledge & Kegan Paul, 1975), 140-148. See now Herbert Bannert, "Die *editio princeps* der *Dionysiaka* des Nonnos von Panopolis *ex bibliotheca Ioannis Sambuci*," in *Iohannes Sambucus / János Zsámboki*, 161-204. See also Francesco Tissoni, "Jean Dorat lecteur des Dionysiaques de Nonnos de Panopolis," in *Jean Dorat, poète humaniste* (as in note 124), 167-183. On the provenance of the manuscripts see also *Humanistes du bassin des Carpates II. Johannes Sambucus*, 124-125, note 623. See also *Brill's Companion to Nonnus of Panopolis*, ed. Domenico Accorinti (Leiden: Brill, 2016). Although Utenhovius offered himself as a translator, he did not finish the job. Sambucus's *Dionysiaca* manuscript was later published by Gerhard Falkenburg in 1569 with Plantin. See also "Nonnus-edition" under "Sambucus" in the Index.

aliis eo excuso ullam faciat. Nihil enim non poetice, apte, condite, καὶ μεθ᾿ ἁπάσης σπουδῆς τε καὶ δεινότητος[126] exprimit. Cuius partem laudis et in omnes meritorum ille, si quorum ἐξ ἀκανθώδων δυσκρίτων καὶ λοξῶν[127] ope amicorum expeditur, effuse et gratissime attribuit ac nihil non cum eorundem subsidio prestitum confitetur. In quam societatem si te perpetua observantia depacisci et memoria nunquam obscura, imo si precibus adducere posset, beatum se, felices alios diceret, qui tua opera in rebus a poeta involutis, in verbis adeo caecis adiutos Nonnoque ipso auctos videret. Plurima sunt in eo scriptore difficillima et angusta exemplarium, hoc est, unici eiusque etiam non satis probi nec vetusti depravata, quae nisi oculatissimi commoditate atque alterius codicis praesidio sanari numquam poterunt. Rogat igitur verecundia singulari et memoria prope divina hic iuvenis primum, ut se admittas, tum, si molestum non est, lucem ingenii tui ad quaedam loca illustranda porrigas, postremo si ullum exemplar apud illos extat,[128] illud nobis edas, aut cum his locis et aliis conferas. Quae si omnia impetrabit, est quod ego quoque laeter, sin vel unum obtinuerit, gratias agemus, pro aliis, ut semper habeant, spondere non desinemus. Sed pertinax est Uthenhovius, nihil de spe remittit, quidvis per me et communi studiosorum nomine a tua se humanitate consecuturum iam aliis etiam narrat. Quae spes ne ipsum tanto ardore et cupuditate in omnium usum incredibili et modo non impotenti fallat, a se quidem ille rudimenta non exigua habet; si tu voles, omnia perficiet et absolvet, nec minus, quam si hunc tu laborem totum suscepisses, vel potius ut Hercules ἀνίκητα[129] qui superaris, commendationem ab eruditis invenies. Haec ego, Volffi, non a me tot verbis, sed Carolo nostro ita contendente atque dictante. Et scis, in vestibulo etiamsi difficultas et molestia interdum parva sit, precibus tamen ac solicitudini locum relinqui.[130] Epigramma funebre nondum acceperam, alioqui tibi iam pluribus exemplis reddidissem.[131] Vale, ad nos, si amas, rescribe. Lutetia Parisiorum pridie Idus Decembris 1560. Tuus Ioannes Sambucus.

31.

Sambucus to Henri de Mesmes[132]
[1561][133], Paris

The original is kept in Paris, Bibliothèque Nationale, Latin 10327, f. 120[r]. Published in Gerstinger, "Die Briefe," 54-55; Bach, *Un humaniste hongrois*, 85.

---

[126] and with all industriousness and talent
[127] thorny, hard to discern and ambiguous [words/sentences]
[128] The reference is made to the Fuggers.
[129] invincible
[130] This sentence, exaggerating his role at court, suggests that Sambucus may already have approached Wolf from Vienna, probably in the period between late 1557 and early 1558.
[131] The funerary epigrams to which Sambucus is referring here were most probably requested for the volume commemorating Georgius Bona's death in late 1559 (see letter 21).
[132] Henri de Mesmes (Memmius) (1532–1596) was a French noble bibliophile, numismatist, chancellor and councillor who worked in close association with Jean Grolier (cf. letter 33), a good portion of whose famous library he bought. His memoirs were published by Édouard Fremy in 1886 (republished in Genève: Slatkine, 1970). Sambucus addressed an emblem to him (*Emblemata* 1564, 125). See Janet Espiner-Scott, "Notes sur le cercle de Henri de Mesmes et son influence," in *Mélanges offerts à M. Abel Lefranc* (Paris: E. Droz, 1936), 354-361; Bach, *Un humaniste hongrois*, 44, 56-59.
[133] These undated letters to Mesmes were most probably written at the end of 1560 or the beginning of 1561.

Mesmes's learned nobility demands that Sambucus address him also in a more familiar manner. He does not doubt that Mesmes is ready to dedicate a few hours to him, when he would show him some very rare coins. He would then find out if Mesmes wanted to add his catalogue of coins and other books into Gesner's Bibliotheca, *which will have a new edition.*

S. D.

Nobilitas literata singularisque humanitas tua facit, ut familiarius etiam te compellem atque rogare non dubitem, velis commoditate negociorum tuorum aliquam mihi horulam tui accedendi praescribere, qua illa tibi aliquot rarissimos et antiqui operis historicique numos ostendam simulque intelligam, indicem tuae multorum numorum *Bibliothecae* num inseri catalogo Gesneri καὶ τῶν καταλογοποιῶν[134] velis. Dignus enim es una cum tuis libris, qui locupletiorem ornatioremque indicem denuo recudendum efficias. Vale. Tuus totus Ioannes Sambucus.

Responsum, si nunc domi tuae non es, poteris Bernardo Turisano denunciare.[135]

32.
Sambucus to Henri de Mesmes
[1561], Paris

The original is kept in Paris, Bibliothèque Nationale, Cod. lat. 10327, f. 117ʳ. Published in Gerstinger, "Die Briefe," 55-56; Bach, *Un humaniste hongrois*, 86.

Sambucus confirms that he got his coins back as well as those of Mesmes but without any book. He asks Mesmes for the books by (Pseudo)Castor of Rhodes and Isaac (Monachus) Argyros that Mesmes has promised. Mesmes is free to consult anything he has. The epitome of Herodotus, given to him by someone, is not interesting.

S. D.

Recepi numos meos ac item tuos, sed sine ullo libro, quod scio tibi tum minus fuisse otii ad quaerendum. Rogaram te, nobilissime domine, de Castore Rhodio,[136] qui de metris rhetorum quiddam conscripsit, aut saltem Isaac Monachum *De metris*,[137] quos tu mihi humanissime, ubi reperiisses, missurum dixisti. Ignosce, si humanitate tua abutor, id enim incredibilis in omnem vetustatem sensus meus tecum communis facit. Ἀλλὰ διὰ τὸ ἐπιεικὲς καὶ καλοκαγατίαν σοῦ σύγγνωθι τῇ παρρησίᾳ καὶ πίστευσον ἀνδρί σε χάριν γνωστικῷ ταύτην εὔνοιαν ἕξειν καὶ

---

[134] and of the catalogue-makers
[135] Bernard Turisan was a Venetian typographer working in Paris.
[136] The manuscript *Opusculum de metris rhetorum propriis* by (Pseudo-)Castor of Rhodes is preserved in Paris, Bibliothèque nationale, Grec 2929. It was published as Castor Rhodius (Pseudo-Castor), *Excerpta ex Hermogenis περὶ ἰδεῶν*, in *Rhetores graeci*, vol. 3, ed. Christian Waltz (Tubingae: Cotta, 1835), 712-783.
[137] Isaak Monachus, Περὶ μέτρων ποιητιχῶν. Printed in *Anecdota graeca*, vol. 2, ed. Ludwig Bachmann (Lipsiae: J.C. Hinrichs, 1828), 167-196.

προσοίσειν.[138] Quidquid mihi dederis inspiciendum, id tutum fore recteque commissum sancte credito. Vale, meque benevolentia et gratia complectere. Ex Museolo. Tuae magnificentiae deditissimus Sambucus.

Antea significavi, mi domine Memmie, si quid est penes me, quod aut videris aut videre aliquando voles, omni conditione in tua fore potestate, etsi meis te ineptiis indigere nunquam cogitavi. Hanc Herodoti epitomen quidam mihi dedit, eam percurri, sed non est magni momenti, etc.

33.
Sambucus to Henri de Mesmes
[1561], Paris

The original is kept in Paris, Bibliothèque Nationale, Latin 10327, f. 118[r]. Published in Gerstinger, "Die Briefe," 56-57; Bach, *Un humaniste hongrois*, 86.

Sambucus gratefully sends back a manuscript of Hephaestion. If Mesmes does not have the time to look for [Pseudo-]Castor of Rhodes's work, he should at least in the meanwhile send him the book by Isaac (Monachus) Argyros, which Sambucus would send back that very day or the day after. If anything of his stuff that Mesmes saw the day before should interest him, like rings or the like, he is ready to loan them to him without any conditions. He is sending Mesmes the coins which he forgot to bring along the previous day for his inspection: he has not shown them to Jean Grolier yet and would rather not do so for some time. Sambucus announces that he is working on a book that he will dedicate to Mesmes but he will reveal details later in person.

Salutem.

Remitto tibi Hephestionem, habeo gratiam.[139] Si Castorem Rhodium de metris rhetoricis invenisti, te summopere oro, eum mihi tantum inspiciendum credas, sin eum quaerere non vacat, saltem interea libellum Isaci Monachi *De metris poeticis* commodes, eum tibi summa fide adhuc hodie vel cras remittam.[140] Si quid mearum rerum est, quod tibi placeat, sive annuli, sive aliud est aliquid, quod heri vidisti, modo significes, sine exceptione habebis et condicione, quamcumque praescripseris. Mitto simul numos, quos heri oblitus eram deferre, hos tu inspicias; domino tamen Grolierio nondum ostendi et propter certas causas id differam.[141]

---

[138] But because of your fairness and noble character forgive the frankness and trust that the man who is conscious of your favour will have and provide this goodwill.

[139] Hephaestion was a grammarian of Alexandria (second century AD). For his manual on Greek metres see *Hephaestion on Metre*, ed. Johannes M. Ophuijsen (Leiden: Brill, 1987).

[140] See notes 136 and 137 to the previous letter.

[141] Jean Grolier (1479–1565) was one of the most famous sixteenth-century French bibliophiles who was profoundly influenced by Italian humanism (he was of French-Italian origin). He was a well-to-do statesman (Treasurer-General of France) who owned an exceptional cabinet of coins and medals and was also a patron of several humanists of his time. Cf. letter 45. On Grolier see Le Roux de Lincy and Adrien Jean Victor, *Recherches sur Jean Grolier: sur sa vie et sa bibliotheque* (Paris: L. Potier Libraire, 1866, republished: Hildesheim-New York: Olms, 1970). Sambucus obtained some of the coins in his collection through exchanges with Grolier and Mesmes. The prospect of future business may be the reason why Sambucus did not want to show some of his

Et laboro nunc in quodam libello perpoliendo, cuius editionem cum tuo nomine, si patiere, in vulgus dabo, qua de re coram tecum. Vale meque, ut cepisti, complectere. Tuus Sambucus.

Address: Magnifico D. Henrico Memmio.

34.
Sambucus to Henri de Mesmes
[1561], Paris

The original is kept in Paris, Bibliothèque Nationale, Latin 10327, f. 119ʳ. Published in Gerstinger, "Die Briefe," 57-58; Bach, *Un humaniste hongrois*, 86.

Sambucus saw the text by (Pseudo)Castor but it is all taken from Hermogenes. The epitome of Hermogenes by Kamariotes at the end of the book is a decent work, which Mesmes now has in two or three copies. If he could do without one of them, Sambucus would be happy to make an exchange. The book by Isaac (Monachus) Argyros is on unbounded pieces of paper kept together with Heliodorus's Paraphrase of the Nicomachean ethics. *If Mesmes has time, Sambucus would be happy to have a look at it for a single hour to see what he is saying. He can keep the epitome of Herodotus as long as he wishes. It is in Latin, and it is useless for such a great man to keep it.*

Salutem.

Vidi Castorem, sed videtur Pollucis fratris opera destitutus fuisse, dum haec conscriberet. Nihil enim fere quam ex ideis Hermogenis quosdam pedes collegit.[142] Camariotae epitome in fine libri erudite ex Hermogene est composita;[143] hanc tu bis aut ter habes. Si uno carere voles, permutatione utriusque commoda fiet, cum libuerit. Isaac Monachi libellum de metris, quem petebam,[144] est inter cartulas nondum ad ligaturam comparatas et super Heliodori paraphrasim ethicam abs te cum aliis repositas.[145] Quando ocium fuerit, tua humanitas eum mecum ad horam tantum communicabit, ut quid sentiat, videam. Vale et epitomen Herodoti quandiucunque voles, penes te retineto; certe Latina est et frustra suscepta tanto viro. Tuae magnificentiae deditissimus [?] Sambucus.

---

coins to Grolier and "forgot" to bring them to Mesmes's place, where he apparently also met with Grolier.

[142] Reference is made to Hermogenes of Tarsus's *On Types of Style* (περὶ ἰδεῶν). Cf. letter 31, note 136.

[143] *Synopsis Rhetoricae Matthaei Camariotae, a Davide Hoeschelio edita* (Augsburg: [Praetorius], 1595). Kamariotes (fifteenth century) was a scholar from Thessaloniki.

[144] Cf. the preceding letter.

[145] [Konstantin Paleocappa], *Heliodori in Ethica Nicomachea paraphrasis* (Berolini: Reimer, 1889). The name "Heliodorus of Prusa" was probably invented by the sixteenth-century copyist Paleocappa. See Karl Krumbacher, *Geschichte der byzantinischen Litteratur: von Justinian bis zum Ende des oströmisches Reiches (527–1453)* (Munich: Beck, 1891), 431; Paul Moraux, *L'Aristotelismo presso i Greci*, vol. 1 (Milan: Vita e pensiero, 2000), 144-145.

35.
Sambucus to Daniel Rechnitz
11 August 1561, Melun

Dedication in Johannes Sambucus, *Somnium Scipionis luculenta paraphrasi et scholiis breviter commodeque illustratum*, in Sambucus, *De imitatione a Cicerone petenda* (2nd ed.), f. N^{r-v}.

Sambucus knows what Crassus (i.e. Cicero) would think about this kind of writing, and it is difficult to say something better. Still, he hopes he will be appreciated by erudite men and also by Rechnitz, and he does not care if common people have a different opinion. No one who appreciates this art will find fault in the brevity of an interpretation made by a single person, as no one has the time to go through so many commentaries. If he had written more freely and provided less concrete interpretation, he would have given a bad example. He wanted both to make Scipio's dream more easily accessible and to show Rechnitz how he should write paraphrases, applying Cicero's own words and changing their order. Daniel Rechnitz has decided to dedicate himself to the learning of eloquence and languages in order to provide an example of a virtuous and pious life–like his father, the most noble Vitus, who is adored by great men–and make fame with his sharp mind. This way, his father will not regret Daniel's stay in France and Italy.

Sambucus Danieli Rechnitz[146] S. D.

Scio, quid Crassus ore Ciceronis de toto hoc genere scripturae atque exercitationis sentiat,[147] neque enim optimis fieri aut substitui meliora, si occupentur, facile possunt. Quia tamen ista quaedam contentio non tam in verbis, quam rerum intelligentia posita est tuaque causa horulis aliquot suscepta, credo me ab eruditis veniam, abs te etiam gratiam habiturum. Vulgus si aliter loquetur, praestare nequeo. Certe nemo intelligentis et exercitati iudicii huiusmodi planas, ex eodemque autore transcriptas interpretationes in rebus brevitate et sententia obscuris reprehendet. Neque enim tempus et spacium cuilibet suppeditat evolvendi tot commentarios, et quorundam in studiis nondum firmi progressus molestissime eam moram ferunt, difficillimeque notant definitos sensus. Quod si vel paradoxis, vel aliis pariter illustribus et expositis disputationibus stilum hunc liberiorem applicuissem, vitiose id maloque exemplo fecissem. Nunc ista opella sum adnisus, ut meis somniis Scipionis commentum dilucidius fieret magisque ad percipiendum prompta narratio, et simul ostenderem, quemadmodum abs te paraphrases informandae celebrandaeve sint, ex eodem nempe Cicerone verbis et sententiis comportatis et recta permutatione appensis. Quod si utrumque forte perfecimus, nam studium et conatus minime defuisse non ignoras, obsequii me mei non poenitebit, sin minus, voluntatem id consequendi ac edendi aliis etiam probabis. Tu vero omnino in literarum elegantia pergendum tibi esse et laborem in linguarum cognitione urgendum putabis, ut Viti a Rechnitz,[148] optimi et nobilissimi senis, qui te genuit et quem principes viri amant et

---

[146] Daniel Rechnitz was apparently Sambucus's private student from 1561. His name suggests that he was of Austrian origin. Rechnitz wrote a Latin preface addressed to the Genoan nobleman Francesco Gentile for Sambucus's *Ars poetica Horatii* dated 13 January 1564, which suggests that they were also together on their way to Naples. Sambucus addressed an emblem to him (*Emblemata* 1566, 227).

[147] Cf. Cicero *De oratore* 2.90-96.

[148] We have no information on Vitus of Rechnitz (Veit von Rechnitz), Daniel's father. Sambucus addressed an emblem to him: *Emblemata* (1564), 18.

colunt, maiorumque vestigiis alacriter ingressus pietatis et virtutum exempla egregia nobis et futuris exhibeas et luce ingenii celebritatem omnemque memoriam cum posteritate acquiras. Ita enim salutarem te patriae dignumque expectatione tuorum praestabis, ita absentiae in Italia et Gallia tuae parentem nunquam poenitebit fidemque liberatam apud me fatebor. Vale. Meloduni in Gallia 3. Idus Augusti MDLXI.

36.
Sambucus to Conrad Gesner
13 February 1562, Paris

The original is kept in Chur, Archiv dal stadi dal Grischun, D V/37 C 36.06.11.

Despite the mutual silence, the love between them kept growing no less than had they exchanged meaningless letters to keep their friendship up. By meaningless he is not referring to Gesner's letters, but to such of his own which contain only greetings and affectation. Friends really do not need such letters. Sambucus was away from Paris for six months because of the plague, travelling across France and searching through several libraries, something Gesner also loves to do. Sambucus has recorded the rarer or unique books, this will be of use to the catalogue-maker of Gesner's Bibliotheca. *Gesner will be especially glad that Sambucus has found a very old codex with some Tironian notes for simple herbal remedies. Gesner can insert those signs where they belong in his book on pharmacology. Three days ago, Sambucus found Palladius's thorough and methodical commentary on the sixth book of* Epidemics, *the most difficult and obscure part of Hippocrates. As far as he knows, there are no other copies of this text. Giovanni Ferrerio sends his greetings and begs him to excuse his silence. He preferred to remain silent, as he has not yet received the things from Scotland which he intended to send to Gesner. If Gesner answers, he should send his letter to Augsburg, hence it will be forwarded to Italy, where Sambucus intends to return in April for the summer. Sambucus's young ward sends his greetings.*

S. D.

Diuturnum quidem et mutuum silentium fuit, doctissime Gesnere, eo tamen non minus crevit amor noster, si pristino quae accessio fieri potest, quam si inanibus literis memoriam necessitudinis tueri voluissemus. Voco inanes non quidem tuas, nam meas etiam nugas vocabo, sed quibus salutationes tantum et interdum ostentatio continetur. Quae ab amicibus longe aliena esse debent. Ego, mi optime Gesnere, ob luem publicam sex menses abfui ab urbe, pervagatus sum multa Galliae loca, excussi aliquot Bibliothecas, quarum inspectio tibi etiam voluptatem affere solet. Quae rariora sunt aut proprie sola, annotavi, quibus καταλοφοποιῷ τῆς βιβλιοθήκης[149] tuae subsidio eris. Sed quod tibi praecipue gratum fore scio, inveni quendam vetustissimum codicem, in quo aliquot simplicium notas antiquitatis reperio, quibus Tiro[150] libertus dicitur[151] βραχυγράφος[152] usus. Eos characteres inseres locis suis libri

---

[149] to the catalogue-maker of the *Bibliotheca*
[150] Cicero's freedman Tiro is credited with invention of a shorthand writing system.
[151] crossed out: *scribendo*
[152] as a stenographer

materiae tuae¹⁵³ medicae.¹⁵⁴ Ante triduum incidit in manus meas Palladius medicus sophista in sextum *Epidemiorum*, partem Hippocratis, ut nosti, difficillimam et adhuc obscuram. Qui quam diligenter et methodice singula persequatur, aliquando videbis.¹⁵⁵ Hoc tibi confirmo, eius exemplum nuspiam, quod sciam, extare. Dominus Ferrerius¹⁵⁶ noster, vir doctissimus et communis pater amicusque noster tibi salutem plurimam ascribit, utque se tibi excusarem de silentio rogavit. Maluit enim tacere, quam vacuas et non onustas rebus e Scoctia nondum allatis, quas ad te missurus erat, mittere.¹⁵⁷ Vale et, si posthac ad me scribes, literas Augustam mittito ad Fuggeres, ut in Italiam ad me mittantur. Nam mense Aprili istuc rediturus sum et hanc aestatem σὺν θεῷ¹⁵⁸ transacturus. Ubicumque ero, te certiorem faciam. Iterumque vale. Salutat te generosus adolescens meus.¹⁵⁹ Luteciae Idibus Februarii 1562. Tuus Sambucus.¹⁶⁰

37.
Sambucus to Paolo Manuzio
19 June 1562, Genoa

The original is kept in Rome, BAV, Vat. lat. 3434, f. 60ʳ; a copy is kept in Bibl. Estense, Fondo Estense, Ital. 1827, Beta 1,3,1, pp. 120-121. Published in Gerstinger, "Die Briefe," 58-59.

Sambucus profoundly agrees with Manuzio's choice to publish books for the Christian public in Rome. He has seen some examples of Manuzio's editions in Genua, books by Theodoretus and on the Constantinople Council. He hopes that Manuzio's efforts will be in accord with the pope. He can affirm that even Transalpins–perpetrators of religious divisions–extol his work, but he hopes to say more about this in person, as he is longing to visit Rome and Manuzio, waiting only for better travel conditions. He has no news of Dudith at all and no news of his parents either. He left Muretus in Paris, but he was about to leave for Italy. Turnebus is preparing to publish his variae lectiones. *If Manuzio wants to respond, which he does not expect, as Manuzio is undoubtedly busy, he can send his letter to the noble merchant David Otto in Venice at the Fontego. For a few more days, he will continue to enjoy the company of Matteo Senarega and Stefano Sauli. Finally, Sambucus is sending his greetings to Antonio Augustín.*

---

[153] Gesner intended to publish an edition of *De materia medica* by Dioscorides. The addition (*corollarium*) to Gesner's *De libris a se editis epistola* published in Iosias Simlerus, *Vita clarissimi philosophi et medici excellentissimi Conradi Gesneri* (Zürich: Froschouerus, 1566), mentions (31r) among the unpublished works: "Emendavit [...] Dioscoridem de materia medica et quaedam alia, quae, si vixisset, editurus erat."

[154] Gesner's marginal note: "Simplicium notae."

[155] Gesner's marginal note: "Palladius medicus in sextum Epidemiorum."

[156] The Piemontese humanist Giovanni Ferrerio (1502–1579) spent thirteen years in Scotland and became an expert on the land, writing several books on its history. Sometime after his return to Paris in 1545, he became a correspondent of Conrad Gesner and provided him with information on Scotland for his works on natural history, also acting as an intermediary with learned Scots. Cf. John Durkan, "Giovanni Ferrerio, Gesner and French affairs," *Bibliothèque d'Humanisme et Renaissance* 42 (1980), 349–360.

[157] Gesner's marginal note: "A Ferrerio salutem."

[158] with God

[159] This is probably a reference to Daniel Rechnitz (see letter 35, note 146).

[160] Gesner's marginal note: "Nota."

S. D.

Vehementer probo consilium, quo in edendis atque Christiano vulgo libris communicandis nunc Romae uteris.[161] Vidi nuper Genuae tuae industriae aliquot exempla, Theodorettum [!],[162] *De concilio* Poli sanctissimum librum et quaedam alia, in quibus et diligentia tua illustris est et carta probanda. Utinam hoc instituto et singulari in rem Christianam voluntate cum pontifice proficias![163] Illud tibi confirmare possum vel Transalpinos, a quibus religionis perturbatio manavit atque in sectas abiit, operam tuam laudaturos atque studium cum infinita memoria propagaturos, imo vero allectos tua elegantia et praefationibus, reliqua cupide lecturos. Sed de his spero me propediem pluribus coram tecum acturum. Omnino enim in Romae tuique desiderio sum, mi Manuti, eoque potior, ubi se calores hi infesti non nihil fregerint mitioresque itineri praebuerint. De Duditio prorsus nihil audio, minus de parentibus nostris. Muretum Parisiis reliqueram, parantem tamen in Italiam abitionem.[164] Turnebus sedecim variarum lectionum apparat libros, e cuius officina quid nobis sperandum sit, tute intelligis.[165] Si quid rescribere voles, quod minime in tanto negotio abs te requiro, Venetias mittito ad Davidem Otthonem, mercatorem nobilem in fontego.[166] Hic Genuae consuetudine domini Senaregae ac inprimis Stephani Saulii,[167] senis antiqui exempli, aliquot

---

[161] Paolo Manuzio moved to Rome in 1561. See Barberi, *Paolo Manuzio*.

[162] Cf. *Theodoreti urbis Cyri episcopi in visionem Danielis prophetae commentarius, Ioanne Baptista Gabio Veronensi interprete* (Romae: Manutius, 1562); *Beati Theodoreti episcopi Cyrensis in Ezechielem prophetam commentarius, Ioanne Baptista Gabio Veronensi interprete* (Romae: Manutius, 1562); *De concilio liber Reginaldi Poli cardinalis* (Romae: Manutius, 1562). On his Genovan stay (with little more information than provided here) see Várady, "Relazioni di Giovanni Zsámboky col'umanesimo italiano."

[163] Giovanni Angelo Medici (1499–1565), Pius IV (1559–1565).

[164] Marc Antoine Muret (Muretus) (1526–1585) was one of the best Latinists of the sixteenth century, famous for his poetry, letters and orations, which remained models to be imitated until the end of the eighteenth century. His talents were noticed early by Julius Caesar Scaliger, while later in Paris he joined the circles of Jean Dorat. His success and early fame brought him trouble in France, where he was charged several times with the crime of homosexuality and also for harbouring Protestant sentiments. In 1559, he moved to Italy at the invitation of Cardinal Ippolito d'Este and settled in Rome, where he became a professor. In 1561–1563, he was in France. He was a pioneer in Tacitism, and held advanced ideas about politics. Charles Dejob, *Marc-Antonie Muret, un professeur français en Italie dans la seconde moitié du XVIe siècle* (Paris: Thorin, 1881); Jill Kraye, "The Humanist as Moral Philosopher: Marc-Antoine Muret's 1585 Edition of Seneca," in *Moral Philosophy on the Threshold of Modernity*, eds. Jill Kraye and Risto Saarinen (Dordrecht: Springer, 2006), 309-330; Jean-Eudes Girot, *Marc Antoine Muret: des Isles fortunées au rivage romain* (Geneva: Droz, 2012).

[165] Adrien Turnèbe (Tournèbe or Adrianus Turnebus) (1512–1565) was one of the most significant Greek scholars in sixteenth-century France. He was professor (royal reader) of Greek at the Collège Royal from 1547 and professor of Greek philosophy from 1562. See John Lewis, *Adrien Turnèbe (1512–1565), a Humanist Observed* (Geneva: Droz: 1998); Jean Letrouit, "Turnèbe (Adrien) (Tournebus Adrian) (1512–1565)," in *Centuriae Latinae*, vol. 1, ed. Colette Nativel (Geneva: Droz: 1997), 761-766. The reference here is probably to the 1564 edition of his *Adversaria*.

[166] The quarters for German merchants in Venice, the Fontego/Fondaco dei Tedeschi. See letter 183, note 1081.

[167] Little is known about Matteo Senarega (1534–1606), who studied law among other subjects in Leuven and was a good friend of Paolo Manuzio, with whom he published translations of Cicero's letters. He followed in the footsteps of his father, became chancellor and later secretary of the State of Genova and finally doge in 1595. Stefano Sauli is another relatively little known contact of Manuzio (cf. with Pastorello, *L'episoltario Manuziano*). He was similarly a person of high prestige in different important positions in the Republic of Genova, and he was also a patron of humanism. See his *Lettera di monsig. protonotario Sauli ambasciadore de la ill. eccel. Repub. di Genoua appresso la maestà cathol. sopra le cose de la detta repub. scritta à l'illustriss. sig. Gio. Andrea Doria, a 15. d'aprile 1575 con un discorso del medesimo* (Milan: Pontio, 1575) and Cesare Vasoli, "Un discorso sull'imitazione' attribuito a Stefano Sauli," in *Omaggio a Gianfranco Folena*, vol. 2 (Padua: Programma, 1993), 1153-1170.

dies fruor tuique memoriam numquam ex ore dimittimus. Vale ac D. Antonium Augustinum a me non moleste salutabis.¹⁶⁸ Genuae 13 Calendas Iulii 1562. Tuus ex animo Sambucus.

Address: Excelentissimo viro D. Paulo Manutio, Sanctae Sedis apostolicae typographo etc., domino suo observandissimo. Romae.

38.
Sambucus to Aldo Manuzio Jr.
30 December 1562, Naples

The original is kept in Milan, Biblioteca Ambrosiana, E 37 inf., f. 118ʳ-118ᵛ. Published in Ester Pastorello, ed., *Inedita Manutiana: 1502–1597: appendice all'Inventario* (Florence: Olschki, 1960), 159-160.

Sambucus thanks Aldo for his letter and the attached index. He cannot add much to it. His resources will not be of much help for Aldo, who has all the virtues and is more erudite than his age would suggest, but he can count on all his resources. Aldo should freely tell his opinion of Sambucus's dialogues and whether they are worthy of publication. And if Aldo has already printed them, he will be immensely grateful. He sends his greetings to Aldo's father, Paolo, and to a certain Scipio.

Sambucus Aldo Manutio¹⁶⁹ S. D.

Cum indice literas tuas accepi, quibus ortam inter nos benevolentiam non mediocriter cumulasti. Libenter agnosco praecipua te voluntate ac studio quidvis in meis rebus ac prolixe cupere. Ago gratias vicissimque id senties. Ac etsi, quod ad usus tuos a me proficisci possit, per est exiguum, ut de tuo exhaurire, quam addere me posse confidam (habes enim patrem cuius praeceptis et consiliis te praeter aetatem eruditum ac beatum ostendis, opes autem, si quae meae sunt, tibi, cui cum virtute ista deesse nihil potest, parum proderunt) quicquid tamen ingenii vel patrimonii suppetit, comune id atque in promptu fac putato. De dialogis libere, quod videbitur, statuetis.¹⁷⁰ Quos si dignos luce pronunciaveritis, non ego me autorem, sed in societatem eiusce opinionis admissum fatebor. Sin vero etiam prelo vestro in manibus et cognitione omnium posueritis, officium tanti aestimabo, ut vos adhuc dilexisse in omne posterum tempus amaturus videar. Vale et patrem omni liberalitate et memoria dignum itemque Scipionem¹⁷¹ salutes. Neapoli 3 Kalendas Ianuarii 1562¹⁷².

---

¹⁶⁸ Antonio Augustín (1517-1586) was a Spanish humanist, bibliophile and antiquarian and a member of Fulvio Orsini's Roman circle. Having studied law in Salamanca, Padua and Bologna, he joined the court of the pope and the Roman Church. See Juan Francisco Alcina Rovira, "El Humanismo de Antonio Agustín," in *Mecenazgo y Humanidades en tiempos de Lastanosa*, eds. Aurora Egido and José Enrique Laplana (Zaragoza: Institución Fernando el Católico, Instituto de Estudios Altoaragoneses, 2008), 31-50.

¹⁶⁹ On Aldo Manuzio, who was fifteen years old at the time and who moved to Rome with his father in 1561, see letter 14, note 62.

¹⁷⁰ Sambucus might have been aiming to reprint his Ciceronian dialogues in Venice, where the press would soon be overtaken by Aldo and his mother.

¹⁷¹ We do not know the Scipio in question.

¹⁷² This must be a dating error on the part of Sambucus, as "3. kl. Ianuarii" refers to 30 December of the previous year.

> Hoc tibi Sambucus Iano renovante Kalendas
> Mittit inoffensae pignus amiciciae.
> Cur maiora negat? Cupidus quia perferet ipse,
> Neve odisse putes, non solet obruere.

Address: Al molto Magnifico Signore Aldo Manutio, Fratello Carissimo, Roma.

39.
Sambucus to Archduke Maximilian, King of Bohemia
18 January 1563, Naples

The original is kept in Vienna, HHStA, Familienkorrespondenz A, Kart. 3. Published in Gerstinger, "Die Briefe," 60-62.

Sambucus apologises for having been silent for so long; this was not because of negligence or disrespect, but because of his continuous search for antiquities and books over the course of the last four years. Maximilian surely remembers his zeal and desire to be of value to the fatherland, the entire world, and, most of all, to the cause of Christ. He has already given evidence of this, and Maximilian kindly approved of his intentions. Spurred by this, Sambucus returned to France, Italy and elsewhere, motivated to collect Latin and Greek books that are rich in content, testimonies of both humanity and religion, and publish them in corrected versions. He promises to present the results of his antiquarian project (the result of hard work and tireless travel) to Maximilian in the summer. He offers his talents, industry, network, language knowledge, his life to Maximilian. He has shown several signs of his loyalty but also has encouraged others to adore and serve Maximilian, who has already been offered the crown of the Romans and the imperial crown. He excuses himself again for his late letter and congratulation (for Maximilian's crowning) and promises to say more in person. He wishes for the coming of a new golden age, asks God to protect Maximilian, soothe the religious divisions and the internal and external wars, and give him divine counsel and help him become the greatly desired light of peace and the founder of universal harmony.

Serenissime Rex etc., domine mihi clementissime etc.

Diuturni silentii non aliqua negligentia aut immutata observantia erga tuam maiestatem causa fuit, sed perpetua variaque per hosce quatuor annos in conquirendis antiquitatibus et libris peregrinatio. Meminit enim tua maiestas, quanto animi ardore, qua cupiditate studeam patriae totique orbi terrarum, imprimis vero Christi rebus prodesse; quod ego coram tuam maiestatem pluribus verbis et vero exemplis testatus sum, ac tua maiestas benignissime atque clementissime voluntatem meam comprobavit.[173] Ea re velut calcari vehementius incitatus

---

[173] This happened in the spring of 1558. In the beginning of 1558, Sambucus returned with Georgius Bona to Vienna and was immediately appointed *aulae familiaris*. A little later, he was entrusted the task of sorting through a certain Viennese library (either the University Library or the imperial collection). There must have been some personal conflict concerning this job, to which Sambucus refers in the dedication to Ransanus's *Epitome rerum Ungaricarum* (see letter 16). For this important letter see Almási, *The Uses of Humanism*, 171-172; idem, "Humanisten bei Hof: Öffentliche Selbstdarstellung und Karrierenmuster," in *Funktionen des*

denuo Gallias, Italiam et alias regiones peragravi, ut libros Graecos et Latinos locupletes et idoneos, cum humanitatis, tum religionis testes colligerem atque eis vel corrigendis, vel edendis ad communem utilitatem ac tuae maiestatis nomen celebrandum iuste uterer. Quod meum consilium ex aliqua parte me consecuturum hoc labore et solicitis itineribus omnino spero, ac tuae maiestati brevi vel potius hac futura aestate declarabo. Quicquid enim ingenioli et industriae, quicquid amicitiae multorum eruditorum, quicquid linguis, quas varias novi, possum, denique totum, quod tot laboribus et sumptibus conquiro, id ad nutum, imperium ac, si quid eiusdmodi fuerit, ornamentum maiestati tuae conferam vitamque dedicabo meam. Cuius clientelae indicia propria et aliena non pauca per hosce annos demonstravi, dum omnes eruditos virtutum maiestatis tuae admiratione cohortor, urgeo, ut sua monimenta et lucubrationes tuae maiestati consecrent. Quod eos merito facere videmus, praesertim divinitus Romani quoque imperii corona tibi oblata sit, et propediem alias regiones gratia et imperio ad maiestatem obtinendamque fidem Christianam et amplificandam auxilio iussuque Dei immortaliter adiunges.[174] Quod ego ex animo dies noctesque precor, aurea ut saecula redeant, longis laetemur et annis. Haec pauca ad tuam maiestatem velut serae gratulationis quandam significationem scribere volui moramque excusare. Quam excusationem pro lenitate et clementia perpetua supplex oro, ut accipiat meque in gratia et patrocinio semel suscepto conservet. Brevi tuam maiestatem humilime revisam et pluribus verbis de omnibus rebus ipse conatus et obsequium exponam. Deus optimus maximus tuam maiestatem tantis religionis discordiis bellisque tam exteris, quam domesticis sedandis una cum suis liberis posterisque in omne reliquum tempus conservet, divina consilia suppeditet, urgeat, ornet, tueatur, ut te crescentem ac florentem videamus, optatissimum lumen pacis, universae concordiae autorem, Ad nutumque tuum vesper et ortus eant. Datum Neapoli 18 Ianuarii 1563. Tuae maiestatis cliens minimus, Ioannes Sambucus Tirnaviensis Pannonius.

40.

Sambucus to Emperor Ferdinand I.
[first half of September, 1563[175]], Antwerp

Dedication in Goltzius, *C. Iulius Caesar sive historiae imperatorum*, f. c v[r-v].

The uses and pleasure of the past are readily noticeable from antique coins and their relation to historical works. Coins bring to light and give sense to historical examples. They have primary importance for the history of the consuls, which until now, with the loss of Livy's books, has relied on Cassiodorus, but can now rely also on antique inscriptions and coins. Sambucus has also collected, as Ferdinand knows, with great zeal and much travel antique coins useful for history both for the benefit of his country and himself and for the glory of Ferdinand. Those who want to understand military standards and the symbolism of triumphal marches and rely only on historical books

---

Humanismus. Studien zum Nutzen des Neuen in der humanistischen Kultur, eds. Gerrit Walther and Thomas Maissen (Göttingen: Wallstein, 2006), 155-165.

[174] Maximilian was crowned King of the Romans on 24 November 1562. In fact, Sambucus was rather late in congratulating him, as he acknowledges in the next sentence.

[175] Although the letter is dated to 23 September, it was written earlier. The letter was post-dated in order to appear to the emperor as recent as possible. As in the next letter of 22 September Sambucus is complaining about printing errors of the dedication, it must have been already printed by then.

and do not consult coins and marble inscriptions are laughed at by the experienced. Sambucus goes on to emphasise the essential importance of material testimony to the knowledge of antiquity. The fact that Ferdinand invests greatly in numismatics also inspires many to see great value in it. This is the case also with Goltzius, who, although a German, is entirely Roman in his striving and industry and has achieved much in numismatics with his talents and travels and through his industry and manual skills. This is not only his opinion, which has considerable weight in this field, but a common opinion of learned men all over Italy (where they are in the greatest number), France and Germany. When Sambucus returned to France and visited Italy the third time, everyone was praising Goltzius's diligence, since he did not neglect anything pertaining to numismatics. He searched through the houses of noblemen, all imaginable corners, and noted down and systematised everything. Goltzius is now offering his work to the emperor, and Sambucus believes that much greater works will still be offered in the future, if Goltzius's life and Ferdinand's favour should last. This immense study cannot be sustained by private men without the financial help of the emperor and his like. Sambucus therefore asks Ferdinand to take Goltzius in his patronage and promises that he will soon make great advances in the study of antiquity. He has recently personally witnessed Goltzius's attitude and many samples of his enterprise in Bruges, in the house of Marcus Laurinus.

Imperatori Maximo Ferdinandi Augusto, Ioannes Sambucus Pannonius Tirnaviensis.

Quanta sit monimentorum vetustatis utilitas atque etiam voluptas, non solum memoria litterarum, sed quoque antiqui operis numorum studium et cum historiis contentio satis ostendit. Quot enim historiae et praeclara exempla aut valde obscura essent aut, nisi horum testimonio ac lumine accenderentur, prorsus laterent, ut merito ἀντίσποφος[176] cognitio ταῖς ἱστορίαις[177] esse videatur? Consulares historiae damno de Livii libris accepto fuissent caecae, nisi Cassiodori quaedam diligentia, nunc vero etiam marmorum reliquiae nobis animum addidissent, atque in copulandis cum annalibus numorum testimoniis spem ostendissent brevi, ut pauca lateant, fore.[178] Multas ego et memoria reliqui temporis dignas historias vel de meis numis, ut tua maiestas optime novit, amore et tot peregrinationibus collegi, quae commoditate patriae rerumque mearum aliquando et cum tua celebritate legentur. Certe qui de ratione militari, et signis eius, de triumphis etc. scripsere ipsisque libris tantum, non etiam pervestigationi marmorum et numismatum studuerunt, dum obeuntis Solis imperium cum Oriente miscent, nec consuetudini mutatae plus, quam vocum notionibus tribuunt, longe interdum a scopo aberrare cum intelligentium risu[179] animadverto, quod ipsi aliquando nec admoniti varia et pertinaci sua professione corrigent. Atque illud tua maiestas testatum firmumque habeat, nisi diuturna inspectione universae antiquitatis et ad lectionem recta et artifici comparatione laudem ab hoc nomine qui ferat iustam, fore neminem. Perpetuum enim a libris subsidium illustrem et iucundam reddit cognitionem, sed inspectio et tractatio monimentorum adeoque iudicium dextrum et facile nisi illa efferat inque vitam probam

---

[176] opposite
[177] histories
[178] Michael Klaassen has recently argued that "to construct his consular list Cassiodorus used a now-lost consularia extracted from Livy and Aufidius Bassus from 509 BCE to 27 CE, the Cursus paschalis of Victorius of Aquitaine (from 28 to 457), and a now-lost extension of Victorius' work (from 458 to 519)." M. Klaassen, *Cassiodorus' "Chronica": Text, Chronography and Sources* (PhD Dissertation, University of Pennsylvania, 2010).
[179] Print: *visu*. See Sambucus's complaints about typographical errors in letter 41.

revocet, ut a fictoribus hodie avaris secura sit scriptio, aeternitatem labor non modo non intuebitur, sed ne diuturnitatem quidem assequetur ullam.

Ea re tua maiestas in cogendis omnis generis numismatibus[180] non levem curam, maximos sumptus ponit, multosque suo exemplo ad has cogitationes indies excitat. Quos inter hic Hubertus Goltzius est, homo Germanus, sed voluntate ac industria media in Roma natus, qui ingenio, longinquis itineribus, singulari industria, manuum facilitate usuque plurimum est consecutus. Idque non meo testimonio, quod in hac professione non omnino nullum est, sed omnium per Italiam, ubi ista praesertim vigent, Galliam et Germaniam virorum, celebri fama atque literis autoritatem qui sibi constituere. Nam cum in Gallias rediissem, tertioque Italiam inviserem,[181] apud omnes eius diligentiam gratam, et memoriam frequentem sentiebam. Ac nihil quod ad illustrandam hanc pulcherrimam totque annis desertam cognitionem pertinere ratus est, uspiam neglexit. Ilico aedibus nobilium pervestigatis, omnia inspicere, intima et quae pro foribus et temere locata sunt, voluit, annotavit, inque usum atque ordinem sevocavit. Ut nullum in Europa locum sciam, quem sibi reliquum fecerit, et ubi praesens non fuerit, multo vero magis accurata eius et multis extollenda nominibus inquisitio quo non pertinuerit.

Offert tuae maiestati specimen illustre et (nisi me indulgens amor fallit) hoc in genere adhuc praecipuum longeque maiora daturus est, si vita illi tuaeque maiestatis gratia, ad quam hoc suo opere nititur, commode suppetat. Varium est studium et amplissimum, sed quod a privatis, nisi tua maiestas similes accedant, sustineri vix queat.[182] Commendo igitur maiestati tuae Goltzium, utque patrocinio iusto comprehendat, supplico ac spondeo multis partibus rem ac investigationem antiquitatis Hubertum brevi cumulaturum, cuius ego sensus et conatuum indicia non pauca nuper Brugis apud nobilissimum et vetustatis amantissimum Marcum Laurinum dominum a Watervliet ipse vidi. Tuam maiestatem Deus nobis conservet, utque perpetuus sit erga τὰ παλαιὰ καὶ ἀξιομνημόνευτα favor,[183] Deum comprecor. Datum Antverpiae. IX. Kalendis Octobris MDLXIII.[184]

---

[180] Print: *numismatis*.

[181] Sambucus first arrived in Padua in October 1553 and returned to Vienna in late 1557. He returned from Vienna to Padua and Venice at the end of 1558 and left for France in the spring of 1560. Finally, he arrived from Paris in Genova in mid-1562, where he remained until the summer of 1563. Cf. 'Várady, "Relazioni di Giovanni Zsámboky," 17-20 (who rejects Gerstinger's thesis about Sambucus's fourth trip to Italy).

[182] It was considerably bold to ask for Ferdinand's patronage for Goltzius. As *aulae familiaris*, Sambucus was at the time only at the lowest level of the court hierarchy. At the same time it was a strategy, characteristic of Sambucus's social skills, that could confirm and enhance his own position.

[183] old and memorable things

[184] There is a variant of the same letter, which was a shorter, first version, printed on the last leaf of the book (ddiiii^r) with a different date (10 September): "Quanta sit monimentorum vetustatis utilitas, atque etiam voluptas, non solum memoria litterarum, sed quoque antiqui operis numorum studium et cum historiis contentio satis ostendit. Quot enim historiae et praeclara exempla aut valde obscura essent aut, nisi horum testimonio ac lumine accenderentur, prorsus laterent, ut merito ἀντίστροφος cognitio ταῖς ἱστορίαις esse videatur? Ea re tua maiestas in cogendis omnis generis numismatibus non levem curam, maximos sumptus ponit, multosque suo exemplo ad has cogitationes indies excitat. Quos inter hic Hubertus Goltzius est, homo Germanus, sed voluntate ac industria media in Roma natus, qui ingenio, longinquis itineribus, singulari industria, manuum facilitate usuque plurimum est consecutus. Offert tuae maiestati specimen illustre et (nisi me indulgens amor fallit) hoc in genere adhuc praecipuum longeque maiora daturus est, si vita illi tuaeque maiestatis gratia, ad quam hoc suo opere nititur, commode suppetat. Varium est studium et amplissimum, sed quod a privatis, nisi tua maiestas similes accedant, sustineri vix queat. Commendo igitur maiestati tuae aiestati Goltzium, utque patrocinio iusto comprehendat, supplico, ac spondeo multis partibus rem ac investigationem antiquitatis Hubertum brevi cumulaturum, cuius ego sensus et conatuum indicia non pauca nuper Brugis apud nobilissimum et vetustatis amantissimum Marcum Laurinum dominum a Watervliet ipse vidi. Tuam maiestatem Deus nobis conservet, utque perpetuus sit erga τὰ παλαιὰ καὶ ἀξιομνημόνευτα favor, Deum comprecor. Datum Brugis. IIII. Idus Septembris MDLXIII." See Sambucus's complaint about the erroneous print of this text in the preceding letter.

41.
Sambucus to Abraham Ortelius[185]
22 September 1563, Ghent

The original is kept in Cambridge, Mass., Houghton Library, Ms. Lat. 225. Published in Ortelius, *Epistulae*, 28-30; Gerstinger, "Die Briefe," 62-65.

Sambucus has received the package from Hubertus Goltzius with two bound and three unbound volumes; one volume is for Sambucus, but there are four superfluous pages in it (which he is sending back), while a page is missing from Goltzius's letter to Marcus Laurinus (which he is demanding). He is surprised by the presence of his letter of dedication at the end of the volume. Sambucus calls attention to other errors concerning his letter and asks for their emendation and offers to pay for it. The package is not suitable for transportation by postal service or a horseman, not even for ten ducats would anyone bring it to Augsburg. Sambucus could have the package brought to Augsburg and then to Vienna via the Fuggers' agents, but it would take longer. He has already written to Johannes Keller, the Fuggers' agent in Antwerp, and is sending him the little box, Keller could forward it to Antwerp. If Goltzius wants to make this process go faster, he can get the package back from the agent. Since Sambucus will be in Vienna in two months' time, he could also bring it personally to the emperor and ask for a reward. If it is too much of a delay, at least the emperor should have his copy, together with a letter by Goltzius, from Keller. Johann Birckmann should make sure Ferdinand gets this copy and should assure him of the arrival of others. Ortelius should ask Libertus Malcotius to add immediately an errata to his book (i.e the second edition of his De imitatione a Cicerone*) and send him four leather-bound copies to Ghent.*

S. D.

Accepi sarcinam ab Huberto missam, in qua sunt duo exemplaria ligata, tria non ligata, unum pro me, sed superfluae sunt in meo quatuor paginae et pagina deest epistulae Huberti ad M. Laurinum, ubi incipere debet "maximo tuo merito."[186] Mitte hanc paginam mihi aut istic

---

[185] Abraham Ortelius (1527–1598) was humanist, antiquarian and map-maker of Antwerp, famous for his *Theatrum Orbis Terrarum*, the first modern atlas. Ortelius, a nicodemite and enemy of religious enthusiasts like his friend Plantin, was appointed geographer to the king of Spain on the recommendation of Benito Arias Montano in 1575. See Cornelis Koeman, *The history of Abraham Ortelius and his Theatrum orbis terrarum* (Lausanne: Sequoia, 1964); Robert W. Karrow Jr., *Mapmakers of the Sixteenth Century and Their Maps: Bio-Bibliographies of the Cartographers of Abraham Ortelius* (Chicago: Newberry Library–Speculum Orbis Press, 1993); *Abraham Ortelius, 1527–1598: cartograaf en humanist*, eds. R.W. Karrow, Jr. et al. (Turnhout: Brepols, 1998); Joost Depuydt, "'Vale, verum antiquae historiae lumen': Antiquarianism in the Correspondence between Justus Lipsius and Abraham Ortelius," in Gilbert Tournoy et al., eds., *Iustus Lipsius Europae Lumen et Columen* (Leuven: University Press, 1999), 34-47; Jason Harris, "The Religious Position of Abraham Ortelius," in *The Low Countries at the Crossroads of Religious Beliefs*, eds. Arie-Jan Gelderblom et al. (Leiden: Brill, 2004), 89-139; Tine Luk Meganck, *Erudite Eyes: Friendship, Art and Erudition in the Network of Abraham Ortelius (1527–1598)* (Leiden: Brill, 2017). For Sambucus's maps in the *Theatrum orbis* see Laszlo L. Grof, "Ortelius' maps of Hungary," *The Map Collector* 6 (1979), 3-11. On Ortelius's relationship to Sambucus see letter 154, note 912 and consult the Index.

[186] Hubertus Goltzius (1526–1583) was an antiquarian, numismatist, poet and publisher living in Antwerp. For a bibliography on Goltzius see C.E. Dekesel, *Hubertus Goltzius: the Father of Ancient Numismatics: Venlo-Weertsburg 30.10.1526 – Bruges 24.10.1583: an annotated and illustrated bibliography* (Ghent: Bibliotheca Numismatica Siciliana, 1988). The numismatic work in question is Goltzius, *C. Iulius Caesar sive historiae imperatorum*. On Sambucus's role in the publication see also the next letter. The page beginning with "Maximo

reserva, ego superfluas tibi quoque mittam. Miror vos epistolam meam in fine etiam reliquisse, quid opus est duabus?[187] Nonne risum alicui movebit? Quaeso te, ut aut configatur ultima epistola atramento, aut, quod ego mallem, recudatur tota ultima pagina meis sumptibus, ne ita risui sit negligentia, et scribe, quantum petat typographus. In ea vero mea epistola, quae aucta est, duo sunt errata (omnium visu) pro risu et (numismatis) pro numismatibus.[188] Rogo ut mea causa et amore in omnibus exemplis pro v facias r, et ex s fac b_9, hoc est bus, ut sit numismatib$_9$.

Caeterum sarcina est inepta postae aut equiti nec quisquam eam pro decem aureis aut pluribus saltem Augustam ferret.[189] Itaque scribe Huberto, me, si velit, Augustam curru missurum et illinc deinde Viennam per dominos Fuggeros curaturum, sed tarde perferetur, ut vix ante tres menses eo perventura sit. Ego scripsi Antverpiam ac cistulam remitto ad Ioannem Keller, qui est in aedibus Fuggerorum, ut is, si vos voletis, occasione per currum data Augustam mittat; sin Hubertus citius mittere volet, ut recipiatis ab Ioanne Keller, is sarcinam vobis restituet. Si Huberto videbitur non incommodum expectare, ut curru transferatur Augustam, ego mittam. Et quoniam ego ipse Deo volente intra duos menses omnino Viennae in curia caesareae maiestatis ero, ipsemet offeram postea et de premio urgebo suam maiestatem et Regem Maximilianum. Quod si tanta mora nocere videretur, saltem ut caesarea maiestas suum exemplar ligatum aliquo modo habeat et literas Hubertus addat, cures.

Per Deum, ex animo doleo me equo aut per postam non posse mittere. Quod si Birkmanus unum tantum exemplum ad caesarem mitteret et per fratrem offeri curaret, bonum esset et significaret caesari Hubertum propediem plura exempla missurum.[190] Haec nollem Hubertus aliter, quam sentio, acciperet. Expiscare tu ipse Antverpiae, intelliges neminem equo hanc vel etiam minorem sarcinam recepturum unquam, ut longe vehat. Itaque ut dixi, haec statim Huberto significa: sarcina est in aedibus Fuggerorum apud Ioannem Keller, qui, si voletis, eam restituet.

Mi Abrahame, dic bibliopolae Liberto,[191] ut errata et indicem missum statim meo libello adiciat et quatuor in corio ligata exemplaria mittat ad hospitium Rosae Gandavum. Ego pretium persolvam. Dic illi quoque me iam in Emblematum argumento versari et propediem aliquid ostensurum. Tu literas tuas ad hospitium Rosae mittito. Vale et statim haec Huberto scribito et mihi rescribas. Gandavo 22 Septembris 1563. Ioannes Sambucus.

---

tuo merito" is f. K^r. The preface is addressed to Marcus Laurinus, Lord of Watervliet (1525–1581), Goltzius's patron and collector of antique coins, the person who initiated the foundation of the printing press "Officina Goltziana" by searching out Goltzius as an illustrator for his manuscript book on Caesar and who thus also contributed to the book, being probably the author of the texts accompanying the coins. Sambucus dedicated an emblem to Goltzius (*Emblemata* 1564, 113) and devoted one of his emblems to Marcus Laurinus and to the flowers in his garden (*Emblemata* 1564, 196). The family of Laurinus belonged to the intellectual elite. His father (with the same name) was friends with Erasmus, Vivés and More. Cf. Herman de la Fontaine Verwey, "The first private press in the Low Countries. Marcus Laurinus and the Officina Goltziana," *Quaerendo* 2 (1972), 29-310.

[187] On the recto of the last leaf Goltzius printed the first shorter version of Sambucus's dedication addressed to Ferdinand, which is cited in note 184 to letter 40.

[188] See the next letter. Also see Hessels's smart note in Ortelius, *Epistulae*, 892.

[189] Apparently, Ortelius and Goltzius asked Sambucus to send the copies to the emperor, but Sambucus was reluctant to pay for the postage costs, which were significant since the package was "oversized".

[190] Johann Birckmann (1527–1572) was a member of the famous publishing firm, which was based in Cologne, Antwerp and Louvain. It had been founded by his father, Arnold, and was actually run by his mother, Agnès von Gennep. See Victoria Christman, "The Coverture of Widowhood: Heterodox Female Publishers in Antwerp, 1530–1580," *The Sixteenth Century Journal* 42 (2011), 77-97, at 90. See the biography of Johann Birckmann by Josef Benzig in *NDB* 2 (1955), 254 and letter 42, note 192.

[191] Libertus Malcotius was an Antwerp publisher. The book in question is Sambucus, *De imitatione a Cicerone petenda* (2nd edition).

Address: Domino Abrahamo Ortelio cosmographo Antverpiensi amico suo. Tot Antwerpen in de Vette hinne,[192] in die Cammestratt.

42.
Sambucus to Emperor Ferdinand I
28 September 1563, Ghent

The original is kept in Vienna, ÖNB, Cod. 9736, f. 3ʳ⁻ᵛ. Published in Gerstinger, "Die Briefe," 65-66.

Sambucus praises Goltzius's Iulius Caesar sive historiae imperatorum. *It will be joyful for Ferdinand to inspect it. Goltzius is sending the first printed copy and is asking for the emperor's patronage. Sambucus knows that the emperor appreciates such endeavours, and he is asking him to provide financial support for Goltzius as Goltzius works to complete the remaining eleven parts of the same project. Having ten years of experience of laborious touring, Sambucus cannot but admire and recommend Goltzius's enterprise. Goltzius could not bring his work to Ferdinand personally because of the distance that divides them and because of his continuous work on writing and illustrating the history of consuls. As for Sambucus, he hopes to return to Vienna next winter and show the results of his research and express his gratitude.*

Sacra Caesarea Maiestas, domine, domine clementissime.

Prodiit tandem liber Huberti Goltzii antiquarii singularis et per universam prope Europam hoc in genere professionis et diligentia celeberrimi.[193] Quo historiam Iulii Caesaris sociorumque rerum interpretando aversas partes atque symbola varie ac docte complexus est. Diu a multis hic labor, ut appareret, expetitus est spemque Italiae non parvam hoc rudimento seu potius exemplo ille concitavit. Sed tuae quoque maiestati gratos fore eius conatus et iucundam horum inspectionem quis dubitat, qui hodie ista laude inter principes Christianos primum locum studio ac sumptibus facile obtines? Mittit ad tuam maiestatem exemplum omnium, quod vulgo conspectum sit, primum et patrocinium humillime implorat, se suamque operam supplex dicat vovetque. Scio, qua gratia tua maiestas me, qua eiusdem voluntatis alios accipiat, itaque pro Huberto communiter tuam maiestatem oro, facile et clementer istud primum consilii volumen acceptet, utque reliqui eiusdem argumenti undecim ab eodem informati citius et felicius lucem videant, sua congenita benignitate urgeat, liberalitate provocet. Multa Hubertus vidit, conquisivit infinita, non pauca informavit, quae cum tuae maiestatis laude coniunguntur.

    Ego per hosce annos decem, quibus ista tracto, atque non ociosa peregrinatione, quod uspiam rarum et nobile est, vidi (absit a verbis in cuiusquam iniuriam gratia). Goltzii institutum nisi probare, mirari, omnibus commendare nequeo. Quod vero ipse, uti volebat, ad tuam maiestatem exiguum hoc nominique tuo consecratum opus non detulerit, itineris et temporis longitudo in causa fuit. Est enim assiduus in signandis, sculpendis, exponendisque fastorum consulariumque simul historiis, ut cum reliquiis ac notis marmorum capitolinorum res et magistratus ipsosque adiunctos numos habeas.

---

[192] Hessels claims that this house was the residence of the bookseller Arnold (II) Birckmann († c. 1576) (Ortelius, *Epistulae*, 892), who was Johann's brother (see letter 41, note 190).

[193] The letter accompanied the gift copy of Goltzius's *C. Iulius Caesar sive historiae imperatorum*. See letters 40-41.

Quod ad me, tuae maiestatis clientulum attinet ac reditum, tua maiestas sciat me hac proxima hyeme, Deo volente, Viennam rediturum ac tuae maiestati diligentiam et, quod tot itineribus et vigiliis sumptibusque coegi, subiectissime ostensurum atque gratiae tuae maiestatis omnia ex animo delaturum. Cuius me clementiae humiliter etiam ac etiam commendo.

Tuam maiestatem Deus integram et salvam custodiat. Datum Gandavi in Flandria, 28 Septembris 1563. Tuae caesareae maiestati deditissimus cliens et aulicus Ioannes Sambucus Tirnaviensis Pannonius.

43.
Hadrianus Junius[194] to Sambucus
[c. November–December 1563[195]], Haarlem

Late 16th century copy with corrections in another contemporary hand in Utrecht, Universiteitbibliotheek, Hs. 829, 167^r-169^r. Published in Junius, 403-408.

Junius thanks Sambucus for his letter, and since he understood from it that Sambucus has not received his letters sent from Amsterdam, he has quickly had a copy made. He was surprised that the pack of books did not contain Goltzius's Iulius Caesar sive historiae imperatorum *with Sambucus's preface, a draft of which Sambucus has previously given Junius. Junius is afraid that Rembertus Dodonaeus's vernacular book on plants may have been crammed in the pack as a substitute, in case Goltzius's work has not yet been printed, however, he was eager for Sambucus's preface. He loved Sambucus's book on Ciceronian imitation, but he lost it before he got it, as Bishop Gulielmus Lindanus, who was visiting him, took it with him for a few days, as he was greatly impressed by Junius's praise of Sambucus's learning. The list of Greek books that Sambucus recently gave to Junius made a strong impression on him; of the listed books, he only desires Eunapius, whom he deeply loves, showing thus Sambucus the respect he feels for him. In return, he accepts Sambucus's offer to mediate at court and obtain patronage for Junius. He would write the history of Austria (which he reckons Sambucus has already started) or the history of other lands, or translate from Greek into Latin. A yearly stipend would really do him good. If*

---

[194] Hadrianus Junius (Adriaen de Jonghe) (1511-1575) was a significant Dutch humanist, physician and historiographer. Born in Horn, he attended the local Latin school of Haarlem, where he settled in 1550 as city physician and private tutor. Junius was a very prolific editor of Latin and Greek authors who was much interested in lexicography. Sambucus's activity (especially his collection of manuscripts or his *Emblemata*) was an important motivation for the much older Junius. In 1567, he became historiographer of the States of Holland, and unlike Sambucus (who became imperial historian a year before) he made significant historical research, producing a book entitled *Batavia*. On Junius's encyclopaedic learning and his fondness of philological miscellanea see *The Kaleidoscopic Scholarship of Hadrianus Junius*. Sambucus and Junius mutually dedicated emblems to each other. Cf. with Hadrianus Junius, *Emblemata ... eiusdem aenigmatum libellus* (Antverpiae: Plantin, 1565), 27, and Sambucus, *Emblemata* (1564), 140. Junius also figures in Sambucus, *Icones veterum aliquot*, no. 48. On Junius and Sambucus see *Humanistes du bassin des Carpates II. Johannes Sambucus*, liv-lvii.

[195] With regards to the date of this letter, one of the *termini ante quem* seems to be Junius's reference to his emblems (see the last sentence: "mittam ad te propediem Emblemata quinquaginta") and cf. with letter 44 ("intelligo te nihildum Emblematum meorum accepisse binis iam literis ad te destinatorum") and letter 46 ("nunc reliqua ad te Emblemata in universum numero quinquagena mitto"). On the other hand, the middle part of the letter, in which Junius contemplates the dignities and salary Sambucus could obtain for him in Vienna (in particular, the reference to the title of *comes palatinus*, which Sambucus himself obtained only in 1567), might appear to suggest Sambucus was already back in Vienna. Yet, he had only recently given Junius his catalogue. Also see *Humanistes du bassin des Carpates II. Johannes Sambucus*, lvi.

Sambucus could arrange this for him, he would be god for Junius. Obtaining the title of comes palatinus, *which is the habit of the times, as Sambucus has explained him, would be the icing on the cake. Junius praises Sambucus's letter concerning the* Stromata *by Clement of Alexandria and expresses his derogatory opinion of Ravisius Textor's chaotically organised collection of epithets. He goes on to explain its weaknesses, using the example of "sambuca" and "sambucus" and several other examples. Junius lists as an example a series of epithets, which he will explain in a different manner. He is going to send Sambucus 50 emblems, which he is currently copying.*

Literas tuas postremas, singularis erga me amoris et benevolentiae testes locupletes et muneris chartacei, eiusque liberalissimi, comites accepi, ὦ μουσῶν εὐκόλων ἀνθρήνιον Sambuce,[196] in quibus cum altissimum sit silentium de literis meis Amsterdamo missis, seu potius αὐτοσχεδίῳ carmine[197] ad te misso, non potui, quin eius exemplum tibi describendum curarem in ipsa temporis angustia.

In libraria vero sarcina miratus sum, cur abessent Commentarii Iulii Caesaris et de numismatis opus, tua praefatione exornatum,[198] et improbis votis a me saepe expetitum, cuius tu specimen ad me pridem dederas. Itaque suspicio animum subiit, eius loco ut subditivus liber de stirpibus Dodonaei, vernacula nostra lingua scriptus[199] eo in fasce stipatus fuerit, nisi forte nondum reliquerit praelum. Quicquid sit, tu scrupulum ex animo facile exemeris, quanquam etiam primorem paginam et praefationem in historias Caesaris[200] desiderabam.

Libellos tuos de imitatione exosculatus sum,[201] sed amisi ferme priusquam accepi (quod Terentiana Thais ominatur Chremeti[202]), quod Lindanus Ruremundensis episcopus, qui mihi tum forte in musaeo adstabat,[203] admiratione eruditionis tuae ex meis verbis tactus, desiderium legendis illis ut expleret, secum eos abstulerit ad dies aliquot, quamvis excusarem mihi nunquam etiam lectos aut visos. Sed quid agerem? Sic homo est.

Catalogus authorum Graecorum, quem nuper ad me dederas, θαῦμα, ἢ ὡς σαφέστερον λέγειν ἔκπληξίν τινα[204] mihi peperit, avertat Deus βασκανίας[205] omen, quam tu amuleto

---

[196] Philostratus Iunior, *Imagines* 13 (884.25): wasp's nest of friendly muses.
[197] improvised
[198] Goltzius, *C. Iulius Caesar sive historiae imperatorum.* See the three preceding letters.
[199] Reference is made to Rembert Dodoens's *Cruydeboeck* (Antwerp: van der Loe, 1554). Rembertus Dodonaeus (Rembert Dodoens) (1517–1585) was a Flemish physician and a distinguished botanist. His father was physician to Margaret of Austria in Mechelen. He studied in Leuven and made a long grand tour, which included a sojourn in Basel. He worked as city physician, refusing prestigious job offers from princes like Philip II of Spain, and became Maximilian II's physician in 1574 (probably thanks to his friendship with Carolus Clusius, who was the French translator of his *Cruydeboeck*), coming into conflict with Johannes Crato (see letter 272). He apparently preserved his office also under Rudolf II, and he accepted the chair of medicine in Leiden only in 1582. See W. F. Vande Walle, "Dodonaeus: A bio-bibliographical summary," in *Dodonaeus in Japan: Translation and the Scientific Mind in the Tokugawa Period*, ed. idem (Leuven: University Press, 2001), 33-43.
[200] Print: *Ciceronis.*
[201] Sambucus, *De imitatione Ciceroniana.*
[202] Cf. Terentius, *Eunuchus.* 4. 6.13.
[203] Gulielmus Lindanus (William van der Lindt) (1525–1588) was a Catholic theologian of Dordrecht and a staunch defender of the Catholic faith and Trento. He became royal counsellor and inquisitor in Friesland and bishop of Ruremonde (on Philip II's appointment), which was a newly established seat; however his bishopric activity was wrecked by protests of the Protestants. He was the author of *Panoplia Evangelica, sive de verbo Dei evangelico libri quinque* (Paris: apud Guilelmum Iulian, 1564), mentioned here. Lindanus later visited Sambucus in Ghent (see letter 48). See P. Th. van Beuningen, *Wilhelmus Lindanus als inquisiteur en bisschop: Bijdrage tot zijn biografie (1525–1576)* (Assen: Van Gorcum, 1966); Antonio Davila, "La polémica Arias Montano-Wilhelmus Lindanus: un nuevo documento (AGR I 115, 3714)," *Humanistica Lovaniensia* 49 (2000), 139-165.
[204] some surprise, or to say it more clearly, some consternation
[205] evil eye

praesenti facillime averteris, certe si tantum operae mihi (id quod non dubito, obtestari dum fas sit, quin impetrem) praestare lubeat, meo ut aere descriptis frui detur Eunapii vicenis illis Sophistarum vitis (quas ego prorsus depereo, ne te amoris nostri ardorem clam esse patiar),[206] nihil unquam gratius feceris. Quid aio? An vero quicquam mihi esse possit gratius, καὶ προφερέστερον ἠδὲ καὶ εὐμαρέστερον [207] quam quod tute mihi modo offers de conditionis ratione, ut alendis studiis, sublevandis (ut tuo utar verbo) lucubrationibus honorificum ac luculentum industriae subsidium deposcatur a maximis laudatissimisque principibus. Nosti vetus illud, non defuturos Marones, si sint Maecenates. Velim equidem quidvis subire oneris in tantorum heroum gratiam, sive Austriacae historiae (quam te exorsum esse telam autumo) texturam mandent, sive alterius provinciae curam delegent, sive interpretandi aut e Graeca in Romanam coloniam traducendi munus credant, quo immortalitate nominis argumentis exilioribus partam illustriore via tuerer. Quod tunc animo incrementum, quam studiis industriaeque accessionem futuram auguraris, si honoraria stipe eaque annua cohonestari me talium principum beneficentia dignaretur? Quod si fiat (potes autem in ea re plurimum), nae tu mihi Deus fueris in universum, οὐ μόνον ὁ ἐκ μηχανῆς.[208] Ad id, si comitis palatini iustus, haud trivialis iste titulus accederet, ut nunc sunt mores et vita (quod tu prudenter edisseris) quid me beatius?[209] Te mihi praesidium, ornamentum, Aiacis clypeum esse deputo. Perfice, quantum potes, et ubi potes, non omnino specto illud: bis dat, qui cito.

Epistola tua in *Stromatum* (quod librorum de epithetis, in locos communes digestis, indigitamentum erit) editionem servabitur.[210] An tu quidquam insulsius, ineptiusve Ravisii, vere rabidi et Athamante tragico vesanioris hominis collectaneis vidisti, obsecro?[211] Credo equidem idem te mecum sentire de eo opere, quod nullo iudicio indigestu quoddam epithetorum chaos congessit. Velut, ubi sambucam (recreor enim tui nominis fausta recordatione) epithetis insignit medullatae, olentis et triangulae, hoc postremum tam sambuco competit, quam illi ipsi; nec enim in arborem illam notissimam cadit, sed in sambucam, instrumentum musicum triquetrum, fidibus tendi solitum. Rursus Iberiae, quam ab Ibero amne Hispaniam recte vocari annotat, quid congruunt illa epitheta venenorum ferax, venenifera, quum haec Iberiae, Ponti regionis ad Colchidem sitae, propria sint? Itaque sit, ut et a latae culpae crimine exsolvere se nequeat, et tamen eadem opera iuvenes et semidoctos altissima erroris caligine involvat libere citra iudicii amussim[212] epithetis rei incongruis abutentes. Exemplii gratia, avenam pro sati genere levem, gracilem, sterilem dici patiar, non itidem argutam, septiformem, Phoebeiam, docilem, quae in avenam pro fistula quadrant aptius. Quanquam e classicis et maiorum gentium scriptoribus retexuisse illum suas corollas, nunc parum rite lemniscatas, mallem. Neque enim statim epithetorum ordini adscribendum, si oceanum fertilem vocet Faustus quispiam. Expenso hic iudicio opus est, et Critolai bilance.[213] Velim potius explicari mihi, cur Pythagoras

---

[206] On Sambucus's Eunapius-manuscript and its edition by Junius see "Eunapius-edition" under "Sambucus" in the Index.
[207] at the same time both more excellent and more convenient
[208] and not only ex machina
[209] Sambucus handed in a petition for the title of *comes palatinus* only in 1567, but he used this title a month earlier in his marriage contract. See letter 101.
[210] Junius called his collection of adjectives *Stromata* (patchwork) after Clement of Alexandria's *Stromata*. The manuscript book was never published. See Van Miert, "Epilogue," 297. See also letters 49 and 56.
[211] Junius also epithomised Johannes Ravisius Textor's *Specimen epithetorum*, a book on adjectives, which appeared posthumously. *Epithetorum Ioannis Ravisii Textoris epitome, ex Hadriani Iunii medici recognitione. Accesserunt eiusdem Ravisii Synonyma poëtica, multo quam prius locupletiora* (Londini: [Ex officina H. Ioannes Iacksoni], [1588 or 1595]).
[212] Print adds: *ac pormiscue.*
[213] Peripatetic philosopher Critolaus of Phaselis (c. 200–c. 118 BC) used a parable of scales, reported by Cicero

vocetur Panthoïdes, cur ab Ausonio renatus²¹⁴. Et id genus alia. Ego in meis *Stromatibus* aliam rationem sequar. Verbi gratia, cur navim μιλτοπάρηον²¹⁵ et κορωνίδα²¹⁶ vocet Homerus, ἰουλόπεζον,²¹⁷ πελαργοχρῶτα²¹⁸ Lycophron, ποικιλόστολον²¹⁹ Sophocles, εὔσκαρθμον²²⁰ Q. Calaber²²¹, κυανώπιδα²²² Aeschylus, ὑλότομον²²³ Sibylla, εὐστείραν²²⁴ Apollonius, ἀμύαλον²²⁵ Theocritus, ἁλίδρομον ²²⁶ Nonnus, δουροπαγῆ,²²⁷ λινοπτέρυγα²²⁸ et βαθυτέρμονα²²⁹ Oppianus, θοὴν²³⁰ Callimachus, ἐυεργέα²³¹ Dionysius, ποντοπόρον²³² Orpheus etc. Addam alterum exemplum, apes βουγενεῖς²³³ Porphyrius, βουπαίδας,²³⁴, εὐαγέας,²³⁵ σιμβλήϊδας²³⁶ Epigrammata, ὑμηττίδας,²³⁷ διαθρύπτους²³⁸ Nicander, ἡεροφοίτους, ἀριστοπόνους²³⁹ Phocylides, σιμὰς²⁴⁰ Theocritus, ξουθὰς²⁴¹ Sophocles, ἀνθομουργοὺς²⁴² Aeschylus, ξουθοπτέρους²⁴³ Euripides, ἐργάτιδας²⁴⁴ Pisides, φιλέργους²⁴⁵ Nazianzenus, ἐριβόμβους²⁴⁶ Orpheus. Habes, quam insistam viam, ab indocto grammatista alienam, quam te non improbaturum spero, mutaturus vela, si aliud suadeas. Mittam ad te propediem emblemata quinquaginta, quae describo, praeter ista historiarum aliorumque argumentorum emblemata.²⁴⁷ Vale. Harlemi.

---

[213] (*Tusc.* 5.51), to contrast inner and external goods.
[214] This is explained by, for instance, Jean Baptiste Dugas-Montbel, *Observations sur l'Iliade d'Homère*, vol. 2 (Paris: Didot, 1830), 98; Ausonius, *Epistolae* 25.38–39.
[215] red cheeked. *Ilias* 2.637.
[216] curved. *Ilias* 18.332.
[217] many-oared. Lycophron 23.
[218] stork-coloured. Lycophron 24.
[219] with variegated prow. Sophocles, *Philoctetes* 343.
[220] swift-springing. Quintus Smyrnaeus 14, 10
[221] In the sixteenth century, Quintus of Smyrna was mostly known as Quintus Calaber, as Aldus had referred to him in his *editio princeps* of 1504, because the only manuscript of his work had been discovered in Otranto.
[222] dark-looking. Aeschylus, *Supplices* 743; *Persae* 559.
[223] cut in the wood. *Oracula Sibyllina* 3.824.
[224] with good keel. Apollonius Rhodius, *Argonautica* 1.401.
[225] marrowless. Manuscript and print: ἀκύαλον. Neither variant seems to occur in the surviving text of Theocritus.
[226] running over the sea. Nonnus, *Dionysiaca* 43.281.
[227] compact of beams. Oppianus, *Halieutica* 1.358.
[228] sail-winged, Oppianus, *Cynegetica* 1.121; 4.61.
[229] deep-edged, Oppianus, *Cynegetica* 2.87.
[230] quick. Callimachus, *Epigrammata* 17.1.
[231] well-made. Dionysius Thrax, *Ars grammatica* 6 (7b).
[232] seafaring. *Argonautica Orphica* 53; 1100.
[233] born from cow. Porphyrius, *De antro nympharum* 15; 18.
[234] children of the ox. *Anthologia Graeca* 7.36.3
[235] pure. *Anthologia Graeca* 9.404.7
[236] hive-children. *Anthologia Graeca* 9.226.1.
[237] children of Hymettos. Nicander, *Alexipharmaca* 446. Mount Hymettos near Athens was famous for its honey. Cf. Plinius, *Naturalis historia* 11.32 (XIII).
[238] Nicander, *Alexipharmaca* 445.
[239] air-wandering; excellently working. Pseudo-Phocylides 171.
[240] flat-nosed. Theocritus, *Idyllia* 3.8.
[241] nimble. Sophocles, frg. 398.5.
[242] working in flowers. Aeschylus, *Persae* 612.
[243] with nimble wings. Euripides, *Hercules* 487; frg. 467.4. Manuscript: ξυνθοπτέρους.
[244] female workers. Georgius Pisides, *Hexameron* 1150.
[245] industrious. Gregorius Nazianzenus, *Oratio* 44.11.
[246] loud-buzzing. Orpheus, frg. 220 (154 K).
[247] Junius, *Emblemata*. Cf. with letter 45.

44.
Hadrianus Junius to Sambucus
[December 1563], [Haarlem?]

Late 16th century copy in Utrecht, Universiteitbibliotheek, Hs. 829, 56ʳ. Published in Hadrianus Junius, *Epistolae selectae*, 67.

Junius received Sambucus's letter of 26 November with his epigrams and the engraved emblems, from which he understands that Sambucus sent his letter before he had received two of Junius's letters, which included his emblems. He has also received Goltzius's book with copper engravings by a Dutch engraver, to which four copies were attached. He does not know if these are to be sold by Goltzius or by Laurinus. He would fly to Sambucus if he could take Pegasus's wings. If it is good for Sambucus and the weather allows, he will visit him in January in order to meet him personally and discuss the edition of Nonius with Plantin.

Epistolam tuam ad VI. Calendas Decembris datam, epigrammate tuo, ceu emblemate quopiam adsculpto, locupletem accepi heri,[248] e qua intelligo te nihildum emblematum meorum accepisse binis iam literis ad te destinatorum,[249] semel per affinem meum, secundo per tabellarium Amserodamaeum, sed earum adventum antevertisse tuam epistolam ex inscriptione diei suspicor aut hariolor. Iulii Caesaris historiam a formarum sculptore insigni nostrate, qui eius libri τὸ πρόσωπον τηλαυγὲς[250] in aere expressit, accepi mutuo.[251] Ad quem quaterna missa fuerant exemplaria vendenda, haud scio ab Hubertone an a D. Laurino.[252] Equidem si Pegaseas possem asciscere mihi alas iam ad vos advolarem, cum lucubratiunculis aliquot meis iisque νεοτευχέσι καὶ ἔτι γλυφάνοιο ποτόσδουσιν,[253] ut cum Theocrito ludam. Certe animus eo anhelat nisi brumae incommoda et sumptuum immanitas deterreret. Sub Ianuarium tamen, si calculus accedat tuus, illuc iter paro, cum ut amicissimum caput semel adhuc ante obitum exosculer,[254] tum ut cum Plantino[255]

---

[248] Sambucus's *Emblemata* came out in August 1564. On the work see Visser, *Johannes Sambucus*. See also Zoltán Erdős, "Machtsymbole und politisches Programm in den *Emblemata* des Johannes Sambucus," in *Iohannes Sambucus / János Zsámboki*, 331-355.

[249] Junius, *Emblemata*. See letter 49.

[250] far-shining face

[251] Goltzius, *C. Iulius Caesar sive historiae imperatorum*. See the four preceding letters.

[252] Hubertus Goltzius and Marcus Laurinus, see letters 40-41.

[253] newly made and still smelling of the chisel. Cf. Theocritus, *Idyllia* 1.28.

[254] According to an anecdote Sambucus had once visited Junius in Haarlem, but when "he was told that Junius was having a drink with a couple of coachmen he was so shocked that a scholar of Junius's standing spent time with such people" that he left Haarlem immediately. The anecdote is quoted by Van Miert, "Epilogue," 293. "M. [Isaac] Vossius m'a conté que Sambuc, plus célèbre par la publication de plusieurs manuscrits que par son savoir, estant venu exprès en Hollande pour voir Hadrianus Junius, il apprit à son logis qu'il beuvoit avec des Wourmans, [voermannen in Dutch], c'est-à-dire des Charretiers; Ce qui luy donna tant de mépris pour ce grand Critique, qu'il s'en retourna sans le voir. Le départ de Sambuc estant rapporté à Junius, il s'excusa fort, disant qu'il ne s'estoit trouvé avec ces Wourmans, que pour apprendre d'eux quelques termes de leur métier, qu'il vouloir metre dans son Nomenclator qu'il faisoit alors." Paulus Colomesius, "Particularitez," in id., *Opuscula* (Parisiis: Mabre-Cramoisy, 1668), 132-133.

[255] Christophe Plantin (1520-1589) was one of the most influential and successful humanist publishers of the sixteenth century, and he was Sambucus's most important publisher (publishing also his "best-seller" *Emblemata*). He was famous for the high quality of his prints, his strong aesthetic sense, his large and important network and the religious middle-way that he represented. See Visser, *Joannes Sambucus and the Learned Image*, 49-84; Sandra Langereis, *De woordenaar: Christoffel Plantijn, 's werelds grootste drukker en uitgever* (Amsterdam: Uitgeverij Balans, 2014); *Ex officia plantiniana: Studia in memoriam Christophori Plantini*, eds. Marcus de

de Nonio aliquid certi statui possit,²⁵⁶ nisi brumalis ista tempestas transmittendis rebus incommoda me forte excludat. Breviorem me esse cogit subitus istius negotiatoris superventus et festinatus eiusdem discessus.

45.
Sambucus to Jean Grolier
3 January 1564, Ghent

Published in Sambucus, *Emblemata cum aliquot nummis* (1564), 232; republished with some interesting modifications (indicated in the notes below) in *Emblemata* (1566), 256.

Sambucus remembers how Grolier had once received him and how he esteemed him. Sambucus passed two years in daily conversation with Grolier inflamed by the study of antiquity, although he was very busy otherwise. He is indebted to Grolier for his benevolence, and he owes him the debt of dedicating one of his works to him. Although there is nothing to add to Grolier's fame, he wanted to pay tribute to him with his coins, some which he has collected over the course of the past two years, when he also greatly enlarged his library. These rare coins were also admired by Roman cardinals and Italian princes. He will try to make sure that no one in a similar state as his (modest but independent, and a diligent student of antiquity) supersedes him.

Magnifico domino Ioanni Groliero, thesaurario regio Lutetiae, salutem.

Scio, quanti me facias, quo animo semel comprehenderis, quem quotidie in tuis colloquiis et omnis antiquitatis delectationibus biennium fere, licet aliis quoque studiis ac negociis occupatissimum, esse me paterne volueris.²⁵⁷ Eius igitur voluntatis erga me prolixae ac singularis nomine tibi omnia debeo, sed imprimis, si quae ex meis scriptis aliquando tam gravi tamque illustri viro digna posset existere, memoriam. Quae quoniam ita dudum celebris, ita in omnium auribus ac simul animo posita est, nulla ut ex commendatione illi quicquam addi queat, in tuo aere me futurum semper hisce aereis aliquot nummis testari volui.²⁵⁸ Per hoc vero biennium scias me multis modis bibliothecam auxisse ornasseque meam, atque nummos, quos tantopere extollebas, maxime raris cumulasse, ut vel summis cardinalibus admirabiles Romae fuerint et per Italiam principibus. Doque operam, ne meae conditionis, satis angustae, liberalis tamen atque illius studiosae vetustatis quisquam me superet.²⁵⁹

Schepper and Francine De Nave = *De Gulden Passer*, vol. 66-67 (Antwerp: Vereeniging der Antwerpsche Bibliophielen, 1989); *Christophe Plantin, 1520-2020: Studies of the Officina Plantiniana at the Quincentennial of Plantin's Birth*, eds. Nina Lamal and J. Christopher Warner = *De Gulden Passer*, vol. 98:2 (Antwerp: Vereniging van de Antwerpse Bibliofielen, 2021).

²⁵⁶ Nonius Marcellus, *De proprietate sermonum*. On this project, cf. the Index.
²⁵⁷ In the 1566 edition Sambucus changes the end of the sentence, making the structure clearer: "quem quotidie in tuis colloquiis et omnis antiquitatis delectationibus esse toties, licet aliis quoque occupatissimum, more patris volueris."
²⁵⁸ In the 1566 edition Sambucus underlined that he published only a small selection of his coins in the *Emblemata*: "nam si plures, quos alii etiam pro insignibus produnt, et non nulla argentea ponere vellem, iustus libellus vix sufficeret."
²⁵⁹ In the 1566 edition, the end of the letter is considerably changed. Sambucus highlights one of his coins; mentions that in his fatherland there is hardly anyone interested in antique coins, and better explains his condition, describing it as a little impoverished by many years of touring and the deceit of some merchants: "Per hoc quippe triennium multis modis bibliothecam auxi ornavique meam ac antiqui operis numismata, quae tu adeo extollebas, maxime raris cumulavi, ut vel summis cardinalibus admirabiles Romae, et per Italiam principibus fuerint. Praesertim Otho hic aereus cum circo Hadriani et Pescennio, unicis, quod sciam, in Europa.

Vale, dominoque Henrico Memmio,[260] si grave non est, a me salutem. Gandavi, III. Nonas Ianuarii. MDLXIIII.

46.
Hadrianus Junius to Sambucus
[January 1564], Haarlem

Two late 16th-century copies[261] in Utrecht, Universiteitbibliotheek, Hs. 829, 55[r-v] and 151[v]-152[v]. Published in Junius, *Epistolae selectae*, 65-66.

From Sambucus's letter Junius realises that Sambucus also wrote a letter confirming he had recieved the emblems, but it got lost. Now he is sending Sambucus the remaining fifty emblems he made, and Sambucus should decide whether to burn or publish them. Although many think that they are not to be rejected and thrown away like dung, Sambucus's opinion will be decisive. He agrees with Sambucus's good opinion on Plantin. He very much likes his types and would not like to see delays in publishing his emblems. Junius lists his other books in preparation: a volume of poetry and his Nomenclator. He wants to dedicate his edition of Nonius to the emperor, provided Plantin will back this tedious work, but he still does not know how his emendations should be made typographically visible. Finally, Junius gives some examples of his conjectures and asks for Sambucus's opinion.

Literas tuas, vir doctissime, vicesimo Decembris scriptas, sub atrocissimum istud gelu accepi, in quibus video mentionem fieri epistolae a me non visae, qua scribis certiorem me reddidisse te de acceptis emblematibus, ea haud dubie naufragium passa videtur. Nunc reliqua ad te emblemata in universum numero quinquagena mitto, de quibus statue quod lubet, sive ea publicum tentare velis, sive mari flammisque aboleri iubeas, susque deque ferendum putabo: tametsi non prorsus reicula καὶ κοπρίων ἐκβλητότερα,[262] ut Democriti verbis utar, ea iudicent esse nonnulli, sed tui iudicii ἀκριβεία[263] momentum omne hac in re trahet.[264]

Plantini fidem, diligentiam et in deferendo mihi omni officio studium magnopere praedicas et id obviis ulnis ut defertur, amplector: certo typi placuerunt olim impense et quod

---

Doque operam, licet paucos, seu potius nullos in patria huiusce studii esse in desiderio admodum videam, ne meae conditionis et patrimonii satis angusti quidem ac tot peregrinationibus, impostura etiam quorundam mercatorum diminuti, mediocris et honesti tamen, homines voluntate atque conatibus hoc in genere professionis omnisque adeo antiquitatis longius superent. (Dated: Vienna tertio Iduum Martii. 1565.)

[260] Henri de Mesmes, cf. letters 31-34.
[261] Beside the two copies listed above, the same manuscript (Utrecht, Universiteitbibliotheek, Hs. 829) preserves an earlier version of this letter on folio 54v, with the content corresponding to the first paragraph only. The text was subsequently crossed out by the copyist, who was preparing the Hs. 829 as the fair copy for the printer, when he came across the longer version of the letter. The short version also identifies Haarlem as the place of dispatch. "Sambuco. Literas tuas, vir doctissime, vicesimo Decembris scriptas sub atrocissimum istud gelu accepi, in quibus video mentionem facis epistolae, quam (!) de acceptis emblematibus me certiorem reddideris, at eam ego non vidi. Mitto ad te emblemata reliqua in universum quinquagena, de quibus, si ad stomachum facient nec plane reiicula καὶ κοπρίων ἐκβλητότερα iuxta Heraclitum videbuntur, statue quod libet, sive flammis ea dedi velis, sive publicum tentare malis, susque deque ferendum putabo. Vale. Harlemo."
[262] [thrown away] quicker than dung. The expression goes back to Heraclitus, frg. B 96: νέκυες γὰρ κοπρίων ἐκβλητότεροι ("corpses should be thrown away quicker than dung"), not Democritus. In the shorter version of this letter in the same manuscript on folio 54[v], the quote is correctly ascribed to Heraclitus.
[263] accuracy
[264] Sambucus's good opinion of Junius's *Emblemata* was based on these epigrams. Cf. letter 49.

ad Emblematum editionem attinet, moram praecipitari velim. Poematia mea in decem aut duodecim libellos distributa brevi in publicum lucemque venire patiar.²⁶⁵ Item nomenclaturas rerum omnium in classes statosque locos digestas, nunc quaternis olim etiam octonis linguis expressas iam in procinctu habeo.²⁶⁶ Nonium Marcellum, qui et ab aliis doctis cum flagitio etiam deposcitur, quam primum ad editionem concinnatum caesareaeque maiestatis nomini inscriptum non denegabo,²⁶⁷ modo Plantinus molestam operam liberalitate nonnihil iuvet, sed exerceor cura dubia, quo potissimum pacto restituta loca praestiterit procudi, an margini adiici variata et interpolata lectio, an dissimulanter vel studiose praeteriri corrupta debeat, at hoc si fiat, parum momenti accessisse operi restituto videbitur. Exempli gratia. In dictione *Ramices* legitur περὶ ἀρετῆς,²⁶⁸ quum lectio verior sit περὶ τῆς κυήσεος [!].²⁶⁹ Ibidem *senex appetitus ac podagrosus,* quum legendum sit *senex arthriticus.* Si simpliciter emendatior lectio supponatur, vides multum gratiae decedere, quando ignoratio discriminis lectorem otiosum transmittit. Item in *Austrum* vulgati codices habent σὺν δ' εὔροστε νότοστε²⁷⁰ etc., vetustus recte legit κατὰ δὲ νότιος ῥέεν ἴδριος.²⁷¹ Odoraris, arbitror, quid velim. Tu sententiam tuam perscribe. Quid si exilioribus characteribus interpollis lectio addito asterisco interseratur? Miseram olim ad te oden ad Maximilianum Caesarem, ea an interciderit, dubito, quod illius haud memineris. Nunc oden strenae loco missam boni consule, tenuia damus tenues. Wolfio non invideo gloriam in mustaceo quaesitam.²⁷² Vale.

47.
Sambucus to Abraham Ortelius
19 January 1564, Ghent

The original is kept in Cambridge, Mass., The Houghton Library, Ms. Lat. 225.²⁷³ Published in Gerstinger, "Die Briefe," 66-67.

As for the poems that Ortelius wanted to include in his book, this is what Sambucus produced for now, before the muses supply him with something better. Regarding the coins, he has given his answer to Laurinus.

S. D.

Quod a me petiisti, ut aliquod Epigramma tuo libro adiungemus, id utcumque nunc feci, donec ocium et Musae aliquid melius suppeditarent. Vale, 19 Ianuarii 1564. D. Laurino rescripsi de numis, quid velim.

---

[265] A book of Junius's poetry was only published by his grandson, Albertus Verlanius, in 1598: *Poëmatum Hadriani Iunii* (Lugduni: L. Elzevirius, 1598).
[266] Hadrianus Junius, *Nomenclator, omnium rerum propria nomina variis linguis explicata indicans* (Antverpiae: Plantin, 1567). Cf. note 363 to letter 59.
[267] Nonius Marcellus, *De proprietate sermonum.* Cf. the Index.
[268] on virtue
[269] on the pregnancy
[270] Cf. *Odyssea* 5.295.
[271] *Ilias* 11.811 and 23.715; ἴδριος is an erroneous transcription of ἱδρώς.
[272] The suggestion that Hieronymus Wolf seeks glory in the laurel is probably a reference to Wolf's desire to be crowned poet laureate.
[273] We thank William Stoneman for sending us the manuscript of this letter.

De Durerio[274]
Dureri aeternum celebratur nomen, honosque,
Divina cuius praestitit arte manus.
Praxiteles si quid potuit, Lysippus, Apelles,
Atque alii, quorum nomina tanta vigent:
Omnia coniunxit, dedit exemplarque futuris,
Quodque sequens numquam consequeretur opus.
Huius avum genuit quondam pulcherrima tellus
Pannoniae,[275] gethicus quam premit usque furor.
Extulit ingenio ad dites Pegnesidos undas,[276]
Quas adeo ornatas reddidit inde nepos.
Cuius ab insigni cartis quodcumque relictum est
Arte, liber furto hic non removendas habet.
Ortelius precio multis quem cogit et annis
Mirari ut possis μέτρον ἐπουράνιον.[277]
Idem Sambucus.

Οὐ μόνον οἰκείαν μορφὴν Δουρήριος ἡμῖν
Ἀλλὰ γραφῇ θείως φύσιν ἔδειξεν ὅλην.
Τοῦ γένος ἦλθε κλυτῶν ποτε Πανονίης ἀπ' ἀρουρῶν
Νορικίας αὐτὰρ τοῦτον ἔδωκεν πόλις.
Εὗρε πόνοιο βάρους κῦδος καὶ πείρατα γαίης
Τοὔνομ' ἔχει, πᾶσιν θαύματα πολλὰ λιπών.[278]
Αὐτοσχεδιαστὶ ὁ Σαμβοῦκος.[279]

Address: Abrahamo Ortelio amico suo.

---

[274] Ortelius was an expert on and collector of contemporary paintings. By 1562 he had assembled a significant number of Dürer's woodcuts, placed in a separate album, which is one of the earliest collections of works by an individual artist to have survived. This album (without the woodcuts) is preserved in the Rijksmuseum. Ortelius also put together another, finer album of Dürer in two volumes, now in the Louvre (Rothschild coll.). It is introduced by poems and notes by Pirkheimer, followed by Ortelius's portrait, engraved by Philip Galle, and then by Sambucus's Latin poem. Iain Buchanan, "Dürer and Abraham Ortelius," *The Burlington Magazine* 124 (1982), 734-741. (Buchanan does not mention the inclusion of Sambucus's Greek poem.)

[275] It was not Dürer's grandfather but rather his father (Albrecht Dürer Sr.) who was born in Hungary and migrated to Nürnberg. He was a great goldsmith and a very fine artist himself. He came from Ajtós, which is why in Hungary the second family name "Ajtósi" is often attached to Dürer's name.

[276] Pegnitz, close to Nürnberg.

[277] "Dürer's name and fame may be celebrated forever, whose hand was pre-eminent in divine skill. Whatever the talents of Praxiteles, Lysippus, Apelles, and the others, whose fame is so great, he combined them all, and gave a model for the future, and an achievement that no one will ever match in time to come. His grandfather was born in the once very beautiful land of Pannonia, which Gothic violence continues to ravage. He brought his family to the rich waters of the Pegnitz, which his grandson later rendered so splendidly. Whatever has been left on paper from his outstanding skill, this book contains, which must not be stolen. Ortelius has collected this book for many men at expense of money and time, so that you might wonder at the 'divine perspective.'" Translation by Iain Buchanan and William Barnes.

[278] In his drawing Dürer showed us not only the familiar form, but, divinely, the whole nature. His kin once came from the famous fields of Pannonia, subsequently the city of Nuremberg produced him. Gain the glory for the abundance of your work and your name, which left many wonders to all, reaches the limits of the earth!

[279] Extempore, Sambucus.

48.
Hadrianus Junius to Sambucus
20 January [1564], [Haarlem?]

Late 16th century copy in Utrecht, Universiteitbibliotheek, Hs. 829, 157ᵛ. Published in Junius, *Epistolae, quibus accedit eiusdem vita*, 267-268.

The person who brings this letter to Sambucus is Bishop Gulielmus Lindanus, who asked for Junius's mediation. Junius hopes that Sambucus will be ready to show his library to the bishop, whom he knows to be open to new friendships.

Qui has ad te prefert, ornatissime Sambuce, in illustri positum habet nomen, tum titulo, tum scriptis evulgatis orbi notus: est enim Ruremundensis episcopus, theologiae doctor, *Panopliae*, quam haud scio an videris, scriptor, Guilelmo Lindano nomen est.²⁸⁰ Is per me muniri sibi aditum ad tuas aures expetiit, cui ut in officio deesse nequeo, ita etiam per se clara doctrina facile tibi commendabit. Novi enim tuam liberalis institutionis comitem individuam, facilitatem in admittendis ad amicitiam et complectendis eruditis viris. Illi nihil magis in votis esse intelligo, quam ut librarias tuas divitias aliqua ratione cognoscere possit ac frui, quam illi operam non denegabis, ut confido, humanissimo, tu ipsa humanitas, quod sine tuo studiorumque dispendio aut incommodo fieri queat, pro amicissimo mihi olim capite intercedo, ut saltem aliquod apud te pondus mea habuisse scripta intelligat. Vale, pridie Agnetis.

49.
Sambucus to Hadrianus Junius
10 February 1564, Antwerp

Published in Junius, *Emblemata*, f. A3ᵛ.

Sambucus has received Junius's Emblemata *and believes that they will be successful and will win the author and the publisher more renown. His own emblems will not be published before April because of the engravers' delay, but when Junius will see them, his desire to read it will diminish and he will claim that the book should be thrown away more quickly than dung. Junius is restoring the text of the Suda, writing a book on Greek epithets and editing Nonius. He hardly finishes a work before jumping to another in order to equal Erasmus not only in his talents (which he already does) but also in the number of his publications.*

Ioannes Sambucus Hadriano Iunio suo salutem.

Accepi tua Emblemata,²⁸¹ de quibus etsi tu nimium modeste sentis, aliud tamen fore publicum iudicium videbis, nam et sana, et varia elegantiaque sunt et facile auctorem officinamque testabuntur. Quod vero mea tantopere expetis, ante Aprilem ob sculptoris et pictorum moram vix apparebunt, quae si videtis, minuetur desiderium legendi ea, et vere τῶν κοπρίων

---
²⁸⁰ See letter 43.
²⁸¹ Cf. letters 43 and 46.

ἐκβλητότερα²⁸² dices.²⁸³ Tu vero tandem nobis Sudam restitutum,²⁸⁴ epithetorum Graecorum explicationes,²⁸⁵ Nonium²⁸⁶ et alia extrudas; nec, quasi nondum absolveris, otium differendo quaeras teque ad alia accingas, ut, quando Erasmum vestrum ingenio aequare coepisti, numero quoque lucubrationum inferior ne sis,²⁸⁷ dumque aetas viresque permittunt, τὴν τοῦ χρόνου συνέχειαν συναφείᾳ quadam καὶ εἱρμῷ²⁸⁸ velut librorum, qui nisi eruditi esse nequeunt, posteris repraesentes. Vale, et Sambucum amare pergito, sed minus laudato: quis enim, quam ego, me novit melius? Antverpiae, IIII. Idus Februarii. Anno MDLXIIII.

50.
Hadrianus Junius to Sambucus
[February 1564], [Haarlem?]

Late 16ᵗʰ century copy in Utrecht, Universiteitbibliotheek, Hs. 829, 51ᵛ-52ʳ. Published in Junius, *Epistolae selectae*, 57-58.

Junius has already asked twice for Sambucus's coins, now he repeats this request for a third time. He does this not because he has not received the gift but because it would distress him if someone had intercepted it. He will not forget about Nonius. This very day he has submitted to the press a book on the mushroom genus Phallus, which grows only in the sandy areas of Holland. Sambucus should give the book, as soon as it comes out, to Pietro Mattioli. Junius praises him in the book, because he owes him more than he owes any other scholar, especially for his description of the Cervinus mushroom. Sambucus should also informally recommend Junius to Mattioli.

Scripsi iam bis ad te sollicitum de nummis, iam tertium repeto eandem cantilenam, nisi etiam obtundo, me nihil dum accepisse, non tam dono (quod tua liberalitate dignum, mea exspectatione maius erat) indolens, quam quod gravate feram perfidia hominum interceptum esse absentis tui suavissimum monumentum.²⁸⁹ De Nonio ero memor,²⁹⁰ dedique hoc ipso die libellum de Phallo,²⁹¹ fungini quidem generis, sed nusquam nisi in Hollandiae nostrae sabuletis nascente germine, oratione et soluta et ligata textum, quem, ubi primum prodierit in lucem, id quod brevi fiet, communicabis cum Petro Matthiolo Senensi,²⁹² in re herbaria

---

²⁸² more fitting to be thrown away than dung. Cf. Heraclitus, frg. 96. Cf. also letter 46.
²⁸³ Sambucus refers to his own *Emblemata*, which were finally printed only in late August 1564.
²⁸⁴ Junius greatly admired, profoundly knew and very extensively used the Suda, this massive tenth-century Byzantine Greek historical encyclopaedia. Although he was preparing an edition (and was wondering about the dedicatee already in 1562), his work never saw light. See Van Miert, "Epilogue," 297. The reason of not publishing his Suda may be the appearance of Oporinus's edition in 1564, of which Sambucus could still not have known when this letter was written.
²⁸⁵ Reference to Junius's *Stromata*. See letter 43, note 210.
²⁸⁶ Nonius Marcellus, *De proprietate sermonum*. Cf. the Index.
²⁸⁷ A comparison between Junius and Erasmus was prompted also by Junius's supplement to the *Adagia* of Erasmus. See Chris Heesakkers, "From Erasmus to Leiden: Hadrianus Junius and his Significance for the Development of Humanism in Holland in the Sixteenth Century," in *The Kaleidoscopic Scholarship of Hadrianus Junius*, 16-37.
²⁸⁸ the continuity of time by certain combination and (quasi) sequence (of books)
²⁸⁹ It is unclear what kind of sustenance Junius demands from Sambucus. Cf. with letter 56.
²⁹⁰ Nonius Marcellus, *De proprietate sermonum*. Cf. the Index.
²⁹¹ The book was later dedicated to Sambucus. See the next letter.
²⁹² The botanist Pietro Andrea Mattioli (1501–1578) was employed as imperial physician. He was famous for his

coryphaeo, principibus tuis addictissimo, quem honoris caussa nomino, quod illi cum omni studiosorum gente plurimum me debere libens agnoscam, tantoque magis, quod in suis ille epistolis cervinum fungum posteritati descripserit,[293] cui etiam de nota interiore commendari tuis verbis cupio ultro atque ambio. Vale vir doctissime.

51.
Hadrianus Junius to Sambucus
1 March 1564, Haarlem

Dedication in Hadrianus Junius, *Phalli, ex Fungorum genere in Hollandiae sabuletis passim crescentis, descriptio* (Delphis: Schinckel, 1564), f. Aii^r-Aiii^r. Published in Junius, *Epistolae, quibus accedit eiusdem vita*, 413-417.

Junius gladly follows the authority of Anaximander, seeing that the hidden workings of nature are better and better understood all the time through efforts of talented men. Pietro Mattioli has played the leading role among them. Mattioli is devoted to the princes Sambucus serves and has published a commentary on Dioscorides. Junius found the description of the Cervinus mushroom (unknown in Italy) in the edition of Mattioli's medical letters, which he received as a gift from Sambucus. This reminded him of the mushroom Phallus, of which he had once been joking, which can only be found in some sandy areas of Holland, and he thought the subject was worthy of more serious consideration. He decided to publish an illustrated description of the mushroom. Pythagoras preferred simple words to polished rhetoric. He could have brought together much Greek and Latin wisdom on this type of mushroom, however he did not want to intrude into the territory of others and look for glory with plagiarism. His ambition was to provide illustrations by great painters. He was more generous in this than Hipponicus had been, who did not want to engage the sculptor Polycletus as the artist for a monument he was about to sponsor, as he was worried that the artist would take greater glory than the patron. He did not care about vulgar opinion concerning efforts spent on less important subjects but wanted to make the mushroom known. He dedicates this book to Sambucus in recognition of his generosity. He would soon dedicate Nonius Marcellus to him, corrected in infinite places.

Eruditissimo Ioanni Sambuco Pannonio suo, Hadrianus Iunius medicus, S. D.

Non invitus accedo Anaximandri Milesii auctoritati,[294] infinitatem rerum atque naturae, e qua cuncta gignantur, invehentis, Sambuce doctissime, postquam video omniparentis illius inexhaustas opes indies magis ac magis e tenebris, quibus mersae latent, existere, novas erumpere, solertia hominum investigari et ingeniis illustrari, in quam rem studium omne et operam certatim conferre debere censeo, quotquot aciem ingenii clariorem, industriam solertiorem et (uti poetae fabulantur) Promethaeum illud lutum defaecatius nacti sunt.[295] Quos inter palmam, et quidem lemniscatam (absit dictis invidia) meretur Petrus Matthiolus, in rei herbariae cognitione pentathlus quispiam, principibus tuis addictissimus, qui restibilem illam segetis herbariae

---

commented edition of Dioscorides's *Materia medica*. See letter 155, note 922.
[293] Petrus Mattiolus, *Epistolarum medicinalium libri quinque* (Pragae: Georgius Melantrichus, 1561), 252.
[294] Anaximander (c. 610–c. 546 BC) was a pre-Socratic Greek philosopher who lived in Miletus.
[295] Martialis, *Epigrammata* 10, 39.

foecunditatem accuratissime asseruit ac a tenebris vindicavit.[296] Cuius *Medicinales epistolas*, nuper abs te mihi dono missas, quum percurrerem, incidi forte in fungi cervini descriptionem, Italiae (ut ipse attestatur) ignoti.[297] Ibi tum in mentem mihi venit, quam de phallo fungini quidem generis, sed regionibus aliis, praeterquam Hollandiae sabuletis, ignoto, lusisse me olim memineram,[298] dumque altius rem mecum animo voluto, et apud me maiorum nostrorum sedulam in habenda posteritatis ratione curam pressius considero, ne quid venturis seculis lateret incognitum, visus sum mihi pretium operae facturus, si rem, cognitione non indignam, publici iuris facerem. Itaque nihil habui prius aut antiquius, quam planioribus verbis historiam cognitionemque non modo scripto prodere, verum etiam aptis iconibus repraesentare.

Pythagoras Samius dictitabat anteferendas esse Sirenibus Musas,[299] significare volens simplicem veritatis orationem praestare comtis ac phaleratis sermonibus. Nimirum Sirenibus assimilavit ille orationis structuram, lenociniis verborum fucatam, ut Musis nudam orationem, nullo artis mangonio medicatam. Licuisset mihi isthic myrothecia Graecorum Latinorumque, et pigmentarias arculas omneis consumere, onerando et chartas pariter et aures variae lectionis divitiis et commentationibus, undecunque aggestis de fungis, boletis et, quae huc faciunt, aliis. Verum nolui alienis in laboribus stulte ingeniosus vindemiam cogere aut e plagio gloriam aucupari. Deinde studui etiam praestantissimi pictoris manu expressas icones dare, liberaliore animo, quam Hipponicus olim, qui cum haberet in animo votivam statuam patriae erigere consultumque illi esset, ut nobilissimo plastae Polycleto fingendam locando auctoritatem operi communiret, repudiavit consilium, dictitans se nolle simulacrum, cuius gloria ad fictorem redundatura esset, eo quod artificis nobilitas plerunque obscuret auctoris nomen.[300] At nihil ego tale veritus, non gloriolae fumis inhians, sed propagandae disseminandaeque huiusce rei cognitioni incumbens, contemto vulgo, inepto iudice, quod sui similibus impensius afficitur et quod forte laborem in re tenui consumtum criminabitur, prodire in publicum foetum istum volui.

Quem nostrum laborem cui rectius nuncuparem, quam tibi, Sambuce, decus meum? Cuius animi magnitudo atque liberalitas erga immerentem ea extitit, ut ingratitudinis notam incursurus ac tibi etiam decocturus videar, ni beneficiolum aliquod tenue reponere adnitar, quod ipsum pulchre foeneratum abibit, dum tui nominis celebritas commendationis plurimum opellae nostrae apud eruditos lectores conciliabit. Vale, et levidensae munus benigna fronte metire, et ab aemulorum virulentis morsibus tutare. Nonium Marcellum, quod te velle video, infinitis locis interpolatum et a squalore suo detersum, brevi, annuente conatibus Deo, dabo tuis votis.[301] Harlemo, Kalendis Martiis.

---

[296] Reference is made to Mattioli's Dioscorides-editions. Cf. with the preceding letter.
[297] Mattiolus, *Epistolarum medicinalium* (as in the preceding letter), 252.
[298] Junius might have made obscene jokes about this mushroom type, which took its name from its phallus-like shape.
[299] Clemens Alexandrinus, *Stromata* 1.10.48.
[300] Aelianus, *Varia historia* 14.16.
[301] Nonius Marcellus, *De proprietate sermonum*. Cf. the Index.

52.
Sambucus to Fulvio Orsini[302]
13 April 1564, Augsburg

The original is kept in Rome, BAV, Vat. lat. 4103, I, f. 44ʳ⁻ᵛ. Published in Gerstinger, "Die Briefe," 67-69.

Sambucus believes Fulvio Orsini was eagerly expecting his letter, but if he knew the story of his recent activity and the jealousy aroused by some of his endeavours, he would understand his silence. But he would not like to accuse anyone. He only wants to greet Fulvio and recommend to him the learned Philipp Apianus, the son of Petrus, the mathematician of Charles V, who is bringing this letter. Sambucus knows that his recommendation will have great importance with Fulvio. He asks him to show Philipp his library, especially his mathematical manuscripts, which he will well understand. He should see the antiquities which Orsini deems worthy. Since Sambucus left Rome, he passed a few months in Antwerp in order to publish his Dialogues on Ciceronian imitation, Ars poetica *and his collection of 200 emblems. Now he is returning to Vienna, where he will with pleasure see again, as if they were his children, all those things he had gathered on his journeys, turn his library into a testimony to his love of Italy and soon write some works worthy of the expectations of those around him. He is sending his greetings to Cardinal Ranuccio Farnese.*

Domino Ursino Fulvio Sambucus S. D.

Credo te summo in desiderio et expectatione mearum esse literarum adeoque non parum et iure mirari, quid hoc silentium atque moram iniecerit. Sed si negociorum vel potius molestiarum historiam, quae invidia quorundam ob studium nostrum commune antiquitatis excitatorum fuit, exponerem, nae tu iustam excusationem cessationis admitteres. Sed neminem accusare institui neque litium tabellas proponere, sed potius te amantissime salutare huncque nobilem et eruditum virum, veterem meum sodalem, diligentissime commendare. Cuius ego caussa quicquid apud te atque tui similes cupio, ingenio eius ac monimentis imprimis mathematicis debeo, hancque communem fere omnium erga ipsum cognitum voluntatem non dubito. Is est Philippus Apianus, illius tot nominibus et libris atque gratia Caroli Quinti celebris mathematici filius, cuius memoria sola omnem omnium benevolentiam complecti deberet eiusque haeredibus bonorum adiungere gratiam, quem de colloquiis intime cognosces, ac nisi me iudicium praeceptum fallit, etiam sermonibus delectabere.[303] Cupit is videre Italiam

---

[302] Fulvio Orsini (1529–1600) was one of the most famous sixteenth-century antiquarians who worked as an art dealer and librarian in the service of the Farnese family. At the time he was still under the patronage of Cardinal Ranuccio Farnese as his librarian. See Pierre de Nolhac, *La bibliothèque de Fulvio Orsini: contributions à l'histoire des collections d'Italie et à l'étude de la Renaissance* (Paris: F. Vieweg, 1887); Giuseppina Alessandra Cellini, *Il contributo di Fulvio Orsini alla ricerca antiquaria* (Roma: Accademia nazionale dei Lincei, 2004); Jörn Lang, "Orsini, Fulvio," in *Geschichte der Altertumswissenschaften. Biographisches Lexikon*, eds. Peter Kuhlmann and Helmuth Schneider (*Der Neue Pauly, Supplemente* 6) (Stuttgart: Metzler, 2012), 909-912. Sambucus dedicated him an emblem: *Emblemata* (1564), 56.

[303] Members of the Apianus family were among Sambucus's earliest scholarly contacts. He met them in Ingolstadt in 1548 after his enrolment at the university on 17 July 1548 (cf. letters 2-3). The father, Petrus Apianus (Peter Apian-Bennewitz) (1495–1552) was a distinguished humanist, astronomer, cartographer and professor of mathematics at the University of Ingolstadt from 1527. See *Peter Apian: Astronomie, Kosmographie und Mathematik am Beginn der Neuzeit; mit Ausstellungskatalog*, ed. Karl Röttel (Eichstätt: Polygon-Verl. Buxheim, 1995); Christian Kahl, "Peter Apian," in *BBKL* 24 (2005), 107-114. For Petrus Apianus's possible influence on

sed praecipue urbem Romam, ad cuius memoriam semper ingemiscit. A me igitur persuasus proficiscitur ad vos, cui has meas ad te dare volui, quas scio pondus apud te habituras magnum. Amabo te, mi optime ac doctissime Fulvi, da operam videat bibiothecam vestram, videat antiquitates, commendatione tua, quod dignum inspectione atque perpetuo sermone dignum putas, istic observet. Si qui libri aut manu factae demonstrationes mathematicae sunt, ostendas, iudicium non vulgare istius aetatis intelliges. Ego a discessu ex Urbe aliquot menses Antverpiae haesi, istic *Dialogos de imitatione a Cicerone petenda*, in *Artem poeticam* et *Emblematum* praelo subdidi,[304] et de his quaedam nomen quoque tuum praeferent, quae propediem videbis. Nunc in patriam redeo Viennam, et quae tot peregrinationibus et sumptibus coegi, libentissime tanquam faetus videbo atque Italiae amorem bibliotheca mea mihi posthac representabo et brevi aliquid expectatione meorum dignum elucubrabo. Vale, mi carissime et amantissime Ursine, et Sambucum illustrissimo cardinali S. Angeli commenda, quem mihi bene velle aliquot exemplis teque interprete sum expertus.[305] Datum Augustae,[306] Idibus Aprilis 1564.

53.
Sambucus to Jean Matal[307]
6 May 1564, Vienna

The fragment is taken from Jean Matal's letter to Georg Cassander of 6 June 1564 published in *Sylloges epistolarum*, 2:289.

[Sambucus wrote the following to Matal from Vienna:] *Matal should give his greetings to Georgius Cassander and Cornelius Valerius. The emperor and the king are said to have given the books to their councillors to read and to have praised the eagerness, the variety of learning and*

Sambucus's education see István Borzsák, "Ein Copernicus-Exemplar aus der Bibliothek des Joannes Sambucus in Debrecen," *Magyar Könyvszemle* 85 (1965), 133-138. His son, Philipp Apian took over the printing press and the mathematical professorship at the University of Ingolstadt from his father at the age of 22. However, in 1569 the Jesuits forced him to leave the city because of his Protestant sentiments. He came to Vienna and spent three months in the city. In his effort to obtain a commission of land measurement he relied (next to his good references in Bavaria) probably on Sambucus. Maximilian offered him no appointment but only 100 thalers and not even the commission by Archduke Karl materialized in the end. Apianus moved to Tübingen and dedicated himself mostly to cartography, measuring different German lands with extreme precision. The early friendship of Sambucus and Philipp in Ingolstadt is documented also by their common trip to France (see more in letter 2, note 11). See Adam, *Vitae Germanorum philosophorum*, 349-352; Almási, *The Uses of Humanism*, 211-213. Sambucus dedicated him an emblem in *Emblemata* (1564): 23.

[304] Sambucus, *De imitatione a Cicerone petenda* (2nd edition); idem, *Ars poetica Horatii*; idem, *Emblemata cum aliquot nummis* (1564).

[305] Cardinal Ranuccio Farnese (1530–1565), Fulvio's patron, who died in the following year.

[306] Sambucus came from Antwerp to Augsburg in the company of Clusius. See Clusius's letter to Lipsius of 20 September 1591 in *Sylloges epistolarum*, 1:319.

[307] Jean Matal (Metellus) (c. 1517–1597) was a French legal humanist, a student of Alciato. From 1563 he lived in Cologne. He corresponded with most major humanists and irenic thinkers of his times, among others with Petrus Ximenius. See Anthony Hobson "The 'iter italicum' of Jean Matal," in *Studies in the Book Trade: in Honour of Graham Pollard*, eds. R. W. Hunt et al. (Oxford: The Oxford bibliographical society, 1975), 33-60; Heuser, *Jean Matal*. On Matal's relationship with Cassander and other humanists in the Cologne circle see Heuser, *Jean Matal*, 256-289, 317-372, 430-439; Carlos Gilly, *Spanien und der Basler Buchdruck bis 1600: ein Querschnitt durch die spanische Geistesgeschichte aus der Sicht einer europäischen Buchdruckerstadt* (Basel: Helbing & Lichtenhahn, 1985), 197-200. See also his letters in *Illustrium et clarorum virorum epistolae*.

the love of truth found in it. He has not yet been able to speak with the emperor personally, either because he was lying ill or because Sambucus was staying away for three weeks. Matal should greet Sifanus and tell him that Sambucus will send him Theophylact of Ochrid within ten days, as he has told Birckmann.

[Sambucus ad me Vienna scripsit pridie Nonas Maii in hunc modum.] "Saluta diligentissime, dominos meos et eruditos viros D. Cassandrum[308] et Gualterum[309]. Libellosque imperatorem et regem suis consiliariis legendos dedisse.[310] Et valde studium et varietatem laudasse doctrinae καὶ τὴν φιλαλήθειαν.[311] Ego nondum cum imperatore loqui potui, tum quia decumbit, tum quia tres septimanas abfui. Saluta D. Gifanium[312] et me intra X. dies Theophylactum misurum significato,[313] quemadmodum ad Bircmannos quoque scripsi.[314]" [Haec ille.]

---

[308] Joris (Georg) Cassander (1513–1566) was a Flemish theologian of deeply Erasmian spirit, who devoted his life to the question of how to reconcile Catholic and reformed churches. He was critical of the papacy and sought concord in rituals. From c. 1549 he lived in Cologne until his death. Maria Elisabeth Nolte, *Georgius Cassander en zijn oecumenisch streven* (Nijmegen: Centrale Drukkerij, 1951); John Patrick Dolan, *The Influence of Erasmus, Witzel and Cassander in the Church Ordinances and Reform Proposals of the United Duchees of Cleve during the Middle Decades of the 16th Century* (Münster: Aschendorff, 1957); Erika Rummel, *The Confessionalization of Humanism in Reformation Germany* (Oxford: OUP, 2000), 144-149; Van der Schoor, "Georgius Cassander: searching for religious peace in his correspondence (1557–1565)," in *Between Scylla and Charybdis*, 127-147. Cf. with his letters in *Illustrium et clarorum virorum epistolae* and in Georgius Cassander, *Opera quae reperiri potuerunt omnia* (Parisiis: Drovart, 1616).

[309] Cornelius Valerius (Gualterus/Wouters) (1512–1578) was another Flemish humanist and schoolteacher who also lived longer in Cologne, but was apparently mostly away in 1563 and 1565. His publications comprised several kinds of school textbooks. See the article by Daniel Jacoby in *ADB* 39 (1895), 469-470. Cf. his letters in *Illustrium et clarorum virorum epistolae*.

[310] Several books were published by Cassander in the early 1560s. Among the books Cassander might have sent to the imperial court was a manuscript published only posthumously with the following title: *De Articulis Religionis inter Catholicos et Protestantes controversis: ad invictissimos imperatores Augustos, Ferdinandum I. et Maximilianum II. eius successorem consultatio...* (Lugduni: Zetzner, 1612). On this work see Howard Louthan, "Johannes Crato and the Austrian Habsburgs: Reforming a Counter-Reform Court," in *Studies in Reformed Theology and History* 2 (1994), 27-28. See also *Georgius Cassander's 'De officio pii viri' (1561): Critical edition with contemporary French and German translations*, eds. Rob van de Schoor and Guillaume H. M. Posthumus Meyjes (Berlin: De Gruyter, 2016); *De sacra communione Christiani populi in utraque panis et vini specie* ([Cologne]: [Cervicornus?], 1564); *De baptismo infantium, testimonia veterum ecclesiasticorum scriptorum* (Coloniae: Cervicornus, 1563).

[311] and love of truth

[312] Laurentius Hubert Sifanus (Cifanus, Gifanus, Siffanus etc.) (1510–1579) was a German humanist born in Brunsfeld. He was a preceptor of the Fuggers, tutoring Markus and Hans Fugger for almost ten years (c. 1539–1549), and also preparing for them a manuscript Greek grammar. Financed by Anton Fugger he finished his education in Italy. From 1556 he also settled in Cologne, teaching at the Tricoronatum as professor of Greek and history. Later he moved to the Strasbourg Academy and ended up at the University of Ingolstadt (changing religion accordingly). His main opus was his publication of Gregorius Nyssenus's *Opera omnia* (1562, 1571). See the article by Heinz Schmitt in *BBKL*, 24 (2005), 1366-1376; *Humanistes du bassin des Carpates II. Johannes Sambucus*, lxvi-lxix.

[313] Theophylactus, *Explicationes in acta Apostolorum*. Cf. the Index.

[314] Reference is made to Arnold (II) Birckmann. The letter in question is also mentioned by Matal in his letter to Cassander of 23 June 1564: "Arnoldi Bircomanus epistolam a Sambuco die Maii XIV datam accipit, qua scribit, te brevi a Maximiliano ac Ferdinando caesaribus adcersitum, in Pannoniam superiorem iri, ut de constituenda religionis reformatione sententiam tuam iis exponas. [...] Scribebat Sambucus, ut te ad iter una cum comitibus comparares, tam putavit certam tuam profectionem. [...] Litteras autem Sambuci ad te mitto, quas remittis. Mitto vero, ne non rem, uti ad me perscripta fuit, intelligas." Leiden, Rijksuniversiteit, Codices Papenbroekiani, Pap 2., no. 2. Cited by Heuser, "The correspondence," 248.

54.
Hadrianus Junius to Sambucus
24 May 1564, Antwerp

Late 16th century copy in Utrecht, Universiteitbibliotheek, Hs. 829, 142ʳ-143ʳ. Published in Junius, *Epistolae, quibus accedit eiusdem vita*, 385-386.

Junius's bad memories of the trip to Denmark are tempered by the visits of friends. The salary would be attractive but he reprimands the harsh customs of the Danes, the high prices and the diet. He is sending Sambucus two copies of his book (on the mushroom Phallus), which he has dedicated to him, and he will send more as soon as the publisher gets hold of the copyright permission. He is discussing the publication of Nonius and the Nomenclator, *which is an octolingual dictionary, with Plantin today. He wants to dedicate Nonius to the emperor and the* Emblemata *to the treasurer of Holland. He has still not decided about the* Nomenclator. *He will write more before leaving for Brussels and make sure to write more frequently via Plantin, and he asks Sambucus to do the same. Sambucus should have Eunapius's work transcribed for Junius, and if possible also Nonnus's* Dionysiaca, *which seems most useful for his edition of epithets.*

Ioanni Sambuco Pannonio.

Liberet mihi Polydori exemplo erumpere in haec verba "Adsum profectus Danica e caligine,"[315] nisi longinqui ac molesti itineris, ceu partus, recordationem obliterasset iucundus amicorum reduci quotidie gratulantium suisque salutationibus fastidium illud lenientium occursus. Stipendium honestum facile me illectum traheret, sed coeli morumque gentis inclementia absterret, ingens rerum caritas accedit et aeris (quid dico aeris, quum hoc moneta omnis abundet) penuria, huc adde victus infelicitatem.[316] Sed quid haec apud te, quasi feriatis auribus depono importune garrulus?

En tibi foetum nostrum tuo nuncupatum genio, quem, si merebitur, hospitem haud gravate accipies.[317] Mitto duo tantum exemplaria, missurus proxime plura, ubi typographus privilegium, quod hic nullum extat, obtinuerit, adeo religiose formidolosus aegre bina longuinquae peregrinationi parata concessit. Tu boni consules. Egi hodie cum Plantino praesens de Nonio excudendo, de Nomenclatore, qui rerum omnium vocabula variis linguis (nempe Latina, Graeca, Gallica, Germanica, Belga, Italica, Hispana, Anglica) reddet.[318] Nonium caesareae maiestati destino,[319] *Emblemata* quaestori nostro,[320] epigrammata diversis,[321] *Nomenclatorem* principis alicuius filio, quod nondum satis constitutum habeo. Scribam prolixius proxime, eo quod Bruxellam expedito mihi proficiscendum sit. Daboque post hac operam, ut per Plantinum nostrum frequentius ad te commeent literae, quod ipsum

---
[315] Cf. Vergilius, *Aeneis* 3.44, where Polydorus, a young Trojan prince sent by his father to the neighbouring kingdom of Thrace, says "Heu fuge crudelis terras, fuge litus avarum."
[316] In April 1564 Junius travelled to Copenhagen to become a physician to King Frederick II and to succeed a professor of medicine who had died in January 1564. See *The Kaleidoscopic Scholarship of Hadrianus Junius*, 9.
[317] Junius refers here to his book *Phalli ... descriptio* dedicated to Sambucus (see letter 51), which he apparently attached to the letter.
[318] Junius, *Nomenclator*. Cf. letter 59, note 363.
[319] Nonius Marcellus, *De proprietate sermonum*. Cf. the Index.
[320] Arnoldus Cobelius, treasurer of the province of Holland.
[321] Martialis, *Epigrammaton*. See Chris Heesakkers, "Junius' Two Editions of Martial's Epigrammata," in *The Kaleidoscopic Scholarship of Hadrianus Junius*, 136-187.

ut tu quoque praestes, dum Iunii non te pudebit, obnice rogo. Eunapium ut describendum cures,[322] et si fieri potest etiam Nonni *Dionysiaca*,[323] quod ad *Epithetorum*[324] meorum editionem maxime necessaria videantur, obsecratum te velim. Vale, et Iunii patrocinium, ubi poteris, ne desere. Raptim Antverpia, nono Kalendas Iunias. 1564.

55.
Georg Cassander to Sambucus
[July 1564], Cologne

Published in Cassander, *Opera omnia*, 1180.

Cassander already wrote to Sambucus a few weeks before, explaining to him why he could not accept Ferdinand's invitation and travel to Vienna. He also presented his reasons (concerning his feebleness) to the archbishop of Cologne. He was also happy to see the support of great princes for religious moderators in the letter of King Maximilian to the archbishop of Trier, who sent a copy of it to Cassander with one of his councillors. Yet, he would not know how to fulfil their expectations, and he understands that whatever remedy he would suggest for the problems of the Church, he is not an equal of the princes. He would nevertheless go if he were not ill and did not expect his sickness to reach another culmination and force him to stay in bed. He had to hurry writing the letter to the emperor, as the person who was to carry it away from Duisburg, where he spends the summer sometimes, wanted to leave at noon. As a consequence, where he wrote that the Church should be restored to the form it had after Constantine the Great, he should have added "till the time of Saint Augustine or Pope Leo", or even until Saint Gregory, a time limit also agreed on by Protestants. He recommends that Petrus Ximenius, who is presently staying in Cologne, be invited to Vienna in his place.

Domino Ioanni Sambuco, viro et genere et literis claro.

Misi ad te ante paucas hebdomadas epistolium, clarissime domine Sambuce, una cum literis ad caesaream maiestatem, quibus me excuso et causas adfero, cur ipsius maiestatis voluntati et mandato in suscipienda tam longinqua profectione obsequi, ut velim, non possum.[325] Quas causas etiam archiepiscopo Coloniensi praesenti praesens exposui,[326] qui eas, cum huius corpusculi infirmitatem videret, nimis esse iustas agnovit. Cum autem alterae literae a potentissimo rege Maximiliano allatae essent ad episcopum Trevirensem,[327] qui earum exemplum una cum suae celsitudinis literis per quendam consiliarum suum ad me misit, equidem gaudebam, cum

---

[322] Eventually, Eunapius came out in Junius's edition. See the story of this publication in *Humanistes du bassin des Carpates II. Johannes Sambucus*, lvi-lvii; Gerstinger, "Zusammenfassung," 303-305. See also "Eunapius-edition" under "Sambucus" in the Index.

[323] For Nonnus's *Dionysiaca* see letter 126 and consult the Index. For the story of its publication see *Humanistes du bassin des Carpates II. Johannes Sambucus*, lix-lxi.

[324] Junius refers to his *Stromata*. See letter 43, notes 210-211.

[325] This letter to Emperor Ferdinand of 28 June is published in the same volume of Cassander's *Opera omnia* on pages 1176-1177. Ferdinand was already sick and died less than a month later. In the middle of May Sambucus was already expecting Cassander's arrival. He was prompted to write this letter by Jean Matal a few days before. See letter 53, note 310.

[326] Friedrich IV. von Wied, Archbishop of Cologne (1562–1567).

[327] Johann VI. von der Leyen, Archbishop of Trier (1510–1567). See Cassander's letter to him, published ibid. on p. 1179.

tantum studium potentissimorum principum iuvandae opera doctorum et moderatorum virorum ecclesiae perspicerem. Dolebam vero, cum nihil in me esse cognoscerem, quo tantorum principum aliorumque excellentissimorum virorum expectationi respondeam. Nam ut me iuvandae ecclesiae studio flagrare, et quibus remediis sanari possit, utcumque animadvertisse profitear, tamen vires tanto negotio pares deesse mihi intelligo. Neque tamen haec imperitiae meae conscientia tam me deterruisset, nisi haec valetudinis tenuitas hanc profectionem prohibuisset. Nam in singulos dies paroxysmum expecto, qui ad aliquot dies lecto me affigit, et cessantibus etiam cruciatibus articulorum gravissimum morbum ad aliquot hebdomadas relinquit. Si quid interea, dum aliqua ab his doloribus et morbis interspiratio et recreatio conceditur, vel scribendo, vel conferendo, quod ecclesiae iuvandae serviat, conferre possim, haud gravatim sum facturus. Id quod in literis ad caesaream maiestatem adieci, quas literas nimia celeritate conscribere coactus sum, cum is, qui mihi eas Duisburgi Clivorum, ubi per aestatem aliquando commorari soleo, ante meridiem traderet, a meridie sibi abeundum esse diceret. Quare veniam mihi dari peto, si quid negligentius et minus accurate in iis scriptum sit, quamquam et haec infirmitas, quae omnes ingenii vires deterit et debilitat, hanc veniam mereretur. In iis ad caesaream maiestatem literis postea deesse aliquid, quod obscuritatem parere possit, deprehendi. Scripseram enim, "Ecclesiam esse instaurandam ad formam et exemplum potissimum illius Ecclesiae, quae ab aetate Constantini floruit,"[328] quo loco addendum erat, "usque ad aetatem Augustini vel Leonis."[329] Nam ad eam usque aetatem, imo usque ad Gregorium I.[330] etiam illi, qui praesentem Ecclesiam aspernantur, apostolicam doctrinam incorruptam, et Ecclesiae constitutionem et gubernationem legitimam fuisse fatentur. Illud autem admonendum duxi, si fortassis caesarea ac regia maiestas nostram operam in aliqua deliberatione et consultatione de constituenda Ecclesia uti velit, esse hic Coloniae virum quendam summo ingenio variaque, eaque eximia, eruditione, praesertim rerum divinarum, acerrimo iudicio, incredibili modestia, ardentissimo studio pacificandae ecclesiae praeditum atque ornatum, cui Petrus Ximenius[331] nomen est, quem si caesareae et regiae maiestati ad hanc deliberationem admittendum et adiungendum videatur, opere pretium futurum sperem.

56.

Hadrianus Junius to Sambucus
23 August [1564], n.p.

Published in Junius, *Epistolae, quibus accedit eiusdem vita*, 273-279.

It would be against all laws of decency, if Junius were not to extol as much as he can Sambucus's courtesy toward him. He cannot himself claim the great erudition that Sambucus has ascribed to him. Junius remembers that Sambucus made liberal promises already in their first conversations,

---

[328] Constantine the Great (c. 272–337). See Cassander, *Opera omnia*, 1177.
[329] Augustine of Hippo (354–430); Pope Leo I (c. 400–461).
[330] Pope Gregory I (Saint Gregory the Great) (c. 540–604).
[331] See the letter of Petrus Ximenius to Cassander of 10 August 1564: "Oblitus eram tibi scribere de eo, quod ad Sambucum non tu solum, sed etiam Metellus ac Bircmanus, ut arbitror, de me scripsistis. Usque adeone me honorare cupitis, ut ea mihi tribuatis, quae tanto intervallo superant et ingenii mei et eruditionis tenuitatem." *Sylloges epistolarum*, 2:268. Cassander's response is in Cassander, *Opera omnia*, 1181-1182. On Petrus Ximenius (Pedro Ximénez) (1524–1595) see García Pinilla, I. J. "Paz religiosa, libertad religiosa: la apuesta por el pacifismo de Pedro Ximénez en el Dialogus de pace (1579)," *Hispania Sacra* 70 (2018), 39-50.

but he far superseded the hopes he had generated. Junius owes no one as much as to Sambucus. If only he could pay Sambucus back with refined words, lasting regard and persistent work, which is the most shabby and common way of compensation. Junius claims (with reference to Greek concepts) that the origins of Sambucus's friendship must lie in his knowledge of virtue. Junius goes on to rhapsodise about the honour Sambucus has rendered him, although he would not like to exaggerate. As for Sambucus's urging that he should publish his works, he could rightly return it to him but will nevertheless make sure to keep to Sambucus's advice and dedicate the edition of the Suidas *to Maximilian. His* Stromata *is similar in its character, and wealthier than Erasmus's* Adages. *Sambucus will shortly get a copy of it. He will probably dedicate some books of his* Animadversa *to Ulrich Fugger, and he is asking for Sambucus's mediation with him and with Fugger's typographer Henri Estienne, to whom he will write soon. Nonius Marcellus will be dedicated to Sambucus but he has not decided about his* Nomenclator *yet. The books of Martialis's* Epigrammaton *will be dedicated to various people in accordance with their arguments.*

Omnia pudoris officiique repagula perfregisse videri possem, doctissime Sambuce, si singularem istam et inauditam tuam in me complectendo humanitatem et in ornando munificentiam, tacitam praeterirem; si verissimis iustissimisque laudibus non eam in coelum extollerem, si non omni dicendi scribendique vi ac copia, qua possem, eam enarrarem, ne dicam exornarem.[332] Verum quum neque usu satis valeam, atque ingenio parum possim, qua ratione id pro meritis praestare queam, nullus scio, neque vero in impudentiae scopulos impingere velim prudens, ut id mihi eruditionis arrogem, quod tu tantus Encomiasta tribuis, quod si addesset, nae ego plenis velis in tuae liberalitatis laudes efferrer, a quo nunc instituto tenuitatis meae conscientia me retrahit, quanquam etiam in Salustianas illas salebras angustiasque praeceps incurrere periclitor,[333] ut nihil quam pauca dixisse satius fore videatur. Memini quidem prolixe mihi ipsi de tua voluntate et liberalitate promisisse a primo colloquii nostri rudimento, sed votum illud ita superasti, ut cumulatissime mihi satisfactum et supra spem videam, ita, ut nulli hominum plus propemodum quam tibi debere me agnoscam. Atque utinam pro ingentibus istis in me beneficiis supersedere mihi liceat tam vili, tam inerti, tam ἀγεννεῖ καὶ βλακώδει[334] orationis muneri, ac potius observantia et assiduitate officiorum praesens possem memorem me tibi approbare, proque amplissimis tuis erga me meritis pertinacem operam studiumque navare, quandoquidem nihil iam sit extritius, nihil vulgatius communi ista agendi gratias lege ac via. Contra si istam amicitiae, quae te erga me adeo liberalem et profusum facit, rationem atque originem ad fontes suos revocare velim atque a capite arcessere, ad trivium illud decurrendum mihi fuerit, quod amicitiae genera dispescit in τὸ κατ' ἀρετήν, τὸ κατ' ἀμοιβὴν καὶ τὸ ἐκ συνηθείας[335] (quae obscurius paulo Pythagoraeus Hippodamus τὰν ἐξ ἐπιστάμας θεῶν, τὰν δ' ἐκ παροχᾶς ἀνθρώπων,[336] τὰν δ' ἐξ ἁδονᾶς ζώων indigitat[337]) in quibus cum nullum

---

[332] Junius thanks in this letter for the emblem Sambucus has dedicated to him, which extolled his erudition and industry (the *Emblemata* came out in Plantin's Antwerp press, as its last page indicates, on 25 August). On Sambucus's *Emblemata* see Visser, *Joannes Sambucus and the Learned Image*; idem, "Why did Plantin publish Emblem books?" in *Emblems of the Low Countries: A Book Historical Perspective*, eds. Alison Adamsa and Marleen van der Weij (Glasgow: Glasgow Emblem Studies, 2003), 63-78.

[333] Next to brevity, the style and language of Sallust has a large number of grammatical oddities.

[334] low-born and lazy

[335] based on virtue, based on reciprocity, and out of habit. Cf. Clemens Alexandrinus, *Stromata* 2.101.

[336] Print: ἀνῶν, probably a misunderstood abbreviation.

[337] from knowledge of the gods, from benefit of humans, from pleasure of animals. Clemens Alexandrinus, *Stromata* 2.102.

habeant locum vel beneficii a me orti conscientia, vel consuetudo prior, reliquum est, ut aliqua virtutis perspicientia hos tibi amoris fonticulos aperuerit, quae cuiusmodi sit, ex tuo iudicio coniectare magis, quam de me ipse praedicare possim. Videor hercle mihi hariolari posse, te ex eorum numero esse, qui me in re literaria praestitisse aliquantum, monumentisque editis et iuventuti utilitatis, et nomini meo gloriae nonnihil peperisse autumant, unde τὸ τοῦ πόνου τέκνωμα κλέος, ut Aeschyli verbis dicam, consecutum sit.[338] Quae certe in re gaudeo si quid feci, aut facio subcisivis operis, quod non segnibus iudiciis placere, quod amorem multorum conciliare, quod posteritatem demereri queat: nec enim usqueadeo corneam alicui, non ignavo homini, fibram innasci existimo,[339] ut amplissimum illud virtutis praemium gloriam respuat. Quis enim tandem fastidium illud ingenii aequis ferat vel auribus, vel animis, qui id repudiet, quod caeteri per ferrum, per ignes quaerere solent? Sed a diverticulo regredior ad illud amicitiae seminarium, quod aut necessitate, aut occulta aliqua ratione coaluisse opertet, nam qui coisset alioqui horulae unius auspiciis ingeniorum non omnino compar conditio? Quod coagmentum tam solide coniunxisset, quae naturali regionem divortio dissederunt? Itaque ferruminis firmi laudem suo iure sibi vendicabunt, opinor, literae virtutum omnium fundamenta, omnis humanitatis, omnisque industriae fomites, alumnae, matres denique. Eaedem tamen, nisi fallor, te propenso quodam mei studio efferri (absit ut hallucinari dicam) faciunt, qui laudis plus iusto ficulneo ingenio meo affuas, nisi forte ἐνδόσιμόν τι[340] mihi accinis, quale remigibus praeire solet. Quanquam quid pulchrius, quam viro literatissimo placere? Si Naevianus Hector praecipua in laude ponit a viro laudato collaudari,[341] ego vero non omnino semissis homo quam non lauream, quas non triumphales quadrigas assecutum me putem, cui a laudatissimo viro, et eius regis, qui nostro hoc saeculo idem audit, quod Sol (absit dicta invidia) oculus nimirum et fax orbis, familiari et praeconium amplissimum obtigit, et cum beneficiis haud postremis, ultronea amicitiae arctissimae necessitudo honorifice delata est?

Sed heus mihi Sambuce, cave cum Stesichoro palinodia Helenes tibi cantanda sit, laudesque intra modi cancellos revocandae.[342] Quod me ad editionem mearum vigiliarum provocas, nempe cursurum sua sponte, nec stimulis opus habiturum (si abesset ergastulum illud, quod me plane conficit) instigas, facisque ut te decet ἄνδρα πάσης εὐμουσίας τε καὶ χαρίτων γέμοντα,[343] quanquam eodem ego te iure in campum istum provocare debeam, ut Hesiodiana illa ἀγαθὴ ἔρις apud nos locum haberet, quae mutuis exhortationibus immortalitatis amorem utrinque accenderet.[344] Dabo tamen operam ut tuis monitis obtemperem, utque tuo arbitratu *Suidas* in augusti et re vera maximi Maximiliani manus inscriptione transeat;[345] cuius genio etiam cudentur nocturnis diurnisque operis eandem incudem tundentibus *Stromata* mea, quo opere Graecorum epithetorum rationem explico, opus altero tanto copiosius, quam sint Erasmi *Chiliades*, cuius specimen propediem tibi dabo.[346] Miscellaneorum libri aliquot forte Hulrico Fuggero, Mecoenati olim in Italia meo, quum Senae ageret puer;[347] cui commendatione tua

---

[338] glory is the child of the toil. Cf. Aeschylus, frg. 315.
[339] Cf. Erasmus, *Adagia* 645, "Cornea fibra."
[340] some kind of signal
[341] Cf. Cicero, *Tusculanae disputationes* 4.67.
[342] Stesichorus (640–555 BC) was a Greek lyric poet. He was the first to write a palinode, in which he retracts his negative statements about the role of Helen in the Trojan War.
[343] a man brimming with thorough sense of beauty and art and with graces. Cf. Iulianus, *Epistulae* 4 (427 A).
[344] good strife. Cf. Hesiodus, *Erga* 11-26.
[345] See letter 49, note 284.
[346] See letter 43, notes 210–211.
[347] A new edition of his *Animadversa* never appeared in his life. Junius lived probably with the young Fugger boy

charior notiorque fieri cupio, ut et typographo eius τῷ πάνυ[348] Henrico Stephano,[349] nostri saeculi ἀκριβεστάτῳ πάσης εὐμαθείας γνώμονι,[350] ad quem meditor propediem literas. Nonius Marcellus, si videbitur, in tuam familiam adoptabitur.[351] Nomenclaturas rerum omnium, variis linguiis scriptarum, haud dum statui, cuius parem patrocinio.[352] *Epigrammaton libri* variis pro argumentis diversis nuncupabuntur.[353] Vale praesidium et decus meum, decimo Kalendas Septembris.

57.
Sambucus to Karl II, Archduke of Austria
1 September 1564, Vienna

Dedication in Johannes Sambucus, *Oratio cum epigrammatis aliquot epitaphiis in obitum Imperatoris Ferdinandi primi* (Vienna: Zimmermann, 1564), f. Aii[r].

Although his talents and style are insufficient for the praise of Ferdinand's virtues, he felt it was his duty to conserve the memory of such a great emperor. Thus he has only produced a sketch, outlining things but not fully expounding or refining them. Nevertheless, Sambucus promises to write a history of Ferdinand's rule someday. This piece of writing wants to be only a gesture of observance and his position as a client, so that Karl and his brothers should not only be heirs to Ferdinand's virtue and power but also to his generosity toward Sambucus.

Serenissimo atque illustrissimo principi, domino, domino Carolo archiduci Austriae, duci Burgundiae, comiti Tyrolis, etc., domino suo clementissimo.[354]

Lucubratiunculam tibi hanc, Serenissime Princeps, offero, non quia paternis illis virtutibus ac praeconiis ingenium vel stilum suffecturum meum arbitrer, sed quia debiti est ac pii officii memoriam tanti caesaris conservare tibique eorum qualemcunque significationem

---

[347] Ulrich Fugger (1526–1586) in 1538 in Sienna. See Chris L. Heesakkers, "'Italia optima morum ingeniorumque officina,' Die Früchte einer Italienreise in den Wirken des Hadrianus Junius," in *Margarita amicorum. Studi di cultura europea per Agostino Sottili*, eds. Fabio Forner et al. (Milan: Vita & Pensiero, 2005), 2:473.

[348] the famous

[349] Born as a son and heir of the Paris publisher Robert Estienne, Henri (II) Estienne (1528/1531–1598) spent the major part of his active life outside Paris, in Lyon and Geneva. Ulrich Fugger was indeed a major patron of Estienne, who considered himself typographer of the Fuggers. His daughter married Isaac Casaubon. Despite his enormous significance and talents as a humanist, Hellenist (e.g. publisher of the *Thesaurus graecae linguae*), as a supporter of the French language movement and the Huguenot movement, several aspects of his secretive life are still unknown to us. See *Henri Estienne [actes du Colloque...]* (Paris: Presses de l'École normale supérieure, 1988); *La France des humanistes. Henri Estienne, éditeur et écrivain*, eds. Judith Kescsméti, Bénédicte Boudou and Hélène Cazes (Turnhout: Brepols Publishers, 2003); Denise Carabin, *Henri Estienne, érudit, novateur, polémiste* (Paris: Honoré Campion, 2006).

[350] the most precise yardstick of all learning

[351] Nonius Marcellus, *De proprietate sermonum*. In January he still wanted to dedicate it to Emperor Ferdinand (who would die in July). See letter 46 and cf. the Index.

[352] Junius, *Nomenclator*. See letter 59, note 363.

[353] Martialis, *Epigrammaton*. See letter 54, note 321.

[354] Karl II Franz, Archduke of Austria, ruler of Inner Austria (1540–1590) was the third son of Emperor Ferdinand. Franz was a patron of arts and music, and the founder of the University of Graz. See the article by Regina-Bianca Kubitscheck in *BBKL* 22 (2003), 701-705.

representare.³⁵⁵ Attigi igitur, non detexui, indicavi, non exposui, primis quasi lineis deformavi, non illustravi, minus expolivi, quae hoc in genere scriptionis solent commemorari. Verumtamen universam divini pientissimique parentis vitam resque immortaliter gestas a me quoque descriptas aliquando leges.³⁵⁶ Hoc vero ad funus elogium observantiae atque clientelae indicium esse velim, ut cuius in virtutum ac ditionum possessionem cum fratribus successisti, eiusdem clementiae atque erga me voluntatis copiosae sis deinde haeres. Quod ipsum te haud difficile facturum spero, utque facias vehementer ac demisse oro. Viennae, Kalendis Septembris 1564. Tuae illustrissimae serenitatis clientulus, Ioannes Sambucus.

58.
Sambucus to the Mayor and the Council of Trnava
10 September 1564, Vienna

The original is kept in Trnava, SAT, Magistrát mesta Trnava, Missiles. Published in Vantuch, "Die Sambucusbriefe," 329-330.

Sambucus read the letter of 6 September during the night of the ninth. He could not do anything on that very day but this morning he approached the apostolic legate on the matter, who was hurrying to the emperor, so he said he would have the matter resolved by lunch. Sambucus did the same with the bishop of Gurk, who also promised a response by lunchtime. He could not be faster than this. Sambucus is sorry that the city did not communicate about this with Archbishop Nicolaus Olahus. They should aim for concord, and he will pray to God that he finally bring some peace to the conscience of everyone and create universal concord under a Christian flag. As a postscript he adds that he compared the articles sent to him with the copy of the papal legate and there are no differences except for some additions, as they can see. Another copy was given to him by the bishop of Gurk. It is not his job to judge it, everyone is responsible for himself and his conscience to God.

Egregii et circumspecti domini et amici honorandissimi.

Quas vos literas 6. Septembris ad me misistis, eae 9. die mihi sub noctem sunt redditae. Eo die nihil efficere potui. Hodie, qui est dominicus dies, mane cum nuncium apostolicum ea de re appellassem,³⁵⁷ respondit se mecum omnia libentissime communicaturum, sed ad caesaream maiestatem illi nunc properandum, a prandio igitur rem paratam habiturum. Item feci de Gorycensi,³⁵⁸ qui a sua concione humaniter mihi negocium ostendit seque a prandio mihi id

---

³⁵⁵ It is curious that Sambucus dedicated his work to Archduke Karl and not to the imperial heir Maximilian. On their relationship see Almási, *The Uses of Humanism*, 181.
³⁵⁶ This promise was not fulfilled.
³⁵⁷ Papal nuncio Zaccaria Delfino (Dolfin) (1527–1583) stayed in Vienna in 1561–1565. He studied in Padua and later was sent to diverse missions in the Holy Roman Empire. In 1565 he was created a cardinal. See Helmut Goetz, "Einleitung," in *Nuntiaturberichte aus Deutschland*, vol. 1.17, ed. Helmut Goetz (Tübingen: Niemeyer, 1970), vii-xv, xli-lv, *Venetianische Depeschen vom Kaiserhofe*, ed. Gustav Turba (Vienna: Tempsky, 1895), 3:633 and the voice by Gino Benzoni in *DBI* 40 (1991), 576-588. The issue on which Sambucus had to meditate, as Anton Vantuch supposes (Vantuch, "Die Sambucusbriefe," 330), may be a confession drafted by the city of Trnava (Nagyszombat). Alternatively, Trnava demanded permission for using communion in both kinds.
³⁵⁸ Slip of the pen for "Gurzensi". The bishop of Gurk was Urban Sagstetter (1529–1573), who was another learned man, competent even in Hebrew. A close advisor of Emperor Ferdinand, he held moderate views, worked

descriptum daturum pollicitus. Citius igitur mittere nequivi. Itaque si quid in mora peccatum est, eius, qui literas pertulit, et celebritatis diei dominicae culpa est. Vobis cum reverendissimo archiepiscopo minus de publicatione convenisse intelligo et non parum doleo.[359] Vestra tamen prudentia, quatenus per dominationem licuerit, moderabimini omnia ad concordiam. Ego hanc operam et alia maiora in gratiam vestram facturus sum. Dominationes vestrae valeant, Deumque omnipotentem precor, ut tandem conscientiis omnium aliquid satisfiat et universa sit in Christiano nomine consensio. Viennae, raptim 10. Septembris 1564. Vester servitor Sambucus.

Contuli cum nuncii apostolici articulis vestros ad me missos,[360] nulla est differentia praeter quaedam adiecta ex ipso exemplari, ut videtis. Alterum exemplum est mihi datum ab ipso episcopo Gurzensi. Meum non est de his pronunciare, quisque pro se et conscientia Deo respondebit. Iterum valete.

Address: Egregiis et circumspectis, iudici iuratisque civibus civitatis Thyrnaviensis, dominis et amicis observandis. Thyrnaviam. Cito, cito, citissime.

59.
Hadrianus Junius to Sambucus
[November-December] 1564, [Haarlem?]

Late 16th century copy in Utrecht, Universiteitbibliotheek, Hs. 829, 169^r. Published in Junius, *Epistolae, quibus accedit eiusdem vita*, 408-410.

Junius received Sambucus's laconic but gentle letter, in which he assured him of the good will of Maximilian and the Archdukes. But Junius remembers that Sambucus gave several times reason to hope for an annual stipend funding his studies without the need of being present, which would be very handy, also because a long trip would be too tiring and expensive for him. The Danish king agreed to pay him 40 thalers as a small stipend but he and his wife deeply dislike the spirit of that region. Nonius, dedicated to the emperor, will go to press in a week, it is hard to say how much fatigue it took him. He had never thought that those corrections would take so long and give him so much trouble, but urged by friends, like Sambucus, it has now been finished with much perseverance. As soon as it is sent out, it will be followed soon by the Nomenclator, *dedicated perhaps to Maximilian's children. Junius understands from the letter Sambucus sent to Plantin that he is looking for someone to translate Eunapius. He is greatly upset, since he had demanded this text more than once in his letters, hoping to make a translation, but perhaps Sambucus thinks he is unfit for the task. If so, let it be. Meanwhile, he would not decline a job offer as a historian or doctor. What matters is that the emperor, who created so high expectations toward his person, liked him. Sambucus should obtain for him either the job or the stipend, whichever seems easier to him.*

---

on conciliation with the Protestants and fought for the permission of communion in both kinds not only in individual bishoprics but also on a larger scale. See Karl Kranner, *Bischof Urban Sagstetter von Gurk und das Religionsproblem in Innerösterreich* (University of Innsbruck, Ph.D. Diss., 1958); Jakob Obersteiner, *Die Bischöfe von Gurk. 1072–1822* (Klagenfurt: Verlag des Geschichtsvereins für Kärnten, 1969), 310-331.

[359] Nicolaus Olahus.
[360] See note 357 above.

Literas tuas laconicas, sed perhumanas, Octobri mense scriptas, accepi, quibus liberaliter de Imperatore Maximiliano et regulorum erga me studio polliceris. At heus tu: memini te olim non semel iniecisse spem pensionis annuae, qua absentis studia ali possent, id quod commodius in hac aetate mihi eveniret, cui tam longinqua peregrinatio fastidiosa et impendio sumptuosa accideret. Alioqui Danus rem quaedringentis Daleris stipis loco appendendis mecum pactus erat.³⁶¹ Sed eius regionis genium ego et uxor abhorremus.

Nonius, caesareae maiestatis auspicio proditurus, infra octiduum meam custodiam deseret, alieni iuris futurus, in quo quantum exantlaverim laboris, nullus facile dixero.³⁶² Nunquam enim speraram tandiu, atque ad eum modum me castigationes illas exercituras fuisse, sed tentatum laborem atque improbis cum tuis, tum aliorum votis toties expetitum, pertinacius ursi et (gratia superis) iam perfeci. Ubi ille evolarit hinc, mox subsequetur *Nomenclator*, liberis Maximiliani imperatoris consecrandus fortassis, ut tuo iudicio et voluntati acquiescam, quae opera non tam longum extrahetur ut ista, quod istic de antiquitate altissime obruta divinandum fuerit, hic meo iudicio scribendum aut potius iam perscriptum sit.³⁶³

Intelligo ex literis ad Plantinum tuis Eunapio interpretem te quaerere. At nescis, quam me ea res commorit, quando iam olim non semel Eunapii copiam describendi in spem versionis per literas depoposcerim, nisi imparem me illi provinciae iudicaris, in quo libens tuae censurae ἀκριβείᾳ³⁶⁴ stabo.³⁶⁵ Interim historici munus, aut medici, aut qualecunque tandem non abnuero, modo imperatori tanto, qui iam olim orbem terrarum latissime sui expectatione implevit, approbari atque placere queam.³⁶⁶ Tu sive istud, sive pensionem impetrabis, fac quod videbitur expeditius, ὠκεῖα χάρις γλυκερωτέρα,³⁶⁷ ut nosti, quem mihi non fronte, sed mente mihi studere persuasum habeo. Vale.

---

³⁶¹ See letter 54.
³⁶² Nonius Marcellus, *De proprietate sermonum*. Cf. the Index.
³⁶³ Junius, *Nomenclator*. The book was finally dedicated (31 December 1565) to Philip William, the later Prince of Orange (1554–1618), the eldest son of William I (the Silent, 1533–1584). Apparently, by the end of 1565 Junius had given up hope of getting a stipend or position in Vienna.
³⁶⁴ accuracy
³⁶⁵ See letter 54, note 322. However, Junius did not state in this letter that he wanted to do the job, but rather kept emphasising how busy he was with all sort of other projects. Sambucus may have believed that Junius was too busy for this "tedious" job and certainly did not want to ask more from his elderly friend as he increasingly realised that he would not be able to fulfil any of his promises that he made to Junius earlier. As the next sentence suggests, Junius must have understood that this was the issue behind. Finally, Junius did the job but his friendship to Sambucus rapidly deteriorated in the following period. Sambucus is mentioned only on the title page of the Greek text ("ex bibliotheca Ioannis Sambuci Pannonii Tirnaviensis"), although he warmly remembers him in the dedication to Elizabeth I of England. Eunapius, Βίοι φιλοσόφων καὶ σοφιστῶν. E bibliotheca Ioannis Sambuci Pannonii Tirnaviensis (Antverpiae: Plantin, 1568). See more in *Humanistes du bassin des Carpates II. Johannes Sambucus*, ad indicem.
³⁶⁶ The positions Junius was hoping to obtain using Sambucus's help were exactly those that Sambucus, who had just returned to Vienna, was eager to acquire. See Almási, *The Uses of Humanism*, 157-158.
³⁶⁷ a quick favour is sweeter

60.
Sambucus to Johannes Listhius[368]
11 November 1564, Vienna

Dedication in Petronius, *Satyrici fragmenta*, f. A2ʳ⁻ᵛ. Published in *Humanistes du bassin des Carpates II. Johannes Sambucus*, 45-46.

61.
Sambucus to Jean Matal
11 November 1564, Vienna

A copy (by Matal's hand as the back of the letter reads) is kept in Leiden, Rijksuniversiteit, Codices Papenbroekiani, Pap 2. no. 49. Published in *Illustrium et clarorum virorum epistolae*, 303-305.

Sambucus has received Cassander's defence and presented it to Emperor Maximilian. He is really surprised that the letter he wrote to Matal two months before, addressing it to the Birckmanns, did not arrive. He spoke again to Andreas Dudith concerning Matal's business, who promised to help in case these matters are still in Maximilian's competency. The emperor has not forgotten about Cassander's case either, but for several reasons he always preferred the Augsburg Confession. Matal should warn Cassander to build his argument on the latter next time. This is Sambucus's advice, not the emperor's order. Sambucus sends his greetings to Cassander, the Birckmanns and Sifanus. The lord of Lansac is in Vienna. Sambucus is not sure if the books required by Matal are in the imperial library. The prefect has never put it in order and the Greek books ended up in chests.

Ioanni Metello Sambucus salutem.

Accepi responsum pro Cassandro, et imperatori Maximiliano obtuli.[369] Quod tibi meae prolixae ad Bircmannos ante duos menses missae non sint redditae, vehementer miror.[370] Nec me tam

---

[368] Johannes Listhius (János Liszthy, Listhi), (?–1577) had an outstanding career. Starting as a royal Hungarian secretary and councillor he became vice-chancellor, bishop of Weszprém, chancellor, bishop of Győr and a baron (1576). His career was supported by Archbishop and Hungarian Chancellor Nicolaus Olahus, who came from the same Transylvanian city Sibiu (Szeben, Hermannstadt) as Listhius. Listhius was a learned patron of Sambucus and other Viennese humanists (cf. e.g. letters 162 and 170) with a profound interest in Hungary's history. He also collected manuscripts himself, wrote some Latin poems and a Latin description of Maximilian II's coronation as king of Hungary. Sambucus dedicated to him an emblem: *Emblemata* (1564), 205. See the article by Gábor Barta in *NDB* 14 (1985), 700; István Fazekas, "A Magyar Udvari Kancellária leltára 1577-ből" [The inventory of Hungarian Court Chancellery in 1577], in *Tanulmányok a 60 éves Gecsényi Lajos tiszteletére = Fons* 9 (2002), 227-248; idem, "Egy 16. század közepi kancelláriai formuláriumos könyv tanúságai" [A study of a mid-sixteenth-century formularium of the Chancellery], in *Universitas – Historia*, eds. István Draskóczy et al. (Budapest: Magyar Levéltárosok Egyesülete, 2018), 551-566; Almási, *The Uses of Humanism*, passim; and the article by Dávid Molnár in *Companion*.

[369] Reference is made to Bartholomaeus Nervius, *Responsio ad calumnias quibus Georgius Cassander in Germanico quodam libello Viae commonstrator inscripto petulanter impetitur, in qua et de eucharistia, quae veterum sit sententia, obiter exponitur* (Coloniae: apud haeredes Arnoldi Birckmanni, 1564). See the next note.

[370] We could not identify this letter. However, it may have been a response to one of Jean Matal's letters written to Sambucus in August or September 1564, to which Matal refers in his letters to Georg Cassander. See Matal's letter to Cassander dated 10 October 1564: "Sambuci nullas litteras, praeter eas quas tibi Ximenius

oblitum officii atque humanitatis putes, qui erudito ac singulari amico, cuius mihi familiarem consuetudinem saepe optabam, respondere nolim. Denuo allocutus sum dominum Sbardellatum, episcopum nunc Quinque Ecclesiarum, de negotio tuo. Is totus esse cupit tuus, suamque operam, modo si quae facultas eiusce rei in Maximiliano sit relliqua, promptam pollicitur. Monere non desistam, et quid sperandum sit, postea significabo. Cassandri memoria non excidit etiam Maximiliano, sed is Augustanae Confessioni multis de causis magis semper favit.[371] Quare, si Cassandrum monueris, ut, quemadmodum indicasti, sua ad illam proxime rationem instituerit, gratiam ab eo et Republica Christiana auferet omnibusque salutariter consulet. Haec ex me dico, non imperatoris nomine ac iussu. Vale et me domino Cassandro, Bircmannis itemque Syffano commendato. Viennae est dominus a Lansacco.[372] In die Martini 1564. Raptim. Vale et salve. De libris nihil certi scio, an sint in bibliotheca imperatoris, quos quaerebas. Nondum enim sunt digesti in ordinem a praefecto, et Graecos scio esse conclusos in arcis.

Address: Clarissimo iurisconsulto D. Ioanni Metello amico suo. Coloniae, apud Bircmannos.

---

coram ostendit, accepi. Ei misi Nervii tui defensionem. Siquid tibi scripsit, fac intelligam, et si rescripseris, mei memineris, obsecro." Leiden, Rijksuniversiteit, Codices Papenbroekiani, Pap 2., no. 68. Published in *Illustrium et clarorum virorum epistolae*, 348-361. There is also another (undated) letter, in which Matal refers again to the letter he had sent to Sambucus: "Ei Nervii pro te responsionem miseram tamquam amico. Is vero eam Maximiliano caesari obtulit. Scripseram te valde dolere Ferdinandi imperatoris obitum, qui tamen tibi adtulisset aliquam a tibi commisso negotio, cum Maximilianus te in eo, ut pergeres, non monuisset, respirandi facultatem. Sed is, qui cum Maximiliano collocutus de te, ut videtur, fuit, rescribit, tui memoriam non excidisse. Suspicor, eum legisse meas caesari." Cited by Heuser, "The correspondence and casual poetry of Jean Matal," 249. See Cassander, *Opera omnia*, 1193-1194.

[371] In a letter to Matal, Georg Cassander explains that Matal forwarded him Sambucus's words too late. He finished the *Consultatio de articulis religionis inter Catholicos et Protestantes controversis* in mid-December (he could have finished already in November, had he not fallen sick), and the bishop of Cologne forwarded it to Maximilian by 1 January 1565. He then continues: "I believe that a major reason of why Maximilian has always favoured the Augsburg Confession—as Sambucus writes regarding the *Consultatio*—is to be found in the fact that in that Confession some disorders and errors of the present Church seem to be pointed out and improved but without going so far as to remove and abolish what is good and healthy and what the present Church shares with the early Christian Church, which was the true Bride of Christ. It is for that reason—as Sambucus points out—that I have sought rapprochement in my book with the Augsburg Confession: my work, as I have said, therefore genuinely contains no warning, because in this book I have followed only the dictates of my conscience and I did not find it necessary to deviate therefrom out of consideration to each of the two confessions." Quoted in Van der Schoor, "Georgius Cassander: searching for religious peace" (as in letter 53, note 308), 132. The translation is based on Van der Schoor.

[372] Louis de Lusignan de Saint-Gelais, lord of Lansac (1513-1589) was a diplomat, political councillor under the regency of Catherine de' Medici and Henry III. Lansac's mission to Vienna was to procure unity of action between France and the Empire in matters of religion. He was also supposed to encourage dynastic alliance between French and imperial ruling families. See "Elizabeth: November 1564," in *Calendar of State Papers Foreign: Elizabeth, Volume 7, 1564-1565*, ed. Joseph Stevenson (London: Longman, 1870), p. 242, no. 789 (11 November).

62.
Obertus Giphanius[373] to Sambucus
1565, no place

Published in T. Lucretius Carus, *T. Lucreti Cari de rerum natura libri sex. Mendis innumerabilis liberati, et in pristinum paene, veterum potissime librorum ope ac fide ab Oberto Gifanio Burano* (Antverpiae: Plantin, 1565), f. 2-8; *Humanistes du bassin des Carpates II. Johannes Sambucus*, 49-60.

63.
Hadrianus Junius to Sambucus
[January–February 1565], Antwerp

Published in Junius, *Epistolae, quibus accedit eiusdem vita*, 262-263.

Junius wrote at greater length to Sambucus a month before. He reports now that he came to Antwerp in the great cold. He brought the manuscript of Nonius Marcellus, corrected in more than a thousand places to Plantin. His corrections won the admiration of several learned men. Last week Laurinus urged him to print it in a press of Bruges, promising him a nice royalty. Junius wants Sambucus to confirm if he is fine with his dedication to Maximilian (who is upgrading his library in imitation of the Alexandrian one, as Sambucus has written), which will be followed by a letter to Sambucus. Theodor Poelmann is sending his greetings.

Scripsi ad te ante mensem prolixius, Sambuce doctissime, de rebus omnibus, responsum a facili ac votis amicorum deditissimo expectans.[374] Hoc te nunc scire velim interim, me inter initia gelus saevissimi non sine vitae discrimine Antverpiam venisse, ac Nonium Marcellum[375] (quem Laurinus[376] scriptis ad me praeterita hebdomada literis Brugensi praelo efflagitabat cum honorarii insignis pollicitatione) Plantino attulisse, locis supra bis mille a me restitutum, cuius restitutionis specimen doctis hic viris nonnullis exhibui cum incredibili admiratione,

---

[373] Obertus Giphanius (Hubert van Giffen) (1534–1604) was a Dutch legal humanist naturalised as German. He studied first in Leuven, then with famous French legal humanists in France, and finally toured Italy. His first humanist publication was this edition of Lucretius, which was followed by many others. He also wrote numerous legal works. From 1571 he was employed at the Strasburg Academy, from 1583 at the University of Altdorf and from 1590, after his scandalous conversion to Catholicism, in Ingolstadt. He corresponded with several of Sambucus's contacts (e.g. Crato, Ellebodius and Blotius) and finally managed to obtain an office at the imperial court. Sambucus dedicated him an emblem: *Emblemata* (1566), 223. See Theodor Schirmer's article in *ADB* 9 (1879), 182-185; R. von Stintzing, *Geschichte der deutschen Rechtswissenschaft*, vol. 1 (München: R. Oldenbourg, 1884), 405-414; C. L. Heesackers, "Le Procurateur Obertus Giphanius (5 november 1566–4 januari 1567)," *Etudes Néerlandaises de droit et d'histoire* 1985, 133-153; Martin Mulsow, "Mehrfachkonversion, politische Religion und Opportunismus im 17. Jahrhundert. Plädoyer für eine Indifferentismusforschung," in *Interkonfessionalität – Transkonfessionalität – binnenkonfessionelle Pluralität. Neue Forschungen zur Konfessionalisierungsthese*, eds. Kaspar Greyerz et al. (Gütersloh: Gütersloher Verlagshaus, 2003), 132-150, at 135-144.

[374] See letter 59.

[375] Nonius Marcellus, *De proprietate sermonum*. Cf. the Index.

[376] Marcus Laurinus lord of Watervliet. See letter 41, note 186.

adeo θάμβου³⁷⁷ omnes tenuit ἀπέραντον.³⁷⁸ Unus nos solicitos habet scripulus, an te lubente ac patiente Maximiliano Augusto (quem olim instructissimam prorsusque Ptolomaicae illius aemulam bibliothecam adornare scripseras) opera ingentibus ac tantum non herculeis (ut ille inquit) laboribus mihi exantlata nuncupari possit, subsecutura a tergo ad te epistola. Qua de re primo quoque tempore voluntatem tuam ut perscribas, te etiam atque etiam pro summo tuo erga me studiososque omnes studio obsecro. Salutem tibi plurimam officiose D. Pulmannus adscribi iussit.³⁷⁹ Vale. Antverpia.

64.
Hadrianus Junius to Sambucus
10 March 1565, Haarlem

Published as a letter to Sambucus following the dedication to Emperor Maximilian in Nonius Marcellus, *De proprietate sermonum*, f. A6ᵛ-A7ʳ. Late 16ᵗʰ century copy in Utrecht, Universiteitbibliotheek, Hs. 829, 169ᵛ-170ʳ. It also appeared in Junius, *Epistolae, quibus accedit eiusdem vita*, 410-413.

When he took the job of restoring the text of Nonius Marcellus, he thought that many learned men had already invested efforts in it. Although in many things they were successful, it may appear as a work done in the fog. Frequently urged by Sambucus, he embarked on restoring this very corrupt text in order to win some glory in the Republic of Letters. He will not deny that several corrupt places may have remained unnoticed, as happens even to the greatest experts, since he is only a human too. Yet he can claim without boasting that he did more than what has been done in the previous hundred years. Junius praises the richness of Nonius's book. Encouraged by Sambucus to publish his work, he wanted to have it nicely printed so as to merit a worthy place in the imperial library, enriched by Sambucus, who travelled through Europe for many years in order to buy coins, antiquities and old manuscripts with much money and great fatigue. Sambucus should nicely present Junius's small gift to the emperor.

Cum unice mihi placuerit semper Lucilii illud, "Eum laborem sumas, laudem qui tibi ac fructum ferat",³⁸⁰ Sambuce doctissime, sumpseram mihi in manus repastinandum Nonii Marcelli vinetum, cui labori propterea lubentius institi, quod hoc tempore in repurgandis restituendisque eius aliquot locis doctissimos quosque viros multum operae posuisse animadverterem.³⁸¹ Quae res tametsi non infeliciter plerisque cessit, attamen veluti per nebulam tentata videri potest. Itaque honestissima studiorum altrix aemulatio faces animo subdidit, ut auctorem corruptissimum a mendis, hoc est Augiae stabulum, repurgare sim aggressus.³⁸² Eodem accesserunt multorum doctorum hominum, atque inter eos frequentes tuae efflagitationes, ut Nonio lucem suam ac recidivae gloriae usuram permitterem, et laudem

---
³⁷⁷ amazement
³⁷⁸ infinite
³⁷⁹ Theodorus Pulmannus (Theodoor Poelman) (1512–1581) was a prolific Dutch philologist collaborating with Plantin. See Max Rooses's article in *Biographie nationale publiée par l'Académie royale … de Belgique*, vol 17 (Brussels: Bruylant, 1903), 874-884.
³⁸⁰ Lucilius, frg. 713 Warmington.
³⁸¹ Nonius Marcellus, *De proprietate sermonum*. Cf. the Index.
³⁸² Cf. Erasmus, *Adagia* 1321, "Augiae stabulum repurgare".

gratiamque a litteratorum coetu ὥσπερ Πανιωνίῳ[383] quopiam expectandam occuparem. Eam ob rem ingentes ac tantum non Herculeos (ut ille inquit[384]) labores in urgendo pertinacius incoepto exantlavi tuaque fretus auctoritate aliquo prodii tenus.[385] Nosti Philemonis comici illud, Ἐκ τοῦ φιλοπονεῖν γίνεθ' ὧν θέλεις κρατεῖν,[386] quanquam accepi esse, qui eandem telam texant, quorum editionem non tardaturos conatus nostros spes est. Neque vero infitias ivero multa nos fugere potuisse, quod in profundissima et captum nostrum fugiente vetustatis cognitione nemo usque adeo Lynceus reperiatur,[387] quin alicubi caliget atque hallucinetur. Nec sum adeo humanitatis exsors, nec sciolus aut philautus.[388] Ausim tamen gloriari citra iactantiae suspicionem plus Nonio accessisse lucis hac opera nostra, quam omnium, quotquot a centum retro annis huic auctori medicam manum admoverunt, studiosis et immortalibus laboribus effectum sit. Non te latet, quam Nonius iste uber sit Amaltheae cornu καὶ παγκτησία,[389] vel, si mavis, apotheca quaedam, omnis generis fructibus cum veteranis, tum novellis, nonnullis etiam vietis instructa et tanquam per cellas et loculamenta ab diligente patrefamilias digesta.

Hunc quia toties extrudi et publici iuris fieri cupivisti vel efflagitasti verius, eo consilio nitidioribus typis excudendum dedi, ut in bibliotheca caesareae maiestatis, quam didici incomprabili sumptu et diligentia adornari, locum tua commendatione mereatur atque obtineat, qui ipse βιβλιοθήκη es ἔμψυχος καὶ μουσεῖον περιπατοῦν[390] (neque enim abnues, opinor, elogium, quod de Longino extulit Eunapius, de te praesagiisse videri potest[391]) quippe qui peragrata bona Europae parte peregrinationes longinquas decurso iam multorum annorum curriculo susceperis (egregio periculorum sumptuumque contemptus testimonio), ut numismata, antiquitates, veterum scripta conquireres. Quod tuum institutum honestissimum ut secundabit Deus, ita cum aeternitate coniunctum provocabit amorem tui et perennem laudem apud studiosos omnes. Vale, vir doctissime, munusculumque verbis apud caesaream maiestatem orna. Harlemi, VI. Idus Martias.

65.
Guglielmo Sirleto to Sambucus
[c. April] 1565, Roma

A copy is kept in Rome, BAV, Vat. lat. 6946, f. 36^{r-v}. Published in Várady, "Relazioni di Giovanni Zsámboky," 28.

---

[383] as if to Apollo (Panionios was an epitheton of Apollo)
[384] It is a reference to Erasmus who advertised his Herculean labours in many places (among others in one of his longest adages). See Oren Margolis, "Hercules in Venice: Aldus Manutius and the Making of Erasmian Humanism Author," *Journal of the Warburg and Courtauld Institutes* 30 (2018), 97-126.
[385] This sentence echoes the thought expressed in the preceding letter.
[386] from the hard work emerges mastery of that which you desire. Philemon, frg. 174 (238).
[387] Lynceus was one of the Argonauts, famous for the sharpness of his look. He could even see through the walls, trees and the ground.
[388] Manuscript: φίλαυτος.
[389] and aquisition of everything
[390] a living library and a walking museum. Eunapius, *Vitae sophistarum* 4.1.3 (456).
[391] Cassius Longinus (213–273) was a Hellenistic rhetorician, Platonist philosopher, and teacher. Junius was apparently already working on the edition of Eunapius Sardianus's *Lives* (cf. Eunapius, Βίοι φιλοσόφων). Accoding to Eunapius, "Longinus was a living library and a walking museum," who was "entrusted with the function of critic of the ancient writers." Philostratus and Eunapius, *Lives of the Sophists*, trans. by Wilmer Cave Wright (London: Heinemann, 1921), 354.

Sirleto wishes that Sambucus's congratulations for his election to the College of Cardinals were rightly founded. Sambucus attributes to him qualities that are needed for the cardinalship, but which, he realises, he does not have. Concerning the book required by Sambucus, he will need to wait until Sirleto, presently overwhelmed by work, can get to it. He encourages Sambucus to publish the works he possesses by ancient authors.

Vellem, quam vere, pro tuo in me amore, meo hoc honore laetatus mihique ex animo gratulatus es, pari scilicet ratione causas commemorasses, quibus merito meo in cardinalium collegium cooptatus essem.[392] Sed, cum eas humanissimis literis tuis amice collegeris, mihique tantum tribueris, quantum certe postulat hic dignitatis gradus, non etiam quantum ipse mihi possim assumere, profecto intelligo, quam longe absim ab ea facultate, quam mei officii munus requirit. Quod nisi Dei benignitatem considerem, qui me a cardinalatus cogitatione, non solum a cupiditate, remotissimum in hunc locum vocavit, sane venerer, ne gravissimo oneri succumberem. Huc igitur, pro nostra benevolentia, tua de nobis optata, huc tuae preces incumbant, meam ut imbecillitatem suae gratiae adminiculo fulciat beneficentissimus Deus. Illud vero, quod neque tu pie neque mihi utiliter precari potes, remove, quaeso, ab optatis tuis. Nam suo id Deus consilio reservavit, ut ne cupiditate quidem aut cogitatione cuiquam hoc praecipere liceat.

De libro, quem requiris, quominus obsequar studio tuo, sit multis magnisque occupationibus, quibus, quomodo nunc est, ita distineor, ut verendum sit, ne obruar, cum primum me ex his impedimentis relaxaro, tibi morem geram. Tu praeclara ista veterum hominum ingenii monumenta, quae sunt in manibus, quaeso, pervulga. Ego et virtutis atque doctrinae nomine et tuae in me benevolentiae causa tibi eximium amorem ac studium meum semper praestabo. Vale.

66.
Sambucus to the Imperial Chamber
26 April 1565, Vienna

The original is kept in Vienna, ÖStA, FHKA, Alte Hofkammer, Hoffinanz Ungarn, Vermischte Ungarische Gegenstände, r. Nr. 6B (alt Fasc. 15373), f. 250^r-251^r. Published in Károly Tagányi, *Magyar erdészeti oklevéltár*, vol. 1. (1015–1745) (Budapest: Pátria, 1896), 91-94; Gerstinger, "Die Briefe," 69-71.[393]

With the emperor's knowledge, the Imperial Chamber sent Sambucus an edict on forests to be translated into Latin three days before. Despite his present engagement with writing histories and other things Sambucus would happily take the job. However, he is not perfectly experienced in the German language, but even if he were, he has no practice in the subject matter. Having read twice the

---

[392] Guglielmo Sirleto (1514–1585) was made cardinal on 12 March 1565. In 1570 he became custodian of the Vatican Library and later also collaborated with the Congregation of the Index. He had many connections with members of the Republic of Letters and a profound interests in Greek cultural heritage and manuscripts. For his relation to Sambucus see Várady, "Relazioni di Giovanni Zsámboky," and Gerstinger, "Die Briefe," passim. See Georg Denzler, *Kardinal Guglielmo Sirleto (1514-1585). Leben und Werk. Ein Beitrag zur nachtridentinischen Reform* (München: Hueber, 1964); *Il cardinal Guglielmo Sirleto: (1514–1585); atti del convegno di studio nel IV centenario della morte*, ed. Leonardo Calabretta (Catanzaro: Istituto di Scienze Religiose, 1989).

[393] We are grateful to István Fazekas for providing us a copy of this letter.

text he reckons that it is fully impossible to translate some terminology. It would not be fatiguing for other learned courtiers, experienced in mountain issues. Another problem is that the corresponding Latin terminology is missing. Using the language of Cicero and Livy, understood by common people, would be difficult. If he used the language of Varro and similar ancient authors (provided he well understood the German), it would be incomprehensible to most. If he paraphrased the mountain and forest terminology, people would understand it in different ways, so he would more happily translate some Greek or even Hebrew texts than this one. Hence Sambucus asks the Chamber to exempt him from this job and entrust it to Paulus Rubigallus or other more experienced men, who would do it hundred times better. If it were about some historical or other job, he would do it as soon as possible, even if it were hundred times lengthier. If the Chamber is in no hurry, he can nevertheless translate it in two or three months, as he pointed out to the emperor the day before. According to the secretary's notes on the letter, the emperor accepted Sambucus's apologies.

Der Römisch kayserlichen Majestät Hochlöblichen Hofkamer-Rätt, Wolgeborn, Gestrengen, Edl und Vest etc.

Gnädige Hern. Euer gnaden haben mir vor drey tägn aus andern information und an Ir Maiestät, unsers allergnedigisten hern bericht, die Waldordnung lateinische zu machen, gnedighlich zuegeschikt. Welche mue ich auffs untertanigist und treulichist ghar ghern thätt (wiewoll ich mitt historien und andern schreyben zimblieh beladen), es wern dan dise gwysse und genugsame ursachen. Die erst, das ich der deutsche sprach nicht so gar woll erfarn bin, und wan ichs glaych weer, so istes das ein matery, darinnen ich gar nieht geybet bin, und wie ichs zwaymall schon yberlesn hab, etliche termin und perkhwörtlein gar schir unmuglich zu latein machen, weyll sonst andre dinen in perkhstättn wolgeybten und glerte laytt solche mue nicht inen haben, vertrautt anzunemen. Die ander ursach ist, das da nicht desgleyche wörtlein in der latein vorhanden sein, und wan der Cicero oder Livius vorhanden wern, das sies mächtn, das dinen die gmain versteen khundt, ist es schwörlich. Mach ichs dan, wan ich das deutsch recht verstiend, wie etliche wörtlein bey den Varrone und andren alten desgleychen lateinische sein, so wurds die gmeyn gar nicht verstenn. So ichs dan mitt vill wörtlein umbschreyb die terminos der perkh und waldwörtlein, so versteets ainer also, der ander also, dass ich lieber etwas khriechisch oder gar hebraysch vertieret als dieses.[394]

Derhalben gnadige, gebüttende hern, bütt untertäniglich, wollet dise ursachen und meine untertagnichliche information bedenkhen, und so man dise ordnung woll und mitt Ire Majestät ehrn und gmainen nutz will an tag geben, diser version mich erledigen, dan als der her Rubigallus und andre dinnen hundertmall solchen sachen pesser als die wollgeybtn vermugen.[395] Wan es sonst ein historie oder, wes es sey, weer, so wolt ichs auffs untertanigist

---

[394] As far as we know, this is the only evidence of Sambucus's elementary Hebrew knowledge.
[395] The translation job was in fact taken over by Paulus Rubigallus, who had some sort of court office, as documented by one of his letters to the Chamber (see Gerstinger, "Die Briefe," 71). Paulus Rubigallus (1510?–1585?) was a humanist from Northern Hungary of ethnic German origins, coming from a wealthy family of the mining centre Kremnica (Kremnitz, Körmöcbánya). His *Hodoeporicon itineris Constantipolitani* was published in Wittenberg in 1544, perhaps during a second stay there. He was also author of a *Querela Pannoniae ad Germaniam*, similarly published in Wittenberg (1537). He was responsible for the mines (as "bányabíró") in Banská Štiavnica (Schemnitz, Selmecbánya). See *Pauli Rubigalli Pannonii Carmina*, ed. Miloslav Okál (Stuttgart: Teubner, 1980); Imre, Mihály, "Der Topos 'Querela Hungariae' in der Literatur des 16. Jahrhunderts. Paulus Rubigallus–Ursinus Velius," in *Iter Germanicum. Deutschland und die Reformierte Kirche in Ungarn im 16–17. Jahrhundert*, ed. András Szabó (Budapest: Kálvin, 1999), 39-117; and the article by Gábor Förköli in *Companion*.

und auffs nächst machen, als es muglich weer, wans hundertmall so vill weer, dan ich khainer mue weych. So es aber, gnädige hern, nicht ayll hatt, und ich des termin halben woll informiert wird, so will ich in zwayen oder drey monaten, als vill mir muglich ist, diese sache verfertigen, wie ich auch gestern ir Majestät auffs allerunterteniigst hab angezaigt. Damitt mich gäntzlich Euer gnaden befelch. Den 26 April. Im 1565. Wien. Euer gnaden untertanigster dienner alzeitt, Johannes Sambucus D.

Address: An die Römisch Khayserlichen Majestät hochlobliche Hoff Chammerrätt untertanige bericht der lateinische Waldordnung etc. D. Sambucus etc.
Secretary's note: D. Sambucci Entschuldigung pro Neusolerisch Waldordnung Vertierung. H. Maius, Anno 65.
Die khai. Mt. sei mit dieser entschuldigung zufriden: sollen die schriftn vom D. Sambuco wider herein erfordert werden. 4 Maii 65.

67.
Sambucus to Philipp von Winneberg[396]
13 July 1565, Vienna

Dedication in Aristaenetus, Ἐπιστολαὶ ἐρωτικαί, f. A2[r-v]. Published in *Humanistes du bassin des Carpates II. Johannes Sambucus*, 72-73.

68.
Sambucus to Karl II, Archduke of Austria
11 August 1565, Vienna

Dedication in Diogenes Laertius, *De vita et moribus philosophorum libri X.*, 3-6. Published in *Humanistes du bassin des Carpates II. Johannes Sambucus*, 74-76.

69.
Sambucus to Christophe Plantin
23 August 1565, Vienna

Dedication in Plautus, *Comoediae viginti*, f. A2[r]-A4[r]. Published in *Humanistes du bassin des Carpates II. Johannes Sambucus*, 77-80.

---

[396] Little is known of Philipp Freiherr von Winneberg (1538–1600), head of the Imperial Chamber of Justice (Reichskammergericht) in Speyer.

70.
Hadrianus Junius to Sambucus
2 September 1565, Amsterdam

Late 16th century copy with corrections and additions in another contemporary hand in Utrecht, Universiteitbibliotheek, Hs. 829, 165ᵛ-167ʳ. Published in Junius, *Epistolae, quibus accedit eiusdem vita*, 399-403.

The last letter, which Junius wrote after his return from home (i.e. Haarlem), where he stayed for ten days, may seem curious to Sambucus after the letter Sambucus wrote on 27 August, which gives new testimony to Sambucus's generosity. In exaggeratedly pompous language, Junius goes on to praise Sambucus, who always keeps his word and even gives more than what he has promised while nonetheless remaining uniquely modest. Junius owes no one as much as he owes him. He avidly read his history on the successful war against the Turks and praises Sambucus's knowledge of ancient writers. He asks for a list of Sambucus's collection of old books, once promised to him. If there can be no way to get him out from the school where he is reduced to teaching some noble students, and if he needs to be excluded from all other honest occupations, Junius would at least like to dedicate himself to literary projects. Before this can happen, Sambucus, staying on the stage of the theatre of the world, should help Junius to come out of his cave. Sambucus should provide him substance for glory, be his light in the darkness. He is sending to Sambucus his Emblemata, *which were printed in Haarlem.*

Literis meis ad te post reditum e patria meum (ubi ad decem dies peregrinatus fueram) scriptis, sed supino quodam otio iam requietis, dum in omnem eventum paratae primi tabellarii occasionem operiuntur, supervenere postremae tuae, ante diem VI Kalendas Septembris scriptae, quae me novo beneficiorum auctario onerarunt, ita ut iam amicitiae benignitatique non leviter pressa vestigia posuisse, sed monumenta quaedam, ad perpetuitatem trabali quodam clavo fixa, apud me depangere voluisse, nedum studuisse videaris.[397] Alii primoribus solum labris pollicentur, nec fidem promissis adiiciunt. Tu, quae spondes, praestas, et verba re ipsa sancibus et cumulo insuper auges, ita ut in par pro pari referendo omnem adimas atque intercidas spem. Absit enim ut tantorum beneficiorum, cuiusmodi iam tertio in me luculenta contulisti, vel nomen sperare fuerim ausus. Qua ergo ratione σε τὸ μέλημα τοὐμον, ut cum Sappho dicam, περιπτύξομαι,[398] qua amici ἦθος ἀκαπήλευτον[399] exosculer? Quomodo immoderatam istam in ornando me benignitatem humanitatemque celebrem? Ut de modestia singulari ac prope unica taceam, qui, cum individua sit felicitatis comes et assecla superbia, cum vix ulli contigerit simul et fortunis abundare et fastu carere, ingenium ab omni fastus suspicione alienissimum prae te feras, id quod et vultus (tacitus quidam mentis sermo) praesentis loquebatur et scripta (nec ipsa ignava testimonia) fidem faciunt. Etsi vero plurimi interesse, cui quid debeas, non sim nescius, nemini tamen debere plus fateor, quam tibi, viro literatissimo, quem literarum communium amor arctissimo vinculo quondam mihi conciliavit atque coniunxit. Eam necessitatem, quae per se sola satis esset, insuper accessario beneficiorum cumulo adauges atque instauras.

Inter quae historiolas tuas cupide devoravi rerum superioribus annis in Turcam feliciter καὶ εὐκλεῶς[400] gestarum, ubi pulchre navata est abs te opera, qui memorabilem cognitionem

---
[397] The eulogistic voice of the letter is decidedly pompous. Junius places Sambucus so high and himself so low that it is difficult to miss the irony.
[398] will I embrace you, my beloved. Cf. Sappho, frg. 163.
[399] sincere manner
[400] and gloriously

scriptorum monumentis consignaris, ὅτι τὰ τῶν ἔργῶν μεγάλα ἂν μὴ τύχῃ λόγων κηρύκων, τῆς μνήμης ἀπορρεῖ καὶ λήθην ἀμπίσχεται.[401] Postularem abs te veterum librorum, indefesso studio et inexhaustis laboribus tibi conquisitorum indicem, quem olim pollicitus fueras, nisi vererer mihi totidem oculorum vulnera καὶ δακεθύμους ἄτας[402] deposcere.

Quod si liberiori mihi apud te esse concessum foret, oratum te velim, candidissime Sambuce, ut quando reperire mihi vix liceat rationem extricandi me e phrontisterio isto, cui me propter redituum angustiam ad instituendos aliquot nobilium pueros mancipavi, et quidem ita, ut a caeteris laboribus honestissimis distinear prorsus et excludar libenterque a sordido et inglorio labore respirare et ad literarium otium transire cuperem, quo inchoatae operae χρυσῆν κορωνίδα[403] imponam vindemiasque meas omnes, quas cum Platone senii oblivioni subsidium paravi, plenis manibus effundam, ut, inquam, momenta omnia, quoad eius fieri potest, per occasionem observes, nullumque praetermittas iuvandi Iunii atque e specu isto in lucem evehendi locum, tu, qui velut edito in orbis terrae theatro regum principumque in oculis versaris. Fac obsecro, ut tu mihi seges ac materia gloriae, vel lumen potius et ornamentum in obscuritate ista facem praeluceas; tu loco prorae puppisque sis rationesque impeditas commendatione tua explices, sicubi patebit non indigna meo loco conditio. Hanc tibi palmam vere lemniscatam depangito, haec somnii fides tibi arrogetur. *Emblemata* aliquot, isthic Harlemi typis expressa, ac a me versibus illustrata, levidense munus accipito serena fronte, qua turbidam aquam Artaxerxes,[404] qua Dii molam salsam ab egenis.[405] Vale Amsterodamo, quarto Nonas Septembris.

71.

Hadrianus Junius to Sambucus
[Autumn? 1565], Antwerp

Late 16th century copy in Utrecht, Universiteitbibliotheek, Hs. 829, 159[r-v]. Published in Junius, *Epistolae, quibus accedit eiusdem vita*, 272-273.

Plantin has written to Junius, urging him to edit Eunapius and [Pseudo-]Hesychius. He has almost finished translating Hesychius, who plagiarized Diogenes Laertius. There is more work to be done with Eunapius, as the copy of this work is full of errors; moreover, he understood from collating Porphyry's biography that it was also mutilated in some places, and something was missing right on the first page. Junius is asking for Sambucus's interpretation of this place. Eunapius's language has a special obscure brevity so one cannot read it superficially (as people in "Germania" do). He presumes that Sambucus has already presented Nonius Marcellus to the emperor, in the edition of which there have remained several errors because of the hurry. He asks for Sambucus's opinion on the Nomenclator *and sends his congratulations to the emperor on his minor advances in Transylvania, of which he would like to hear more.*

---

[401] that the great deeds, if they do not secure words as their harbinger, disappear from memory and are covered in oblivion. Synesius, *Epistulae* 99.
[402] and the heart-eating anguish. Cf. Sophocles, *Philoctetes* 706.
[403] golden crown
[404] The story of Darius finding turbid water exceptionally good after a battle is related by Cicero (*Tusculanae disputationes* 5.97); the same is told of another Persian king, Artaxerxes by Plutarch (*Artaxerxes* 12.3-4) and then Maximus Tyrius (*Dissertationes* 34.6). Junius must have purposefully referred here to the less known version of the anecdote.
[405] Junius, *Emblemata*.

Scripsit ad me hisce diebus Plantinus te Eunapium et Illustrii editionem valde urgere,[406] qua in re mos tibi geretur. Nam Illustrium prope verti, simium Laertii.[407] Maius opus restat in Eunapio, quem vitiosissime descriptum, et, ut ex collatione vitae Porphyrii[408] deprehendi, alicubi mutilatum nosse potuisti, quin statim prima pagina desidero aliquid, ὁ γοῦν μέγας Ἀλέξανδρος οὔκ ἂν ἐγένετο μέγας, εἰ μὴ Ξενοφῶν καὶ τὰ πάρεργά φησι δεῖν τῶν σπουδαίων ἀνδρῶν ἀναγράφειν.[409] Quem locum quomodo tu reddideris velim scire. Eunapius peculiari quadam phrasi et brevitate tenebrosa ac subtilitate quiddam habet immutabile,[410] ut mihi videtur, alioqui nitore verborum et adagiorum raritate atque elegantia illustris. Itaque nec potest, nec debet levi quodam brachio (quo vitio Germania laborat) percurri, sed acurata dicendi ratione exprimi. Igitur, si plusculum illi temporis detur, inter beneficia referendum puto. Nonium Marcellum arbitror iam a te caesareae maiestati exhibitum,[411] quem, dum festinant operae, eo complusculis mendis resperserant.

De *Nomenclatoris* nuncupatione velim sententiam tuam promas.[412] Caesari gratulor, quod Transylvaniae locis aliquot oportunioribus potitus sit,[413] qua de re, si placebit, tribus poteris verbis μάλα λακωνικῶς,[414] et quid de belli eventu, et num decumani illi a Turca fluctus sint metuendi. Vale et Iunium ama.

72.
Georg Cassander to Sambucus
[c. 28 October 1565[415]], [Cologne]

Published in Cassander, *Opera omnia*, 1217.

Since their mutual friend, Jean Matal, has shown Cassander Sambucus's letter and explained how to reach him via correspondence, he wanted to write him, although suffering of joint pains. As Matal was also going to write Sambucus, Cassander asked him for some words of recommendation. It became also clear that Sambucus addressed to Cassander a letter the summer before which did not arrive. Cassander wants to let Sambucus know about his great desire to see the Rite of

---

[406] Eunapius, Βίοι φιλοσόφων; [Pseudo-]Hesychius, Περὶ τῶν ἐν παιδείᾳ.
[407] See Junius's opinion in his preface to the textual emendations added to the Latin translation in [Pseudo-]Hesychius, Περὶ τῶν ἐν παιδείᾳ, 61, where he criticizes Hesychius for his reliance on Diogenes Laertius.
[408] Porphyry's life is the second in the series of Eunapius's *vitae*.
[409] Alexander would never have become great, if Xenophon had never existed. He says that one should write down even the less important deeds of virtuous men. Eunapius, *Vitae sophistarum* 1.1.2. Junius could not discern where the first sentence ended and the next one began.
[410] Another hand crossed out *immutabile* and wrote *inimitabile* in the copy.
[411] Cf. letter 64. Nonius Marcellus, *De proprietate sermonum*. (It was printed between January and March 1565.) Cf. the Index.
[412] Junius, *Nomenclator*.
[413] Junius refers to the war against the Transylvanian Prince János Zsigmond led by Lazarus von Schwendi, who successfully re-conquered some North-East Hungarian territories for Emperor Maximilian. His first success, the conquest of the Castle of Tokaj in February 1565 was described by Johannes Sambucus (who was not yet a historian, (cf. Almási, *The Uses of Humanism*, 166), and later published in his Bonfini-edition (1568) as *Expugnatio Arcis Tokay*.
[414] very laconically
[415] The dating of the letter is helped by the editor of Cassander's *Opera omnia*, who placed it right after Cassander's letter to Maximilian of 28 October 1565, which concerns the unpaid honorarium of 200 talers, which Cassander only mentions shortly at the end of this letter.

Toledo, that is, the Mozarabic Rite, which had been used during the mass by Christians who lived among Arabs all over in Spain and is still observed in Toledo and other places. He talked about its history to Matal, the way it was replaced by the Gallican Rite, which he collected from works on Alfonso XI of Castile and Archbishop Roderico of Toledo. The only description of this rite he has found is in Vasaeus's history. He wants to know more about it partly because it is missing from his catalogue of liturgical traditions of all Christian churches, and partly because Isidore of Seville's book on ecclesiastical offices clearly indicates that this was the rite used in Latin Christendom before Saint Gregory. Isidore's description of the order of the mass seem to coincide with Vasaeus's description of the Toledo or Gothic Rite. The fact that this mass was universally applied can be concluded not only from Isidore but also from Jerome (and Pseudo-Jerome). Cassander has understood that Sambucus had a manuscript book on Mozarabic Rite; he would like to have a copy of it, made at his expense. Once Caspar Nidbruck had raised hopes about a copy of the works of Hincmar, Archbishop of Reims, which he had seen in the library of Liège. If Sambucus has them, in particular the work written against Hincmar, Archbishop of Laon, he would be grateful to have it. Sambucus should also let Emperor Maximilian know that he has never received the 200 thalers for the work on sermons, which he wrote for Ferdinand at the advice of the archbishop of Cologne via Matthias Sittard, and which was donated to him by Ferdinand and Maximilian. Georg Lang the treasurer claims he has not received any order to pay it.

Domino Ioanni Sambuco Pannonico viro et genere et literis clarissimo S. P.

Cum mihi hisce diebus communis amicus dominus Ioannes Metellus literas a tua dominatione ad se scriptas ostenderet[416] simulque viam ad te recta literas dandi indicaret, nolui praetermittere, quin inter has articulorum dolorum, quibus assidue affligor, molestias haec pauca tamen ad tuam dominationem describerem et meam erga tuam dominationem observantiam manifestius declararem. Nam cum nuper idem dominus Metellus se ad tuam dominationem scripturum diceret, rogavi, ut iisdem literis meam quoque vicem sustineret, meque tuae dominationi quam officiosissime commendaret simulque significaret, ut quas hac superiore aestate ad nos scripsisse literis tuis affirmabas, nos nullas accepisse, quod nobis non parum doluit.

Ad haec ab eodem Metello petii, ut illud literis suis adiiceret, quod ipsum et his literis vehementer abs tua dominatione contendo, miro me videlicet desiderio teneri visendi Officii Toletani, quod vulgo Mosarabes vocatur, quo olim Christiani Arabibus, inter quos habitabant, permixti per Hispaniam utebantur in divinis officiis, et praesertim missae, et adhuc hodie Toleti in sacello quodam et aliis locis observatur, cuius officii cum Gallicano officio commutati historiam[417] ex historia generali Alphonsi XI. regis Castellae[418] et Roderici archiepiscopi Toletani[419] eidem D. Metello communicavi. Cuius officii descriptionem integram nondum nancisci potui, neque plus de eo cognoscere, quam a Iacobo [!] Vasaeo Brugensi in priori libro *Chronicorum Hispaniae* commemoratur.[420] Eo autem ardentius illud cupio, tum quod illud

---

[416] Cf. letter 61, note 370.
[417] Cf. Roger Reynolds, "The Visigothic Liturgy in the Realm of Charlemagne," in *Das Frankfurter Konzil von 794* (Mainz: Koblenz, 1997), 919-945.
[418] Alfonso XI of Castile (1311–1350).
[419] Rodrigo Jiménez (Ximénez) de Rada (c. 1170–1247) Archbishop of Toledo, historian. Among others he is the author of *De rebus Hispaniae* and *Historia arabum*. Rada believed the "officium Toletanum" went back to Isidore of Seville.
[420] Johannes Vasaeus, *Chronici rerum memorabilium Hispaniae tomus prior* (Salmanca: Ioannes Iunta, 1552),

solum ad integrum plenumque liturgiarum omnium Christianae professionis gentium, quas studiose collegi, corpus desidero,[421] tum etiam quod existimem non modo per Hispaniam, sed per alias plerasque omnes ecclesias Latinas hunc ritum divina mysteria celebrandi ante Gregorii tempora usitatum fuisse,[422] id quod ex Isidoro libro I. cap V. de ecclesiasticis officiis haud obscure colligitur.[423] Describit enim ordinem missae, seu orationum, quibus Deo oblata sacrificia consecrantur; atque eum ordinem cum ordine Toletani, seu Gothici officii, ut vocatur, quo modo a Vasaeo describitur, prorsus convenire deprehendi. Affirmat idem Isidorus eam celebrationem divinorum mysteriorum uno eodemque modo ab universo orbe peragi. Idem probari potest ex Hieronymo *Ad Rusticum*,[424] ex *Libro de septem gradibus*, ubi diaconi officium describit,[425] qui in divinis officiis, ut aures habeamus ad dominum, clamat,[426] quod in libro illo Mosarabum aperte fit.

Huius igitur Officii cum apud vos exemplum esse intellexissem, tuamque humanitatem, quae huiusmodi piis desideriis libenter obsequi soleat, perspectam haberem, putavi neminem istic esse, per quem commodius quod volebam perfici possit.[427] Quare si hoc officium, ut vel nostro sumptu describatur, curare digneris, rem et tua ista insigni humanitate et pietate dignam et mihi harum rerum ecclesiasticarum studioso quam gratissimam et optatissimam feceris. Iamdudum quoque a clarissimo viro Casparo a Niedbruuck piae memoriae spes nobis facta fuit operum Hincmari archiepiscopi Remensis,[428] cuius quaedam opuscula ex bibliotheca Leodiensi vidimus, sed insigne illud opus, quod scripsit contra Hincmarum episcopum Laudunensem de provocatione ad Ecclesiam Romanam, desideramus,[429] quo si per te, vir clarissime, potiri possemus, esset quo nos plurimum tibi debere fateremur.[430] Vale, vir clarissime, et nos, quod facis, ama, et ubi occasio tulerit caesareae maiestati nos quam obsequentissime commendatos habe, quam ex consilio archiepiscopi Coloniensis per dominum Matthiam Sittardum[431] eius maiestati a concionibus sacris monendum curavi,[432] me ducentos illos aureos, quos pro opella nostra in opere illo ab augustae memoriae parente eius Ferdinando et ab ipsius maiestate mihi iniuncto conficiendo insumpta per literas donavit, nondum accipere potuisse. Nam Georgius ille Lanngh rationum praefectus,[433] cum a nobis interpellaretur, nullum se mandatum illius pecuniae numerandae accepisse asseverabat.

[—] f. 115ʳ–117ʳ. Johannes Vasaeus (1511–1561) was a Flemish humanist and historian, who spent his working life in Spain and Portugal.
[421] Cf. Georgius Cassandrus, *Ordo Romanus de officio missae* (Coloniae: Birckmann, 1561).
[422] Saint Gregory the Great (c. 540–604).
[423] Isidorus, *De ecclesiasticis officiis* 1.5.
[424] Hieronymus, *Epistulae* 2.14 (*Ad Rusticum monachum*).
[425] Pseudo-Hieronymus, *Epistula XII seu opusculum de septem ordinibus ecclesiae* [PL 30, 148-162].
[426] Cf. Isidorus, *De ecclesiasticis officiis* 2.8.3.
[427] It does not appear that Sambucus had any manuscript of the Rite of Toledo.
[428] The works of Hincmar (806–882), archbishop of Reims, which were first published in the seventeenth century.
[429] Hincmarus (i.e. Hincmar bishop of Laon, † 879), *Libellus expostulationis adversus Hincmarum Laudunensem* (in *Patrologia latina* CXXVI). First published in Ludovicus Cellotius, *Concilium Duziacense I, anno domini DCCCLXXI celebratum, cum aliis Hincmari utriusque opusculis* (Parisiis: Cramoisy, 1658), 69-209.
[430] It does not appear that Sambucus had any manuscript by Hincmar.
[431] Friedrich IV of Wied (1518–1568) was the Archbishop-Elector of Cologne from 1562 to 1567, often accused of Protestant sentiments. Matthias von Sittard (1522–1566) was a Dominican theologian, chaplain of Emperor Ferdinand.
[432] He may be referring here to *De Articulis Religionis inter Catholicos et Protestantes controversis*. See letter 53, note 310.
[433] Georg Lang zu Speyer († c. 1582) was Maximilian's Hofpfennigmeister probably from 1563 (ÖStA, HHStA HausA Familienakten 99-18).

73.
Sambucus to Emperor Maximilian II
22 November 1565,[434] Vienna

The original is kept in Vienna, ÖNB, Cod. 9039, f. 32r.[435]

The historian should not make or judge history, he should not persuade or express his opinion but only teach. He should rely only on true and proven facts, otherwise he will deceive people, like in the case when one learns about something false or unknown and then either subjectively justifies it or excuses it. This is the job of philosophy and the courts. We want to leave it to posterity and to the readers to decide what value the facts have. The narrations should be written as simple, truthful, fitting to the relevant age, without so many reflections and not over-elaborate. Sambucus does not care why Ulloa offered exaggerated judgements in the biographies of two the emperors that he published, but he must say that Ulloa made a patchwork rather than proper history, relying in spirit and facts but also often word-by-word on the works of Guicciardini, Guazzo, Giovio and others. At the emperor's order, Sambucus shortly noted down some critical points regarding Ulloa's history as they came to his mind, which may once be developed into a history, if life and the emperor's generosity allows for it.

Maximiliano II. domino suo clementissimo Ioannes Sambucus.

Historia pars ea est rhetoricae, quae narratio dicitur. Cuius cum orator minime esse author possit, sed ad ipsum res exponendae afferantur, quanto minus historicus suarum narrationum factor esse debet atque etiam iudex, qui non persuadere nec peragere quemquam, sed docere tantum constituit.[436] Itaque alterum in mendacii vitio, in morbo animi atque particulari studio alterum ponitur. Vera et quidem vere testataque sunt stilo suscipienda, ne temporibus et rerum gestarum authoribus fraus fiat ulla, quod certe accidit, cum vel falsa, vel ignota nobis prodimus, atque si diis placet, ut hodie fit, iudicio nostro rationibusque approbamus quidque vel excusamus. Quod ipsum est philosophiae atque iudiciorum. Posteritati et lectoribus, ut illa valeant, disceptanda relinquamus, simplices, verae, tempori congruae, sine tot epilogis narrationes contexantur et non affectae. De Ulloa vero qui de duorum potentissimorum imperatorum et fratrum vita libros edidit,[437] nihil pronuncio, minus curo quo animo quaedam et iudicio exaggerarit, sed tamen tacere non possum, centones esse potius, quam integrum corpus historiae, et ad verbum exscriptas paginas de Guiczardino, Guazzo, Iovio et aliis,

---

[434] Dated according to the entry in Sambucus's hand at the end of the list of the coments on folio 36v.

[435] This is a preface to Sambucus's critical comments concerning Alfonso Ulloa's historical writings. The handwriting of the critical notes does not seem to be Sambucus's, but some notes and additions are by him.

[436] Nevertheless, in his critical comments the first thing Sambucus points out is Ulloa's cool (impartial) voice in narrating Ferdinand's occupation of Hungary.

[437] Ulloa, *Vita del potentissimo e christianissimo imperatore Ferdinando I*; idem, *Vita dell'invittissimo e sacratissimo imperator Carlo V.* (Venice: V. Valgrisio, 1566). Alfonso Ulloa (1529–1570) was a Spanish humanist making his living mostly as a professional translator, historian and spy. Having moved to Italy between 1546–1549, he wrote numerous historical works and transmitted a wealth of literature between Italy and Spain. After the death of the imperial historian Wolfgang Lazius (summer of 1565), he obviously aspired for the position of historian. The fact that his greatest competitor Sambucus was asked to assess his work already signals the chances of the Spaniard. On Ulloa see Othón Arróniz, "Alfonso de Ulloa, servidor de don Juan Hurtado de Mendoza," *Bulletin Hispanique*, 70 (1968), 437-457; Antonio Rumeu de Armas, *Alfonso de Ulloa, introductor de la cultura española en Italia* (Madrid: Gredos, 1973).

quorum et mentem et res prorsus sequitur.⁴³⁸ Idque ut aliquot locis mandato tuae maiestatis confirmem, brevissime et velut praetereundo quaedam, ut in mentem venerint annotabo, quae aliquando si vita tuaeque maiestatis liberalitas adiungetur, copiose fideliterque contexam.⁴³⁹

74.
Christophe Plantin to Sambucus
12 January 1566, Antwerp

The original is kept in Vienna, ÖNB, Cod. 9736, f. 5-6. Published in *Supplément à la Correspondance de Christophe Plantin*, 25-27.

Plantin asks Sambucus to send his Greek manuscript of Theodoret of Cyrus's commentaries into the Pentateuch (Plantin is quoting the relevant Latin translation) to the Frankfurt book fair. Concerning Laertius he will do as Sambucus desired in his last letter. He asked Birckmann concerning Theophylact of Ochrid, and got the response that the translation was not yet ready. Despite his urgings and Junius's promises, Junius does not send him Eunapius. Junius is sending him pages of Nonius Marcellus and the Nomenclator *separately, but he cannot begin to print it before he gets all the copy. He will send copies of Sambucus's* De imitatione ciceroniana, *which is worthy of him and his friends, to the Frankfurt book fair. Plantin explains that the ideal way to sell his books, which are much demanded, would be to leave more copies with the booksellers, who could sell them at more than one book fair and then make the balance. He has found out after long research that Philo's* On the virtues *had been printed by Robert Estienne more correctly than could be printed from Sambucus's manuscript, which Plantin sent to him in order to attach it to Aristaenetus's letters.*

---

⁴³⁸ References are made to the historians Francesco Guicciardini (1483–1540), Marco Guazzo (c. 1480–1556) and Paolo Giovio (1483–1552). Sambucus possessed many works by Guicciardini and Giovio (cf. with Gulyás, *Sámboky János könyvtára*). Giovio had several Hungarian connections, and was not only informed but also criticised by Sambucus's friend, Antonius Verantius.

⁴³⁹ Sambucus's criticism was successful. The most irritating for the emperor must have been Ulloa's fiercely anti-Protestant attitude, very distant from his own irenic spirit. His book on Ferdinand represented an entirely Catholic interpretation of the Reformation. Maximilian, in fact, sent a letter to the Venitian ambassador of Philip II, where the book on Ferdinand's life was being printed, claiming that correcting Ulloa's history was more difficult than starting it over. He asked the ambassador to stop the publication of the book until the errors were corrected. However, he was late, the book on Ferdinand had already been printed. Nevertheless, Ulloa's failures did not stop Maximilian from recommending him to the Spanish king as a courtier (Vienna, HHStA, Familienarchiv, Sammelbände, box I, vol. 2, f. 18.). Ulloa had apparently no success in his patria, and continued to cherish the ambition of serving the Austrian Habsburgs as a historian. Later, he passed as his own a description of the battle of Sziget (*Historia di Zighet, ispugnata da Suliman, Re de'Turchi, l'anno 1566*, Venice: Bolognino Zaltieri, 1569), which was actually a work by Fran Crnka, who had published it a year before in Turin with Giovanni Criegher. In 1570 he published a history of recent Ottoman wars in Hungary, which was again a plagiarised version of Pietro Bizzarri's *Historia della Guerra fatta in Ungheria*. Ulloa dedicated it to a Genoan banker so that the work could have a powerful patron who would protect it against plagiarism, as he asserted in the preface. Alfonso Ulloa [Pietro Bizzarri], *Le historie de Europa… nelle quali principalmente si contiene la guerra ultimamente fatta in Ungheria tra Massimiliano imperatore de' Cristiani et sultan Solimano re de' Turchi* (Venice: Zaltieri, 1570). See Massimo Firpo, "Pietro Bizzarri e la storia della Guerra d'Ungheria," in *Venezia e Ungheria nel Rinascimento*, ed. Vittore Branca (Florence: Olschki, 1973), 449-467 (at 461-467). At the same time, Ulloa also tried to make himself useful to Maximilian by reporting on people in Venice he suspected to be Turkish spies. Consequently, Maximilian ordered his Venetian ambassador to look into the matter. See Gorizia, Biblioteca del Seminario Teologico Centrale, Fondo Strassoldo-Villanova, Busta 216, f. 87-90. See also Almási, *The Uses of Humanism*, 160-161.

So Plantin will only print the first leaf of Sambucus's letter of dedication to Aristaenetus. He will not print some of the epigrams sent to him either, because they had already been printed by Aldo. Plantin also found out that some verses in Sambucus's manuscript by Plautus were simply misplaced. In these places he just put a note indicating their different place in Sambucus's copy. He wants to have the figures of the emblems engraved by the next book fair but the engravers are negligent.

Monsieur, ie nay sceu [...][440]

le livre *De quaestionibus ambiguis in Genesim* Theodoreti[441] lequel aussi ie nay pas trouve en grec; le latin commence ainsi

In principio creavit Deus coelum et terram   Gen. I.
Scriptura sacra docendi rationem metiri consuevit ex discipulis ac perlatis perfecta proponere, rudibus autem elementa eorumque facultati convenientia. Quum ergo conspicuam creaturam Deum constituerent Aegiptii, quibuscum Israel diutissime conversatus impietatem hanc inbiberat, necessario quae de creatura scire expediat illis proponit ac diserte docet, illam habuisse initium, et ab universitatis Deo creatam esse. Nec tamen etc.

Les dernieres lignes de la fin sont

Et inde dominus reprehendit Saduceorum incredulitatem quum inquit: Quod autem resurgant mortui, non legistis, Ego Deus Abraham, Isaac, et Iacob? Deus non est Deus mortuorum, sed viventium. Ipsi gloria in secula, Amen.
In Exodum.
Quomodo est intelligendum, est ista: Creverunt ut plebs multa? Non contumeliose posuit hoc, ut quidem intellexerunt, sed numerosam multitudinem declaravit. Sic enim ait: Adeo creverunt ut per universam illam terram etc.

Les dernieres lignes sont

Tunc quoque primum festum hoc erant celebraturi in deserto. Nam secundus agebatur annus, ex quo vindicati erant a servitute.

Apres quoy suict in Leviticum in Numeros in Deuteronomium et puis finablement in Judicum qui finist

Ego vero nec instar hominis opus habeo cibo, nec honorem Deo debitum capio. Unde perspicuum est Angelos humaniter ab Abraham exceptos modo quodam altero propositam escam consumpsisse.

Monsieur sil vous plaist me le mander ie vous envoyeray lentier livre a la foire de Francfort. Je desire aussi que ceux qui peuvent et le doibvent faire eussent la volonte demployer deniers

---

[440] The beginning of the letter is missing.
[441] A part of Εἰς τὰ ἄπορα τῆς θείας γραφῆς κατ' ἐκλογήν by Bishop Theodoret of Cyrus (c. 393–c. 466), an influential theologian, one of the principal actors in the Nestorian controversy (on the side of Nestorius) and author of several works on church history. See *RE* V.A (1934), 1791-1801. Sambucus had many manuscripts by Theodoret, among others his commentaries in the Pentateuch (Vienna, ÖNB, Cod. Theol. gr. 153).

a secourir ceux qui travaillent a mectres les anciens aucteurs en lumiere tant en leur langue grecque comme latine. Quant au Laertius ie ne faudray a faire cela que me commandes par vos lectres le 19 du mois de Decembre en envoyant bien relié.[442] J'ay parle au Birkmans[443] touchant le Theophilactus in Acta Apostolorum[444] qu'ils m'ont respondu ne pouvoir estre faict encores de quelque temps qu'ils ne m'ont sceu limiter a cause de la traduction non achevee et qu'ils ne scavent le temps qu'ils la pourront avoir, ce qui me desplaist aussi grandement en la longueur de Monsieur Junius qui ne nous expedie point aussi la traduction d'Eunapius[445] nonobstant que ie limportune souvent par mes lectres et que ia plusieurs fois il m'ayt promis lexpedier. Vray est qu'il a este aucunnement empesche a son Nonius Marcellus[446] et depuis a son *Nomenclator*[447] duquel il m'a ia delivre une partie de lexemplaire ascavoir quelque 40 cahiers et ne reste plus ainsi qu'il m'a escrit de long temps quenviron 7 cahiers lesquels il m'a promis envoyer de bref et moy de le commencer incontinent que i'auray lentiere copie et non pas devant a cause qu'il m'est tousiours mal succede davoir commence aucun livre devant qu'avoir toute la copie en mon pouvoir [...] n'est si grand que non pouvoir [...] bien entreprendre. Et mesmes si l'oeuvre m'est trop pesante iespere bien de trouver assistence et aide. Parquoy Monsieur s'il vous plaist m'envoyer l'exemplaire par la premiere occasion ie satisferay volontiers a ce que mordonneres pour iceluy. Car i'ay delibere dentretenir un compositeur a ne besongner autrement qu'en grec. Et si ie trouve qui me veille assister aux frais i'y mettray davantage douvriers en besongne.

Je vous envoyray par la voye de Francfort vostre exemplaire de Imitatione[448] avec ce que i'estimeray digne de vous ou que prendries plaisir de voir ou de communiquer a vos amis. Et pourtant que m'avies quelquesfois escrit que les livres de mon impression sont bien desires par dela ne fust la cherte que les libraires y tiennent s'il y avoit libraire par dela dont ie fusse asseure de fidelite pour me payer de foire en foire ie luy en conterois a prix raisonable tel nombre quil voudroit et mesmes sil ne les vendoit durant le temps dentre la foire les rapportans a ses despents sains et nets et me les restituant a lautre foire ou deuxiesme ensuivante ie les reprendrois pour autre telle marchandise qu'alors il pourroit estre mienne en ma boutique qui luy duiroit, bien entendu qu'il devroit payer la somme arrestee entre nous desdicts livres prins quil raporteroit et pour lesquels il prendroit autres livres dont il penseroit mieux faire son proffict.

Ac reste, Monsieur, soyes adverti que iay trouve apres longue recherche que le Philo *De Virtutibus* que maves de vostre grace envoye pour adiouxter aux Epistres d'Aristenetus est imprimé plus correctement par Robert Estienne[449] que n'est vostre copie parquoy i'en feray rimprimer la premiere feille et Espistre dedicatoire desdictes Epistres Aristeneti[450] pour ne vendre chose pour non imprimee qui le soit par un tel imprimeur ains les oeuvres dudict

---

[442] Diogenes Laertius, *De vita et moribus philosophorum* (see letter 68).
[443] Johann Birckmann.
[444] Theophylactus, *Explicationes in acta Apostolorum*.
[445] Eunapius, Βίοι φιλοσόφων.
[446] Nonius Marcellus, *De proprietate sermonum*. Cf. the Index.
[447] Junius, *Nomenclator*.
[448] Sambucus, *De imitatione a Cicerone petenda* (2nd ed.). Apparently, Sambucus ran out of copies and asked Plantin to send him a few.
[449] We were not able to identify Robert Estienne's edition of Philo. See Antoine Augustin Renouard, *Annales de l'imprimerie des Estienne, ou, Histoire de la famille des Estienne* (Paris: Jules Renouard, 1837). There was a large edition of Philo's works printed by Adrien Turnèbe using Robert Estienne's types in 1552, which he inherited as new royal printer. Sambucus had several manuscripts by Philo, but the ones mentioned in the letter are not in the holdings of the ÖNB.
[450] Aristaenetus, Ἐπιστολαὶ ἐρωτικαί.

Philo sous le tiltre de *Περὶ ἀνδρίας*[451] ce que je vous supplie ne trouver mal et aussi que iay delibere de non imprimer aucuns des Epigrammes envoyes qui sont aussi imprimes per Aldum in libro *Epigrammatum Graecorum*.[452] Jay trouve aussi de cas fortuit quelques vers in Plauto qui navoyent change que de place dun feillet ou deux parquoy ie les ay laissés, ayant annote simplement en chaicun lieu que vostre exemplaire les avoit en un autre endroict.[453] Je poursuy et presse les tailleurs des figures de vos Emblesmes pour les pouvoir imprimer devant ceste foire de Francfort, ce que ne pouvant estre ie vous prie de croire quil naura tenu a moy mais a la negligence et mauvaise foy du pourtraiteur et des tailleurs qui non seulement me travaillent et font dommage mais aussi a eu mesmes. Que sera lendroict, Monsieur, ou ie prieray Dieu vous avoir en sa saincte grace et me maintenir en la vostre. D'Anvers le 12 Janvier 1566. Entierement vostre a iamais [?] serviteur et ami, Plantin.

Address: A Monsigneur Monsieur Sambucus.

75.

Sambucus to Paolo Manuzio
1 February 1566, Vienna

The original is in Rome, BAV, Vat. lat. 3434,[454] f. 88. A copy is held in Bibl. Estense, Fondo Estense, Ital. 1827, Beta 1,3,1, 120. Published in Gerstinger, "Die Briefe," 71-73.

The death of Pius IV must be sad for Manuzio and the Republic of Letters, although Sambucus knows both from others and from the conversations he has witnessed personally that Pius V is a pope who values learning and the learned men, as he was raised to his rank from humble standing because of his philosophical and theological learning and morals. Andreas Dudith's diplomatic mission in Poland is becoming longer than thought. If he accomplished it successfully, he would be fortunate and have many friends. Since the recent death of his father Sambucus was busy with family affairs but he will soon finish and return to publishing his Pannonian history. Since the time he saw Manuzio, he has published a numismatic work in addition to some emblems, explained the poetry of Horace, corrected Laertius, Plautus, Petronius, edited Eunapius and [Pseudo-]Hesychius, all with Plantin. He is avidly waiting for Manuzio's works. He is sending his greetings to Aldo Manuzio, whose talents he expects to be worthy of the Manuzios.

Paulo Manutio Ioannes Sambucus salutem.

Pontificis Pii IIII obitum,[455] etsi tibi omnibusque elegantia literarum et studio antiquitatis claris permolestum non dubitem, quia tamen hunc etiam V. e tenui loco ad hunc gradum

---

[451] Recently, it is understood that Philo's work *De caritate* should be considered as an attached part of *De specialibus legibus*.
[452] *Florilegium diversorum epigrammatum in septem libros* (Venetiis: Aldo, 1503). The edition of Aristaenetus's *Love espistles* contained also some unpublished epigrams by Aristaenetus, which appeared almost contemporaneously in Henri Estienne's *Ἀνθολογία διαφόρων ἐπιγραμμάτων παλαιῶν* in the same year.
[453] Plautus, *Comoediae viginti*. See letter 69.
[454] We have not managed to find the original letter indicated in Gerstinger.
[455] Pope Pius IV died on 9 November 1565.

philosophiae ac theologiae commendatione morumque probitate evocatum cum ex omnibus audio, tum ex eius crebris sermonibus praesens colligere potui.[456] Cogitat ille salutaria nec amantes linguarum et scriptis eloquentiaque corroboratos negligit, quod tuum tuique similium, hoc est sapienti et pura scriptione spectabilium, consilium non parum confirmare debet nec ullo metu stilum vel animum contrahere.

Sbardellatus noster Polonica legatione praeter opinionem diutius detinetur, qui si rempublicam feliciter gesserit, beatus ille et copiosus etiam amicis.[457] Ego mortuo nuper patre domesticis constituendis occupatus fui, sed brevi expeditus, quae caepi, publice dabo historias nostras Pannonicas.[458] Dum a vobis absum, praeter numismatum opus edidi Emblematum ludos,[459] Horatii *Poeticam* illustravi,[460] Laertium, Plautum, Petronium correxi,[461] Eunapium cum Illustrio et alia edo,[462] omnia ex officina Plantini. Tuas ego lucubrationes cupide expecto, neve illarum cognitione me prives, vehementer oro. Aldum nostrum salutabis,[463] cuius ego de ingenio haud minora quam omnium Manutiorum spero, quod ipsum prima quidem eius exempla, sed egregia multaque laude cumulata, docent. Vienna, Kalendis Februarii 1566.

76.
Sambucus to Guglielmo Sirleto
20 February 1566, Vienna

The original is kept in Rome, BAV, Vat. lat. 6792, f. 127ʳ. Published in Gerstinger, "Die Briefe," 73-75.

Sambucus is gratefully sending back Ptolemy of Ascalon's book on Greek lexical differences. He notes that the title of the work is false, and it is in fact a confused excerpt from the work of Ammonius Grammaticus, who has already been published together with other Greek lexicographers, so Sambucus did not care to make a copy. Supported with a decent salary by the emperor and also by friends he is now working on some histories of Hungary. He is also engaged with the books of ancient authors, either emending or commenting them. He is now publishing Eunapius and [Pseudo-]Hesychius, a Greek work on rhetorical figures and his own works. Three years before he approached a few times the present pope in private and called his attention to the importance of publishing old codices, of which the Vatican has so many. He used to respond: "My Sambucus, I wish it depended on me. I would publish those good Greek books and would not let them be consumed by moths. But I am a poor little monk and it is not in my power." Sambucus wishes that now someone took the pope at his word.

---

[456] Antonio (or Michele) Ghislieri (1504–1572), Pope Pius V (1566–1572). He was born into a poor family and had to work as a shepherd in his childhood before he joined the Dominicans at the age of fourteen.
[457] For this mission of Dudith see Almási, *The Uses of Humanism*, 252-257.
[458] Sambucus's father died on 14 August 1565. The Hungarian history is a reference to the edition of Bonfini's *Rerum Ungaricarum decades*. See letter 93.
[459] Sambucus, *Emblemata cum aliquot nummis* (1564).
[460] Sambucus, *Ars poetica Horatii*. Cf. letter 35, note 146.
[461] Diogenes Laertius, *De vita et moribus philosophorum* (cf. letter 68); Plautus, *Comoediae viginti* (cf. letter 69); Petronius, *Satyrici fragmenta* (cf. letter 60).
[462] Eunapius, Βίοι φιλοσόφων; [Pseudo-]Hesychius, Περὶ τῶν ἐν παιδείᾳ.
[463] Aldo Manuzio Jr.

Illustrissimo cardinali Schirleto, patrono suo Ioannes Sambucus.

Accepi libellum Ptolemei Περὶ διαφορᾶς λέξεων,[464] quem remitto, atque tuae illustritati gratiam habeo de benevolo erga me sensu, quo mihi amplissimo eo et ad exornandos conatus locupletissimo nihil optatius potuisset accidere.[465] Illud tamen tuae reverendissimae illustritati significare volui vel potius in memoriam reducere, falsam esse hanc libelli ἐπιγραφήν,[466] et quicquid est, ex Ammonio Grammatico confuse ad verbum excerptum,[467] qui Ammonius editus est olim cum *Lexicis Graecis*, itaque ne describendum quidem curasse.[468] Verumtamen tua illustritas me isto beneficio communicandi totum clientelae devinxit suae. Utinam aliquando tuae illustritati emetiri aliquo exemplo grato voluntatem queam, profecto studium atque opera nulla in parte deforet.

Ego honesto salario caesareae maiestatis et amicorum ope adiutus texo res Pannonicas et per ocium in vetustis scriptoribus versor tum emendandis, tum illustrandis, quorum exempla credo ad vos brevi allatum iri. Nunc Eunapium cum Illustrio edo atque grammaticos Graecos περὶ σχημάτων[469] itemque meas quasdam nugas.[470] Cum, ut scis, aliquoties hunc pontificem familiarissime ante 3 annos accessissem atque de studiis et vetustis codicibus edendis admonerem, quorum copia tanta apud vos delitescit, memini illum mihi aliquoties respondisse:[471] "Mi Sambuce, utinam per me staret, ego ederem optimos quosque libros Graecos neque hic eos tineis absumendos paterer. Sed sum pauper fraterculus, in meis viribus id situm non est."[472] Utinam, mi optime atque Illustrissime Schirlette, hanc vocem illi aliquis repeteret atque ad sanctos literatosque conatus excitaret, quod non dubito sponte ipsum ac prolixe facturum. Vale. Vienna, X Kalendas Martii MDLXVI.

---

[464] on lexical differences. Cf. Sirleto's letter to Sambucus (no. 65), promising him to send the book desired by Sambucus to Vienna.

[465] This work was published as *Ptolemaei P. Ascalonitae de differentia vocum Graecarum specimenque Glosarii νομικοῦ* in *Bibliothecae Grecae*, vol. 4.2 (Hamburgi: Liebezeit, 1711). On Ptolemy of Ascalon the grammarian (active at around Christ's birth), who was, in fact, not the author of this later compilation, see Max Baege, *De Ptolemaeo Ascalonita dissertatio inauguralis philologica* (Hallis Saxonum: Karras, 1882); Joseph Geiger, "Ptolemy of Ascalon, Historian of Herod," *Scripta Classica Israelica* 31 (2012), 185-190.

[466] attribution

[467] Ammonius Grammaticus was a fourth-century Egyptian priest who fled to Constantinople and became the tutor to the church historian Socrates. He is the supposed author of a lexicon of Greek synonyms and antonyms. Sambucus is right to point out the close relationship between his work and the Περὶ διαφορᾶς λέξεων. See Eleanor Dickey, *Ancient Greek Scholarship: A Guide to Finding, Reading, and Understanding* (Oxford: OUP, 2007), 94-95.

[468] Sambucus is referring here to Aldo Manuzio's *Dictionarium Graecum cum interpretatione latina* (first published in 1497 and many times enlarged and republished). Also see Gerstinger, "Die Briefe," 74-75.

[469] on figures

[470] Eunapius, Βίοι φιλοσόφων; [Pseudo-]Hesychius, Περὶ τῶν ἐν παιδείᾳ. For the planned edition of Greek grammatical figures see his *Catalogus librorum*.

[471] Antonio (or Michele) Ghislieri (1504–1572), Pope Pius V (1566–1572). See the preceding letter.

[472] Three years earlier, Michele Ghislieri was already a cardinal.

77.
Sambucus to Johannes Crato[473]
23 March 1566, Vienna

Published in Gerstinger, "Die Briefe," 75-76.

Sambucus has forwarded Crato's letter to a certain Gottfried. Everyone talks about the Ottoman danger and if Crato does not intervene, the rest of Hungary will cease to exist. The garrisons are rare, the provisions of Lazarus von Schwendi are inadequate, the lords are confused and disheartened, all is bad because of "our sins." The diet of Pressburg ended, the nobles promised to pay 2 florins per gate rather reluctantly, and the archduke returned to Vienna. When they wanted to move some gunpowder, of which there is great shortage, from Krems to Vienna, it exploded and caused a great fire. A hundred gunboats have been added to the imperial fleet. Some claim that the Ottoman army returned from Edirne to Constantinople. The "voivode" is preparing for something. 7,000 Polish horsemen are approaching the Zips, but Schwendi will attack them soon. It is rumoured that the "voivode" will marry the princess of Muscowy and that the prince of Muscowy will marry the sister of the Polish king.

Salutem dicit Ioannes Sambucus.

Ad Godefridum tuas misi.[474] Apud nos graves illi et constantes de periculosis et universis malis Thurcici rumores extiterunt ac, nisi secundum Deum vos istic aliquid ingens impetraveritis, actum de reliquiis Pannonicis fuerit. Praesidia tenuia et rara, commeatuum apud Schwendium inopia,[475] nervorum exigua vis, animi consternati et pene fracti baronum καὶ ἅπαντα λυπηρά[476]

---

[473] Johannes Crato von Krafftheim (1519–1585) was one of Sambucus's principal contacts at the imperial court. Crato was a descendant of a patrician family in Wrocław. He studied in Wittenberg under Luther and Melanchthon (living in Luther's household for six years) and later obtained a doctoral degree in Padua. After his success in countering the plague in Wrocław, he managed to join the imperial court, serving Ferdinand, Maximilian II, and Rudolf II. Apart from his great expertise, originality and connections, it was his conciliatory character that won the recognition of his patrons. Crato was a very prolific correspondent and a productive author of medical writings. Maximilian made him an imperial counsellor and granted him the title of nobility. See Gillet, *Crato von Crafftheim*; Louthan, *The Quest for Compromise*, 85-105; Ralf Böer, "Friedenspolitik durch Verketzerung Johannes Crato (1519–1585) und die Denunziation der Paracelsisten als Arianer," *Medizinhistorisches Journal* 37 (2002), 139-182; Charles D. Gunnoe, Jr. and Jole Shackelford, "Johannes Crato von Krafftheim (1519–1585): Imperial Physician, Irenicist, and Anti–Paracelsian," in *Ideas and Cultural Margins in Early Modern Germany*, eds. by Robert Barnes et al. (Farnham: Ashgate, 2009), 201-216; Almási, *The Uses of Humanism*, passim; *Girolamo Mercuriale et Johann Crato von Krafftheim. Une correspondance entre deux médecins humanistes*, eds. Jean-Michel Agasse and Concetta Pennuto (Geneva: Droz, 2016).
[474] We do not know the person in question. He might be one of Crato's brothers-in-law.
[475] For Lazarus von Schwendi (1522–1583) military commander, politician and religious thinker see Roman Schnur, "Lazarus von Schwendi (1522–1583). Ein unerledigtes Thema der historischen Forschung," *Zeitschrift für historische Forschung* 14 (1987), 27-46; Thomas Nicklas, *Um Macht und Einheit des Reiches. Konzeption und Wirklichkeit der Politik bei Lazarus von Schwendi (1522–1583)* (Dissertation) (Husum: Matthiesen 1995); Louthan, *The Quest for Compromise*, 13-23, 106-122; Kaspar von Greyerz, "Un moyenneur solitaire: Lazarus von Schwendi et la politique religieuse de l'Empire au XVIe siècle tardif," in *Frömmigkeit und Spiritualität: Auswirkungen der Reformation im 16. und 17. Jahrhundert*, eds. Matthieu Arnold and Rolf Decot (Mainz: P. von Zabern, 2002), 147-160; Alexander Schmidt, *Vaterlandsliebe und Religionskonflikt: politische Diskurse im Alten Reich* (Leiden: Brill, 2007), 193-200.
[476] and everything is sad

ob peccata nostra Διὸς μεγάλοιο ἕκητι,[477] nisi ad sanitatem redierimus. Conventus Posoniensis dissolutus est, promissi sunt satis aegre bini floreni ostiatim.[478] Archidux heri 21. Martii rediit Viennam.[479] In oppido Cremps 20. Martii, cum pulvis sclopetarius Viennam esset devehendus, flamma temere correptus caedem edidit miserabilem ac incendium. Ita nostra vino curamus. Imperator id molestissime audiet, magna enim erat necessaria copia eius nitrati pulveris. Vale. 23. Martii 1566. Vienna.

Classem nostram 100 nassadinis[480] velocibus auctam adornamus. Thurcae exercitum rediisse Constantinopolim ex Hadrianopoli quidam confirmare volunt. Vaivoda multa molitur.[481] Accurrerunt Scepusium[482] versus in confinia nostra 7000 Polonorum equitum, quorum consilium incertum est, sed audio Schvendium eos aggressurum brevi.[483] Nuptiae audiuntur inter vaydam et Moscoviticam, alterae inter Moscovitam et sororem Poloniae regis.[484]

Address: Clarissimo et excellentissimo domino Ioanni Cratoni, medico sacratissimae caesareae maiestatis, domino et amico honorando.

78.
Sambucus to Johann Andreas von Schwanbach
31 March 1566, Vienna

Published in Iohannes Sambucus, *Epistola et epitaphia de obitu magnifici herois ac baronis Sigismundi ab Herberstain etc observantiae ac memoriae ergo* (Augsburg: Matthaeus Francus), f. A2ʳ-B3ʳ. Contemporaneously it also appeared in Vienna by Stainhofer.

Man is inclined to all evil, which is proven by the recent cases of even great lords. Yet, what is happening now was already foreseen in antiquity, when people, who reckoned that humans were inferior to animals in many things, already knew that fate was inconstant and changing. They

---

[477] on account of great Zeus. Hesiod, *Opera et dies* 4.
[478] I.e. after each peasant house and lot.
[479] The diet convened on 2 February. The Hungarian nobility was demoralised and discouraged, as Sambucus claims, and only unwillingly offered the 2-florin military tax. Maximilian sent his brother Archduke Karl to the diet. For the history of the 1566 campaign and the military failures of Hungary and the Monarchy see Bibl, *Die Korrespondenz Maximillians II. Band 1*, passim; Gerstinger, "Aus dem Tagebuch," 5-7; Georg Wagner, "Maximilian II, der Wiener Hof, und die Belagerung von Sziget," in *Szigetvári Emlékkönyv*, ed. Lajos Rúzsás (Budapest: Akadémia Kiadó, 1966), 237-268; Fichtner, *Emperor Maximilian II*, 126-134.
[480] "naszád" means gunboat. Cf. Bibl, *Die Korrespondenz Maximillians II. Band 1*, 455.
[481] Szapolyai (Zapolya) John Sigismund, elected King of Hungary, Prince of Transylvania (1540–1571). John Sigismund was planning to pay a visit to the sultan in Constantinople and was organising a diet to Torda, where he also invited the estates of the Kingdom of Hungary. To call Szapolyai a "vaivoda" or "vayda" was derogative for most Hungarians and a clear sign of Sambucus's pro-Habsburg standpoint, which offened many of his Hungarian compatriots.
[482] Zips (Szepesség), a region in today's north-eastern Slovakia and south-eastern Poland.
[483] It does not seem that there was any serious danger of invading Polish cavaliers. Cf. Bibl, *Die Korrespondenz Maximillians II. Band 1*, 448 and 479.
[484] We have no other information about marriage plans between John Sigismund and female relatives of Ivan (IV) the Terrible (1533–1584). On the possible plans of Ivan the Terrible to marry Anna Jagiellon, the sister of Sigismund II Augustus (1548–1572) see Isabel de Madariaga, *Ivan the Terrible. First Tsar of Russia* (New Haven: Yale Univ. Press, 2005), 215.

consoled themselves with the idea that the mind was eternal and with the hope of immortality [through fame] but had no idea of the eternity or afterlife for the mind. In the present, however, surrounded by greater and greater superstitions if we do not want to feel inferior to men of the antiquity, we need firmer faith in the afterlife and God's teaching and should attribute everything to God. We should not think that it follows from the teaching of Aristotelians, who claim to be ignorant about divine things and want us to suspend judgement in anything that lacks a clear proof, that we do not know anything and are denied any kind of guidance. The death of Siegmund von Herberstein greatly increased the general sorrow caused by the recent string of deaths of great and loyal clients of Maximilian II. Sambucus calls attention to the death of Bohemian Chancellor Joachim von Neuhaus, and Imperial Vice-Chancellor Georg Sigismund Seld. The latter had just met Maximilian to talk about important businesses and was leaving for the Augsburg diet in order to ask for imperial subsidy when he fell into a river and died, crossing a ruinous timber bridge with his coach not far from Vienna. The wound Maximilian felt was then reopened by the death news of Joachim von Neuhaus. Sambucus thinks it is natural to be moved by the fate of one's clients even among princes. This is also what Christian religion demands from us. We share in the good and the bad all the same. The desire to survive in the memory of posterity is a driving force for many, while the memory of the deeds of the dead is a lesson for posterity. Herberstein served the Austrian House for 58 years, performing so many missions in Europe and Asia, which would suffice for ten others. He had incredible diplomatic skills in appeasing the minds of others and making peace. Sambucus compares Herberstein to Ptolemy in his diligence. He enlarged our geographical knowledge and made Moscow known to everyone. Sambucus praises Herberstein for his erudition; skill in quoting the ancients; diligence in counselling at the Austrian Chamber; and speed in making notes while reading. These come from personal observations made during Sambucus's frequent meetings with Herberstein who completely opened up to him, offering not so much his patronage but friendship. Herberstein talked to him about his collections and observations, and Sambucus always left his place cleverer than before. He also showed Sambucus the genealogical tables and the histories he had prepared of his family and a register of these writings on four pages. It is better to remain silent than to write sketchily about the antiquity of his family. This will be, however, remembered in funeral orations, which are rightly dedicated to great patriots. Sambucus will not be deterred by Pericles's thoughts (as described by Thucydides) about the difficulties to praise in the right manner a deceased hero. Herberstein died at the age of eighty during the night of 29 March because of difficulties of urinating, the urethra's irritation and the three stones in the kidney. His passing away was not so much death but the liberation of his mind. He did not debase himself with luxury, idleness or adulation; even foreigners will adore his memory. Herberstein remains an example of great hopes also for his promising descendants, especially his nephew Caspar. Sambucus goes on to ponder about the example given by Herberstein and his happy state in the paradise. The letter is ended with reference to gossip about an Ottoman attack. He wishes that Schwanbach also contributed financially to the defence of the empire, and he promises to prepare a fuller oration.

Ioanni Andreae a Schvanbach,[485] secretario caesareo, amico carissimo, Ioannes Sambucus salutem. Vita hominum a prima labe, quam sponte ac inique, ut nosti, suscepimus, conditionem reliquam invenit sibique constituit, ut quomodo antea cunctis animalibus et a Deo Maximo opifice creatis praefuit, deque imaginis authoris tanti similitudine vices in omnia gessisset, ita nunc nihil tam imbecillum, nihil miserum, nihil etiam calamitosum excogitari potest, cui non simus obnoxii. Quod cum, proh dolor, quotidie tot malis videmus involuti, tum praesens magnifici quoque baronis importunus, sed tamen casus debitus, quo a nobis digreditur, abunde comprobavit. Veruntamen mi Ioanne Andrea, quid tam insolens aut adversum nostris rebus occurrat, quod non quisque antea providere animo et sperare ausit? Non ignorarunt vel a sensu beato remoti et obscuri hanc vitae rationem mobilem atque nusquam constantem, qui cum omni genere animantium partes nostras ac robur componens inferiores nos multo maxima parte viderunt. Unde mentem suo modo aeternam deprehendentes sese, ut potuere, spe posteritatis atque immortalitatis consolabantur, si modo eam consolationem dicas, quae caeca et ignara sempiternorum, quibus innitatur, haereat, nec a disiunctione istius molis et animi quis bonorum status sit futurus emetiri, suo iudicio aut informare valuerunt. Nobis vero superstitibus longe malis indies gravioribus, nisi firmior expectatio felicitatis restantis ostenderetur, nisi bonorum exemplis et voce non vana Dei roboraremur, non illis solum nos inferiores, sed abiectissimos arbitraremur. Dum igitur in illam formam aeterni domicilii et perpetuitatis negotium intuemur, spiritu coelesti, quibus de causis abitio haec paranda sit, cunque melioribus vita commutanda erudimur. Iis dico, qui a sana fide muniti universa Deo contribuunt salutareque desiderium, unde profectum est, eodem recurrere, scopumque unicum proponi sibi persuaserunt. Quin vel Peripatetici docent in divinis nescire, vel dubitare quibus in rebus ac locis demonstratione sit opus, summam esse ignorantiam, nec tam ubique exigendam, quod negetur omnium posse dari ἀπόδειξιν.[486] Si hoc illi inambulando fatentur, quid nobis firmis et χριστονύμοις[487] de sempiternis non credendum?

Atque intra aliquot mensium decursum maximorum virorum atque caesaris Maximiliani Secundi, domini nostri clementissimi intimorum obitus res communes non parum exacerbavit, horrenda eventa etiam terruere. Quae omnia cumulat recens, qui vulgo percipitur ex morte prudentissimi atque sancti senis, domini ab Herberstain dolor,[488] cuius nomine omnes posteri

---

[485] Johann Andreas von Schwanbach († 1575), coming from a noble Catholic family from the Bodensee area, was imperial secretary at the time, the second after Mark Singkmoser at the Latin secretariat. Later he became member of the imperial council (Reichshofrat). He studied law in Orléans and Bologna and also received a degree. Later he became close to the Jesuits. Schwanbach wrote to Onofrio Panvinio from Vienna (23 April 1564): "la descrittione delle antichità di Roma, che V. S. a miei preghi m'ha mandata, tanto cara et desiderata m'è stata, che fra le piu degni et preciosi thesori ch'io habbia merita d'esser riposta." (Vat. Lat. 6412, f. 121ᵛ.) cited by Jean-Louis Ferrary, *Onofrio Panvinio et les antiquités romaines* (Rome: École française, 1996), 15. In Italy he also collected a few legal manuscripts, which he apparently left for the University of Freiburg im Breisgau. Vera Sack, *Die Inkunabeln der Universitätsbibliothek*... (Wiesbaden: Harrassowitz, 1996). Also see *Die Amerbachkorrespondenz*, 10 vols., ed. Alfred Hartmann (Basel: Verlag der Universitatsbibliothek, 1942–1995), 10:233-237; Nicolaus Mamerarus, *Kurtze und eigentliche verzeychnus der Römischen Kayserlichen Mayestat, unnd ihrer Mayestat Gemahels Hofstats, unnd aller anwesenden Churfürsten, Fürsten Gaistlichen und Weltlichen, Graffen, Herren und Stenden des heyligen Röm. Reichs* ([S.l.]: [s.n.], 1566), f. Ciiᵛ; Gisela Becker, *Deutsche Juristen und Ihre Schriften auf den Romischen Indices* (Berlin: Duncker & Humblot, 1970), 226.
[486] guidance. This may be a reference chiefly to Pietro Pomponazzi and his followers.
[487] who carry the name of Christ
[488] Siegmund von Herberstein (1486–29 March 1566), imperial councillor and diplomat, famous author of the *Rerum Moscoviticarum Commentarii* (1549), died only three days earlier, on the 28ᵗʰ of March. See recently *450 Jahre Sigismund von Herbersteins 'Rerum Moscoviticarum commentarii': 1549–1999. Jubiläumsvorträge*, eds. Frank Kämpfer and Reinhard Frötschner (Wiesbaden: Harrassowitz, 2002). On his family, learning and

in admirationem ducentur, et exemplum: tantum est republica bene gesta diu floruisse. Vellem preces ac vota nostra pondus habuissent, magnanimum adhuc senem haberemus nostrisque commoditatibus retinuissemus. Invitus in memoriam funesti et gravissimi casus D. cancellarii Bohemici redeo[489] nec sine lachrumis subita Seldii mors[490] itemque D. Puchleri[491] cogitatione ex atra bile perpetuisque studiis turbata animo meo succurrit, quorum consiliis temperatio et lumen afflictis rebus his accommodabatur. Ille enim paulo antea de rebus magnis cum caesare pertractatis, valentissimo habitu, laeta appellatione omnium amicorum ad suos revisurus, constitutis iam ad iter Augustanum cunctis, descriptis etiam sumptibus, apparatu idoneo, in ipso ingressu itineris, equis iugum et flagellum recusantibus, vix aliquot a Vienna passibus infeliciter, ponte non nihil sublicibus laxo partibusque ruituro, ante et post ipsum aliis ultro citroque commeantibus ac salvis, curro suo transiturus, qui alioqui pedibus eiusmodi loca transmittebat, cum familiarissimis praeceps medio alueo hauritur inundationeque suffocatur. Ecquis eo die hoc malum praedixisset vates? Quis auspicatis et primis comitiis tantum subsidium imperatori subtractum iri minus antea Seldium putasset? Hae sunt nimirum illae lachrymae aspersae labis, haec documenta, quibus nihil perpetuum in communibus rebus, quodque violari nequeat transverse incurrentibus adversis, monemur. Certe cum vix Seldii fatum et memoriae dolor anxium caesarem remisisset, nuncio domini a Nova domo[492] in vulnus recruduit, eamque animi commotionem fidelissimo consultationum socio Maximilianus impertivit, ut in mediis hostibus et fulminum per tentorium minis nunquam ita fuerit infractus notamque perturbationis ipso ore et vultu adeo insignem edidisse multis sit visus. Ac sane, ut scis, non temere id principibus viris usu venit, ut enim laetissimi successus ac victoriae plus quam gregarii militis aut centurionis animum exhilarant et gaudio effundunt, ita adversa et subita exempla solent vel cordatos maxime ferire atque maerore attentare. Nugentur stoici quantum velint, accusent in Homero τὸ πρέπον [493], quod ducibus metum lacrymasque concesserit. Ergo vero eos a sensu bonorum maximaque fortunarum humanarum parte relictos pronuncio, qui non suorum periculis et gaudio moventur nullumque perturbationibus aditum et locum permittunt. Christiana pietas, ut contra faciamus, nos

---

(mediocre) Latin knowledge see Marija Wakounig, "'... hab ich teutsch und winisch gelernt ...' Zur Herkunft und zu den kulturellen Wurzeln von Sigismund von Herberstein," in *Russland, Polen und Österreich in der Frühen Neuzeit. Festschrift für Walter Leitsch zum 75. Geburtstag*, eds. Christoph Augustynowicz and Andreas Kappeler (Vienna: Böhlau, 2003), 1-24.

[489] Joachim von Neuhaus (Jáchym z Hradce) (1526–13 December 1565). Joachim died in December, when a bridge collapsed under him in Vienna. He was returning from the emperor, whom he persuaded to sign an edict against the Bohemian Brethren. But the document got providentially lost in the river and Maximilian never signed a new one. John Holmes, *History of the Protestant Church of the United Brethren* (London: printed for the author, 1825), 1:113.

[490] Georg Sigismund Seld (1516–26 May 1565) was imperial vice-chancellor and one of the most learned and influential courtiers of emperors Charles V and Ferdinand I. He was instrumental in shaping the imperial politics at the Council of Trent. On Seld see the article by August von Druffel in *ADB* 33 (1891), 673-679; Ernst Laubach, *Ferdinand I. als Kaiser: Politik und Herrscherauffassung des Nachfolgers Karls V.* (Münster: Aschendorff, 2001), passim; and the dissertation by Walter Vogel, *Der Reichsvizekanzler Georg Sigmund Seld, sein Leben und Wirken* (Leipzig: Fischer, 1933).

[491] On Leonhard(t) (Lienhart) Puchler (Püchler/Pichler) von Weitenegg (Weiteneck) († 1567) we have little information except that he was a Catholic (he was to found a monastery before his death). Sambucus calls him chancellor in his dedication of Diogenes Laertius (see letter 68). One of his daughters married Ruprecht von Stotzingen. See Gedeon Borsa, "Die Familien Püchler und Stotzingen und die Ortschaften Wimpassing und Stotzing," *Burgenlandische Heimatblätter* 57 (1995), 117-124; Michael Denis, *Wiens Buchdruckgeschicht bis MDLX* (Vienna: Wappler, 1782), 571-572.

[492] Joachim von Neuhaus (see note 489).

[493] resemblance

confirmat, nec illos adeo ἀπαθεῖς⁴⁹⁴ et indolentes duroque animo et undique ad affectus clauso fuisse crediderim, quin rebus ex sententia laeteque et optate affluentibus significationem simul animi commodi praebuerint. Nonne amor in prole relinquenda, producenda memoria ultimae voluntatis expositione fuit? Unde, quaeso, amicitias, clientelas, patrocinia foverunt? Unde spem victoriae, metum adversariorum conceperunt? Quis amorem sine odio vel invidia, felicitatem sine periculis, maerore gaudium, absque amaro dulce absque cogitatione mortis vitam potiorem duxit? Cur illi ipsi tam rigidae ac pertinacis sectae professores suis monumentis titulos praeponi curarunt? Cur nomen philosophiamque suam duram ad nos pertinere cupierunt, si ambitio, si φιλονικία⁴⁹⁵ et admiratio consequentis omnis temporis eos non titillasset? Sed longius horum stipitum animo carentium errore digredior. Superest ille, qua vivere quisque potissimum parte cupit, viget memoria, non interitura monumenta canent, eumque representabunt, ingenii praestans effigies relucet, aliisque viam monstrat, imitandi studium et aemulatio existet, tot beneficia gratiam illi deberi testabuntur. Officium igitur si vulgare est dolorem et lamenta nobis caris et amicis tribuere, quid eis debemus, qui loco et gradu eo fuerunt, unde regnorum salus pendere solet, unde summa et certa consilia manant, spes pacis, bellorum timor proficiscuntur.

Quis non indicium doloris bonus et patriae amans comiter efferat, qui Sigismundum baronem his praecipue tempestatibus et diris furoreque conceptis barbarorum conatibus (quos Deus eludet inque ipsorum caput convertet) ereptum audiet, in privato fuere non publicum luctum sordesque fatebitur? Operam hic senex per quinquaginta octo annos, et fidem dominis Austriae per Europam et Asiae fines integram et inauditam praebuit, tot legationibus exercitus eam prudentiam collegerat, quae aliis decem sufficeret. Quibus artibus, qua facundia ipsum commotos et iam caedem vicinis spirantibus animos regum flexisse, et ut pacem vel inducias admitterent persuasisse credis? Alii oratores uni reipublicae studuerunt, atque e plurimis vix duo satisfecerunt. Hic tot regnorum periculis consilio et legationibus profuit, ab omnibus collaudatus variisque immunitatibus clarus, muneribus auctus octoagesimum annum vidit aetatis.

Diligentiam Ptolemaei et historicorum alii decantent: Germania hunc singularem habuit, qui et illorum scripta tenebat, et multa loca, flumina non audita adiit, inspexit, veterum nominibus patefecit, Moscoviam in cognitione omnium posuit et stilo illustravit.⁴⁹⁶ De eruditione varia et solida, de colloquiis et verbis, sententiis crebris refertis, de amabili morum feveritate, in consiliis et obeundis fisci Austriaci negociis fide expeditaque solicitudine, in annotandis inter legendum adversariis celeritate et iudicio esse testis ipsam possum, quem non ita pridem complecti quidem ceperat, et in clientelam vel, ut ipse volebat, amicitiam admiserat: sed frequentibus congressibus totum se mihi aperuerat. Ultro ad me, quae olim collegerat et observarat, missitabat, suavissima oratione recenti et vetusta memoria aspersa me nutriebat, nec nisi doctior ab eo unquam discedebam. Reliquit ille varias genealogiarum tabellas, multa in commentariis habuit, suae gentis sobolem universam et nominatim edidit, de suisque rebus et vita non semel et vere scripsit. Postremo vero libello quatuor paginarum cuncta breviter, velut indice, nobis prodidit, nec quicquam φιλαύτως⁴⁹⁷ commisit. De familiae vetustate, praecipuis eiusdem exemplis, gratia omnium ordinum et amicitia, doctorum memoria, et ad eum missis tot, ut apellant, praefationibus satius est tacere, quam levius scribere.⁴⁹⁸ Cui tamen vacat et de

---

⁴⁹⁴ emotionless
⁴⁹⁵ contentiousness
⁴⁹⁶ Sigismundus Herberstein, *Rerum Moscoviticarum Commentarii* (Viennae: n.d., 1549). Cf. *Rerum Moscoviticarum commentarii: synoptische Edition der lateinischen und der deutschen Fassung letzter Hand, Basel 1556 und Wien 1557*, ed. Hermann Beyer-Thoma (Munich: Osteuropa-Institut, 2007).
⁴⁹⁷ self-lovingly
⁴⁹⁸ Herberstein was an important patron of Viennese humanism. For an idea of the number of his clients see his

eius vita orationem ad funus est habiturus, innumera suppetent et multa propria. Vehementer enim morem epitaphiorum probo eosque, laudandi, qui operam publice ingeniumque patriae ac regibus prompte et sine excusatione suppeditarunt. Nec difficultate, quam sibi obiectam Pericles apud Thucydidem cogitabat,[499] me absterreri sinerem, odium in omnes partes satis, sive minus, sive nimium laudes provocari auditorum, nec vererer ea praeconia conservatori et amplificatori patriae, quam eius authoribus, et ipsi, quae tales tulisset, patriae concedere.

Mortuus autem est felicissimus senex nocte vigesimam nonam Martii proxime antecedente, ad duodecimam facile, et velut penuria fomenti elychnium solet, extinctus est octuagenarius, non tam alicuius externi vi morbi aut virium lacertorumque tenuitate, vel aetatis quoque confectae, quam familiari quidem, sed expressione molestissima urinae, viis iam exacerbatis, vesicae quoque a tribus calculis affectione, compositissime via ad optatum et coelestem caetum Christiane communita, opibus non vulgaribus ad concordiam suorum, nulla prole relicta, caute et liberaliter definitis, emigravit et cum Christo vivit. Non itaque obiit, sed in vitam secessit clariorem, de corporis nexu ad libertatem spiritus diffugit. Facta eius cum omni aevo adaequabuntur, quod ipsum hic praemium summum videtur. Haud ventri, luxui, inertiae, non ocio, pompae, adulationibus, levitate sese abiecerat, sed ingenii viribus, abstinentiae, continentiae, modo gravitatique decenti inserviens diuturnum sui desiderium reliquit, ut loca ubi genitus est, vestigia quae pressit, sepulchrum quo reliquum eius conditur etiam exteri sint veneraturi. Profecto pueri mitem parentem requirent, senes coaevum iocundum, pauperes facilem et copiosum largitorem, consilii prolixium causarum benignumque patronum, pii exemplum vitae innocentis, ut si qui forte in eo naevi fuissent, vel imbecillitas deprehensa in virtute ea sibi multi ducere possint.

Sed alius panegyrici locus erit. Interea pignus vitaeque imaginem et documenta in nepotibus reliquit, quos inter extat bellica, consiliorumque commendatione et authoritate generosus dominus Casparus,[500] fratris filius, aliique multi, et longa serie nepotes agnatique, de quibus non minor spes est possessionis avitae tuendae ornandaeque. Tantorum a nobis digressus heroum quid enunicent, non tam ab astrologis, quam statu praesenti rerum eo periculoso perpetuisque historiarum exemplis petendum est. At senibus hanc quietem exoptandam velis et illorum aetati inserviendum. Ego vero, quia usuram diuiturnae vitae non pollicentur, dum licet, molestias et curam illis afferendam censeo, etsi enim ista aetate quod caeperunt, ut finem simul consiliorum videant, vix sperare debent, cogitatione tamen, quid sit consecuturum, praecipere solent. Ut cum parentes liberos vel editos tantum et susceptos aliis alendos tradunt, cum eos annis et viribus corroboratos aspiciunt, a se illos vires et incrementum accepisse rentur. Quod initium et fomentum confirmandorum et augendorum membrorum videantur cum nascendi ortu contulisse, ita satis emolumenti auferunt annis confecti, si fundamenta recte construendorum iecerint. Sed beatus nunc triumphos videat sanctis aggregatus, perlustret perspiciatque, antea quorum vix umbram vel extremitatem cernebat. Distincta enim sunt apud Deum universa, nihil turbatum, multae mansiones, cuiusque meritis a Deo profectis certa et constituta praemia, nec animae confunduntur, aut propter insignem ad corpora propensionem in quaevis subiecta sese ingerent, quicquid Plato somniat.[501]

---

    memoirs *Gratae posteritati ... actiones suas ... brevi commentariolo notatas reliquit* (Viennae: Hofhalter, 1560).
[499] Thuc. 2.35.2. Pericles argues that the speaker of the oration has the impossible task of satisfying the associates of the dead, who would wish that their deeds be magnified, while everyone else might feel jealous and think of the orator's exaggeration.
[500] Caspar von Herberstein († 1572) was a military leader and high steward (Obersthofmeister) of the court.
[501] Reference is made to the myth of Er which concludes Plato's *De re publica* (10.614–621).

Hic graves sunt et metu pleni de Turca sermones, sed rumoribus nunciis.[502] Utinam vos opem subito et salutem afferatis inque societatem defensionis Imperii subsidium adiungatis, quod ipsum sperant multi, optant omnes, ego vero etiam confirmare soleo. Vale, et memoriam domini Herberstanii libenter usurpes, talesque ut aliquot habeamus comprecare, τὸ γὰρ ἰσχυρὸν[503] ἀνόητον, καί τὸ ἔμφρον ἀδύνατον[504] quantum ad opem et res obtinendas separatim valeant, didicisti. Atque de his, hoc est ipso generoso barone, pleniorem a me orationem, cui mora cultum et copiam fortasse non denegabit, expectabis: haec observantia et amor exarare lugentem iussere.[505] Pridie Kalendas Aprilis, MDLXVI. ex Museolo nostro Viennae.[506]

79.
Sambucus to Johannes Crato
1 April 1566, Vienna

Published in Gerstinger, "Die Briefe", 76-78.

Sambucus has previously written about the rumours concerning the Ottomans. He believes that the danger is much less than is generally believed, but the Viennese, who should already have been hardened by past attacks, are worried for their wives and treasures and shamefully think of an escape. If only someone like Lycurgus, who took action against Leocrates, did something against those who say they want to sell their belongings, while they are in fact deserting their country, though it is not in actual danger. The pasha of Buda gathered 8,000 horsemen to harass the mining towns of northern Hungary, but when he heard that an imperial legate had left for Constantinople he decided to wait and not violate the "jus gentium". Selim is in Edirne with a second-rate army, but even if his father, the sultan, little believes in his wicked son, Selim can still be dangerous for Hungary. He will head toward Transylvania, where the "voivode" will take the side of the Habsburgs and block his entrance in case he arrives with forces that are too strong. Food is in such short supply in the Balkans that an attack can hardly be expected before the autumn. Sambucus hopes that there will soon be a large army to push the Ottomans back. In Vienna four monasteries unfit for defence will be razed to the ground.

S. D.

Antea scripsi hic gravia de Thurcae consiliis circumferri, sed rumore tantum nuncio.[507] Ego qui etiam intelligo et audio aliquid, longe minora duco quam vulgo fit, atque Viennenses, qui tamen iam ad tot vicina pericula roborato animo et dextera esse firma deberent, coniugibus et opibus metuentes fugam turpiter parant. Contra quos utinam aliquis Lycurgus, quomodo contra Leocratem, existat, qui ad mercatus res suas exportare se aiunt, cum deserant et quidem

---

[502] Maximilian's diligently prepared but fruitless encounter with the Ottomans happened in the summer of 1566, when Szigetvár was tragically lost. Cf. with letter 77, note 479.
[503] Print: ἰαγυρὸν.
[504] the strength without reason and the prudence without power. Synesius, *De dono astrolabii* 2.5.
[505] We have no other information on any lengthier oration on the death of Herberstein by Sambucus.
[506] The funerary epistle is followed by one Greek and five Latin epitaphs.
[507] See letter 77.

sine presenti periculo patriam.⁵⁰⁸ Budensis ὕπαρχος⁵⁰⁹ convocarat Pesthum 8000 equitum ad infestandas civitates montanas, sed audito adventu nostri legati ius gentium non violandum putavit atque imperium hoc internuncio a nobis misso a Thurco caesare expectandum.⁵¹⁰ Selimus est Adrianopoli cum mediocri apparatu,⁵¹¹ sed tamen non tantum credit pater filio exoso et iniquo, quantus nobis molestus esse ac perniciosus possit. Transylvaniam ille petet, sed audio vaydam⁵¹² eius esse animi, ut, si nimis magnis copiis, quam ipsum una haurire possent, venerit, se ad nos transiturum nec aditum in Septemcastra⁵¹³ permissurum. Commeatus ea ubique ad Savum et Istrum tenuitas,⁵¹⁴ ut ante autumnum nihil sit moliturus. Vos brevi numerosissimo milite auctos expectamus et anteversuros haec speramus. Scis enim illud: καὶ τὸ ἰσχυρὸν ἀνόητον ⁵¹⁵καὶ τὸ ἔμφρον⁵¹⁶ ἀδύνατον,⁵¹⁷ quid valeant. Viennae quatuor in angulis latentia coenobia ad propugnandum inepta solo aequabuntur. Vale. Kalendis Aprilis 1566. Ioannes Sambucus.

Address: Clarissimo viro domino Ioanni Cratoni, sacratissimae caesareae maiestatis medico, domino et amico observando. Augustam.

80.
Sambucus to the Mayor and the Council of Trnava
15 April 1566, Vienna

The original is kept in Trnava, SAT, Magistrát mesta Trnava, Missiles. Published in Vantuch, "Die Sambucusbriefe," 330-331.

Sambucus has heard the Council's verdict on the request of Albertus Viennensis, concerning the house where his brother-in-law Mr Panithy used to live, for which Albertus is going to deposit

---

⁵⁰⁸ The attic orator Lycurgus of Athens charged the blacksmith Leocrates with treason. Leocrates's crime was that he left Athens with his entire household for Rhodes immediately after news of the defeat of Chaeronea in 338 BC. Lycurgus's speech "Against Leocrates" has survived complete; it was first published by Aldo Manuzio.
⁵⁰⁹ governor. Referring to the pasha of Buda, Arslan, who fell out of favour and was killed in August. See Gerstinger, "Aus dem Tagebuch," 7, n 23.
⁵¹⁰ We do not know anything about the origin and education of György Hosszutóthy/Hosszútóti (?–1572), who we find first in the service of Archbishop Nicolaus Olahus. In 1557 he was sent to the Diet of Regensburg. Two years later he entered the service of Emperor Ferdinand as secretary of the Chamber; from 1564 he was councillor of the Chamber. Hosszutóthy was sent to Suleiman in February in order to steal time and send fresh news about the plans of the Ottomans (although initially Maximilian had some hopes in a larger effect of his mission). It was clearly a dangerous legation, as Hosszutóthy was not even duly supplied with money and could not pay the annual tax. Suleiman put him in jail where he stayed for a year. Sambucus was very well informed as Hosszutóthy dated his letter from Buda on 28 March. See ÖStA, HHStA, Turcica, 1566. III. 28. See Bibl, *Die Korrespondenz Maximillians II. Band 1*, ad indicem. Also see Gerstinger, "Aus dem Tagebuch," 5, note 9.
⁵¹¹ Selim (1524–1574) was Suleiman's son and heir as Selim II.
⁵¹² John Sigismund Szapolyai, prince of Transylvania.
⁵¹³ The Latin translation of the German name for Transylvania (Siebenbürgen), frequently used by Germans like Crato.
⁵¹⁴ The rivers Sava and lower Danube.
⁵¹⁵ Gerstinger: αιοτητον.
⁵¹⁶ Gerstinger: ἄ[μετ]ρον.
⁵¹⁷ both the strength without reason and the prudence without power. Synesius, *De dono astrolabii* 2.5. Cf. the last paragraph of the preceding letter, where Sambucus used the same quote.

100 florins. The councillors must know that Albertus owes Sambucus from the part of Panithy 50 florins, and another 50 florins which he lent him. He asks the Council to secure the repayment of the debt.

Salutem ac debitam filialemque commendationem.

Audivi dominationes vestras denuo pro Alberto Viennensi de domo,[518] quam sororius meus quondam D. Panithy inhabitabat,[519] sententiam vestram et iustam pronunciasse. Qui Albertus, ut audio, his diebus 100 fl. deponet. Sciunt autem multi ex dominis senatoribus mihi deberi 50 fl. ratione Panithy ab Alberto ob restitutum illi ius et a me mutuatam pecuniam 50 florenorum. Quare dominationes vestras supplico, velitis, quicunque deposuerit eos 100 fl. pro Alberto, ad rationem debiti mei, pro quo ab Alberto habeo chirographum, retineri facere in pecunia vel pro domo ipsa 50 fl. Ungaricos, atque iniungere domino notario inscriptionem inhibitionis, cuius ego mercedem solvam debitam et usitatam domino iudici ac notario.[520] Quam rem ego dominationibus vestris in maioribus compensare conabor et me filialiter commendo. Datum Viennae, 15. Aprilis 1566. Servitor et filius dominationum vestrarum Ioannes Sambucus.

Address: Egregiis et prudentibus dominis, iudici iuratisque civibus civitatis Tyrnaviensis, dominis suis honorandis. Tirnaviae.
Another hand above the address: Szamboky Yano.

81.
Sambucus to Imre Kalmár, Mayor of Trnava
12 November 1566, Vienna

The original is kept in Trnava, SAT, Magistrát mesta Trnava, Missiles. Published in Vantuch, "Die Sambucusbriefe," 331-333.

Sambucus repeats his request (made in front of the Council) about holding back the 400 florins that Mr Mager needs to pay in accordance with the father's testament to his father's widow Sophia (Sambucus's stepmother) on behalf of his niece, little Sophia (Zsóka), daughter of Mr Panithy. He is following the wishes of his father, so far as they do not harm his niece, to whom he is a kind of guardian. This money cannot be entrusted to the stepmother, who shared no children or possessions with his father and who was already given enough of movables and estates. She also has taken dresses and jewellery that were due for little Sophia, and even the belongings of Sambucus's deceased sister Magdalena, which Magdalena had not even received from her father, but from her husband, Mr Gávay, as everyone knows. Sambucus hardly wants to sue his stepmother out of his

---

[518] Albertus Sambucus, who was also called Albertus Viennensis. He was the owner of fields and a vineyeard on the hills. See Vantuch, "Die Sambucusbriefe," 330.
[519] Sambucus's brother-in-law János (Johannes) Panithy († 1565), married to his sister Katalin, was already dead by the time. See the next letter. Sambucus addressed a Latin poem to Panithy at his wedding with his sister, published in the *Poemata*, f. 28ʳᵛ. Sambucus also dedicated him an emblem: *Emblemata* (1564), 101.
[520] Sambucus used his prestige and good relations to the Council in order to get back a debt, going back partly to Panithy, which Albertus was obviously reluctant to pay back to him. Finally, he resigned of Panithy's former debt. See letter 137.

own interest but he demands back at least a part of the things she has taken from his sister. If little Sophia (the heir of his sister) does not receive anything, he will start a judicial case. The Council should publicly communicate this to his stepmother as he does not want to be considered malicious. He is sending a map (i.e. of Hungary) to the city, corrected by him but badly executed by the mapmaker. If the deadline of 16 November will be changed, he should be warned. Sambucus attaches a short note addressed to the mayor in Hungarian. If they set a date for his judicial case, he should be warned beforehand so that he can either be present in person or through a representative. He has written to his brother-in-law István Nyilas about the clothes and the letters held by Georg Jo. The mayor should give in exchange for the letters the one by Markó Horváth.

Salutem et mei commendationem.

Quomodo antea dominationes vestras[521] praesentibus aliis et notario rogavi, ut, quos 400 fl. dominus Mager[522] depositurus est, ex testamentoque patris dominae Sophiae novercae meae deberent exhiberi, ut arestentur et inhibeantur nomine Sophiolae, filiolae quondam domini Panithy, eiusque haeredum legitimorum, ita misericorditer iterum oro, ut ex officio vestro solemniter fiat.[523] Ego enim ex animo domini patris mei piae memoriae promissis sto et satisfacio in omnibus, uti transactum est inter nos, sed ea conditione, ut nepticulae meae ego tanquam tutor bonae fidei et frater numquam noceam, nec ipsa me vel eius aliqui haeredes possent de mala tutela accusare. Caussas vobis antea significavi: primo quod pater novercae, quae nullos prorsus liberos habet et quae cum illo nihil bonorum immobilium lucrata est in damnum et praeiudicium suorum filiorum filiarumque, cum quarum matribus vel matre immobilia et possessiones domum acquisivit, non potest legare, cum satis illi donarit ex mobilibus et pecunia, aut eius ad res mobiles aut immobiles debet manus noverca applicare. Utrumque non potest ullo iure nec bona consuetudine. Altera causa est inhibitionis ex parte quoque neptis meae Sophiolae, quod domina mater noverca non solum vestes matris et aliarum sororum Sophiolae neptis, sed etiam dominae quondam Magdalenae[524] bona, vasa argentea, annulos, aliquot cingula argentea habeat, quae non pater meus piae memoriae illi Magdalenae dederat, sed habuit a marito domino Gavay,[525] ut omnes norunt. Quae me non concernunt quidem, sed Sophiolam Panithy tamquam

---

[521] Imre Kalmár (whose name means "merchant") got rich on cattle trade and soon became a very important member of the Trnava patriciate and the Council. Starting from 1554, he was city mayor five times till 1576, when he was imprisoned because he invited a Hungarian Protestant priest (next to the German and Slovak ones) into the city. The Catholic archbishop (Miklós Telegdi), who resided in the city, managed to have this person banned and punished for his disobedience by Emperor Rudolf II. See Bakonyi Zsuzsanna, "Majd' három évtized a város élén: Kalmár Imre Nagyszombat bírája (1547–1576)" [Almost three decades among the first ones of the city: Imre Kalmár Mayor of Trnava], in *"Serpentarius viginti quatuor stellis decoratus" Baráti ajándék Farkas Gábor Farkasnak*, eds. Péter Ekler and Bernadett Varga (Budapest: the authors' publication, 2015), 7-8; Bakonyi, "Nagyszombat város követei," 433-434 (where there is more on religious tensions).

[522] This may refer to Peter Mogor, an important merchant and member of the City Council. He was sent to the diet of 1567 in Pressburg as a delegate of the city together with István Nyilas and was later twice elected as mayor. In 1567 it was his merit that the twelve-member Council reached ethnic parity. Its members were "ex hungaris: Emericus Kalmar, Michael Kys, Stephanus Nyilas, Philippus Kadas, ex germanis: Petrus Mogor, Christophorus Prwkner, Michael Swaar, Christophorus Lyngel, ex sclavis: Joannis Pellio, Iwan Horwath, Joannis Seratir, Georgius Slegel." See Bakonyi, "Nagyszombat város követei," 436.

[523] For János Panithy see also the previous letter. Sambucus's dearest niece Zsóka (Sophia) Panithy died in 1569. See letter 137 and Kóssa, "Adatok Sámboky János életéhez."

[524] Magdalena (Magdolna) was Sambucus's sister.

[525] István Gávay (Balaskó) was Sambucus's brother-in-law. Sambucus dedicated to him a poem in his *Poemata* (f. 29[r-v]). For details see Illésy, "Sámboky János történetíróról."

haeredem sororis propriae et eiusdem postea veros haeredes. Absit a me, bona conscientia dico, quod ego de his bonis contra dominam novercam ex parte mea unquam litem vellem movere, ita Deus novit, sed conscientia tutelae me adigit et bonorum virorum consilium, ut haec repetam, vel saltem partem bonorum. Nam aliquando Sophiolae maritus liberique a me vel meis haec possent repetere et meo sanguini tantum debeo, quantum aliis. Ideo haec scribo aperte, et si nullum ius sororcula eiusque haeredes in hac inhibitione habebunt, vos et iustitia ipsa videbit et decernet, ego nihil inique postulabo nec accipiam, sed iuri caussam submitto. Haec dominatio vestra poterit in ipsa pecuniae inhibitione dominae matri publice significare et etiam ipse et alii significarunt, ne me malo animo et ingrato erga quemquam esse putent, quibus per Deum verum alioqui honorifice cupio in omnibus satisfacere et servire. Dominatio vestra valeat et huius meminerit, quia terminus pecuniae adest dies 5. Martini. Eidemque me commendo et mitto civitati mappam unam a me nonnihil correctam, sed a pictore non ita belle illustratam.[526] Viennae, 12. Novembris 1566. Dominationis vestrae filius et servitor Ioannes Samboki.

Si dominatio vestra diem causae huic nostrae posuerit, oro, in tempore per certum hominem et literas significate, ut ipse adsim vel procuratorem plenarium constituam.

Byro uram keg[yelmének] es Nylas[527] uramnak soghoromnak irtam vala ruharol ky az Jo Jorgh kezenel vagyon; hogh az leveleket, ky ot az boldban vagyon Horwath Marköet erette ky adnatok hogh ha meg még nem leth kerem kegel[med] hogh megis zerezhetek megh, hogh az ruhe megh ne vesszen, es az en penzemis. Megh zolgalom kegeletekeknek S.[528]

Address: Egregio domino Emerico Kalmar, iudici civitatis Tyrnaviensis, domino suo et amico observandissimo. Naghzombath.

82.
Sambucus to Johannes Crato
[1566],[529] Vienna

Published in Gerstinger, "Die Briefe," 78-79.

As soon as the bookseller, who is now in Vienna, is back in Augsburg, he will leave for Basel and look after Sambucus's businesses. Sambucus is asking Crato to write a preface addressed to the reader for his corrected edition of Paulus Aegineta and let him know if he finds something about the text. Crato could also mention the potential future edition of Hippocrates, corrected with much fatigue, together with Palladius's commentaries, which he also collected with much travel, investment and energy with the single goal to publish them. He is now publishing Eunapius and [Pseudo-]Hesychius, and will publish greater things if succoured by princes. There are clear evidences of his past achievements, but he lets Crato judge it for himself. Since he is going to send

---

[526] On Sambucus's map of Hungary, see letters 41 and 189.
[527] István Nyilas was Sambucus's other brother-in-law. He came to Trnava from Esztergom and married Sambucus's sister, Anna, in 1548. A Hungarian song for their wedding was written by the Lutheran bishop Péter Bornemissza. Nyilas died before 1579, when the sources present Anna Zsámboky as a widow. See Bakonyi, "Nagyszombat város követei," 434-435. This data, however, contradicts Sambucus's claim that all his sisters died before his father's death, made in his preface to his edition of Plautus (letter 69).
[528] We were not able to identify these citizens of Trnava and do not understand clearly the issue at hand.
[529] We have dated this letter to 1566, because Sambucus claims in a letter to Zwinger of 23 March 1567 to have sent the manuscript of Paulus Aegineta to Basel long before. Cf. letter 88.

the book without a preface, Crato might want to add one and let the readers know about his judgement. He asks Crato to send him back the manuscript of Paulus Aegineta together with the preface still in the evening as the bookseller will leave the day after. Crato's notes on the letter express his annoyance about Sambucus's self-conscious assiduity.

Salutem.

Est hic bibliopola, qui, ubi Augustam domum suam rediit, recta se Basileam profecturum affirmat seque meo nomine, quod optem, curaturum. Rogo epistolium ad lectorem Aegyneticae correctioni meae edendae praeponas, quaeque in eo vides, significato.[530] Poteris mentionem facere Hippocratis quoque tot laboribus meis et locis non parum correcti et facile, si impressores velint, communis futuri una cum Palladii medici vetustissimi in *Epidemiarum* 6[531] et Περὶ ἀγμῶν[532] commentariis,[533] quod nihil sit tot peregrinationibus, sumptibus, studio et sudoribus meis comparatum, quia publice illud prodesse velim atque conspici etc. Quod ipsum nunc in Eunapii etiam historiis et Illustrii excudendis faciam, et, si principum benignitas iuvaret, longe maiora brevi daturus essem; quod adhuc, mi Crato, quod per ingenium et sumptus potui, non obscure nec paucis exemplis sum testatus. Sed haec tuo iudicio promittam nec φιλαύτως[534] tractabo. Ego sine mea praefatione mittam, tu, si vacat, lectorem tui iudicii monebis. Vale et Aegynetam cum praefatione vesperi remittito, nam is perendie vel cras est discessurus. Tuus totus Sambucus.

Under the letter Crato's autograph notes: Mone ac quidem Duo quod edicto libri d[a]mnati, et quisquam quod vix legit, ut iubetur, remittam. Quod discedens in recentioribus scriptis vel doctorum notis cognoscam. Incurvatum de industria. Versamur in rebus exulceratis et exagitatis.[535]

Address: Doctori Ioanni Cratoni clarissimo viro, physico caesareo etc., domino et amico observandissimo Sambucus.

83.
Sambucus to the Mayor and the Council of Trnava
1 January 1567, Vienna

The original is kept in Trnava, SAT, Magistrát mesta Trnava, Missiles. Published in Vantuch, "Die Sambucusbriefe," 333-334.

Sambucus has resolved the question of the customs office. Letters will be sent by both Chambers to Kielmann still during the week. Concerning the tax exemption of the wine hills of Smolenice

---

[530] On the unrealised edition of Paulus Aegineta see Gerstinger, "Zusammenfassung," 307-309.
[531] The sixth book of *Epidemics* of the Hippocratic Corpus was written in the late fifth century by the same author who wrote books II and IV.
[532] On fractures. The work *De fracturis* was probably written in the same period. It is sometimes attributed to Hippocrates I. On these unrealised editions see Gerstinger, "Zusammenfassung," 307-309.
[533] On Palladius the physician and Greek medical author of late antiquity (sixth century?) see *RE* XVIII (1949), 211-214.
[534] selfishly
[535] Cf. Almási, *The Uses of Humanism*, 179.

(Szomolány) and Modra (Modor), the emperor responded that he would gladly be helpful but Smolenice is occupied by the Bánffys, because of some transfer by the widow of László Országh with whatever right, so he will have to call Bánffy to court to clear the matter. Modor is not in the hands of the emperor so he cannot donate it to anyone. Maximilian asked Sambucus to come back to these issues in due course.

Salutem et felix auspicium Kalendarum Ianuarii totiusque anni et servitiorum commendationem.

Negotium telonii ad finem produxi, non sine importunitate magna, et literae ex consensu utriusque camerae ad Khielmanum hac septimana, ut spero, expedientur in forma convenientes etc.[536] Quod ad libertates vinearum sub Somolyan etc., Modor etc., caesarea maiestas clementissime respondit, se libenter in omnibus vos tueri velle et debere, sed Somolyan occupasse Banfium[537] ex traditione viduae domini Orzagh[538] et praetexere nescio quod ius. Ideo se coactum iri vocare in ius ipsum Banffy, ut videatur, quem respiciant illa bona. Modor et alia se in manibus ex pacto non habere nec imperare velle, ubi quid adhuc non possideat nec aliis donavit. Ubi vero tempus fuerit, iussit sua maiestas, ut ipsum moneamus iterum, se generosissimum responsum daturum. Quibus me commendo. Vienna prima Ianuarii 1567. Servitor Sambucus.

Address: Egregiis dominis, iudici senatuique Tyrnaviensi, dominis et patronis honorandissimis. Tirnaviam. Cito.

84.
Sambucus to Pompilio Amaseo
13 January 1567, Vienna

The original is kept in Parma, Biblioteca Palatina, Ms Parma 1019, fasc. IX, f. 13ʳ.

Sambucus received Amaseo's letter of 9 December from Bologna on 8 January. Amaseo should not excuse himself for his silence as Sambucus does not press seriously busy men for letters. Sambucus highly praises the way Amaseo restored Polybius's text. If he had called Sambucus's attention to his project earlier, he might have been able to check some places in his codices. He encourages Amaseo to discuss with him his philological questions. He also did well to add some military diagrams. Concerning the Viennese adolescent, Sambucus and the parents of the student are grateful for the news. Sambucus cannot say much about his historical works, which are all just drafts, as nothing worthy happened in the past few years. He has collected seven rare authors on rhetorical figures, commented on Xenophon's assembly speeches, corrected Laertius, while Eunapius and [Pseudo-] Hesychius are being published in Amsterdam. They would already be out if there had been no civil wars over religious questions among the Belgians. He is sending his greetings to Carlo Sigonio.

---

[536] Vantuch calls attention to the many charters kept in the archives of Trnava, in which the emperor affirmed the city's right to collect taxes from neighbouring noblemen who refused to respect customs charges. See also letters 103–104, 109 and 191.

[537] On Sambucus's long legal case with the Bánffys see Illésy, "Sámboky János történetíróról."

[538] Anna Pekry, the widow of László Országh. The castle of Smolenice was apparently successfully taken back from the Bánffy, as it was later owned by her son, Kristóf Országh.

D. Pompilio Amasaeo[539], Sambucus salutem.

Quas tu V Idus Decembris Bononia ad me scripsisti, eas ego VI Idus Ianuarii accepi, quibus prolixe silentium tuarumque moram excusas. Verum ego, mi doctissime Pompilie, non ex eorum numero sum, qui vel ab occupatione gravi studiorum literas exigere soleam, vel ob moram in suspicionem aliquam necessitudinis leges vocare. Memoria tu Polybii cuncta sarcisti,[540] nec citius neque gratius responderem unquam antea, quam tuarum in eo[541] excolerem: ac restituendo lucubrationum significationem, quod inieceris [?], potuisses [?]. Scio te iudicio praestare, ad huiusmodi labores nostra et domestica laude excellere, non defuisse tibi chirographa vetustissima. Sed si tamen huiusce praeclari tui conatus antea meminisses, nae ego te fortasse in quibusdam locis observationibus de codicibus omni exceptione maioribus iuvare aut certe confirmare potuissem. Ac si quid adhuc errorem obiicit, aut dubium tibi animum, annotato, cum meis conferam, nec quicquam communicare tecum recusabo. Recte atque commode de adiungendis schematibus militaribus cogitasti nec parum vigilias eo consilio apud omnes tuas ornabis.

De adolescente Viennensi: nuncius mihi et ipsius parentibus testimoniumque tanti viri gratissimum fuit. Utinam pergat esse diligens, nec, ubi opus videris, solicitudinem et curam ob adversariam illi constitutam importare cessabis.

De historiis meis nihildum indicare possum. Rudia omnia, nec res elapsi annis posteris quicquam dignum suppeditavit. Quid deinde sit futurum, videbimus.

Ego septem authores δυσευρήτους περὶ σχημάτων[542] collegi, illustravi παρεκβολαῖς δημηγορίας[543] Xenophontis,[544] Laertium correxi,[545] Eunapii philosophi et Illustrii poetae sub praelo sunt Antverpiae,[546] ac nisi civile hoc calamitosumque ob religionis novae opinionem bellum in Belgicis arderet, iam absoluta fuissent omnia. Vale, et doctissimo Sigonio nostro a me salutem [da], cuius in rebus ego omnia cupio et, quod antea significavi, ut exemplo periculum faciatur, oro. Vienna, Idibus Ianuarii 1567.

Address: D. Pompilio Amasaeo viro clarissimo amico veteri, Bononiam.
1567 Idibus Ianuarii.

---

[539] Pompilio Amaseo (1513–1586) was son of the humanist Romolo Amaseo. Born in Bologna, he studied first with his father, then served as secretary to various cardinals. In 1540–1543, he taught humanities in Bologna and published his single philological work, *Fragmenta duo e sexto Polybii libro* (Bologna: Ioannes Baptista Phaellus) in 1543. With the help of some cardinals he obtained the chair of Greek and despite complains about his negligence he kept it until 1582 when he was forced to leave. Sambucus probably knew Amaseo through the Manuzios and from his sojourn in Bologna in 1556. See the article by Rino Avesani in *DBI* 2 (1960), 658-660.
[540] This must concern an unpublished, now probably lost work of Amaseo, *Lucubrationes Polybianae*.
[541] Instead of the crossed-out *Polybio*.
[542] rare (authors who wrote) about rhetorical figures
[543] assembly speeches with notes
[544] See letter 2.
[545] Diogenes Laertius, *De vita et moribus philosophorum*. See letter 68.
[546] Eunapius, Βίοι φιλοσόφων; [Pseudo-]Hesychius, Περὶ τῶν ἐν παιδείᾳ.

85.
Joachim Camerarius Sr.[547] to Sambucus
21 January 1567, Leipzig

Published in Camerarius, *Epistolarum libri quinque posteriores*, 408-410.

One of Johannes Crato's merits is that he wins many friends for Camerarius. Crato reinforced Sambucus's good feelings toward Camerarius and gave him an excuse to write an elegant letter to Camerarius, from which he understood that Sambucus never received his letter. He had informed Sambucus about having both his work and the book of Hephaestion and that he would do his best to get the former published and send back the latter. He was happy about Sambucus's letter also because it raised high hopes about musical sheets, which he saw on the list of Sambucus's books. Although times interfere with the studies and he is getting feeble, the only pleasure he can still take is in these studies. So Sambucus can be sure that his treasures, when entrusted to Camerarius, will be profitably used and shared with him. He is sending this letter to his son Joachim, a doctor in Nuremberg, who will quickly forward it to Sambucus, who can also use him as a middleman. Aphthonius's textbook was published in Leipzig for the use of schoolboys. It is an old work that needed to be finished although his explanations are not full. Camerarius saw the edition of Aristaenetus. It is easy to notice that Sambucus was not there when it was printed.

S. D.

Cum multa ac magna merita clarissimi viri Ioanni Cratonis in me exstent, non parvum duco hoc, quod ille mirifico quodam amore mei praedicando de me et nonnullorum studia mihi conciliavit et tuam erga me benevolentiam ac iampridem cognitam humanitatem non modo confirmavit, sed etiam auxit occasionemque dedit cum eleganter, tum perquam amanter scriptae ad me epistolae, quam his diebus accepi. Exque ea visus sum mihi intelligere meas literas, quas studuissem tibi mitti, nequaquam omnes ad te pervenisse. Significavi enim tibi unis et tuum scriptum et Hephaestionis librum penes me esse[548] meque in hoc operam dare diligentem, ut tuum scriptum exprimatur; alterum vero librum cupere ad te per opportunitatem remittere. Sed excepta hac significatione non magna iactura mearum literarum facta est. Tuas autem mihi esse redditas luculenti lucri instar duco, non solum quanti me facias declarantes, sed spem facientes opulentae copiae musicae.[549] Itaque animus meus, cum chartam illam, librorum tuorum indicem

---

[547] Joachim Camerarius Sr. (1500–1574) was a highly important Greek scholar and humanist. He was a follower and friend of Melanchthon. After teaching in Nuremberg and Tübingen, he moved to the University of Leipzig in 1541, where he remained until the end of his life. His sons, Joachim Jr., Ludwig and Philipp all became important scholars. On the basis of a poem by Sambucus addressed to Camerarius in his *Poemata* of 1555 (f. 29ʳ), in which Sambucus claims to have carried a letter to Camerarius from Vienna, it has been suggested that he had studied with Camerarius already in Leipzig. However, this letter implies that there had previously been no personal contact between Camerarius and Sambucus (see also *Humanistes du bassin des Carpates II. Johannes Sambucus*, viii, note 10). On Camerarius Sr. see Stephan Kunkler, *Zwischen Humanismus und Reformation. Der Humanist Joachim Camerarius (1500–1574) im Wechselspiegel von pädagogischen Pathos und theologischen Ethos* (Hildesheim: Olms, 2000); *Joachim Camerarius*, eds. Rainer Kössling and Günther Wartenberg (Tübingen: Gunter Narr Verlag, 2003); *Camerarius Polyhistor. Wissensvermittlung im deutschen Humanismus*, ed. Thomas Baier (Tübingen: Gunter Narr Verlag, 2017).

[548] See letters 33, 92 and 111.

[549] Sambucus had a considerable number of books on music and music sheets in his collection. See Gulyás, *Sámboky János könyvtára*.

legerem, gaudio exultare, praesertim te benigne offerente nobis communem illorum usum. Et si enim et tempora illa sunt, quibus vel possessio, vel certe ususfructus studiorum nostrorum admodum conturbatur ac intercipitur et in me vires tam animi, quam corporis fiunt aetate ingravescente languidiores, sola tamen tractatio horum mihi terrenae voluptatis aliquid affert et saepe abiectum atque iacentem erigit ac recreat. Quapropter id quod liberaliter pollicere, mi Sambuce, praestabis, et meae fidei credes divitias tuas, quae vel ita collocabuntur a me, ut praeclare foenerentur, vel erunt certe mecum communicatae, nihilo minus propriae tuae. Misi autem has literas Norimbergam ad filium meum Ioachimum[550] medicum δημεύοντα ἐκεῖ,[551] a quo tibi curarentur, et eidem scripsi, ut rationem reperiat et viam, qua et hae tibi celeriter tradi et ad ipsum abs te, quicquid visum fuerit, tuto perferri possit. Edebantur modo hic Aphthonii *Progymnasmata*, ut scholae pueriles hoc libello instruerentur,[552] in quibus saepe aqua, ut dicitur, haesit. Sed opus incoeptum fuit perficiendum, quamvis nostrae explicationes nondum etiam absolvi potuerint. Implicui his literis nuper hic proposita, quorum arbitrabar lectionem tibi non iniucundam fore. Te, vir clarissime, bene valere opto. Tuum Aristaenetum vidi,[553] sed inter exprimendum te abfuisse facile deprehendi. Tu velim tibi persuadeas me, si quid tua hoc refert, esse studiosissimum nominis tui. Vale. Lipsiae 21. die Ianuarii 67.

Address: Clarissimo viro D. Ioannis Sambuco, historico ac medico caesareo, etc.

86.
Sambucus to Ferenc Forgách[554]
1 February 1567, Vienna

Dedication in Iohannes Sambucus, *Reges Ungariae, ab anno Christi CDI. usque ad M.D. LXVII. Item Iani Pannonii episcopi Quinquecclesiensi Eranemus nunc repertus* (Viennae: Stainhofer, 1567), f. Ai^v. Published in *Humanistes du bassin des Carpates II. Johannes Sambucus*, 81-83.

---

[550] Joachim Camerarius Jr. (1534–1598) was a famous doctor and botanist. Born in Nuremberg, he studied medicine at Wittenberg under his father's close friend Melanchthon and then practiced with yet another friend of his father, Johannes Crato in Wrocław. On Crato's advice he took up medical studies in Padua and finally became a doctor in Bologna in 1562. Upon his return to Nuremberg he started practicing as a physician and established the first scientific botanical garden in the city. Unlike his father, he was not very prolific (although he disserted among others on the plague). His most famous publications were collections of emblems and enigmatic texts: *Symbola et emblemata* (1590) and *Hortus medicus* (1598). See Svenja Wenning, *Joachim II. Camerarius: (1534–1598). Eine Studie über sein Leben, seine Werke und seine Briefwechsel* (Duisburg: WiKu-Wiss.-Verl., 2015). The *Symbola et emblemata tam moralia quam sacra* has a recent commented edition by Wolfgang Harms and Gilbert Hess (Tübingen: Max Niemeyer, 2009).

[551] who lives there

[552] Aphthonius, *Libellus progymnasmatum, id est praeparantium exercitationum in sermonem Latinum conversus, Graeco scripto et exemplis compluribus additis a Joachimo Camerario* (Leipzig: Voegelin, 1567).

[553] Aristaenetus, Ἐπιστολαὶ ἐρωτικαί. Cf. *Humanistes du bassin des Carpates II. Johannes Sambucus*, 71-73.

[554] Ferenc Forgách (1535–1572) was an erudite Hungarian nobleman educated in Padua. His Latin history of contemporary Hungary remained unpublished for centuries because of its gloomy, "Tacitean" tone. He had an ecclesiastical-political career in the service of the Habsburg dynasty (as bishop of Várad and royal councillor), but as his career progressed too slowly he left the court in 1567, departed for Venice, but finally joined the service of the Transylvanian prince. Eventually he left the Transylvanian court as well, and died in Padua, where he had settled to cure his chronic sickness. See Almási, "Variációk az értelmiségi útkeresés témájára," 1405-1440; Gábor Petneházi, "Párhuzamos történetek. Egyéniség, politika, hitelesség Istvánffy Miklós és Forgách Ferenc történeti műveiben" [Parallel histories. Singularity, politics and authenticity in the historical works of Nicolaus Istvánffy and Ferenc Forgách], in *"A magyar történet folytatója"*, 141-164; and the article by idem in *Companion*.

87.
Sambucus to Koloman Egerer Jr.[555]
13 February 1567, Vienna

Dedication in (Pseudo-)Demetrius Phalereus, *De epistolis doctrina: rhetoricae, dialecticaeque summa*, ed. Iohannes Sambucus (Antverpiae: Plantin, 1567), f. A2ʳ. Published in *Humanistes du bassin des Carpates II. Johannes Sambucus*, 83-86.

88.
Sambucus to Theodor Zwinger
23 March 1567, Vienna

The original is kept in Basel, Universitätsbibliothek, Frey Mscr II 26, no. 209. Published in Gerstinger, "Die Briefe," 79-80.

Sambucus has received Zwinger's letter affirming his agreement with Johannes Crato's ideas. He sent Zwinger his manuscripts of Hippocrates, Paulus Aegineta and others long ago, the marginal notes of which Zwinger will find particularly useful for his work. He wishes that Hippocrates came out in Zwinger's edition together with his structural overview. There are also marginal notes in the German edition, but with unique spelling differences characteristic of his codex. Sambucus warns Zwinger that he lends him and Oporinus his books with the condition of getting them back undamaged. He is happy about the epitaphs; he is sending one to Zwinger discovered in Turin. If he had time, he would send more. Had he known about Zwinger's edition of Aristotle, he could have supplied much material.

Sambucus Zvingero suo salutem.

Accepi tuas 21. Martii, quibus tuas cogitationes et conatus a Cratone comprobatos significas.[556] Misi dudum Hippocratem meum cum Aegineta et aliis, quibus consilii tui usus non parum subsidii sentient.[557] Sunt enim in margine voculae variae, quarum singulae multum ponderis sunt et salutis.[558] Utinam tuo labore Hippocratis textus ederetur, adiungeres tuam methodum ordinatam.[559] Sunt quidem multa in margine vel in Germanica editione observata, sed plura vel syllaba vel vocali etc. in meo codice quam in ullius alterius. Eaque lege Oporino et tibi meos libros communico, ut vos adiurem per fidem integros mihi eos redditum iri. De epitaphiis universis laetor. Mitto nuper Taurini[560] repertum, si ocium fuerit, plura mittam.

---

[555] Koloman Egerer Jr. was the brother of Sambucus's future wife Cristinna Egerer. See more on his family and father in letter 97, note 593.

[556] Sambucus probably refers here to Zwinger's edition of Hippocrates (*Viginti duo commentarii*). See Gerstinger, "Zusammenfassung," 307. and the notes below.

[557] In the case of Hippocrates, it was not a manuscript but an Aldine edition, in which Sambucus annotated his variant readings. See ibid. and letter 82.

[558] Zwinger's marginal note: "Aegineta emendatus a Sambuco."

[559] Sambucus makes reference to the usual Ramist tables attached to Zwinger's works, in which he summarised and structured the message of the book. His edition of Hippocrates came out only much later with 22 Ramist tables as also the title indicated: Hippocrates, *Viginti duo commentarii*.

[560] Possibly Zemun (Semlin/Zimony) across the Danube opposite Belgrade. Its usual Latin name was Taurunum (or Taururum, as on *Tabula Hungariae*).

Vale, mi Zvinggere. In Ethicis edendis multa tuis annotationibus et lectionibus, si scivissem, suppeditassem, sed aliquid fiet.[561] Viennae, 23 Martii 1567.

Address: D. doctori Theodoro Zvingero etc. amico suo veteri.

89.
Sambucus to Joachim Camerarius Jr.
25 March 1567, Vienna

The original is kept in Munich, BSB, Clm 10367, f. 295ʳ. Published in Gerstinger, "Die Briefe," 81-82.

Sambucus received the letters of both younger and elder Camerarius with a month of delay as he had been at home in Hungary. He could not understand who has delivered Camerarius's letter nor whom Camerarius has tasked with transport of Sambucus's codex. Camerarius should appoint someone to whom Sambucus can entrust this unique codex in return for a pledge of 200 thalers. He would not deny any book to the Camerarius, as he collected his library with the goal of making it useful for everyone. He asks Camerarius not to be offended by his demand for a surety, but he has never seen anything like this geometrical codex. It contains the most correct text of Euclid with diagrams and marginal notes, and other unknown geometrical explanations, the index of which he had sent to Joachim's father. He wants the pledge of 200 thalers or a person who guarantees the loan in order to get back the book exactly after 10 months of the day of receipt. Sambucus does not mind if whatever Camerarius Sr., to whom this letter should be forwarded as soon as possible, deems to be of value in the codex is published. They will get Laertius, carefully corrected by Sambucus, at the next Frankfurt book fair. He is sending his greetings to his old friend Daniel Canter, with whom he could well discuss things of classical interest.

Sambucus salutem.

Accepi tuas et parentis viri doctissimi literas,[562] verum tardius, quod in patria fere mensem haeserim, nec quis eas attulerit, vel cui negocium perferendi codicis dederas, intelligere potuerim. Da igitur aliquem, mi Ioachime, cui tuto librum singularem et preciosum, qui pro eo ad 200 talleros hic spondeat reddendo, committam. Nihil vel tibi, vel optimo clarissimoque patri a mea bibliotheca denegabitur unquam.[563] Ea enim re hanc mihi suppelectilem comparavi, ut publico usui per alios etiam inserviat. Quod autem sponsorem peto, ne moleste feras, nec difficili a me vel dubio vobis animo codicem suppeditari iccirco arbitremini, sed quia in tota Europa lustratis omnibus bibliothecis haud meminerim eiusmodi volumen geometricum simul extare. Euclides enim totus emendatissimus schematibus, in margine scholiis et, quorum indicem patri miseram, aliorum geometricas continet lucubrationes raras necdum cognitas. Ut igitur ipsum sine difficultate et ulla exceptione ab eo die, quo eum misero, intra 10 menses rehabeam, ideo

---

[561] Aristoteles, *De Moribus ad Nicomachum Libri decem [...] Opera et studio Theodori Zvinggeri Basiliensis medici et phiosophi* (Basileae: per Ioannem Oporinum et Eusebium Episcopium, 1566).
[562] We could not identify the letter sent by Camerarius Jr.
[563] Cf. with letters 85 and 91.

200 pignus seu sponsorem ego postulo.⁵⁶⁴ Quicquid in eo boni fuerit, parentis exercitatissimi iudicio et opera per me facile vulgabitur ac spero eius licet iam tot vigiliis affectum laborem codicis nobilitate non parum excitatum iri, cui hasce meas quamprimum mitte et, quid fieri et per quem velitis, cito me reddite certiorem. Laertium a me non negligenter correctum et alia ex his nundinis Francfortensibus accipietis.⁵⁶⁵ Vale, mi domine Ioachime, ac meo nomine D. Daniel Cantero veteri amico salutem plurimam,⁵⁶⁶ qui eum si congredi possim, de mul[tis] antiquitatibus mutuo nos possemus monere. Iterum vale. 8 Kalendas Aprilis Vienna 1567.

Address: Dem Edlen und hochgelehrten Herrn D. Joachim Camerarius der Statt Nurnberg Artzt etc. seinen gunstigen Herrn und guetten froudt. Nurmberg bey dem herrn David Chauler zuerfragen.⁵⁶⁷ Cito, Cito.

90.
Sambucus to Johannes Sturm⁵⁶⁸
1 April 1567, Vienna

The original is kept in Zofingen, Stadtbibliothek: Pa 14/1. cart. Misc. f. 182. Copies are held in Basel, Universitätsbibliothek, Handschriften, Mscr. G2 I 15, no. 43; Zürich, Zentralbibliothek, Simler Sammlung, Joh. Sambucus 1567–1568; a German summary is kept in Aarau, Staatsarchiv, Ms BNQ 32,2. Published in Gerstinger, "Die Briefe," 80-81 (based upon the Basel copy).

Human studies without moral discipline, which is a strength of the Strasbourg academy, are less fertile. Sambucus persuaded this boy (coming from a respected and rich family) to go to Strasbourg, since his former tutor, taken from Wittenberg, had inadequate manners. He is asking Sturm to put the boy up in his house if possible or find another place for him. Sturm should find out advanced his knowledge is and select the right class for him so that his work remain even. If he runs out of money,

---

[564] See Almási, *The Uses of Humanism*, 218-219; Gerstinger, "Zusammenfassung," 302-303. The Euclid-manuscript, which had once belonged to Bessarion, was apparently one of his most precious manuscripts. It was finally entrusted to Camerarius, who passed it on to Conrad Dasypodius (or perhaps sent it to Dasypodius via Eusebius Episcopius), who for many years neither published it nor sent it back, as Sambucus repeatedly complained (see "Euclid" in the Index). See also Gerstinger, "Zusammenfassung," 302-303.
[565] Diogenes Laertius, *De vita et moribus philosophorum*. Cf. letter 68.
[566] We have no information on Daniel Canter.
[567] We have no information on David Chauler.
[568] Johannes Sturm (1507–1589) was one of the most significant educators of mid-century Europe. He established a Protestant gymnasium in Strasbourg in 1537 and directed it for 43 years. His educational system became famous and a model for grammar schools elsewhere (also influential for Zamojsky's academy). He was a man of moderate religious views, but his position became controversial in the face of accelerating confessionalisation. See Pierre Mesnard, "La 'pietas litterata' de Jean Sturm et le développement à Strasbourg d'une pédagogie oecuménique," *Bulletin de la Société d'Histoire du Protestantisme Français* 111 (1965), 281-302; Anton Schindling, *Humanistische Hochschule und freie Reichsstadt – Gymnasium und Akademie in Straßburg 1538 bis 1621* (Wiesbaden: Franz Steiner Verlag, 1977); Lewis W. Spitz and Barbara Sher Tinsley, *Johann Sturm on Education: The Reformation and Humanist Learning* (St. Louis: Concordia Publishing, 1995); Simona Negruzzo, "L'Alsace et Jean Sturm. Réforme et modèles pédagogiques au XVIe siècle," in *Protestantisme et éducation dans la France modern* ([Lyon]: Équipe religions, 2014), 53-72. Sambucus spent a short period of time in Strasbourg in 1550, where he certainly got to know Sturm. In 1555, he dedicated to him a poem in his *Poemata* (f. 32ʳ⁻ᵛ) and later also the emblem "Ordo" in *Emblemata* (1566), 190.

Sturm can assume responsibility of a debt up to 300 ducats without any worry. Sambucus is either working on Pannonian histories or restoring corrupted texts with the help of manuscripts from his noteworthy library. He is not going to speak about his original works. He is now editing the works of Eunapius and [Pseudo-]Hesychius. Sturm can send his response through Leonard Weis in Augsburg.

Ioannes Sambucus salutem.

In laudibus vestri gymnasii quoque ponitur disciplina morum observantiaque iuventutis, qua sine progressus in literis parum sunt fructuosi, minus laudabiles. Fui igitur huius adolescentis parentibus honestissimis et illis copiosis author multisque aliis ad vos proficiscendi. Habuit praeceptorem non indoctum, quem secum Viteberga adduxerat, sed moribus iniquis et huic aetati non adiungendis. Pollicitus sum de vestris classibus et exemplis diligentiam et mores optabiles. Nosti enim illud vetus: ἑλοῦ βίον τὸν ἄριστον, ἡ συνήθεια δὲ ἥδιστον ποιήσει.[569] Itaque hunc, in cuius rebus valde cupio, tibi etiam atque etiam commendo, ut vel in aedibus tuis communi mensa uti possit, vel alio in loco honesto et literato eum colloces tuaque authoritate iuves aut confirmes, cuius te beneficii non paenitebit, meque, cui multum antea debeo, totum obstrinxeris. Exquiretis, uti soletis, quantum profecerit propriaeque classi destinabitis, ut non vagus sed constans sit utilisque labor. Quod si etiam sumptus aliquando illi deficeret, ad 300 aureos pro eo spondere sine iactura vel fidei, vel pecuniae tuto poteris.

Ego, mi clarissime Sturmi, Pannonicas hic texo historias veterumque authorum corruptos vel mutilos locos e chirographis meaque non contemnenda bibliotheca, quod possum, restituo.[570] Cuius voluntatis atque etiam conatus exempla non pauca iam prodiere. De meis propriis lucubrationibus taceo. Edo nunc Eunapii Philosophos et Milesii Poetas, etc.[571] Vale. Kalendis Aprilis 1567.

Cum rescribere quid volueris vel adolescens noster, Augustam litterae mittantur ad Leonardum Weys,[572] qui eas mihi curabit reddendas.

Other hand: Hic est imperatoris historicus vir insignis.

91.
Joachim Camerarius Sr. to Sambucus
24 April 1567, Nuremberg

Published in Camerarius, *Epistolarum libri quinque posteriores*, 410-411.

When Camerarius came to see his son in Nuremberg, he received Sambucus's letter and realised Sambucus's severe conditions concerning his books, regarding which he appeared once to be most generous. In his age and standing these conditions are not to be accepted. He wishes that Sambucus would publish these works so that more people would profit from them and his name could be spread wider. He has no doubts about Sambucus's benevolence, there may be other occasions in the future. Camerarius complains about his old age and waning strength.

---

[569] Choose the best life you can and the habit will make it most sweet. Cf. Plutarchus, *De exilio* 8.
[570] A reference to Bonfini, *Rerum Ungaricarum decades quatuor*.
[571] Eunapius, Βίοι φιλοσόφων; [Pseudo-]Hesychius, Περὶ τῶν ἐν παιδείᾳ.
[572] We were not able to identify the person in question.

S. D.

Cum superioribus diebus Norimbergam venissem ad filium meum Ioachimum, allatae fuere literae tuae ad ipsum scriptae, in quibus de libris, quorum usum aliquando humanissima liberalitate mihi visus esses offerre, conditiones quaedam feruntur graves neque mihi hoc loco et ista aetate mea accipiendae.[573] Itaque facio gratiam de officio isto tuo neque te mittendi tam praeclaros libros molestia atque cura onerare neque mihi periculum in copia hac acquirenda creare volo. Te tamen, qua es cupiditate studia bonarum artium augendi et ornandi, operam dare velim, ut ista scripta in lucem typis expressa proferantur, ut quam plurimi illorum lectione frui possint et tua fama celebretur tanquam Musarum θεράποντος καὶ ἀγγέλου,[574] secundum Theognidem, libenter communicantis cum aliis sapientiae suae eximia munera. Nam quemadmodum ille ait, τί σφιν χρήσηται μοῦνος ἐπισταμένος.[575] Sed cum de tua voluntate non dubitem, in temporis scilicet opportunitate erunt reliqua. Ego et aeate debilitante et curis defatigantibus sentio me fieri indies languidiorem, propius iam accedentibus annis ad eam summam, in qua ponitur πρεσβυτικὸς ὄκνος,[576] cum etiam valetudo morbis affligi incipiat, τοῦ γήρως καθ' αὐτὸ ὄντος νόσου φυσικῆς.[577] Sed haec alieniora sunt. Bene igitur valebis et benevolentiam erga me humanitatemque tuam conservabis. Vale. Norimbergae. 8. Calendas Maii. 67.

92.
Sambucus to Joachim Camerarius Sr.
1 June 1567, Vienna

The original of the letter is held in Munich, BSB, Autogr. Cim. Sambucus, Johannes. (The date of the letter is misread as 1561.) Published in *Virorum doctorum epistolae selectae ad Bilibaldum Pirckheymerum, Ioachimum Camerarium, Carolum Clusium et Iulium episcopum Herbipolitum datae*, ed. Theodor Friedrich Freytag (Lipsiae: Teubner, 1831), 70-71 (dated to 1562).[578]

Sambucus repeats what Camerarius said about his old age, feebleness and inability to accept his conditions of loan. He would entrust anything to Camerarius without testimonies, it was all about the question of delivery. He wrote Camerarius Jr. more fully about it. Had Crato told him about a way of delivery earlier, he would not have needed to say all of it either. Sambucus wonders about Camerarius's opinion of his collection of epithets and his Hephaestion-manuscript. It is a juvenile work, hastily done while reading. Camerarius should give it to someone to get it systematised and enlarged. He should send back Hephaestion in time.

---

[573] See letter 89.
[574] minister and herald (of the Muses). Cf. Theognis, *Elegiae*, 769.
[575] what will it avail him, if only he knows it? Theognis, *Elegiae*, 772.
[576] the laziness and inactivity of the elderly
[577] since the old age is by its nature an illness
[578] In the catalogue of the BSB the date of the letter is misread as 1561, in the published version as 1562.

Salutem.

Ὄκνον[579] affectae morbisque iam obnoxiae aetatis facere scribis, quominus codicem promissum requiras, conditiones vero etiam graves arbitraris.[580] Ego vero, vir doctissime Ioachime, non hunc modo codicem, sed quicquid habeo, id totum sine testibus tibi crederem, sed qui librum recepisset perferendum, eius gratia quosdam adsciscerem. Qua de re nuper copiosius ad filium Norimbergam: neque his, nisi commoditatem mittendi D. Crato significasset, opus erat. Quod vero me confirmas ad lucubrationes, ac ne tot veterum scripta latere patiar mones, habeo gratiam, itaque faciam. De puerili epithetorum farragine quid futurum sit atque Hephestione vehementer cupio ex te intelligere.[581] Fassus sum antea leviter atque inter legendum obiter collecta a me admodum adolescente. Tu erudito alicui eas recognoscenda, ordinanda, augenda trades atque, quod voles, de eis statues. Hephestionem tuo commodo remitti velim per Norimbergam, vel aliter. Vale, mi optime ac doctissime Ioachime, tibique persuadeas nihil mihi accidere posse carius, quam si quid in meis rebus iubear. Vienna, Kalendis Iunii 1567. Tuus Ioannes Sambucus.

Address: Domino Ioachimo Camerario viro clarissimo. Leyptzig.

93.
Sambucus to Emperor Maximilian II
24 June 1567, Vienna

Dedication in Bonfini, *Rerum Ungaricarum decades quatuor*, 3-8. Published in *Humanistes du bassin des Carpates II. Johannes Sambucus*, 102-113.

94.
Sambucus to István Nyilas
27 June 1567, Pressburg

The original is kept in Trnava, SAT, Magistrát mesta Trnava, Missiles. Published in Kóssa, "Adatok Sámboky János életéhez," 372; Vantuch, "Die Sambucusbriefe," 334.

Sambucus got to writing to his brother-in-law only in the evening. He had the last will of the widow of Sibrik officially acknowledged. She did not want to believe (?) that no one should worry about a judicial case, unless one wants a case with the emperor. He asks Nyilas to present his case to the councillors and let him be free of his debts. Nyilas should rather give those goods of little value to the poor (the victims of the fire), or lend them to someone or give them to God. He should tell Philep that Sambucus is in Pressburg. The bills of debt, which Sambucus left there, should be given to him. He wishes that Nyilas would come to Pressburg.

---

[579] hesitation
[580] See letters 89 and 91.
[581] The fate of Sambucus's collection of Greek epithets is unknown; it certainly did not get published (cf. letters 8, 111 and 221). Sambucus's Hephaestion-manuscript has not survived. Cf. letters 33, 85 and 111.

Kezenetemet mint Soghor uramnak, czak ez estwe iuték. Kegyelmednek ielentem hogh az Sibrikne[582] testamentomat nem czak ex gratia confirmaltattam, de ugyan vytotta azont, hogh semmi peurtul ne fellyen senky: hanem ha czasarral akar peureulni. Azertan kerem kegyelmedet hogh ez dolgot az uraimnak eleybe aggya, az en adossaghimat megh zabaditza: kegelmetek inkabban ozza az keves marhat az zeghineknek, ielesben kik megh eghtenek vagh költzen, uagh Istennebe. Kerem kegyelmedet Philep[583] uramnak izend megh hogh itt vagyok: az ados leveleket ky adassatok, kiket ott hattam, hogh Sivaron megh vehessem, mert elegh gondal liszen megh: es ha tuddya, hogh kegyelmednel [kegyelmeddel?] vagyon, kevessebbet gondol rea. Akarnam kegyelmet ide iöne. Isten tartza megh kegyelmedet mind haza nepevel. Anno 27 Juni Posonii, 1567. Kegyelmednek J. Samboky.

95.
Sambucus to the Mayor and the Council of Trnava
3 July 1567, Pressburg

The original is kept in Trnava, SAT, Magistrát mesta Trnava, Missiles. Published in Vantuch, "Die Sambucusbriefe," 334-335.

Eight days earlier Sambucus sent them the testament of the widow of Sibrik acknowledged and confirmed by the emperor. This should be sufficient against any assailer. The Council should distribute those things among the poor victims of the fire or give them as a loan to someone. He has had no response to his letter about the remaining 600 florins debt so he wants a response within three days, that is, by Saturday. The captain held back 8 florins as a house tax. He would not discuss it if it had been at the order of the Council. But he hopes he can do them some services of 8 florins worth, since Ferenc Szeghedy did not pay him anything as rent. He also asks the mayor to take over the stuff and clothes left by János Panithy with Imre Kalmár as he has discussed in the chapter house with Georg Jo. The Council should send him the cloths either by Saturday or have them shaken out and sent to Vienna later, for which he will pay in kind. He will in any case need to leave for Vienna on Monday.

Salutem servitiorumque debitam commendationem.

Misi ante 8 dies confirmationem et innovationem caesaream testamenti Sibrikne, quae sine dubio vestris dominationibus tute satis erunt contra impetitores ac satius esset vestras dominationes res eas pauperibus distribuere et igni afflictis vel dare, vel mutuo dare. Responsum nullum habui de meis litteris penes dominationes vestras relictis de 600 fl. debitis.[584] Quare rogo dominationes vestras mihi intra triduum, hoc est, ad diem sabbathi vel

---

[582] Veronika Pechy, the widow of Georgius Sibrik. Vantuch reports that a testament of 26 April 1552 by Georgius Sybryk is held in the city archive of Trnava, in which Sibrik left "unam sedem" as an estate to Sambucus's father. Among the witnesses there was also Sambucus's father. The testament was apparently contested for decades and the case was only brought to a close by Emperor Maximilian on 15 April 1567, that is, not much before the letter was written. Vantuch, "Die Sambucusbriefe," 336. See also the next letter.
[583] Fülöp (Philep) Kádas was several times councillor of Trnava. See ibid., 334.
[584] See the preceding letter.

litteras per vestros concives mittantur, vel responsum aliquid. Ceterum dominus capitaneus[585] mihi 8 fl. ratione domus taxae retinuit. Si vestro mandato fit, non recusabo, sed spero me dominationes vestras tantum posse inservire quantum 8 fl., cum Zeghedy Franciscus[586] ne obolum mihi dederit ex aedium habitatione. Rogo quoque dominum Judicem, ut res et vestes apud dominum Emericum Kalmar[587] Ioanni Panithy depositas ad se accipiat, quia negocium totum coram Capitulo hinc nobili domino Georgio Jo confeci. Et eas dominus iudex[588] vel hac die sabbathi mittat, vel curet eas excuti bene et postea Viennam mittere per occasionem; quod beneficium suae dominationis omni genere officiorum compensabo. Quibus me commendo responsumque expecto. Nam omnino die lunae Viennam discedendum mihi erit. Valere easdem opto. 3 Iulii Posonio 1567. vestrarum dominationum filius et servitor, Ioannes Sambucus.

Address: Egregiis ac prudentibus dominis, domino iudici, totique senatui Tyrnaviensi etc., patronis meis observandissimis. Nagh Zombath. Cito, cito.

96.
Sambucus to Johann Sommer, Mayor of Trnava
4 July 1567, Pressburg

The original is kept in Trnava, SAT, Magistrát mesta Trnava, Missiles. Published in Vantuch, "Die Sambucusbriefe," 335-336.[589]

Sommer should believe him; he looked after the whole issue with Georg Jo very well and the chapter house provides testimony. He asks Sommer to send that letter back together with the cloths to doctor Georg Purkircher, living on the square (in Pressburg). The register of the cloths was given to Imre Kalmár, as the clothes have been delivered to him. Sambucus demands an answer concerning the widow of Sibrik. He will go back to Vienna either on Monday or Friday.

Salutem et commendationem.

Gunstigen herren und frondt:[590] butt wollet mir auch glauben geben: dan ich ye alhie kräfftiglich mit dem Jo Jorg alle sach richtig gemacht, und Zeugnis das Capitel gibt.[591] Derhalben ich butt, wollet diss brieflein wider schikhen, und auch den punkl mitt dem Klaidern auffs nechst hieher schikhen zu dem heren doctor Purkircher am platz.[592] Das register hatt darfor der her

---

[585] Vantuch asserts that he was "J. Mohr" at the time. Vantuch, "Die Sambucusbriefe," 335.
[586] Ferenc Szeghedy was a citizen of Trnava. See Vantuch, ibid.
[587] On Kalmár's debts to Sambucus see letters 206-207, 209 and 211.
[588] Johann Sommer. See the next letter addressed to him.
[589] The address is missing but it was clearly addressed to Johann Sommer (cf., for example, letter 98). See Vantuch, "Die Sambucusbriefe," 336.
[590] Johann Sommer was several times Mayor of Trnava. He must have been fully bilingual as Hungarians usually corresponded with him in Hungarian (addressing him as Szomer). See Bakonyi, "Nagyszombat város követei."
[591] For the context of this letter see letters 81 and 94-95.
[592] Georg Purkircher (1535–1577) was a physician, botanist and a significant poet from Pressburg. He studied in the famous grammar school of Bartfeld (Bártfa), in Wittenberg with Melanchthon and from 1561 he took up medicine in Padua. Upon his return to his hometown he started practicing as a doctor and became a key figure

Emrich von mir empfangen, da die klaider ime sein zuegestelt worden. Bütt auch wellet die herren ansprechen umb ain andtwort der Sibrikin halben, damit ich mich darnach richtn wiss: wils umb euch treulich verdienen: worein irs die Klaider werdet ausmachen, soll euch alles wider zuegeschikt werden. Damit Gott befolchen. Ich zieh an montag oder Erichtag auff Wien zurück; nichti weniger schikt ir die Klaider dem heren doctor zue gen Prespurg. Damit Gott befolchen. Prespurg den 4. Julii 1567. Euer Diener Samboki.

97.
Sambucus to the Mayor and the Council of Trnava
10 July 1567, Vienna

The original is kept in Trnava, SAT, Magistrát mesta Trnava, Missiles. Published in Vantuch, "Die Sambucusbriefe," 337-338.

Sambucus invites the Council of Trnava both collectively and individually to his wedding with Cristinna, daughter of Koloman Egerer, who is a common acquaintance of the councillors, on 4 August 1567 in Vienna. He implores them to send at least some representatives for the sake of his honour.

Salutem et servitiorum commendationem debitam.

Cum reliqua hominis causa sint creata, earum vero usum unicus Adam vix omnium percepisset nec videbatur maiestatis divinae laudibus is solus et ornamento sufficere, Evam illi ad propagationem generis prolisque ad eiusdem gloriae amplificationem curam addidit. Dei igitur mandato et instituto me in matrimonium contuli filiamque amici vestri communis Colimani Egreri Christianam nomine connubio adiunxi.[593] Ad celebritatem igitur nuptiarum vos universos et singulos de senatu valde oro, ut vestro commodo ad 4. Augusti hic Viennae

---

of the city's intellectual life. He dedicated an epithalamion to Sambucus for his wedding in August 1567. See Vilmos Frankl, "Egy XVI-ik századi magyar fűvész és orvos emlékezete," *Századok* 8 (1873), 529-530; Mária Kneifel, *Purkircher György* (Budapest: Egyetem, 1942); Georg Purkircher, *Opera quae supersunt omnia*, ed. Miloslav Okál (Budapest: Akadémia, 1988); and the article by Áron Orbán in *Companion*.

[593] Koloman (Kálmán) Egerer († c. 1587) was a rich Viennese merchant, originating probably from Pressburg or Trnava. He became citizen of Vienna in 1542 but apparently kept his contacts with Trnava, as also this letter proves (cf. with letter 141). His choice of Sambucus as his son-in-law was an investment into political power. Sambucus was relatively poor (he got to know Cristinna very probably as a house tutor to her brothers), but was a nobleman and a well-connected member of the court. Koloman and his family meant financial security for which Sambucus paid in kind. Already in 1568 Sambucus must have attempted to back Koloman's supplication to Maximilian for tax exemption of his Viennese house, which was refused. However, it was probably also thanks to Sambucus that in 1572 Koloman became a nobleman. Moreover, in 1575 the palace which he built–and named Egereck–on a piece of land attached to Linz received the status of "Freihaus" (which was quite extraordinary in Linz). The diploma stressed that the exemption happened "aus kaiserlicher unnd landtsfürstlicher Machtvollkhommenhait." Cristinna (Christianna) Egerer's († c. 1609) surviving letters and testament suggest that she was relatively learned. In her testament of 1609 she commemorated Sambucus as a noble and highly learned doctor, councillor and historian of the Holy Roman Emperors Maximilian and Rudolf. See Franz Wilflingseder, "Geschichte des einstigen Freisitzes Egereck in Linz," *Jahrbuch der Stadt Linz* (1954), 455-484 (at 456-463). For her testament see Robert Matt, "Die Wiener protestantischen Bürgertestamente von 1578-1627," *Mitteilungen des Vereines für Geschichte der Stadt Wien* 17 (1938), 29.

adsitis, de hospitio bene provisum vobis fuerit meque vestra praesentia beabitis.[594] Quod si per negotia omnibus, totique senatui interesse non licuerit, saltem vestro nomine aliquem honoris caussa mittite, quam ego gratiam perpetuis servitiis et obedientia erga civitatem vosque senatores perpetuo promereri conabor. Utque precibus meis faciles vos praebeatis, obsecro. Easdem valere opto et, ut mihi quamprimum respondeatis, ut de hospitio commoditatem habeatis, valde oro. Vienna, 10 July 1567. Vester servitor et filius Sambucus.

Address: Egregiis ac prudentibus domino iudici totique senatui, singulis senatoribus Tyrnaviensibus dominis et amicis honorandissimis. Tirnaviam.

98.
Sambucus to Johann Sommer, Mayor of Trnava
10 July 1567, Vienna

The original is kept in Trnava, SAT, Magistrát mesta Trnava, Missiles. Published in Vantuch, "Die Sambucusbriefe," 336-337.

Georg Jo surprised him when he asked either for a document about the 200 florins or a quittance. He has no letter and God knows that they already sorted it out at the chapter house. He has given the quittance to Márton Deák. If Jo does not have trust, Sommer or his brother-in-law (Nyilas) should guarantee it and send the cloths through Deák and Pajzsgyártó to Purkircher in Pressburg. He is worried that the cloths will be damaged after so much time and has already spent 64 florins on them. Sambucus invites Sommer and his wife to his wedding on 4 August and hopes that also the city will delegate some people and Nyilas and Kádas will turn up. One cannot find capons in Vienna, so Sambucus asks Sommer to send him 20 pieces 10 days before the wedding. He has asked the same from the captain and his brother-in-law. Finally, he asks for an answer regarding the testament of the widow of Sibrik and calls attention to the future services he can do for the city.

Gunstiglicher herr, mein vertrauter frondt: mich hatt verwundert an dem Jorg Jo der Klaider halber, das er eintweder ein briff von 200 fl., oder quittung begert.

Ich hab khain briff, wayss gott, und habens doch mit ainander vor dem Capitl alles beschlosshen. Quittung hab ich zuegestelt dem Marton Deakhn.[595] Und wan derselben niht trauett, verhoff werdt ir und der her Schwager fur ein quittung dieweyll guett sein, und die Klaider nechst ghen Prespurg den her Marton Deakhen, und Paysgiarto[596] zueschikhen, damit sie die dem hern doctor Purkirchern zu Prespurg zuestellen, wie ichs ime auch hob

---
[594] On Sambucus marriage also see Liebl, "Der Heiratskontrakt"; Almási, *The Uses of Humanism*, 167.
[595] Very little is known of Márton Nagy Deák ("deák" means scribe), who was a scribe of the city, an agent representing the city in Pressburg (and deputy at the diet of 1569), where he had a house. Bakonyi, "Nagyszombat város követei," 436.
[596] It is probably Mátyás Pajzsgyártó (of Szeged origins), who was an important citizen of Trnava, twice member of the twelve-member Council. In 1560 he was garantor for a minor sum of money in a case also involving Sambucus. In 1561 he was *magister hospitalis*, head of the hospital of the poor and the sick. While his son studied in Wittenberg, he got Márton Deák write his letters to him. See Bakonyi, "Nagyszombat város követei," 436; Vantuch, "Die Sambucusbriefe," 337. We also know of an Elek Pajzsgyártó of Nagyszombat, see *Régi Magyar nyelvemlékek*, 3:70-71.

anzaigt. Dan ich furcht die Klaider vom schaden so lange Zeytt, und hab woll 64 fl. drauff verrechnet wider gelt.[597]

Demnach ist mein butt, als guetten vertrautten here wöllet auff den 4 Augusti mitt sambst euren liebe hausfrau alhie zu meiner hochzeytlichen freyd euch erzaigen so es muglich ist, welchs ich umb euch treulich verdienen will. Hab auch der Statt geschriben, verhoff sie wirt etwa einen in iren namen senden. Verhoff der Nylas und Kadas werden gwislich auch khomen.[598] Die Kapaun sein hie gor niht zufinden, butt den heren das er auff den thörn [?] etwa lass auff khauffen ein 20, und ein 10 tag darfor schikhen, wie ich auch den hern Hauptman und Schwagern gepetten. Damit gott befolchen, und bütt umb ein andtwort der Statt halben, und sonst, damit ich Zeytlich herberig find. Wien den 10 Julii 1567. Euer Diener Samboki.

Bütt seer, wellet der Sibrikhne testament halben[599] von rott [Von Rott?] mir ein andtwort lassen wissen. Damit ich betzalt werd an schaden. Bin ich doch euer, solt mich niht also lang auff ziehen. Khan der Statt wider dienen.

Address: Egregio domino Ioanni Sommer, iudici Tyrnaviensi, amico observandissimo, Tirnaviam.

99.
Sambucus to Emperor Maximilian II
27 July 1567, Vienna

The original is kept in Vienna, ÖStA, Allgemeines Verwaltungs-, Finanz- und Hofkammerarchiv, Familien Akte, S-15, f. 2.

Sambucus repeats his invitation to his wedding: Maximilian should send a representative to his wedding, as is customary in the case of imperial clients. This would fully oblige Sambucus and his father-in-law Koloman Egerer.

Sacratissima Caesarea Maiestas, domine, domine perpetuo clementissime.

Non ambitione aliqua, aut loco, authoritatisque alicuius spe, quem omnium vestrae maiestatis servitorum minima est, vestram maiestatem ad nuptias meas 4. Augusti futuras antea humillime vocavi, ac nunc quoque iterum supplex oro, sed more aulae vestrae maiestatis familiorum: dignetur eadem vestra caesarea maiestas erga infimum Sambucum suum clementissime memor esse, ac si unquam meis vigiliis ac servitiis promereri possim, aliquem, quemcumque suorum vel minimorum gratiosissime ad eum diem nuptiis destinare, quo vestrae maiestatis humillimi clientis hilaritas tanta authoritate extollatur. Magnum est quod supplico, sed vestra maiestas clementissime sentiet, Sambucum perpetua fide et vigiliis partem aliquam tantae gratiae fauturum, socerum vero meum Colimannum Egrer devotissima obedientia

---

[597] On the issue of the cloths, see letters 81 and 94-96.
[598] Fülöp Kádas must have been a relative of Sambucus. See letters 135 and 137.
[599] On the issue of the testament see letters 94-96.

ac perpetuo adhuc praestita fide agniturum beneficium. Cuius me clementissimae maiestati totum commendo ac subiectissime voveo. Ac si quid hic maius peto, quod personam minimi servitoribus non decet, vestra maiestas mihi gratiosissime ignoscat. Vestram maiestatem Deus conservat plurimos in annos. Amen. Vienna 27 Iulii 1567. Vestrae sacratissimae maiestatis infimus clientulus et servitor Iohannes Sambucus etc.

Address: Sacrae caesareae maestati etc., domino, domino semper clementissimo.[600]

100.
Laurentius Sifanus to Sambucus
13 August 1567, Steinfeld Abbey

Dedication in *Theophylacti... Explicationes in Acta Apostolorum*, f. 4^r. Published in *Humanistes du bassin des Carpates II. Johannes Sambucus*, 93-95.

101.
Sambucus to Emperor Maximilian II
1 September 1567, Vienna

The original is kept in Vienna, ÖStA, Allgemeines Verwaltungsarchiv, Adel RAA 359.51, Johannes Sambucus Palatinatsverleihung. Published in Liebl, "Der Heiratskontrakt des Johannes Sambucus," 185.

Just as it is characteristic for princes to decorate their weapons with coats of arms and their states with laws, they also usually grant men of letters immunities and other favours. Sambucus says nothing about his already published works of the previous 15 years. However, what he is presently elaborating (for the emperor's honour) has been highly praised by his friends. He is now applying for the title of comes palatinus *with the usual rights: the right to distribute the titles of baccalaureate, doctorate, poet laureate and notary in the presence of two expert witnesses and to hold lectures in his fields of expertise. In the latter he can rely on his library, which provides him books to be commented and edited.*

Sacratissima Caesarea Maiestas, domine, domine clementissime.

Imperatorum ac principum virorum est, ut arma insignibus, respublicas legibus munire ac decorare, ita, quorum diuturnae lucubrationes et scriptiones vulgo nota sunt ac posteritati sunt profuturae, immunitatibus ornare atque maiora clementissima benignitate excitare.[601] De meis adhuc editis vigiliis nihil pronucio, multae annis 15 et variae apparent, sed, quae in manibus supersunt cumque laude vestrae caesareae maiestatis coniugentur, amicorum iudicio non sunt contemnendae. Supplex oro eandem vestram maiestatem, dignetur me

---
[600] The supplication was countersigned by Vice-Chancellor Johannes Zasius on 1 August 1567. In his German notes addressed to Maximilian on the verso of the letter Zasius summarises Sambucus's request.
[601] See Almási, *The Uses of Humanism*, 167-168.

palatinatus honore eiusque singularibus privilegiis donare, ut etiam notarios, poetas, doctores aut praesentibus duobus examinatos, aut alioqui iam exemplis cognitos et praxi creare, ac si a vestra caesarea maiestate vel gymnasiis fieret, ratumque id haberi.[602] Praeterea in usum iuventutis vestra authoritate praeter theologiam et, in quibus non sum ita versatus, legere docereque queam sine impedimento, quam ad rem non exiguum mihi subsidium ad multos authores illustrandos ac edendos bibliotheca suppeditabit.

Quam vestrae caesareae maiestatis gratiam perpetuis vigiliis de perpetua domo Austria promereri enitar. Cuius me clementissimae gratiae humillime voveo. Viennae, Kalendis Septembris 1567. Vestrae sacratissimae caesareae maiestatis humillimus clientulus, aulae famulus et historiographus, Iohannes Sambucus.

102.
Sambucus to the Hungarian Chamber
11 September 1567, Vienna

The original is kept in Budapest, Magyar Nemzeti Levéltár, E 41 22. cím, 1567, Mf. 7603, No. 63.

Sambucus is writing in the interest of a Trnava citizen Mihály Kis, who has been innocently accused because of the fault of others. He has testimonies and has never been caught cheating, and he has much contributed to the emperor's treasury during many years. He hopes the Chamber will close his case without referring it to the Viennese authorities. Moreover, Sambucus humbly asks for some regular stipend to sustain his everyday life, since his costly wedding emptied his wallet. He hopes the Chamber will not forget about him, as he is planning to visit them in the company of László Mossóczi.

Reverendissimi, magnifici ac egregii domini et patroni observandissimi, salutem et servitiorum commendationem.

Innocens hic civis Tyrnaviensis, perpetua fide cognitus, quo ante annum casu et alieno lapsu Mihael Kys vexabatur;[603] eodem malo inspectoris mertium errore ad dominationes vestras supplex advolare cogitur. Habet locuples testimonium, praestare alienam culpam tanto suo damno nequit. Reprehensus in dolo nondum est, multorum annorum negociationibus non parum fisco suae maiestatis addidit. Idque ut deinceps possit, hac eum molestia gratiose liberetis. Et quia ego intellexi neminem, qui crocum a caesare adhuc more satis iniquo et avaro impetrarit,[604] sperat reverendissimas magnificas egregias vestras dominationes sine tot Viennam recursibus omne negocium expedituros. Cuius benignitatis ac iustae gratiae partem meis servitiis aliquando emetior, eumque vobis ex animo commendo.

---

[602] The diploma of *comes palatinus* (dated 14 September 1567) must have costed Sambucus some money. Eventually, he received even more priviledges than demanded. Curiously, Sambucus called himself "Pfalzgraf oder comes Palatinus" already in the marriage contract, although, as we can see, it was only a month later that he made an appeal for the title. See Liebl, "Der Heiratskontrakt."

[603] We lack further information on this Trnava citizen.

[604] As the note on the verso of the letter suggests, the Kis might have been accused of embezzling or smuggling some 46 pounds of saffron.

Praeterea rogo, reverendissimae magnificae egregiae dominationes vestrae dignentur sui quoque Sambuci rationem aliquam ducere ac tandem nonnihil pecuniarum concedere. Quotidianae enim necessitates, cura domestica, initio praesertim sumptuosa, ipsae nuptiae marsupium satis exhauserunt. Spero reverendissimae magnificae dominationes vestrae mei gratiosam habituros memoriam, nam cum domino Ladislao Moschotzi Posonium ad vos cogito.[605] Quibus me totum dedo ac voveo. Vienna, 11 Septembris 1567. Reverendissimarum magnificarum egregiarum dominationum vestrarum servitor et [...] Iohannes Sambucus etc.

Address: Reverendissimo, magnifico, egregiis dominis praefecto et consiliariis camerae sacrae caesareae regiaeque maiestatis Posonii etc., dominis et patronis observandissimis, Sambucus.
Posonium
Other hand: XIII. Settembris Anno 67. De 46 libris croci.

103.
Sambucus to the Mayor and the Council of Trnava
2 November 1567, Vienna

The original is kept in Trnava, SAT, Magistrát mesta Trnava, Missiles. Published in Vantuch, "Die Sambucusbriefe," 338-339.

There was no need to send others in the matter of this supplication. As Sambucus had earlier written, he would have told them if it had been needed. It will be debated today. Sambucus talked to councillors, he hopes to attain something but not concerning the estates, which are in the name of the widow and belong to Jókő (Dobrá Voda). It will be very difficult to attain anything concerning the customs due at Komárom, since the exemption is coveted also by other communes and by many in Trnava, and people share their exemption certificates with other passengers in the ship, with great damage for the Chambers. Sambucus will try to do what he can through his contacts from the Austrian Chambers. He asks the mayor to send him the clothes of János Panithy together with 30 florins and to give 12 florins to his brother-in-law István Nyilas for the sustenance of his little Zsóka (Sophia).

Salutem et servitiorum debitam commendationem.

Nihil erat opus alios huc pro supplicatione sollicitandos nunc mittere: nam scripsi me, si opus erit, significaturum. Vestra supplicatio hodie omnino proponetur. Locutus sum cum consiliariis, spero dominationes vestras aliquid impetraturos, sed de bonis dubito. Nam inscripta sunt viduae,[606] dum ita manet nec separabantur, cum ad Jokw pertineant.[607] De telonio Comaroniensi impetare [!] admodum erit difficile, nec quidquam polliceor, nam et aliae civitates idem cuperent, et multi Tyrnaviensium. Communicant aliis in navi suas litteras telonias cum camerae magno detrimento. Sed mihi credite, ita dabo operam per camerarios

---
[605] László Mossóczi was a tax collector of the Hungarian Chamber from 1539. His son Zakariás, Bishop of Nyitra, was a learned man who edited with Miklós Telegdi the laws of Hungary, which was published by Sambucus as an attachment to Werbewcz [Werbőczy], *Tripartitum opus iuris consuetudinarii*.
[606] The widow of László Országh. See letter 83, note 538.
[607] Jókő (Dobrá Voda) was a castle and village north of Trnava.

Austriacos, ut, quod possibile fuerit, nihil negligam. Quibus me commendo. Vienna, 2 Novembris 1567. Vobis deditus servitor Sambucus.

Rogo dominum iudicem, ut vestes Panythy una cum 30 fl. mittat quamprium;[608] duodecim vero det domino sororio Nylas, pro Sophiola mea sustentanda.[609]

Address: Egregiis et prudentibus dominis, iudici senatuique Tyrnaviensi, dominis et amicis honarandissimis. Tirnaviam.

104.
Sambucus to the Mayor and the Council of Trnava
2 December 1567, Vienna

The original is kept in Trnava, SAT, Magistrát mesta Trnava, Missiles. Published in Vantuch, "Die Sambucusbriefe," 339-340.

Concerning the issue of the customs, he still could not obtain a letter of order addressed to Andreas Kielmann by the (Hungarian) Chamber, as the secretaries are slow. The noble majordomo of the English ambassador wants four horses of the same colour and if possible also a horseman, who will be well paid, Sambucus asks the mayor to help him. It will be a service to the emperor and they should make sure that Viskelety, who claimed to have nice horses, should have them. Also Archduke Karl may be grateful if he hears about the origins of good horses from the ambassador. Sambucus asks the councillors to free the clothes of Panithy from the jaws of so many wolves. They should give this letter to Mihály Komornik. Even the imperial marshal asked him carefully to look after this business. They will do well if they prepare some gift of wine, reed and fish for the majordomo of the English ambassador in view of the emperor and the archduke.

Salutem et debitam comendationem.

Scripsi nuper de telonii negotio confecto, sed literas mandatorias ad Kilmanum ex camera nondum potui extorquere. Valde sunt tardi et difficiles isti secretarii.[610] Nunc nihil est quod scribam, quam me hunc nobilem Angliae legati[611] magistrum curae vobis commendare in conquirendis bonis quatuor equis unius coloris, et si fieri potest una etiam servum bonum qui gubernet, bonum habebit salarium. Oro dominationes vestras, velitis illum omnibus modis apud concives vestros iuvare nec, quod fieri poterit, denegare facietis. Caesareae maiestati quoque gratissimum officium certo scio. Dixit mihi dominus Viskelety se pulchros habere, date operam ut habeat.[612] Archidux Carolus quoque habebit pro officio grato, si legatus se vestro beneficio bonos equos consecutum dixerit. De pretio conveniet et bonis conditionibus,

---

[608] On the issue of the clothes see letters 81, 94-96 and 98.
[609] On his niece Zsóka (Sophia) see letter 81, 135 and 137.
[610] Andreas Kielmann (Khielmann, Khielman) was imperial councillor and military commander at Komárom.
[611] Thomas Radclyffe (or Ratclyffe), 3rd Earl of Sussex (c. 1525–1583) was sent to Maximilian II by Queen Elizabeth I in order to negotiate a marriage with Archduke Karl (his mission failed). On the mission see the relevant British state papers and Bibl, *Die Korrespondenz Maximilians II. Band 2.*
[612] Viskelety (Vizkelety) was a citizen of Trnava. See Vantuch, "Die Sambucusbriefe," 340.

et tolerabilibus. Quare si suae maiestati, si archiduci, si denique tantae reginae legato gratum praestare vultis, efficite, ut pulchros equos aequales illi reperiatis. Quibus me commendo et ut tandem vestes Panithii ex faucibus tot luporum liberetis, ne pereant, obsecro. Vienna, 2 Decembris 1567.

Has oro Mihaeli Komornikh per aliquem iubeatis reddi.[613] Ipse magnificus dominus marescalcus caesaris[614] quoque me rogavit, ut negotium de equis vobis diligenter commendarem.

Dominatio vestra recte fecerit, si huic domino magistro curiae legati Anglici honorem munusculo vini, avenae, piscium vel etc. fecerit, idque propter caesarem et archiducem, ut sciat domino legato de vestra humanitate loqui et mihi gratias agere.[615] Valete. Sambucus.

Address: Egregiis ac circumspectis dominis iudici senatuique Tyrnaviensis, dominis et amicis optimis.

105.
Hadrianus Junius to Sambucus
[Beginning of 1568?], no place

Late 16th century copy in Utrecht, Universiteitbibliotheek, Hs. 829, 34r-v. Published in Junius, *Epistolae selectae*, 31-32.

That Junius has not written for longer is due to his reverence for Sambucus, but also to the fact that Sambucus seems to have forgotten about him. Still, it is not nice to let a stable friendship break down without announcing its end. In exchange for his edition of Nonius, Sambucus should at least obtain the honorary title of comes palatinus for him. He is publishing Eunapius in Greek and Latin, a sample is attached. It will be finished during the month, with an afterword praising Sambucus and explaining the long delay. The book by [Pseudo-]Hesychius will be out by the next book fair. Meanwhile they should repair their friendship.

Quod ad te non scripserim quicquam a multo tempore, Sambuce doctissime, fecit cum reverentia tui, tum oblivio quaedam in te mei, quam unde biberis, ignoro. Videtur tamen illa mihi mandragorae vires, ne dicam Stygis virus, secum traxisse. Equidem reserari mihi fontem sive τῆς ληθοσύνης sive τοῦ κοτοῦ[616] candide optarim, a Sicambrone an Cecrope[617] quopiam emanarit, an veritus es improbum (ut Marcellini verbo utar[618]) repostorem? Attamen haud decebat amicitiae ita constabilitae loricam καὶ θριγκόν τινα[619] disrumpi absque tesserae confractae denunciatione. Quin tu, siquidem nihil meretur Nonius, pro quo stipulator intercedebas, ut non in ius eat, effice tua authoritate saltem, uti titulum aliquem honorificum et qui aliquando usui esse possit et

---
[613] Mihály Komornik was very probably a relative (brother-in-law?) of János Panithy. See letters 137-138.
[614] We could not find out who held this office in December 1567, which was primarily held by Johann (III) Trautson.
[615] This last sentence, adopted from Vantuch's publication, is not on the same sheet of paper. It must be on a separate slip, which we have not seen.
[616] of either oblivion or grudge
[617] Print: Cyclope.
[618] We were not able to identify this allusion.
[619] and a fence

emolumento (cuius modi est comitem palatini) ab imperatoria maiestate per te impetrem, quod ut facias τρὶς καὶ τετρακὶς oro.[620] Eunapium Graecum et Latinum edimus,[621] cuius specimen hic vides, hoc mense finiendi, cum insigni cum tuis virtutibus elogio,[622] quod ante castigationes[623] locorum aliquot prius Graecum exemplar excudendas honorificum, ut me teque dignum fuit, leges, additae tantae morae rationibus. Milesius sequetur nundinas,[624] quod operae finem illi imponere non possint ante id tempus. Interim ut amicitiae pristinae foedus interruptum reparemus aut ferruminemus potius, si videbitur, legem statue. Vale.

106.
Sambucus to Johannes Oporinus
8 February 1568, Vienna

The original is kept in Basel, Universitätsbibliothek, Frey Mscr II 26, 210. Published in Gerstinger, "Die Briefe," 85-87.

Oporinus must have already received the imperial copyright privilege for six years for the indicated titles. If the Augsburg booksellers have not received a sufficient number of copies, he should send Sambucus 60 for the usual price and he will sell them for a better price than the booksellers. Two copies should be sent to the (Imperial) Chancellery. One cannot find in Vienna the book by Riccardo Bartolini, which must have been printed either by Scottus or Soterus. The Cardinal has promised him his travel notes. For an anthology of Ottoman matters Oporinus may use the work by Raphael Maffei or the publications of the Venetian Soncinus. Oporinus could also print Sambucus's battle descriptions (added to Bonfini) and Sambucus will send him soon a long letter on Ottoman matters. There are interesting appendices in a recent edition of Chalcondyles. He also has the work of a Sicilian author on Ottoman matters, of which he has already written. Oporinus should not forget about Sambucus's own works. If he invests in paper, Sambucus will pay it back. He is waiting for Oporinus's delayed letter concerning Baumius, with which he can go to court. He is playing the fool and is unreliable with the money and things with which he had been entrusted. Oporinus should tell Zwinger that next to working on his histories this winter he corrected Quintilian, so he cannot send his conjectures regarding Plato, but will have more time in April when the emperor will be away will offer some results. Oporinus should not despise his Aegineta and Hippocrates if he wants to make sure Sambucus continue in his philological enterprises. If he decides to print them, other texts will be added. He was admonished by Crato, and the letter was written in a hurry.

---

[620] three times and four times
[621] Eunapius, Βίοι φιλοσόφων (1568). See the story of this curious publication in *Humanistes du bassin des Carpates II. Johannes Sambucus*, lvi-lvii; Gerstinger, "Zusammenfassung," 303-305. Cf. the Index.
[622] Eunapius, Βίοι φιλοσόφων, 199-200.
[623] Ibid., 201-213.
[624] [Pseudo-]Hesychius, Περὶ τῶν ἐν παιδείᾳ (1572).

Sambucus salutem.

Scius significavi privilegium esse certum pro libris annotatis in sexennium ac ipsum te iam accepisse credo. Perge igitur et da nobis, quae tantopere expetimus. Quo ad exemplarium numerum, quod quaeris, quid velim abs te fieri, respondeo: si videris bibliopolas Augustanos non valde multa exemplaria accepisse, per quos huc mittuntur, mitte 60 exemplaria et pretium istic solitum, quo citius distrahantur per me meliori pretio, quam bibliopolarum.[625] Duo vere exemplaria pro privilegio in cancellariam mitti debent, ut nosti. De Richardo Bertolino[626] ad Maximilianum I. scias hic non reperiri, nam Argentinae a Sottero credo vel Scotto fuere impressa.[627] Quo ad Hodopericon cardinalis,[628] quidam mihi pollicitus est exemplum suum daturum. Caeteroqui si uno volumine omnia Thurcica [vis] complectere, poteris ex Volaterano,[629] Venetorum historiis, libro Italico Soncini Veneti multa et vere petere.[630] Orationes contra Thurcas aliquot habentur, quas colligam. Poteris quoque obsidiones meas, quas Bonfinio adiicimus, addere,[631] et brevi summam Othomanicorum longa epistola ad te mittam.[632] Scis in Chancondyla prius impresso quoque esse adiecta quaedam Thurcica variorum authorum.[633] Habeo Siceliotam historicum de Thurcis multum et copiosum sed adhuc distractum opus, de quo antea scripsi.[634]

Mi domine Oporine, conciones meas ne prorsus negligito. Si quid te iacturae in carta facturum putas, bona fide restituam. De Baumio tuas serias, quibus tribunal accedamus muniti, expectamus.[635] Nam nugator videtur et varie rem et pecuniam, ut audio, missam excusat. Domino Zvinggero significa me hac hyeme occupasse operam in Quintiliano purgando et praeterea historiis meis,[636] itaque in Platonis quaedam varias lectiones non potuisse[637] mittere, sed Aprili mense caesare absente plus ocii futurum,[638] quo eius laboribus

---

[625] Sambucus is speaking about the copies of Bonfini's *Rerum Ungaricarum decades*.

[626] Riccardo Bartolini († c. 1529) was a humanist from Perugia who moved to Germany after 1513. See F. H. Schubert, "Riccardo Bartolini. Eine Untersuchung zu seinen Werken über den Landshuter Erbfolgekrieg und den Augsburger Reichstag von 1518," *Zeitschrift für bayerische Landesgeschichte* 19 (1956), 95-127.

[627] *Guntheri poetae clarissimi, Ligurinus, seu opus de rebus gestis imperatoris caesaris Friderici I. augusti libris X absolutum. Richardi Bartholini, Perusini, Austriados libri XII Maximiliano augusto dicati* (Argentorati: apud Ioannem Schottum librarium, 1531). Cf. with Gulyás, *Sámboky János könyvtára*, 1617/3.

[628] The Cardinal in question may be Guglielmo Sirleto.

[629] Raffaelo Maffei (Raphael Maffeus Volaterranus) (1451-1522) Italian humanist. His most important historiographical work is his *Commentariorum Urbanorum Raphaelis Volaterrani libri XXXVIII.* (Roma: Ioannes Besicken, 1506). See Gulyás, *Sámboky János könyvtára*, 1593.

[630] The Soncino family was an Italian Sephardic Jewish family of printers. Hieronymus Soncinus did not publish many historical works. Joachim Kirchner, *Lexikon des Buchwesens*, vol. 2. (Stuttgart: Hiersemann, 1953), 722.

[631] Sambucus attached several of his historical essays on battles against the Ottomans to Bonfini's *Rerum Ungaricarum decades*.

[632] Reference may concern Sambucus's manuscript *De Thurcis*, published in Gerstinger, "Aus dem Tagebuch," 45-46.

[633] Laonicus Chalcondyles (Chalkokondyles) (c. 1430-1490) was a Greek historian from Athens, a student of Gemistos Plethon. He completed many diplomatic missions. His *Historiae* (c. 1464) were published also by Oporinus in *Nicephorus Gregoras, Romanae, hoc est Byzantinae historiae libri...* (Basileae: Oporinus, 1562), but Sambucus may think here of the 1567 Paris edition by Chaudière, which had many attachments on Ottoman matters.

[634] Glycas, *Annales*. Glycas was also known as Siculus or Siceliotes, an erronoeus interpretation of the name Michael Sicidites. It is probable but not proven that Glycas and Sicidites were the same person.

[635] Theodor Baumius (Baum) was a Cologne printer, who worked as a partner of Johann Birckmann in 1556-1585 and 1568-1571. See Leonhard Ennen's article in *ADB* 2 (1875), 152.

[636] On Sambucus's work on Quintilian see Gerstinger, "Die Briefe," 86.

[637] ms: *possem*.

[638] This unusual statement suggests that during Maximilian's stay at Vienna the imperial historian either was engaged with specific tasks or had to assume representative duties.

aliqua parte inserviturum me polliceor. Aegynetam et Hippocratem, oro, ne contemnite, ut me in diligentia et labore contineatis.[639] Addentur plura, si animum ostenderitis praelique consilium. Haec subito ad Cratonis nostri admonitionem. Vale, 8 Februarii 1568. Vienna.[640]

Address: Illustrissimo Ioanni Oporino typographo Basiliensi amico honorando. Basell.

107.
Sambucus to Emperor Maximilian II
21 February 1568, Vienna

Dedication in Eunapius, Εὐναπίου ... Βίοι φιλοσόφων.[641]

Although historical and rhetorical writings give abundant instruction on how to live a life virtuously and regulate a state, and thus their authors can be called living philosophy and walking museums, it is the philosophers who have always excelled at explaining these things. No one who discusses these questions will deny that the philosophers through their deeds and lives demonstrate important points and (as much as poets, as it is claimed in that old comedy) improve the morals of the citizens with their dexterity and advice. The discussions and opinions of learned men should not pertain only to private men and the scholars but also to the magistrates and the princes, helping them to better control political matters and preserve their office. Although virtues should be defined through deeds and no praise should be given for what is feigned or simulated, it is easy to be deceived in our judgements. Hence, it should not be seen as bold if Sambucus, when publishing the long awaited Eunapius, links it to Maximilian's name so that it may gain larger circulation.

Invictissimo potentissimoque caesari Maximiliano II. Germaniae, Hungariae, Bohemiae, etc. regi, archiduci Austriae, duci Burgundiae, comiti Tyrolis etc., domino, domino semper clementissimo, salutem.

Quae ad mores vitamque cum virtute degendam, rerumpublicarum temperationem cum maiestate faciunt, etsi ea historicorum et oratorum scriptis cumulate sint testata exemplisque doceantur, ut philosophia ἔμψυχος καὶ μουσεῖον περιπατοῦν[642] dici queant, regulis tamen, fontium naturae propria explicatione, unde dubia solvuntur, certa liquent, in utramque sententiam suppetere iudicio necessaria solent, philosophi semper excelluere. Quare nemo negabit, qui intelligentia, observatione ac disputationibus hoc genus doctrinae diligenter tractarunt (alioqui nuda professione, ut cythara tantum alios oblectarent) eosdem actionibus et vita sua non minima voluisse repraesentare, ut, quod in veteri comoedia Aeschylo de

---

[639] Cf. letters 82, 88 and 119. Also see Gerstinger, "Die Briefe," 307-309.
[640] The letter contains the following marginal notes: "[...] privilegium pro libris Sambuci etc. excudendis; Richardus Bertolinus; Turcica unde petenda; Chalcondyla; Siceliota historicus; Sambuci [conciones]; Quintilianus purgatus a Sambuco; Hippocrates Agyneta."
[641] This dedication is printed only in an honorary copy meant for the emperor, given as a gift by Sambucus, and held today by ÖNB: 74.K.128, f. [2ʳ-3ᵛ] (unnumbered pages), preceeding the Greek text of Eunapius. For this letter see *Humanistes du bassin des Carpates II. Johannes Sambucus*, lvi-lvii and 348-350, where an image of the dedication is reproduced.
[642] a living philosophy and a walking museum. Cf. Eunapius 4.1.3 (456).

poetis quaerenti fuit responsum,⁶⁴³ de philosophis et sophistis pronuncies: dexteritate et admonitionibus eos civium mores reddere meliores. Etenim, ut tua maiestas probe novit atque tenet, sapientum accuratae disceptationes ac sententiae non ad privatorum modo rationes atque scholarum subsellia umbrasque pertinent, sed apud magistratus etiam principesque viros, quod prudentiam acuant, consilia summis negotiis moderandi praebeant, adeoque in officio contineant, valere debent. Quaquam enim virtutum laus actionibus definiatur et quidquid ficte ambitiosaque simulatione apparet, in laude non ponatur, nisi tamen prudenter illa diiudicemus, leviter in tribuendis premiis ornandisque factis ac memoriae celebritate inepteque peccamus, opinione in aliorum rebus gestis labimur velutque pueri aut caeci aberramus. Itaque haud temere cum vestrae sacrae maiestatis nomine tot saeculis Eunapium desideratum philosophiae illum scriptorem acutum, in negotiis versatum, accuratum et planum denique in lucem profero, quem vestrae maiestatis dignatione exemploque alii libentius amplexi, saepius in manibus cum versione docti amici habebunt. Vestram sacram maiestatem Deus salutariter omnibus diutissime conservet, cuius me clementiae subiectissime dudum vovi. Viennae, 9. Kalendas Martiis 1568. Vestrae sacrae maiestatis humillimus clientulus etc. Ioannes Sambucus

108.
Johannes Oporinus to Sambucus
31 March 1568, Basel

The original is kept in ÖNB, Cod. 9737^{z14-18}, I, f. 5^r, Published in Gerstinger, "Die Briefe," 94.

Oporinus is sending Sambucus in a package 90 copies of Bonfini, printed by his associate. Sambucus can take as many as he wants and give the rest to the Chancellery and to Mr Singkmoser and Mr Tanner, to whom he is sending his greetings. If Sambucus wants to sell extra copies, he should sell them for at least 2 florins. In Frankfurt they are sold for a price of one French crown (Écu). He hopes to receive the manuscripts of Glycas and Nonnus, promised by Sambucus. Oporinus has already received the manuscript of Manasses, but it is very corrupt. He has found another copy in Italy and Johannes Löwenklau has started collating them and emending the text. Several things happened to Bonfini's publication in a manner different than he wanted, so it is truly badly printed. As he could not print it in house, he needed to trust others, who did not work as well as promised. He tried to make sure that it got well printed but he could not always be there, especially as it was winter. It will not happen again. Sambucus will receive the index, which was badly printed, from Willer, a certain book agent of Augsburg.

---

⁶⁴³ In Aristophanes's *Frogs* (*Ranae* 1008-1010) Aeschylus asks Euripides "for what quality should a poet be admired," to which Euripides replies "skill and good counsel, and because we make people better members of their communities." Quoted by Jonathan Hart, *Textual Imitation: Making and Seeing in Literature* (New York: Palgrave, 2013), 19.

Salutem.

Historiae Bonfinii a sociis nostris excusae 90 exemplaria proprio vasi inclusa ad te mittimus.[644] Ex quibus, quotquot voles, pro te servabis, reliqua dabis cancellariae et D. Singkmosero[645] et D. Thannero, quos officiosissime meo nomine salutabis. Quos deinde distrahendos curare voles, non minoris quam 2 florenis vendendos curabis, coronato enim Gallico Francofordiae distrahentur. Ego, qui nundinis praesentibus non sum interfuturus, si quid literarum miseris, alio tempore respondebo. Spero autem omnino me Siculum accepturum et Dionysiaca, quae pollicitus es.[646] Manassem iam accepi, sed corruptissimum.[647] Ex Italia aliud exemplar nacti sumus, eius collationem Leoclavius, quia tractare iam coepit, ut longe emendatior in publicum prodeat, curaturus est.[648] In Bonfinii impressione multa mihi praeter animi sententiam acciderunt, adeo male excusus est. Nam quia domi nostrae fieri non potuit, tota editio et magna pars per alios facta est, qui fidelem tamen operam ipsi quoque pollicebantur, multa negligentius, quam vellem, curata sunt. Oro autem, ut eius culpam mihi non imputes. Cavi pro virili, ut bene fieret, sed adesse semper, praesertim per hiemem non potui. Haec excusare ut necesse habeo, ita alio me tempore diligentiorem fore polliceor. Bene vale et nos, ut facis, amare perge. Basileae, pridie Calendas Aprilis 1568. Iohannes Oporinus, tuus ex animo.

Indices, quia serius excusae sunt, post missum iam Francfordiam vas, proprio fasciculo indices inclusimus, quem a Willero Augustano bibliopola accipies, qui se probe et cito ad te missurum recepit.[649]

Address: Doctissimo viro D. Ioanni Sambuco caesareae maiestatis historico, domino et amico suo colendo. Viennae Austriae.
Other hand: Ultima Aprilis

---

[644] Bonfini, *Rerum Ungaricarum decades*. While on the title page it is written that the book appeared in the edition of Oporinus ("ex officina Oporiniana"), the colophon at the end of the book says that it was printed by Bartholomäus Franck and Paul Queck, and the book apparently also needed an investor: "Basileae, per Bartholomaeum Franconem et Paulum Quecum, sumptibus partim successorum Oporini, partim Sigismundi Feirabent. Anno Domini MDLXVIII. Mense Martio."

[645] Mark (Marcus) Singkmoser (Sinckmoser, Singkhmoser) (c. 1522–1569), educated in Tübingen and Bologna, was the Latin secretary of the Imperial Chancellery from c. 1555. Already in 1554 he took part in the preparation of the "Reformatio Nova" of the University of Vienna. He was sent as a diplomat to Constantinople in 1549 and 1550 (from where he sent manuscripts of Greek poems to Wolfgang Lazius). Very soon he became instrumental in imperial diplomacy and religious policy. Singkmoser had many learned friends from the Republic of Letters. Sambucus commemorated his death with a funerary epistle (see letter 132). See Paul Moeller, "Marcus Singkhmoser: The Contributions to History by a Secretary of Ferdinand I." Available at https://paulkarlmoeller.wordpress.com/article/marcus-singkhmoser/ (accessed on 4 December 2022). Also see Almási, *The Uses of Humanism*, passim.

[646] Glycas, *Annales*; Nonnus, *Dionysiaca*. For the story of their publication see *Humanistes du bassin des Carpates II. Johannes Sambucus*, lix-lxi.

[647] Manasses, *Annales*.

[648] This suggests that it was originally Oporinus who contacted Johannes Löwenklau, the editor of the book, who would become the most diligent editor of Sambucus's manuscripts. Cf. *Humanistes du bassin des Carpates II. Johannes Sambucus*, lxiii.

[649] Georg Willer (Wyler) (1514–1593) was an Augsburg bookseller and bibliophile. He issued catalogues of the Frankfurt Book Fair from 1564. See Gerstinger, "Die Briefe," 86 and the article by Karl Steiff in *ADB* 43 (1898), 268-269.

109.
Sambucus to the Mayor and the Council of Trnava
3 April 1568, Vienna

The original is kept in Trnava, SAT, Magistrát mesta Trnava, Missiles. Published in Vantuch, "Die Sambucusbriefe," 340-341.

He did all he could in helping Joseph, an old friend. If some of the mandates were issued late, it was not the fault of the person in charge (Joseph). Joseph will also do his best with regards to the concession of the customs, issued twice by the emperor but sent back to Pressburg as inadequate. Sambucus will also keep doing what he can to get the exemption for them. Joseph's prudency and efficiency need to be duly compensated. They should consider giving a present to the majordomo of the English ambassador, so that the Emperor can praise them to the ambassador.

Salutem et debitam commendationem.

Quibus in rebus adesse domino Iosepho, veteri et cognito amico potui, id non moleste feci, quod vero serius fortasse pars mandatorum aliquibus videbitur curata et expedita, meo testimonio et exemplo veniam curatori tribuetis, cuius diligentiam nemo requisierit, tarditatem per quos stetit, facile accusarit. De th[e]lonio a sua maiestate bis concesso editoque diplomate[650] nuncque inepte Posonium remisso pro informatione omnia navabit dominus Iosephus. Qua tamen cumque via libertatis vestrae salva habebitur ratio, meumque in ea re studium certe numquam defuit, dumque impetratis, non deerit. Proximis meis de Iosephi conditione quiddam ad vos scripseram et salario, cuius quia doctrina in negotiis non vulgaris prudentia in conficienda sedula celeritas vobis antea nota est, pluribus eum non commendabo. Negocia illum vestra expetent, premioque decenti ornabunt atque tuebuntur, quibus me meaque commendo. Vienna, 3 aprilis 1568 Vienna. Vester servitor et filius Sambucus.

Dominationes vestrae recte fecerint, si huic domino magistro curiae legati anglici honorem munusculo vini, avenae, piscium, vel etc. fecerit, idque propter caesarem et archiducem, ut sciat domino legato de vestra humanitate loqui et mihi gratias agere. Valete. Sambucus.

Address: Egregiis dominis iudici senatuique Tyrnaviensi, dominis et amicis suis observandissimis. Tirnaviam.

110.
Sambucus to Archdukes Matthias, Maximilian, Albrecht and Wenzeslaus
5 April 1568, Vienna

Dedication in Gregory of Nazianzus, *Sententiae et regulae vitae ex Gregorii Nazanzeni scriptis collectae. Eiusdem iambi aliquot, nunc primum in lucem editi. Per Ioannem Sambucum Pannonium* (Antwerp: Plantin, 1568), f. A2ʳ-A5ʳ. Published in *Humanistes du bassin des Carpates II. Johannes Sambucus*, 121-124.

---

[650] On the issue of the customs exemption see letters 83 and 103-104.

111.
Joachim Camerarius Sr. to Sambucus
5 April 1568, Leipzig

Published in Camerarius, *Epistolarum libri quinque*, 411-412.

Camerarius was very grateful to get Sambucus's poem and letter, even if received with delay. He is also looking forward to the edition promised by Sambucus, especially the mathematical works. Concerning the edition of Hephaestion and Sambucus's epithets he cannot promise anything, because the local publishers prefer more marketable works. Even his books are queuing up, waiting for publication. But he will try to do something, also with the poems of Gregory of Nazianzus, to which he is eagerly looking forward. Oporinus might be a good choice if Sambucus wants a good edition. Camerarius is worried about the news concerning future French wars and possible attacks on Hungary.

S. D.

Vir clarissime! Versus tui una cum epistola, quamvis sero redditi, fuere mihi gratissimi. Atque exspecto avide ea, quae tuo studio iam edi significas. Utinam et alia, inprimis mathematica, quae penes te sunt, aliquando prodirent in lucem. Hephaestion et *Epitheta* tua adhuc penes me sunt deque illo nihil omnino polliceri possum. De his vero etiam nunc experiar aliquid.[651] Ea autem est, mi Sambuce, fortuna mea, ut non facile officinae hic typographorum vacent iis libellis, quos ego elaborari cupio, occupatae aliorum scilicet magis vendibilium editione. Itaque nostra quoque, quae interdum emitti studeo, apud me delitescunt et nonnulla etiam obsolescunt. Sed tentabimus aliquid, quemadmodum et de Nassianseni versibus, quorum editionem mirifice expeto, si miseris. Quod opus tamen, si vellet recipere ad exprimendum Oporinus noster, fortasse proferretur maturius.[652] De quo tua consideratione id fiet, quod optimum esse putaveris. De voluntate quidem mea meoque studio omnia, quae praestari a me poterunt, tibi velim pollicearis. Hic rumores belli Gallici parientes alios, sane ingratos, hominum animos nonnihil sollicitant.[653] Vobis quoque a vicinis hostibus periculi aliquid impendere creditur. De quo si videbitur, facies me certiorem. Vale. Lipsiae. 5. die mensis Aprilis 68.

112.
Antonius Verantius[654] to Sambucus
12 May 1568, Vienna

---

[651] On Hephaestion see the Index, on Sambucus's epithets see letters 11, 92, 221 and 241

[652] Camerarius apparently did not know about the imminent publication of Gregory of Nazianzus's book by Plantin.

[653] In reaction to the Peace of Longjumeau (1568), which granted significant religious rights to Protestants, Catholics rose up throughout France and Huguenot leaders soon had to flee the court.

[654] Antonius Verantius (Antal Verancsics, 1504–1573) was a diplomat and bishop of Dalmatian origin, one of the most learned churchmen and politician of sixteenth-century Hungary, who left behind a large corpus of Latin correspondence, poems, historical descriptions, notes, choreographies etc. His church career started in 1553, when Ferdinand sent him to Constantinople as one of his ambassadors. After Olahus's death, from 1569, he was archbishop of Esztergom. On Verantius see Birnbaum, *Humanists in a Shattered World*, 213-240;

A copy is kept in Budapest, OSZK, Fol. Lat. 1681/4, f. 14. Published in Antal Verancsics, *Összes munkái*, eds. László Szalay and Gusztáv Wenzel, vol. 9, 1563–1569 (Pest: Eggenberger, 1870), 222 (Monumenta Hungariae Historica, Scriptores 20).

Verantius gives his thanks for Sambucus's congratulatory poem written upon his return from Constantinople, which praises his attempts to arrive at a peace treaty. Likewise he has been happy about everything Sambucus published in recent times and highly appreciates his friendship and learning, which their nation should reward and recompense with offices. He hopes that others will also share his sincere appreciation for Sambucus. He sends him a carpet, but will show him the bezoar stone only personally.

Magnifice domine et frater charissime.

Carmina tua de incolumi reditu meo gratulatoria et plena etiam laudis, qua industriam meam de obtenta pace extollis, fuere mihi quidem gratissima, ut alia tua solent omnia, quae ad multorum utilitatem successivis temporibus excudis, maxime autem, quod primus omnium veteri officio comprobare maturaveris, quam me constanter ames et quanti etiam facias. Cuius erga me tam praeclaram voluntatem quanti ipse quoque faciam, ne vivam, si non pluris, quam multorum aliorum, qui se amici mihi profitentur. Delector enim ex eruditione tua et ingenio tuo, quod quidem certe dignum esse iudico, ut illud gens nostra et ornet praemiis, et honoribus cumulet. Atque ego, ut et simpliciter et sinceriter profero de te hanc sententiam, ita etiam velim me omnes in te amando et ornando sequantur, qui in te agnoscunt, quod ego. Ut autem retineas apud te mnemosinon fuisse me in Turcia et ibi tui meminisse, misi tibi tapetem, Bezaarem[655] vero ipsemet manu mea exhibebo. Vale et sis felix. Viennae XII. Maii 1568.

Address: Ad dominum Sambucum.

113.
Johannes Oporinus to Sambucus
20 May 1568, Basel

The original is kept in ÖNB, Cod. 9737^{z14-18}, I, f. 6^r.

Sambucus surely has received the package with Bonfini's history sent from Frankfurt. Oporinus hopes that Sambucus will like the edition more than he does. Löwenklau has already finished the translation of Manasses's chronicle. He also corrected Sambucus's Greek copy by collating it

---

Gál-Mlakár Zsófia, "Verancsics Antal korának humanista hálózatában. Vázlat egy kapcsolati háló modellezéséhez" [A. V. in the humanist network of his age], *Publicationes Universitatis Miskolcinensis. Sectio Philosophica* 14 (2009), 115-144; Éva Gyulai, "Verancsics Antal," in *Magyar művelődéstörténeti lexikon* 12 (2011), 395-399; idem, "Turcissare – Verancsics Antal török-képe" [Turcissare: Antonius Verantius' Image of Turk], in *Humanista történetírás*, 91-108; and the article by Áron Orbán in *Companion*. For a full bibliography of his works see Kulcsár, *Inventarium de operibus litterariis ad res Hungaricas pertinentibus ab initiis usque ad annum 1700* (Budapest: Balassi–Studiolum, 2004), 569-572.

[655] A stone or a solid object found in the intestines of animals to which curing powers were usually ascribed. The word had many meanings at the time. See Caspar Bauhin, *De lapidis bezaar orientalis et occidentalis cervini item et germanici ortu, natura, differentiis, veroque usu* (Basel: C. Waldkircher, 1613).

with another copy found in Italy. He wishes to have also Glycas's book, as promised by Sambucus. Plantin started to print Nonnus. Oporinus would have preferred if Carolus Utenhovius could also have contributed to the publication. Utenhovius is thinking about writing a preface, mentioning Sambucus's name with respect, if Sambucus agrees. Oporinus wonders about the 50 florins that should be collected from Theodor Baumius in his name. He asks Sambucus to submit the two copies that are due for the imperial privilege to the Chancellery.

Salutem.

Accepisse te vas plenum *Historiarum* Bonfinii Francfordia ad te missum non dubito, mi D. Sambuce.[656] Atque utinam tibi impressio melius placeat, quam mihi. Sed ferendum est, quod mutare iam nequeas. Mihi recte semper adesse impressioni non licuit, adeo multis occupationibus totam hieme fui obtentus. Manassis *Chronicon* iam a Leoclavio absolutum est versione Latina[657] et collatione alterius exemplaris, quod ex Italia accepimus, innumeris in locis Graecum tuum emendatum. Utinam Siculum quoque haberemus, quam es etiam pollicitus, et ut adhuc mittas, vehementer te oro.[658] Nonnum Plantinus excudere coepit, et tuo se exemplari uti gloriatur.[659] Sed vellem Utenhovii etiam opera in excudendo eo uti ipsum potuisse.[660] Cuperet etiam Utenhovius praefari, si per te sibi liceret et honorificam se tui mentionem facturum pollicetur. Si id ferre potes, quaeso prima occasione ad nos scribe. De 50 taleris a Paumio extorquendis meo nomine quid actum sit, spero me item ex litteris tuis intellecturum. Bene vale et libellos alios, quos eidem vasi cum Bonfiniis inclusimus una cum Bonfiniis duobus, cancellariae reddendos pro iure impetrati privilegii, quaeso te, bene cura nosque amare, ornare, beare (ut coepisti) perge. Basileae, 20 Maii 1568. Ioannes Oporinus tuus ex animo.

Address: Doctissimo viro D. Ioanni Sambuco Tirnaviensi cesareae maiestatis historico, venerando domino et amico suo inprimis colendo. Viennae Austriae.
Other hand: 3 Iunii.

---

[656] See letter 108.
[657] Manasses, *Annales*. Johannes Löwenklau (Leunclavius/Leonclavius) (1541–1594) was a Greek scholar and a historian of the Ottomans and the Byzantine period. He was born in Westphalia but spent his early years in Lübeck and Livonia. He studied in Wittenberg and became interested in the Ottomans and the idea of a Protestant mission at a very early age (he personally knew Jacob Heraclides). He was a vagabond humanist living several years in Basel, spending two years in Turin, several in Vienna and also at the court of Karel Žerotín, the famous learned Moravian aristocrat. He also travelled to Constantinople in 1584–1585. He learnt some Viennese patrons partly through Sambucus (e.g. Lazarus von Schwendi and Hieronymus Beck von Leopoldsdorf). He was the most important editor of Sambucus's manuscripts, publishing seven works "ex bibliotheca Sambuci." On Löwenklau see Franz Babinger, "Johannes Lewenklaws Lebensende," *Basler Zeitschrift für Geschichte und Altertumskunde* 50 (1951), 5-26; Dieter Metzler, "Johannes Löwenklau," in *Westfälische Lebensbilder*, ed. Robert Stupperich, vol. 13 (Münster: Aschendorff, 1985), 9-44; Pál Ács, "Pro Turcis and contra Turcos: Curiosity, Scholarship and Spiritualism in Turkish Histories by Johannes Löwenklau (1541–1594)," *Acta Comeniana* 25 (2011), 1-22; *Humanistes du bassin des Carpates II. Johannes Sambucus*, lxiii-lxvi, 204-234; Almut Höfer's article in *Christian-Muslim Relations. A Bibliographical History. Vol. 7.*, eds. David Thomas and John A. Chesworth (Leiden: Brill, 2015), 481-488; and Stolte, "Joannes Leunclavius."
[658] Glycas, *Annales*.
[659] Nonnus, *Dionysiaca*.
[660] Carolus Utenhovius was preparing an edition of the *Dionysiaca*, but the project was completed by Gerhard Falkenburg, who duly acknowledged Utenhovius's contribution. See letter 126.

114.
Sambucus to Conradus Hubertus
12 June 1568, Vienna

A copy of the letter is kept in Zurich, Zentralbibliothek, MS S 118, Nr. 16 (16–17th c.).

Regarding the death of Matthaeus Collinus, Sambucus informs Hubertus that he died two years earlier. He excelled with his learning and religious morals at the University of Prague. Sambucus goes on to praise his religious and intellectual coherence. Collinus was a "politicus", a man of exceptional modesty, whose company made young people better. Sambucus has never read his poems. He would happily help Hubertus in his work on ecclesiastical high offices if he knew more about it. What he has is not worthy to be added, but he can send it to Hubertus. He is sending his greetings to Conrad Dasypodius and others.

Sambucus Conrado Huberto,[661] amico suo veteri, salutem.

Quod de Collini[662] morte quaeris: is ante biennium fere, quo eius mens vitaque adspirabat, domicilium aeternum profectus[663] est. Praefuit scholae Pragensi cum ornamento literarum, tum religionis verae constanti professione. Quae aliquoties illi molestias, sed spe maiorum non graves attulit, mutationem animi et consilii nullam. Fuit in omni vita politicus, modestia rara, et cuius consuetudine iuvenes emendabantur. Haec de eo breviter. Carmen eius nondum vidi. Ita est, ut scribis, pietatem eius numeri et gratiam habent insignem. Tueher bene habetur,[664] quod ex ipsius hic fratre nuper cognovi. Libenter tuos labores in cogendis sacris primatibus iuvarem, nisi suppeteret tibi eius generis argumenta plurima scirem. Mea vero vix digna sunt, quae adiungantur. Si voles tamen, aliquot mittam. Vale et Dasypodium[665] nostrum aliosque de me saluta. Vienna, pridie Idus Iunii 1568.[666]

---

[661] Conradus Hubertus (Konrad, Conrad Hubert) (1507–1577) was a learned Protestant theologian and author of hymns. He studied in Heidelberg and Basel, and maintained a relationship with Oporinus. He was an assistant to Johannes Oecolampadius and later for eighteen years to Martin Bucer in Strasbourg. After Bucer's death he became isolated in Strasbourg and, just like Johannes Sturm, he came into conflict with Strasbourg's new, disciplinarian Lutheran leader Johannes Marbach. He published some of Bucer's works posthumously with the help of Sturm. See the article by Carl Bertheau in *ADB* 13 (1881), 261-263.

[662] Matthaeus Collinus (1516–1566) was a Bohemian Neo-Latin poet and humanist. After his long study in Wittenberg (1530–1540) he became professor of Greek and Latin at the University of Prague. He also opened a private boarding school for wealthier students in his home. On him see Lucie Storchová, "Collinus, Matthaeus". In Companion to Central and Eastern European Humanism. Volume 2. The Czech Lands. Part 1 (Berlin: Walter de Gruyter, 2020), 298-316.

[663] Copyist: *perfectus*.

[664] We were not able to identify this person. It may also be that the copyist misread Sambucus handwriting.

[665] Conrad Dasypodius (Rochefass, Rauchfuss, Rauchfuss, and Hasenfratz) (c. 1530–1600) was professor of mathematics in Strasbourg. He was famous for his astronomical clock constructed for the cathedral of Strasbourg, which apparently reflected heliocentric views, and which he also described in German and Latin. He edited Euclid and several other ancient mathematicians. His father Petrus was famous for his German-Latin dictionary. See Johann Georg Ludolf Blumhof, *Vom alten Mathematiker Conrad Dasypodius* (Göttingen: Schneider, 1796); Wilhelm Schmidt, "Heron von Alexandria, Konrad Dasypodius und die Strasbourger astronomische Münsteruhr," *Abhandlungen zur Geschichte der Mathematik* 8 (1898), 175-194.

[666] Hubertus refers to his exchange of letters with Sambucus in a letter addressed to the Bohemian humanist publisher Thomas Mitis (1523–1591), dated 1 July 1568, printed in *Thomae Mitis Hymnodiae in Messiam libri II* (Pragae: Georgius Nigrinus et Georgius Daczicenus, 1576), f. Aʳ: "Interea tamen ad clarissimum virum D. Iohannem Sambucum caesareae Maestatis historicum Viennae scripsi, si quid ex eo certi de statu vestro

115.
Sambucus to Theodor Zwinger
8 July 1568,[667] Vienna

The original is kept in Basel, Universitätsbibliothek, Frey Mscr II 26, 206. Published in Gerstinger, "Die Briefe," 83-84.

Sambucus does not doubt that Oporinus is in a better place; but he feels sorry for the infant son and the friends. He will do what he can in the case of Konrad Hubert, but he wants his books sent back to him (also the ones kept by Zwinger) through Georg Willer, the bookseller in Augsburg. Zwinger should to talk with (Oporinus's) heirs to send him back his Xenophon with commentaries, Apollonius's Syntax, Bonfini's dialogue, Manasses etc. If Episcopius or others want to print any of them, they should do it indeed, but he lets Zwinger decide about it. Georg Tanner could not help him in obtaining the 50 thalers from Baumius, one will need to go to court. The texts of Nonnus and Stobaeus are being printed by Plantin. He sent epigrams and epitaphs to Jagicius.

Sambucus salutem.

De Oporino quis dubitat, quin bene salutariterque habeat. Filioli amicorumque iacturam doleo.[668] Quod potero, Huberti caussa ex animo faciam,[669] sed ita, si meos libros salvos restituetis.[670] Tu itaque, quos habes, cura Francfortum deferri et ad manum Willeri tradi bibliopolae Augustani,[671] de aliis quoque oro, cum haeredibus agito diligenter. Nam Xenophontis *Conciones* commentariolo illustratas,[672] Apollonii *Syntaxin*,[673] Bonfinium *De pudicitia* etc.,[674] Manassem etc. repeto.[675] Si Episcopius[676] vel alius quid horum imprimere vellent, meo nomine illis deferas, verum non verbis illa excudi sed typis velim. Tuo igitur iudicio, quod videbitur, facies. A Baumio 50 talleros cum Tannero non possum exigere.[677] In foro cum illo nobis res erit necesse. Vale. Scis Nonni Διονυσιακά[678] et Ἐκλογὰς φυσικὰς Stobaei nunc a Plantino imprimi et alia brevi.[679] Vale. Vienna 8. Iulii 1568 raptim.

---

 cognoscere possem. Is mihi superioribus diebus respondit ante biennium fere optimum Collinum pietate constanti ad aeternum domicilium profectum esse."
[667] This letter was dated in Gerstinger to 8 January as he misread July. However, this date is also problematic in as much as Oporinus is supposed to have died on 6 July. Oporinus may have died a month earlier (which we could not verify).
[668] See the preceding note.
[669] Sambucus might refer here to Hubertus's demand for help, alluded to in the preceding letter.
[670] Zwinger's marginal note: "Sambucus libros aliquot ad Oporinum missos repetit."
[671] See letter 108, note 649.
[672] Sambucus may have planned a re-edition of his Δημηγορίαι, or rather he simply never got back the manuscript printed in 1552 by Oporinus (see letter 2).
[673] Apollonius Dyscolus (2nd c. AD) was one of the greatest Greek grammarians in Alexandria. Sambucus's collection of grammatical manuscripts (including Apollonius's work) survives in ÖNB as Cod. Phil. gr. 237 but it is not sure whether this is the book he was demanding back.
[674] Bonfini, *Symposion trimeron* (cf. letters 181-182).
[675] Manasses, *Annales*.
[676] Eusebius Episcopius (1540–1599) was a member of the Episcopius publisher family of Basel. From 1565, his name appeared on books, sometimes together with his brother Nicolaus, at other times independently. He later also bought the printing business of Herwagen. Charles William Heckethorn, *The printers of Basle in the XV. & XVI. centuries* (London: Unwin, 1897), 126-128. Among his major authors were Theordor Zwinger and François Hotman.
[677] See letter 106, note 635.
[678] Nonnus, *Dionysiaca*. See Gerstinger's notes in "Die Briefe," p. 86.
[679] *Stobaeus et Plethon, Stobaei eclogarum libri duo ... et Plethonis de rebus Peloponnesiacis orationes duae.*

Address (verso): Clarissimo viro Theodoro Zvinggero amico optimo. Basell. Epigramata, epitaphia diu misi Iasicio nostro.[680]

116.
Piero Vettori to Sambucus
14 August 1568, Florence

A copy of the letter is kept in Munich, BSB, Clm 791, f. 116ʳ-117ʳ (no. 147) (16ᵗʰ c.). Published in Várady, "Relazioni di Giovanni Zsámboky," 34-35.

Vettori has loved Sambucus for a long time. He especially appreciated Sambucus's praise of him. It was high time to pay back Sambucus for his kindness (which he happily does, as Sambucus deserves it), especially as the Florentine men sent to Vienna told him that he took all possible occasions to express his admiration for Vettori. He now asks Sambucus to support at court the Tuscan Bishop Antenoreo and his young companion Belisario (Vinta), a lover of fine literature, as both are his friends. A second volume of his Variae lectiones *is going to appear soon.*

Petrus Victorius Ioanni Sambuco salutem.

Dilexi ego te iam pridem, Sambuce mi optime et multis magnisque virtutibus commendatissime, ac merito quidem necessitateque mihi huius rei non parva imposita id feci. Quomodo enim non amare potui, ut praeteream alias singulares animi tui dotes, quae facile omnes ad se suspiciendas colendasque trahunt, illum, a quo viderem me tantopere diligi atque ornari. Noli enim putare obscurum mihi ignotumque fuisse testimonium, quod mihi magnum dedisti mediocris mei ingenii et tenuis eruditionis, et quod praeterea in claro et illustri loco posuisti,[681] et si satis negligens tardusque fui in te remunerando, neque tamen id factum est, quia beneficium istud tuum (ita enim appellandum est) parvi duxerim. Contra enim praeclarum semper ipsum eximiumque existimavi, ac merito id quidem. Quae namque res magis grata acceptaque potest esse illi, qui omnem curam suam studiumque consumpsit in honestis artibus persequendis laboreque suo ceteris cupidis litterarum adiuvandis, quam intelligere operam suam non contemni ab illis, qui summum locum in ipsis tenent ac vere existimare de ipsis possunt. Ignosces igitur naturae meae: inde enim profecto hoc, quidquid est incommodi, natum est, quae iners pigraque est admodum in huiuscemodi officiis obeundis ac satis habet consciam sibi esse grati animi expectatque tempus rei isti apte efficiendae, et pari munere, si potest, compensandae idoneum. Sed cum ad vetus istud tuum humanissimum officium erga me accedant cotidie alia ab eodem amore profecta plenaque cuiusdam incredibilis benevolentiae, quomodo ego possum non aliquando expergisci et eniti corrigere pristinam tarditatem. Pervenit enim ad aures meas significatione nostrorum hominum, qui istic sunt missi a duce nostrae reipublicae, te saepe, quavis occasione arrepta, mentionem mei facere atque in omni sermone me plurimum ornare. Cum igitur praeclare huius tuae voluntatis in me ab his honestissimis viris ac mei amantissimis certior factus sim, non putavi ulterius hoc officium proferendum esse et hac mea epistola testare volui me tibi valde obligatum esse ac

---
[680] We were not able to identify the person in question.
[681] Vettori may refer here to the emblem addressed to him by Sambucus: *Emblemata* (1568), 189.

cupere toto animo tibi honorique tuo servire. Quod si maiorem aliquam facultatem aliquando adeptus ero me tibi gratum ostendendi, ipsa libenter utar. Id autem facere videor debere non tantum, ut tibi me probem, verum etiam ne offendam apud alios graves et honestos viros, qui me iure insimularent, nisi luculentum tuum praeconium laudis meae, illo, quo possem, genere honoris compensarem, praesertim cum id recte et sine suspicione ulla assentationis facere possim. Ut autem sentias quantopere tibi confidam, dum de reddenda gratia tecum loquor, venit mihi in mentem te rogare, ut cumulum addas superiori illi tuo officio. Hoc autem est, ut ames oratorem nostri ducis, Ludovicum Antenoreum,[682] honestissimum sacerdotem et singularis prudentiae virum nec non comitem etiam ipsius Bellisarium adolescentem probum et politarum litterarum studiosum,[683] qui ambo mihi amicissimi sunt, nec tantum ames, verum etiam gratia et auctoritate, qua flores in ista splendidissima aula, ipsos iuves. Erit hoc mihi vehementer gratum.[684] Ut autem aliquid tibi narrem, quod ad nostra studia pertineat, exciditur hic nunc alterum meum volumen *Variarum Lectionum*, quod ego superiori illi meo adiunxi.[685] Cum vero absolutum opus erit, statim exemplar eius unum ad te mittetur. Tu vero in optimo isto tuo erga me animo perseverabis. Vale. Florentiae, XIX. Kalendas Septembris 1568.

117.
Sambucus to Johannes Crato
25 August 1568, Vienna

Published in Gerstinger, "Die Briefe," 87-88.

As Greek language and philosophy teaching is in vogue in the Saxon grammar schools, Crato may want to send the attached Greek letters by Manuel Chrysoloras to Camerarius, who is planning an edition of Latin correspondence of learned men, as Crato has told him. The oration by Polemon of Laodicea could be added to it, which was corrupted by someone but collated by Sambucus. The only old copy of it he saw with the abbot of Barletta in Apulia. The edition of these works will be the most useful at schools. Crato should urge Camerarius to add to them his letters and similar letters of others. He must also add that there is surely hope of finding pieces of Menander's remaining comedies with the bishop of Konya. Nonnus's Dionysiaca *will be out by the time of the coming Frankfurt book fair.*

---

[682] Ludovico Antenoreo was bishop of Volterra. He was apparently the only translator to the Florentine legate.

[683] Belisario Vinta (1542–1613) from Volterra had a spectacular political career in the service of the Duke of Florence, marrying into the family of the first secretary (Bartolomeo Concini), then succeeding to the office of his father-in-law. He was instrumental in bringing Galileo to Florence. See Paola Volpini's voice in *DBI* 99 (2020), 124-126.

[684] This was the point of the letter. Vettori asked the same from Johannes Crato in a letter written on the same day. Petrus Victorius, *Petri Victorii ad Cratonem, Thomam Rehdigerum et Hieronymum Mercurialem epistolae*, ed. Franciscus Passow (Vratislaviae: n.d., 1823), 13-14.

[685] Petrus Victorius, *Petri Victorii Variarum Lectionum XIII. Novi Libri* (Florentiae: Filii Laurentii Torrentini et Carolus Pettinarius, 1568 [appeared in 1569]). A Giunta-edition also appeared in 1569. In the 1580s a joint edition of the 38 books appeared, collecting the 25 books published in 1553 and the 13 books from 1568.

I. Sambucus doctori Cratoni suo salutem.

Cum praesertim in Saxonicis gymnasiis graecae philosophiae et linguae studium vigeat, cuius consilii Μουσαγέτου ὄντος τοῦ Ἰωαχείμου ἡμετέρου[686] praeclara exempla in dies prodeunt, si tibi videbitur, has Chrysolorae Atticas et sententiis gravibus plenas epistolas ad ipsum mittes,[687] cum ex te intellexerim, Latinas doctissimorum virorum ipsum edere constituisse. Poterit adiici Polemonis Sophistae[688] depravatae quidem ab aliquo sed a me collatae orationis exemplum, cuius vetus apud solum Barletanum abbatem in Appulia vidi. Gratissimam horum editionem fore scholis non dubito, tu vero Ioachimum[689] hortabere suas et aliorum similes addat, quo iuventus ad veterum et ab illis non alienorum imitationem constanter nitatur. Non possum hic non adscribere μετὰ χάριτος[690] Menandri reliquiarum certam spem factam et apud Iconii episcopum extare. Nonni Διονυσιακά hoc Francfortensi mercatu habebimus.[691] Vale. 8. Kalendas Septembris 1568. Ex Museolo nostro Viennae. Camerariumque ex me salutato.

Address: Clarissimo doctissimoque domino doctori Ioanni Cratoni etc.

118.
Sambucus to Piero Vettori
1 September 1568, Vienna

The original is kept in Munich, BSB, Clm 734, Nr. 191. Published in *Clarorum Italorum et Germanorum epistolae*, 2:19-23; Gerstinger, "Die Briefe," 88-91.

Sambucus is grateful for Vettori's acknowledgement, especially that he is a unique scholar of all times. However, for judging Sambucus's merits there is no need for an orator; he strived more than excelled and rightly acknowledges and loves Vettori and his like as his master. If Vettori's praise were only partially true he would already feel that he had accomplished enough. Even if he himself cannot write anything extraordinary, he has worked a great deal on correcting and divulging texts, as Vettori must have realised from the catalogues of the Frankfurt book fairs. In two months Vettori will have Nonnus's Dionysiaca *elegantly printed and in many places corrected. He was happy to see the book*

---

[686] the guide for the Muses is our Joachim
[687] Manuel Chrysoloras (c. 1350–1415) was a pioneer of Greek learning, a very important figure for Italian humanism. He was invited to Florence by Coluccio Salutati in 1396 and passed several years also in Venice and Rome, visiting also Germany. His Greek letters are in Migne's *Patrologia graeca*, vol. 156. See Lydia Thorn-Wickert, *Manuel Chrysoloras (ca. 1350–1415): eine Biographie des byzantinischen Intellektuellen vor dem Hintergrund der hellenistischen Studien in der italienischen Renaissance* (Frankfurt am Mein: P. Lang, 2006); Ruth Webb, "Describing Rome in Greek: Manuel Chrysoloras' Comparison of Old and New Rome," in *Villes de toute beauté*, eds. Paolo Odorico and Charis Messis (Paris: Centre d'Études Byzantines, 2012), 123-133. Sambucus's collection of Manuel Chrysoloras's letters was never returned. For a fuller account see note 1999 to letter 351.
[688] Polemon of Laodicea (c. 90–144) was the head of one of the best schools of rhetorics in Smyrna. His only fully preserved works are his funeral orations in the memory of Athenian heroes who died at the Battle of Marathon in 490 BC. Sambucus's manuscript apparently did not get back to Vienna. See Gerstinger, "Johannes Sambucus als Handschriftensammler," 330.
[689] Two weeks later Joachim Camerarius came to Vienna and stayed in Crato's house. See Gerstinger, "Johannes Sambucus als Handschriftensammler," 344, note 1.
[690] with grace
[691] Nonnus, *Dionysiaca*.

of Hipparchus published, but he has a better manuscript of it. The bishop of Volterra and Belisario are the most learned men. Sambucus adores them and will do for them whatever little he can. He much desires to see the second book of Vettori's Variae lectiones. *Sambucus complains about men who abuse this kind of philological works, give annoyance to great men because of typo mistakes and make conjectures without having consulted old codices. Sambucus joins to the letter some of his philological observations and asks what Vettori thinks of them. Vettori may add them to his observations (i.e. the* Variae lectiones*), if this is not too ambitious to ask.*

Domino Petro Victorio Ioannes Sambucus salutem.

Ego vero de ista humanitate praeter meritum effusiore tua sensuque erga me liberali, nisi aliquando gratus sim, ἀνάξιος ἂν εἴην τοσαύτης φιλίας.[692] Prolixa sunt, mi Victori, quae Sambuco tribuis eoque ampliora, quod abs te, hoc est omnium literatorum nostra memoria exemplo singulari, proficiscantur. Sed quantus sim, paucis emetiri quisque vel non tantus ῥήτωρ[693] poterit, qui ab ineunte aetate ad literarum elegantiam non quidem excellens verumtamen studiosus et cupidus tantum videor assecutus, ut te tuique similes in praeceptoribus agnoscam, diligam, omni observantia colam. Quod si umbram ego tantae commendationis obtinuero, navasse operam satis putabo, qui, quando a me ipse nihil egregii lucubrare queam, in alienis eruendis, sanandis divulgandisque adhuc fere sum versatus, quorum nomina ex indice Francfortensi vos percepisse non dubito. Nonni quoque *Διονυσικὰ* [!] intra duos menses elegantissime impressa typis, non paucis locis correctis habebis.[694] Hipparchum vidi libenter, sed ego exemplar integrius possideo.[695] Interpretem vestrum Volateranum episcopum, una et Belisarium, ob mirificam humanitatem, eruditionem raram, usum copiosum, suaves et sententiis plenos et aptos sermones ita complector ut reve[re]or, quibus de authoritate mea nihil polliceor, opera, si quid efficere poterit, absque exceptione praestabit. Secundum *Lectionum* tomum discupio videre et quamprimum ex eo locupletior ornatiorque fieri.[696] Multi hodie tuo praecipue exemplo id genus scriptionis arripuere, sive potius corrupere, qui levissime summis viris ob syllabulam infesti esse caeperunt, cum ex aliis audita coniecturisque eorum, qui nullos viderunt veteres codices, sua vestiunt. Ἐρρωμένος εὐδαιμόνησον[697] et Sambucum, licet Tomitanis paene vicinum patria, tuis tuorumque rebus omnia velle et cupere tibi persuadeas. Vienna, Kalendis Septembris 1568.

Dum has exaro, venit mihi in mentem adscribere aliquot observatiunculas, quas tuo iudicio permitto et, si quid esse putaris, facile etiam in extremo alicubi tuorum patiar adiungi, si tamen id non ambitiose a me fieri apud tantum virum cogitaris vel potius inepte.

    1. In Arati *Phaenomenis* 161: δεινὴ γάρ κείνη etc. et sequens versus, ἀστέρες οὐκ ἂν τοὺς etc., hic versus sequi iste addique debet: ἀστέρες οἵ μην[698] ὄπισθεν ἑλισσόμενοι τυπόωσιν. Deinde excusus habet ibi: ποσσὶ δὲ ἀμφοτέροισι; legendum omnino ex vetere codice ὀπισθοτέροισιν.[699]

---

[692] I would be unworthy of such a frendship
[693] orator
[694] Nonnus, *Dionysiaca*.
[695] *Hipparchi Bithyni in Arati et Eudoxi Phaenomena libri III. Eiusdem liber asterismorum. Achillis Statii in Arati Phaenomena. Arati vita et fragmenta aliorum veterum in eius poema* (Florentiae: Giunta, 1567). Sambucus's manuscript of Hipparchus is preserved in Vienna, ÖNB, Cod. Phil. gr. 14 (f. 193ʳ-221ʳ).
[696] Cf. letter 127, where he expresses his disappointment about the new volume of Vettori's *Variae lectiones*.
[697] be strong and happy
[698] Sambucus writes μην without an accent, as it was most probably just a slip of a pen for μιν transmitted in the younger manuscripts of Aratus.
[699] Aratus, *Phaenomena* 141–149.

2. In Plutarchi libello paene initio *Περὶ δεισιδαιμονίας* mendum est non ferendum, cum legitur: ἐκβολαὶ ἀνθρώπων; legendum, ut sit sensus aliquis, ἄρθρων, et facile abbreviatio librariis imponit.[700]

3. In Halicarnasseo meo *Περὶ συνθέσεως ὀνομάτων* additur initio προσφώνησις:[701] ᾧ φίλε Ῥοῦφε Μηλέτιε.[702]

4. Eleganter Vergilii illud *ignavum fucos pecus a praesepibus arcet* ex *Oeconomia* Xenophontis expressum κηφῆνας ἀχρήστους ὄντας et paullo post ἐκ τῶν σμηνῶν ἀφαιρεῖν. Quomodo etiam Horatius illud *Multa tulit fecitque* etc. ex *Συμποσίῳ* eiusdem de Autolyco πολλοὺς μὲν πόνους πολλὰ δ' ἄλγη ἀνέχεται.[703]

5. Quem hodie Josephum Graecum habemus, non de Hebraeo est translatus, a quo plurimum differt, sed omnino credo de interpretatione omnium prima Latina Ruffini Graecam translationem factam, idque observaturo patebit. Quomodo nec Plinii *De viris illustribus* librum esse credo sed Asconii Pediani, stili oratorii ratione et quia Asconius fatetur se quoque de urbe Patavina scripsisse. Quomodo nec dialogos vel disputationem Athanasii esse contra Eutychum et Nestorium puto, sed eius nomine Vigilius fatetur se eum librum scripsisse, Graeci demum transtulerunt. Sic ἀνώνυμα σχόλια in Theocritum quidam prodidit esse Triclinii, cum Tzetzes expresse in 2. *Iliados* confirmet esse Ἀμαράνθου τοῦ γραμματικοῦ. Nec ἀποδείξεις illae geometricae in Euclidem sunt Theonis, sed ipsiusmet auctoris. Theon tamen illa disposita ordinate locupletioraque edidit, ut in exemplari meo, qui Bessarionis fuisse fertur, apparet.

6. Pindarus in *Pythiis* pulchre ἀφοριστικὸν[704] illud Hippocratis explicat, ὀξὺς καιρός etc.: Καιρὸς πρὸς ἀνθρώπῳ βραχὺ μέτρον ἔχει.[705]

7. Initio fere *Παραινετικοῦ* Isocratis omnes legunt: σὺ μὲν ἀκμὴν φιλοσοφεῖς. Vetustissimus codex legit melius: σοὶ μὲν ἀκμὴν φιλοσοφεῖν etc.[706]

8. Non possum reticere particulam *et* pro *et tamen* usurpari a Cicerone elegantissime Graecorum more, qui καὶ pro ὅμως ponunt. Demosthenes in *Corona* σὺ τοίνυν τοιοῦτος εὑρεθεὶς καὶ βλέπειν εἰς τὰ τουτωνὶ πρόσωπα τολμᾷς;[707]

9. Quarto *Ὀδυσσείας* de Pharo insula dum fit narratio, Εἰδοθέην nominat filiam Protei, sed reperio non male Εὐρυνόμην legisse etiam Zenodotum.[708]

10. In primo *De generatione animalium* Aristotelis folio 350 basiliensi asterisco recte suppletur locus, sed cum legitur ἐν τῷ γήρᾳ, adde τοῦ ἀφροδισιάζειν. Leve est, quod in θ' περὶ ζώων initio τὰ δ' ἤδη pro ἤθη legitur. Et in fine quinti περὶ ζώων distinctione prima, ibi οἷον μέλιττα καὶ σφήξ, adde ἐπὶ τὸ ἐν τοῖς ποταμοῖς. Initio vero secundi, cum legitur τὰ μὲν κοινὰ πάντων ἐστί insere ἀπολελυμένα τῶν ἀνθρώπων etc.[709]

Sed haec ἐξ ἀσυσκευάστων[710] aliquot, faciem papyri ut compleant, obiter adieci nugasque ipse aio. Vale.

---

[700] Plutarchus, *De superstitione* 164f.
[701] an address
[702] Dionysius Halicarnassensis, *De compositione verborum* 1.
[703] Vergilius, *Georgica* 4.168; cf. Xenophon, *Oeconomicus* 17.14; Horatius, *Ars* 413; Xenophon, *Symposium* 8.37.
[704] aphorism
[705] Hippocrates, *Aphorismi* 1.1; Pindarus, *Pythia* 4.286.
[706] Isocrates 1.3.
[707] Demosthenes 18.282-283.
[708] *Odyssea* 4, 366; Cf. Eustathius, *Commentarii ad Homeri Odysseam* ad loc.
[709] Aristoteles *De generatione animalium* 725b20; *Historia animalium* 588a18; 489a32; 497b6. Sambucus is quoting the third Basel edition, Ἀριστοτέλους ἅπαντα (Basileae: per Ioannem Bebelium et Michaelem Isingrinium, 1550), however the passage in question and the asterisk he mentions are on p. 354, not 350.
[710] from among random

119.
Sambucus to Theodor Zwinger
20 September 1568, Vienna

The original is kept in Basel, Universitätsbibliothek, Frey Mscr II 26, 211. Published in Gerstinger, "Die Briefe," 92-95.

Hieronymus Wolf wrote Sambucus from Augsburg that he knew nothing for certain about Oporinus's library, and he did not even know if Löwenklau was in Basel, to whom Sambucus wanted to send something. Zwinger knows how much he and Oporinus loved and honoured each other, but Oporinus' printing press, busy with the works of others, was too slow for him. Sambucus lists his books that Zwinger will find in Oporinus's library (Bonfini, Apollonius, Xenophon, Manasses, Hippocrates, Aegineta, Palladius etc). Oporinus sent him 90 copies of Bonfini. He needed 8 copies, distributed 12 to Oporinus's friends as he wished and to the Chancellery in return for the privilege and to Ulrich Zasius, Georg Tanner, Mark Singkmoser etc. He sold 70 to the bookseller Schiller for 2 florins and 8 kreuzers each, who sold no more than 40 volumes, since some other booksellers also took some copies. As soon as they are all sold, he will send the money to Oporinus's heirs, but three copies were destroyed by water. The rest he will keep himself. He loves Zwinger's works and does not doubt that they will also sell for a profit. He is, however, surprised to see that Zwinger abandoned Hippocrates and Aegineta. Camerarius (who is in Vienna) and Crato are sending their greetings. If Zwinger sees Sambucus's Greek epitaphs on Oporinus's death, he should correct a mistake.

Ioannes Sambucus salutem.

Hieronymus Volfius ad me Augusta scribens significat se de Oporini bibliotheca nihil certi adhuc cognovisse, minus an Leonclabius istic sit, ad quem missurus quaedam eram.[711] Testis locuples es, mi Zuingere, quantum ego Oporinum amarim, vicissim ille me quanti fecerit, eiusque honorificae ingenii opinionis, quando potui, exempla etiam cum eo facile communicabam, sed typi aliorum occupati vigiliis serius mihi inserviebant. Reperies igitur, nisi omnino fallor, salvos in eius libris haec mea, quae ut quam primum reddantur aut per alios edi curentur, valde oro:

 1. Bonfinium *De pudicicia coniugali*.
 2. Apollonii *Syntaxim* a me auctam commentatamque.
 3. *Conciones* Xenophontis rhetorico artificio recognitas et oratiunculas funebres et epitomen rhetorices Graecam.
 4. Manassis *Chronica*.[712]
 5. Hippocratem, Aegynetam, Palladium[713] etc., quos nosti.

Caeterum miserat Bonfinii exempla 90 ad me; ex iis 8 pro me servavi, duodecim distribui amicis eius, uti iusserat, et in cancellariam nomine privilegiorum itaque Zasio, Tannero, Synkmosero etc.[714] Septuaginta vendideram bibliopolo Schillero nostro binis florenis 8 kruceris, sed quoniam alii bibliopolae mediocrem numerum quoque attulerant, non plus

---
[711] Cf. letter 115.
[712] See ibid.
[713] Cf. the Index.
[714] Cf. letter 108.

quam 40 adhuc vendidit, reliqua in spe sunt. Ubi distracta erunt, pecunia haeredibus erit parata, sed tria exemplaria aquis et defectu corrupta sunt, reliqua apud me habeo. Amo lucubrationes tuas nec dubito te aliquid hoc quoque mercatu egregium produxisse,[715] sed miror Hippocratem et Aegynetam deseruisse te, etsi ἀντιβαλλόμενον[716] erit labor platonicus. Camerarius apud nos est Viennae,[717] is te quoque salvere et Crato iubent. Ἔρρωσο εὐτύχει [718] Vienna 12. Kalendas Octobris 1568.

Si ad vos pervenerunt duo epigrammatia mea de obitu Oporini in Graeco versiculum illum οἳ γὰρ Ὀπορίνου etc. ita: πῶς τιν᾽ Ὀπορίνου θυμὸς πραπίδες τε λαθοῖεν vel pro οἳ ἤ tantum posito;[719] uti voles.

120.
Joachim Camerarius Sr. to Sambucus
[Late September 1568[720]], Vienna

Published in Camerarius, *Epistolarum libri quinque*, 412-413.

"Greetings.[721] Some old author says that a certain Diotimus, when sitting among boys and reciting the alphabet for them, was lamenting. Now I am sitting here bewailing in the same way that I have been so long away from the place where I used to teach, holding lectures about the alphabet, that is, about grammar. I wish I had the opportunity to return immediately to our institute, but not before I have spent time, in some way, with the treasures in your library, certainly as long as the flow of your benevolence and our occupations, or rather, to tell the truth, our laziness permits. As a matter of fact, I am taking sweet amusement in turning the pages and spending time with the books I have taken from you, from the banquet where you welcomed me so kindly and generously. Thus, a great desire has grown in me to watch at least the labels and titles of the rest; I would like to delight in them. I wish, if God wants it as well, that it be convenient for you before long. I have already sent to you something of our work, about which we talked recently. Although it has been prepared with eagerness for certain studies, I worry that in erudition and elegance it is not matching my eagerness. However, you will make a sound judgment in a friendly but fair way of it, and will tell me what seem to you as correctly or misguidedly done. Farewell." The letter continues with *"a noble maxim very much appropriate for our times",* which Camerarius is sending to Sambucus together with his translation: *"The one who is obstinate and loves noisy quarrels has*

---

[715] Sambucus probably refers to Zwinger's *Theatrum humanae vitae*, which first appeared in 1565. He received the new edition as a gift in 1571, see letter 174. (Sambucus's catalogue does not indicate it, see Gulyás, *Sámboky János könyvtára.*)
[716] excuse
[717] Camerarius stayed with Crato but was Sambucus's guest not much before. See Gerstinger, "Die Briefe," 95.
[718] good bye and good luck
[719] how could anyone fail to recognize Oporinus's spirit and mind. Cf. letter 115.
[720] The letter should be dated right after Camerarius's and Crato's visit of Sambucus on 21 September (of which Sambucus took note in his diary). Sambucus, in his response (see the next letter) remarks, that he is sending some peaches (!) to Camerarius as a gift. Camerarius arrived to Vienna in early September and stayed in Crato's place until mid-December. On his Viennese stay see recently Steinmann, "Camerarius' *Libellus Gnomologicus*" 102-106.
[721] We provide a translation of the Greek text and a paraphrase of the Latin parts.

known during all his life how to fuel discord and cherish hatred and hostility. The person who is fond of truth uses his conscience as kind of scales in a balanced way for the thing, which we are told, and thus he does not want to be superior using all his wickedness, but in some things he easily accepts being inferior with honesty."

Ἰωάννῃ Σαμβύκῳ.

Χαίρειν. αἰάζειν τις τῶν πάλαι φησὶ Διότιμόν[722] τινα ὅπου καθήμενος παισὶν βῆτα καὶ ἄλφα λέγει. ἐγὼ δ᾽ ἐνθάδε κάθημαι ὀδυρόμενος, ὅτι ἄπειμι τοσοῦτον ἤδη χρόνον ἐκεῖθεν, ὅπου τὰ ἀλφαβητικὰ τοντέ ἐστι τοὺς γραμματικοὺς λόγους ἀσκήσαιμ᾽ ἂν διδάσκων, καὶ βουλοίμην ἄρ᾽ ἐξουσίας τοαυτίκα τυχεῖν τοῦ πρὸς τὸ ἡμέτερον ἐπιτήδευμα ἀπερχόμενον ἀναστρέψασθαι, οὐ πρότερον μέντοι ἤπερ τοῖς τῆς βιβλιοθήκης σοῦ θησαυροῖς ἐμφιλοχωρῆσαι πως ἐφ᾽ ὅσον γε τό, τε τῆς χρηστότητός σου πρόθυμον καὶ αἱ ἡμέτεραι ἀχολίαι ἢ μᾶλλον, ἵνα τ᾽ ἀληθὲς φράσω, νωθεῖαι συγχωρήσουσι. νυνὶ μὲν οὖν ἃς διαψιλῶς θ᾽ ἅμα καὶ φιλοφρόνως ἐστιαθεὶς παρά σοι βίβλους ἐκομισάμην ἀπιών, ἐκείνας ματαχειριζόμενος διέρχομαί τε καὶ ἐνδιατρίβων αὐταῖς ἡδέως ψυχαγωγοῦμαι. ἐγείρεται δ᾽ οὕτως μᾶλλον καὶ τῶν ἐπιγραφῶν μόνον ἀπολαύειν. γενήσεται δὲ τοῦτο, θέλοντος τοῦ θεοῦ, καί σου εὐκαιροῦντος, ὅσον οὐκ ἤδη. ἔπεπεμψα δέ σοι νῦν τῶν ἡμετέρων ἐκπονήσεων τι, περὶ ὧν πρώην εἴπομεν, οὐ μὲν ἀσπουδεί γε, δέδια δὲ ὡς οὐκ ὁμοίως ἐμμούσως τε καὶ ἐμμελῶς συντεθέν. ἀλλὰ περὶ τούτου σὺ γνώμην οἴσῃ, φιλικῶς ὁμοῦ καὶ δικαίως, ἀποφαίνων περὶ τῶν εὖ τε καὶ ἡμαρτημένως ἐχόντων. ἔρρωσο.

Mitto ad te sententiam praeclaram et nostris temporibus admodum congruentem, una cum mea versione. Hoc enim te velle fieri animadverti. Iterum vale.

Ἐξ Ἀνδρονίκου τινὸς Κομνηνοῦ *Κατὰ Ἰουδαίων*.[723]
ὁ μὲν γοῦν φιλόνεικος διὰ πάσης μεμάθηκε τῆς ἑαυτοῦ ζωῆς διαφέρεσθαι τὴν ἔχθραν καὶ ἀσπάζεσθαι, ὁ δὲ φιλαλήθης καθάπερ πλάστιγγα τὴν ἑαυτοῦ συνείδησιν ἀρρεπῶς ἐπιβάλλων τοῖς λεγομένοις, οὐ πάντα νικᾶν κακῶς βούλεται, ἀλλ᾽ ἔστι εἰς ἃ καὶ ἡττᾶσθαι καλῶς ἀνέχεται.

Qui contentiosus est et rixas amat, is toto vitae suae tempore novit dare operam dissidiis, et amplecti odia atque inimicitas. Veritatis autem studiosus applicando veluti trutinam conscientiae suae aequabiliter ad ea, quae dicuntur, ita non ipse superior esse vult per omnia improbitate sua, sed in nonnulus facile patitur se esse inferiorem cum honestate.

---

[722] Diotimus of Adramyttium was a Greek grammarian teaching in the town of Gargara, probably in the third century BC. He was known to Camerarius through an epigramm by the poet Aratus, in which he lamented Diotimus's lot, transmitted by Stephanus of Byzantium in the entry Γάργαρα.

[723] "From the work of a certain Andronicus Comnenus against the Jews." Andronicus Comnenus Ducas Palaeologus, *Dialogus contra Iudaeos*, 37. The work is occasionaly attributed to the byzantine emperor Andronicus I Comnenus, but was written by a nephew of the emperor Michael VIII (see *Prosopographisches Lexikon der Palaiologenzeit*, eds. E. Trapp et al. (Vienna: Österreichische Akademie der Wissenschaften, 1976–1996), nr. 21439. See A. Lukyn Williams, *Adversus Judaeos. A Bird's Eye View of Christian Apologiae until the Renaissance* (Cambridge: University Press, 1935), 181-187; Andreas Külzer, *Disputationes graecae contra Iudaeos* (Stuttgart-Leipzig: Teubner, 1999), 195-199 (here the work is ascribed to an otherwise unknown nephew of the Emperor Andronicus II). The Greek text, which is transmitted only in very few manuscripts, has not been edited yet, while a Latin translation is found in *Patrologia Graeca* 133, 797-924. Sambucus's manuscript of Andronicus, from which Camerarius probably had this quotation, is held in Vienna, ÖNB, Cod. theol. gr. 118.

121.
Sambucus to Joachim Camerarius Sr.
[Late September 1568[724], Vienna]

The original is kept in Munich, BSB, Clm 10363, f. 29ʳ. Published in Gerstinger, "Die Briefe," 154-155.

"I read your letter, o most venerable Camerarius, full of certain fatherly benevolence and true friendship. At the same time I am grateful to you for the things published ever so wisely and learnedly. I agree with you that the basic education matters are as you say. I would wish that you unreservedly take advantage not only of the bible manuscripts, but of all that I have, if you, a man so great, and polished to precision in arts, and much spoken of, now even in imperial business above all other illustrious men, think that I possess something useful. For among the first, without flattering the physicians and the soundly earnest works of piety, we promote and praise both what concerns faith and the errors of the Christians, and we hope that you will correct the struggling, so to say, church, which suffers with sedition, and that you will bless this land forever with your treasures. So do not mention any composition or grammar disputation like some cantankerous person, but rather help to complete the defence of the Lord that you have taken in hand, as the one who will instead receive an everlasting gift in return. For you know that the road to heaven opens up for those who are careful and capable of recovery in such things. Rescue therefore what is public good, o most blessed old man at the edge of the grave, and be strong, and excuse the one who in a puerile Latin fashion writes Greek in an unaccustomed way. Yours, Johannes Sambucus. As a present I send you some peaches."

Ἀνέγνων τοὐπιστόλιον σοῦ, ὦ αἰδεσιμώτατε Καμεράριε, πατρικῆς τινος εὐνοίας τε καὶ ἀληθοῦς φιλίας γέμον· ἅμα δὲ καὶ τὰ νῦν σοι σοφῶς καὶ πάνυ φιλολόγως ἐκδοθέντα χάριν γινώσκω. Συνομολογῶ σοι τὰ περὶ τῶν ἀλφαβετικῶν, ὡς γράφεις, ἔχοντα. Οὐ μόνον δὲ τῶν βιβλικῶν ἐπιγραφῶν σε ἀπολαύειν, ἀλλὰ καὶ ἁπάντων τῶν παρ' ἐμοὶ διακορῶς ἂν βουλοίμην, εἴπερ ἡγῇ τόσος ἀνὴρ καὶ ἐπὶ τῶν μουσικῶν ἐς ἀκριβὲς ἀπεξεσμένος πολυθρύλλητός τε, νῦν δὲ καὶ αὐτοκρατρικαῖς πραγματείαις διαφερόντως λαμπρῶν, κατέχειν με ὀφέλιμόν τι. Ἐν πρώτοις γὰρ ἄνευ κολακίας τῶν ἰατρῶν καὶ ὑγιεινῶς σπουδαίων τῶν θεοσεβείας ἔργων προτίθεμεν, ἐγκωμιάζομεν καὶ τὰ περὶ πίστεώς τε καὶ χριστιανῶν σφάλματα, καὶ σφαδάζουσαν, ὡς εἰπεῖν, στασιαστικῶς τε τυχοῦσαν τὴν ἐκκλησίαν σε ἐπανορθώσοντα ἐλπίζομεν καὶ θησαυροῖς ἐς ἀεὶ ταύτην χώραν μακαρίσοντα. Μὴ οὖν μηδεμίας ἀναστροφῆς νῦν ἢ γραμματικῆς σχολῆς μεμψιμοιροῦντι ἐοικὼς ὑπομνήμισκε [!], ἀποτελεῖν μᾶλλον βοήθει μεταχειριζόμενος τὴν κυριακὴν προβολήν, ἀντιληψόμενος ἀντίδωρον αἰώνιον· Οἶσθα γὰρ τοῖς ἐπιμελῶς καὶ σωτηρίως περὶ τοιούτων ἔχουσιν ἄνοδον εἰς οὐρανὸν ἀναπέτασθαι· σῶσον οὖν τὰ κοινά, ᾧ μακάριστε τυμβογέρον, καὶ ἐρρωμένως εὐτυχῶν, παιδαριωδῶς ῥωμαϊστὶ τὰ ἑλληνικὰ ἀπειθισμενῶς τε γράψαντι σύγγ(ν)ωθι· ὁ σὸς Ἰωάννης Σαμβῦκος.

Δῶρόν σοι πέμπω περσικὰ ἐνιά τινα μῆλα.

Address: Clarissimo viro domino Ioachimo Camerario etc., praeceptori et amico suo.

---

[724] This letter is a direct answer to the preceding one and should be dated not later than the end of September 1568, as Sambucus mentions sending some peaches along with the letter in the postscript. Cf. also note 720 to the preceding letter.

122.
Sambucus to Piero Vettori
11 November 1568, [Vienna]

The original is kept in Munich, BSB, Clm 734, no. 199. Published in Gerstinger, "Die Briefe," 95.

By inserting among his observations some of those of Sambucus, Vettori is offering him more than private acknowledgment, he is blessing him with a public token of his friendship, which is difficult to pay back. Sambucus asks Vettori to secure for him while still living a place in heaven through his writings by selecting the observations he just sent to him: it will be useful for many and an honour for him. Sambucus goes on to encourage Vettori to continue with his philosophical and philological studies; he will do whatever Vettori thinks he can do for him. He is sending him a coin, commonly called "Dacicus" in Transylvania.

Χαίρειν.

In beneficiis, doctissime Victori, summa esse duco, quae posteritatem intuentur. Non privatum igitur me modo ornasti, dum quaedam meorum tuis inserenda putas, sed publice amicitia praestita memoria beasti.[725] Sed unde gratiae occasionem captem? Quid tibi non debebo, qui me tuo praeconio vis esse aliquid? Atque cum scias in laude poni, de quo bene meritus sis, amplius velle, patere vel vivum adhuc in caelo collocari tuis monumentis, quod ipsum abunde fore spero, si quaedam ex his subito annotatis nuncque missis delegeris, quod utile sit multis, honorificum mihi futurum.[726] Perge vero ὡς Ἡρακλῆς ἀνανταγώνιστος[727] tueri philosophiam et philologiae averte a finibus barbariem imminentem. Quid enim melius de civilibus periculis est expectandum? Si quid ego tuo iudicio potero, non cessabo. Vale et dum melius quid consequatur, nummum hunc in Transylvania Dacicum vulgo apellatum,[728] quod tribus regibus primis insignis sit, μνημόσυνον[729] accipito, cui me semper debere plurimum fatebor. Vale. Die Martini 1568. Totus tuus Sambucus.

Address: Doctissimo et clarissimo viro domino Petro Victorio etc. Florentiam.

123.
Sambucus to Piero Vettori
26 November 1568, Vienna

The original is kept in Munich, BSB, Clm 734, no. 202. Published in Bandini, *Clarorum Italorum et Germanorum epistolae*, 2:32; Gerstinger, "Die Briefe," 96-97.

---

[725] See letter 118 and Visser, *Joannes Sambucus*, 118.
[726] Gerstinger believes that it is a reference to the observations listed in letter 118 but the word "nunc" suggests that he sent some new philological observations. Cf. Gerstinger, "Die Briefe," 95.
[727] as a Hercules who has no rival
[728] Dacicus was a gold coin issued by Emperor Domitian in honour of his peace treaty against the Dacians in the first century, which obliged the Romans to pay an annual subsidy of 8 million sesterces to Decebalus. See Gerstinger, "Die Briefe," 95.
[729] memorial offering

Sambucus feels honoured by Vettori's frequent letters. He would send Vettori the commentary on the Odyssey, but he does not have and has never seen the type of commentary Vettori is looking for. He has two very old copies of Homer, which could be profitably used for emending the text, but Vettori certainly has more copies and better ones. Vettori would be hailed as the discoverer of the Odyssey *if he published his materials on the poem. If only Vettori told him where Antiphon's arithmetic is to be found. Finally, Vettori should decide if he wants to publish the observations Sambucus recently sent him.*

Salutem.

Indies crebritate literarum amorem in me tuum sensusque crescere deprehendo, cui nulla praebita occasione tamen facile tuas cogitationes aperis, quodque in publicum excudis, amanter significas. Ego vero, si eiusmodi commentariolos in Ὀδύσσειαν vidissem aut haberem, sine ulla exceptione ad tuos usus imperiumque accommodarem, sed quibus ea tu conditionibus scholia definis, ego nusquam vidi.[730] Duo exempla Homeri vetustissima, quae suppeditare quiddam emendationi textus possent, habeo, sed vos maiora pluraque possidere non dubito.[731] Tu etiam si alteram thesauri tanti partem edideris, omnes laudabunt, ac sicubi latuerit Ὀδύσσεια, ex prelo teque authore prodibit. Utinam, mi doctissime Victori, Antiphontis *Arithmeticam* indices,[732] de quo studio cuncta tibi deberem. Quas nuper observatiunculas obiter ista tua humanissima officiique plena liberalitate adductus misi, tuo arbitrio abiicies vel proferes.[733] Vale. Vienna, 6. Kalendas Decembris 1568. Tuus Sambucus.

124.
Joachim Camerarius Sr. to Sambucus
4 January 1569, Lipsiae

Published in Camerarius, *Epistolarum libri quinque*, 414.

Camerarius reports his return to Leipzig. He is now dealing with the works borrowed from Sambucus, seeing if they can be published. The problem is that the publishers do not happily take the job of editing such material. There are also school texts that Camerarius needs to work on. Even if they are not important, they take time from other studies, yet he will not forget about them. He is grateful to both Sambucus and his father-in-law. Finally, he is sending him a book written for Christmas, as is usual at the University of Leipzig. If Sambucus wants, he can show it to Thomas Jordan as well, whom Camerarius is greeting.

---

[730] On Vettori's commentaries on the *Odyssey* see the notes in Gerstinger, who claims that a copy may still be found in the BSB in Munich. Gerstinger, "Die Briefe," 97.

[731] These are probably the ones held in Vienna: ÖNB, Cod. Phil. gr. 50 and 56.

[732] The mathematical writings of the Greek sophist Antiphon (fifth century BC) are lost. They are known only from a few references by later authors. Antiphon made advances in calculating the circumference of the circle, imagining that it was made of many small straight lines. See Samuel Sambursky, *Physics of the Stoics* (Princeton: University Press, 1959), 90.

[733] This sounds strange after the affirmative tone of the preceding letter. Sambucus may be wondering about Vettori's opinion of the newly sent observations, attached probably to the preceding letter.

S. D.

Reversi sumus huc, Christo gratia, salvi et incolumes, sane ita mea valetudine et anni tempore postulante in itinere morati diutius. Nunc ea, quorum nobis usus abs te benigne concessus est, tractabamus, si quid edi forte posset. In quo obiicitur nobis nonnihil difficultatis, quod officinae non facile talia scripta elaboranda recipiant. Me etiam occupant scholastica negotiola, cumulata dum absumus. Quae et si parvi sunt momenti, tempus tamen ipsa quoque aliis studiis praeripiunt. Sed cura ab nobis ista non abiicietur. Tibi maximas ago gratias nec non ornatissimo viro socero tuo, cum omnia eximiae humanitatis officia nobis studiosissime praestistis. Mitto tibi hic proposita vetere consuetudine academiae nostrae γενεθλίοις[734] Iesu Christi,[735] quae si videbitur, etiam clarissimo viro domino Iordani legenda dabis[736] eumque officiose salutabis nomine meo et valebis. Vale una cum tuis. Lipsiae, die 4. mense Ianuarii, 69.

125.
Sambucus to Eusebius Episcopius
20 January 1569, [Vienna]

The original is kept in Basel, Universitätsbibliothek, Cod. Fr.-Gr. II 27, f. 226ʳ-226ᵛ. Published in Gerstinger, "Die Briefe," 97-98.

As Sambucus needed to write to Konrad Hubert, he wanted to take the opportunity and ask Episcopius whether he was willing, as he has promised, to print the treasure that Sambucus will give him, worthy of his publishing house: a 24 books digest of the 60 books of the Basilica, *which has never been published. It will not be much longer than Theophilus's paraphrases (of Justinian's* Institutes*) or the edition of Justinian's* Novels. *The 60 books are not found anywhere in their entirety and would be too long to publish and too expensive to distribute anyway. Sambucus will send him a clearly written manuscript which could be directly used for printing. Episcopius should respond him as soon as possible via (Johann Andrea) Schwanbach in Frieburg or through Strasbourg, and not talk about this offer to others because of some reasons. He will obtain a treasure and glory. Sambucus does not want anything for the copy.*

---

[734] on birthday feast. In the margin of the edition: "Feriis Natalitiis."

[735] This may be a reference to J. Camerarius, *Historiae Iesu Christi filii Dei nati in terra matre sanctissima sempervirgine Maria summatim relata expositio* (Lipsiae: Voegelin, 1566).

[736] Thomas Jordan (Jordanus or Jordanes) (1540–1585) was one of the most learned doctors of the Habsburg Monarchy of the day. Born in Cluj (Kolozsvár) he studied extensively all over Europe (1555–1565), in Wittenberg (with Melanchthon), in Paris (with Louis Duret and others), in Montpellier (with Guillaume Rondelet and Laurent Joubert). Despite the doctoral degree obtain in Montpellier, he continued his studies in Basel, Padova, Pisa, Bologna and Rome, making contacts with learned men in each place. After his diploma was recognised by the University of Vienna he was first appointed as army doctor in 1566, then accepted a job offer as "protomedicus" of Moravia in Brno. See Robert Offner, "Neue Daten zur Biographie des Klausenburger Artztes Thomas Jordanus (1540–1586). Epidemologe, Balneologe und Protomedicus von Mähren," *Sudhoffs Archiv* 102 (2018), 89-112; and the article by idem in *Companion*.

Sambucus salutem.

Cum mihi ad D. Conradum Hubertum scribendum esset, eadem commoditate significare tibi volui, si velis atque pollicitus fueris, quamprimum te impressurum thesaurum a me tibi datum ingentem, rarum tuaque officina omniumque bibliothecis dignum: sexaginta librorum Βασιλικῶν σύνοψιν 24 librorum, desideratam tot seculis a iureconsultis sanioribus.[737] Codex non excedat multum[738] Theophili Παράφρασιν[739] vel potius Νεαράς Geneve excusas.[740] Nam sexaginta illi nuspiam integri simulque extant et volumen ingens ineptumque esset nec cuiusvis usibus et crumena aptum, etiamsi extaret. Ego exemplum mittam perspicue descriptum, quo utere ad praelum. Quod si diligenter edideris, gratiam non vulgarem feres.[741] Tu quam citissime ad me rescribe tuasque Friburgum ad dominum Schvambach vel qua via libuerit, etiam Argentoratum, mittes, ut sciam. Nec velim te vulgare hanc voluntatem certas ob causas. Crede te θησαυρὸν καὶ δόξαν[742] comparaturum. Ego pro exemplo nihil cupio. Vale. 20. Ianuarii 1569.

Address: Domino Episcopio, typographo Basiliensi, amico ad manus proprias. Cito, cito.

126.
Gerartus Falkenburgius[743] to Sambucus
22 February 1569, Antwerp

Original is kept in Vienna, ÖNB, Cod. Phil. gr. 45,[744] f. 1ʳ-2ʳ. Dedication in Nonnus Panopolites, *Νόννου Πανοπολίτου Διονυσιακά. Nonni Panopolitae Dionysiaca, nunc primum in lucem edita, ex Bibliotheca Ioannis Sambuci Pannonii. Cum lectionibus et coniecturis Gerarti Falkenburgii Noviomagi et indice copioso*, ed. Gerhard Falkenburg (Antwerpen: Plantin, 1569), f. 2ʳ-8ᵛ. Published in *Humanistes du bassin des Carpates II. Johannes Sambucus*, 124-135.

---

[737] Zwinger's marginal note: "Basilica iuridica pollicetur." The Basilica are a Greek version of the *Corpus Iuris Civilis*, first published entirely in the middle of the seventeenth century. Sambucus's manuscript (from the mid-tenth century) is an anthology of the Basilica under alphabetically arranged keywords. The manuscript was published in 1575 as *LX librorum Βασιλικῶν, id est, universi iuris Romani ... ecloga sive synopsis* by Johannes Löwenklau. It is not identical with the manuscript called "Basilicorum synopsis minor," held in Vienna, ÖNB, Cod. Iur. gr. 14, which Sambucus bought in Taranto for 10 ducats (Gerstinger, "Johannes Sambucus als Handschriftensammler," 326). See more in Stolte, "Joannes Leunclavius"; Gerstinger, "Zusammenfassung," 289-291.

[738] Löwenklau's emended and commented edition was 752 folio pages.

[739] Theophilus [Antecessor], *Institutiones iuris civilis in Graecam linguam per Theophilum Antecessorem olim traductae ac fusissime planissimeque explicatae* (Basileae: H. Froben and N. Episcopius, 1543).

[740] Iustinianus, *Novellae constitutiones*, ed. Heinrich Scrimger (Genevae: H. Stephanus, 1558).

[741] Sambucus apparently did not think of a critical, emended and commented edition, as it was done eventually by Löwenklau, but only a faithful edition of his copy.

[742] treasure and glory

[743] Little is known of Gerartus Falkenburgius (Gerhard/Gerard Falkenburg/Falckenburg) of Nijmegen (1535–1578). He studied law in Bourges and carried on his studies in Italy as it also appears from this preface. His only publication is Nonnus's *Dionysiaca*. In 1571 he stayed in Cologne as a secretary (or paid companion) of the Wrocław patrician Thomas Rehdiger. Among others he corresponded with Carolus Clusius, Justus Lipsius, Bonaventura Vulcanius and Janus Dousa Sr. (the later published some of his epigrams in 1582). He died in a horse accident. See the article by Conrad Bursian in *ADB* 6 (1877), 555. Also see letter 295.

[744] This is the first part of Sambucus's codex of Nonnos (the second part is Cod. Phil. gr. 51), which Falkenburgius used for the editio princeps.

127.
Sambucus to Joachim Camerarius Sr.
6 March 1569, Vienna

The original is kept in Boston, The Houghton Library, Ms. Lat. 307.

Sambucus received two of Camerarius's letters, in which he told him about his wellbeing but also about the stubborn theologians. The second one was brought to him by the student that Camerarius recommended to him. Everything that he and his friends have would have been accessible to the student if he had ever returned. He gave Camerarius's greetings to Lazarus von Schwendi. Although the Ottomans have real troubles, the Monarchy wants the easier way by paying much in tributes. The Persian king has died and his son is most inimical to the Ottomans and will certainly invade the area of the Euphrates. Although David Chytraeus is in Vienna, there is no advance on the question of religion. Camerarius should decide about his little books. Concerning the greater ones, he would not like to have vain hopes. Nonnus is ready. He has given Stobaeus to the presses. He thoroughly read and corrected both. He has sent to Basel the epitome of the Basilica, *which will be printed soon by Eusebius Episcopius. Vettori's* Variae lectiones *came out, he expected something greater. Sambucus, his father-in-law and family are sending their greetings to Camerarius's son-in-law and Ludwig (Camerarius's son).*

S. D.

Binas tuas easque optatissimas nuper accepi, quibus de tua valetudine, non nihil ea incommoda, theologis αὐθάδεσι[745] et aliis significas.

Posteriores scholasticus, quem commendasti, attulit, cui omnia mea amicorumque patuissent, si unquam fuisset reversus. Schwendium, ut iussisti, honorifice salutavi grataque illi fuit memoria. Nos Thurcam, licet gravissimis propriisque periculis occupatissimum, amplis muneribus faciliorem quaerimus. Persarum rex mortuus est, cuius filium Thurcis infensissimum ad Euphratem negocium praebiturum cumque maleficio invasurum non dubitamus. De religionis negotio, licet Chytraeus adsit,[746] nullum amplius verbum καὶ κατὰ τοὺς Μεγαρεῖς οὔτε ἐν ἀριθμῷ οὔτε ἐν λόγῳ.[747] De meis libellis quod voletis honorificumque mihi ac publice utile videbitur, istic statuetis. De epistolis tamen et aliis nollem spem omnino

---

[745] stubborn

[746] David Chytraeus (1530–1600) was a Lutheran theologian, disciple of Melanchthon, a historian and an important Greek scholar from Baden-Württemberg. He enrolled at the University of Tübingen at the age of nine, where he studied with Camerarius and moved to Wittenberg in 1544. From 1548 he taught in Wittenberg, but in 1550 he moved to Rostock, where he became a central figure of the university. He was co-author of the Formula of Concord. He founded several Lutheran gymnasia and was author of a series of pedagogical works. As a humanist historian his most significant contribution may be his *Oratio de statu ecclesiarum hoc tempore in Graecia, Asia, Africa, Ungaria, Boëmia etc* (Francofurti: A. Wechel, 1580). See Daniel Benga, *David Chytraeus (1530–1600) als Erforscher und Wiederentdecker der Ostkirchen* (PhD Dis., University of Erlangen, 2001); Harald Bollbuck, *Geschichts- und Raummodelle bei Albert Krantz (um 1448–1517) und David Chytraeus (1530-1600): Transformationen des historischen Diskurses im 16. Jahrhundert* (Frankfurt am Main–Vienna: Lang, 2006).

[747] and, after the fashion of the Megarians, nowhere in the reckoning. This is a reference to the people of Megara, who in their vanity once asked an oracle, whether anyone was mightier than them. It answered that they were not the third, not the fourth, not the twelfth, and not at all in the reckoning. Cf. *Scholia in Theocritum vetera*, ed. Karl Wendel (Lipsiae: Teubner 1914), 302-303. Cf. also Plutarchus, *Quaestiones conviviales*, 682.

esse vanam. Nonnus est absolutus,[748] Stobaei Φυσικὰς ἐκλογάς[749] utrimque a me perlectas et multis locis emendatas praelo quoque subieci.[750] Misi ante mensem Basileam ἐπιτομὴν τῶν Βασιλικῶν,[751] Episcopius formis suis brevi magna omnium doctorum expectatione reddet. Victorii *Lectiones* prodierunt: maiora cogitabam.[752] Vale, tuoque genero[753] et Ludovico[754] a me, socero meisque mille salutes. Vienna, VI. Martii 1569. Totus tuus Sambucus.

Address: D. Ioachimo Camerario, viro clarissimo, praeceptori et amico suo. Lipsiam.

128.
Sambucus to Johannes Listhius
15 March 1569, Vienna

Dedication in Ianus Pannonius, *Illius antiquis vatibus comparandi, recentioribus certe anteponendi, quae uspiam reperiri adhuc potuerunt, omnia. Opera Ioannis Sambuci consiliari et historici caesaraei* (Vienna: Stainhofer, 1569), f. ii^r-iiii^r. Published in *Humanistes du bassin des Carpates II. Johannes Sambucus*, 143-150.

129.
Sambucus to Piero Vettori
6 April 1569, [Vienna]

The original is kept in Munich, BSB, Clm 735, no. 11. Published in Gerstinger, "Johann Sambucus als Philologe," *Wiener Studien* 78 (1966), 551-556; idem, "Die Briefe," 98-101.

He has received Vettori's gift copy, which made him more cautious and learned in philological observations. It is like having gained the rules for this kind of work. Everyone must be grateful to him and posterity will acknowledge this more than the bad poets of their times. Vettori should not get upset if Sambucus wants to continuously learn, yet what follows are Sambucus's thoughts on Vettori's philological observations, for instance concerning the astrological sign of the wolf, to which, Sambucus confirms, Ptolemy attributes 19 stars, or concerning the poetry of Vergil, calling attention to the poet's use of hendiadyoin. Sambucus searched through a certain little library and found

---

[748] Nonnus, *Dionysiaca* (see the preceding letter). The book had just been published, as the censor's permission dates to 19 February 1569.
[749] Stobaeus and Plethon, *Stobaei eclogarum libri duo ... et Plethonis de rebus Peloponnesiacis orationes duae*.
[750] Concerning Sambucus's philological contributions see the introduction of *Humanistes du bassin des Carpates II. Johannes Sambucus*.
[751] See letter 125.
[752] Petrus Victorius, *Variarum lectionum XIII novi libri* (Florentiae: Iunta, 1569).
[753] Esrom Rüdinger (1523–1591) acted as a tutor in Camerarius's houshold and later married his daughter Anna. In 1557 he began lecturing on physics at the University of Wittenberg. He also took over the chair of Greek but as he was arrested because of his alleged Crypto-Calvinism in 1575 he had to flee from Wittenberg. He found employment in Moravia as the director of a school of the Moravian Brethren in Eibschütz (Andreas Dudith also sent his son to this school). See the article by Franz Machilek in *BBKL* 8 (1994), 952-956.
[754] Ludwig Camerarius (1542–1587) was the third son of Joachim Camerarius. He was a doctor, just like his elder brother Joachim Jr. Not to be mixed up with Joachim Jr.'s son Ludwig (1573–1651).

some dramas of Aeschylus, including the Libation Bearers. *He is sending Vettori some results of his collation, using his very old codex, and encourages Vettori to edit the drama. He does not have the two lives by Dionysius Halicarnasseus demanded by Vettori, who does well to edit them. He has given to the printing presses Stobaeus's* Physical and Moral Extracts *and the epitome of the 60 books of the* Basilica. *The Dionysiaca has already come out but he still has not received a complete printed copy. He asks Vettori to send him back his notes as he wrote them rashly and hurriedly. If Vettori needs, he will send him the scholia of Triclinius and others concerning Aeschylus.*

Petro Victorio Sambucus salutem.

Munus ego tuum accepi, quo uno quasi contento spiritu hausto cautior in multis observandis atque eruditior sum factus, videorque mihi regulas quasdam collegisse in eo praeclaro genere scripturae.[755] Debent igitur tibi omnes memoriam sempiternam idque posteritas copiosius, quam forsan hodie Suffoeni[756] agnoscet. Illud significare volui tuamque humanitatem, quam numquam deseris, orare, ne moleste feras, si discere perpetuo cupio. Est pagina 115 de lupa signo locus, de quo nonnihil ἐπέχω.[757] Lupa certe signum est et pars itidem Centauri ex Ptolemaei *Almagesto* .8., ubi Lupo XIX stellas attribuit in Libra et Scorpione.[758] Idem Firmicus transtulit in 8. c. 19,[759] qui, inquit, in ore Lupi nascuntur, saltatores fient, canibus praeda futuri etc. In Virgilio quae non vulgaria observavi, nescio an tibi placeat idem sentire: saepe illum duabus vocibus coniungendis per se interponere eleganter copulas, ut 7., *fronde et oliva*.[760] Et *pateris libamus et auro*[761] et 8., *squamis et auro*,[762] pro fronde olivae, pateris aureis etc. Gramen vero in Martis sacrificio imponi aris solitum sit,[763] fortasse quia Plinius de humano sanguine id nasci confirmet.[764] Nec dissimulare possum Servium male in Vergilio *Athon*[765] pro *Athos* substituere velle ob quantitatem syllabae, cum certum sit saepe sequentem brevem iuvari a longa proxima, ut: *tibi pampineo gravidus autumno*.[766] Et Ovidius: *In liquidum rediit aethera Martis opus* etc.[767] Sed haec mitto, περιαυτολογικά[768] enim sunt.

Excussi bibliothecam, in qua Aeschyli aliquot fabulas reperi, sed in diversis libris illigatas, quas inter Χοηφόρας[769] sine ἀρχῇ[770] habeo et ipse, verum τὰ πρόσωπα[771] adsunt:

---

[755] Victorius, *Variarum lectionum XIII novi libri* (as in letter 127, note 752). Cf. with Sambucus's opinion expressed there.
[756] Suffenus was a poet ridiculed as "caprimulgus" in Catullus 22.10.
[757] I offer. It refers to Vettori's discussion of a passage in Cicero, *De natura deorum* 3.16: "Disputatio de loco Ciceronis, qui simulachrum quoddam coeleste vocat lupam, cum effigies lupae non videatur in sideribus collocata." See the relevant note by Gerstinger, ("Die Briefe," 100).
[758] For Ptolemy the sign is the wild beast and not the wolf (Ptolemaius, *Almagest* 8.H171).
[759] Julius Firmicus Maternus (c. 300–c. 350), a Roman senator born in Sicily was a convert to Christianity. Sambucus refers here to his pre-conversion: *Mathesis* 8.29.13.
[760] Vergilius, *Aeneis* 7.751.
[761] Vergilius, *Georgica* 2.192.
[762] Vergilius, *Aeneis* 11.771.
[763] Vergilius, *Aeneis* 12.119.
[764] See the reference in Gerstinger, "Die Briefe," 100).
[765] Vergilius, *Aeneis* 12, 701. Maurus Servius Honoratus was a late fourth-century grammarian of Rome, author of a set of commentaries on the works of Virgil. Sambucus owned two Vergil-editions with Servius commentaries from 1551 (Basel) and 1552 (Venice). See Gulyás, *Sámboky János könyvtára*, 1322 and 1729.
[766] Vergilius, *Georgica* 2.5.
[767] "In liquidum rediit aethera Martis equis [!]" Ovidius *Remedia amoris* 6.
[768] boastings
[769] *Choephori* (*The Libation Bearers*) is the second play of Aeschylus's Oresteia trilogy.
[770] beginning
[771] characters, dramatis personae

Ὀρέστης.	Κείλισσα Ὀρέστου τροφός.
Χορὸς ἐκ γυναικῶν	Παῖς.
χοηφόρων	Αἴγισθος.
Ἠλέκτρα	Κλυταιμνήστρα.
Θεράπαινα	Πυλάδης⁷⁷²

In meo vetustissimo illud: δι' αἰῶνος διοιγμοῖσι βόσκεται κέαρ legit δ οἴτοισιν nec male.⁷⁷³ Et ἰὼ γαῖα γαῖα μωμένα μιλλεῖ etc. ἰάλλει ut ἰάλλον postea.⁷⁷⁴ Et φεύγων Ὀρέστης etc. ὑπερκόπως: meus ὑπερκόμπως.⁷⁷⁵ Et ἐκ τῶν πατρῴων: meus ματρῴων.⁷⁷⁶ Et πράσσουσα δίκη etc.: meus codex δίκης.⁷⁷⁷ Et extremus versus: θεόθεν δὲ φραδαῖς duo mei εὖ φραδαῖσιν, licet in margine ῃσι γρ.⁷⁷⁸ Sunt etiam alia tenuia, quae observavi. Digna vero fabula est, quod omnes ex tua recognitione tentant, utque eam edas, valde rogo.

De Halycarnassei libello, quo duorum optimorum oratorum vitam colligavit, apud me nihil extat.⁷⁷⁹ Tu vero, mi doctissime Victori, cum adhuc benemerendo publice alios innumeros superaris, fac illa quoque reliqua vel manca legamus. Ego Φυσικὴν ἐκλογὴν Stobaei praelo subieci itemque ἐπιτομὴν 60 librorum Βασιλικῶν dictorum.⁷⁸⁰ Διονυσιακὰ mea iam exiverunt, sed impressum integrum exemplum ad me adhuc non pervenit.⁷⁸¹ Quod vero fere praeterieram: si grave non est, oro mea σχεδίολα⁷⁸² tibi missa, hoc est, obiter et subito aliquot adversa, uti remittas. Ex plurimis enim illa temere descripsi et festinatione ad te misi, nec bene memini, quae illa sint. Fortassis brevi libellus somniorum meorum talium se propinandum omnibus dabit et illudendum. Ἔρρωσο,⁷⁸³ vir humanissime ac doctissime. 6. Aprilis 1569.

Si opus fuerit, scholia varia Triclinii et aliorum παλαιὰ⁷⁸⁴ in Aeschylum mittam, modo gratum tibi sit, cui ego debeo ob memoriam praestitam non parum.⁷⁸⁵ Vale.

Address: Petro Victorio, doctissimo viro et publice optime merito. Sambucus

---

[772] Dramatis personae from *The Libation Bearers*.
[773] Aeschylus, *Choephori* 26.
[774] Aeschylus, *Choephori* 45.
[775] Aeschylus, *Choephori* 136.
[776] Aeschylus, *Choephori* 284.
[777] Aeschylus, *Choephori* 311.
[778] Aeschylus, *Choephori* 941. Some of Sambucus's solutions became part of modern editions. See the notes in Gerstinger, "Die Briefe," 100-101.
[779] The reference to Dionysius Halicarnasseus's lives of Isaeus and Dinarchus (which were parts of his work on ten attic orators), edited later by Vettori: Διονυσίου Ἁλικαρνασσέως Ἰσαῖος καὶ Δείναρχος. *Vitae Isaei et Dinarchi, magnorum Graeciae oratorum* (Lugduni: Ioannes Tornaesius, 1581).
[780] Stobaeus and Plethon, *Stobaei eclogarum libri duo ... et Plethonis de rebus Peloponnesiacis orationes duae; LX librorum Βασιλικῶν.*
[781] Nonnus, *Dionysiaca*.
[782] notes
[783] farewell
[784] old (scholia)
[785] Vettori apparently did not want the manuscript (although he edited and annotated Aeschylus's tragedies in 1557), as five years later Sambucus sent this manuscript (perhaps Cod. Phil. gr. 334 of the ÖNB) to Plantin. See letter 235 and Gerstinger, "Die Briefe," 101. Demetrius Triclinius (c. 1300) was a Byzantine scholar who annotated and analysed the metrical structure in the works of Aeschylus and others. See Ole Langwitz Smith, *Studies in the Scholia on Aeschylus: The Recensions of Demetrius Triclinius* (Leiden: Brill, 1975).

130.
The Council of Trnava to Sambucus
14 April 1569, Trnava

The original is kept in Trnava, SAT, Magistrát mesta Trnava, Missiles. Published in Anton Vantuch, "Nové dokumenty k životu a dielu Jána Sambuca," *Historické Štúdie* 13 (1968), 251-252.

With respect to the lack of learned men, the Council of Trnava has decided to send Georgius Bánchay, the noble youngster of good intellectual abilities, to Wittenberg. They now ask Sambucus to write a letter of recommendation to the professors of Wittenberg and others, as they know how much it would matter for them.

Egregie domine, frater et amice nobis observandissime, salutem et servitutis nostrae officiosam commendacionem.

In tanta literatorum hominum penuria decrevimus nobilem adolescentem Georgium Banchay, quem ad capescenda bonarum literarum studia suapte natura promptum et idoneum cognovimus, Wytebergam mittere.[786] Qui ut commodiori faciliorique via in suis studiis versare possit, dominationem vestram Egregiam tanquam dominum et fratrem observandissimum rogamus, doctoribus Wytebergensibus et quibus dominatio vestra magis necessarium cognoverit, in commendationem huius adolescentis suas dare ne gravetur litteras. Scimus etenim nihil ambigentes scripta diminiationis vestrae egregiae huic Georgio Banchay multum profectura. Quod nos vicissim dominatione vestra egregia omni officio promereri studebimus. In reliquo dominationem vestram egregiam una cum suis quam felicissime valere optamus. Thyrnavie 14. die mensis Aprilis. Anno domini 1569.

Address: Egregio domino Ioanni Sambuco, historiographo et consiliario sacre cesaree et regie maiestatis etc., domino amico et fratri nobis observandissimo.

131.
Sambucus to István Nyilas, Mayor of Trnava
14 May 1569, Pressburg

The original is kept in Trnava, SAT, Magistrát mesta Trnava, Missiles. Published in Kóssa, "Adatok Sámboky János életéhez," 373; Vantuch, "Die Sambucusbriefe," 341-342.

Sambucus understood that in the lawsuit concerning the house, Jacab the scribe wants to get away. Sambucus believed that Bálint the scribe took a copy of the transaction but he did not. Sambucus scolded him, but Bálint claimed Nyilas could obtain a copy. Sambucus asks Nyilas to levy low tax on the house and when the upper court (tárnokszék) gathers, he will send Jacab. Nyilas should tell Jacab or the renters to keep the house in good condition ("not to ruin it"), as he wants to earn

---
[786] Georgius (György) Bánchay was a student from Trnava. We have no other information on him apart from Sambucus's correspondence. See also letter 143.

money on it also later. Nyilas should make this an order "ex officio." Sambucus will probably leave Pressburg on Tuesday.

Zolgalathom utan minden iott kegielmeteknek. Meghertettem az haz pewr dolgat, hogh Jacob deak zabadittya magat.[787] Byzon hogh az tuttam hogh Walint deakh az transmissionak massat vette volna, de nem leth. Elegeth pyrongattam es azt monda hogh kegyelmeteknek iryak, es ottan ky vezzy az masaat, mint az Ellensiges az transmissionak. Es miert hog arua dolog, hallom hogh minden feel arkozert fel latt. veznek. Kerem kegyelmeteket hogh io keves iaro lighen az taxaban; es mihent Tarnokzeek liszen, rea hivom az Jacab deakot. Addigh kerem kegyelmeteket megh izennye Jacab deaknak, vagh az hazy zellyereknek, hogh az hazat ne puzticzyak, mert megh keresnem azutannis raytok. Eztett pedigh kegyelmetek ex officio meg porantzyolhattya nekyek. Isten tarza megh kegyelmeteket. En talan kedden el fogok innen mennem. Posomban 14 May 1569. Kegyelmednek s[oghora] J. Samboky.

Address: Nylas Istwan uramnak Zombathy byronak, nekem io uramnak es tiztelendó zoghornak kezehez. Naghzombath.

132.
Sambucus to Michael Otrer
15 May 1569, Vienna

Published in *Elegia de angelis cum precatiuncula quadam et epistola de obitu magnifici D. Marci Singhmoseri, etc.* (Vienna: Steinhofer, 1570), f. D3^v-E2^v.

Sambucus is responding to the question of Otrer, who has often used the patronage of Mark, about Singkmoser's sickness and whether the doctors have any hope. One who does not think of death as something bad has no need of advice how to stay alive. Singkmoser's fever was dangerous even on the fourth day and he had all kinds of other problems like the unability to digest and some general edema, so he died at the age of 46 on the first of May. Sambucus praises Singkmoser's cooperation and benevolence, which is now missing, adding to the miseries of the century. He is leaving behind an honest wife and a daughter. Moreover, Singkmoser had a great intellect and a peaceful nature, easily got over his anger, and followed the piousness of the ancients. His numerous official letters sent to all the parts give testimony of his virtues as a diplomat (also among the Ottomans), of his shrewdness in counsel and dedication to the interests of his two imperial masters. Some, especially foreigners, had some complaints about his stalling, reproaching him that he reciprocated many greetings in spirit only, rather than according to ceremony, when he was under pressure. But he seemed to be painstaking in difficult tasks, which he rightly preferred to the routine, knowing with Socrates that life is made perfect by wisdom and pleasures. Whatever Latin missives were sent to Italy, France, Spain, Poland, even Turkey, they were all perfectly written thanks to his trustworthiness, experience and language skills; even the emperor grieved over his death. Sambucus hears that even those who unjustly blamed him were struck by the death of such a great man. This is the commonly held and objective view of Singkmoser, which coincides with truth, for

---

[787] Vantuch believes that this concerns the house of Sambucus's former brother-in-law János Panithy. See letter 80. Vantuch, "Die Sambucusbriefe," 342.

no one has gained praise through pleasures, as the comic poet said, and neither does rest come from work or work from idleness, as Plato said in the Laws. If a case took him longer, the result was all the better. The longer Singkmoser is missed, the more his talents will be appreciated. But Otrer is no need of arguments to be consoled, as he usually provides them to others. Singkmoser cannot miss anything in that heavenly abundance, where there is truth and is also recognised as truth (in contrast to Democritus's opinion). They had better congratulate him on his heavenly home and value earthly, transient things less. Sambucus wonders about the useless efforts invested in the cult of the dead even among the common people, seeing that everyone must turn into dust; obviously people cannot confront God without superstition. Meanwhile Otrer should tell Sambucus what he should think of all this bloodletting, the attempts to create a common doctrine, and the disruptors of peace, and what he should hope for.

Ioannes Sambucus N. S.

De Singhmoseri,[788] cuius tu patrocinio et opera usus es prolixe, morbo et, an eius restituendi spem medici aliquam ostendant, quod requiris, paucis accipe.[789] Nullum ipsum habere malum et, qui ne mortem quidem in malis posuit, consilio, in vita uti retineatur, opus ei minime fore.[790]

Diu quarto quoque die recurrens ei febricula infesta erat, quodque omnes aliae, ut denique ventriculi robur vimque cibos conficiendi laedant, haec praesertim effecit itaque evaluit, ut cruditatibus in abdomen deinceps tributis alimentorumque commeatibus impeditis non sine aquae subter universam cutim illapsae suspitione magno omnium moerore ipsis Kalendis Maii, aetatis XLVI. extinctus sit.

Hoc scilicet multis aliis reliquum huic saeculo incommodi defuit, haec ad miserias aggreganda erat calamitas, ut domi et publice singulariter meritum, officii et humanitatis nunquam oblitum, erga omnes voluntate benefica, laboribus ad credendum vix facilibus, praestantem virum mors iniqua etiam eriperet, carere tanto subsidio caesaris comitatum importunius vellet, tot clientes in lachrimas coniiceret.

Verum haec magnificentiae humanae conditio est, haec vana fraudulentaque altorum spes affert, qua cum in horas ludamur, tamen non resipiscimus, ad sanitatem purae semperque valentis frugis aegre adducimur. Reliquit ille honestissimam foeminam uxorem cum filia, quarum disciplina omnisque vitae ratio amabilis extat inque ore familiarium cum laude versatur.

Fuit in Singhmosero, ut hoc quoque addam, mens cunctorum nata atque illa usibus dedita, sensus vel de immerentibus Christianus, vindictae nullius cupidus, bile interdum subito effusa, mox remissa, exemplum pietatis antiquum, arduis tractandis iudicium subactum, humanae artes ab eo compraehensae mores, quos, qui recte intuitus est, nisi laudare nequivit, corpus etiam non ad quosvis casus erroresque tenuiculos moleste subiectum. Quantum eius virtutes (ἔργον δ᾽ οὐδὲν ὄνειδος[791]) in legationibus vel ad Thurcas iterum obita diligentia, in consiliis acumen, duorum imperatorum secretis et authoritatibus conservandis industria valuerit, quid

---

[788] For Mark Singkmoser see letter 108, note 645.
[789] Unfortunately, we do not know anything about the Otrer family. This letter suggests that Sambucus was tutoring Michael Otrer's son Johannes. See letter 139.
[790] Cf. Cicero, De finibus 3.29: "ut enim qui mortem in malis ponit non potest eam non timere, sic nemo ulla in re potest id, quod malum esse decreverit, non curare idque contemnere."
[791] work is no disgrace. Hesiodus, Erga 311.

ingenue salutariterque cupierit, in amicorum contentionibus praestiterit, tot imperatoriae literae de illius officina expeditae ubique locorum abunde profitentur.

Equidem scio quosdam, praesertim exteros, de mora eius quiddam conquestos, difficultatem, cum gravissimis obrueretur, obiectam, aliorum tot salutationes animo potius, quam ceremoniarum gestibus metitum. Sed morosus videbatur in arduis, quae ille quibusdam commendaticiis, aut in tutum addendis literis, mandatis privatim satisfacientibus, privilegiis gratiose impetratis iuste praeferebat vereque norat cum Socrate vitam sapientia et voluptate consistere fierique perfectam.

Certe quidquid per Italiam, Gallias, Hispanias, Poloniam Latine, etiam Thraciam literis committebatur, huius praecipue fide, usu, linguarum peritia est perfectum. Nec parum eius a nostro convictu digressum vel caesar ipse doluit. Ego vero tanti viri obitu, vel qui iniquius eum accusabant, vehementer turbatos audio. Haec non mea, sed communis de Singhmosero vox et opinio testata est, quam non amicitiae aut doloris impotentis memoria expressit, sed exempla et veritas pronunciant, nec fraudandum ista commendatione iubent, quae illa in horas absens vires sumet, posteri quaerent, similes exoptabunt multos, οὐδεὶς γὰρ ἔπαινον ἡδοναῖς, ut comicus ait, ἐκτήσατο[792] ac recte ille in Platonis *Legibus* quietem a laboribus venire, e turpi ocio nasci labores prodidit.[793]

Quo igitur magis in tanti viri desiderio sumus, eventaque negociorum longius precedent, hoc Marci dotes amplius vigebunt, eaque re tibi lenius casus ferendus, quo propius imortalitatem intueri licet. Neque hic opus est ullis ad te consolandum argumentis, qui a te ipse maiora petere aliisque deiectis suppeditare levationem soles. Qui cum bene fit, nec deesse quidquam in coelesti copia iure potest, ubi non modo est verum, contra Democritum, sed cognoscitur quoque verum, eius conditioni ne invidere velle videamur, domicilium sempiternum nullis cohibitum finibus fruitionemque divinorum congratulemur, una sancte esse longinque caduca ista despectare minusque aestimare cupiamus. Sic demum vitae a labe sordibusque remotae ratio beate constabit, sic Christi sententiis confirmabimur, qui ad perpetuum revocari gaudium expetunt. Non magis iis, quam sementi terrae credito (si modo ager cum foenore acceptum reddere debeat) eandem faciem et naturam licere tueri.

Ut interdum in mentem veniat mirari, cuivis, etiam de plebe, vitio in cinerum ossiumque condendorum tam solicitam incidere accurationem (de principum sancteque meritorum exemplis non loquor, nec huius est loci), cum illa in pulverem abire necesse sit, nisi si, ut qui solem sine nubibus aspicere nequeunt, item isti divinitatem citra hanc suam umbram et superstitionem haud ferant. Coeterum quid de inaudita passim αἱματοχυσίᾳ καὶ ὑποκρίσει συνεσκευασμένῃ διδασκαλίᾳ[794], adeoque ἰδιογνώσταις[795] tranquilli status perturbatoribus, de quibus et ipse significas, sentiam et quid hoc rerum profligatarum loco sperandum sit melius, id vero tu expertus longo usu praecipere animo informareque, et nos docere potes.

Oro, ut denique e Graecia senex quispiam fiat, nec semper sint pueri, quod ad Solonem ab Aegyptio quodam sacrifico non in disimili re fuit dictum.[796] Vale, Idibus Maiis 1569. Vienna.

---

[792] no one won glory by pleasures
[793] Plato, *Leges* 6.779A.
[794] bloodletting and forged by hypocrisy doctrine
[795] self-aware
[796] Plato, *Timaeus* 22b.

133.

Sambucus to István Nyilas, Mayor of Trnava
16 May 1569, Pressburg

The original is kept in Trnava: SAT, Magistrát mesta Trnava, Missiles. Published in Kóssa, "Adatok Sámboky János életéhez," 373; Vantuch, "Die Sambucusbriefe," 342-343.

The bill of debt and the letter of appeasement are with the attorney. Sambucus is surprised that the councillors, not having seen the book, think that it is Sambucus's fault if he had no copy of Jacab's transaction. He talked about it with both the "masters" and the personalis *(royal judge) who were surprised and believed that it was no problem if Jacab scribe lost the appeal, the previous decision of the court was valid. And there was no need for Sambucus to take a copy of Jacab's transaction if his case was strong enough. The argument that Sambucus waited too long after the lost appeal is not right. The money Jacab has put in deposit at the City Council because of the house is no problem either, he did it with cunning, but Sambucus can pay it back to him. Sambucus is advised by everyone to get hold of the verdicts of the judge and he would be assigned the house. The two "masters" laughed at this claim. Sambucus will stay in Pressburg until Friday to see what is needed to be done. And why was Jacab scribe sent to him? Jacab knows his job and could have newly found Sambucus when he was in the house. It would have been better than sending an enemy to Sambucus. But God should keep Nyilas safe.*

Salutem et servitiorum commendationem.

Az ados level, es quietantiales az procatornal vagyon. Es czodalom hogh az Uraim nem latvan az könweth, es ha Jacab deaknak transmissio[já]val volt-e, ugy iteltenek hogh en bewnem, hogh massam annak nem volt. En ez dologh felol zoltam mind Mesterekkel, mind personalis urammal, de czodalkoznak rayta. Azt mondiak ewk, hogh ha az appellatiot el hatta Jacab deak, mi gondom ennekem vele, az itelett kyt az elwt miveltetek ugyan io. Es my züksig nekem masat az ew transmissiojaval vennem, ha io caussam, es pewrem vagyon, es inkabb ewneky kellene, ha nekem volt volna, ollyat vennye. Hogh pedig azt mondya: zokaig vartam, es hallaztottam az dolgot az elhatt appellatio utan: kinek my gondya vagyon arra, ugyan transiit in rem iudicatam. Es az my penzt Jacab deakh az haztul addigh le tett az varoznak es az nem arthatt[797] mert ravassaggal mivelte, hanem le tehetem azt neky. Azwthan azt aggiak tanatzul mindnyaian, hogh egg parantzolatot vegyek kiuel az adiudicatat kyaddyak, es ugyan en nyertem az hazat. Byzon nevettek ez dolgot ketten az mestereknek. Isten tartza megh kegyelmeteket meg itt moradok[798] pentegik, es addig meg latom mitt kel mivelnem. Oztan mire volt zewgsig Jacob deakot rea hiwna, hizem tuddya dolgot vezelni, es engemet uyonnan meg lelny mikor az hazba voltam volna. Az keggyelmeteknek nem artott volna, nem inkabb az en ellensigemet kwlteni ream etc. Isten tarcza megh kegelmeteket. 16 May 1569, kegyelmeteknek sógora, Sámboky.

Address: Nemes es tiztelendo Nylas Istwan uramnak, Nagh zombathy byronak zoghor uramnak kezehez. Naghzombath.

---

[797] deleted word: *hanem.*
[798] deleted word: *egh.*

134.
Sambucus to Theodor Zwinger
31 May 1569, Vienna

The original is kept in Basel, Universitätsbibliothek, Frey Mscr II 27, no. 225; a copy is kept in Mscr. G II 37, 145. Published in Gerstinger, "Die Briefe," 161-162.

Sambucus received Zwinger's letter of February on 31 May. He is grateful for his efforts concerning a certain official (praetor) but wonders why these men are so worried about foreign things, since their continuous exchange of letters should already have cured them of that illness. But he will urge them through some official warning, unless they pay back the loan. Zwinger should know that he had never been interested in this kind of profits. Having committed a horrible crime, Baumius escaped, so there is no hope to get the 50 thalers left by Wolfgang Lazius. He sent another copy of the chronicle of Manasses to Löwenklau, but could not send the rest of what he wanted to send because of the couriers, but after the (Frankfurt) book fair of the Pentecost, he will send some other books. He pleads Zwinger to ask Episcopius or Löwenklau whether they received the books of the Basilica and what they intend to do with such great treasure. Zwinger should also ask Episcopius or whoever else to edit Bonfini's dialogue on chastity in matrimony, which he had sent to Oporinus and is now presumably with Zwinger. He should decide about this matter but make sure to have the scribal errors corrected without damaging Sambucus's codex.

Sambucus salutem.

Tuas Idibus Februarii scriptas pridie Kalendas Iunii accepi. De opera apud praetorem habeo gratiam. Miror eos tam suspiciosos esse posse in re aliena, cum perpetuo literarum cultu dudum omnem eius generis morbum exuisse debebant.[799] Sed urgebo publico mandato brevi, nisi mutuum reddiderint; scis enim nihil me faenori unquam talium collocasse. Baumius horrendo facinore commisso profugit, nuspiam, si deprehendetur, salvus futurus, ut de 50 taleris legatis Lazianis nihil sit sperandum.[800] Leonclavio miseram alterum exemplum nuper Manassis,[801] quae alia voluissem, per tabellarios non licuit, sed post mercatum pentecostes dabo quaedam perferenda etc. Oro te, mi domine Zviggere, de Episcopio quaere aut Leonclavio, an συλλογὴν τῶν Βασιλικῶν[802] acceperint, et quid de tanto fiat thesauro. Rogabis item Episcopium vel quem voles, ut, si ad manus Bonfinii *Dialogos de pudicitia coniugali* a me missos Oporino habetis,[803] ille a nostris desideratum librum edat, et quidquid de reliquis voles, statues, modo sciam. Sed librarii in dialogis aliquot orthographicos errores describendo emendabitis, nec exemplar corrumpi velim.[804] Vale. Vienna pridie Kalendas Iunii 1569.

Address: Clarissimo viro domino Theodoro Zuingero etc., amico suo honorando. Basell.

---

[799] This may refer to some kind of temporary interception of their letters because of sanitary precautions.
[800] On efforts to recuperate 50 thalers from Baumius see also letters 106, 113 and 115.
[801] Manasses, *Annales.*
[802] *LX librorum* Βασιλικῶν. Cf. the Index.
[803] Bonfini, *Symposion trimeron.*
[804] I. e. the emendations should not be written directly into his codex.

135.
Sambucus to the Mayor and citizens of Trnava
30 August 1569, Pressburg

The original is kept in Trnava: SAT, Magistrát mesta Trnava, Missiles. Published in Vantuch, "Die Sambucusbriefe," 343-344.

Sambucus reminds the councillors of his past and future offices toward his patria *and asks them to send a cart of wheat from the common reserves to Vienna tax-free, where there is scarcity. People do not get to bread for days, while he is feeding his family in a mediocre way. Since Sir Kádas also promised to send one cart of wheat from his, they could send both in a large cart, he will pay honestly for the transport. Sambucus came together with the men of Trnava, whom he presented to Johann Baptist Weber, who will be of great help in the business of the tax exemption. He asks his brother-in-law István Nyilas in Hungarian not to forget about him and about the poor little Zsóka. He would be happy if she were taken away from the woman.*

Salutem et servitiorum commendationem. Egregii domini et amicissimi.

Cum semper debito meo vobis et patriae libenter inservierim idque officium non sum facile desertus, hoc vero tempore tanta sit difficultas Viennae tritici et panis, ut multi aliquot diebus careant pane, ego vero, ut sciunt dominationes vestrae, familiam alam mediocriter, oro, velitis unum currum tritici e publico conferre, hoc est, Viennensem Mutt[805] dictum vel quid dominationibus vestris placuerit idque per aliquo curru cum scheda tricesimatoris libera Viennam mittere. Et quia dominus quoque Kadas alterum mutt est ex suo pollicitus, poterit unus currus vestras magnus simul adferre. Qui advehet, habebit in expensas honorarium a me honestum. Locutus sum hic cum dominis concivibus, deduxi eos ad dominum Beberum,[806] commendavi eorum negocium. Is non parum negocio ipsorum proderit aditumque liberum habebunt. Dominationes vestrae eos, qui hic sunt, omnes consentientes de tritico habetis. Ego vero meis officiis compensare, uti hactenus, beneficium vestrum enitor meque commendo et triticum quamprimum expecto. Valeant dominationes vestrae. Posonio 30 Augusti 1569. Vestrarum dominationum servitor et filius D. Ioannes Sambucus.

Nylas uram, Soghor uram, el ne feletkezzetek regy zolgatokrol, ky tuddya hon halalhatom megh. Schwor Mihalnak[807] adassa meg ezennel az levelet. Az szeghin Sokaczkat semmiben

---

[805] "Mutt," usually spelled "Muth," was an Austrian unit of volume used to measure wheat.

[806] Johann Babtist Weber (1526–1584) was imperial vice-chancellor, one of Sambucus's important patrons at court. He was an accomplished careerist with great talent for making a fortune through his diplomatic contacts and for securing his place in the imperial administration through marriage politics. Both later vice-chancellors, Jakob Kurtz and Johann Wolfgang Freymon, were Weber's son-in-laws while the Latin secretary Mark Singkmoser became his brother-in-law. Having bought some estates in Austria, Weber retired in 1577 but as a member of the Privy Council he continued to receive a yearly pension of 1500 florins until his death in 1584. See Andreas Edel, "Johann Baptist Weber (1526-1584). Zum Lebensweg eines gelehrten Juristen und Spitzenbeamten im 16. Jahrhundert," *Mitteilungen des Österreichischen Staatsarhivs* 45 (1997), 111-185; Lothar Gross, *Die Geschichte der Deutschen Reichshofkanzlei von 1559 bis 1806* (Vienna: Selbstverlag des Haus-, Hof- und Staatsarchivs, 1933), 307-321; Goetz, "Die Geheimen Ratgeber," 479, 487-488; Fichtner, *Emperor Maximilian II.*, 85-89; Almási, *The Uses of Humanism*, 133-134; Almási and Molino, "Nikodemismus und Konfessionalisierung," 121-122.

[807] Michael (Mihály) Schwor, citizen of Trnava owed 80 Hungarian florins to Sambucus's father at the time of his death. See the notes in Vantuch, ("Die Sambucusbriefe," 344)

ne haggya kegyelmetek.⁸⁰⁸ Ha el vehetnűk az azzontul, hitemre nagh örömem volna. Kegyelmektektül közönetemet azzaöak [asszonyomnak?]. Es valaztot varok kegyelmetektul.

Address: Egregiis, prudentibus ac circumspectis dominis, iudici civibusque Tyrnaviensibus, dominis et amicis honorandis Tyrnaviam.

136.
Simone Galignani to Sambucus
1 September 1569, Ingolstadt

Dedication by the publisher in Ioannes Paulus Pernumia, *Philosophia naturalis ordine definitivo Tradita, quod a nullo hactenus factum est* (Padua: Apud Simonem Galignanum de Karera, 1570), f. †2ʳ.

Plato put it well that we are not born only for ourselves, but that our country, parents and friends all claim a part of our existence. It is almost a natural instinct to help and benefit each other. People who are not only useless to others, but also hinder others in helping each other are reprehensible and same as beasts. Galignani has always made an effort not to be counted among them. As far as it was possible, he has tried to help others, either by printing books or in other ways. While thinking about which useful work he should publish, he chanced upon a work on natural philosophy by Pernumia, an expert in both medicine and philosophy. As it has been written by a serious man and it deals with the most admirable things, he had to publish it, although it had been lying hidden for some years and was riddled by booklice. What can be more excellent or desirable than philosophy, which is universally seen as the mother of all other arts, detecting hidden causes of things and proving the divine element in humans? Everyone will agree that he is doing right in publishing this book, especially as unlike most other books on natural philosophy it does not deal in a convoluted way with obscure details, but is extraordinarily straightforward and clear. Sambucus possibly wonders why the book is dedicated to him. He has often seen how much Galignani esteems him. Since Galignani has met him, he has loved, cherished and venerated him more than anyone else. Sambucus's humanity, talent, integrity and sincerity have drawn Galignani to join him in an eternal bond of love and veneration. Searching for a gift worthy of Sambucus, he found Pernumia's work, which will not only be useful to students from Sambucus's land, but is also necessary to all who want to reach the pinnacle of philosophy. Although he is obliged to many other people, no one will begrudge the fact that he dedicates it to Sambucus. Sambucus should accept this little present benevolently.

Peritissimo viro D. Ioanni Sambuco, sacratissimae Romanorum imperatoriae ac Germaniae, Hungariae, Bohemiae etc. regiae maiestatis rerum pronunciatori syncero, Simon G.⁸⁰⁹ S. D. P.

---

⁸⁰⁸ On Zsóka (Sophia), see letters 81, 103 and 137.
⁸⁰⁹ Simon Galignanus de Karera (Simone Galignani) was the official librarius (bookseller) of the Padovan university. He was also active as an editor and publisher in Padua and later in Venice, cooperating with various printing establishments. He died probably around 1583, when the imprint "Apud haeredes Simonis Galignani de Karera" first appears. Cf. the article by Mario Infelise, in *DBI* 51 (1998), 466-467. On his further dealings with Sambucus cf. the Index.

Optime a gravissimo illo tum intellegendi, tum etiam dicendi auctore et magistro Platone dictum esse arbitror, vir quam elegantissime, nos non solum nobis natos esse, sed ortus nostri partem patriam, partem parentes, partem etiam amicos sibi vendicare.[810] Etenim cum hominum inter homines societas (ut disertissime Cicero nobis prodidit) artibus, opera, facultatibus et mutatione officiorum devinciri soleat,[811] necesse est, ut quasi naturae quodam instinctu, alius alii prodesse laboret atque alter in alterius emolumentum suos actus et operationes referre quodammodo teneatur. Quare et repraehendos plurimum et brutis animantibus adaequandos esse iudico eos, qui, cum aequissima natura suadente hominum generi et praesertim iis, quibuscum necessitudo aliqua intercedit, utiles esse debeant, tantum abest, ut id efficiant, ut etiam, ne alii quoque id faciant, multis rationibus impedire conentur. In quorum quidem numerum ne ullo modo adscriberer, certe (ut scis Sambuce doctissime) omnem et dedi operam et dandam esse maximopere semper ego existimavi. Nam quandocunque vel potui, vel occasio sese mihi obtulit (quod tamen arroganter dictum esse nolo), qua excudendo libros, qua alia industria, omnibus, omni tempore, qualitercunque potui, fructum affere desideravi. Atque cum proximis etiam hisce diebus eius animi essem, ut exquisitissimo illi naturae muneri, pro exigua ingenii mei facultate, satisfacerem cogitaremque, quidnam, quod et necessarium et maxime utile hominibus esset, in lucem proferre deberem, incidi tandem in opus quoddam naturalis philosophiae Ioannis Pauli Pernumiae,[812] viri tum in medica arte exercitatissimi, tum etiam multum in philosophiae rebus versati. Quod, quoniam ut a gravissimo viro, ita de rebus admodum praeclaris scriptum videbam, certe, quin[813] illud (quamvis aliquot annos in tenebris latitaret et a tineis fere consumptum esset) in lucem non proferrem, facere nulla ratione potui. Quid est enim, quaeso, quod aut praestantius aut optabilius esse possit hac toties ab eruditissimis quibusque viris laudata philosophia? Nonne etenim haec mater omnium disciplinarum atque donum et inventum deorum esse dicitur? Nonne laudandarum artium omnium procreatrix et parens esse ab omnibus admittitur. Nonne haec ea est, quae rerum caussas quaeque maxime abdita sunt aperiens lucemque iis, quae obscuriora sunt, adhibens hominumque cognoscentem vim illustrans, eos coeleste ac divinum aliquid in se continere omnibus probat? Quamobrem non immerito me hunc pulcherrimum librum recte in manus hominum adduxisse omnes profecto confitebuntur, praesertim autem, cum is non, quemadmodum plurimi forsan alii de naturali philosophia hactenus editi libri (pace omnium dixerim) tricis quibusdam et obscuritatibus involutus sit, sed ita perspicuus itaque dilucidus, ut magis perspicue aut clarius scribi quidem vix potuerit. Verum miraberis forsitan, Sambuce prudentissime, atque quaeres, quam ob rem haec a me ad te modo adferantur quidve sit, quod tam alte repetita utar narratione. Nosti bene, nosti, inquam, et saepissime, nisi fallor, perspexisti, quanti te semper ego fecerim quantaque veneratione prosecutus fuerim. Tu si quidem et charissimus mihi, et praeter caeteros omnes, quos summopere amavi, cum primum

---

[810] Plato, *Epistola* 9, in a translation by Cicero, *De officiis* 1.22.
[811] Cicero, *De officiis* 1.22.
[812] Giovanni Paolo Pernumia (died before 1564, when his work was published posthumously) was a Paduan physician and an Aristotelian philosopher. Apart from the information in the paratexts included in the prints of his works, very little is known about him. In his writings he tried to organize natural philosophy and therapeutic medicine in a systematic way. His *Therapeutice sive medendi ratio affectus omnes praeter naturam* (Venetiae: Apud Simonem Galignanum de Karera, 1564) was reprinted several times. See the article by Gregorio Piaia in *DBI* (https://www.treccani.it/enciclopedia/giovanni-paolo-pernumia_(Dizionario-Biografico)/, accessed on 12 March 2024); Bruno Nardi, *Saggi Sull'Aristotelismo Padovano Dal Secolo XIV Al XVI* (Florence: G. C. Sansone, 1958), 402-404.
[813] Print: *quum*.

te cognovi, maxime collendus fuisti, te, inquam, unice semper dilexi, te colui, te observavi teque integerrime veneratus sum. Neque iniuria. Tanta etenim est in te humanitas, tantum ingenii acumen, tanta vitae integritas tantaque animi synceritas, ut profecto totum me tibi obstrinxeris vinculoque quodam venerationis et amoris perpetuo devictum reddideris. Quas ob causas quaerenti mihi, quidnam tibi conferre deberem, quod tua auctoritate et munificentia dignum foret, quodque meum erga te officium, si non, ut vellem et par esset, at aliquomodo declarare posset, id mihi occurit Pernumiae opus, id, inquam, volumen, tam patriae tuae studiosis maxime utile, quam etiam (ut ipsemet iudicare poteris) omnibus ad philosophiae culmen conscendere conantibus multum maximeque necessarium. Quod quidem, licet multis aliis, quibus plurimum me debere existimo, dicare potuerim, attamen cum ipsos id omnes facile permittere viderem, ut tibi plus quam illis devinctus viderer, tibi illud consecrandum esse putavi. Quare, aequo ac benevolo animo, vir clarissime, id a tuo Simone suscipias nec ita ipsius munusculi rationem habeas velim (exiguum enim admodum est), quemadmodum animi, quo tibi confertur et quo te ego adeo certe prosequor, ut verbis explicare non possim. Vale et me, ut soles, plurimum ama. Patavii, die primo mensisi Septembris anno domini MDLXIX.

137.
Sambucus to István Nyilas, Mayor of Trnava
6 September 1569, Vienna

The original is kept in Trnava: SAT, Magistrát mesta Trnava, Missiles. Published in Kóssa, "Adatok Sámboky János életéhez," 373-374; Vantuch, "Die Sambucusbriefe," 345-346.

Sambucus was very confused by the death of little Zsóka. He was about to bring her away despite Madam Veni's fury and keep her until God decided about her fate, but the debt (for life) needs to be repaid and one cannot protest against this. He is sure that Zsóka is in God's lap, and has his mercy. The little quantity of cloths and stuff she used to have can stay with madam (Veni), as they are poor, but they have nothing to do with the cloths sold by Márton Szabó [Tailor],[814] and for which Sambucus had spent 60 florins, as Mihály Komornik knows it well. Moreover, he had lent 50 florins to his brother-in-law Panithy for the house, but they should squabble about it themselves, he has spent and bothered about it sufficiently, and also gave Albert (Sambucus) 8 florins in Vienna later. He would happily go to Trnava but he has some things to do both in Vienna and Pressburg. Sambucus will leave for Pressburg the following day and asks Nyilas to let someone search for Mihály Komornik and send him to Pressburg so that he could have a talk with him. It can bring no harm to Komornik, as Sambucus has always been and wants to be a friend to him. He thanks Nyilas for intervening in the case of the cart of wheat, if he has not served for it, he wants to do so. They should send the wheat in strong sacks at least to Pressburg if not to Vienna. Philepp Kádas also promised to send a portion of wheat, but it has not been threshed yet. Nyilas would do a great favour for Sambucus if he lent a cart of wheat to Kádas, and send him both. Sambucus should deserve more from Kádas, as he owes him 100 florins, but he never demanded it, so Nyilas should not worry about also sending the part of Kádas. If Kádas does not keep his word, it does not mean that Sambucus would not pay for it and remain also obliged. If he can linger a few days in Pressburg, he would pay a visit to Nyilas, who should tell Márton Szabó that Szabó's letter arrived.

---

[814] We could not identify Márton Szabó.

Zerelmes soghor uram, byzon ighen megh haborodam az en edes Sokaczka halalan. Kyt zinthe mostan nagh haraghiaval nagh akarattyaval az Veny azzonnak el akartam hoznya, es nalam tartani,[815] migh az Ur Isten zerenzyet paranczyoltha volna, de ez adossagnak megh kell lennye fizetise, es semmy okh, gondolath ellen nem tehet: semmi ketsighem benne, hogh az Ur Istennek ewlebe vagyon, es kegyelmeben. Tovabbam az mi kewes portecaczka volt az azzonnal, es Panythy ruhaczka, azzal nem banthatom, sem kewanom, mert Zeghinek. De az my ruhat Zabo Marthon el adoth, ahhoz semmi gondyok, es azra en kewltöttem 60 fl, minth tuddya Mihal comornik. Azmelleth Panythy zoghoromnak 50 fl attam volt az hazra kewltzen; ha azt megh addyak, am pewröllyenek ewk erette, en elegheth kewltettem, vezottem erette, es annak felötte adogattamis Albertnek itfen [itt fenn] 8 fl. azutan. En eremest ala mennek, de ielez nehan dolgom, nem magame vagyon mind itfen, mind Posomban. Holnap ala Posomba kezdek mennem; kegyelmedet kerem, kerestesse megh Komornik Mihalt, es kewldye fel nehan zora Pozomban kegyelmet. Nem arthatna nekyek, es megh esmerik, hogh barattyok voltam, es akarok lennem. Az egg' szeker gabonarol hogh kegyelmed ir, közönem, es ha megh nem zolgalam, megh akarom zolgalny, kegyelmed valamy ewrös szekerrel zagokban [zsákokban], hanem sinthe ide fell akaryatok, ottan Posonigh kewldyetek.

Kadas Philepp azt mondya, hogh egg itvalo Muttal ewys ad, de nem czepeltettett megh.[816] Ha kegyelmed addigh kewltzyen adna nekye, es eggiwt kwldene fel, nagh baratsagott tenne kegyelmed es megh halalnam az uraimnak. Tobbetys erdemlek Kadas uramtul, merth 100 fl. tartoz<ik>nek, de nem kivannam soha. Isten tartza megh kegyelmedet, es az Kadas rizetis [részét is?] batoron kwldye fell kegyelmed. Ha ew nem allana megh fogadasat, en embersighemre fogadom, hogh az arrat kegyelmednek azuntol meg adom, es meghis kewzönem. Datum Viennae 6 Septembris 1569. Kegyelmed zoghora Samboky.

Ha Posonban nehany napoth kezhettem, megh visitalom kegyelmed Isten akarattyabol. Zabo Marthonnak mondassa megh kegyelmed, hogh az ew levelet megh attak etc.
1569. 6. Septembris.

Address: Nylas Istvan uramnak, Naghzombathy byronak, nekem zerelmes zoghor uramnak kezehez. Nagh Zombathban.

138.
Sambucus to István Nyilas, Mayor of Trnava
15 September 1569, Pressburg

The original is kept in Trnava: SAT, Magistrát mesta Trnava, Missiles. Published in Kóssa, "Adatok Sámboky János életéhez," 374 (postscript is missing); Vantuch, "Die Sambucusbriefe," 346-347.

Sambucus would unpretentiously let it go; he has made a pact with Anna Panithy and Mihály Komornik that they would never go to court because of the bequest of János Panithy or because of or Zsóka Panithy. Sambucus let them have the cloths as well but they should give him the upper

---
[815] See letter 135. We could not identify Madam Veni.
[816] See ibid.

dress and rock of bluish colour and the 25 florins which is with Nyilas; he has spent three times more before. He let the 50 florins of debt of (János) Panithy go and the price of the vineyard. Nyilas should keep the 25 florins, give the tailor Márton Szabó the rest of the cloths, the taffeta bluish upper dress with the red velvet, add the rock to it, and possibly also send them to Vienna. He should also send the letter of the family pact with Albert; God should let him win this (debate). They also tore up the bill of debt of 50 florins of poor Panithy. This happened in the presence of Matthias Graecus, who can testify to this last and ultimate mutual agreement.

Zerelmes Soghor Uram, en jamborol, eligeth engednem, meg zerzottem Panythy Anna azzonal es Komornik Mihallyal,[817] hittönkre, embersegöenkre, hogh soha eggikünk sem keres masikon semmit, sem peröllünk valahon mi volt Panythy Janos marhayval Sokatzkarol [Zsókácskáról], kwltzigröl, es egg' zoval minden dolog, öröksig felol ky lehetne. Az ruhatis nekiek engettem, hanem az felsö sederyes ruhat, es zoknyat ky addyak, es 25 fl. ky kegwdevel [kegwdnel?] vagyon aztis nekem addyak, az ellete en koltettem harom anyit. Az 50 fl. kiwel tartozot Panythy es az zölö arrat mert hogh be vettem, megh engettem. Azwthan kegyelmednek vallom, es kerem, hogh az 25 fl. megh tarcza, Zabo Marthonnak[818] haggya hog anny [ami] ruha maradot, vagh az arra mi maradot addyak nekiek, az sederies taffta felsö ruhat verös barzonval vettet, es zoknat veghe hozza, ha lehet kwldye felys valakitül. Az hazy pactum leweletis Albertell, megh ighertven, es megh köldyen, Isten engeddye hogh nyerhessek. Az seghin Panythy ados leweletis az 50 fl. el zaggatuk,[819] de kerhessem raytok. Datum Posonii in praesentia reverendi domini Matthiae Graeci etc. 15 Septembris 1569. Johannes Sambucus mp.

Ego Mathias Grecus praepositus maior et vicarius fateor me in hista [!] ultima et plenaria concordia praesentem fuisse.[820] Idem manu propria me subscripsi.

Address: Egregio domino Stephano Nylas, iudici civitatis Tyrnaviensis, domino et affini honorando. Tyrnaviam.

139.
Sambucus to Michael Otrer
1 October 1569, Vienna

Published in Sambucus, *Elegia de angelis*, f. A2[r-v].[821]

When Otrer invited him for lunch to celebrate the name day, although he had more pressing matters at hand and felt that this artistic task would be too difficult for him, he wanted to make a contribution and rapidly wrote down what came to his mind on angels. Otrer's son Johannes recognising that

---

[817] It appears from this letter that Anna Panithy was a close relative (perphaps sister) of Sambucus's former brother-in-law and her husband was Mihály Komornik.

[818] Szabó means tailor in Hungarian, which actually seems to be his profession as well. See the preceding letter on Szabó's involvement in the matter of the cloths.

[819] He demanded earlier this money from Albertus Sambucus. See letter 80.

[820] Matthias Graecus (Görög) was vicar of the archbishop Nicolaus Olahus. See István Fazekas, "Oláh Miklós reformtörekvései az esztergomi egyházmegyében 1553–1568 között" [The reform attempts of Nicolaus Olahus in the diocese of Esztergom in 1553–1568], *Történeti Szemle* 45 (2003), 139-154; Károly Péterffy, *Sacra Concilia Ecclesiae Romano-catholicae in Regno Hungariae celebrata* (Posonii: Kaliwodianis, 1742), 2:147.

[821] Cf. letter 132.

Sambucus would be ready to publish it, he took care of it. As it is a difficult argument, it has rarely been treated in poetry. It was certainly troublesome to find copious and powerful words. He preferred content to superstitious expressions; the majesty of the angels to the variability of the expressions and classical references; simple words to obscurity. Sambucus added to his poem a short prayer based on Matthew 8, accommodated to modern times, and a letter on the death of Mark Singkmoser.

Ioannes Sambucus Michaeli Otrer, civi Viennensi, amico veteri salutem.

Cum ob diei celebritatem, memoriamque nominis, ad prandium me vocasses, etsi, quod magis urgeo, prae manibus erat καὶ τὴν εὐμουσίαν[822] mihi difficiliorem fore sentiebam, adferre tamen symbolam volui arreptoque calamo istud, quidquid est, de angelis subito exaravi. Quod ipsum filius tuus Ioannes intelligens commune uti esse pateretur, impetravit. Argumentum ipsum ut arduum, nec ita vulgo numeris tractatum, satis certe ad verborum copiam vimque proprietatum adhibendam fuit molestum. Rebus igitur potius, quam vocum superstitioni, angelorum maiestati, quam varietati phrasium, aut imitationi ad veteres alludenti, ut omnes intelligerent, verbis planis, quam obscuritati hac opella inserviendum putavi. Cui precatiunculam ex Math. VIII. hisce accommodatam temporibus addidi, una cum Epistola de obitu domini Singhmoseri. Quae tu, mi Otrer, amori nostro, iussui partim amicorum, filiique postulationibus, cui vel maiora vix negarim, tribues. Viennae Kalendis Octobribus 1569.

140.
Sambucus to Piero Vettori
13 November 1569, Vienna

The original is kept in Munich, BSB, Clm 735, Nr. 19. Published in *Clarorum Italorum et Germanorum epistolae*, 2:47; Gerstinger, "Die Briefe," 102-103.

Sambucus justifies his silence with reference to his stay away for more than two months because of businesses and judicial cases. He would not forget about Vettori, who showed fatherly feelings toward him. He wonders what Vettori is working on, what he will publish next. Busy by commenting and collecting Hungarian histories, he hardly has any time to look at the authors who were so familiar to him earlier, but during the coming winter he wants to engage with the emendation of Quintilian and Hermogenes of Tarsus. He recently saw a French edition by Francesco Porto of the latter, but it hardly offered more than some references. He is now publishing Stobaeus's Physical and Moral Extracts *in Antwerp and the epitome of the councils collected by Zonaras. The emperor will leave for Prague at the end of the month, as Vettori may have heard from others.*

Clarissimo viro Petro Victorio Sambucus salutem.

Diuturni silentii non mutatus sensus aut negligentia, sed duorum et amplius mensium absentia negociorum vel in foro patriae disceptatorum causa fuit.[823] Qui enim tui obliviscar,

---

[822] and the sense of beauty
[823] Concerning Sambucus's legal troubles, see also Illésy, "Sámboky János történetíróról," which regards still another judicial case, going back to his father's times.

quem erga me paterna voluntate, studio et amore singulari aliquot exemplis didici? Cupio intelligere, quid modo lucubraris (qui numquam ociosus es), quid brevi nobis sis ex officina illa erudita plenaque daturus. Ego annotandis colligendisque historiolis Pannonicis occupatus antea familiares vix inspicere scriptores iam possum, vellem tamen hac hyeme in Quinctiliani emendationem quiddam conferre,[824] itemque Hermogenis, quem in Gallia recusum a Francisco Porto nuper vidi, sed praeter exemplorum loca addita non multum praestitit.[825] Stobaei Φυσικὰ nunc Antverpiae imprimi curo,[826] et epitomen synodorum a Zonara collectam.[827] Ἔρρωσο[828] Vienna Idibus Novembris 1569.

Imperator Pragam hinc discessurus est sub fine mensis huius, quod ex aliis plenius et alia soles doceri.

Address: Clarissimo viro domino Petro Victorio, praeceptori et amico singulari. Florentiam.

141.
Sambucus to István Nyilas, Mayor of Trnava
26 December 1569, Vienna

Published in Vantuch, "Die Sambucusbriefe," 347-348.[829] [These are in fact two letters addressed to Nyilas, the first one is by an elder relative of Sambucus, as he calls Sambucus his son.[830]]

The author wishes his friend Nyilas a happy new year. He sent his man to Trnava because of some business and the debt. He sends a bolt of lint to his wife not as a payment but as a reminder of his friendship. He claims to rightly complain about the furrier Mihály Szűcs who has owed him money for so long and now demands another loan for leather, in case he wants to be paid back. He is not used to keep his money idle for so long, he wants to get it back and does not care about the interest. He will make sure to get it back. The more he does and the more he is liberal, the more ungrateful the world becomes. But he does not reprove Szűcs, as he will need him on other occasions.
Sambucus, together with his wife and little daughter, wishes his brother-in-law a happy new year. He does not know if Mihály Schwor has given back the 300 florins ordered to be paid by Johannes

---

[824] On Sambucus's study of Quintilian cf. the Index.
[825] Aphthonius, *Hermogenes et Dionysius Longinus, praestantissimi artis rhetoricae magistri, Francisci Porti Cretensis opera industriaque illustrati atque expoliti* ([Genevae]: Crispinus, 1569). The edition has a few marginal explanatory and referential notes. Francesco Porto (1511–1581) was a Greek humanist, a student of Arsenio di Monemvasia, who taught Greek at the academy of Geneva. See M. Manoussakas, "L'aventure vénitienne de François Portus," *Bulletin de la Société d'Histoire et d'Archéologie de Genève* 17 (1980–1983) [1985], 299-314.
[826] Stobaeus et Plethon, *Stobaei eclogarum libri duo ... et Plethonis de rebus Peloponnesiacis orationes duae*.
[827] We do not know of any edition of Zonaras by Sambucus. Johannes Zonaras (c. 1074–after 1159), a Byzantine chronicler and theologian, was first secretary to the emperor Alexios I Komnenos. An edition of the work in question was published in 1613: *Ioannis Zonarae monachi In canones veterum conciliorum commentarii, nunquam antea Graece, aut Latine editi*, ed. Antonius Salmatia (Mediolani: apud B. Lantonum, 1613). The work was included in Sambucus's codex "Collectio canonistica," which is held by the ÖNB as Cod. Hist. gr. 12, f. 10ʳ-32ʳ.
[828] farewell
[829] The original kept in Trnava (SAT) could not be identified, so we relied on Vantuch's edition.
[830] The author might be Sambucus's father-in-law Koloman Egerer, which would prove his good knowledge of Hungarian (although it is difficult to tell more in the absence of an autograph).

Sommer (the former mayor of Trnava). If he needs to travel to Trnava in order to get it back, he will also demand money for the expenses and the damage. He asks Nyilas to tell this to Michael Schwor and Sommer, who keep silent after so many of his letters. Nyilas should not let the wolf become needy, and Sambucus will pay back the favours.

Nagh sok ewduesseghes uyestendoben etc.

Zerelmes uram io barathom kiwanok kegyelmednek mind Samboky fiammal egyetemben. Ime ualamy dolgokert, es adossagertis esmegh ala kwldem emberemet, kyt kegyelmed ne haggyon, es erten mindenkeppen ualo io akarattya kegyelmed kyt meg akarok zolgalnom. Ime azzonyomnak egg uegh gyolczot kwltem, kiuel nem akarok fizetnem, hanem czak emlekeznem baratsagodrol. Zewcz Mihairol meltan panazzolkodhatom, kyt adossemal nem ighen zoktam, hogh enny idewtul fogua tartozuan, nem czak nem fizet, hanem egh kewes bewrre meg annak feulette 1000 latten kert kwltzen, ha azt akarom hogh az elwbbit megh fizesse. Nem zoktam az en penzemet nyergelny oknekwl, es nem kiwanom bewnyt czak addyemeg enny idewtul fogua valo penzemet. Hogh meg nem czeleszy ez uttal, gondot vyzelek rea. Mentewl tewbbet miuelek es engedek, attul halalatlanib az vylagh. De nem diczyrem, mert maszoris kell az ember. Isten tarcza megh kegyelmed mind a azzonyommal, gyermekywei velouk es zok eztendeig, minden kegyelmes anandekyual. Beczbol Zent Istwan napyan. 1569. Kegyeimetnek io barathya.

Zerelmes zoghor uram Istentul kiwanok kegyelmednek nagh zok io uy eztendwt eghyssiget, mennyey malaztot azzonyommal eggyetemben mind felesegemtul, leanyoczkamtul, amen. Az mesterrol nem iratok tewbet, elys ment imaran kermendo kyt kwldek vala. Az Schwor nem tudom ha meg atta az 300 fl., kyt Sommer bezedete, fogadasora hattam uolt nala, es mint kwzre biztam uolt. Byzon ha ala kell mennem, az kwltsziget, mind karral eggiwt megh kiwanom. Kerem kegyelmed izennye meg Sommernek es Schwornakis mert enny leueleimre czak halgatnak. Kegyelmed az farkazt szwgsigibe ne haggya, kepes dolgaban kyt enis megh zolgalok kegyelmet. Kegyelmet zoghora Samboky.

Address: Nemes es tiztelendo uramnak barathomnak Nylas Istuan uramnak. Zombathy byrona' tulaydon kezehez. Nagh Zombath.

142.
Joachim Camerarius Sr. to Sambucus
22 January 1570, Leipzig

Published in Camerarius, *Epistolarum libri quinque*, 414-415.

Camerarius received Sambucus's letter from his fellow countryman Georgius (Bánchay), who up to now lived with Camerarius but his health did not let him stay longer. He knows from Camerarius's son-in-law Esrom Rüdinger that meanwhile Bánchay has suffered much and seriously of his sickness. So he thinks to return to Sambucus and offered to bring a letter, and Camerarius wanted to take advantage of the opportunity. Camerarius is worried for Sambucus and his Viennese friends because of the news of the plague in Vienna. His region is peaceful, except for some neighbouring people who continue roar against them and give reason for new strife. His health is the same but the medicine he recently took made his problem worse. Printing Sambucus's manuscripts is not only hindered by his feebleness but also by the fact that publishers are busy and prefer to publish other books. Nevertheless, he promises to do something sometimes. He gave some (books) to Georgius to bring them to Sambucus, who should say hello to Camerarius's old friend Paulus Fabritius, Thomas Jordan, and a certain Lehmann and Zimmermann, and Sambucus's father-in-law, Koloman Egerer.

S. D.

Attulit mihi aliquando literas abs te popularis tuus Georgius, qui apud nos hactenus vixit et fuit eius consuetudo omnibus bonis grata atque iucunda.[831] Sed valetudo eum diutius illo in loco permanere non est passa. Atque significat mihi gener meus Esromus multum et interdum graviter illum laborasse. Itaque necessitate coactus hac loca reliquit et se reverti ad te cogitare et, si quid literarum ad te dare vellem, ad perferendum se esse paratum mihi ostendit. Sane gavisus sum offerri occasionem mearum aliquid ad te mittendi, quae longo iam tempore nulla appareret. Sed Georgii vicem, ut par erat, dolui, cuius probitas meliorem fortunam merebatur. Verum Dei scilicet aeterni haec voluntas est, cui parere nos omnibus modis decet, et tua humanitas benigne recipiet Georgium nostrum, quem aliquando studiose nobis commendasti.

Fama est hic cum magna nostra de te et tuis aliisque amicis istic solicitudine sparsa vestram urbem contagionibus pestilentiae esse infestam. Itaque commendare precibus nostris salutem vestram Χριστῷ Ἰησοῦ σωτῆρι[832] non cessamus. In his regionibus nullus esset magnopere singulari querelae locus, nisi in vicinia obstrepentes maledicendo nostris quidam non desinerent novarum rixarum indies causas dare. Cumque importunitas istorum sane animadvertenda sit, equidem vereor, quo tandem evadant contentiones istae.

Mea valetudo antiquum obtinet et fieri hanc infirmiorem non est mirandum. Nuper usu medicamentorum valde fuerat irritatum malum. Nunc ἀνέχεσθαι καὶ ἀπέχεσθαι[833] soleo. Quo minus accepta abs te quaedam hic exprimantur, non solum obstat mea languiditas, sed officinarum etiam occupatio, quae aliis editionibus operam dare malunt. Studebimus tamen aliquando aliquid effici.[834] Tradidi quaedam afferenda tibi Georgio nostro, quae tua humanitas boni consulet. D. Fabricium[835] veterem amicum meum per occasionem meis verbis salutes

---

[831] Georgius Bánchay was sent for a study tour by the city of Trnava. See letter 130.
[832] to Jesus Christ the Saviour
[833] to hold up and keep away. In the margin: Sustinere et abstinere.
[834] The same was repeated in most of Camerarius's previous letters.
[835] Paulus Fabritius (Schmid) (1529–1589) born in Lubań/Lauban (Silesia) and studied probably with Camerarius in Leipzig. He arrived to Vienna in 1553. In 1557 he became doctor of medicine and probably soon joined the university as professor of mathematics, while also working as imperial physician. In 1555 he married the daughter of Georg Rithaymer, Sambucus's former university professor. As an astronomer, he observed three comets during his life as well as the new star of 1571, published astronomical tables, constructed a clock (in Olomouc), and engaged in cartography. He was the first to climb the mount Ötscher in 1574 in the company of Johann Aichholz and Carolus Clusius. See Tino Fröde, "Paulus Fabricius – ein universaler Humanist aus Lauban: Sein Leben, seine Schriften und seine Beziehungen zur Oberlausitz," *Neues lausitzsches Magazin* 13 (2010), 55-70; Kaufmann, "Astronomy, Technology, Humanism"; Almási, *The Uses of Humanism*, passim.

velim. Itemque dominos Iordanem, Lemanum[836] et Zimmermanum[837] et tuum socerum inprimis. Bene vale. Lipsiae, die 22. mensis Ianuarii 70.

143.
Sambucus to the Council of Trnava
27 February 1570, Vienna

The original is kept in Trnava: SAT, Magistrát mesta Trnava, Missiles. Published in Vantuch, "Die Sambucusbriefe," 348-349.

Sambucus informs the members of the Council about Camerarius's letter on the forced return of Georgius Banchay, justified also by the doctor, and asks them to accept it prudently, inform his father Mathias and continue to support the adolescent. Georgius is of rare talent and diligence, and he will be useful for the city someday.

Salutem et commendationem servitiorum.

Scripsit ad me vir clarissimus Ioachimus Camerarius, cui Georgium vestrum commendaram, ex testimonio doctoris generi sui[838] caussas, quare Georgius istic degere non potuerit diutius, prout cupiisset vosque mandastis.[839]

Quas ego caussas sufficere apud vestram prudentiam puto ipseque coram omnia copiosius narrabit. Commendo eum vobis porro, ne patrocinio suscepto deferatis, qui adolescens ingenio et studio rarus est vestrisque usibus brevi profuturus est. Itaque ut faciatis, vos pro vestra humanitate et iusta liberalitate oro, patrique Mathiae excusetis simul. Valete meque commendatum habeat vestra prudentia. 27. Februarii 1570. Vestrae humanitatis et prudentiae servitor, Sambucus.

Address: Prudenti ac humanissimo senatui Tyrnaviensi etc., dominis et patronis observandissimis. Tirnaviam.

144.
Sambucus to Piero Vettori
30 April 1570, Vienna

The original is kept in Munich, BSB, Clm 735, Nr. 35. Published in *Clarorum Italorum et Germanorum epistolae*, 2:52-53; Gerstinger, "Die Briefe," 104-105.

As Crato von Krafftheim was called back to Vienna by a sick Hungarian noblewoman, he entrusted his letter and that of Johannes Caselius to Sambucus and urged him to send them to

---

[836] This might be Zacharias Lehmann, later printer in Wittenberg.
[837] This might be the son of Michael Zimmermann (Cymbermannus) († 1565?), who was a Viennese printer, printing books in various languages (German, Latin, Greek, Italian, Spanish, Arabic, Syriac and Hebrew).
[838] Esrom Rüdinger.
[839] See the preceding letter.

Vettori. He wishes that by virtue of his talents Caselius were wealthier, as common people think philosophy to be needy if money is lacking. If only he sustained his studies with the practice of the medical or legal profession or took care of himself through some good marriage or position. But such people find happiness in virtue itself. Sambucus has learnt about Vettori's new book on the cultivation of olive trees. He hopes to read it soon all the more so as he is fully immersed now in the emendation of the Greek text of Dioscorides. He asks Vettori for any annotation he may have done on the subject in Italian libraries. Vettori's "Politica" is expected by all.

Domino Petro Victorio Ioannes Sambucus salutem.

Valetudine illustrissimae cuiusdam faeminae pannonicae Viennam Crato noster evocatus has mihi suas itemque Caselii commendavit interesseque non parum, ut quam primum tuteque ad te perferrentur, dixit.[840] Quod ipse vel nomine tuo inspecto, cui privatim quoque semper debebo, solicite curassem. Caselii fortunae ingeniique meritis cuperem ampliora; sed nosti philosophiam indigam, ubi χρήματα[841] desint, vulgo censeri. Utinam cum studiis tam reconditis suis medicinae aut iuris professionem suscepisset, consuluisset rebus suis copiosiore aliquo matrimonio vel loco etc.; ἀλλ' ἡ ἀρετὴ τοῖς τοιούτοις αὐταρκὴς εἶναι πρὸς εὐδαιμονίαν[842] absque comitatu externo δοκεῖ.

Audio te libellum eruditum et universae Italiae probatissimum de oleae cultu edidisse,[843] quem brevi me lecturum spero, idque eo cupidius fiet, quod in Dioscoride Graeco purgando nunc totus sim,[844] ad quem, si vel ipse vel per alios ex bibliothecis vestris quiddam annotasti, oro, mecum communices; cuius beneficii memoriam non patiar latere. Politica omnes expectant.[845] Vale mihique per ocium rescribito. Vienna. Ex Museolo, pridie Kalendas Maii 1570.

Address: A Molto Mag. Signor Pietro Vittorio Gentilhuomo fiorentino etc., patron suo et amico. In Fiorenza.

---

[840] Johannes Caselius (Kessel) (1533–1613) was a philologist of Göttingen, who studied in Wittenberg under Melanchthon and in Leipzig under Camerarius. After 1560 he also studied in Bologna, where he became doctor of law in 1566, and in Florence, where he became a student and friend of Vettori. He returned home through Vienna in 1568 (where Crato managed to get his diploma of nobility renewed), taught first rhetoric in Rostock, then tutored princely heirs and became professor of philosophy in Helmstedt. Caselius held irenic religious views, like Sambucus and most of his friends. See Heinrich Julius Kämmel's article in *ADB* 4 (1876), 40-43; Mario Scattola, "Gelehrte Philologie vs. Theologie: Johannes Caselius im Streit mit den Helmstedter Theologen," in *Die europäische Gelehrtenrepublik im Zeitalter des Konfessionalismus*, ed. Herbert Jaumann (Wiesbaden: Harrassowitz, 2001), 155-181.
[841] money
[842] but for such people the virtue seems to be sufficient for their happiness (without external trappings)
[843] Piero Vettori, *Trattato delle lodi e della coltivazione degli ulivi* (Firenze: Giunti, 1574). First published in 1569.
[844] See Gerstinger, "Zusammenfassung," 297-302.
[845] Petrus Victorius, *Commentarii in VIII. libros Aristotelis de optimo statu civitatis* (Florentiae: Giunti, 1576).

145.
Benito Arias Montano[846] to Sambucus
[early May 1570], [Antwerp]

A draft of the letter is kept in Stockholm, Kungliga Bibliotek, Engeströmska Samlingen, A 902. cart. Misc. XVI. f. 196ᵛ.[847] Published with a Spanish translation in *La Biblia Políglota*, 192-195.

Since the study of literature and religion also fortifies friendships, it has always been considered a good way to establish and confirm friendly contacts between people who have never met. Montano now addresses Sambucus as someone unknown to him, believing that like studies have the power to make people friends and seeing that Sambucus is pious and erudite, which is proven also by his own writings and classical editions and testified by their mutual friend Christophe Plantin. There is no one else who burns with more of a passion and love for studies than Montano, and to no one does Plantin matter more than to him. No one is therefore more eager to get close to Sambucus, whose erudition, talents and religious zeal are well proven and are also testified by great men. Montano thought that their mutual friendship toward Plantin may be a good occasion to address a letter to Sambucus, and he looked for a worthy argument suitable for initiating communication. It is about the preface into the Bible, which he was writing in the last days following the topic given by Philip II of Spain. This Bible is being published by Plantin at the advice and with the authority of the king and Montano is the chief editor. However, Montano wanted to have first the critical comments of the most learned and purest men, to whom also Sambucus belongs, so he is asking him to put his notes and corrections into the copy.

Iohanni Sambuco salutem.

Cum pietatis et bonarum literarum similibus studiis amicorum etiam communio accedit, eae res satis idoneae semper optimis viris existimatae sunt ad novas inter eos, qui se mutuo antea alias non viderint aut cognoverint, amicitias, consuetudines ac necessitudines ineundas et confirmandas. Quippe cum ipsa religionis communio et fraterna dilectio homines vinciat, studiorum preterea similitudo amorem mutuum, etiam inter absentes, conciliet et amicorum

---

[846] Benito Arias Montano (1527–1598) was a polymath from Spain. He studied initially in Seville, then in Alcalá de Henares, where next to medicine he took up theology and philosophy. He also studied Oriental languages (Arabic, Hebrew and Syriac). Having received holy orders he started studing the Bible more profoundly. In 1562, he participated in the Council of Trent, and in 1566 he was made chaplain of Philip II. Montano's life achievement was the new polyglot edition of the "Royal Bible," published in eight volumes (1569–1572) by Plantin, realised on the commission of the king (see note 849). Montano also published works concerning individual books of the Bible and provided numberless erudite commentaries on Hebrew idioms, chronology, geography, archaic languages and customs. A Salamanca professor of Oriental languages denounced him for using rabbinical works too liberally but was freed from the charges by the Inquisition in 1580. See *Anatomía del humanismo: Benito Arias Montano, 1598-1998*, ed. L. G. Canseco (Huelva: Universidad de Huelva, 1998); Sylvaine Hänsel, *Benito Arias Montano, humanismo y arte en España* (Huelva: Universidad de Huelva, 1999); Ronald W. Truman, "Justus Lipsius, Arias Montano and Pedro Ximenes," in *The World of Justus Lipsius: A Contribution Towards His Intellectual Biography*, ed. Marc Laureys (Turnhout: Brepols, 1998); Antonio Dávila Pérez, "New documents on Benito Arias Montano and Politics in the Netherlands," in *Between Scylla and Charybdis*, 233-262; Guy Lazure, "Becoming an Antwerp Humanist: The Culture of Friendship and Patronage in the Circles of Benito Arias Montano (156–1598)," *Erudition and the Republic of Letters* 6 (2021), 270-298.

[847] This letter and the next one are two drafts of the same letter. Apparently only the second one was sent to Sambucus. They are preserved in a Stockholm codex dedicated to the publication of the Polyglot Bible.

communia pignora necessitudines efficiant certissimas. His igitur nominibus omnibus, quod a me iam diu est, quamvis alias tibi ignoto, plurimum animo dilectus atque etiam cultus existens, ut ego vicissim a te amer, hac prima conciliationis epistola postulatu dignum duxi, quippe cum te et egregio pietatis studio flagrantem et multiplici bonarum literarum eruditione ornatum tum res ipsae et eorum scriptorum, quae a te vel composita, vel explicata, vel ex antiquorum scriptorum thesauris in lucem edita sunt, rationes plurime docent et communis utriusque nostrum amici eiusdemque optimi viri Christophori Plantini testimonium assiduum confirmat. Nemo autem mortalium est, quem ego, et bonarum literarum, non dico usu et facultate (his enim partibus tenuem admodum me esse confiteor), sed studio et amore flagrantiorem quam me esse arbitrer. Nemo etiam hominum est, cui Plantinus noster charior quam mihi sit. Quamobrem nullum ego esse mortalium puto, qui maiore in te studio et dilectione affectus sit, quam ego, cui quantum virtute et doctrina valeas, quantum etiam Plantinum diligas nostrum satis fuerit exploratum. Id quod ubi tibi expositum fuerit, mihi esse a te rependendum minime ambigo, quandoquidem ea honestae et ingenuae amicitiae vis est, ut vel unica tantum sui gratia eius, qui dilectus fuerit, animum ei, qui prior amaverit, simili vinculo et charitatis iungat iugo. Cupio igitur [...][848].

Diu enim est, quod virtutum artiumque tuarum exemplis et multorum, quos ego summos viros habeo, testimoniis, quantum et ingenio et eruditione valeres, quantum pietatis studio flagrares, aperte cognovi teque ob eam rem plurimum, iam diu est, dilexi et, ut mihi vehementer dilectum tibi confirmarem, ocassionem commodam captavi, quam iam mihi communis amicitia Plantini nostri obtulit et rei eius, de qua nunc te appellaturus sum, dignitas confirmavit. Quantum enim tibi Plantinus, vir optimus et de omni literarum republica benemerentissimus, tibi charus sit, probe novi. Eundem autem mihi charissimum esse omnibus, quibus potui, argumentis testatus sum et omnibus officiis perpetuo me testaturum profiteor, ut amicitiam, quam ego, tibi nondum notus, exoptabam, communicatis etiam rationibus inirem. Occasionem nactus sum et virtute tua et honestissimae caritatis causa dignam. Ea huiusmodi est: prefationem in sacrum bibliorum[849] opus, quod Philippi Catholici regis[850] consilio et auctoritate Plantinus noster cudit, ego, ut ei operi procurator legatus, hisce proximis diebus accepto a rege ipso argumento scribebam. Eam autem non antea ego probare decrevi, quam doctissimis et candidissimis viris ad legendum, corrigendum censendumque traderem, in quorum numero unum te semper habui, cuius ingenio et iudicio plurimum tribuerem cuiusque et in rebus meis suscipiendis humanitatem, cognoscendis candorem, iudicandis diligentiam et integritatem mihi ipse promitterem, quibus omnibus [...], quam publica ecclesiae clavis opus hoc est, causa regendae et pro arbitrio iudicioque tuo additis in margine notis et adscriptionibus corrigendae impenderis, cui etiam efficiendae rei amicorum doctorum, quibus tu uteris quorumque magnus in ista ecclesia numerus est, operam adhibebis, si placeat, et exemplum abs te notatum et correctum, quam primum id tuo commodo fieri possit, ad Plantinum nostrum mihi reddendum remittes. Vale et me ama, amoremque erga te meum quocumque officii genere expectando experire.

---

[848] The sentence cuts off.
[849] *Biblia sacra Hebraice, Chaldaice, Graece et Latine, Philippi II. regis Catholici pietate et studio ad sacrosanctae ecclesiae usum* [8 volumes] (Antverpiae: Plantin, 1569–1572).
[850] Philip II (1527–1598), king of Spain in 1556–1598.

146.
Benito Arias Montano to Sambucus
6 May 1570, Antwerp

A draft of the letter is kept in Stockholm, Kungliga Bibliotek, Engeströmska Samlingen, A 902. cart. Misc. XVI. f. 198ʳ.[851] Published with a Spanish translation in *La Biblia Políglota*, 202-205.

Although Montano may not be the earliest among Sambucus's followers, as for his emotions and zeal, he is among the first. Sambucus may expect any kind of help from him and Montano is sure that it is also true vice versa. He reports about the publication of a quadrilingual edition of the Bible on the commission of Philip II of Spain and printed by Christophe Plantin in the close future. He is now thinking about an apt preface, the topic of which has been prescribed by the king, which he will develop into a longer speech. Since this work required nothing but philological expertise, the preface has a particular importance. Montano thus wanted to make sure that he and his writings are welcomed by the pious and the learned, Sambucus included, and he asks him to check not only the content but also the style of the preface. In order to leave space for comments he had the text printed by Plantin with larger margins. He will not be ungrateful, and spread the news about Sambucus's piety and erudition among all who know him and also in front of the king.

Ego tametsi tempore non primus omnium quibus charus es dici possim, affectu tamen et studio inter primos censeri. Id quod si tibi persuaseris, omni officiorum genere ex me expectando, cum opportunum fuerit, experiri poteris. Eadem autem ego animi mei fiducia fretus amiciatiae fructus ex te, cum res postulaverit, suavissimos percepturus exigere non dubitabo.

Bibliorum quadrilinguium opus illud maximum et dignissimum, quod a Philippi Catholici regis consilio et auspiciis Plantino nostro imprimendum commissum est cuique ego procurando regis auctoritate legatus sum, ex divino beneficio foeliciter atque ex animi sententia procedere atque non longe nimium a fine distare scias, volo.[852] Id autem oportuna praefatione instruere ex eiusdem Catholici regis auctoritate meditamur. Ipse autem rex argumentum nobis prescripsit, quod longiore oratione etiam ex illius mandato persequeremur. Quoniam vero nihil a nobis in toto opere exigebatur praeter summam versionum fidem et correctionis diligentiam, quam pro ingenii ac facultatis nostrae tenuitate studiose praestitisse videmur, una tantum reliqua cura est praefationis, cuius rationem non meo unius ingenio aut iudicio constare volui, sed eorum omnium arbitrio et calculo, quibus et pietatis, et doctrinae nomine me ipsum meaque omnia ad examen, correctionem et probationem proponere et summittere debeo. Ex quibus te unum, ut amicum diligo, ita quoque meorum studiorum censorem adiutoremque appellare constitui in re praecipue non mea tantum, sed tua, sed communi omnium Christianorum et doctorum virorum, qualis tu es, cuiusmodi hanc sacrorum bibliorum aeditionem existimare oportet. Te igitur, mi Sambuce, vehementer oro atque obsecro ut, inter caetera studia tua, aliquot saltem horas huic praefationi impertiri

---

[851] See note 847 in the preceding letter. Note that Montano prepared a meeker, more submissive version of the same letter, and a more affirmative and elegant one (the present letter). Either he prepared originally two versions, not knowing the style that could best fit the taste of the "imperial historian" (leaving the decision for Plantin) or was told to use a more affirmative style and rewrite the letter having showed the first draft to Plantin.

[852] Cf. note 849 to the preceding letter.

velis pro arbitrio iudicioque tuo eximio, non in rebus, quae in ea tranctantur solum, sed in verborum etiam proprietate, elegantia et castimonia examinandae, corrigendae, et si commodum videatur, immutandae. Ideo enim latiores margines in exemplo relinqui curavi ut idoneus adnotationibus et correctionibus adscribendis esset locus. Gratissimum autem mihi et te dignissimum feceris officium ac me tui amantissimum perpetuo beneficio devinxeris. Nec ingratum experiere aut immemorem, utpote qui cum apud alios omnes, quibus notus sum, tum apud regem meum pietatem doctrinamque tuam sim libenter perpetuo praedicaturus. Vale. Antverpiae, pridie Nonas Maii 1570.

147.
Sambucus to Joachim Camerarius Sr.
7 May 1570, Vienna

This funerary epistle was published in Johannes Sambucus and Johannes Crato, *Epistolae duae duum clarissimorum virorum V. D. Iohannis Sambuci et D. Iohannis Cratonis a Crafthaim, etc. de lugubri et reipublicae damnosa ex hac vita migratione magnifci viri D. Iohannis Udalrici Zasii Procancellarii Imperii Augusti. Una cum epitaphiis* (Leipzig: n.d., 1570), f. A2^r-A5^r.[853]

Sambucus excuses himself if he describes with inflated words what the death of some great men means in these miserable times of horror, slaughter and overall disagreement. The unfortunate death of Johann Ulrich Zasius destroyed the hope of better fortunes for his clients, left his friends deprived of his help and caused general consternation. Are diverse current troubles and the death of great courtiers Georg Sigmund Seld, Joachim von Neuhaus, Mark Singkmoser and now of Zasius not the sign of something more terrible? Zasius's diligence compensated for the absence of the other three, but it will not be easy to find a replacement for his industry and experience. Sambucus is not indebted to anyone, except God, for all the lasting good that he has, but also understands what he owes to humans. He would not lie publicly, he avoids adulation, but why would he not speak of something obvious? He does not want to react to the petty voice of the common people with contempt but wants to confront it with the truth, and he disagrees with those who belittle others, especially the dead, whose merits tend to get obscured by the vice of many and the zeal for acquiring new patrons. He knows that there are indeed great, talented and useful men in the retinue of the king. Secret affairs are entrusted to them and the emperor happily takes their advice. Sambucus praises the talents of Zasius, the son of a great father, in managing imperial administration, showing benevolence and moderation and appeasing commotions. He was sincerely religious, even if in such confusion of religious opinions he could not appear to satisfy everyone. Sambucus's knew Zasius's religious attitude well and closely observed his words. He was always tending to religious concord and moderation considering those who wanted discord, who he called tyrants and arsonists, and hoped they would perish. He openly talked about these things to Sambucus and did not keep silent about what he disliked. Sometimes he also added how ugly it was to hesitate in professing Christ and not to be able to take sides. (Once) encouraged by Zasius's words also Sambucus talked more freely about the need to do something about the disrespect for religion and close the field in front of religious sects and aberrations, and that, if not counteracted, the free rein will make everything even worse. One needs to stay with the one and attested faith,

---

[853] Cf. letter 151.

which should be adjusted to Christ's teaching and to the apostles. Zasius responded seriously and sadly, saying that he appreciated concord more than anything else. The accusations concerning Zasius's lack of humanity or (religious) impotence are obviously false. On the contrary, Zasius openly confirmed in the company of learned men what he thinks about not having communion in both kinds or the invocation of the saints, and prayed that no one should be worse than those who are joined by the Augsburg Confession. He hardly thought he could take another path. In short, Sambucus is missing great and unrestrained protection, from which many have profited. Zasius never got involved in quarrels and fights, was modest and pious, prudent and accurate in work, eloquent and persuasive, had great communicational skills, was friendly, noble and grave, helpful, incorrupt, happy with his family and distinguished by his origins. He alone estimated the losses of people affected by the warring princes and safeguarded their rights. He had great knowledge of history and expertise in law. If his work had left him any time for scholarly activities, his glory in jurisprudence would have equalled that of his father. He digested and put in practice what others knew only from books, the habit of ruling well. Zasius had a deep knowledge of all liberal arts, philosophy, and all legal matters. He easily applied the language of earlier jurists, inventively used an elevated style, wrote in a most polished German, and had Latin and other languages. These skills of Zasius are acknowledged by all princely legates. His actions, judgements and advice all speak for his sense of justice and diligence as imperial officer. And when he could steal time from work and get away from worries he found solace and peace in talking with others, washing all the troubles away with cheerfulness. Georg Sigmund Seld, who is gladly remembered but whose virtues are rarely followed, also highly esteemed Zasius. He avoided sycophants and embraced the uncertain and the desperate. He so eagerly embraced the organisation of education that he could justly be called the father of schools. Zasius fell sick after a little dinner with a pain in the sides, followed by stiffness and fever in the night, and an inflammation of the head. The inflamed substance could not evacuate through ear, which was blocked by the wrongly applied medicine, resulting in swelling, which neither the scalpel nor drugs could alleviate. He died at 8 o'clock in the morning on 27 April as a good Christian, steadfast and confident in afterlife. Sambucus intends to speak more extensively about his excellent qualities and to rebuff his critics another time. A more detailed account of his sickness is offered in Johannes Crato's letter, attached to Sambucus's one. If Crato had been present in time, he could have prolonged Zasius's life for several days. Sambucus cannot keep silent about the memory of such a Maecenas, and the pain caused by his death will never abate. He knows that Camerarius also suffers due to the loss of such men as Zasius, but being tough, he should also know the remedy for it. Nevertheless, Sambucus does not think his own pain can alleviate Camerarius's pain, and does not want to appear an alarmist. Whatever will be the end, these are bad times. He finishes his epistle with a prayer to God. God should unite the princes in concord and in the love of their subjects; let religion, for the salvation of all, be freer. God should be praised by one faith, one baptism and one church only. People who deserted the good cause should be driven back; schisms and tumults should disappear; vain religious services should not turn bloodthirsty people against each other; they should recognize, confess and remedy their sins; and those who cannot deceive God should not take the light away from others.

Clarissimo viro Ioachimo Camerario Ioannes Sambucus S. D.

Praecipuus hic dolor meus, Ioachime, cum publico iunctus, minae, tempora (liceat nunc vel initio quae turbant, conglobate affectiusve narrare), mores, horrores, bella, rapinae, caedes, flamma et, ut ille ait, urbium et regionum cadavera,[854] universa querelae, urgentia pericula non epistolam aut orationem, sed volumina, lachrimarum poene dicam flumina, requirerent. Tot mala nobis summorum aliquot virorum obitus religionisque dissidium ac vulnera intestina contulere. Sed praesertim Zasii mors importuna spem clientibus meliorum, amicis opem extinxit omnem, luctum ac moerorem plurimum auxit, ipsius quoque caesaris et imperii animis perculsis solicitudinem obiecit non exiguam.[855] Quid? Non astra minatur? Difficultas oppressae annonae? Contagiones, πολύθεοι, πλαναί, βλακικὰ σχίσματα,[856] vicinorum acies, Seldii, Novodomensis, Singhmoseri,[857] iam denique Zasii mors nihil terreant? Haec scilicet vana sint, non gravius obnuncient? Ac illorum quidem absentiam et desiderium huius prompta subactaque tot negotiis industria leniebat, ipsius, qui loco diligentiaeque respondeat, quod tute nosti, haud facile nec cito reperias. Nullius praeter Deum gratia et beneficiis non caducis meam conscientiam obligatam teneo, quid homini vel saluti perpetuae debeam, sentio. Publice mentiri nolim, adulatione mentem notatam fugio. Quod tamen in oculos incurrit, certumque est, cur sileam? Voculas imperitae plebis et morbos non contemptu, sed veritate metior nec ilico cuivis assentior alii detrahenti, praesertim mortuo, quorum merita vitio multorum studioque accidentium novorum patronorum solent obscurari.

Equidem esse plaerosque scio usu et ingenio laboribus in caesaris comitatu viros magnos, quibus occultae res committuntur quorumve consiliis summus princeps libenter acquiescit, agendi dicendique magistros. Verum in Zasio tanto patre genito[858] amabilis confirmataque erat δεξιότης[859] quaedam conficiundi res expediundique facultas, tractandorum supplicum ratio copiosa et sensus benevolus, animi temperata magnitudo, sedatio perturbationum εὖ καὶ φιλοπροσηγορίᾳ,[860] in rem Christianam mens propensa, non levis pietas, etiamsi non ilico in tanta occupationum mole vel potius opinionum divortio cuivis satisfecisse sit visus.

Novi ego Zasii voluntatem, sermones collegi, vota comparavi, nihil a concordia alienum, nihil ignem ferrumque spirans, aequa et moderata omnia cupiebat, qui secus animati essent, illos aperte tyrannos, facium subiectores vocabat, rerum ac temporum praesentem faciem inspiciundam, primi, qui dissidia velint, uti perirent optandum.[861] Non obscure, minus simulate mecum hisce interdum loquebatur, pectus et sinum aperuit, separatim cum de uno

---

[854] "Semirutarum urbium cadaver" was an expression by Saint Ambrose (*Epistolae* 39, *Patrologia Latina* 16, col. 1099).

[855] Johann Ulrich Zasius (1521–1570), born in Freiburg, was the son of the humanist jurist Ulrich Zasius. He studied in Freiburg and Ingolstadt, among others under Veit Amerbach and at Italian universities. He became doctor of law in 1541 in Freiburg. In 1544, he was invited to Basel to teach law (Goetz claims he had to leave Basel because of his Catholicism but this seems unprovable in view of Sambucus's epistle). He joined the service of King Ferdinand in 1546, who used him as diplomat in missions to German courts and at imperial diets. Zasius established particularly strong relationships to the court of Bavaria. He settled in Vienna in 1562 and became imperial vice-chancellor after the death of Georg Sigismund Seld in 1565. See Walter Goetz, "Zasius von Rabenstein, Johann Ulrich," *ADB* 44 (1898), 706-708; idem, "Die Geheimen Ratgeber," 477-479; Almási and Molino, "Nikodemismus und Konfessionalisierung," 120-121.

[856] heathens, errors, stupid religious divisions

[857] Cf. letters 132 and 108, note 645.

[858] Ulrich Zasius (1461–1536) lived mostly in Freiburg, teaching law at the university and working as a jurist in the service of the city and the bishop. He mantained contacts with many humanists and was a prolific author of legal texts. After hesitations he took sides against the Reformation. See August Ritter von Eisenhart, "Ulrich Zasius," *ADB* 44 (1898), 708–715; Steven Rowan, *Ulrich Zasius: a Jurist in the German Renaissance, 1461–1535* (Frankfurt am Main: Klostermann, 1987).

[859] dexterity

[860] well and through affability. Print: φιλοπροσηγορία.

[861] Cf. Almási and Molino, "Nikodemismus und Konfessionalisierung."

accersendo, de altero solicitando, eiusque formula, deliberatio incidisset. Quid displiceret, quam proba, non sucis imbuta aut tincta coloribus optaret, deprompsit, aliquando addidit, quam turpis in Christi professione omnis esset haesitatio, medicorum exemplo doceri, qui ad evertendum stomachum tepida uterentur, cruditates alentibus et in utramque sententiam propensis, non sanis talia convenire. Conquestus interim ipse sum liberius religionis curam iacere, sectis patefieri campum et aberrationibus propositam audaciam nisique occurratur, licentia cuncta fore deteriora, unam, probam, contestatam, Christi sententiis affixam, apostolorum innocentisque Ecclesiae et consensus beatorum normam ad pacificandum restare. Ad quae ille serio ac dolenter pro sua in me singulari humanitate sancteque respondebat, concordiam coelestiaque honoribus et muneribus praetulit. Quid etiam alii reprehendant, optent expressumque velint, voces, clamores non reticui, nihil inhumanum aut impotentius in ipso haerere deprehendi. Imo ad mensam non raro magnis doctoribus praesentibus non clam tulit, vel quid de altera parte coenae domini ablatae, vel largis operum conductoribus, vel sanctorum invocatione sentiret, nulli ut deteriores essent, quam quos confessio Augustae oblata coniunxit, precabatur, viam, qua animi dissidentium coalescant, praeter illam, vix se inire meliorem posse fatebatur, de quibus hic locis non est disputandi.

Tantum scribo amplum me liberumque patrocinium amisisse, unde ad multos beneficium redundabat, aditu et familiaritate orbatum non vulgari nec me vel in hac animi contractione in sinu, quod alii decantant, posse continere. Nihil ipsum in lites et dimicationes dedisse, pietatem cum modestia coluisse, prudentiam expediundique accurationem, artem eloquentiae, vim persuadendi in eo extitisse admirandam, cordis et linguae Crassi nullum dissidium, authoritatem ad caesarem summam, in clientibus accipiendis fovendique domicilium religiosum, integrum auscultatorem, respondendi artificium consultissimum, hospitalitate copiosum, amicitiis florentissimum, gravem nobilemque apud omnes, profusum officii, omnium rebus natum ac deservientem, suorum minus solicitum, auri et, qua vel dii minorum gentium flecti solent, δωροληψίᾳ,[862] quod audierim, nunquam verberatum, minus expugnatum, coniugiis et prole felicem, parentibus et maioribus illustrem, aliorum semper laudatorem, patronum, advocatum, ipsum nunquam φιλεγκώμιον.[863] Unus sibi hasce laudes vendicat, unus fractorum domesticisque armis principum infirmatorum causas aestimavit, iura per caesarem tutatus est.

Iam quid de historiarum ego memoria, iuris cognitione, facultate interpretandi, severa ad aequitatem vocandi eiusque lectionibus dicam? Speculatores, indices, repertoria, summae, Bartholi distinctiones,[864] cautelae, subsellia possident. Sed si Zasio omne ocium negocia non subtraxissent, si ad commentandum respondendumque tempus aula non eripuisset, nae illi patri aegre, nisi honoris causa, vel hoc praeconio cessisset. Qui quod alii de literis tantum et libris cognorunt, velut probiorem cibum tractandum confecerat inque succum et habitudinem redegerat ac principum operis partitis, illud senis ad Cyrum observarat, ὑπερμέγεθες ἔργον εἶναι τὸ καλῶς ἄρχειν.[865] Orbem artium, philosophiae mysteria, ortus occasionesque legum, edictorum, responsorum, rogationum, tabularum, fixarum, refixarum, regionum, novellarum modos intime callebat, quod ipsum docent eius acta in omni varietate exemplorum, hisque alios superabat. Verbis ille veterum iureconsultorum, cum locus fuit, commode utebatur et vel stylus elatus perque ipsum auctus et Germanice expolitus, quid in Latina caeterisque potuerit,

---

[862] taking of presents
[863] craving praise
[864] Bartolus of Sassoferrato (1313–1357) was one of the most prominent jurists of medieval Roman law.
[865] it is an immensely difficult task to rule well. Xenophon, *Cyropaedia* 6.8.

demonstrant [!]. Agnoscunt has eius dotes omnium principum internuncii. Nec a vero et gratia, nisi abiecti servilisque sit et omnia fastidientis animi, quenquam fore adeo seiunctum arbitror, quin hasce laudes et maiores deferat mortuo vitaque ipsum longiore dignum fuisse confiteatur. Loquentur, Ioachime, ipsius curae, loquentur actiones, iudicia, consilia in omne tempus, quanto studio ad aequitatem incubuerit, quanta contentione, vigiliis, caesarum secreta sit tutatus aut illustrarit, omnis posteritas ad pacem animum inclinatum susceptosque conatus in coelum extollet, authoritati et iudicio testimonium non recusabit, a se hausisse gloriam, non claritate domestica peperisse, clamabit. Caeterum si quid inter quietis a solicitudine scripturisque aliquando impetrabat, cum amicis communicabat, suspicionem mutati ab ipsis animi silentio, allocutioneque diuturniore praeditam omnemque molestiam hilaritate diluebat, fractus laboribus in sermonibus quietem quaerebat. Seldius ipse, quantum testem adduco, Seldius, inquam, cuius memoriam libenter omnes audiunt, virtutes assequntur paucissimi, magni Zasium faciebat, parem se et ad labores promptiorem vix unquam expertum aiebat, quem, si tranquilla senectus exceperit, Delphico oraculo non inferiorem evasurum summumque arcanorum caesaris moderatorem fore praedixit.

Adulatorum pestem, mimos excludebat, timide accedentes constituebat, dubios instruxit, desperatos erexit, quod sequi iter ad ius persequendum et decus cuique restaret, sincere admonuit, ad alienos usus porrigi suam perpetuo industriam passus est. Literatos σιωπᾶν γὰρ τά γε δίκαι᾽ οὐ χρή ποτε[866] ordinemque scholasticum quam sit complexus, quibus praesidiis elucesere voluerit, neminem latet, ut gymnasiorum patrem iure, curatoremque pronuncies. Tantum humanitatis virtutumque simulacrum, doctissime Ioachime, repente nobis ereptum est.

Etenim lateris a coenula oborto dolore consecutum nocte rigore aestus ingens accepit capitique infesto incendio, quod aliquando ex gravissimo casu cum Seldio debilius factum erat, materia ad defluxum liquefacta perque alias familiarem aurem ad excernendum viam quaerente, sed inepte medicinis clausam, paulo post tumori collecto nec scalpellum profuit neque tot remediis periculum avertitur. Verum pure fauces et pulmones repetente spiritusque viis ac domicilio praecluso omnibus rebus ad caput solutis sedemque Christi directis V. Calendas Maii ante meridiem octava lumen aulae, exemplar veteris disciplinae, abiectis opibus, honorum specie ambitionisque illecebris remotis constanter abiit, in vitam se rediturum ociique receptum nunc proficisci testatus est. Certe hanc ille lucem, ut mortem contemsit, quae subesset, vitam duxit, nullamque medicinam ad aeternitatem praeter hunc abitionis morem superesse credebat. Siquidem tanta est perpetuorum vis coelestiumque amoenitas, nihil ut incerti admittat, laetis et gratissimis omne aevum mulceat et compenset. Sed ἐκ δρόμου πεσὼν τρέχω,[867] cum alias copiosius de amplitudine, fide, integritate, doctrina eiusdem sim dicturus, canumque morsus et ingratum officium reiecturus, quando τοῦ ζῴου χάριν μᾶλλον διωκόμενον.[868] Caeterae morbi περιστάσεις καὶ συμπτώσεις[869] ut malum presserint, praesentemque mortem velut cervici gladium inhibuerint, ex epistola D. Cratonis nostri hisce coniuncta intelliges. Cuius quidem viri manus si tempore adfuissent, usuram aliquot dierum (nisi omnino fallor) eius medendi commoditas Zasio addidisset.

---

[866] [The litterati] should not keep quiet about what is just. Euripides, frg. 1037.
[867] I am thrown off the track. Aeschilus, *Agamemnon* 1245: τὰ δ᾽ ἄλλ᾽ ἀκούσας ἐκ δρόμου πεσὼν τρέχω.
[868] rather searching for the sympathy of the living one
[869] circumstances and incidents

Profecto tam prolixi mecaenatis memoriam latere non patiar, ac sensibus colam intimis nec temere dolorem ex animo ullum tempus delebit. Si enim non tam est necessarium male meritis referre quod debeas, quam ut benemeritos colas, quantum onus evehendi celebrandique Zasii mihi incumbere putas? Te quoque vel ob communem legis humanae sortem sensumque luctu carere nec simul adduci in societatem moeroris posse, qui orbitatem tantorum virorum intelligis, minime persuadebor. Remedia tibi relinquo, qui fortissimus tot annis factus es antagonista. Hac nihilominus scriptione te appellare non sum veritus, quo ut maius lumen officit minori, meus luctus allevaret tuum, nec omnia dixi, ne ἐπιτάσει καταστροφὴν[870] constituere velle videar aut plus, quam rerum eventa ferent, significationes metuere. Gravibus certe fluctibus iactamur, quicunque finis sequetur.

Omnibus igitur studiis, intimo collectoque desiderio ac precibus aeternum patrem domini nostri Iesu Christi oremus, spiritu suo corda nostra penetret ac muniat, quae tristia pro foribus astra minantur, longe removeat, principes concordia suorumque amore coeant, religio pateat et cum salute omnium liberius constet: una fides, unum baptisma, una ecclesia laudes sui capitis beneficiaque per mortem obtenta concinat, qui ab optima causa descivere, in ordinem revocentur, secessiones, turbae, scandala facessant, κεναὶ ἐθελοθρησκεῖαι τοὺς αἱμοχαρεῖς [871] non effrenes differant, agnoscant vicia, fateantur, emendare conentur, qui fallere Deum nequeunt, aliis lucem ne adimant, via ingrediantur regia et coelesti, eleganti et abundantissimo patrimonio aggregati fruantur per Iesum Christum, Amen. Vienna, Nonis Maiis MDLXX.

148.

Sambucus to Johannes Crato
9 May 1570, Vienna

Published in Gerstinger, "Die Briefe," 105-106.

Sambucus has no news from Lakner concerning Crato's books, which have already been paid for. He is urging Lakner, but tradesmen care only about their own business. His physician Ladislaus (Stuff) died in a two-day fever, many friends will miss his medical knowledge and remember his piety. He asks Crato to write something detailed on the death of Zasius as he wants to memorialise his benevolence and remember him in a letter addressed maybe to Crato. He knows about the gossip about the departed, but he wants to shortly and modestly note down what was obvious to everyone. If Antonio Abondio comes to Crato, Crato should ask him not to forget about Sambucus's business. (In his marginal notes Crato seems to complain ironically about the way in which Sambucus demands from him a letter on Zasius's death).

Sambucus salutem.

De Laknero tuisque redemptis iam libellis nihil dum certi scio, moneo, urgeo, sed nosti mercatorum in literas mentem: sua curant, sedulitate propria metiuntur.[872] Heri doctor

---

[870] [so that I do not seem to want to create] a catastrophy by stretching [my narrative].
[871] pointless (κεναὶ), religious services (ἐθελοθρησκεῖαι), the bloodlusty (τοὺς αἱμοχαρεῖς)
[872] The Lakner (or perhaps Lackner) in question must have been a bookseller, we could not identify him, see also letter 256.

noster Ladislaus e vita digressus est bidui febricula confectus,[873] cuius paratam sine exceptione medicinam multi amici requirent, pietatem non obliviscentur. De Zasii morbo et obitu aliquid singulariter annotatum requiro, non quod profusior aut ineptus παραδόξως[874] in cuiusquam laudes efferri cupiam, sed beneficiis ipsius nonnulla ut contester memoriam idque consilium epistolio fortassis ad te consequar.[875] Scio, quae voces passim et opiniones mortuo supersint, sed quae nota omniumque oculis exposita fuere, brevissime καὶ ἀνακεφαλαιώσει[876] comprehendam, nec fines τῆς ἀληθείας[877] nullius gratia vel authoritate ductus excedam. Ἔρρωσο,[878] et si ad te Abondius venerit,[879] negocii ut mei aliquando meminerit, admonebis. 9. Maii 1570.

Address: Clarissimo viro domino doctori Ioanni Cratoni, caesareae maiestatis medico, τῷ ἐν πρώτοις[880] consiliario et comiti palatino, domino et amico singulari. *Prag. Herrn D. Krafft*.
Crato's remark: Magnae atque singularis benevolentiae indicium esse puto expectare alicuius literas. Esse autem benevolentia et humanitate grave, non tam illius ratio, qui molesta afficit, qua qui afficitur, cuaito [?] puto."[881]

149.
Sambucus to Theodor Zwinger
17 May 1570, Vienna

The original is kept in Basel, Universitätsbibliothek, Frey Mscr II 26, no. 212. Published in Gerstinger, "Die Briefe," 106-108.

Sambucus expresses his thanks for the package, which Zwinger sent back to him, and hopes that it has served him well in his work. If Zwinger suspects anything to lurk among his manuscripts that can serve his studies, he is happy to provide all that he has. He responded to the heirs of Johannes Oporinus concerning the money and his books and allowed them to print, if they want, Apollonius's Syntax *and Bonfini's* Dialogues. *He is happy for the news about Zwinger's* Theatrum

---

[873] Ladislaus Stuff de Kellinkensis († 8 May 1570), of Transylvanian origin, enrolled at the University of Vienna in 1549 and obtained a doctoral degree in 1554. He was many times elected the president of the "Hungarian nation" of the university until 1566. In 1570 he compiled a basic book on medication used in Viennese pharmacies *Dispensatorium pro Pharmacopaeis Viennensibus in Austria*, which remained unpublished. See Robert Offner, "Erdélyi szász orvos- és sebészprofesszorok Bécsben" [Professors in medicine and surgery in Vienna of Transylvanian Saxon origin], *Bécsi Posta* new series 10.6 (2015 Sept.), 1.
[874] contrary to expectation
[875] On Zasius's death and the funerary letters by Sambucus and Crato, published in his memory, see the previous letter.
[876] as a summary
[877] truth
[878] farewell
[879] Antonio Abondio (1538–1591) was an Italian sculptor and medallist in the service of the Habsburgs. See Stefania Schir, "Antonio Abondio: una produzione artistica poco nota," *Atti della Accademia roveretana degli Agiati. A, Classe di scienze umane, lettere ed arti* 261 (2011), 221-241. "Sambucus's business" concerned the prepareation of the images for the *Icones veterum aliquot*. See letters 149,154 and 210.
[880] among the leading ones
[881] The transcription by the eighteenth-century copyist is corrupted. Gerstinger proposes: *Esse autem benevolentia et humanitate grave*[m?] *non tam illius ratio*[nem?], *qui molesta afficit, qua*[m?], *qui afficitur, cuaito* [?] *puto*, which hardly improves the text.

vitae humanae, *but hears that Zwinger, persuaded by someone, has omitted many examples. As long as the headings are there, people will be able to supplement what is missing by their own effort. Zwinger's idea about publishing the philological observations of some learned men is good, but it is difficult to find someone who would do the tedious work of proofing and cleansing their texts. He has not much to offer but what he has is not to be condemned. Zwinger would soon receive the images of ancient and some recent doctors accompanied by epigrams. Sambucus is sending Zwinger Vegetius's* Mulomedicina, *asking him to have it printed by someone. Forty years earlier the corrupt and incomplete text had been printed. Sambucus now compared two manuscripts, indicated their differences but did not add any comments or conjectures since there are many obscure, corrupt and senseless places. Sambucus asks Zwinger to go through it and, if time permits, study it. The printer may print the earlier edition with marginal notes about the textual variants or insert the emendations into the text in places where Zwinger holds them to be clearly the better solution or print the notes at the end of the book as it seems more convenient and useful to Zwinger.*

Sambucus salutem.

Habeo gratiam de fasciculo remisso, utque is tuis lucubrationibus inservierit, opto. Si quid in meis latitare suspicaris, quod deinceps aliquid subiecerit vel ornarit tuas vigilias, omne expedietur, liberique impera, profusum me senties. Respondi Oporinianis de pecunia et meis libris dedique libertatem, si velint, Apollonii *Syntaxeos* et *Dialogorum* Bonfinii imprimendorum.[882] De *Theatro* laetor,[883] sed audio te commotum ab aliquo multa praeclara exempla subduxisse; sed nihil oberit, modo enim capita rerum constant, locupletatio a quolibet suorum studiorum conscio fieri poterit. De adversariis clarorum virorum scriptis non male cogitas, sed moleste aliquis fortasse eam sarmentorum castigationem ac putationem faciet. Tu videris, mea non negabo, pauca quidem illa, sed non contemnenda. *Icones veterum medicorum et aliquot recentium* brevi accipies cum tetrastichis aptis.[884] Mitto tibi Vegetii *Mulomedicinam*, mi Zvingere, quam alicuius prelo tradito.[885] Ante annos 40 mutila et misere habita est excusa;[886] ego duobus manuscriptis adhibitis varietatem adnotavi sine tamen ἐπιλόγῳ seu ἐπικρίσει[887] vel meis coniecturis, quod pleraque sint obscura et omnino mendosa et inepta. Tu percurrito et per ocium, si voles, examina. Poterit typographus vel textum pristinum sequi et varietatem in margine addere vel inserere, quae manifeste saniora excusis tuo iudicio videbuntur vel ad extremum libri opportunius reicere, ut commodius operis et vobis videbitur. Quam vero utilem sibi et studiosis operam sit typographus navaturus, ipse vides. Vale et rescribe. Vienna 17. Maii 1570.

---

[882] Zwinger's marginal notes: "Apollonii syntaxis. Bonfinii dialogi–Theatri exempla–Medicorum veterum icones cum tetrastichis pollicetur–Vegetii mulomedicina a Sambuco ex codicibus raris revisa auctaque." The comment on money concerns Sambucus's debt for the copies of Bonfini's *Rerum Ungaricarum decades*. Cf. letters 163, 227 and 233. On Apollonius's *Syntax* see Gerstinger, "Zusammenfassung," 285. "Bonfini's *Dialogues*" is a reference to Bonfinius, *Symposion trimeron*. Cf. the Index.

[883] Theodorus Zwingerus, *Theatrum vitae humanae* (Basileae: ex officina Frobeniana, 1571).

[884] Sambucus, *Icones veterum aliquot* (see note 879 to the preceding letter). Since not even the images were ready, Sambucus must have known that the book was not going to be out very soon.

[885] Vegetius, *Mulomedicina*. In view of the title either Zwinger (or someone else) still managed to compare it with a further manuscript, or Sambucus calculated Johann Fabri's edition as a further manuscript. Cf. with *Humanistes du bassin des Carpates II. Johannes Sambucus*, xlvii-xlix; Gerstinger, "Zusammenfassung," 317-318.

[886] Reference to the Basel edition by Johann Faber of 1528. Perna reprinted his preface in the edition of 1574.

[887] reasoning or judgement

150.
Piero Vettori to Sambucus
20 May 1570, Florence

The original is kept in Munich, BSB, Clm 791, f. 156.[888]

It was Johannes Crato, who gave Vettori an opportunity to write to Sambucus, whose letters Vettori always welcomes. He reacts to Sambucus's worries about Johannes Caselius's future, whose present state does not match his learning. He was surprised to hear of his interest in his book on the cultivation of the olive tree. He encourages Sambucus's work in Dioscorides.

Debeo multum hoc etiam nomine Cratoni, viro optimo, cesareo medico, qui tibi ansam dedit ad me scribendi. Litterae namque tuae mihi semper iucundae sunt et hominis doctissimi meique amantissimi.[889] Noli igitur, quacumque occasionem huius rei nactus eris, eam omittere. Quod doles fortunam non admodum respondere doctrinae meritisque Caselii nostri humaniter et amice facis. Est ille quidem et propter eruditionem et propter vitae probitatem singularem dignus honesto quovis amplo loco. Ego autem opto illi multa prospera in vita: sperabamque ipsum commendatione tanta ingenii et morum apud suos facile summa omnia consecuturum. Planum apertumque est eum via ista, quam dicis, minorum negotio fortunas suas multo minores, quam oportere, aucturum fuisse, sed Deus optimus det [?] nobilem ipsius animum ne magis laudis tuae honorisque cupidum, quam [...] adiunctio [?]. Quae mihi narrasti de libello meo, quo laudari dicis domique meum cultum ipsarum, fuerunt mihi inexpectata neque enim putabam aliquam huius rei [...] tum [?] [...] meum laborem, patrio nostro sermone script(ti) tum, ad curas nostras Pernae missum.[890] Sed tamen cum facultatem aliquam habuero mittam ad te ipsum [...] ut te ipsum postquam significas te librum tui facturum esse. Gratum autem mihi fuit audire te incumbere toto animo in Dioscoridis Graecum exemplar [?] dandum, si operam aliquam enim utilem navabis, magnam profecto laudem adipiscis. Sit opus [...] est propter [...] antiquorum librorum dignum [...]
Ego indurabo, postquam me hoc diligenter rogas, si opus aliquid ubi adferre possum ad hoc grave inprimis onus sustinendum. Vale. Florentiae XIII. Kalendas Iunii 1570.

151.
Johannes Crato to Sambucus
26 May 1570, Prague

Sambucus and Crato, *Epistolae duae duum clarissimum virum* (see letter 147), f. a5ᵛ-(b1ʳ).

Crato would never allow Sambucus to claim that he was more obliged to Johann Ulrich Zasius than he was. It is the habit at court that we only hastily preform things for which the most conscientious execution was proposed, and great benefices are repaid by some oration of little consequence.

---

[888] Old Vettori's hand is hardly legible. Unfortunately, we have not been able to transcribe the other drafts preserved in the same codex.
[889] This is a reaction to letter 144.
[890] See letter 144, note 843. (This edition was however printed in Italy.)

However, he lacks time and is too much overburdened by the misery of others (not to mention his own fragility) to write peacefully. Yet, he will put together what he really knows in order not to delay Sambucus's writing and not to leave the task to some potential enemy of virtue. Five years earlier, when Sigismund Seld died, Zasius also travelled in the same coach and badly injured the right side of his head. Since then his health has been broken and he was liable to develop catarrh. When they were together in the army camp at Belgrade he had great pains and fever because of the catarrh in that part of the face and was preparing for death but they managed to drive out the catarrh through the ear. He was able to live with a purulent ear, but was then cured badly by someone else. When they were later in Silesia, the fluid went onto his eyes then moved on to the ears. Back in Vienna he repeatedly wanted to get his head cleaned and took different medicines for that, despite Crato's objection, and a few times blood was drawn off, so in the end he could hardly breathe. Crato warned against losing his natural heat and let the catarrh go down to the breast but he preferred to listen to others. When at the beginning of March Crato approached him in Prague in an official matter he tried to dissuade him from using those bad medicines again. Zasius admitted that Crato had foreseen the way his sickness developed. Thereafter Zasius broke down, went to court and complained to the high steward of the court, Crato was present by chance, and newly tried to dissuade him of the use of frequent medication. Later, on the day when he had to leave Prague he talked again with Zasius about his health and the dangers of medication. He heard that six days later, on the 10th of April, Zasius fell ill with fever. It seemed that he would develop pleurisy but the catarrh got blocked in the throat so much that he could not speak. So he could hardly speak when he died three days later, although he did not lose hope, despite the doctors' despair. Despite a deep cut of the surgical knife nothing flew out of it and his condition aggravated afterwards, so he piously died on 17 April a little after 7 o' clock in the morning. He has not yet passed the climacteric year (i.e. 49), as he claimed to be born in 1521. Before his fatal illness broke out he was so weak from work, pains and medication that he could not make the thirty steps that divided his home from the court without a horse. The vast responsibility made his mind sick and the people for whom he worked so hard only made his task worse, but he followed the businesses of the emperor with enthusiasm. If in certain cases people think his work was unsatisfying, one should remember that he was only human. His loyal and sober work should be appreciated and Crato thinks high of it. Crato praises Sambucus for his work in memorialising Zasius. He started writing a poem but could not finish it, perhaps when he will be travelling he will have some inspiration. He will leave on 29 May for the imperial diet, for the success of which there is much to pray. Dated on 26 May, which is the day of the accident of Seld and Zasius five years before.

Iohannes Crato a Crafftheim sacratissimae caesareae maiestatis etc. consiliarius et medicus intimus Iohanni Sambuco artis medicae doctori excellentissimo consiliario et historico sacratissimae caesareae maiestatis fidissimo S. D.

Nunquam tibi clarissime Sambuce concedam, ut te summo, dum in hac vita esset, viro D. Iohanni Udalrico Zasio ad gratiae debitum obstrictum verius profitearis, quam ego, et libenter me illius meritis ac beneficae naturae debere plurima fateor et meritam gratiam referre cupio. Quo magis mihi elaborandum existimo, ut non minus accurate officium meum, quam tu, facere voluisse videar. Verum in aula saepe hoc usu venit, ut ea, quae diligentissime exequi propositum est, deinceps quasi praecipitanda nobis sint et maxima beneficia levi orationis munere compensanda. Nunc autem non solum tempore egebam, sed ex alienis miseriis ita propriis cooperiebar, ut animo quieto nihil scribere possem. Accedebat et valetudo capitis reipublicae Christianae, quae minime firma erat,[891] ut de mea debilitata atque fracta nihil dicam. Veruntamen, ne scriptiones tuas remorarer et εὐεργέτην[892] nostrum dissipatis atque dispersis sermonibus, virtuti etiam fortasse inimicis, relinquerem, αὐτοσχεδιάζων[893] potius, quae mihi vere nota atque explorata sunt, perscribere, quam officium hoc differre volui.

Meministi, cum ante annos quinque tristissimo casu vir optimus et praestantissimus D. Georgius Sigismundus Seldius singulare reipublicae Christiane et aulae imperatoris ornamentum extingueretur, quid D. Zasio acciderit, cum ipse quoque magno cum periculo e curru desiliisset et dextram capitis partem graviter laesisset.[894] Ea igitur deinceps invalida et distillationibus obnoxia remansit et non semel iis graviter tentata atque afflicta est. Cum enim in castris ad Taurinum essemus,[895] febricula primum correptus, magna deinceps vi catarrhus in eam capitis affecti partem irruit, et tantos dolores fecit, ut de iis, quae ad brevi morituros spectant, cogitaret et loqueretur. Sed beneficio Dei maturata materia, qua decubuerat, eo rem perduximus, ut large ex aure illa deflueret. Itaque multis mensibus sine ulla gravi de valetudine querela purulentas aures habuit, quas deinceps nescio cuius consilio, vel quibus medicamentis sane infeliciter sanavit. Defluxit enim paulo post ad oculos, cum in itinere Silesiaco essemus, et gravissimis oculorum doloribus oppressus est, abscessu iam ad angulum maiorem, quem κανθόν[896] dicimus, periculose orto. Verum illud quoque malum divino auxilio et opera nostra diligente effugit, dum rursus per aurem materia fluere cepit. Viennam autem reversus, persuasit quidam, vacuationibus repetitis posse caput sanari et deformitatem purulentae auris tolli. Itaque crebro, me repugnante, medicamentis catharticis usus est et aliquoties singulis annis sanguinem detraxit, cum quidem ita occupationibus distineretur, ut vix respirare posset. Hoc cum animadverterem, saepe eum amicissime pro mea fide et rectissima vonuntate admonui, ne calorem naturalem isto modo debilitaret et exhauriret, denique catharrum in pectus praecipitaret, sed plus aliorum subiectiones, quam meae rationes valuerunt. Caeterum cum ineunte Martio Pragam nuper in aulam revertissem et officii caussa eum accessissem, medicationi huic malae atque perversae rursus operam dare cognovi. Quae igitur tum dixerim, nolo commemorare, cum ipse deinceps aliis gemens dicta sibi a me recitarit. Meas vaticinationes vero non fuisse falsas exitus, proh dolor, declaravit. Egressus enim post curationem illam domo et forte me praesente cameram caesaream ingressus spiritum sibi eripi, decumbens quasi in scamnum, generoso aulae imperialis praefecto[897] conquestus est. Iterum igitur multis verbis et exemplis etiam veris recitatis eum deterrere a frequenti medicamentorum usu sum conatus, et sermonum meorum gravissimum testem illustrem D. praefectum aulae imperialis habeo. Nihil igitur amplius addo. Ad extremum vero eo nimirum quo in Pannoniam[898] mihi discedendum fuit, die, etiam atque etiam per quicquid potui obtestatus sum, ut valetudini suae bonam rationem haberet, et plus saepe a medicina periculi esse, quam a morbo existimaret. Quid effecerim tot fidissimis monitis et quid post sit factum nescio. Sexto a meo discessu die X. nimirum Aprilis in dolorem capitis atque febrim incidisse audio. Illa quidem remissior paulo post visa est, verum haud scio quomodo tanta catarhi moles in musculos atque glandulas colli

---

[891] This is probably a reference to Maximilian II's bad health, which was cause for worry and much work from the part of Crato, who served him as physician.
[892] benefactor
[893] improvising
[894] See letter 78.
[895] Cf. letter 88, note 560.
[896] corner of the eye
[897] On High Steward Johann Trautson see letter 276, note 1607.
[898] I.e. for Vienna.

irruit et parotides excitavit, quae nullo modo ad maturitatem pervenire potuerunt. Aliqua quidem pars diebus insequentibus ad costas delapsa pleuritidis suspicionem praebuit, collum tamem, quae remansit, ita obsedit, ut sermonis etiam usum adimeret. Itaque triduo, quam e vita discessit, pauca verba proferre potuit, bonam vero spem semper, etiam desperationem quandam medicis ostendentibus, habuit fore melius. Alte igitur scalpellum in tumorem adigi passus est, verum nihil nisi pauca cruda effluxerunt. Aucto itaque subinde malo, cum spiritum amplius ducere non posset, magno cum reipublicae Christianae detrimento et suorum luctu ex hac misera et aerumnis plena, cum suspiriis pietatis religiosae, cuius cultum foris alii instituerant, declarasset, in beatam atque quietam vitam XXVII. Aprilis paulo post septimam horam matutinam evocatus est.

Nondum superaverat annum clymactericum: vigesimo primo enim supra 1500. se natum mihi recitasse memini. Laboribus autem, et quod intempestive aberrationes a molestiis quaereret, dum amicis operam daret, et medicationibus ita fractus erat, ut non multis ante morbum diebus, sine equo triginta passus, quibus ab aula aberat, vix posset conficere. Animus vero curis ingentibus aeger erat, quas ii, quorum caussa facere studebat omnia, altius etiam infigebant. Caesarea quidem negotia cum alacritate agebat et in iis fidem summam demonstrabat. Inter singulares rerum tractatus, si forte non satisfecit omnium iudicio vel voluntati, hominem eum fuisse non meminisse decet, et in lubrico faciles esse lapsus existimandum. Certe illius fidissimi et moderatissimi labores et tolleratae difficultates approbationem bonorum merentur. Ego quidem cum de illius virtutibus et summo de omnibus bene merendi studio cogito, expressam in clarissimo Zasio nostro imaginem veteris versus κοινὸν ἀγαθὸν χρηστός ἀνήρ[899] video et eum his difficilimis temporibus reipublicae ereptum summo dolore afficior.

Tibi autem non minori studio et diligentia, quam M. Cicero res suas Luceio commemorandas commendat,[900] nomen summi viri D. Zasii scriptis tuis illustrandum et virtutes illius celebrandas ingeniumque et singulare εὐεργεσίας[901] studium laudibus verissimis efferendum committi, atque ut huic meae festinationi ignoscas, et epistolam ita scriptam, ut describenda esset, siquidem legere te eam vellem in maiorem modum peto. Coepi facere versus quosdam, verum non potui perficere. In itinere vacuo animo fortasse aliquid poetari conabor, si modo meliuscule mihi fuerit, quam dum haec scriberem erat.[902] Nos ut opinio est ad XXIX. diem Maii iter ingrediemur, ut Deus hoc et ea quae in comitiis imperii suscipientur et agentur benigne fortunet maximas et gravissimas precandi caussas habemus.[903] Interea absentis memoriam coles et literis mittendis desiderium meum lenies. Bene vale, Pragae 26 Maii, quo ante annos quinque praestantissimus D. Seldius infelicissimo casu extinctus et Zasius noster lethalem huius morbi ἀφορμὴν[904] contraxit.

---

[899] a useful man is a common good
[900] An allusion to Cicero's letter to Lucius Lucceius (*Ad familiares* 5.12), in which he tasked Lucceius with preserving his memory in writing.
[901] patronage
[902] Crato's epigram follows after this letter in the print.
[903] The Imperial Diet of Speyer opened on 13 July.
[904] origin

152.
Sambucus to Benito Arias Montano
1 June 1570, Vienna

The original of the letter is kept in Stockholm, Kungliga Bibliotek, Engeströmska Samlingen, A 902. cart. Misc. XVI. f. 168. Published with a Spanish translation in *La Biblia Políglota*, 192-194.

Sambucus read the erudite, pious and ornate preface by Montano without a break. He praises its message, which comes from real religious principles, and its clear structure. He does not want to offend anyone, but has never seen so much style in the work of a Spaniard, especially of a theologian. He similarly lavishly praises the Spanish king Philip II. Yet Montano is misled by Plantin's love toward Sambucus in thinking that he might somehow improve the preface, although he is glad to be praised so highly by such a great man. If he can use the liberty of a friendship, he would affirm that he and others in Germany believe that learning and understanding of the sacred books in the vernacular language is indispensable. However, the prefects of the church should have the privilege of interpreting the scripture, but the audaciousness to teach and comment on it should be generally supressed, and while love should dominate religious arguments, private passions and hate should be tamed. Yet Christian authority or divine gifts are not restricted to any place, not even to Toledo. Likewise, when the rest are in agreement, the Pope is not considered to be greater. It is nevertheless necessary to have a head and principal members, who then sustain the religious community, whom, after God, we follow. If these opinions seem a bit tough, there have already been much said in their defence, so Sambucus stops here. Montano should make his feelings about Plantin clear to the public. He would say more if it were possible. He would be grateful if Montano found out, when meeting the Spanish king, what the king wants concerning him, or if Montano achieved something. Sambucus finishes his letter politely, and promises to write more frequently in the future. In the postscript he mentions some notes he made on the New Testament using some old codices, which he could send to Montano in his next letter.

Reverendo Benedicto Ariae Montano etc. Iohannes Sambucus salutem.

Praefationem non modo sanam, eruditam et piam, sed omnis generis ornamentis et artificii politam flosculis iterum opera non intermissa perlegi. Cuius dignitas tanto consilio et operi facile respondebit. Laudo studium et adhibitas vigilias, amplector sensus e veris principiis salutis coelestisque disciplinae profectos, progressus ordinatos, rationes expedite confectas, consectaria non ἀνακόλουθα.[905] Ac sine ullius offensa dico me in homine Hispano, theologo praesertim, vix tantam rerum tractationem stilo exquisito deprehendisse. Nemo est, Aria, qui summi regis altam et solidam in rem Christi voluntatem et impensas non in coelum extollat, omnibus omnino victoriis, insulis recens vel antea repertis aut ad navigationes notatis non anteferat. Sed de me iudicium te fallit quod ex amore et sermonibus Plantini hausisti, qui a me putes aliquid prolegomenis addi aut demi posse. Conscius mihi sum et Euripidis illud tueor: βάρος δὲ καὶ τόδ' ἐστίν, αἰνεῖσθαι λίαν.[906] Verumtamen qui a puero linguarum commendationem philosophiamque sum secutus, a tanto viro laudari mihi non iniucundum est. Et quando

---
[905] inconsistent
[906] even that is a burden, to be praised too much. Euripides, *Orestes* 1162.

amicitiae libertatem concedis, illud non reticebo: nos in Germania ὡς πλείστους[907] tenere nullo pacto aut conditionibus obiectis neque tollendam neque negligendam esse sacrorum vernacula lingua intelligentiam et lectionem, cum hoc tamen, ut scripturae interpretatio et mysteriorum enunciatio perfectis ecclesiae salva sit, audacia temere docendi aut commentandi vulgo reprimatur, caritatis in monendo arguendoque vis valeat, odium et morbus privatus minuatur, secessiones et idiognostae non plus quam universus sanctorum spiritu Dei munitorum sensus possit. Sed neque dona caelestia et authoritatem Christianam unico loco aut sede concludimus, etiamsi Toleti sit. Modo caetera conveniant, non maioris Pontificem aestimamus. Necessarium tamen caput praecipuaque membra, quibus nitatur coetus divinus, quos sequamur nosque committamus, secundum Deum, omnes boni profitentur. Haec si non nihil duriora videntur, rationes copiosae sunt a defensoribus expositae; nec meum est pluribus tractare. Amo te de sensu in Plantinum, quidquid in eum contuleris, publice feceris. Utinam per facultates illius rebus copiosius liceret consulere, prolixe illud declararem. Vestrum est, quibus expeditiora sunt omnia, ornare iuvareque tales, per quos beneficii gratia in omnem redundat posteritatem. Si quid apud regem, quod sponte velle videris, de me inveneris aut aliquando effeceris,[908] prosequar officium memoria constanti. Verum qui amicitiam non utilitatibus metior, sustinebo me atque oblectabo tuis eleganter et amantissime scriptis literis, cui, nisi saepius scripsero, provocatus indignus necessitudine optata fuero. Vale. Kalendis Iunii 1570. Vienna.

Post scriptum: Si ingratum tibi non erit, aut significabis, mittam fortasse proxime aliquot meas in *Novum testamentum* observationes, obiter dum veteres codices verso, annotatas. Iterum vale, mi optime et doctissime Aria, meque diligere pergito.

Address: Reverendo et clarissimo viro domino Benedicto Ariae Montano, domino et amico observando. Antverpiam.
Montano's hand: Iohannis Sambuci. Calendis Iunii 1570. De praefatione.

153.
Sambucus to Piero Vettori
31 August 1570, [Vienna]

The original is kept in Munich, BSB, Clm 735, Nr. 40. Published in *Clarorum Italorum et Germanorum epistolae*, 2:54; Várady, "Relazioni di Giovanni Zsámboky," 38; Gerstinger, "Die Briefe," 108-109.

Sambucus is responding late to Vettori's very kind letter with promises about Dioscorides, because he left Vienna while the plague was raging. Vettori will get his publication of [Pseudo-]Hesychius together with his new maps of old Hungary and ancient Greece and Italy. He is delaying the printing of Dioscorides as he hopes that by including Vettori's notes and Crato's observations he will make it a nice publication. He asks Vettori to send him his notes as soon as possible.

---

[907] as most (either: the majority of us in Germany believes, or: we in Germany, as do most people, believe ...)
[908] We do not know to what Sambucus is referring here.

Domino Petro Victorio Sambucus salutem.

Serius ad tuas plenas amoris et optatissimi de Dioscoride promissi respondeo.[909] Quam moram secessioni a Vienna et bibliotheca ob grassantem saevius pestem frequentissimamque urbem misere depascentem tribuas, oro. Illustrium de poetis e mercatu proximo Francfortensi accipies[910] una cum nova πινακογραφίᾳ[911] Ungariae veterisque Graeciae et Italiae nostra.[912] Dioscoridem premo, quem spero tuo subsidio et lectionibus, itemque Cratonis observationibus non ignobilem fore. Sed amabo te, quam primum tua ad nos mittas, quo officio et beneficentia omnes tibi obstrictissimos plurimum cumulabis, a me perpetuam inibis gratiam et memoriam. Tibi tuisque quam optime semper esse cupio, utque spei de Dioscoride factae satisfacias, vehementer oro. Pridie Kalendas Septembris 1570.

Address: Clarissimo viro D. Petro Victorio, amico observatissimo. Florentiam.

154.
Sambucus to Johannes Crato
1 September 1570, Perchtoldsdorf

Published in Gerstinger, "Die Briefe," 109-111.

Since Sambucus, worried about the plague, moved to the suburbs and left his library at home, he has fallen behind on his book projects, which he had vainly promised to others for the coming Frankfurt fair. Punishments and chance occurrences (if there are any according to Christian teaching) should be tolerated. In his last letter he failed to tell Crato that he did not understand what Zwinger needs or why he complains about Hippocrates. Zwinger held Sambucus's notes and observations on Hippocrates for two years and then copied them out and sent the volume back with particular gratitude. So Crato and Zwinger should accept this as his excuse. Sambucus asks Crato to encourage Antonio Abondio to carry on with the engravings and make the look of dead (doctors and philosophers) appear lively. If the printers are to be believed, [Pseudo-]Hesychius's and (Zonaras's) epitome of the councils together with his notes are printed now. Dioscorides, corrected to a certain degree by Sambucus, is waiting now for the work of Vettori and Crato to be fully correct. The Strasburg publisher Josias Rihel would be happy to cure and print it but Crato should urge Vettori. Sambucus is sending his greetings to the Camerarius and Thomas Jordan, and asks about the results of the legislation (i.e. at the Imperial Diet of Speyer). Finally, he asks Crato to forward his letter to Conrad Dasypodius by the legates of Strasburg, as he still does not know anything about certain mathematical manuscripts that he has sent him.

---

[909] See Vettori's letter of 20 May (letter 150).
[910] [Pseudo-]Hesychius, Περὶ τῶν ἐν παιδείᾳ. The book appeared only in 1572. See *Humanistes du bassin des Carpates II. Johannes Sambucus*, 155-161.
[911] map
[912] Sambucus contributed to the 1570 edition of Abraham Ortelius's *Theatrum orbis terrarum* ([Antwerp]: Apud Aegidium Coppenium Diesth, 1570) with a map by Wolfgang Lazius, which he must have thought better than his *Ungariae Tanst[etteriana] descriptio nunc correcta* (Viennae: Stainhofer, 1566), which was based on the oldest map of Hungary called "Lázár-map" (1528) with only minor modifications. His new map of Hungary ("Ungariae loca praecipua" of 1571) came out in the 1579 edition of *Theatrum orbis terrarum*. In his bibliography of 1583 Sambucus wrote "Italiam veterem et Graeciam eiusdem Ortelius adhuc detinet". Sambucus, *Catalogus librorum*.

Sambucus salutem.

Labes contagione et metu horrenda in suburbium ad II. lapidem me expulit carissimamque bibliothecam, ut deinceps tutius ea uterer, mecum esse noluit, ut, quod multi per Francfortensem mercatum de meis conatibus praeceperint, ipse etiam confirmarim, vix sint lecturi. Poena et casus, si quis casus in Christiana disciplina est, ferendi communiter sunt. Proximis ad te omiseram me non satis intelligere, quid de Hippocraticis Zvinggerus noster requirat aut per te conqueri possit, qui Hippocratem meum cum meis observationibus et varietatibus biennium tenuerit,[913] eo sit proprie usus, quae selecta sunt, testibus eiusdem binis descripserit, cum gratiae non vulgaris indicio remiserit. Proinde nisi aliud velitis, hoc nomine causam accipietis, a quibus nihil unquam meorum abditum patior. De Abondio, quaeso, hoc est μονογραμμικοῖς εἰκόσι[914] curam sine incommodo sustine, ut, quem vivum in oculis omnes ferunt, aliqua suffiguratione et lineis etiam mortuum intime et memoria usurpent.[915] Illustrius et, nisi perpetuo sunt nugaces typographi, Epitome synodorum mea cum variis παραπομπαῖς,[916] ut iuris consulti loquuntur, nunc extrudentur.[917]

Dioscorides utcunque purgatus Victorii tuamque opem, ut prorsus sanetur, expectat. Richelius[918] Argentinensis impressor valde solicitat, pollicetur quodvis μῦκτρον [?], si foetum ei committam nutriciumque et procuratorem constituam. Tu quoque Victorium urge, qui liberalissime se obtulit. Camerariis plurimam salutem et Iordano. Si quid decreto publico salutariter transegistis et quando vobis propius fruituri simus, significaris, gratissimum fuerit. Pettersdorfii, Kalendis Septembris 1570.

Oro hasce Argentinam Dasypodio per legatos urbis eius quamprimum curato, nam de certis mathematicis a me fasciculo ad ipsum missis nondum sum certior.[919]

Address: Dem Edlen und Hochgelerten Herrn Doctor Johan Krafft von Krafthaim, Khaiserlicher Majestät Ratt und fürnembster Leibarzt, meinem günstigen Herrn und Freund zu handen. Speyr. Cito, cito, cito.

155.
Sambucus to Piero Vettori
12 September 1570, Vienna

The original is kept in Munich, BSB, Clm 735, Nr. 39. Published in *Clarorum Italorum et Germanorum epistolae*, 2:53-54; Gerstinger, "Die Briefe," 112-113.

---

[913] On Sambucus's studies of Hippocrates see Gerstinger, "Zusammenfassung," 307-308 and cf. the Index.
[914] engraved pictures.
[915] Reference is made to the preparations of the woodcuts of the *Icones veterum aliquot*. Cf. the Index.
[916] notes. This may refer both to marginal notes and interlinear glosses for the epitome of the councils collected by Zonaras, see letter 140, note 827.
[917] [Pseudo-]Hesychius, Περὶ τῶν ἐν παιδείᾳ. On Zonaras's epitome see letter 140, note 827.
[918] Josias Richel (Rihel) (1525–1597), printer active in Strasburg from 1556. There is hardly any information available on him. See Josef Benzing, *Die Buchdrucker des 16. und 17. Jahrhunderts im deutschen Sprachgebiet* (Wiesbaden: Harrassowitz, 1963), 418 and 421.
[919] See letter 89, note 564.

The emendations of Dioscorides that Sambucus has are not only annotated in books of his library but have been written out and are print-ready. He begs Vettori to share with him the textual variants he has collected which deviate from the Aldine and the Parisian Greek-Latin edition. Vettori's help, acknowledged by Sambucus, will be known immediately to all. Crato has also promised something and will join in at once, if Vettori truly sends (his notes), which would be for the good of all. He is urging Vettori because he is himself being urged. He is going to publish the 120 images of the plants, also those missing from Pietro Mattioli's commentary. The letter was written rapidly, so Vettori should forgive him for this.

Domino Petro Victorio Sambucus salutem.

Non solum in studio et commentariis, quae ad integritatem ac lucem Dioscoridis pertinent, sed etiam ad praelum descripta habeo.[920] Tuam opem atque manum imploro, ut quam primum, quae collegisti ab editione Aldina et maxime illa Parisiensi Graecolatina diversa cum omnibus communices.[921] Cuius beneficium nullius temporis fama deseret, Victorii in adversis et corruptis locis medicinam ac victoriam meo testimonio cantabit. Pollicitus quiddam est Crato noster, qui, si tu, quorum spem omnibus extuli, miseris, simul coniunget. Amabo te, mi doctissime Victori, ne pulcherrimam cunctis inserviendi occasionem dimittas, consule aliquot observationibus, quae multorum saluti prosint. Urgeo, quia urgeor; plantarum effigies 120, Mathiolo[922] invisas, identidem sum editurus.

---

[920] Sambucus planned a Greek and Latin edition of Pedanius Dioscorides's *De materia medica*. It was essentially a philological project, demonstrating his scholarly superiority to members of both the imperial court and the Republic of Letters. With the arrival of previously unknown codices from Constantinople (most famously the Codex Aniciae Julianae, i.e. the Codex Vindobonensis, brought by Augerius Busbequius) there was in fact a good opportunity for an improved edition. Moreover, because of the beauty and size of its illustrations, publishing Dioscorides was a highly prestigious endeavour, fitting Sambucus's ambitions. The importance of the project is made clear by the very frequent mention of it in his letters (see "Dioscorides-edition" under "Sambucus" in the Index) and by Sambucus's investment into images of plants, missing from Dioscorides (cf. with letter 174). Nevertheless, probably because of the enormous competition and investment, for many years Sambucus failed to convince any publisher to publish a new text based on his emendations. When Henri Estienne eventually embraced the project (Sambucus also paid him for the publication, see letter 312), he entrusted it to the learned doctor and botanist Jean-Antoine Sarasin (see letter 302). In preparing an edition and translation Sarasin went much further than Sambucus. Eventually, Sambucus's collations and annotations played only a secondary role in Sarasin's edition, which came out only posthumously: Πεδακίου Διοσκορίδου τοῦ Ἀναζαρβέως τὰ Σοζόμενα Ἅπαντα. *Pedacii Dioscoridis Anazarbaei Opera quae extant omnia. Ex nova interpretatione Jani-Antonii Saraceni Lugdunaei, medici* ([Frankfurt am Main]: Haeredi Wecheli etc., 1598) (next to this bilingual edition, there was a contemporaneous Latin edition published as well). See Olivier Reverdin, "Exposé, en forme de causerie, sur le Dioscoride de Jean-Antoine Sarasin," in *Médecine et morale dans l'Antiquité*, eds. Hellmut Flashar and Jacques Jouanna (Vandœvres-Genève: Fondation Hardt, 1997), 365-381; *Humanistes du bassin des Carpates II. Johannes Sambucus*, xxix-xxxii; Gerstinger, "Zusammenfassung," 297-302; Siraisi, *History, Medicine*, 219-220. For the Codex Aniciae Julianae see *Dioscurides: Codex Vindobonensis med. Gr. 1 der Österreichischen Nationalbibliothek*, ed. Hans Gerstinger (Graz: Akademie, 1965–1970), 5 vols.

[921] Pedanius Dioscorides's *De materia medica* appeared in Greek first in 1499 from the Aldine press. The Paris bilingual edition in the translation of Jean Ruel is from 1516, but Sambucus used a copy of 1549 published by Arnold Birckmann (Vienna, ÖNB, *69.J.141), in which he put down notes of the textual variants from six different codices (cf. Gerstinger, "Die Briefe," 112). See also Várady, "Relazioni di Giovanni Zsámboky," 37; and in general John Riddle, "Dioscorides," in *Catalogus translationum et commentariorum*, eds. F. Edward Cranz and P. O. Kristeller (Washington, DC: Catholic University of America Press, 1980), 4:1-142.

[922] Pietro Andrea Mattioli (1501–1578), humanist, botanist and physician was the personal doctor of Ferdinand and Maximilian II. Born in Siena to a family of doctors, he studied in Padua. After a few years of medical practice in Rome he moved to Trento, then to Gorizia. In 1555 he moved to Prague and finally retired to Trento in

Ἔρρωσο et δημοσίων ἀγαθῶν,⁹²³ ut soles, facile memineris ac rescribe quando etc. Pridie Iduum Septembris 1570. Haec raptim a Vienna ad secundum lapidem, itaque ignosce.

Address: Clarissimo viro domino Petro Victorio, amico observatissimo. Florentiam.

156.
Sambucus to Johannes Crato
31 October 1570, [Pressburg]

Published in Gerstinger, "Die Briefe," 109-111.

(The publication of) Dioscorides depends only on Crato and Vettori. Whatever Vettori will send to Sambucus will be the ultimate contribution. Sambucus asks Crato to urge Vettori, even if there is no danger in delay. Crato has not responded concerning Abondio's snatching some images of doctors. If Abondio is in Speyer, too, Crato should warn him to restore (Sambucus's) faith in him and give back the images. He does not care if Abondio is touching up the images, as long as he has the rough versions that he has ordered. He never thought Abondio was so unreliable. He is in Pressburg at the session of the jury of the lord chief justice, hoping for some kind of ending of a 15-year-long case.

Sambucus salutem.

Dioscorides a vobis tantum pendet. In Victorio, si quid miserit singulare, pro eo ac pollicitus est, victoria pensumque ultimum erit.⁹²⁴ Mone meo nomine, urge, obsecra, obtestare. Etsi enim in mora non subsit periculi, tamen cupidius a tantis viris vel minima soleo repetere. De Abondio illo, qui aliquot icones medicorum abstulit, nihil rescribis. Si istic est, oro, mone et exige, liberet fidem, restituat, quod abstulit. Non curo eius manum et expolitiones, modo rudia illa commissa habeam. Numquam cogitassem hominem tam esse vanum. Ego nunc Posonii sum in conventu iudicum Ungarorum de lite et causa 15 annis producta sperans aliquem finem.⁹²⁵ Novi nihil est. Vale. raptim ultimo Octobris 1570.

Address: Clarissimo viro domino doctori Ioanni Cratoni, archiatro caesaris et consiliario, amico et patrono suo. Speyr.

---

923 1571. His greatly successful and popular, thickly commented and augmented Dioscorides-publication, which was already much more than the original *De materia medica* (which became his life project) came out first in 1544 after ten years' work and was augmented and published many times: 1550, 1563, 1568, 1570 in Italian, and 1554, 1558, 1559, 1565 in Latin all in Venice; in 1561 and 1566 in French, 1554 and 1567 in Latin all in Lyon (cf. letter 163, note 984). The success of this work must have been an important reason behind Sambucus's zeal to publish a new edition. See Giuseppe Fabiani, *La vita di Pietro Andrea Mattioli*, ed. Luciano Benchi (Siena: G. Bargellmi, 1872); *I giardini dei semplici e gli orti botanici della Toscana in appendice saggi su Pietro Andrea Mattioli*, ed. Sara Ferri (Perugia: Quattroemme, 1993); *Pietro Andrea Mattioli (Seca 1501–Trento 1578): la Vita, le Opere con l'Identificazione delle Plante*, ed. Sara Ferri (Ponte San Giovanni: Quattroeme, 1997); Daniela Fausti, "Su alcune traduzioni cinquecentesche di Dioscoride: da Ermolao Barbaro a Pietro Andrea Mattioli," in *Sulla tradizione indiretta dei testi medici greci: le traduzioni*, eds. Ivan Garofalo et al. (Pisa–Rome: Fabrizio Serra, 2010), 181-205; Luca Ciancio, "'Per questa via s'ascende a magior seggio'. Pietro Andrea Mattioli e le scienze mediche e naturali alla corte di Bernardo Cles," in *Studi Trentini di scienze storiche. Storia* 94 (2015), 159-184.
923 good bye [and think of the] common good
924 See the preceding letter.
925 It is a reference to the judicial case with the Alaghys, which had been peacefully concluded in 1571, but was renewed by Sambucus in 1573 (apparently without a conclusion). See Illésy, "Sámboky János."

157.
Carolus Utenhovius to Sambucus
1 November 1570, Düsseldorf

The original is kept in Vienna, ÖNB, Cod. 9736, f. 7ʳ-10ᵛ.

Sambucus may understand the distress and the inconvenience of Oporinus's death for Utenhovius. It is tragic, especially as Oporinus worked selflessly for the scholarly community for more than forty years with his typographic press. Oporinus wanted to be useful to as many as possible, and not having children, he cared for those who had original enthusiasm, who were low-born but ambitious. Among these men were Hieronymus Wolf, Sebastian Castellio and many others, who can thank the beginning of their career to Oporinus but there is hardly any learned men not indebted to him. Utenhovius has written more about this argument but since Sambucus never responded he started having doubts whether he received his letters. Yet, Utenhovius does not believe that Sambucus is alienated from him. He sends him epithalamia he received for his wedding and asks Sambucus to add a few distichs of his own. Sambucus should have them copied and distribute them among his learned friends, so they would follow the lead of Jean Dorat and himself and add their own poems, and Utenhovius would return the favour whenever they want. In particular, he asks Sambucus to send a copy of it to Giulio Alessandrini, Andreas Dudith and Jan Kochanowski, who imitates Callimachus so well. Others have also written some equally good poems, but he chose to have only those of famous authors transcribed. On his shelves there are also some Hebrew and Greek poems on the same topic, which he will keep for a while, until the duke of Alba leaves Flanders. Utenhovius is wondering about Sambucus's recent publications of the type Aldus had used and older than the one on which Palntin had relied. He would also be glad to have a copy of any especially old manuscript of the Dionysiaca *by Nonnus. He would confer the copy Plantin had used more accurately with his manuscript copies, if Sambucus could send it to him.*

Eruditissimo viro domino Iohanni Sambuco suo, Carolus Utenhovius filius.[926]

Quam grave vulnus atque incommodum ex Iohanni Oporini clarissimi typographi decessu non ego tantum, qui candidissimi hominis optimeque compatris necessitudine sum privatus, acceperim, tu vel imprimis, mi Sambuce, (longinquis licet a nobis regionibus absis) omnium lucupletissimus testis esse potes. Ad cuius enim tanti fama viri penetravit aures, cuius item animum non incredibili moerore perfuderit? Nam et doloris acerbitatem nostri duplicare debet non parum, quod, cum post exantlatos tot laborum (ut eius ad me verbis utar) fluctus, in senecta tranquillum portum divina benegnitate consecutus iam esset iamque adeo et ad rem literariam magno aliorum compendio, suo (paucis ut plurima dicam) periculo atque dispendio quasi natus, ingenii sui lucubrationibus literarum studia iam sexagenarius deinceps non minore studio quam quadraginta ab hinc amplius annis typographicam ornare porro et illustrare et coepisset et posset,[927] nobis ex hoc emigrans ergastulo perpetuum eruditionis suae candoris et industriae prope singularis incredibili desiderium reliquerit. Praeterquam enim quod huius etiamnum lucis usura perfruens, eruditis et piis omnibus cum hominibus ita vivere consueverat, prodesset ut quam plurimis, nullius enim laudibus obtrectando

---

[926] In order to distinguish him from his father of the same name, Karel Utenhove the Elder.
[927] In reality, Oporinus had been working as a publisher for little more than thirty years. He set up his printing shop (with Robert Winter) first around 1535. Previously, he had been working as a proofer for Froben.

(tantum abest quenquam ut laeserit unquam) officeret, non homines ingenio tantum et doctrina praecellentes, fortunis opibusque affluentes, sed et tenui in re, qui iam inde a teneris (ut Graeci dicunt) unguiculis spei et expectationis vel exiguissimam de suo, ut ita dicam, ingenio scintillulam excitare viderentur, tanto semper studio complexus aluit, fovit ac prope paterna pietate (cum liberis ipse careret) adoptavit, ut (dum nihil fere sibi ipse reliquum facit), quorum virtutibus res alioqui angusta domi obstatura videbatur, quo minus eam, quam dixi, scintillulam illustribus doctrina viris unquam praeferrent, nobilissimorum ipsi obscuro loco nati luminibus obstruxerint; quorum e numero (neque enim illi idipsum non fateri tantum dignantur et praedicare) Hieronymus Wolf, Sebastianus Castelio et innumerabiles alii, quorum illi multis hi fere omnibus eruditissimis viris exiguae huius, quam Oporinus accendit faculae, beneficio praeluxerunt. Quid, quod neminem vel mediocriter eruditorum (quos gremio Europea suo doctissima fudit hactenus) invenias, quem non insigni aliquo beneficio ἀμπελοέσσης, ut ita dicam, ὀπώρης δίκην sibi demeruerit.[928] Tu, si mentior (quando Augustissimi imperatoris historiographus es), verioris narrationis penicillo hoc tanti viri elogium exteres, sed non exteres, si te, mi Sambuce, novi, ut quicum tibi non multo minor quam mihi necessitudinis usu intercesserit. Etc.

In hanc, mi Sambuce, sententiam plura me ad te scribere memini (quorum periodum unam et alteram vel hoc nomine famulum describere volui), quod, an ea receperis, cum nihil respondeas, incipiam dubitare. Neque enim persuadere mihi possum alienatum a me animum tuum, quae ne me spes fallat, placuit hic nonnulla epithalamiola tibi describenda curare, quibus ut unum et alterum saltem distichon appingas, te, per quicquid tibi est carum, vehementer etiam atque etiam rogo.[929] Eo enim sum ingenio, ut non cuiusvis ore cani gaudeam, eoque nomine non nisi praestantissimos quosque compellem, in quibus cum et Sambucus nomen profiteatur suum, ne diffidere tuae erga me benevolentiae multis indiciis mihi cognitae penitusque perspectae videar, pono deque manu tabulam, de tabulaque manum[930] ut nuper tuum in Bonfinium lusi.[931] Vale Dusseldorpio 1570 Calendis Novembribus.

Quando vero, mi Sambuce, cum nemine non eruditorum necessitudo tibi intercedit, velim, ut pluribus haec epithalamiola exemplis describenda cures, eorum singula doctissimis quibusque viritim ea conditione didas, ut et Aurati tuoque exemplo suis a musis quod his accinant, aliquam appingere dignentur, par officii genus a me quando volent reportaturi. Quos vero per te potissimum compellari inprimis cupiam hi sunt: D. Iulius Alexandrinus, qui cum cygno maxime canoro certare carminis suavitate meo iudicio valeat; D. Andreas Duditius, cuius ingenio nihil exagitare queat vel tersius vel candidius;[932] N. Kochenhovius Polonus, qui Romanum Callimacum mirifice exprimit,[933] sed charta me deserit.[934] Alioqui nihil erat

---

[928] in a manner of a wine-rich autumn (a wordplay on Oporinus's name)
[929] The attached poems have been included into the letter, the last paragraph follows the poems. A poem by Sambucus to Utenhovius (Cod. 9736, f. 26ʳ-27ᵛ, published in Gerstinger: "Die Briefe," 53-54) was written already in 1560 in Melun.
[930] Cf. Erasmus, *Adagia* 219 "Manum de tabula."
[931] Reference is made to Utenhovius's poems in the 1568 edition of Bonfini's *Rerum Ungaricarum decades quatuor cum dimidia*. See *Humanistes du bassin des Carpates II. Johannes Sambucus*, 119-120.
[932] On the doctor and medical author Giulio Alessandrini (1506–1590) see the very rare conference volume: *Giulio Alessandrini personaggio illustre del Cinquecento trentino* (Civezzano: Scuola media Giulio Alessandrini, 2000).
[933] Filippo Buonaccorsi (Callimachus) (1437–1496) moved to Poland in 1468 and as tutor to the king's sons, diplomat and councillor he soon became a fundamental promoter of Polish humanism.
[934] He must be referring here to Cochanovius, that is, Jan Kochanowski (1530–1584), the greatest Polish

iucundius, quam cum Sambuco meo prolixas serere fabulas. Intimo tuus ex animo Carolus Utenhovius filius. ΚΑΡ-ΟΛΟΣ ΟΥΘὲΝ-ᾧ-ΒίΟΣ[935]

Scripserunt et innumerabiles alii nec aspernanda, sed nec his deteriora epithalamiola, sed eorum tantum modo, quorum nomen isthic innotuisset, consulto describere placuit. Nam et Hebraica et Graeca eodem scripta argumenta meis in pluteis tantisper asservo, dum Flandria cesserit ille, qui niveum penitus nil nisi nomen habet.[936] Quod prae manibus habeat Sambucus, nam eius musae cessare ἀδύνατον,[937] aveo cognoscere. Praeterea si quod Nonni *Dionysiacon* exemplum antiquius eo, quod imitatus est Plantinus, uspiam esset non sine παραφράσεως[938] eiusdem archetypo, quod Aldus primus est aemulatus, eorum mihi copiam fieri πολλῶν ἀνὰ χρημάτων πριαίμην ἄν.[939] Quin et illud quod expressit Plantinus exactius cum meis exemplaribus conferre gestiam, si qua via Sambucus illud ad me commode possit transmittere, sed cum nihil non mihi spondeat eius vel ingeniutas vel candor, eo longiore scriptione supersedebo, eumque valere μουσικώτατα hoc est εὐδαιμονέστατα[940] iubebo. 3 [?] Calendis Novembribus. Tuus qui supra Carolus Utenhovius.[941]

Address: Clarissimo doctissimoque viro domino Iohanni Sambuco, caesaris invicti historiographo, amico singulari et veteri.
Another hand: Vigilia Andreae Uthe...
Another hand: Caroli Utenhovii epistula ad Sambucum. Ubi ubi erit.

158.
Sambucus to Johannes Crato
20 November 1570, Mannersdorf

Published in Gerstinger, "Die Briefe," 114-116.

Sambucus never had doubts about the polished style of their friend. He is glad about being listed in the same index together with Crato. If he produces nothing worthy of Crato's honour, his memory might at least be preserved by association. Friendship should be based on divine philosophy and pious sentiments; when it is not, it often changes, and can easily appear feigned. In his seclusion, which is wearisome in the winter, he is working on several texts and polishing Dioscorides, but with regard to Vettori he will not urge Crato again. Abondio foolishly retards the edition (of the Icones*). He is sending his greetings to Camerarius and asking for a copy of Manuzio's letter, as he is happy to follow*

---

[935] Renaissance poet.
[935] I.e. Carolus Utenhovius. On fols. 8ʳ-10ʳ Utenhovius has copied congratulatory poems on his wedding with Ursula Floderiopa (Ursula von Vlodrop), written by Jean Dorat, Hermannus Comes a Nuenar (Neuenahr), Petrus Ximenius and Jean Matal.
[936] "the one about whom nothing is snow-white, except his name" is probably a reference to Duke of Alba.
[937] impossible (for it is impossible that his Muses should stop)
[938] [is not without] the paraphrase
[939] I would buy for lots of money. Utenhovius had also planned to publish the *Dionysiaca* (with Oporinus) but eventually Sambucus decided to work with Plantin and the edition was prepared by Gerhard Falkenburg. See letter 126 and cf. the Index.
[940] most artistically (i.e.) most happily
[941] Note that the postscript is dated earlier than the letter.

Manuzio's doings. Unless the Christians occupied Selim's powers at sea, the Habsburgs may need to face war with the Ottomans. The heirs of Oporinus are asking him to obtain a copyright privilege for "these books" but as he is away, he cannot help, so he asks Crato to obtain it for them. He does not believe they could get a universal privilege (as their activity, as Crato knows, is considered suspicious), but only for "these titles." He will pay the five thalers back to Crato.

Doctori Cratoni Sambucus salutem.

De amici eleganti politoque stilo et ad epistolas nato potius quam confecto nunquam dubitavi. Eodem vero indice meum nomen cum tuo aliquando coniunctum iri valde laetor, ut, quando a me tuis officiis et dignitati ornandae nihil proprium emanet, alterius saltem beneficio ac interventu memoria frui liceat.[942] Sed mallem eam copiam distinctam prudentia omnique humanitate decoratam [?] seriis amicis tandem redderet, insigni aliquo thesauro et argumento posteritatem collectam tueretur. Philosophia quoque divina et coelestibus sensibus necessitudinem constitutam velim, quae, nisi eo fundamento nitatur, facile cogitationes mutat, si spei fructus mora succedat, voluntatem damnat, ficta omnia clamat, eludit.[943] Ego in isto secessu satis per hyemen difficili aliquot libellos tero, Dioscoridem dolo et polio. De Victorio te amplius non exercebo.

Abondius inepte editionem τῶν ἰατρικῶν εἰκόνων impedit,[944] a quo exige debitum, in cuius promissis hanc vanitatem haerere nunquam putassem. Vale et Camerario aliquod verbum. Epistolae Manutii,[945] ita me amabis, si exemplum miseris. Libenter enim eius studii memoriam recolo, vestigia, quod possum, persequor, qui assecuti sunt, mirari soleo.

Nova hic nulla. Sed tamen nisi Selymi vim mari aliter occupaverimus, bellum nobis metuendum videtur etc. Maynersdorffo. 20. Novembris 1570.

Haeredes Oporini, typographi non vulgares, ut se in hisce libris[946] impetrando iuvem, valde orant, qui, quia longissime absum, incommodo illis satisfecero. Tuam igitur humanitatem oro, et studium in hisce non remissum nomine Μουσῶν[947] posco. Ut universum privilegium Basiliensibus detur, quos scis suspectos esse, vix credo. Satis igitur hisce libris privilegium impetrare. V talleros ego vestrae excellentiae restituam.

---

[942] We do not know to which friend and publication project Sambucus is referring here. It might also be *Symbolum Iacobi Monawi Ipse faciet, virorum clarissimorum, et amicorum clarissimorum versibus celebratum et exornatum*, which came out only in 1581.
[943] These two sentences seem to have been heavily corrupted in the transcription used in Gerstinger.
[944] of the pictures of the physicians
[945] We could not identify the letter to which Sambucus is referring here.
[946] There must have been a list attached to the letter.
[947] of Muses

159.
Sambucus to Theodor Zwinger
20 November 1570, [Mannersdorf]

The original is kept in Basel, Universitätsbibliothek, Frey Mscr II 26, no. 213. Published in Gerstinger, "Die Briefe," 113-114.

Sambucus complains that living far away from his library he cannot help Zwinger with work on the Politics *(of Aristotle) as he was asked. He will do so as soon as he is back (in Vienna) but meanwhile Zwinger should take his situation into account. He has finished the great work on Dioscorides, hopefully for the good of the people. He is urging Löwenklau again. If he does not get him to act now, then the whole thing is over. He has not seen the Manasses-manuscript of Pierre Pithou and does not normally use the codices in possession of others, unless he can become the owner. He sent two or three copies of Manasses to Löwenklau two years before and believes that he has already translated and edited the work. Zwinger should give his greetings to Pithou, whose talents and works deserve the praise of posterity. He should let him know if Löwenklau will edit the history of Glycas.*

Sambucus Zvingero salutem.

Iniucunde vivo, dum a bibliotheca per λοιμικὰς στάσεις[948] urbis absum, nec parum augent molestiam tuae preces honestae inque *Politicis* illustrandis studium egregium,[949] cui, si ad Musas rediero, quiddam subiciam. Interea voluntatem re metiare. Dioscoridem absolvi opera non vulgari, utilitate hominum, ut spero, maxima. Leonclabium denuo urgeo, quem si nunc non commovero, actum est. Pythaei Manasses mihi visus non est, nec soleo alienis manum adhibere, nisi herus factus.[950] Misi ego ante biennium fere duo vel tria ex[em]plaria Manassis Leonclavio,[951] qui conversum et varietatibus distinctum credo iam edidit.[952] Pythaeo salutem a me, cuius ingenium et labores, uti dicis, laude posterorum digna sunt. Glycei historias an Leonclabius edat, oro significes.[953] Ἔρρωσο.[954] XX. Novembris 1570.[955]

---

[948] pestilential situation
[949] Zwinger had most probably asked for Sambucus's contribution to his planned edition of Aristotle's *Politica*. His edition came out as *Aristotelis Politicorum libri octo ex Dionysii Lambini et Petri Victorii interpretationibus* (Basel: Episcopius, 1582).
[950] Pierre Pithou (1539-1596) was a significant philologist and collector of manuscripts. He was also the author of several historical and juridical works. He came from an important Parisian family of advocates but he had to leave his office because of his Calvinism in 1562. He withdrew to Basel and returned to Paris only in 1572, miraculously escaping the Saint Bartholomew's Day Massacre. See Louis De Rosanbo, "Pierre Pithou érudit," *Revue du Seizième siècle* 16 (1929), 301-330; Klaus Malettke, "Pierre Pithou als Historiker," in *Humanismus und Historiographie*, ed. August Buck (Weinheim: DFG, 1991), 89-103; *Les Pithou, les Lettres et le Royaume*, ed. Marie-Madeleine Fragonard (Paris: Champion, 2003).
[951] Löwenklau mentions in the preface to his Latin translation that Sambucus has sent him two copies. Manasses, *Annales*, f. a2ᵛ.
[952] Manasses, *Annales*. See Gerstinger, "Zusammenfassung," 309-311.
[953] Glycas, *Annales*. See Gerstinger, "Zusammenfassung," 306-307.
[954] farewell
[955] Zwinger's marginal notes: "Pestis Sambucum impedit libris illustrandis; Dioscorides; Manassis edita per Leonclavium; Glycei historiae."

160.
Sambucus to Johannes Crato
[1570?][956], Vienna

Published in Gerstinger, "Die Briefe," 111.

Sambucus sent Crato the summary of the argument he intends for the preface, in which he explains things at greater length. He hopes this work will not be disappointing, as his friends have praised his writings before. He does not think that anyone's written style should be accepted unless it is grounded in ancient usage and supported by the recommendations of better rhetors. He thinks that the natural form is preferable to affected effort. He does not criticize carefulness, as long as the style is consistent and the inherent vigour (of words) is not deformed, fractured, inflated or in a bad taste. He wishes Crato a good trip and safe return. Had he not met the servant with Crato's new letter at the door, he would have given him this leaf of paper.

Clarissimo domino doctori Ioanni Cratoni amico suo observandissimo.

Summam tibi et praecipua argumenta eorum, quae ad praefationem cogito, miseram, ubi pluribus verbis rem declaro. Spero me λέξει καὶ συνθήκῃ,[957] ut in aliis adhuc studium extitit nostrum, magis satisfacturum, cui eius laudis nonnullam et professionis partem amici aliquando mihi contribuerunt. Nec probo, si ita sentis, cuiusque genium esse in scribendo acceptandum, nisi ex vetustatis proba ratione formaque συντηρήσεως καὶ μιμήσεως[958] ducta eluceat commendationeque meliorum artificum nitatur. Illud, quando familiarissime inter nos agitur, addo, differre quaesitam diligentiam a naturae forma; illam non negligendam, haec si artifex sit, praeferendam, dissimilem saepe a se illam, hanc constantem deprehendi, hanc confecta meditari et propria, illam accersita cogere. Voco tamen propria et confecta Latina, plena, significantia, Ciceronis aetate trita et repetita. Solicitudinem non vitupero, modo labore unius sit stili nec consilio perpetuo Nizolii[959] δήναμις,[960] in qua Hermogenes universam idearum laudem constituit,[961] difformis, separata, inflata καὶ κακόζηλος[962] sit. Tibi vero iter felix, omnibus rebus incolume abituro redituroque precor, de assidua scriptione nihil querare. Vale ex Museolo nostro, hancque schedulam illico famulo dedissem, nisi pro foribus mihi non lecta tua obtulisset. Totus tuus Sambucus.

---

[956] This letter has been dated in Gerstinger to the spring of 1570, supposing it was written before Crato's travel to Prague and Speyer. However, since Crato was often on the way, this dating is not entirely convincing. We cannot be sure in the year 1570 either.
[957] words and compound / by choice of words and composition
[958] of preservation and imitation
[959] Mario Nizolio (1488–1567), humanist of Brescia, was famous for his dictionary on Ciceronian Latin and his criticism of scholastic Aristotelianism. Nizolio denied the validity of universal concepts, questioned the philosophical significance of several of Plato's and Aristotle's works (especially the latter's metaphysical and dialectical texts). See Quirinus Breen, "The Observationes in M. T. Ciceronem of Marius Nizolius," *Studies in the Renaissance* 1 (1954), 49-58; idem, "Marius Nizolius: Ciceronian Lexicographer and Philosopher," *Archiv für Reformationsgeschichte* 46 (1955), 69-87; Matthias Wesseler, *Die Einheit von Wort und Sache: der Entwurf einer rhetorischen Philosophie bei Marius Nizolius* (Munich: Fink, 1974).
[960] power
[961] A reference to *On Types of Style* (*De ideis*) by Hermogenes of Tarsus (second century BC).
[962] having bad taste

161.
Claude Aubery[963] to Sambucus
1571, Basel

Dedication in Theodorus Ducas Lascaris, *De communicatione naturali libri VI, admiranda philosophia referti. Nunc primum in lucem prolati et Latinam in linguam versi a Claudio Auberio Triuncuriano. Ex Ioannis Sambuci viri celebris bibliotheca* (Basileae: E. Episcopius, 1571), 3-7. Published in *Humanistes du bassin des Carpates II. Johannes Sambucus*, 151-155.

162.
Sambucus to Hugo Blotius
27 April 1571, Vienna

The original is kept in Vienna, ÖNB, Cod. 9737^{z14-18}, V, f. 257^r. Published in Menčik, "A Páduában tanuló," 48; and Gerstinger, "Die Briefe," 118-120.

Sambucus has received Blotius's letter and forwarded the one addressed to Ellebodius to Pressburg. He wishes he could do something for Blotius. He cannot write securely about the unexpected peace, but Blotius will understand from others what he thinks about it. It does not seem to be conductive to the cause or the prestige of Christendom, but the peacemakers will find it out. Georgius Ursinus is with him, and on Blotius's request asked him to speak with bishop Listhius about calling back Márton Berzeviczy and offering him some better position. The previous day Sambucus dined with Listhius and discussed the question. The bishop would not be against such move and will write more in detail about it in his next letter to Blotius. Blotius should say hello to Aldo Manuzio and do Sambucus the favour of searching out Andreas Darmarios in the boutiques of the Greeks at the church of San Giorgio in Venice, if he is still there. Four years before that impostor received 150 scudi from Sambucus (of which he has a written acknowledgment) and was supposed to send books demanded by Sambucus but he sent no books but left with his manuscripts for Lérida in Spain to visit Antonio Augustín. If he were back, Sambucus would put pressure on him through friends in order to make him respect his word. Blotius should not mention Sambucus' name, as Andreas's brother, Joannes, already suspects that he is planning to bring a lawsuit against him. Blotius may learn about Darmarios with the pretext of buying books. Sambucus would anyway need very much the Bibliotheca *of Photius, so he asks Blotius to buy it from the Greeks either in a new or an old transcript. The price is 25 coronati or 30 "mutilated" ducats.*

---

[963] The little-known philologist Claude Aubery (Aubry) (c. 1540–1596) came from Triaucourt (Meuse), a little French village. Later he moved to Lausanne where he worked as a physician, and from 1576 taught philosophy. He was scarcely twenty when he published a new Latin translation of Theophrastus's *Characteres* with erudite comments, and later also edited Aristotle. In the 1580s he published several orations in religious subjects, which were condemned by the City Council of Bern on Theodore Beza's demand (c. 1586). As a result, he returned to Dijon, where he converted to Catholicism. See *Biografia universale antica e moderna* (Venice: G. B. Missiglia, 1822), 3:406; Thomas Frognall Dibdin, *An Introduction to the Knowledge of Rare and Valuable Editions of the Greek and Latin Classics Including an Account of Polyglot Bibles*, 3rd ed. (London: Longman Group Limited, 1808), 500.

Sambucus salutem.

Tuas accepi,⁹⁶⁴ Ellebodio suas Posonium misi.⁹⁶⁵ De copiosa tua in me measque res et usus voluntate nunquam dubitavi. Quod eiusdem memoria sensum confirmare cupis, id vero officiosi et integri amici semper duxi. Utinam tua caussa aliquid efficiam; parum vires possunt. Si opinio authoritatis quid ab aliis impetraverit, libere scribito, impera, nihil est, quod neglectum querere. De pace praeter omnium spem ac vota quid scribam tuto, ignoro, quid sentiamus, ex aliis intelliges.⁹⁶⁶ Importuna rei nominique Christiano videtur, sed autores viderint. Ursinus nobiscum est.⁹⁶⁷ Is abs te me petiit, cum reverendissimo tractarem de revocando B. eique loco commodo prospiciendo.⁹⁶⁸ Heri inter prandendum reverendissimo negocium exposui, qui ut redeat sibique melius caveat prolixiusque prospiciat, nunquam impediturum se ait, imo sibi consilium placere ad teque proxime de ipso expediundo scripturum. Aldum Manutium a me saluta. Cumque tam facile tuam operam mihi deferas, te valde etiam atque etiam rogo, ipse aut per alios ad S. Georgii aediculas Graeculorum subeas atque expiscere, num adsit Andreas dal

---

⁹⁶⁴ Hugo Blotius (1534–1608) was a Dutch humanist, who studied in Leuven, Orlèans, Basel and Padua, and became the first imperial librarian in 1575. The first time Blotius visited Vienna was in late 1570. In 1571 he returned to Padua with the elder son of the Bishop of Veszprém and Hungarian Vice-Chancellor Johannes Listhius. On Blotius see Louthan, *The Quest for Compromise*, 53-66; Paola Molino, "Die andere Stimme." *La formazione di un intellettuale erasmiano nell'Europa del tardo Cinquecento: Hugo Blotius. (1534–1574)* (MA thesis, University of Florence, 2006); Almási, *The Uses of Humanism*, 186-190; Molino, *L'impero di carta*.

⁹⁶⁵ This letter of Blotius to Ellebodius is now lost. Nicasius Ellebodius (1535–1577) was a Flemish philologist, who studied in Leuven and later lived a few years in Rome under the protection of Cardinal Granvelle. In 1557 he came to Vienna, where he met Nicolaus Olahus, archbishop of Hungary. By 1560 he was made canon of Trnava. He passed the next ten years in Padua, living mostly in the house of Gian Vincenzo Pinelli. In 1571 he moved to Pressburg and lived in the house of his new patron István Radéczy, bishop of Várad. His major work was an edition of Aristotle's *Poetics*. He is probably the author of a biography of Michele Sofianos. Curiously, Sambucus did not have a very good relationship with him. See Tibor Klaniczay, "Contributi alle relazioni padovane degli umanisti d'Ungheria. Nicasio Ellebodio e la sua attività filologica," in Vittore Branca, ed., *Venezia e Ungheria nel Rinascimento* (Florence: Olschki, 1973), 316-333; Anna Meschini, *Michele Sofianòs* (Padova: Liviana, 1981); Almási, *The Uses of Humanism*; Nicasius Ellebodius, *In Aristotelis librum De poetica paraphrasis et notae*, ed. Zsuzsanna Maurer (Budapest: Typotext, 2014); Áron Obán, "Nicasius Ellebodius and the 'otium litterarum': The vicissitudes of a Flemish humanist in Pozsony (1571–77)," *East Central Europe* 48 (2021), 1-22, idem, "Clusius, Ellebodius and Purkircher: A Cross-Section of Humanist-Naturalist Cultural Exchange Between Vienna and Pozsony," *Erudition and the Republic of Letters* 8 (2023), 1-35; and the article by idem in *Companion*.

⁹⁶⁶ Sambucus seems to have been opposed to the conditions of the religious concessions made to the Austrian nobility, but he did not dare to commit his criticism to writing. The "Assekuration" of 14 January 1571 granted the right to the Lower Austrian nobility to worship according to the Augsburg Confession (use the Lutheran practice in their castles and lands together with their servants). See Grete Mecenseffy, *Geschichte des Protestantismus in Österreich* (Graz: Böhlau, 1956), 52-53; Louthan, *The Quest for Compromise*, 50, 103.

⁹⁶⁷ We hardly know the person in question. Johanna von Ernuszt claims there was an Ursinus in the environment of Johannes Listhius who travelled to Padua. He may be Georgius Ursinus (Georg Bähr ?), who returned to Padua in 1571 and became doctor of medicine in Ferrara in 1572. Johanna von Ernuszt, "Die ungarischen Beziehungen des Hugo Blotius," *Jahrbuch des Graf Klebelsberg Kuno Instituts für ungarische Geschichtsforschung in Wien* 10 (1940), 7-53. at 24; Zonta, *Schlesische Studenten*, 168.

⁹⁶⁸ Reference is made to Márton Berzeviczy (1538–1596), later chancellor of Transylvania, who became Polish nobleman and baron under Stephen Báthory's rule. He studied in Wittenberg, joined the Hungarian court in Vienna but quitted and continued his studies in Padua with the protection of Bishop of Várad Ferenc Forgách in 1568–1572. This letter suggests that Listhius's (vain) promises for a position at court might have played a role in his return to Vienna next year. See Endre Veress, *Berzeviczy Márton (1538–1596)* (Budapest: Mayar Történelmi Társulat, 1911); Barlay Ö. Szabolcs, "Egy humanista pályakezdése – Berzeviczy Márton [The beginning of the career of a humanist – M. B.]," in *Irodalom és ideológia a 16–17. században*, ed. Béla Varjas (Budapest: Akadémia, 1987), 135-150; Almási, "Variációk az értelmiségi útkeresés témájára"; and the article by Gábor Förköli in *Companion*.

Mar.[969] Is enim impostor a me ante 4 annos 150 scutatos accepit certis promissis et syngrapha data, missurum se mihi quamprimum libros a me requisitos, sed nihil dum vidi, profectus erat Ilerdam cum libris manuscriptis ad Antonium Augustinum[970] in Hispaniam. Si reversus esset, cogerem illum per amicos ad liberandam fidem. Sed dissimula nomen meum, nam frater Ioannes dal Mar subolfecit me quiddam in eos iure moliri. Poteris praetextu librorum emendorum talia cognoscere. Est praeterea mihi valde opus Photii patriarchae *Bibliotheca*.[971] Te obsecro, descriptum illum recens vel antiqua manu mihi compares apud eosdem Graecos. Venit 25 coronatis 30 ducatis mutilis, ut vocant. Vale, 27. Aprilis 15[71].

Address: Al molto Magnifico et Excellentissimo Signor Dottor Hugo Blotius Guvernator del Illustrissimo Signor Giovanni Listio, Barone Ongaro, Amico osservandissimo. In Vineggia.

163.
Sambucus to Theodor Zwinger
7 June 1571, [Vienna]

The original is kept in Basel, Universitätsbibliothek, Frey I 12, f. 328. Copy: ibid., Mscr G2 II 8, no. 160. Published in Gerstinger, "Die Briefe," 116-118.[972]

Sambucus is sorry to hear that his manuscript of Apollonius's Syntax, which he restored with so much work, has gone lost. He is upset about Bonfini's work on chastity being so ignored; it has neither been published nor resent to him. The heirs of Oporinus should make sure it does not get lost. The money Sambucus owes them after the sold copies of Bonfini's history will not get there by the next market day. He gave this task to a merchant called Ammanus, but it didn't work out. He would send the money, if he only knew whom to trust it. He keeps the money safely and Zwinger should let the heirs know that they will be paid, even if he owed them twenty times. Sambucus wonders about the (publication of) Vegetius. He once sent Johannes Herwagen a book on usury by some old jurist but he does not know if Herwagen will publish it. For his part, Dioscorides is ready. It needs a sponsor and a suitable publisher. He would like to have it printed in folio format because of the many comments, in Latin and Greek, together with the skilfully made coloured images of 124 plants, which are partly exotic, partly disputed and unknown. He has corrected innumerous

---

[969] Andreas Darmarios (1540–1587) was a manuscript trader and Greek copyist, who prepared hundreds of transcripts of rare Greek manuscripts in Venice. He was a major contact for Sambucus. The catalogue of the ÖNB lists 63 manuscripts that Sambucus bought from him. See Otto Kresten, "Die Handschriftenproduktion des Andreas Darmarios im Jahre 1564," *Jahrbuch der Österreichischen Byzantinistik* 24 (1975) 147-93; Otto Kresten, "Der Schreiber und Handschriftenhändler Andreas Darmarios. Eine biographische Skizze," in *Griechische Kodikologie und Textüberlieferung*, ed. Dieter Harlfinger (Darmstadt: Wissenschaftliche Buchgesellschaft, 1980), 406-419; Mark Sosower, "A Forger revisited: Andreas Darmarios and Beinecke 269," *Jahrbuch der Österreichischen Byzantinistik* 43 (1993), 289-306; Kersten Hajdú, "Andreas Darmarios in München? Über einen Handschriftenverkauf an die Herzogliche Bibliothek," *Bibliotheksforum Bayern* 22 (1994), 118-128.

[970] Antonio Augustín y Albanell (1516–1586), Bishop of Lleida (later Archbishop of Tarragona), was a humanist interested primarily in the history of canon law.

[971] The *Bibliotheca* of the patriarch Photius I of Constantinople (d. 893) is a collection of abridgments of 280 volumes of (to a great extent lost) classical works, in the majority Christian patristic texts, but also historical and literary writings. On Sambucus's attempts to find copies of it and publish it, see letters 162, 245, 257 and 261. See Gerstinger, "Zusammenfassung," 312.

[972] Gerstinger relied on the copy of the letter.

corrupt places in the text which have caused problems and error for Mattioli and others. He talked several times about it with Josias Richel but when he heard about Sambucus's minor condition of (the payment of) 500 florins, he changed his mind. Zwinger can imagine how much effort it took Sambucus. He would be very grateful if Zwinger talked with some quality publisher. If the honorarium (of 500) seemed too much, it can also be 300. Publishers can be sure that it will be as lucrative as Mattioli's edition. Zwinger will soon receive the map of Hungary and maps of ancient Rome and Greece prepared by Sambucus. The books Plantin has from him are unjustly laid aside because of the printing of the Polyglot Bible.

Sambucus salutem.

Apollonii σύνταξιν⁹⁷³ tot meis restitutam sarctamque vigiliis, pro eo ac publice omnia cupio, vehementer doleo periisse. Bonfinii autem philosophum eruditumque opus *De pudicitia coniugali* ita temere abiici nec excudi nec remitti ad me nonnihil molestum est.⁹⁷⁴ Admone Oporini haeredes seu potius, qui socii officinae procurandae fuere, ut caveant, ne pereat. Nescio, quo ipsorum fato, forte bono, quam ex Bonfinii exemplariis pecuniam illis debeo, his nundinis ad eos non pervenerit,⁹⁷⁵ [dederam Ammano mercatori⁹⁷⁶ non ignobili negocium cum literis, sed frustra. Pecuniam,]⁹⁷⁷ quam bona fide salvam teneo mittamque, modo sciam, cui recte dederim, imo et quod interea lucri illis apportasset, non recusabo compensare, idque ut illis significes, valde te oro, inque certa spe retineas et confirmes, vel si vicies tantum deberem. Quid Vegetius noster, nonne aliquando consulet agasonibus et equisonibus? Miseram Hervagio de faenore iuris consulti cuiusdam vetusti librum, nescio an excuderit.⁹⁷⁸ Dioscorides meus σὺν θεῷ⁹⁷⁹ absolutus a me est, quaerit patronum et officinam idoneam. Vellem impressum folii forma et quidem ob lucubrationes impensas, Latine et Graece simul cum insertis 124 plantis externis partim,⁹⁸⁰ controversis et ignotis partim, quarum imagines artificiose coloribus et μονογράμμους⁹⁸¹ expressas habeo, menda innumera, quae Mathiolo et aliis dubitandi et errandi obiecere ansas. Richelius aliquoties mecum egit, sibi mitterem, sed cum conditiunculam 500 florenorum adiecissem, ilico mutavit consilium. Quanti mihi labor constiterit, quanti plantarum εἰκόνες⁹⁸² et alia, tu ipse aestimes. Tu igitur si cum eleganti typographo et diligenti velut a te ipse de hac re tractaris, non erit parum gratum. Si de honorario gravius videbitur, sit 300 florenorum.⁹⁸³ Illud confirmare poteris, non minus gratum et lucrosum fore opus quam Mathioli eruditis bibliothecis etc.⁹⁸⁴ Ungariam et veterem

---

973 Syntax. On Apollonius's *Syntax* cf. the Index.
974 Bonfini, *Symposion trimeron*.
975 This regards the money Sambucus owed for the copies he sold of Bonfini's *Rerum Ungaricarum decades*. See letters 149, 227 and 233.
976 We were not able to identify this tradesman.
977 This part of the sentence appears to be crossed out, especially the last word, *pecuniam*.
978 Johann Herwagen Jr. (1530–1564?) was a printer in Basel. Episcopius took over his firm in 1571. We do not know more about the manuscript in question. Benzing, *Die Buchdrucker*, 38.
979 with god's help
980 Cf. letters 155 and 174.
981 delineated
982 images
983 Ironically, Sambucus was eventually ready to pay to the publisher Henri Estienne 60 florins to get the book published. See letter 312.
984 On the lucrative business of Mattioli's botanical manual see Ilaria Andreoli "'A voi gran lodi e allo stampatore gran guadagno.' Vincenzo Valgrisi stampatore e libraio del *Dioscoride* del Mattioli," in *I discorsi di P.A. Mattioli:*

Graeciam cum Italia a me descriptas brevi cum aliis habebis.⁹⁸⁵ Quae Plantinus habet, ob biblia sua incohata et papismos latere inique patitur.⁹⁸⁶ Tu ad me brevi de omnibus. Ἔρρωσο⁹⁸⁷ 7. Iunii 1571.

Address: Viro clarissimo domino Theodoro Zuinggero, medico et philosopho etc., amico singulari. Basileam.

164.
Sambucus to Emperor Maximilian II.
1 July 1571, Vienna

Dedication to Sambucus, Περὶ πανανθεντείας,⁹⁸⁸ *sive maiestate imperatoris, et quorundam praeiudicio sive donatione Constantiniana*, preserved in Vienna, ÖNB, Cod. 9534, f. 4-5. Published in Chmel, *Die Handschriften der K. K. Hofbibliothek in Wien*, 1:708-709; Gerstinger, "Die Briefe," 120-122.⁹⁸⁹

Sambucus knows that this argument (about the Donation of Constantine and papal power), which has gone ignored for long, can rouse hatred against him. But he thinks it is of general importance and he always cared more about the truth than about offending someone. No one doubts that truth is important also for the emperor. Sambucus used an epistolary style, simple language, and numbered not the pages but the arguments, since Maximilian has little time for reading. What he said is not against the pope but the emperor will see what to think about the dignity of the emperor (ruling in the name of entire Christianity) and the role of Rome: the (secular and ecclesiastical) offices need to be kept separate and vain ambition (of individuals), detrimental to the public, should be kept at bay. He wants to bring back the old freedom and does not demand new ones. The emperor's sword (i.e. power) needs to be in proportion with the greatness of the world. If the pope is believed to deserve more (power) it is because of the rights given by Constantine and others and not because of divine law. It is the emperor's task to emend corrupt religion and safeguard the established one, while the pope, with imperial backing, needs to elevate faith. Finally, Sambucus asks Maximilian that he leniently receive his work on the diploma attributed to Constantine, conserve the country against the Ottomans and liberate Hungary.

---

l'esemplare dipinto da Gherardo Cibo, eds. Duilio Contin and Lucia Tongiorgi (Sansepolcro: Aboca, 2015), 2:69-85. Cf. with letter 155.

⁹⁸⁵ See letter 153, note 912.

⁹⁸⁶ The first volume of the eight-volume Polyglot Bible appeared on 1 March 1569, the last came out on 31 March 1572. See Ángel Sáenz-Badillos, "Arias Montano y la Biblia Políglota de Amberes," in *Encuentros en Flandes*, eds. Thomas Werner and Robert A. Verdonk (Leuven: Presses Universitaires, 2000), 327-340.

⁹⁸⁷ farewell

⁹⁸⁸ On universal authority.

⁹⁸⁹ Chmel also transcribes the full address, the motto, Sambucus poem, as well as the first and last paragraphs of the essay (*Die Handschriften der K. K. Hofbibliothek*, 1:708-711). See Christian Gastgeber, "Johannes Sambucus und die *Donatio Constantini*," in *Iohannes Sambucus / János Zsámboki*, 241-268. Cf. Imre Téglásy, "Über das Schicksal der Donatio Constantiniana im 16. Jahrhundert. Ein unbekanntes Werk des Johannes Sambucus (Zsámboky) über die kaiserliche Plenipotenz," in *Geschichtsbewustsein und Geschichtsschreibung in der Renaissance*, eds. August Buck et al. (Budapest: Akadémia; Leiden: Brill, 1989), 85-96; Viktor Bibl, "Die Erhebung Herzog Cosimos von Medici zum Grossherzog von Toskana und die kaiserliche Anerkennung, 1569–1576," *Archiv für österreichische Geschichte* 103 (1913), 1-162.

Potentissimo invictissimo clementissimoque caesari Maximiliano II. etc., domino, domino suo longe benignissimo salutem.

Scio me multorum odium et voces excitaturum, qui nullis partibus neque iudicio neque lectionum varietate ad quosdam aggregandus, tamen grave, lubricum, tamque diu invise iactatum argumentum hodie sumpserim tractamdum. Ego vero, clementissime Imperator, hanc rem ad omnes pertinere valde ratus, cum natura et disciplina, tum, conscientiam qui rectam tuentur, exemplo. Veritatem omnibus omnium opibus ac offensis semper praetuli. Hanc tuae maiestati caram primoque constitutam loco nemini dubium est. Nihil quidem hisce pagellis offero singulare. Scripseram ad amicum epistulae in modum. Caeterum leget tua maiestas quaedam ab aliis non lecta, neque fortassis observata. Cumque in hac imperii mole ocium multa legendi vestrae maiestati desit, plane et apto stilo non folia sed argumenta numeravi, argutias et coniecturas ociosis reliqui.[990] Non sum extra septa lapsus. Si quid de pontifice incidit, honoris utriusque caussa factum est, ut tua maiestas videret, quanti Germanici, hoc est, universi nominis Christiani imperii dignitas aestimanda, quo loco res Romanae sint habendae, distincta esse munia debere, vanas ambitiones nec accersandas neque admittendas publico detrimento cogitaret. Libertatem veterem repeto, novam non fingo, finibus sacros teneo, gladium tuum orbis amplitudine metior. Si quid opinione vulgi maius Romanis est concedendum, iure Constantini aliorumque beneficio tribuo, aeternis legibus ac sententiis non tueor. Tuum est et religionem perversam emendare et constitutam tueri. Pontifici res fidei tuo subsidio augenda, si recte sentiat, relinquatur: caetera a Deo accipis, ornata confirmataque egregia voluntate et moderatione sarta defendes. Caput sit praecipuum membrum utroque in statu reipublicae, sic tamen, ut aliorum usu membrorum ne prorsus eximatur. Imperii firmitudo electione consistat divina suffragioque coelo delectorum, unde coronae auctarium speretur. Quod quis nunquam habuit nec acceptavit a patronis, cliens in officio maneat, gratus erga benefactores sit, elemosinae conviva et curator idoneus sit, humanitate et vitae innocentia vincat, superque sit, qua de re alii et nos alibi copiosius. Adscripsi Graecum θέσπισμα[991] Constantino tributum, quod nec annos nec caudam alitis superbae nec alia pleraque Latine prodita contestatur. Tuam maiestatem oro supplex, opellam maiestatis functioni accommodatam clementissime accipiat adeoque contra icterum, hoc est, quibus bile et odio suffusi cuncta aurea et irata apparent, facillime tueatur. Quam Deus optimus maximus tot coniugiis celeberrimis, fratris et filiarum applausu omnium bene effuseque beet exhilaretque, sceptro imperii Germanici tuendo, regundis contra Thurcam regnis et finibus, constantem et vividum conservet. Tua maiestas libertatem Pannoniae vindicet, asserat, propaget ad aeterni Dei, cuius vices geris, religionisque salutaris laudem, tuorum nostrumque omnium subiectorum usum et diutissimam laetitiam. Amen. Viennae Kalendis Quinctilibus 1571. Tuae clementissimae maiestatis subditissimus clientulus, consiliarius et historicus Ioannes Sambucus.

---

[990] This is not even true of this very dedication. Apparently, Sambucus was not willing to use simple Latin apt for his princely patron, not even in cases where he knew he should. His concise and often allusive style was also a good way to avoid saying what he meant in absolute terms.

[991] imperial constitution, decree

165.
Sambucus to Emperor Maximilian II.
5 August 1571, Vienna

This note, which accompanied the previous manuscript, is preserved in ÖNB, Cod. 9534, f. 4ª. Published in Chmel, *Die Handschriften der K. K. Hofbibliothek*, 1:709; Gerstinger, "Die Briefe," 121.

Sambucus asks Emperor Maximilian to take and read his booklet and graciously help him out in his household expenses in these times of high prices.

Allergnadigister, Grossmachtigister khayser und herr, herr etc.

Mein untertanigist suppliciern E. M. wölle gnadigist ditz mein büchlain de Maiestate imperatoris annemen, auch lesn: und meine schwäre zerung und haushaltung bey disen teuern zeyten gnadigist und guetigist, mit einer hilff bedenkhen und erheben: welchs ich die Zeytt meins lebens untertanigist will verdienen. Thuend mich, und mein nott, und mue befelhennd. Den 5 Aug. 1571. E. M. Untertänigster gehorsamister D. Joan. Sambucus.

166.
Sambucus to Karl II, Archduke of Austria
1 September 1571, Vienna

Dedication on the map *Ungariae loca praecipua recens emendata atque edita per Ioannem Sambucum MDLXXI Viennae*, preserved in Vienna, ÖNB, Kartensammlung AB 9 A 1.

As there is no need for a detailed description, Sambucus has made only some more important corrections, used only single, better known place names, identified ecclesiastic seats by crosiers and crosses, towns and villages by their magnitude. He dedicates this work, which he hopes to present in a bigger format in the future, to the Archduke.

Serenissimo principi domino Carolo archiduci, Maximilliani II fratri Sambucus.

Cum ad potiores historias descriptione illa minuta opus non sit, praecipua emendavi, nominibus singulis et vulgatioribus nunc utor, sacra lituis et cruce, loca amplitudine distincta sunt. Hoc quidquid est, tuae serenitatis in Pannoniam meritis, patrocinio reliquo nuptiisque illustrissimis dicatur, quod plenius maiore alliquando forma sum praestiturus. Vestra serenitas opellam clientis ut clementissime accipiat supplex oro. Viennae Kalendis Septembribus 1571.

167.
Antonius Verantius to Sambucus
19 October 1571, Vienna

Copies are kept in Budapest, OSZK, Fol. Lat. 1681/4, f. 19 (16th century); Eger, Főegyházmegyei Könyvtár, Y.V.22, f. 167ʳ (19ᵗʰ c.). Published in Antal Verancsics [Verantius], *Összes munkái*, ed. László Szalay and Gusztáv Wenzel, vol. 10, 1569–1571 (Pest: Eggenberger, 1871), 311. (Monumenta Hungariae Historica, Scriptores 25.)

Verantius expresses his thanks for the poems. He will respond to them, if not with something greater, at least with some Georgian wine. He will make sure that the wine is good enough to serve as a gift in return for all the praise he got. He is not yet thinking about the cardinalship but takes Sambucus's show of good will with the usual mind. The answer about the house was that it has already been promised to someone else, hence, Sambucus should look for another lodging close to the centre without any lodger. It should have much space, many bedrooms and have only one entrance.

Anthonius Verantius electus Strigoniensis Ioanni Sambuco fratri salutem.

De carminibus habeo maximas gratias easque etiam referam, si non re alia quapiam maiore at vino saltem Georgiano curaboque, ut sit tale, quod promereatur tanti munus encomii. De purpurae amictu nondum cogito.[992] Accipio utique tamen tuae erga me tam praeclarae voluntatis ac studii significationem eo animo, quo tua soleo omnia. De domo autem datum est responsum, quod iam antea promissa fuerit alteri nec duobus licere illam elocari.[993] Rogo itaque te, mi Sambuce, cures mihi aliam, quae et arci vicina et nulli inquilino sit obnoxia. Curiaeque laxitate et habitationum copia polleat nec duabus portis pateat. Vale. Viennae 19. Octobris Anno 1571.

168.
Marco Mantova Benavides[994] to Sambucus
[Late October–early November 1571], [Padua]

Published in Marcus Mantua Benavidius, *Epistolae familiares et nuncupatoriae simul* (Patavii: Lorenzo Pasquale, 1578), f. 58ᵛ-59ᵛ.

---

[992] Verantius, who was archbishop of Esztergom from 15 October 1569, eventually became cardinal only ten days before his death in June 1573.

[993] Verantius was looking for lodging in Vienna, see letter 176.

[994] Marco Mantova Benavides (1489–1582) was a revered professor of law at the University of Padua, a scholar of wide erudition, a remarkable antiquarian and collector. He was a friend of many famous humanists and literati in Padua and Venice, like Pietro Aretino, Sperone Speroni, Bernardino Tomitano, Francesco Sansovino etc. His legal scholarship and aesthetic views were influenced among others by Alciato. See Luigi Polacco, *Marco Mantova Benavides nella storia e nella cultura del Cinquecento* (Padova: Grafiche Erredici, 1984); *Marco Mantova Benavides: il suo museo e la cultura padovana del Cinquecento*, ed. Irene Favaretto (Padova: [Erredicci], 1984); Charles Davis, "Titian, 'A singular friend'," in *Kunst und Humanismus. Festschrift für Gosbert Schüßler zum 60. Geburtstag*, eds. Wolfgang Augustyn and Eckhard Leuschner (Passau: Dietmar Klinger, 2007), 261-301; *Un museo di antichità nella Padova del Cinquecento: la raccolta di Marco Mantova Benavides all'Università di Padova*, eds. Irene Favaretto and Alessandra Menegazzi (Rome: GB, 2013).

Benavides gently received the young men who carried Sambucus's letter and the son of the Hungarian Chancellor Listhius, recommended by Sambucus. But Sambucus might have given them an untrue image of him, and they might disappear soon, as happens to many who arrive with such letters of recommendation. But if they come for help, he will be most happy to do anything for them. If they want to study Roman law, which he has been teaching for 55 years, he is available. Unfortunately, he has no rare golden coins of Roman emperors, he only has many common ones. But he has around 200 silver coins, which he is happy to give as a gift to Maximilian II, as soon as he understands from an imperial decree that he would not disdain such a gift. He is not a merchant but a collector of antiquities, a rather extravagant person, said without arrogance. He will send an inventory of the statues and paintings decorating his library, as Sambucus wished.

Ioanni Sambuco, a secretis regis Ungariae, viro amplissimo virtutumque omnium genere praestantissimo salutem.

Adoloscentes,[995] quos mihi tuis literis magno affectu commendasti, amplissime vir, Listhiumque cancellarii regii Ungarici filium benevole et amanter, ut mores mei est, mirifice sum amplexatus eisdemque omnem meam operam polliceri haud praetermisi, si ea uti non indigne voluerint nec fuerint aspernati. Sed cum non sim ego talis, quem iis fortassis deliniasti, vide ne aegre ferant et conquerantur, quod sane dubito, eoque fit, ut alii quamplures mihi literas eiusmodi, commendatitias scilicet, perferant, postea tanquam canes Aegyptii bibentes nos auditoriumque nostrum, ut illi, Nili aquas epoti, fugiant nec amplius conspici (ut ita dicam) velint vel alloqui patiantur.[996] Non deero tamen, (quicquid sit) quantum in me est, et officii, et humanitatis, quominus praesto sim semper et ad omnia eorum commoda promptissimus, si me (ut dixi) accersierint.[997] Sique edoceri voluerint inque iure caesareo, quod profitemur, iam annus (nec ignoras tu) quinquagesimus quintus agitur, erudiri, mihique satis erit tuis humanissimis iussibus et literis benevolentia fraterna abunde plenis paruisse. Quoad aereos nummos caesarum, qui et rari sint (ut scibis et optas) nullos habeo, communes et vulgares, multos: Adrianos, Antoninos, Traianos, Caracallas, Augustos, Tiberios, Aurelios, Titos, Vespasianos, Domitianos et id genus plura, quae scribere longum foret. Argenteos etiam circiter ducentos plus minus, quos omnes si tibi tuoque regi non displicuerint, gratuito ad vos confestim mittam, cum primum diplomate regio intellexero (non enim sum ego nec unquam fui horum venditor seu mercator, sed emptor homoque profusus potius, verbo arrogantia absit) munuscula levidensia haec libenti animo et hilari fronte ac regia non dedignari, qualiacunque sint, excipere, et id quidem de statuis deque picturis et aliis omnibus, dictum putabis bibliothecam nostram exornantibus, quorum insuper (ut petiisti) ad te indicem mitto. Vale meque in tuo aere computa.

---

[995] Next to a certain Balthasar Praetorius, there were some other unnamed youngsters in the group of Blotius and Listhius Jr., probably György Dobos from Nagyszombat, whose stay was financed by the city (see letter 218). See Bakonyi, *Magyar nyelvű írásbeliség*, 68. It is a question if Johann Wilhelm Schwendi was already present in Blotius's group (see letter 234).

[996] It is a reference to Aesop's fable *Crocodilus et canis*, which is also the origin of the proverb: "sicut canis ad Nilum: bibens et fugiens."

[997] In fact, Listhius Jr. and Blotius would live in Benavides's house in the coming period. See, for example, the address in letter 177.

169.
Sambucus to Don John of Austria[998]
1 November 1571, Vienna

Dedication in Sambucus, *Arcus aliquot triumphales*, f. A2^r.

What should Sambucus do in such universal joy? As a private citizen, he expresses through this work what others have displayed by sending envoys and erecting triumphal arches. While some friends will happily read it, to others his striving will seem to serve the common good. This work will not offend anyone and hopefully will please Don John until he can describe the events themselves and Don John achieve a final victory over the Ottomans.

Serenissimo principi[999] Iano Austrio, Caroli V filio, domino suo clementissimo, Ioannes Sambucus.

In tanta omnium laetitia universoque applausu, quid ego privatim agam? Doleam? Inauditam victoriam invideam? Sileam? Absit, absit procul; cuius desiderium omnesque preces et vota in Christianorum triumphis et spoliis de immani barbarie versantur. Quod igitur alii tot allegationum concursu ostendere, tot arcuum substructionumque molibus atque magnificentia sunt passim contestati, id ego privatus animo et voluntate emensurus, hasce nugas intra parietes mihi effingens, cuncta repraesento, et quibusdam amicis dum satisfacio, persuadeor, alii quoque ut cogitationes inque salutem communem studium meum videant legereque possint. Qua opella neminem offensurum me spero tuaeque serenitati minimi clientuli ac ignoti factum non ingratum fore credo, dum res ipsa aliquando narratione nostra etiam ad posteros celebretur, communemque voraginem et pestem Christiani nominis prorsus conficiatis. Amen. Cuius me clementiae commendo. Vienna, Kalendis Novembribus 1571.

170.
Sambucus to Hugo Blotius
1 November 1571, Vienna

The original is kept in Vienna, ÖNB, Cod. 9737^{z14-18}, I, f. 70^{r-v}. Published in Menčík, "A Páduában tanuló," *Erdélyi Múzeum* 5 (1910), 26; Gerstinger, "Die Briefe," 122-123.

Blotius must have safely arrived in Padua and received the good news of the triumph of Lepanto. Sambucus wishes that the Christians carry on with their liberating fight and use the victory well. He recommends Georgius Ursinus to Blotius, a student of medicine and expert on Greek. Anything Blotius does for him is a favour to Sambucus personally, which will be duly compensated. He is sending his greetings to Johannes Listhius Jr. and the bookseller Simon, who should give him a response concerning books and other things. He is happy that Márton Berzeviczy got back into

---

[998] Don John (Juan) of Austria (1547–1578) was the illegitimate son of Charles V. After his father's death, his half-brother King of Spain Philip II officially acknowledged him and made him supreme commander of the royal forces in 1569. In May 1571 he became commander-in-chief of the naval army of the Holy League and defeated the Ottoman fleet at Lepanto on 7 October.
[999] Don John of Austria never received a princely title.

royal favour thanks to the intervention of Johannes Listhius Sr. and Johannes Crato and the fatherland my soon feel the benefit of his work. Sambucus is sending his greetings to him.

I. Sambucus salutem.

Credo ego vos,[1000] licet aliquandiu vagos, omnibus rebus incolumes Patavium pervenisse, cumulatos etiam ex itinere gaudii nuncio insigni de triumpho ex Thurcica relato classe.[1001] Qua occasione utinam deinceps et constanter ad libertatem universam nitamur, utique sciamus victoria. [...][1002] Nisi te facilem in amicorum rebus et solicitum nossem, nunquam abs te contenderem, hunc medicinae studiosum, Graecae linguae peritia et scripturis haud vulgarem Ursinum uti commendatissimum haberes.[1003] Quidquid in eum abs te idonee ac tempore proficiscetur, vel tua caussa ab aliis tuoque interventu, privatim in me collatum noveris, officium a me mutuo fore comparatum. Listhium a me et alios diligenter salutato. Simonem bibliopolam salutes et moneto me responsum exspectare de libris et aliis.[1004] Ipsis Kalendis Novembris 1571 Vienna.

Berzevitium gratulor autoritate Listhii et solicitudine Cratonis in gratiam repositum, cuius studia et conatus non ignobiles uti patriae rebus omniumque negociis quamprimum adhibeantur, exopto. Dic eidem salutem.[1005]

Address: Clarissimo iuris consulto doctori Blotio praefecto disciplinae Listhi etc., amico optimo. Patavium.
Blotius's hand: Ioannes Sambucus Vienna. 1571. Kalendis Novembris.

171.
Sambucus to Paolo Manuzio
1 December 1571, Vienna

The original is kept in Rome, BAV, Vat. lat. 3433, f. 27[r-v]; a copy is held in Modena, Biblioteca Estense, Fondo Estense, Ital. 1827, Beta 1,3,1, 121-122. Published in Gerstinger, "Die Briefe," 123-125.

Sambucus understood from reading the latest edition of Manuzio's letters that he desires to return to Venice to stay with his family and spend his time in much desired tranquillity. Not to mention Manuzio's personal reasons, also the public will profit of this decision and enjoy the benefits of Manuzio's great knowledge more widely. Sambucus was wondering why Manuzio did not respond to three of his laboriously written letters sent to Fulvio Orsini. He was worried that Manuzio, not helping him in his work in Dioscorides, neither personally nor through his friends, ceased to think of him as a friend. Now all the blame is on Fulvio, who did not inform Sambucus about Manuzio.

[1000] Hugo Blotius and his student Johannes Listhius Jr. left Vienna on 4 October 1571. On 2 November Listhius matriculated as a law student at the University of Padua. See Ernuszt, "Die ungarischen Beziehungen," 10.
[1001] See the previous letter.
[1002] Illegible word.
[1003] On Ursinus see letter 162.
[1004] This must be Simone Galignani, cf. letter 136.
[1005] See letter 162.

Sambucus's friendly feelings toward Manuzio have not changed and seeing Manuzio's merits they could not indeed. Manuzio will see that Sambucus thinks of his interests also at court. He is sending an example of his petty efforts (in a draft form), aimed at spreading the news of this universal joy, which will be a mosaic of emblems in the ancient style, which he will send to Manuzio (when printed). He sends his greetings to Aldo, who should buy him a manuscript of Photius's Bibliotheca. *Aldo will be repaid by the (Venetian) agent of the Polish post service. As a postscript he calls Manuzio's attention to an alternative reading of a place in Cicero's* For Murena. *This place has always bothered him and in fact his old codex gives a much more probable solution than the one usually accepted.*

Paulo Manutio Sambucus salutem.

Ex epistolis tuis, eis aliquot nuper libris auctis, quod nesciebam, intellexi certis ac expeditis consiliis te in dulcissimam patriam reversum in osculis et amplexibus carissimorum ocioque diu optato velle acquiescere. Nae tua ista deliberatio sana rebusque communibus utilis futura est. Ut enim, quas tu firme et rectissime privatim commemoras, causas omittam, certe a multis annis lucubrationes incohatas omnium desiderio sic perpolies usibusque vulgo trades, cuius nimirum pectus omnis generis doctrinarum et antiquitatis abundans liberius patebit, ut ad alios emanent, facilius assequere: πόνος γάρ, ὡς λέγουσι, εὐκλείας πατήρ.[1006] Mirabar equidem non sine quadam molestia ad ternas Romam scriptas et ad Fulvium nostrum missas nihil te rescripsisse, alienatam a me pristinam voluntatem silentio metuebam, quod haerenti mihi et in Dioscoride purgando laboranti neque ipse neque per amicos succurreras. Nunc in Fulvium omnem culpam redigo, qui nihil de te significavit. Me vero, mi Manuti, nihil immutatum, constantem in te amando colendoque esse minime dubites, nisique id tuis meritis porro faciam, fallax sim et minime vir bonus, tuaque indignus amicitia, idque adeo ἀναμφισβήτως[1007] habeas, ut nihil eorum, quae ad cuiusdam amici non obscuri curiosas literas suspicionis expediendae ergo respondisti, ad sensum nostrum pertinere existimem. Qui sim, fac periculum, aeque ac de aliis in caesaris aula meas cogitationes in tuis tuorumque rebus tuendis, ornandis, si possum, augendis etiam fixas reperies. Mitto exemplum nugarum universa laetitia effusarum, cuius generis varia et antiquo more emblematis, ut ille,[1008] vermiculata ad te mittam.[1009] Aldo tuo itemque dudum meo salutem, quem nomine meo rogabis, ut istic apud librarios Graeculos Photii *Bibliothecae* exemplar sive olim sive recens proba descriptum manu mihi curet, pecunia erit in promptu apud magistrum cursus publici Polonici,[1010] et gratiam feret mutuam. Vale, Kalendis Decembris 1571. Vienna.

Iam haec scripseram, cum in manus cecidit vetus codex orationum Ciceronianarum, in quo locus suspectus mihi semper sed a nemine sanatus in oratione *Pro Murena*: "Et ab ipsis cautis iureconsultorum sapientiam compilavit." Sic legitur: "Et ab ipsis capsis iureconsultorum" etc.[1011] Quid verius aut ad sensum et facilem in literis labem emendatius? Haec te scire, cuius praecipue interest, volui.

[1006] the effort is, as they say, the father of prestige. Euripides, frg. 474.
[1007] indisputably
[1008] Cicero, *De oratore* 3.171 and *Orator* 44.149: "emblemate vermiculato."
[1009] Sambucus, *Arcus aliquot triumphales*. Cf. letter 172.
[1010] A few years later, this Polish postal agent in Venice was Antonio Mazzuola. *Monumenta Poloniae Vaticana, tom. 4.: I. A. Caligarii nuntii apostolici in Polonia epistolae et acta, 1578–1581*, ed. Ludovicus Boratyński (Cracoviae: Sumptibus Academiae Litterarum Cracoviensis, 1915), 270, 397. On Photius cf. the Index.
[1011] Cicero, *Pro Murena* 11.25. In the recent edition of Elaine Fantham (*Cicero's Pro L. Murena Oratio*, Oxford: OUP, 2013) it reads "et ab ipsis his cautis iuris consultis eorum sapientiam compilarit [!]". Sambucus knew how to impress Manuzio, whose life project indeed was the edition of Cicero's works.

172.

Sambucus to Piero Vettori
1 December 1571, [Vienna]

The original is kept in Munich, BSB, Clm 735, Nr. 54. Published in *Clarorum Italorum et Germanorum epistolae*, 2:59-60; Gerstinger, "Die Briefe," 125-127.

If Vettori wonders what Sambucus is doing in this common happiness about this unheard-of triumph, well, he is giving thanks to God. He is sending Vettori the first draft results of it, and will soon send him a booklet with ancient inscriptions and triumphal arches. He is wondering what Vettori is working on. He is trying to correct some places in the poetry of ancient poets; he has finished with Dioscorides and the Physical and Moral Extracts *by Stobaeus. The book by [Pseudo-]Hesychius has already been printed. As a postscript Sambucus repeats the same note concerning the emendation of Cicero's* For Murena *as in the previous letter to Manuzio. He wanted to let Vettori know about it, as this place has not yet been corrected by anyone. Finally, it is the common opinion of the erudite that Vettori should follow others in publishing his familiar letters, which would not be a sign of vanity. Moreover, these kinds of (philological) arguments are more freely expressed in letters.*

Domino Petro Victorio Ioannes Sambucus salutem.

Quid in hac publica laetitia inaudito thriumpho demptoque universo metu ipse agam, si forsan quaeris, ex animo grates Deo authori cano, quorum autem interventu tam strenue res sunt gestae, elogiis, quod licet, orno. Cuius mei consilii exordium rude mitto,[1012] brevi libellum inscriptionibus antiquis et thriumphalibus, ut ille ait,[1013] vermiculatum missurus. Semper, mi optime Victori, illud Erechtei apud Euripidem verum fuit οὐδεὶς στρατεύσας ἄδικα σῶς ἦλθεν πάλιν.[1014]

Tu quid meditare aut etiam emiseris ex Μουσείῳ περιπατοῦντι[1015] et reconditis doctrinis bibliotheca abundanti, oro, significes, ego secundum historias in purgandis quibusdam locis veterum poetarum adeoque prodendis πινακογραφίαις[1016] versor, Dioscoridem et Stobaei Φυσικά absolvi.[1017] Illustrius Milesius de antiquis poetis iam formis expressus est.[1018] Ἔρρωσο,[1019] decus literarum et omnis vetustatis antistes, et Sambuco tuis meritis obstricto aliquando rescribito. Kalendis Decembris 1571.

Superiora scripseram, cum forte mihi codex vetus orationum Ciceronis occurrit, in quo illa in Mureniana: "Et ab ipsis cautis iureconsultis eorum sapientiam compilarit"[1020] sic legitur: "Et ab ipsis capsis iurisconsultorum etc." Quid verius, quid ad literarum labem et syllabarum similitudinem facilius proditur? Hoc te scire volui, quod a nemine locus vitiosus adhuc visus sit aut emendatus.

[1012] Sambucus, *Arcus aliquot triumphales*. Cf. the Index. On the distribution of the booklet also see Gerstinger's note in "Die Briefe," 126.
[1013] See note 1009 to the preceding letter.
[1014] No one who unjustly waged a war came back safe. Euripides, frg. 353.
[1015] out of the walking museum
[1016] maps
[1017] Stobaeus et Plethon, *Stobaei eclogarum libri duo ... et Plethonis de rebus Peloponnesiacis orationes duae*.
[1018] [Pseudo-]Hesychius's Περὶ τῶν ἐν παιδείᾳ appeared with the date of 1572.
[1019] farewell
[1020] See note 1011 to the preceding letter. Note that Sambucus quotes here the text correctly, while in the letter to Manuzio he only relied on his memory.

Addo ex eruditorum colloquio et de tua eximia eruditione iusta opinione, quando multi iam suas epistulas ad familiares cum laude edant, quando non inflata et inani sed ὀγκώδει[1021] scriptione et ποικιλία[1022] praestas, debere item de tuis iudices. Scis enim in eo genere argumenti de magnis rebus semper familiarius et liberius scribi solere.

Address: Clarissimo viro domino Petro Victorio, nobili Florentino, domino suo observandissimo. Fiorenza.

173.
Conrad Dasypodius to Sambucus
2 December 1571, Strasbourg

Published in *Sphaericae doctrinae propositiones graecae et latinae, nunc primum per M. Cunradum Dasypodium in lucem editae, quorum authores sequens indicat pagina* (Strasbourg: Mylius, 1572), f. A6ᵛ-A8ᵛ (it follows the dedication addressed to Johannes Crato).[1023]

Dasypodius claims Sambucus had told him five months before that Andreas Dudith would soon decide about a Diophantus-manuscript, but in the last eleven months he has not received any letters from Dudith. He does not think there is any better manuscript of Euclid than Sambucus's ancient codex, as Bessarion himself has also indicated. While he made use of six other manuscripts, Sambucus's codex served him as a yardstick to evaluate their readings. He thus noted down the readings from his manuscript, which will make all posterity grateful to Sambucus. He responds to Sambucus's question about Sambucus's Euclid-manuscript and fragment by Hero of Alexandria the following. Sambucus will soon see Euclid edited, corrected and commented in Greek and Latin. Dasypodius has not yet translated Sambucus's fragment by Hero, as he would like to get hold of the other two works of the author. He asks Sambucus to search for them. Sambucus can see that Dasypodius was busy with editing the works of Theodosius of Bithynia, Autolycus of Pitane and Barlaam of Seminara, which will also be useful for students of mathematics. Theodosius proves with the most solid demonstrations everything that can be taught about the "first motion"; Autolycus deals with the rise and set of each star; and Barlaam claims to be proving things that have never been proven. Sambucus can now see that the goal of the publication was not to place himself in the foreground but to show his contemporaries that the ancients are to be preferred to the moderns. In the same way, mathematical education should be raised through knowledge of great Greek mathematical texts and hence by getting rid of the barbarian past. Dasypodius is sending his greetings to Georg Tanner.

Clarissimo atque doctissimo viro domino Ioanni Sambuco, caesareae maiestatis a consiliis, amico suo antiquo, Cunradus Dasypodius S. D.

[1021] grandiose, well-rounded.
[1022] varied
[1023] The book contained the following works: *Theodosii de sphaera libri III; Theodosii de habitationibus liber I; Theodosii de diebus et noctibus libri II; Autolyci de spaera mobili liber I; Autolyci de ortu et occasu stellarum libri II; Barlaami Monachi Logisticae astronomicae libri VI.*

Ad me literis tuis postremis scribis, magnificum D. Sbardellatum brevi aperiturum animum suum de Diophanto,[1024] in quintum nunc mensem usque expecto responsum nec quicquam intelligo, nisi quod binas vel etiam ternas ad me dederit literas, quibus mecum omnibus de rebus agit. Ego vero ne unas quidem D. Sbardellati ad me ab undecim mensibus accepi, itaque nihil certi tibi rescribo.

Euclidis vero illud tuum antiquum exemplar, de quo scribis, clarissimam authori lucem adferet nec facile crediderim ullum aliud inveniri posse correctius teste Bessarione.[1025] Nam praeter sex alia, quibus sum usus exemplaria, nullum aliud habui quam tuum, quod mihi instar normae geometricae fuerit. Singula itaque, quae in tuo sunt codice, notavi, ut omnis posteritas tuae bibliothaecae pro hoc beneficio gratias agat. Quia vero me rogas, quid Euclides noster agat et cur non prodeat, aut quid causae, quod Heronis fragmenta latitent, quae omnia viri eruditi avide a me expectant, sic velim habeas: te intra paucos menses, Deo iuvante, visurum Euclidem Graecum et Latinum una cum commentariis Graecis et Latinis atque correctionibus eorum locorum, qui depravati esse exisitimantur aliisque ad geometriae cognitionem pertinentibus. Heronis vero fragmenta, etsi paulo accuratius inspexerim, nondum tamen verti, quia omnia huius authoris cupio habere opera, et si iam nactus essem, Ἀριθμητικὴν στοιχειώσιν [1026] et librum Περὶ ὑδρείων ὡρολογείων[1027] tuis meisque adiungerem.[1028] Fac, rogo, ut haec duo nancisci possis exemplaria, et erit mihi gratissimum. Vides me nunc occupatum fuisse in his propositionibus edendis Theodosii, Autolyci, et Barlaami,[1029] quae ideo literatis et disciplinarum studiosis gratae erunt, quia magnam in se continent doctrinam et paucis hodie notam. Theodosius enim firmissimis demonstrationibus confrimat omnia ea, quae de primo tradi possunt motu.[1030] Autolycus diligentissime singula de ortu et occasu stellarum persequitur.[1031] Barlaamus denique in sua testatur praefatione se ea demonstrasse, quae a nemine unquam fuerunt demonstrata.[1032]

Hinc ergo facile tibi erit iudicare, quis meus fuerit animus, dum haec in lucem edidi scripta, non ut magni quiddam praestarem, verum nostris ostenderem hominibus nos non esse eius eruditionis aut nostros libellos eius praecii, ut his praeferantur aut praeferri debeant

---

[1024] Dasypodius refers here to the *Arithmetica* of Diophantus of Alexandria, which he expected from Andreas Dudith, who had a Greek copy obtained most probably from Gian Vincenzo Pinelli. He sent the copy to Joachim Camerarius Sr., who refused to publish it. Sambucus might have recommended Dasypodius to Dudith as a possible editor, but Dudith did not apparently decide about the book and failed to ask Camerarius to have the manuscript sent over to Dasypodius. The latter included his letter to Dudith in the *Sphaericae doctrinae* (f. F2ʳ-F4ʳ.) This printed letter and the relevant correspondence with Camerarius is published in Dudithius, *Epistulae*, 2:124, 283 and 322-324. See letter 341 for Dudith's low opinion of Dasypodius.

[1025] Sambucus's manuscript of Euclid, which had once belonged to Bessarion, was given to Dasypodius before 1570. (See letter 154 to Johannes Crato.) See also Dasypodius's other letter to Sambucus of 1578 (letter 300) and letter 89, note 564.

[1026] Elements of arithmetic (a reference to Hero's work)

[1027] about the water-clocks

[1028] Dasypodius developed a special interest in Hero of Alexandria. See letter 300, note 1759.

[1029] See letter 173, note 1023.

[1030] Theodosius of Bithynia (c. 160–c. 100 BC) was a Greek mathematician and astronomer. See *RE* V.A (1934), 1930-1935. The "first motion" was commonly thought to be generated by the outermost sphere and the daily risings and settings of the Sun.

[1031] Autolycus of Pitane (c. 360–c. 290 BC) was another Greek astronomer and mathematician. See *RE* II (1896), 2602-2604.

[1032] Barlaam di Seminara (1290–1348) was a Calabrian philosopher and mathematician, who moved to Constantinople and became an abbot. See Martin Jugie, "Barlaam de Seminara," in *Dictionnaire d'histoire et de géographie ecclésiastiques*, eds. Alfred Baudrillart et al. (Paris: Letouzey and Ané, 1932), vol. 6, cols. 817-834.

authoribus. Ideoque idem faciendum esse in scholis nostris mathematicis, quod ii faciunt, qui dum in tenebris palpitant adminiculo candelae incensae et ardentis vias quaeritant. Sed postquam sol exortus est candelae opera nullo modo indigent, quae ipsamet claritate et splendore solis offunditur et iam qui ambulant, in luce clarissima versantur. Removeamus ergo nostra et quae barbara sunt, seponamus atque haec antiquorum Graecorum excellentissima scripta recipiamus nostrasque adornemus scholas mathematicas.[1033] De caeteris alias. Vale et D. doctorem Tannerum, amicum meum antiquum saluta. Postridie Calendas Decembris 1571. Argentinae.

174.
Sambucus to Theodor Zwinger
8 December 1571, [Vienna?]

The original is kept in Basel, Universitätsbibliothek, Handschriften, Fr.-Gr. I 12, no. 329. A copy is kept in ibid., Mscr G2 II 8, no. 161.

Sambucus wrote recently to Löwenklau and warned him of his promises. He believes that Löwenklau will eventually do something; Zwinger should urge him in Sambucus's name, especially to work on the edition of Manasses and the Sicilian. The situation has not changed regarding Dioscorides. The 130 images of the plants have been carefully designed; there will be no need for other images from elsewhere. They can be inserted in their place in the text or at the end of the book. His effort in purging the text of errors would surely be apparent to erudite experts. In the preface he would point out the many textual variants and corruptions and people will be able to make numerous emendations when relying on his observations. He saw a book printed in England; the authors appropriated Dioscorides as if his text were theirs. Sambucus is sending his greetings to Löwenklau; he appreciates him a lot and will try to recommend him to higher circles. He is sending his greetings to Claude Aubery and will publicly thank for his letter of dedication and send him soon something greater than that. He is very grateful for Zwinger's Theatrum humanae vitae, paid three florins for the carriage. Johannes Crato is in his fatherland.

Sambucus salutem.

Scripsi nuper ad Leonklavium, monui officii promissi. Credo tandem aliquod facturum, idque quo citius fiat, adde calcar meo nomine, praesertim Manassis, Siceliotae etc. editionem.[1034] Dioscoridis, quam antea significavi, eadem est ratio. Icones plantarum μονογραμμικῶς[1035] diligenter sunt simulatae, nec opus erit ex alio quopiam, praeter has 130 inserere suis locis, vel in extremo libro.[1036] Operam certe videor quibusdam eruditis iudicibus eo in purgando navasse. In praefatione aperiam quibus occasionibus tot sint opinionum varietates et lapsuum.

[1033] In fact, Dasypodius is arguing for a humanistic mathematical education in the place of a medieval syllabus, which would be based on the reading and interpretation of Greek mathematical authors.
[1034] Manasses, *Annales*; Glycas, *Annales*. Cf. letter 106, note 634.
[1035] in line-drawing
[1036] This letter suggests that Sambucus must have invested much money in this publication. On the failed project of a new edition of Dioscorides see letter 155, notes 920-921.

Multi multa poterunt istis meis obsservationibus emendare.[1037] Vidi nuper in Anglia excusum librum, sed Dioscoridem non iuvant, sua videntur tractare, tamquam propria. Et maledicendo consequuntur, male ut audiant.

Saluta Leonklavium a me, et promissorum mone, cuius ingenium magni facio, industria si constans fuerit, dabo operam, ut aliquando altiore loco conspiciatur, si voluerit. *Dialogos* Bonfinii pollicetur se proxime editurum. Aubero salutem, de cuius epistola ad me publica me gratum declarabo, si ubi sit rescivero, et alia maiora ad ipsum brevi mittam.[1038] Vale 8 Decembris 1571.

Pro *Theatro* tuo immortali studiosorum panoplia mille gratias.[1039] Solvi pro vectura 3 fl. Crato noster in patria sua amicis carissimis fruitur.[1040]

Address: Clarissimo viro domino doctori Theodoro Zvingero etc., amico suo optimo. Basell ad Hern Episcopio...

175.
Sambucus to Johannes Crato
10 December 1571, [Mannersdorf/Pressburg]

Published in Gerstinger, "Die Briefe," 127-128.

In the package sent to him by Plantin Sambucus found a letter by Lipsius addressed to Crato. Lipsius is seeking patronage from Crato. Sambucus does not know what he wants in his letter written to Crato but from the letter he received he guesses that Lipsius wants to be recommended for his literary studies to the emperor and receive some kind of imperial acknowledgment. Crato should not forget to do what he can for Lipsius without much hassle. He has heard that Crato wants to move to Pressburg in eight days, where he will happily meet him. He complains about someone's slow work on an unnamed book and wonders how long it will take, as the indices alone require two years, but he is ready to wait, as long as someone supports him materially.

Magnifice domine et amice, salutem.

Fasciculo Plantini has Iusti Lipsii inclusas reperi, qui tuam magnificentiam de patrocinio amat colitque ac beneficii summam aliquo testimonio redditurus est.[1041] Quid te velit, ignoro. Ex meis colligo vehementer ipsum cupere caesaris literis studia commendata esse inque sua

---

[1037] This also proves that Sambucus wanted only to offer the textual variants he found in his old codices, writing them in the margin, and did not intend to emendate the text or make conjectures. Cf. with his general philological method as explained in *Humanistes du bassin des Carpates II. Johannes Sambucus*, i-lxxii.

[1038] See Aubery's letter of dedication (letter 161).

[1039] Zwingerus, *Theatrum vitae humanae*. Cf. letter 149.

[1040] Crato's hometown was Wrocław.

[1041] Justus Lipsius (1547–1606) left Holland for Jena in late 1571 and arrived to Vienna in July 1572, where he was looking for an employment at the imperial court. See on this period of his life Jeanine De Landtsheer "Pius Lipsius or Lipsius Proteus?" in *Between Scylla and Charybdis*, 303-350. On his ambiguous relationship to Sambucus see Almási, *The Uses of Humanism*, 207 and *Humanistes du bassin des Carpates II. Johannes Sambucus*, 188.

familia eiusmodi testimonium clementiae ἀρχισύμβολον[1042] extare. Quod citra molestiam poteris atque commode, oro, eius ne obliviscare. Audio vos intra 8 dies Posonium cogitare, quod si est, istic vos desiderio convenimus. Vale, mi patrone. Si biennium indices postulant, quid τὰ ἔνδον ἢ ἐν μέσῳ κείμενα[1043] librorum exegerint?[1044] Sed bene est, tacebo, fruor, dum licet ac dum aliquis liberalitate in vetustatem me expugnet. X. Decembris 1571. Vestrae magnificentiae totus tuus etc. Sambucus.

Address: Magnifico et clarissimo viro domino doctori Cratoni ab Craffthaim, caesareae maiestatis consiliario et medico primo, domino et patrono singulari. Viennae.

176.
Antonius Verantius to Sambucus
13 December 1571, Trnava

A copy is kept in Eger, Főegyházmegyei Könyvtár, Y.V.17–27 (19th c.). Published in Verancsics, Összes munkái, 10:349-351. Partially quoted in Nicolaus Schmitth, *Episcopi Agrienses* (Tyrnaviae: Typis collegii academici Societatis Iesu), 3:68-69.

Verantius liked the monument Sambucus erected in verse and prose to the victory in the Gulf of Corinth. But how can Sambucus go so far to affirm that it is the end of the Ottoman Empire? Even when they initially arrived from Asia in foreign ships and did not know how to sail, they already ruled on two continents, and now they control more than twelve rich countries. Sambucus should reconsider how the Ottoman Empire could be overthrown by a single defeat. It is not that their defeat was not disastrous, but if Sambucus considers the naval and land forces that have remained for them (and which are their strength), how does he think they can collapse so fast? This is wishful thinking. But he does not want to be annoying; it was really a great victory, all the more so, as God put the Christian arms finally in concord, hence all the merit is His. It was a very fortunate battle, which has had hardly any parallel in history: a devastating victory in eight hours over a huge fleet, which was triumphant for so many years. They captured all the military leaders except for Occhiali and freed almost 12,000 Christian captives. It should be all the more clear that the victory was a message from God: Hungarians will not always be exposed to the Ottomans, who are God's punishment, sent in order to turn them towards God, obey his orders, be reconciled among one another and return to the Catholic faith and no longer follow false and sectarian churches. What regards the lodging (in Vienna), Verantius sent his client Galassus. Sambucus should show him the place, and Verantius will accept Galassus's decision. He would be content also with the lodging Sambucus primarily described, if it was pleasing and had the qualities he mentioned in his previous letter. As for his health, he is fine. He is taking care of the Church and the ordination of the priests. He would return to Pressburg after Christmas and wait there for the diet. On the second of the month in Nitra he received the pallium due to the archbishop. If in the meanwhile the Ottomans can be expelled from Esztergom, he will pray to God to carry on helping Christians in their fight.

[1042] main symbol
[1043] that which lies inside or in the middle
[1044] Sambucus refers here to a future publication that we could not define. See letter 158.

Ad Ioannem Sambucum.

Placuit nobis admodum sacrae nostrae classis tropheum, quod imperatoriae maiestati erexisti, pulcherrimo elogio tum prosaico, tum poetico, de profligata Turcica in sinu Corinthiaco.[1045] Sed heus tu! Quonam provectus es tam repente, ut ausus fueris ita hanc victoriam efferre, ut affirmes iam de Turcae actum esse imperio? Qui vel adhuc initio, quo ex Asia alienis navibus in Europam traiecerit, nec sciverit, quid sit carinis altum secare, utrique tum continenti potentissime imperabat. Nunc supra XII amplissimis et opulentissimis regnis auctus, scire ex te cupio, num una clade deiici, prosterni, atque extingui possit, consideres. Nec alioqui parum est, tota classe fuisse spoliatum exutumque et viris et instrumentis navalibus. Verum si cetera expendas diligentius, quae supersunt illi, quum ad vires maritimas reparandas, tum ad terrestres commovendas, quae ipsi semper fuere genuinae et propriae, putasne tam cito collapsurum, quam nos tam diuturno iugo eius pressi et optamus et ex desiderio, quo quietis ac securitatis tenemur, nobis pollicemur? Quod enim miseri volunt, hoc haud dubie facile credunt. Sed ne molestius de his disputem, haec sane ingens est victoria. Atque eo etiam amplior et augustior primum, quod Deus exercituum caelitus concordes nostros fecerit, qui iam diu concordiam ignoraverant, et deinde sic pro nobis pugnaverit, ut quicquid felicium eventuum hoc conflictu datum est nostrae classi, ut ei soli deferendum esse pronunciem. Neque scio, an unquam ille felicius dimicaverit, qui de se dixit: „Veni, vidi, vici." Rarum est enim et vix etiam in omnibus historiis inventu facile classem tam grandem et iam a tot annis triumphantem horis VIII debellatam et totam in potestatem fuisse redactam, ex summis eius ducibus nonnisi uno Occhali nuncupato[1046] et quatuor vel quinque triremibus fuga servatis,[1047] reliqua tota tum militum, tum classiariorum turba partim caesa et mari obruta, partim vero capta et XII ferme Christianorum millibus, qui in captivitatem agebantur, liberatis. Quo magis nobis iam enitendum est, ut hoc praesenti divinae maiestatis ac potentiae beneficio moniti meminerimus, non omnino nos in sempiternum Turcae esse traditos, sed ab eodem paterne castigari, ut ad eum convertamur, legem eius observemus, mandatis pareamus et diligamus mutuo demusque operam, ut eandem reconciliemus ad Catholicam fidem reversi et ecclesiis commentiis atque angularibus destitutis. Sic demum nos florebimus, et Iesus noster pugnabit pro nobis, quibus non certe reliquit gladium testamento, quod sibi Mahometes arrogavit, sed pacem et cum unitate charitatem. Nec de his plura modo.

Et ad novum hospitium quod attinet, misi istuc Galassum meum,[1048] cui domum ostendes, eique si placuerit, mihi non displicebit. Novit enim in hoc, quicquid animi habere soleam. Stabo itaque eius iudicio. Neque ea illius stipe gravabor, de qua scripsisti mihi, modo domus arrideat, neque in ea desiderentur, quae superioribus meis attigeram.[1049] De mea valetudine si quaeris, bene habeo. Curo res ecclesiae, clericorum ordinationes paro, festisque natalitiis absolutis Posonium redibo diemque ibidem comitiorum expectabo,[1050] iam tandem Nitriae

---

[1045] The Battle of Lepanto took place west of the Gulf of Corinth, in the Gulf of Lepanto, which is called Gulf of Patras today.

[1046] Occhiali or Uluj Ali (1519–1587), born in Calabria and taken as a captive at the age of 17, converted to Islam and gradually became one of the best corsair captains. His military prowess secured him ever higher offices; in the Battle of Lepanto he took part as Pasha of Algiers. The only success of the Ottoman fleet was his work, as he managed to flee with c. 40 vessels. Joining other survivors he arrived to Constantinople with 86 vessels. Salvatore Bono, *Corsari nel Mediterraneo* (Perugia: Oscar Storia Mondadori, 1993), passim.

[1047] In actual fact, many more managed to escape, see the preceding note.

[1048] On Vince Galassus see Verancsics, *Összes munkái*, 9:299.

[1049] See letter 167.

[1050] The diet of 1572 was called together for 6 January but was then postponed to 2 February, among other reasons

secunda huius sacro pallio insignitus donatusque archiepiscopali plenitudine. Si tamen interim et Strigonio potiemur et hostes hinc etiam summovebimus, quorum iam petulantiam ut terra quoque divina vis comprimere non gravetur, et oremus altissimum et laetemur moderate de tam donis gratuitis, ut maiora in nos conferat et quos hostes tam fortiter nostra causa coepit frangere, in finem usque conterat. Vale. Tyrnaviae XIII. Decembris 1571.

177.
Sambucus to Hugo Blotius (and Márton Berzeviczy)
21 December 1571, [Vienna]

The original is kept in Vienna, ÖNB, Cod. 9737^{z14-18}, I, f. 78^r. Published in Menčík, "A Páduában tanuló," 27; Gerstinger, "Die Briefe," 129-130.

Sambucus has received the package. Blotius seems to be bothered by two things: the frequent contact with some people and the insolence of his administrator. He can resolve the first issue through his own diligence, and as for the second one, Listhius will take care to see that the administrator stops urging Blotius so hard. As nothing concerning him was specified in Blotius's mandate, Sambucus would reject the administrator's account to the bishop. Listhius will send money by post as long as there is hope for safe exchange. Blotius should carry on and not let himself be hindered by anything; signs of gratitude will not be missing. An attached letter should be given immediately to Doctor Mantua (i.e. Marco Mantova Benavides), and his response sent to him. Sambucus produced some triumphal arches in the style of the ancients but he did not want to burden the messengers, who charge extraordinary rates. Sambucus attaches to his letter some notes regarding Márton Berzeviczy, whom he appreciates a great deal. If Berzeviczy continues the way he started, a great future will await him. Blotius should warn him not to forget his fatherland, where his zeal will bring its fruits. Sambucus had no doubts about Berzeviczy's friendly feelings toward him, which he shares. Finally, he asks Blotius not to send so great packages to his address. He should either send them to Listhius or divide them. Had he not referred to his courtly tax exemption, he would have needed to pay two thalers.

Sambucus salutem.

Fasciculus mihi redditus est. Duae sunt, quae tibi molestiam exhibere videntur: consuetudo nonnullorum frequentior et vicarii tui importunitas, quarum illi ipse tua diligentia mederi poteris, huic patronus, ne urgeat importune, providebit; cumque nihil praecipue de eo in mandatis receperis, ex praescripto eius rationem ad reverendissimum reicerem. Pecuniam mittit dominus per veredarium, dum colybi certi spes fiat. Tu vero caetera perge nec ullis impedimentis iniici moram progressibus patiere: feres gratiam non vulgarem. Hasce domino D. Mantuae nostro statim. Si quid responderit, mitte. Scripsi aliquot arcus triumphales more antiquo etc., sed cursoribus onere nollem esse iniquus, qui animam exigunt. Vale, festo Thomae 1571.

Bertzevitio.

---

because Emperor Maximilian wanted to find out if there was hope for a new anti-Ottoman league, of which there was much talk after the Battle of Lepanto. See *Magyar országgyűlési emlékek* 5, 279-312.

Domino Berzevitio Sambucus salutem. Cuius rationem scribendi et quos exprimendos putat, laudo, ut vero pergat, cohortare. Ita enim rem aggressus mihi videtur, ut, si eandem viam porro diligenter et vestigia persequi velit, facile aliquid egregium et quod miremur brevi assequatur. Tum ut patriae memor sit, moneas, in cuius segete et area studiorum fructus eluscescent uberiores, gloria cum omni reliquo tempore coniuncta erit, ὡς ἀνδρὸς ἐν ἀρχῇ.[1051] De mente illius et erga me mutua voluntate cum numquam dubitavi tum vero nunc eo nobis reddito prolixa quaeque mihi polliceor. Iterum vale. Ἔρρωσο.[1052]

A tantis fasciculis ad me deinceps abstineas. Reverendissimo inscribas vel partite mittas. 2 talleros volebat exigere, nisi libertatem aulae obduxissem.

Address: Al Molto Magnifico Signor Dottore Hugo Blotius gentilhuomo Fiammengo etc. come fratello. Padoa, appresso il Signor Dottore Mantua[1053] in Porzia[1054].

178.
Sambucus to Johannes Crato
[1571–1572], [Vienna?]

Published in Gerstinger, "Die Briefe," 128-129.

Sambucus cannot find the edition of the history of Paulus Aemilius by Johannes Thomas Freigius. He had it in his hands for a while and suspects that he has lent it to someone who unfairly did not return it. He does not know where Giovanni Michele Bruto, whom he appreciates highly, is staying. He is sending Bruto the (accompanying) manuscripts of Sallust, which are better than the previous two. He will do everything to dig out the history of Aemilius or find out who has borrowed it and taken it for so long. The book has been published by Thomas Guérin.

Clarissimo viro domino doctori Ioanni Cratoni, imperatorio medico ἄρχοντι[1055] Sambucus salutem.

P. Aemylii Freigianam editionem,[1056] quam aliquandiu ad manum habebam, non reperio. Si cui eam utendam commodavi, iniquum in restituendo se praebet idque suspicor. Brutus noster,[1057] quem ego libenter usurpo, non sine collaudationis sensu et honorifico

---

[1051] as of a man standing at the beginning
[1052] farewell
[1053] Marco Mantova Benavides.
[1054] Today it is called via Porciglia, next to the Chiesa degli Eremitani.
[1055] to the chief [imperial physician]
[1056] Paulus Aemilius Veronensis, *Historiae iam denuo emendatae [...] de rebus gestis Francorum...*, ed. Johann Thomas Freigius (Basileae: Sixtus Henricpetri, 1569). See Gulyás, *Sámboky János könyvtára*, 1683. Johann Thomas Freigius (1543–1583) taught Aristotelian philosophy in Freiburg und Altdorf. During his study years, which included a sojourn in Basel, he met among others Zwinger, Blotius and Petrus Ramus, and adopted Ramus's method. See Roderich von Stintzing, "Freigius, Johann Thomas," *ADB* 7 (1877), 341-343.
[1057] Giovanni Michele Bruto (1517–1592) was a Venetian humanist, author of a history of Florence and an unpublished history of contemporary Hungary. Originally a deacon of the *canonici regolari* he abandoned the convent and grew close to the Valdesians and the Italian Evangelicals. Bruto fled Venice several times due to religious persecution, the last

in amplum elegansque ingenium praeconio, ubi diverterit, ignoro. Velim hosce Sallustios acciperet duobus prioribus, nisi fallor, probiore manu et tempore.[1058] Perquiram omnes angulos, latebras Museoli nec cessabo, dum Aemylium aut eruam aut, ubi hospes tam diu se terendum heri et mancupii oblitus fruendumque invito me patiatur, intelligam, nec nisi tua caussa manumittam, sed sine pileo rasoque vertice. Vale et ignosce! Tuus Sambucus. Editio Basileensis est apud Thomam Guerinum in folii forma.[1059]

179.
Sambucus to Augerius Busbequius
[1572], [Vienna]

Dedication in [Pseudo-]Hesychius, Περὶ τῶν ἐν παιδείᾳ, 3-5. Published in *Humanistes du bassin des Carpates II. Johannes Sambucus*, 156-158.

180.
Justus Lipsius to Sambucus
1572, [Vienna]

Published in Justus Lipsius, *Epistolicarum quaestionum libri V. In quibus ad varios scriptores pleraeque ad T. Livium notae* (Antwerp, 1577), f. 131-132.[1060]

Both the emperor's gift and Sambucus's ring with the image of Augustus have been well looked after. He is grateful for both; the ring struck him as a surprise. He might have been waiting for some imperial benefice, but was satisfied with Sambucus's good opinion of him. In the remaining part, the letter offers various readings of classical authors.

---

time in 1565. From 1552 he was frequently on the move around Europe, tutoring students and publishing on different subjects. In 1572 he was in Basel, where he finally accepted the invitation of Ferenc Forgách to come to Transylvania. When he arrived to Vienna, Maximilian II wanted to entrust him the writing of the history of his father Ferdinand I. Bruto, however, returned to Lyon and settled in Transylvania only at the beginning of 1574 as the historian of Prince of Transylvania Stephen Báthory (1571–1586), whom he also followed to Krakow. In 1585 Bruto abjured the protestant faith and in 1589 joined Emperor Rudolf II as a historian. Sambucus knew Bruto already from Venice (he dedicated to him an emblem: *Emblemata*, 1564, 230). Having joined Báthory, Bruto apparently started looking at Sambucus from the perspective of the Transylvanian court as a Habsburg client disloyal to the Hungarian cause. An alleged goal of his history of Hungary was to counter the "lies" of Sambucus and demonstrate that John Sigismund Szapolyai (Zapolya) was a king. On their later relation, see letter 323. See Endre Veress, "Il veneziano Giovanni Michele Bruto e la sua storia d'Ungheria," *Archivio Veneto* 6 (1929), 148-178; Mario Battistini, "Jean Michel Bruto, humaniste, historiographe, pédagogue au XVIème siècle," *De Gulden Passer* 32 (1954), 29-156; Domenico Caccamo, *Eretici italiani in Moravia, Polonia, Transilvania (1558-1611). Studi e documenti* (Florence: Sansoni; Chicago: Newberry Libr., 1970), 145-151; Gábor Petneházi, "How to write History? The *Rerum Ungaricarum libri* and Neo-Latin historiography in Hungary in the 16th century," *Humanistica Lovaniensia* [forthcoming].

[1058] Sambucus had several Sallust-manuscripts, see Gerstinger, "Johannes Sambucus als Handschriftensammler," 389.
[1059] The publisher was not Thomas Guérin, but Sixtus Henricpetri, as in letter 178, note 1056.
[1060] Although it is most probably a fictive letter, it contains some specific information as well. The *Epistolicae Quaestiones* was a series of fictive letters, through which Lipsius published his collections of emendations and variant readings for classical authors, addressed often to influential friends and patrons.

Iustus Lipsius Ioanni Sambuco, viro clarissimo.

Et munus caesaris recte curatum est et anulus tuus cum effigie Augusti.[1061] Utrumque gratum, alterum etiam inexpectatum. Nam, ut olim non inscite Passienus,[1062] a caesare beneficium fortasse exspectabam, a te satis erat iudicium. Quod idem in his Agellii[1063] locis adhibere te volo.

Lib. IX, cap. XIII. De pugna Manlii Torquati.

I. [1064] *Sed quis hostis, et quod genus, et quam formidandae vastitatis, et quantum insolens provocator, et cuiusmodi fuerit pugna decertatum.*[1065]

Membranae Victoris Giselini *et cuiusmodi pugna*, et ante *sed quid hostis*. Verissime.[1066]

II. Is maxime proelio commoto atque utrisque summo studio pugnantibus, manu significare coepit utrique ut quiescerent pugnare. Pugnae facta pausa est.[1067]

Ibi scribitur *atque utris summo*. Dium fidium appello eam germanam *Quadrigarii* scripturam esse. Antiqui enim *Plerus, plera, plerum; Uter, utrim; Alterutrim*, haec talia sine copula efferebant. Pacuvius *Plera pars pessundatur.*[1068] Et notant Grammatici veteres. Suetonii etiam illud in optimo codice ita scriptum, Tiberii capite paenultimo *Conclamantibus pleris Atellam potius deferendum*, non ut obtinuit, *plerisque.*[1069]

Apud Livium, Lib. XXVI.[1070]

Ita aequatae res ad Tarentum. Romanis victoribus terra, Tarentinis mari. Frumenti spes quae in oculis fuerat, utrosque pariter frustrata est.[1071]

In veteri codice reperio *utros pariter*. Et melius de Livio sentio quam ut id mutem. Sed ad Quadrigarium:

III. Extemplo silentio facto cum voce magna inclamat.[1072]

Scidae *cum voce maxima conclamat*.

Deinde Gallus irridere coepit atque linguam exertare.[1073]

Nae audax nebulo, qui priscam lectionem immutavit. Ea est *atque lingua exerrare*. Et sic etiam Buslidianus codex.[1074] *Exerrare lingua*, nimium apte et signate, linguam extra os proiectam per irrisum reciprocare. Verbum id Statius quoque usus VI. Thebaidos:

[1061] Lipsius received an honorarium of 30 florins on the intervention of Crato and Sambucus, which could hardly compensate for his hopes for a position or stipend at the imperial court. See Almási, *The Uses of Humanism*, 128-129.

[1062] Gaius Sallustius Passienus Crispus was twice consul and stepfather to the future emperor Nero. For Lipsius's reference, see Suetonius, *Vita Passieni Crispi* (part of *De oratoribus* in *De viris illustribus*).

[1063] Aulus Gellius was sometimes erroneously referred to as Agellius.

[1064] marginal note: "Quadrigarius apud Agellium emend."

[1065] Gellius. 9.13.4.

[1066] Victor Giselinus of Ghyselinck (1543–1591), a humanist and corrector for Plantin, was a very close friend of Lipsius. See Christiaan L. Heesakkers, "Janus Dousa and Victor Giselinus: a correspondence around the literary debut of Janus Dousa," *Lias* 2 (1975), 5-54, 191-248; Lipsius, *Epistolae*, passim.

[1067] Gellius 9.13.8-9.

[1068] The same is quoted by Adrien Turnèbe in his commentary to Cicero (*M. Tullii Ciceronis de legibus libri tres, cum A. Turnebi commentario*, Parisiis: ex officina Turnebi, 1552), 140.

[1069] Suettonius, *Tiberius* 75.

[1070] marginal note: "Livius item. "

[1071] Livius 25.39.

[1072] Gellius 9.13.10.

[1073] Gellius 9.13.12.

[1074] Hieronymus van Busleyden (1470–1517) was a humanist from the Low Countries. See Henry de Vocht, *Jerome De Busleyden Founder of the Louvain Collegium Trilingue: His Life and Writings* (Turnhout: Brepol, 1950) (*Humanistica Lovaniensia* 9). Unfortunately, this very precious manuscript of Busleyden was lost after the sixteenth century.

Plectiur in gyros dexterque exerrat Arion.[1075]
A Giselini membranis abest etiam τὸ *coepit*. Recte.
IV. Manlius iterum scuto scutum percutit atque de loco certo hominem iterum deiicit.[1076]
Vetus *iterum proiecit*. Et omittit vocem *certo*, quae certa inserta est.
V. Eo pacto ei sub Gallicum gladium successit atque Hispanico pectus hausit. Dein continuo humerum dextrum eodem concussu incidit neque recessit usquam donec subvertit, ne Gallus impetum icti haberet.[1077]
Illic est *eodem concessu* et probant sequentia. Id valet, eodem impetu, eadem aggressione. Quod autem in Buslidiano est *impetum istius haberet* male est. Nisi forte Quadrigarius scripsit *impetum ictuis*, antique, ut *senatuis, anuis*. Stant tamen a vulgata optimae scidae.
VI. Ubi eum evertit, caput praecidit.[1078]
Membrana *caput praecedit*. Et scio veteres ita scripsisse, unde et *concaedes silvae*.

181.

Sambucus to Antonius Verantius
5 February 1572, Vienna

Dedication in certain copies of Bonfini, *Symposion Trimeron, sive de pudicitia coniugali et virginitate dialogi III*, f. 2ʳ-3ᵛ. Published in *Humanistes du bassin des Carpates II. Johannes Sambucus*, 161-162.

182.

Johannes Löwenklau to Sambucus
8 March 1572, [Basel?]

Dedication in certain copies of Bonfini, *Symposion Trimeron, sive de pudicitia coniugali et virginitate dialogi III*, f. 2ʳ-3ᵛ. Published in *Humanistes du bassin des Carpates II. Johannes Sambucus*, 162-165.

183.

Sambucus to Hugo Blotius
16 April 1572, [Vienna?]

The original is kept in ÖNB, Cod. 9737^{z14-18}, I, f. 117ᵛ. Published in Menčík, "A Páduában tanuló," 34; Gerstinger, "Die Briefe," 130-132.

A year ago, Sambucus bought from the bookseller Simone Galignani seven marble busts. He is now sending their price and asking Blotius to help Galignani and place the busts in boxes, one

---

[1075] Statius, *Thebais* 6.444.
[1076] Gellius 9.13.17.
[1077] Gellius 9.13.17.
[1078] Gellius 9.13.18.

or two of them in each so that the ears and noses will not be damaged. The expenses, including the delivery to Venice, should be covered by Galignani or Blotius. Blotius should get a certificate from the prefect of Padua or from the customs officers that the marbles are for the imperial court so that the boxes will not be opened in the Fondaco dei Tedeschi, creating further expenses. He would do Sambucus a great favour if he got one of his men to go to Venice in order to make sure that the marbles are given over in the Fondaco to an agent of Andreas and Sebastian Eiseler, who are well-known Viennese merchants, who are related to Sambucus, and have imperial exemption from customs duty. If Blotius needs, he should contact Hoffmann and others. The expenses will be paid back. Listhius will be in Pressburg the day after, where Rudolf was elected king of Hungary.

Sambucus salutem.

Emi 7 marmora ante annum a doctore Cavino Patavino,[1079] negociator est Maesser Simon librarius.[1080] Mitto nunc pretium. Oro, mi Bloti, omnibus rebus ei adsis, curetis capsulas vel binis capitibus singulas vel singulas singulis, quo sine offensa narium vel auricularium huc pervehantur. Impensas curabit et vecturam Venetias ipse Simon vel vos interea. A magnifico praefecto Patavino vel daziariis testimonium Venetias impetrabitis esse tantum marmora pro curia caesareae maiestatis, ne Venetiis in Fontigo[1081] capsulae solvantur et molestis iterum impensis componi cogantur. Facies mihi rem gratissimam, si vestrum hominem una Venetias conductorem in tutum mandaris, ut in Fontigo tradantur negociatori et factori Eyslerorum, qui in Fontigo cameram suam habent. Sunt celebres mercatores Viennenses, Andreas et Sebastianus Eysleri,[1082] affines mei. Ii caetera curabunt. Habent iidem literas a sua maiestate pro libera ab oneribus viarum vectura. Vale et hoc officio me nostramque necessitudinem cumulabis. Si opus est, accerse quoque Hoffmannum et alios.[1083] Quodque impensum erit, restituetur. Vale. 16 Aprilis 1572. Reverendissimus noster cras Posonio aderit. Electus est Rodolphus in regem Ungariae.[1084]

Address: Al Molto Magnifico Signor il Doctor fingo Blotius Precettor de Signor Giovanni Listhio etc. Amico observando. Padoa appresso il Signor Dottor Mantua.

[1079] Giovanni da Cavino (1500–1570) is mostly known as a medallist and sculptor of Padua. He reproduced the portraits of many contemporaries and was also famous for his very credible imitation of antique coins and medals. See Andreas S. Norris, "Giovanni da Cavino," *DBI* 23 (1979), 109-112.

[1080] Simone Galignani.

[1081] On this German commercial centre at the Rialto see Carolin Wirtz "'Mercator in fontico nostro' mercanti tedeschi fra la Germania e il fondaco dei Tedeschi a Venezia," in *Presenze tedesche a Venezia*, ed. Susanne Winter (Roma: Edizioni di Storia e letteratura, 2005), 1-48.

[1082] The Eiselers (Eyseler) were an important merchant family in Vienna who came from Buda in c. 1512. Several of their members were part of the City Council, including Sebastian Jr., while Sebastian Eiseler Sr. was also mayor. Sambucus may have been related to them through the family of his wife. Source https://www.geschichtewiki.wien.gv.at/Sebastian_Eysler (accessed on 3 May 2023).

[1083] Sambucus might be referring to one of the members of the Hoffmann zum Günbühel family. For his relation to them see letter 15.

[1084] Rudolf's election was discussed and accepted by the Diet of Pressburg on 1 April and announced to Rudolf on 2 April. *Magyar országgyűlési emlékek* 5, 307-308.

184.
Sambucus to Hugo Blotius
25 June 1572, [Vienna]

The original is kept in Vienna, ÖNB, Cod. 9737^{z14-18}, I, f. 136^r. Published in Menčík, "A Páduában tanuló," 39; Gerstinger, "Die Briefe," 132-133.

Sambucus is responding late as he was away. Meanwhile, Blotius must have received the money. He keeps on lobbying for Blotius's salary and in support of his case, and hopefully not without results. Listhius is seriously sick, he himself was already worried for his life the day before, but today he has gathered some strength and puts his hope in a better physician to keep death away. Sambucus has replied to Simone Galignani, sent 123 ducats and 3 Portuguese reals, which make 127 ducats, which is worth 6 lire, there remain 33 ducats to be paid. If Simone objects, Blotius should vouch for the rest and he will not incur damages. There is a reason why he wants it this way (i.e. keeping some money back) as long as the busts do not arrive in Vienna. Blotius should make sure to pack the busts without the fitting torsos so that the Eiseler could easily send them from the Fondaco dei Tedeschi to Vienna in two horse loads. Sambucus would compensate Blotius for this favour. He wrote the letter hurriedly, and is now off to see Listhius. Simone writes (to have received) 100 ducats, whereas he entrusted 123 to the Polish postmaster and had previously sent 3 reals as a deposit.

Sambucus salutem.

Serius rescribo, quod absens fuerim, interea vos pecuniam accepistis. Ego solicitare omnibus modis sumptus et causam tuam soleo. Credo me aliquid profecturum. Reverendissimus dominus, quod tibi scribo, lethaliter laborat, ut heri de vita fuerit eius desperatum, sed hodie nonnihil se colligit. Ostendit spem medicis meliorem. Absit Θ [mors]. Simoni rescripsi,[1085] misi hactenus 123 ducatos et tres portugalenses, facit ad 127 ducatos per 6 libras; reliqui sunt 33.[1086] Pro iis, si Simon recusarit, spondeas, sine damno tuo facies. Caussa est, cur id velim, dum marmora huc pertineant. Efficite oro in eis includendis sine illis adhibitis pectoribus, ut duobus somis[1087] commode Eysleri[1088] in fontigo huc queant mittere; beabis me, beneficium non levidense gratia emetiar. Vale, raptim, dum eo ad visendum reverendissimum. 25 Iunii 1572. Simon scribit de 100 ducatis, cum ego postae Polonico[1089] 123 dederim et antea miserim arram 3 portugalenses.

Address: Al Excellentissimo e Magnifico Signor Dottor Hugo Blotius etc. amico suo honorando. Padoa appresso il S. Dottor Mantua, con Signor Ongaro Giovan Listhio. Cito. Cito.

[1085] On the purchase of marble busts from the bookseller Simone Galignani see the preceding letter, and cf. the Index.

[1086] On Venetian money see Frederic C. Lane, Reinhold C. Mueller, *Money and Banking in Medieval and Renaissance Venice*, 2 vols. (Baltimore: The Johns Hopkins University Press, 1985, 1997).

[1087] Soma was a measurement for volume, ca. 150 liter. The word is derived from *sauma*, vulgar Latin for "packsaddle," denoting approximately a package a horse can carry.

[1088] On the Eiseler see the preceding letter.

[1089] Sambucus used the services of the regular Polish post between Krakow and Venice via Vienna. See note 1010 to letter 171.

185.
Sambucus to Marcus Antonius Muretus
15 July 1572, Vienna

The original is kept in Rome, BAV, Vat. Lat. 11590, f. 112ʳ.

This is a letter of recommendation for Giovanni Battista Fonteo, in which Sambucus refers to his old acquaintance with Marcus Antonius Muretus, who should know that Sambucus has praised highly his "museum" in front of many people. He is waiting for some news as usual.

Sambucus Mureto.

Fonteio[1090] non tam mea caussa, volo, quantum ubi sese tibi aperuerit ac de consuetudine cognoris, tribuas. Nos eius discessu maeremus, vos uti eo fruamini, non invidemus, ipsius praesertim commodo. Te pro veteri nostra necessitudine eodemque in literas sensu oro, eruditum iuvenem uti ad amicitiam admittas et familiariter eo utere. Ita fiet, ut me idoneum tuo museo coram multis ornasse hisce litteris tibique et per te omnibus literatis commendasse sentias. Vale et aliquid novi, quod soles,[1091] ad nos e tuo penu mitte. Idibus Quinctilibus 1572, raptim. Vienna.

186.
Sambucus to Piero Vettori
15 July 1572, Vienna

The original is kept in Munich, BSB, Clm 735, Nr. 60. Published in *Clarorum Italorum et Germanorum epistolae*, 2:60-61; Gerstinger, "Die Briefe," 133-134.

Sambucus is warmly congratulating Vettori on his new book and his continuous productivity in his old age. He saw the book in Crato's place but could not go through it. He has not yet published Dioscorides but there is no hurry. Meanwhile, he hopes that it will be emended and enlarged. Twenty triumphal arches and figures of the naval victory at Epirus together with [Pseudo-] Hesychius's antique poets are now printed in Antwerp. As soon as he gets them, he will send copies. One might want to wrap fish in them.

[1090] Giovanni Battista Fonteo († 1579/1580) was a young humanist of Milan, who had been educated by his uncle Primo Conti (that is why his chosen name, Fontana de' Conti). From 1568 we find him in Vienna where he collaborated with Giuseppe Arcimboldo, explaining in a poem the allegorical meaning of his famous pictures. In 1570 he dedicated a manuscript treatise on laughter (*De risu*) to Michele Frangipani, Venetian ambassador to the emperor (today held in ÖNB). In 1571 he wrote a 90-page manuscript funeral oration on the death of Melchior Biglia, apostolic nuncio to the imperial court (1565–1571). Sambucus's recommendation may have helped him find employment in Rome, probably with the Cesi family, writing their genealogy, in which he also refers to Muretus (*De prisca Caesiorum gente Ioannis Baptistae Fonteii primionis commentariorum libri duo*, Bononiae: Rossius, 1582.) See Thomas DaCosta Kaufmann, *Arcimboldo: Visual Jokes, Natural History, and Still-Life Painting* (Chicago: University of Chicago Press, 2009), 81-83, 106, 112; Robert Lindell, "The wedding of Archduke Charles and Maria of Bavaria in 1571," *Early Music* 18 (1990), 253-270.

[1091] The very direct and familiar tone of the letter also suggests that there was, in fact, some kind of regular correspondence between Muretus and Sambucus.

Domino Petro Victorio Sambucus salutem.

O te beatum senem, felices nos, qui tot ingenii tui monumentis fruimur, tu vero, qui numquam cessas egregii aliquid prodere. Quid ad beatas sedes et immortalitatem tibi restat? Ecquis est omnium vel a veterum memoria, cuius industria tot praeclara pectora vatum et aliorum spiritus e tenebris et tumulis extiterint vitamque et lucem sint adepti? Nunc Atticanis tuis οὐ μόνον εὐδαιμονίαν[1092] sed ipsum τὸ γάλα τῶν ὀρνίθων,[1093] ut est apud comicum, dedisti θαλείαν,[1094] χοροὺς[1095] etc. Percurrere tam insigne opus nondum licuit, tantum apud Cratonem inspexi.[1096] Ego Dioscoridem nondum edidi, mora nil nocebit, spero dum emendatus et auctus conspiciatur.[1097] Museum Sambuci itemque triumphi 20 Epirotici de navali victoria figuris et arcubus varii, antiquis etiam inscriptionibus non vulgares Antverpiae imprimuntur cum Illustrii poetis antiquis.[1098] Quae ubi accepero, non omittam, quin ilico nugas nostras habeas, quae fortasse laxas scombris dabunt tunicas.[1099] Vale, τρισμακάριστε γέρον,[1100] et Sambuco aliquando responde. Idibus Quinctilibus 1572. Vienna.

Address: Clarissimo viro Petro Victorio etc., amico et praeceptori. Florentiam.

187.
Sambucus to King Rudolf
1 October 1572, Vienna

Published in Werbewcz [Werbőczy], *Tripartitum opus iuris consuetudinarii*, f. aii[r-v].

If some people reprehend him for having allowed this work to take his time from more serious studies or for having pillaged the professional field of others, they have three reasons to do so. First, because he is not an expert on civil law; second, because it seems to be far removed from the interests of a philosopher and doctor; and third, because he has neither clients nor patrons at the Hungarian law courts. He responds to them that everyone measures himself according to his own conscience. He once spent four years studying civil law intensely and with profit. And it is an error to think that law has no relation to philosophy. Finally, he also gathered personal experience in legal matters unintentionally. If it was needed, he could aptly respond during a legal case, satisfying anyone. If they still object, he would add, that he understands laws, sees their sources, can gather similar opinions and the decisions recognized in those statutes. But this would be annoying for his people and their lords, who do not want to change or reject anything of the law and esteem

---

[1092] not only happiness
[1093] literally: the birds' milk; proverbially: perfect happiness. Aristophanes, *Aves* 733. For classical parallels see Gerstinger, "Die Briefe," 134.
[1094] in abundance
[1095] dances
[1096] M. Tullius Cicero, *Epistolae ad Atticum, ad M. Brutum, ad Q. fratrem. E bibliotheca Petri Victorii* (Florentiae: apud Iuntas, 1571).
[1097] Sambucus may already have realised that for a new edition he needed a good philologist to go through the entire text again. Cf. "Dioscorides-edition (planned)" under "Sambucus" in the Index.
[1098] Sambucus, *Arcus aliquot triumphales*; [Pseudo-]Hesychius, Περὶ τῶν ἐν παιδείᾳ.
[1099] Cf. Catullus 95.8.: "et laxas scombris saepe dabunt tunicas".
[1100] thrice happiest old man

even the jurisprudence of Sulpicius as not severe enough. He will not argue against their customs, which derive from the similarity of feelings and goals; but in agreement with Justinian's Novels he adds that badly introduced laws should not be tolerated. There are many good and appropriate, regularly used legal rules which have not been written down. Together with the summary of legal provisions he is now editing these customary laws at the demand of many and with the special approval of Rudolf. He highly appreciates the endeavour of István Werbőczy, who diligently collected the customary law of Hungary, neglected for 360 years, and approved by the father of Rudolf's grandmother, King Ladislaus. Werbőczy published it in Latin, in accordance with the terminology of the church archives and French customary law, from which the Hungarian seems to be borrowed. While he was searching for an experienced printer he prepared an index and described the contents, in order to make it easily searchable. He is dedicating these short hours (of work) to Rudolf and the nobility of his crown, as the kings are the embodiment of the living law. Sambucus will write about Rudolf's virtues on a later occasion. He is only begging him now to take notice of this mark of loyalty and to respect some (both divine and human) rules, taken indeed from the Twelve Tables and leading to peace and immortality. (Seven motto-like maxims follow: respect God, show piety, exercise just power etc.)

Serenissimo principi Rhodolpho,[1101] regi Ungariae etc., archiduci Austriae, duci Burgundiae, comiti Tyrolis etc., comino suo clementissimo, salutem.

Si qui forte hanc opellam, Serenissime Rex, a gravioribus impetratam studiis reprehendent meque in alienam raptum messem querantur, tribus, credo, potissimum rationibus ad tantam scilicet rem illi nitentur. Quod iuris civilis scientiam non sim professus, quod a philosopho et medico remota haec videantur, tum, in iudiciis foroque Pannonico duntaxat neque clientela, neque patrocinio esse me cognitum. Quibus ego brevissime: scitum esse, sua quemque metiri conscientia et veritate, non modo vulgata opinione. Falli tamen eos, aut nescire dicam, si negarint, olim publice me quadriennium in civilis prudentiae, canonumque auscultatione utiliter posuisse. Labi et errare, si legum et consuetudinum rationem ex philosophia profectam ignorent, si etiam τὸ ἐν πλάτει καὶ τὴν ἐπιείκειαν[1102] aliunde, quam ex illius subselliis, acciundam formandamque arbitrentur, prorsus insanire. Nam qui affectae parti salutariter, nisi universo rite constituto, medeare? Ad tertium: me aliis palam nec tuendis, nec communicando patrocinio quidem inserviisse, aliquot armorum tamen molestiis, litium quoque privatarum necessitate, contra voluntatem et naturam, invito genio ac renitente assecutum, ut, si opus sit, et cognoscere multas controversias, et respondere in medium haud fortassis inepte, quibusdam etiam satisfacere possim. Addam, si stomachum fecerint, intelligentiam me hac tenus legum habere, videre fontes, accumulare posse similes sententias, hisque statutis cognata praeiudicia. Sed scio, quam id nostris hominibus, et magnis illis patronis futurum esset molestum: qui nec immutandum, nec demendum quicquam a praescriptis vel antiquandum, ut nomophylaces[1103] illi Athenienses candidi, censent lenioremque non nihil Sulpitii apud

---

[1101] Rudolf (1552–1612) was crowned king of Hungary on 26 September (four years before Maximilian II's death). This publication, dedicated to Rudolf, was Sambucus's tribute to the young Hungarian king. After the dedication, Sambucus addresses the Hungarian estates with a short essay "on Rudolf's crown" (ibid. aiii[r-v]), which also appeared as a separate broadsheet: *De corona serenissimi Rudolphi regis Ungariae etc., archiducis Austriae etc. 25. September 1572 ad status Regni et alios Ioannis Sambuci oratiuncula* (Viennae: Blasius Eberus, 1572).

[1102] that which is taken in a broad sense and the fairness

[1103] The duty of the *nomophylaces* (νομοφύλακες) in ancient Greece was to see that nothing unconstitutional was proposed, and to punish those who acted unconstitutionally. In Athens this was originally the job of the

Ciceronem iureconsulti disciplinam existimant.[1104] Quorum usibus et consuetudini, quod ex similitudine affectuum ac studiorum manare secundum Demosthenem soleant, libenter concedam, minus pugnabo, dum illud ex *Novellis* Iustiniani addam: male introducta nullo tempore posse praescribi nec esse ferenda. Multae sunt, Inclyte Rodolphe, constitutiones aliae item probae ac idoneae, ut testamentariae, exceptionum, cautelarum typorum formis nondum proditae, quarum usus in foro alioqui passim communique temperatione causarum adhibetur. Quas brevi, multorum precibus, te separatim annuente, sum editurus eque capsulis cautorum advocatorum cornicum oculos confixurus. Quod vel nunc fecissem, nisi boni et industrii typographi conditio, tenuitasque modo emergens seseque luci committens tuaeque Serenitatis in corona recipienda celebritas consilium moramque exclusissent omnem.[1105]

Vehementer probo voluntatem Stephani Werbewczii, amo praeclaros conatus, qui, non secus atque Iustinianus ius Romanum per mille et quadringentos confusum annos, et inculcatum, ita consuetudines ille et articulos, ut vocant, Pannonicos per 360 annos neglectos sedulo collegit redactosque in ordinem et ab aviae tuae parente, Rege Ladislao, comprobatos, vulgo legendos, tractandosque dedit, et quidem Latine, ob archivorum sacrorum litiumque vetustarum authoritatem atque Gallicorum, unde nostra deportata et mutua videntur, terminorum receptam haerentemque in animis et subactam prorsus opinionem, qua de re alibi. Interea, ut rudioribus peritoque ac solerti typographo studerem, verba et res praecipuas serie literarum ad inveniendum apta coegi; non pauca illustravi, ne ob quidvis toties omnes tituli pervolutandi, in primis exteris percurrendi forent. Tibi autem, clementissime Princeps, hasce horulas (quoniam exemplaria excusa valde desiderabantur) tuaeque amplissimae coronae nobilitati offero tanquam tutelari numina. Cuius est talia et maiora condere, nec dubito haec ipsa, quibus adhuc, secundum reges, hoc est, leges animatas in terris, salutem referimus libertatemque reliquam, firmissima semper et expedita cuique fore. Ἰσχυρὸν γαρ ὁ νομὸς, ἤν ἄρχοντα ἔχει.[1106]

De tuis vero propriis clarisque virtutibus, quarum expectationem longe animi magnitudine et constantia vicisti, ut omnes te ament suscipiendumque et exoptandum vulgo ducant, de dignitatum hoc applausu omnium in spectaculo diadematis laetitia effusa, inaudito apparatu, inviso concursu, ipsa coeli benigna in tuis progressibus facie omnique omnino preconio alias et suo loco plenius verba faciam, quippe qui brevi divinitus aliorum quoque regnorum imperia et maiestatem capesses. Et quidem merito, quod, qui archidux archiregnum, sic olim appellatum, facile nunc sis adeptus, reliqua pateant, tuamque opem et moderationem nacta, suaviter sint quietura.

Areiopagus, and when it was deprived of its power they established a board of seven nomophylaces, chosen annually by lot.

[1104] Cicero very highly esteemed his colleague and friend Servius Sulpicius Rufus, orator and legal expert. See Cicero, *Ad Brutum* 41.152.

[1105] The *Tripartitum*, in which Werbőczy collected and organised Hungary's customary law, was one of the most important books in early modern Hungary, often nicknamed as the bible of the nobility. Most importantly, it fixed the nobility's cardinal privilges for the coming centuries and was regarded (although it was never sanctioned) as their definitive law shortly after it was presented to the diet in 1514. See *The Customary Law of the Renowned Kingdom of Hungary: A Work in Three Parts Rendered by Stephen Werbőczy (The "Tripartitum"). The Laws of the Medieval Kingdom of Hungary*, ed. and trans, János M. Bak and Martyn Rady (Idyllwild, CA: Schlacks, 2005); Martyn Rady, *Customary Law in Hungary: Courts, Texts, and the Tripartitum* (Oxford: OUP, 2015). On the first editions see István Csekey, "A Tripartitum bibliográfiája" [The bibliography of the Opus tripartitum], *Acta Iuridico-Politica* 2 (Kolozsvár/Cluj 1942), 141-194.

[1106] a strong thing is the law, if it has a ruler

Nunc, potentissime Rhodophe, tantum supplex oro, clientuli hoc obedientiae testimonium uti clementer habeas et foveas, adeoque legum, tam divini, quam humani, summam vel ex *XII tabulis* hanc esse ad pacem et immortalitatem, quod facis, attente memineris:

Ad divos iuste adeunto. ET Iusta Imperia sunto.
Pietatem adhibento.   Iisque cives modeste ac
Opes amovento.   sine recusatione parento.[1107]
Qui secus faxit, Deus vindex erit.[1108]

Vale, decus Austrium, tuique sceptri initia et processus Deus optimus maximus, quo sine nihil constans et laudabile, nihil ad aeternitatem paratur, indies omnibus commodis augeat, memoria posterorum ornet, totamque hanc gentem, singulare non Ungariae solum praesidium, sed universi nominis Christiani asylum, perpetuo feliciterque communiat. Kalendis Octobris M D LXXII. Viennae ex Museolo. Vestrae serenitatis et clementissimae infimus clientulus, D. Ioannes Sambucus, caesareae maiestatis consiliarius et historicus.

188.
Sambucus to Hugo Blotius
8 October 1572, Vienna

The original is kept in ÖNB, Cod. 9737[z14-18], I, f. 167[r]. Published in Menčík, "A Páduában tanuló," 45; Gerstinger, "Die Briefe," 134-135.

Their common patron (Listhius) is regaining health thanks mainly to Sambucus's advice. He was in bad shape for a long time, his nerves and spirit were worn out, now he only needs careful recovery. The feast of Rudolf's coronation was rich and remarkable, Blotius will get Sambucus's narration of it. He is sending 9 ducats, each of 6 liras, which remain from the total of 180 ducats. He asks Blotius to urge Simone Galignani and place two or three busts in a box, as it suits the carriers and the horses. They will be carried tax-free as the Eiselers already have the imperial permission from him. If Blotius needed any help in the future, he should turn to Sambucus. He is sending his greetings to Listhius Jr. and the others. The apostolic nuncio (Zaccaria Delfino) could not say much about a second naval battle (if only it were the last). Sambucus's 16 triumphal arches for the first victory are in print in Antwerp. After the crime in France (i.e. Saint Bartholomew's Day massacre) there is great anxiety in the Low Countries, calling for divine vengeance.

Sambucus salutem.

Patronus communis meo imprimis consilio convalescit, satis malum fuit diuturnum, nervos et spiritus absumpserat, nunc modo ἀναλήψει[1109] accurata opus habet. Celebritas coronae

---

[1107] Cicero, *De legibus* 3.6.
[1108] Cicero, *De legibus* 19.2. "Ad divos adeunto caste [!], pietatem adhibento, opes amovento. Qui secus faxit, Deus ipse vindex erit." The last part of this archaic legal idiom means "Improper treatment of the gods is punished by the gods themselves." See Andrew Roy Dyck, *A Commentary on Cicero, De Legibus* (Ann Arbor: The University of Michigan Press, 2004), 292.
[1109] recovery

Rhodolphi copiosa fuit et omnibus partibus admirabilis, cuius historiam accipies aliquando.[1110] Mitto novem ducatos senarum librarum, reliquos ad summam 180 ducatorum.[1111] Praeter alia etc. Te pro necessitudine valde oro, Simonem cohortare tua opera marmora apte capsulis bina vel terna, pro ut commodo gerulorum equorum videbitur, componatis. Libere absque impedimento teloniorum autoritate diplomatis caesarei, quod Eysleri in fontigo iam a me habent, conduci poterunt. Quacunque in parte tuo subsidio fuerit opus, Sambuci praesto adsis, beneficium non peribit. Saluta Listhium a me et alios. Ioinus ille vester nunc est ad cancellariae opus redactus estque apud reverendissimum nostrum Listhium.[1112] Vale. 8. Octobris 1572.

Nuntius cladis secundae, utinam ultimae, nihildum singulare attulit.[1113] De prima victoria 16 arcus mei sunt typis aereis Antverpiae editi,[1114] adiungam ex rebus nunc gestis plures. In Belgio post Gallicum facinus omnia solicitudinis plena et ad vindictam divinam spectantia.

Address: Clarissimo Hugoni Blotio doctori et amico suo observandissimo. Padoa. Cito.

189.
Sambucus to Abraham Ortelius
25 October 1572, Vienna

Printed as a legend on the map *Illyricum*, which was included as a fourteenth map in Abraham Ortelius, *Additamentum theatri orbis terrarum* (Antwerp: Ortelius 1573).[1115]

Sambucus sends a map of Hungary. He has corrected several features of Hirschvogel's map and added new ones thanks to Angielini's efforts. If taken together with Hirschvogel's map, it leaves nothing to desire.

[1110] Cf. the preceding letter, note 1101, but Sambucus might have also intended to write a more proper history of the coronation.

[1111] Cf. letter 184, where the total to be paid to Simone Galignani was only 160 ducats. 180 ducats may have included the expenses of the spedition. Sambucus is talking about "lira di piccoli" here.

[1112] János Joó, was tutor to Faustus Verantius, the nephew of Antonius Verantius. He was in Padua from 1569 to 1572, when he found employment at the Hungarian Chancellery under Listhius. He was not happy with the job, as also Sambucus's words suggest in his letter to Verantius of 21 November. He held positions as scribe or translator at the imperial court. In 1575 he was promoted to a position at the Hofkriegsrat with a salary of c. 300 guldens. In 1581 he was promoted to the position of secretary at the Hungarian Chancellery with a salary of 400 guldens, in 1587 he became chief justice ("királyi személynök") of Hungary. See Gombáné Lábos Olga, "Joinus–Joó János padovai Aristoteles-példánya" [The Paduan Aristotele copy of János Joó], in *Magyar Könyvszemle* 93 (1977), 354; also see Vienna, ÖNB, HHStA, Ungarische Akten, Allgemeine Akten, Fasc. 106. Konv. A. 1575.I-II., 30-31; Fasc. 113. Konv. C. 1581. I-XII. 189; Fasc. 118. Konv. A. Konv. 1587. I-II. 42, etc.

[1113] The apostolic nuncio was Zaccaria Delfino. Still in 1572, there was repeated attempt by the part of the Catholic League to achieve another naval victory but the Ottomans managed to evade its fleet. See John F. Guilmartin, *Galleons and Galleys: Gunpowder and the Changing Face of Warfare at Sea in the 16th Century* (Cambridge: Cambridge University Press, 1974), 149-50; Alberto Tenenti, "La Francia, Venezia e la Sacra Lega," in *Il Mediterraneo nella seconda metà del '500 alla luce di Lepanto*, ed. Gino Benzoni (Florence: L. S. Olschki, 1974), 393-408.

[1114] Sambucus, *Arcus aliquot triumphales*.

[1115] From 1573 onwards the map was included in the editions of Abraham Ortelius's *Theatrum orbis terrarum* (Antverpiae: Ortelius).

Ioannes Sambucus Ortelio suo salutem.

Mitto hanc quoque tabellam, qua necessaria confinia Pannoniae declarantur. Fluviorum et aliquot locorum situs Hirschvogelii[1116] recte mutavi, Angelini[1117] autem studio plurima adieci et intervalla correxi, ut parum quis, si cum Hirschvogelii haec coniungat, desiderarit. Si qui errores sint, dies certiora docebit. Viennae, Vale, 25. Octobris 1572.

190.
Sambucus to Piero Vettori
8 November 1572, [Vienna]

The original is kept in Munich, BSB, Clm 735, Nr. 64. Published in Gerstinger, "Die Briefe," 135-138; and partially in Bandini, *Clarorum Italorum et Germanorum epistolae*, 2:64-65.

Sambucus discovered that Vettori's package stayed with the fast carrier for a long time; he expresses his thanks for Vettori's book. He is collecting rare and unusual spelling variants in order to harvest them in the future, and he goes on to discuss orthographical questions from a historical point of view. In a learned, Ciceronian Latin he would happily insert words used by Ennius or Varro and not rigidly insist on homogeneity. At the Frankfurt book fair one finds books coming from his little museum ("Museolum"): Bonfini's Dialogue on chastity in matrimony; Glycas's Byzantine history; [Pseudo-]Hesychius's work on good writers; and Theodore Ducas Lascaris's natural philosophy. The books of the Basilica are in press. Vettori will soon receive his booklet on Rudolf's crowning; meanwhile, he can read Sambucus's oration. Sambucus has received only two copies of his printed triumphal arches, which he has given to the emperor. They will send more, and he will give one to Vettori. He would send all his (new) books to Vettori if the books published in Basel were not in suspect in Italy. The gods should prolong Vettori's old age. He tried to help Pál Szegedi, recommended by Vettori, as much as he could. Finally, he is apologising for the ugly script. He wrote the letter lying in bed and suffering stomach pains.

[1116] Augustin Hirschvogel (1503–1553), artist and mathematician, worked as a cartographer for Ferdinand I, traveling, measuring and documenting his domains. Sambucus refers to his map *Schlavoniae, Croatiae, Carniae, Istriae, Bosniae finitimarumque regionum nova descriptio*, which had been used in the older editions of Ortelius's *Theatrum*, and kept being reprinted in the later editions alongside Sambucus's *Illyricum*.

[1117] Nicolò Angielini was a fortification architect and cartographer in the service of the Viennese War Council. Sambucus used his manuscript map *Croatia et Sclavonia* (preserved, among others, in Vienna, ÖNB, Cod. 8609 Han, Nr. 2*), but may also have had other information provided by Angielini. On Angielini and his brother and nephew, likewise military architects and cartographers, see Géza Pálffy, *Die Anfänge der Militärkartographie in der Habsburgermonarchie. Die regelmäßige kartographische Tätigkeit der Burgbaumeisterfamilie Angielini an den kroatisch-slawonischen und den ungarischen Grenzen in den Jahren 1560–1570 / A haditérképészet kezdetei a Habsburg Monarchiában. Az Angielini várépítész-família rendszeres térképészeti tevékenysége a horvát–szlavón és a magyarországi határvidéken az 1560–1570-es években* (Budapest: Magyar Országos Levéltár, 2011), and Ferdinand Opll, Heke Krause and Christoph Sonnlechner, *Wien als Festungsstadt im 16. Jahrhundert. Zum kartografischen Werk der Mailänder Familie Angielini* (Vienna: Böhlau 2017).

Petro Victorio viro clarissimo Sambucus salutem.

Fasciculum tuum apud celerum magistrum serius latuisse deprehendi. Habeo gratiam de Atticanis et raris monimentis advectis.[1118] Equidem ut faeneratores τὰ δυσεύρητα[1119] vel literulam insolentem in alveolos comporto, unde aliquando mellificemus apes. Verumtamen, mi doctissime Victor, multis exemplis aeque, credo, vetustas docuerit C. et G. et Q. separata fuisse, consonantes geminatas appellationem et congressus mitiores, ut nec grammaticis aliquot παραδείγμασιν[1120] fidam nec a lenioribus usu facile abducar et in notionibus peregrinarum vocum nugatos grammaticos olim putem. Nunc enim demebant, nunc addebant consonantes, ut in discipulina, tempulum etc. poplo, nunc biginti, pelbis, nunc e pro i, u pro b, o pro u, f inversum pro v sic ɟ ponebant. In his quoque tuis, quod alias video in coniunctis originem custoditam, ut obsedeo, consaciatas, decaptus, Sicelia etc. Notam D alias post dictiones positam memini, sed sexto casui tantum et gerundivis significatis, quo modo hic, fortassis διακρίσεως ἕνεκα[1121] popularis, quod non tunc subiectores epigramatum valde docti nec Latini grammatici fecisse omnino videantur. Ac cum de hac veterum differentia in scriptionibus cogito, succurrit illud vulgare vestrum, quos audio una cum Gallis Latina et Graeca eadem via secutos et ante 100 annos scripturas Latinoitalicas et Graecoitalicas viguisse secus quam hodie, dum occultantur aliena dumque propria efficiuntur.[1122]

Et quando, a Cicerone et aliis lingua sit excultissima, agnosco, veneror antiquitatem, auctoritatis ergo voculam Ennii,[1123] Varronis[1124] amplectar, inseram, non omnem sequamur disciplinam. Quae est enim in setum pro sed, in rehapse et huius generis suavitas? Haec non scribo, ut res et memoriam antiquam neglegendam censeam, cuius me sedulo fuisse studiosum non nulli sciunt, sed ne superstitiose eadem celebremus. Id vero hisce apud te innuere volui. E Francofortensi mercatu nuper prodiere ex Museolo nostro Dialogi de pudicicia coniugali, M. Glyceus de Byzantina historia, Hesichius Milesius de claris scriptoribus, Constantinus Ducas de philosophia naturali; sub praelo sunt τῶν Βασιλικῶν[1125] libri, qui iuris consultorum sunt.[1126] De celebri coronatione Rodolphi libellum brevi accipies, interea istam oratiunculam legito. Arcuum meorum duo modo exempla acceperam, quae imperatori obtuli. Mittuntur plura, quae tecum communicabo ac, ut, quod animus fert, enunciem, meas nugas omnes ad te mitterem, nisi libri ex officinis Basileae expediti apud vos improbi omnes et suspecti haberentur. Dii hanc vegetam et nullis partibus ab annis imminentem senectam tibi nobisque diuturnam esse concedant.

[1118] See letter 186.
[1119] hard to find
[1120] patterns, models
[1121] for the sake of differentiation
[1122] "elementa dissimulant" deleted by Sambucus.
[1123] Quintus Ennius (c. 239–c. 169 BC) is often considered the father of Roman poetry.
[1124] Marcus Terentius Varro (116–27 BC).
[1125] of the royal
[1126] Bonfini, *Symposion trimeron*; Glycas, *Annales*; [Pseudo-]Hesychius, Περὶ τῶν ἐν παιδείᾳ; Ducas Lascaris, *De communicatione naturali* (see letter 161); *LX librorum Βασιλικῶν*.

Paulo Segedeo tuarum laudum et viciniae praeclaro encomiastae tua quoque caussa, quod potui, praesto fui.[1127] Vale. 8. Novembris 1572. Ignosce manui! Scripsi haec in lecto intestinis doloribus moleste attentatus.

Address: Clarissimo viro Petro Victorio, amico et tamquam fratri observatissimo. Florentiam.

191.
Sambucus to Johann Sommer
13 December 1572, [Vienna?]

The original is kept in Trnava: SAT, Magistrát mesta Trnava, Missiles.[1128] Published in Vantuch, "Die Sambucusbriefe," 349-350.

Sambucus did not have anyone to whom he could entrust the letter, now he is sending it to Sommer, fully finished and nicely written. He received the trousers and three shirts. Concerning the 24 thalers of tax to be paid, Sambucus indicates how much to pay to whom. He will send the money when there is a good occasion. Part of it (?) should be paid by Imre Kalmár.

Mein dienst etc. hab niemandt zu schikhen bishero khuenne funden. Schikh euch den Briff wolgefertigt und herlich geschriben. Seytt mir yber die 30 taller und 2 dukaten, 14 khreuzer rest. Hob die Hosn, und 3 Riempfhemde [?] mit großen dankh empfangn, und bitt hinfiro [?] auch, doch umb betzollung der taxen 24 taller: 2 taller umb schmer [?], wachsen und siglen, 4 fl. in die Cantzley, damit sie ainandermall lustig seyen, 3 fl. dem Mutth [?] 30 khreuzer umb die pichsen, 24 khreuzer porgomen. Den unterlauffen auff der Cantzley 20 khreuzer schlafstehl [?] 6 khreuzer.[1129] Mitt dem Mutt traidt werdt ir verhoff ich mitt guetter gleghaitt

---

[1127] Pál Szegedi was the coach driver for the duke of Florence and from 1572 his courier ran between Florence and Vienna. In the beginning of the same year, he published a long Italian poem on the subject of the coach, signing it as "Paolo Zeguedi di Pest": *Capitolo in lode de cocchi molto ingegnioso, con un sonetto per il contrario, cosa degua di essere veduta et letta. Novamente posta in luce* (Florence: [Giorgio Marescotti], 1572; Bologna: Alessandro Benacci, 1572). The poem was not his work, he only published it, probably written on occasion of the Florentine carnival, when also coach drivers had a role. Since the dedicatee of the poem was his "patron" "la signora (E)Leonora Cibba, Marchese di Cittone," we may suppose that he found employment with the duke only in the spring of 1572. As we learn from Vettori's letter to Crato, in the summer of 1572 Szegedi lived in the duke's house (*Petri Victorii ad Ioannem Cratonem, Thomam Rehdigerum et Hieronymum Mercurialem epistolae*, ed. Franciscus Passow, Breslau: n.d., 1823, 21). Recommended by Vettori both to Sambucus and Crato, he travelled to Vienna in the entourage of the Florentine ambassador to Vienna. Sometimes in 1572-1573 he met Hugo Blotius; two of his interesting letters, written in bad Italian to Blotius still survive (published by Kovács). From these letters we learn that Szegedi had an Italian wife and also children. Because of his postal services his name keeps turning up in the correspondence between Vettori and Sambucus. This Pál Szegedi is not to be mixed up with another Pál Szegedi, who studied in Bologna in the same period, preparing for an ecclesiastical career and later became bishop of Csanád, and similarly put his name in Blotius's *album amicorum*. There was even a third Pál Szegedi in the same period, who studied in Wittenberg in 1578 and then found employment as lector at the Protestant boarding school of Sárospatak. Cf. Zsuzsa Kovács, "Szegedi Pál(ok) Italiában" [Pál(s) Szegedi in Italy], in *Régi és új peregrináció: magyarok külföldön, külföldiek Magyarországon*, eds. szerk. Békési Imre et al. (Szeged–Budapest: Scriptum Nemzetközi Magyar Filológiai Társaság, 1993), 2:605-616.

[1128] Dated to 31 December.

[1129] It is probably the price of the diploma of tax exemption, cf. letter 109.

heruff schikhen. Den ain mutt mocht ir beholten, weyll mir Calmar Imre will zolln. Bin etwas gott lob pesser auff. Euch zu gfalln all Zeitt den dreizten [?] December 1572.
Euer Diener J. Sambok.

Address: Dem Ehrnvesten Hern Hannsn Sommer, burger und Handlsman zu Thierna, meinem guett frondt zuh[anden]. Tierna. Mitt einem plechen buchsen und briff.

192.
Sambucus to Piero Vettori
1 January [1573], [Vienna]

The original is kept in Munich, BSB, Clm 735, Nr. 65. Published in Gerstinger, "Die Briefe," 255-256; and partially published in Dekker, "Ein unbekannter," 92-93.

When Sambucus answered concerning Duilius's column, he was ill and now cannot remember what he wrote. As soon as he started feeling better, he took a closer look at it and was able to correct some corrupt places. In the first book of Quintilian's (Institutio Oratoria), *in the place where he discusses the superfluous letter 'd'; 'D. Iulio' is a corrupt place as it should be written as Duilio. The same in Sextus Rufus. In Pliny's* (Naturalis Historia) *34 it is C. Duilius, as in Silius, end of the sixth book (of his* Punica*) and in the* Fasti (Capitolini). *Sambucus explains another strange term from the inscription of the column with reference to Pliny and analyses its scriptural characteristics with reference to Quintilian. With reference to the (false) etymology of duellum–bellum, he explains that the word 'Bilium' is a corruption made by the stone-cutters and should be written 'Duilium'. While he respects antiquity (i.e. antique varieties in spelling), he thinks such inscriptions were incised in a manner of the plebs. With reference to the fragments of the* Lex Thoria *he lists some deviating spellings and goes on to speculate about the origin of the numeral L. He wrote the letter, while Pál Szegedi was departing, whom he had supported in every way. If similar inscriptions will turn up, Vettori should write about them. He is sending Vettori his work, corrupted by minor typographical errors, which Vettori should correct. Vettori should warn Paolo (Manuzio?) not to forget about the promised theriac and mithridate.*

Salutem καὶ εὐμοιρίαν παρὰ θεῷ εἰς ἀεὶ cum mille Kalendis Ianuarii.[1130]

Cum de Duilii columna rescriberem,[1131] acerbissime in lecto intestinis malis cruciabar nec satis memini, quid fere scripserim. Ubi commodius haberi coepi, diligentius singulis extimatis, occasionem aliquot locis antiquis corrigendis praebuit. Nam in 1. Quintiliani, ubi de litera D tractat superflua, corruptus est locus D. Iulio, cum Duilio sit scribendum;[1132] ita in Sexto Ruffo.[1133] Plinius quoque in 34 de columna C. Duilium nominat cum Silo in fine

---

[1130] Health and good fortune from God forever with 1000 new year days.
[1131] On Duilius's column see letter 216 and Dekker, "Ein unbekannter Brief"; Gerstinger, "Die Briefe," 256.
[1132] "[...] ut a Latinis veteribus d plurimis in verbis ultimam adiectam, quod manifestum est etiam ex columna rostrata, quae est Duilio in foro posita..." Quintilianus, *Institutio oratoria* 1.7.12. Note that in the manuscript tradition in the place of "Duilio" there is often "iulio," and in the first editions "(D.) Iulio" is the most frequent solution. See Dekker, "Ein unbekannter Brief," 94-95.
[1133] Sambucus refers here to the author of the "Chronography of 354," which was attributed among others

sexti, quo modo et *Fasti*.[1134] Luceis bovibus puto istud, quod Plinius ait de lucanis bubus, hoc est, Elephantis.[1135] Nec modo observatur in hoc epigrammate singularitas consonantum, sed quoque semivocalium, qua de re quoque Quintilianus 1. meminit.[1136] Quod autem Bilium habet, mendum omnino est sculptoris.[1137] Nam cum Cicero duellum licentia pro bello,[1138] duis pro bis et per synecesim Duîs pro Dis, omnino Duilius debet scribi. Quod ad reliqua, vetustatem veneror, agnosco libenter, sed cum inter i et e interque alia elementa iam tum discrimen fuerit, credo talia plebiscita ad vulgi consuetudinem incisa fuisse. Moenitam pro munitam grammatici quoque annotarunt. In fragmento *Legis Thoriae* meo[1139] aheneo legitur semper Paperius, ioudicium et pro quinquaginta non L sed ↓ velut anchora; unde L fictum post fuisse credo, licet in *Fastis* quoque L sit, nam centum C dimidium ↓ recte fit. Sed sus Minervam! Haec urgente et abituriente Zeghedeo scripsi, cui non solum tuo iudicio sed voluntate et sponte, ut voti hinc compos ad vos redierit, praesto fui nec ulla in parte officium deserui. Vale, doctissime Victori, et si quid epigrammatum similium acciderit, ad me quoque. Mitto nugarum exemplum, a typographo aliquot erratulis corruptum, quae corriges. Kalendis Ianuarii etc. Ioannes Sambucus. Oro, mone Paullum nostrum,[1140] ne theriacae et Mithridati promissi obliviscatur etc.

Address: Clarissimo viro domino Petro Victorio, amico et tamquam patri. Florentiam.

193.
Sambucus to Samuel Grynaeus
5 January 1573, [Vienna]

The original is kept in Basel, Universitätsbibliothek, Handschriften, Mscr G2 I 30, no. 149. A copy is kept in ibid. G II 34, no. 8. Published in Gerstinger, "Die Briefe," 138-139.

Johannes Thomas Freigius handed Grynaeus the translation of Sambucus's Basilica a long time ago, and the translation is much awaited by many in Italy, France and Germany. Why is Grynaeus not publishing it? Sambucus's friends claim the delay is Grynaeus's fault. He asks Grynaeus to place public interest before less weighty matters that hinder him at work. It will be a good investment both in terms of work and money. Sambucus urges Grynaeus not to let others come out with an edition earlier

---

to Festus [Sextus / Rufus]. Sambucus's information goes back to a 1558 edition of the text by Onophrius Panvinius: *Reipublicae Romanae Commentarium* (Venetiis: ex officina Erasmiana, 1558), 239. See Dekker, "Ein unbekannter Brief," 95-96.

[1134] Plinius, *Naturalis historia* 34.11; Silius 6.663-665. For an edition of the *Fasti consulares* see Attilio Degrassi, *I fasti consolari* (Rome: Edizioni di storia e letteratura, 1954), 54, 55, 58 and 100. See Dekker, "Ein unbekannter Brief," 94.

[1135] Plinius, *Naturalis historia* 8.6.16.

[1136] Quintilianus, *Institutio oratoria*. 1.7.14.

[1137] See Dekker, "Ein unbekannter Brief," 92.

[1138] Cicero, *Orator* 153 (cf. with Quint. *Inst.* 1.4.15).

[1139] On the agrarian law *Lex Thoria* see Cicero, *Ad Brutum* 36.136; and Cicero, *De oratore* 2.284 (70). The fragments of the law were first published by Fulvio Orsini in 1584 (apparently Sambucus had his own bronze fragment). For the history of Orsini's edition see Adolfus Fridericus Rudorff, "Das Ackergesetz des Spurius Thorius," *Zeitschrift für geschichtliche Rechtswissenschaft* 10 (1839), 1-194 (at 1-5).

[1140] Gerstinger suggests that this is a reference to Paolo Manuzio, although he dates the letter to 1581. It was more probably a reference to Pál Szegedi.

(although he does not know about anyone in particular), and leave the glory of this first edition for him. If he can offer something to Grynaeus's press from his library, he will be happy to do so.

Ioannes Sambucus salutem.

Basilica mea vobis[1141] cum interpretatione sua dudum communicavit Fregius,[1142] quorum in editionis desiderio cum plurimi sint, Itali, Galli et Germani, cur, quaeso, non extruditis, quid in optatissimo authore, diligenti interprete requiritis? Spem fecerat nobis Fregius ante annum eum librum recepturos, sed amici et qui familiares vestri sunt, in vos moram coniciunt. Oro vos per autoritatem typorum, per fidem, per commoda publica, nonnihil privatis cedatis, rationem omnium quibusdam leviculis impedimentis anteponite; non vos operae aut sumptuum paenitebit. Ubi is prodierit, si quis alius manum ei tabulae ausus erit admovere, faciat, fruatur sui laboris gloria. Hanc primam editionem nobis concedite. Cumque ad multos scripserim de hac re, ne me vana et ficta scripsisse putent aut moram non ferendo ipsi aliquo modo antevertant editionem, providete, etsi scio neminem adhuc eam cogitationem suscepisse.

Si quid praelo vestro idoneum mea bibliothecula porro adhibere poterit, si ingeniolum, credite Sambuco non defore vobis studium et promptam in remetiendo officio voluntatem et exempla. Iterum oro, quamprimum excudite, scio venalem fore librum et nobilitaturum fortasse vestros labores et sumptus. Haec subito scripsi. V. Ianuarii 1573.

Address: Domino Samueli Gryneo, Episcopiorum praecipuo typographo eleganti et industrio, amico singullari. Basileam.
Other hand: Accepi 29. Ianuarii 1573.
Iohannes Sambucus urget editionem τῶν Βασιλικῶν.

194.
Sambucus to Johann Baptist Weber
[8 January 1573]

The original is kept in Vienna, ÖStA, HHStA, HausA, Familienakten 17-4.

Sambucus has received the imperial decree sent by Weber. Although he is so weak that he can barely stand, he has carried out the order as good as it was possible. The actual titles and seals are seldom described in historical works. They are usually found in tournament books and kept by

---

[1141] *LX librorum Βασιλικῶν.* See letters 127 and 134 for Sambucus's *Basilica*-manuscript and the context of this letter and cf. the Index under "Sambucus." Samuel Grynaeus (1539–1599), son of Simon Grynaeus the elder, studied in Basel, Strasburg, Tubingen and Dole (Franche-Comté), and obtained his masters degree in 1565 and doctoral degree in 1569 in Basel. From 1571, he taught Roman law in Basel and was elected several times as rector of the university. See Adam, *Vitae Germanorum iureconsultorum,* 337-339. He seems to have intensely collaborated with the Episcopius press.

[1142] As we know, the *Basilica*-edition eventually appeared in the translation and edition of Johannes Löwenklau (*LX librorum Βασιλικῶν*). This letter suggests that it was Grynaeus's decision not to accept Freigius's translation, who later claimed that Löwenklau had stolen it. Löwenklau defended himself in the preface to the edition, without naming Freigius. The great legal humanist, who had already published a book of the Basilica, Jacques Cujas later took sides with Freigius and strongly criticised Löwenklau's translation. See more in letters 120 and 196, and note 1231 on Cujas in letter 205.

heralds, but Sambucus has followed the order and had the coats of arms painted truthfully. In the case of the French mother (Anne of Foix-Candale) of Queen Anna of Bohemia and Hungary he cannot confirm the coat of arms with certainty, but only provide what he had heard. If something is amiss, Weber only has to tell him. Sambucus commends himself and wishes a happy New Year. The painter has placed the coats of arms wrongly, as the drawing on the back shows.

Gnädiger [?] Gebiettender Herr etc.

Es ist mir vor fünff tag ain Decret zukommen von Euer gnaden in Irer Maiestät namen.[1143] Unnd wiewoll lang schwach gelegen, das ich noch khaum auff den fuessen stee, jedoch hab ich in der als vill muglich ist, Irer Maiestät befelch nachkhommen. Die aigen titell, vnd sigill fündt man selten in historiis beschriben: in Turnier büchern, und bey den Herolden pflegt mans hietten: Jedoch Weyll es mir auffgelegt ist: hob ich die Wappen als vill die Warhaitt ist, lassen mallen zu einem muster: aber in der hochloblicher Khunigin Anna Muetter aus Franckraich khan ich nicht gar gwiss das Wappen confirmiern, allain wie ichs vernomen hab. Manglet was, Euer gnaden befelch mir alzeytt. Derer ich mich vntertaniglich comendier, mitt winschung vill glukselig Neus Jar.
 Der Maller hatt die Wappen etwas versetzt, wie dan der [...]rich anzaigt.[1144] den 8. Jan. 1573. Euer gnaden Vnterthänigster diener D. Sambucus.

Address: Dem Wohlgeboren meinem gnädigsten Herrn etc. D. J. Baptista Beber etc. Irer Mayestät Hoff vicekantzler vnd geheim Ratt.
Zu Handen.

195.
Sambucus to Emperor Maximilian II
[8 January 1573]

The original is kept in Vienna, ÖStA, HHStA, HausA, Familienakten 17-4.

Sambucus has received Maximilian's order to supply information on several related families and their coats of arms five days ago. Because he is still ill and cannot consult his library, he has to rely on his memory. He asks Maximilian to be lenient, in case he has forgotten something, and to attribute it to obscurity of historical accounts and to scarcity of documents. In following he presents what is proven by history. There follows genealogic and heraldic information on Maximilian II's ancestors Philip I (of Castile), Maximilian I, Mary of Burgundy, Casimir IV Jagiellon, Anne of Foix-Candale, Vladislaus II of Hungary, and Elisabeth of Austria. Coats of arms are not printed in books of history, but are found in the archives, from where clerks can get them.

[1143] This was in connection with the project of the creation of the cenotaph for Maximilian I in the Court Church in Innsbruck. The emperor ordered Sambucus to provide genealogical and heraldic information on his ancestors.
[1144] The letter accompanied a sheet with a gouache rendering of eight coats of arms on the front side and additional heradic and genealogical information on the back (Vienna, ÖStA, HHStA, SB Kartensammlung T, Ke3-6/8). The painter erroneously positioned the coat of arms of Mary of Burgundy at the side of Philip I (of Castile), and that of Joanna of Castile at the side of Maximilian I. Sambucus drew the lines to connect the correct pairs.

Sacratissime Caesar, domine, domine clementissime et cetera.

Decretum vestrae maiestatis ante quinque dies redditum subiectissime accepi, de aliquot familiis agnatis et cognatis cum insignibus suis annotandis. Utinam vires ex diuturno morbo suppeterent, vel haec morula non fuisset interiecta. Nondum firme insisto, minus conscendem ad Museolum, licet, quod tamen memoria subiecit, adscripsi, suppliciter orans, si in quo offendi, vel historiarum obscuritati, vel diplomatum inopiae, in quibus tituli integri cerni legique solent, adeoque arma propius conspici etc. clementissime nunc annuat et ignoscat. Quae vero historica sunt et testata memoria, breviter ita habent:

Pater Ferdinandi augusti vestrae maiestatis Philippus Austrius Flandriae comes fuit, Maximiliani I. filius, Friderici IIII. nepos, qui ob parentis ingentem vulgi spem ostensam preclaras res vel[1145] patre vivo nondum imperio eius incepto passim gestas obtinuit, ut Ioannam Ferdinandi ultimi Arragonis et Elizabethae reginae filiam unicam in matrimonio foveret Hispanias et viciniam possideret.

Arma Philippo integra sunt appicta, simul et coniugis non tamen aquila est, sed vultur occidentalis, accipiter Bethicus. Titulos certos cancellaria prodent.

Pater Philippi Maximilianus I. fuit, ex Maria Caroli Burgundi ultimi ducis filia unica. Qui Carolus post tot acria bella et in Gallos fulmina, ut ad eius nomen Franci cohorrescerunt, tertio prelio ad Nancium caesus, filiam reliquerit tot Belgii ditionibus ad Austrios collatis. Titulus Mariae fuit ducissa Burgundiae, comitissa Flandriae et cetera. Carolus utramque Burgundiam, planam et submontanam tenebat, multa prelia [!] per Maximilianum cum Gallis ea de re atrocia comissa, denique pactis et induciis res constitit, ut plana sive maior feudum Galliae agnosceret, comitatus vero imperii sceptra [?].

II

Quid ad matrem, avum aviamque maternam et cetera pertinet, eorum hic insignia usitata posui: De familia Candales nonnihil est dubii: nondum legi qui nominatim parentes [aviae] maternae fuerunt.[1146]

Casimirus Polonus frater fuit Vladislai regis Ungariae, eius qui ad Varnam 1444 misere occubuit religionis amore, vix 22 aetatis suae. Is Casimirus duxerat sororem Elizabetham, regis Ungariae et Bohemiae Ladislai, nepotis Sigismundi caesaris, filii Alberti Austrii, sororem, quem puerum Fridericus IIII. detentum Ciliae comiti reddiderat.

Suscepit hic Casimirus praeter alios Vladislaum regem ilico Poloniae factum et Bohemiae et ab Ungaris ob familiaritatem Olomutio conventu constitutam exoptatum. Cuius fortunam Albertus frater diu, sed suo dedecore oppugnavit. Minimum natu fratrem is habuit Sigismundum Poloniae regem, Sigismundi Augusti patrem et cetera. Hic Vladislaus Casimirus spreta Beatrice consilio Florentinorum et aliquot legatorum, ne ob leves caussas connubium Beatricis neglexisse videretur seque non tam gentis amplitudinem, quam spem sobolis alere significaret, Hludovici principis Aquitanici de Candales, familiae apud Guascones nobilissimae et vetustissimae filiam duxit Annam. Quae illa sanctissima regina et insignis, ut ita loquor, mater familias primo partu Annam matrem vestrae maiestatis in lucem edidit, altero nixu, quo est mortua, Lodovicum, quem Mater omnino Iulium ad sacrum fontem

---

[1145] Crossed out: *patre vivo*.
[1146] Sambucus's main source on the house Candale seems to have been *Genealogia illustrium familiarum Dalbert, Foix et Candalles* (Vienna, ÖNB, Cod. 3324, 1ʳ-5ʳ).

nominandum voluit,[1147] sed vicit praelatorum opinio, qui Lodovicum appellandum censuere. Arma Casimiri Lituanica et Polonica sunt, post Borrussis in fidem et tutelam omnino deditis aquilam ipsorum armis addidit, ut Sigismundus crucferorum et aliorum.

Arma uxoris eius Boemica, Ungarica et Austriaca, quod Alberti Austrii fuerit filia. Arma aviae maternae audivi fuisse Aquitaniae, uti hic pictura monstrat, certius nondum comperi.

Vladislai vero Polonica, Lituanica cum Ungaria coniuncta, ut vel aurei eius numi docent.

Ceterorum arma, et sanctissimae matris imperatoris Annae nota sunt, nec tituli et arma expressa in monumentis historiarum poni solent. In autoritatibus et scriniis literisque mutuis latent, unde a condis promi, requiri solent.

Vestrae sacratissimae maiestatis subdidissimus [!] clientulus Sambucus.

196.
Sambucus to Emperor Maximilian II
[January 1573]

The original is kept in Vienna, ÖStA, HHStA, HausA, Familienakten 17-4, 5.

Sambucus sends to Maximilian the inscriptions (for the statues of his ancestors). Some historians are not in agreement, but he thinks that he was quite accurate. If Maximilian wants something to be corrected or changed, he should let Sambucus know. The abbreviations are explained. He is not sure about the dates of birth and death of Philip I of Castile's wife, Maximilian will know this better.

Schikh dem Herrn die tumulorum inscriptiones mitt sambt der Zeytt, vnd örter, auch khertz. Es sein etlich historici nicht ains, aber ich hab glaub ich das nechst troffen. Ist was zu pessern, andern etc. laße michs der Herr wissen. Das θ ist Mortuus est. VIX. ist lebens Zeytt. F. Filius vel filia. N. Nepos. Nept. Neptis. Pron. Pronepos, vel proneptis. M. Mensis. D. Dies. H. hora. Des Khunigs Philippi, vatters Caroli V. et Ferdinandi Frauen todt vnd lebens Jar zweiffl ich etwas, Ir Khayserliche Maiestät wird's gwisser haben. Eurer Khayserlichen Maiestät Diener Sambucus.

197.
Sambucus to Hugo Blotius
12 January 1573, [Vienna]

The original is kept in ÖNB, Cod. 9737[z14-18], I, f. 199[r-v]. Published in Menčík, "A Páduában tanuló," 47; Gerstinger, "Die Briefe," 139-140.

Sambucus was suspecting what Blotius wrote about the negligence of the postal officers: he paid already six months earlier. He scolded the brother of Petrus, who promises that the money will be delivered at the next dispatch to Simone Galignani or Doctor Cavino himself. Blotius should meanwhile urge Galignani to send the busts. Blotius has full authority and his expenses will be

---
[1147] Instead of *censuit*, which is crossed out.

repaid. A Venetian nobleman "Hieronymus Leon" will help with the shipping; he lives close to the Fondacco dei Tedeschi. If someone will bring the busts on Sambucus's expense to Venice, there should be a person sent to Venice to give the package over to the Eiselers, who will carry them tax-free, as they have already received the imperial permission for the route. Sambucus asks Blotius to show the busts to Alessandro Bassiano and other antiquarians to find out if it is worth sending them together with the chests rather than only the heads. If it costs more than 10 florins, he is happy with the heads alone. Blotius should decide and not spare expenses. Sambucus is happy about the progress of Listhius Jr. The Basilica has been printed in Latin and Greek in Basel, and he is planning a better edition of Harmenopoulos's work and a synopsis of all laws. He wrote the letter in bed because of stomach pains, Blotius should apologise to Galignani for that and tell him that he would write more later on.

Sambucus salutem.

Dudum suspicatus sum, quod scribis de negligentia veredarii, nam pecuniam dissolvi totam ante sex menses.[1148] Acrius cum magistro hinc Petri fratre egi,[1149] qui serio mandat, ut proximo cursu apocha mittatur et Simoni vel ipsi doctori Cavino numeretur.[1150] Tu igitur vel Simone non aperto urge bonam et commodam in missionem marmorum, interpone autoritatem. Quidquid in sumptu fuerit, ilico fide integra recipietis. Est Venetiis nobilis insignis Venetus in vicinia Fontigi ad S. Iohannem Chrysostomum, aediculam [!],[1151] Hieronymus Leon,[1152] qui officium nullum in expediendo deseret. Si meis sumptibus Venetias, qui deducat, mittendus erit aliquis, ut in Fontigo Eyslerorum negociatori tradantur et ab omnibus teloniorum liberentur, gratus erit. Habent illi mandatum caesareum per iter iam acceptum. Illud te unice oro, adhibito Bassano Alexandro[1153] et aliis antiquariis consulito, an cum pectoribus afficits mitti debeant et vecturae pretium mereantur. Nam X florenos non respicio, sin minus, sola capita mittantur. Facietis, quod voletis, nec parcite numis.

Memoriam et progressus discipuli amplector, cum renunciabis mille Kalendas Ianuarii. *Basilica* mea Graece et Latine fere typis sunt absoluta.[1154] Harmenopulum[1155] correctiorem quoque editurus sum cum omni iuris codicum parapompes[1156] [!] etc. Haec in lecto intestinis malis scripsi, excusa me Simoni et pollicere a me omnia copiosa et pro officiis gratiam. 12 Ianuarii 1573.

[1148] See letter 183.
[1149] We do not know the person in question.
[1150] Sambucus did not know about Cavino's death, which happened two and a half years before. Sambucus's words suggest that the marble busts were his work. See letter 183, note 1079.
[1151] The church dedicated to Saint Chrysostom is little to the north of the Fondaco dei Tedeschi.
[1152] We could not identify Hieronymus Leon (Girolamo Leon).
[1153] Alessandro Bassiano (1503/4–1587) was a Paduan antiquarian with numismatic interests, a close friend of Cavino. He is held to be Cavino's collaborator and the person who inspired the artist to create his copies of antique coins.
[1154] Cf. with the preceding letter.
[1155] In his bibliography Sambucus claims to have corrected the "storehouse of laws" by the fourteenth-century Byzantine scholar Constantine Harmenopoulos: "Harmenopuli Πρόχειρον iuris emendavit, scholia temere cum textu confusa separavit, Falkenburgio tradiderat." See Sambucus, *Catalogus librorum*. He is probably not talking of the manuscript preserved in Vienna, ÖNB as Cod. Jur. gr. 14, since it only has some excerpts from Harmenopoulos's *Hexabiblos* or *Procheiron*.
[1156] escort ("with the whole accompanying stuff of the codices of law")

Address: Al Magnifico et Excellente Signor Dottor Hugo Blotius Maggior Domo del Signor Giovanni Listio Ongaro Amico osservandissimo. Padoa in Portia appresso l'Excellente Bonavito[1157] Overo in botega del Simon librario al Bo.[1158]

198.
Sambucus to Theodor Zwinger
6 February 1573, Vienna

The original is kept in Basel, Universitätsbibliothek, Frey Mscr II 27, no. 227. A copy is kept in ibid., Mscr G II 37, no. 146. Published in Gerstinger, "Die Briefe," 140-141.

Sambucus had some stomach pains and is not completely over them, so he writes only briefly. Crato has told him about (Zwinger's) edition of Aristotle; Sambucus will be able to contribute with something. He has collected some important textual variants. He will also send Zwinger Georgius Trapezuntius's autograph of Aristotle's History *of animals, which may help him emend the text. If only he could send more manuscripts of the same type. For him alone, this work of comparing texts with attention to minute details would be the most annoying. With reference to their old friendship he suggested that Pietro Perna publish Vegetius. Zwinger should urge Grynaeus and Episcopius to publish his* Basilica, *translated by Johannes Thomas Freigius and given a long time ago to Episcopius, or to publish at least its first two pages for the next book fair (of Frankfurt) so that others not publish it earlier. He is getting letters from France and Italy that remind him of his promise to publish it. He promised them (the publication of) Aristotle and other authors. The* Basilica *would get an imperial privilege for ten years.*

Sambucus salutem.

Intestino malo[1159] καὶ πόνοις πνευματώδεων ὑποχονδριῶν[1160] aliquamdiu laboravi necdum omnino liber sum. Ideo brevis nunc tecum sum. Crato significavit de editione Aristotelis,[1161] cui consilio praeclaro et satis arduo quiddam addere potero. Nam collegi varias lectiones, imo supplementa lacunarum aliquot non vulgaria.[1162] Mittam quoque versionem Trapezuntii[1163] numquam

---

[1157] Marco Mantova Benavides, who was a friend of both Bassiano and Cavino.
[1158] Simone Galignani was the official bookseller of the university and had his shop at Palazzo del Bo, the seat of the university.
[1159] Zwinger's marginal note: "Sambucus flatibus hypochondriacis torquetur," that is, Sambucus is tormented by abdominal bloating.
[1160] pain of the gassy abdomen
[1161] This might be a reference to the planned *Politica*-edition of Zwinger (and Episcopius) (see letters 159 and 205), although the promise to send a manuscript of the *Historia animalium*, suggests that it may have been another project concerning Aristotle. Crato may have heard about it from Episcopius, as Gerstinger claims in "Zusammenfassung," 286.
[1162] Zwinger's marginal note: "Labores eius in Aristotelis editionem".
[1163] Zwinger's note above Trapezuntii: "Georgii". Georgius Trapezuntius (George of Trebizond) (1395–1486) was a Greek philosopher from Crete, who moved to Italy probably already as a mature man. See John Monfasani, *George of Trebizond: A Biography and a Study of His Rhetoric and Logic* (Leiden: Brill, 1976); James Hankins, "George of Trebizond's life and character," in idem, *Plato in the Italian Renaissance* (Leiden: Brill, 1990), 1:173-193 (on his translation method: 186-188); idem, "George of Trebizond, Renaissance Libertarian?" in *Essays in Renaissance Thought and Letters. In Honor of John Monfasani*, eds. Alison Frazier and Patrick Nold (Leiden:

editam *Historiae animalium*, ipsius ἰδιόγραφον,[1164] quo plurimum iuvari poteritis. Utinam ipsa mea exemplaria varia mittere possim, plura collegeritis. Nam mihi soli is labor conferendi minute molestissimus esset. Vegetium commendavi[1165] Pernae eumque ad editionem hortor veteris amiciciae erga etc.[1166] Te, optime Zvingere, oro, Gryneum et Episcopios meo nomine saluta ac omnibus modis impetra, urge, *Basilica* mea a Ioanne Thoma Freigio versa cum Graecis quamprimum excudant aut saltem ad has nundinas duo prima folia cum ἐπιγραφῇ[1167] tamquam specimen deportent, ne mora ista aliqui editionem tam desiderati operis antevertantur.[1168] Freigius dudum Episcopiis dedit. Scias ex Italia et Gallia de iis libris ad me ab eruditis scribi literas et, ut fidem liberem, instare. Pollicere illis a me Aristotelica et alia. Vale. 6. Februarii 1573. Viennae. Decennii privilegium *Basilicis* apponant; tot enim ob tuum etc.

199.
Sambucus to Guglielmo Sirleto
9 February 1573, Vienna

The original is kept in Rome, BAV, Vat. lat. 6191 II, f. 448. Published in Gerstinger, "Die Briefe," 141-143.

One of Sirleto's outstanding virtues is his readiness to support anyone who has the right qualities. This is what also Fonteo must have experienced. Sambucus found him really worthy of recommendation. After a very hard winter, the snow suddenly melted and the Danube is flooding, yet the food imports are sufficient and generally there is hope of a rich harvest. He is writing a letter to attain Sirleto's support for an edition of Dioscorides, of which he has often written to Fulvio Orsini. It will be the fourth year since he launched this project, starting by hurriedly collating some old manuscripts. Many learned men sent him their lists of textual variants. Only Rome is missing: his Roman friends should also give him their collations, made according to the pagination of the Parisian Greco-Latin edition. He asks Sirleto to grant this favour and let Orsini or someone else do this work for him. If he had no hope for it, he would have long ago given Dioscorides, enlarged with 100 very rare plants, to the presses. In a postscript Sambucus claims to have written three times to Paolo Manuzio of the same thing, but Manuzio does not respond. From his part, he would be happy to share whatever he has with others.

Brill, 2015), 87-106. For Sambucus's appreciation of Trapezuntius see letter 293 and Gulyás, *Sámboky János könyvtára*, 315/3, 356, 518, 771, 943, 1017 and 2347.

[1164] autograph
[1165] Zwinger's note above *Vegetium commendavi*: "de Mulomedicina".
[1166] See letter 149, note 885 (the book came out finally with Perna in 1574). Curiously, Zwinger did not manage to find a publisher for the book, which he received several years before, although he was in excellent terms with Perna and functioned as his consultant and closest collaborator. On the Basel publisher Pietro Perna (1519-1582) see Peter G. Bietenholz, *Basle and France in the Sixteenth Century* (Geneva: Droz, 1971), passim; Antonio Rotondò, "Pietro Perna e la vita culturale e religiosa di Basilea fra il 1570 e il 1580," in *Studi e ricerche di storia ereticale italiana del Cinquecento* (Turin: Giappichelli, 1974), 273-394; Gilly, "Zwischen Erfahrung und Spekulation"; and Leandro Perini, *La vita e i tempi di Pietro Perna* (Rome: Edizioni di storia e letteratura, 2002).
[1167] titlepage
[1168] See letter 187.

Illustrissime atque amplissime Cardinalis, patrone singularis, salutem.

In praeclaris tuis virtutibus, positis iis summa in dignitate et orbis specula, illud quoque singulare inest, non modo ut bonus ac eruditus sis, sed humanitate admiranda quosvis idoneos benigneque foveas. Quod ipsum animadverto Fonteium quoque expertum,[1169] qui tam sedule de commendatione gratias agat. Profecto dignum censui, quem in notitia et patrocinio tuo collocarem, nec spem fallet. Nos hic post acerrimam hyemem nivibus subito solutis et ripas Danubii superantibus quasi diluvio conflictamur, annonae tamen importatio non est angusta vulgoque spes ostenditur in agrorum ubertatem omne cessurum. Cuius autem praecipue causa ad vestram illustrissimam amplitudinem scribo, est, ut suppliciter exorem aliquod subsidium in editionem Dioscorideam, qua de re saepe Fulvium Ursinum monui, impetrem.[1170] Quartus instat annus, cum id consilium coeperim, ursi coeptum collatione aliquot manuscriptorum vetustissimorum codicum, a multis adiutus sum viris doctis, qui lectiones suas indicibus perscriptas ad me miserunt. Sola Roma deest, hoc est, commoditas bibliothecarum et aliquorum amicorum, qui cum scriptis editione Graecolatina Parisiana per paginas collatis observationes submittant.[1171] Obsecro, doctissime Cardinalis, confer huc sensus aliqua ex parte tuos, da negocium Fulvio vel aliis, qui aliquid comunicent, nisi hac spe me sustentarem, dudum Dioscoridem 100 plantis rarissimis auctum typis tradidissem.[1172] Cuius beneficii tui celebritatem vel posteri ut laudent, efficiam, privatim vero omnia tibi deberi profitebor. Vale. 9. Februarii 1573. Viennae. Vestrae illustrissimae amplitudini deditus cliens, Ioannes Sambucus etc.

Paullo quoque Manutio ternas de ipso hoc negocio scripsi, nihil respondet.[1173] Credo in meis rebus nihil est, quod non aeque aliorum esse cupiam.

200.
Sambucus to Theodor Zwinger
10 February 1573, [Vienna]

The original is kept in Basel, Universitätsbibliothek, Frey Mscr II 26, no. 214. Published in Gerstinger, "Die Briefe," 143–144.

Sambucus is recommending Giovanni Michele Bruto, who is going back to visit his dear ones. He is not only erudite but also good, which is a great thing, as Zwinger knows from his reading of Plato and Aristotle. He has entrusted some fragments by Michael Marullus and others to Bruto so that they may be printed in due course, and he may give him similar texts in the future. He has already indicated that he is ready to give his opinion on Aristotle and offer what his library has on this question. He asks Grynaeus to publish the Basilica, as he has long ago received Freigius's translation. As a postscript Sambucus gives a sample of his annotations on Aristotle. His manuscript of Stobaeus's

---

[1169] See letter 185.
[1170] For the Dioscorides-project see among others letter 155. Sambucus's letter had no effect. Cf. letters 253 and 291.
[1171] *Dioscoridis libri octo Graece et Latine. Castigationes in eosdem libros* (Parisiis: Petrus Haultinus, 1549), see letter 155, note 921.
[1172] Note that the number of planned illustration changes once again. Cf. letters 155, 163 and 174.
[1173] We know only of letter 171 addressed to Manuzio on this subject.

Physical and Moral Extracts *will appear in Antwerp, with the help of which many places will be emendable, as Stobaeus piled up in it quotes from Aristotle and sentences by many others.*

Sambucus salutem.

Brutum, qui ad suos revisit, tibi vere commendo, qui sine Sambuco, quod caelestibus amicis debet vovitque, offeret.[1174] Non modo eruditus est sed etiam bonus, qua in voce, quantus sit thesaurus, ex Platone et Aristotele tuo nosti. Equidem in eius rebus omnia volo et cupio, item esse animatum non dubito. Marulli et aliorum nondum vulgata quaedam ἀποσπασμάτια,[1175] ut commode imprimantur, ei dedi, quod consilium eius, ubi operae pretium fuerit et paratos typos videro, cumulabo et confirmabo aliis similibus scriptis. De Aristotele meum iudicium et bibliothecae subsidium promptum antea significavi nec muto animum, dum uti velitis.[1176] Gryneum quaeso de Basilicis edendis moneto, quorum interpretationem cum Graecis Freigius dudum illi tradidit. Vale. 10. Februarii 1573.

Gustum aliquot locorum breviter praebebo:[1177]

Nicomachearum in extremo paginae 7 editionis Isingrinianae[1178] nonne verba transposita?[1179] ἐθίζομεν γὰρ καταφρονεῖν τῶν φοβερῶν καὶ ὑπομένειν αὐτά lege γενησόμεθα ἀνδρεῖοι καὶ γενόμενοι μάλιστα lege ἐθιζόμεθα ὑπομένειν etc.[1180]

Paginae 15 tertii libri in extremo, χείρους δ' ὅσῳ ἀξίωμα οὐδέν ἔχουσι alienus [!] est glossema, textus veteris codicis χείρους δ εἰδότες ὑπερορῶσιν, ὥσπερ ἐκεῖνοι, διὸ καὶ μένουσι etc.[1181]

In *Magnorum moralium* 76, 8, περὶ τύχης,[1182] τὸ μὲν γὰρ ἀγαθὸν λαβεῖν ὃ καὶ καθ' αὑτὸ δόξειν εὐτύχημα εἶναι, haec sequentia tamquam ἐπισύναψις[1183] sunt omissa: καὶ ἐν τὸ κακὸν μὴ λαβεῖν εὔλογον· ἀλλὰ μᾶλλον.[1184] ἔστιν οὖν ἡ εὐτυχία τῷ ἀγαθόν τι ὑπάρξαι παρὰ λόγον, adde: καί ἐν τῷ κακὸν μὴ λαβεῖν εὔλογον, ἀλλὰ μᾶλλον etc.[1185] Paullo post: δόξειεν ἂν

[1174] Zwinger's marginal note: "Brutum commendat".
[1175] scattered pieces. Michael Tarchaniota Marullus (c. 1458–1500) was a humanist and neo-Latin poet of Greek origin. His family escaped from Constantinople to Ragusa, when it was captured by the Ottomans. Later, Marullus studied in Italy, travelled through the country and campaigned for war against the Ottomans. Sambucus, among others, obtained an annotated Lucretius-manuscript from Piero Vettori, originally belonging to Marullus. *Humanistes du bassin des Carpates II. Johannes Sambucus*, lviii, 58, 60. The manuscript sent to Zwinger with Bruto was probably his *De principum institutione* (identical with Cod. 9977, f. 107ʳ-122ᵛ, in Vienna, ÖNB), which later got published in Palaeologus, *Praecepta educationis regiae*. On Marullus see Yasmin Haskell, "The Tristia of a Greek Refugee: Michael Marullus and the Politics of Latin Subjectivity after the Fall of Constantinople (1453)," *Proceedings of the Cambridge Philological Society* 44 (1999), 110-136; Karl Enenkel, *Die Erfindung des Menschen: Die Autobiographik des frühneuzeitlichen Humanismus von Petrarca bis Lipsius* (Berlin: De Gruyter, 2008), 368-428; *Michael Marullus: ein Grieche als Renaissancedichter in Italien*, eds. Eckard Lefèvre and Eckart Schäfer (Tübingen: Gunter Narr Verlag, 2008).
[1176] See letter 198.
[1177] Zwinger's interlinear note: "Ethices Aristotelicae loca quaedam prava emendat".
[1178] Zwinger's marginal note: "Ethica σφάλματα corriguntur".
[1179] Ἀριστοτέλους ἅπαντα (Basileae: per Ioannem Bebelium et Michaelem Isingrinium, 1550).
[1180] Aristoteles, *Ethica Nicomachea* 1104b, 1-2.
[1181] Aristoteles, *Ethica Nicomachea* 1117a, 23-24.
[1182] about luck
[1183] a continuation
[1184] Aristoteles, *Magna moralia* 1207a 33-34. Sambucus crossed out this part and in the following applied the same correction to the sentence preceding this one in Aristotle.
[1185] Aristoteles, *Magna moralia* 1207a 30-32.

εὐτύχημα εἶναι adde τὸ δέ κακὸν μὴ λαβεῖν κατὰ συμβεβηκὸς εὐτύχημα· ἔστιν οὖν etc.[1186]
Pagina 289, principium β. περὶ ψυχῆς: τὰ μὲν δὴ etc. Veteres codices tres ita: ἐπεὶ τὰ δὲ παραδεδομένα περὶ ψυχῆς παρὰ τῶν ἄλλων, ἐφ᾽ ὅσον ἕκαστος ἀπεφήνατο, πρότερον εἴρηται σχεδόν, νῦν ὥσπερ ἐξ ἀρχῆς ἐπανίωμεν etc. incipiunt.[1187]

Prodibit Antverpiae propediem Stobaei *Physica* mea,[1188] ex quibus multa quoque loca corrigi poterunt; qui Stobaeus loca Aristotelis et aliorum sententias coacervat. Liber rarus ex mea bibliotheca manavit. Vale.

201.
Antonius Verantius to Sambucus
25 February 1573, Pozsony

Copies are kept in Budapest, OSZK, Fol. Lat. 1681/4, f. 316 (16th century); Eger, Főegyházmegyei Könyvtár, Y.V.21. f. 168. Published in Verancsics [Verantius], Antal, Összes munkái, eds. László Szalay and Gusztáv Wenzel, vol. 11 (Monumenta Hungariae Historica, Scriptores 26), 1572-1573 (Pest: Eggenberger, 1873), 244.

Verantius sent some wine to Sambucus, it will be satisfying. It is appreciated by many and he believes it is worthy of Sambucus's palate. He wanted to make sure Sambucus would not remain disappointed in him. It was sent with delay because of the unusually cold winter; Verantius was worried that the wine would spoil because of freezing. He has received all Sambucus's letters but did not want to answer before he could send the wine from Pressburg once the ice on the Danube had melted. He expresses his thanks for the news that Sambucus sent to him; he should make sure to send news more frequently, especially good news from Poland and about the fleet (of the Holy League). Sambucus should enjoy the Georgian wine and not forget to compose the history of the century with all its confusion and disorder unworthy of Christians.

Ad Ioannem Sambucum.

Misi tibi vinum diu iam donatum, quod, credo, arridebit.[1189] Est enim ex pluribus delectum et mea ipsius censura dignum palatu tuo iudicatum. Adhibui enim peculiare studium, ne te falleret opinio, qua es de mea erga te benevolentia. Quod autem serius sit missum, hyberno tempore, quod frigidissimum habuimus habemusque etiam modo ad stuporem omnium mortalium, prohibitus sum, quemadmodum antea etiam scripsi tibi, metuens, ne vectura gelu fuisset viciatum, quo fere omnia elementa obriguerant.

Litteras tuas, quas ad me dedisti, omnes accepi nec ad eas prius tibi respondere volui data opera, quam Posonium redissem et vinum mittere potuissem Danubio glaciebus resoluto. Ignosce itaque huic tarditati, quae in te non tui incuria, sed iam enumeratis causis commissa est.

[1186] Aristoteles, *Magna moralia* 1207a 34-35.
[1187] Aristoteles, *De anima* 412, 3 and the *app. crit. ad loc.*
[1188] Stobaeus et Plethon, *Stobaei eclogarum libri duo ... et Plethonis de rebus Peloponnesiacis orationes duae.* Cf. "Stobaeus-edition" under "Sambucus" in the Index. This was certainly wishful thinking, perhaps incited by Plantin, since Willem Canter, the editor finished his job only by the end of 1573, as it appears from one of his letters sent to Johannes Crato, in Biblioteka Uniwersytecka we Wrocławiu, R 246, no. 415 (dated 30 December 1572).
[1189] On the Georgian wine promised by Verantius see letter 167.

De novis rebus, quas ad me perscripsisti, habeo gratiam petoque, ut cures, quo in posterum quoque saepius hanc promereare gratiam, et maxime, si quid laeti habueris, quod et ex Polonia expectamus et de classe speramus.[1190] Vale, et Georgiano felix fruere, nos ames, tibi non desis et praesentis saeculi statum cum omnibus suis turbis atque indignissimis Christiano nomine tumultibus memoriae commendare non omittas. Posonii 25. Februarii 1573.

202.
Sambucus to Hugo Blotius
6 March 1573, [Vienna]

The original is kept in ÖNB, Cod. 9737[z14-18], I, f. 218[r]. Published in Menčík, "A Páduában tanuló," 48; Gerstinger, "Die Briefe," 145-146.

A student recommended by Blotius has given Sambucus the letter by Blotius. He has learned enough of the malice of the courier. He complained to courier's brother, who was surprised and confirmed that the money had been delayed the month before. Blotius and Simone should have the opinion of Bassiano and others whether to send the busts together with the chests, if they are not too heavy and nice enough. The statues and the boxes should not be too heavily tied up, as in Venice, as he has heard, they normally open up all the parcels unless one has a certificate from the Paduan magistracy or the tax office. There is Hieronymus Leo, his old friend, close to the Germans' house at Saint Chrysostom Church, who will do anything for Sambucus in Venice. Pál Szegedi erroneously claims that he sent Vettori the (description of) the coronation process; it was about the 16 triumphal arches printed in Antwerp, of which he has no copy at the moment, but will send one to Blotius after the Frankfurt book fair. Finally, Sambucus lists the books that his "library published" since Blotius has been away: Glycas's 126 oriental histories, Manasses's Chronicle and others –but the courier would ask 2 or 3 ducats from Blotius (for their transport). He sends his love back to Listhius Jr., and is happy about Blotius's good opinion of his virtues. His father will pay Blotius back for his efforts. There is some news but it is uncertain and he is not happy to write about it.

Sambucus salutem.

Reddidit mihi studiosus quidem tuas, quem tua caussa et iudicio et mea quoque sponte ac voluntate complexus sum omni officio. De veredarii malitia satis sum edoctus, significavi et obieci fratri iniquum facinus, de quo melius et copiosius essem meritus. Miratur, confirmat pecuniam esse immoratam ante mensem etc.

Amabo te, quem in meis rebus observo esse solicitum, adde ad diligentiam Simonis tuam quoque operam et in pectoribus marmorum simul mittendis vel, si vecturam nimium onerarent nec valde sunt pulchra, istic abiciendis, iudicium amicorum, Basani et aliorum.[1191] Collocatio eorum et in arcas conclusio Patavii non est penitus funibus absolvenda etc., nam audio Venetiis apertum iri eas more solito, nisi a praetore vel telonianis Patavinis testimonium simul demittatur.

[1190] In the aftermatch of Sigismund II Augustus's death in the summer of 1572 Poland was preparing for royal elections, in which Maximilian II was also a candidate.
[1191] See Sambucus's last letters to Blotius in the same subject.

Est prope domum Germanorum ad S. Chrysostomum insignis nobilis Hieronymus Leo, humanus, meus vetus amicus, qui omnia Venetiis mea caussa faciet. Oro, adesto, quoad per alia necessaria licet, his mutis et surdis monimentis; quicquid impenderis, mihi expensum ferto, reddam omnia. Quod Paullus Zegedeus me coronationis pompam Victorio misisse dixerit, errat: est liber Antverpiae excusus meus, in quo sunt 16 arcus triumphales, more antiquo inscriptionibus illustres etc., quorum exemplaria nunc desunt, sed post Nundinas Francfortenses accipiam et alia, mittam vobis.[1192]

Dum abes, edidit bibliothecula nostra Michaelis Glycei 126 orientales historias, Manassis *Chronicon*, de viris illustribus Hesichium, item ad coronationem regis decretorum et consuetudinum librum emendavi, indice et vocum insolentium expositione, praefatione, oratione de coronatione illustravi et auxi,[1193] sed veredarius 3 aut 2 aureos abs te exigeret. Listhium nostrum redamo, iudicium tuum et testimonium de ipsius virtutibus gratissimum est, nec operam ludes apud patrem, si tot promissis responderit. Vale, raptim 6. Martii 1573. Nova varia, sed incerta nec libenter scribo propter certas caussas.

Address: Al Molto Magnifico Dottor Hugo Blozio Maggior Domo del Signor Giovanni Listio Illustre Baron Ongaro. Amico suo. Padoa, in Porczia arente il Signor Dottor Mantua. Cito, Cito. *Blotius's hand (above)*: Ioannes Sambucus Vienna 6. Martii 1573. Patavium. De Capitum marmoreorum missione. *(Underneath)*: Redditae Patavii 14. Martii 5 h[ora?].

203.
Sambucus to Nicasius Ellebodius
26 March 1573, Vienna

The original is kept in Milan, Biblioteca Ambrosiana, D 196 inf., 126[r-v].[1194]

Since Ellebodius received the package with the codex via Philippe de Monte, Sambucus got Ellebodius's letter from De Monte, in which he asks if Sambucus interprets a passage from Gregory of Nazianzus in the same way as Ellebodius. A year ago he sent the printed letters of Nazianzus to Plantin, together with letters by Gregory of Nyssa and John Chrysostom and 500 letters of others, but he does not know what will happen to them. He gives his take on the meaning of the passage from Gregory of Nazianzus and explains some rhetorical terminology.

[1192] See letters 186, 188 and 190 on the same.
[1193] Glycas, *Annales*; Manasses, *Annales*; [Pseudo-]Hesychius, Περὶ τῶν ἐν παιδείᾳ; Werbewcz [Werbőczy], *Tripartitum opus iuris consuetudinarii*; *De corona serenissimi Rudolphi regis Ungariae* (see for the latter two letter 187).
[1194] This letter survived among Pinelli's documents. Ellebodius must have attached it to one of his letters, as it concerned the question about Gregory of Nazianzus, raised by Pinelli. Ellebodius's letters will be published soon by Ádám Szabó, Áron Orbán, and Zsuzsa Kovács.

Sambucus salutem.

Post missum fasciculum Philippo Montano[1195] inscriptum, atque scedula ilico exarata cumque codice prisco vestro tradita, mihi tuae a Philippo aliae mittuntur, quasi ἀντίμετρον[1196] vel potius ἐπίμετρον[1197] in quibus de loco Nazanzeni, ut quidem tu significare vis,[1198] addubitas, ut vero ego arbitror, an tecum sentiam, a quo, si discedam, nisi falli et errare nequeo, explorare vis.[1199] Gregorii epistolas excusas, et alias eiusdem cum Nisseni,[1200] Chrysostomi[1201] et aliorum 500 ante annum Plantino misi. Quid de eo θησαυρῷ[1202] fiat, necdum intelligo.[1203] Itaque ex verbis in epistola tua et harum rerum quadam cognitione atque tractatione mediocri itemque consensu τῶν τεχνογράφων[1204] puto esse sensum:[1205] Qui dilucide res obscuras et ad intelligentiam eorum, quorum intersunt negocia, velit accommodare, legem illi propositam, non modo, ut verborum copia et splendore redundet quasique inflatus sit ac tumeat, sed potius ad persuadendum argumentis docendumque nitatur. Λογοειδὲς[1206] enim ornatum speciemque verborum atque adeo rationum non firmam moventemque adversarium confectionem interpretor; τὸ λογικώτερον δὲ,[1207] argumentosam, pleniorem fidei κατασκευὴν καὶ ἐνέργειαν[1208] nec tam inani et prolixo sermone τὴν σαφήνειαν, καὶ rerum ἑρμηνείαν[1209] constare, quam conglobata caussisque probabilibus coacta ἐργασία.[1210] Huncque sensum esse

---

[1195] Philippe de Monte (1521–1603) Flemish composer active at the imperial court. On Monte see Robert Lindell, "Die Neubesetzung der Hofkapellmeisterstelle am Kaiserhof in den Jahren 1567-1568: Palestrina oder Monte?" *Studien zur Musikwissenschaft* 36 (1985), 35-52.

[1196] compensation (a measure in turn)

[1197] addition (something added in excess)

[1198] Gregory of Nazianzus (c. 329–389 or 390) was Archbishop of Constantinople, widely considered the most accomplished rhetorical stylist of the patristic age. As a classically trained orator and philosopher he infused Hellenism into the early church.

[1199] A month before, Ellebodius wrote the following lines to Gian Vincenzo Pinelli: "Sono infelice di non poter trovare Nazianzeno per veder il luoco che V. S. mi scrive. Pur per quanto posso congetturare de le poche parole che V. S. mi scrive, pare che voglia dire che la oratione debba essere chiara, di modo però, che non sia come il parlare quotidiano, ma più erudita. Perché, si bene la oratione a[v]rà τὸ σαφὲς accostandosi a la κοινὰ λεξία, a[v] rà però τὸ ταπεινὸν, che bisogna fuggere. Ma non posso bene giudicare, si non veddo tutto il luoco." 8 February 1573, Pressburg. Milano, Biblioteca Ambrosiana, D 196 inf., f. 43ʳ⁻ᵛ. In the same letter Ellebodius writes the following words concerning Sambucus: "io credevo di potere mandare a Vostra Signoria le Epitome di Polybio, corrette, che sa Vostra Signoria quanto siano scorrette; et il Sambuco me gli aveva promesso, ma fin ora non ha fatto niente, scusandosi la sua malatia. Io pur insisto e spero che otterrò, et a Vostra Signoria mandarò ogni chosa. Ho mandato a Vostra Signoria certe poche correttioni sopra i primi libri di Polybio, havute pur da Sambuco."

[1200] Like Gregory of Nazianzus, Bishop Gregory of Nyssa (c. 335–c. 395) was one of the Cappadocian Fathers. His theology was influenced by Plotinus and Origen. Laurentius Sifanus published different manuscripts by Gregory of Nyssa from Sambucus's collection. See *Humanistes du bassin des Carpates II. Johannes Sambucus*, lxvi-lxix, 96-101.

[1201] John Chrysostom (c. 349–407) was among the most prolific authors in the early Christian Church. See recently J. H. W. G. Liebeschuetz, *Ambrose and John Chrysostom. Clerics between Desert and Empire* (Oxford: OUP, 2012).

[1202] treasure

[1203] On this failed publication project see letter 289, note 1686.

[1204] writers on the art of rhetoric

[1205] The passage in question is from Gregory of Nazianzus's 51ˢᵗ letter (3-4), where he discusses the art of letter-writing.

[1206] prosaic

[1207] but rather argumentative

[1208] preparation and working out

[1209] clearness and the interpretation of things

[1210] work, exercise

posteriora duo verba testantur, τὰ μήκη συνιζάνειν,[1211] qui audiri[1212] volunt et persuadere, quae redundant, esse castiganda, fusa debiliter contrahenda sistendaque esse fide. Συνιζάνειν[1213] enim constituere, certo loco ponere, velutque locare sede significo. Videturque, ut Synesius alicubi, affectationem καὶ τὸ γοργιαῖον ἢ γοργιάζειν notare[1214].

Atque hanc esse mentem theologi ex rhetorum de his praeceptis quoque patet. Qui inter καθαρότητα,[1215] quae τῇ περιβολῇ[1216] est contraria, καὶ εὐκρίνειαν σαφήνειαν[1217] ponunt, ὡς ἀκρίβειαν[1218] temperatam ad credendum, non vanis rebus, et praeter rem accersitis nugis longiusque ductis, sed domi natis argumentis etc. Haec obiter, dum tibi vicissim satisfacere cupio, occurrere. Ἔρρωσο εἰς εὐγηρίαν ὡς εὐμηκεστατήν.[1219] 26 Martii 1573.

Address: Clarissimo viro domino doctori Nicasio Ellebodio, amico singulari. Posonium apud reverendissimum Agriensem.

204.
Antonius Verantius to Sambucus
20 April 1573, Pozsony

A copy is kept in Eger, Főegyházmegyei Könyvtár, Y.V.17-27. Published in Verancsics, *Összes munkái*, 11:306-308.

Verantius received Sambucus's letter of the 4th April and gives thanks for the news in it. He is especially happy that the emperor got better. The Ottoman legate demanded faster shipping of the (annual) "gifts" and wanted to know, if anything was going on in Styria. He should not be allowed to go to Friuli through Styria, he can travel through Dalmatia, if he wants to. The Danube starts flooding and Verantius is worried that it may cover the Csallóköz and form a lake. The Polish royal election is far too long. Hopefully it will not be like in the case of women; the longer they deliberate the worse decision they take. One cannot even tell if they will stay with the Austrian House. If they accept a Russian, they will be slaves; if a native one, there will be civil wars, as after John Zápolya's crowning in Hungary. It will be the same, whether they elect among the Habsburgs Ernest, Matthias, or Maximilian. Verantius favours Archduke Ernest for this role. He believes that the rumours about a Tartar or Ottoman campaign are ominous. But if the Ottomans really make an unfortunate peace with Venice, they will make sure to regain their strength in two years both at sea and on the ground. This is his opinion. The peace between Venice and the Ottomans is certainly painful for the Christians. But God should punish those (i.e. the Venetians) who cause public disaster because of private interests. If only Christian states stopped fighting among themselves and prepared more seriously against the Ottomans. This was in reply to Sambucus's last letter. He is now performing missions that take ten times more energy than the prestige they bring him. He is too old for such tasks.

[1211] to compress what is long
[1212] Instead of the crossed out *percipi*.
[1213] settle down
[1214] Gorgias's style, or to speak like Gorgias
[1215] purity
[1216] exaggeration
[1217] and limpidity of style, perspicuity
[1218] precision
[1219] Be strong well into a green old age, as great as possible.

The emperor and the local nobility, however, should be served and gratified. He needs some rhubarb in order to preserve his good health and asks Sambucus to obtain one or two pieces for him.

Ad Sambucum.

Litteras tuas 4. Aprilis datas accepi, tibique habeo gratias de novis rebus. Atque imprimis laetatus sum allevari caesarem ab aegritudine. Turcae nuntius duo curavit, ut coniicio: muneris honorarii celeriorem expeditionem et si quid per Styriam hinc moliatur. Iter ei in Forum Iulium per Styriam non est concedendum. In Dalmatiam, quum vult, per Bosnam semper potest descendere, cui imminet a monte Scardo, in quo Bosna est sita. Illuvies Danubii nimis et hic apud nos latissime grassari, idque quotidie coepit. Ac vereor, ne nobis insulam Challokewz obruat,[1220] et in lacum diffundatur. Polonia nimis iam diu regem sibi parturit. Utinam illi non contingat, quod mulierum ingenio, quae diuturnius delectui rerum inhaerentes deteriora deligunt. Nec sapiet, si excidet ab Domo Austriae. Et si Moscum admittet, serviet; si indigenam, seditionibus ardebit, ut Hungaria Ioanni Scepusiensi collatis sceptris.[1221] Idem autem erit illi, aut Hernestum, aut Mathiam, aut Maximilianum deligat et cooptet. Ut tamen et parentis censura locum habeat, et ordine tanti fratres promoveantur ad regna, existimarem rite facturam, si Hernestum deliget, iam et aetate et iudicio maturum populis moderandis.[1222] De rumoribus vero Tartarorum, immo et de ipsorum Turcarum terrestribus apparatibus, minas esse arbitror, quam quod serio talia machinentur. Quoniam si revera pax eis constiterit cum Venetis, curabit initio, ut vel ad biennium quiete et otio vires instauret. Idque tam mari, quam terra. Haec mea est de his opinio. De pace tamen Venetorum et Turcae dolendum est haud dubie Christianitati. Deus tamen illis male faciat, qui privatae passionis causa publico ruinam struunt. Utinam quidam Christiani status desinerent aliquando inter sese bellis decertare et sincerius in communem hostem armarentur et coniungerentur, quam nunc. Et haec ad tuas proximas.

Hinc ego, quod ad te possem, nihil habeo. Nisi quod Epergesium[1223] ad iudicia celebranda iter paro, non admodum libenter. Sed necessitas muneris cogit. Quod quantum honoris et authoritatis mihi attulit, decuplo pluribus laboribus, curis et vigiliis exercet, nullis compensat utilitatibus et satis lucri faciam, si quampiam aegritudinem non contraxero, valde iam senior et imbecilior factus ad negotia. Caesari tamen inserviendum est et nobilitati earum partium gratificandum. Ut autem valetudinem curem, bono ac recenti indigeo rhabarbaro teque peto diligenter, da operam, ut aut unum aut duo frusta quam optimi emas et mittas mihi quam primum per hunc meum iuvenem, cui pecuniam quoque credidi ad emendum.[1224] Quod totum fiet tuo iussu. Et bene valeas. Posonii 20. Aprilis 1573.

[1220] Csallóköz (Žitný ostrov) is a long isle on the Danube south-east of Bratislava.
[1221] John Szapolyai (Zapolya) was king of Hungary (1526–1540), elected and crowned by a part of the nobility in 1526. Since the nobility of the western regions acknowledged Ferdinand I as their king, the Battle of Mohács was followed by a long civil war between the two kings.
[1222] For a while, Archduke Ernest of Austria (1553–1595) was a popular candidate among aristocrats, but the szlachta did not back him. See Almut Bues, *Die habsburgische Kandidatur für den polnischen Thron während des Ersten Interregnums in Polen 1572/1573* (Phil. Diss., Univ. of Vienna, 1984).
[1223] He might mean the Eperjes (Prešov) church district.
[1224] Cf. letter 354.

205.
Sambucus to Theodor Zwinger
1 July 1573, [Vienna]

The original is kept in Basel, Universitätsbibliothek, Frey Mscr II 26, no. 215. Published in Gerstinger, "Die Briefe," 146-148.

He repeats what he wrote earlier concerning the edition of Aristotle: he would send Zwinger all that he has, when a good occasion to send it safely arises. He hardly has time to look for the variants himself, so he will send the codices in order that the edition suffer no delay. He would happily entrust the books to a public courier but they usually charge a lot of money. He will speak with the Cologne post master and Crato and do what he can. He has not heard of the Hippocrates-edition. If Pietro Perna published Vegetius, he would not mind. The military tract that Perna wants to add to it is not by Publius but Flavius Vegetius. Sambucus asks Zwinger to help Perna, if he publishes Vegetius. If Giovanni Michele Bruto is in Basel, Zwinger should greet him in his name. Bruto should write to Sambucus what he wants to publish. He has not seen letters from Perna but has heard that Perna is also working on emendation of Aristotle. Zwinger should greet him and the Episcopius. He should tell Episcopius that Jacques Cujas's codex is worse than his; he knows where Cujas has taken it from. Cujas wanted to hide his own involvement in getting the variants via some Paduan friends, but Sambucus rejected this request; but this is meant only for Zwinger and Episcopius. It is strange that publishers are so lazy about such things. But Episcopius should at least print the first few pages for the Frankfurt book fair.

Clarissimo viro domino Zvingero Sambucus salutem.

Et antea significavi pluribus de Aristotelis editione,[1225] quis sit meus sensus, et nunc idem cupio meaque omnia subsidia mittam.[1226] Sit modo ratio et tuta per certos homines occasio mittendi. Nam ut singula ex codicibus exscribam, conferam, mihi vix nunc tantum ocii esset, moram vero editio fortassis etiam vix ferret. Si iubetis, cursori publico committam, id libenter faciam, sed multum exigere solent. Loquar hac etiam de re cum magistro Coloniensi et expeditore atque adeo Cratone his diebus nihilque negligam, quae commodo publico debere me amicisque intelligo. De Hippocrate nihil audio.[1227] Perna si Vegetium ediderit, non perdet operam. Quod autem de re militari addenda censet, nisi ipse fallor, in autore aberrat, quod ille alius sit, hoc est, Publius Vegetius, hic Flavius Vegetius.[1228] Si manum adhibuerit, oro te pro amicitia, quod poteris, iuva. Si Ioannes Michael Brutus istic est, salvere iubeto, quidque pariat, edat, ad me scribat.[1229] Pernae literas non vidi, audio tamen et ipsum moliri

---

[1225] Cf. letter 198.
[1226] Zwinger's marginal notes: "Sambucus Aristotelis editionem iuvare paratus est."
[1227] See Gerstinger, "Zusammenfassung," 307-308 and cf. the index under "Sambucus. Hippocrates-edition" Zwinger's edition of Hippocrates finally came out in 1579.
[1228] Zwinger's marginal note: "Distinguuntur Vegetii quoad materias." Today, the two have been proven to be one person, Publius Flavius Vegetius Renatus (4-5th c. A.D.), author of both the *Mulomedicina* and the *Epitoma rei militaris*. Flavius was only a honorific title, conferred for his civil or military services. See Sabin H. Rosenbaum, "Who was Vegetius?," published in https://www.academia.edu/5496690/Who_was_Vegetius (accessed on 01 May 2023), where Rosenbaum also provides an analysis of the *Mulomedicina*. Cf. "Vegetius-edition" under "Sambucus" in the Index.
[1229] This sentence is written on the bottom of the page and inserted into the text with an asterisk. See letter 200.

Aristoteleam emendare impressionem.[1230] Vale et Pernae Episcopianisque salutem. Kalendis Quinctilibus 1573.

Dic Episcopianis Cuiacii codicem esse nostro deteriorem,[1231] nam unde ille habuerit, scimus, et ex meo tecto nomine quaedam corrigi per amicos Patavinos cupiit, ego negavi. Sed haec tibi et Episcopio tantum. Miror tam esse dites vel potius lentos typographos, ut talia non curent. Metuo, si mora longior inciderit, ne alii antevortant editionem. Sed mone unam atque alteram paginam frontis tamquam incohatae editionis specimen proferant Francforti, si ad nundinas non exierit. Iterum vale.

206.
Sambucus to Johann Sommer, Mayor of Trnava
2 July 1573, Vienna

The original is kept in Trnava, SAT, Magistrát mesta Trnava, Missiles. Published in Vantuch, "Die Sambucusbriefe," 350-351.

The 100 florins had not been paid to him by the feast of Saint John the Baptist. Sambucus received a short letter, in which (Imre Kalmár) says he does not have the money but wants to give him an adequate pledge and the yearly interests that go with it. Sambucus is wholly against pledges with interests, which the Jews use. He asks instead for the help of the Council to have the money paid back as soon as possible, since Kalmár swore in front of the magistracy. If he has such a good pledge, he will also find the money paid for it, or sell it. If Sambucus does not get the money in eight or ten days, he will do what is right and force him to pay with an imperial mandate. It is time to pay a debt going back to 15 years earlier, also because he has debts too. (The letter is addressed to Sommer, but if he is not there, it should be read to István Nyilas.)

Edler gunstiger Her und vertrauter froundt:

die 100 taller hatt mir seinem angelob noch gor niht richtig gemacht auff Johanys.[1232] So schreybt er mir erst ein brieflein er hob das gelt niht,[1233] und wöll mir ein gnugsams pfandt geben, und järlich darfon Zinzen. Ich bin gor nicht des sins, daz ich mitt pfandt verzinzens, wie ain Jud, umbgee, wierts auch nicht erfare. Sondern ich beger mitt eurer herren Richter und pillikhait anriffung und hilff, mein gelt alspald, wie er dan vor euch angelobt hatt. Hatt er

---

[1230] Perna was planning a complete edition of Aristotle's works from at least 1569, but except for the publication of the *Poetics* in the edition of Lodovico Castelvetro in 1576 (and Vettori's *Politica*-edition in 1582, see letter 159), it remained unrealised. See Perna's letter to Vettori from 1569 in *Clarorum Italorum et Germanorum epistolae*, 2:33-36.

[1231] Zwinger's marginal note: "Cuiacii codex qualis." Although Sambucus does not name Cujas earlier, his worries about a rival edition of the *Basilica* concerned probably worries about Cujas's activity, who had already published some fragments of it (like in 1566) and also used it for the different editions of his *Observationes et emendationes*. See Stolte, "Joannes Leunclavius." On one of the most celebrated French legal humanists, leader of the "historical school," Jacques Cujas, distinguished philologist, owner of a large library and teacher of many of Sambucus's contemporaries and friends see Xavier Prévost, *Jacques Cujas (1522–1590), Jurisconsulte humaniste* (Geneva: Droz, 2015).

[1232] 24 June.

[1233] See letters 191, 207, 209 and 211.

so guette pfandt, wirtt woll gelt drauff finden, oder zu verkhauffen wissen. Wo ich mein gelt von dato 8 oder 10 tag niht hab, so wier ich thuen wos recht ist, und meine unkhostn schadn etc. vorwortn mitt einbringen mussen, irre khaiserliche Majestät befelch nach. Verhoff herr Richter, die Herrn werden solchen furkhomen, und in zu der zollung nöten. Dan ich auch schuldig bin, und ein solchs gelt von 15 jaren woll zeytt zu endtrichten. Solches hob ich den herrn mitt bitt, weyterer schadens und unglimpf zu verhietn, wolln schreybn und bitt, verhoff gantzlich von herrn, und durch den herrn das gelt zu nachst zu empfahen. Schikh ich dan darumb, so wiert der unkhost, und schadn nur sein. Datum 2 Iulii 1573. Eurer Herrschaften Diener und allzeit D. Sambucus manu propria.

Address: Egregio domino Ioanni Sommer, iudici Tyrnaviensi etc. domino et amico honorando. Tyrnaviam. Eo absente domino Stephano Nylas legantur.

207.
Sambucus to the Mayor and councillors of Trnava
22 July 1573, Vienna

The original is kept in Trnava, SAT, Magistrát mesta Trnava, Missiles. Published in Vantuch, "Die Sambucusbriefe," 351-352.

Sambucus complains about the unjust way Imre Kalmár treats him, not paying the debt of 100 florins by the promised date, and he wonders why the Council does not make him pay. Sambucus would have accepted payment in wine and wheat, but Kalmár refused and promised to pay in money. If the Council has no problem with Kalmár's delay, what can he do? Now, in the middle of the harvest and close to grape-gathering it is certainly not timely to transport wine and wheat to him. He asks the city to pay him the debt. If he had no faith in their help, he would know how to get paid. He knows how to get his money, but has not yet acted out of respect for the city. If he does not even merit to be repaid what belongs to him, how can he hope for more from the city? He begs the city to get Kalmár to pay him, otherwise he will attain it himself, which may be a nuisance for some people.

Egregii domini, amici observandissimi, salutem et mei commendationem.

Quam inique et immerite tracter a domino Emerico Kalmar vestro iudicio permitto[1234] ac valde miror, cum sit dominationum vestrarum concivis, et isti 100 floreni a vobis quasi proficiscantur, seseque ad festum Ioannis iureiurando de pecunia parata obilgavit, tamen non cogatis ad solutionem. Antea et vinum et triticum accepissem, tunc noluit et presenti pecunia mihi satisfacturum ad intercessionem amicorum est pollicitus. Nunc nihil fit ac dominationes vestrae ipsius nuda dilatione contenta est [!]. Si vestrae dominationes nolunt ad paratam pecuniam cogere taliter obstrictum, ego quid agam? Certe mihi vini et tritici huc vectandi tempus non est, minus si initio recusavit, nunc in messe et vindemiae vicinis talibus occupari possum. Rogo dominationes vestras per humanitatem et iustitiam, ut mihi 100 floreni numerentur. Nam in vobis spes est tota, qui certo talem summan apud eum mihi consignastis. Libentissime amicis parco, sed ista nimia est pacientia, et quibus haec narro, non omnino factis probant. Nolo res

---
[1234] See letters 206, 209 and 211.

eius et utensilia aestimentur, nam id prius fieri debebat. Sed ducit me spe satis molesta et, nisi respectum vestri haberem, scirem omne damnum et sumptus recuperare. Si de dominationibus vestris nihil plus meritus sum, quam ut meum mihi non curetis reddi, quid ulterius de vestra liberalitate et patrocinio mihi sperandum est? Oro igitur ilico 100 florenos imperetis et ad iusiurandum et promissum coram iudice liberandum cogatis, aut aliter providebo et forte non parva molestia aliquorum. Quibus me commendo 22 Iulii 1573. Dominationum vestrarum egregiarum cliens et amicus D. Sambucus manu propria.

Address: Egregiis ac circumspectis dominis iudici iuratisque civibus civitatis Tyrnaviensis, dominis et amicis observandissimis. Tyrnaviae.

208.
Abraham Ortelius to Sambucus
1 August 1573, Antwerp

Dedication in Abraham Ortelius, *Deorum dearumque capita. Ex vetustis numismatibus in gratiam antiquitatis studiosorum effigiata et edita* (Antwerp: Ex musaeo Abrahami Ortelii, 1573), Aii^r.

Since his childhood, driven by his nature or some kind of "genius" and despite his modest situation, Ortelius has collected and taken delight in antique coins. He dedicates these first common fruits of his collection to Sambucus in memory of his visit to Antwerp, when he was coming back from Italy and aiming for England. It is not because these coins can be useful to Sambucus, who has many of this type and has collected so many antiquities (including metal and marble statues of this kind of gods and goddesses) in Italy and elsewhere that he has almost despoiled Italy of them, as he claims, but to serve as a memorial to their friendship.

Clarissimo viro, domino Ioanni Sambuco imperatoriae maiestatis historico, Abrahamus Ortelius salutem.

Quum ego ab ineunte aetate, naturae quodam, an cuius genii nescio ductu, citra mea studia et occupationes, etsi mihi fortuna satis tenuis et ingenium exile fuerit, semper mihi tamen soleam huiusmodi antiqua numismata comparare iisdemque tanquam studiorum delitiis, (nam sic ea libenter et non immerito (ut mihi videtur) recte appellaverim) oblectari. Tibique eo nomine, doctissime Sambuce, quum tu ex Italia rediens hinc Albionem petebas,[1235] primum innotuerim, non potui non has nostras eius generis primitias, ex iisdem nostris antiquitatis monumentis productas, tuae humanitati dedicare. Non quod haec tibi aut tuis Musis utilitati aut ornatui esse posse putaverim, ut qui ipsa numismata (sive prototypa), unde haec ectypa sumpta sunt, abunde possideas et praeter omnem venerendae antiquitatis supellectilem, quam tanta copia in Italia aliisque tuis peregrinationibus, ut iis ipsam Italiam quodammodo expilasse dicebaris,

---

[1235] This is the only source for Sambucus's desire to visit England. On the first contact between Ortelius and Sambucus see letter 41. We do not know if they kept in touch in the second part of the 1560s, before Sambucus started sending Ortelius some maps, of which Ortelius published a few in his *Theatrum Orbis Terrarum* (see letter 153, note 912). In 1580 Sambucus sent his engraved portrait of four years earlier to Abraham Ortelius, which also held the legend of his full title engraved. See Ortelius, *Epistulae*, 892.

etiam ex aere et marmoribus huiusmodi deorum dearumque statuas, signa et sigilla tibi ad miraculum usque congesseris, sed ut hic noster partus qualis qualis sit, duntaxat amicitiae et benevolentiae mnemosynon inter nos extaret. Vale, vir ornatissime. Antverpiae, MDLXXIII. Kalendis Augusti.[1236]

209.
Sambucus to the Mayor and the Council of Trnava
21 August 1573, Vienna

The original is kept in Trnava, SAT, Magistrát mesta Trnava, Missiles. Published in Vantuch, "Die Sambucusbriefe," 352-353.

Sambucus asks if this is his fate or the consequence of Kalmár's negligence or malevolence that his 100 florins have not been paid. He pleaded with the Council, the payment was promised by 24 June, but despite his merits with regard to the city and some of its inhabitants in particular, he has seen nothing of the money. It is in the hands of the Council. If Kalmár has properties, he can make money out of them. How could Sambucus sell anything from the distance? When earlier he asked for properties from Kalmár, Kalmár had not wanted to give him any, and the Council had advised Sambucus to wait for the money.

Salutem et servitiorum debitam commendationem.

Nescio fatone meo, an vestra iniuria vel potius negligentia, ne dicam malevolentia, Emerici Kalmar 100 florenos non impetro.[1237] Toties supplicavi vobis, tot termini sunt dati, maior vestrum pars pro eo ad certos dies intercessit, pollicita est pecuniam paratam, fide publice promisit ad festum Baptistae summam integram: nihil video magna admiratione et praeter merita mea in rempublicam vestram et singulos. Est in manibus vestris. Vos eum ad liberandam fidem cogere et satisfactionem cur non potestis? Quod si agris, vineis et aliis similibus satisfacere velit, ubi fides, vestramet promissa, ubi mea paciencia, respectus et autoritas vestra? Adhuc oro per ius et vestram amiciciam, meum uti quamprimum habeam, ne cogar contra moram et damnum alia via procedere. Si fundos, vina, triticum habet, nonne potest invenire pretium? Quomodo ego venderem absens, qui cum talia antea ab eo petii, numquam dare voluit et vos simul, ut moram exiguam expectarem de pecunia numerata, admonuistis. Rogo responsum dominationum vestrarum, quid spei sit de pecunia sciatis [?][1238], quibus me in maioribus commendo. 21. Augusti 1573 Viennae. Vestrarum dominationum servitor et amicus Ioannes Sambucus manu propria.

Address: Egregiis, prudentibus ac circumspectis dominis, iudici totique senatui Tyrnaviensium, dominis et patronis observandissimis. Tyrnaviam. Byro uramnak.[1239] Cito, cito.

[1236] In the copy of the ÖNB (ZALT PRUNK 45.S.67) Sambucus's handwritten note reads "Maximilliano II. domino, domino suo semper clementissimo. Clientulus Ioannes Sambucus MDLXXIII."
[1237] See letters 206-207 and 211-212.
[1238] Gerstinger: *scietis*.
[1239] "To the mayor."

210.
Sambucus to Abraham Ortelius
2 September 1573, Vienna

Published in *Abrahami Ortelii et virorum eruditorum... epistulae*, 104-105.

Sambucus is very grateful for the extraordinary gift of the Theatrum Orbis Terrarum *and for the* Deorum dearumque capita. *If Ortelius is of the same mind as Sambucus was many years before, he should add other images to a next edition. If Ortelius's colleagues, especially in Bruges, do not have them, he will send copies of the gods Bacchus and Harpocrates and different illustrations of Zeus from different regions. Sambucus goes on to list other images of virtues and gods illustrated by his coins. He has an elaborate map of Poland, indicating the dioceses and other chief places, which was elegantly made by friends and which he emended himself. It was meant for Archduke Ernest in case he won the election. He will send the map to Ortelius the next time, or from time to time in several parts. He asks Ortelius to urge the person who has his "museum" (i.e. the* Icones*) in his hands. If the money runs out, Sambucus will send more. He is sending Ortelius a ring with an uncommon gem. Ortelius should ask Plantin to buy for Sambucus Ximenes's history of Spain printed four years ago and ask again the son of the English doctor about the manuscripts and their price.*

Sambucus salutem.

De *Theatro*, non vulgari, ut tu extumes, munere, itemque deorum imaginibus te vehementer amo habeoque gratiam, dum beneficio maiori redimam.[1240] Et quando in istam mentem ductus es, quae mea quoque ante multos annos fuit, oro, proximae editioni, plures si tibi sunt, addas, sin istis, quod non opinor, vestri carent, praesertim Brugenses, rescribe, exempla curabo de meis, habens Bacchum, Harpocratem silentiosum, Magnum Deum aliter, aliquot regionum, ut Siciliae, Hispaniae, Parthiae, Latii, Ocii, Pomonae, Libitinae, Furiarum etc. Deinde secus factas effigies Victoriae Augusti alatae, Spei, Virtutis seu Fortitudinis, Trium dearum Monetarum cum metallis, Aequitatis, Iani, Apollinis, Aesculapii, Pudicitiae ex Faustina, Iovis Capitolini, Iovis Anxurii barbati, nam tuus imberbis est contra notionem, ut videtis etc.

Poloniam iustissimam, et vere integris locorum potiorum sitibus et fundamentis ad vivum expressam, dignitatibus dioecesium et palatinatus sacrorumque distinctam habeo. Quam non levi amicorum opera et labore emendationeque nostra passim adornavi, depingendam, elegantissime curavi. Quam si suffragia nobis successissent, Ernesto archiduci destinaram.[1241] Sed eam mittam proxime ad te totam, aut pluribus partibus per vices. Preterea si quid erit, a me prompta vobis semper erunt. Oro te, cohortere eum, qui *Museolum* nostrum prae manibus habeat, ut urgeat opus.[1242] Ubi ad extremum erit, munus illi denuo mittam. Tibi vero nunc

---

[1240] The *Theatrum Orbis Terrarum* was first issued in 1570, Ortelius must have sent him the second edition of 1572. In his library we find only the 1579 edition (Gulyás, *Sámboky János könyvtára*, 1839).

[1241] During the election of 1573, Archduke Ernest was the Habsburg candidate in Poland. See letter 204.

[1242] The original etcher of the *Icones veterum aliquot* (of which Ortelius received a copy from Plantin on 28 September 1574) was Antonio Abondio, yet we do not know whether any of his woodcuts were eventually included in the album (see letters 148, 154, 156 and 158). A note preserved in Plantin's collections suggests that the illustrator was Pieter van der Borcht the Elder, but Rooses believes that he was not the only etcher. See the introduction in the facsimile edition of Max Rooses (*Icones veterum aliquot*, Antwerp: Nederlandsche Boekh, 1901). Also see Vida, "A reneszánsz orvostörténeti."

levidense δωρημάτιον[1243] istum annulum mitto, auro non copiosum, lapillo non vulgari, et ad studia cogitationumque occupationes usitato proprioque, quem ornabo proxime aliquo numo vetusto aureo. Vale et mone Plantinum, ut Ximenii Hispanicas historias mihi emat, Compluti ante 4 annos excusas,[1244] et medici Angli filium de libris manuscriptis iterum moneat, qui libri et quo pretio sint. 2 Septembris 1573.

Address: Domino Abramo Ortelio, cosmographo industrio amico suo. Ad Cervulum non procul a Fuggeris.[1245]

211.
Sambucus to Johann Sommer
6 September 1573, Vienna

The original is kept in Trnava, SAT, Magistrát mesta Trnava, Missiles. Published in Vantuch, "Die Sambucusbriefe," p. 353.

Sambucus has still not received an answer from Imre Kalmár. The letter (attached) should be shown only to Sommer's brother-in-law. His wife asks the wife of Sommer to buy for her "hair" for spinning for 2 florins, which is rare in Vienna and is in good quality in Trnava, and she will return the big favour in the future. He wrote to István Nyilas long ago but has not received any reply.

Mein dinst zuvor:

Hob noch khain beschaidt von dem herren oder Kalmar Imre:[1246] ich hob gnug gepettn: wills glaich dorbei lassn beruen. Das Briflein allen auff eures schwagers anzaigen. Wunsch yberall glukh. Meiner hausfraw gor hochvertrautte bitt an eure hausfrawn, die wöll umb ain 2 fl. schön har zu spinnen khauffen: den man hieher yetzo gor seltn bringt und man hatt sie yberredt, der har daniden bey euch und umb auch sey gor guett etc. Wert mir grossn dinst thuen, und mein hausfraw hatt sich erpatt, eurer hausfrawn in grössern zu gffallen widerumb zu sein. Hob den hern Nylas längst geschriben: siech aber nihts. Khumbt dan etwas, ist es pesser. Khundt bey den M. Egidi oder pust herauff shikhn.[1247] Damit wos euch und den euren lieb ist. Den 6 September 1573. Euer vertrauter allzeit D. Sambucus.

Address: Dem edlen ehrnvesten Herrn Hansn Sommer etc., meinen gunstigen froundt zuhänden Tierna.

[1243] a small gift
[1244] *De rebus gestis a Francisco Ximenio, archiepiscopo Toletano, libri VIII* (Compluti: Andreas de Angulo, 1569). Sambucus needed the book for his planned edition of *De rebus gestis a Francisco Ximenio Cisnerio*.
[1245] I.e. the Fugger agents in Antwerp.
[1246] See letters 207, 209 and 212.
[1247] We do not know the person in question.

212.

Sambucus to Johann Sommer
8 September 1573, Vienna

The original is kept in Trnava, SAT, Magistrát mesta Trnava, Missiles. Published in Vantuch, "Die Sambucusbriefe," p. 354.

Sambucus cannot do without the payment of 10 florins. This would mean that he only loses on the affair. The man (i.e. Kalmár) claimed to have given 20 florins of (the debt) to Márton Szabó, but he should only have received 15, since 5 should be given to Martin Scoda. The rest, i.e. 80 florins, should be sent to Vienna, as Sambucus has been made a fool of for long enough. If Márton Szabó remains in his trade, he can surely make a living.

Mein dienst zuvor:

die 10 fl. khan ich gor niht nachlassn, dan ich woll mer unkhost und verdruss gehabt; derhalben ich die 10 taller[1248] hoben will;[1249] das aber der Her 20 taller dem Sabo Marton dorfon gegebn: hob 15 gesagt,[1250] doch weyll es geschehn ist, so geb er dem Martin Scoda die 5 darfon.[1251] Das rest, bitt ich, das ist 80 fl. shikt mir auffs ehst, dorffs woll selbst und bin gewitzigt gnug worden. Pleyb Sabo Marton bei seinem handtwerkh, er khan sein narung woll gevislich gewinnen. Damit [?] was den herrn lieb ist. Den 8. September 1573. Den Herrn vertrauter allzeit [?] J. Samboki.

Address: Dem Edlen Ehrenvesten Herrn Hansn Sommer etc. meinem gunstigen Herrn und froundt zuhänden.

213.

Sambucus to Piero Vettori
26 October 1573, Vienna

The original is kept in Munich, BSB, Clm 735, Nr. 73. Published in Bandini, *Clarorum Italorum et Germanorum*, 2:69-70; Gerstinger, "Die Briefe," 148-149.

Friendships joined together by common intellectual interests do not break because of the interval of time or minor offenses. So he gives this letter to the young and noble secretary (of the duke of Florence, Belisarius Vinta) with whom he spent great time together in order to encourage Vettori in his edition of the much awaited Politica *(of Aristotle). If Vettori did not get his books from Frankfurt, Sambucus will send them by fast courier. He recently "divulged" the images of gods and goddesses taken from antique coins together with some Greek annalists coming from his "Museum" and from cosmographic tables. Next time Vettori will receive the* Basilica, *the*

[1248] I.e. Hungarian florins.
[1249] Since Sambucus wrote his last letter (see the preceding letter) he must have received an answer concerning Imre Kalmár, in which he was offered 90 florins. See letters 207 and 209.
[1250] Cf. with letter 191.
[1251] We do not know either Márton Szabó or Martin Scoda.

emended Mulomedicina *of Vegetius and Stobaeus's* Physical and Moral Extracts. *He is sending his greetings to Pál Szegedi, Vettori's neighbour.*

Domino Petro Victorio Sambucus salutem.

Quae animorum συμμετρίᾳ[1252] studiorumque similitudine quadam necessitudo semel coiit, nullis intervallis ea neque silentio aut impedimentis incurrentibus deminui solet, ut, si quid leviter offensiunculae interdum acciderit, amoris eam potius, quam irae fuisse redintegrationem videamus. Itaque discessuro nobilissimo iuveni secretario vestro, qui, cum mihi suavis et prolixa fuit consuetudo, has adiunxi, ut ad *Politicorum* editionem, in quorum exspectatione diu sumus, te cohortarer.[1253] Meas nugas, si ad vos Francforto non pertinere scirem, vel per celeres mitterem. Nuper deorum dearumque gentilium effigies e numis expressas divulgavi, cum quibusdam chronographis Graecis, meo *Museo*[1254] et cosmographicis tabellis.[1255] Proxime τὰ Βασιλικὰ[1256] et veterinariam Vegetii emendatam accipies ipsiusque Stobaei τὰ´ Φυσικά.[1257] Ἔρρωσο, γέρον, περὶ ἁπάντων μὲν τ᾽ ἀγαθὰ καὶ καλὰ ἀκριβῶς ἔχον, τὰ δὲ τῶν παλαιῶν συγγράμματα ἐξονυχίζον καὶ εὖ μάλα φρονῶν καὶ εὖ αὐτοῖς ἀεὶ ὁμιλήσας.[1258] 7. Kalendas Novembris 1573 Viennae.

Paullum Zeghedeum vicinum, ut audio, tuum, a me, si libet, salvere iubetis.

Address: Clarissimo viro domino Petro Victorio, amico observandissimo. Florentiam.

214.
Sambucus to Hubertus Goltzius
13 November 1573, Vienna

Published in Hubertus Goltzius, *Caesar Augustus sive historiae imperatorum caesarumque Romanorum ex antiquis numismatibus restitutae liber secundus* (Brugis Flandrorum: [Goltzius], 1574), f. Nnii^r.

Sambucus praises the thick numismatic volume by Goltzius and his talent and efforts in general, of which he learned ten years earlier when he spent time with him. In the cult of antiquity Germany now equals Italy, and first place goes in particular to Belgium; an example is provided by the industry of Goltzius and the Laurinus brothers, lords of Watervliet Clinckerland, Goltzius's patrons, whom Sambucus had met personally. Goltzius is the complete opposite of petty antiquarians, who out of snobbery collect (or rather pile up) antiquities without judgment and learning, coaxing them out of the aristocrats. He wishes that Goltzius would publish at least ten

---

[1252] right proportion, symmetry
[1253] Victorius, *Commentarii in VIII. libros Aristotelis* (as in letter 144, note 845).
[1254] *Icones veterum aliquot.*
[1255] This seems to be an unrealised project, probably motived by Ortelius's recent publication (see letter 208), still it is curious that Sambucus is using past tense.
[1256] *LX librorum Βασιλικῶν.* Cf. the Index.
[1257] Stobaeus et Plethon, *Stobaei eclogarum libri duo … et Plethonis de rebus Peloponnesiacis orationes duae.*
[1258] Be well, old man, above all act exactly in a manner that is good and beautiful, scrutinize the writings of the ancients, be of sound judgement, and always be their good friend.

other similar books for the delight of everyone He would then merit a statue, together with the Laurinus brothers. Sambucus is ready to help in any way he can.

Ornatissimo viro Huberto Goltzio Herbipolitae Venloniano civi Romano, historico et totius antiquitatis restauratori insigni, amico optimo suo, Ioannes Sambucus Pannonius Tirnaviensis plurimam salutem.

Quid, doctissime Goltzi, de tuo Augusto copioso eo[1259] totque aversis ab imagine historiis illustri, vel potius omnino ego de tuo ingenio et conatibus sentiam, iam ante annos decem, ni fallor, cum vobiscum suavissime essem, intelligere potuisti. Tum certe opinionem non vulgarem excitaras, nunc vero id ipsum totius orbis testimonio locuplete comprobatum vehementer laetor. Italiae quidem omnis antiquitatis et elegantiae parenti nihil non tribuendum censeo, sed non minus (absit quidquam offensionis aut gratiae ergo mihi excidat) Germaniae studiis, praecipue Belgico, nunc concedendum praeconium arbitror, in quo ab aliquot annis principum et nobilium egregia et ad veterum exempla formata pectora exstitere, quorum cum propria cognitione, tum liberalitate ac subsidio universa poene laus commendatione priscorum ex Italia deportata ac veluti Herculi clava extorta iam visitur. Quod si aliud nullum immortalitate dignum exemplum ac nobile suppeteret, profecto industria tua et fratrum Laurinorum dominorum a Waterfliet et a Clinckerland,[1260] unicum pro millibus sufficeret. Quos ipsos nisi coram et variis colloquiis καὶ συζητήσει[1261] nossem, difficile tot laudes in eos iuste collatas crederem. Horum tu in primis quoque, ingeniosissime Goltzi, beneficentia, hospitio, in omnes huius consilii partes voluntate prolixa tuos thesauros promis polisque ac edis. Nimirum longe te dissimilem ac nonnullos istius cognitionis et cogitationum leviculos iactatores animadverto, quibus cum ambitiose et praetextu modo nominis aliquot nummi, picturae, epigrammata longo usu et praxi magis coacervata sunt, quam iudicio collecta. Aliquot argumentis circumforaneis holosericati et torquati magnatum limina terunt, sumptus ad θαυμαστὰ[1262] illa et abdita sua aliquando divulganda emendicare solent, ubi loculos complerunt, benefactores rident. De quibus alias. Ad tuum Augustum Goltzii redeo, quem fere formis absolutum nobis te daturum brevi ex animo gaudeo. Utinam vita et auctores tibi ad decem saltem reliquos sufficiant. Nae tu cunctos beabis et statua publica dignus pronunciabere una cum patronis Laurinis. Si quid in meis est, quod institutum vestrum iuverit, nihil denegabo; quod vero possidebam, cum apud vos essem, id facile tibi, Goltzi, me impertitum meministi. Vale vir clarissime, et dominis Laurinis a me mille salutes. Vienna Austria[e], Idibus Novembris MDLXXIII.

[1259] The reference to the second volume of Goltzius's illustrated numismatic album (dedicated to Maximilian II), in which the letter appeared. Since the first volume contained a letter by Sambucus addressed to Emperor Ferdinand I, mistakenly published in two versions both in the front matter and at the end (see letters 40-42), apparently Goltzius wanted to have something from Sambucus in the second volume also and published this letter on the last page of his book.

[1260] Marcus Laurinus, lord of Watervliet, patron of Goltzius (see letter 40), and his brother, Guido Laurinus (1532-1589), who had similar antiquarian interests. See Tine L. Meganck, "Abraham Ortelius, Hubertus Goltzius en Guido Laurinus en de studie van de Arx Britanicca," *Bulletin KNOB* 98 (1999), 226-236.

[1261] through discussion

[1262] things worthy of admiration

215.
Sambucus to Johannes Crato
20 November 1573, [Vienna]

Published in Gerstinger, "Die Briefe," 149-150.

While Sambucus was in Pressburg because of court cases for eight days, his son was born at home. On the evening when he was going to the treasurer, two courtiers came at imperial behest to examine his codices, Augerius Busbequius and Martin Gerstman. They said they wanted to see the books; there was only an hour left before dusk. Sambucus responded that if they wanted to judge and estimate the books, it was not an hour's work. Gerstman agreed, but Busbequius said he rarely had time, but then he said he would soon return, meanwhile Sambucus should prepare the books for inspection. If they do not want to conform to the imperial mandate by only looking at the books as if through a lattice-work, they will not do right by Sambucus. If he can be frank, he cannot see much use of Busbequius, and besides, he perhaps prefers to get his own codices sold to the emperor rather than to recommend Sambucus's ones. They can come back whenever they want, it is the same for Sambucus, what matters is to understand the emperor's intentions. He showed them also some marbles but they were either worthless or the two courtiers were incompetent to appraise them. This is all only for Crato.

Salutem.

Dum litibus octiduum Posonii confictor,[1263] auctus sum domi filiolo, cui te bene ominari et salva diuturnaque precari certe scio. Eo ipso vesperi, quo me in viam dabam ad quaestorem, ecce veniunt equites aulici de mandato caesaris codices inspiciundi, dominus Busbekh[1264] et Gerstmann.[1265] Unica et subita hora, quod nox subesset, libros videre velle aiunt.[1266] Respondi

---

[1263] On Sambucus's litigation see Illésy, "Sámboky János." Although his long case with the Alaghys had a peaceful conclusion in 1571, Sambucus reopened it in 1573. (This might be also related to the financial crisis he was going through, which was also the motive for selling his library.)

[1264] Augerius Busbequius (Ogier Ghiselin de Busbecq) (1522–1592) was a Flemish nobleman born in Flanders. He studied extensively in Leuven and elsewhere in Europe and joined the court of Ferdinand I in c. 1552. He served three Habsburg rulers as a diplomat, most famously taking part in a mission to Constantinople from 1555, where he collected many precious manuscripts and botanical rarities. In 1564–1566 he was marshal of the hall to Maximilian's elder sons in Spain. From 1567, he was seneschal and chamberlain to Maximilian's younger sons. From 1575 he served Emperor Maximilian and Rudolf II as their Parisian diplomat, this was the time he wrote the famous *Turkish Letters* (see letter 273). On Busbequius see Charles Thornton Forster and F.H. Blackburne Daniell, *The Life and Letters of Ogier Ghiselin de Busbecq* (London: C. Kegan Paul, 1881); Zweder von Martels, "On his Majesty's Service. Augerius Busbequius, Courtier and Diplomat of Maximilian II," in *Kaiser Maximilian II.: Kultur und Politik im 16. Jahrhundert*, eds. Friedrich Edelmayer and Alfred Kohler (Vienna: Verl. Für Geschichte und Politik, 1992), 169-181; Ignace Dalle, *Un européen chez les Turcs. Auger Ghiselin de Busbecq* (Paris: Fayard, 2008); Almási, *The Uses of Humanism*, passim; Maria Petz-Grabenbauer, "Die Beziehung Ogier Ghiselin de Busbecqs zu Carolus Clusius Charles de l'É(s)cluse und deren Einfluss auf erste botanische Gärten in Wien," *Erkunden, Sammeln, Notieren und Vermitteln – Wissenschaft im Gepäck von Handelsleuten, Diplomaten und Missionaren*, eds. Ingrid Kästner et al. (Aachen: Shaker Verlag, 2014), 177-204.

[1265] Martin Gerstman (1527–1585), canon of the cathedral of Wrocław, was imperial secretary (he was Mark Singkmoser's successor). Gerstman studied with church benefices in Frankfurt an der Oder and in Padua (c. 1556–1561), where he also obtained a doctoral degree. He must have known Sambucus already from Padua. In 1574, he became bishop of Wrocław. See Bibl, *Maximilian II.*, 333; Zonta, *Schlesische Studenten*, 235.

[1266] On the story of the visit of Busbequius and Gerstman and on Sambucus's attempts at selling his library see Gerstinger, "Johannes Sambucus als Handschriftensammler," 281-282; Almási, *The Uses of Humanism*, 184, 193-196. Since these initial attempts to sell his library did not succeed, Sambucus also tried to sell his library

non unius horulae, si probitatem eorum iudicare aestimareque cuperent, id esse opusculum. Assensus est Gerstmann, sed alter sibi non semper vacare, brevi tamen, cum libros ad inspiciendum seposuissem, rediturum. Si aliter caesaris mandato satisfactum nolunt quam per transennam aspexisse,[1267] mihi minus satisfacerent, et aperte dicam, usum Busbekhio deesse video, praeterea suos fortassis codices caesari venditos malit quam meos commendare. Redeant, quando volunt, aeque ducam, modo ego caesaris voluntatem intelligam. Ostendi quoque marmora, sed aut nihil sunt aut isti nihil vident. Haec ad te autorem et patronum solum scribo, cui esse mea et amicorum curae non minus quam sua novi. Vale. 20. Novembris 1573. Tuus Sambucus.

Address: Magnifico domino doctori Ioanni Cratoni, suo patrono et amico Sambucus.

216.
Sambucus to Stephanus Pighius[1268]
December 1573, [Vienna]

The original is kept in Berlin, Staatsbibliothek Preussischer Kulturbesitz, Ms. Lat. F. 61 (Codex Pighianus), unpaginated slip bound behind the index. Published in Dekker, "Ein unbekannter Brief," 90-91.

Sambucus informs Pighius that he has found the right solution for the question of Duilius. The context and the script of three of his old codices make clear the errors, as before the eyes of Rufus and Quintilian. Sambucus will tell Pighius the rest and also (the story of) Vonones's captivity during a meal. Bilios should be Duilios. It is the error of stone-cutters.

Sambucus salutem.

Εὕρηκα τὴν ἀποσημείωσιν ἀληθῆ Duillianam.[1269] Contextus et manus vetus tribus meis in locis expresse, et hinc, πρὸς ὄμμα[1270] Ruffi et Quintiliani mendas produnt. Reliqua in symbolam, καὶ

---

elsewhere. See letter 238, note 1380 and cf. letters 227, 240, 242, 244-245 and 310.

[1267] Cf. Cicero, *De oratore* 1.162: "quasi per transennam praetereuntes strictim aspeximus."

[1268] Stephanus Pighius (1520–1608) was a Dutch humanist and antiquarian. He studied in Leuven, travelled to Italy and became librarian of Antoine Perrenot de Granvelle in 1555. In 1571–1575, he accompanied Karl Friedrich of Jülich-Cleves-Berg on his European grand tour as his tutor, stopping in Vienna in 1572. In 1574, they moved on to Rome, where Karl Friedrich died in smallpox in February 1575. Pighius later commemorated his patron and their tour in the *Hercules Prodicius, seu principis iuventutis vita et peregrinatio* (Antwerp: Plantin, 1587). See Jan Hendrik Jongkees, "Stephanus Winandus Pighius Campensis," *Mededelingen van het Nederlands Historisch Instituut te Rome* 8 (3rd series) (1954), 120-185; Pighius, *Epistolarium*; Robert Lindell, "*Hercules Prodicius* and the Coronation of Rudolf II as King of Hungary," in *Mito e realtà del Potere nel Teatro: Dall'antichità classica al Rinascimento*, eds. Maria Chiabò and Federico Doglio ([Viterbo]: Centro studi sul teatro, 1988), 335-354; Howard Louthan, "The Imperial Court of Maximilian II: Two Excerpts from Hercules Prodicius," *Comitatus* 23 (1992), 101-110; Marc Laureys, "Lipsius and Pighius. The changing Face of Humanist scholarship," *Filologie en literatuurgeschiedenis* 68 (1998), 329-344. For the interpretation and translation of the entire letter see Dekker, "Ein unbekannter Brief."

[1269] "I have found the right solution of the Duilius-question." Translation by Dekker, *idem*, 98. In about 260 BC, on the forum of Rome a rostral column was raised in the memory of the wars against Chartage by Consul Gaius Duilius. Parts of this monument were found in 1565 during the Roman stay of the young Aldo Manuzio Jr., who published the inscriptions in 1566 in his *Orthographiae ratio ... collecta*. The key question of this short letter is the correct spelling of Duilius's name. See more in letter 192.

[1270] in front of the eyes

Vononis[1271] συντήρησιν[1272] servo. Bilios igitur sit Dvîllíos, et per Duîs, DÎs, Dillíos.[1273] Error lithoglyphorum, καὶ λατόμων ἔστω.[1274] Ἰωάννης ἔγραφον Σαμβῦκος[1275]

Pighius's hand: Ioannis Sambuci. 1573. Decembri.

217.
Sambucus to Johannes Crato
3 December [1573], [Vienna]

Published in Gerstinger, "Die Briefe," 151-152.

The auditors of his library have not come back. Sambucus asks Crato to mention the case of his offer to the emperor (who once took great delight in the number and antiquity of his books). Crato can refer to the testimony of Camerarius and others when affirming that no one in Germany has a larger collection as regards the number of manuscript rarities, not even the Fuggers. There are 360 Greek manuscripts (out of which c. 70 unpublished) and c. 140 great Latin classical authors. He would sell them for 2,500 Hungarian florins and swear that they cost him more. There are also twelve exquisite marble pieces; if the emperor was not interested in those, he would be happy. If the emperor has doubts, he should send whomever he wants, even the entire university can come, he will be happy.

Salutem.

Nondum ἐκληκτικοὶ κριταὶ βιβλιοθήκης[1276] venere neque curo.[1277] Tantum te pro nostra mutua benivolentia, imprimis tua doctrina et humanitate oro, apud caesarem huius, si tibi videbitur, libelli oblatione (nam olim numerorum et vetustatis memoria valde oblectabatur) negocii uti memineris. Poteris teste Camerario et aliis plurimis confirmare,[1278] in Germania, quoad tot manu exaratos et raros nulli hanc cedere et quidem Fuggerianae, quam vir Bavarus habet

---

[1271] Vonones I of Parthia († 19) ruled the Parthian Empire from about 7/8 to 11 AD. He was sent to Rome as a hostage in 10 or 9 BC as surety for a treaty his father made with Augustus and was only let go home when the Parthian king died. Disliked for his pro-Roman attitude, he had to escape in 12 AD, and was later killed in Antiochia. See *RE Suppl.* IX (1962), 1865-1867. The reference to his captivity (συντήρησιν) concerns his imprisonment in Antiochia. Interestingly, Vonones is also mentioned in the *Res Gestae Divi Augusti* (see Dekker, "Ein unbekannter Brief," 97), a copy of which was preserved by the so called *Monumentum Ancyranum*, found in Constantinople in 1555, in which Pighius became keenly interested. In fact, this letter suggests that Pighius's interest in the question of Duilius was raised by the *Monumentum Ancyranum*, hence he supposedly already knew the text in 1573, but this is problematic (cf. letter 230). The question of Duilius could have also emerged during Pighius's studies for his commentary on the *Fasti Capitolini*. See Tardy and Moskovszky, "Zur Entdeckung" and Von Martels, "The discovery."
[1272] preservation
[1273] Sambucus corrected *Dvíllíos* to *Dvílíos*, and *Dillíos* to *Dilíos*.
[1274] let it be (the error of the engravers) and stone-cutters. Bilios was added arbitrarily to the beginning of the text by Petrus Ciacconius Toletanus (published posthumously in 1586) and Dekker argues that both Sambucus and Pighius knew Toletanus's text and remained influenced by it. Dekker, "Ein unbekannter Brief," 92. So it was Toletanus's error and not of the stone-cutters.
[1275] I, Johannes Sambucus, wrote this.
[1276] the picky judges of the library
[1277] See letter 215 for the visit of Busbequius and Gerstman in Sambucus's place.
[1278] Joachim Camerarius Sr. visited his library in 1568.

δυσευρέτων[1279] numero antelatam. Sunt 360 Graeci, in his ad 70 non vulgati, Latini optimi classici etc. ad 140. Hos simul 2500 Pannonicis, hoc est singulos quinis vendam ac iuriurando asseverare possum mihi pluris constitisse. Marmora sunt 12 non vulgaria, quae si negligit sua maiestas, laetabor etc. Vale, et si dubitat imperator, mittat, quos voluerit, adhibeat totum Viennae gymnasium, id mihi peresset gratum. 3. Decembris. Tuae excellentiae totus quantus D. Sambucus.

Address: Magnifico et excellentissimo domino doctori Cratoni ab Craffthaim, domino, amico singulari Sambucus.

218.
Sambucus to Johann Sommer Mayor of Trnava and István Nyilas
18 December 1573, Vienna

The original is kept in Trnava, SAT, Magistrát mesta Trnava, Missiles. Published in Kóssa, "Adatok Sámboky János életéhez," 375; Vantuch, "Die Sambucusbriefe," 354-355.

Sambucus is offering his services to his friends. He examined Dobos's learning and knowledge: Dobos had not studied much. Sommer and Nyilas know what they want (to do with him). They should examine him, decide and let him know; he and Mr Lessenprandt will do whatever they can. If they want to send him up (to Vienna), it is fine. He will also let them know what he thinks. God should preserve them in good health. This young man needs now the bridle so that he would remain thankful later.

Tiztelendo Uraim, Baratym, zolgalathomath ayanlom kegyelmeteknek.

Tovabba ez Dobos tanulasat, tudomanyat, akarattjat alkolmasson examinaltam:[1280] elegh kewezzet tanut, my lighen tovabba valo akarattya, kegyelmetek megh erty. Kegyelmetek examinalnya, azutan valamyre intesy kegyelmetek akarattyat, az myben my zolgalhatunk Lessenprandt uramnal,[1281] eremest mynden promotioval liszunk czak kegyelmetek ielencze megh, es kwldye fell, ha teczendik. Enys az mi zandekomot meg mondom. Isten tarcza megh kegyelmeteket. Ez zabla kell zinthe mostan az ifiwnak, hogh azutannis megh közönye. Datum Viennae 18 Decembris 1573. Kegyelmeteknek baratya etc. Samboky Janos.

Address: Egregiis dominis, domino Ioanni Sommer iudici Tyrnaviensi ac domino Stephano Nylas sororio, amicis observandissimis. Tirnaviam.

[1279] not yet found, not yet published
[1280] György Dobos studied in Vienna from 1567 but apparently not at the university. When his father Gergely died, the executors of his will asked Sebestyén Lessenprandt (see the next note) to supervise his studies in Vienna. Lessenprandt wonders about the heritage of György in a Hungarian letter addressed to Johann Sommer, Mayor of Trnava, in 1567. See *Régi Magyar nyelvemlékek*, 3:71-72.
[1281] Sebestyén/Sebastian Lessenprandt was Mayor of Trnava in 1556. See Bessenyei József, "A Magyar Királyság központja - Buda - és Nagyszombat kapcsolatrendszere a Mohács utáni évtizedekben" [The relationship between the centre of the Kingdom of Hungary – Buda – and Nagyszombat in the decades after Mohács], *Tanulmányok Budapest múltjából* 40 (2015), 107-120.

219.
Sambucus to Nicolaus Reusner
1 March [1573–74?][1282], Vienna

Published in Nicolaus Reusner, *Emblemata partim ethica et physica, partim vero historica et hieroglyphica* (Frankfurt am Main: Feyerabend, 1581), 355.

Sambucus greatly approves of Reusner's style in his work on the emperors. Even if Reusner lived another lifetime as long as he has lived until now, he could hardly be expected to produce anything better. Johannes Mylius wrote good poems on secular and religious heroes but Sambucus prefers the grandeur of Reusner's poems. Crato's good words about Reusner were right. Sambucus once also wrote emblems and has always encouraged those who excelled in that art. Now he is less impassioned and does not write poems. As for the poem Reusner has requested, he, the frog among the swans, does not want to interfere.

Ioannes Sambucus N. Reusnero[1283] S. P. D.

Et σαφήνειαν τῇ δεινότητι[1284] iunctam in tuis *Imperatoribus* et genium scribendi amplector. Si totidem lustra, quot excurrere, aetatem (quod opto) istam sequentur, vix ausim polliceri de te meliora. Descripsit Mylius heroas sacros et profanos haud iniquo carmine, sed gravitatem cum venustate tuorum antepono.[1285] Testimonium Cratonis egregium et verum de te agnosco. Colui ego aliquando haec studia, et quos ad ea excellere natura aut voluntate, non invito genio, sensi, cohortatus sum libenter. Nunc illo ardore remissiore nihil pango, miror tantum tui similes. Quod vero a me requiris epigramma, nae ego rana inter olores, tibi obsecutus, interstrepo. Tu boni consule meque in tuis familiaribus repone. Cuius ego honoribus atque monimentis posteritatem gratam memoriamque precor sempiternam. Viennae. Calendis Martii.

220.
Sambucus to Johann Heinrich Herwart
1 January 1574, Vienna

Dedication in Sambucus, *Icones veterum aliquot*, f. B1ʳ.

[1282] This letter seems to be the first one addressed by Sambucus to Reusner, this is why we date it before their letter of 1575 (letter 237), however, it might also be dated earlier.

[1283] Nicolaus Reusner (1545–1602) was a Silesian legal humanist and Neo-Latin poet. He was born into a wealthy and learned family, which had recently moved from Transylvania to Silesia. He travelled and studied for long and was later mostly employed as teacher and professor of law. He was widely learned and allegedly published 83 works on a variety of subjects, emulating Sambucus in many ways. Available biographies of Reusner all go back to Adam, *Vitae Germanorum iureconsultorum*, 379-384.

[1284] clearness (combined with) brilliance

[1285] Johannes Mylius (1535–1575) was a Neo-Latin poet. Born to a family of pastors, he studied in the convent school of Ilfeld with Michael Neander and in Leipzig with Camerarius. He apparently tried in vain to establish himself at the Polish and at the imperial court (he was crowned poet laureate in Vienna in 1565). He published in Leipzig his 560-pages *Poemata*, went back to study in Wittenberg in 1568, and finally became professor of Greek in Jena. See Flood, *Poets Laureate*, 1398-1400.

Sambucus praises Herwart's interest in antiquity and learning, to which all of Europe testifies. As Herwart supported the creation of images of princes and lords, he should not neglect the images of philosophers and doctors either. Although Sambucus knows many such portrait collections, their authenticity is neglected, as it had once been the case also with Homer. However, the images of the Icones go back to statues, paintings, coins, and contemporaries are represented according to their age at the time. If Herwart does not find the images in the book authentic, he should not blame Sambucus, who made all the efforts to find authentic documents and material representations.

Ioanni Henrico Herwarto,[1286] patricio Augustano, in primis magnifico viro litteratorumque fautori Sambucus salutem.

Nae tu Minervius es iusteque γλαῦκα[1287] pro insignibus domus nobilitateque praefers, qui aliis amplius vides. Quanto enim studio cunctam vetustatem et impensis initio sis complexus, quanto post singula iudicio tum discreveris, tum interpretatus sis, universa paene Europa locuples testis est. Cumque non minimam partem soliciti consilii tui effigies principum et heroum esse intelligam, philosophos quoque et medicos ne negligas oro, vel potius σπεύδοντα ὀτρύνω.[1288] Ac scio multos hoc ipso argumento libellos hodie in vulgus produci, sed quod Plinius et Aelianus de Homero fatebantur,[1289] idem censeo de multorum editionibus: icones ad historiarum descriptiones penicillo informatas, non de protypis ectypa reddita. Quod si in his quoque nostris eius aliquot generis deprehenderis, mihi id vitio non vertes, qui ista, amicorum fide ac testimonio, de statuis, signis, tabellis, partim numis haud recentis memoriae atque vetustissimorum codicum vestibulis comportarim, superstites ad cuiusque aetatem simulandos curaverim. Quidquid est operae, tibi dono, cuius ego semper ingenium, humanitatem, doctrinam commemorare soleo, splendorem, opes, nobilitatem canendam aliis, ne in aliquo offendam, relinquo. Meque cum hacce, velut strenula, tibi commendo. Vale, Vienna ipsis Kalendis Ianuarii MDLXXIIII.

221.
Sambucus to Joachim Camerarius Sr.
1 February 1574, Vienna

The original is kept in Munich, BSB, Clm 10363, f. 28[r-v] (no. 14). Published in Sadoletus, *Philosophicae consolationes*, 122-124[1290]; Gerstinger, "Die Briefe," 152-154.

[1286] Johann (or Hans) Heinrich Herwart (1520–1583) was a patrician of Augsburg, business associate of the Fuggers and member of the City Council. He was a generous patron of many humanists and renowned for his botanical garden and his collection of music sheets. Among his humanist friends and clients we find Wilhelm Xylander (see Bayle's *Dictionary*), Johannes Crato, Abraham Ortelius, Conrad Gesner and Hugo Blotius. See Almási, *The Uses of Humanism*, 230, note 117; Joann Taricani, "A Renaissance Bibliophile as Musical Patron: The Evidence of the Herwart Sketchbooks," *Notes* 49 (1993), 1357–1389. On Herwart and the *Icones* see Arnoud Visser, "From the republic of letters to the Olympus. The rise and fall of medical humanism in 67 portraits," in *Living in posterity: essays in honour of Bart Westerweel*, eds. Jan Frans van Dijkhuizen et al. (Hilversum: Verloren, 2004), 299-313; Vida, "A reneszánsz orvostörténeti."
[1287] little owl
[1288] I spur on the one who hastens. Cf. *Ilias* 8.293–294.
[1289] Aelianus, *Varia Historia* 13,22; Plinius, *Naturalis historia* 35.2.
[1290] Cf. letter 223.

Sambucus was agitated by the news of the death of Camerarius's wife, which he got from the most famous and virtuous Hubert Languet. He was agitated because of Camerarius, who is afflicted by old age and sicknesses. (The death of) such an excellent wife, the number of children, the love between wife and husband, and such long uninterrupted intimacy naturally agitate friends. How could Sambucus offer consolation to such a man who always faced dangers with Christian discipline and managed to console others in even greater troubles and bring them back from desperation? Camerarius should gather strength from his own "treasury" and be loyal to himself. Sambucus finishes his letter with a poem. In a postscript he reminds Camerarius of the letters of Chrysoloras. He is doing no work on the (collection of Greek) epithets. He asks Camerarius to publish the consolation of the young Sadoleto, which was his first Ciceronian exercise, together with similar arguments, or send the manuscript back to him. It is an elegant text, which has not yet been published.

Domino Ioachimo Camerario Ioannes Sambucus salutem.

De obitu uxoris, foeminae singularis exempli, nuncius quam me turbarit, Languetum habebis confitentem, cuius in laudum virtutumque commemorationi eidem nihil concessi.[1291] Illud quidem tua caussa, quem cum tot labores, affecta aetas, morbi paene reipublicae aliquoties eripuerint, isto quoque casu profecto debilitarunt. Hoc vero, coniugis praestantia, tot liberorum procreatio, amor inter vos, tot annorum nulla umquam intermissa offensa consuetodo cur non ab amicis impetrarit? Iam, optime mi Ioachime, si te vel paullum consolari aut confirmare coner, nonne ineptus fuero, plurimis periculis a recto sensu et Christiana disciplina virum numquam demotum, qui alios modo non maerore confectos ad memoriam mortis universae condicionis revocarit, a desperatione ad frugem traduxerit meliorem? Te ad te ipsum ablego, paenum illud πάγκοινον[1292] scilicet quaestorem ad locuples firmumque aerarium, a quo nisi cuncta lenia et moderata, nihil confeceris. Suppedita te ipsi, representa τῇ φρονήσει, ἣ πάντα δοῦλα καθίσταται,[1293] quod alii longo tempore vix queunt. Da hoc opinioni de te clarissimae, da rei publicae, domui, populo. Non dico, omnino nihil doleas, nam id humanum est, sed ne tui obliviscare. Valeant ἀπαθεῖς[1294] illi stipites nec persuadebunt verbis, ubi res aliter urget aut poscit.

> Quod si dolentem nec Phrygius lapis
> Nec purpurarum sidere clarior
> Delenit usus nec falerna
> Vitis Achaemeniumque costum.[1295]

Simula dumtaxat in hoc tempore. Sed ne te aliter, ac speramus, acceptum morte rarissimae matronae putemus aut quiddam amplius nos posse aut voluisse subiicere, quam tu valeas, ad consolandum quispiam suspiretur, epistolam aliquot ad tumulum versiculis concludo teque valere diu cupio.

[1291] Hubert Languet (1518–1581), born close to Dion, studied in Poitiers then at Italian universities. He was especially influenced by Melanchthon. His consolidating Protestant beliefs brought him finally to Wittenberg in 1549. Ten years later he became a diplomat in the service of the Elector of Saxony, an office he held until 1577. From early 1574, he was a Saxon ambassador in Vienna, where he apparently arrived little before this letter was written. He was a convinced supporter of the idea of a Protestant union and fought for religious tolerance all through his life. See Nicollier, *Hubert Languet*; Gillet, *Crato von Crafftheim*, 1:272-358.
[1292] common to all
[1293] wisdom, which opposes all that is servile
[1294] free from emotions
[1295] Horatius, *Carmina* 3.1.41-44.

Sedibus haec divum, quae est illachrimabilis ora,
Gaudet et aerumnis libera sceptra colit
Sat soboli, mundo, sat vixit et illa Marito,
Quam sequitur constans et sine labe decus.
Mortua nunc superat, quam forte latere sepulchro
Credimus, hos cineres, ossa iterumque feret.
Quin potius capti illecebris vigilemus in horas.
Nos cito, se raptam serius ista dolet.
Matronae illustres tumulum celebrate quotannis,
Vestra idea iacet delitiaeque viri.
Aliud.
Αἴθερος ἐν κόλπῳ παλινάγρετος οὖσα χορεύει
Ζῆ τ ἄλοχος χρυσῷ Σοῦ Ἰωαχεῖμε χάρις.[1296]

Caeterum ut aliquando Chrysolorae epistolarum memineris,[1297] nam de *Epithetis* nihil laboro,[1298] atque hanc Sadoleti admodum iuvenis consolationem,[1299] in qua primae exercitationis Ciceronianae indicia apparent, πρὸς ὁμοδίαιτόν τε καὶ ὁμόδουλόν ποτε[1300] praesulem, uti commodo tuo edas cum argumentis similibus, te valde oro, aut salvam quamprimum remittito. Est enim elegans necdum cum aliis eiusdem scriptis excusa. Vale. Kalendis Februarii 1574. Vienna, ex Museolo nostro et amicorum.

222.
Sambucus to Theodor Zwinger
7 February 1574, Vienna

The original is kept in Basel, Universitätsbibliothek, Frey Mscr II 26, no. 207. Published in Gerstinger, "Die Briefe," 155-156.

Sambucus will keep his word given to Zwinger and Episcopius with regard to Aristotle, but he also wants to be good to others who demand the same: he is negotiating with Wilhelm Xylander and Henri Estienne. He is ready to give himself to more people, as long as it serves the public. Xylander is going to bring together the Latin translators, read them together with the Greek and emend what he can. Zwinger should work on the Greek texts, to which Xylander can hopefully

---

[1296] The spouse, your delight, oh Joachim, dances and lives, recalled in the golden bosom of the ether.
[1297] See letter 117.
[1298] For his work on Greek epithets see "Greek epithets-edition" under "Sambucus" in the Index and cf. with Gulyás, *Sámboky János könyvtára*, 328 and 2610.
[1299] Jacopo Sadoleto (1477–1547) was a churchman, humanist and poet. Joining the court of Rome he met humanists like Pietro Bembo and became a famous Latinist, developing a Ciceronian style. After the Reformation Sadoleto fought for conciliation and was ready to adopt some of the reformers's demands. See Richard M. Douglas, *Jacopo Sadoleto, 1477–1547. Humanist and Reformer* ([s.l.]: Harvard University Press, 1959). His letter of consolation on the death of a mother (Sambucus's manuscript) was eventually printed in Sadoletus, *Philosophicae consolationes* by Joachim Camerarius Jr. who also included Sambucus's present letter to his father and apparently also sent the manuscript back to Sambucus (held in Vienna, ÖNB, Cod. 3272). See the notes of Gerstinger, "Die Briefe," 153-154. Cf. "Sadoleto" in the Index.
[1300] to (a bishop) who lived and served together with him

accommodate the Latin. He is congratulating for Girolamo Mercuriale's observations, but he made literally the same ones in Rome and also in a book by Agostino Gadaldino, he believes that nothing is from Mercuriale; if Zwinger wants, Sambucus can send it to him. He will send his own annotations with page numbers soon. He muses that it does not help one to be just. Sambucus finally wittily asks Zwinger to speed up the publication of Vegetius's Mulomedicina. *In a postscript we learn that Mercuriale through the apostolic nuncio Delfino to Vienna "extorted" Sambucus's manuscript of Georgius Trapezuntius's translation of Aristotle's* History of animals, *written in Trapezuntius's own hand and containing his comments as well. If Mercuriale does not publish it, Sambucus will be upset.*

Sambucus salutem.

Quod tibi et Episcopio de Aristotele sum pollicitus, nisi tueor, officium et fidem deservero, quod vitium, si in quemque cecidit, apud me numquam locum habuerit. Sed, mi Zvingere, sensus meos benevolos et occasione plurium, qui urgent idem, ut aeque partire velim, nescio, qui recte possim. Xylander mecum valde exigit,[1301] ὁ Ἕρρικος Coronatus[1302] idem. Sed me edam pluribus, dum publice prosit. Xylander latinos Interpretes conferet et, quae poterit, de Graecis lectionibus castigabit. Vos Graecis vestram operam navabitis, ut vobis Graeca, deinceps de his Xylandro accommodaturum Latine quidem me posse sperem, itaque conabor. De Mercurialis[1303] observationibus gratulor, sed easdem ipse ante multos annos

---

[1301] Wilhelm Xylander (1532–1576) was a humanist of Augsbrurg of modest origin. He studied in Tübingen and from 1558 he taught Greek and later logic at the University of Heidelberg. He was a very prolific editor and translator of classical works, translating among others Dio Cassius, Plutarch, Strabo and Euclid (the latter into German). Already Pierre Bayle had a high opinion of him. Fritz Schöll's biography in *ADB* 44 (1898), 582-593 is still the best.

[1302] Henri Estienne (1528–1598) (Coronatus is a wordplay with the name Estienne, since etymologically Stephen derives from stephanos, meaning "crown, wreath, garland"). Estienne was one of France's most remarkable publishers and humanists, famous among others for his *Thesaurus linguae graecae* (1572). As member of a great family of typographers, he studied Greek at an early stage and travelled widely in Europe, before joining his father's office in Paris and establishing his own. Estienne published most of his books in Paris or Lyon, but his itinary is not easy to follow. He wrote many books himself and probably several very important works (concerning politics and religion) also anonymously. He was an extremely critical philologist. At the time this letter was written he probably lived in Geneva, where he presumably established close contacts with Huguenot leaders like Beza and Hotman. See *La France des humanistes. Henri II Estienne, éditeur et écrivain*, eds. Judit Kecskeméti et al. (Turnhout: Brepols, 2003); *Robert et Charles Estienne: des imprimeurs pedagogues*, eds. Bénédicte Boudou et al. (Turnhout: Brepols, 2009).

[1303] Girolamo Mercuriale (1530–1606) was an influential Italian doctor and philologist. His famous *De arte Gymnastica* first appeared in 1569, when he took the chair of practical medicine at the University of Padua. In 1573 he was invited to the court of Maximilian II to treat the emperor's gout. For his successes he got the title of *comes palatinus*. The bad relationship between Sambucus and Mercuriale (documented also by this letter) probably goes back to the latter's Viennese sojourn. See *Girolamo Mercuriale medicina e cultura nell'Europa del Cinquecento*, eds. Vivian Nutton and Alessandro Arcangeli (Florence: Leo S. Olschki, 2008); Massimo Rinaldi, "Tradizione encomiastica e modelli pedagogici nell'inedita Oratio de re medica di Girolamo Mercuriale," in *Girolamo Mercuriale: medicina e cultura nell'Europa del Cinquecento*, eds. Alessandro Arcangeli and Vivian Nutton (Florence: Olschki, 2008), 319-341; Jean-Michel Agasse, "Girolamo Mercuriale – Humanism and physical culture in the Renaissance," in *Girolamo Mercuriale, De Arte Gymnastica*, ed. Concetta Pennuto (Florence: Olschki, 2008), 863-872; idem, "Cardia ou Cor? Une polémique entre Girolamo Mercuriale et Piero Vettori à propos de la peste d'Athènes," *Medicina & Storia* 6 (2011), 21-44; Vivan Nutton, "With Benefit of Hindsight: Girolamo Mercuriale and Simone Simoni on Plague," *Medicina & Storia* 6 (2011), 5-19; Nancy G. Siraisi, *Communities of Learned Experience: Epistolary Medicine in the Renaissance* (Baltimore: Johns Hopkins, 2013), 134-146; *Une correspondance entre deux médecins humanistes: Girolamo Mercuriale, Johann Crato*

Romae et a Gadaldino per indices ad verbum habui nec proprium istic quicquam est, ut credo, Mercurialis.[1304] Si vis, eadem mittam. Quae vero nostra sunt, accipies per foliorum numerorumque annotationes proxime.[1305] Τρόπος γὰρ δίκαιος κτῆμα κενώτατον.[1306] Excita quaeso omni contentione fatigatos, claudos equisones et dormientes veterinarios,[1307] quos si expedieritis, referent eadem celeritate nuncios vobis optatos. Vale sine mora 7. Februarii 1574.

Humanitate simulata Mercurialis per pontificium nuntium[1308] a me Trapezuntii versionem *Historiae animalium* extorsit cum eiusdem Trapezuntii lectionibus, librum idiographum Trapezuntii. Nisi ediderit, malam gratiam feret.[1309]

Address: Clarissimo domino, domino Theodoro Zwingero Basilium, amico optimo. Basell.

223.
Joachim Camerarius Sr. to Sambucus
19 February 1574, Leipzig

The original (draft) is kept in Munich, BSB, Clm 10367, f. 14ᵛ, attached to Sambucus's letter (no. 220). First published in Sadoletus, *Philosophicae consolationes*, 125.[1310] Second edition: Camerarius, *Epistolarum libri quinque*, 416-417.

Camerarius gratefully received Sambucus's letter of 1 February together with Sadoleto's consolation. But neither can others console him because of the death of his wife nor can he himself find solace. He was delighted by the elegance of Sambucus's funerary epigrams. He sends back one of his poems, which he wrote during the night as he could not sleep. He has already worked on the publication of the letters (by Chrysoloras) for some years, but he is running short of publishers. Nonetheless, he will make sure that they appear, no matter in what way. He hopes to convince one of them to publish Sadoleto's consolation together with the epitaph he wrote and other poems, which could be collected by his son Ludwig. He is happy that Sambucus welcomed Hubert Languet and asks Sambucus to love this virtuous person also for his sake.

Von Krafftheim, eds. and trans. Jean- Michel Agasse and Concetta Pennuto (Geneva: Droz, 2016). Note also Mercuriale's correspondence with Nicasius Ellebodius, preserved in Milan, Biblioteca Ambrosiana, D 196 inf.

[1304] We could not identify Sambucus's reference. The only book published by Gadaldino was a translation of a commentary of Galen (*Stephani Atheniensis Explanationes in Galeni priorem librum therapeuticum ad Glauconem*, Venetiis: Juntae, 1554). We have not found a corresponding book by Mercuriale. Nevertheless, Sambucus may refer here to *Melchioris Guilandini Papyrus, hoc est commentarius in tria C. Plinii maioris de papyro capita / Accessit Hieronymi Mercurialis Repugnantia, qua pro Galeno strenue pugnatur* (Venetiis: apud A. Ulimum, 1572). Zwinger's marginal notes ("Mercurialis lectiones") show that he believed Sambucus was referring to Mercuriale's *Variae lectiones* (which among many other texts also uses Stephanus's commentary) but this book appeared already in 1570 (Venetiis: G. Perchacinus). More recent and fascinating was his *De morbis cutaneis et omnibus corporis humani excrementis tractatus* (Venetiis: Meietos, 1572), of which there is a modern edition (*Mercurialis "On diseases of the skin": a Sixteenth-century Physician and his Methods* by Richard L. Sutton, 1986).

[1305] These seem to be annotations concerning the author of Mercuriale's text.
[1306] A just habit is the most empty possession.
[1307] Zwinger's marginal note: "Vegetius".
[1308] Zaccaria Delfino, see letter 58.
[1309] Note that this manuscript was already promised to Zwinger (cf. letter 198). See on this manuscripts Gerstinger, "Zusammenfassung," 286-287; idem, "Johannes Sambucus als Handschriftensammler," 346-347.
[1310] Cf. letter 221.

S. D.

Literas tuas plenas humanitatis et benevolentiae erga me tuae, Calendis Februarii scriptas his diebus accepi, una cum Iacobi Sadoleti elegantissima consolatione.[1311] Quod me in acerbissimo luctu propter defunctam coniugem meo consolaris, facis tu quidem amanter. Sed neque ab altero ullo neque a me ipso, cui tuae litterae tantum tribuunt, meo dolori medicina afferri potest estque hic pariter ac morbus in hac aetate meus tibi non ignotus τῶν συναποθνησκόντων.[1312] Tu autem benigne facis, quod doloris usuram mihi concedis, in tristissimi casus patientia, cui quidem dolori ita moderor, quemadmodum possum. Epigramma utrumque tuum in moerore me elegantia sua delectavit. Atque unum meum remittendum duxi, quod noctu, dum somnus me destituit, sum commentatus. De epistolis et aliis quibusdam, ut mihi videtur, non inutilibus scriptis proferendis iam aliquot annos laboro, sed officinae operis deficimur.[1313] Cuiusmodi enim iam libri edantur videmus. Spero me tamen impetraturum ab uno, ut exprimendum Sadoleti consolationem accipiat, cui addentur epitaphia nostra epigrammata, quae colligere dispersa et a me temere in diversas cartas coniecta Ludovicus filius meus potuerit.[1314] Quod Hubertum Languetum complecteris, utriusque vestrum causa laetor. Nam et illi tuam consuetudinem esse iucundam scio, et tu usum amici tibi concilias, viri eximia pietate, fide, virtute, rerum bonarum multiplice scientia praediti, quem abs te meo etiam nomine diligi cupio. Tu, ut facis, me diligere perges, et una cum tuis omnibus bene valebis. Vale. Lipsiae die XIX. mensis Februarii 74.

224.
Sambucus to Aldo Manuzio
5 March 1574, Vienna

The original is kept in Milan, Biblioteca Ambrosiana, E 37 inf., f. 119[r-v]. Published in Ester Pastorello *Inedita Manutiana: 1502-1597: appendice all'Inventario* (Florence: Olschki, 1960), 375.

Sambucus claims it was not necessary for Aldo Manuzio to thank him for his help with regards to his planned edition of Galen. Manuzio can have anything his library has on medicine. Likewise he has a translation of Aristotle's History of animals *in the translation and handwriting of Trapezuntius and Paulus Aegineta, which Sambucus emended long ago. He wants to know the fate of Manuzio's edition of Galen. He is spending his free time on his old emendations of Quintilian. He is sending his greetings to Aldo's father Paolo Manuzio, his old friend.*

[1311] Cf. letter 221.
[1312] of those who die together. In the margin of the 2nd edition of the letter: "unus ex iis qui commori solent" (one of those who would die with the other). In fact, Camerarius Sr. survived the death of his wife only for a short while. He died two months after he wrote this letter, on the 17th of April.
[1313] This is probably a reference to the letters and other manuscripts Sambucus had sent to him. See letters 12, 92 and 111, and cf. with Gulyás, *Sámboky János könyvtára*, 328 and 2610.
[1314] Ludwig Camerarius.

Iohannes Sambucus Aldo Manutio Pauli filio salutem.

Literae, quibus de mea voluntate et accommodato quodam ad Galeni editionem et consilium vestrum subsidio gratias agis, gratissimae, non tamen ita necessariae fuere. Cumque de phisicorum disciplina ὠφελία[1315] nisi quaedam sit, ἰσότης εὐνοίας ἀντιστροφή.[1316] Quidquid mea bibliothecula reliqui tenet, id omne vestro imperio, industriae usibusque publicis patebit. D. Mercuriali simul *Historiam animalium* Aristotelis ex interpretatione Trapezuntii proprioque chirographo itemque Aegynetam a me diu multumque emendatum dederam.[1317]

Quid de illis et Galeno vestro fiat, cum poteris cupio abs te intelligere.[1318] Cuius ego nunc alicui vel potius mediocri valetudini salutaria et diuturna cuncta precor, laudes vero domesticas, quod tua industria ornes augeasque, plurimum laetor. Ego antiquas meas lectiones verso. Quintiliani emendationi ocium reliquum adhibeo. Parenti tuo, viro optimo et amico veteri meis verbis mille salutes. III. Nonas Martii 1574. Viennae.

Address: Aldo Manutio Paulli filio, amico optimo. Venetiae.

225.
Sambucus to Johann Sommer, Mayor of Trnava
19 March 1574, Vienna

The original is kept in Trnava, SAT, Magistrát mesta Trnava, Missiles. Published in Vantuch, "Die Sambucusbriefe," 355-356.

The servant of Sambucus's brother-in-law (?) has come to him, complaining about the will, the terms of which have not been properly enforced. Sambucus asks the members of the Council to do what they can. At the chapter house there is a letter waiting for Sambucus, which the Council should send to him in Vienna as he knows no trustworthy person he could ask at the moment. He promises that in the diet the interests of Trnava will be diligently represented.

Mein dienst alles guetts, Gunstiger herr, unsers Schwehers dienner ist khomen und dem alten vill klagt, das man weder auszug der Vertröstung nach, heraus gegeben, weder verpott auffs Fekete Ferentz angenommen, alls noch khinftigs und ungwiss.[1319] Der Schweher maint, es wor gor ain unbraylich sach neben einem mandat niht mich auff alle gfar anzunemen, es sey doch darmit nihti khains entzogen.

Ich ways dem herren khain ordnung zu geben: doch was braichlich unnd fürderlich ist, bitt wollets niht abschlagen. Darneben mein butt an herrn auff alle vertraw; es ist ein briff im Capitl fur mich, den wirt der Ghoda [?] herauss geben;[1320] was der Herr darfur gebt, soll richtig mitt grossen dankh werden. Der herr schikh mir solchen briff zunechst herauff. Hab yetzo gor niemandt unten, den ich etwas bitt oder traue. Alspald der Landtag fur ist, soll

---

[1315] help
[1316] impartiality is the opposite of a favour
[1317] Cf. with letter 222.
[1318] As far as we know, Aldo Manuzio has produced no edition of Galen.
[1319] We have no information either on the matter in question or on Sambucus's brother-in-law (?) and Ferenc Fekete.
[1320] We were not able to identify the person in question.

des herren sachen vlayssig und von hertzen triben und angehalten werden.[1321] Damit gott befolchen den 19. Martii 1574. Des Herrn Diener allzeit [?] D. Sambucus.

Address: Dem Edlen Vesten hern Johannes Sommer, Richter zu Thierna etc. meinem gunstigen, vertrauthen hern und froundt. Tierna.

226.
Sambucus to Theodor Zwinger
20 March 1574, Vienna

The original is kept in Basel, Universitätsbibliothek, Frey Mscr II 27, no. 229. A copy is held in ibid., Mscr G II 37, no. 147. Published in Gerstinger, "Die Briefe," 156-158.

Sambucus will soon send his emendations of Aristotle (written in) Isingren's edition to Zwinger. If he can arrange it with "Master Centhar", he will send it via Reinhausen as he knows how carelessly they handle things in Augsburg (but if Centhar does not want to take it, then via Augsburg). He asks Zwinger to urge the publication of the Greek and Latin edition of the Basilica, *much awaited by the erudite, and to make sure the translation is correct so that there would be no need for a new edition. The edition of the* Mulomedicina *is slow. As soon as the* Basilica *is out, he will send Zwinger the Greek manuscript summary of an old book with a new order of the titles of the book. Already François Duaren and Andrea Alciato complained about the confusion of the titles. He sends his greetings to the heirs of Oporinus and promises to send them the 35 thalers he owes them. He would have paid it back long ago had he not been taken in by the promises of the Feyerabends. Zwinger should also tell them that he examined Bonfini's (history) again and added his narration on (the battles of) Lazarus Schwendi. If they are considering a reprint, they should let him know.*

Sambucus salutem.

Ego emendationes non paucas nec inanes brevi una cum ipso Aristotelis impresso codice meo Isingreniano mittam ac vestra caussa quidvis et publica faciam.[1322] Si per Cantharum magistrum impetraro, uti tuto per Reinhausen ad vos codex perferatur, nam per Augustam scio quam res negligenter procuretur, mittam. Vos illi satisfacietis.[1323] Sin ille recipere fasciculum recusabit, per Augustam. Te valde oro, Episcopios urgeas de Basilicis, quas tantopere eruditi exspectant Graece et Latine, ne ulli fraus interpretatione fiat aut occasio sit aliis traductionis et simul editionis.[1324] *Mulomedicina* nostra lenta est et prorsus autoris nomini adversa, qui Vegetius dicitur.[1325] Ubi *Basilica* prodiderint, mittam epitomen veteris codicis Graece, rarum librum, et titulos codicis alio ordine cum paraphrasi; nam et Duarenus et Alciatus semper conquesti sunt titulos confusos, transpositos, incertos.[1326] Vale et haeredibus Oporinianis meo

---

[1321] The diet of 1574 convened in early March. *Magyar országgyűlési emlékek* 6, 3-7.
[1322] On the promise of sending his emendations on Aristotle to Zwinger see letters 198, 200, 205 and 222.
[1323] We were not able to identify this postmaster.
[1324] On the *Basilica* cf. the Index.
[1325] On the *Mulomedicina* cf. the Index ("Vegetius-edition" under "Sambucus").
[1326] Zwinger's marginal note: "Iuridica". François Duaren (1509–1559) was a French jurist teaching at Bourges.

nomine salutem. De reliquo adhuc quod debeo, ad 35 talleros, dic me satisfacturum fuisse dudum,[1327] si Feyerabenti promissa me non fefellissent.[1328] Solvam brevi aut mittam illis, quod tanti et maioris sunt aestimaturi. Te rogo, istud illis significa quamprimum atque adeo me Bonfinium recognovisse, auxisse non contemnendis narrationibus Schvendianis.[1329] Si quid consilii de iterando eo prelis habent, faciant me certiorem. 20. Martii 1574. Viennae.

Address: Clarissimo viro D. doctori Theodoro Zuingero etc., amico optimo. Basileam.

227.
Sambucus to Johannes Crato
19 April 1574, [Vienna]

Published in Gerstinger, "Die Briefe," 158.

If there has not yet been a good occasion to remind the emperor of his mandate, Crato should wait for it. Above all, Sambucus wants the emperor to send expert inspectors who can read old scripts and judge their rarity and merits. He has c. 60 books and booklets that have not been published, 300 manuscript Greek codices and c. 150 Latin poets and orators etc. for which he asks 5 golden florins each. If Crato wants to, he can show this message to the emperor as a reminder.

Clarissimo domino et patrono salutem.

Si occasio plus quam opportuna commonefaciendi suam maiestatem ex eiusdem mandato nondum accidit, inservies tempori.[1330] Ante omnia velim, sua maiestas mitteret inspectores intelligentes harum rerum et cum characterum vetustatisque probitatum eorum peritos, tum qui norunt, qui sint rari et prelo adhuc idonei. Nam ad 60 fere sunt libri et libelli omnis professionis nondum vulgo typis usi. Trecenti sunt codices Graeci manu exarati, ad 150 latini, poetae, oratores etc. Horum singulos quinis aureis pannonicis nec minoris suae

---

[ ] Sambucus may be refering here to his *Commentarius in librum xxiiii Pandectarum.* Andrea Alciato (1492–1550) was one of the greatest legal humanists of the sixteenth century, who made a career in France and had a decisive influence on French and northern legal humanism. His most famous books were his collections of emblems (the first one appeared in 1531), which became a model also for Sambucus. Among others he published *Digestorum seu Pandectarum libri 50* (Basileae: Joan. Hervagius, 1541), to which Sambucus may be referring here. (See Gulyás, *Sámboky János könyvtára*, 1815, 1816.) On Alciato see Donald R. Kelley, *Foundations of Modern Historical Scholarship: Language, Law, and History in the French Renaissance* (New York: Columbia UP, 1970), 90-106; Annalisa Belloni, "Andrea Alciato fra simpatie luterane e opportunismo politico," in *Margarita amicorum: studi di cultura europea per Agostino Sottilia*, eds. Fabio Forner et al. (Milan: Vita e Pensiero, 2005), 117-143; *Andreae Alciati contra vitam monasticam epistula = Andrea Alciato's letter against monastic life*, ed. and trans. Denis L. Drysdall (Leuven: Leuven UP, 2014).

[1327] On the debt see letters 149 and 163.

[1328] The Frankfurt publishers Sigmund (1528–1590) and Johann Feyerabend (1550–1599). See Heinrich Pallmann, *Sigmund Feyerabend – Sein Leben und seine geschäftlichen Verbindungen* (Frankfurt a. M.: Völcker's Verlag, 1881); Benzing, *Buchdruckerlexikon*, 53 and 57.

[1329] The second edition of Bonfini's *Rerum Ungaricarum decades quatuor* appeared eventually in Frankfurt in 1581 (see letter 336, note 1922). It had more attachments than the edition of 1568 (for example on the battle of Gyula of 1566), but there was no new attachment on Schwendi's achievements. Cf. letter 77.

[1330] Cf. letter 215 (esp. note 1266).

maiestati humillime ac ex animo defero. Vale et, si voles, hanc ipsam schedulam memoriae ergo ostendes. XIX. Aprilis 1574. Totus tuus χρήσει καὶ κτήσει[1331] Sambucus.

Address: Clarissimo domino doctori Cratoni Sambucus, de codicibus manuscriptis pro sua maiestate.

228.
Sambucus to Aldo Manuzio
1 May 1574, [Vienna]

The original is kept in Milan, Biblioteca Ambrosiana, Cod. E 37 inf., f. 115ʳ. Published in Gerstinger, "Die Briefe," 159.

Sambucus was greatly upset by the news of the death of Aldo's father, Paolo Manuzio. What was lost in a single hour could hardly be compensated for in thousand years. Sambucus was only consoled in these sad pondering by thinking of Aldo. He heard recently from the Spanish legate Pedro Fajardo that Paolo had had commentaries and other pieces of texts ready for print, which Fajardo asks Aldo to publish. Sambucus asks the same. If Aldo should ever print the letters of illustrious men, he should let Sambucus know about it. He has a collection of rare and autograph letters by Giovanni Pontano, Jacopo Sannazaro, Jacopo Sadoleto, Pietro Bembo and others.

Ioannes Sambucus Aldo Manutio, Pauli filio, salutem.

De parentis tui ad sempiternas sedes, quas ille dum vixit intuebatur, secessu nuncius quam me turbarit, dici non potest.[1332] Quid, tantum virum tot annorum usura, summorum principum largo patrocinio, omnium bonorum amicicia florentem, literarum et eloquentiae recuperatae decus, horula eripuit, quam mille anni vix compensarint? Haec et similia animo meo dolenter occurrebant, sed, ut in memoriam tuarum virtutum domesticarumque possessionum discedere potui, cuncta leviora repperi, quod non imaginis externae modo, sed intestinae ac propriae in te exemplum liceret intueri.

Audio ipsum multa in commentariis fovisse et adversariis plurima ad praelum comparata tenuisse, quod ex eiusmet literis nuper illustris orator Hispanus, marchio Petrus Faggaiardus mihi recitavit.[1333] Is te rogat et hortatur, communem luctum illius monumentis in lucem missis primo quoque tempore leves, nec mora longiore speque ducas opinionem praeclaram. Utque ita facias, itidem te rogo, cuius ingenium et industriam laudare libenter soleo. Me vero,

---

[1331] by usufruct and possession. Cf. Erasmus, *Adagia* 4026.
[1332] Paolo Manuzio died on 6 April.
[1333] Pedro Fajardo y Fernandez de Córdoba (1530–1579) was Spanish legate to Vienna in 1572–1576. He was the third marquis of los Vélez from 1574. After his return he became the queen's high steward and state councillor but in 1578 he fell out of grace. He was an erudite figure and particularly interested in the Bible. In c. 1570, he compared the Vulgate with the Greek text and wrote in the margins of a Greek New Testament around 2000 variant readings, which happen to be his translations taken from the Vulgate. See Jan Krans, "Stronger than Fiction. The 'Velesian Readings' of the Greek New Testament," in *Scriptural Authority and Biblical Criticism in the Dutch Golden Age: God's Word Questioned*, eds. Dirk van Miert et al. (Oxford: Oxford UP, 2017), 73-88. Also see Ruben Gonzalez Cuerva and Alexander Koller, *A Europe of Courts, a Europe of Factions: Political Groups at Early Modern Centres of Power (1550–1700)* (Leiden: Brill, 2017), 118-120.

mi Alde, quem pridem nosti, eodem sensu et benevolentia erga te fore nec in tuis progressibus et laudibus quicquam neglecturum facile, tibi omnino velim, persuadeas. Vale, Kalendis Maiis 1574.

Si clarorum virorum epistolas aliquando formis recuderis, fac sciam. Augebo editionem multis clarorum virorum epistolis, Pontani, Sannazarii, Sadoleti, Bembi et similium,[1334] quorum sylvam habeo raram καὶ ἰδιόγραφα.[1335]

229.
Justus Lipsius to Sambucus
July 1574, Cologne

Published as a dedication in C. Cornelius Tacitus, *Historiarum et annalium libri qui exstant, Iusti Lipsii studio emendati et illustrati* (Antverpiae: Plantin, 1574), 561. Republished in Lipsius, *Epistolae*, 141-142; *Humanistes du bassin des Carpates II. Johannes Sambucus*, 188.

Lipsius left Vienna reluctantly. He was held back by the city, the court, and especially by Sambucus. He was delighted by Sambucus's humanity and erudition. In the memory of this, he dedicates to Sambucus Tacitus's Germania *and* Agricola, *and the* Dialogus de oratoribus *of uncertain authorship. Sambucus should accept this gift with patience until something better comes up.*

Ad clarissimum virum Iohannem Sambucum Pannonium.

Vienna vestra, clarissime Sambuce, invitus discessi. Tenuit me urbs ipsa et optimi imperatoris aula, tenuisti praecipue tu. Urbis amoenitatem, aulae splendorem admiratus sum, in te singularem humanitatem cum singulari eruditione coniunctam dilexi, vel ut magis proprie loquar, amavi. Cui amori meo testificando hos Taciti duo libros, alterum *De moribus Germanorum*, alterum *De vita Cnaei Agricolae*,[1336] et incerti scriptoris tertium *De oratoribus sui temporis*,[1337] nomini tuo inscripsi et benevolentiae perpetuae, monumentum libens merito dono dedi. Tenue munus, fateor, et quod nullam partem sit gratiae exsolvendae, sed in quo spero me facturum, quod benigni creditores solent, ut hac quasi particula soluti debiti tantisper sustenteris, dum meliore ingenii mei proventu sortem ipsam cum usuris dependam. Id quod brevi, si Musae adnuent, futurum confido. Vale.

[1334] This is a reference to Paolo Manuzio's edition *Epistolae clarorum virorum* (1556). Giovanni Pontano, Jacopo Sannazaro, Jacopo Sadoleto, Pietro Bembo were characteristic models for Sambucus's humanism. In a codex held today in Vienna (ÖNB, Cod. 9977), we find poems by Pietro Bembo, Michael Tarchaniota Marullus, Petrus Lotichius, Giovanni Pontano and others, but there are no letters. In 1579, Sambucus sent the poems for publication to Perna but they did not get published. See Sambucus, *Catalogus librorum*.

[1335] autograph

[1336] Tacitus, *Germanica* and *Agricola*

[1337] The *Dialogus de oratoribus* was not always attributed to Tacitus.

230.
Sambucus to Stephanus Pighius
30 August 1574, [Vienna]

A copy is kept in Hamburg, Staats- und Universitätsbibliothek Sup. ep. (4°) 7, f. 179ᵛ-180ʳ.
Published in Pighius, *Epistolarium*, 342-343; Gerstinger, "Die Briefe," 160.

Sambucus informs Pighius about a distinguished poet of modest circumstances (i.e. Johannes Secervitius) staying in Vienna, writing heroic and lyric poetry and living on the support provided by patrons. He will receive the magisterial grade from the university. Secervitius composed an elegant poem addressed to the lord of Pighius (Karl Friedrich of Jülich-Cleves-Berg), hoping for compensation. He asks Pighius to recommend him to Karl Friedrich and announces that in four days they will have the text of the Monumentum Ancyranum.

Iohannes Sambucus Pighio S. D.

Est hic poeta insignis, quem ante vero [?] Germania celebrem duxit, praesertim heroo et lyrico numero.[1338] Sorte communi poetarum tenui et museo angusto. Is hic Viennae magisterii gradum est suscepturus. Sumptibus destituitur, quod amici et patroni suppeditant, habet. Scripsit hoc elegans et non vulgari genio carmen ad vestrum illustrissimum ducem, ut necessariis sumptibus aliquantulum sublevetur. Hoc ei testimonium recusare nequivi. Te oro, illustrissimo duci ipsum una cum carmine commendes, tuum enim tuique similium patrocinium meretur. *Ancyranam* omnino intra 4 dies habebimus.[1339] Vale et in negocio istius poetae clari et multis editis libellis noti facilem te nobis praebeas, oro. Totus tuus Sambucus.
30. Augusti 1574.

Address: Doctissimo viro domino Stephano Pighio, amico singulari Iohannes Sambucus.

[1338] Johannes Secervitius (Seckerwitz, Seckervitz, Seckerbickius) (1520–1582) of Wrocław studied theology in Wittenberg, then history and poetics in Tübingen. He made his name as a talented author of occasional poetry. From 1574, he was professor of poetics at the University of Greifswald. See Theodor Pyl, "Johann Seckervitz" in *ADB* 33 (1891), 523-524. The information on his position at the University of Vienna is contradictory, see Gerstinger, "Die Briefe," 160 and cf. with the information of this letter, and also see the following one.

[1339] Apparently, Pighius was informed about the *Monumentum Ancyranum* (see letter 216, note 1271) by Busbequius not long time before (see Martels, "The discovery," 151), and right away understood the significance of the discovery from his reading of Suetonius. It is improbable that Sambucus's copy of the *Res Gestae Divi Augusti* came from Antonius Verantius's erudite nephew Faustus, as argued by Tardy and Moskovszky("Zur Entdeckung," 375-395, taken over in Almási, *The Uses of Humanism*, 122), since according Carolus Clusius's testimony this latter was different and better than the one Sambucus showed him (see also the precious notes to Clusius's letter to Lipsius in *Sylloges epistolarum*, 1:311-313). It may have been the copy made by (or for) Hans Dernschwam. In any case, it remains a curious fact that Pighius was the first to recognise the importance of this inscription, earlier than Sambucus or anyone else in Vienna, and that almost twenty years after the discovery Sambucus had still no copy of it. This was principally because neither Busbequius nor Verantius and their entourage recognised that this was the *res gestae* to which Suetonius had referred. It is similarly curious that when in 1584 Löwenklau asked Busbequius for his copy, he responded that he had lent it to someone and did not get it back (*Sylloges*, ibid.). Once Pighius obtained the text, he called the attention of the Republic of Letters to this sensational discovery. Among the middle men there were Fulvio Orsini, with whom Pighius left a copy later in Rome; Lipsius, who got the copy made by Verantius (or more precisely his secretary Johannes Belsius) from Clusius; and Andreas Schottus, who first published a detail from it (see Martels, "The discovery").

231.
Stephanus Pighius to Sambucus
[September 1574], Vienna

A copy is kept in Hamburg, Staats- und Universitätsbibliothek Sup. ep. (4°) 7, f. 180[r-v]. Published in Pighius, *Epistolarium*, 360; Gerstinger, "Die Briefe des Johannes Sambucus," 161.

Pighius is delighted by the poem and talents of Johannes Secervitius and recommended his poem to the prince (Karl Friedrich of Jülich-Cleves-Berg), who did not read it yet, as he expects the legates of the Duke of Florence for lunch. Meanwhile, he approached the secretary of the prince, without whom nothing can be done, but one can easier shear the wool of a donkey than obtain money from him for the part of a scholar, especially now, as they are preparing for the next trip. And he is so irritated by the high number of supplicants that he rejects them all. Pighius is sorry about this, and as he did not want to send a reply without anything, he gave some money of his own. He is happy about the news concerning the Monumentum Ancyranum *and hopes to be able to compare it before his departure. He will visit Sambucus in four days and bring back his Livy.*

Sambuco salutem Pighius.

Iohannis Seccervitii carmen et ingenium mirifice placet.[1340] Carmen principi commendavi, sed nondum legit, habet enim convivos et a prandio expectat oratores ducis Florentiae.[1341] Egi interea cum Panurgo [?],[1342] sine quo nihil hic. Verum ex asino citius lanam detondes, quam ab hoc vel nummum unum emungas ad subsidium alicuius studiosi, hoc maxime tempore, quo maximi sumptus faciendi sunt. Et is prorsus offenditur multitudine petacium libellorum, qui in hac aula in dies a diversis offeruntur, ideoque repellit statim quoscumque. Doleo certe, quod tuae commendationi et Secervitii votis hac vice satisfacere nequeam. Prorsus vacuum tamen ipsum ad te remittere nolens ex mea tenuitate, quod potui, dedi. De *Ancyranis* laetissima nuncias, atque utinam hic ante discessum meum videre et simul obiter conferre liceat! Post quartum diem igitur te visitare cogito et Livium referre.[1343] Vale, ex hospitio.

232.
Sambucus to Stephanus Pighius
16 October 1574, Vienna

A copy is kept in Hamburg, Staats- und Universitätsbibliothek, Sup. ep. (4°), 7, f. 184[v]-185[r]. Published in Pighius, *Epistolarium*, 360; Gerstinger, "Die Briefe," 161-162.

[1340] See the preceding letter.
[1341] These were Ludovico Antinori (1531–1576) bishop of Volterra and Giovan Battista Concini (1532–1605) learned secretary and diplomat of the duke of Florence. See the biography by Paola Malanima in *DBI* 27 (1982), 731-733. See Marcello del Piazzo, "Il carteggio della Legazione Toscana presso l'Impero," in *Studi in onore di Arnaldo d'Addario*, eds. Luigi Borgia et al. (Lecce: Conte, 1995), 1:165-217, and idem, *Gli ambasciatori toscani del principato: 1537–1737* (Rome: Istituto Poligrafico dello Stato, 1953).
[1342] This is a learned reference to the crafty figure of Panurge in Rabelais' *Pantagruel* (πανοῦργος means rouge.) Apparently, Pighius expected Sambucus to know *Pantagruel*.
[1343] Sambucus did not get the copy of the inscription of the *Monumentum Ancyranum* in time, see the notes of De Vocht in Pighius, *Epistolarium*, 343.

Sambucus reports that ten copies of Valerius Maximus arrived the day before and that he is sending two of them, as Pighius desired, to the courtiers who follow the duke (i.e. Prince Karl Friedrich of Jülich-Cleves-Berg) because of his sickness. There was also a richly illustrated book with the distichs of Benito Arias Montano included, which he keeps for himself in return for the postal fee, which he had to pay to the Frenchman. Pighius should write him about the antiquities or inscriptions he finds on his way. He is writing this letter in a hurry without Clusius's knowledge, as he learned about their early morning departure. According to the address, the letter was accompanied by two copies of Valerius Maximus.

Sambucus salutem.

Heri allata sunt Valerii exemplaria,[1344] idque X. Mitto ex mandato tuo duos [!], idque commoditate vestrorum aulicorum, qui ducem sequuntur morbis expediti.[1345] Caetera distribuemus ex sententia tua. Erat libellus figuris plenus, distichis Ariae Montani insignis sacris literis,[1346] quem mihi servo pro vecturae redemptione, quam Gallo huic pro tuo fasciculo coactus sum solvere. Vale et scribe, ubi sitis, ut habeatis, quod vetustatatis repereris aut rari epigrammatis. Quorum significatione et coindicatione me beabis. Haec subito et sero scribo inscio[1347] Clusio,[1348] quod commodum de vestrorum mane discessum intellexeram. Vale, mi optime Pigghi, et Sambucum redama. 16. Octobris Viennae 1574.

Address: Clarissimo domino Stephano Pighio Campensi, praefecto studiorum illustrissimi ducis Clivensis, amico optimo. Cum duobus exemplaribus Valerii Maximi.

233.
Sambucus to Theodor Zwinger
18 November 1574, [Vienna]

The original is kept in Basel, Universitätsbibliothek, Frey Mscr II 27, no. 228. A copy is kept in ibid., Mscr G II 37, no. 148. Published in Gerstinger, "Die Briefe," 163-164.

Staying at home because of problems with his kidney, he looked through his notes and found his former annotations on Plato. Henri Estienne would like to have them. When Zwinger is ready with Aristotle, Sambucus will think of Plato and Quintilian. One of the Gemusaeus brothers was convinced that Oporinus should have received 90 coronas for the 90 copies (of Bonfini's

---

[1344] A second, corrected and enlarged edition of Valerius Maximus's *Dictorum factorumque memorabilium libri IX* (Antverpiae: Plantin, 1574), edited by Pighius, which originally appeared in 1567.
[1345] This letter reached Clusius in Ferrara. See Clusius's letter to Plantin, quoted in Gerstinger ("Die Briefe," 162): "Libros a te missos Viennam Sambucus accepit post nostrum discessum. Icones Montani ipse retinuit, Valerios distribuit inter amicos [...] duo tamen exemplaria incompacta ad me misit in Italiam, quae Ferrariae accepi."
[1346] It was Philippe Galle's *Virorum doctorum de disciplinis benemerentium effigies xliiii* (Antverpiae: Galle, 1572) or the 1574 reprint of it. A modern edition was published by the press of the University of Huelva in 2005.
[1347] *Inscio* is ommitted in De Vocht's transcription.
[1348] Carolus Clusius (Charles de l'Écluse) (1526–1609) was one of the most influential sixteenth-century botanists. Initially, he studied law and theology in Leuven, Marburg and Wittenberg, then medicince in Montpellier. Serving as a tutor to rich noblemen he collected rare plants from many parts of Europe. In 1573, he settled in Vienna where he was appointed as the prefect of the imperial medical garden, thanks to the patronage of Busbequius, but he was discharged from his office after Maximilian's death in 1576. He knew Sambucus from

Decades*), which Sambucus had once received, but Sambucus informed him that this was not the case. Gemusaeus makes no further demands, even the 35 thalers, obtained from Sambucus, will remain with Episcopius and he will provide greater favours to Sambucus. Sambucus had received 90 copies, seven or eight of them were damaged and incomplete, 20 were donated to him, while he distributed some among Oporinus's friends and the Chancellery, sold 35 and still has a few. If only it had been printed more diligently, he would not spare his efforts. He asks Zwinger to bring the issue to an end and hopes that Episcopius and the creditors of which he hears will be happy. He will send Wolfgang Lazius's books on Roman history and antique coins, requested by Gemusaeus. He is sending his greetings to Löwenklau and wants him to finish the* Basilica. *The distance from the publishers and their delay make him sluggish.*

Sambucus salutem.

Per hos dies renum molestiis vexatus domique eo ocio quosdam commentariolos recognoscens multa me variis lectionibus in Platonem collegisse reperio.[1349] Henricus Stephanus cupit Platonica habere,[1350] quando Aristotelicis vesci nequit. Si vos Aristotelem expedieritis, cogito de Platone et Quintiliano.[1351]

Ab Gemuseo responsum accepi.[1352] Sibi fuisse persuasum Oporinum pro singulis exemplaribus missis, quae 90 fuere, singulos coronatos accepturum, quoniam vero a me aliter de illis certior sit factus et edoctus, nihil petiturum, quorum intersit 35 talleros apud Episcopium a me impetratos relicturum et rebus longe maioris momenti mihi gratificaturum.[1353] Ego 90 acceperam, 7 vel 8 corrupta erant et non integra quaedam; 20 Oporinus mihi donarat testibus litteris ipsius. Distribui aliquot amicis eius et cancellariae, habeo adhuc aliquot. Vendidi ad 35. Utinam aliter, hoc est, diligentius excusus fuisset, nullius me laboris paeniteret. Quare te pro amicitia oro, conficias negocium; spero Episcopium, quos creditores audio et alios contentos fore. Mittam proxime Lazii Romanorum et numorum,[1354] ut ab authore sunt

---

1561 (see Almási, *The Uses of Humanism*, 75) and remained in touch with him both in Paris in 1562 and Amsterdam in 1564. See the letter by Johann Banno (who later also visited Sambucus, as he tells in a letter to Reinerus Reineccius in 1568) in the digital edition of Clusius's correspondence (http://clusiuscorrespondence.huygens.knaw.nl/, accessed on 12 March 2024) and letter 52, note 306. See *Charles de l'Escluse; Carolus Clusius. Towards a Cultural History of a Renaissance Naturalist*, eds. Florike Egmond, Paul Hoftijzer and Robert Visser (Amsterdam: Koninklijke Nederlandse Akademie van Wetenschappen, 2007); Florike Egmond, *The World of Carolus Clusius: Natural History in the Making, 1550–1610* (London: Pickering & Chatto, 2010). Also see letter 215, note 1264.

[1349] Zwinger's marginal note: "Sambuci in Platonem variae lectiones"

[1350] On Henri Estienne's Viennese stay, see letter 238, note 1376. His edition of Plato's complete works appeared in three volumes in Geneva in 1578 and remained for several centuries the reference edition (see letter 306, note 1790). Even today, Plato is cited according to the Stephanus-pagination going back to this edition.

[1351] With regards to Aristotle see the previous letters to Zwinger (222 and 226). In general, on Sambucus's philological efforts regarding his manuscripts of Aristotle, Plato and Quintilian see Gerstinger, "Zusammenfassung." Cf. the Index.

[1352] The brothers Hieronymus and Polykarp Gemusaeus together with Balthasar Han bought the press from Oporinus's heirs after his death and ran it as "Officina Oporiniana" until 1600. See Benzing, *Buchdruckerlexikon*, 27.

[1353] On the payment for the copies of Bonfini's *Rerum Ungaricarum decades* see letters 106, 149, 163 and 226.

[1354] Zwinger's marginal note: "Wolfgangi Lazii Roma et nummi," which is a reference to Wolfgang Lazius's *Commentariorum reipub. romanae illius in exteris provinciis...* (Basileae: Oporinus, 1551), which was later re-edited as *Reipublicae Romanae in exteris provinciis, bello acquisitis, constitutae* (Francofurti: Claude de Marne and Jean Aubry, 1598), and his *Commentariorum vetustorum numismatum* (Viennae: Mich. Zimmermann, 1558). On Sambucus's efforts to publish these books see letters 262, 266, 271, 283, 326-327 and Gerstinger,

relicta; petit Gemuseus, mea quoque non recuso. Leonclavio salutem. Utque ἔκτυπα Βασιλικὰ fiant, cupio.[1355] Me, qui longius a typographis absum et prelis, mora illorum negligentiorem et languidiorem reddit. Vale. 18. Novembris 1574.

234.
Sambucus to Johannes Crato
20 November 1574, Vienna

Published in Gerstinger, "Die Briefe," 164-165.

Following Pighius's order given to him before his departure from Vienna, Sambucus is sending a copy of the corrected edition of Valerius Maximus by Stephanus Pighius, which arrived from Frankfurt, to Crato as well. The tenth book of Valerius Maximus comes from Sambucus. The son of Lazarus Schwendi, returned with Blotius from Italy, came to visit him during the day and will also visit Crato.

Salutem.

Stephanus Pigghius, in quo non vulgaris est antiquitatis effigies, hinc cum Clivensi suo discipulo profecturus iussit, ubi Valerius a se iterum correctus Francforto allatus esset, exemplum tibi quoque communicarem, quod facio.[1356] Quoad decimum libellum, a me praecipue habet.[1357] Etc.

Lazari Schwendi filius ex Italia cum Blotio reversus hodie me accessit.[1358] Iuvenis amore patris et patrocinio, nisi fallor, largiore dignus, qui te inviset etc.[1359] Vale et me fove, in cuius benevolentia dudum coepi acquiescere mihique satisfactum adhuc abs te humanissime confiteor, me nullam gratiam redditam doleo; ἀλλά ποτε κρειττόνων ἐπονοιῶν [ἑπομένων] κρείττοσι καὐτὰ ἐψόμεθα. Ἔρρωσο.[1360] Ex Museolo 20 Novembris 1574. Totus tuis meritis Ioannes Sambucus.

Address: Clarissimo domino et patrono D. Ioanni Cratoni.

"Zusammenfassung," 311-312. Curiously, he made no attempt to publish Lazius's work on the history of contemporary Hungary, the fifth decade of his *Rerum Austriacarum decades*, which will be first published only in the near future by Péter Kasza.

[1355] royal outline. Zwinger's marginal note: "Basilica ἔκτυπα iuris." For the Basilica-edition cf. the Index.

[1356] See letter 232.

[1357] In the edition of 1574 of Valerius Maximus's *Dictorum factorumque memorabilium libri IX* (see letter 232, note 1344) Pighius added a chapter he did not attribute to Valerius, as indicated on the title page: "Hac altera recognitione fragmentum de praenominibus antiquum incerti auctoris, quod decimi libri locum in multis exemplaribus occupat." After the end of book 9, Pighius inserted a new letter to the reader dated 1 January 1574, in which he explained his views about this alleged tenth book, consisting of a few pages and found in several manuscripts (mentioning also Sambucus's one). Although Pighius was convinced that it was not by Valerius, he claims that Plantin nonetheless insisted on attaching it to the edition (p. 388), see also more abundantly on pp. 98-99.

[1358] Johann Wilhelm Schwendi (1557–1609) studied in Italy together with Johannes Listhius Jr., tutored by Blotius. Cf. letter 168, note 997.

[1359] From June to December Crato was away in Ebersdorf with the ailing emperor. See Gillet, *Crato von Crafftheim*, 2:9.

[1360] but if something better follows, we will follow this also with better things. Farewell.

235.
Sambucus to Piero Vettori
17 December 1574, [Vienna]

The original is kept in Munich, BSB, Clm 735, Nr. 79. Published in Bandini, *Clarorum Italorum et Germanorum*, 2:82-83; Gerstinger, "Die Briefe," 165-166.

Sambucus thanks Vettori for his benevolence expressed in his last letter. The news about the making of a new eight-year treaty with the Ottomans brought great relief to the regions in conflict. Hopefully, the Ottomans will not use the peace with the emperor to harass Italy. He sent to Plantin the annotations to Aeschylus by Triclinius and Thomas Magister. He is presently "caressing" his old annotations and wants to work on Plato's manuscripts in the way he worked on Aristotle. The Basilica *is being printed in Basel.* Stobaeus's Physical and Moral Extracts *are printed by Plantin. Vettori must know well how important Photius's* Bibliotheca *is. He made plans and worked much on its edition but cannot proceed without the aid of other old manuscripts. There is no lack of a printer for it. He asks Vettori to supply a manuscript from some Florentine library and promises to send it back safe and intact.*

Ioannes Sambucus salutem.

Tuae mihi plenae humanitatis, amoris ac perspectae benevolentiae sunt redditae. Novi ingenium, pectus, quae illic polliceris, dudum publice honorifica mentione comprobasti, de qua commendatione adhuc tibi debeo, sed emetiar mutuum aliquando etc. De induciis octennio productis Byzantio nuper nuncius has regiones mirum est quam recreavit, tot malis et perpetuis rapinis αἱματοχυσίᾳ τε[1361] conflictatas.[1362] Sed veremur, mi optime Victori, ne istam nostram requiem ac ocium neglegentia accipiat inque Italiam tyrannica iniuria et vis excedat, quod procul absit etc. Ego Triclinii et Thomae Magistri scholia in Aeschylum Plantino misi, non displicebunt fortasse eruditis.[1363] Meas antiquas observationes lambo ut ursus faetum ac polio, in Platonicis, quod in Aristotele feci, subcesive cupio. Τῶν Βασιλικῶν 24 libri Basileae excuduntur.[1364] Ἐκλογὰς φυσικῶν γνωμῶν[1365] Stobaei Plantinus absolvit.[1366]

[1361] bloodshed

[1362] Despite the 1568 Treaty of Edirne the Ottomans continued to vex the borderlands and also captured minor castles. Eight years before the death of Selim II (which happened on 12 December 1574), the Ottomans already sent out their legate to Vienna to signal their desire to renew the peace. A new treaty for another eight years was finally negotiated in the middle of 1575 by Freiherr von Preyner (Breuner) but signed only after the arrival of the promised amount of money on 22 November. See Joseph Hammer-Purgstall, *Geschichte des osmanischen Reiches* (Pest: Hartleben's Verlag, 1840), 2:450-451. For the borderland fights of these years see Sz. Simon Éva, "Várfoglalás vagy illúziókeltés?: az 1574. évi Kanizsa elleni oszmán támadás és következményei" [Conquering a castle or making illusions? the consequences of the Ottoman attack on Kanizsa in 1574], *Zalai múzeum* 23 (2017), 201-215.

[1363] Sambucus offered to send this manuscript (perhaps Cod. Phil. gr. 334 of the ÖNB) to Vettori already in 1569 (see the postscript of letter 129), who apparently did not want it. Thomas Magister was a Byzantine scholar who wrote among others scholia on Aeschylus, living in the same period as Triclinius (c. 1300). It appears that Plantin could not make any use of Sambucus's manuscript and did not think it was worthy of publication. He makes no reference to it in the 1580 Greek edition of Aeschylus by William Canter.

[1364] *LX librorum* Βασιλικῶν. Cf. the Index.

[1365] Extracts from the physical and ethical deliberations

[1366] Stobaeus and Plethon, *Stobaei eclogarum libri duo ... et Plethonis de rebus Peloponnesiacis orationes duae*. Cf. the Index.

In Photii *Bibliotheca* qui thesauri lateant, quanta sit antiquitatis effigies, quam eius editio multorum desiderium atque iacturam reficeret, nosti.[1367] Eam ego diu in animo habui imprimendam; perlegi, multa notavi, plura, nisi subsidio veterum codicum, sanari posse non video. Typographus non deest. Tuo consilio et auxilio opus est tamquam summi artificis καὶ ἀνταγωνιστοῦ ἢ ἀντισχολαστοῦ[1368] contra omnem exceptionem. Oro te, mi Victori, da publicis rebus, da benevolentiae singulari ἀντίγραφον[1369] aliquod vestrum, suppedita sine incommodo tuo, quod omnes iuverit; potes enim et habetis in vestris apothecis Florentinis exemplaria, reddentur tuta et integra, fidem et praedes habebitis. Vale atque Sambuco fide, istud beneficium fore cum tuo honore perpetuum. Vale! 17. Decembris 1574 festinanter.

Address: All Molto Magnifico et Dottissimo Signor Pietro Vittorio Fiorentino, Amico suo osservatissimo. Fiorenza.

236.
Sambucus to Johannes Crato
23 January 1575, [Mannersdorf]

Published in Gerstinger, "Die Briefe," 166-167.

Despite the plague, Sambucus was already preparing to return to Vienna when a servant informed him that the sewers and the toilets are being cleaned, so he postponed the departure for a few days. He has still not received the books from Plantin except for a single copy of Stobaeus, which has no index. He has heard that the package is with the Frenchman (Jean Aubry) and includes five copies. Crato should feel free to take a copy and any other potentially included books. Henri Estienne may answer about Dioscorides. Sambucus asks Crato to let him know when Olbracht Łaski and the other Polish legates are going to leave Vienna and if there is anything worth seeing or doing which can relieve his solitude.

Magnifice domine, salutem.

Non me coeli urbisque contag[i]es amplius, quominus ad vos redeam, tenent. Cum omnia ad iter composuissem, nunciat famulus cloacas et foramina (auribus et scripto sit honor) in aedibus nostris expurgari reditumque differendum in aliquot paucos dies. Libros a Plantino missos praeter Stobaei unicum exemplum et quidem sine ullo indice et literis nondum accepi.[1370] Audio apud Gallum esse fasciculum, in quo V sunt exemplaria. De iis et, si quid aliud est in eo, quod tuae excellentiae placeat, oro κτήσει καὶ παγκτήσει[1371] accipiat. Henricus

---

[1367] On Sambucus's efforts concerning Photius cf. the Index. See Claudio Bevegni, "La Bibliotheca di Fozio nei secoli XV-XVI e l'edizione mancata di Giovanni Sambuco," *Studi Umanistici Piceni* 20 (2000), 183-195.
[1368] as a competitor and a rival student
[1369] copy
[1370] Stobaeus and Plethon, *Stobaei eclogarum libri duo ... et Plethonis de rebus Peloponnesiacis orationes duae*.
[1371] in possession and full ownership. Gerstinger suggests to correct Samuel Klose's transcription παγητήσει to χρήσει or παγχρήσει.

forte rescribet de Dioscoride.[1372] Audio esse Laskium et alios Polonos ad caesarem legatos.[1373] Oro, quando ii sint discessuri, si intelligis, mihi significes, et si quid est, quod citra molestiam et publice licet συνιδεῖν[1374] aliud, ut interea hanc solitudinem eis sublevem. 23. Ianuarii 1575. Totus meritis tuis Sambucus.

Address: Magnifico et excellenti domino doctori Ioanni Cratoni ab Craffthaim, caesareae maiestatis consiliario et archiatro, domino patrono et amico observando. Viennae.

237.
Sambucus to Nicolaus Reusner
13 February 1575, Vienna

Published in Nicolaus Reusner, ed., *Epistolarum turcicarum variorum* (Frankfurt am Main: Ioannes Collitius, 1608), liber XI, 154.

Sambucus excuses himself for his silence, which cannot affect a friendship based on virtue and learning. He informs Reusner of the death of Selim II. As a prince, Selim was devoted to pleasures, never conducted wars in person and ruled less than eight years, which was foretold by some diviners. It is held that weakened by Venus and wine, he died of fever. They say that Murad III started his rule in the barbaric way of his forefathers by having five of his younger brothers strangled in his own presence.

Ioannes Sambucus caesaris historicus Nicolao Reusnero Leorino.

Ita est, ut scribis, silentio non dissui firmas amicitias, quarum conciliatrix est virtus et doctrina, praesertim si inopia tabellariorum, aut etiam ipsarum rerum scribendarum interveniat. Itaque mutua nobis excusatione opus esse non puto. Et sane quod scribam hoc tempore, nihil habeo. Illud fortassis ab aliis ad te scriptum est: mense Decembri anni superioris Selymum Turcarum Tyrannum diem obiisse suum.[1375] Princeps fuit voluptarius, bella non nisi per legatos gessit, annos regnavit octo non integros. Imperii hoc tempus (ut aiunt) nescio a quibus suis divinatoribus praedictum fuit, quod cum breve et angustum videretur tyranno, voluptatibus impendendum esse solitus fuit dicere. Sic nimirum Venere et vino exhaustus, tandem febre

---

[1372] In a letter dated 8 June (which may also have been written many years later), Henri Estienne tells Crato that Sambucus should not give up hope concerning the publication of Dioscorides. See *Praemissae sunt Henrici Stephani*, 25: "Ad Sambucum scribo ne me de Dioscoride edendo mutasse sententiam existimet, quem mihi pollicitus erat." On the Dioscorides-project, which would finally be realised thanks to Henri Estienne, who delegated the job to Jean-Antoine Sarasin, see the Index. It is curious that Sambucus did not get an answer from Estienne during his Viennese sojourn in the autumn of 1574.

[1373] Count Olbracht (Albert) Łaski, Palatine of Sieradz (1536–1604) was an adventurer, diplomat and alchemist, sometimes acting as a pro-Habsburg agent. He was important to the imperial court because of his influence in Poland and North Hungary. He worked together with Jacobus Basilicus Heraclides on securing the Moldavian throne in 1559–1561. In 1575, after Henry Valois's escape from Poland he was suspected of plotting to seize the Polish throne. See *Olbracht Łaski wojewoda sieradzki: wizerunek historyczny dziejów Polski XVI wieku. 2: Drugie bezkrólewie: 1574–1876*, ed. Alexander Kraushar (Warszawa: Gebethner i Wolff, 1882); Miklós Istvánffy, *Historiarum de rebus Ungaricis libri XXXIV* (Coloniae Agrippinae: Antonius Hieratus, 1622), 538-542.

[1374] to see

[1375] Selim II died on 12 December 1574.

extinctus scribitur. Imperium Amurathes filius more maiorum barbarico auspicatus esse perhibetur, quinque fratribus suis natu minoribus in praesentia sua strangulatis. Sed de his alias plura et certiora. Interim vale. Viennae. Idibus Februarii MDLXXV.

238.
Sambucus to Johannes Crato
[January–February 1575[1376]], [Vienna]

Published in Gerstinger, "Die Briefe," 170-171.

When Henri Estienne was leaving Vienna he told Sambucus to communicate with him through Crato. Now he is sending Gemistus Pletho's booklet On destiny *requested by Estienne so that he can add it to the writings of other writings concerning Plato, and he asks Crato to forward it to him. He will publicly thank Crato for his intervention with the emperor, meanwhile he should urge him by giving him a memo. He repeats the summary of the same in the little book (meant for the emperor) so that the emperor, if he does not read the other memos, remembers at least Sambucus and hence makes up his mind.*

Clarissimo viro domino doctori Ioanni Cratoni etc., patrono et amico observandissimo.

Henricus noster hinc profecturus, si quid ad se recta vellem, tuae humanitati committerem. Mitto ad ipsum requisitum libellum Περὶ εἱμαρμένης Plethonis,[1377] ἀνεύρητον[1378] et quem cum aliis Platonicis coniunget.[1379] Oro, si commodo veredariorum aut alia via mittere poteris, ad ipsum mittito. De singulari et optatissimo ad imperatorem officio et interventu tuo quantum tibi debeam, palam aliquando omnes intellegent; adhuc urge, cum occasio dabitur, una cum schedula ad memoriam scripta suae maiestati.[1380] Vale, mi optime Crato. Ex Museolo etc. Totus tuis meritis Sambucus.

[1376] The dating of this letter depends partly on Henri Estienne's Viennese sojourn, which apparently took place in the autumn of 1574. Although much of Estienne's itinerary is still unknown, from a letter he addressed to Crato "ex Heliconio nostro" on 18 January 1575 we can now date his departure to December 1574: "Domum satis ex animi sententia confecto itinere (qua in re, sicut in aliis multis, Dei benignitatem agnosco) sum reversus aliisque iam literis de hoc meo felici reditu certiorem te feci [...]" *Praemissae sunt Henrici Stephani*, 11. On his Viennese and Hungarian stay (he also visited Pressburg) see in general Bach, *Un humaniste hongrois*, 23-24; Michael Maittaire, *Stephanorum historia, vitas ipsorum ac libros complectens* (Londini: Benj. Motte, 1702), 370-372; and cf. letter 236. As this is only a note without a proper address, Sambucus probably wrote it before Crato's departure in late February, although its dating to March or April cannot be excluded either. Cf. other undated letters on the following pages.

[1377] Pletho's *De fato* was published first in 1722. Sambucus's manuscript cannot be found in the holdings of the ÖNB in Vienna.

[1378] unpublished

[1379] Cf. Estienne's letter to Crato, where he explicitly asks for the book: "Caeterum de Platone commodum mentionem fecisti in tuis literis, quod et antea de illo excudendo cogitassem, et illam voluntatem confirmaverit nova interpretatio quae mihi paulo post meum reditum oblata fuit: quo magis D. Sambucum ut exemplaria vetera si nondum Augustam misit inde ad me perferenda (sicut inter nos convenerat) ut quamprimum mittat, rogatum volo." *Praemissae sunt Henrici Stephani*, 11. Crato must have informed Sambucus of Estienne's desire still in January.

[1380] It concerns Crato's intervention regarding Sambucus's attempt to sell his library to the emperor. Cf. letter 215, note 1266. Note that Sambucus made contemporaneous efforts to sell the library elsewhere (cf. letters 234-235), offering it also to Augustus, Elector of Saxony, using the mediation of Hubert Languet.

Summam repeto in libello, ut rei meminerit, et si alias schedulas non legit, saltem ex aliqua inspecta animum patefaciat.

239.
Sambucus to Johannes Crato
[February 1575[1381]], [Vienna]

Published in Gerstinger, "Die Briefe," 171-172.

Sambucus has taken the book apart. He is sending its first part, in which he corrects Diogenes Laertius's life of Aristotle, to Episcopius, duly mentioning Crato's name in it. He asks Crato to send it with the courier of the next day. The publishers demand this kind of works to come out as soon as possible. In Basel the couriers ask three guldens for the transportation. Three days earlier, he had a private conversation with the emperor among other things about the ongoing business of buying his Greek manuscripts. The emperor asked him to be reminded of it later and expressed his wish to have the matter concluded. He said that his and Sambucus's hopes had been frustrated because of the many duties he had.

Sambucus salutem.

Dissolvi librum, priorem partem mitto σὺν θεῷ,[1382] in quo vitam quoque Aristotelis Laertianam correxi, iudicium de numero, serie et proprietate, τῇ συνεχείᾳ ἤτοι καὶ ἁφῇ[1383] meum edidi, eum nominis apta tui mentione ad Episcopium.[1384] Oro, iuva nos, ut veredarius cras mittat omnia ad praelum, quamprimum similia exeunt et efflagitant typographi. Qui perferent cursu, μισθὸν[1385] habebunt 3 fl. Basileae. Vale et me de officio non communiter sed privatim publica debere scito. Ex Museolo.

Since this offer is much more detailed than all that has been previously known, and amply illustrates that it concerned more generally Sambucus's "museum," it is worth quoting it here: "Summa eorum quae dixi esse venalia: / - Codices manuscripti graeci 355 in quibus sunt ad 60 scripta nondum evulgata, Latini miscui poetarum historicorum et aliarum artium 245. Venditor aestimat quemlibet codicem quinque aureis Hungaricis. / - Marmorea capita magnarum statuarum 8, singula aestimatur 25 ducatis. / - Statuae integrae duae Veneris et Priapi, 300 ducatis. / - Solis imago in forma pueri aenea elegantissima, 200 ducati. / - Veneris in balneo tabella aenea rara, 50 ducat. / - Numus triumphalis L. Veri et M. Antonini insignis 100 ducat. / - Calix insignis figuris scuplits ex iaspide continens veterum sextarium, 100 ducat. / - Numi magni aerei probi et rari ad 150, 300 ducatis. Numus unicus de donatione Constantini 100 ducatis" (Sächsisches Hauptstaatsarchiv Dresden, loc. 9083, LM III, f. 224.) Quoted by Nicollier-De Weck, *Hubert Languet*, 354, note 51. The refusal by Augustus of Saxony is dated to 27 April 1576, ibid.

[1381] As it appears from the text, this letter (or note) was written still before Maximilian II's departure to Prague. See the previous and the next letter and cf. with letter 242.
[1382] with God's help
[1383] about the sequence or even touch
[1384] We do not know of which book Sambucus is talking here. It may have been a contribution to Episcopius's planned Aristotle-edition, see Gerstinger, "Die Briefe," 172.
[1385] fee

Cum caesare nudiustertius separatim sum locutus cum de aliis rebus tum coepto initoque consilio de libris Graecis.[1386] Iussit se moneam et discupere, ut rebus concluderem, dixit, sed multa negocia adhuc transversa spem suam itemque meam remorantur.[1387] Ἔρρωσο.[1388] Totus etc. Sambucus.

Address: Magnifico domino Ioanni Cratoni, caesaris consiliario et medico singulari et in primis.

240.
Sambucus to Johannes Crato
[Late February 1575[1389]], [Vienna]

Published in Gerstinger, "Die Briefe," 167-169.

Sambucus has heard that the court is openly preparing for departure. Meanwhile, he would like to find out what the emperor thinks about his little library. It does not matter if he decides against it, he would like to close this matter and not offend the emperor if he finds another buyer. He asks Crato to mention it a second time. He would not lower the price but the terms of payment can be set by the emperor provided a small interest is included. Urged by Henri Estienne, he spends several hours a day with Plato's works but has found only a few errors in his three manuscripts. He has collected some rare foreign plants, adding to his notable emendations in Dioscorides, which he will these days show to people, who think themselves to be experts on Crateuas and Dioscorides. He will send to the press very soon two volumes of Variae lectiones, *i.e. his miscellaneous observations. Sambucus complains about that ungrateful Italian (i.e. Girolamo Mercuriale) to whom he entrusted Palladius's Hippocrates-commentary, Trapezuntius's translation of Aristotle's* History of animals *and Paulus Aegineta's books to no avail, as he is neither publishing them nor sending them back. He is said to have copied the interesting parts and left it with someone in Venice so that this person will send them back to Sambucus. "What a nice company!" These people should go to hell, "we are Germans"!*

Salutem.

Audio abitionem vulgo parari.[1390] Discupio antea, quid animi caesar de bibliothecula habeat subintelligere. Sive eam acceperit, sive non, ἐλαχίστου ποιήσω,[1391] modo ista cura liberer, ne, ubi alium herum nacta fuerit, caesar offendatur, quod non puto, qui talia curare desiit.[1392] Obsecro te per elegantiam doctrinae, per humanissima paratissimaque cuique amico officia tua, occasione

---
[1386] See also the previous and the next letters.
[1387] Sambucus returns to the encounter in letter 242.
[1388] farewell
[1389] Since Sambucus's letters to Zwinger suggest that Crato moved with the court to Prague sometimes in late February, this letter should be dated before his departure (by 4 March Crato was in Prague, see the next letter). It was a note (Billet), like the other undated letters of this period which Sambucus addressed to him mostly while both were in Vienna.
[1390] The court moved to Prague in late February, where Rudolf was crowned king of Bohemia on 12 March 1575. See Bibl, *Maximilian II*, 383-385.
[1391] I will not care in the least
[1392] Cf. letter 238, note 1380.

commoda iniicies et iteres mentionem. De pretio nil imminuam, de solutione tempus sua maiestas constituere, modo fiat cum aliqua specula lucelli intercurrentis, poterit. Ego precibus Henrici adductus quotidie in Platonicis aliquot horas pono, pauca in tribus χειρογράφοις[1393] adhuc repperi mendosa.[1394] Ad observationes meas haud vulgares in Dioscoridem coegi undique aliquot raras plantas externas, quas his diebus magistris eius cognitionis et arbitris, qui se familiam ducere existimant Crateuae et Dioscoridis,[1395] ostendam ac in omnem eventum iudiciaque emittam.[1396] Ilico *Variarum lectionum* duo libri [i.e. duos libros], quas adversaria et miscellanea vocant, prelis mandabo. Vale, mi doctissime Crato, meque, quod potes et facis, iuva.

Ingratus ille Italus, cui Palladium in 6 Ἐπιδημιῶν[1397] et Trapezuntii de *Animalium* Aristotelis *historia* [et] partibus nostram versionem etc. commisi una cum Aegyneta, nihil dum edit nec remittit.[1398] Audio exscripsisse illum potiora et cuidam Venetiis negocium dedisse, libri ad me redeant. Das sein feine Gesellen! Sed εἰς κόρακας[1399] abeant, nos germani sumus.[1400] Vale. Totus tuus Sambucus.

Address: Magnifico et clarissimo viro domino doctori Ioanni Cratoni etc.

241.
Sambucus to Joachim Camerarius Jr.
4 March 1575, Vienna

The original is kept in Munich, BSB, Clm 10367, Nr. 176.

Sambucus has belatedly received the letter, in which Camerarius renews the friendship Sambucus had with his father and writes that he has Sadoleto's book. Sambucus approves of his plan for the edition and offers his own writings of the same kind. He has entrusted Camerarius's father with two books. The first one contains Greek letters of Chrysoloras and some others, which Camerarius Sr. has promised to publish alongside his own letters. The second contains some Greek epithets which Sambucus once collected through casual reading and which he liked and also wanted to publish and provide with a preface. Sambucus has asked him to correct what he did not like or what the scribe has misspelled. Sambucus asks Camerarius to return the books if he does not intend to publish them, and he encourages him to keep up his father's work.

[1393] manuscript
[1394] See letters 233, 235, 238 and 257.
[1395] Crateuas was a Greek pharmacologist, artist, and physician to Mithradates VI, king of Pontus (120–63 BC). His herbal and work on root cutting survived only in quotations by Dioscorides. In fact, some of the botanical illuminations in Busbequius's Anicia Juliana-manuscript (Cod. Med. gr. 1), to which Sambucus is referring here, are supposedly based on Crateuas's drawings, although direct borrowing is denied by John M. Riddle (*Dioscorides on Pharmacy and Medicine*, Austin: Univ. of Texas Press, 1985, 190-1).
[1396] It is rather curious that Crato was not included among these experts, especially in the light of his greater earlier involvement into the project. Cf. letters 154 and 156.
[1397] (commentary on the sixth book) of the *Epidemics*.
[1398] See letters 224 and 226.
[1399] to crows (= to hell)
[1400] Germanus also means here brotherly, true and sincere, in contrast to the untruthful Mercuriale.

Sambucus salutem.

Accepi tuas longo licet intervallo dierum, quibus memoriam veteris necessitudinis cum patre tuo, clarissimo viro gratiosissime repetis, itidem Sadoleti te libellum possidere significas. Consilium in edendo tuum probo. Si quid mearum nugarum simul esse voles, non recuso, cuius ista quoqe sunt generis. Sed, mi Ioachime, credideram ego duos alios libros patri, cuius laus cum omni reliquo tempore aequa vigebit, epistolarum Graecarum Chrysolarae cum aliis aliquot Bessarionis, Planudis, Gemistii, quibus se suas ille additurum, et publicas facturum est sancte pollicitus. Alter habet quaedam epitheta Graeca, olim a me citra delectum et seriem rerum lectione temeraria conlectum, quem ille a me ostensum probare videbatur, seque prelo cum prohemiolo suo adhibiturum. Sed rogabam, quae disciplicerent [!] aut a meo puero negligentius essent descripta, ne negligeret. Hos ego mihi restitui, si non edis, cupio atque obsecro, ne sibi iniuriam fieri aut fraudem Bibliothecula queratur. Tu vero et nomine et laborum molem paternam fortiter exceptam urge ac tuere meque ama. IIII Martii 1575 Vienna raptim.

Oro rescribe, si quid miseris, vicino meo civi vestro Sigemondo Richtero[1401] inscribas, qui ilico mihi restituet. Am alten Vlayschmarkt[1402] Zu Wien H. Sigmondt Richter.

Address: Clarissimo viro domino doctori Ioachimo Camerario, physico reipublicae Norinbergensis, amico suo singulari. Nurnberg H. D. Camerario zu handen. Cito cito. *Camerarius's note:* 25. Martii anno 75.

242.
Sambucus to Johannes Crato
4 March 1575, [Vienna]

Published in Gerstinger, "Die Briefe," 172-173.

Since the departure of the emperor they are entirely abandoned. Sambucus is happy about the emperor's wellbeing and asks Crato to mention (the case of) his books to him. The point is that he should receive a donation of 1,000 florins from the Hungarian Chamber in order to be helped out in his difficulties and with regards to his service of many years, for which he never asked for anything in exchange. As the emperor was getting on the chariot, he noticed Sambucus watching, he called him over and giving his hand told him: "Well, Sambucus, write to me in time. I have your supplication in mind, let someone remind me of it in Prague, and I will not forget about your case; can't you see, how many negotia *have taken my time." Sambucus thanked him and mentioned Crato as the person who would remind him. Ten days earlier Juraj Zrinski (György*

[1401] Possibly the Nuremberg merchant Sigmund Richter (1529–1587), who was ennobled in 1560 together with his brothers (Vienna, Staatsarchiv, AVA Adel HAA AR 793.1). Richter had a portrait medallion of himself coined in 1562 (preserved e. g. as an application on a silver double cup now in New York, Metropolitan Museum of Art, accession number 17.190.607a–b) and another one, of himself and his wife, in 1576 (see Arthur Suhle "Neuerworbene Medaillen des Münzkabinets," *Berliner Museen* 64.3/4 [1943], 34–41, at 34–35). The years of his birth and death are indicated on a portrait engraving of him preserved in several collections.

[1402] It seems that in this period, Sambucus lived on the Fleischmarkt in the northern part of the city.

Zrinyi) took a nice booty from the Ottomans and killed the bey of Szeged. If they had been able to capture him alive, they could have enriched Zrinski with 10,000 florins. Count Eck zu Salm was buried without any pomp by his brothers and wife in their burial vault at St Dorothea. Sambucus asks Crato to forward a letter to (Conradus?) Hubertus.

Salutem.

Nos hic pene in solitudine a discessu imperatoris degimus. Imperatori commodam valetudinem ex animo comprecamur, apud quem, si recte poteris sine offensione, oro, mei libelli memineris, cuius summa fuit, ut, quid de libris iubeat, clementer patefaciat, tum ut me mille florenorum donativo ex camera Ungarica measque difficultates sublevet ac annorum servitia augeat ornetque, qui nihil umquam adhuc a sua maiestate eo nomine petii. Cum concensurus currus esset, me illico conspecto ad se vocavit, dextra porrecta his verbis: *Nunc Sambuce, schreybt mir zu Zeytten. Eurer Supplication bin ich ingedenkh, lasst mich manen zu Prag, will euer nicht vergessen; seht, wievill negocia mich gehalten habem.* Ego humillime gratias egi perque te negocium ursurum dixi. *Ist guett,* dixit.

Zerinius Canisiae praedam ex hoste non ignobilem retulit ante 10 dies et agam Zegediensem interfecit,[1403] quem si vivum abducere potuissent, X milibus Pannonicis comitis rem auxissent. Comes Eccius sine ulla pompa suorum conditorio est per fratres cum uxore ad Dorotheae illatus 26. Februarii.[1404] Me tuae excellentiae commendo, hosque [i.e. hasque] ut Huberto reddi curet, oro. IIII. Martii 1575. Tuae magnificentiae totus tuus Sambucus.

Address: Magnifico et clarissimo viro domino doctori Cratoni a Craffthaim. Maximiliani caesaris archiatro et consiliario, domino patrono et amico observando. Prag. Herrn Cratoni. Cito, cito, cito.

243.
Sambucus to Johannes Crato
9 March 1575, [Vienna]

Published in Gerstinger, "Die Briefe," 173-175.

Sambucus forwarded the letters sent by Crato to the right persons. Guillaume Arragos travelled to Reichard Strein. Sambucus will contact the Fuggers through Henri Estienne but, considering the high number of books they have, they will have no ambition to buy more. Estienne demands Sambucus's four manuscripts of Plato, asking him to send them via Augsburg, using "Mr Herbort" so that Estienne can publish a new bilingual edition, using the new translation of an erudite man. Sambucus is in no hurry; first he wants to be sure about the person he can entrust the books to, and not bother the couriers with so much weight, i.e. of 36 books. He does not either know if it

---

[1403] Juraj (IV) Zrinski (György IV Zrinyi) (1549–1603), the son of the hero of Szigetvár Miklós Zrinyi/Nikola Zrinski, was Western Hungary's most important and successful military leader, supremus capitaneus from 1574, and captain of Kanizsa from the mid 1570s. He promoted both Lutheranism and book culture in Croatian language. See László Nagy, "Kanizsa nagyhírű kapitánya, gróf Zrínyi György," *Zalai múzeum* 7 (1997), 23-26. We do not know the name of the bey of Szeged.

[1404] By the end of his life Eck Graf zu Salm (1527–1575) served as supremus capitaneus of Transdanubian Hungary.

will suite Mr Herbort and worries about the codices' eventual condition or loss. Crato may want to excuse him for the delay and warn him if there is an opportunity for transport; he should also tell Estienne to publish (the already) borrowed books. If there will be no other way, he will send some of his emendations on Plato but he could only find a few with respect to the last edition. Episcopius finally published the Basilica *in the translation of Johannes Löwenklau, although the same was also prepared by Thomas Freigius. Plantin releases Stobaeus's* Physical and Moral Extracts *together with some other works. He had sent Willem Canter something which the latter promises to finish for the coming book fair (in Frankfurt). At the moment, he is preparing some Transylvanian history about Bebek. Estienne has not said anything about editing Dioscorides, so to avoid empty promises in the future Sambucus may publish his emendations own their own. Different stories circulate of the emperor's entry into Prague; about an eagle seen in the air with a sword; the threats of the emperor; and about the particular attention paid to not letting any Bohemian nobleman leave Prague without the emperor's permit. They say the emperor prefers to return to Vienna by Pentecost and that the king (Rudolf) will visit his bride in Dresden. Sambucus hopes that Crato will soon return to Vienna, but he sees little hope of that in the next two years because of the imperial diets.*

Salutem.

Distribui tuas, quibus voluisti. Arragosius ad Streinium erat profectus, Henrico Stephano omnibus modis ad Fuggerum [i.e. Fuggeros] adero.[1405] Sed tam sunt contracta non modo manu sed animo quoque erga literas, ut numero librorum territi nihil amplius benigne faciant. Henricus Platonis 4 Codices meos urget,[1406] ut per Augustam et dominum Herbortum ad se mittam,[1407] accidisse occasionem edendi utraque lingua egregiam, nova eruditaque interpretatione cuiusdam maximi viri etc. Ego vero, uti debeo et soleo, nihil urgebo, dum sciam, qui tuto recteque transmittam, ne cursores tanto onere, hoc est librorum 36, sumptusque vexem, nec scio, an id domino Herborto placeret. Possent quoque codices tanto intervallo aut perire aut serius redire. Si tuae excellentiae videtur, excusabis moram et me consilium ex occasione capturum significabis; hortabere simul, uti libellos mutuos publicos faciat. Si aliter nequiero, aliquot lectiones in Platonem missurum me, nam pauca adhuc repperi, quae ab ultima editione discedunt. Episcopius tandem Βασιλικῶν 24 libros ex interpretatione Leonclavii, licet Freggius idem praestiterit, mea causa edidit.[1408] Plantinus absolvit Φυσικὰς γνώμας Stobaei cum quibusdam aliis.[1409] Cantero aliquid miseram, qui idem

---

[1405] Guillaume Arragos (Aragos/Arragosius) (1513–1610) was a Huguenot doctor and hermetic thinker of Toulouse, who came to Basel in c. 1571, and became a friend of Theodor Zwinger. He believed in alchemy, in the Kabbalah, and made research into Paracelsism. In November 1574, he arrived to Vienna in the service of the ailing emperor, but as it appears, he did not follow him to Prague. See Gilly, "Zwischen Erfahrung und Spekulation." R(e)ichard Strein (Streun) von Schwarzenau (1538–1600) studied law in Padua and Strasburg, joined the court in 1564 and became president of the Imperial Chamber in 1567. He was a loyal follower of Maximilian II, trying to mitigate between the religious parties and having an important role in the 1568 religious settlement. See Karl Großmann, "Reichart Strein von Schwarzenau," *Jahrbuch für Landeskunde und Heimatschutz von Niederösterreich und Wien* 20 (1927), 1-37.

[1406] Gerstinger thinks ("Die Briefe," 175) that these were Cod. Phil. gr. 21, 80, 109, and Cod. Suppl. gr. 20 in the ÖNB. On Estienne's plan to publish Plato see letters 233, 235, 238 and 240.

[1407] This might have been the Augsburg patrician Johann Heinrich Herwart (see letter 211) or probably his brother Paulus Herwart, who was a patron of Crato, as Gerstinger suggests ("Die Briefe," 175).

[1408] *LX librorum* Βασιλικῶν.

[1409] Stobaeus and Plethon, *Stobaei eclogarum libri duo ... et Plethonis de rebus Peloponnesiacis orationes duae*.

se hoc mercatu liberaturum fidem pollicetur.[1410] Ego rerum Ungaricarum Bebekiana polio et Transylvanica etc.[1411] Henricus de Dioscoridis editione nihil scribit, cogar meas variantes et emendationes separatim prodere, ne diutius tot flagitatores promissis ducam.[1412] Hic varia de caesaris Pragensi ingressu, de aquila cum gladio minace in aëre conspecta, de imperatoris minis et, quod extremo caverit, ne quis baronum Bohemiae absque eius consensu se illinc commoveat etc.[1413] Suam maiestatem palam praeferre ad Pentecostam ad nos reditum. Regem Dresium [!] ad sponsam visendam iturum.[1414] Utinam quamprimum ad nos revertatis, publicis rebus commodis, nam de comitiis imperii hoc proximo biennio exigua spes ostenditur. Vale meique memineris, valde oro. 9. Martii 1575. Tuae excellentiae totus Sambucus.

Address: Magnifico et clarissimo viro domino doctori Cratoni a Craffthaim etc., caesaris protophysico et consiliario, domino patrono, amico colendo. Prag. Herrn Doctori Crato. Cito. Cito.

244.
Sambucus to Johannes Crato
[Spring 1575[1415]], [Vienna]

Published in Gerstinger, "Die Briefe," 169-170.

Sambucus responded to Markus Fugger using the arguments mentioned by Crato, which will hopefully convince Fugger. He accepts Crato's reasons and does not think that Henri Estienne had the same solid reasons. He thanks Crato for his intervention regarding (the selling) of his little library. If only the emperor decided about it. But if he decides to join it to his library, Sambucus is ready to accept even the mediocre conditions. He would gladly send Episcopius a Greek booklet on Aristotle, which argues against Gemistus Pletho and other Platonists. He gave some rare books to Henri Estienne (who wants to publish Plato), arguing for Plato and the Platonists; now he would like to have something published against Plato and for Aristotle. If Crato were to help him send this work to Xylander (in Heidelberg) or to Basel, he would do a service to all.

[1410] This appears to be a reference not to Stobaeus, edited and translated by Canter, but to another book. Gulielmus Canterus (Willem Canter) (1542–1575) is a little known but extremely productive and talented Dutch humanist, related to the circle of Plantin. Still the best source on his life is Melchior Adam, *Vitae Germanorum philosophorum*, 272-288. Also see Gábor Almási, "The Work Ethic in Humanist Biographies: the Case of Willem Canter," *Hungarian Historical Review* 8 (2019), 594-619.

[1411] This could be a reference to the powerful aristocrats of Transylvania Ferenc Bebek († 1558) or György Bebek († 1567). On both of them see Ildikó Horn, *A hatalom pillérei. A politikai elit az Erdélyi Fejedelemség megszilárdulásának korszakában (1556–1588)* [The pillars of power. The political elite during the consolidation of the Transylvanian Principality] (Academic Doctoral Thesis) (Budapest 2012), passim. Unfortunately, we do not know this work by Sambucus.

[1412] See letter 236.

[1413] On the Bohemian diet, which just started, see Bibl, *Maximilian II*, 384.

[1414] Gossip held that Maximilian II's son, Rudolf, could feel interest in the daughter of Augustus, Elector of Saxony. See ibid.

[1415] Gerstinger dated the letter to the spring of 1575, which seems correct because of its mention of the Fuggers (see the preceding letter) and Sambucus's attempts at selling his books.

Clarissimo viro domino doctori Ioanni Cratoni etc. suo observandissimo salutem.

Rescripsi Marco Fuggero et adspersi argumenta abs te recte notata, quibus, credo me quiddam profecturus, nisi omnino suam dignitatem et officium deserere velit.[1416] Causas tuas accipio nec putarem tam firmis Henricum niti etc., cui non minus quam tu et omnes boni eruditique volunt omniaque ampla ex meritis cupio.[1417] Habeo de memoria bibliothecae singularem gratiam. Nihil gratius egeris, quam si me expeditum denique sensero, quod omnino spero tuo interventu fore. Modo sua maiestas nutu aut verbulo significet se nolle, in coelo fuero. Sin adiungere suae constituerit, ad mediocres conditiones subiectissime facilis ero. Episcopio libellum Graecum ad Aristotelem ex animo mitterem, qui contra Plethonem et alios Platonicos disputat. Dedi pro Platone et Platonicis aliquot rara scripta Henrico Platonem edituro. Vellem vicissim quid contra Platonica pro Aristotele extaret. Si, ut perferantur ad Xylandrum vel Basileam me iuveris, publice inservieris, ut facis. Vale. Totus tuus Sambucus.

245.
Sambucus to Johannes Crato
6 April 1575, Vienna

Published in Gerstinger, "Die Briefe," 175-177.

Sambucus finds solace in the news about Crato's (and the emperor's) return by the middle of the year, since without Crato he is in complete lack of contacts and information. Let Crato do what he wants concerning his copies of Plato. If Crato wants him to, he will even send them to the Garamantes, but the distance is great and he does not know to whom to consign them in Augsburg to send them on. He hopes that Estienne will understand it. He is sorry that the sale of his books can in no way be urged; the delay is tiring him. If the emperor had brought the issue to an end, which he for the last three years frequently said and hoped to do, he would have taken on the special responsibility for the imperial library. He would have restored it in order and size so that it could have justly surpassed many other collections in number, quality and arrangement. He would have known well where to look to enrich it with old and new books. Not to praise himself, but there are few who have studied the appropriateness and authenticity of the characters, the paper and the age of books as long as he has. But he neither cares nor wishes anymore; from now on he can take care of his own books exclusively, without being suspected by someone of stealing from the emperor's store-room when sizing a book in order to make it accessible to everybody or having his family forced to sell his books cheaply after his death. He never feared something like this and does not think about it. If the heirs of Camerarius convene, he would like to have the Greek letters that were given to the father and Sadoleto's consolation either published or sent back to him.

[1416] Most probably, Sambucus was trying to sell his books to the Fuggers. Markus Fugger (1529–1597) was the eldest son of Anton Fugger. He held the most prestigious offices in the empire and the city of Augsburg and was connected to German aristocracy through marriage. His father's patrimony was divided between him and his two brothers in 1575. He was the author of a German book on horse-keeping. Sambucus, who was once tutor to his younger brother Jakob Fugger, knew Markus from the 1550s and also dedicated an emblem to him (*Emblemata*, 1564, 78). See also letter 238, note 1380.

[1417] The debate between Crato and Henri Estienne probably took place during Estienne's stay in Vienna.

Salutem.

Adhuc nos vulgi sermones de vestro ad nos reditu post semestre solantur. Utinam vera, si ominantur, enuncient vosque cito praesentes constituant, adeo omni congressu et communicatione careo. De Platonis exemplaribus, quod voles, fiet.[1418] Mittam vel ad Garamantas,[1419] si e re publica futurum putas et iusseris, sed longum est iter, difficilis mittendi ratio, nec ad quem Augustam mittam, ut libenter facileque transmittat perveniatque, certo scio. Nisi omnino fallor, Henricus causas accipiat, sin minus, passa. De meo negocio, cuius me mora fatigat, nullam esse occasionem reliquam urgendi doleo nec parum res meas turbat. Sed graviora et diutius aliis multa aeque ferenda. Si caesarea maiestas benigne rem mecum confecisset, quod saepe iussit et voluit ante triennium et alias, bibliothecae augustae curam in me praecipuam recepissem ac iis modis illam in ordinem et copiam redegissem, ut et numero et dignitate et serie aliis multis anteponi iure posset.[1420] Novi enim, unde ea esset locupletanda recentioribus et vetustis codicibus. Qui characterum, cartarum aetatumque probitatem et fidem tot annorum exemplis tractassent, paucos vides, absit gloriari. Sed nunc nec curo nec velim dum mea proprie mihi colenda sit et tractanda, ne, si quid depromo cumque omnibus communico, suspicetur quisquam me ex imperatoris apothecis sumsisse [!] etc., aut a mea morte mei quoque istuc concedere aliqua occasione non sufficiente aut preciolo cogerentur. Etsi nihil eiusmodi umquam nec metui nec cogito. Si Camerarii haeredes convenerint, oro, ut traditas patri epistolas Graecas et Sadoleti Consolationem elegantissimam edant aut reddant.[1421] Vale et me fove inque patrocinio haud vulgari positum serva. 6. Aprilis 1575. Viennae. Totus tuis meritis Ioannes Sambucus.

Address: Magnifico et clarissimo viro domino doctori Ioanni Cratoni a Craffthaim, caesareae maiestatis archiatro etc., domino patrono et amico summe colendo. Pragae aut Dresdae.

246.
Sambucus to Hugo Blotius
23 April [1575], [Vienna]

The original is kept in Vienna, ÖNB, Cod. 9737^{z14-18}, II, f. 46^{r-v}. Published in Gerstinger, "Die Briefe," 177-178.

Sambucus is sorry that Blotius is in bed. He understood the letter sent from Strasburg: it offers a good opportunity, if Blotius wants to grab it. He cannot see any reference to 200 (guldens) in it. If Blotius takes the place of Valentin Erythraeus, he would certainly get his salary. And this could be raised

---

[1418] See letter 243, note 1406.

[1419] A Lybian tribe mentioned by Herodotus 4.174 and 183, and Strabo 17.835.

[1420] The context of these sentences is provided by the next letter. Although Sambucus had apparently never thought of assuming the position of the imperial librarian, he felt deeply offended by Hugo Blotius's potential nomination. This seemed especially embarrassing in case his library got eventually included into the imperial collection, hence taking a book from his former library could seem to the new librarian as stealing (see below). Ironically, it was later Blotius who furthered the purchase of Sambucus's library. See Almási, *The Uses of Humanism*, 186-190 and 193.

[1421] On the letters of the Greek church fathers cf. letters 289, 351 (note 1998) and 368; and Gerstinger, "Zusammenfassung," 294-295. On Sadoleto's *Consolationes* cf. the Index.

during the years and Sambucus hopes that a good marriage and other sources can further increase his income. If Blotius wants, he will also be able to take part in prestigious diplomatic missions. Blotius should let him know what he wants without hesitation and tell his decision to the ones in Strasburg. It is an important city and to first promise something and then to disappoint would have an impact on the tribunal, the city and his honour. Carolus Lorcher sent a package of 5 April, with a letter to Blotius and to Mr Stornberg. The courier of Strasburg left the package at the pharmacy of Rappius, who forwarded it to him. He does not know where the courier is, but Lorcher may be waiting for a response.

Salutem.

Doleo te in lecto esse. Literas Argentoratenses intellexi. Occasio egregia oblata, si tibi ipse deesse nolueris. Non video 200 nominatos. Si locum Erythrei possederis, eodem salario te habitum iri non dubito.[1422] Quod si primo anno quiddam desideraris, sequentibus sacietur, ac spero et matrimonio et aliis rebus tibi abunde provisum iri. Imo si voles, elatus etiam legationibus satisfeceris illustribus [?].

Proinde quid tui sensus est, plane mihi aut illis citra haesitationem significato. Scis tibi cum amplissima republica et pacis amante, in eruditos prolixa esse negocium, quam pollicitis ducere, post fallere interesset et subselii et reipublicae honorisque tui. Aie [!] vel nega! Quo proximis literis illorum expediere.

Lorcherus[1423] ad me fasciculum scriptum 5 Aprilis misit una cum tuis et ad dominum Stornberg.[1424] Tabellarius Argentinensis ad officinam Rappii pharmacopolae hodie fasciculum detulit, pharmacopola ad me.[1425] Ubi tabellarius sit, ignoro. Fortasse per hunc ipsum responsum exspectat. Resciemus aliquid cras. Vale et valetudinem curato. 23 Aprilis. Tuus Sambucus.

Address: Domino doctori Hugoni Blotio amico meo.
Blotius's hand: Ioannes Sambucus Viennae 23. Aprilis 1575. De professione Argentoratensi.

[1422] Valentin Erythraeus (1521–1576), taught at the Academy of Strasburg and was later rector of the gymnasium of Altdorf, the later university. See Karl Ritter Halm, "Erythraeus, Valentin," in *ADB* 6 (1877), 335-336; Véronique Montagne, "Jean Sturm et Valentin Erythraeus ou l'élaboration méthodique d'une topique dialectique," *Bibliothèque d'Humanisme et Renaissance* 83 (2001), 477-509. Blotius was finally offered as much as 400 guldens in Strasburg. See Franz Unterkircher, "Hugo Blotius und seine ersten Nachfolger (1575-1663)," in *Geschichte der Österreichische Nationalbibliothek*, ed. Josef Stummvoll (Vienna: Prachner, 1968), 1:82-120, at 85.

[1423] Johann Karl Lorcher (1528–1588) was a prominent Augsburg patrician, a patron and correspondent of Blotius, later also rector of the Strasburg Academy. See Judith Jungo, "Briefe an den Straßburger Ratsherrn Johann Karl Lorcher, Abgeordneten der Stadt auf dem Augsburger Reichstag von 1566," in *Mittelalterliche Literatur im Lebenszusammenhang*, ed. Eckart Conrad Lutz (Freiburg, Switzerland: Univ.-Verl., 1997), 387-421.

[1424] We were not able to identify this person (he may be a member of the Sternberg family).

[1425] We have no further information on the Viennese pharmacist Rapp (or Rappius).

247.
Sambucus to Joachim Camerarius Jr.
26 April 1575, Vienna

The original is kept in Munich, BSB, Clm 10367, Nr. 177.

Whatever they decide concerning Chrysoloras's letters, Sambucus agrees, but he would prefer Camerarius keep to his father's plan, who wanted to add his own published and unpublished letters to them to serve as a benchmark of the art and to show what the present times are capable of. He has not yet received the copy of Sadoleto from Ludwig Camerarius and hopes it did not perish. They should not forget his collection of epithets when they find it. He has many letters and orations by Planudes, but they are full of contentious topics, which he will postpone for later times. Dioscorides will soon appear. Sambucus has spent many perhaps not futile hours collecting and commenting on Dioscorides's text. He has emended the Greek text of Aristotle in many more passages than anyone could have hoped or dared to promise. It will be published in Basle. He is working on Plato and on variae lectiones. Basilica *and the military writings will have been published by now. Camerarius should love Sambucus both of his own accord and for his father's sake.*

Sambucus salutem.

Quodcumque de Chrysolora et aliis statueris, per me licebit. Sed vellem consilio parentis quoque rationem in illis edendis duceres, qui pollicitus erat, se suas Graecas cum editas, tum alias additurum, quo naturae vis et artis διάκρισις[1426] quoque deprehendatur nostrique seculi ingenia studiumque extarent, tamquam ἀνταγωνία καὶ ἀντικαταλλάξις[1427] quaedam. Sadoleti exemplar nondum accepi a Lodovico, nec perditum velim. De epithetis, ubi ad manus venerint, ne obliviscitor. Planudis multas epistulas et orationes habeo, sed infestis et invisis argumentis refertas, quas in aliud tempus differremus. Dioscoridea mea brevi apparebunt, in quibus cogendis et annotandis non paucas, nec fortasse vacuas horas posui. Aristotelem Graecum infinitis locis restitui et pluribus, quam sperare quisquam potuisset, minus polliceri. Edetur Basileae. In Platone nunc secundum χρονικόγραφον[1428] versor et variis lectionum libellis. Βασιλικῶν 24 libri[1429] καὶ πολεμικὰ[1430] nunc exierunt.[1431] Vale, et me tum proprio [!] necessitudine, tum optimi et clarissimi viri patris tui nomine, quem ego unice colui, amore pergito. Viennae 26. Aprilis 1575.

Address: Clarissimo viro, domino doctori Ioachimo Camerario, physico reipublicae Noribergensis, amico singulari. Nurnberg, Herrn Jochm Camerarius doctor.
Camerarius note: 16. Maii anno 75.

[1426] determination.
[1427] adversity and profit.
[1428] chronicle writer.
[1429] *LX librorum Βασιλικῶν* was published by Episcopius in 1575.
[1430] militaria
[1431] Sambucus had Andreas Darmarios (on him see letter 162, note 969) prepare a collection of writings on military and mechanical topics (now in Vienna, ÖNB, Cod. Phil. gr. 55), containing works of Hero of Alexandria, Apollodorus Damascenus, Philo Mechanicus, Sextus Iulius Africanus, Constantinus VII, Nicephorus II Phocas and several anonymous works. He paid 12 Ducats for the manuscript (entry on f. 2ʳ). Later he entrusted the manuscript to Episcopius for publication and the accompanying translation was to be prepared by Wilhelm Xylander (on him see letter 222, note 1301), but the project was never brought to fruition. See letters 257, 266, 271, 291, 301, 361 and Gerstinger, "Die Briefe," 195.

248.
Gulielmus Canterus to Sambucus
[May] 1575, Leuven

Dedication in *Ioannis Stobaei eclogarum libri duo: quorum prior physicas, posterior ethicas complectitur, nunc primum Graece editi, interprete Gulielmo Cantero. Una et Georgii Gemisti Plethonis de rebus Peloponnesiacis orationes duae, eodem Gulielmo Cantero interprete. Accessit et alter eiusdem Plethonis libellus Graecus De virtutibus. Ex bibliotheca clari viri Ioannis Sambuci* (Antverpiae: Plantin, 1575), f. *2^r-3^r. Published in *Humanistes du bassin des Carpates II. Johannes Sambucus*, 192-201.[1432]

249.
Sambucus to Joachim Camerarius Jr.
17 June 1575, [Vienna]

The original is kept in Munich, BSB, Clm 10367, Nr. 178.

Sambucus urges Camerarius to publish the books, which are expected by many friends, with his own and his father's additions. He has read the epigram dedicated to him by Posthius, who flatters him too much. He has improvised an epigram dedicated to Posthius's coat of arms, which Posthius will receive with this letter.

Ioannes Sambucus salutem.

Etsi, quod responderim ad tuas, nil magnopere reor, quia tamen urgebat tabellarius, has reddere volui, quibus iterum te rogo et, si pateris, hortor, uti libellos, in quorum editionis desiderio non pauci sunt amici, cum tuo et parentis optimi et clarissimi viri, auctario divulges. Posthii[1433] ad me epigramma legi. Musis adblandientibus et fortasse me ad pristinum museum tuum invocantibus, ea in me confert, quae non agnosco. In eius veredum inscripsi temere epigramma, quod cum his accipiet.[1434] Vale, mi optime amice, meque tuam amicitiam multorum gratiis anteponere certo tibi persuadeas. 17. Iunii 1575.

Address: **Clarissimo physico et medico reipublicae Noribergensis, Domino Ioachimo filio,** amico suo optimo. Nürnberg. Herrn Doctor.
Camerarius's note: 13. Iulii 75.

[1432] Although the printing was finished on 26 May, Sambucus gave a copy to Maximilian II only on 23 March 1576. See the dedicated copy with Sambucus's poem in Vienna, ÖNB, ZALT PRUNK, 74.B.54.

[1433] Johannes Posthius (1537–1597), physician and humanist, *poeta laureatus*, befriended Sambucus during his visit to Vienna in the winter of 1574-75. Sambucus gave Posthius a manuscript with the *Elegies* of Propertius. See letter 367 and Klaus Karrer, *Johannes Posthius (1537–1597). Verzeichnis der Briefe und Werke mit Regesten und Posthius-Biographie* (Wiesbaden: Harrasowitz, 1993), 83–84.

[1434] On 2 June 1575, Posthius sent a letter to Camerarius (received on 5 June) and asked him to forward the enclosed letter to Sambucus. See Karrer, *Johannes Posthius* (as in the preceding note), 158. The epigram was probably in the letter. It was probably the same epigram Posthius published in *Ioannis Posthii Gerrmershemii, archiatri Wirzeburgici Parerga poetica* (Würzburg: Henricus Aquensis, 1580), 140^v. Posthius asked his correspondents to write poems dedicated to his motto or his coat of arms (depicting a postal courier on his horse, *veredus*). Sambucus's epigram was published, alongside other poems on the same topic, in Christianus Egenolphus, *Anthologia gnomica* (Frankfurt: Georgius Corvinus, 1579), 183^v. See also Karrer, *Johannes Posthius*, 71–72.

250.
Sambucus to Hugo Blotius
30 August 1575, Mannersdorf

The original is kept in Vienna, ÖNB Cod. 9736, f. 11ʳ. Published in Gerstinger, "Die Briefe," 178-179.

If Blotius wants Sambucus's assistance in reviewing the books (of the imperial library) for half a year than he does not seem to understand (the depth of) Sambucus's potential contribution or (the limitedness) of his free time. He often saw the books of the emperor. If Blotius wanted to have his opinion about the superfluous books or the books to be obtained, he would happily help as much as the time spent in the country allows him. For the actual cataloguing of the library Blotius can find other assistants, who will do the work in a few months. If Blotius seeks to involve Sambucus in this, he will not be doing him any favour, especially considering his suspicion about many missing books. He would think the same even if Blotius sustained his ideas with a letter from the emperor. He never happily took over the duties of others except when it was about family or private matters, especially everyday tasks, as a simple cataloguing without in-depth analysis of the books. If Blotius loves him, he should resolve the duty himself, he will help him in more important matters. Blotius should pass a letter on to Crato. On the cover Blotius noted: "refusal of the task of cataloguing, biting."

Sambucus salutem.

Ad recensionem librorum si testimonium oculorum Sambuci sex mensium adhibitum velis, parum te, vel quid elucubrem aut ocii supersit, videre dixerim. Saepe ego caesaris libros vidi. Si qui vel probi sint vel superflui vel substituendi meliores vel aggregandi rariores, meum iudicium accieritis, libenter faciam idque commodo temporum meaeque rusticationis.[1435] Sunt, mi Bloti, alii, qui indicem descripserint et paucioribus mensibus. Hac igitur molestia si me sponte involveris, exiguam feres gratiam, praesertim ista tua suspicione et querela, multos libros subtractos desiderari [...][1436]. Si caesaris literae tuo iudicio venerint, idem sentiam et uberius perscribam nec citra caussas.

Onus alienum nisi fiat privatim et familiariter, numquam libenter sustinui, praecipue vulgare, cuius generis fuerit ista annotatio nuda sine epicrisi, sine iudicio. Vale et si me amas, tali onere expedi sponte, potero maioribus tibi adesse et satisfacere. 30. Augusti 1575. Ex Villula Manerstorfensi, raptim.

Domino Cratoni has diligenter transmittito.

Address: Clarissimo domino doctori Hugoni Blotio iurisconsulto et bibliothecae caesareae praefecto, amico meo singulari.
Below: Wienn. In der Walstrass. Ins hern Ungrischen Cantzler hauss[1437]
Blotius's Hand: Io. S. Ambucus.[1438] Mannersdorffio. 30. Augusti. De reiectione oneris recensionis in bibliotheca imperatoris etc. mordax.[1439]

[1435] The letter was sent from Sambucus's country house in Mannersdorf in Burgenland (close to Neusiedler See), which Sambucus owned at least from 1570.
[1436] Deleted words.
[1437] The house of Hungarian Vice-Chancellor Johannes Listhius.
[1438] Play with words.
[1439] Curiously, this letter survived (with the notes of receipt and the comment on style: "mordax") among Sambucus's

251.
Sambucus to Hugo Blotius
10 September 1575, Mannersdorf

The original is kept in Vienna, ÖNB Cod. 9737^z14-18, II, f. 118^r-119^v. Published in Gerstinger, "Die Briefe," 179-181.

Sambucus considers it an honour that the emperor passed the task of cataloguing the books (of the imperial library) to another person, since the emperor well knows that his books give him sufficient work. He is glad that the emperor appreciated Blotius's ideas about the order and place of the library. The complains of Blotius about people's jealousy and faked feelings does not concern their relationship. God should punish the suspicious and the malevolent who neither correctly judge Blotius's nature nor respect the laws of friendship. Why should he not congratulate him on the many patrons Blotius obtained in a few months with his learning and fame as a diligent person? He accuses himself all the more for the 22 years passed hidden among four walls making no friends other than Weber from the Privy Council, and by this restriction he foolishly harmed his interests. Living in the country, he is now especially held back by the family problems. For his part, he never envied anyone progressing because of his virtues or tried to go in the footsteps of learned men like Blotius, as his nature is such that he wanted to be happy even with little honours. As soon as Sambucus returns to Vienna, he will happily share his long experience with him and Blotius can generally be sure that he will want good for him and could never suffer that Blotius be offended by him. If Blotius thinks that Sambucus has other things in mind, he is ungrateful, goes against Christ's teaching and shows an example of unjust friendship to his learned friends. Blotius should love Sambucus, who would not harm his friends thoughtlessly. He will tell him personally what he wants to do with his manuscript books. He edited Pletho's commentary on Peloponnesian matters, he does not know if Blotius has seen it. It will be understood someday, or soon, what else he is preparing for publication next to the book on plants. Blotius's comment: "He is excusing himself for jealousy and hatred."

Salutem.

Iudicium caesaris de conficiendo indice nudo librorum inque alium translato onere per mihi honorificum duco, quippe cuius maiestas optime norit, mihi satis negocii cum meis superesse.[1440] Tuas autem cogitationes de ordine, loco bibliothecae principi adeo placere laetor, idque institutum tuas virtutes illustrabit.

Quod vero, mi Bloti, μεμψιμοίρως[1441] de nonnullorum invidia fictisque sensibus et ad rem praesentem compositis solicite comemoras, ad nostram necessitudinem nihil pertinere puto. Dii male faciant suspiciosis et malevolis, qui nec ingenium aestimant tuum recte nec amiciciae leges vere et tantum προσχήμασιν[1442] sequuntur. De tot tantisque patronis, quos intra paucos menses doctrina et opinio industriae non vulgaris tibi adiunxit, cur non congratulor? Me gravius etiam accusem, qui mea me ἁπλότητι[1443] mensus intraque parietes et latibula coniciens

---

papers. Either Blotius gave it back to Sambucus (who must have apologized for his biting tone) or Sambucus got it from someone else (Crato?) to whom Blotius showed it.

[1440] Cf. the preceding letter, where Sambucus claims not to care about the emperor's intention, which the emperor was expected to tell Blotius in a letter. Meanwhile, this letter seems to have arrived, and confirmed Sambucus, who lobbied probably via Crato.

[1441] criticizingly

[1442] in outward appearance

[1443] sincerity, simplicity

decursum 22 annorum nullum fere praeter Weberum ex intimo senatu vel compellarim vel ad mensam eorum fuerim, istaque animi contractione inepte mihi nocuerim.¹⁴⁴⁴ Nunc, ut ruri ago, praecipue rei familiaris molestiis prorsus deterreor.

Equidem nullius virtutibus et progressibus honorem viamque invidi, ut vero similium tui et doctissimorum vestigiis insisterem, vel cum tenuitate dignitatum mea me natura contentum esse iussit. Ubi ad urbem accessero, si quid tot annis collecta industriola tenet, libenter tecum communicabo, nec modo speres sed quoque credas omnino initiis et auspiciis amoris nostri profectus tuos responsuros rerumque et commodorum Blotii me studiosum fore aperte. Eaque sum animi inductione et amore erga te, ut nullam offensam illabi a me ad animum tuum sim passurus.

Sin aliter mentem Sambuci acceperis, ingrate feceris inque disciplinam Christi, bonos mores, exempla amicitiae, doctores denique philosophos tuos inique commiseris. Vale, et me, qui te amo carumque habeo nec leviter contra amicos impellor, redama, mutuum reddam omnibus oficiis. De libris manuscriptis vetustis meis coram, quid animi habeam. Ἔρρωσο.¹⁴⁴⁵ X. Septembris 1575 raptim.

Plethonis *De Peloponneso* commentariolum edidi et alia, nescio an videris.¹⁴⁴⁶ Quid prae manibus habeam praeter herbarium,¹⁴⁴⁷ dies posterique, si non praesentes, docebunt. Tuus Sambucus.

Address: Doctissimo viro D. D. Hugoni Blotio, caesareae bibliothecae praefecto, amico singulari. Viennae. In aedibus reverendissimi Listhii Iaurinensis.
Blotius's hand: 1575 Ioannes Sambucus Mannersdorf 10. Septembris, Purgat se de invidia et odio etc.

252.
Sambucus to Johannes Crato
12 September 1575, Mannersdorf

Published in Gerstinger, "Die Briefe," 181-182.

Since Sambucus was in doubt as to whether a copy of Tacitus was offered to the emperor in Lipsius's name, Lipsius sent him another copy. Lipsius asked him to give it to the emperor in his name and to plead with the emperor to include Lipsius among his clients. As Sambucus appreciates Lipsius's talents (which appears no smaller than Hadrianus Junius's), and knows Lipsius's respect for Crato, he promised him to use Crato's mediation in offering the volume to the emperor. So he asks Crato to give it to the emperor (even if he had already received a copy, as rulers tend to forget about these things) with an attached note, or give it personally and take the emperor's words of gratitude

---

[1444] On an interpretation see Almási, *The Uses of Humanism*, 187-188.
[1445] farewell
[1446] "Edidi" is curious in this place since the publication of Stobaeus and Plethon (*Stobaei eclogarum libri duo... et Plethonis De rebus Peloponnesiacis orationes duae*) was the work of Willem Canter (see letter 248). The orations entitled *Ad regem Emanuelem De rebus Peloponnesiacis oratio* and *Ad principem Theodorum De rebus Peloponnesiacis* concerned the right way of governing the Peloponnese.
[1447] By "herbarium" Sambucus means his intended Dioscorides-edition.

on the spot. Lipsius published ten books of Variae lectiones *recently, he is working on Plautus and emending Tacitus. Written from the solitude of Mannersdorf. Sambucus will respond to Xylander in his next letter, and send Dioscorides to Henri Estienne within a month with Crato's help, for which he is grateful. Plantin urgently wants an imperial diploma of free access to the Frankfurt book fair. Crato can easily get such diploma from Weber. He will pay for the shipping and has already drafted the permission, which he attaches.*

Salutem.

Quia dubitabam Taciti exemplum nomine Lipsii doctissimi iuvenis caesari oblatum, transmisit idem hoc meque rogat, uti caesari reddendum curem cum commendatione plena suae clientelae subditissimae speque maiorum brevi offerendorum etc., utque se caesarea maiestas in clientibus ponat et patrocinio haud vulgari, suppliciter agit.[1448] Ego vero, qua amo carumque habeo praeclarum eius ingenium, a quo non minora quam Hadriano iunio ostenduntur, et quia tuum nomen praedicat et auctoritatem iuste doctrinamque colit, pollicitus sum me accurate ad te cum libro scripturum atque obtenturum, ut princeps quamprimum Tacitum habeat conatusque et nomen eius clementissime intelligat, tum maiestate sua et benignis sensibus complectatur. Itaque te, mi optime et communis Musarum patrone, sinas exorari, ut sive antea acceperit, sive non (nam princeps saepe talium obliviscitur vel [...] oblatorum), quod prorsus timeo, hunc codicem de optima nota expedias et Lipsio gratiam et patrocinium eiusdem sacrum adiungas, vel prorsus, quod summopere probaret, duobus verbis ab eodem principe accepti codicis memoriam auferas. Beatum se duceret Lipsius tuoque beneficio perpetuo auctum ornatumque. Quod si feceris, reddet ille mutuum publice et quod studium tuum exornet etc. Edidit nuper X libros *Lectionum*,[1449] in Plauto est totus et Tacito multis locis emendando. Vale et in aliena re tam officioso ignoscito. XII. Septembris 1575. Ex solitudine Mannerstorffiensi. Xylandro proxime persolvam,[1450] Henrico Stephano intra mensem Dioscoridea omnino σὺν θεῷ[1451] tuo subsidio curabo deque tua liberalitate καὶ τῷ κοινωνικῷ[1452] gratias ago. Totus tuis meritis Sambucus.

Plantinus anxie solicitat, ut sibi a caesare diploma impetremus, liceat Francfortum sibi et suis commeare, pro alienis debitis nuspiam impediri. Tu hoc facile apud Beberum et, offerre[1453] qui talia potest, obtinebis et Plantino mittes. Pro redemptione ipse spondeo, formulam ipse confinxi[1454] et his inclusi. Vale et me etc.

Address: Clarissimo viro domino doctori Ioanni Cratoni ab Crafftthaim, caesareae maiestatis consiliario et archiatro, domino patrono et amico colendo. Prag.

[1448] Tacitus, *Historiarum et annalium libri qui exstant* (see letter 229).
[1449] Justus Lipsius, *Antiquarum lectionum commentariolus, tributus in libros quinque: in quibus varia scriptorum loca, Plauti praecipue, illustrantur aut emendantur* (Antverpiae: Plantin, 1575).
[1450] Cf. with letter 222.
[1451] with God's help
[1452] sharing, friendliness
[1453] Gerstinger's transcript reads *offeru*. Gestinger suggested the reading *Offnerum*, a supposed name of another, unidentified member of the Chancery.
[1454] Corrected from *conscripsi*.

253.
Sambucus to Fulvio Orsini
16 September 1575, Mannersdorf

The original is kept in Rome, BAV, Vat. lat. 4105, f. 90ʳ. Published in Gerstinger, "Die Briefe," 182-183.

Sambucus received Fulvio's letter of 4 September. He has already responded twice to this question to Giovanni Battista Fonteo: he is happy to give the two copper (plates?) as a gift. A copy of them was given to Stephan Pighius, Orsini may have seen it. The plague is severe in Vienna, he will hardly return to his library in less than a month. As soon as he returns, he will send everything that Fulvio demands. If the courier refuses to bring the load, he will send a copy before he finds an opportunity for transport of the original. He would be grateful to have (Orsini's) Dioscorides. Although he already submitted it to his publisher, it will be complete with Orsini's variant. Fulvio should greet Sambucus's old friends Achilles Statius and Fonteo.

Molto Magnifico Signor et Amico Salute.

Ho riceputa la Vostra alli 4 d'Settembrio, ho anchora risposto di questa dimanda doi volte al Dottor Fonteio, che sia contentissimo da donarvi li pezzi doi di rame e che ne alliegro, che porraio sodisfar in publicum. La copia havevo dato al Signor Pigghio, non so si l'habbiate havuto o visto.[1455] La peste e grande a Vienna, ante mensem vix accedam bibliothecam. Ubi id licuerit, absque exceptione mittam;. Si onus cursores recusarint, dum alia occasio venerit, descripta mittam, post ipsa ἀρχέτυπα.[1456] De Dioscoride magnas gratias, si comunicaris, licet iam miserim typographo meo,[1457] sed tamen integra erit editio vestrorum, si quid rari attulerint. Vale et Sambucum ama. Saluta Statium,[1458] veterem meum amicum, et Fonteium. 16. Kalendas Ottobris 1575. Ex Villula nostra Mannerstorff. Tutto di Vostra Signoria, Giovanni Sambuco.

Address: Clarissimo viro domino Fulvio Ursino, secretario illustrissimi et Romani cardinalis Farnesii etc., amico optimo. – Romam, al Signor Fulvio Ursino appresso il Reverendissimo [?] Farnese.[1459]

[1455] We do not know if Sambucus refers here to plates (see letter 253), coins or statutes.
[1456] archetypes, models
[1457] See the preceding letter.
[1458] Achilles Statius (Estaço, Stazio) (1524–1581) was a Portugese humanist famous for his commentary on Catullus, Horace, Suetonius and his private library. From 1555, he lived in Rome, in 1557 he was in Padova, where he may have met Sambucus. See Gerstinger, "Die Briefe," 183, Jozef Ijsewijn, "Achilles Statius, a Portugese Latin poet in late sixteenth-century Rome," in *Humanismo Portugués na época dos descobrimentos Coimbra* (Coimbra: FLUC, 1993), 109-123; and idem, "Petrus Nanius and Achilles Statius," *Humanistica Lovaniensia* 43 (1994), 288-294.
[1459] Fulvio Orsini was librarian to Cardinal Alessandro Farnese.

254.
Sambucus to Hugo Blotius
3 November 1575, [Mannersdorf]

The original is kept in Vienna, ÖNB Cod. 9737[z14-18], II, f. 140[r]. Published in Gerstinger, "Die Briefe," 183-185.

Together with Blotius's letter Sambucus received two letters from Bruges, written by Hubertus Goltzius and Marcus Laurinus of Watervliet 18 months earlier. There is no problem concerning Nicasius Ellebodius's letter, since these things often happen by accident. He received also the letter by Johannes Listhius three days earlier, which mentioned the same thing using almost the same example. Sambucus complains about the (courier) boy, who did not return to Blotius and neglected his job. The goldsmith confirms he would pay everything to the person of Sambucus's choice until Saint Martin's Day, but now Sambucus lives in such poverty in the country that he is almost ashamed of it; he hopes it will turn better soon. If he received his salary after this delay, he could provide for everyday expenses. But despite his insistence and use of patrons he just cannot achieve anything. He sent his wife to look after their common businesses in Vienna and meet her father. She will certainly raise some money. He ordered the goldsmith through the boy to pay Blotius 10 florins, on the extended deadline. In only the last three months he thinks to have spent more than 200 florins (which he regrets among all these unfriendly rumours); he will be more careful in the future. He is looking forward to the emperor's return.

Salutem.

Accepi cum tuis literis binas Brugi exaratas ante 18 menses, Goltzii antiquarii non vulgaris et patroni eiusdem domini de Watterflied. Quod ad literas Nicasii, quia temere saepe id accidere solet, nulla est iniuria. A reverendissimo Iaurinensi ante triduum cum diplomatibus certis alias, quae harum meminere, habui, et paene eodem exemplo. Habeo gratiam. Quod puer ad te non redierit, praeter voluntatem certe meam admisit, qui, quod ei mandare soleo, ne impedite aut negligenter exsequatur, soleo mandare. Aurifex sanctissimus confirmat, se ad Martini absque exceptione numeraturum, cui voluero. Ipse vero, mi Bloti, hoc tempore et ista rusticatione ita anguste domi vivo, ut fere pudeat, sed τῇ ἀνάγκῃ[1460] cedo ac brevi meliora spero. Profecto, si salarium ista mora ab aerario edetur, aliter rebus quotidianis providebo. Nil conficio, quamvis premam et obtester patroncinia et caput obligem, nil cogo. Misi hodie coniugem Viennam, ut res istic nostras inspiciat et patrem salutet, non dubito illam aliquid allaturam. Aurifici vero per puerum commisi, ut tibi 10 florenos omnino numeret ad diem productum. Credo mihi hoc trimestri in fabricas et alia ultra 200 florenos (quod me valde his rumusculis adversis currentibus paenitet) insumpsisse, sed in dies cautior ero. Vale. Caesaris reditum cupidissime exspecto. 3. Novembris 1575. Tuus totus Sambucus.

Address: Clarissimo viro D. doctori Hugoni Blotio, caesareae bibliothecae praefecto, amico meo singulari. Viennam.
Blotius's hand: 1575 Ioannes Sambucus Mannersdorfio. 3. Novembris. De magistro Henrico aurifico, ut mihi numeret die Martini 10 florenos.

[1460] to necessity

255.
Sambucus to Joachim Camerarius Jr.
9 November 1575, Vienna

The original is kept in Munich, BSB, Clm 10367, Nr. 179.

He implores Camerarius to forward the included package to Estienne in Geneva as soon as possible. He will be shown gratitude in public. Sambucus is sending readings in Dioscorides, for which Estienne and others have called. Soon he will send the rest. Then Camerarius will easily be able to send it to Geneva through merchants from Nuremberg, who do a lot of business in Lyon and have two permanent couriers on the route to Lyon. He hopes to settle many controversies, especially with his additions and notes. He entrusts this portion of the work to Camerarius. He wishes to know what will happen with the writings of Camerarius Sr. The answer should be sent to his neighbour Sigmund Richter. Estienne urges that this be sent as soon as possible so he can publish it alongside the text of Dioscorides corrected by Sambucus. Sambucus will pay whatever the courier demands. Camerarius can add his own letter to Estienne.

Salutem.

Te per Aesculapium et omnem βοτανῶν φιλίαν[1461] oro, hunc fasciculum tuto recteque Geneuam ad Henricum Stephanum quam primum curato. Feres publice gratiam. Nam in Dioscoridem lectiones mitto, quas tantopere ille et alii exigunt. Caetera mittam brevi. Tum vero per Noribergenses, qui Lugdunii [!] plurimum negociantur et habent duos perpetuos tabellarios in vestra urbe concurrentes Lugdunum, facile Geneuam mittetis, aut Lugduno istuc curabitis. Spero multorum altercationes et dissidia hisce meis compositum iri, praesertim quae corollaria subicio, seu notas meas non vulgares. Hanc igitur partem tibi mitto, credo, sancte committo. Quid de bibliotheca Cameraria fiat, quid depromas paterni in lucem, oro mihi significes ac tuas Viennam ad dominum Sigismondum Richter, meum vicinum, concivem vestrum tuas dirigito. Vale, raptim, 9. Novembris 1575. Totus tuus Sambucus.

Henricus Stephanus orat, ut cito, citissime ad se haec mittam, quo hac hyeme cum textu Dioscoridis etiam a me emendato absolvat. Quidquid tabellarius exegerit, bona fide sumptus feram. Tuas vero adiunges aut fasciculum tutius involves σὺν ἐπιγραφῇ[1462] ad Henricum Stephanum.

Address: Clarissimo viro domino Ioachimo, illius quondam filio, amico optimo.
Camerarius's note: 75. 26. Novembris.

[1461] friendship of plants
[1462] with the address

256.
Sambucus to Johannes Crato
30 November 1575, [Mannersdorf]

Published in Gerstinger, "Die Briefe," 185.

This letter is written in haste because Lakner's agent is already on his horse. He is more or less over some problems with kidney stones. He means to return to Vienna before Christmas, if the plague allows, or go to Pressburg to Crato. Henri Estienne has hopefully received Dioscorides, Crato should urge its edition if he writes to him. He wishes that Christians had firmer peace with the Ottomans or opposed them more boldly and break down the madness of war once and for all. No news from the French bookseller. He will soon send his servant to Crato. Finally, he asks Crato to remind the emperor of his books.

Magnifice domine et amice, salutem.

Epistolam exarare hanc subito Lakneri negociator, qui equum iam conscenderat, fecit, qua te diligenter saluto tuamque familiam incolumem omnibus rebus exopto. Scio te in meis velle mutuum. Ego mediocriter ex renum sentina et arena convalui. Ante ferias Christi in urbem cogito, si leniora erunt ἐπιδεμικά vel potius ἐνδεμικά[1463] (de qua re oro aliquid ad me), aut Posonium ad vos.[1464] Henricus spero Dioscoridea accepisse, tu vero, mi clarissime patrone, cum hisce ad eundem serio scribas, urgebis editionem. Fiet non obscura tuae magnificentiae et idonea memoria. Prorsus hic omnia silent, nil audimus. Thurcae tamen furores et minae non ita procul absunt. Utinam in rem Christianam pacem firmam impetremus aut animosius nos temporariusque opponamus beluaeque rabiem fractam in aeternis monumentis ponamus! A Gallico[1465] bibliopola nildum.[1466] Mittam his diebus famulum ad vos. Vale, mi patrone, et si opportuna res esset de libris caesarem submonere, gratissimum accideret. Pridie Kalendas Decembris 1575. Vale. Totus tuus Sambucus.

Address: Clarissimo viro domino doctori Ioanni Cratoni a Craffthaim, caesareae maiestatis consiliario et archiatro, domino patrono et amico colendo. Viennae.

257.
Sambucus to Fulvio Orsini
8 December 1575, [Vienna]

The original is kept in Rome, BAV, Vat. lat. 4105, f. 91^{r-v}. Published in Gerstinger, "Die Briefe," 186-187.

Sambucus sends as a gift via apostolic nuncio Zaccaria Delfino (two) copper (plates?) of the Lex Thoria. *He would have sent his copy along with some text reconstruction but could not find it right*

[1463] epidemic; endemic
[1464] Crato may have gone to Pressburg because of the coming diet, which was convoked for 13 December but which convened only in January of the following year. *Magyar országgyűlési emlékek* 6, 21-24.
[1465] Gerstinger's transcript: *Galliae*. Gerstinger proposes *Gallico* or *Gallo*.
[1466] This may be a reference to Jean Aubry.

now. If Orsini wants, he will send it soon. They cost him 18 ducats but would not ask a penny even if it had cost him 100; he only begs Orsini for his observations in Dioscorides. Although he has already sent his Dioscorides-edition to the presses corrected with the use of seven old manuscripts together with his own precious observations on rare plants and some notes on debates among the botanists, if Orsini has any worthy observation, he would immediately send it to Henri Estienne so that he can attach it to the end. He found many credible (illustrations) of plants not seen by Dioscorides and several nice "relics" from Crateuas, as Orsini will see perhaps next Easter. He did the same (philological study) in the works of Aristotle and is doing it in Plato. He collected some emperors and military writers to be printed in a single volume. He has not seen Orsini's book on coins, he asks him to send a copy. He also asks Orsini to find him an old or new copy of Photius's Bibliotheca. He has an old and a new copy, but this is a much corrected Venetian one. A printer has still another copy. He looked through it, and it will be a great edition, a printer has already made a promise. He hopes that there will be a corrected edition of Aulus Gellius very soon. He is sending his greetings to Achilles Statius, Giovanni Battista Fonteo and Cardinal Guglielmo Sirleto.

...[ho (?) om]. Sambucus Salutem.

Mando per il Reverendissimo Vescovo Delphino, Nonsio di Sua Santità quelli rami di *Lege Thoria*,[1467] alle opinione mia simplice in don. gratis amore vetustatis et amiciciae memoria nostrae, haveria mandato la copia mia, con qualche supplemento mio in certi logetti: ma non li trovato cosi subito: mandaro si vorrete praesto. A mè hanno costato. 18. [kk] ma si fosse 100 non vorrià un quatrineto. Solamente priego, che mi mandiate quelle osservatione in Dioscoride. E benche il mio Dioscoride ho gia mandato alla stampa corretto par 7 copie antiche é miei altre osservatione rare delle piante e notis adiectis de controversiis herbariorum καὶ ῥιζοτόμων;[1468] tamen si mandarete, e si sarà qualche cosa digna, subito mandarò al Henrico Stephano, che li metta in extremo.[1469] Io ho trovato molti capi legitimi non visti del Dioscoride: et molte belle reliquiae del Crateua antichissimo et altri, come vederete forse questo paschate etc. Cosi ho fatto in Aristotelis operibus et adesso in Platone etc. Ho condotto anchora certi imperatori e scrittori de re militari rari; si stampano in d'un uolumine etc.[1470] Lo libro di V. S. delle medaglie non ho visto, si sarà occasion di mandar mi, farete gran favor.[1471] Non meno supplico di far trovar mi un exemplo vecchio o moderno iusto della *Bibliotheca* del Photio.[1472] Perche ne ho una vecchia e moderna, ma Vinneggiana assai corretta.[1473] Una copia ha un stampatore anchora. Ho rivisto, fariamo stampar un thesoro grande, et un stampator mi ha gia promesso. Supplico adiutate noi presto, sarà con grande lode del beneficio et ma obligo a pagar subito qualche [...]. Spero che in puochi di haveremo un Aullo Gellio emendato. Ma ricomando comè à fratello et amico singolare. Salutate il nostro Statio dottissimo et Fonteio: ante omnes reverendissimum cardinalem Schirlettum patronum literatorum literatissimum. 8. Decembris 1575.

[1467] On the *Lex Thoria* and Orsini's edition of it, see letter 192, note 1139.
[1468] and of herbalists (root-pickers)
[1469] Cf. letter 155, note 920.
[1470] See letter 247, note 1431.
[1471] Fulvio Orsini, *Imagines et elogia virorum illustrium et eruditorum ex antiquis lapidibus et nomismatibus expressa cum annotationibus* (Venetiis: In aedibus Petri Deuchino Galli, 1570).
[1472] On Photius cf. the Index.
[1473] Venezia, Biblioteca Marciana, Cod. Marc. 450, formerly owned by Cardinal Bessarion. See Gerstinger, "Die Briefe," 187.

Address: Al Dottissimo é Nobilissimo I Signor il S. Fulvio Ursino Gentilhuomo Romano etc. Patrono et amico Singolari. Roma in Casa del Illustrissimo Cardinal Farnesi con doi petzi de rame antique.

258.
Sambucus to Johannes Crato
[1575[1474]], [Vienna]

Published in Gerstinger, "Die Briefe," 170.

It is strange how neglectful that "ungrateful adolescent" (i.e. Vitus) is. He looked for Sambucus twice in his house and when Sambucus bumped into him in the street, he followed him to his place. Tucher has owed him 70 florins for a year, which he had accepted on Sambucus's behalf. When Sambucus was urging his agent on that same day, he saw the ruby ring of 80 florins which Tucher obtruded on him. He told the agent, while Vitus was following him, to bring and show it to the next goldsmith. Otherwise, he does not know what Vitus wants to do, he heard that he plans to visit his parents, until his cousin Rechnitz comes back here from Moravia. He thanks Crato for his friendly service.

Salutem.

Miror ingratum adolescentem tam officii oblitum.[1475] Hodie bis me domi quaesivit. Cum in via illum offendissem, secutus me ad aedes usque est. Tuecherus 70 fl. mihi ab anno debebat, quos nomine meo acceperat;[1476] cumque eius negociatorem hodie ursissem, vidi annulum rubinum, quem 80 fl. mihi obtrudit. Eum ipsum, cum Vitus me consequitur, ut proximum aurificem diverteret et ostenderet, iussi. Caeteroqui quid agat aut animi habeat, ignoro, audio ipsum ad suos revisurum, dum Rechnitzius patruelis ex Moravia huc revertat. Habeo gratiam vestrae excellentiae de amica commonefactione.[1477] Vale. Tuae magnificentiae deditus Sambucus.

Address: Magnifico et clarissimo viro domino doctori Ioanni Cratoni, patrono et amico.

259.
Johannes Löwenklau to Sambucus
[January/February 1576], [Basel]

Dedication in *Zosimi comitis et exadvocati fisci historiae novae libri VI, numquam hactenus editi, quibus additae sunt historiae Procopii Caesariensis, Agathiae Myrrinaei, Iornandis Alani.*

[1474] It is difficult to date this letter or note. Gerstinger dated it to 1575, from the year of other surviving notes ("Die Briefe," 170). If it was written in 1575, it must have been either in January-February or in December, as Crato and Sambucus spent only a few months together in Vienna during that year.

[1475] We were not able to identify the adolescent named Vitus. Gerstinger suggests he was from the Rechnitz family, nephew of Daniel Rechnitz (whose father was also called Vitus), but this seems to be no more than a guess.

[1476] Tuecherus seems to be a reference to Paul IV Tucher (1524–1603), the head of a famous goldsmith family in Nuremberg. See also letter 254.

[1477] Gerstinger claims this refers to Crato's mentioning the case of Sambucus's books to the emperor.

Zosimi libros Iohannes Leunclaius primus ab se repertos de Graecis Latinos fecit, Agathiam redintegravit, ceteros recensuit. Adiecimus et Leonardi Aretini rerum Gothicarum commentarios, de Graecis exscriptos. Omnia cum indicibus copiosis (Basileae: Perna, [1576]). Published in *Humanistes du bassin des Carpates II. Johannes Sambucus*, 205-213.

260.
Sambucus to Johannes Crato
3 January 1576, [Mannersdorf]

Published in Gerstinger, "Die Briefe," 188-189.

Before New Year's Day he thought to go to Crato with his family, but he did not dare to embark on the journey with his small children who were just over the flu in that cold weather. He heard that the king (of Hungary, Maximilian II) went to Pressburg the day before to urge the Hungarian nobility to meet and discuss Ottoman affairs. If it is true, he may go there two days later, and then to Vienna to Crato when the cold has abated. Joachim Camerarius has still not answered concerning the package for Henri Estienne. If Crato receives something he should let Sambucus know about it. Reading Saint Augustine and Pliny he starts casting doubt on Conrad Dasypodius's being truly a hare, as in Aristotle. He neither gives back the Euclid manuscript nor publishes it, only gives promises and wants Sambucus to get Plantin to publish his mathematical works. He is happy that Poland finally procured Austria's protection and hopes that this gain will result in victories against the Ottomans, and he prays that it will ease the situation of Hungarians ("nosque Ungaros") a little.

Salutem cum mille Kalendis Ianuariis.

Omnino cogitabam ante Kalendas Ianuarias ad vos cum familia, sed frigoris inclementia tanta intervenit, ut liberos tenellos et vixdum catarrho molesto soluto coelo rigido et itineris molestiis non sim ausus committere. Audio regem Posonium heri profectum, accurrere nobilitatem Pannonicam, de Thurcicis negociis senatum coiturum. Quod si est, fortasse istuc ad biduum excurram post remisso fractoque nonnihil algore Viennam ad vos.[1478] Camerarius nildum de fasciculo ad Stephanum rescripsit. Si quid accepisti, oro fac me certiorem. Dasypodius an sit λαγωός, fere cum Augustino et Plinio dubitare incipio contra Aristotelem.[1479] Diem et promissa e promissis ducit et vane exspectant Euclidem, nec reddit nec prodit.[1480] Solicite mecum agit, Plantini officinam eius mathematicis concilem, sed quam apte, ipse nosti. Poloniae regnum denique Austriae patrocinium impetrasse laetor,[1481] eaque accessio ut diuturna laetitia et contra Thurcas victoriis plena manu reportatis constet, ex

---

[1478] Maximilian II did not go to the diet. See letter 256, note 1464.
[1479] λαγωός (hare) is a play with Dasypodius's name. In Aristoteles it is δασύπους = λαγωός, while in Pliny it means *caniculus*. See the article in *RE* I.7 (1912), 2477. See Gerstinger, "Die Briefe," 189.
[1480] On the Euclid-manuscripts see letter 89, note 564.
[1481] Sambucus was little behind with news on the Polish election. Although the senate elected Maximilian as Polish king, and he was unconstitutionally declared as King of Poland and Grand Duke of Lithuania on 12 December 1575, the Polish gentry (the szlachta) did not accept the result and elected Stephen Báthory on 22 December. His election was confirmed on 1 February. See Sándor Gebei, *Az erdélyi fejedelmek és a lengyel királyválasztások* [The Transylvanian princes and the Polish elections] (Szeged: Belvedere Meridionale, 2007), 31-33.

animo opto, nosque Ungaros aliqua periculi parte societas sublevet, precor. Vale. 3. Ianuarii 1576. Totus tuis meritis Sambucus.

Address: Dem Edlen, Hochgelehrten Herrn Johanni Cratoni von Crafftthaim, Khayserlicher Maiestät Ratt und Obristen Leibphysico, meinem insonders gunstigen Herrn und Freunde. Wien.

261.
Sambucus to Theodor Zwinger
1 March 1576, Vienna

The original is kept in Basel, Universitätsbibliothek, Frey Mscr II 26, no. 216. Published in Gerstinger, "Die Briefe," 189-190.

Sambucus received letters from the Oporinus office and from Pietro Perna in the same bundle with Zwinger's letter but these letters disagree as regards the receipt of 35 thalers paid to Gemusaeus. He does not know what is owed to Perna, but he would not like to pay the debts of others. He sends his greetings to Episcopius and wants him to finish the affair with the Gemusaeus brothers and to have his Bonfini-dialogues sent back from Frankfurt. Henri Estienne is taking his Dioscorides and other books. He wants to know where his Aristotle and his very rare Euclid manuscripts are, the latter corrected by Dasypodius. Yet he does not much trust the latter, as he fails to send back the autograph and excuses himself with Episcopius's negligence. Zwinger should make sure that Sambucus gets it. Henri Estienne is printing Plato. Sambucus did not have time to compare his three manuscripts; he would keep his contribution, which is not contemptible, especially on the Laws and the State, for an edition that suits him. He wonders what Zwinger is working on. He is still thinking of an edition of Photius's Bibliotheca, but he cannot carry it out on his own and the circumstances are often adverse (to the project). He finished some historical work, a book on tombs, and reworked his jottings on Horace's Ars Poetica. He is sending his greetings to Perna, Episcopius and Gemusaeus, Zwinger should call their attention to his things and not forget about Aristotle and Euclid. If patrons and publishers were not lacking, he would abound in rare books, but he sees only avarice and bad luck.

Sambucus salutem.

Accepi tuas cum Oporinianis et Bernae eodem fasciculo sed diversis sententiis de apocha et 35 talleris Gemuseo solutis.[1482] Nescio, quid Bernae debeatur, alieno et circumforaneo debito meum persolvi fidemque laborare nolim. Episcopio a me salutem et urge cum Oporinianis res confiat denique tam parvi aeris,[1483] longae syngraphae molestiaeque importunae, atque Bonfinii dialogi mihi remittantur Francforto.[1484] Henricus Stephanus meum Dioscoridem accepit et alia. Aristoteles quo loco sit, cupio scire et, an Euclides de meo thesauro rarissimo emendatus per Dasypodium ubi lateat, pro amicitia nostra perquire. Nam Dasypodio non

---
[1482] See the next letter, note 1495.
[1483] Cf. letter 233.
[1484] Bonfini, *Symposion trimeron*.

satis fido, necdum ἀντίγραφον[1485] restituit, Episcopii negligentia se excusat.[1486] Fac quaeso rem ipsam percipiam. Henricus Platonem sub prelo habet.[1487] Mihi ocium defuit tria mea exemplaria vetusta conferendi, differam eam farraginem non contemnendam, praesertim de Legibus et Politia, in opportunam mihi editionem. Tu vero, doctissime Zvingere, quid lucubres cudes, de officina tam erudita et copiosa moliare, item significa. Photii *Bibliotheca[m]* adhuc cogito, sed non omnia solus possum et quae incurrunt transverse, saepe impediunt. Absolvi quaedam historica, et *Tumulorum* cum vetustate certantium librum;[1488] retexui in *Artem* Horatii ἐκβολάς[1489] meas etc.[1490] Vale. Kalendis Martii 1576. Vienna.

Bernae et Episcopio Gemuseoque salutem, et de his meis, si commode occurrent, eos moneas, itidem de Aristotele, Euclide etc. quam primum. Mi Zvingere, si maecenates et typographi non deessent, libris abundarem rarissimis, sed avaritia et omen adversum cuncta occupant.

262.
Sambucus to Theodor Zwinger
12 March 1576, Vienna

The original is kept in Basel, Universitätsbibliothek, Frey Mscr II 26, no. 217. Published in Gerstinger, "Die Briefe," 190-193.

Sambucus is happy that the Basilica *are finally being published. He has a high opinion of Claude Aubery, and asks Zwinger to greet him. If he will send Photius's* Bibliotheca *(to Basel), he would like it to be published in Greek not to derogate from the authority of Greek and let its study decline because of the many translations. He will decide about shipping when there is an occasion. Meanwhile, he is sending Abu ʿMa'shar's (Albumasar), which is not an entirely superstitious work, as noted in the front, singular for preserving antique views on dreams. Two of its front pages are missing as is clear from the contents, but it is not a real loss. He wrote to all the libraries but the missing part does not seem to exist. Aubery could translate it in a few hours and publish the Latin. It would have greater authority in Latin than in Greek, which is a translation from Arabic. But Zwinger should do as he wishes. He recently sent to Zwinger Lazius's work on the* Republic of Rome, *which the author corrected in many places persuaded by friends and Sambucus's frequent visits. Episcopius and Gemusaeus could publish it together, or Gemusaeus, as he desired, on his own. Sambucus will send an appropriate foreword. It is good that they accept the condition of 35 thalers but Zwinger should procure a receipt and make sure that twenty entire copies of Lazius be sent to Sambucus. Zwinger should also ask them to return his manuscript of Bonfini's* Dialogue *and Apollonius's* Syntax, *(also because) he heard that Estienne is planning to publish Apollonius using Franciscus Portus's emendations. He is sending his greetings to Löwenklau. While the emperor is away, he is working on Hungarian history. He would be ready to publish (his emendations in)* Dioscorides *on their own, if he was not disgusted by the avarice of the publishers. Zwinger should*

[1485] copy
[1486] On the Euclid-manuscript see letter 89, note 564.
[1487] See letter 233, note 1350 and letter 243, note 1406.
[1488] See "Tumulorum Heroicorum et miscelaneorum librum suum, una cum Heroicorum Symbolorum a se inventorum appendice iam expolit." listed in his bibliography. Sambucus, *Catalogus librorum*.
[1489] offshoots
[1490] Sambucus, *Ars poetica Horatii*.

find out whether Euclid is being published in Greek or only in Dasypodius's Latin translation. Six years ago, he entrusted him with Bessarion's rare manuscript, but he does not send it back and blames Episcopius in an uneducated manner.

Sambucus salutem.

Laetor tandem Basilica prodire.[1491] Aubrio, viro doctissimo, a me salutem, cuius doctrinam raram puto, iudicium philosophum et varium. Photii volumen,[1492] si misero, Graece edi tantum vellem, non Latine, ut autoritas Graecorum integra maneret, tot interpretibus scholae studiumque linguarum ne contraheretur. Consilium tamen ex occasione captabo mittendi. Mittam interea Albumasoris,[1493] ut in fronte annotatum est, libellum non omnino superstitiosum et vestigiis antiquarum opinionum de insomniis egregium et rarum; cui duo priores pagellae desunt, ut ex indice capitum deprehendetis, citra iacturam rerum aliquam. Scripsi ad omnes bibliothecas, reliquum nusquam reperiri video. Poterit Aubrius paucis horis absolvere et praelo subiicere latina. Ita enim maior erit libelli autoritas quam Graeci ex Arabico interpretis. Ut voletis, facietis. Misi nuper opus Lazii ad vos *De Republica Romana* ab ipso multis partibus amicorum admonitione meisque frequentibus congressibus emendatum.[1494] Poterit Episcopius cum Gemuseo aut solus, ut petiit, Gemuseus edere. Mittam praefationem postea meam non alienam a libro.[1495] Quod conditionem 35 tallerorum acceperint, bene est, apocham exigatis, et 20 exempla Lazii integra mihi expeditaque cupio sint. Praeterea Bonfinii *Dialogorum* ἀντίγραφον[1496] cum Apollonii mei *Syntaxi* repetite,[1497] oro, et mittatis aliquando; nam Henricus Stephanus nuper significavit se ex Porti emendatione Apollonium excusurum, sed nescio, an supplementa tot paginarum habeant uti meus.[1498] Leonclavio salutem plurimam. Ego Pannonica mea nunc texo et polio,[1499] dum caesar abest.[1500] Dioscoridea vel separatim edam a textu, si avaritia impressorum mihi stomachum moverit, ne diutius cupidos earum lectionum promissis fraudem. Vale. Vienna, XII. Martii 1576.

Oro te, mi optime Zwiggere, expiscere apud vos, num Euclides Graecus sit sub prelo aut Latinus ex Dasypodii lucubrationibus.[1501] Nam ante 6 annos ei rarum et copiosiorem aliis

---

[1491] *LX librorum* Βασιλικῶν.

[1492] Zwinger's note above *Photii*: "Patriarchae Constantinopolitani."

[1493] Zwinger's marginal note: "Albumasor [i]nsom." Abu Maʿshar (Albumasar) was a 9th-century early Persian Muslim astronomer and astrologer. Probably his most influential work in the Middle Ages was his "Book on religions and dynasties." Sambucus's manuscript of Abu Maʿshar's dream-book was published in the translation of Löwenklau in Frankfurt: [Pseudo-]Albumasar [Abu Ma'shar], *Apotelesmata*.

[1494] See letter 233.

[1495] The work eventually appeared in the edition of the Wechel press in 1598 (see letters 233 and 359). Cf. the Index. On the history of 35 thalers see letters 226, 233, 266, 271, 358 and 376.

[1496] copy

[1497] Bonfini, *Symposion trimeron* (see the preceding letter). For Apollonius's *Syntax* cf. the Index. Curiously, Sambucus seems to have forgotten or ignored Zwinger's note about the loss of his Apollonius's *Syntax*, see letter 163. Cf. with Gerstinger, "Zusammenfassung," 285 and "Die Briefe," 193.

[1498] Franciscus Portus (1511–1581) was a Greek humanist from Crete, who studied in Padua, lived in Modena and Ferrara and finally became a citizen of Geneva in 1562. His emendations were later used in the edition of Friedrich Sylburg in 1590. Estienne had just published an edition of Apollonius in 1574.

[1499] See Gerstinger, "Zusammenfassung," 291-292.

[1500] Here again, Sambucus gives the impression that as a busy courtier he only has time to work when court business does not occupy him.

[1501] See letter 89, note 564.

Euclidis ἀντίγραφον[1502] Bessarionis communicaram, qui nec mutuum remittit nec liberat fidem, semper me spe et mora Episcopii ducit seque excusat satis frigide.

Address: Clarissimo domino doctori Theodoro Zvingero Basiliensi physico, in primis amico singulari[1503]

263.
Sambucus to Aldo Manuzio Jr.
21 March 1576, Vienna

The original is kept in Milan, Biblioteca Ambrosiana, Cod. E 37 inf., 116ʳ. Published in Gerstinger, "Die Briefe," 193.

Sambucus is happy to hear people praise Aldo Manuzio's virtues and see his publications in the hands of people of his land. This is natural in view of their 15-year-long friendship, which was first for Aldo's sake and then for his father (Paolo's) sake, who much loved Sambucus. Aldo should continue this nice family tradition and publish commentaries on Cicero. If he hears of anything that Sambucus has in his possession that could be useful for his press, he should let him know and he will get it. He recommends to Aldo a youth (Rubigallus) of most noble and wealthy parents and his tutor and hopes that his recommendation will have an effect.

Ioannes Sambucus salutem.

Vehementer laetor, mi Alde, cum tuas virtutes laudari audio nec vulgaria ingenii monimenta passim in nostratium manibus versari video. Cur enim id non feram, cuius indolem iam a 15 et amplius annis complexus sim sponte, amicitia denique paterna, cuius in me sensus qui fuerint, tibi nondum excidisse puto, officiis et memoria vulgo praestita confirmavit? Perge vero, cuius avita initia domi hausisti, amplitudinem familiae perpetuitate cum reliquo tempore coniungere. Ede, tum quae ipse lucubras egregie, tum quorum te pater dixit constituitque patronum ipse, clarissima in Ciceronem varieque conducta commentaria. Si quid ex amicis forte audies Sambucum in suis libris habere, quod te quiddam iuvare officinamque exercere possit, impera, totum καὶ χρήσει καὶ κτήσει[1504] tua reperies.

Hunc vero[1505] singulari indole, parentibus nobilissimis et copiosis una cum praeceptore suo tibi commendo, utque eis te accedentibus de humanitate accommodes tuaque facile patefacias, quae cum aliis communiter habes, te vehementer rogo. Ferent amoris et beneficiorum acceptorum aliquando prolixam gratiam, Sambuco vero gratissimum fuerit, si suam commendationem ad Aldum suum aliquid impetrasse senserit. Vale, mi frater. 12 Kalendas Aprilis 1576 Vienna. Calamo subito.

Address: Aldo Manutio Paulli filio, viro clarissimo, amico optimo.

[1502] copy
[1503] Zwinger's notes below: "Lazius, Martius [?], Albumasar, Euclides."
[1504] in usufruct and possession. Cf. Erasmus, *Adagia* 4026.
[1505] Contemporary marginal note (perhaps by the hand of Aldus): "Rubigallum." This must be the son of Paulus Rubigallus, mentioned in letter 66.

264.
Sambucus to István Radéczy
7 April 1576, Vienna

The original is kept in Budapest, MOL, E 211 XXXII. Lymbus II. series 1552-1848. 113 cs. f. 21.[1506]

Sambucus is sorry about the unjust consequences of the fire, although some causes made the damage smaller, as he heard from his patron, the bishop of Győr (Listhius). Nevertheless, he regrets the destruction of the cherished objects for the sake of the art, and that the neighbourhood experienced this evil, but Radéczy will be able to remedy this. One will see how the Polish affairs will end; one needs to turn to God, who will not abandon his people. Sambucus asks Radéczy to carry on sustaining him. Sambucus complains that he has not seen any of his court stipend for three years, while he has a middle-size family to sustain and would not like to go into debt, as it would be difficult to pay it back. He asks Radéczy to pay 100 florins to the young courier of the letter: he has a blank sheet signed and stamped by Sambucus (for a receipt). He knows that the treasuries cannot satisfy more urgent demands either, but (will accept) whatever "little part of the republic" Radéczy means for Sambucus. He will see if Sambucus is worthy to be his client. He already wrote about his request to István Hosszutóthy. He hopes that Nicasius Ellebodius has solved Radéczy's gout problem and that it is cured. The Bishop of Eger (Győr?) decided to follow the medical advice of Giulio Alessandrini. He recommends certain Pertelius and expects the answer with 100 thalers.

Reverendissime domine domine semper patrone gratiossissime, salutem.

Incendii temere dati iniuriam valde doleo, etsi, quae damnum extenuent, non exiguae sint causae, quas vestrae reverendissimae dominationes[1507] patrono meo reverendissimo Iaurinensi perscripsit. Tamen doleo delitiarum Apollinis ergo, doleo viciniam sensisse malum. Quibus vestrae reverendissimae dominationes mederi poterit. Res Polonicae itemque nostrae quo loco sunt, quam laboraturae, nisi prospiciatur, ipsi videtis. Sed Deus negocium suum haud deserat, aliquos afflictos et paene extinctos proprius respiciet, si nos in illum intuebimur pectusque ad gratiam et sensus eius praescriptos adduxerimus, quod omnino faciundum erit, nisi universe periclitari volemus.

Supplice vestram reverendissimam dominationem oro, Sambucum beneficiis tueri atque ornare suis pergat, qui tuam reverendissimam dominationem in oculis, animo et ore fert, cum non vulgari laudum memoria, iustisque semper praeconiis et sermonibus. Valde impensae quotidianae me urgent, alo mediocrem familiam, ex aulica pensione triennio ne tertium [!] abstuli: molestus aliis esse nollem, minus me aere circumforaneo implicare,[1508] unde

---

[1506] We thank Kees Teszelszky for his enthusiastic search for Sambucus's letters and for communicating this letter to us.

[1507] István Radéczy (Stephanus Radezius) († 1586) came from the same city in Transylvania (Sibiu, Nagyszeben) as Nicolaus Olahus (who was his major patron) or Johannes Listhius. Sustained by ecclesiastical benefices, he was educated by the Jesuits in Vienna, but remained religiously moderate and attracted to learning. In 1559, he was already sent on a diplomatic mission to Rome, a year later he was ennobled and soon received further ecclesiastical benefices and titles. From 1569, he was the prefect of the Hungarian Chamber and after Verantius's death one of the most trusted and well paid members of the court. From 1573 he was bishop of Eger. See István Sugár, *Az egri püspökök története* [The history of the bishops of Eger] (Budapest: Szent István Társulat, 1984), 275-283.

[1508] Cf. Cicero, *Ad Atticum* 2.1.11: "aere [...] circumforaneo obruerunt."

emergere difficile foret. Supplico huic iuveni 100 vestra reverendissima dominatio conficiat. Habet membranam aptam meoque idiographo et sigillo testatam, quod cumque acceperit, inscribi poterit, dum vacuus ne recurrat. Nisi reverendissima dominatio vestra me iuverit, qui consistam, nescio.

Video gravibus negociis aerarium non suppetere, sed partem me quoque minimam reipublicae statuatis, si dignum clientela, quod adhuc sensi, vestra iudicaveritis. Qua de re ad consilium vestrum, et separatim etiam domino Hosszuthotii scripsi cuius me gratiae subiicio,[1509] meque uti iuvet sive ex aerario sumptis 100, sive aliunde, subiecte obsecro. 7. Aprilis 1576. Vestrae reverendissimae dominationis clientulus [?], Sambucus etc.

Podagram spero sanuisse satis operaque Nicasi solutam. Reverendus Agriensis[1510] de consilio Alexandrini et aliorum valetudini suae inservire medicorum disciplina constituit. Pertelium[1511] optimum virum quoque commendo: meretur favorem coronae.

Responsum cum 100 talleris expecto.

Address: Reverendissimo domino, domino Stephano Radezio, episcopo Agriensi et sacrae caesareae regiaeque maiestatis camerae praefecto, consiliario et per Ungariam locumtenenti etc., domino meo et patrono semper generoso. Posonium.
Scribal note: Sambucus petit 100 florinos.

265.
Sambucus to István Radéczy and the Hungarian Chamber
8 May 1576, Vienna

The original is kept in Budapest, MOL, E 211 XXXII. Lymbus II. series 1552-1848. 113 cs. f. 22^r-23^v.[1512]

Sambucus is pleading with the emperor to pay attention to him. He knows that he is asking something for which powerful antagonists are much agitated, but he is not one who would like to harm anyone or pounce on the possessions of others. At the beginning, when Jakab Was and Torda's biological brother publicly claimed that they were the heirs to Sigismund Torda, they came to Sambucus and asked him to help them, having the most legitimate hereditary rights. In compensation they separated the library (from the bequest) and gave it to Sambucus in the presence of the bishop of Veszprém. Sambucus (in return) introduced their case at court and lobbied for them with powerful councillors. Eventually, Jakab Was, with the authority of the other heirs, collected the bequest of Torda. Sambucus at this point asked the emperor to resign of his part for his sake, a part which is too little to be worthy for the emperor, who agreed and communicated it with Sambucus's patron (Vice-Chancellor) Johannes Listhius. Sambucus knows that they will sue him and he will go into expenses; he would therefore like to have a mutual agreement through Radéczy and the emperor. He would be grateful if Radéczy could achieve something, but will accept his decision whatever it is. He never asked anything from the emperor "gratis." He talked

---

[1509] István Hosszutóthy was councillor of the Hungarian Chamber in Pressburg. His testament is published in *Történeti Tár* ser. 4, vol. 5 (1904), 97-102.
[1510] Sambucus must have thought of Győr and Listhius, since the bishop of Eger was Radéczy.
[1511] We were not able to identify this person.
[1512] We thank Kees Teszelszky for communicating this letter to us.

about it with the emperor, who showed himself to be very affable. All he is doing is done because of the humble requests of Jakab Was. As many know well, he never does things in secret, and he is far from being a fraud or someone with any desire to do harm.

Reverendissime, egregii domini, domini patroni observandissimi, salutem et perpetua obsequia.

Supplex oro caesaream maiestatem, ut denique aliquid mihi speratae tandiu clementiae impartiatur rationemque servitiorum ac meae tenuitatis generose in oculis ferat ducatque. Scio rem turbatam satis importunorum et potentum adversariorum diuturnisque processibus obnoxiam me petere. Non is tamen sum, qui iniuria ullius et damno contra ius ire involareque in aliena cupiam. Occasio autem huius meae contentionis est, initio, ut Iacobus Waz [!] cum fratre germano Tordae sese haeredes Tordae palam docuissent,[1513] me accessere obsecrant.[1514] Impetravere in iustissima haereditate iacente, partim distracta consilio et omnibus legitimis adhibitis modis, se iuvarem. In manifesto iure sibi vim fieri. Bibliothecam divisam, quam ilico mihi muneris et praetii ergo coram reverendissimo Vesprimensi detulerunt etc. Introduxi eos in forum, adfui subsidio apud magnos consiliarios comparato, rem visere non segniter, sed adhuc lento caesaris, seu vestro auxilio, quod tamen reverendissimae dominationes egregiae vestrae absque causa gravi facere puto.

Tandem his diebus Iacobus Was de potestate sibi a caeteris cohaeredibus producta cogat, urget, quam res suae, tam Tordae et extremis impensis sui et aere alieno progrediantur. caesarem subiecte compellem, ut sua maiestas sibi collatam partem patrocinii nomine generose mihi concederet. Me ita habiturum ipsius iuvandi occasionem pleniorem, nihil hac exigua re caesaris maiestati decessurum, imo tam tenue lucrum ineptum esse maiestatis amplitudine etc. Persuasit, re communicata satis cum reverendissimo nostro domino patrono Listhio etc. Scio litibus me conflictatum iri, et aliquibus impensis, si obtinuero. Sit res morae ad exitum haud tolerandae, tentarem tamen aliquid, si per vos et caesarem liceret et viam quaererem, utrique parti haud impeditam, qua demum causa modo finiretur aut coitione leniretur.

Si aliquando quid aequo iure obtinueritis, erit cur caesari vobisque gratias agam. Certe hoc negotio caesari nil incommodi afferatis vos et ego fortasse ad negocium diligentius vobis perquisitiusque [?] citra haeredum pauperum sumptus et molestias, quibus hucusque graviter laborarunt, incumbam. Quidque statueritis, aeque feram. Aut vos miseros solicitius iuvate, aut alios volenter ne moremini.[1515]

Nil unquam a caesare gratis petivi. Locutus sum suae maiestati de hoc negotio, cuncta grata et facilia prae se tulit. Vos, si Musas et servitia Sambuci fovete, suffragiis ne deseratis. Per plena est dubitationis causa aliquot annorum, sumptuum non vacua, molestiis cumulata.

[1513] Initially, after Sigismundus Torda Gelous's death in 1567 there seemed to be no direct heirs. Sambucus lobbied for the interests of a certain relative Jakab Was, but he apparently failed. Later, new "heirs" appeared on the scene. See Illésy, "Sámboky János történetíróról," 529-530.

[1514] The subject of the sentence may be Torda's relatives, Ferenc and Miklós. See Illésy, ibid.

[1515] Sambucus also appealed to the Imperial Chamber. See his petition registered in ÖStA, FHKA, Alte Hofkammer, Hoffinanz, Band 327-R [1576], f. 210ᵛ (5 May). Little later a report of the Hungarian Chamber sent to the Imperial Chamber suggests that Sambucus's petition was successful at least with Radéczy: "Camer in Hungern bericht, waßgestalt Sigißmundi Tordae guetter auf Martinum Spazai und von dannen auf Jacoben [!] Sambucum khumben sei, ligt da also anzuzaigen." ÖStA, FHKA, Alte Hofkammer, Hoffinanz, Band 321-E [1576 June], f. 7ᵛ (see http://rudolphina.com/Regesten/A1576-06-00-02984.xml, accessed on 22/05/2023.) However, the affair did not stop here (see Almási, *The Uses of Humanism*, 186, note 165) and apparently Torda's relatives won against Sambucus, and managed to obtain his part of the inheritance (probably without the library, which might have already been given to Sambucus).

Propter caesaris et camerae dignitatem vos videritis. Quibus me subiecte commendo adque obsequia submitto cliente idonea et meritis vestris plurimis debita. 8. Maii 1576. Vestrae reverentiae egregiarumque dominationum servitor et cliens Ioannes Sambucus.

Quidquid facio praecibus et paene lachrymis Iacobi Was adductus, ut norunt multi, facio, nil clam molior, absit a me fraus et nocendi voluntas.

Address: Reverendissimo ac egregiis dominis, dominis praefecto consiliariisque camerae Posoniensis sacrae caesareae regiaeque maiestatis, dominis meis et fautoribus semper gratiosissimis.
Scribal note: XII. Maii 1576. Doctor Ioannes Sambucus pro bonis olim Sigismundi Tordae.

266.
Sambucus to Theodor Zwinger
14 May 1576, Vienna

The original is kept in Basel, Universitätsbibliothek, Frey Mscr II 26, no. 218. Published in Gerstinger, "Die Briefe," 194-195.

Sambucus wrote to Episcopius about the 35 thalers not yet paid and about Gemusaeus's annoying letter. If he is unsatisfied when so little money is concerned, what would happen if there were more money involved? If Sambucus had thought of it earlier, he would have chosen another way. He asks Zwinger to remind them of their interests, of Aristotle, the Greek military writers provided to Xylander and Lazius's Republic of Rome, *which he all spontaneously and generously gave and will give to others soon. Sambucus highly appreciates Löwenklau and the public testimony he gave of his love for Sambucus. He has not yet seen the edition of Zosimus. The French bookseller says he has not yet received Löwenklau's books from Regensburg. As soon as he receives them or sees them, he will send Löwenklau some worthy gift, meanwhile Zwinger should greet him in his name. The emperor will leave for Regensburg before the end of the month, which will provide an occasion to send an honorarium through Johannes Crato, as is it not safe at all these days to include anything blindly in letters. If Zwinger starts working on Hippocrates, he should let Sambucus know. He is now sending him 60 or 80* variae lectiones *made in Hippocrates's works which he compiled two years before using someone else's codex. He is sending greetings to Claude Aubery.*

Sambucus salutem.

Scripsi Episcopio de 35 talleris nondum solutis et importunis scriptionibus Gemusaei.[1516] In tam exigua summula non satisfit, quid de maiori speraris? Si hoc credidissem, aliam viam iniissem. Te oro, mone quorum interest, itemque de Aristotele et polemicis a me Xylandro suppeditatis Graecis[1517] et *Republica Romana* Lazii,[1518] quae omnia sponte libereque communicavi, et missurus sum brevi alia, si volent. Leonclavio, viro doctissimo, cuius iudicium

---
[1516] On the history of 35 thalers see letters 226, 233, 262, 271, 358 and 376.
[1517] Zwinger's marginal note: "Polemica," see letter 247, note 1431. On Aristotle see Gerstinger, "Zusammenfassung," 286-287, and letter 292.
[1518] On Lazius see letter 233, note 1354.

magni facio, amorem et publicum de meis studiis testimonium amplector. Praefationem et librum Zosimi[1519] adhuc non vidi, necdum bibliopola Gallus se Ratispona libros suos accepisse ait.[1520] Ubi accepero aut videro, literis et munusculo idoneo statim benevolentiam redimam. Cui interea a me salutem plurimam. Caesar intra mensem Ratisponam est profecturus,[1521] istinc occasio per dominum Cratonem literas et honorarii mittendi occasio commodissima est futura, nam temere literis quicquam includere hodie vix tutum est. Vale et si in Hippocratem incumbitis, significate. Mittam 60 vel 80 lectiones ante biennium ex alio codice manuscripto obiter descriptas.[1522] Auberio salutem. 14. Maii 1576. Vienna raptim.

Address: Clarissimo viro D. doctori Theodoro Zwingero etc., amico optimo suo. Basell.

267.
Sambucus to Joachim Camerarius Jr.
14 June 1576, Vienna

The original is kept in Uppsala, University Library, The Waller Manuscript Collection, Ms hu-00064.

Sambucus wonders why Camerarius the Younger does not publish the textual bequest of his father, like his Greek letters, which could be printed together with the letters of Chrysoloras, provided by Sambucus. Camerarius Sr. also wrote several Greek prefaces and (letters) addressed to Antonios Eparchos, Michele Sofianos etc. If the son could also add his father's poems, it would be a volume that would stand the test of time. He is sending one of Camerarius's letters. He is surprised that Sadoleto's oration has not yet been printed. If Camerarius publishes Chrysoloras's letters only in the far future, he would like them back. Henri Estienne promises to publish Dioscorides and other works soon, but he is slow due to the number of editions he is working on. Finally, he asks Camerarius to forward a letter to Henri Estienne. If he also writes a letter to Estienne, he could mention the Greek works of his father.

S. D.

Scio te, mi Ioachime, nisi oblitus virtutum, educationis omnisque humanitatis sis, in primis paternarum laudum cupidissimus et amplitudinis esse studiosum, qui ipse non mediocribus extas. Cur igitur eius reliqua non edis, quae scio esse nec vulgaria, nec pauca? Cur non editas Graecas et domi latentes eius epistolas coeres? Cur non cum Chrysolorae epistolis, quas a me habetis, producis?

[1519] See letter 259.
[1520] This may be a reference to Jean Aubry.
[1521] To the Regensburg diet, where Maximilian II eventually died on the 12th of October.
[1522] Zwinger's marginal note: "lectiones variae in Hippocratem." On Hippocrates see Gerstinger, "Zusammenfassung," 307-308.

Scis, credo, olim parentem tuum multis libellis editis Graece praefatum, astrologicis et aliis opusculis, item ad Eparchum, ad Sophianum, etc.[1523] Imo si versus eiusdem adhibere possis, volumen conficeris omnibus saeculis dignum, et simulachrum veteris Ἑλλάδος.[1524]

Mitto unam ad me quoque. Non deerunt typographi. Sadoleti *Consolatoria* adhuc haeret, miror.[1525] Chrysolorae epistolas meas si diutius presseris, repetam, vel etiam exigam, nam mutuas dederam.[1526]

Vale, et scio de te quoque illud vetus esse ἀληθέστατον,[1527] ἅπαν τὸ χρηστὸν τὴν ἴσην ἔχει φύσιν[1528] et ut Euripides in Hecuba ὅδε ἐσθλὸς, ἐσθλὸς etc.[1529] Raptim, 14. Iunii 1576. Tuus semper Sambucus etc.

Dioscorides et alia Stephanus brevi se editurum pollicetur. In tanta varietate et quadam segete librorum non nihil tardior est.[1530] Mitto ἰδιόγραφον [1531] patris, quod ubi descripseris, oro, remittito.

* Has oro ad Henricum Stephanum nostrum cito curato. Si ad eundem tuas adiunxeris, poteris de Graecis parentis scriptis meminisse. Non dubito illum recepturum opus exoptatissimum.

Address: Dem Edlen Hochgelerten Herrn Jo[a]chim Camerario der Ertznay Doctorn etc. meinem Jugendten guetten Herrn und Freundt. Nurnberg. Cito, cito.
Camerarius's note: 76, 26 Iunii.

268.
Sambucus to Theodor Zwinger
9 July 1576, Vienna

The original is kept in Basel, Universitätsbibliothek, Frey Mscr II 26, no. 219. Published in Gerstinger, "Die Briefe," 195-196.

Sambucus will receive Löwenklau according his merits. Sambucus has made everything he has available to him and his companions. He is sending some further annotations on Hippocrates. Previously he sent many to Zwinger. These ones are from a Byzantine codex. They seem minor but

---

[1523] Antonios Eparchos (1491–1571) was a Greek humanist from Corfu, who later came to Italy and taught Greek in Milan. Michele Sofianos (c. 1530–1565) was a Greek humanist of Chios, where he received solid education from Listarchos and others. He moved to Padova in c. 1550-1552, where he frequented the university and soon became an acknowledged authority of ancient Greek, moving in the circles of Paolo Manuzio and Gian Vincenzo Pinelli. Sambucus dedicated to him an emblem: *Emblemata* (1564), 31. His biography, published by Meschini, was probably written by Nicasio Ellebodio. Camerarius Jr. established contact with him during his studies in Padua in 1562. See Anna Meschini, *Michele Sofianòs* (Padova: Liviana, 1981). A Latin letter by Camerarius Sr. to Sofianos was indeed printed in *Ioachimi Camerarii Epistolarum familiarium libri 6* (Francforti: A. Wechel, 1583), 528-529.
[1524] Greece
[1525] Sadoletus, *Philosophicae consolationes* (1577). Cf. the Index.
[1526] See letter 117, note 687.
[1527] is most true
[1528] all the useful things are of the same nature. Sophocles, *Fr.* 87, 2: The wording here is based on the faulty transmission in Clemens Alexandrinus, *Stromata* VI 2.10.
[1529] Euripides, *Hecuba* 597: this good (man) is good.
[1530] On Dioscorides see letter 155, notes 920 and 921.
[1531] autograph

in Hippocrates even single syllable can matter. Zwinger should send them to Claude Aubery. He is sending his greetings to Episcopius and Perna and lets them know that he has received the two copies of Zosimus, and he should also get his manuscript back at the next book fair.

Sambucus salutem.

Leonclavium, virum doctissimum, suis meritis complexurus sum omni genere officiorum; patuere illi Sambuci cuncta eiusque comitibus.[1532] Mitto quaedam quasi postspicilegia in Hippocratem obiter annotata.[1533] Antea tibi miseram non pauca.[1534] Haec vero ex codice quodam Byzantino exscripseram. Etsi etiam levia videntur, quia tum sunt Hippocratica, in cuius singulis syllabis, non dictionibus modo, singulae salutares sententiae latent, cum Auberio communicabis meoque nomine illum salutabis. Episcopio et Bernae, amicis nostris, salutem et significabis me duo Zosimi exemplaria accepisse et,[1535] uti pollicentur, proximis nundinis Francforto me omnino συγγραφὴν[1536] meam exspectare. 9. Iulii 1576. Viennae.

Address: Clarissimo viro domino doctori Theodoro Zwingero etc., amico singulari. Basell.
Zwinger's note: Accepit duo Zosimi exemplaria; Syngraphen [...] et Bonfinium.

269.
Sambucus to István Radéczy
13 August 1576, Vienna

The original is kept in Budapest, MOL, E 211 XXXII. Lymbus II. series 1552-1848. 113 cs. f. 24.

Knowing the general shortage of money Sambucus would not trouble Radéczy but God knows how little he has for everyday life. He therefore makes a petition for 200 florins. He knows he is owed up to 450 florins. If they ever cared for him, they should help him now. The receipt will be provided by Nicasius Ellebodius, to whom he entrusted the whole matter, as he trusts his true friendship.

Reverendissime, Egregii domini domini et patroni semper observandissimi, salutem et servitiorum perpetuam commendationem.

Nisi me summa necessitas undique arctaret, nisi multis nominibus essem obaeratus, in ista, ut audio, aerarii angustia vestrae reverentiae egregiis dominis minime importunum me ostenderem. Sed is, qui omnia intuetur, novit, solusque tuetur, scit, quam tenuis sit meae rei familiaris ratio, quam curta suppellex. Quare, si unquam patrocinio me tutati estis, beneficiisque fovistis, hanc supplicatiunculam de 200 florenis non difficile admittetis. Scio restare mihi istic

---

[1532] Zwinger's marginal note: "[com]mendat [Le]onclavium."
[1533] Zwinger's marginal note: "Hippocra[tis] spicilegia [e]x codice [pe]rantiquo."
[1534] See letter 266.
[1535] This is a reference to printed copies of Zosimus, published by Löwenklau (Sambucus's single manuscript of Zosimus cannot to be found in Vienna, ÖNB).
[1536] book

ad 450 florenos. Cur non possitis dimidium presto et laboranti vestra benevolentia imperare? Itaque, Vestra Reverentia, Egregii domini, si unquam Sambucum amastis, sustinuistis usus eius quotidianus, ab aerario 200 mihi concedetis. Apocham D. Nicasius exhibebit, cuius industriae et amicitiae totum negocium commisi, nec vanum advocatum fore omnino mihi persuadeo. Quorum patrocinio me humilime commendo. 13. Augusti 1576. Vestrae reverentiae, egregiarum dominationum vestrarum servitor etc. Sambucus.

Address: Reverendissimo ac egregiis dominis, dominis, praefecto consiliariisque camerae sacrae caesareae regiaeque maiestatis Posoniensis, dominis patronis gratiosis et observandissimis. Posonium.
Note: D. Sambucus petit pecuniam.

270.
Sambucus to Johannes Crato
15 September 1576, [Vienna]

Published in Gerstinger, "Die Briefe," 196-197.

Sambucus has informed Löwenklau about the benevolence (waiting for him in Vienna). They say that the emperor is considering visiting Wrocław before returning to Vienna. Archduke Karl wants to go to Wiener Neustadt in two days and move on to Graz in ten days. They are waiting for the return of Archduke Ernst. Twenty chariots loaded with select wine are sent to the king. The Ottomans demand the due tribute but Sambucus saw that the money is still lying in the Chamber. He is happy that the emperor feels well. He asks Crato to forward a letter to Dasypodius with complaints about his impertinence.

Magnifice domine, salutem.

Leonclaio de humana et prolixa benevolentia significavi. Hic rumusculi non certo autore extitere caesaream maiestatem Vratislaviam cogitare, ad nos serius redituram. Carolus archidux perendie in Novam Civitatem cogitat, illinc intra 10 dies Graeciam revisurum aiunt. Ernestum exspectamus.[1537] Regi hodie 20 currus onusti vino selecto mittuntur.[1538] Thurca cupide urget honorarium, sed in camera latere adhuc hodie omnia oculatus vidi. Cum caesare bene esse laetamur ex animo. Vale. 15. Septembris 1576. Totus tuis meritis Sambucus.

Has oro commodo tuo ad Dasypodium cum [...] expostulatione ac mea repete serius eiusque ignaviam et moram nota haud inique nec citra stomachum.

[1537] Archduke Ernst (1553–1595) was the second son of Maximilian II, educated together with his brother Rudolf in Spain. He was candidate for the throne of Poland in 1573. In 1576, he became governor in the Archduchy of Austria, hence the most powerful Habsburg in Vienna, where he promoted the case of the Counter-Reformation. In 1590, he became governor of Inner Austria and in 1594 of Spanish Netherlands, where he died. See Bibl, "Erzherzog Ernst und die Gegenreformation".

[1538] This may be interpreted in two ways, either the "king" refers to Maximilian, hence the wine was sent from Hungary (to Vienna) or it refers to Rudolf, hence from Vienna to Prague.

Address: Magnifico et clarissimo viro domino doctori Ioanni Cratoni a Craffthaim, caesaris consiliario et archiatro fideli etc., domino amico observando. Regenspurg. Herrn Doctor Crato zu handen.

271.
Sambucus to Theodor Zwinger
13 October 1576, [Vienna]

The original is kept in Basel, Universitätsbibliothek, Frey Mscr II 26, no. 220. Published in Gerstinger, "Die Briefe," 197-200.

Sambucus thanks Zwinger for forwarding the 35 thalers to Episcopius. His testimony is sufficient for Sambucus, a receipt from the Oporinus office will be fine later. He has neither received the Bonfini-manuscript nor the one provided to Zwinger, they might come with the package of the bookseller. He is sorry that work on Aristotle has stopped. Henri Estienne does not publish his own edition of Aristotle and asks Sambucus to write to Episcopius and Perna, if they are associates, and obtain from them "our Aristotle", that is, by dividing the expenses Estienne would print it in a most emendated version on nice paper. Sambucus will publish Photius. He is surprised how fierce the Oporinus office is toward him. Lazius's work on the migration of peoples was banned by the emperor because of protests by the Austrian nobility, as he wrote to the Oporinus office, although he had managed to obtain a two-year allowance for its sale. But those good men (i.e. the heirs of Oporinus) forget about these things. Sambucus sent Lazius's Roman Republic, a rare and huge book, corrected and enlarged by the author, which he had bought, obtaining the imperial permission for its print, as they (i.e. the Oporinus office) desired, which they neither publish nor resend, while the delivery cost him 3 thalers. If they do not admit their responsibility he will stop this business. He asks Zwinger to inquire from Episcopius what should happen to his manuscript on military things translated by Xylander. Likewise, they keep his Euclid-manuscript unpublished, provided to Dasypodius, which he values at 100 florins. This is all Episcopius's fault. Löwenklau sends his greetings to Zwinger, they are united day by day. Löwenklau is using all his books, collecting things for a second volume of the Basilica *and translating Manuel II Palaeologus's counsel to his son John. He also provided him with the rare* Lexicon of Zonaras, *from which he is collecting many legal terms. Zwinger should mediate between Henri Estienne and Episcopius and let Estienne know what they think about the project of publishing Aristotle.*

Salutem Sambucus.

Habeo gratiam de opera ad Episcopium navata pro 35 talleris. Sufficit mihi tua manus et testimonium, liberatum me ab Oporinianis, quandocumque tandem apocha sequetur. Nec Bonfinium[1539] nec tua dum accepi, fortasse cum sarcinis bibliopolae reddentur. Aristotelem iacere doleo. Henricus Stephanus suum[1540] non edet ac me urget amore et beneficio publico, ad Episcopium et Bernam, si socii sunt, diligenter scribam ac exorem, ut sibi nostrum Aristotelem

---
[1539] Zwinger's notes among the lines: "de rebus Ungaricis." In fact, it probably refered to Bonfini, *Symposion trimeron* (cf. letter 182).
[1540] Zwinger's notes above the line: "Aristotelem."

impetrem, hoc est, dimidio sumptuum onere se typis suis editurum emendatissime, carta proba, ut laudem ferant. A me responsum vel a vobis exspectat quamprimum, utque iuves, si Episcopius cessat, valde oro, ac illis persuade. De Photio[1541] mihi cura est, crede, nec latebit diu. Valde miror Oporinianos tam duros in meis rebus, quibus plus profui fortasse, quam obfui. Caesaris edicto vendicio Transmigrationum gentium ante annum ob supplicem nobilitatem Austriae,[1542] cui in multis iniuria fit nominis et familiae, erat prohibita, uti perscripseram ad illos, tamen impetravi, ut horum distractio per biennium concederetur.[1543] Talium non recordantur boni viri. Misi eiusdem Lazii *De Republica Romana* et cetera ingens volumen ab authore ipso emendatum et multis partibus auctum, a me redemptum et permissu caesaris mandatum ad editionem,[1544] uti expetiverunt, nec edunt nec remittunt; qui detulit, constitit mihi Augustam 3 talleris. Haec nisi et alia serius agnoverint, de tabula manum levabo. Mi optime amice, quaere ex Episcopio, quid de libris a Xylandro ex meis ἀντίγραφοις[1545] de re militari[1546] conversis fiat, cur premant adeo. Itemque Euclidem detinent meum, quem 100 florenis aestimo, per Dasypodium suppeditatum, nam hic omnem culpam in Episcopium reiicit.[1547] Leonclaius te salutat,[1548] quotidie una sumus, fruitur omnibus meis, collegit non pauca apud me ad secundum volumen *Basilicon* apta. Palaeologi Manuelis παραινέσεις[1549] ad Ioannem filium nunc vertit a me datum [!] et alia.[1550] Dedi etiam Zonarae Λεξικὸν[1551] rarum, ex quo multae [i.e. multas] voces rarae [i.e. raras] et ad ius quoque facientia colligit.[1552] Summa non cessat. De Aristotele quaeso cum Henrico communicando expedi negocium, contra me non erit et non paenitebit. Si consenserint, significate illi Genevamque scribite, aut si recusarint, item tu illi significato, ne diutius et tam longinque a me responsum ille exspectet.[1553] Haec, oro, perfice, mi amice, ac vale. 13. Octobris 1576.

[1541] Zwinger's notes above the line: "et eius bibliotheca."
[1542] Zwinger's notes among the lines: "Querela nobilitatis Austriae de W. Lazio"
[1543] Apparently, the Oporinus office was considering the republication of Lazius's *De gentium aliquot migrationibus* (Basileae: Oporinus, 1555). Unfortunately, we have no other information on the imperial ban on Lazius's work. To be sure, Lazius was aware of the danger of the nobility's possible anger, as it appears from a short postscript added to the book.
[1544] Zwinger's marginal note: "Lazii volumen de Republica Romana."
[1545] copies
[1546] Zwinger's marginal note: "de re militari." See letter 247, note 1431.
[1547] See letter 89, note 564.
[1548] On Löwenklau's activity in Sambucus's library during his stay in Vienna see the note of Gerstinger in "Die Briefe," 199; *Humanistes du bassin des Carpates II. Johannes Sambucus*, 63-66.
[1549] counsel
[1550] Palaeologus, *Praecepta educationis regiae*. Manuel II Palaeologus (1350–1425) was a Byzantine emperor. Troubled by Ottoman attacks and conquests, his rule meant an opening toward the West. He was a prolific author who wrote on various subjects.
[1551] lexicon
[1552] The *Lexicon* attributed to Zonaras was not published by Löwenklau, although Sambucus expected its print as his bibliography testifies: "Leontii scholia historica in novum Testamentum [...] Zonarae et Philotei Λεξικὰ a se credidit Leonclaio excudenda. 1579" (Sambucus, *Catalogus librorum*). This popular Byzantine lexicon was, in fact, from the thirteenth century and is today not considered as Zonaras's work. See Klaus Alpers, "Zonarae Lexicon," in *Brill's New Pauly. Antiquity*, vol. 15, ed. Hubert Cancik (Leiden: Brill, 2010), 722; Gerstinger, "Die Briefe," 200. Cf. with letters 298 and 359.
[1553] See Gerstinger, "Zusammenfassung," 286-289.

272.
Johannes Crato to Sambucus
20 October 1576, Augsburg[1554]

Contemporary copies are held in Vienna, ÖNB, Cod. Ser. n. 56205, 1^r-4^v and 9^r-10^r, and Cod. 11049, f. 1^r-9^v, and in Wolfenbüttel, Cod. Guelf. 864 Helmst, 94^r-100^v. Published as "Joannis Cratonis... Nachricht von der letzten Krankheit und Tode Kaisers Maximiliani II de Anno 1576," in *Nützliche Sammlung Verschiedener Meistens ungedruckter Schrifften*, ed. Christian Gottlieb Buder (Frankfurt–Leipzig: Ch. Heinrich Cuno, 1737), 589-599 (reprinted in *Historische Denkwürdigkeiten und Sittengemälde*, ed. Christian H. R. W. Spiller von Witterberg, Rudolfstadt: Frödelschen Hofdruckerei, 1830, 17-25); *Ioannis Cratonis a Krafftheim... epistola ad Ioannem Sambucum medicum... de morte Imperatoris Maximiliani Secundi*, ed. Christian Gottfried Gruner (Jenae: Litteris Mavkii, 1781), 13-24;[1555] and in German translation by Becker, "Die letzten Tage," 338-343.

Crato was so shaken by the emperor's death and his son's sickness that he had difficulty writing a letter to Sambucus about Maximilian's death. Sambucus must have already received different news, as fake and dissonant news usually shamelessly circulates in Vienna. So he is now writing the truth. Following the emperor on this journey, he was very sick and consequently had personal access only rarely to the emperor but was informed by men who dined together with him. The emperor ate fish in those days, which he often did not do for an entire year. When they reached Straubing, he had kidney pains but after three days he got rid of them by ejecting a big stone. (At this time) he was close to the emperor day and night, but when they arrived to Augsburg, he fell seriously sick again and stayed in bed. Meanwhile the emperor ate much fruit. As soon as he gathered some strength, he warned him. The emperor was over the seventh climacteric year of his life (i.e. 49), but in Crato's experience the years after the climacteric ones were more dangerous. From the beginning of August Archduke Ferdinand stayed with the emperor for eight days, while Crato suffered his usual eye pains. On 7 August, the emperor drank cold wine for dinner and had breathing problems right after, so he lay down and sweated; Crato does not know what medicine he took, as he was at home. Dodonaeus, who stayed with the emperor at dinners, did not tell him. Dodonaeus gave him candied borage but he did not touch it. When the pharmacist informed him that the emperor was badly effected he wanted to go and see him in the evening but was ordered to

---

[1554] In a letter of 1 December 1576, Hubert Languet informs Crato about the circulation of a writing by Rembert Dodonaeus, concerning the death of Maximilian II. Since it is malicious with regards to Crato, Languet appears to suggest that Crato should write a neutral description of the event without being harsh on Dodonaeus: "Versantur hic in plurimum manibus quoddam scriptum de morbo Imperatoris Maximiliani foelices memoriae, cuius author dicitur esse Dodonaeus. Quo scripto quoniam videtur te perstringere et id agere, ut tibi invidiam conflet, putavi nostram amicitiam et meam erga te observantiam exigere, ut illud ad te mitterem. Tu pro tua prudentia, quid in ea re faciendum tibi sit, tecum mature deliberabis. Nam testantur historiae, contentiones de eiusmodi rebus adiunctum periculum saepe habuisse. Obsecro te, ne quid in hac re fervide agas, et considera potius, quaenam sit res, de qua agitur, quam quis sit is, qui te oppugnat." Gillet, *Crato von Crafftheim*, 2:533-534. By the time, Crato's response to Dodonaeus might already have been written (and in a style suggested by Languet). Compare this letter with Rembertus Dodonaeus's rather different description of the event and Crato's role in it (f. 10^r-12^v in the Viennese manuscript Cod. 11049), with his notes concerning Maximilian's autopsy (f. 13^r-14^r), and finally with Crato's funeral oration (Crato, *Oratio funebris*). See also letter 279.

[1555] There are minor textual differences between the surviving manuscripts and prints, which suggest that the text circulated more widely. In our edition we followed the Viennese Cod. Ser. n. 56205, which gives the best text, except where indicated.

stay home. Early in the morning the emperor told Crato that if the severe pain had lasted longer he would have called for him. From then on, the emperor could not urinate even as much as half a decilitre, but he got better on 13 August, but as he lunched on nuts and cherries, he vomited at night, so, as was his habit, he stayed away from lunch in the following days. Crato never saw him well afterwards, although he still met a few great men and even showed some gaiety. Crato heard that he was annoyed by kidney pains but does not know what medication he used. Sometimes he took juniper seeds and wanted them also candied. He coughed heavily. On 29 August, at 10 pm he had very bad kidney pains and heavily vomited and they confirmed that his heart got disturbed, neither could the emperor feel the pulse. He would not like to mention names, but some men, who do medicine out of books and not by practice, think differently. He himself confirmed that the problem was that the heart and lungs were blocked by the mucus or humours, and indicated the cure. Yet, some who cared more about their prestige than the emperor's health, objected and their method prevailed. So the heart was kept warm, against Crato's will, and thus enfeebled, while poultice was applied on the kidney, which he approved. Some days later the emperor ejected five rather big stones. A messenger was sent to fetch Giulio Alessandrini. Before he arrived, Georg Ilsung, bailiff in Swabia recommended a woman from Ulm, from the Streicher family (i.e. Agatha Streicher), who was also praised by Franz Prinzenstein and by Günther of Schwarzburg, whose gout pains she allegedly cured. He was heard to imprudently say that the emperor would not have lived more than three days unless she came for his help and promised a fast recovery. She took away wine, in which all the hope of regeneration lay. She brought different herbal drinks, often he drank four different types in one day, one Crato saw was traditionally used for epilepsy, but he does not know if the emperor drank them or not, he knows only about the false gossip in town about the emperor's two epileptic feats. He never noticed any sign of this sickness in twelve years of service. He vainly tried to intervene and stop the audacity of the woman and suggest a cure to get rid of the mucus. Now the emperor wanted meat and was not averse to wine, even if sour. He got so calm that he ordered Crato to stay some nights at home. Giulio Alessandrini arrived on 22 September and the emperor described him the treatment of the woman (without Crato's presence), which he wanted to continue at least for three more days, of which Alessandrini approved. Observing the cure for six days, Crato could not support any longer this womanly fraud and pleaded the emperor to stop it in front of all the consulting doctors. The emperor's select doctors were present, all thought to understand the sickness and were ready to take the cure in their hands. While Crato made clear that he wanted to take it into his hands, dishonesty won. That deceitful woman gave him a purgative medicine and some balm, as she called it. The emperor started rejecting food and drink and had a haemorrhoid pain and could not sleep. Everyone saw that he was getting worse, but they did not want to offend him and many praised that old-womanish cure. Crato turned to Adam von Dietrichstein in letter. He omits the long story that happened after Rudolf's arrival. On the night of his death the emperor complained of a benevolent pain of the upper abdomen. The impudent woman persuaded the wife of the Bavarian Duke, Queen Anna that the emperor suffered from pleuritic pain, putting off a (real) cure for good. On 12 October, he could not stop himself from protesting against all these bad cures. So they asked his opinion. He responded that the emperor either needed sudorific or diuretic cure but admitted that he did not know if his state was still curable. When he was led to the emperor in order to feel the pulse, the emperor told him that there was no pulse to be felt. As he hardly felt it and during the sickness it was highly irregular, he spoke to everyone present: instead of human help one needs here divine remedy. Two hours later the bishop of Wiener Neustadt, who had been already there without the emperor's knowledge, was let to enter, but the emperor was deep in his thoughts or praying. When an hour later he bravely affirmed that his time was up he agreed to the bishop's visit on condition that he will only speak about Christ our only saviour. The bishop encouraged the emperor to place his hopes in Christ, who redeemed all sinners of the world, and in eternal life. The emperor agreed and soon after died on 12 October at 9 am, exactly when in the Imperial Council Rudolf was about to ask the chancellor, the archbishop of Mainz to read the decrees of the imperial diet as advocated by the estates. Rudolf who entered the Council as king left it as emperor. There were many who falsely claimed that the emperor had died much before. The following day, Crato's man Petrus Suma did the autopsy but could not find signs of inflammation, of which some foolishly talked. The lungs and other organs swam in a yellow humour, while the cavity of the heart was so much hardened that it seemed as if it were bone. He removed some matter, which was hardened into a stone from the heart, and showed it to Mr Dietrichstein. The heart was somewhat white at the cone. In the belly there was some black humour, either coming from the spleen or the result of the woman's cure, from which he vomited before he died. Despite his frequent kidney problems the kidney looked fine, except for some sand in the left one, which damaged a little the ureters. From all this, a medical expert can easily reveal the right cure. He never doubted, especially when he saw the emperor having breathing difficulties, that the problem was that he hardly drank, a pint in a whole week. But Dodonaeus, who had not been able not drive out that watery humour, claimed that it was the cause of his death. Crato did not want to argue next to the corpse, he only called his attention to a quote by Hippocrates that anything can cross a living body. Giulio Alessandrini commented to have noticed the presence of pleuretic pus in his urine. A sure verdict is difficult to make but he will make sure to avoid conflict with these people in the future. He could not write earlier because of the grave sickness of his son.

De morte Imperatoris Maximiliani. Ioanni Sambuco, viro doctissimo, salutem.

Incredibilis meus dolor, quem ex obitu sacratissimi imperatoris et morbo gravissimo filii mei accepi, ita me afflixit et omnes animi atque corporis vires abstulit, ut nulla in re cogitationem locare atque figere possim. Itaque de morbo et vitae exitu sacratissimi Imperatoris Maximiliani II. domini nostri benignissimi saepe[1556] me ad te scribere conantem doloris acerbitas remoratur.[1557]

Non dubito autem, quin multis litteris plurima vobis nunciata sint. Vera et certane omnia, cum in hac urbe non dissentanea tantum, sed conficta atque falsa sine pudore proferantur, haud scio. Inscribam igitur pauca, et quibus tu atque omnes homines tuto fidem adhibere possint. Meministi vero, quam gravi morbo confectus in viam me dederim, ut imperatoriam maiestatem huc sequerer. Proinde raro caesarem in toto itinere accessi. Ex iis autem, qui mensae affuerunt, cognovi prolixius his paucis diebus, quibus in itinere fuimus, usum piscibus, quam multis annis proxime praeteritis. Saepe enim toto anno ne gustare quidem piscem memini. Straubingam cum venissemus in nephriticum dolorem incidit, eo triduo post satis grandi eiecto calculo liberatus est. Supra vires tunc die noctuque caesari praesto fui et, simul ac huc veni, in gravissimum morbum, quo pene confectus sum, incidi. Cum iacerem, non temperasse sibi imperatorem a fructibus parum etiam maturis, in ore omnium fuit. Vix vires collegeram, meum officium monendo, quantum potui, feci.

[1556] While the Viennese Cod. Ser. n. 56205 transmits capital letters S. M. (sacratissimae maiestatis), in this instance we chose to follow other textual witnesses, who all read saepe me.
[1557] On Maximilian's death see Becker, "Die letzten Tage" and Leopold Senfelder, "Kaiser Maximilian's II. letzte Lebensjahre und Tod," *Blätter des Vereines für Landeskunde von Niederösterreich* 22 (1898), 47-75.

Videbatur autem sibi caesar annum climactericum septimum superasse (Calendis enim Augusti quinquagesimum ingressus fuerat).[1558] Verum, id quod non raro observavi, plus periculi annus climacterico proximus habuit. Ineunte enim Augusto, cum octiduum apud caesarem fuisset serenissimus archidux Ferdinandus[1559] et mihi dolor auris, quo nimium saepe iam propemodum enecor, graviter molestus esset; die 8. Sextilis in coena vinum refrigeratum caesar hausit, et subito quasi spiritum sibi intercludi sensit. Coniecit igitur se, discedens a mensa, in lectum et nescio quo medicamento hausto (domi enim tunc me continebam) sudare, idque caesar rarissime facere solebat et poterat, coepit.

Nihil mihi Dodonaeus, qui coenanti imperatori affuerat, significavit, sed ad flores boraginis[1560] zarcaro conditos confugit, quos tamen imperator nunquam attigit. Cum nunciatum mihi esset a pharmacopaeo caesarem male affectum, sublata iam die volui accedere, verum domi remanere ea nocte iussus sum. Mane cum lecto imperator surgeret, *saevum,* inquit, *me heri malum oppressit. Si durasset, tibi non pepercissem.* Ex eo vero tempore numquam (quod sciam) integrum cyathum exhaurire potuit, XIII. tamen die ad ingenium quasi rediit, et cum in prandio et persica, et cerasa largius comedisset, sub noctem vomuit. Et ut auxilium naturae ferret (quod superioribus annis saepe fecit), in sequenti die a prandio abstinuit. Nunquam autem mihi deinceps recte valere visus est, etsi quosdam principes viros accederet et hilaritatem etiam prae se ferret. Sperni excellentes nam se nolunt. Nihil a me quidem auditum praeter illud, nephriticum dolorem sibi molestum esse, quem nescio quibus conquisitis remediis avertere studebat. Aliquoties granis iuniperi est usus, zuccaro etiam ea incrustari voluit. Graviter deinde et cum magna difficultate tussivit.

Itaque iam tum morbi exitialis factum initium non dubito, XXIX. autem Augusti die, quem divus Ferdinandus pro nephasto habebat, sub noctem hora X. nephriticus dolor imperatorem optimum gravissime invasit. Vomuit supra modum. Ex hac comotione cor comotum, πάλμον[1561] esse omnes arbitrabantur. Verum pulsus non ostendit cor palpitare, et ipse caesar non esse veram palpitationem affirmabat. De nomine numquam odiose contendere volui, licet quidam, qui doctrinae suae annos numerant et iactitant atque in deliberationibus medicis lecta magis de morbis, quam recte cogitata et intellecta adferunt, aliter sentiant. Obsessum vel a pituita, vel humore cor et pulmones affirmavi et confirmavi atque vera remedia ostendi. Verum praevaluit error et obstinata voluntas adversandi eorum, quibus pluris fuit sua existimatio, quam caesaris salus. Continuo igitur fotu cor contra meam voluntatem est debilitatum, et renibus cataplasmata me quidem approbante adhibita. Ita intra paucos dies 5 calculos satis grandes imperator excrevit.

Missi sunt celeris nuncii, qui D. Iulium acerrserent (!). Priusquam vero is huc venit, mulier quaedam Ulmensis, Stricheriana,[1562] re et nomin, operatione D. Georgii Ilsingii,[1563] praefecti Sueviae, mirifice commendata fuit. Appulit enim, urgentibus nos fatis, fatuitate quadam ea

---

[1558] Maximilian II was born on 31 July 1527. The "seventh" climacteric years means year 49 (seven times seven years).
[1559] Archduke Ferdinand II (1529–1595), governor of Bohemia (1547–1567) and ruler of Further Austria and Tirol (from 1564), famous for his art collection at the Ambras Castle.
[1560] The leaves of the plant borage have been traditionally used for gastrointestinal, respiratory and cardiovascular disorders.
[1561] palpitation
[1562] Agatha Streicher (†1581) was celebrated by Paracelsians as "endowed by God with great medical understanding." See Tilmann Walter, "New Light on Antiparacelsianism (c. 1570–1610): The Medical Republic of Letters and the Idea of Progress in Science," *The Sixteenth Century Journal* 43 (2012), 701-725, at 712 with further literature on Streicher.
[1563] Georg Ilsung von Tratzberg was a member of the Imperial Court Council already at the 1547 Augsburg diet.

huc navigio. Et cum Ilsingum ἄποδα¹⁵⁶⁴ esse scias, internuncio D. Francisco Prinzenstaeinio,¹⁵⁶⁵ quem praepositum Tridentinum etiam nunc appellant, conquisitis laudibus ornata est. Accessit comitis Guntheri a Schwartzburgk et cetera,¹⁵⁶⁶ cui dolores podagricos ademisse perhibebatur, testimonium et fatales machinae sapientissimo imperatori ad istum modum admotae, ut firmissimum quemque evertere possent. Primo cum impudentissimae et confidentissimae mulieri ad caesarem aditus fuit, dixisse fertur non supervicturum fuisse caesarem triduum, nisi illa auxilio venisset, et, ut solent mendaces impudentes, de valetudine intra paucos dies recuperanda ineptissime promisit. Vino interdixit, in quo omnis propemodum virium conservandarum spes erat et nescio quas cocturas vino praetulit. Saepe igitur uno die quatuor potus genera attulit. Vidi descriptionem quandam ex herbulis, quibus vulgo ad epilepsiam utuntur, nescio, an imperator biberit. Hoc scio in tota urbe rumorem falsissimum sparsum caesarem duabus horis correptum epilepsia iacuisse. Vere autem affirmare possum me totis his XII annis, quibus continuo imperatori affui et suae maiestatis valetudinis curam optima conscientia et rectissima voluntate gessi, ne minimum quidem huius morbi indicium unquam a me animadversum. Conatus sum nefariam audaciam mulieris comprimere, quantum in me fuit, et aliqua remedia, quae humorem in pectore assumere possent, proposui. Sed nescio quomodo, imo bene scio, quomodo eorum usus est impeditus. Appetebat tunc caesar carnes. Vinum, etsi insuave erat, non abhorrebat. Ita quiescebat, ut me aliquot noctibus domi remanere iuberet. Nequeo de his scribere plura et haec ipsa gravissimum dolorem mihi faciunt.

Advenit D. Iulius 22. Septembris, cui, cum imperator consilia muliebria, me absente, exposuisset, et quibus illa remediis triduo saltem uti vellet, locum muliebri medicationi concessit. Inspector fui huius acerbissimae fatuitatis sex diebus. Cum vero istius imposturas et muliebres fraudes ferre amplius non possem audientibus omnibus medicis supplex suam caesaream maiestatem oravi, ne sibi impudentem mulierem verba dare pateretur, me non velle videri mutum canem, qui silentio domini sui salutem prodat. Adesse suae maiestati medicos eximios, qui et morbum intelligant, et quilibet in se curam recipere non dubitet. Si quis addubitaret (me quidem ea, quae divina voluntate fiunt, non posse ad meum iudicium revocare, neque avertere) verum si concederetur, solum velle curationem in me recipere. Vicit fatalis improbitas. Mulier enim purgans medicamentum dedit, et aliis multis, ac vero balsamo, ut mendacissima foemina appellabat, usa est. Abhorrere statim a cibo et potu sacratissima caesarea maiestas coepit et gravissimus haemorrhoidum dolor, qui somnum ademit, invasit. In oculos incurrebat omnium, valetudinem caesaris in peius ruere, tamen ne in offensionem incurrerent, plurimi anilia ista collaudabant. Recensere de his omnibus neque possum, neque debeo. Ad generosissimum D. Dietrichsteinium, summum palatii caesarei praefectum, ἡμερόλεγδον¹⁵⁶⁷ scripsi.¹⁵⁶⁸ Si ea saltem, quae post adventum caesaris Rudolphi augusti II. facta sunt, nunc recensere vellem, longa epistola futura esset.

---

¹⁵⁶⁴ lame
¹⁵⁶⁵ ms: *Sprinzeinsteinio*; E1737: *Pinckenstenio*. We were not able to identify this person.
¹⁵⁶⁶ E1737: *Swartzburgk*; E1781: *Schwartburgk*. Johann Günther Count of Schwarzburg (1532–1586).
¹⁵⁶⁷ daily report
¹⁵⁶⁸ Adam von Dietrichstein (1527–1590), educated in Padua, was a learned diplomat and councillor of Maximilian II. He served as seneschal to young Rudolf and Ernst (being responsible for their education in Spain). From 1573 he was master of the Chambers (Oberstkämmerer) and secret councillor, and under Rudolf also high steward of the court (Oberthofmeister). When Crato supposedly wrote this letter, Dietrichstein probably still did not have this title. See the article by Heinrich Ritter von Zeißberg in *ADB* 5 (1877), 197-198; Friedrich von Edelmayer, "Ehre, Geld, Karriere. Adam von Dietrichstein im Dienst Kaiser Maximilians," in *Kaiser Maximilian II.: Kultur und Politik im 16. Jahrhundert*, eds. Friedrich Edelmayer and Alfred Kohler (Vienna: Verl. Für Geschichte und Politik, 1992), 109-142; Almási, *The Uses of Humanism*, 137.

De dextri hypochondrii[1569] dolore nocte ea, quam mors consecuta est, caesar conquerebatur. Ibi foemina impudens Reginae Annae, ducis Bavariae coniugi,[1570] persuasit pleuritide caesarem laborare. Infinita igitur remedia prolata. Ut primum 12. Octobris illucescere coepit, continere me non potui, quin multa fieri, nihil rectum affirmarem. Voluerunt igitur me, quid recte fieri posset, proferre. Respondi me in ea esse sententia, si iuvari natura debeat, vel diaphoretica, vel diuretica adhibenda, atque de radicum petroselini decocto peculiari ita monui, ut me ignorare, sitne vitalis virtus integra adhuc, significarem. Biduo enim muliebris medicatio explorandi potestatem non concesserat. Naturalem iacere manifestum erat. Me igitur prostratae naturae, et quae nullo modo medicum adiuvare queat, auxilium ferre posse testabar. Itaque ut arteriae motum explorarem, ad caesarem deductus sum. Cum optimus imperator carpum[1571] mihi praeberet: *Crato*, inquit, *nihil est pulsus*. Deprehendi autem vermicantem, ut medici loquuntur, pulsum, et vix quasi repere arteriam, cum quadam intermissione elationis. Fuit toto morbi tempore et inaequalis et intermittens pulsus, interdum ordinate. Itaque omnibus, qui aderant, audientibus dixi: humanis auxiliis nullum iam esse locum, divina imploranda, et, quae pro mea parte potui, optima fide monui.

Accersitus est episcopus Neapolitanus,[1572] inscio imperatore, verum duabus fere horis post admissus. Nam aliquamdiu vel in ardua cogitatione vel invocatione Dei imperator iacuit. Paullo post horam suam adesse magno animo atque excelso affirmavit. Admonitus de praesentia episcopi, eum posse accedere dixit hac conditione, ne qua alia de re, quam Christi salvatoris nostri unici merito loqueretur. Non defuit officio suo episcopus et cum ad extremum caesarem hortaretur, ut pluris valere apud Deum Iesu Christi domini nostri innocentis sanguinem, quam totius mundi nocentis peccata certo statueret atque in hac fiducia se suamque salutem aeterno Deo committeret et in spe vitae beatae atque aeternae usque ad extremum spiritum constanter acquiesceret. Ibi imperator clara voce respondit: *Non aliter faciam* ac mox quasi obdormiscens animam pie et cordate egit.[1573] Ea ipsa hora, quae 12. diei Octobris (qui divo Maximiliano inscriptus est in calendario) IX. erat, in curia senatoria patrem repraesentante Rudolpho II. caesare, decretum conventus imperii coram statibus promulgatum est, cumque finem legendi Moguntinus cancellarius fecisset,[1574] vivere quoque in his terris Maximilianus imperator desiit et filius, qui paulo ante in senatum imperii ut Germanorum rex venerat, imperator discessit. Non defuerunt homines improbi et leves, qui affirmare audebant, multo ante Imperatorem Maximilianum e vita migrasse. Sed cum illis contendere, qui tanquam suavi esca mendaciis delectantur, ineptum est.

Insequenti die XIII. noster Petrus Suma,[1575] industrius et officiosus vir, cadaver aperuit, neque in ullius ullum membrum insigniter laesum, nec ullum exulcerationis vel inflammationis signum, de qua inepte quidam loquebantur, reperit. Pulmones et illa omnia, quae Diodorus

---

[1569] ms: *hypocundrii*.

[1570] Anna of Austria (1528–1590), Duchess of Bavaria, Maximilian II's sister, wife of Albert V the Magnanimous (1528–1579), Duke of Bavaria. She was not a queen.

[1571] I. e. καρπός, wrist (offered by the Emperor to Crato to feel the pulse).

[1572] Lambert Gruter, born in the Low Countries, educated in Leuven, was bishop of Wiener Neustadt in 1574–1582. He was one of Maximilian II's court preachers from 1569. See Theodor Wiedemann, "Lambertus Gruter," *Österreichische Vierteljahrschrift für katolische Theologie* 7 (1868), 241-262; Louthan, *The Quest for Compromise*, 138.

[1573] Cf. with Louthan, *The Quest for Compromise*, 134-140; Almási, *The Uses of Humanism*, 344-345.

[1574] Daniel Brendel of Homburg (1522–1582) was archbishop-elector of Mainz from 1555. See Walter Goetz, "Daniel, Kurfürst von Mainz," in *Realencyklopädie für protestantische Theologie und Kirche* 4 (1898), 441-445.

[1575] On Petrus Suma's findings see Cod. 11049 in ÖNB (see Senfelder, "Kaiser Maximilian's II" - as in note 1557 - p. 47).

ἐντοστηθίδια πνεύματα¹⁵⁷⁶ appellat, humore subflavo innatabant et pulmo nativum colorem amiserat, φρένες¹⁵⁷⁷ etiam et cordis involucrum plus iusto humoris aquei continebant, et ad orificia cordis membranae ita induruerant, ut osseae viderentur. Materia autem quaedam in lapidem quasi in ipso corde concreverat, quam exemtam illustri domino Dietrichsteinio exhibui. Cor nonnihil ad conum propter redundantem humorem albicabat. In ventriculo ater humor conspiciebatur, qui vel e splene in eum in[gur]gitavit, vel ex medicamentis muliebribus ortus erat.

Nam pituitosi humoris crassi et viscidi plane in morbo supra libras sex vomitum reiecerat. Huius autem atri humoris paulo ante vitae finem ad unciam unam evomuit, neque deinceps quicquam assumsit. Allatae quidem quasi in articulo beatae migrationis sorbitiones fuerunt, verum illas non attigit. Renes minime male, cum saepe hoc decennio nephriticus fuerit, affecti erant et dexter sanus omnino videbatur, in sinistro materia arenosa, pauca, nondum tamen concreta reperta. Ureteres tamen in ea parte aliquo modo laesi. Satis ex his medicae artis peritis, quae morborum causa fuerit, et quae sanationis via, perspicuum qui non videt, infeliciter in arte medica occaecatus est. Ego quidem numquam dubitavi, ut saepe frustra monui, cum difficultatem spirandi eam viderem, ut sorbendo paululum vix cyathum exiguum exhaurire posset, atque cum integra septimana sextarium biberet, singulis vero diebus naturalibus ad conchium fere urinam redderet, eo ducendum, quo natura nobis viam monstrabat. Sed Dodonaeus noster nescio quae somnia fingebat, et non potuisse aquosum istum humorem medicamentis educi de mortuo etiam imperatore affirmabat. Nolui contendere ad cadaver. Hippocraticae saltem sententiae, qua in corpore vivo omnia posse permeare et vias nobis ignotas transire docemur, admonui. Clarissimus etiam D. Iulius, vir ad levitatem animi singularem factus, et vere ἄρεσκος, ¹⁵⁷⁸se observasse pleuriticium pus minxisse subiiciebat. Sed difficile est μηχανορράφους¹⁵⁷⁹ ad rectam sententiam perducere. Ego de his recordationibus nunc fugio, et ἐγγήραμα¹⁵⁸⁰ quaero ac, ne cum istis ingeniis mihi deinceps unquam sit conflictandum, sedudulo cavere studebo. Utinam iterum, utinam Deo atque nostris Musis, quod reliquum est vitae, vivere concederetur. Bene vale. Augustae Tiberii 20. Octobris. Citius enim propter gravissimum morbum filii animum ad scribendum applicare non potui. Anno MDLXXVI. Johannes Crato.

273.
Sambucus to Hilfreich Guett
20 October 1576, [Vienna]

The original is kept in Vienna, ÖNB, Cod. 9737^{z14-18}, II, f. 216ʳ. Published in Gerstinger, "Die Briefe," 200-201.

Sambucus complains about the general loss for the republic and Christianity caused by Maximilian's death and praises his moderation and tempered mind. Sambucus will worship his memory so that Maximilian's sons can understand his gratitude. He asks Guett to order the payment of 100 thalers to him, if his colleague agrees. He has not received the book by Guillaume

---
1576 breathing intestines
1577 heart
1578 obsequious
1579 schemers. Marginal note in ms: *fraudum consutores.*
1580 employment for old age

du Choul on antiquities; Guett's book was accidently thrown in its place. He is sending back the Turkish letters. Finally, he invites Guett to visit his "museum" sometime.

Magnifice domine, salutem.

Scis, quem invitissime amiserimus, quanto patrocinio communis res et Christi negocium sit diminutum, quam sit orandum, ut subsistamus et sine motu et labe nostra tueamur.[1581] Habuimus eo sensu imperatorem, qui neminem turbarit, moderatione, alacri vultu, temperato animo sustinuerit vel adversa. Sed nec sine spe nos deseruit, qui talem tantumque praesidem [?] maiestatis ac loci, tot pignora exempla virtutum posteris reliquerit. Valeat igitur et floreat suis divinitus comparatis meritis et ornamentis. Colam eius memoriam, ut me gratum filii patronum habuisse sentiant. Tuam magnificentiam oro, potes enim, si cum Collega[1582] velis: 100 Sambuco imperetis, nisi squalori et luctui tabem addere cupiatis. Librum Gulielmi Schoul Lugdunensis de antiquitatibus non recepi,[1583] eius loco tuum libellum temere meis iniectum. Thurcicas Epistolas remitto.[1584] Vale, patrone et amice observande. 20. Octobris 1576. Ex Museolo, quod ut ocio aliquando inspicias, oro. Totus tuae magnificentiae Sambucus.

Address: Magnifico domino, domino Helfercho Guett, caesareae maiestatis consiliario et camerae praefecto patrono observando.
Blotius's hand: Ioannes Sambucus 20. Octob. 1576 D. Helf. Gutt. Petit 100 flor.

274.
Sambucus to King Rudolf
21 October 1576, Vienna

Dedication to *In moerore funeris D. Maximiliani II. Laudatiuncula cum schediasmate epitaphio. Authore Ioanne Sambuco etc.* Autograph manuscript held in Budapest, MOL, I. 45 (copies of Böhmisch-Österreichische Hofkanzlei), f. 84^r.[1585] Copy is held in Bern, Burgerbibliothek, Bongarsiana, Cod. 139, f. 2^r.

[1581] Little is known of Hilfreich Guett (Helferich/ Helfrich Gütt/Gutt) who joined the court as imperial councillor in 1561 and worked later at the Imperial Chamber (as *Hofkammerrat*) under Reichard Strein, and apparently became president himself in c. 1576 (see Sambucus's address). From a letter preserved in HHStA it appears that he, like Strein, also studied in Italy (before 1562) and may have obtained a doctoral degree (see Molino, *L'impero di carta*, 64). Sambucus's letters addressed to him testify to his erudition and learned interests. He certainly helped Blotius with practicalities and apparently even with cataloguing the books of the library (ibid., 62-63). He may have established good relationship with Blotius, which should explain why Sambucus's letter ended up in Blotius's collection (i.e. Sambucus probably asked Blotius to forward his letter to Guett). Sambucus's play with words in letter 328 indirectly testify to Guett's erudition. Also see Oswald von Gschliesser, *Der Reichshofrat: Bedeutung und Verfassung, Schicksal und Besetzung einer obersten Reichsbehörde von 1559 bis 1806* (Vienna: Holzhausen, 1942), 104.

[1582] This might be a reference to Reichard Strein.

[1583] This might be a reference to Guillaume du Choul (1495–1560), an antiquarian from Lyon, author of *Discours de la religion des anciens Romains* and *Douze livres des antiquitez de Rome*, see Gulyás, *Sámboky János könyvtára*, 1562 and 1768[/2].

[1584] This might be a reference to Augerius Busbequius's *Turkish Letters*, although it was first published only in 1581, when it was still entitled as *Itinera Constantinopolitanum et Amasianum*.

[1585] This draft manuscript (full with marginal additions, f. 84^r-95^r) was found by Kees Teszelszky, to whom we are infinitely grateful. It was actually the draft of the version that Sambucus sent to Prague to be censored, as the notes on the top of the first page (above the dedication) indicate: "Misi Censori Pragam, 9 Martii. Sepultus in Curia [?]." It was actually the copy used for its eventual print in 1581 (without the dedication to Rudolf), in the

Sambucus knows that there will be several others who will commemorate Maximilian II's life and death. As he will publish later in more detail on Maximilian's acts, plans and ideas, he asks Rudolf to read this short writing and keep him in his patronage, following the example of his father, who showed signs of particular favour toward him. If some parts of his writing, based on the more outlying learning of antiquity, should appear strange to those less learned, they should keep in mind that there must be a difference between the praise of the men of merit and that of the common people.

Rudolpho II. Romano imperatori electo, Ungariae Bohemiaeque regi I., archiduci Austriae etc. domino suo clementissimo.

Scio non defore, qui maximi ac optatissimi caesaris parentis tuae[1586] maiestatis vitam, funus copiose lectoque stilo infinitis eius meritis suffragantibus ad posteros honoribus sint affecturi, idemque a me exigi vulgo iure posse non diffiteor. Quia tamen res eiusque gestas, acta, conatus, consilia, quantum illa mihi meique similibus cognita sunt, plenius aliquando sum editurus. Breve hoc testimonium, idoneo suo ornamento necessariisve haud instructum, clementissime uti legas, dum longiorem in eis orationem ponam, subiecte oro, meque exemplo parentis, avi, magni patrui, quorum non obscura, sed testata, nec vulgaria in me beneficia extant, uti comprehendas auraque adspirabili foveas, suppliciter obsecro. Quod si hoc in genere lucubratiuncularum mearum quiddam e remotiore eruditaque vetustate minus exercitatis forte insolentius occurrerit,[1587] mirentur illi sane, dum viderint in summe honoratorum laudibus et plebeiorum recensendis, loco apteque discrimen esse ponendum. Tuae maiestatis praeclaris sceptri auspiciis divinum adsit numen, succesibus et eventis coelum arrideat precibusque ac votis intonet.[1588] Amen. Vienna, XII. Kalendas Novembris 1576.[1589] Tuae sacrae maiestatis subditissimus clientulus etc. Iohannes Sambucus.

275.
Sambucus to Johannes Crato
17 November 1576, [Mannersdorf]

Published in Gerstinger, "Die Briefe," 201-203.

Sambucus is glad about Crato's return. He retired to the village not only to flee the plague but also to work on some commentaries and send the results to the press. While Crato was away, he sent a Dioscorides (manuscript?) to Joachim Camerarius Jr. in Nuremberg and hopes that he would realise his promises regarding the traders of Leiden. He knows that when compared to the writings of great men his works are like the turtle compared to the rabbit, yet he gives great attention to his works so that he himself might be satisfied with them, and will strive with all his talent to

---

    new edition of Bonfini's *Ungaricarum decades quatuor* (Francofurti: Wechelus, 1581), 816-827. See Almási, *The Uses of Humanism*, 347-350 and cf. the Index.

[1586] Originally, Sambucus used the formal V. (Vestrae), then replaced it with T. (Tuae).

[1587] Sambucus attached originally to his oration many poems in the style of emblems or in the imitation of Roman epitaphs. However, he did not attach them to the copy he sent to Prague.

[1588] These last four words and the following (illegible) words are cancelled in the autograph manuscript and are missing from the copy.

[1589] The dedication may have been predated, see the next letter.

be open for even a little praise, to which not even the Gods are averse, as Euripides testifies. He is working on his Dialogues, *which are neither of the Stoic nor of the Peripatetic school, but are apt for the imitation of the ancients. He will also collect funerary orations and inscriptions for an edition when he gets back to his "museum." He wonders what Crato is doing, how long the emperor is staying in Vienna and whether he will not move soon to Linz, and he asks for gossip and second-hand news. He thinks to travel to Vienna in the coming days. He has not received copies of Stobaeus yet, or got back what he lent to Henri Estienne. He does not know where his manuscript on the art of war ended up in Basel. Seeing that Obertus Giphanius stopped working on Aulus Gellius, he thinks to give his own emendations on Gellius to Plantin. He asks Crato to forward his letters to mutual friends.*

Salutem.

Quam me reditus vester ipsi mihi restituerit, desiderium et literae ad amicos confitebuntur, quibus tuo patrocinio vel molestia tua prolixe adesse soles. Ego me subduxi in villulam non modo, uti pestem fugerem, sed commentariolos varios excuterem atque frugem aliquando expedirem. Dioscoridea te absente ad Camerarium Norimbergam misi, quem spero sua diligentia apud negociatores Lugdunenses[1590] votis et optatis satisfacturum. Scio me velut χελώνη ad δασύπουν,[1591] si cum magnorum virorum scriptis mea comparantur unquam, celeritate et cursu, qui vires agnoscam, fore. Ita tamen vigilias meas lambere soleo, ut aliquando mihi ipsi non displiceant, ac enitor omni contentione ingenioli, ut me non prorsus alienum ostendam ab collaudatiunculis,[1592] a quibus nec Deorum familiae sunt aversae,[1593] ἀχρημάτως[1594] tamen: οἱ γὰρ τιμώμενοι χαίρουσι,[1595] ut scenicus[1596] prodidit. In *Dialogis* meis nunc versor, non academicis nec peripateticis illis, sed subselliis et concionibus aeternis promissisque certis ad imitationem veterum institutis, denique in orationibus et tumulis funebribus libro uno comprehendendis, dum ad Museum accedam.[1597] Te, mi optime patrone, vehementer oro, quid agas, quamdiu caesar istic sit mansurus, an Linzium cito cogitet, ut rumusculi non firmi ferunt, si grave non est, significes. Cogito enim Viennam hisce diebus. Si quid praeterea ab amicis habes, quod commune fieri cum aliis potest, communicato. Stobaei

---

[1590] It is unclear to what Sambucus is referring here. The term "negotiator" suggests that Camerarius was going to find some traders and not publishers, with whom Sambucus could also have had contact (cf. letter 260). Gerstinger, on the other hand, suggests in "Zusamennfassung" (p. 300) that Sambucus simply sent his emendations, as he was frustrated by Henri Estienne's delay. This is what he promised to do in letter 149, written to Zwinger. If this was the case, he must have made a copy of the emendations sent to Estienne, which were written in the margins of an edition of Dioscorides.

[1591] tortoise [to] hare. This is a reference to Aesop's famous story, in which, however, the tortoise wins.

[1592] This must be a reference to his work on the funeral oration for Maximilian II. His reluctance to engage in such work may be felt also in the first lines of the dedication addressed to Rudolf II (see the preceding letter).

[1593] Gerstinger's reading (*a quibus me Deorum familiae sunt aversae*) makes no sense. Gerstinger suggests ("Die Briefe," 202-203) that there are transcription errors in this part, since Sambucus's letters to Crato survived only in the copy of Samuel Benjamin Klose, which are now lost. This is an allusion to Eur. *Hipp*. 8, which is partly quoted in Greek in the following.

[1594] without a monetary reward

[1595] Those who are honoured rejoice. Cf. Euripides, *Hippolytus* 8. It is characteristic even for the family of gods that they enjoy receiving honours from humans.

[1596] Euripides.

[1597] This must be a reference to his (unpublished) "Tumulorum Heroicorum et miscellanorum librum suum una cum Heroicorum Symbolorum a se inventorum appendice iam exploit." See Sambucus, *Catalogus librorum*.

nullum adhuc exemplum ad me pervenit,[1598] minus quae Henrico Stephano credideram. Τὰ πολεμικὰ[1599] quo loco sint Basileae, etiam ignoro. De Aristotele non dubito.[1600] Ad Gellium meas notas et obscurorum aliquot expositiones, quia cessare Gyphanium video, cogor cum Plantino conferre.[1601] Has ad communes amicos cum tuis, cum recte poteris, committito. Vale. 17. Novembris 1576. Tuis meritis semper Sambucus.

Address: Magnifico atque clarissimo viro domino doctori Ioanni Cratoni ab Craffthaim, caesareae maiestatis consiliario et archiatro, patrono et amico observando. Wien.

276.
Sambucus to Johannes Crato
10 December 1576, [Vienna]

Published in Gerstinger, "Die Briefe," 203-206.

Sambucus thanks Crato for his report on Maximilian II's medical treatment in Augsburg, which he failed to do in his previous letters. He understood that Crato did things right. Crato will soon see what Sambucus intends to publish about Maximilian's life. He thinks to publish his oration and epigrams in Vienna. He would have already done so if difficulties with the Greek characters had not caused delay. He is hesitating but will resolve it and may also send a manuscript copy to Crato to judge them and let him decide, whether to publish in Leipzig or elsewhere. If he wanted to publish anything in Vienna, it would have to be censored and censors always refused his works. Sambucus is astonished that no one at the Viennese university memorialises the death of Maximilian with an epigram or oration [...] He has heard that the emperor wants to go to Prague with his mother and brothers. The Bohemians are pleading with him to move the court to Prague at least for five years but there are many obstacles to this. The Ottomans leave the Hungarian border in peace. Johann Trautson managed to get exempted. Adam von Dietrichstein will be high steward of the court and was named first member of the Privy Council. Siegmund Vieheuser is claimed to take the place of Johann Baptist Weber soon. Sambucus has still not seen the list of confirmed courtiers, nominations are done one by one, Rudolf is constantly in the Privy Council where they say he makes decisions only slowly and timidly but once a decision is made he severely makes sure that it is executed. Hans Rueber comes to the emperor to complain about soldiers' destitution and desertions. The son of Dodonaeus is coming back without having seen Italy. His father, who is said to be rather stern, does not want to see him. There is some sad but uncertain news about the sack of Antwerp by the Spanish, the fault of Germans and the troops of (Filips van) Egmont. The emperor will travel to Prague, then to Crato (to Wrocław) and Olomouc, and he will return to Vienna by Easter.

[1598] Stobaeus and Plethon, *Stobaei eclogarum libri duo ... et Plethonis de rebus Peloponnesiacis orationes duae.*
[1599] militaria
[1600] On Aristotle see Gerstinger, "Zusammenfassung," 286-289, and "Aristotle-edition (planned)" under "Sambucus" in the Index.
[1601] He was probably not very serious about this plan, as he does not mention it in his bibliography. Cf. letter 257.

Salutem.

Gratissimum fuit ex tuis reliquum curationis Augustalis, quod prioribus omiseram, intelligere, quod abs te recte factum aliquando leges.[1602] Quae de caesaris vita rebusque gestis in Commentariis habeo et brevi sum editurus, videbis.[1603] Orationem bene longam de obitu cum variis et 28 epigrammatis prelo subiicere hic cogito idque pridem fecissem, nisi difficultas Greacorum characterum, quorum passim in funebribus usus requiritur, consilium moraretur. Adhuc haereo, sed me expediam et fortassis ad tuam magnificentiam manu exarata mittam, ut iudicio tuo stent aut cadant Lipsiaeque imprimantur aut ubi voles. Si quid excusum Viennae cupiam, sunt inspectores scriptorum et varia iudicia, quorum arbitria[1604] meas nugas semper recusarunt.[1605] Profecto cum molestia demiror adeo ab isto gymnasio negligi officia et scriptiones Maximiliani II. memoriam servatura.[1606] Nondum quicquam eorum prodiit, qui oratiuncula aut epigrammatio tanti principis laudes annotassent, qui aliquid cuperent, quantum possint, sua mora et mensura abstinere velint, uti audio. Sed vale etc.

Caesarem ad 20. huius cum Augusta et fratribus Pragam cogitare intelligo. Bohemi suppliciter ac solicite agunt, uti aula Pragam transferatur saltem ad quinquennium, sed multa sunt, quae impediunt etc. A Thurca sicut ocium et benevolentia in confiniis Pannoniae. Dominus Trautson vacationem impetravit.[1607] Dominus Dietrichsthainus palatii praefectus et arcanorum consiliorum particeps imprimis nominatus. Fiechhauserum audimus paulo post Bebero successurum.[1608] Nondum aulicorum officiorum et ministeriorum series ad nos venit, ordinata esse commode singula, caesaremque assiduum in senatu esse omnes fatentur pedetentim ad ardua accedere et timide, sed quod statutum forte est, ut exitu et exemplis constet, ipsum diligenter severeque procurare novimus. Rueberus hinc ad caesarem currit de militum clandestina fuga et inopia conquesturus.[1609] Dodonei filius his diebus rediit non visa Italia, quem pater aspicere non vult. Audio eum satis esse durum καὶ ἀστοργόν.[1610]

[1602] The ending of the sentence "aliquando leges" suggests that Sambucus was going to publish Crato's letter on Maximilian's death (letter 272), which was certainly what Crato expected him to do. However, its publication was banned by the emperor. See letter 279, note 1626.

[1603] See letter 274.

[1604] Gerstinger's transcript: *arbitrium*.

[1605] On the story of Sambucus's funeral oration and the reaction of the censors see Almási, *The Uses of Humanism*, 347-350.

[1606] Gerstinger's transcript: *servaturis*.

[1607] Johann Trautson (1507–1589), coming from a noble family of Tirol, was among the most influential courtiers of Ferdinand I and Maximilian II. He studied in Padua, spoke several languages, and rose to the highest ranks at the court, ending his career as marshal and high steward. He served for 49 years in the Privy Council, also presiding over it. See Franz Hadriga, *Die Trautson. Paladine Habsburgs* (Graz–Vienna–Cologne: Styria, 1996); Goetz, "Die Geheimen Ratgeber," 477-479, 481-483; Franz von Krones's biography in *ADB* 38 (1894), 522-524; Almási, *The Uses of Humanism*, passim.

[1608] Siegmund Vieheuser (1545–1587), of bourgeois origins, was a doctor of law who studied in Ingolstadt and Freiburg im Breisgau, became councillor at the Bavarian court, joined the Imperial Chamber Court in 1567 and finally became imperial councillor in 1572. He was also member of the Privy Council and replaced Weber as imperial vice-chancellor in 1576. See Bibl, *Maximilian II*, 388 and http://rudolphina.com (accessed on 12 March 2024).

[1609] Hans Rueber zu Pixendorf (1529–1584) was a soldier in the service of a number of European rulers. After schooling in Vienna he took a long study tour in Europe. His first battle against the Ottomans in the service of the Habsburgs goes back to 1556. From 1568 he became military captain of North Hungary, following Lazarus Schwendi in the office. See https://de.wikipedia.org/wiki/Hans_Rueber_zu_Pixendorf (accessed on 22 May 2023), which is by far the best source on Rueber.

[1610] and lacking natural affection

Tristis rumor hic sed incerte iactatur de Antverpiensi direptione calamitosa per Hispannos ope operaque Germanorum et Egmondani vinculis, 4. Novembris ad X milia in urbe pugna commissa cecidisse etc.[1611] Sed haec vos melius. Vale. X. Decembris 1576. Tuae magnificentiae deditus [?] Sambucus.

Caesar Pragam, inde ad vos, post Olomutium, sub Pascha Viennam omnino rediturus dicitur.

Address: Magnifico et clarissimo viro domino doctori Ioanni Cratoni a Craffthaim, caesareae maiestatis consiliario et archiatro, domino amico singulariter observando. Bresla.

277.
Sambucus to Johannes Crato
31 December 1576, [Vienna]

Published in Gerstinger, "Die Briefe," 206-207.

Sambucus wishes Crato a happy New Year. He gave (Crato's letter) to Carolus Clusius and told him about Crato's advice, which cheered him up. Crato's colleague managed to obtain the second position (as physician) through entreaties and is thinking about writing an apology against Crato. Count Juraj Zrinski marries the daughter of Wolfgang Stubenberg and wants to have a magnificent wedding in Vienna. Johannes Listhius wants to leave for Prague the day after. Count Julius stays at home. Archduke Ernst has very few men in his entourage. Rueber hastened back to Košice/Kassa, but there is no worry from the "voivode" (prince) of Transylvania (Stephen Báthory). The siege of Danzig/Gdańsk has been abandoned. The voivode of Podolia (Mikołaj Mielecki) also subjected himself to his majesty (Báthory). The Russians want to draw the Lithuanians on their side. The Ottomans are using all their force against the Persians, if only they were ruined there. Finally, Sambucus is sending his greetings to Jacobus Monavius.

Salutem et mille Kalendas Ianuarii!

Clusio reddidi et, uti scribis, monui. Has tuis eodem quasi spiritu reddo.[1612] Collegam tuum audio magis precibus secundum locum obtinuisse et ad quasdam tuas apologiam meditari.[1613] Si id est, experiemur, quid ille patrio aere dignum sonuerit aut oraculi ediderit. Comes Zerinius Wolffgangi baronis Stubenbergii filiam duxit ac de nuptiis magnifice hic cogitat et versatur.[1614]

[1611] The Sack of Antwerp, which eventually led to the city's decline, was the greatest massacre in Belgian history with the loss of 7000 lives. Contrary to Sambucus's information, the city was defended by German troops but abandoned by the Walloons, led among others by Filips van Egmont (1558–1590). See Pieter Génard, "Les poursuites contre les fauteurs de la furie espagnole ou de sac d'Anvers de 1576," in *Annales de l'Académie d'archéologique de Belgique* 5 (1879), 25-170; Etienne Rooms, "Een nieuwe visie op de gebeurtenissen die geleid hebben tot de Spaanse furie te Antwerpen op 4 november 1576," *Bijdragen tot de geschiedenis* 54 (1971), 31-54.

[1612] Despite Crato's help, Clusius's contract was not renewed and he was left in uncertainity for long. See Carolus Clusius, *Ad Thomam Redigerum et Ioannem Cratonem epistolae. Accedunt Remberti Dodonaei, Abrahanii Ortelii, Gerardi Mercatoris et Ariae Montani ad eumdem Cratonem epistolae*, ed. P. F. X. Ram (Brussels: Hayez, 1847), 63-66.

[1613] This must be a reference to Rembert Dodonaeus.

[1614] Zsófia/Sofija/Sophia Stubenberg was the second wife of Juraj Zrinski. Her relative, Jacob, was once Sambucus's student in Padua, upon whose death he published a funeral oration: *Oratiuncula in obitum generosi adolescentis*

Listhius cras Pragam cogitat. Comes Iulius domi cum sua haesitat,[1615] admodum exiguus comitatus Ernesti etc. Rueberus heri cum mandatis Cassoviam recurrit, sed a vayvoda nil periculi subesse scimus. Soluta est et reiecta a Gedanis obsidio.[1616] Podoliae regulus tamen se eius maiestati quoque subiecit nuper.[1617] Moscus Litavos in rem suam urgebit. Thurca omnibus viribus in Persae vindictam ruit, utinam corruat! Haec non relegi. Dominum a Monaw officiosum atque in scribendo diligentissimum a me saluta,[1618] cuius amicitiam amplector [...].[1619] Vale. Ultima Decembris 1576. Tuus Sambucus. Niphus ne νέφος ex nivibus fiat, vereor.[1620]

Address: Magnifico et clarissimo viro domino doctori Ioanni Cratoni a Craffthaim, caesareae maiestatis consiliario et archiatro etc., domino et amico observandissimo. Bresla.

278.
Henri Estienne to Sambucus
[1577] [Geneva]

Published in Henricus Stephanus, *Pseudocicero. Dialogus* ([Genevae]: Henricus Stephanus, 1577), f. ii^{r-v}.

Sambucus surely remembers when during their talks in Vienna Estienne told him that no one had greater merits, not only among Latin authors but in all human studies, than Cicero and that the writings of hardly any author had been (and partly were) in a worse condition, while

---

[ ] *Iacobi a Stubenberg* (Patavium: s.t., 1559).
[1615] Count Julius von Salm (1531–1595), the son of Niklas von Salm, was imperial councillor from 1576. Sambucus dedicated to him an emblem: *Emblemata* (1564), 93. He had many Hungarian connections, since he received the estates of the Thurzós as a dowry and also lived in Hungary for a while. His first wife was Erzsébet Thurzó (1532–1574). For a period they employed the famous Lutheran priest and author Péter Bornemissza. His second wife was Anna Maria von Dietrichstein (1557–1586). For his learned interests, see also letter 376, note 2171.
[1616] Stephen Báthory attacked Danzig/Gdańsk, which contested his election as king of Poland. Although the city hired mercenaries in the spring of 1577, it failed and eventually had to recognize Báthory and pay a substantial sum of money as a tribute, while he reconfirmed its privileges. John Brown Mason, *The Danzig Dilemma. A Study in Peacemaking by Compromise* (Stanford: University Press, 1946).
[1617] Podolia was part of the Polish-Lithuanian Commonwealth from 1568, and like Danzig/Gdańsk also resisted Báthory's election.
[1618] Gerstinger's transcript: *salutes*.
[1619] Jacobus Monavius (Monau) (1546–1603) was a citizen of Wrocław, who studied in several German Protestant universities and in Padua. He became a central figure of Silesian humanism with contacts to men like Lipsius, Ortelius, Crato, Blotius and many other Central European humanists. His brother Petrus became imperial physician. He was a Crypto-Calvinist dedicated to religious via media. See Adolf Schimmelpfennig's voice in *ADB* 22 (1885), 162-163; Theodor Wotschke, "Aus Jacob Monavius Briefwechsel mit Beza," *Correspondenzblatt des Vereins für Geschichte der evangelischen Kirche Schlesiens* 16 (1919), 314-348.
[1620] cloud. The reference is to Fabio Nifo († later than 1599), who was the son of Agostino Nifo, the famous philosopher. He must have studied medicine as he later practiced as a physician and taught at the medical faculty in Padua. In 1565 we find him in Paris, and we know that in 1567 he attempted to move to Geneva but was rejected because of his bad character. In 1572 he returned to Italy and in 1575 he became second professor of practical medicine in Padua, but was denounced and imprisoned a year later because of his religious beliefs, which made him to escape to Vienna. By September 1577, he joined Stephen Báthory's army at Danzig/Gdańsk as military doctor and consequently found employment as court physician. Due to his controversy with Niccolò Buccella he had to escape again, now to London, from where he eventualy had to flee to Oxford. At the end, he found refuge in the Low Countries. Cf. Margherita Palumbo's voice in *DBI* 78 (2013), 552-554.

emendations often made them worse. When facing more difficult Ciceronian texts, one needs to consult both old and recent editions and pay attention to both the ignorance of the earlier editors and the audacity of the recent ones, as well as to the negligence and ignorance of the printers. One should not go to the other extreme either and consider places of Cicero as the work of Pseudo-Ciceronians. Others are deceived by the antiquity of books (codices), although it is just as reckless to trust books blindly just because they are old. No one knows this better than Sambucus, whose work in his very rich library is for the benefit of scholars of both languages. Although Sambucus needs no lessons of the sort, he will hopefully enjoy Estienne's dialogue. Sambucus may respond that he was waiting for his Dioscorides and not for this book. However, offended by Dioscorides's delay he should not be angry with Pseudocicero, *since the delay will be for the benefit of medical scholars, as the text will appear not only restored by Sambucus's emendations but also in a new translation.*

Clarissimo viro, Ioanni Sambuco, Henricus Stephanus S. D.

Non dubito, vir clarissime, quin tu cuiusdam mei sermonis tecum Viennae Austriae habiti recorderis:[1621] quum dicerem nullum esse scriptorem non solum de lingua Latina sed etiam de humanitatis studiis melius meritum Cicerone, et vix tamen ullius scripta peiore loco partim fuisse, partim esse, quod multa ex vulneribus, quae ignorantia ei intulisset, quorundam sive medicorum sive chirurgorum audacia maiora reddidisset ita, ut in eius scriptis illud ingeniosi poetae experiremur,

Curando fieri quaedam maiora videmus
Vulnera, quae melius non tetigisse fuit.[1622]

Eo certe res rediit, ut quum aliquid ex Cicerone nobis afferendum est, ex iis praesertim locis qui aliquid paulo difficilius vel minus usitatum habent, multas prius editiones non solum ex vetustioribus, verum etiam ex recentioribus consulere necesse sit atque operam dare, ne vel illarum ignorantiam non animadvertere, vel ad harum audaciam connivere videamur, simulque cavere, ne vel ea, quae librariorum incuria simul et inscitia Ciceroni affinxit, nos quoque illi affingamus: vel, quae vere sunt illius, ideo quod a nostris auribus abhorreant, ei detrahamus, ut denique nec illa, quae Pseudociceronis sunt, pro Ciceronianis, nec, quae sunt Ciceronis, pro Pseudociceronianis habeamus. At multi contra, quicquid in aliquo exemplari vetustatem prae se ferente offendunt, ἀβασανίστως[1623] (ut Thucydides loquutus est) recipient et in hunc vel illum Ciceronis librum, perinde ac si oraculum aliquod sermonem Ciceronis purum putum esse testaretur, intrudunt, quum tamen veteribus libris non minus temerarium sit fidem subito adhibere, quam derogare. Hoc autem nemo melius te novisse potest,[1624] qui tam multos quotidie in ista tua instructissima et locupletissima bibliotheca non sine magno utriusque linguae studiosorum fructu pervolutas. Sed quanvis tu non modo monendus hac de re non sis, sed optimus aliorum monitor esse possis, meum dialogum *Pseudociceronem*, qui alios quamplurimos monendi munus suscepit, non indignum, ut spero, censebis, cui aurem paulisper commodes.

[1621] See letter 238, note 1376.
[1622] Ovidius, *Ex Ponto* 3.7.25-26.
[1623] without due examination; Thucydides 1.20.1.
[1624] One wonders if this is not Estienne's veiled criticism of Sambucus's exaggerated insistence on old manuscripts.

At ego (dices) meum Dioscoridem a te expectabam, cum quo nihil commune habet tuus Pseudocicero. Ne igitur in immerentem *Pseudociceronem* longiore expectatione tui Dioscoridis offensus stomachum erumpas, huius editionem cum magno studiosorum medicinae commodo differri scito, ut uno eodemque tempore et tuis illis utilissimis castigationibus velut renovatus et nova interpretatione Latine donatus prodeat.[1625] Vale.

279.
Sambucus to Johannes Crato
16 January 1577, [Vienna]

The original is kept in Wrocław, Stadtbibliothek, Cod. Rehdiger. 248 (Klose 166), Nr. 85. Published in Gerstinger, "Die Briefe," 207-209.

Sambucus went through Crato's refutation with the chancellor and agreed with its conclusions. He has not seen the text of the accuser (Rembertus Dodonaeus), but it is probably like his office and garden: ostentatious and full of sham. He will defend Crato in case he comes across anyone suspecting his trustworthiness. The emperor does not want to make a detour to Wrocław any longer but will return to Vienna sooner than expected. There is dead silence on the part of Theodor Zwinger, hopefully he has no serious problems. Henri Estienne does not write to him. He neither publishes his texts nor sends them back. When Crato writes Estienne the next time, he should remind him of his promises. Crato will soon receive the funerary oration and epigrams either printed or in manuscript copy.

Salutem.

Irenaei tui recusationem cum domino cancellario percurri, narrationem et rationes conclusionum probo.[1626] Accusatoris scriptum nondum vidi, credo esse affinia [!] eius officinae hortisque, hoc est, expositionem ambitione et calumniis corruptam, argumenta irrigua et brassicana, quantum ex tua ἀνταπολογία[1627] coniicio, quae, si nimium coxerit, fortasse aliquibus stomachum facient. Si audiero suspicionem de te tuaque opinione et fide ex eo aliquibus leviter conceptam, faciam, quod mones, diligenter tuisque meritis.

Nova hic nulla. Caesarem ad vos non diversurum citius, quam putabamus, huc exspectamus. De Zvingero mortuum silentium, absit aliquid a vita eius gravius! Henricus nil scribit, mearum nil effert, minus reddit. Quaeso te, qui scribendi et mittendi occasiones habes expeditiores, promissorum καὶ τῶν ἐνεχύρων[1628] acceptorumque moneas. Quaevis enim

---

[1625] On Dioscorides see letter 155, notes 920 and 921, and the Index.

[1626] The refutation in question appears to be a new piece of writing, not the one addressed to Sambucus (see letter 272). In his previous letter Sambucus informed Crato that Dodonaeus was thinking about writing an apology. Nevertheless, the fight between the two of them apparently continued and involved now also higher courtiers (the chancellor in question is probably not the new vice-chancellor Siegmund Vieheuser but still Johannes Weber, a friend of both Sambucus and Crato). Soon the debate was ended by an imperial ban, which prohibited both of them to come out with written attacks, as Hubert Languet informed Joachim Camerarius Jr. on 1 March (commenting that Crato is frustrated about the ban, especially as back at home in Wrocław he has too much free time). See Hubertus Languetus, *Epistolae ad Ioachimum Camerarium patrem et filium*, ed. Ludwig Camerarius (Lipsiae et Francofurti: impensis Mauritii Georgii Weidmanni, 1685), 177; Gillet, *Crato von Crafftheim*, 2:206-207.

[1627] anti-apology

[1628] and of pledges

in propriorum desiderio mora cuique molestior accidit. Vale, mi doctissime Crato, meque, ut soles, redama. Laudatiunculam in moerore funeris Divi Maximiliani cum schediasmate epitaphio nostro excusam aut descriptam brevi accipies. 16. Ianuarii 1577. Totus tuis meritis Sambucus.

Address: Magnifico et clarissimo viro domino Ioanni Cratoni a Crafftheim, sacratissimae caesareae maiestatis consiliario et archiatro etc., domino patrono et amico observandissimo. Breslaw etc. D. Cratoni zu händen. Cito, cito.

280.
Sambucus to Johannes Crato
1 February 1577, [Vienna]

Published in Gerstinger, "Die Briefe," 209-210.

Sambucus has received Crato's letter on 21 January. The courier Sigismund gave him the package two days ago. He read Crato's refutation, and responded to it shortly the day before. He really wishes for Crato's happy return to the court. Having experienced the "liberality" of the court he could speak about it to others. Concerning his office and title, he still does not know anything, but he does not care. Tunner, on the other hand, speaks about the generosity of Rudolf II and his high steward (Adam von Dietrichstein), who seems to have left for Rome. Finally, he asks Crato to mention his case to these great patrons too, if he finds the occasion.

Salutem.

XXI. Ianuarii tuas scriptas accepi. Tabellarius Sigismundus ante biduum fasciculum reddidit. Recusationem tuam legi, ad eam, quid sentiam, breviter nuper respondi.[1629] Tibi ad aulam reditum felicem et citra ullam nugatorum iniuriam laudis perpetuitatem exopto.[1630] De liberalitate aulica doctus aliis etiam narrare possem. Quo sim loco et nomine, quia nildum significatum est, nescio nec curo.[1631] D. Tunnerus tamen larga, copiosa, benigna a caesare et magistro palatii nunciavit, quem Romam discessisse puto.[1632] Te per amicitiam rogo, si quae opportuna mei alicubi mentio apud magnos istos patronos iniecta fuerit, solito ut favore commendes. Vale. Kalendis Februarii 77. Tuus Ioannes Sambucus.

[1629] See the preceding letter.
[1630] Crato was called back to court service only in September 1578, when Rudolf fell badly sick (cf. letter 309, note 1804). See Gillet, *Crato von Crafftheim*, 2:213.
[1631] On the confirmation of the courtiers and Sambucus's feigned nonchalance see Almási, *The Uses of Humanism*, 190, note 181.
[1632] A certain imperial councillor Hieronymus Tunner and Philipp Flacchen (Flacchius) master of the Hospitallers were sent as legates to Rome, in order to express the emperor's obedience toward the Catholic Church in the usual ritual (but not toward the pope, as Gregory XIII had demanded). See Innocent Gentillet, *Speculum Iesuiticum pontificum Romanorum erga imperatores Germanicos perfidiam* (Ambergae: [Joachimus Ursinus?], 1609), 180-182; Christianus Gottlieb Buderus, *De legationibus obedientiae Romam missis* (Ienae et Lipsiae: Ritter, 1737), 50-51.

Address: Clarissimo viro doctori Ioanni Cratoni a Craffthaim, suae caesareae maiestatis consiliario et archiatro, domino patrono et amico observando. Vratislaviam aut Pragam.

281.
Sambucus to Johannes Crato
8 March 1577, [Vienna]

Published in Gerstinger, "Die Briefe," 210-211.

Sambucus enjoyed reading Crato's funerary oration on the death of Maximilian. Concerning his oration, he is doing what Crato may also have done: trying to get it authorised by the emperor and the Council in order not to offend anyone. He has not yet received Johann Weber's opinion, neither urged it, but should get it within days. Here and there he said a few (but true) things more freely. Hans von Häusenstein has not yet given back Crato's second apology. Concerning the damages of an explosion caused by lightning in (the castle of) Kanizsa, Crato will hear from others. If they do not urgently mend the situation, the people will flee the country everywhere and go as far as Sopron. No letters from Henri Estienne, but this is his style. As soon as he gets hold of something he treats it as if it were his, and thinks only of his little dirty gains from it. Johannes Löwenklau is sending his greetings to Crato and Sambucus is sending his greetings to Jacobus Monavius.

Salutem.

Orationem, qua mores, vitam, ab hac exitum divi caesaris luculenter comprehendisti, equidem libenter legi.[1633] Quid dicam? Tanto praeconio et argumento dignum ingenium, officina idonea. Quod vero mea premo, ne putas me id alia re facere, quam fortasse et ipse fecisti, qui arbitrio caesaris et senatus obtulisti, ne quem offenderes. Nondum iudicium et voluntatem a Webero intellexi nec ursi, sed in dies tamen exspecto, quod pauca, licet vera et testata, liberius tamen inseruerim.[1634] Dominus a Haysenstain nondum alteram mihi, tuam apologiam reddidit.[1635] Canisia quantum ruinae traxerit ex fulminis ictu, quanto in horrore misera multitudo in vicinia haereat, ex aliis cognosces.[1636] Profecto nisi cito et serio providerimus, universae plebiculae deditio ad Sompronium [!] usque vulgo metuenda est. Nil prorsus ab Henrico. Sed facit suo more. Ubi aliquid extorsit, proprium esse vult et captat fere sordidus et avarius ex nugis lucellum etc.[1637] Vale, mi optime Crato, meque constanter amato et foveto. 8. Martii 1577. Totus tuis meritis Sambucus.

[1633] Crato, *Oratio funebris*. It contemporaneously came out in Pressburg, Strasbourg and Wrocław. See Almási, *The Uses of Humanism*, 348.

[1634] Ibid., 347-350.

[1635] Hans von Häusenstein was an officer of the Imperial Chamber under Maximilian II. See Eduard Vehse, *Geschichte des österreichischen Hofs und Adels und der österreichischen Diplomatie* (Hamburg: Hoffmann und Campe, 1851–1853), 2:281-282.

[1636] On 10 February, a lightning hit the tower storing gunpowder in the strategic castle of Kanizsa. The explosion and fire killed 300 people.

[1637] This is fairly unjust toward Henri Estienne, who lived in rather straitened circumstances, dependent on patronage, and was much more famous for the quality of his prints than for any longing for profit.

Leonclaius vestram magnificentiam salutat. Idem domino a Monaw ipse cupio eique nunciabis, si non conveneris etc.

Address: Magnifico et clarissimo viro domino doctori Ioanni Cratoni ab Craffthaim, consiliario et archiatro caesareae maiestatis, domino et amico colendo. Vratislaviam.

282.
Sambucus to Johannes Crato
13 April 1577, [Vienna]

Published in Gerstinger, "Die Briefe," 211-213.

Sambucus read Crato's letter while he was having a modest dinner with Löwenklau, who had recovered from a sickness, and is warmly sending his greetings to Crato and Jacobus Monavius. Soon after he wrote this letter, urged by the courier and the pharmacist. He has heard that the Jesuits presented a drama of several acts on the death of Maximilian II. Nothing else came out, except for some unenthusiastic poems by Paulus Fabritius and Elias Corvinus. Sambucus recently let Crato know about the reason why his oration has not yet appeared through Crato's brother-in-law. Kanizsa is in danger, in the lack of protection. Andreas Kielmann is going to take over the defence. If it is not better provided, the defenders will abandon it. The wedding of Juraj Zrinski is so luxurious that one worries that it can lead to the ruin of Radkersburg. Karl Zelking received the office of military commander of the County of Győr from the part of the Austrian nobility. The pasha of the district of Fülek is too troublesome towards the highlanders. The Bey of Sziget again attempted to fraudulently raid Kanizsa, which had been destroyed by the explosion. He is sending some epitaphs written by someone on the death of Johannes Listhius. He sent Perna, who demanded it, an emendated Greek codex of Plotinus collated with Ficino's edition. Ficino had used a corrupt manuscript for his edition, missing even entire pages. Also included are rare unpublished manuscripts of Numenius, Asclepius and others. Löwenklau finished with Abu Ma'shar's (Albumasar) dream-book and is now translating Manuel II Palaeologus's counsel to his son. Sambucus is sending his greetings to Monavius. Hans von Häusenstein still has not given back Crato's apology, he is not in Vienna, but Sambucus will make sure to get it back.

Sambucus salutem.

Tuae mihi redditae sunt, cum Leonclaius accepta salute mecum tenuiculum coenulae apparatum sumebat, qui se tuae excellentiae et domino Monau proxime persoluturum et quidem plene est pollicitus.[1638] Has paulo post exaravi tabellario et pharmacopeo ita urgentibus. Iesuitae fabulam in actus et scenas dimensam, ut audio, de obitu Maximiliani ediderunt.[1639] Hic nil praeter aliquot Fabritii versiculos et invitos Corvini vulgo adspectum

---

[1638] See *Humanistes du bassin des Carpates II. Johannes Sambucus*, lxiv-lxv.
[1639] This was published as Νεκύσια *D. Maximiliano II Romanorum imperatori* (Viennae Austriae: Stephanus Creuzer, 1577).

est.¹⁶⁴⁰ Mea cur nondum vulgata sint, nuper per uxoris tuae fratrem D. significavi.¹⁶⁴¹ Nova hic nulla quam Canisiam periclitari, praesidium destitutum necessariis, Khielmanum ingressurum custodem,¹⁶⁴² nisi tutius et copiosius fuerit provisum, signis replicatis impositos discessuros. Zerinii nuptiae nimium sumptuosae ne quid ad Raklspurgum perniciei sua pompa afferant, metuendum.¹⁶⁴³ Dominus Carolus a Celting cras nobilitatis Austriacae comitatu Iaurini praefecturam inibit.¹⁶⁴⁴ Filekiensis Bassa nimis montanis est importunus et praeter meritum.¹⁶⁴⁵ Iterum Bekus Zygethiensis Canisiam fulmine deformatam et ictu depositam intus, 7000 praedonum et velitatione ad fraudem attentavit. Mitto epitaphiola cuiusdam in obitum Listhii, digni praeconis.¹⁶⁴⁶

Misi Plotini codicem Graecum emendatum et collatum ad Ficini editionem Pernae flagitanti.¹⁶⁴⁷ Non aliquot verbis modo aut lineis sed totis pagellis mutilo et mendoso libro Ficinus manum applicuerat. Adsunt praeterea Numenii, Asclepii et aliorum libelli ἐριστικοί,¹⁶⁴⁸ rari, nondum typis vulgati. Leonclaius Apomazaris ὀνειροκριτικοῖς¹⁶⁴⁹ absolutis Palaeologi ad filium παραινετικά¹⁶⁵⁰ Latine transcribit. Vale. 13. Aprilis 1577. Salutem domino a Monau, cuius ingenio et studiis non servilibus et avare institutis delector. Tuus Sambucus. Dominus ab Heyssestain nondum Apologiam tuam mihi reddidit et abest ab urbe, sed curabo.¹⁶⁵¹

Address: Clarissimo viro domino doctori Ioanni Cratoni a Craffthaim, caesareae maiestatis consiliario et archiatro, domino et amico singulariter colendo.

[1640] Curiously, these two university professors were also the censors of Sambucus's funerary oration. See Almási, *The Uses of Humanism*, 348. Elias (Joachim) Corvinus (1537–1602), originally called Raab, was born to a Lutheran family in Jáchymov (Joachimstal) but apparently converted to Catholicism early (perhaps in order to sustain his studies). He studied in Vienna and Padua, where he already wrote long epic poems and made numerous learned contacts. He joined the University of Vienna in 1557, became poet laureate in 1558, competed with Sambucus for the position of historian, retired from his university chair in 1578 and became senator in Lower Austria in 1581 and chancellor in 1591–1592. As a member of the Teutonic Order he received estates in Carinthia and the golden chain from Archduke Matthias. On Corvinus's life see the introduction to Elias Corvinus, *Ioannis Hunniadae res bellicae contra turcas. Carmen epicum*, ed. Oscarius Sárkány (Lipsiae: Teubner, 1937); Szabolcs Ö. Barlay, "Elias Corvinus és magyarországi barátai" [E. C. and his friends from Hungary], *Magyar Könyvszemle* 93 (1977), 345-353.

[1641] Crato was married to Maria Scharf, whose brothers were called Johann, Gottfried and Friedrich. See Gerstinger, "Die Briefe," 213.

[1642] Andreas Kielmann von Kielmansegg (c. 1530–1590) was "Hofquartiermeister" (subjected to the high steward) and member of the War Council. See Ernst Birk, "Materialen zur Topographie der Stadt Wien in den Jahren 1563 bis 1587," *Berichte und Mitteilungen des Altertums-Vereines zu Wien* 10 (1869), 82; Gerstinger, "Die Briefe," 213.

[1643] Sambucus meant that spending so much money may badly influence the defence of Radkersburg, which was in possession of the Zrinski/Zrinyi family and was the southern and easternmost garrison of Styria.

[1644] Karl Ludwig Zelking (1531–19 August 1577) was chamberlain of Maximilian II. See Gerstinger, "Die Briefe," 213.

[1645] Hassan, the bey (not pasha) of Fülek. See *A budai basák magyar nyelvű levelezése I. 1553–1589* [The Hungarian correspondence of the pashas of Buda], ed. Sándor Takáts (Budapest: Akadémia, 1915), 134-137.

[1646] Johannes Listhius died on 5 March in Prague.

[1647] The manuscript in question is Cod. Phil. gr. 102 (Vienna, ÖNB). Sambucus collated it with Ficino's Latin translation and commentary in *Plotini ... De rebus Philosophicis libri LIIII in Enneades sex distributi* (Basileae: Perna, 1559). The resulting *editio princeps* of the Greek text, accompanied by Ficino's translation, was *Plotini Platonicorum*. It was based on Sambucus's codex and three manuscripts from Italy. Sambucus recieved the codex back from Perna on 15 April 1581 (note on f. 3ʳ). See *Humanistes du bassin des Carpates II. Johannes Sambucus*, xxvi; Gerstinger, "Zusammenfassung," 313-314. See also letters 283, 289, 295 and 322-323.

[1648] polemical. Gerstinger's transcript: ἀριστικοί.

[1649] oneirocriticisim (the art of dream interpretation). [Pseudo-]Albumasar [Abu Maʿshar], *Apotelesmata*.

[1650] exhortations. Manuel Palaeologus, *Praecepta educationis regiae*.

[1651] See the preceding letter.

283.
Sambucus to Theodor Zwinger
14 April 1577, Vienna

The original is kept in Basel, Universitätsbibliothek, Frey Mscr II 26, no. 221. Published in Gerstinger, "Die Briefe," 213-214.

Sambucus is sending back Zwinger's letter to Guillaume Arragos because he does not know where Arragos is staying. He is sending a nicely corrected Greek codex of Plotinus to Pietro Perna, as he would like it to be printed alongside with Ficino's translation, which lacks entire pages of text. He wrote in detail about it to Perna, who will tell Zwinger the rest. He asks Zwinger to urge the edition of Aristotle, blaming publishers for not aiming at eternity but being interested only in best-sellers and neglecting antiquity. Zwinger should also urge the publication of Plotinus, which he is sending to Augsburg, to Georg Willer, who should keep it for Perna. He complains about the silence concerning the edition of Lazius's book and asks Zwinger to take care of Löwenklau.

Sambucus salutem.

Remitto ad Arragos literas tuas, quia, ubi sit, ignoro. Mitto Pernae Graecum Plotinum, optime correctum et rarum Codicem, quem cum Ficini versione collatum velim.[1652] Nam deprehendi non lineis tantum aliquot sed totis pagellis Ficini editionem mutilam, uti obiter notavi. De toto negocio et consilio copiose ad Pernam, qui tibi caetera exponet. Aristotelem, quaeso, urgete.[1653] Quae istaec cessatio, sive melius avaricia, perversa ratio aeternitatem factis consequendi, libellos famosos et in diem proditos excudere, vetustatem in damno ducere? Plotinum quoque urge, quem Augustam mitto, ut illic apud Willerum Pernae reponant. De historiis Lazii silentium, quem certe non in hoc redemi ab haeredibus nec istuc ea re miseram.[1654] Vale, mi optime Zwingere, et Leonclavii negocia tuae accurationi et amiciciae commendo. 14. Aprilis 1577. Vienna.

Address: Clarissimo domino medico, domino Doctori Theodoro Zwingero, amico singulari. Basell.

284.
Sambucus to Johannes Crato
22 April 1577, [Vienna]

The original is kept in Wrocław, Stadtbibliothek, Cod. Rehdiger. 248 (Klose 166), Nr. 86. Published in Gerstinger, "Die Briefe," 214-215.

Sambucus already sent two letters to Crato in the days before confirming that there was no need anymore to solicit help from the military paymaster. Rudolf II is said to depart on 27 April.[1655]

[1652] See also letters 282, 289 and 295 and cf. *Humanistes du bassin des Carpates II. Johannes Sambucus*, xxvi.
[1653] On the edition of Aristotle see Gerstinger, "Zusammenfassung," 286-289 amd cf. the Index under "Sambucus".
[1654] See letter 233, note 1354 and cf. the Index and Gerstinger, "Zusammenfassung," 311-312.
[1655] Probably to Wrocław. In reality, he arrived there only on 24 May. See Robert Lindell, "Music and Patronage

Juraj Zrinski spent madly 30,000 florins on his wedding. Poor unarmed peasants, who are continuously plagued by their lords and the Ottomans, need to compensate for the wasted money. Rueber also led his men out into a camp, because those of Szolnok castle (Ottomans) were said to be preparing an attack on Eger. The day before the Frenchman (Jean Aubry) opened his parcel (of books) from Frankfurt, in which he saw prefaces by Henri Estienne, some books of poems and other things, nothing of greater worth but Sambucus expects another two parcels. The attached letter is by Fabio Nifo.

Salutem.

Bis intra paucos dies ad tuam excellentiam scripsi, ut solicitudine quaestori bellico importata non fuerit opus.[1656] Caesarem ad 27. huius moturum se audimus. Magna hic numorum et ad fines tutandos necessariorum penuria. Zerinii celebritates insanae nuptiarum ad 30000 exhaurient.[1657] Miseri coloni, qui perpetuo inermes ab heris suis et Thurca vexantur, plectuntur et sumptus iniquissimo tempore productos [?] compensare coguntur. Rueberus quoque in castra suos eduxerat, quod dicebatur Zolnokiense castellum ad Agriam moliri.[1658] Gallus heri vas aperuit Francfortense,[1659] in eo obiter vidi interpretationem Περίπλους [!][1660] Arriani cum commentario Genevae excusam,[1661] Henrici Stephani praefationes, poemata varia et alios libellos, nil solidi et maiorum gloria digni. Sed exspectat 2 praeterea vasa. Has ad te Niphus denique verbis exquisitis commendatas mittit. Vale, 22. Aprilis 1577. Vestrae magnificentiae totus tuus Sambucus.

Address: Clarissimo viro domino doctori Ioanni Cratoni ab Crafthaim, suae caesareae maiestatis consiliario et archiatro, domino patrono et amico observando. Bresla, Herrn Doctor Cratoni zu Handen.

285.
Sambucus to Johannes Crato
19 May 1577, [Vienna]

Published in Gerstinger, "Die Briefe," 215-217.

---

at the Court of Rudolf II," in *Music in the German Renaissance: Sources, Styles and Contexts*, ed. John Kmetz (Cambridge: CUP, 1994), 258-259.

[1656] The paymaster (Kriegszahlmeister) was Egidius Gattermayr (Gattermaier).
[1657] See letter 282.
[1658] This information must have come from István Radéczy, bishop of Eger.
[1659] Jean Aubry (brother-in-law to André Wechel) regularly supplied books for Boldizsár Batthyány and also for others at court (see letter 285). He worked for the Wechel Press and was also Carolus Clusius's contact. See Szabolcs Ö. Barlay, "400 éves francia levelek és könyvszámlák. Batthyány Boldizsár és Jean Aubry barátsága" [400 Years Old French Letters and Book Bills. The Friendship of Boldizsár Batthyány and Jean Aubry)], *Magyar Könyvszemle* 93 (1977), 156-164; Hunger, *Charles de l'Escluse*, 29, 134, 169-171.
[1660] i.e. περίπλου: of the circumnavigation
[1661] Arrian of Nicomedia (c. 86/89–c.146/160 AD) Greek historian, philosopher and military commander. See *RE* II (1895), 1230-1247. The book in question is *Arriani historici et philosophi Ponti Euxini et maris Erythraei periplus ad Adrianum caesarem* (Genevae: Vignon, 1577). It is listed on the bill of Aubry for Batthyány. See Barlay, "400 éves francia levelek" (as above), 163.

Since Jean Aubry has not turned up, Sambucus still has not seen the parcels meant for him and others. He sent a nicely written shortened version of his funerary oration (on the death of Maximilian II) together with epigrams to Prague two months before to Mr Johannes Weber so that he and Adam von Dietrichstein present it to the emperor and tell him the decision of the emperor and their opinion on its publication. In the present corrupt climate of false accusations he does not want to publish anything without their approval. He vainly asked Weber again to give some response, his office is said to have been taken over by Siegmund Vieheuser. He begs Crato to inquire from Weber or Vieheuser, and Dietrichstein, in case he meets them, what they want to do with his oration. Henri Estienne promises to publish Aristotle, restored through Sambucus's commentaries, at his own and Episcopius's expenses. In the preface to Pseudocicero *Estienne announces the delay of Discorides. They expect Rudolf II's arrival in Vienna soon and hope he will bring help. The elephant strangely kneeled down in front of his keeper, asking for help, and an hour later died on 16 May. The same happened to the lion the same day. A certain old Ottoman legate, who is often in Buda, talked with Hilfreich Guett, councillor of the Imperial Chamber, on the very same day. He will bring back the demanded tax and an answer. He has not seen Löwenklau. He sending his greetings to to Jacobus Monavius and will soon send the requested book, too.*

Salutem.

Aubrius nondum visus est nec meos fasciculos nec aliorum vidi. Orationem meam breviorem illam, qua summam τῶν ἐνταφίων[1662] et historiarum complexus sum, una cum epigrammatis ita suadentibus amicis Pragam ante duos menses ad dominum Weberum elegantissime descriptam miseram, ut is et dominus Dietrichstainius caesari offerrent meque de caesaris mandato ipsorumque iudicio monerent, an publica velint, me citra illorum voluntatem ita nunc animis et linguis corrupte ad calumnias conversis nil editurum.[1663] Iterum monui humiliter dominum Weberum, ut aliquid responsi daret, sed nil exprimo et audio Fiechauserum successisse. Oro vehementer, si commoda occasio alloquendi et salutandi Weberum aut Fiechauserum aut etiam dominum praefectum palatii fuerit, obiter uti de mea oratione quaeras, quid velint, statuerint iubeantve. Si libet licetque, significes. Henricus se Aristotelem meis observationibus restitutum suis et Episcopii impensis excusurum significant [?].[1664] Dioscoridis moram in praefatiuncula *Pseudociceronis* nunciavit.[1665] Caesarem ad nos brevi exspectamus, uti viciniae sibique provideat nec desertorum alienis locis misereatur, praesens opem ferat; quod nisi accurarit, nil salutarius speramus. Elephas 16. Maii praefecto insolenter genibus flexis supplex factus post horam exspiravit, idem de leone eodem die accidisse. Czobantzius Czaus senex saepe Buda hic allegatus hodie apud Guett, camerae consiliarium, ad horam 2. responsum et munuscula quaesita cum comitatu auferet.[1666] Vale et rescribe. 19. Maii. Exaudi. Utinam exaudiam! 1577. Leonclaium prius non vidi. Domino a Monau salutem, ad quem brevi exemplum Synodi et patrum etc., quod petit, mittam. Totus tuus Sambucus.

[1662] exequies
[1663] See Almási, *The Uses of Humanism*, 348-349.
[1664] Cf. letters 271, 283, 298 and the Index.
[1665] See letter 278.
[1666] We were not able to identify this Ottoman legate.

286.
Sambucus to Johannes Crato
25 May 1577, [Vienna]

The original is kept in Wrocław, Stadtbibliothek, Cod. Rehdiger. 248 (Klose 166), Nr. 87. Published in Gerstinger, "Die Briefe," 217-218.

As soon as Sambucus finds Zwinger's book, he will take a look at it as Crato asked him to do. There is the same lack of such books in Vienna. He is warning Estienne to publish Aristotle (with Eusebius Episcopius) and Dioscorides as soon as possible. Now that the court is in Wrocław, Crato certainly does not have the opportunity to write Estienne and Simon Grynaeus. To the latter he gave Michael Psellos's commentary on Euclid with a new translation and many illustrative notes. He promises to publish it, together with some of Sambucus's notes on it, because publishing Conrad Dasypodius's work is being delayed. Strange that Dasypodius neither sends him back his codices nor cares about his threats. The Ottoman (legate) will leave within four days. He is sorry for the defeat of those of Danzig/Gdańsk but hears that the day after they took revenge on the Poles for their slaughter. He asks Crato to inform himself about his funerary oration with Weber and Vieheuser.

Salutem.

Theodori librum, ubi videro, tua caussa respiciam. Eadem hic difficultate et maiore talium scriptorum premimur. Henricum moneo, ut Aristotelem, quem cum Episcopio communiter edet, atque Dioscoridem quamprimum imprimat. Non dubito caesaris aula apud vos praesente occasionem defore mittendi Henrico et erudito viro Gryneo, cui Pselli commentarios in Euclidem et demonstrationes cum nova interpretatione Euclidis innumerisque novis demonstrationibus communicaram.[1667] Is brevi se editurum una cum meis quibusdam notis in Euclidem promisit, quando Dasipodea haeret. Miror me meos codices ab eo non recipere nec curare ullas minas. Vale. Thurca[1668] intra quatuor dies discedet. Vale. 25. Maii 1577. Totus tuis meritis Sambucus.

Cladem a Gedanis acceptam dolemus,[1669] sed audio eam postero die maiori caede Polonorum et internecione compensatam. Oro, apud Weberum et Fiechhauserum de mea funebri oratione aliquid exploratum significato.

Address: Clarissimo viro domino D. Ioanni Cratoni ab Craffthaim, sacrae caesareae maiestatis consiliario et archiatro etc., domino patrono et amico observando. Wroslae. Herrn doctori Cratoni zu Handen.

[1667] Michael Psellos (1018–after 1081) was an intriguing highly erudite Byzantine philosopher who wrote on a number of different subjects. See Denis Walter, *Michael Psellos – Christliche Philosophie in Byzanz. Mittelalterliche Philosophie im Verhältnis zu Antike und Spätantike* (Berlin: De Gruyter, 2017). Sambucus's manuscript is not in Vienna anymore. See Gerstinger, "Zusammenfassung," 303, and letter 372.

[1668] The Ottoman legate, cf. the preceding letter.

[1669] See letter 277, note 1616.

287.

Joachim Camerarius Jr. to Sambucus
1 June 1577, Nuremberg

Published as a dedication in Sadoletus, *Philosophicae consolationes*, 3-6.

Camerarius believes that Sambucus must have been avidly waiting for the publication of Jacopo Sadoleto's letter, which he had generously offered from his well-supplied library to Camerarius's father together with other writings. Sambucus also offered consolation over the death of his mother, with whom his father had lived in total harmony without any argument for forty-six years, and thought to apply Sadoleto's writing to his grief. Before his death, his father, as it also appears from a letter written to Sambucus and attached here, wanted to publish Sadoleto's letter in the company of other similar arguments. Camerarius embraced the project, urged also by Sambucus, but as he found presses that were busy printing more popular books, he could satisfy Sambucus's request only later than was expected. The benefit of the delay was that Camerarius had more time to augment the book. The treatise (of his father) is short but to the point, his father gave it the title: Meditation for bad times. *Johannes Crato, his friend, liked it so much that he recently wanted to copy it in Regensburg. Finally, Camerarius promises the publication of the Greek letters of Chrysoloras and his father, and he encourages Sambucus to let him know of potential publication projects.*

Clarissimo viro D. Ioanni Sambuco, medico et historico caesareo, Ioachimus Ioachimi filius Camerarius S. D.

Iamdudum, ut arbitror, a me cupide expectas editionem epistolae elegantissimae Iacobi Sadoleti, quam ante aliquot annos ex ista tua instructissima bibliotheca patri meo piae memoriae cum aliis quibusdam scriptis bonis liberaliter communicasti.[1670] Ea autem fuit tum humanitas tua, ut non solum orbatum optima et fidelissima coniuge, matre mea carissima (cum qua in summa concordia et sine omni querela vixit annos integros quadraginta sex) ac in maximo luctu versantem patrem meum peramice et officiose admodum consolari studueris, sed insuper quoque valde convenientem medicinam, nimirum hoc παρηγορικὸν[1671] scriptum ipsius aegritudini applicare volueris. Quamvis vero pater meus piae memoriae dum in vivis eum esse aeternus Deus voluit, quemadmodum quoque ex literis ad te eo tempore scriptis, quas una cum tuis adiungere hic placuit,[1672] apparet, paulo post ad editionem adornare tam Sadoleti epistolam, quam alia nonnulla huic argumento non discrepantia, in animo habuerit, morte tamen et ipse praeventus et ex hac misera vita in meliorem a misericordi Deo avocatus illam absolvere non potuit. Eandem postea editionem inter varias occupationes meas ego pariter, abs te etiam crebro admonitus, urgere diligenter coepi, sed contra meam opinionem et tuam expectationem offendi officinas typographicas nescio quibus aliis scriptis (quibus vulgus scilicet iam delectatur maxime) subinde ita occupatas, ut tuae petitioni serius forsitan, quam oportuit, satisfieri a me potuerit, quod te sane in optimam accepturum esse partem confido. Habuit autem haec mora nihilominus commodi quoque in se aliquid. Nam cum interea mihi paulo plus temporis et ocii concessum fuerit ad conquirenda alia nonnulla, quae huc quadrare videbantur, ita libellum

---

[1670] Cf. "Sadoletus" in the Index.
[1671] consolatory
[1672] See letter 223. Also see letter 289, esp. note 1691.

reddidi nonnihil auctiorem, et ut spero, doctis viris non minus gratum acceptumque futurum. Commentatiuncula certe illa brevis quidem, sed satis, ut ita dicam, nervosa, cui pater meus titulum fecit, *Meditatio in adversis*, ita placuit clarissimo viro, D. Ioanni Cratoni a Craffthaim, medico et consiliario caesareo, amico meo observandissimo et patris loco colendo, ut etiam sibi eam Ratisbonae nuper describi voluerit.[1673] Tu boni haec consule, et brevi, volente Deo, Chrysolorae quoque et patris mei piae memoriae Graecas epistolas, nisi nos rursum typographus fallat, et alia quaedam paterna lectione tua et eruditorum virorum forsitan non omnino indigna expecta.[1674] Tu vicissim, quid iam in manibus habeas et publicae utilitati, ut soles, profuturum pares, si non molestum est, significare mihi non gravaberis. Bene vale, et pristinam benevolentiam erga me, ut facis, conserva. Norimbergae, Calendis Iunii, anno Christi. MDLXXVII.

288.
Sambucus to Johannes Crato
13 June 1577, [Vienna]

The original is kept in Wrocław, Stadtbibliothek, Cod. Rehdiger. 248 (Klose 166), Nr. 84. Published in Gerstinger, "Die Briefe," 218-219.

Sambucus has not yet forgotten his interest and will now urge men concerning his funerary oration. He attributes the due importance to what Crato has written. Johannes Allegri died in custody three weeks earlier, Nicasius died of the plague on 4 June at 2 pm, which he got when curing the daughters of Christoph Ungnad, earning 100 thalers in three days. Sambucus is sorry for the death of such talent and the interruption of great work. On the 8 June, the emperor sent an unexpected mandate to the city of Vienna on religious change, prohibiting (Lutherans) the practice of communion in both kinds, absolution in private houses, baptism or funerals in their own churches. Those who do not abide should be identified and arrested. Further deliberations will drag the whole issue on and it may have a better end, except if there will be no new developments. The mandate is not subjected to the Viennese Council, but its authors are unknown to Sambucus. While there is confusion, the Ottomans use their peace only to look for an opportunity for war. They have been well fed thus far. The great ambitions of the Polish king (Stephen Báthory) are no secret to him. He is constantly praying for the liberation of Danzig/Gdańsk.

Salutem.

Nondum sum mei oblitus, nunc urgebo de oratiuncula Maximiliani.[1675] Novi, quem adscripsisti, quanti est, tanti eum facio. Vale.[1676]

[1673] Camerarius, *Meditatio in adversis*, in Sadoletus, *Philosophicae consolationes*, 100-121.
[1674] See letter 117, note 687 and letter 351, note 1998. Cf. "Chrysoloras" in the Index.
[1675] See *In moerore funeris Maximiliani II* under "Sambucus" in the Index.
[1676] In the copy of Samuel Klose we can read the following words in the margins (their origin is unknown): "Autumno longe hic praestantiora esse in Deo, videre Deum, ut est, cum animo meo cogito, ad altiora erigor et ista humana quasi oblectamenta mitto. De adiunctione nostra cum Christo." See Gerstinger, "Die Briefe," 219.

Allegrius noster ante 3 septimanas in custodia mortuus est,[1677] Nicasius 4. huius secunda a meridie bubonibus lethalibus, quos e cura filiarum Christophori Ungnadii in triduum 100 talleris acceptis sibi accivit.[1678] Doleo tantum ingenium, labores praeclaros institutos in medio relictos. Respublica Viennensis 8. huius infelix nec speratum mandatum a caesare accepit de religione mutanda, hoc est, nec communionem corporis et sanguinis Christi nec absolutiones in aedibus nec baptismum nec funerum ad al[tar]em [?] consuetum exsequias celebrandas, paroecialibus propriis esse utendum, qui obedire nolint, comprehendendos et in vinclis continendos nec laxandos citra mandatum imperatoris.[1679] Res deliberatione extrahetur, et meliore fine, quam principio expedietur, nisi prorsus nil viderimus. Adiiciunt quidam mandatum extra ordinem, et senatum hinc subiectum expeditum, sed auctores nescio. Censum caesaris effigie insignum caesari dandum profitemur. Thurca nil aliud sua pace, quam occasionem belli quaerere videtur, dum tumultuantur. Verum isti Thurcici adhuc saginantur. Poloniae regem multa cupere haud ignoramus. Dantiscanis constantiam et mentem sanam precor, dum liberi sint. Vale et me ama. 13. Iunii 1577. Tuus Sambucus.

Address: Magnifico et clarissimo viro domino Ioanni a Craffthaim, suae caesareae maiestatis consiliario et archiatro etc., domino patrono et amico observando. Bresslaw, Herrn Doctor Cratoni zu Handen. Cito. Cito.

289.
Sambucus to Joachim Camerarius Jr.
7 July 1577, Vienna

The original is kept in Munich, BSB, Clm 10367, f. 303^r. Published in Gerstinger, "Die Briefe," 221-222.

Sambucus asks why he should be mad at Camerarius. He is not angry about the delay of publishing some books (Sadoleto's Consolation*) and knows well the avarice of men (i.e. publishers) and their disinterest in antiquity. He has other projects which neither money nor prayers seem to further. Camerarius should encourage the publisher (André Wechel) and tell him that by publishing Sadoleto he will acquire future projects undertaken by Sambucus, which will bring him some nice profit. He is greatly enthusiastic about the idea of having the letters of Chrysoloras edited by Bonaventura Vulcanius. Conrad Dasypodius does not publish or give him back his Euclid-manuscript, which Camerarius's father had so much appreciated. The almost 600 later Greek*

[1677] Johannes Allegri was a doctor in the court hospital. After his death, his library was bought by the court. See Paola Molino, "The library, the city, the empire: de-provincialising Vienna in the early seventeenth century," in *Knowledge and the Early Modern City. A History of Entanglements*, eds. Bert De Munck and Antonella Romano (London and New York: Routledge, 2020), 235-6.

[1678] Christoph Ungnad von Weissenwolff (1527–1587) was the son of Hans Ungnad, the patron of Croatian Reformation and literary culture. Christoph studied among others in Wittenberg. In 1569–1575 he was captain of Eger, in 1576–1583 he was Croatian ban but actually in office only from 1578. His wife was Anna Losonczy (from 1567) , the lover of the famous poet Bálint Balassa. We only know of one daughter, Anna Ungnad (1564–1611). See Péter Kőszeghy, "Az 1578-as év Balassi Bálint életében" [The year 1578 in the life of B. Balassi], in *Rod Balašovcov v 13. až 19. storočí. Zborník z medzinárodnej konferencie*, ed. E. Antolová H. Ferencová (Bratislava: SNM, 2013), 225-236.

[1679] See Bibl, "Erzherzog Ernst und die Gegenreformation"; Almási, *The Uses of Humanism*, 345.

letters he collected with much expenses are lurking in Antwerp, as also his collection of "Polemica" sent to Eusebius Episcopius and made available to Wilhelm Xylander. Dioscorides will finally come out, hopefully what Pietro Perna promised to Löwenklau for his Plotinus-codex will also be realised. In a postscript Sambucus affirms that Camerarius can also attach this letter to his edition. He is sending his letter back, which he emended.

Sambucus Ioachimo filio Camerario salutem.

Ego vero, mi amantissime Ioachime, tibi subirascar?[1680] Moram edendorum aliquot libellorum accusem? Non etiam quasvis causas accipiam potius, quam ut minimum de tuo in me studio ac egregia voluntate detraham? Absit. Prorsus enim vulgarium rerum cursum, avaritiam, mores hominum a veteri disciplina et in literas voluntate relictos ignorarim? Haerent etiamnunc quaedam mea passim, quae nec precio expediuntur nec precibus laxantur ullis. Tu vero typographum de Sadoleti scripto elegantissimo confirma.[1681] Adde, si libet, mea fide et periculo, ista liberali sui preli opella ipsum assecuturum, ut a me lucello pleniori cumulata brevi accipiat. Caetera tui iudicii sunt, cui acquiescam. Chrysoloram impressum diligentia inprimis Vulcanii, viri clarissimi, cupidissime sum amplexurus.[1682] Dasypodius in codice illo meo Euclidis rarissimo, et quem parens tuus omnibus omnium ἀντιγράφοις[1683] praetulit, nondum curat nec mea reddit, non citra molestiam bibliothecae[1684] nostrae.[1685] Volumen illud a me tot impensis epistolarum seriorum Graecorum ad 600 numero comparatum Antverpiae latitat,[1686] quomodo etiam σύνταγμα[1687] illud nostrum πολεμικῶν[1688] scriptorum Xylandro olim suppeditatum et Episcopio missum.[1689] Dioscorides tandem prodibit, utinam idem, quod Perna de Plotino nostro Graeco correcto pollicitus certe est Leonclaio, praestet.[1690]

[1680] Cf. letter 287.
[1681] André Wechel (Andreas Wechelus) († 1581) was a humanist publisher and bookseller in Paris (1554–1572) and in Frankfurt (1572–1581). His father had also been a printer. Being a Huguenot, he escaped from Paris after St. Bartholomew's Day Massacre with the help of his tenant Hubert Languet. See R. J. W. Evans, *The Wechel Presses: Humanism and Calvinism in Central Europe 1572–1627* (Oxford: Past and Present Society, 1975); Ian MacLean, "André Wechel in Frankfurt, 1572–1581," in idem, *Learning and the Market Place: Essays in the History of the Early Modern Book* (Leiden: Brill, 2009), 163-225.
[1682] For Chrysoloras's letters see letter 117, note 687 and cf. the Index. Bonaventura Vulcanius (1538–1614) was one of the leading Greek scholars in the Low Countries. After his education in Leuven and Cologne he worked as a secretary to a Spanish bishop and his brother in Spain. For some years he worked for various publishers (e.g. Henri Estienne), and was finally offered the chair of Latin and Greek in Leiden in 1578, which he eventually accepted only in 1581. On Vulcanius, see Alfons Dewitte, "Bonaventura Vulcanius en de Officina Plantiniana (1573–1600)," in *Ex officina Plantiniana: studia in memoriam Christophori Plantini (ca. 1520–1589)*, eds. Marcus de Schepper and Francine de Nave (Antwerp: Vereeniging der Antwerpsche bibliophielen, 1989), 565-597; and Harm Jan Van Dam, "The Blacksmith and the Nightingale: Relations between Bonaventura Vulcanius and Daniel Heinsius," in *Syntagmatia: Essays on Neo-Latin Literature in Honour of Monique Mund-Dopchie and Gilbert Tournoy*, eds. Dirk Sacré and Jan Papy (Leuven: Leuven Univ. Press, 2009) (Supplementa Humanistica Lovaniensia), 557568; *Bonaventura Vulcanius, Works and Networks. Bruges 1538–Leiden 1614*, ed. Hélène Cazes (Leiden: Brill, 2010).
[1683] copies
[1684] It was written originally with capital B, just like Museum, stressing its character as an institution.
[1685] See letters 89, 91 and 92 on Camerarius Sr.'s failed attempt to borrow the same Euclid-manuscript.
[1686] On the story of his collection of Greek letters see Gerstinger, "Die Zusammenfassung," 295; *Humanistes du bassin des Carpates II. Johannes Sambucus*, xxxiii. See also letter 351, note 1998.
[1687] collection
[1688] military
[1689] See letter 247, note 1431.
[1690] On Dioscorides see letter 155, notes 920-921. On Plotinus see letter 282, note 1647. It is unclear, whether

Vale et me ornare perge, mutuum brevi emetiar. Nonis Quinctilibus 1577 Vienna.

Post scripta. Si hanc quoque subiicere tuae voles, non curo. In epistola mea abs te communicata quaedam emendavi, itaque edenda cogites, uti remitto.[1691]

Address: Clarissimo viro domino doctori Ioachimo Camerario etc., archiphysico reipublicae Norimbergensis etc., domino et amico singulari. Nürnberg. Hern Doctor Camerario zu handen.
Camerarius's hand: 77. 18 Iulii.

290.
Sambucus to Johannes Crato
18 July 1577, [Vienna]

Published in Gerstinger, "Die Briefe," 219-221.

Magister Zoppelius brought Sambucus Crato's funerary oration. He read it in one breath and noticed its purity and cleverness; it will satisfy even the detractors. He asks why he should want to publish his delayed text rendered obsolete by such splendid writings published day by day. Still, he does not bother. The emperor entered the city the day before at five in the evening in the presence of 5,000 soldiers. There was an expensive triumphal arch raised in the vegetable market. There were a few inscriptions in prose, not in verse placed on it. Depicted on the front of the arch was Maximilian to the right, Rudolf to the left, with moving images of a celestial and a terrestrial globe under their feet. On both sides there were the four virtues made of pottery, and Pegasus on the top of the arch. On the top of the tower of Saint Stephen church there was a standard-bearer who feigned fire out of a dragon's mouth, and an eagle flew on the door of the church when the emperor approached it. There is no hope for a diet in Hungary before October. Lazarus Schwendi arrived with his wife two days before by boat. Sambucus has never seen so many people in Vienna. There is no news about the Ottomans. Count Julius Salm and his wife remain in Vienna for some time. As soon as he can, he will present Rudolf II six triumphal arches adorned by different stories in order to inquire whether they still need his service and for what salary and in which position. He is saying hello to Jacobus Monavius.

Magnifice et clarissime vir, salutem.

Reddidit mihi orationem abs te recognitam et de cuius aura et portu[1692] addubitas, magister Zoppelius. Eam licet ἀπνευστὶ hauserim,[1693] duo tamen in ea praecipua egregie extare deprehendi, τὴν καθαρότητα καὶ δεινότητα,[1694] ut vel invidis sit luculenter satisfactura. Cur

---

Löwenklau was in any way involved with the editon of Plotin, or was just given information, that it is coming soon by Perna. .

[1691] It appears from Sambucus's postscript that Camerarius sent him the texts of the preface to Sadoleto's *Consolationes* and Sambucus's letter (see letter 287) so that he could check them before publication.
[1692] Cf. "portus et ara fugae" in Ovidius, *Ex Ponto* 2.6.68.
[1693] without breathing
[1694] purity and cleverness

igitur deinceps hoc in genere scriptum meum publicum cupiam, nescio, quando mora ista et in dies similium scriptorum exeuntium splendore nil obtentura [!] sit pristinae commendationis ac dignitatis? Nec valde curo. Heri vesperi ad 5. horam effusa obviam universa provincia et urbe hominum armatorum ad 5000 caesar Viennam est ingressus. In olitorio[1695] ara sive arcus sumptibus et opere raro extructus fuit.[1696] Epigrammata pauca soluta non numerosa. In fronte arcus conspicui fuere Maximilianus dexter et Rodolphus adversus, quorum ad pedes globi coelestibus et Terrae imaginibus mobiles subiecti caesarem vicinum accepere. Utroque in latere binae ex figulina eductae moles forma 4 virtutum, in summa Pegasus. In summa turri Stephani vexillifer arte confictos ignes per os draconis excitavit, accessuro caesari valvas templi aquila se demisit. De conventu Pannonico ante Octobrem nulla spes. Schvendius cum uxore nudiustertius applicuit. Nunquam hic frequentiam istam notavi. Ab Thurca mediocre silentium. Comes Iulius cum uxore aliquandiu hic est mansurus. Si quid novi fuerit, cum tua magnificentia communicabo. Ego prima occasione caesarem cum sex arcubus triumphalibus varia historia et rebus ornatis compellabo, quid porro meam operam velint et quo salario, loco, omnino exquiram.[1697] Vale. 18. Quinctilis 1577. Dominum claris simum a Monau salvere iubeto. Vestrae magnificentiae totus Sambucus.

Address: Clarissimo viro domino Ioanni Cratoni ab Crafftheim, caesareae maiestatis consiliario et medico etc., domino amico observandissimo. Bresla.

291.
Sambucus to Guglielmo Sirleto
29 July 1577, [Vienna]

The original is kept in Rome, BAV, Vat. lat. 6180, f. 100. Published in Gerstinger, "Die Briefe," 221-222.

Sambucus is praising Sirleto's merits and position. He asks for his financial support in a matter on which he has written in more detail to Fulvio Orsini. The patrons of studies became less generous, the publishers are greedy, investing only in trifles and best-sellers, which chills the passion for old books. Sirleto is almost the only exception in his rank. As much as possible, he will also cling to the old ways and do and help in what he can.

Illustrissime ac Reverendissime Cardinalis, domine Maecenas observandissime, salutem ac obsequiorum paratissimam oblationem.

Nisi tuam celsitudinem nescirem, quantus sis, quo te loco merita tua in rempublicam salutaria posuerint, quo iudicio omnes humanitatem celebrent, de cunctis vel immerentibus quanto ardore benemereri studeas, pluribus in tuis laudibus versarer. Sed ὄνος πρὸς λύραν,[1698] cuius amplitudinem vix quisque calamo aut sermone emetiretur. Itaque duobus verbis illustrissimam reverendissimam dominationem vestram observantiae veteris nomine saluto, ac de quibus

---

[1695] According to Gerstinger (p. 221) it was in today Kohlmarkt street.
[1696] On Rudolf II's entry see Kaufmann, "Astronomy, Technology, Humanism."
[1697] These triumphal arches (possibly designed by Sambucus) were ephemeral structures and have not survived.
[1698] donkey in front of a lyra. Cf. Erasmus, *Adagia* 335.

ad Fulvium nostrum copiosius scripsi, in quo tuae celsitudinis subsidio opus fuerit, id uti benignum facileque sit, supplex oro.[1699] Videt tua illustrissima dominatio, quam contracta sit maecenatum liberalitas, quam typographos avaricia occuparit, ut in nugacibus libellis et lucrosis typos conterant[1700], quam denique passim frigeant animi ad veterum scriptorum edendorum labores. Tu igitur fere de vestro ordine solus es, qui vias non teneas modo, sed libenter admonitus et rogatus ingredieris, expedias, quo sacra antiquitas a tineis vindicetur, omnium in manibus gestentur. Mea opella, si quod potest, nondum discessit a consuetudine pristina, facit, iuvat, quod potest. Me vestrae illustrissimae reverendissimae dominationi humillime commendo. 29. Quinctilis 1577. Vestrae illustrissimae celsitudinis servitor Ioannes Sambucus.

292.
Sambucus to Piero Vettori
23 August 1577, Vienna

The original is kept in Munich, BSB, Clm 735, Nr. 108. Published in Bandini, *Clarorum Italorum et Germanorum*, 2:111-112; Gerstinger, "Die Briefe," 224-225. Reproduced in Várady, "Relazioni di Giovanni Zsámboky," 40-41.

Their mutual silence should be no sign of diminishing relations. Sambucus does not usually want to annoyingly push people engaged in great works of common use. He expresses his reverence for Vettori, whose Politica *he has not yet seen, but its quality cannot be questioned. As soon as Crato receives a copy, he will provide it for Sambucus. His Aristotle, corrected in infinite places is in print, Dioscorides will be published for the next book fair. Vettori must have already seen his edition of Zosimus's history of the Goths and knows that Sambucus was going to publish Photius's* Bibliotheca, *but he only has a copy of the Marciana. If only Vettori had an older manuscript. He will receive Abu Ma'shar's (Albumasar)* Apotelesmata *very soon, together with his funerary oration and inscriptions for Maximilian II.*

Clarissimo viro domino Petro Victorio Sambucus salutem.

Silentium mutuum satis diuturnum est, sed eo nil in nostra necessitudine diminutum credito, nec soleo urgere molestius eos, quorum opera et vigiliae maioribus et publicis rebus et commodis sunt occupatissimae.

Te uti adhuc semper veneror, memoriam frequentem tuis meritis usurpo, cuius nominis splendore Sambuci quoque lucubraciunculae sunt illustratae. Politica tua nondum contigit, licet cupidissimis, videre, sed qualia sint, facile officina vetus et omnem aeternitatem ementiens iudicium arguunt.[1701] Ubi Crato exemplum acceperit, mecum communicabit. Aristoteles Graecus nostris infinitis notis purgatus sub praelo est. Dioscorides hoc mercatu prodibit![1702] Zosimi Exadvocati *Historias Gothicas* te vidisse nostra industriola proditas

---

[1699] We do not know to which project he refers here.
[1700] corrected from "atterant"
[1701] See letter 144, note 845 and letter 213.
[1702] Note that neither of these projects were realised. On the failed Aristotle-project see "Aristotle" under "Sambucus" in the Index, and see Gerstinger, "Zusammenfassung," 286-289. On Dioscorides see letter 155, notes 920 and 921.

credo, uti alia nonnulla.[1703] De *Bibliotheca* Photii edenda consilium nostrum antea nosti, sed codice Marciano tantum utor. Utinam vos istic vetustius habeatis. Apomazaris Ὀνειροκριτικὰ ἀποτελέσματα[1704] his diebus accipies cum oratione funebri καὶ ἐνταφίοις[1705] elogiis Maximiliani II. etc.[1706] Vale, clarissime vir, et ubi quid ocii nactus es, Sambuco rescribe. X. Kalendas IIVbris [!] 1577. Vienna.

Address: Domino Petro Victorio, nobili Florentino, viro clarissimo, amico observandissimo. Fiorenza.

293.
Sambucus to Piero Vettori
13 September 1577, [Vienna]

The original is kept in Munich, BSB, Clm 735, Nr. 111. Published in Bandini, *Clarorum Italorum et Germanorum*, 2:118-120; Gerstinger, "Die Briefe," 225-227.

Emperor Rudolf called Johannes Crato back to Vienna from Wrocław because his doctors were in disagreement about his stomach problems. He received Vettori's Politica *and will give it to Sambucus. He praises Vettori's commentaries of Aristotle's* Rhetorica, *which Vettori will certainly augment with comments for the benefit and exercise of young men. Among those who claim some oratorical achievements there are few who can match Aristotle's style. One of them is Johannes Sturmius, who was the first to introduce in German schools the art of Aristotle and Hermogenes of Tarsus. It was thanks to him, the teacher of many, who openly showed the rules of imitation, that some Germans and Poles are hardly behind the Italians, who want to be the purest (in style). Two years earlier, Sturm translated and provided commentary on these three books, just like the entire Hermogenes and Dionysius of Halicarnassus's* The Arrangement of Words *and his remarkable work on sentences and general rhetoric. Nevertheless, he is sure that Vettori will be able to add much to it and make new corrections. As an adolescent, fond of eloquence and the rules of imitation, influenced by Georgius Trapezuntius's works, he had also tried to write such a work, but with no success, so he quit. However, he still has some old notes and readings, which he is happy to send to Vettori. He only wants to point out how he provided the first sentence (of Aristotle's* Rhetorica*) taken from an old codex, which is better than the solution of many. There are good commentaries by uncertain Greek authors published 50 years earlier in Paris, which Vettori certainly has, and those of "Heliodorus of Prusa," which he saw in France. Finally, he hopes that Vettori's stay in the country will render him stronger that he may accomplish his great plan.*

[1703] See letter 259.
[1704] oneirocritical outcomes. [Pseudo-]Albumasar [Abu Ma'Shar], *Apotelesmata*.
[1705] and funeral
[1706] See "In moerore..." under "Sambucus" in the Index.

Salutem.

Cratonem imperator his diebus Wratislavia diligenter cumque cura accivit, quod medicos praesentes nonnihil de suo malo intestinorumque levitate dissidere forsan senserit. *Politica* tua eo itinere accepit, mecum communicabit.[1707] Cogitationes tuas, quae nisi egregiae atque omnium lectione et applausu commendabiles esse aliis nequeunt, valde probo, quod eius[1708] *Rhetorica* τεχνικώτατα[1709] sint, et vel ignota, vel minus exemplis adhuc τῶν τεχνικῶν[1710] tractata.[1711] Non dubito lectionibus et commentariis te cuncta aucturum et ad usum exercitationemque iuventutis accommodaturum. Profecto, mi optime Victori, raros videas, qui cum sibi nescio quid oratoriae artificiosaeque laudis usurpent, qui vestigia aliqua tanti philosophi stylo suo ostendant. Unus est in Germania, cui hoc in genere laudis est multum concedendum, Ioannes Sturmius, qui primus in Germanicas scholas Philosophi[1712] et Hermogenis artem induxit, multos ita instruxit, imitationis norma aperta expolivit, ut aliquot Germani et Poloni vix Italis, qui puriores esse volunt, concesserint. Is ante biennium cum hosce tres libros conversione sua apta et eleganti tum commentariis illustravit,[1713] quomodo etiam totum Hermogenem et Halicarnassaei Περὶ συνθέσεως ὀνομάτων[1714] libellum, adiuncto singulari suo de periodis et universa arte dicendi scripto.[1715] Verumtamen qua es varietate observationum munitus, nil dubito te plurima additurum atque purgaturum. Ego iam adolescens eloquentiae laudibus imitationisque regulis quibusdam captus quiddam Trapezuntii *Rhetoricis* admonitus tentaram, sed frustra, deque tabula manum abduxi.[1716]

Retinui tamen aliquot notas et lectiones antiquas, quibus te abundare scio. Si tamen inspicere voles, facile mittam. Illud hic dissimulare nequeo ex antiquissimo codice primam sententiam eorum librorum me ita supplevisse[1717]: ἡ ῥητορική ἐστιν ὕλη ἀντίστροφος τῇ διαλεκτικῇ[1718] etc., quae vocula multorum expositiones et ambages superat. Extant Commentarii ante L annos Lutetiae excusi, haud inepti, Graeci incerti auctoris, quos te habere puto, tum etiam Heliodori Prusiensis,[1719] quem in Gallia vidi etc. Vale, utque villicatio tua te solidiorem et firmiorem ad praeclarum consilium expediat, ex animo precor. Eidibus Septembris 1577. Tuus Sambucus.

Address: Clarissimo viro domino Petro Victorio, amico observatissimo suo. Florentiam.

[1707] See the previous letter. In December, Crato was still not back. See letter 297.
[1708] Aristotle's
[1709] most artful
[1710] of the specialists
[1711] Cf. with Petrus Victorius, *In tres libros Aristotelis de arte dicendi* (Florentiae: Giunti, 1548 and Basileae: Oporinus, 1549). The new edition, to which Sambucus alludes, appeared in 1579.
[1712] I.e. Aristotle.
[1713] This book appeared seven years earlier: Ioannes Sturmius, *Aristotelis Rhetoricorum libri III* (Argentinae: Theodosius Rihelius, 1570).
[1714] the arrangement of words (i.e. *De compositione verborum*).
[1715] Hermogenos Tarsensis, *Partitionum rhetoricarum liber unus, qui vulgo de statibus inscribitur, Graece. Latinitate donatus et scholiis explicatus atque illustratus a Ioanne Sturmio* (Argentorati: Josias Rihelius, 1570); Ioannes Sturmius, *Libri duo, Iohannis Sturmii de periodis unus, Dionysii Halicarnassaei de collocatione verborum alter* (Argentorati: Vendelin Rihelius, 1550).
[1716] It is unclear to which of his early works he is referring, perhaps to *De imitatione Ciceroniana*. On Trapezuntius's *Rhetoric* see Monfasani's book cited in letter 198, note 1163.
[1717] In the place of *emendasse*, deleted by Sambucus.
[1718] Rhetoric is a matter counterpart of dialectic. The most textual traditions ommit the word ὕλη.
[1719] See letter 34, note 145.

294.
Sambucus to Joachim Camerarius Jr.
17 September 1577, [Vienna]

The original is kept in Munich, BSB, Clm 10367, f. 304^{r-v}. Published in Gerstinger, "Die Briefe," 227-228.

Although Sambucus learned of the death of Camerarius's wife only later, he is sorry about it both because of its general cause, invoked by man's sins, and because Camerarius and his wife had lived in peace with each other. Camerarius' beautiful children can temporarily lessen his grief. Sambucus received the legates of Nuremberg with friendliness, they spoke a lot about Hungary and other matters. He gave Mr Julius Geuder some peaches from the species that is very fragrant and small and matures in July, also three-headed mespilus, which is from Naples, also called azarole. In Venice and Florence they call it wild strawberry. He wrote about the melon, which is red inside, to Hungary. They can be preserved in the autumn in jars. Finally, he is wondering what happened to a certain book or to the consolatory writings.

Sambucus salutem.

De obitu praestantissimae faeminae uxoris tuae, licet serius intellexerim, tamen vehementer doleo tum ob casum universum, quem vitio nobis accersivimus, tum, quia inter vos nulla umquam offensa intervenit. Sed te solabere liberis belissimis, qui minuere brevi quoque tempore, si non evellere maerorem solent.

    Legatos reipublicae vestrae complexi sumus familiarissime. Multi sermones de Ungaricis, de allis mutui fuere. Amo eos colamque ob egregias virtutes et quia a philosophia et ὕλῃ ἰατρικῇ[1720] non abhorrent. Dedi domino Gaidero[1721] persici genus odoratissimi, minimi, quae Iulio mense maturescent. Dedi quoque mespili tricocci genus Neapoli allatum, quod azarolis (Venetiis et Florentiae fraga quoque) vocatur. De melopeponibus prorsus intus carne rubea scripsi in Ungariam. Possunt nunc autumno in ollas condiri. Quid de libello illo ἢ περὶ τῶν παραμυθητικῶν[1722] fuit, fac sciam et vale.[1723] Raptim, 17. Septembris 1577.

Address: Clarissimo viro domino doctori Ioachimo Camerario, reipublicae Norimbergensis physico etc., amico in primis. Nurnberg.
Camerarius's note: 77. 2. Octobris.

[1720] medical matter
[1721] Julius Geuder of Herolzberg (1530–1594) was a patrician of Nuremberg, councillor, mayor, superintendent of the University of Altdorf (in 1578), third chief captain of the city. He was frequently sent on diplomatic missions. His father was a brother-in-law and student of Willibald Pirckheimer. He was also connected to Carolus Clusius. See Clusius's letter to Camerarius on 17 september 1585, in Hunger, *Charles de l'Escluse*, 2:406. His wives were Maria Hallerin (1534–1583) and Ursula Tucher (1556–1594). For his missions see Franz von Soden, *Kaiser Maximilian II. in Nürnberg: zur Geschichte des sechzehnten Jahrhunderts* (Erlangen: Eduard Besold, 1866), passim.
[1722] or about consolations
[1723] A reference to Camerarius's edition of Sadoleto, see letter 287.

295.
Sambucus to Theodor Zwinger
12 November 1577, Vienna

The original is kept in Basel, Universitätsbibliothek, Frey Mscr II 26, no. 222. Published in Gerstinger, "Die Briefe," 228-230.

Sambucus praises Zwinger's Methodus apodemica. *Who would reject anything from Zwinger's pen and press? His Euclid lies buried. He cannot believe that it is in such darkness. He is writing a letter of accusation to Conrad Dasypodius and another one to Eusebius Episcopius concerning the Aristotle manuscript and other texts he sent to him. Zwinger can also send their responses to Camerarius in Nuremberg. Johannes Löwenklau is in Vienna and also Gerhard Falkenburg stays with him for a while, representing his count in a matter of receiving some estates. Löwenklau, worthy of any patronage, is totally frustrated by false hopes. Zwinger should at least obtain for him the 50 coronati often promised by Pietro Perna. Jean Aubry, the book dealer of the court, with whom Perna talked, does not do anything. If Perna cannot do it otherwise, he should at least give a voucher, provided with Zwinger's testimony, to Aubry about the future payment of 80 florins. Sambucus would then make sure that someone give the money to Löwenklau in advance. If Zwinger meets Perna, he should warn him about sending back his rare Plotinus codex, which was compared to three copies. Even if it lacks some books, it also has parts that Ficino had not had, and it is richer in many places.*

Salutem.

Ἀποδημικὰ laudo.[1724] Quid enim ex tua officina et lucubrationibus quis reiiciat? Euclides meus sepultus est.[1725] Non ego profecto hisce tenebris ac compedibus, quos inditos video, credideram. Scribo ad Dasypodium gravius eius cessationem accusans, scribo Episcopio quoque de Aristotele et aliis a me acceptis. Si quid responderint, poteris, qua soles, aut Norimbergam ad Ioachimum Camerarium mittere etc. Leonclaius Viennae est, est quoque Falkenburgius nobiscum aliquandiu mansurus, a suo comite feudorum recipiendorum caussa legatus.[1726]

Te valde oro, quando Leonclaius, omni patrocinio et favore dignus ita frustratus est spe Allobrogica,[1727] apud Pernam 50 coronatos ei procures toties promissos.[1728] Nam Aubrius,

---

[1724] Theodorus Zwingerus, *Methodus apodemica in eorum gratiam, qui cum fructu in quacunque tandem vitae genere peregrinari cupiunt* (Basileae: Episcopius, 1577). See Paola Molino, "Alle origini della Methodus Apodemica di Theodor Zwinger: la collaborazione di Hugo Blotius, fra empirismo ed universalismo," *Codices Manuscripti, Zeitschrift für Handschriftenkunde* 56/57 (2006), 43-67.

[1725] See letter 89, note 564.

[1726] Count Hermann von Neuenahr (1520–1578) the Younger was lord of Moers and administrator of the Kölner Erbvogtei. Maximilian II made him imperial councillor in 1566. He was highly erudite and promoted the Reformation and the publication of numerous books, and was patron to many learned men, including Jean Matal and Georg Cassander, hosting them in his house in Cologne. We do not know when Falkenburg joined his service. See https://de.wikipedia.org/wiki/Hermann_von_Neuenahr_der_Jüngere (accessed on 22 May 2023).

[1727] Savoyard.

[1728] Löwenklau stayed in Vienna between October 1576 and April 1577. From April, he must have looked for patronage elsewhere, probably among lords related to the imperial court. See *Humanistes du bassin des Carpates II. Johannes Sambucus*, 65 and cf. the Index. Perna may have owed money to Löwenklau either because of his contribution to Zosimus (which was, however, probably paid before his departure from Basel) or possibly for his

bibliopola noster aulicus, cui Berna locutus erat, nil facit. Quodsi aliter nequit, Berna saltem firmam syngrapham munitam testimonio tuo mittat se praesenti pecunia Aubrio satisfacturum, aut qui Leonclaio 80 florenos dederit meamque operam quoque addam, ut aliquid fiat.

Si quando Berna occurrerit, de Plotino admoneas, quem codicem non frustra istuc misi, rarum, ad tria exemplaria adhibitum, licet aliquot libellis mancum, sed non refert; habet hic quoque, quod Ficinus[1729] non habebat, et multis locis copiosius. Vale et mihi scribe quamprimum. 12. Novembris, Vienna. 1577. Totus tuus Sambucus.

Address: Clarissimo viro domino doctori Theodoro Zwingero Basilium, amico singulari. Basell.

296.
Sambucus to Piero Vettori
20 November 1577, Vienna

The original is kept in Munich, BSB, Clm 735, Nr. 112. Published in Bandini, *Clarorum Italorum et Germanorum*, 2:110-111; Gerstinger, "Die Briefe," 230-231.

Sambucus has heard that the Biblioteca Laurenziana has a Greek codex paraphrasing the Codex Justinianus, *he does not know by whom. He asks Vettori to describe shortly the work and if his copyist has the time, to make a copy of the beginning and end of it. Sambucus wishes that the* variae lectiones *of Lelio Torèlli in the* Digest *would be made available by the heirs. He recently saw Vettori's oration on the death of Maximilian II, which confirms (the quality of) Vettori's "publishing house." He will send his oration with the next letter. He thinks that Vettori has already returned from his farm to his books because of the cold weather and has the time for an answer. He hopes that Vettori has received Abu Ma'shar's (Albumasar) dream-book and other edited books from his library. Vettori's* Politica-*edition is read by people; the French publisher André Wechel from Frankfurt wants to republish it. If Vettori wants to add or change anything, Sambucus will do it. He did not want to hide it, but Vettori should be quick.*

Salutem.

Audio in Bibliotheca Laurentiana Codicis Iustinianei paraphrasi explicatum volumen Graecum extare, auctorem ignoro.[1730] Quid sit, mi doctissime Victori, oro, duobus verbis perscribas et, si vacat librario tuo, initium et finem libri. Utinam aliquando haeredes consultissimi Taurellii

---

work on Plotinus. However, in the latter case, Perna may have thought that Löwenklau's contribution was not worth the money, as the edition came out without acknowledging his work, mentioning in the preface (written in Perna's name but probably by Zwinger) simply the use of three other manuscripts: "Plotinum [...] quatuor Graecorum exemplarium manuscriptorum, trium quidem Italicorum, quarti vero Io. Sambuci Tirnaviensis, caesaris historici, liberalitate, literaria privatis omnibus praeferendi, principibus etiam plerisque conferendi, fide ac subsidio, sua nunc lingae loquentem et auctiorem et emendatiorem dare voluimus" (*Plotini Platonicorum* [as in letter 282, note 1647], f. α4ʳ).

[1729] Zwinger inserted "Marsilius" before *Ficinus*. See letters 282-283.

[1730] Sambucus refers here to the Greek translation and paraphrase of Justinianus's *Institutiones* by Theophilos, of which there are five copies in the Biblioteca Laurenziana. See Bandini, *Clarorum Italorum et Germanorum*, 2:110; Várady, "Relazioni di Giovanni Zsámboky," 42.

lectiones varias in *Pandectas* eius rarissimas et maxime utiles extrudant.[1731] Dignum manibus officium debitum tanto viro certum iustumque exsolverent. Orationem tuam, qua meritis sanctissimi Maximiliani II satisfacis, nuper vidi. Quid pronunciem? Officinam Victorii, ex qua tot tantaque prodiere, arguunt, meas quoque nugas eius argumenti proxime mittam. Vale, clarissime vir, et quia e ruro te ad libros redactum per frigora non dubito, commodo tuo rescribe! Vienna 20. Novembris 1577. Tui nominis et virtutum admirator Ioannes Sambucus.

Apomazarem *De insomniis*, in quo multa sunt hieroglyphice, et alia e libris nostris edita spero te accepisse.[1732] Vale!

Politica tua leguntur. Est insignis impressor Francforti Gallus, qui regiis typis eadem vult recudere, nomine Andreas Wechelius. Si quid addere aut emendatum velis, ad me recta mittito, quod volueris cumque efficiam. Haec te celare nolui. Sed cito velim mandes.[1733]

297.
Sambucus to Johannes Crato
4 December 1577, [Vienna]

The original is kept in Wrocław, Stadtbibliothek, Cod. Rehdiger. 248 (Klose 166), Nr. 88. Published in Gerstinger, "Die Briefe," 231-232.

Crato claimed that Sambucus had been silent for an entire year, to which he agrees in case a year means two months for Crato. He heard what happened to Fabio Nifo, who had an insult for all, and whose name was already hateful. He intends to return as a friend to his lot, with doubtful merits. Crato's return is greatly desired by everyone, especially his patients. He does not know where Carolus Clusius is heading, the fruit of his diligence, his botanical garden, has been turned into a circus and riding school. He forwarded Crato's letter to Padua. He knows that the military paymaster and others have already informed Crato about the latest news. Many see in the appearance of the comet the end, but the "Turks" are sufficient "for us", more than hostile comets. He prays that God judge men not according to their merits but with compassion and clemency.

Clarissime domine, salutem.

Toto me anno siluisse scribis, quod lubens admitto, si mensis aut duum intervallo annos emetiris, nisi meae perierint. Quis sit Niphus, pridem vel nomine exosus, in omnes contumeliosus, didici, sed recte Lyricus ἀκέρδεια λέλογχεν θαμινὰ τοὺς κατηγόρους.[1734] Amicus ad suos revisurus est, quo

---

[1731] In light of an edition of the monumental work of Lelio and his son Francesco Torèlli, which came out as *Digestorum seu Pandectarum Libri quinquaginta ex Florentinis Pandectis repraesentati* (Florentiae: Vettori, 1553), also relying on the Greek expertise of Vettori, it is unclear to what exactly Sambucus is referring here. Lelio Torèlli (1489–1576) was secretary to Cosimo I de' Medici. His son Francesco Torèlli died in 1579. On the prehistory of their highly appreciated edition of the *Pandects* see *Correspondance de Lelio Torelli avec Antonio Agustín et Jean Matal (1542–1553)*, ed. Jean-Louis Ferrary (Como: New press, 1992).

[1732] [Pseudo-]Albumasar [Abu Ma'Shar], *Apotelesmata*.

[1733] Cf. with letters 213, 304 and 306.

[1734] often the lot of the accusers is lack of profit. Cf. Pindarus, *Olympia* 1.53. See letter 277, note 1620. Andreas Dudith informed Thomas Jordan already on 19 July that Nifo was said to have drowned in a shipwreck on the way to England. Dudithius, *Epistulae*, 6:231.

suo merito, novimus.[1735] Exoptatissimus tuus est omnibus reditus, clientes etiam a Deo suplices exorant. Clusius nescio quo cogitat, indicia eius industriae atque hortus in circum conversus est, καὶ ἱππικῶν προγυμνάσματα[1736] etc. Literas tuas Patavium curavi. Nova scio te ex quaestore bellico et aliis acceptare.[1737] De cometa variae voces multorum quoque nugae excitatae, exitus docebunt.[1738] Sufficiunt nobis Thurcae plus quam infesti cometae. Deus nobiscum commiseratione non iudicio meritorum uti clementer agat, comprecor. Teque cum tuis optime habere cupio. Vale, 4. Decembris 1577. Totus tuis meritis Sambucus.

Address: Dem Edlen, hochgelehrten herrn Doctor Johanni Craton von Craffthaim, Khayserlichem Ratt unnd Protophysico et cetera meinem gunstigen Herrn und freunde zu Handen. Breslae. Cito.

298.
Sambucus to Theodor Zwinger
8 January 1578, [Vienna]

The original is kept in Basel, Universitätsbibliothek, Frey Mscr II 26, no. 223. Published in Gerstinger, "Die Briefe," 232-233.

Johannes Löwenklau is going back to Basel, Sambucus hopes he will be more diligent there. He is astonished that Conrad Dasypodius does not send him back his manuscripts of Euclid, Hero and Doxopatres. He wrote often but in vain. He wrote more vigorously to the printers (Eusebius Episcopius and Henri Estienne) concerning the Aristotle-edition. No one will be moved to great projects by their avarice. He asks Zwinger to approach them again. Löwenklau will tell Zwinger about Sambucus's future projects. He entrusted manuscripts concerning Polybius, Zonaras's very rare Lexicon *and some legal texts to Löwenklau. He asks Zwinger to write to Dasypodius, urging him to send back his codices. Otherwise, he will go to court.*

Salutem et felices annos.

Leonclaius ad vos redit, spero ipsum minus in ocio quam hic futurum. Demiror, quid Dasypodius Euclidem meum, Heronis quaedam et Doxopatrem in Ideas Hermogenis detineat.[1739] Scripsi saepe, nil obtineo. De Aristotele et aliis ad typographos vehementius

---

[1735] If Nifo was believed to be dead this might have been a reference to his father, Agostino Nifo.
[1736] a riding school.
[1737] Egidius Gattermayr (Gattermaier).
[1738] The comet appeared on 9 November and caused great excitement. In view of the more than hundred publications that appeared in reaction to the comet of 1577, this is a rather laconic comment. See Clarissa Doris Hellman, *The Comet of 1577: its Place in the History of Astronomy* (New York: Columbia University Press, 1944). See Gábor Almási, "Astrology in the Crossfire: The Stormy Debate after the Comet of 1577," *Annals of Science* 79 (2022), 1-27.
[1739] Zwinger's marginal notes: "Euclides. Heronis quaedam. Hermogenis ideae cum Doxopaterni scholiis." On Euclid and Hero of Alexandria cf. the Index. On Johannes Doxopatres's *Commentarius in Hermogenis De ideis* see letter 27, note 110. In this latter codex (today in Vienna, ÖNB, Cod. Phil. gr. 145) it is noted that it came back from the heirs of Valentin Erythraeus: "Redditus ab Erythrianis 12 Maii 1578." Gerstinger suggests it was originally sent to Johannes Sturm in Strasburg in "Die Briefe," 50.

scripsi. Quae isthaec iniqua cessatio? Quis ad plura et maiora illorum avaritia sordibusque excitetur? Si me amas, iterum aggredites, lacesse etiam convitiis? Quae in manibus habeam, et de allis coram Leonclaius noster. Cui in Polybium non pauca commisi cum Zonarae *Lexico* rarissimo et Νεαραῖς[1740] variis constitutis.[1741] Vale et scribe a me Dasypodio, ut meos Codices remittat, aut iure me experturum et publica querela. 8. Ianuarii 1578. Totus tuus Sambucus.[1742]

299.
Sambucus to Joachim Camerarius Jr.
31 January 1578, Vienna

The original is kept in Budapest, National Széchényi Library, Levéltár, Levelezések, S. Published in Gerstinger, "Die Briefe," 233-234.

Sambucus is sorry for the death of Sebald Kraus, a relative of his wife, and he promises to send something that will please Camerarius and Julius Geuder in the early spring. He is sending some notes on Dioscorides, taken from two Roman codices and some "Florentine fragments," which are worthy of attention, and he asks Camerarius to forward them to Henri Estienne. His emendations will mitigate, if not resolve, the difficulties of four textual places. He wishes he had collected something better. Camerarius knew how to carry burdens even in praiseworthy circumstances, not only in pitiful ones. He urges and will continue to urge Jean-Antoine Sarasin (concerning the edition of Dioscorides); they should put an end to these delays, and asks Camerarius to do the same, when he sends his notes to Estienne.

Salutem.

Regia vestra itemque nostra moerore de obitu optimi viri et affinis nostri Sebaldi Crausii perculsa graviter decumbit, cui opella nostra non desit.[1743] Πρώτη ἐαρῷ[1744] mittam tibi et Geydero[1745] aliquid, quod voluptates vestras iuvet; cui a me salutem. Mitto velut spicilegia quaedam ad Dioscoridem e codicibus duobus Romanis et fragmentis Florentinis non omnino contemnenda, quae ad Henricum recte tutoque mittas, valde oro.[1746] Scio quatuor loca cum

---

[1740] novella. A part of the *Corpus Iuris Civilis*.
[1741] Zwinger's marginal notes: "Polybius. Zonarae Lexicon. Iuridica." Concerning these unrealised projects see the notes in his bibliography (Sambucus, *Catalogus librorum*): "Leontii scholia historica in novum Testamentum et Nazianzeni libros. Item Harmenopulom de canonibus sacris cum quibusdam nauticis novellis et Hermopolitae Paratila. Zonarae et Philothei λεξικά, Polybium multis locis saniorem ac suppletum a se credidit Leonclaio excudenda. 1579." Cf. letter 271, note 1552.
[1742] Zwinger's notes underneath: "Aveo et cupiam [...]"
[1743] Sebald Kraus (b. 1514) was a Viennese patrician and merchant. He was a relative (or contact) of Sambucus's father-in-law, and worked (also) as an agent of the Österreicher family. See Attila Tózsa-Rigó, *A dunai térség szerepe a kora újkori Közép-Európa gazdasági rendszerében. Délnémet, osztrák, (cseh-)morva és nyugat-magyarországi városok üzleti és társadalmi hálózatai* [The role of the Danube-region in the economy of early modern Central Europe. Commercial and social networks of Southern German, Austrian, (Bohemian-)Moravian and Western Hungarian cities] (Miskolc: Egyetemi Kiadó, 2014), passim. See also Gerstinger, "Die Briefe," 234.
[1744] at the beginning of spring
[1745] Julius Geuder of Herolzberg (1530–1594). See letter 294, note 1721.
[1746] On Dioscorides see letter 155, notes 920 and 921, and cf. the Index.

meis ἐπικριματίοις¹⁷⁴⁷ quorundam dissidia laxatura, si non solutura. Utinam aliquid melius conquisierim! Πόνου γὰρ πόνον φέρειν¹⁷⁴⁸ nosti etiam in τοῖς ἐπαινετοῖς,¹⁷⁴⁹ non ἐλεεινοῖς¹⁷⁵⁰ modo. Saracenum¹⁷⁵¹ urgeo et urgebo, me denique ista mora liberent fideque vulgo edita expediant, tu idem facies, dum haec ad ipsum miseris. Vale, meque tuum tuorumque constantem fore credito. Pridie Kalendas Februarias 1578. Totus tuus Sambucus P[annonius?].

Address: Clarissimo doctissimoque viro domino doctori Ioachimo Camerario, reipublicae Norimbergensis Physico etc., amico optimo. Nurnberg, hern Doctori Camerario. Cito.

300.
Conrad Dasypodius to Sambucus
1 February 1578, Strassburg

Dedication in Conradus Dasypodius, *Brevis doctrina de cometis et cometarum effectibus* (Argentorati: Wyriot, 1578), f. Aii^r-Aiii^v.

Sublunar phenomena have been abundantly described by Aristotle and others, but they have not done justice to some recent occurrences. Time changes everything, including humans. This is particularly true for sublunar phenomena, of which one has only conjectural knowledge, based on the senses, as in the case of winds, lightning, hail etc. As a result, descriptions of comets differ from one another and also from historical observations, so they have never been well described and explained and there is no certain knowledge about them. Dasyposius provides here a few of his and others' observations of comets in order to make the understanding of other comets easier, and he gives a summary of what has been taught about comets and also some brief astronomical rules. Dasypodius asks Sambucus to receive this booklet positively and informs him that he had submitted his manuscript of Isaacus Monachus's commentaries into Euclid's Elements *to a publisher, as he also edited from the same codex the works of Theodosius and Autolycus a few years before. He had given Euclid's collected works, corrected and commented, to the publisher (Eusebius Episcopius) five years earlier, as he often complained about to Sambucus, but the publisher continues to delay and keeps the work with himself. He has his own geometrical commentary still at home, waiting for the occasion to publish it with his other works, while Sambucus will soon see his Hero of Alexandria appear.*

Clarissimo viro Ioanni Sambuco, caesareae maiestatis historico atque consiliario. S. D.

Meteorum quam varia et multiplex sit natura, vis et efficatia, quamve mutationi multiplici ac diversae obnoxia, ab Aristotele caeterisque philosophis diligenter et accurate explicatum est ita, ut nihil videatur in rerum sublimium varietate maxima esse, quod non erutum, non

---
¹⁷⁴⁷ little decrees
¹⁷⁴⁸ To carry the burden of burden. Cf. Sophocles, *Ajax* 866.
¹⁷⁴⁹ praiseworthy
¹⁷⁵⁰ finding pity
¹⁷⁵¹ Jean-Antoine Sarasin (1547–1598) was a humanist, physician and botanist of Geneva. His father Philibert was a doctor and expert of Greek, a friend of Calvin and many famous learned men. Sarasin studied in Lyon and Montpellier, where he developed an interest in botany and also taught medicine. On his return to Geneva, he started practicing medicine and sometimes also taught (unpaid) at the academy. See Reverdin, "Exposé, en forme de causerie, sur le Dioscoride de Jean-Antoine Sarasin" (as in letter 155, note 920). See letter 302.

traditum, non patefactum a summis istis philosophis sit. Verumtamen video in quibusdam meteoris nondum satis esse factum nostrorum temporum experientiis.

Communi enim dicto fertur tempora mutari, nec tempora tantum, verum et nosmet ipsos, quodve de nobis dicitur, etiam de caeteris naturalibus rebus intelligendum est. Maxime vero de meteoris, quia sunt imperfecta corpora et multis variisque ac diversis et continuis mutationibus obnoxia, ut nobis satis sit coniectura adsequi, quae sensibus patent et diuturnis observationibus multorum temporum annotantur atque ad rationem nostram allata verisimilitudine quadam percipiuntur, ut flatuum ventorumve natura, grandinum, tornitruorum, fulminum, ignitarum quoque impressionum vis et efficacia atque proprietas vera, talia sint, necne, non nisi coniecturis physicis adsequimur et a multis diverso traduntur modo, sicuti etiam de cometis, cometarum natura, proprietate, vi atque efficacia diversae sunt doctorum sententiae. Dum alii aliter eos generari in aere aut in aethere iudicant, formas quoque magnitudines, splendorem, motum, locum, tempora et reliqua eorundem accidentia in historiis aliter, quam praecipiant philosophi, annotari videmus. Unde etiam colligimus nondum esse exquisite tradita et explicata, quae de cometis, cometarum natura dici possunt, sed tantum iuxta Aristotelicum δυνατὸν[1752] investigata.

Aristoteles duo facit cometarum genera, alii tria, sunt, qui plures species et differentias enumerant. Motus etiam cometarum sunt varii, diversa annotantur quibus apparent tempora, loca quoque non conveniunt, genera effectum discrepant, ut nullam quis existimet in his esse certitudinem aut perceptionem. Verum si, quae nos experientia docet et quae frequenti diuturnaque observatione deprehendimus, ad praecepta rerum naturalium referemus, quod antiquos fecisse philosophos legimus, tum certiora et veriora naturaque magis consentanea proferemus, imo talia, quae locum habere possunt in acuratis et eruditis rerum probationibus.

Ut ergo eos, qui haec perscrutari volunt, pro tenuitate mea iuvarem, ea, quae ipsemet in apparentiis aliquot cometarum observanti et ab aliis doctis viris observata et annotata deprehendi, in hoc libello propono. Non quidem omnia, sed tantum praecipua, ut his perceptis reliqua, si quae sunt, facilius comprehenderentur. Spero etiam me hac tenui opella id adsequuturum, quod exopto, ut quae sparsim a nostris et antiquis tradita sunt, in hoc exiguo libello comprehensa studiosis usui esse possint in doctorum virorum scriptis cognoscendis. A quibus haec omnia melius et prolixius atque maiori diligentia et eruditione explicantur in his enim paginis, περιοχὴ[1753] tantum breviter continetur astrologicarum praeceptionum, quam meis praelegi discipulis, cum superioribus mensibus cometa appareret.

Tibi vero haec ob veterem nostram amicitiam, animorum coniunctionem multaque tua in me merita mitto, ut cum multum delecteris rerum naturalium cognitione, qualiacunque haec mea sint, animum tamen tuum post graviora tua studia recreent. Te etiam atque etiam oro, ut hasce meas pagellas boni consulas et animo benigno legas, mea etiam studia, ut semper, tibi commendata habeas.[1754] Nuper ex tuo antiquo codice typographo imprimenda dedi Isaaci Monachi antiqua in Euclidea *Elementa* scholia,[1755] ut ex eodem superioribus annis Theodosii et Autolyci opera edidi.[1756] Euclidea opera omnia (ut saepe tibi sum conquestus) ante quinquennium

---

[1752] possible
[1753] summary
[1754] The real reason behind this dedication was Sambucus's growing anger about Dasypodius's withholding his manuscripts. See letter 298 to Theodor Zwinger, where he even threatens to sue Dasypodius.
[1755] Isaacus Monachus Argyrus, *Scholia in Euclidis elementorum Geometriae sex priores libros*, ed. and trans. Conrad Dasypodius (Argentorati: Wyriot, 1579).
[1756] Dasypodius, *Sphaericae doctrinae propositiones* (as in letter 173).

correcta et emendata atque exornata typographo tradidi,[1757] qui moram morae nectit et adhuc illa penes se retinet. Commentaria mea geometrica adhuc mecum habeo,[1758] nactus occasionem cum aliis meis scriptis in publicum emittam; Heronem tuum brevi videbis.[1759] Tu, ut facis, me meaque studia iuva et, quo semper erga me fuisti animo benevolo, eodem etiam esse pergas. Vale. Calendis Februariis. Anno MDLXXVIII. Argentinae. Cunradus Dasypodius.

301.
Sambucus to Joachim Camerarius Jr.
7 March 1578, [Vienna]

The original is kept in Munich, BSB, Clm 10367, Nr. 182.

Sambucus wanted to give this letter to Regius, who is returning to his folks. His sorrow will disappear through prudence and his return home. Here, it is very cold, but the seeds are secure under the cover of snow. He is astonished that Estienne has forgotten his promises and has set aside many diverse and rare texts given by Sambucus while taking care instead of pointless pamphlets. But he will demand in earnest if Estienne does not have something ready by the time of the coming fair. He is also annoyed that Dasypodius holds on to Euclid, Athenaeus, Hieron and others. This is the gratitude of the times. He asks what Camerarius and the printers have decided concerning the letters of Chrysoloras and his father's Greek writings. Sambucus has finished a Habsburg genealogy, eight triumphal arcs and the rules for military commanders. He has sent Wechel some of his writings, because poor Plantin will have completely perished by now. There is no good news and nothing better can be expected. One must bear it and mitigate it by prayers. He has written to Julius Geuder of some widely publicized news, Camerarius can get this news from him.

Regio[1760] vestro ad suos revisuro has dare volui, cuius maerorem cum prudentia leniet, tum forte reditus optatus delebit. Apud nos frigora et glacies durant. Geminum hyemem reperimur, sed sata cuncta nivibus tecta inoffensa sunt. Miror Henricum nostrum adeo promissorum oblitum, ut, quae a me ad prelum suum non pauca, nec unius generis raraque acceperit, seponat ac praeter decorem nugacibus libellis incubat. Sed expostulabimus, nisi his nundinis aliquid comparuerit. Euclidem cum Athenaei mechanicis, Hieronis opusculis et ceteris Dasypodium continere miror. Haec, scilicet, est gratia nostri saeculi. De epistolis

---

[1757] See letter 89, note 564.
[1758] He may be referring here to his *Institutionum mathematicarum voluminis primi erotemata, logisticae, geometricae, sphaerae, geographiae* (Argentinae: Rihelius, 1593).
[1759] Hero of Alexandria (c. 10–70 AD) was a Greek mathematician and engineer. See *RE* XV (1912), 992-1080. Dasypodius wrote a long treatise on Hero and the mechanical arts (Cunradus Dasypodius, *Heron mechanicus, seu de mechanicis artibus atque disciplinis*, Argentorati: Nicolaus Wyriot, 1580), and also published Hero's geometrical work in 1571 (included in Euclid's *Elementorum liber primus* of the Strasbourg edition, which was issued later separately as *Heronis Alexandrini vocabula quaedam geometrica*, Argentorati: Christianus Mylius, 1580).
[1760] Probably the Nuremberg syndic Joachim Regius (or König, 1532–1616), on whose help in sending his correspondence Camerarius Sr. was relying already in 1565 (see *Ioachimi Camerarii Bapenbergensis Epistolarum familiarium libri VI* [Frankfurt: Wechelius, 1583], 322). He was often in Vienna on diplomatic or commercial missions (see e. g. the passports recorded in Viennese Staatsarchiv, HHStA, Reichhofsrat, Passbriefe 9-1-49 to 9-1-51). On his mission in 1573–74 to secure corn for Nuremberg in Vienna cf. Erich Landsteiner, "Trübselige Zeit? Auf der Suche nach den wirtschaftlichen und sozialen Dimensionen des Klimawandels im späten 16. Jahrhundert," *Österreichische Zeitschrift für Geschichtswissenschaften* 12.2 (2001), 79–116, at 102–103.

Chrysolorae, de pare[n]tis variis et eruditissimis Graecis scriptis quid consilii tui, quae voluntas typographorum sit, aliquando perscribito. Ego genealogiam Habspurgicam cum 8 ar[c]is thriumphalibus absolvi, itemque canones imperatorios seu bellicos.[1761] Misi etiam ad Wechelum quaedam mea nuper, quod Plantinus totus perierit miser.[1762] Nova nulla, quae grata esse queant, nec meliora sunt vel in religionis tot dissidiis, vel republica exspectanda. Ferenda tamen et precibus continentissimis mitiganda. Vale. Nonis Martiis 78. Vienna. Totus tuus Sambucus.

Scripsi ad D. Gayderum[1763] quaeda[m] vulgata nova et cetera, de quo, si veles, intelligas.

Address: Clarissimo viro domino D. Ioachimo Camerario, physico reipublicae Norimbergensis et cetera, amico optimo. Norimbergam.
Camerarius's note: 78. 25. Martii.

302.
Jean-Antoine Sarasin to Sambucus
[Spring–early summer 1578], [Geneva]

The original is kept in Vienna, ÖNB, Cod. 9736, f. 23ʳ-24ᵛ.

Sarasin would have responded to Sambucus's letter much sooner if he had found the occasion. Sambucus is urging and entreating him to leave no stone unturned to persuade him to publish Dioscorides as soon as possible. However, his medical practice and the management of the household leaves him hardly any time for translating or commenting on it. Meanwhile he is sending a partial proof copy of the edition, the errors are due to the hurry of the printer. He is also sending a list of contents. Sambucus should let him know his opinion. If he cannot suffer any more delay, he should get Henri Estienne to publish Jean Ruel's translation with his variae lectiones. *He prefers publishing the next year to letting something inelaborate come out. The letter concludes with a list of the contents of the planned edition.*

Si commodam fuissem nactus occasionem, vir clarissime, iam dudum ad literas tuas respondissem. Nos hortabaris, imo etiam flagitabas, ut Dioscoridem Graeco-Latinum quamprimum praelo subiiceremus, omnemque moveas lapidem, nobis id uti persuaderis.[1764] Cuperem equidem desiderio tuo satisfacere, vir clarissime, ac certe, quotiescunque vacat, opellam meam Dioscoridi tribuo. Sed tum consultationibus medicis domi forisque, tum etiam quotidianis domesticis occupationibus ita distineor, vix ut mihi tantillum otii supersit, quod illi vertendo illustrandoque suppeditem. Interea vero editionis nostrae specimen mitto; errata, quae observare licebit plurima typographi festinatio excusabit. Mitto etiam elenchum eorum quae illa editione contineri cupio. Ut placeant omnia, velim nos certiores facias. Quod si moram longiorem ferre minime potes, agita quaeso cum D. Stephano, ut Ruellii

---

[1761] Probably a reference to his collection of military authors (see letter 247, note 1431).
[1762] After the sacking of Antwerp in late 1576, Plantin's press ran into financial difficulties.
[1763] Julius Geuder of Herolzberg (1530–1594). See noteletter 294, note 1721.
[1764] On the project of publishing Dioscorides see letter 155, notes 920 and 921 and cf. the Index.

versionem[1765] cum tuis variis lectionibus notisque primo quoque tempore emittat in lucem, equidem nihil morer. Malo enim editio nostra novum prematur in annum, quam permittere, ut inelaboratum opus e manibus nostris dimittatur. Vale, vir clarissime, et ignosce tarditati nostrae. Tuae excellentiae addictissimus Saracenus.

Pedanii Dioscoridi Anazarbii 6 librorum *De materia medica*, itemque duorum *De venenis* contextus Graecus quam emendatissimus.[1766]
Eorundem nova interpretatio Latina Graeco contextui ex adverso respondens autore Ioanne Antonio Saraceno.
Clarissimi viri Ioannis Sambuci in contextum Dioscoridis Graecum variae lectiones attigunt ad marginem interiorem.
Aliorum complurimum variae tum lectiones, tum emendationes ad marginem exteriorem.
Ioannis Antonii Saraceni in Dioscoridem scholia ad capitum calcem addita.
Dioscoridis notha, tum Graece, tum Latine.
Dioscoridis appendices duae, Graece et Latine.
Fragmenta Crateuae.
Ioannis Sambuci in Dioscoridem observationes et notae.
Index Graecus omnium quae in Dioscoride continentur simplicium.
Idem Latinus.
Simplicium medicamentorum quae in Dioscoride habentur temperamenta et temperamentorum ordines.
Simplicium medicamentorum vires ex Dioscoride ad corporis partium varios affectus tum internos, tum externos a capitis affectibus ducto exordio.
Stirpium differentiae ex Dioscoride secundum locos communes, opus ad ipsarum plantarum cognitionem admodum conducibile, autore Benedicto Textore Segusiano.[1767]
Εὐπορίστων[1768] Dioscoridis ad Andromachum libri duo iam nunc secundo tum Graece, tum Latine in lucem editi.[1769]

Address: Eximio viro D. Ioanni Sambuco historiographo caesareo. Viennae.

[1765] The physician and botanist Jean Ruel (1474–1537) is famous for his treatise on botany, *De Natura Stirpium* (1536) and his Latin translation of Dioscorides' *De materia medica*: *Pedacii Dioscoridis Anazarbei de medicinali materia libri quinque* (Parrhisii: Estienne, 1516). Sambucus put his annotations into a later edition of this work (see letter 155, note 921).

[1766] Sarasin's monumental publication of Dioscorides's *Opera omnia* of 1598 (as in letter 155, note 920) did not include all the listed works. Sambucus's observations, for example, had no place in it, only his collations were placed in the margins.

[1767] Benenedictus Textor, *Stirpium differentiae ex Dioscoride secundum locos communes: opus ad ipsarum plantarum cognitionem admodum conducibile* (Parisiis: Apud Simonem Colinaeum, 1534). This was not included in the edition.

[1768] easily prepared

[1769] First published as *Pedacii Dioscoridis Anazarbei ad Andromachum, hoc est De curationibus morborum per medicamenta paratu facilia, libri II. Nunc primum et Graece editi, et partim a Ioanne Moibano, partim vero post huius mortem a Conrado Gesnero in linguam Latinam conversi* (Argentorati: Josias Rihelius, 1565). The work was actually published by Sarasin as a part of the *Opera omnia* in 1598, but was often bound separately.

303.
Sambucus to Piero Vettori
22 April 1578, Vienna

The original is kept in Munich, BSB, Clm 735, Nr. 116. Published in Gerstinger, "Die Briefe," 234-235.

Sambucus recommends a certain Nicolaus Valens, who wants to study law in Sienna and asks Vettori to recommend him to some Sienese friend of his. He forwarded Vettori's letter to Frankfurt. The book dealer (Jean Aubry), who brought it to his father-in-law in Frankfurt, has not yet returned from the book fair. He gives his thanks for the information on the Greek translators of the codex, but he was thiking of others. There is great grieving over the death of Archduchess Joanna of Austria, and Sambucus knows that Vettori will memorialise her life.

Domino Petro Victorio Sambucus salutem.

Nicolaus hic Valens, iuvenis indole, moribus et litterarum progressibus haud vulgaris, Italiam vestram inspicere cupit, et ni quid impedierit, Senis aliquandiu ad legum studia haerere constituit.[1770] Si te convenerit, oro mea caussa illum amplectare et Senas alicui familiari commendes. Cuius beneficii gratiam ille declarabit, ut te de officio, cui commendasti, etiam amarit. Francfortum tuas, uti iussisti, diligenter curavi.[1771] Bibliopola, qui pertulit ad socerum Wechelium, nondum e mercatu rediit; spero nil neglecturum. De Graecis interpretibus codicis etc. habeo gratiam, sed alios putabam ex aliorum sermone.[1772] Obitum illustrissimae reginae Ioannae lugemus immoderate.[1773] Cuius vitam te egregio monumento exaraturum adque memoriam omnium ornaturum scio.[1774] Vale! X Kalendas Maii Vienna 78.

304.
Sambucus to Piero Vettori
19 May 1578, Vienna

The original is kept in Munich, BSB, Clm 735, Nr. 117. Published in Gerstinger, "Die Briefe," 235-236.

Occupied by court affairs, the Florentine legate (Orazio Capponi) gave Sambucus Vettori's letters only recently. Sambucus appreciated him not only for his office but also for his own virtues, and he would be happy to engage in correspondence with him. He is not surprised by the Florentines'

[1770] We do not have further information on the student in question.
[1771] See letters 296, 304 and 306.
[1772] See letter 298.
[1773] Joanna of Austria (1547–1578) was Ferdinand I's youngest daughter. By marriage to Francesco I de' Medici she became Grand Princess of Tuscany and later the Grand Duchess of Tuscany.
[1774] Vettori had already published a book about Joanna of Austria of 1566 (both in Latin and Italian), *Orazione ò vero libro ... delle lodi della serenissima Giouanna d'Austria* or *Liber de laudibus Ioannae Austriacae*. He did not publish any funerary oration over her death, which is not so surprising in view of her conflicted relation to Francesco de' Medici, so much so that even her death (caused by prematurely giving birth to a baby as a result of her fall of the stairs) was gossiped to be intentional. Cf. the next letter.

sorrow at the death of Joanna of Austria, as she is much mourned also in Vienna: what reasonable and pious person would not be moved by the misfortune of the House of Austria? Sambucus praises Vettori's earlier publication about Joanna of Austria and believes that he would follow it up with a new one in "these miserable times." Sambucus asks Vettori, if he has already published something, to send it to him, where they may also publish something in the same argument. The book dealer (Jean Aubry) appears to have seen Vettori's Epistolae familiares *published somewhere, but perhaps he is only dreaming. Concerning Vettori's* Politica-*edition, his message will be told by Capponi.*

Petro Victorio Sambucus salutem.

Occupationibus publicis et salutationibus vulgo aulae usitatis distractus nobilissimus vester legatus mihi serius tuas reddidit.[1775] Quem ego illustrem non allegationibus modo, sed propriis virtutibus et humanitate plane amabili ita diligere pariterque colere coepi, ut me magni viri amicicia per te auctum profitear. Memoriam tuebor, si volet, crebris litteris etc. Quod vos tantopere serenissimae Ioannae obitum lugeatis, non miror, quando nos quoque in partem maeroris casus tantus trahat. Quis enim recta mente constans, pietate optabili, sensibus Christianis, consiliis in medium dandis idoneus, caritatis praeconiis et exemplis ductus, quis inquam Austriae domus adversis non moveatur, non simul lachrimis amorem et observantiam declaret? Laudo consilia tua, quibus in praeconiis sanctissimae faeminae et principis tum antea usus fuisti, tum hoc miserabili tempore usurum te arbitror.[1776] Si quid a vobis profectum est, quod omnes scire velitis, fac ut ad nos perferantur, fortassis hinc quoque ex aetheriis incudibus aliquid eiusdem argumenti excudetur, quod proprie harum regionum dolorem ostendat. Nisi omnino fallor, audieram a bibliopola nostro tuas se aliquot *Epistolas ad familiares* typis alicubi impressas vidisse.[1777] Nildum ad manus venit, requisivi, ait et negat, fortasse somnia narrat. Ego non cessabo, dum reapse cognoro. De *Politicis* tuis per Caponium.[1778] Vale et me ama, tui observantissimum, ac festinanti manui σύγγνωθι.[1779] Vienna 19. Maii 1578.

305.
Sambucus to Johannes Crato
20 May 1578, [Vienna]

Published in Gerstinger, "Die Briefe," 239-240.

The driver has given Sambucus the books of Matthias Wesenbeck on the day he writes this letter, and claimed that it was agreed that Sambucus paid him one florin. The books confirm Wesenbeck's

---

[1775] Orazio Capponi (1552–1622) was born in Florence. Hardly anything is known about his early career. From at least 1576, he was a friend of Tasso. Later he made a career at the papal court, became governor of the Macerata and bishop of Carpentras (in 1596), spending his time between Carpentras and Rome, where among others he published a work in defence of the Venetian Interdict. See the article by Francesco Agostini in *DBI* 19 (1976), 86-87. See also letter 306 and Jules de Terris, *Les évêques de Carpentras: étude historique* (Avignon: Seguin, 1886).

[1776] From the previous sentences it appears that Sambucus encouraged Vettori to publish something about Joanna out of religious motives. Joanna could have been celebrated as a pious, religiously moderate person in the midst of Viennese confessionalisation and revealed as a counter-example.

[1777] Petrus Victorius, *Epistolarum ad Germanos missarum libri III nunc primum editi ab Ioanne Caselio* (Rostochii: Iacobus Lucius, 1577).

[1778] Cf. letters 213, 296 and 306.

[1779] forgive

talents. Sambucus distributed the books to Rumpf and others, who thank him for them and promise to be helpful. Vice-chancellor Siegmund Vieheuser is with the imperial committee in Worms. He gave the parcel to Johann Weber, who after opening the letter said that it was none of his business, but that he wishes to consider Wesenbeck and his books in a notable manner as soon as possible. He is afraid that the emperor will not respond in Vienna, as he is leaving for Linz on 3 June. As soon as he arrives in Prague, Crato and Sambucus may remind him of Wesenbeck. They will certainly achieve something, the question is for what price. Crato must know the nature of the chancellor and the secretaries, who care more about getting their palms greased than about books, especially the tax collector and the treasurer need to be bribed. "Things are miserable for the courtier!" He will do what he can and is saying hello to Wesenbeck.

Salutem.

Libros Wessenbecii auriga mihi hodie reddidit.[1780] Coactus sum illi numerare florenum 1, id se ex pacto velle aiebat. Ingenium Wessenbecii nobile et copiosum amo. Praeclara tot monumenta, quid velit aut possit, abunde probant. Domino Rumpfio et caeteris suos[1781] obtuli, qui gratiam habent atque operam suam apud caesarem non defore pollicentur.[1782] Dominus procancellarius Viechauserus Vormatiae in conventu istuc allegatorum est.[1783] Fasciculum domino Webero obtuli, qui resignatis literis respondit ad se nihil eorum pertinere, verumtamen cupere haud obscure Wessenbeccio ac libelli fore memorem quamprimum. Sed vereri, ut hic Viennae responsum habeamus, quod caesarea maiestas hinc Lintzium ad 3. Iunii cogitet. Pragam ubi venerint, et tua excellentia et ego poterimus monere. Si quid obtinuerimus, nec despero, quod precii erit (taxaret[1784]), componatur. Nam scis, quae cancellarii sit et notariorum conditio, qui τὰ χρήματα, οὐ βιβλία[1785] curant, praesertim exactor et quaestor unguetur. Res est misera aulicorum![1786] Quidquid mea industriola et opera poterit, non deerit. A me domino Wessenbeccio multam salutem. 20. Maii 1578. Tuus Sambucus.

[1780] Matthias Wesenbeck (1531–1586) was a Flemish jurist. He studied in Leuven but moved to Germany in 1558 because of his Lutheranism, and became doctor of law at the University of Jena, from where he moved to Wittenberg in 1569. He published, among others, a commentary on the *Digest* and eight volumes of his own legal opinions. See the article by Johann August Ritter von Eisenhart in *ADB* 42 (1897) 134-138.

[1781] Gerstinger supposes that instead of *suos* (scil. libros) one should read *tuas* (scil. literas), i.e. that Sambucus delivered Crato's letter to Rumpf and others. See Gerstinger, "Die Briefe," 239-240.

[1782] Wolfgang Rumpf (1536–1605) was chamberlain under Maximilian II, following the young Rudolf and Ernst during their years of education (1563–1571) to Spain. He became high chamberlain and member of the Secret Council under Rudolf and remained his most influential courtier for long but after 1596 he gradually fell from grace. See the article by Felix Stieve in *ADB* 29 (1889), 668-669.

[1783] A *Reichsdeputationstag* (meeting of an ad hoc imperial commitee of invited members) was held in Worms, starting on 12 April 1578. See Helmut Neuhaus, *Reichsständische Repräsentationsformen im 16. Jahrhundert* (Berlin: Duncker & Humblot, 1982), 478-479.

[1784] *taxaret* is written above *erit*.

[1785] (care) about money, not about books

[1786] Cf. with Almási, *The Uses of Humanism*, 191-192.

306.
Sambucus to Piero Vettori
23 May 1578, Vienna

The original is kept in Munich, BSB, Clm 735, Nr. 118. Published in Bandini, *Clarorum Italorum et Germanorum*, 2:125-126; Gerstinger, "Die Briefe," 236-238.

Sambucus found Orazio Capponi's talents greater than he had anticipated on the basis of Vettori's recommendation, and he established a relationship with him that he believes will last forever. He opened up his library for him and showed him his different notes and observations. Capponi persuaded him to write some epitaphs on the death of the duchess (Joanna of Austria) and send them to the duke. Sambucus informs Vettori about books that appeared on the book fair of Frankfurt, of which Capponi will give a fuller account. Concerning Vettori's edition of Politica, *Sambucus tells Vettori that Andreas Wechel, who recently published Aristotle's all works, lost his wife, with whom he spent together many years and raised many children. Now that he had immediately remarried, he has become much less diligent and generous. He nevertheless promises to republish Vettori's book but with time, since he claims these philosophical texts lost their appeal in Germany and other works sell better. Sambucus will nonetheless urge him and not accept his excuses. Sambucus wishes that Vettori will live long and enjoy the fruits of his labours, and he sends greetings to Pál Szegedi in case Vettori meets him.*

Petro Victorio salutem.

In Horatio Caponio, nisi fallor, plures dotes quam tua commendatio praefert, repperi.[1787] Non tua igitur modo caussa verum eius meritis complexus ita ipsum sum, ut necessitudinem constitutam in omne reliquum vitae nostrae tempus valituram mutuo credam. Quod potui, cum illo communicavi: aperui bibliothecam, varia mea σχεδιάσματα[1788] et observationes lectionum. Nonnulla etiam liberius egi. Persuasit enim dudum a musis museisque relicto, ut Graece et Latine aliquot tumulos de obitu serenissimae reginae effuderim et ad magnum vestrum ducem miserim.[1789] Sed post nugas aliquid accuratius meditabor. E mercatu Francfortensi multa prodiere. Imprimis Platonis opera Serrani viri clari et elegantissimi philosophi interpretatione aucta ex officina H. Stephani;[1790] prodiere Clementis Romani Διαταγαί;[1791] *Variae lectiones* H. St[ephani];[1792] *Omnia opera* Iovii;[1793] Sadoleti Παραμυθητικά[1794] de obitu matris ex bibliotheca nostra etc.,[1795] de quibus Caponius noster coram. De tuis *Politicis* quid fiat, audi. Typographus Andreas Wechelius, qui omnia opera Aristotelis in quadrata forma typis regiis

---

[1787] See letter 304.
[1788] improvisations, drafts
[1789] See letters 303-304.
[1790] Πλάτωνος ἅπαντα τὰ σωζόμενα. *Platonis Opera quae extant omnia*, 3 vols. (Genevae: Henricus Stephanus, 1578).
[1791] constitutions. *Apostolicarum constitutionum et catholicae doctrinae Clementis Romani libri VIII* (Antverpiae, Christophorus Plantinus, 1578).
[1792] Henricus Stephanus, *Schediasmatum variorum et observationum, expositionum, emendationum, disputationum, alii libri tres* (Genevae: Henricus Stephanus, 1578).
[1793] Paulus Iovius, *Opera, quotquot extant omnia a mendis accurate repurgata* (Basileae: Pietro Perna, 1578).
[1794] consolations
[1795] Sadoletus, *Philosophicae consolationes*. See letter 221.

nuper recudit,[1796] amissa uxore, quacum multos annos exegerat pluresque liberos susceperat, mutato subito consilio vidui status ad iteratas nuptias reversus, de diligentia et liberalitate haud parum remisit, pollicetur se quidem impressurum sed temporibus commodioribus, quod philosophicae hae disputationes in Germania refrixerint minusque vendibiles aliis sint etc. Sed urgebo et vel incommodo eius caussis non acceptis premam, ut exprimam. Vale, mi optime et clarissime vir, tuaque vegeta senecta ut diu laborumque fructibus et honoribus fruare, ex animo precor. Si in Zegedinum incideris, a me saluta. X Kalendas Iunii 1578 Vienna.

307.
Sambucus to Joachim Camerarius Jr.
12[1797] June 1578, [Vienna]

The original is kept in Munich, BSB, Clm 10367, Nr. 180.

He has heard nothing about Chrysoloras's letters, but one must bear what printers' avarice or negligence demands. Estienne has not started the work on Dioscorides, which is no wonder, as he is also infected by the common ailment and lets his press be of little use to others, who have nothing but trouble, hard work and costs. He mentions this only between themselves. Recently, Estienne has sent him his edition of Plato, and he otherwise acts generously. Sambucus has decided to express his thanks, as he believes that Estienne wishes this, and to encourage him to publish Dioscorides. If Camerarius knows of a secure way to send Estienne 40 gold pieces through a banker or a money-changer, he should let him know as soon as possible. Otherwise he could entrust them to the merchants from Nuremberg. He implores Camerarius to get the included letters to Basel and to Estienne. He sends greetings to Julius Geuder. They will get the news from others, everything is dangerous for those who write. He has received Glycas's Annals through Dasypodius and extends his thanks.

Salutem.

De Chrysolora nil audio. Sed feramus, quod typographorum seu avaritia, seu negligentia imperat. Henricus Stephanus nondum est aggressus Dioscoridem, sed non miror, qui labe communi adsepersus, parve redimi suorum typorum usum ultra molestias et operas aliorum impensas solet. Haec tibi et cetera. Misit nuper ad me Platonem suum et alias semper liberalius mecum agit. Constitui ei gratiam aliquam reddere, quod velle ipsum animadverto, simulque excitare ad Dioscoridis editionem. Itaque, si quae tuta via est, si qui mensarii, aut colybei, quorum opera 40 aureos illi Geneuam perferendos aut reddendos scis, quamprimum

---

[1796] In his series of Aristotle-editions Wechel also published Vettori's version of Aristotle's *Politica*, but only the Greek text: *Aristotelis Politicorum, sive de optimo statu reipublicae libri octo. Ex castigationibus Petri Victorii emendatiores facti* (Francofurti: Andreas Wechel, 1577). Vettori's *Politica*-edition was bilingual and supplied with a densely written commentary, which was inserted among the paragraphs and was much longer than the actual text. This commentary was finally published in Zwinger's edition of the *Politica*, with the collaboration of Jean de Sponde: *Aristotelis Politicorum libri octo ex Dionysii Lambini et P. Victorii interpretationibus purissimi Graecolatini, Theodori Zvingeri argumentis atque scholiis, tabulis quinetiam in tres priores libros illustrati, Victorii commentariis perpetuis declarati. Pythagoreorum veterum Fragmenta Politica a Iohanne Spondano conversa et emendata* (Basileae: Episcopius, 1582).

[1797] According to the Julian calendar, in the year 1578 the solstice fell on 12 June.

mihi significes. Curabo istuc eos, aut credam hinc Norimbergensibus tantum, ut aureis Henrico reddantur. Facies mihi rem gratissimam. Haec raptim. Te pro veteri amore posco, has perferendas Basileam et Henrico Stephano cures, vicissim impera. Ipso solstitio aestivo 78.

Domino Iulio Gaydero, viro inprimis humano et mei studioso multas salutes. Nova ex aliis malo accipiatis. Nil enim modo tutum est, omnia infesta scribentibus. I. Sambucus. Glycei comentarios per Dasypodium remissos accepi. Ago magnas gratias.

Address: Clarissimo viro, medico reipublicae Norimbergensis in primis, domino, D. Ioachimo Camerario et cetera, amico observando. Nurmberg. Herrn Doctor Camerario zuhanden. *Camerarius's note:* 78 28. Iunii.

308.
Sambucus to Adam von Dietrichstein
28 July 1578, Vienna

The original is kept in Vienna, ÖStA, HHStA, Spanien Diplomatische Korrespondenz, Fasc. 7, Mappe 161 "Verschiedene an Adam von Dietrichstein 1568–1571," f. 24-25.[1798] Published in Gerstinger, "Sambucus als Handschriftssammler," 279-280; idem, "Die Briefe," 238-239.

"The die is cast" and Sambucus prays that it moves forth. Having examined diligently his manuscript books and prepared an index, the agents of the emperor set the price the day before. It is not to agree about details of the payment. It does not matter to whom the emperor gives the job of writing a contract, what matters is to get 300 ducats as a deposit to satisfy his urgent needs. He added (to the books) an artistic statue of Priapus, for which he had frequently been offered 400 scudos, as he understood the emperor's fascination about it. The emperor will be able to compensate him for it in other, more important ways. He is happy that the emperor will have such select books and that they remain in the fatherland. He emphasises that these are first-class books, for which foreigners were ready to pay much more than what he is going to have in Vienna. But he will never regret something which he owes to the emperor. He kept only five small rather common books as a memento and a few books which he has recently had copied in Florence and Venice for his personal need and use, as it is known by the agents. He has no news from Vienna unknown to Dietrichstein. He will pray for the success of Archduke Karl's mission and that internal conflicts or the news of Belgian events not be turned to the advantage of the Ottomans and other enemies of the Christians.

Illustris et magnifice heros, maecenas benignissime, salutem, servitutem.

Iacta est alia [!], quod exeat, precor, ad honorem Dei publicique meam meorumque laetitiam et usum. Heri commissarii caesaris excussis antea diligenter libris meis vetusta manu exaratis et indice rite confecto, denique de pretio conclusum est. De ratione solvendi aut assecurandi reliquum est nogocium. Cui autem sua maiestas negocium syngraphae dederit, mecum facile convenietur, modo nunc mihi pro extremis pene necessitatibus 300 ducati deponantur. Addidi

---
[1798] We thank András Oross and István Fazekas for finding this letter (misplaced since the time of Gerstinger) and sending us a copy.

admirandam et artificio longe lateque nobilem statuam Priapi,[1799] pro qua saepe oblati fuere 400 scutati. Sed ego pretio librorum addidi, quod caesarem ea valde captum intelligam, et sua maiestas in maioribus compensare poterit etc. Laetor, quod tam selecti libri [!] 500 princeps noster sit habiturus, exulto eos in patria mansuros.[1800] Scio, qui libri et quam famosi sint, quam exteri hos longe maiori pretio expetiverint, quam habiturus sum. Sed cum vitam et bona suae maiestati debemus, nil paenitet. Nil mihi ex tot antiquis libris quam parvulos quinque servavi eosque vulgares, tantum in memoriam aliorum. Et quos cotidie describi curo curavique manu recenti Florentiae, Venetiis etc. aliquot pro meo gustu et usu, uti norunt commissarii. Nova hic nulla sunt, quae vos ignoretis. Oremus Deum toto corde, uti haec expeditio optimi et sanctissimi archiducis Caroli victoria memorabili et clade hostium eveniat.[1801] Res quoque Belgicae sapiantur,[1802] ne domesticum malum in Christianorum universam perniciem excedat Thurcarumque et aliorum Christi inimicorum robur et exultationem. Me vestro illustrissimo patrocinio humiliter commendo. 28. Iulii 1578. Vienna. Vestrae illustrissimae magnificentiae clientulus etc. Ioannes Sambucus.

Address: Illustri et magnifico heroi, domino, domino Adamo baroni a Dietrichstain, Hollenburg etc., sacratissimae caesareae maiestatis palatii praefecto eiusdemque secretissimo consiliario etc., domino mecenati meo generoso. An Herrn von Dietrichstain, Prag. Cito. Cito.

309.
Sambucus to Johannes Crato
29 July 1578, Vienna

Published in Gerstinger, "Die Briefe," 240-241.

Sambucus wishes Crato and his family a pleasant journey to Prague. He must know that princes often demand such annoyances from their followers and are almost jealous of their time spent freely, so either one should never attach oneself to the court or one should come to rest deep in its bosom. He does not know the jurist who made the confusion and only knows the men who

---

[1799] Priapus was a minor rustic fertility god in Greek mythology.
[1800] See Almási, *The Uses of Humanism*, 192-196. On his attempts to sell his books abroad see, for example, letter 244.
[1801] As a reaction to the incursion of Ottomans from Bosnia, Rudolf II entrusted military leadership to his uncle Archduke Karl II (ruler of Styria, Carniola and Carinthia) on 12 February, and made also sure about adequate revenues, yet action was taken only much later. For the military events see Rudolf Horvat, *Povijest Hrvatske* [History of Croatia] (Petrinja: Dragutin Benko, 1904), 379-382; Isthvanfius, *Historiarum de rebus Ungaricis*, 338. For the whole military reorganisation with the fundamental leadership and support of Styria see Johann Loserth, *Innerösterreich und die militärischen Massnahmen gegen die Türken im 16. Jahrhundert: Studien zur Geschichte der Landesdefension und der Reichshilfe* (Graz: Styria, 1934); Géza Pálffy, "A Bajcsavárig vezető út. A stájer rendek részvétele a Dél-Dunántúl határvédelmében a 16. században" [Before the construction of Bajcsavár. The contribution of the Styrian estates to the defence of Southern Transdanubia], in *Weitschawar. Bajcsa-Vár. Egy stájer erődítmény*, ed. Gyöngyi Kovács (Zalaegerszeg: Zala Megyei Múzeumok, 2002), 11-26.
[1802] After the Battle of Gembloux in January 1578 the Spanish armies won a crushing victory over the army of the States General of the Netherlands, which forced Prince William of Orange, the leader of the revolt, and Archduke Matthias, the Governor-General installed by the States General, to leave Brussels. See James D. Tracy, *The Founding of the Dutch Republic: War, Finance, and Politics in Holland 1572–1588* (Oxford: Oxford University Press, 2008), 135-141.

initiated the whole affair a bit. God will decide, but one may fear about unexpected outcomes, as Crato writes. He recommends to Crato Petrus Johannes Crapidel who taught Sambucus's son for some time in the Silesians' boarding school in Vienna. Concerning Matthias Wesenbeck's affair it is up to Crato to accomplish something.

Salutem.

Pragam tibi cum tuis iter felicissimum precor. Scis has molestias a principibus saepe obiectari ociumque eos bene meritis quasi invidere, ut verum sit illud: aut nunquam attigisse eorum consuetudinem, aut penitus in sinu conquievisse praestet. De iurisconsulto, qui turbas dederit, non intelligo. Qui sint authores, eos mediocriter novi. Deus caussam suam[1803] [?] aget fovebitque, contra quem nil valent consilia nec conatus hominum, metuendum tamen, ut scribis, ne oblata temere occasione quaedam praeter omnium opinionem accidant.[1804] Hunc iuvenem popularem tuum, Petrum Ioannis Crapidel,[1805] commendo suaque negocia, qui aliquandiu meum filiolum in schola hic seu contubernio Silesiorum eruduit. Oro ipsius et mea caussa, in quo tuam opem commodo implorarit, facile adsis. De Wessenbeccii negocio tu confeceris.[1806] Vale. 29. Iulii 1578. Viennae. Tuae magnificentiae totus deditus Sambucus.

Address: Magnifico et clarissimo viro domino Ioanni Cratoni a Craffthaim, caesareae maiestatis consiliario et physico, domino et amico colendissimo. Vratislaviam.

310.
Sambucus to Emperor Rudolf II
2 August 1578, Vienna

The original is kept in Vienna, ÖStA, Allgemeines Verwaltungs-, Finanz- und Hofkammerarchiv, Alte Hofkammer, Niederösterreichische Herrschaftsakten, W 61/A/1 [Karton 766], f. 42[r-v]. Published in Franz Kreyczi, "Urkunden und Regesten aus dem K. und K. Reichs-Finanz-Archiv," *Jahrbuch der kunsthistorischen Sammlungen des Allerhöchsten Kaiserhauses Wien* 15 (1894), x (Nr. 11578); Gerstinger, "Die Briefe," 241-242.

Sambucus adjoined 30 worthy manuscript books to the 500, already exposed for sale, leaving for himself nothing but some recent books needed for his future studies. Moreover, he added an admirable statue of Priapus and asked 3,000 ducats for all. However, 500 was taken off the price as the emperor's agents confirmed that the emperor could not offer more but did not doubt that

---

[1803] Gerstinger suspects a transcription error and proposes *tuam* instead of *suam*. See Gerstinger, "Die Briefe," 240-241.

[1804] This period in Crato's life is less well documented. We do not know to what Sambucus is referring here. According to Gillet (*Crato von Crafftheim*, 2:212), Crato was ordered to return to court in the autumn of 1577 but appeared there only in September 1578, after Rudolf fell badly sick, although his presence had also been apparently solicited before 1577.

[1805] Petrus Crapidel, otherwise unknown son of Johannes Crapidel († 1579), who had an ecclesiastical career in Silesia as a Lutheran deacon and minister. See Johann G. Knie, *Alphabetisch-statistisch-topographische Uebersicht der Dörfer, Flecken, Städte und andern Orte der Königl. Preuss. Provinz Schlesien* (Breslau: Grass, Barth & Comp., 1830), 55.

[1806] See letter 305.

Rudolf would grant him a honorarium by his singular grace. Accordingly, Sambucus applies for a honorarium of 500 ducats with respect to both the library sold, in which there are c. 60 codices containing texts which have never before been published, ready to be printed in the honour of the imperial library, and to the eighteen years of service, during which he never made such a request of Ferdinand I or Maximilian II. This would allow him to provide his family with a home and do his scholarly work more easily in his advanced age. He also asks Rudolf to make sure that those whom he is about to entrust with writing the contract act benevolently towards Sambucus. A scribal note on the back of the letter says that the inventory of the books was sent to Hugo Blotius.

Potentissime clementissimeque semper Imperator etc.

Non modo, quos antea quingentos Graece et Latine manu exaratos libros venales indicaram, sed insuper 30 non contemnendos adieci, ut praeter aliquot recentissimorum manus scripta ad usum meum et lucubrationes futuras, nil mihi reliqui fecerim. Praeterea admirandi artificii Priapeii statuam addidi, pro quibus omnibus 3000 aureos denarios petebam.[1807] Sed vestrae maiestatis respectu 500 dempserunt, se amplius nil promittere posse commissarii affirmantes, sese tamen nil dubitare vestram caesaream maiestatem ex gratia singulari honorarii minusculi loco concessuram. Quare, clementissime Caesar, cum bibliothecam scriptam manu amplam et raram, in qua ad 60 codices nondum typis editi magna bibliothecae dignitate imprimi poterunt, atque ego a decem et octo annis servitio humillimo aulae addictus nil profecto unquam nec ab sanctissimo avo Ferdinando I. nec pientissimo domino parente vestrae maiestatis tale petierim, quod boni noverim, supplico, oro vestra maiestas ultra pretium conclusum 500 aureos suo clientulo Sambuco imperet, uti ingravescenti aetati meisque de propria aliqua sede provideam, vigiliisque et scriptionibus institutis expeditius incumbam. Praeterea subiectissime oro, quibus vestra caesarea maiestas de syngrapha et cautione ad breve tempus curam mandarit, clementissime iubeat, mecum uti benigne transigant.[1808] Nil certe importune contendam et cuncta in vestrae maiestatis benigna gratia deponam, cuius mitibus me meaque submisse trado et vovi dudum. Viennae 2. Augusti 1578. Vestrae sacratissimae maiestatis subditissimus clientulus etc. Ioannes Sambucus.

Address: Ad sacratissimam imperialem maiestatem humillima Ioannis Sambuci supplicatio.
(*Other side:*) An die, Rö. Khay.
Secretary's hand: Das Inventarium dem Plotio zugeschickt.

311.
Sambucus to Fulvio Orsini
6 August 1578, [Vienna]

The original is kept in Rome, BAV, Vat. lat. 4104, f. 155ʳ. Published in Gerstinger, "Die Briefe," 242-244.

[1807] See letter 308.
[1808] Cf. with Rudolf II's answer summarised in letter 314, note 1827.

Fulvio Orsini should not give up hope concerning those fragments. Although there is a long debate with the heirs, Sambucus is hoping for a positive answer. He has not found the book on the familia Julia; he (would) pay double (for it), and he will write to Frankfurt. He is not working much, as he is busy with the history of Hungary and some explanation of the Habsburg House. As soon as he is ready, he will do what he has to. He has received fantastic medals from France, of Tiberius, Mark Antony (one of the triumvirs), Antinous, Alexander the Great with Bucephalus (i.e. his horse), Homer with the Trojan horse and Marcus Aurelius and Lucius Verus on horseback, which can still be seen in Piazza Campidoglio. He is missing some three dozen, but he doubts that they could be found in Italy. But there are few who delight in these things. Finally, he asks Orsini to share with him the results of his activity as scholar and antiquarian; and sends his greetings to Cardinal Sirleto. He is sending some epigrams taken from antique marbles, which he recently received from Dacia (i.e. Transylvania) and neighbouring lands. Orsini can use and copy them, or show them to Cardinal Sirleto, but he should send him back the original.

Magnifico Signor, Amico osservandissimo. Salutem.

Vostra Signoria non disperi de quelli fragmenti.[1809] La cosa va in lungo per amor della haeredità hercisconda[1810] et lo hèrede picciolo dell antigitade non vi é capace, ma in brev spetto ottima risposta. Lo libro de la famiglia Julia non trovamo, pagera il doppio ma scrivero à Francfort à posta.[1811] Io faccio puocho, essend'occupato delle historiolae nostrae et certa explicatione di casa d'Habspurg, come sarò spedito, farò il devere. Ho riceputo medaglie d'un luogo di Frantza miracolose, grand medaglione in rame de Tiberio, de Marco Antonio IIIviro, di Antinoi,[1812] Alexandri con Bucefalo, Homero con equo Troiano et altre triumphe di Marco Aurelio et Lucio Vero grande con essi cavalli triumphali, che si vedano in Campidoglio.[1813] Ho fin à tre donzine al manco, che dubito si vi si trovano in Italia. Ma sono puochi qui, chi si dilettano. Si Vostra Signoria lucubra qualche bella cosa, ò si vi fu trova qualche bell marmo, ò ricuperato qualche libro raro, faccia me Vostra Signoria à saper, mutuum praestabo. Vale, mi doctissime Ursine. 6. Augusti 1578.

Illustrissimo domino et patrono nostro communi, decori Collegii Romani, doctissimo cardinali Schirleto mille salutes et me subiecte illi commenda, oro. Tuus χρήσει καὶ κτήσει[1814] Sambucus. Ne nil mitterem per nostrum Diutalevium,[1815] accipe aliquot epigrammata e vetustissimis

---

[1809] See n. 6 below.
[1810] division of inheritance
[1811] See F. Ursinus, *Familiae Romanae quae reperiuntur in antiquis numismatibus* (Romae: impensis haeredum Francisci Tramezini, apud Iosephum de Angelis, 1577). See Nolhac, *La bibliothèque de Fulvio Orsini*, 42-43.
[1812] Antinous (c. 111–130) was the favourite or lover of Emperor Hadrian.
[1813] The golden painted bronze equestrian statue of Marcus Aurelius was standing in Piazza Campidoglio in the sixteenth century. Today, it is on display in the Capitoline Museums.
[1814] in usufruct and possession. Cf. Erasmus, *Adagia* 4026.
[1815] We do not know anything of Francesco Diotelevi, friend of Orsini. However, a letter by Diotelevi to Orsini, quoted in Gerstinger, "Die Briefe," 243, and written in Vienna on 27 December 1577 (BAV, Vat. lat. 4104, f. 156ʳ) helps to understand the context of the letter: "... con dirle che la sua fu gratissima al Signor Sambuco, al quale dispiace, non puoter compiacerla di quel pezzo di Tavola di bronzo, che lei desidera, per havuto prima che ne facesse parte a Vostra Signoria illustrissima del suo, dato al Signor Conte di Monteforte, il quale lo condusse in Augusta, et essendo morto, con havere lasciato un suo figliolo, che e in questa Corte cuppiero della Maiestate Caesarea; speramo insieme di fare si, che ne verrà compiacciuta, et id in particulare me valerò de quei mezzi, che giudicare piu à proposito et, si fara quanto sarà possibile; il dotto Signor Sambuco desidera un de greci libri di

marmoribus eruta et nuper partim e Dacia, partim viciniis nostris ad me missa. In quibus si quid est, utere, describe, sed idiographum hoc remitte et cum cardinale Schirleto, si ita censes, oro, communicato.

312.
Sambucus to Henri Estienne
15 August 1578, Vienna

The original is kept in Staats- und Universitätsbibliothek Bremen, msa 0008, no. 164.[1816]

Sambucus asked Camerarius to make sure that his 60 florins remaining in Geneva be given to Estienne. He responded that he was ready to help and that the money should be sent to the Frankfurt book fair. Of people who will go there, Sambucus only knows Jean Aubry, the book dealer of the court. As Aubry was away in Prague, he gave these 18 Portuguese gold pieces, which amount to 30 florins or 20 scudi, to Aubry's servant, who hurried to his master in Prague. So Estienne should accept now the half of what he promised, and as soon as Dioscorides starts (to be printed), he will get the rest. He took the risk of sending the money and pleads with Estienne not to postpone the edition any longer because of someone else's version. If Jean Sarasin does not hurry with what he promised or abandons his plan, Estienne should publish it with Jean Ruel's translation, which could be corrected in many places using his annotations. Opinions diverge concerning the translation and commentaries of Plato: some people would much prefer Ficino and consider this one (Sarasin) only a grammarian but not a philosopher: they say he is rhetorising and using childish scholasticisms. But they may not be saying the truth out of hostility toward Estienne and those who live there, as Italians and some people who are imbued with pathologically critical opinions usually do. Estienne, if he loves Sambucus, should go ahead with it (i.e. Dioscorides), and he should tell Sambucus when he is almost ready. Sambucus will send a short preface addressed to the greatest of patrons (i.e. Rudolf II). Crato was summoned by the emperor. If the Portuguese gold pieces prove deficient on the scales, it is because of the fraud of Italian merchants. Hungarians or

---

Vostra Signoria ill. la quale, si ben me raccordo, dissiemi in Roma d'haverlene inviato uno, che cosi li ho detto, però la prega di cola prima occasione farlene gratia d'uno, che li sarà gratissimo. Se in questo mentre me verrà alle mani qualche medaglia, non me scordaro punto de l'honorato suo desiderio, et essendosi prolongata questa dieta l'ongaria per six à mezzo febraro, non credere esser'di ritorno prima Pasqua, ma se in questo mentre le soverrà di comandirne cosa alla, lo faccia, se desidera favorir me."

[1816] This letter has been partly published by Melchior Goldast (see Gerstinger, "Die Briefe," 258-259), who cut together two of Sambucus's letters (cf. letter 339) in an arbitrary way, not caring about the large time gap between the two: "Ioannes Sambucus viro clarissimo Henrico Stephano εὖ διάγειν. Fasciculum ad me missum, quod indicium plenum amoris interpretor, accepi. Xenophontis editio ita valde mihi accepta venit, nil ut cupidius exspectarim. Zosimi mutua sunt et suis partibus mutila, graviter affecta plurima. Sed quid agas? Melioribus id malum scriptoribus evenit. Graecum sperabam fore integrius totque locis minus ad sanitatem impeditum. Nil editionem Dioscoridio moretur, oro, cuiusquam nova versio. Mitto tibi ἐπίμετρον non contemnendum. Si Saracenus pollicita non urget aut deseruit, adde Ruellii interpretationem quam meae observationes meliorem multis partibus efficient. De Platone variae voces eiusque versione et scholiis. Sunt qui, si non falluntur iudicio, Ficinum longo praeferant et Saracenum hunc grammaticum tantum non philosophum aiant, rhetorizare et παιδαριωδῶς scholastica interim adhibere. Sed fortasse odio tui et qui istic degitis, uti solent Itali et quidam carpendi morbo suffusi οὐκ ἀληθῶς pronunciare. Egi cum Episcopio de meo Aristotele imprimendo. Sed is tergiversatur. Alloquitur eum sodes, forte persuadebis. Palladii ἀπόσπασμα in VI Ἐπιδημιῶν meum edidit Perna ex interpretatione Crassi, utinam tibi comisissem. Ἔρρωσο atque Saracenum virum clarissimum et magnum ἰατρὸν a me saluta, quem omni praeconio dignum censeo. III. Kalendas Maii, anno 1581. Viennae." *Philologicarum epistolarum centuria una*, 313 (nr. 74).

Italians do not use trick weights. He will compensate Estienne the next time. He wrote to Eusebius Episcopius that he should publish Aristotle together with Estienne, using Estienne's types. Estienne should speak to him, he might be able to persuade him.

Εὖ διάγειν.[1817]

Dederam negocium exorato a me Camerario, uti per aliquem istic ad 60 florenos manentes Genevae tibi meos reddendos procuraret.[1818] Is uti est officiosus et factus ad commoda amicorum respondit, rectissime me facturum, si Francofortum tibi ipse ad mercatum mittam. Ego hinc praeter bibliopolam Aubri nostrum, qui istuc proficisceretur, neminem novi, eoque ipso Pragae absente, hosce 18 portugalenses, qui 30 florenorum sint, seu 20 scutatorum, commisi famulo eius, uti hero suo Pragam statim curreret. Accipies igitur dimidium mei promissi, ubi Dioscoridem incoharis, reliquum accepturus citra ullam haesitationem. Nam et hoc meo periculo misi. Nil editionem moretur, oro, cuiusquam nova versio, si Saracenus pollicita non urget aut deseruit,[1819] adde Ruellii interpretationem, quam meae observationes meliores multis partibus efficient.

De Platone variae voces, eiusque versione et scholiis.[1820] Sunt qui, si non falluntur iudicio, Ficinum longe praeferant, et hunc gramaticum tantum, non philosophum aiant, rhetorizare et παιδαριωδῶς[1821] scholastica interim adhibere. Sed fortasse odio tui et qui istic degitis, uti solent Itali, et quidam carpendi morbo suffusi οὐκ ἀληθῶς[1822] pronunciant. Omnino, si me amas, rem aggreditor. Ubi fere absolveris, fac sciam. Praefatiunculam ipse mittam brevem ad patronum summum, cui plurimum omnes debent. Ἔρρωσο.[1823] Crato a caesare Pragam est accitus. Aurei isti portugalenses, si ad libellam non responderint, mercatoris Itali fraude accidit. Nam nec Pannonicos, nec Gallicos repereris, quod probitati cumque ponderis deerit. Proxime compensabo. 15. Augusti Vienna 1578. Tuus Sambucus.

* Scripsi Episcopio de Aristotelea editione, ut tecum communicet et a vobis edatur typis tuis. Alloquitor eum, oro, forte persuadebis.

Address: Domino Henrico Stephano viro clarissimo et typographo celebri, amico optimo. Francforti, cum ducatis portugalensibus xviii.

313.
Sambucus to Nicolaus Reusner
23 August 1578, Vienna

Published in Nicolaus Reusner, *Emblemata partim ethica et physica, partim vero historica et hieroglyphica* (Frankfurt am Main: Feyerabend, 1581), 356-357.

[1817] Live well.
[1818] Initially, Sambucus asked for an honorarium of 300 florins. Cf. letter 163.
[1819] See letter 299.
[1820] *Platonis Opera* (as in letter 306, note 1790). There are no references to Sambucus's assistance in the book.
[1821] childishly
[1822] not truely
[1823] farewell

Sambucus is happy for Reusner's excelling in all disciplines and for the consequent broad and large knowledge he has. Reusner can judge best of all what one can expect from the advanced age, or rather what anyone should expect from an outstanding talent, as he has extensively dealt with this argument. Reusner may think he is exaggerating, but he should make sure to deserve such praise. Occupied by dense and slow historical work and by correcting the works of others, he cannot enjoy a respite with Reusner's muses. Even if he had the time, he knows his limits and that he has been out of practice for many years. However, as soon as the editions of Aristotle, Dioscorides and some minor works, which he restored with so much night work, appear, he will try better. Reusner should carry on with his projects, and if he might complain about rewards and patrons, he should think of posterity. If Sambucus may help Reusner in his work, he should speak out.

Ioannes Sambucus Nicolao Reusnero S. P. D.

Te ad omne genus scientiarum atque eruditionis excellere laetor, unde scio varietatem istam copiosam manare, in qua τὸ εἰλικρινὲς καὶ ὥσπερ ἐνσώματον δεινὸν[1824] valde probo. Quid affectior aetas, quam diuturnam et vegetam opto, datura sit, vel melius, quid quisque a praestantis ingenii vi exposcere debeat, tute omnium optime, qui tam ample et luculente argumentum, quid quisque sit aut valeat, cognoscendi tractaris, aestimare potes. Scio, qui tuus pudor est ac modestia (ἵνα γὰρ δέος, ἔνθα καὶ αἰδὼς, κατὰ τὸ Στασίμου[1825] in *Euthyphrone*), gratia et amore liberalius me effusum diceres, si te non immerentem coloribus attingerem. Ego spisso ac lento historiarum opere distentus, quibusdam etiam alienis sanandis et ab tineis liberandis occupatus ad amoenitates istas tuas Musarum hortorumque respirare nequeo. Et si tantum ocii impetrarem, agnosco vires et exercitationem longo intermissam intervallo. Ubi tamen Aristotelis et Dioscoridis opera, tot vigiliis meis nonnihil restituta, cum aliquot aliis minorum vigiliarum opusculis, e tenebris claustrisque librariorum expedita fuerint, quam etiam valeo, amplius tentabo. Tu vero, mi praestantissime Reusnere, ab instituto nullis te impedimentis aut divortiis splendidis dimoveri patiere. Si forte gratiam laboribus et patrocinium angustius lucubrationibus propositum querere, posteritatem intuitor, cuius opinione, et memoria omnes laborum fructus exaequari nitique videmus. Si quid Sambuci opella in tuis effecerit, nil reticeto. Vale. Raptim. X. Calendis Septembris MDLXXIIX. Vienna.

314.
Sambucus to the Imperial Chamber
30 August 1578, Vienna

Vienna, ÖStA, FHKA, Alte Hofkammer, Niederösterreichische Herrschaftsakten, W 61/A/1 [Wien, Hof, Bibliothek 1576-1744; Rote Nr. 269/1 Karton 766, f. 40ʳ, 41ᵛ.] Published by Manfred Staudinger at http://rudolphina.com/Regesten/A1578-08-30-00198.xml (accessed on 27 September 2022).

By August, six and half years had passed during which Sambucus did not receive a penny of his small yearly salary of 300 thalers, and this had brought him detriment and debts. His brother-

---

[1824] the pure and so to speak corporeal strength
[1825] for where fear is, there is also reverence, according to the saying of Stasimos. Cf. Plato, *Euthyphro* 12B.

in-law had helped him out (advancing the salary) two years earlier, for which he obtained a certificate of 1,200 florins from the emperor, which remained unsettled, proven also by the attached document. Either they pay his brother-in-law or his brother-in-law rightfully arrests him. Since then, his salary had grown, but despite his repeated petitions, he never got anything and needed to go into debt, which are now higher than 1,000 florins. So he asks for the payment of his pending salary of 1,675 thalers at the latest in three months or a half year. He has given Mr Clee (Khlee) the right to collect the money.

Gnadige, Grosginstig Herren etc.

Es ist nun disen Augusts Monatt Sechthalben Jhar, das ich an meiner geringer besoldung, so per ein Jhar 300 taller zu 68 kr thuett nie khain Haller empfangen hab: mitt meinem schaden, unnd merkhlicher nott, und schulden. Es hatt mich mein Schwager Jacob Egrer woll etwas vertröst gehabt, ehr wolt mich niht lassen, auff welches zuesagung mir vor zwayen Jharen auff 1020 fl. ein gfertigter schain von Irer Khayserlichen Maiestät ervolgt:[1826] hab aber dernach nichti ausgericht, wie dan ich hiermitt den khayserlichen schain unvergruffen yberandtwortt. Und meer ein ding: mein Schwagern zuvergniegen oder das man mirs zugehalten hatt, und richtig mitt dem Rest mache.

Es ist die Somma woll etwas gewachsen, ist mir aber laidt, dan ich auff anzellichs anhalten und gelieferte Supplication nie etwas erhalten, hab darneben mein armutt, und parschafft die sechthalb Jhare müssen verzern, und schulden machen, mheer [...] die Creditoren, als 1000 fl.

Derhalben mein ghor ghorsams, notturfftigs, und vertreulichs Suppliciren: Euer gnaden wöllen mir solchen ausstannd als 1675 taller zu 68 kr lassen machen betzollen: da es aber yetzo khain andre gelegenhaitt gebe: damit ich doch meine glaubiger vertröst, und mein notturfft weytter vergwisse, an den Hern Clee ain furderlichen bevelch ervolgen lasse, der von andern etwa vorfallenden an Ihn bevelchen unverhindert sey: das er mir solchen ausstand (dan ich mitt wenigern ghor nichtij wurdt ausrichten, und weer in grösser nott, als zuvor) die nachst gelegenhaitt, oder aber auffs längst in Einer Cotember, oder unverzogen in einen halben Jhar richtig mache.

Daran werden Euer gnaden die pillikhaitt handln, auch gwiss Ir Maiestät khain misgefallen thuen: und an mir soll es nicht versaumbt werden, das ichs gegen Ir Khayserlichen Maiestät, auch umb die fürderung gegen Euer gnaden gehorsamlich verdienen will. Thuend mich dienstlich bevelchen, den 30. august 1578.[1827] Euer gnaden ghorsamer d[iener] allzeit. Johann Sambucus.

[1826] See on Sambucus's pending salary Almási, *The Uses of Humanism*, 192-195.

[1827] The letter was followed by a summary of Sambucus's petition addressed to the councillors of the Imperial Chamber from Vienna on 4 September (ÖStA, FHKA, Alte Hofkammer, Hoffinanz Österreich, Band 346-R [1578], f. 90ʳ); the summary and receipt of the latter in Prague on 11 Sept. (ibid., Band 339-E [1578], f. 416ʳ); a memorandum of Sambucus's petition concerning the payment of his books in Prague by Georg Zippringer (ibid. f. 418ᵛ); and a decision by Rudolf II sent from Prague to Archduke Ernst on 19 September, signed by Rudolf and Zippringer (ÖStA, FHKA, Alte Hofkammer, Niederösterreichische Herrschaftsakten, W 61/A/1 [Karton 766], f. 36-37). In this letter (transcribed by Manfred Staudinger at http://rudolphina.com/Regesten/A1578-09-19-00905.xml) Rudolf orders Ernst to get Sambucus paid from the thirtieth tax ("harmincadvám"), collected in Mossonmagyaróvár ("auf dem Oberdreissigist Hungerischen Altenburg," cf. letter 328). Ernst should pay the purchase money of 2500 ducats, plus 50 ducats for Sambucus's wife as a tip (*arra*) and take over the books and inventory and give them over to Hugo Blotius. Ernst should also prepare a single certificate of the imperial debt to be paid from the thirtieth tax to Sambucus, which should also include the pending salary of 1020 gulden, which Sambucus had given over to Jakob Egerer but which has still not been paid. Ernst should

Address: An die Römisch Khayserlichen Majestät etc. Herrn HoffCamer Rätt, alhie nachgelassen diemutigen Supplication Joan. Sambuci 30. August 1578. Mitt einen khayserlichen schain von 1020 fl.
Secretary's comment: Den Herr Presidenten und Camer Räthen einzuschliessen 2. Septemb 78.

315.
Sambucus to Johannes Crato
31 August 1578, [Vienna]

Published in Gerstinger, "Die Briefe," 244-245.

Sambucus understood Crato's response to his question and his intentions. He is much thinking about (the qualities of thermal) water. It helps many but can hurt, as Crato claims, in old age, so he would use it moderately. Sambucus has a low opinion of those doctors of great families and kings, with whom the schools of the barbarians are full. They are vauntful and hollow in their long sleeves and birettas. Sambucus wishes that men became newly aware of their bodies, the place, and air, and considered not what India, Egypt or Ethiopia but what our lands demand. He wrote this letter quickly, afraid that Crato would leave his home.
Salutem.

De quaesitis quid sentias fierique rite velis, intellexi. De aquis nonnihil haereo, quarum usum non paucis profuisse audio, licet, quod praenuncias, denique sub affectam aetatem non parum laesi fuerint. Moderabor his et aliis caute σὺν θεῷ.[1828] Pro beneficio ἀντικατάλλαξιν,[1829] dum re emetior, polliceor. De medicis illis maiorum gentium et regiis, nam barbarorum scholae plenae regibus sunt, suum praeferentes, ne aliquando in praecipuum periculum erumpant, videritis. Tumidi sunt et inanes, manicis suis et byretis insignes.[1830] Ubi cum nemini conveniunt, triumphos ducunt. Utinam aliquando resipiscamus nostraque corpora, loca et aerem observemus, ne, quid India et Aegyptus aut Aethiopes, sed nostrae regio nos exposcant, cogitemus. Haec ad tuas raptim, quod te domum discessurum verebar.[1831] Vale. Pridie Kalendas Septembris 1578. Tuae magnificentiae totus Sambucus.

Address: Clarissimo viro domino doctori Ioanni Cratoni a Craffthaim, caesareae maiestatis consiliario et medico, domino et amico observandissimo. Prag. Herrn Doctor Cratoni.

---

establish real deadlines for the payment. Concerning Sambucus's petition for an extra 500 ducats (see letter 310), Ernst should gently deny it, as Sambucus is fortunate enough to have found a buyer for his books sold for such high price: "So achten wir gleichwol darfur, Er muge mit obsteender mit Ime verglichner khauffsuma wol zufriden sein, In bedenckhung das Er nit so paldt ainen funden hoben wurde, der beruerte Püecher von Ime vmb eine so hohe suma angenomben hette, Gesinnen derholber ferner an E. L. freundlich vnd gnediglich, Sy wöllen Ine dauon mit glimpfen abweisen lassen."

[1828] with god's help
[1829] profit, return
[1830] This is very probably a reference to the doctors around Rudolf II, among whom there was still Rembertus Dodonaeus, and probably some doctors of the University of Vienna (see Gerstinger, "Die Briefe," 245).
[1831] Crato went to Prague after 20 of June. See Gillet, *Crato von Craffheim*, 2:208.

316.
Sambucus to Hartmann II von Liechtenstein[1832]
17 September 1578, [Vienna]

The original is kept in Munich, BSB, Clm 10367, Nr. 181.

On the basis of the two documents, Sambucus sees little hope. The missives state that both women are poor widows who must sustain a big retinue and also recently had to send troops to the frontier at their own expense without knowing how long it will last. Lady of Landsee/Lánzsér (widow of Miklós Oláhcsászár, Anna Frangepán) writes that she is owed much. Sambucus knows someone holding 4,000 talers and another one or two holding 7,000 talers. For this reason, Sambucus can provide no comfort. Everyone cries that the times are dangerous and that the Turks will not keep the peace. The ladies keep several secretaries who advise them, and they do everything according to their secretaries' will.

Wolgeborner g[estrenger] g[nädiger] Herr et cetera.

Auss bayden schreiben verstee ich wenig hoffnung: dan das promemoria ist, dz sie arme wittiben beyde sein: vill gesindt mussen halten, auch Neulich etlich fuessvolkh auff iren unkhosten haben mussen auff granitzn schikhen, vnd wissen nicht wie lang es werrn soll. Dernach schreibt die fraue v[on] landsee, das man Ihr hin und wider vill schuldig ist, nicht ein schon. Ich Wayß selbst ein Tutorem von 4000 tallern und andren, oder zween bey 7000 tallern ...ig [?] et cetera. Derhalben, Gnädiger Herr Weyß ich hirrin E[euer] g[naden] khain sonderliche verströstung thuen: Schreyen alle, die Zeytt sey geforlich, der Thurkh Wirr disen frid also nicht halten et cetera. So haben gnedige herr solche Frauen etliche deakhe, oder schreyber die ire Ratt sein, unnd walten alles irem gefallen nach. Thund mich E[uer] g[naden] dinstlich bevolchen. Den 17. Septembris 1578. E[uer] g[naden] gehorsamer d[iener] J. Sambucus

Address: Illustri baroni domino domino Hartmanno a Liechtenstain et cetera, domino patrono singulari.
Another hand: Von Herrn D. Sambuco.
Another hand: Bei den Laugben zum vrissten zuebehalten.
Another hand: Februarius [!] 1578.

317.
Sambucus to Theodor Zwinger
18 October 1578, Vienna

The original is kept in Basel, Universitätsbibliothek, Frey Mscr II 26, no. 224. Published in Gerstinger, "Die Briefe," 245-246.

[1832] Baron Hartmann II von Liechtenstein-Feldsberg (1544–1585) was an imperial councillor of Protestant persuasion. As an art and book collector, he laid the foundation of the famous Liechtenstein collections. His sons later converted to Catholicism, distinguished themselves in service to the Habsburgs and were elevated to princely status. See Thomas Winkelbauer, *Fürst und Fürstendiener: Gundaker von Liechtenstein, ein österreichischer Aristokrat des konfessionellen Zeitalters* (Vienna: Böhlau 1999), 53–55.

Learned men are waiting for Zwinger's Hippocrates-edition. Sambucus wonders why Zwinger is excusing himself with reference to Claude Aubery, being more competent in the field of medicine than Aubery, as he himself writes. He asks him to warn Johannes Löwenklau of his duties undertaken in Vienna. He is surprised about the change of idea in relation to the edition of Aristotle, but they should do as they please. If he meets them, Zwinger should urge them. He asks Zwinger to forward a letter to Dasypodius, who speaks more than acts and does not send him his codices.

Ioannes Sambucus salutem.

Hippocratis editionem[1833] scis exspectari ab eruditis.[1834] Quod obducis Aubri impedimenta, miror, quasi vero non Aubrum praestiteris, qui in tractanda medicina magister es, perinde scribis. Oro te, Leonclaium, si occurrerit, moneas officii et debiti Viennensis. De Aristoteleo consilium varium miror. Faciant, quod libuerit.[1835] Ubi in eos incideris, adhuc urge reipublicae nomine. Te tuosque salvere et optime habere cupio. Has ad Dasypodium mittito,[1836] qui quo plus verborum, hoc minus rei praestat. Meos codices non remittit. 18. Octobris 1578. Viennae.

318.
Sambucus to Archduke Ernst
16 November 1578, [Vienna]

The original is kept in Vienna, ÖStA, FHKA, Alte Hofkammer, Hoffinanz Ungarn, r. Nr. 38, Konv. 1578. XI., f. 113.[1837]

Sambucus presented Ernst's letter to the Hungarian Chamber in Pressburg concerning the pending payment of his meager salary, but they keep postponing it with petty excuses. So Sambucus asks Ernst again to warn the Hungarian Chamber not to let Sambucus down but to pay his due salary in the established time and measure, as they used to do, by 1 January without finding all those excuses.

Serenissime atque Illustrissime Princeps, domine, domine mihi semper clementissime etc.

Obtuli camerae Posonium vestrae serenitatis mandatum de provisiuncula reliqua mihi numeranda et posthac angariatim eadem pro rata portione ad usque quotidiana necessaria exigenda. Sed nescio quibus exceptiunculis rem differunt, magna rei domesticae meae iniuria et difficultate. Quare denuo humillime supplico, vestra serenitas eidem camerae serio iungat [?], ne me pollicitis ductent affligantque, sed proprio quoque tempore, rationibus putatis satisfaciant, et ut antea solitum erat, a Kalendis Ianuariis incohando, angariatim

---

[1833] Zwinger's marginal note: "medici".
[1834] Hippocrates, *Viginti duo commentarii* came out in 1579 with Perna. On Sambucus's efforts and Zwinger's edition cf. "Hippocrates-edition (planned)" under "Sambucus" in the Index and see Gerstinger, "Zusammenfassung," 307-309; Siraisi, *History, Medicine*, 337.
[1835] See the Index under "Sambucus".
[1836] Zwinger's marginal note: "taxat." See letters 295, 298 and 300.
[1837] We thank István Fazekas for finding and preparing a copy of this letter. Sambucus's petition resulted in a new mandate of the Imperial Chamber sent to Hungarian Chamber on the same day, ordering it to pay his pending salary: ÖStA, FHKA, Alte Hofkammer, Hoffinanz Ungarn, Band 346-R [1578], f. 160ʳ.

omnibus modis, quod debetur, adnumerari curet, sine tot caussis et exceptiunculis obiectis, quo mea studia munusque felicius, citra talia impedimenta, porro sint libera expeditaque. Quam gratiam serenitatis vestrae perpetuis servitiis promereri conabor, me humillime subiiciens favori et clementiae vestrae serenitatis. 16. Novembris 1578. Vestrae serenitatis actque illustritatis subiectissimus cliens etc. Ioannes Sambucus etc.

Address: Ad serenissimum illustrisimumque archiducem Ernestum etc., dominum, dominum meum semper clementissimum, Ioanni Sambuci supplicatiuncula de mandato iterum ad cameram Posoniensem expediendo etc.
Camerae Ungariae iniungat, ut ei satisfaciat. 16. Novembris 1578.
Scribal note: Joannes Sambucus pro ausständige Provision. November 1578.

319.
Sambucus to Johannes Crato
19 December 1578, [Vienna]

The original is kept in Wrocław, Stadtbibliothek, Cod. Rehdiger. 248 (Klose 166), Nr. 88. Published in Gerstinger, "Die Briefe," 246-247.

The wedding of Harrach's son was probably as magnificent in Vienna as (it was) in Prague. Archduke Ernst stays in bed because of pains in the leg and the tibia. In Styria the Habsburg army is left in peace, but one worries for the mountain areas (the northern cities), against which the pasha of Buda openly makes preparations. The tax to the Ottomans was sent with a cortege of young men the day before. Crato must have seen Leonhard Krenzheim's chronological conjectures. They are not altogether bad although they incite superstition. Sambucus sent Reusner's package to Crato. Reusner is a very diligent author, but he is liable to please the general public with an easy style. If Crato has attained something for the jurisconsult (Matthias Wesenbeck), he is glad, these people merit much greater things. He has heard that the doctors are still hesitating (about Rudolf's cure), and is sorry that Crato must stay (in Prague) until the 24th of December despite his bad health. There are less news from the Low Countries than from India. The rumours about the heavy losses for Austrians have petered out. Finally he asks Crato to warn Wolfgang Rumpf to mediate, as he promised, with Rudolf in the issue of his request.

Salutem.

Harrachii filii nuptiae die solis hic celebratae sunt non minori celebritate ludorumque spectaculis, quam fortasse apud vos[1838]. Serenissimus Ernestus ob pedem tibiasque offensas in cubiculo se attinet, ut cum Tacito loquar.[1839] In Styria adhuc secura nostroque progressu

---

[1838] This was the second wedding of Leonhard (V) Harrach (1542–1597) (to Anna von Ortenburg-Salamanca († 1602). He he had twelve children from his first marriage. Harrach was secret councillor, chamberlain, marshal of the hall to Archdukes Matthias and Ernst, chairman of the government (*Landeshauptmann*) of Austria. He was the son of the influential imperial marshal, Leonhard (IV) Harrach. Like his father, he studied law in Italy. See Matschinegg, *Österreicher als Universitätsbesucher in Italian*, 404.
[1839] No similar phrase is found in Tacitus. Gerstinger suggests *Annales* 14.4: "cubiculi fores recluderet."

actum.[1840] Sed metuimus montanis locis, quibus aperte Budensis insidiatur. Honorarium heri dimisimus comitatu iuventutis decoro. Credo vestram magnificentiam vidisse coniecturas chronologicas Krenzhemii.[1841] Acumen habent nec synicesis haec omnino nil valet, nisi ad superstitionem vocaris. Fasciculum ad te miseram Reusneri, quem valde in scribendo officiosum et impigrum video. Ingenio tamen praestare ad varietatem videtur, ad numeros facilis, ad stylum, qui vulgo placeat etc.[1842] Si in magni iuris consulti libello quid impetrasti, laetor, longe maiora ultro talibus offerenda essent.[1843] Medicos adhuc istic haesitare audio, forte famelici sunt. Te ad Kalendas IX[1844] detentum iri molestiasque obiectari praeter commodum valetudinis satis adflictae doleo. Ex Belgio minus quam ex Indiis auditur. Rumusculi de accisis Austriis etc. evanuere. Ἔρρωσο.[1845] 19. Decembris 1578. Tuae magnificentiae deditus Sambucus.

Magnifico domino et veteri patrono Rumpfio salutem et servitia. Si occasio venerit, suppliciter mone, Sambuci precum ad caesarem uti diligenter meminerit, uti est pollicitus.

Address: Magnifico et clarissimo viro, domino domino Ioanni Cratoni a Craffthaim etc., consiliario et archiatro imperatoris, domino et fautori amicoque observando. Breslae. Hern Doctor Cratoni.

320.
Sambucus to Joachim Camerarius Jr.
22 December 1578, Vienna

The original is kept in Munich, BSB, Clm 10367, Nr. 183.

Sambucus was away from Vienna for some days due to lawsuits concerning his father's legacy. Camerarius should therefore not consider his silence to be the end of the friendship. Clusius, who is being cheated out of his salary, will stay with Sambucus until Easter. Blessed is Camerarius, who being far from the court can truly possess and enjoy what he has. Sambucus inquires what is happening with the book on the unicorn translated by Camerarius and with the collection of Greek letters. One lives with no or with too little religion. Many see the fault in the disunity of the potentates. May God help, or may he come as soon as possible. He extends greetings to Julius Geuder. He will talk with Clusius and others concerning the exotic seeds in order for Camerarius to get some soon.

[1840] See letter 308, note 1801.
[1841] Leonhard Krenzheim (1532–1598) was a Protestant theologian and priest from Silesia. Educated in Wittenberg he made an ecclesiastical career in Leignitz. His major scientific contribution was his *Chronologia. Das ist Gründtliche und Fleissige Jahrrechnung ... aus heiliger Göttlicher Schrifft und andern glaubwirdigen und bewerten Historien, so wol aus dem Calculo Astronomico genommen, und treulich zusammen gezogen* (Görlitz: Ambrosius Fritsch, 1577). See the article by Adolf Schimmelpfennig in *ADB* 17 (1883), 125-128.
[1842] Cf. Sambucus's praise of Reusner in letter 313.
[1843] See letters 305 and 309.
[1844] I.e. ante diem IX Kalendas Ianuarii.
[1845] farewell

Salutem.

Abfui ab urbe per multos dies ac litibus paternis conflictatus aliquandiu necdum constitutis, nuper redii. Silentium igitur accipias non cessatione aut neglecta amicitia incidisse, sed causis iustis. Clusius ad Pascha usque nobiscum ha[e]rebit, vix dici potest, quam inique tractetur suoque salario hactenus fraudetur. Beatos et vos felices, qui procul a splendore vano aulae, quod datur vare possidetis, et cum velitis, fruimini. Quid de unicornu libello[1846] abs te translato et, ut spero, utiliter illustrato fiat, quae praeterea spes epistolarum Graecarum superfit, fac sciam. Religione nulla, aut perexigua vivimus. Multi culpam in Barones discidiis optionum varios transferunt. Deus his meliora, aut veniat quam primum. Magnifico domino Gaudero salutem. De seminibus exoticis communicabo cum Clusio et aliis, ut quiddam tempore accipiatis. Vale 22. Decembris 78. Raptim. Totus tuus Sambucus.

Address: Clarissimo dominio, D. Reipublicae Norbergensis archiphysico et cetera, domino amico singulari. Nurmberg.
Camerarius's note: 1579[1847] 8. Ianuarii.

321.
Piero Vettori to Sambucus
28 January 1579, Florence

The original is kept in Munich, BSB, Clm 791, f. 287^v. A copy is kept in ibid., f. 240^{r-v}. Published in Várady, "Relazioni di Giovanni Zsámboky," 44.

Vettori is recommending one of his former students of great talent, who won fame with his legal studies and taught for several years in Pisa. As a former student of Vettori, he loved the Latin language (which is disdained by other legal professionals in Italy) so much that he studied the ancient jurists and made a name with it. Since he would happily move to Germany if he found a good position, namely at the "gymnasium," Vettori asks Sambucus to support him in his goal. He is a Florentine of a good family, but what matters more: he is a good man of perfect manners.

Ioanni Sambuco.

Vetus quidam auditor meus, quem semper dilexi, ut magni ingenii adolescentem studiosumque optimarum artium, totum se postea dedit cognitioni legum, qua in doctrina multum profecit laudemque eo[1848] studio non parvam consecutus est. Is postea voluit alios, quae didicerat, docere curavitque, ut in Pisano nobili gymnasio ipsam publice profiteretur, quam personam egregie plures annos substituit. Cum tamen, ut a me olim institutus et eruditus, valde amet Latinum sermonem, quem spernunt fere ceteri apud nos, qui munus id

---

[1846] In 1597, Camerarius wrote to Abraham Ortelius that he was still working hard on the book about the unicorn, to the extent that his other occupations and his age allowed, but that the end was not yet in sight. *Abrahami Ortelii*, 716. Camerarius never finished this work. See Melchior Adam, *Vitae Germanorum medicorum* (Heidelberg: Haeredes Ionae Rosae, 1620), 157.
[1847] corr. from *1578*
[1848] *ex eo*, added by the copy on 240^r

obeunt, scriptaque antiquorum iurisconsultorum diligenter legerit,[1849] qua ratio iuris civilis fideliter percipiendi, praeter quam quod est elegans et polito homine digna, probatur hodie plurimum nostris hominibus. Is igitur si condicionem aliquam honestam apud Germanos[1850] inveniret, praesertim in gymnasio, libenter se in istam terram conferret. Rogo igitur te, mei amantissimum, ut suscipias curam aliquam de hac re, et videas si satisfacere possis desiderio ipsius ac meo. Polliceor tibi te ex hac opera tua, si negotium confeceris, laudem non parvam adepturum. Est autem (quod tibi vehementer commendo) civis meus ex honesto loco natus, inprimisque vir probus et optimis moribus praeditus. Vale, V. Kalendas Februarii 1579.

322.
Sambucus to Joachim Camerarius Jr.
31 January 1579, [Mannersdorf]

The original is kept in Munich, BSB, Clm 10367, Nr. 184.

Perna's letter was wandering around for some time and yesterday Crato finally brought it. Perna seeks advice concerning the preface to his Greek edition of Plotinus, which he does not want to publish without it having the proper appearance. In short, three years ago, Sambucus made many emendations to the text. He admires Plotinus almost as much as Plato and considers him to be the interpreter of the Stoics. He has spent many hours collating the passages and has passed this on to Jakob Schegk and others. He knows not which parts they accepted or rejected, but he guesses that they must not have disliked it entirely, as the edition is forthcoming. So the decision has been made for him, even if he will get little thanks for his labours. Others will see it and posterity will reward him. Camerarius should make a decision about the poems, which those people seem to have cut out without being asked. He asks Camerarius to ensure that Perna gets the letter, so that he can, as far as Sambucus is concerned, dedicate the edition to whomever he wants. It is important that Perna get this before the fair, so that he does not publish the book without a preface and a patron. If Camerarius would like to add an epigram to the edition, he would do Sambucus a favour. Sambucus has also stated his view on Aristotle in few words. He again implores Camerarius to get the letter to Perna before the next fair.

Salutem.

Oberrarunt aliquandiu literae P. Pernae nostri typographi, ac denique per Cratonem heri ad me venere. Petit consilium a me de praefatione Plotino Graeco addenda, quem exscribendum typis suscepit nec ἀμετατωπᾶ[1851] exire velit.[1852] Quid sentiam brevissime declaro. Ante enim triennium quaedam adspersi locis aegris nec bene sanis Plotino Graeco, quem ego philosophum secundum Platonem magni facio et internuncium Stoicorum arbitror. Graeca nondum visa cum aliis eiusdem originali contuli, non paucae horae, haud pauca praestarunt, quae et cum Schekio[1853] et aliis iussi communicanda. Quid laudarint reiecerintve ignoro, tantum divino,

---
[1849] *tracta*, deleted by Vettori
[1850] *vos*, deleted by Vettori
[1851] probably a lapsus calami for ἀμέτωπα, faceless
[1852] See letter 282, note 1647.
[1853] Tübingen professor, physician and philosopher Jakob Schegk (1511–1587) was among the scholars most interested

quia editur, non omnino displicuisse. Iacta ista quoque sit alea Sambuco, licet exiguam his laboribus gratiam adhuc relatam sentiam: Sentient alii, compensent posteri. De carminibus, quae excidisse non exorati videntur, statuetis vestro arbitrio. Has te, mi optime Camerarie, oro tuto candideque via uti curato, ut bonus typographus ad has nundinas Plotinum suo voto, cui volet, dicet, idque ipsi per me integrum fore intelligat. Facies mihi rem gratissimam. Modo ante nundinas habeat, ne dubius ἀκέφαλον καὶ ἄνευ προστατείας[1854] reddet. Si epigrammatio τὸ πρόσωπον[1855] ornare volueris, gratum feceris.[1856] De Aristotele quoque paucis mentem meam persc[r]ipsi. Vale mi carissime Camerarie. Pridie Kalendas Februarii 79. Totus tuus Sambucus.

Oro, obsecro, ad Pernam has meas ante nondinas proximas [?].

Address: Dem Edlen hochgelerten herrn Joachimo Camerario, der Ertznay doctor et cetera, meinem lieben gunstig Herr vnd fröndt Zu handen. Nurnberg. Cito cito.
Camerarius's note: 79 10 Februarii.

323.
Sambucus to Johannes Crato
31 January 1579, [Mannersdorf]

Published in Gerstinger, "Die Briefe," 247-248.

When Sambucus received Crato's letter the day before, he summed up what he thought of Perna's Greek edition of Plotinus. He wonders who might find fault with Crato, so busy with his duties. Sambucus remained in his estate, thingking about how things in the city are going to turn out and change by all those edicts. If it were not illicit to divine, he would confirm that he had felt something in advance. Concerning the Saxon jurist (Matthias Wesenbeck) he is surprised to see that so many works did not get any recognition. He knows the aptitude of both, and wishes that they would both be deprived of their manger. Giovanni Michele Bruto came to Vienna to see his married daughter with the permission of his prince (Stephen Báthory). Sambucus met him only once, as he avoids greater intimacy because of "mores et tempora." He is saying hello to Crato's son. Finally, he asks Crato to forward his letter either by the captain of the cavalry or via Lazarus Schwendi or through Strasburg to Pietro Perna, as he would not like him to remain in doubt about the preface to Plotinus and postpone its edition.

---

in Plotinus. He had been given the Greek manuscript of Plotinus saved from the Bibliotheca Corviniana as a present by Ferdinand I (now Munich, BSB, Cod. graec. 449). On Schegk's ownership of this manuscript see Kerstin Hajdú, "Mit glücklicher Hand errettet? Zur Provenienzgeschichte der griechischen Corvinen in München," in *Ex Bibliotheca Corviniana. Die acht Münchener Handschriften aus dem Besitz von König Matthias Corvinus*, eds. Claudia Fabian and Edina Zsupán (Budapest: OSZK–BSB, 2008), 29–67. It is unclear what role Schegk and the other unnamed recipients of Sambucus's emendations played in the events leading up to Perna's edition. In his autobibliography (*Catalogus librorum*, 8), Sambucus counts himself as the first editor of the Greek text of Plotinus.

[1854] headless and without patronage
[1855] face
[1856] No poems were included as paratexts in Perna's edition.

Magnifico et clarissimo viro domino doctori Ioanni Cratoni a Craffthaim, Sambucus salutem.

Quid de consilio Pernae in edendo Plotino Graeco sentiam vel potius, quid in eodem cum aliis conferendo aliquando meditatus sim ac subiecerim, quo μετώπῳ καὶ προσώπῳ[1857] reddendus sit, breviter tuis heri acceptis significavi.[1858] Te in tantis occupationibus officiose calamo quis turbarit, quis inepte accusarit, cuius pectus apertum rectumque pridem cognovi? Ego his diebus praediolo finibus me continui, quid in urbe fieret, mutetur tot edictis, quo res sint excessurae, cogitavi. Divinare, si liceret, atque visa enunciare, quiddam me praesensisse testarer. Sed etc. De iuris consulto Saxonico miror, tot praeclaris monimentis exiguum testimonium negatum.[1859] Novi utriusque ingenium, saginam utrique exercitatione maiore detractam velim, iudicium de bene meritis copiosius καὶ ἁλὸς ἅλις ἵνα μή σαπῇ τὰ κρέα.[1860] Ioannes Michael Brutus ad filiam matrimonio illigatam videndam se principis sui venia huc ait advolasse. Semel hominem conveni, abstineo familiaritate ob mores et tempora. Ἔρρωσο.[1861] Filio tuo salutem. Pridie Kalendas Februarii 1579.

Oro, per celerum magistrum aut dominum Schuendium aut Argentoratum impetra, ut hac meae Pernae reddantur, saltem ante nundinas, ne de praefatione Plotini dubius haereat editionemque differat.

Address: Caesaris ἰατρῷ[1862] primario et consiliario etc., domino fautori, amico observando. Prag, Herrn Doctor Cratoni. Cito.

324.
Sambucus to Johannes Crato
25 April 1579, Vienna

Published in Gerstinger, "Die Briefe," 248-249.

Sambucus did not write Crato earlier because he was unsure whether he was still in Prague, as people claimed he was going to visit Wrocław. There is uncertainty about the diet (in Hungary), all hope is in the emperor. Austrian translators were sent there (to Pressburg). The (deputies of the) cities and towns, betrayed by the ambition and adulation of a few, intend to split, whereas earlier they were united. The future is unsure. The estates left for the counties, they depend on the will of the emperor. Some believe the emperor will come to this part, but Sambucus does not think so. A young, learned Bohemian gentleman sent him the attached letter from Constantinople, asking him to forward it to Rostock, hence Sambucus asks Crato to entrust it to David Chytraeus. The Hungarian borders are relatively peaceful. Some lightly armed veterans from Eger were killed, which was avenged by Ferenc Nádasdy ten days ago. Everyone says the Ottomans are exceedingly worried about the Persians.

[1857] front and face
[1858] On the Plotinus-edition, which came out in 1580, see letter 282, note 1647. Perna probably offered Sambucus to write a preface for the edition, which he must have refused. See the last sentence of the letter.
[1859] See letters 305, 309 and 319.
[1860] and plenty of salt so that the flesh does not rot
[1861] farewell
[1862] [chief] physician

Sambucus salutem.

Silentii mei diuturni causam obduco, quod dubitarim, num adhuc Pragae esses, quod quidam Vratislaviam secessurum ad aliquot dies affirmabant. Nos haeremus nostro conventu, omnis spes et salus Praga exspectatur. Sunt istuc ablegati interpretes Austriaci. Civitates et oppida, quae ante sensibus et oneribus coibant, quorundam temeritate et adulatione prodita separari volunt.[1863] Quid sit futurum, nescimus. Discesserunt status provinciae, ab imperatoris responso et clementia pendent. Sunt, qui putent suam maiestatem ad nos disgressurum, sed ego non credulus. Has ad me Byzantio nobilis et doctus iuvenis Boemus, secretarius oratoris nostri, uti eas recta tutoque Rostochium curarem, misit. Obsecrat, ne pereant. Equidem nisi tuam magnificentiam, cui eas commendem curandas, ignoro, ad quem commeatus est literarum et officiorum ortus et occasus etc. Rogo igitur, Chytreo has tradendas committas. Fines nostri minus infestantur, Agrienses tamen nuper admodum de suis aliquot veteranos expeditos amisere, quod damnum per Nadasdium ante 10 dies maiori caede et praeda compensatum fuit.[1864] Thurcam anxie praeter consuetudinem occupari solicitudine Persicorum constanter omnes affirmant. Vale, mi optime patrone! Die Marci 79. Vienna.

Address: Dem Edlen und hochgelerten Herr Johann Crato von Craffthaim, Khayserlicher Maiestät Ratt und Physico, meinem günstigen Herrn und Patron zu Handen. Prag oder Bresla. Herrn Cratoni. Cito.

325.
Sambucus to Theodor Zwinger
14 May 1579, Vienna

The original is kept in Basel, Universitätsbibliothek, Frey Mscr II 26, no. 225. Published in Gerstinger, "Die Briefe," 250-251.

Sambucus has received Zwinger's letter but still has not seen the edition of Hippocrates, although Jean Aubry should be back soon. He is greatly hurt that such great philosophers are neglected by such mediocrities; the printers prefer small profit of whatever little source to the beacons of wisdom; he will not urge any longer (Episcopius and Perna to print) Aristotle and Plotinus. Unless they recover from their avarice, they will hear unpleasant things. Zwinger has asked him to provide exempla *for (a new) edition of the* Theatrum humanae vitae. *He would be happy to give some but does not know to which parts of the* Theatrum. *There are some recent* exempla, *but they have been badly received by many and even excluded by slanderers. Vienna is so agitated by religious discord that Sambucus would prefer staying away to hearing and seeing all those inequities, as this*

[1863] After the litigious diet of 1578 a new one was convoked finally by January 1579 but it convened only in February. See the history of these diets in *Magyar országgyűlési emlékek 6*, 187-410.

[1864] In April the market town of Hatvan under Ottoman occupation was burnt down and plundered. Ferenc Nádasdy (1555–1604), comes of Vas, later supremus capitaneus of Transdanubian Hungary, was one of the most important military leaders during the Long Turkish War and most influential aristocrats of Hungary next to Boldizsár Batthyány and György Zrinyi, demanding greater Hungarian influence on Habsburg politics. See László Nagy, *Az erős fekete bég – Nádasdy Ferenc* [The strong black bey – F. Nádasdy] (Budapest: Zrinyi, 1987), esp. p. 128.

nastiness delays his writing. Finally, Sambucus encourages Zwinger, who lacks neither talent nor diligence nor opportunity for publishing, to continue with his work, to scorn the greedy and the petty, and he assures him of his standing with posterity.

Sambucus salutem.

Tuas quidem accepi, sed Hippocratem nondum vidi, sed Aubrium ad nos brevi exspectamus.[1865] Vehementer doleo tantos philosophos a tantillis neglegi, lucellum ex qualibet recula luminibus sapientiae praeferri. Reservent [?] illi Aristotelem, Plotinum, quamdiu volent, ego amplius non urgebo.[1866] Nive resipuerint ab avaritia, audient, quae fortasse nolunt. Exempla petis, quae editioni et genio publico *Theatri* tui adhibeas. Libenter morem gessissem, nisi dubitassem, quibus locis et materiae addideris. Sunt enim, ut scis, quaedam exempla nuper accommodata, sed calumniose et male a nonnullis accepta,[1867] ut Viennae parum abfuerint, quin exclusa sint a Glauciis et similibus.[1868] Nostra dissidiis religionis adeo turbata sunt, ut malim longius abesse quam molesta et iniqua quotidie audire et spectare,[1869] totumque me externa fastidia tardiorem ad scribendum reddident. Vale, mi optime Zuiggere, et quoniam nec ingenium nec industria, minus loci commoditas ad edendum desunt, perge, macte, contemne avaros, ride metum pusiliorum tibique pretium in posteritatis memoria et praeconio statutum certum putato. 14. Maii 1579. Vienna.

326.
Sambucus to Theodor Zwinger
16 August 1579, [Vienna]

The original is kept in Basel, Universitätsbibliothek, Frey Mscr II 26, no. 226. Published in Gerstinger, "Die Briefe," 251.

Sambucus, like many others, appreciates Zwinger's Hippocrates-edition supplied with an index and synoptic tables, although some would prefer to have the tables separated from the text, not to be hindered in reading and taking marginal notes. He thanks him for mentioning his name in the preface, but he could have made it clearer which readings Sambucus supplied with respect to others. Plotinus is not coming out. He has some good Greek authors he would like to make known to the public, but publishers are greedy, ungrateful and tedious and nourish vain hopes. Sambucus does not know what Johannes Löwenklau is doing. Finally, he asks Zwinger to remind the Oporinus press to send back his codex of Wolfgang Lazius's De Republica Romana, otherwise he will go to court.

[1865] See letter 317.
[1866] On Aristotle and Plotinus cf. the Index under "Sambucus."
[1867] Zwinger's marginal note: "Exempla Theatri."
[1868] No such recent *exempla* were added to the new 1586 edition of the *Theatrum humanae vitae*, which has anyway only very few recent *exempla* compared to those taken from ancient authors. Sambucus is comparing here calumnious men in Vienna to the physician Glaucus of Alexandria (the first century BC), who is described in the 1586 edition (vol. 14, p. 2941) in the following way: "animo fuit erga philosophiam parum placido, semperque in disputationibus habebat aliquid confragosi et acerbi: procul etiamnum vociferans, rem eos non exiguam neque levem designasse, qui differendo de victus ratione salubri, terminus confudissent."
[1869] Zwinger's marginal note: "1579 Viennae dissidia religionis."

Salutem.

Hippocratis editionem[1870] tuis indicibus et συνόψεσιν[1871] inlustratam probo et multi mecum, licet sint, qui separatas tabulas tuas a contextu optarint, ne lectio ipsa et per oras notationes quorundam talium cupidorum impedirent. De memoria Sambuci in prohemio habeo gratiam, sed id testatus fuissem pluribus verbis, si quae a me, quae ab aliis subiecta fuere, distinctiora essent.[1872] Plotinus non prodit.[1873] Habeo egregios aliquot scriptores Graecos, quorum cognitionem omnibus esse communem vellem, cumque typographi difficiles, avari, ingrati, longi sint, malo mihi mecum intus canant et [...]. Leonclaius quid agat, ignoro. Oporinianos, oro, *De republica* voluminis Lazii[1874] a me missi moneas, alias iure asserturum me denuncio.[1875] Vale, mi carissime, etc. 16. Augusti 1579. Totus tuus Sambucus.

327.
Sambucus to Theodor Zwinger
1 September 1579, Vienna

The original is kept in Basel, Universitätsbibliothek, Frey Mscr II 26, no. 227. Published in Gerstinger, "Die Briefe," 252.

Sambucus sent a letter to Zwinger via Frankfurt, which he must have received. He asks him to admonish Episcopius and Perna to publish Aristotle, which is much expected by many. He should also call the attention of the Oporinus press to Lazius's enlarged and emended De Republica Romana, *which he bought for some florins from Lazius's heirs against the will of the Viennese Council. If they do not want to publish it, they should send it back. He can find as many as three presses in Frankfurt that would publish it. "What is this insane avarice?"*

Sambucus salutem.

Reversurus est hic tabellio ad vos, cui has ad te addere volui. Scripsi Francfortum ad te, quas te accepturum non dubito. Oro, Episcopium et Pernam moneas de Aristotele edendo, cuius exspectatione et mora video me multorum genium adhuc fraudasse. Sed quid agam? Si amicus es, Oporinianos meis nominibus salutes atque commonefacias voluminis Lazii *De republica*, quod ad eos auctum et emendatum misi, meis impensis ac aliquot aureis ab haeredibus contra senatus Viennensis voluntatem impetravi.[1876] Multi sunt in spe editionis. Si nolent, reddant mihi codicem, reperiam Francforti tres, qui praecario arripient praelisque subiicient. Quae haec beneficiorum oblivio? Quae insana avaritia? Quae mora tot bonis noxia? Haec raptim. 1. Septembris 1579. Vienna. Tu aliquid rescribe, oro.

[1870] Zwinger's marginal note: "Zwingeri". Hippocrates, *Viginti duo commentarii*.
[1871] synoptic tables
[1872] In the dedication to Johannes Crato, Zwinger mentions Sambucus in the following way: "Glossas interea lectionesque varias ex diversis manuscriptis codicibus Hippocrateis diligenter collectas, nobis primus omnium insigni liberalitate communicavit Ioannes Sambucus Tirnaviensis, historicus caesareus, ad veterum auctorum obstetricationem felici sidere, regio certe animo natus." Hippocrates, *Viginti duo commentarii*, β2.
[1873] Zwinger's note above *Plotinus*: "in Platonem."
[1874] Zwinger's note above *Lazii*: "Wolf."
[1875] See letters 233, 262, 266, 271 and 283.
[1876] See letters 326-327.

328.

Sambucus to Hilfreich Guett
Shortly before 29 September 1579, [Vienna]

The original is kept in Vienna, ÖStA, FHKA, Alte Hofkamer, Hoffinanz Ungarn, r.Nr. 40. Konv. 1579. IX, f. 361.[1877]

Starting the letter with playful language Sambucus complains that he has still not been paid. Furthermore, he warmly recommends the case of Lukács Csütörtök, who should finally be released with just conditions to meet personally all the testimonies, and not under conditions invented by the judges. He should be set free upon bail, and some expert reckoners should be selected who can look into the argument. Finally, he asks Guett also to remember his case.

Magnifice comine et patrone observandissime.

Trifolium pratense, mihi satis plagense, nondum quicquam numeravit,[1878] magna rei meae familiaris iactura, creditorum quoque indignatione.[1879] Quid porro agam, prorsus ignoro, nisi succurreritis falce, qua illud demetam. Negocium diligenter commendo Lucae Csotörtök,[1880] ut tandem quibusvis aequis conditionibus miser e cathenis laxetur, cum palam fiat tot testibus, non fuisse conditiones, a iudicibus pactas, servatas etc. Liberetur ergo sub cautionibus et constituantur gnari computatores, qui rationes eorum examinent ac discutiant. Reliquum uterque suo loco persequatur. Sed haec ultra meam crepidam. Vestrae magnificentiae me commendo, utque clee aliquando mihi quoque virescat, oro, imperate. Vestrae magnificentiae servitor [?] Ioannes Sambucus.

Address: Magnifico domino H. Gütti, domino patrono singulari. Sambucus.
Scribal note (by Guett?): d. Sambuccus pro Bezallung Seines Austendiges [?] bey dem dreyssigist Hungerischen Altenburg.[1881] September 29te.
Another hand: 1579.
Camer ernstlich bevelch zustellen.[1882] Septembris 29.

[1877] We thank István Fazekas for finding this letter and providing a copy of it.
[1878] The wordplay is with the name of Mr. Clee (=Klee [clover]) = Hans Khlee, see http://rudolphina.com/Namen/Kleen_Hans.xml (accessed on 12 March 2024). "Clover of the field, very troublesome to me, has not paid anything yet [...] I simply do not know what I should do further, if you do not provide me with a sickel, with which to mow it down." See also letter 314.
[1879] Sambucus is referring to the thirtieth (harmincad) tax office of Mosonmagyaróvár, as it appears from the scribal notes on the back of the letter.
[1880] Lukács Csütörtök came from a wealthy family of cow merchants from Szeged. See Ferenc Szakály, "Török megszállás alatt (1543–1686)," in *Szeged története. I. A kezdetektől 1686-ig*, ed. Gyula Kristó (Szeged: Somogyi Könyvtár, 1983), passim.
[1881] The thirtieth (harmincad) tax office of Mosonmagyaróvár.
[1882] The summary of the scribe mentions only Sambucus's request for payment "through the thirtieth tax office at Altenburg (Mosonmagyaróvár)," saying that a severe order should be sent out (probably to the Hungarian Chamber).

329.
Jan Meller Palmier[1883] to Sambucus
[second half of 1579[1884]]

Published in Ianus Mellerus Palmerius, *Spicilegiorum Iani Melleri Palmerii commentarius primus* (Frankfurt: Apud Georgium Corvinum impensis Sigismundi Feyrabendii, 1580), f. 17^{r-v}.

Those who examine old manuscripts follow a unique way of enhancing erudition. The people who have old books neither know how to use them nor tolerate those who know. If, with much luck, one manages to snatch a book in order to use it and does not return it immediately, they complain and call one a criminal. Why do they think they can possess alone what is public property? However, since these men have recently been ridiculed by Janus Dousa, Palmier rather addresses Sambucus and lavishes praise on him for having saved, collated, annotated and shared with the public so many codices. That is why Palmier, conscious of his temerity, is sending Sambucus a few notes on Sallust, although for Sambucus they are certainly too many. He has not inspected the manuscripts himself. Three were collated by Franciscus Modius in diverse abbeys, another by Janus Gulielmus, and the rest came from the collection of Hieronymus Berchem.

Viro clarissimo Ioanni Sambuco Tirnaviensi Pannonio.

Verum est, Sambuce, quibus hoc primum, hoc postremum fuit, ut vetustos codices, qua cuique proximum esset, anquirerent, viam ad iuvandas literas unicam institerunt. Ita, si etiam communicant, ne isti dictum pro se putent, qui antiquos libros habent atque id hactenus uti neque sciunt ipsi neque, qui sciant, patiuntur. Hoc primum. Deinde, cum diis tuis aequis librum e turba utendum abstuleris, si hoc tantum diem non repraesentes, quiritantur, clamant Deum atque hominum fidem, flagitium, facinus, perfidiam, quicquid ipsis libuit, vocant. At ubi aequum bonum? Tu mihi quo iure, qua iniuria publicum occuparis atque id licere tibi postules, praeter te nemini? Sed de horum hominum, audebo dicere, scelere non addam, ne lacessivisse convitia videar. Et quia pridem sunt, ut scire potes, Duzae nostri Hipponacteo praeconio addicti,[1885] ad te ibam, clarissime Sambuce, dignissimum, qui omnibus, quantum est, poetis carmen esses. Nam quis, o dii, bonum hoc hominum generi dedit? Tantum optimorum codicum vim acervasse laborantibus ac diu extremum spiritum trahentibus musis remedium fuit. Contulisse, adnotasse, emisisse, vita. Quid communicasse? Itaque ergo paucas ad Sallustium notas misi. Paucas, ut hic fabulator errat. Tibi, sat scio, nimium, quam multae videbuntur. Nimirum,

---

[1883] Hardly any information on Jan Meller Palmier (Palmerius, d. 1580) is to be found, except for some hints in the few surviving letters of his correspondence. Aside from his collection of textual emendations (*Spicilegiorum commentarius primus*, dedicated to Crato) he seems not to have published anything. In 1580 Janus Gulielmus (see note 1889) published his *Rosae, epigrammata*, in which most poems were dedicated to Palmier, some of them deploring his death.

[1884] This possibly fictitious letter was written after March 1579 (publication of Modius's Curtius-Edition) and the beginning of 1580 (printing of Palmerius's book).

[1885] Janus Dousa (Jan van der Does, 1545–1604) was an important Dutch statesman, scholar, and poet. See Chris L. Heesakkers and Wilma M.S. Reinders, *Genoeglijk bovenal zijn mij de Muzen. De Leidse Neolatijnse dichter Janus Dousa [Pleasant above all are the Muses to me. The Leiden Neo-Latin poet Janus Dousa] (1545–1604)* (Leiden: Dimensie, 1993). See also letter 180, note 1066. Here his role as a satirical (Hipponactean) poet is stressed. The Greek poet Hipponax (6th century BC) was an archetypal satirical poet, renowned for his scathing wit.

Sic quondam tener ausus est Catullus
Magno mittere passerem Maroni.[1886]

De libris antiquis, ne ignores, nullum inspexi: Tres in totidem abbatiis repertos et accuratissime a se collatos Franciscus Modius[1887] Brugensis, adolescens doctus, quem de edito Curtio nosse potes, mecum communicavit. Unum Sigebergensem[1888] mea caussa diligenter legit amicus meus, Ioannes Guilhelmus Lubecensis.[1889] Reliqui domi clarissimi Hieronymi Berchemi[1890] fuerunt.[1891]

330.
Sambucus to Joachim Camerarius Jr.
7 September 1580, Vienna

The original is kept in Munich, BSB, Clm 10367, Nr. 311. Published in Gerstinger, "Die Briefe," 252-253.

Sambucus would say that the brothers in the office of Vulcan are not really of the heavens: the nice Greek letters of Chrysoloras might have been inflamed by the excessive heat. Hopefully it will not be the fate of the letters of Camerarius Sr. as well, attached to Chrysoloras's ones. He is engaged in antiquarian research on Camerarius's region, encountering sometimes unexpected things. At the instigation of the parents, he has now sent Philipp Crato to live in the vicinity of Camerarius and recommends him warmly. Day by day, he supplied Sambucus with private news and helped him. He is sending his greetings to Julius Geuder, and he also ordered Philipp to do so. The news from Belgium is sad, but the situation is controlled by arms.

Salutem.

De Vulcani officina minus quam aetheri fratres umquam testarer. Chrysolorae bellae Graecae epistolae fortasse nimio aestu conflatae evanuere. Utinam non idem tui clarissimi parentis ad familiares scriptis additis intercedat.[1892] Ego in vestratibus antiquitatibus haereo, commoveo, eruo, quaedam inauspicata averrunco. Utinam genio benigno, bono, eventus tribueretur! Philippum Cratonem,[1893] qui quotidie rei familiaris internuncius et administer secura fide fuit, hunc vicinum vobis a parentibus solicitatum dimisi, quasi invitus. Commendo eum tibi ea vice, qua tu mihi tuos et maiores commendaris. Exceptione, si commodo tuo te compellarit,

---

[1886] Martialis 4.14.13–14.
[1887] On Modius see letter 367, note 2104.
[1888] In the Benedictine abbey in Siegberg near Bonn.
[1889] Janus Gulielmus (1555–1584) studied in Rostock under David and Nathan Cythraeus and Johannes Caselius. He became an accomplished classical scholar and published, among others, on Euripides, Plautus and Cicero. On Guilelmus see Iohannes Mollerus, *Cimbria literata* (Havniae: Sumptibus et typis orphanotrophii regii, 1744) 3.303-315.
[1890] The Cologne jurist Hieronymus Berchem (d. 1597) was a close friend of Franciscus Modius. He was a teacher and a majordomo of Charles II, 7th count of Egmont (brother of Count Filips van Egmont) whom he influenced to accept Modius as a client for a time. Later, Berchem became canon of the cathedral of Ypres.
[1891] There follows a long list of emendations to Sallustius on f. 17ʳ–45ᵛ, which we omit here.
[1892] This is a funny reference to Bonaventura Vulcanius's failure to publish Chrysoloras's letters. Cf. the Index.
[1893] Philipp Crato was probably Johannes Crato's son or nephew.

nec secus. Domino Gaydero salutem, quem ut meo nomine idem Philippus consalutet, iussi. Ἔρρωσο.¹⁸⁹⁴ De Belgis et κοινωνία¹⁸⁹⁵ ἅπαντα¹⁸⁹⁶ tristia, sed causa moderatur bellis et armis.¹⁸⁹⁷ 7. Septembris 1580 Vienna. Tuus totus Sambucus.

Address: Ioachimo Camerario viro clarissimo protophysico reipublicae Noribergensis, domino amic o suo. Noribergam.

331.
Sambucus to Joachim Camerarius Jr.
[December 1580], no place

The original is kept in Munich, BSB, Clm 10367, f. 313ʳ⁻ᵛ. Published in Gerstinger, "Die Briefe," 259-260.

Since Sambucus knows that Camerarius is dedicated to the good of others, and since he has a similar approach, he asks Camerarius to forward a parcel to Simon Grynaeus the Younger in Heidelberg, who will pay for the courier. The classical author of the book sent to Grynaeus will be a nice contribution to mathematics and astrology. Grynaeus will publish the manuscript together with other texts. He asks Camerarius to remind Bonaventura Vulcanius of the (Greek) letters. He is sorry for the death of Hieronymus Wolf. Among other spontaneous writings, he wrote the enclosed Greek poem for him.

Sambucus salutem.

Quia scio te reipublicae omniumque commodis natum factumque, ego vero ab eisdem sensibus numquam abhorruerim, te valde rogo, fasciculum hunc Heidlpergam ad Simonem Gryneum tuto mittas. Tabellario a Gryneo satisfiet.¹⁸⁹⁸ Autor hic vetus gratus erit mathematum et astrologiae lectionibus, quem Grynaeus curabit cum aliis quibusdam edendum. Vale et Antverpiensis scholae moderatorem Vulcanium de epistolis mone.¹⁸⁹⁹ Vale. Volffii mortem doleo,¹⁹⁰⁰ ad cuius tumulum cum alia subito effudi tum hoc quoque παρονομαστικῶς.¹⁹⁰¹

[1894] farewell
[1895] union
[1896] everything [is sad]
[1897] In August 1580, the Prince of Parma and his mother arrived to take control of the situation, while the Dutch States General elected Francis, Duke of Anjou and Alençon to be the sovereign of the United Provinces. See *A Generall Historie of the Netherlands*, 746-747; Mack P. Holt, *The Duke of Anjou and the Politique Struggle during the Wars of Religion* (Cambridge: Cambridge University Press, 1986), 113-145.
[1898] Simon Grynaeus the Younger (1539–1582) was a physician and mathematician. Very little is known of his life. He appears to be a distant relative of Simon Grynaeus the Elder, and a good friend of Thomas Erastus. He was excommunicated for his support of the Antitrintarian Adam Neuser. Around 1580, like Erastus, he also wanted to move back from Heidelberg to Basel, and apparently managed to do it by 1581, see letter 342. See Charles D. Gunnoe, *Thomas Erastus and the Palatinate. A Renaissance Physician in the Second Reformation* (Leiden: Brill, 2011), 238-245.
[1899] See the previous letters to Camerarius.
[1900] Hieronymus Wolf died on 8 October 1580.
[1901] in a manner of wordplay

Βόλφιος οὐ δάκνων ἀρετὴν καὶ πᾶσιν ὀφέλλων
ᾤχετο τῶν ἁγίων δώματα λαμπρὰ ἔχων
Ῥήτωρ, ἰητρός, ποιητής, ἀστρολόγος τε
οὔφυγε τὴν μοῖραν τ' εὐσεβέων ὄναρ εὖ.[1902]

Address: Clarissimo viro domino Ioachimo Camerario reipublicae Noribergensis archiatro etc., domino et amico observandissimo.
Nurnberg. mitt einem pachete auff heydlperg Simon Gryneo etc.
Camerarius's hand: 81 5. Ianuarii.

332.
Sambucus to Ruprecht von Stotzingen
1 January, 1581, Vienna

Dedication in Alvarus Gomez, *De rebus gestis a Francisco Ximenio Cisnerio, archiepiscopo Toletano, libri octo, qui sunt rerum Hispanicarum tomus III. Nunc primum in Germania recusi, quibus inscriptiones aliquot Tarraconenses ex historia Hispanica Ludovici Pontis adiunctae sunt. Omnia studio Ioannis Sambuci Pannonii, caesareae maiestatis consiliarii et historici. Adiectus est in fine rerum memorabilium index* (Francofurti: Ex officina typographica Andreae Wecheli, 1581), f. ii[r-v].

Sambucus often wished that the history of Francisco Jiménez de Cisneros's Spanish regency (representing Charles V in Spain) were reprinted in Germany. When Andreas Wechel, whom Sambucus praises as the first among all publishers, reprinted two volumes of Spanish history, he missed therein the book on Cisneros as well as the works of Pedro de Medina and Lluís Pons d'Icart, and Mendoza's book on noble families, which, however, have not yet appeared in Latin. Before they get translated and appear as a fourth volume, Sambucus wanted to have this book on Cisneros published together with some inscriptions taken from Lluís Pons d'Icart's Spanish history. He dedicates it to Stotzingen, who has provided him the volume on Cisneros, because he admires his merits, his learned nobility furnished with legal knowledge, his polished style neat with poetical rhythms and his generosity toward all. Stotzingen, who is High Steward of the court of Archduke Maximilian and much listened to in the Imperial Council, is greatly admired by everyone. He has been councillor to three emperors, worked as an assessor in Speyer, was sent on a diplomatic mission to Pius IV in Rome, became chamberlain to Maximilian II's daughters sent to Spain, and then to his sons, Matthias and Maximilian.

Roberto a Stozingen,[1903] serenissimi archiducis Maximiliani etc. palatii rectori senatusque aulici imperialis consiliario etc., Sambucus salutem.

[1902] Wolfius, who did not disparage virtue and was supportive of everyone, / went away, he who had shining convictions concerning religion, / an orator, physician, poet, and astrologer, / he did not escape the fate and the sleep of the pious well.

[1903] Ruprecht von Stotzingen (1540–1600) studied law in Bologna and Freiburg im Breisgau. In 1562–1569, he worked in the Reichskammergericht in Speyer and was consequently sent to Spain. Later, he became member of the Imperial Secret Council, high steward (Hofmeister) and high chamberlain of Archduke Maximilian and finally in 1592 *Statthalter* of Lower Austria. See Borsa, "Die Familien Püchler und Stotzingen" (as in letter 78 note 491) and Adolf Mohl, *Geschichte des Ortes und der Pfarre Stozing* (Raab: Diözesan-Buchdruckerei, 1895). Also see his various privileges in Vienna, ÖStA, AVA, Adel RAA 413.18.

Ximenii res prudenter et constanter feliciterque gestas tot annorum interregni variam faciem, quibus Carolo V. nondum ad sceptra idonea aetate longeque absenti Hispanias ille conservavit,[1904] in Germania ut recuderentur,[1905] saepe optavi, quod ipsum modo per typographum sum consecutus.[1906] Nam cum Wechelus, cuius typis ac diligentiae nil praeposueris, ante annum duobus tomis res Hispanorum denuo produxisset,[1907] inque illis Ximenium, cum Petro Medina et Ludovico Ponte,[1908] qui Tarracoviensia separatim comprehendit, Mendozaeque familias nobiliores desiderarem, sed hos nondum translatos scirem, dum Latini fierent (quod brevi succedet quarto tomo, vel potius nunc accuratur) author eidem fui, tertium interim tomum uti adornaret ipso hoc luculento Ximenio et aliquot Tarraconensibus epigrammatis et inscriptionibus ex *Historia Hispanica* Ludovici Pontis adiectis. Tui vero nominis praeclara usurpatione, qui exemplaria nobis suppeditaris, hanc editionem constare volui, cum quia te amo tuis meritis coloque virum nobilitate vetustissima eaque literata iuris cognitione praestantem, stilo polito elegantique numeris poeticis tersum, erga omnes humanitate ac beneficentia prolixum, tum vero quia omnium admiratione ita extas, clientelis flores et amicitiis abundas, denique aulae Maximiliani archiducis moderator cunctorum ferris ac ita in oculis haeres (taceo quantum sententiae tuae luceant in senatu caesaris et imperiali), nemo ut sit, nisi monstro editus ac extrema laborans barbarie, quin in tuis virtutum monumentis libenter copioseque versetur adque te amandum alios facile excitet. Scio eam semper tuam fuisse modestiam, ut lucem fugias, quae in te singularia omnes laudant, tute non agnoscas. Veruntamen haud ego levia duco, dum explico vitae tuae cursum ac nonnullorum excutio memoriam. An tu exiguum censes, consiliis trium maximorum imperatorum excellere, abs divo Ferdinando laribus excitum, Spirae assessorem floruisse, Romam ad Pium IIII. esse missum? Paulo post a Maximiliani II. filiae carissimae in Hispaniam missae comitatui et, ut vocant, salae praefectum ablegatum? Mox Matthiae et Maximiliani filiorum aulae regundisque moribus adhibitum? Haec tu non curas, silentio etiam obrui velis? Absit. Nil ista stoica secta perficies, non evades, ut maxime adnitare, quin te canamus, ac aetas in secquens dotes loquatur sempiternas. Vale. Kalendis Ianuariis, haecque nomine Iani, strenarumque ut accipias, oro, 1581. Viennae, ex Musaeolo nostro.

[1904] Cisneros's second regency lasted less than two years (1516–1517). Charles V, arriving in Spain, hardly appreciated his services; he sent Cisneros home and was later even suspected to have poisoned him.

[1905] The book first appeared with the same title in Alcala (Andreas de Angulo) in 1569.

[1906] Francisco Jiménez de Cisneros (1436–1517) was a controversial figure of Spanish political and religious life. Among others he was archbishop of Toledo, cardinal, twice regent of Castile, Grand Inquisitor (formalising the legal processes and excluding the use of force), persecutor of the Moors, personal leader of a bloody crusade to North Africa, supporter of milder treatment and Christianisation of the indigenous peoples of the Americas, founder of the Complutense University of Madrid, and the person responsible for the edition of the first polyglot Bible in the world, the Complutensian. See Erika Rummel, *Jimenez De Cisneros on the Threshold of Spain's Golden Age* (Tempe: Arizona Center for Medieval and Renaissance Studies, 1999); Joseph Pérez, *Cisneros, el cardenal de España* (Barcelona: Taurus / Fundación Juan March, 2014).

[1907] *Rerum hispanicarum scriptores aliquot ... ex bibliotheca clarissimi viri Roberti Beli Angli*, 2 vols. (Francofurti: Ex officina typographica Andreae Wecheli, 1579). In fact, Sambucus's edition appeared as the third volume of the same series.

[1908] Pedro de Medina (1493–1567) was a Spanish polymath mathematician, cosmographer, historian etc., most famous for his works on navigation. See Juan Fernández Jiménez, "Introducción," in *Suma de la Cosmographia de Pedro de Medina*, ed. idem (Valencia: Albatros-Hispanófila, 1980), 1-24; idem, "La obra de Pedro de Medina (ensayo bibliográfico)," *Archivo Hispalense* 180 (1976), 113-128. Lluís Pons d'Icart (ca. 1518–1578) was a jurist and an antiquarian from Tarragona. See Jaume Massó i Carballido, "Notes per a una biografia del Lluís Pons d'Icart," *Treballs Canongins* (1985), 63-102. Sambucus refers to his *Libro de las Grandezas y Cosas memorables dela Metropolitana Insigne y famosa Ciudad de Tarragona* (Lerida: Pedro de Robles y Iuan de Villanueva, 1572).

333.
Sambucus to Joachim Camerarius Jr.
8 January 1581, [Vienna]

The original is kept in Munich, BSB, Clm 10367, f. 312ʳ⁻ᵛ. Published in Gerstinger, "Die Briefe," 253-255.

There is a learned nobleman close to Sambucus who has a genuine, exceptionally large unicorn. It escaped notice before, no prince or nobleman has seen it. Sambucus knows that it is a rare treasure for great princes or cities. If Camerarius thinks his city may need such outstanding treasure of such measures or knows anyone else who might be interested, he should tell them that the price is 5,000 ducats and alert him. For its rarity and length it is worth even 20,000, and no one would question its originality, they must only agree on the price. There was a shorter one sold for 24,000 thalers seven months before. He writes about it only to Camerarius, who should speak to Julius Geuder, and write back about potential hopes. Rudolf II feels a little better; he is expecting some doctors from Italy. The courier has been paid till Nuremberg. He is reminding Bonaventura Vulcanius of the letters of Chrysoloras and Camerarius Sr. If there is no hope for selling the unicorn in Camerarius's land, it will be sold in Italy at much greater profit. Meanwhile, it should remain between the two of them. He is sending his greetings to Julius Geuder.

Salutem cum mille felicibus annis.

Est apud nobilem et eruditum virum in nostra vicinia unicornu genuinum, probum, huius longitudinis et latitudinis, quantum pictoris rudis manus ruri ibi assequi potuit.[1909] Latuit hactenus nec quisquam principum aut nobilitatis vidit, nec aspectu vilescet. Scio rarum esse thesaurum ac nisi magnorum principum ac rerumpublicarum. Quod si tu putas rempublicam vestram tam eximio thesauro tantaeque magnitudinis carere aut aliquem alium, quibus tu gratam operam ἐνδέξει καὶ ἀποφάνσει[1910] praestitam arbitraris, significes, et 5000 ducatorum precio communicare poteris meque statim facere certiorem. Nam valet 20000 ob raritatem et longitudinem, nec de eius probitate quisquam dubitet, modo de pretio conveniatis. Ante 7 menses 24000 talleris brevius nuper venditum fuit.[1911] Haec tibi soli, ac magnifico Gaydero communicabis, ac si quid spei adfulserit, rescribes. Caesar meliuscule [se] habet et medicos exspectat nonnullos ex Italia. Vale, et quamprimum aliquid, si dignum videbitur, persolve. Tabellario satisfactum est Noribergam usque. 8. Ianuarii 1581. Ioannes Sambucus.

[1909] Sambucus must have sent a life-size picture of the unicorn as an attachment in the letter. For the story of the unicorn see Almási, *The Uses of Humanism*, 194-195. See also the note of Gerstinger ("Die Briefe," 255), quoting from Sambucus's testament, which shows that Sambucus finally bought the unicorn and was in the process of selling it at the time when his testament was written: "Schaff Inen auch den Khindern das lange Einhorn, so 38 Taller schwer wigt, der mich über 3000 Taller gestehet, solches Einhorn, hab Ich neulich dem Herrn Johanni Rogazi laut seines scheins auf Venedig Vertraut, darfür er sol mir geltswert der Lysta nach, die er auch hat aussrichten per 3000 Cronen unnd in Parem 2000 Cronen unnd etliche stuckh Antiquiteten, oder das Einhorn wieder mir zustellen, ohn gefahr unnd schaden."

[1910] by indication and declaration

[1911] See the next letters.

Vulcanum moneo Chrysolorae et vestrarum epistolarum Graecarum.[1912] Si de μονοκέρῳ[1913] a vobis nulla spes praebebitur, in Italiam mittetur longe maiore lucro. Interea ego rem inter nos cohibebo, quantum possum. Domino Geydero salutem et servitia parata.

Address: Clarissimo viro domino Ioachimo Camerario reipublicae Norimbergensis medico in primis etc., amico meo observando. Nürnberg. Hern Doctor Camerario. Ihns Doctor abwesen, dem hern Gayder Zulesen.
Camerarius's hand: 81. 23 Ianuarii.

334.
Sambucus to the Hungarian Chamber
8 February 1581, Vienna

The original is kept in Vienna, ÖStA, FHKA, Alte Hofkammer, Hoffinanz Ungarn 43, f. 9.

The previous year, the Imperial Chamber gave Sambucus a voucher of 2,000 thalers subtracted from the imperial voucher of 6,200, which was to be paid through (the tax offices of) Trnava and Hlohovec, but he received only 81 thalers, although already the third deadline is approaching. Therefore, he asks the Imperial Chamber to get the Hungarian Chamber to give the voucher of 2,000 thalers to two (merchants) of Nuremberg, Georg Schnierle und Andreas Schorger, and document it on the imperial voucher of 6,200. Finally, Sambucus demands that the Chamber see to the payment of the rest of the debt together with interests.

Gnadige, Gebiettende Hern und Patroni etc.

Es ist mir ferten ein abtrub umb 2000 taller in abschlag des Khayserlichen schains (umb 6200 fl. Renisch deutscher werung) durch Eure Gnaden auff Tierna und Freystätt[1914] gnadiglich ervolgt.[1915] Hab aber durch allerlay der ampter beschworung, und andre unglegehaitt nicht meer dan 81 taller erhaltem [...] mitt mein grosthen schaden; weyll der dritt termin auch schon heer nachentt. Ist derhalben mein hoche, nottwendigs Supplicieren Eure Gnaden die wollen wegen fürderung des abtrubs den bevelch auff Georgn Schnierle und Andres Schorger boyde von Nurnberg,[1916] oder werr den Camer Bevelch zu Presspurg derer 2000 taller wegen auff dierna unnd Freystatt dreyssigist inhaben wiert verordnen mitt ernstlich clausell, der sye die abtrub vier fall an abschlag passiern, und abtreyben lassen, und auff den der Camer zu Presspurg bevelch, an den Khayserlichen hauptschain, verzaichnen nach ihren brauch. Den Gnadigen Herrn ich den khayserlichen briff, weyll ehr umb vill meeres ist, niht alzeytt zum abtrub finantz wolt vertrauen. Soll gott, will alles ungefar gehandlet worden etc. So wolt ich auch gern sonst mitt dem rest des khayserlichen brifs weytter sehen, und auch mitt einem merklichen Ynteresse handlen: damit ich doch ein mall meine schulden und Creditores auch abfertigen möchte, thuend mich Euer Gnaden dienstlich und furderlichst bevelch. Den 8 febr. 1581. Euer gnaden gehorsamer diener Alzeit. D. Sambucus.

[1912] See letters 330-331.
[1913] unicorn
[1914] Hlohovec (Freistadt, Galgóc) is a town close to Trnava (Nagyszombat).
[1915] See again Almási, *The Uses of Humanism*, 194-196.
[1916] We have no information about these merchants.

Address: An der Römischen khayserlichen Maiestät etc. Nachgelassen HoffCamer wegen eins Neuen furderlichen abtrubs bevelch an die Prespurgerische Camer etc. Johannis Sambuci untertanigs Supplicieren 7. Febr.

335.
Sambucus to Hilfreich Guett
9 February 1581, Vienna

The original is kept in Vienna, ÖstA, FHKA, Alte Hofkammer, Hoffinanz Ungarn 43, f. 8.

Sambucus repeats the petition of the previous letter: he wants to get paid directly from the customs that the cattle merchants of Nuremberg Georg Schnierle and Andreas Schorger should pay at Trnava or Hlohovec. The scribal note suggests that his petition was accepted and 2,500 thalers of the 6,200 thalers debt (to be paid by the Mosonmagyaróvár tax office) were now transferred to the tax offices of Trnava and Senec (Szenc).

Magnifice domine, patrone observandissime, salutem.

Supplico, oro, rebus meis sic urgentibus et angustiae rei familiaris libellum, uti, peto, cum mandato serio ad cameram Posoninum expediatis, ut tricesimae Tyrnaviensis et Freystadiensis actus boum citra defalcationem Georgio Schnierle et Andreae Schorger Noribergensibus liberos concedant, ac summa abacta dorso mandati camerae Posonium per officiarios rescribantur, absque mea syngrapha imperatoria, ne periclitetur temere commissa ad singulos actus, quem mitto vestrae magnificentiae inspiciendam, quod adhuc ex 2000 talleris tantum 81 acceperim, summo meo incommodo. Valeat vestra magnificentia. 9. Februarii. Vestrae magnificentiae servitor Iohannes Sambucus.

Address: Magnifico domino et patrono meo singulari domino Helfricho Guttn.
Scribal note: Johann Sambucus Zur In abschlag seiner verweisung den 6200 fl. so auf Alltenburg lign 2500 fl. aus Tierna und Wardperg[1917] zulegen. 2. Martii 1581.[1918]

336.
Sambucus to Joachim Camerarius Jr.
10 February 1581, [Vienna]

The original is kept in Munich, BSB, Clm 10367, f. 318[r-v]. Published in Gerstinger, "Die Briefe," 256-258.

Camerarius should not think that Sambucus wrote about the unicorn because of some hope for profit but only because of his respect for Nuremberg, Julius Geuder and Camerarius. If it is not the appropriate time to sell it in Nuremberg, Camerarius should forgive Sambucus. A few months

---

[1917] Wartberg, i.e. Senec in Slovak, Szenc (Szempcz) in Hungarian.
[1918] According to a certificate of 29 September 1581 in the same archival material, 81 florins were paid through Georg Schnierle from the customs at Hlohovec.

before the Prince of Moscow bought one shorter and coarser for 24,000 thalers. He is urging Bonaventura Vulcanius to publish (the Greek letters of Chrysoloras and Camerarius Sr.) and asks Camerarius to do the same. He has given to Andreas Wechel Bonfini's History *supplied with some new appendices and the third volume of* Spanish history. *He is busy emending Quintilian and studying Austrian genealogy but cannot do more because of the political situation ("mores ac tempora"). He is sending his greetings to Julius Geuder. Rudolf II feels better and there is much talk again of a diet in Nuremberg. Jakob Andreae is leaving Saxony.*

Sambucus salutem.

Non lucelli alicuius spe, non alia re, quam observantia erga tam egregiam rempublicam studiumque erga dominum Geyderum et te singulare meum de unicornu tanto tamque raro, pretii satis vilis me scripsisse putes.[1919] Quod si incommodo id ac reipublicae vestrae importuno tempore acciderit, ignoscite. Tamen voluntas stabit immota de vobis benemerendi semper. Paucos ante menses nonnihil brevius, sed ab imo crassius Moschorum princeps,[1920] vera narro, 24000 talleris redemit. Vos arbitrio vestro agite etc. Vulcani officinam audio esse amplam. Moneo, urgeo, quod tu item amore patris piae memoriae facies, uti incude et malleis denique excudat, quod tenet.[1921] *Bonfinii Historias* cum aliquot novis appendicibus[1922] Vechelio dedi, itemque 3. tomum rerum hispanicarum.[1923] In Quintiliano totus sum sanando et genealogia recognoscenda Austriaca,[1924] nam alia nec licet, nec libet nunc, ut sunt mores ac tempora. Nobilissimum dominum Geyderum a me salutes et, si quid seminum rarorum occurrerit, mittam, aut vos praescribite. Vale. 10. Februarii 1581. Caesar melius [se] habet. De dieta Noribergensi denuo multi loquuntur. Iacobus Andreae Saxoniam reliquit.[1925]

Address: Clarissimo viro domino Ioachimo Camerario, reipublicae Norimbergensis protophysico etc., domino amico observando. Nürnberg, herrn doctor Camerario.
Camerarius's hand: 81, 22 Febr.

[1919] See letter 333.
[1920] Ivan the Terrible (1530–1584) bought, in fact, a beautifully decorated unicorn from the Fuggers in Augsburg for quite a fortune, which he later called his "imperial staff." Sambucus, however, may have not known that he bought it partly because of the popular faith in the healing power of unicorns against poison. See Robert Payne and Nikita Romanoff, *Ivan the Terrible* (New York: Crowell, 1975), 427. On the Christian connotations of unicorns see Karl Vocelka, *Die politische Propaganda Kaiser Rudolfs II. (1576–1612)* (Vienna: Österreichische Akademie der Wissenschaften, 1981), 198.
[1921] See letters 333 and 363.
[1922] Antonius Bonfinius, *Rerum Ungaricarum decades quatuor cum dimidia* (Francofurti: Andreas Wechel, 1581). It had the following new attachments: Sambucus's oration *De coronatione Rudolphi II.*; his funerary oration *In moerore funeris D. Maximiliani II.* (cf. the Index under "Sambucus"); *De tribus summis in imperatore virtutibus gnomae generales...*; *De Giulae et Zygethi exitu*; *Decretorum seu articulorum aliquot priscorum Ungariae regum* (with a new title page, sold also separately). See also *Humanistes du bassin des Carpates II. Johannes Sambucus*, 101-102.
[1923] See letter 332.
[1924] For his unpublished notes concernig "Austrian genealogies" see the notes in Gerstinger, "Die Briefe," 258.
[1925] Jakob Andreae (1528–1590) was a Lutheran theologian and priest, teaching at the University of Tübingen from 1541. Later, he worked diligently on the unification of the Lutherans in Germany with the protection of Julius of Brunswick-Lüneburg and then Augustus, Elector of Saxony, who dismissed him in 1580. See the article by Ernst Henke in *ADB* 1 (1875), 436-441; Christoph Weismann, "Auf Kanzeln, Kathedern und in Kutschen. Jakob Andreae als Universitäts- und Kirchenpolitiker," in *Die Universität Tübingen zwischen Reformation und Dreißigjährigem Krieg*, eds. Ulrich Köpf et al. (Ostfildern: Thorbecke, 2010), 119-140.

337.
Sambucus to Nicolaus Reusner
26 March 1581, Vienna

Published in Nicolaus Reusner, *Insomniae, sive noctes Iuniae entheae, in gravi et periculoso articulorum morbo evigilatae, cum epistolis aliquot illustrium et clarorum virorum* (Lauingen: Leonhardus Reinmichaelius,1581), f. D2ʳ-D3ʳ.

By publishing his Emblemata *Reusner has proven his genius. All posterity will praise his ability and diligence. Nature has no secrets which Reusner has not treated in his poetry and explained in a manner that he may be called a storehouse of physiology and philology. It is evident that some exercises by the old sophists will have to cede their place to his works, so much does his Aristotelian poetry encapsulate everything in its propriety and vividness. Sambucus does not always subscribe to the view that if one is very daring, one makes many errors, for Reusner's work is free of rashness which would leave it open to reproof. Sambucus is thankful to Reusner for mentioning him (in the* Emblemata*) and he will remain indebted to him until he can return the favour. The count praises Jeremias and has taken him on as his secretary. The young man is so diligent that he will undoubtedly come to the attention of Italian and French luminaries. Sambucus will try hard to make it happen soon.*

Clarissimo iurisconsulto et vati inprimis divino, D. Nicolao Reusnero Leorino etc., amico suo honorando S. P. D.

Non modo praestantis ingenii vim *Emblematis* tuis indicasti, quod vel ipsum equidem in commendatione eruditorumque nomine semper ponendum censui, sed totum te, quantus es, quantum alii de te pridem iudicarunt, eorum divulgatio prodidit. Quippe quae bibliothecae intimae opes praesentes nobis constituunt omnique insequenti aetati, vel quid possis, vel quantum pensum evigilaris urserisque, egregio exemplo cantabunt. Si cogitationes obiter ad disciplinas primarum artium redigo, ecquid vel ad commentationes, vel declamationes, vel etiam consultationes proposueris, quid abditum natura tenet, cuius tu non indicium extuleris, suavissimis Camoenis ita subegeris, ita explicaris, ut penu te φυσιολογίας τε καὶ φιλολογίας[1926] dixerim, ac si feres merito, quod res ipsa luculente monstrat, aliquot veterum sophistarum progymnasmata lucem aliquando prae talibus sunt fugitura, ita decorum καὶ τὸ πρὸ ὀμμάτων[1927] ποιήσις[1928] Aristotelea[1929] cuncta velut orbe suo comprehendit. Nec semper ego admitto illud veteris fabulatoris: τὸ πολλὰ τολμᾶν, πολλ᾽ ἁμαρτάνειν ποιεῖ.[1930] Abest enim a tuis προπέτεια[1931] illa, quae reprehensionibus conflictatur. De memoria vulgo mihi abs te impertita, et amo te et gratiam habeo. Debeo certe mutuum, dum officio pari reddidero. Ieremiam[1932] nostrum comes[1933] laudat,

---

[1926] of physiology and philology
[1927] and the vivid
[1928] poetry
[1929] Cf. Aristoteles, *Rhetorica* 3.10.7.
[1930] To venture a lot makes one errs a lot. *Menandri sententiae* 774.
[1931] rashness
[1932] Nicolaus Reusner's younger brother Jeremias (1557–1599), who was the editor of the *Insomniae* and several other works of his older brother.
[1933] Sambucus had secured for Jeremias Reusner a position as secretary to count Julius Salm-Neuburg (cf. the letter

conscium secretorum esse et magistrum libellorum patitur. Industriam ita exercet, ut eo loco et fide ad Italiae Galliaeque lumina emersurum eum minime dubitem. Qua in spe ne diu ille haereat, omnem adhibebo operam. Vale. Vienna. 26. Martii 1581. Ioannes Sambucus.

338.
Christophe Plantin to Sambucus
22 April 1581, Antwerp

The draft of the letter is kept in Museum Plantin-Moretus, Antwerp - UNESCO, World Heritage, Archief Officina Plantiniana, X, f. 27^v. Published in *Correspondance de Christophe Plantin*, 6:259-260.

Plantin passed the images of the coins to Abraham Ortelius, who corrected a few letters in some of the descriptions, but wanted Plantin to send them back to Sambucus to be checked once more, because they were so badly transcribed that he did not dare correct them. He could not achieve anything with Vulcanius, who left.

Clarissimo viro domino Iohanni Sambuco.

Communicavi cum Ortelio figuras numismatum.[1934] Is quasdam litteras emendavit in nonnulis. Has vero suasit ut tibi remitterem ad scripturam examinandam in qua putat esse maiora vitia, quam ut audeat manum apponere. Nostri Francofurto redierunt, sed libri non sunt adhuc allati. A Vulcanio nihil potui extorquere. Is hinc discessit.[1935] Bene vale. Antverpiae raptim inter varias occupationes et dificultates innumeras. Deus nos sua misericordia conservet. 22. Aprilis 1581.

339.
Sambucus to Henri Estienne
29 April 1581, Vienna

The original is kept in Bremen, Staats- und Universitätsbibliothek, msa 0008, no. 166. Published in a mutilated way in *Philologicarum epistolarum centuria una*, 313 (nr. 74);[1936] Gerstinger, "Die Briefe," 258-259 (relying on the published version).

Sambucus received the parcel from Estienne and acknowledges it as a sign of love for him. He hardly expected anything more avidly than Xenophon's edition. Zosimus is in great parts seriously mutilated, he hoped it was going to be in better shape, but what could Estienne have done? It happens also to greater authors. Estienne will not only receive what Sambucus had already contributed to

---

of Giacomo Malipiero, the count's counsellor, at the beginning of the *Insomniae* on f. A2^{r-v}). The count also praises Jeremias in his letter to Nicolaus Reusner attached at the end of the *Insomniae* (f. [C7^v]-[C8^v]).

[1934] These might have been images of coins to be included into a new edition of the *Emblemata*. (The Latin original was published in 1564, 1566, 1569, 1576, 1584 and 1599. The edition of 1584 does not have new coins.)

[1935] On Vulcanius, neither publishing nor returning Sambucus's manuscripts cf. the Index.

[1936] Cf. with letter 312, note 1816.

Dioscorides but also some weighty additions. He agrees with the quarto format, but it should be out for the next autumn book fair and Estienne should urge Jean-Antoine Sarasin to prepare the translation. If he cannot have the free time for that, they should follow the translation of Jean Ruel, adding Sarasin's notes to it. If Sambucus had known how many obstacles would arise, he would have prevented many of them already earlier. Estienne should do his best and oblige Sarasin so greatly with his generosity (i.e. money) that he should not be able to slip away and not finish what he started. Theodor Zwinger and Pietro Perna know how much Sambucus quarrelled about (the edition of) Aristotle with Eusebius Episcopius, using also threats. Estienne made everyone excited by his future edition of Galen. Perna published Sambucus's manuscript of the fragments of Palladius's commentaries to (Hippocrates's) Epidemics in the translation of Giulio Paolo Crasso. Sambucus wishes he had entrusted it to Estienne. Sambucus, finally, expresses his admiration for Sarasin and Estienne. He is also expecting other books he entrusted to Estienne.

Sambucus salutem dicit.

Fasciculum ad me missum, quod indicium plenum amoris interpretor, accepi. Xenophontis editio ita valde mihi accepta venit, nil ut cupidius exspectarim.[1937] Zosimi mutila sunt et suis partibus mutila, graviter affecta plurima.[1938] Sed quid agas? Melioribus id malum scriptoribus evenit. Graecum sperabam fore integrius totque locis minus ad sanitatem impeditum. Quod editioni Dioscoridis detuli, non modo accipies, sed cum ἐπιμέτρῳ[1939] non contemnendo. Forma quadrata isthaec placet, modo pergas, ut autumnalibus his nundinis possimus habere. Quid ut certius confirmem amicis, Saracenum urgeto, admoneto publico commodo. Pergat, versionem absolvat. Ni tantum a tot annis ocii a gravioribus obtinet, Ruellium sequimini, modo Saraceni notae adsint ac quadrent.

Si tot divortia, impedimenta interventura cogitassem, tempore multis occurrissem. Quaeso te, mi optime Henrice, praelis et industria in Dioscoridem incumbito, tuos addicito totos. Saracenum ita benevolentia et liberalitatis copia adstringas e nexu ut nostro elabi nequeat, quodque incohavit, perficiat.

De Aristotele quantae rixae cum Episcopio mihi sint, testem habes Zwingerum, Pernam, cum quibus acerbius quoque et minaciter nuper egi. Quo scripto, [...][1940] significet, me non parum profecisse, ipsosque de[nique] impressionem acceleraturos. Iacta est alea [...] minus prudenter, qui moras texit, ac tant[...] nugis querendam commutare omnino veren[tur ...] et ad Dioscoridem te Saracenumque applicato, si me amatis, citra damnum fore tuum scio. De Galeni editione omnes excitasti, breve tibi comprecantur. Palladii ἀπόσπασμα[1941] in VI Ἐπιδημιῶν[1942] meum edidit Perna ex interpretatione Crassi,[1943] utinam tibi commisissem. Εὖγε

[1937] Ξενοφῶντος τὰ σωζόμενα βιβλία. *Xenophontis (viri armorum & literarum laude celeberrimi) quae extant opera. Annotationes Henrici Stephani* (Genevae: Stephanus, 1581).
[1938] Zosimus was printed as an addition to Henri Estienne's edition of *Herodiani Historiarum libri VIII* (Genevae: Stephanus, 1581). Johannes Löwenklau had published only a Latin translation of Zosimus, dedicated to Sambucus (see letter 259).
[1939] addition
[1940] The right margin of the letter is damaged in this part, missing between five and fifteen characters in each of the five lines.
[1941] fragment
[1942] of Epidemics
[1943] *Medici antiqui Graeci Aretaeus, Palladius, Ruffus, Theophilus, physici et chirurgi. ... Omnes a Iunio Paulo Crasso medico et professore Patavino Latio donati. Quibus accesserunt Stephanus Atheniensis et ipsius Crassi Quaestiones medicae et naturales* (Basileae: Perna, 1581). There is very little information on Giulio Paolo Crasso

ἔρρωσο[1944] atque Saracenum, virum clarissimum et magnum ἰατρὸν[1945] a me saluta, quem omni praeconio dignum censeo atque meritis vestris τιμωμένους [?][1946] florere, καὶ πᾶσαν γῆν καλῶς πράσσουσι εἶναι πατρίδα.[1947] III. Kalendas Maii 81. Viennae.

Verso: Libellos alios tibi commissos cum lucis fervore tuique praestantis ingenii vi illustres exspecto, nam ut pereant, bibliotheca nullo modo patietur.
Address: Praestanti et clarissimo viro domino Henrico Stephano, architypographo, amico meo veteri. Genevam. In eius absentia legat doctor Saracenus.

340.
Bonaventura Vulcanius to Sambucus
15 June 1581, Leiden

The original is kept in Leiden, Universiteitsbibliotheek, Bijzondere Collecties, Vul. 36, f. 139.

Christophe Plantin wanted to find out in Sambucus's name what Vulcanius was planning to do with Gregory of Nyssa's Great Catechesis. He did not respond earlier because of other occupations. As soon as he moves to Leiden, Greek classes will steal less of his time from friends. To tell the truth, this work of Gregory is not so suitable for publication in times inflamed by debates on the sacraments. In his opinion, Gregory is exceedingly philosophical here, more than it befits a theologian. Certainly, such a publication would lead to strife. Yet, good arguments can still convince him of the opposite, so he wants to hear Sambucus's opinion, who should, in the meanwhile, not be frustrated by the delay. He asks Sambucus to publish a catalogue of his manuscript books, as it has been done in Augsburg. He knows that Sambucus would then provide copies of his books to literate men who ask for them.

Sambuco.

Interpellavit me non semel tuo nomine Plantinus noster, ut, quid de Nysseni tui *Catechesi* statutum nobis esset, perscriberem.[1948] Id cur hactenus non fecerim, variae rerum mearum iactationes in causa fuerunt. Nunc cum semel Leydae pedem fixerim, non tantum, uti spero, temporis Graecae linguae professio auferet, quin multum sit superfuturum, quo amicis, quod facio libentissime,

---

(† c. 1575), to whom Girolamo Mercuriale entrusted Sambucus's manuscript of Palladius's commentary on book VI of Hippocrates' *Epidemics* (as Celso, the son of Giulio Paolo, writes in the preface). See Gerstinger, "Zusammenfassung," 307-308. The manuscript of Palladius, which Crassus used for his translation, was actually incomplete, so he supplied the missing parts from the commentary by Ioannes Alexandrinus. See Sibylle Ihm, *Clavis Commentariorum der antiken Medizinischen Texte* (Leiden: Brill, 2002), 178.

[1944] now then, farewell
[1945] of Epidemics
[1946] honoured
[1947] and the whole world is the fatherland to those who do well. Cf. Erasmus, *Adagia* 1193.
[1948] Gregory of Nyssa's *Great Catechesis*, a defence of Catholic teaching against the Jews, heathens and heretics, was his most important theological work. Several years before, Sambucus told Nicasius Ellebodius (see letter 203) that he had sent the letters of Gregory of Nyssa to Plantin but did not mention this manuscript. To be sure, it was not this publication that Sambucus so avidly expected from Vulcanius, but the Greek letters of Chrysoloras, mentioned first in letter 117, and in all the previous letters to Joachim Camerarius Jr. See also letter 351.

vacare possim.[1949] Atque ut sincere tibi animi mei sententiam de Gregorii tui scripto aperiam, non video an magnopere expediat, ut hisce temporibus adeo ob controversias de re sacramentaria exulceratis in vulgus edatur. Agit enim hac in parte, περὶ μετρησιήσεως[1950] inquam, philosophum, meo quidem iudicio ultra quam theologum deceat. Neque dubitarim quin, si manus hominum contentiosorum inciderit, maiorem rixis atque dissidiis ansam sit praebiturus, quum de iis componendis serio potius cogitandum esset. Idem crediderim quam plurimos doctos et pios et Christianae tranquillitates mecum sensuros. Neque tamen ita hac in sententia animum meum obfirmavi, quin rationum machinis ab ea[1951] dimoveri possim. Gratissimum certe fuerit tuum ea de re indicium audire, quo semel intellecto non comittam, quin de versione certi aliquid statuam. Te interea ut moram hanc non moleste feras etiam atque etiam rogo. Manuscriptorum codicum,[1952] quorum apud te ingente thesaurum esse audio, velim te exemplo Augustanae reipublicae indicem edere. Facile enim mihi tantum de tuo erga bonas literas studio persuadeo, ut non gravate literatis viris, modo bene tibi caveatur, eorum, quos petent, copiam sis facturus. Bene vale, vir clarissime, et a me omnia studia et officia expectes. 15. Iunii 1581.

341.
Andreas Dudith to Sambucus
22 June 1581, Wrocław

Copies are kept in Wrocław, Biblioteka Uniwersytecka, Akc. 1949/549 (=Kl. 169), no. 12, f. 9^r; Bruxelles, Bibliothèque royale, ms. 19306, cah. 39, no. 60, f. 84^{r-v}; Berlin, Staatsbibliothek - Preußischer Kulturbesitz, R 253, no. 3, f. 4^r. Published in Pierre Costil, *André Dudith*, 44; Dudithius, *Epitulae*, 7:61-63.

Whenever Dudith sees Sambucus's letters sent to mutual friends on a daily basis, he is saddened that Sambucus, being such an old friend, does not even mention his name in them. Even worse is that he does not even respond to his letters, but all this did not cause Dudith to stop loving him. An opportunity for writing this letter was given by the Englishman Henry Savile, who will deliver it, and whom Dudith recommends as a person most worthy for Sambucus's hospitality and for sharing his library with. He is proficient in Latin, Greek, Hebrew and philosophy, and Dudith would swear that he is the best in mathematics. Thaddaeus Hagecius mentions him at the end of his work on the comet and Dudith in his preface to the same book. He heard from Hagecius that Sambucus had sent some mathematical books to Conrad Dasypodius. He begs Sambucus to get them back or have them published by someone else as they will perish there (in Dasypodius's hands), which he will better understand from Savile. Dudith complains that Sambucus's Aristotle, Hippocrates, Dioscorides and "Epistulae sacrae" have never seen the light. Sambucus will learn about the identity of the two noblest adolescents who are accompanying Savile from Savile himself. They are from baronial families of the first rank, one is the brother of Philip Sidney, who was sent some years ago by the queen (Elizabeth I) to Maximilian II, the other is coming from the ancient Neville family.

[1949] Cf. letter 289, note 1682.
[1950] beyond measure
[1951] Instead of crossed out: *facile me*.
[1952] Instead of crossed out: *Bibliothecae tuae*.

Iohanni Sambuco.

Quoties litteras tuas ad communes amicos video, mei me pudet ac sane etiam miseret, quod ne mentio quidem in illis mei inicitur.[1953] Quid commerui, mi Sambuce, ut veteris amici ac sodalis cari omnem prorsus memoriam abiceres? Illud etiam acerbius est, quod ne respondes quidem. Gravia certe haec sunt et perpessu aspera,[1954] sed numquam tamen perficient, ut tui cupidissimus amantissimusque esse desinam. Hanc ad te scribendi et leviter expostulandi occasionem attulit mihi dominus Savile, qui has reddet, nobilis Anglus.[1955] Is, ad te aditum ut sibi patefacerem, petivit, quem tu pro tua bonitate et humanitate nemini bono umquam clausisti.[1956] Sed si quem umquam amice accepisti, oro te pro veteri nostra amicitia, ut hunc hominem accipias. Dignus imprimis est, quem ames cuique bibiothecae tuae thesaurum aperias. Latinae, Graece, Hebraicae linguae, philosophiae, mathematicarum disciplinarum peritissimus est, in quibus quidem mathematicis ausim deierare non vivere quemquam, qui huic merito anteferri debeat, id quod tu facile iudicabis. Hic ille est, cuius dominus Thaddaeus in postremo *Cometa* suo,[1957] ego item in praefatione in illius librum mea[1958] mentionem fecimus. Audivi ex eo, ut id obiter dicam, libros quosdam mathematicos a te Dasypodio commissos esse. Oro te, ut eos retrahas aut aliis excudendos tradas, ibi quidem interibunt, de quo plura ex domino Savile cognosces. Tuus Aristoteles, Hippocrates, Dioscuri[de]s, *Epistolae sacrae* et praeclara alia nondum lucem aspiciunt. Dii male illis faciant, qui tanta nobis bona invident. Duo nobilissimi atque illustrissimi adolescentuli, quos hinc comites nactus est, qui sint, ex ipso cognosces. Primarii barones sunt regni illius, alter Sidneus, Philippi frater,[1959] qui

---

[1953] Their most important mutual friend was Johannes Crato, who had moved to Prague from Wrocław a year before Dudith moved to Wrocław. Sambucus also corresponded with Jacobus Monavius, and Dudith may have referred to him, but perhaps also to his close friend Thaddaeus Hagecius, who lived in Prague (see below).

[1954] Cf. Cicero, *Tusculanae disputationes* 2.20.7: "O multa dictu gravia, perpessu aspera."

[1955] Henry Savile (1549–1622) was a remarkable mathematician and humanist. He is famous for his translation of the New Testament from Greek and his translation of the Histories of Tacitus. He was an avid collector of manuscripts. Later, he endowed the "Savilian chairs of astronomy and of geometry at Oxford University." See Robert Goulding, "Sir Henry Savile," *Oxford Dictionary of National Biography* 49 (2004), 109-118; idem, *Defending Hypatia. Ramus, Savile, and the Renaissance Rediscovery of Mathematical History* (Dordrecht: Springer, 2010); Jan Waszink, "Henry Savile's Tacitus and the English role on the Continent: Leicester, Hotman, Lipsius," *History of European Ideas* 42 (2016), 303-319.

[1956] A significant stop of Henry Savile's study tour was the house of Andreas Dudith in Wrocław. In early January 1581 Savile arrived from Nuremberg (which he visited because of the imperial diet) and stayed with Dudith for more than a half year. On his way to Italy he stopped in Vienna and visited Sambucus, who provided him with a copy of Geminus's *Elements of Astronomy*, which was based on a copy from Busbequius's collection obtained in Constantinople (see Costil, *André Dudith*, 305-306). On his Italian stay see Jonathan Woolfson, *Padua and the Tudors: English Students in Italy, 1485–1603* (Toronto: University of Toronto Press, 1998), 129-130.

[1957] Thaddaeus Hagecius (Thadeáš Hájek) (1525–1600) was a Bohemian doctor, Rudolf II's physician, botanist and one of the leading astronomers of the age. He studied in Prague, Vienna and Bologna, and became professor of mathematics at the University of Prague in 1555. In 1566–1570, he also served as an army doctor in Austria and Hungary. See Clarissa Doris Hellman, *The Comet of 1577: its Place in the History of Astronomy* (New York: Columbia Univ. Press, 1944), 184-206; Josef Smolka, "Briefwechsel zwischen Tycho Brahe und Thaddaeus Hagecius – Anfänge," in *Tycho Brahe and Prague: Crossroads of European Science*, eds. John Robert Christianson et al. (Frankfurt am Main: Deutsch, 2002), 224-236; Josef Smolka, "Thaddaeus Hagicius ab Hayck, aulae caesareae maiestatis medicus," in *"Discourses – Diskurse": Essays for – Beiträge zu Mikuláš Teich & Alice Teichova*, ed. Gertrude Enderle-Burcel (Prague: Nová tiskárna Pelhřimov, 2008), 395-412. The work in question is Hagecius's *Apodixis physica et mathematica de cometis* (Gorlicii: Fritsch, 1581). Hagecius's reference is at the end of his dedication to Dudith.

[1958] Dudith's letter is included into Hagecius's *Apodixis physica* (as in the preceding note), f. A2^r-A4^v.

[1959] Robert Sidney, 1st earl of Leicester (1563–1626) soldier, diplomatist and patron of literature.

ante paucos annos a regina ad dominum Maximilianum caesarem allegatus erat, Hiberniae proregis filius. Alter Nevellus, ex antiquissima et illustrissima Nevellorum, Rosae Rubrae familia.[1960] Doctus uterque et modestus. Eos tibi unice commendo. Vale meque mutuo ama et dominum Isthwanffium ex me officiose saluta. Breslae, 22. Iunii, anno 1581.

342.
Sambucus to Joachim Camerarius Jr.
1 July 1581, Vienna

The original is kept in Munich, BSB, Clm 10367, f. 314ʳ. Published in Gerstinger, "Die Briefe," 260-261.

Sambucus is wondering about the parcel that he sent to Simon Grynaeus through Camerarius. He has heard that Grynaeus returned to Basel, where he became professor of ethics. If Camerarius still has the book, he can take a look at it with Johannes Praetorius and see if they think it worthy of publication. Sambucus complains about Bonaventura Vulcanius's silence, who is holding back (the letters) of Chrysoloras and other writings belonging to Camerarius, and asserts that unless Vulcanius responds through Plantin, he will have to threaten him. Concerning the rest, Camerarius should be informed by others, as in the political situation of the day ("mores et tempora") not even ideas appear to be free any more. This is how they deceive the feelings of the common people and take everything badly.

Salutem.

De fasciculo ad Simonem Gryneum per te misso nil audio.[1961] Gryneum Basileam rediise isticque ethices factum professorem aiunt. Si adhuc tenes, non refert, etiamsi libellum cum Praetorio, viro clarissimo vestro, conferas,[1962] et an luce vestraque opera dignus sit, definiatis. Vulcani silentium miror, qui Chrysoloram et alia tua premit.[1963] Alia via et minis tractandus erit, nisi quamprimum per Plantinum responderit. De aliis malo te ab aliis doceri, quod his moribus et temporibus ne cogitationes quidem satis liberae videantur, ita vulgi sensus ludunt cunctaque in deterius accipiunt. Vale, ipsis Kalendis Quinctilibus 1581. Viennae. Totus tuus Sambucus.

Address: Clarissimo viro domino Ioachimo Camerario, reipublicae Noribergensis physico etc., domino amico observando. Nurnberg.
Camerarius's hand: 81. 16 Iulii.

[1960] Henry Neville (1564–1615) studied in Oxford. Tutored by Henry Savile, he was likewise interested in mathematics. Upon their return to England, he soon joined the parliament as a delegate for New Windsor. The red rose is a reference to Neville's coat of arms.
[1961] See letter 331.
[1962] Johannes Praetorius (Richter) (1537–1616) was a mathematician and astronomer, who studied in Wittenberg, lived in Nuremberg from 1562 and in Vienna in 1569. In 1569–1571 and 1575–76 he stayed in close relation with Andreas Dudith in Krakow. In 1571–75 he was professor of mathematics at Wittenberg and from 1576 in Altdorf. He published calendars with astronomical information and also devised mathematical instruments. See Menso Folkerts, "Johannes Praetorius (1537–1616)–ein bedeutender Mathematiker und Astronom des 16. Jahrhunderts," in *History of Mathematics. States of the Art*, ed. Joseph Dauben (San Diego: Academic Press, 1996), 148-169.
[1963] See letter 117, esp. note 687, and cf. the Index.

343.
Sambucus to the Mayor and the Council of Trnava
18 July 1581, Vienna

The original is kept in Trnava, SAT, Magistrát mesta Trnava, Missiles. Published in Vantuch, "Die Sambucusbriefe," 356.

It is a reaction to Trnava's request concerning the city's search for a doctor. As Sambucus told them before, it would be easy to find good and experienced doctors, provided the city and the church (the chapter) generously pay them. If the city pays an annual salary of 100 (florins) and the chapter does the same, he will make sure that a doctor is found for them.

Egregii et prudentes, patroni obs[ervandissimi, salutem et] debitam servitiorum commendationem.

Exposuit [... ... ...]¹⁹⁶⁴ vester, instituisse ac denuo instruxisse [... ...]atoris commendaticiis medicis suam officinam, sed deesse dominationibus vestris doctorem. Ego antea significavi non defore bonos medicos et peritos, modo liberalitas vestra cum reverendo capitulo desit. Nam si vos 100, capitulum totidem annuos definieritis, cura erit mihi et aliis, ut civitas vestra sit ornata et provisa Deo volente. Quare ubi imperaveritis, diligenter obsequar, meque vestro patrocinio commendo. 18. Iulii 81. Viennae. Dominationum vestrarum servitor et alumnus Ioannes Sambucus manu propria.

Address: Egregiis ac circumspectis dominis iudici senatuique Tyrnaviensi, dominis patronis et amicis observandissimis Tyrnaviam.

344.
Martin Crusius¹⁹⁶⁵ to Sambucus
4 August 1581, Tübingen

The original is kept in Vienna, ÖNB, Cod. 9736, f. 12ʳ. Published in Hans Gerstinger, "Martin Crusius' Briefwechsel mit den Wiener Gelehrten Hugo Blotius und Johannes Sambucus (1581–1599)," *Byzantinische Zeitschrift* 29 (1929), 210-211.

[1964] The manuscript is damaged. Concerning the letter see the commentary in Vantuch's edition ("Die Sambucusbriefe," 356), where he claims that in 1578 Sambucus had already recommended a doctor called Sporischius, coming from Ottenbach (Otmuchów) in Silesia, who referred to Sambucus in his letters addressed to the city of Trnava. For the letters, see Jozef Šimončič, "Príspevok ku korešpondencii Jána Sambuca," *Historické štúdie* 13 (1968), 257-259. Johannes Sporischius (Johann Sporisch, c. 1546–?) graduated at the University of Vienna in 1575. In the same year, he offered his services as a doctor to the city of Olomouc (Ölmutz) asking for an apartment, salary and allowance for his graduation in Vienna. See Archiv města Olomouce, Ref. mark 2277, Sig. 77/1, s.n. 2265. His request was denied, much like the one he made three years later in Trnava. He worked as a physician in Znojmo (Znaim) and Wrocław, later returned to the University of Vienna where he became, for a brief time, a member of the Faculty of Medicine. Eventually he returned to Moravia. See *Rukověť humanistického básnictví v Čechách a na Moravě* 5 (1982), 153-155. We thank Ivan Lábaj for this information.

[1965] Martin Crusius (1526–1607) was one of the most famous German Hellenists of the epoch as well as a historian and classical philologist. He was professor at the University of Tübingen from 1559. He maintained many relationships with contemporary Greeks, and also studied their language and history. See in Franz Brendle,

441

Crusius thanks Sambucus for having taken the time to explain some barbarian (i.e. modern) Greek, which was a great help. He has a modern Greek history of political and ecclesiastical matters, which he has already translated and wants to publish together with some recent vulgar and elegant modern Greek letters, partly written to him, partly written among Greeks. He will provide ample notes in order to make contemporary Greece better known. If Sambucus has any of these kind of letters, modern Greek histories or poets and does not want to publish them, Crusius would add them to his volume and publicly praise him. Finally, at the request of Michael Neander, he asks about Johannes Löwenklau. He hopes that no one will be offended by his work, which is full of references to learned men and omits everything that is not praiseworthy.

Salutem per Christum.

Nobilis et clarissime vir, domine colende! Quod dominatio tua inter plurima, ut non dubito, ardua negotia sibi tamen temporis sumpsit, ut mihi non pauca Barbaro-Graeca explicaret, gratias equidem ago permagnas, quia per mihi quoque gratum officium fuit nec inde nihil sum adiutus.[1966] Habeo enim Barbaro-Graecam historiam in manibus, politicam et ecclesiasticam, quam cum conversione mea iam absoluta cogito edere in publicam ξὺν θεῷ[1967] una cum multis hodiernae vulgaris et politioris linguae epistulis, quas partim ad me, partim ipsi inter se Graeci scripserunt.[1968] Addo copiosas ubique annotationes, ut hodierna Graecia nobis notior fiat. Si ergo dominatio tua etiam aliquas epistulas habet huius temporis (sive politioris, sive vulgaris linguae) nec eas ipsa edere vult, poterit ad me mittere et ego cum hoc opere coniungens non sine elogio (qualecumque parvitas mea dare potest) nominis tui antea clarissimi (sed me εὐχάριστον[1969] esse decebit) simul edam.[1970] Si quid etiam Barbaro-Graecae historiae aut poeseos habes. Nam hisce annis non parum eam linguam didici. Εἰ δέ τι πέμψεις, πέμψειας, ὦ κλεινὲ, ὡς ἂν δύναιο, τάχιστα.[1971] Bene valeat dominatio tua et me venia atque etiam favore suo dignetur. Tybingae, 4. Augusti 1581. Nobilitatis et virtutis tuae studiosissimus Μαρτίνος ὁ Κρούσιος.

"Martin Crusius. Humanistische Bildung, schwäbisches Luthertum und Griechenlandbegeisterung," in *Deutsche Landesgeschichtsschreibung im Zeichen des Humanismus*, ed. F. Brendle (Stuttgart: Steiner, 2001), 145-166.

[1966] This letter is the principal source for Sambucus's knowledge of modern Greek, and interest in the contemporary Greek situation. See also note 1970, which suggests that Sambucus had good relations with contemporary Greeks.

[1967] with god's help

[1968] Martinus Crusius, *Turcograeciae libri octo ... quibus Graecorum status sub imperio Turcico in politia et ecclesia, oeconomia et scholis, iam inde ab amissa Constantinopoli, ad haec usque tempora, luculenter describitur* (Basileae: Leonhard Ostensius, 1584).

[1969] agreeable

[1970] In a letter of 1 August 1581 Crusius tells Michael Neander that Stephan Gerlach, who worked as secretary to the imperial delegate David Ungnad in Constantinople, told him to make sure to obtain from Sambucus any new letters that were sent to him by the Greeks: "Da operam, ut a D. Sambuco, mihi etiam favente, Graecorum literas accipias, cum toties ab ipsis accipiat." Michael Neander, *Bedencken an einen guten Herrn und Freund* (enlarged 4th ed.) (Eisleben: Urbanus Gubisius, 1583), f. 71ᵛ. In the same book (f. 54ᵛ), Neander informs the reader of a long letter by Ioannes Zygomalas (a frequent correspondent of Crusius from the mid-1570s), which Neander received from Sambucus but decided not to transcribe and include into his book because of its length: "Cum istis eas etiam adiungere hoc loco licuisset, quas a Iohanne Zygomala viro septuagenario maiore et plurium linguarum et inter caeteras etiam latinae linguae callente, magnae ecclesiae, quae est Constantinopoli interprete, prolixe et amice scriptas, in ipso autographo legendas nuper Vienna Austriae ad nos misit clarissimus, celeberrimus et doctissimus vir D. Iohannes Sambucus caesareae maiestatis medicus, historicus et consiliarius." On Zygomalas and his contacts, see *Ἰωάννης καὶ Θεοδόσιος Ζυγομαλᾶς*, ed. Stauros Perentidēs (Athēna: Daidalos, 2009).

[1971] If you will send something, on renowned man, may you send it as soon as you can.

Ubi est noster Levenclavius aut quid agit? Quid editurus est? Quaerit ex me D. Neander.[1972] Neminem (spero) hoc opus offendet, sed gratum erit φιλέλληνι παντί.[1973] In annotationibus multos claros viros induco. Quae laudare non possum, omitto, tantum ἐπαινετὰ καὶ φιλικὰ[1974] pono.

Address: Nobili et clarissimi viro, domino Ioanni Sambuco, augusti Romanorum historiographo dignissimo, domino suo officiose colendo. Viennae Austria.

345.
Sambucus to Christophe Plantin
26 August 1581, [Vienna]

The original is kept in Museum Plantin-Moretus, Antwerp - UNESCO, World Heritage, Archief Officina Plantiniana, XCIII, f. 7. Published in *Correspondance de Christophe Plantin*, 6:286-287; Gerstinger, "Die Briefe," 261-262.

Sambucus received the books from Plantin. If Plantin writes him the price, he will get the money from Jean Aubry. Sambucus wants to thank for such benevolence and generosity. He asks Plantin to give Aubry the missing pages from Ludovico Guicciardini's book. He is sending his greetings to Abraham Ortelius and wants to know if he has already published the map of Greece. Sambucus sent back to Plantin the pictures of the back sides of antique coins with the addition of some recently purchased rare ones. He asks him either to attach them to a re-edition of the Emblemata *or to send them back. If he attaches them, the* Emblemata *would have greater success among the French and the Italians. The copies were made of coins that are original and fully made of copper, which is much appreciated among numismatists, so Plantin should warn the readers.*

Sambucus salutem.

Libellos novos una cum Belgiae descriptione accepi,[1975] habeo gratiam. Si pretium adscripsisses, per Aubrium reciperes. Volo enim hanc benevolentiam et liberalitatem erga me sine mutuo καὶ ἐπιμέτρῳ[1976] quoque commemorare. Sed in Guicciardini opere P. ternio deest,[1977] quem

---

[1972] Michael Neander (1525–1595) was the rector of the monastery school of Ilfeld. In 1580 he published the above-mentioned book (*Bedencken an einen guten Herrn*, f. 48ʳ) on the education of children, to which he added some letters on the Ottoman situation. From one of Neander's attached letters we learn that even Sambucus has confirmed to him that Athens was still a great and well-populated city, worthy of a visit. Having toured barbarian Greece Sambucus did not neglect Athens either: "Ac idem plane de Athenis affirmare ac commemorare solere virum clarissimum et celeberrimum D. Ioannem Sambucum Romanae caesareae maiestatis medicum et historicum, qui perlustrata Graecia barbara, Athenas etiam hodiernas inaccessas et inexcussas non reliquit, scribitur ad me diebus superioribus ex Austria." Since no other information confirms Sambucus's journey to Greece, Neander may have misunderstood his letter. Supposing Sambucus did indeed visit Greece, the only time it could have happened was in 1561–1562 with a departure from Southern Italy.
[1973] to every philhellene
[1974] what is praiseworthy and friendly
[1975] *Descrittione di tutti i paesi Bassi per M. Ludovico Guicciardini... riveduta di nuovo ed ampliata* (Antverpiae, Plantin, 1581). See Gulyás, *Sámboky János könyvtára*, 1566/1.
[1976] and with a bonus
[1977] Ternio is a quire consisting of three sheets of paper, which once folded in the middle form 6 leaves, i.e. 12 pages

Aubrio, tuo tamen commodo, dabis. Dominum Ortelium saluta, et an Graeciam absolverit, vellem significares.[1978] Numismatum antiquorum et aereorum omnium aversas partes remisi cum augmento; addo has quoque raras, quas nuper adeptus sum. Oro, ne pereant, et vel addes *Emblematis* extremo aut salva et integra remittes. Verum scio *Emblemata* fore Italis et Gallis longe cariora horum appendice. Vale, raptim 26. Augusti 1581.

In primis scito numos, quorum similitudinem καὶ ἀπόγραφα[1979] ad te misi et mittam forte, si gratum erit, esse genuinos aereosque omnes, nullum alius metalli, ideoque rariores et amantibus talia fore gratiores spero, idque si in fronte numorum admonueris lectorem, recte facies.

Address: Domino Christophoro Piantino typographo regio, amico optimo. Francfortum aut Antverpiam.

346.
Piero Vettori to Sambucus
1 September 1581, [Florence]

The original is kept in Munich, BSB, Clm 791, f. 242.

Old Vettori's hand is hardly legible. In this letter, he recommends Riccardo Riccardi (see the next letter).

Ioanni Sambuco.

Inter occasionem mihi datam, mi Sambuce, scribendi ad te atque eam quidem humanitatem, ut potius tibi voluptatis aliquid allatura sit, quam molestiae aut incommodi [...] enim facio [...] ea, qui libenter video amicos amicorum meorum atque ipsis quacunque ratione possum inservio, modo ad nos minimis [?] probus, nae omni liberali doctrina perpolitus, instruxisses, quam ego valde diligo, ut in quo olim [...]

Est enim θεωρὸς[1980] ac facile potest [?] non abundat, perclarum ratio danda in suum amphora. Nam bonam etiam Graecam partem perlustravit. Gratum igitur mihi feceris, si ipsum comitem acciperis ne aliquo huius generis atte[...]ris. Vocatur autem is Riccardus Riccardius de cuius etiam ingenio et amore magno erga studia bonarum artium ergo iam diu non nihil in meis scriptis praedicavi. Vale Florentiae. Kalendis Septembris MDLXXXI.

---

in a book. In addition to pagination, many early modern prints contained also a quire count in letters at the lower margin of the page (A, B, C, ... AA, BB, CC etc., with the leave count within a quire as in A, A2, A3 etc.). The quire P in Plantin's Guicciardini edition consists of pages 137–148. As the books were often transported unbound in order to save on the shipping costs, Sambucus could include the missing quire afterwards.

[1978] A map of Greece ("Graecia Sophiani") was first included into Ortelius's *Theatrum orbis terrarum* in its 1579 edition. It also appeared as a separate print. This map by Nikolaos Sophianos had originally been printed in 1540 (now lost). Sambucus's question implies that he was the one who sent a copy of the map to Ortelius. See George Tolias, "Nikolaos Sophianos's Totius Graeciae Descriptio: The Resources, Diffusion and Function of a Sixteenth-Century Antiquarian Map of Greece," *Imago Mundi* 58,2 (2006), 150-182.

[1979] (a drawing) and and a transcription

[1980] envoy

347.
Sambucus to Piero Vettori
21 October 1581, [Vienna]

The original is kept in Munich, BSB, Clm 735, f. 157. Published in Gerstinger, "Die Briefe," 262-263.

There was no need for Vettori to recommend Riccardo Riccardi, who Sambucus came to like profoundly for his virtues and talents. He wishes Riccardi could stay longer, but his friends and his fatherland are calling him back, as well the gymnasium (Studio Fiorentino), which should always be adorned by Vettori's presence and writings. Riccardi observed everything that Sambucus keeps in his study, but did not have sufficient time, being kept away by businesses. Sambucus is happy that Vettori brought back from the otherworld the ghosts of two legates (i.e. published their vitae by Dionysius of Halicarnassus), and he hopes that he will soon publish his thoughts about the ethics (of Aristotle).

Sambucus salutem clarissimo domino Petro Victorio.

Richardum vestrum, modo etiam nostrum, suis virtutibus, tua etiam commendatione, qua opus non erat, ita comprehendi itaque intestine ad animum egregias eius dotes admisi, ut, qui cum diu esse velim συζυγεῖν,[1981] συμφιλολογεῖν[1982] perpetuo cuperem.[1983] Hunc prae multis in oculis tulerim, sed revocant ipsum amici, patria, revocant ista vestra urbs literis et humanitate praestans, Mediceorum nunquam interiturum patrocinium, tuis quoque Musis et platano illustrissimum et florentissimum gymnasium. Quod tua luce et voce, stylo et lucubrationibus uti perpetuum sit, iure omnes politioribus literis imbuti expetere debent. Equidem nil apud me vel temere quod pateat, vel studio lateat, ab oculis Richardi fugit. Utinam ad eorum explicationes eius consuetudo fuisset liberior perque negotia subitumque recursum magis diuturna. Non fallit illud, opinor, Democriti: Τὰς μεγάλας τέρψεις ἀπὸ τοῦ θεᾶσθαι τὰ καλὰ τῶν ἔργων γενέσθαι.[1984] Duum summorum oratorum manes tua lyra ab inferis excitatos vitaeque ac lumini suo redditos admodum laetor, quos nondum videre licuit.[1985] De moribus quae tuae sint cogitationes,[1986] quod institutum, brevi nos visuros speramus, hoc est, intimum pectus atque thesauros viri prudentis, boni, officiosi, cauti, omnium commodis ac usibus parati. Vale, utque secundum illud concilium beatorum, quo mens piorum respectat, vires atque animum tuum communia studia mille annis amicorumque familiaritates contineant, demorentur, senectam firment, ex animo precor. 12 Calendas Novembris 1581.

Address: Clarissimo ac praestantissimo viro, domino Petro Victorio etc. Florentiam.

[1981] to get in touch. Ms.: συζηγεῖν.
[1982] to study literature together
[1983] Riccardo Romolo Riccardi (1558–1612) came from an important family of bankers. He was a student of Piero Vettori at the University of Pisa. Later, he established the Biblioteca Riccardiana. See Paolo Malanima, *I Riccardi di Firenze. Una famiglia e un patrimonio nella Toscana dei Medici* (Florence: L. S. Olschki, 1977), 48-103; idem, "Riccardo Riccardi," *DBI* 87 (2016), 176-177.
[1984] that the great satisfaction arises from watching the good doings. Cf. Democritus, Frg. DK B194.
[1985] Διονυσίου Ἁλικαρνασσέως Ἰσαῖος καὶ Δείναρχος. *Vitae Isaei et Dinarchi magnorum Graeciae oratorum... studio ac diligentia P. Victorii* (Lugduni: Ioannes Tornaesius, 1581). See Gerstinger, "Die Briefe," 263.
[1986] Sambucus may be referring here to *Petri Victorii Commentarii in X Libros Aristotelis de Moribus ad Nicomachum* (Florentiae: Giunta, 1584).

348.
Sambucus to the Hungarian Chamber
24 January 1582, Nuremberg

The original is kept in Vienna, Österreichisches Staatsarchiv, FHKA, Alte Hofkanzlei, Hoffinanz Ungarn 44, f. 6.

Four years before Sambucus asked for his seven-year salary. He was directed to get his payment through the tax office of Mosonmagyaróvár, but has received nothing. The unpaid salary of these last four years makes 1,200 thalers. In his present petition, he asks for payment of half of it, while the other half could be placed on a voucher and paid through the tax offices of Hlohovec at Trnava, Pressburg or Senec. Sambucus could at least pay off his debts. An order should be sent to the Hungarian Chamber concerning this debt of 1,200 thalers, because there is no other chance (for payment) than to get some share from the (traffic of) oxen or other goods.

Gnadig, Gebiettende Hern etc.

Ich hab vor vier Jahrn umb 7 Jharige meine Hoffpension suppliciert,[1987] und zuletzt auff das Altenburgische Ampt deruber verwisen worden, da ich noch khain haller hab empfangen, verhoff aber. Alzu sein yetzo weniger eins monatts 4 Jhar widerumb verstrichern, auch khain pfennig empfangen. Solcher 4 Jhar ausständt thuen 1200 taller zu 68 kr. Bitt Euer Gnaden, die wollen mir doch auffs wenigist den halben taill fürderlih in disen meinen nötten verordnen, und das Rest aber auff das Freystattisch zur Thirna, und Presspurgisch oder Warpergisch dreyssig[ist][1988] remittiren auff nächste abtriebe, damit ich doch meine schulden und creditores möge vertrösten, und ein bevelch druber auff die Ungrische Camer expediren, oder umb dies gantzen 1200 taller austand, seyes khain ander glegnhaitt haben khan, will vleysch haben, auch mitt meiner grosser ungelegenhaitt, das man etwas abtreyb, sey mitt ochsen oder andre whar, und handlsmautt solches umb Euer Gnaden untertaniglihste zu verdienen. Euer Gnaden Diener Alzeitlich D. Sambucus.

Address: An die Römisch kayserlicher Majestät Hoffkamer, Johan. Sambuci D. ghorsamste Suppliciren umb seine 4 Jahrige Hoffpension etc.
24 Ianuarii 82 Nurnberg.
Other hand: Camerae Hungaricae pro informatione et consilio. Niernbergae.

349.
Justus Lipsius to Sambucus
15 March 1582, Leiden

A manuscript copy, corrected by Lipsius, is kept in Leiden, Universitaire Bibliotheken, ms. Lips. 3 (5), f. 20^v. Published in Lipsius, *Epistolae*, 338-339.

[1987] Cf. with letter 314 (in which he asks for his six-year unpaid salary).
[1988] "Harmincadvám" (i.e. the thirtieth customs) of Wartberg, i.e. Senec in Slovak, Szenc (Szempcz) in Hungarian.

The reasons for their silence are both the difficult times in which they live and the distance that separates them. Lipsius is in Batavia, which is disturbed by public turmoil, but neither time nor distance could make him forget about Sambucus's pleasing memory. He is not working too hard, but wants to prepare a new full and commented edition of Tacitus. He remembers to have seen a Tacitus-manuscript owned by Sambucus, which could be useful for his work, and he asks him to send it to Plantin at the next book fair.

Clarissime vir Ioannes Sambuce, salve.

Diu mihi nullum alloquium apud te, ne per litteras quidem, caussa et temporum horum, quae nos turbant et ab omni tali voluptate revocant, et locorum, quae seiungunt. Nam nos in Batavis agimus apud Oceanum, vere undosum, iactati publica tempestate tibi non ignota. At nec loca tamen nec tempora gratam mihi memoriam tui excutiunt, quam testari volui per hanc occasionem primo mihi nunc datam. In studiis languide versamur, ita tamen ut cogitemus editionem novam Taciti[1989] cum pleno iustoque commentario ad eius omnes libros. Memoria teneo vidisse apud te eum scriptorem manu descriptum, qui mihi, et publico, possit esse usui inspectus. Quare si gratificari eius usuram mihi volueris, ad proximas nundinas videtur tuto posse transmitti ad Plantinum, qui ex fide curabit remittendum.[1990] Mihi certe gratum feceris, qui coeptam inter nos amicitiam sancte et servo et colo. Vale. Lugduni Batavorum, die qua olim Caesar in curia Pompeii. M. D. LXXXII.[1991]

350.
Sambucus to Theodor Zwinger
31 March 1582, Wien

The original is kept in Basel, Universitätsbibliothek, Frey Mscr II 26, no. 228. Published in Gerstinger, "Die Briefe," 263-264.

Zwinger should not think that Sambucus's silence was a sign of any resentment but rather that of renewed love. He knows that Zwinger is immersed in work, nonetheless, he warmly recommends

---

[1989] For Lipsius's first edition of Tacitus, dedicated partly to Sambucus, see letter 229. For the editions of 1581 and 1585 see note 1995 to letter 351.

[1990] Cf. with letter 351.

[1991] Lipsius revised this letter for the edition of the *Epistolarum centuriae duae* (Cent. I. Ep. 36.), where it first appeared with a changed date: 1 March 1579. Here follows the revised version: "Ioanni Sambuco salutem mitto. Diu mihi nullum alloquium apud te, ne per litteras quidem, causa et temporum horum, quae nos turbant, et locorum, quae seiungunt. Nam nos, ut audisse te credo, in Batavis agimus apud oceanum vere undosum, et iactamur civili tempestate, tibi non ignota. At nec loca tamen nec tempora gratam mihi memoriam Sambuci excutiunt, quam testari volui per hanc occasionem primo nunc datam. Qui enim illuc viam affectaret, praeter hunc adolescentem, nactus sum neminem, et nuncii illi ordinarii, ordines deservere per haec bella. In studiis, dum Mars hic fervet, languide versamur, ita tamen, ut cogitemus editionem novam Taciti cum pleno iustoque commentario in eius omnes libros. Ea in re iuvari me a te posse sentio usu libri manuscripti, quem memoria teneo Viennae olim vidisse. Non illum quidem antiquissimum, sed e quo tamen non dubie aliquid eruamus et critica ista sagacitate indagemus. Quare si eum ad tempus gratificari mihi volueris, amorem in me ostenderis et simul morem tuum tenueris rei literariae adiuvandae. Videtur sub has nundinas tuto transmitti ad Plantinianos posse, quibus mandata dedimus accipiendi, adservandi. Velim voluntas tibi et occasio in mittendo non desit, nobis fides constabit in remittendo. Salve ab eo, qui meritissimo te amat, Iusto Lipsio. Lugduni Batavorum. Kalendis Martiis. M. D. LXXIX."

to him a young and erudite student (but mediocre poet) from Silesia, Valentin Thilo, who wants to spend some years in Basel and who was recommended to him by the imperial physician Petrus Monavius. He may also work for typographers correcting first copies. Sambucus has not received any answer about the publication of Aristotle or Trapezuntius's autograph of the History of animals, *which Zwinger may not have received either, as the courier has disappeared since then. He is sending his greetings to Claude Aubery and asks Zwinger once more to support Thilo in case he wants to work for Episcopius or others.*

Sambucus salutem.

Diuturnum silentium nullius offensae indicium putes, sed amoris potius redintegrationem. Scio te totis voluminibus edendis occupatissimum, quibus vix Hercules suffecerit. Hunc tamen iuvenem eruditum, poetam mediocrem, Graecis scholis quoque exercitatum, morum vero ea temperatione, ut cuivis facile admonitus satisfecerit, Valentinus hic Thilo Silesius.[1992] Is et suo consilio, et voluntate fratris vestri gymnasii desiderio tenetur, vobiscum aliquot annos exigere vult. Eum tibi ita commendo, ut vix diligentius prolixo libello possim. Petrus Monavius, physicus aulicus,[1993] eum mihi totum dedicat; si tuo patrocinio et aliquo beneficio apto et aequo uti voluerit, oro, cum propter eius virtutes, tum nostra quoque caussa commodabis. Fortassis typographis quoque in corrigendis primis ectypis operam navarit. Quidquid erit, mihi, si eum comprehenderis, gratum feceris inque tuis mutuum hinc experiere. Vale. De Aristotelis impressione et Trapezuntii idiographo de historia animalium etc. nildum responsi, nec scio, an acceperitis.[1994] Nam is tabellarius, cui credideram, postea nusquam comparuit. Auberio, viro clarissimo, salutem. Viennae, pridie Kalendas Aprilis 82.

Si Episcopio aut alii cuipiam typographo dare operam velit, oro, itidem tuis verbis promoveas.

351.
Sambucus to Justus Lipsius
1 May 1582, Vienna

The original is kept in Uppsala, Universitetsbiblioteket, Waller Ms. hu-00068. Published and commented in Deneire and Landtsheer, "Lipsiana in the Waller Manuscript Collection 218-220.

Sambucus affirms that Tacitus merits a fully commented edition and what Lipsius has done for this author is greatly acknowledged by everyone. If Lipsius's commentary appears, it will find universal approval. He wishes he could help his work with something coming from the book boxes

---

[1992] Zwinger's marginal note: "Commendatur Valentinus." Valentin Thilo (1564–1616) was born and died in Liegnitz. Little is known of his life, but see Flood, *Poets Laureate*, 2083, who claims he became a distinguished lawyer. In 1584 he published a German history of France, written from the perspective of a German Protestant (*Der erste Theil gründlicher Beschreibung*...s.l.). Thilo's edition of *Icones aliquot clarorum virorum Germaniae, Angliae, Galliae, Ungariae, cum elogiis et parentalibus factis Theodoro Zvingero* (Basileae: Valdkirch, 1589) suggests that Sambucus's recommendation did not remain without an effect and Thilo stayed long in Basel.

[1993] Petrus Monavius (Monau) of Wrocław (1555–1588) was the brother of Jacobus Monavius, a friend of Andreas Dudith. From 1580 he was court physician in Prague. See Gillet, *Crato von Craffiheim*, 2:71-74 and 89-91.

[1994] This is a reference to Trapezuntius's autograph of his translation of Aristotle's *History of animals*. Cf. the Index.

of his little library. On Plantin's encouragement he tried to satisfy Lipsius's needs and sent some variant readings and marginal notes of old codices and a few other notes, but has nothing he could add now. If he has not received them, he should demand them from Plantin, but if he thinks they vanished in the dissaray of papers, as Plantin is wont to say, he should let Sambucus know about it. In return, he only asks Lipsius to warn Bonaventura Vulcanius about the Greek letters, which he had bought for much money. He should give them back to the person from whom he had received them, as the nobleman Andreas Dudith, a man of elegant style, wants to translate them. Next, Vulcanius should either print his letters of Manuel Chrysoloras and those of Joachim Camerarius Sr. or send them back.

Salutem.

Dignus est Tacitus, quem omnes eloquentes et historici non lectionibus modo suis, sed luce similium et commentariis illustrent, quae adfecta sunt, restituant, quae obscura, vetustatis opibus omnium in lectione ponant familiaremque magis reddant. Quae adhuc profecta in eum scriptorem abs te sunt, sana, erudita et idonea omnes confitentur. Si lumen explicationum tuarum accesserit, quis tuas cogitationes improbet, quid reliquum in Tacito haeserit, quod non facile emergat lectoremque expediat?[1995] Utinam, mi doctissime Lipsi, accommodare tuo consilio ac subiicere de meae bibliothecúlae capsulis et lectionibus quiddam possem! Tentavi id ante biennium fere, cum Plantino cohortanti ad eam mentem, quarum meministi, varietatum libri vetusti margines et aliunde accitas aliquot lectiones eidem, ut tecum communicaret, miseram.[1996] Praeterea nil nunc succurrit. Si itaque eum abs Plantino in Tacitum indicem notationesque non accepisti, require meo nomine illius fide in rempublicam officio debito. Sin periisse putas, ut fit in turba cartarum, ut ille ait,[1997] linearumque, fac me certiorem. Unum est quod summopere abs te mutuo praestitum velim, uti Vulcanium moneas de volumine epistolarum seriorum Graecorum, magnis impensis molestiisque a me comportatarum. Reddat unde accepit, quod Andreas Duditius, vir omni elegantiae stilo nobilis, Latine interpretari deposcit.[1998] Alterum, ut idem epistolas Chrysolorae meas cum Camerarii multis

---

[1995] Lipsius's first edition of Tacitus appeared in 1574 (see letter 229). In 1581 he published a reworked edition: *C. Cornelii Taciti opera omnia quae exstant* (Antverpiae: Plantin, 1581) and *Iusti Lipsii ad Annales Cornelii Taciti liber commentarius, sive notae* (Antverpiae: Plantin, 1581). The edition Lipsius was preparing appeared in 1585: C. Cornelius Tacitus, *Opera quae exstant. Ex Iusti Lipsi editione ultima: et cum eiusdem ad ea omnia Commentariis aut Notis* (Antverpiae: Plantin, 1585), which enjoyed the patronage of Andreas Dudith.

[1996] This letter to Plantin is lost, Lipsius apparently did not receive any notes from Sambucus, and this is why he sent him personally a letter not much before (see letter 349).

[1997] This is a reference to Plantin, not to a classical author. Cf. the note in Deneire and Landtsheer, "Lipsiana in the Waller Manuscript Collection," 219.

[1998] Sambucus's collection of Greek letters of the "Fathers" (i.e. the Church Fathers), as he claimed once, were sent to Antwerp, probably to Plantin, who entrusted them to William Canter. After Canter's death, without Plantin's knowledge, they came into the hands of Laevinus Livineius (see letter 368). Sambucus apparently did not know where these manuscripts were lurking and falsely believed that they had ended up with Vulcanius. Dudith's interest in these letters must have been recent (cf. letter 341), but it is very much questionable whether Dudith really desired to translate them. After Sambucus's death Friedrich Sylburg addressed a letter to Andreas Dudith, wondering about the fate of Sambucus's "more than 800 Greek letters" (quoted in *Humanistes du bassin des Carpates II. Johannes Sambucus*, xxxiii), but Dudith probably did not receive them. In other places Sambucus speaks of only 600 letters (800 must be Sylburg's mistake), as also in his bibliography (see the next note). Cf. letters 245, 289 and 368, and see also Gerstinger, "Die Zusammenfassung," 295.

in lumen geniumque producat aut remittat, si me amat.¹⁹⁹⁹ Vale, Kalendis Maiis, Viennae, 82.
Tuus totus Sambucus.

352.
Sambucus to Fulvio Orsini
1 August 1582, Vienna

The original is kept in Rome, BAV, Vat. lat. 4103 I, f. 102ʳ⁻ᵛ. Published in Gerstinger, "Die Briefe," 266-268.

Sambucus and his friends were impressed by Orsini's edition of Polybius's De legationibus; *he should carry on with his work for the Republic of Letters. Sambucus has sent a copy to Andreas Patricius Nidecki, a learned grammarian, who will even in Poland understand more than some in Latium. Concerning Orsini's book on Roman families, Sambucus will have some comments. He is sorry about the theft of Orsini's antique coins and curses the thieves. He has made annotations and some fragmentary conjectures into Velleius Paterculus, but Orsini should wait before something sounder comes up. He has not seen a print or a manuscript version of the medical codex promised by Orsini, who should make sure to keep his word. Sambucus asks Orsini to intervene and reconcile a certain numismatist (Johannes Paulus Hierutius) with his cousin (Horatius Hierutius). He is attaching the letter by Andreas Patricius who is similarly sorry about the theft. Finally, he asks about the fate of the fragments of an (inscribed) copper plate that came to the surface at the Quirinale and pleads with Orsini to let him know about it through the imperial legate or someone else. Sambucus is sending his greetings to Guglielmo Sirleto and the Portuguese Achilles Statius, who, like Orsini, would never exchange his sweet "otium", museum or hobbies with any of the Fuggers.*

Salutem.

Legationibus Polybianis me et amicos,²⁰⁰⁰ quorum studium in antiquitatibus haud obscurum videtur, adeo excitasti, ut quae eius argumenti ἀποσπάσματα²⁰⁰¹ sancte mihique intus quasi

---

¹⁹⁹⁹ For Chrysoloras's Greek letters, sent originally to Joachim Camerarius Sr. in 1568 and forwarded to Vulcanius by Joachim Jr. in c. 1577 see letters 117 (esp. note 687) and cf. the Index. Note that Vulcanius, who fails to mention them in his letter to Sambucus of 1581 (see letter 340), eventually sent them back to Nuremberg to the younger Camerarius (or at least he sent back the Greek letters by his father Camerarius Sr.) only in 1595. Vulcanius's attitude to loaned manuscripts was generally very poor. In Vulcanius's surviving codices we can find both copies and translations of these letters, which reveal his initial interest in editing them. However, by 1583 he must have given up the idea, and excused himself with reference to stylistic considerations, as Plantin explains to Sambucus in letter 368. In his published bibliography from 1583, Sambucus wrote "Chrysolorae Epistolas graecas ad familiares cum Bessarionis, et Planudis. Item S. Patrum ad 600. nondum visas, magnis sumptibus a se collectas. Vulcanius detinet" (Sambucus, *Catalogus librorum*). See more in Deneire and Landtsheer, "Lipsiana in the Waller Manuscript Collection," 220; Gerstinger, "Die Zusammenfassung," 294-296.

²⁰⁰⁰ Ἐκ τῶν Πολυβίου τοῦ Μεγαλοπολίτου ἐκλογαὶ περὶ πρεσβειῶν. *Ex libris Polybii Megalopolitensis selecta de legationibus et alia ... nunc primum in lucem edita ex Bibliotheca Fulvii Ursini* (Antverpiae: Plantin, 1582). This was the first edition of Polybius's fragments "de legationibus," first collected on the order of Constantinus Porphyrogenitus, then discovered and copied by Andreas Darmarios. They were first published by Orsini, who used many conjectures, and then in a remarkable bilingual edition with some additional annotations by Isaac Casaubon. See the preface by Theodor Büttner-Wobst in vol. 4 of Πολυβίου Ἱστορίαι (Lipsiae: Teubner, 1904), iii-xi.

²⁰⁰¹ fragments

tuebar, ilico proiecerim καὶ τὰ χρυσεῖα²⁰⁰² complexus sim. Misi exemplum ad Patricium nostrum,²⁰⁰³ virum elegantem, lectionibus grammaticorum instructum et qui vel in Sarmatis plus interim quam in Latio videt. Tuo ocio, tuae bibliothecae studio in rem publicam toto dato habeo gratiam. Deus genium et operam clementia sua firmet, posteritas voce canora sonet. In Familiis Romanis nonnulla tecum conferam aliquando ac occasionem cogitandi praebebo.²⁰⁰⁴ Et quia in numismatum memoriam incidi, doleo te latronum sacrilegorum manibus tam claro thesauro privatum. Qui scelus sceleratissime patrarunt, eorum mentem Furiae conscie exagitent, manus Vulcani officina vel potius inferorum comburant!²⁰⁰⁵ In Paterculo quaedam obiter notaram, coniecturis subsecivis etiam interpolavi, sed ἐπέχω²⁰⁰⁶ dum saniora occurrant.²⁰⁰⁷ Medicos, quorum manuscriptum exemplar mihi policitus eras, nec formis publicis redditum expressumve vidi, nec exaratum manu. Vide, ut fidem tueare! Caeterum Ioannes Paulus Hierutius ab aliquot annis ob numos antiquos haud vulgares et alia mihi familiaris factus est et aliis illustribus viris. Is citra causam et vinculi sanguinis necessitudinem videtur exosus Horatio Hierutio iuris consulto, patrueli suo,²⁰⁰⁸ quem fortasse nosti. Ac praecipue caussam alienati animi fertur obiicere doctor Horatius, qui in foro Salvatoris Laurino degit,²⁰⁰⁹ quod perpetue hic vagetur, quod se ut caeteri consanguinei non crebrius invisat, observetur. Si haec caussa sola separatave est, non sufficit ad solvendum nexum sanguinis et ne laxandum quidem. Quam, si commodo tuo fieri poterit, facile apud Horatium dilues huncque Ioannem Paulum in gratiam repones illique reconciliabis. Quod ut diligenter facias mea quoque caussa, ni quid gravius intervenit, cur doctor offendatur, te vehementer etiam ac etiam rogatus rogo. Patritii nostri epistolam ad te mitto, qui simul de iactura numismatum condolet. Quid de aenearum tabularum fragmentis fiat, quid modo Romae rari erutum ex faetis visceribus illis Quirinis sit, si me amas, communicato tuasque oratori isthic nostro committas vel cui voles. Vienna, Kalendis Sextilis 82. Totus tuus Sambucus.

Illustrissimum cardinalem Schirletum a me humiliter salutabis, officio viro pleno et veteri amicicia munito Achiliem Statium Lusitanum, qui ocio amoeno ac museo comprehenso suas delitias cum quovis Fuggero non permutarit, quod item de te pronuncio. Vale.

---

²⁰⁰² and as the gold
²⁰⁰³ Andrzej Patrycy (Andreas Patricius) Nidecki (1522–1587) was an important figure of Polish humanism, most famous for his collection of Cicero's fragments. His studies in Padua (where he met Sambucus) were sustained by church benefices, later his career continued at the chancellery. From the 1570s he increasingly oriented himself toward the Catholic Church and also published some polemical writings, but also continued working on Cicero. In the debate over Carlo Sigonio's alleged discovery of Cicero's *Consolatio*, he sided with Sigonio, who had a lasting influence on his humanism. See William McCuaig, "Andreas Patricius, Carlo Sigonio, Onofrio Panvinio, and the Polish nation of the University of Padua," *History of Universities* 3 (1983), 87-100, idem, *Carlo Sigonio*, passim.
²⁰⁰⁴ Familiae Romanae quae reperiuntur (see letter 311, note 1811).
²⁰⁰⁵ See Nolhac, *La bibliothèque de Fulvio Orsini*, 35.
²⁰⁰⁶ I hold onto it
²⁰⁰⁷ For Orsini's interest in the Roman historian Velleius Paterculus (c. 19 BC–c. 31 AD), see his *Fragmenta historicorum collecta ab Antonio Augustino, emendata a Fulvio Ursino. Fulvi Ursini notae ad Sallustium, Caesarem, Livium, Velleium...* (Antverpiae: ex officina Plantiniana, 1595).
²⁰⁰⁸ Except for the fact that two legal consilia by Horatius Hierutius from the 1580s were included in *Francisci Vivii ... Additiones ad decisionum suarum regni Neapolis libros IIII iampridem evulgatos* (Venetiis: Apud haeredem Damiani Zenarii, 1617), 81-86, we have no information on these persons.
²⁰⁰⁹ Piazza San Salvatore in Lauro.

353.
Reinerus Reineccius[2010] to Sambucus
31 August 1582, Helmstedt

The original is kept in Vienna, ÖNB, Cod. 9736, f. 13-14.

Writing in a strikingly polite and formal style, Reineccius addresses Sambucus as "his patron" still "unknown", referring to their common interests in antiquity and history and their mutual friend Jacobus Monavius. He is about to publish the work of which he has already given samples. The publication will be dedicated and financed by Julius, the duke of Brunswick-Lüneburg, but Reineccius needs help with additional sources. He asks for Sambucus's assistance getting documents from others who could be helpful. Sambucus should send his response via Monavius. He promises to remember Sambucus in his works, as he did in his oration on the discipline of history.

Magnifice et amplissime vir, patrone observandissime.

Vereor, temeritatis reprehensionem incurram, quod ignotus, quod officiis nullis commendatus, ad magnificentiam tuam scribam. Sed nescio quod calcar addebat, tum quod in caeteris studiis quibus rem litterariam magnificentia tua mirifice iuvit, ornavit, illustravit, ea quoque summa cum laude excolere ipsam didicerim, in quibus ego praecipue semper desudassem, hoc est antiquitatis et historiarum, tum quod eximia humanitas tua, eruditae doctrinae pedisequa, summopere predicaretur. Et confirmabat me necessitudo, quam Iacobum Monavium, summum meum cum magnificentia tua iunxisse comperi.[2011] Nam in hanc spem veniebam, quae ipsi benevolentiae tuae fores apertae essent, fore, ut nec mihi occluderentur. Quare quicquid huius est importunioris interpellationis, magnificentia tua in bonam partem accipiat, et eum me statuat, qui virtutem, dignitatem, eruditionem et in rem litterariam merita tua amet et magnificaciat, pervelim. Quod si id contra magnificentia tua dederit, ut favore me suo dignetur, beneficio me longe maximo affectum putabo, neque id denegandum existimet, oro. Ego ita vicissim officio studebo, ut ne nostri poeniteat, sed de me ornato laetetur indies vehementius. Nunc quod praeterea commonendum putassem, quam fieri poterit brevissime, perstringam. Habeo in manibus eius operis elaborationem, cuius antehac diversa specimina edidi.[2012] Inscriptio cum hisce coniuncta est. Et patrocinium ac sumtum subministrat illustrissimus princeps Iulius, dux Brunovicensis et Luneburgensis

---
[2010] Reinerus Reineccius (Reiner Reineck) (1541–1595) became professor of history at the University of Frankfurt (Oder) in 1578, from where he soon moved to the University of Helmstedt. He became known as historian of peoples and families, hence most importantly a genealogist, who reconstructed even Hippocrates's family tree. There is no extensive modern biography of him. Recently, his historiographical contributions arose the interest of Anthony Grafton: *What was History? The Art of History in Early Modern Europe* (Princeton: Univ. Press, 2007), 30-33, 140-143.

[2011] Monavius served as a middleman for Reineccius, who tried to enlarge his network toward Eastern Europe. See, for example, Monavius's letter to Reineccius, in which he quotes Sambucus's letter, written in reaction to this letter (cf. letter 357), in Reineccius, *Methodus legendi cognoscendique historiam*, 42^{r-v}, and cf. with f. 36^{r-v}. It was only a year before that he also contacted Andreas Dudith, asking for patronage and help (see Dudith's response, partially published ibid., 35^r-36^r). In the spring of 1583, Reineccius approached Heinrich Rantzau in a similar way, see Peter Zeeberg, "Heinrich Rantzau (1526–98) and his humanist collaborators. The examples of Reiner Reineccius and Georg Ludwig Froben," in *Germania latina – Latinitas teutonica*, eds. Eckhard Keßler and Heinrich C. Kuhn (Paderborn: Fink, 2003), 2:539-553.

[2012] We could not identify the work in question.

etc.²⁰¹³ Sed quibus adhuc aliis adiumentis ad tam arduum argumentum mihi opus sit, magnificentiam tuam non praeterit. Potissimum tamen est monumentorum omnis generis supellex. A qua cum magnificentiam tuam instructissimam esse intelligam, copia sua inopiam meam sublevet atque adeo auctoritate sua apud alios patrocinetur, qui eandem conferre in me opem possint, omnibus precibus et, qua par est, observantia quaeso. Sane si opus esse putarem, non deessent varia eaque honestissima veluti θέλγητρα,²⁰¹⁴ quae ad eum magnificentiae tuae respectum eliciendum afferrem. Summa vero est commodum publicum, cui omnes conatus nostri destinati sunt, praesertim in eo argumenti genere, quod veterum amissis monumentis nondum hac nostra memoria a quoquam pertractatum est. Quapropter magnificentia tua benigne mei rationem habebit et quicquid expectari a se voluerit, significare per litteras, quae commodissime a Monavio curari poterunt, haud gravabitur. Ego meritum hoc memoria colam celebraboque sempiterna, et quod in oratione mea de dignitate et partibus historiae etc. nuper a me recognita et locupletata erga magnificentiae tuae studium testatus sum, id deponam nunquam.²⁰¹⁵ Quam bene feliciterque valere ex animo opto. Ex academia Iulia Helmestadii pridie Calendas Septembris MDXXCII.²⁰¹⁶ Magnificentiam atque amplitudinem tuam cum observantia colens Reinerus Reineccius.

Address: Magnifico viro, eruditae doctrinae copia, virtute et dignitate amplissimo domino Iohanni Sambuco, consiliario et historico caesareo etc., domino et patrono suo perpetua observantia colendo.²⁰¹⁷

354.
Sambucus to Boldizsár Batthyány²⁰¹⁸
10 September 1582, Vienna

The original is kept in Budapest, MOL, Batthyány család, Missilis, Mf. 4929, no. 54267. Published in Ágnes Ritoók-Szalai, "Zsámboky János levelei Batthyány Boldizsárhoz," in idem, *"Nympha super ripam Danubii". Tanulmányok a XV-XVI. századi magyarországi művelődés köréből* [Studies of the culture of Hungary in the 15–16th c.] (Budapest: Akadémia, 2002), 213-214.

[2013] Julius, Duke of Brunswick-Lüneburg (1528–1589), founder of the University of Helmstedt.
[2014] charms
[2015] Reineccius names Sambucus in his *Oratio de historia, eiusque dignitate, partibus, atque in primis ea, quae ad gentilitatibus agit* (Francofurti: Wechel, 1580), 23.
[2016] See Sambucus's response (letter 356) and letter to Monavius (letter 357).
[2017] According to notes on the back of Reineccius's letter, Sambucus seems to have received it on 11 October (the letter travelled through Wrocław, where Monavius stayed), while another date (23 Oct.) seems to be referring to the date of Sambucus's answer, which is different than in the published version; cf. with letter 356.
[2018] Count Boldizsár (III) Batthyány (c. 1542–1590) was one of the most powerful aristocrats of Western Hungary, who was renowned for his learned interests and curiosity for nature, above all for alchemy and botany. He was educated by private tutors and also studied in Graz. Later he spent time at the Viennese court, and then at the court of the Guise princes in Paris in 1559–1561 (when also Sambucus was staying in Paris). He built up an impressive library of c. 1000 volumes, relying partly on the help of the bibliophile Jean Aubry, and kept in touch with physicians, humanists, natural philosophers and like-minded aristocrats. See Bobory Dóra, *The Sword and the Crucible. Count Boldizsár Batthyány and Natural Philosophy in Sixteenth-Century Hungary* (Newcastle upon Tyne: Cambridge Scholars Publishing, 2009); and the article by Dávid Molnár in *Companion*.

Sambucus has gratefully received the horses and wants to know their price, although his wife will hardly be able to use them for the purpose she wanted them for, as they are in great conflict (about) the ban of the (Lutheran) ministers and always surrounded by (Catholic) priests. God should take them in his favour and open his eyes. There is no rhubarb in the entire city, even the doctors complain, however Sambucus sends some to Batthyány, but even the ugly ones are so expensive that 1.5 lots cost 2 florins, which has never happened before. If Batthyány could have some delivered from Venice, it would be great. He is also sending half a lot of manna, which is not as white as it is in Calabria. Batthyány's man did not say anything about the Greek book, only that Batthyány would send it back. He previously wrote that he would have it copied, and send it either to Joachim Camerarius Jr. in Nuremberg or Thomas Erastus in Heidelberg, who was an expert in this matter. If they would like it, they would translate, print, and dedicate it to Batthyány, but it would take one or two years at least. He has had a look at the epigrams of Janus Pannonius; they are rather corrupted copies, and he has (all of) them, but he may come out with a new edition. He does not understand the reaction of Venice; the case is urged by two of his men in the senate and also by the imperial envoy, Veit von Dornberg. If there is no other way, he suggests waiting for the emperor and letting him write once again, because he understands that the young secretaries do not find its copy among the protocols. He has asked Adam von Dietrichstein in a letter to notify him as soon as an answer has arrived. The emperor should arrive by the end of the month. There is some anxiety about the imperial free cities. Fortune is inconstant in Flanders, while the House of Guise is said to have some secret plans. He is also urging the business of the Chamber. The report of the commissary has been handed in to Archduke Ernst by Gall, who promised to be supportive. Archduke Matthias is returning to Linz today, he had much amusement and hunts (in Vienna). The emperor is said to be thinking about sending Maximilian to Košice, but the news at court is unreliable. That piece of metal is still not metal, but can become one over time; Sambucus believes it is asphalt. In a postscript he informs Batthyány about some fresh news: a recent victory of Francis, Duke of Anjou and Alençon, over the Prince of Parma and his chase of the French; and Don Antonio's terror of the people of Philip II, having been defeated at Saint Michael's Isle.

Illustris ac magnifice domine, salutem, servitutem perpetuam.

Equos accepi, gratias ago vestrae magnificentiae perpetuas, ac pretium eorum cupio intelligere. Jollehet ammÿ zeügsegre feökeppen kiwanta felesighem, alegh ha tarthattÿa arra sokaig, merth nagh haboroba vaghiûnk az praedicatorok tiltasban, es eörők papÿ hadban.[2019] Deus adhibeat gratiam, et rectum oculum. Rhabarb[arom] az eghiz varosba io ninczen, és panassokodnak az Doctorokis, Myndazaltal köldek Nagh[ságának]. Ez ollÿ dragais az hytwana, hogh mazfel latot[2020] 2 f[orintért] adnak, kÿ soha nem volt. Ha Nagh[sága] kotol altal Veneczebol hozatna, diczirnem, merth az Rhabarbaromnak az ighen iowa io.

Mannathis fel fontal.[2021] Ezis nem ighen feÿr, mÿnth Calabriaÿnak kellene lennÿ. Mastix io, es az colythonix.[2022] Az görögh könvről semmit nem monda az Naghs[ága] embere, hanem hogh czyak hogh Naghs[ága] vyzza kwldy.[2023] Azuthan valazt varok Naghs[ágától]. Merth

---

[2019] See Almási, *The Uses of Humanism*, 345.
[2020] 1 lot was 17.5 gramm in Vienna.
[2021] This is probably a reference to the sweet liquid gained from fraxinus ornus, the manna ash.
[2022] We could not identify these plants (?).
[2023] Whether Batthyány was going to send the Greek codex back to Sambucus or Ferenc Nádasdy (cf. note 2025) is unclear.

en azt irtham vala, hogh masat le iratnam, azuthan aztot Norinbergaba Camerariusnak, vagy Heÿdlbergaba Erastusnak,[2024] kÿ ezfelehez ieles tŭdos. Hogh ha tetzenek vertalnak, es ha kÿ nÿomtatnak, haat Naghsag[ának] dedicalnak. Ebben nagh idŏ telÿk, az az az vertalasban, es nÿomasban, merth alegh hyzem hogh egg eztendöben, vagh kettöbennis kezöl megh.[2025]

Az Pannonius Epigrammakat conferaltam: ighen hamissan irthak, es megh vadnak nalam, es esmegh megh nÿomtatom talam.[2026] Az Veneczeÿ valaztrol czodalkozom, keet barathom solicitallÿa, harmadik az orator Dornberger ottbenn.[2027] Ha egÿeb nem lehet, hat variúk mĕgh eô felsegeth, es irassûnk esmegh, merth az erthem hogh az protocolomban nem tuddÿak az ifiw secretariûsok, mÿnth volt az dologh, es mÿben masath mŭgh talalnÿ. Irtham Dietrichstain uramnak, hogh ha valamit feleltenek volna, azonal megh ielentene nekem. Nova nulla, quam quod caesaream maiestatem expectamus ad finem huius mensis, et quod cum liberis imperii civitatibus adhuc nonnulli versentur scrupuli.[2028] Flandriaba az Zerencze ide es towa ighen forgattÿa magath. Az Gwisius Nemzetsegh czoda praticaba volna, de kÿ tuddÿa ha igaz.

Az Camara dolgat enis sollicitalom, az comissariûs relatiot Gall ma addÿa be az Herzognek, merth zoltham vele, es fogada mÿnden baratsagath.[2029]

[2024] Thomas Erastus (1524–1583) was a Swiss doctor and philologist. He studied in Bologna and Padova and settled in Heidelberg as the physician of the Elector Palatine Otto Henry and professor of the university. In 1580 Erastus left Heidelberg and moved to Basel. Sambucus's choice of Erastus and Camerarius show that he looked for alchemical experts who had a critical approach to "natural magic" and Paracelsism. Yet, Erastus was more an enemy than an expert of alchemy. Surprisingly, Sambucus did not know about Zwinger's hidden but massive interest in Paracelsus. Charles D. Gunnoe, *Thomas Erastus and the Palatinate. A Renaissance Physician in the Second Reformation* (Leiden: Brill, 2010). On anti-Paracelsianism see Tilmann Walter, "Paracelsuskritische Haltungen oder 'Antiparacelsismus'? 1570–1630," *Würzburger medizinhistorische Mitteilungen* 27 (2008), 381-408.

[2025] The publication of this Greek alchemical manuscript became Sambucus's last (unfinished) project. See letters 355, 365 and 376. The story is reconstructed by Ritoók-Szalai ("Zsámboky János levelei") in the following way. The neatly written manuscript was originally borrowed by Batthyány from Baron Ferenc Nádasdy for a deposit of 200 ducats. Sambucus's first step was to persuade Batthyány to finance the publication, which is documented by this letter. It was probably Erastus's death in early 1583 that stopped him from sending the copy of the manuscript to Basel, which apparently remained with him (and his family) also after his death (see the letter of his widow addressed to Zwinger in 1585, quoted in Gerstinger, "Die Briefe," 275). Batthyány believed that Sambucus had sent the original to Camerarius and asked Carolus Clusius in 1588 to help him get it back, as he needed to return it to Ferenc Nádasdy (see Hunger, *Charles de l'Escluse*, 423). With reference to Sambucus's bibliography (*Catalogus librorum*) Ritoók-Szalai managed to identify the codex in question, which was the work of different authors (among them Stephanus Alexandrinus), of which there are even two copies extant in the ÖNB: Cod. Med. gr. 2 and 3 (probably Med. gr. 2 is the one that came from Sambucus's library via Sebastian Tengnagel). Both were copied in Venice by Kornelios Murmuris in 1564. There are also three Latin manuscript translations in ÖNB (Cod. 11427, 11453 and 11456) from the early seventeenth century.

[2026] Sambucus must have compared a manuscript of Pannonius's epigrams with his own manuscripts and editions and found nothing new. He probably did not seriously plan any new edition of Pannonius, as it is not indicated in his bibliography (*Catalogus librorum*). See Ritoók-Szalai, "Zsámboky János levelei," 213. For his editions of Janus Pannonius, see letters 20, 86 and 128. See also István Borzsák, "Die Janus Pannonius Ausgaben des Sambucus," *Acta Antiqua* 21 (1973), 361-374; Csaba Csapodi, *A Janus Pannonius-szöveghagyomány* [The textual tradition of Pannonius's works] (Budapest: Akadémia, 1981), 12.

[2027] Vito Dornberg (Dorimbergo, Veit von) (1529–1591) was born in Gorizia. From 1553 he received important local political offices from the Habsburgs. In 1567 he became imperial envoy to Venice and remained in the city for twenty years. His job became more difficult from the late 1570s when multiple conflicts haunted the relationship of Venice with the Empire, including several border disputes, which might have been one of the reasons for Batthyány's worries. See the article by Silvano Cavazza in *DBI* 41 (1992), 496-500.

[2028] In the Augsburg diet of 1582 it was decided that the collective vote of the cities should have greater importance in the future, which probably gave reason to worry to aristocratic circles around the emperor.

[2029] We were not able to identify the person and the matter in question. The Chamber in question was probably the Niederösterreichische Kammer. See also the next letter.

Herzog Mathias ma Lintzbe meghÿen vizza, ighen vigadanak, es vadazzanak. Aztis mondÿak hogh kÿkeletre Maximilianot Cassara keoldÿ ew felsighe etc de az udûary hÿrek ighen incertae. Me vestrae magnificentiae valde [?] humiliter commendo. 10 Septembris. Vestrae magnificentiae servitor Ioannes Sambucus.

Az darab ertz nem ertz mēg, hanem czak idôvel valamy ertz lehet. En asphaltumnak mondanam. Huzzar Petert es Isthûanffÿt az Hertzog fel hivatta, hogh baÿra mentenek volt etc.

Post Scripta[2030]
Ma iûtot posta ide bÿzonaûal hog Alanzon mëgh ewtkëzeth volna az parmaÿ herczeggel, es mëg verte volna, es wzte az Frantzősokat.[2031] Esmegh Don Antonio portogal felÿ az Philepp kyral nepet hogh ighen verte volna Zenth Michal Insulanal.[2032]

Address: Illustrissimo ac magnifico domino, domino Balthasaro de Batthyan etc., suae caesareae regiaeque maiestatis etc. consiliario etc., domino fautori generoso. Nemethwywar.

355.
Sambucus to Boldizsár Batthyány
25 September 1582, Vienna

The original is kept in Budapest, MOL, Batthyány család, Missilis, Mf. 4929, no. 54267.

Sambucus confirms that he was grateful for the horses and wants to pay for them. He privately urged Batthyány's case, while Antonius did it publicly. They have both a positive and a negative response, but there is more in the missing books of the Chamber. Batthyány should have reacted more in time, but he still has hope. Sambucus is going to have the book copied, and the old codex will be returned with due gratitude. But its translation and publication will need time. The (ship of the) emperor will land soon. The ships are prepared at the bank (of the Danube) in Ingolstadt.

Illustris ac magnifice domine, salutem, servitutem perpetuam.

De equis gratias egi, uti debui. Nec id moleste accipiat quod de precio adscripserim, nam me obligatum ea re profiteor.[2033]

Negocium vestrae magnificentiae solicitavi ipse privatim, et Antonius publice.[2034] Responsum habemus in utramque voluntatem, sed in libris camerae absentibus plurimum situm est. Id vero

---

[2030] The edition of Ritoók-Szalay does not contain this part.
[2031] In the summer of 1582, there were many skirmishes between the forces of the Duke of Anjou and Alençon (1555–1584) allied with the armies of the States-General and the Prince of Parma but neither side was able to win a decisive or significant victory. See *A Generall Historie of the Netherlands*, 802-808; Holt, *The Duke of Anjou* (as in letter 330, note 1897), 166-184.
[2032] Don António, Prior of Crato (1531–1595) claimed the Portugese throne until 1583, despite Philip II's taking it in 1581. The battle at Saint Michael's, led by Philip Strozzi ended with the total victory of the Spanish fleet under Santa Cruz.
[2033] See the preceding letter. We do not know the reason why Sambucus switched to Latin in this shorter letter. It might have been for the lack of time and his less confidential message.
[2034] We were not able to identify the person in question.

tempestivius potuisset vestra magnificentia significari. Sed non despero in bona causa.[2035] Librum curo describendum, exemplar vetus redderetur cum gratiarum actione, beneficiique memoria.[2036] Sed ad inprimendum et versionem tempore erit opus. Caesar brevi appellet. Quartier magister dominus Gyllis rediere[t].[2037] Ingolstadii in ripa naves apparatae sunt.[2038] Me vestrae magnificentiae humiliter commendo. 25. Septembris 82. Servitor vester Ioannes Sambucus.

Address: Illustrissimo ac magnifico domino, domino Balthasaro de Batthyan etc., sacratissimae caesareae regiaeque maiestatis etc. consiliario etc., domino patrono generoso. Nemethywyor.

356.
Sambucus to Reinerus Reineccius
26 October 1582, Vienna

Published in Reineccius, *Methodus legendi cognoscendique historiam*, f. 42ᵛ.[2039]

Sambucus is the most happy to accept Reineccius's friendship and praises his diligence and work in the interest of all humanity. Similar praise goes to Jacobus Monavius for his constancy, who Reineccius has rightly acknowledged as Sambucus's friend. Reineccius, having generous patronage, is in the right place to publish a work of high density. He should push ahead with his plan and provide the public with a synthesis of so many histories. If Reineccius thinks Sambucus may have read or seen something that may concern his work, he should let him know about it, but he will hardly be able to provide books. Wolfgang Lazius has diligently inspected and cleaned out all the monasteries, and Sambucus does not know where those books are now. He himself conceded the better part of his library, i.e. the manuscripts, to the emperor, who gently asked for it four years ago. Hugo Blotius is in charge of them now. But he had written more about it to their mutual friend (Monavius). Reineccius should not work too hard, so that he might do more work in the future.

Iohannes Sambucus Reinero Reineccio S. D.

Cur ego, praestantissime Reinere, tuam amicitiam non acceptem, vel, ut aiunt, manibus et pedibus non expetam, non prehensem? Quem et litterarum studium ad omnem humanitatem subegit, et tot vigiliae in omnium amore et ore ita posuere, ut qui tuis laboribus non sit aequus aut gratus, lucem non mereatur, ut adspectet. De Monavii necessitudine recte sentis. Est cunctorum χρήσει καὶ κτήσει[2040] vir natus, datusque, qui officium humanitatis nulla ex parte deserit: constantiam ita tuetur amoris, ut inoffensam perpetuis scriptionibus praestet. Tu vero, doctissime Reinere, quia nactus es locum idoneum spissi operis pertexendi, patrocinium expeditum, urge consilium, ut te auctore συνέχειαν καὶ ἐνδελέχειαν[2041] tot historiarum

---

[2035] See the preceding letter.
[2036] Cf. with the preceding letter, note 2025.
[2037] This quartermaster was probably the former Captain of Archers Wolf Georg Gyllis (or Gillus). See http://rudolphina.com/Namen/Gillus_Wolf_Georg.xml (accessed on 12 March 2024).
[2038] Rudolf II was returning from the Augsburg diet.
[2039] See letter 353, note 2011.
[2040] for usufruct and possession. See Erasmus, *Adagia* 4026.
[2041] continuity and persistency

et ἀπογόνων²⁰⁴² habeamus, quod ipsum nisi tua opera et industria, vix a quoquam facile consequemur. Quod si quid apud Sambucum est, quod ad egregiam tuam operam quiddam suppeditarit, vel potius, si quid Sambucum legisse, aut videre opineris, quod tuis lectionibus inservierit, fac sciam, nil recusabo, modo conscium aut memorem appelles. De libris nil, aut parum tibi accommodaro, quod Lazius, vir clarissimus, omnia coenobia²⁰⁴³ pervolitarit, exhauserit et, ubi ii libri lateant, nesciam. Ego vero potiorem bibliothecae partem manu exaratorum caesareae maiestati ante annos quatuor concesserim clementer postulanti, cui Blotius iuris consultus praeest. Qua de re antea communi amico nostro copiosius. Vale, teque tibi nobisque diu incolumem conservet Deus. Tu vero laboribus ita moderare, ut pluribus sufficias. Vienna. XXVI. Octobris MDXXCII.

357.
Sambucus to Jacobus Monavius
31 October 1582, Vienna

Partially published in Reineccius, *Methodus legendi cognoscendique historiam*, f. 42ʳ⁻ᵛ.

Sambucus thanks Monavius for connecting him to Reineccius, whom he abundantly praises for his talents and diligence. His work is impressive, the table of contents seems to require many lifetimes to complete, but the future will reveal how well he can write and organise such mixed historical material. It requires a man of extraordinary stamina. Sambucus explained briefly Reineccius where he could find the help he has been asking for.

Respondi Reineccio nostro,²⁰⁴⁴ cuius tu mihi amicitiam adiunxisti gratissimam. Te enim auctore nescio quam de me opinionem collegit, iudicione an amore, tu pronunciato. Video hominem non modo ingenio ac memoria abundanti, sed etiam ad vigilias diuturnas citra molestiam natum factum posteritati. Spissum opus ille inchoavit, index aetates multas videtur postulare. Ordo quis sit in tanta varietate futurus, quae lux orationis, quis stylus, ubi absolverit ac prodibit, dies docebit. Virum solidorum membrorum, constantis animi, nulla taedia fastidientem esse oportet. Dii illi omnesque aequi bene velint. Quod ad eius consilium suppeditare queam, unde melius petierit, paucis aperui.²⁰⁴⁵ Tu meas ad ipsum tuto curabis. Vale, et me praestantissimorum virorum necessitudine si auxeris, gratum erit, nec desiderari officium a me patiar. Viennae, pridie Kalendas Novembris, 1582.

---

²⁰⁴² descendants. Print: ἀπογεῶν.
²⁰⁴³ The imperial library was kept in the Minoritenkloster in 1558–1613.
²⁰⁴⁴ See the previous letter. Sambucus used Monavius as an intermediary, and sent also to him a letter, of which Monavius (in a letter addressed to Reinerus Reineccius of 20 November) quoted only the part that concerned Reineccius. In his *Methodus*, Reineccius reproduced the entire letter by Monavius, but used larger fonts for the quotation.
²⁰⁴⁵ See letter 356, where he recommends Blotius.

358.
Sambucus to Eusebius Episcopius
1 November 1582, Vienna

A copy is kept in Basel, Universitätsbibliothek, G2 II 37, f. 27^v. Published in Gerstinger, "Die Briefe," 268-269.

Sambucus does not want to conceal his irritation over Episcopius's failure to publish his edition of Aristotle, augmented and emendated with much fatigue. He has been much urging it, likewise Theodor Zwinger, while Perna cannot stand in the way any longer, as he is dead. He gave this work to Episcopius on condition that he would publish it with the help of Jean Aubry as soon as possible but nothing happened. Either Eusebius immediately publishes it or gives it back to him, otherwise Sambucus will leave no stones unturned through the senate of Basel and the emperor. Sambucus threatens Episcopius to enforce his will through the senate of Basel and by using the emperor's letter. Sambucus promises that those 32 thalers that Episcopius paid to the Oporinus family in Sambucus's name will be paid back to him by the family of Wechel. Episcopius should either publish Aristotle together with Aubry, who is a heir of Wechel and could provide him their very elegant Greek fonts, or he should turn the project over to him once his 32 thalers have been paid. Otherwise, Sambucus will take it to court. Episcopius should feel warned. Sambucus has not undertaken the whole work in order to be dependent on Episcopius's judgement, but for the common good. Now everyone considers him a liar, as they cannot believe that this useful undertaking is stopped only because of Episcopius's delay. Concerning the codex of Trapezuntius he demands the same.

Sambucus salutem.

Mi optime amice, ut non facile mihi stomachum fieri patior, ita iram minime ad vindictam retineo, iracunde tamen animus et mens aperienda est moleste admodum me ferre moram tot annorum in Aristotele excudendo, meis non tenuibus vigiliis aucto et purgato.[2046] Moneo, urgeo, saepe idem se officiose Zvingerus factitare ait, Perna mortuus impedire nequit. Equidem in hoc tecum meas operas communicaram, ut pollicitis staretis ac prima quaque occasione Aubrii subsidio ederetis, sed nihil dum video, vel negligi a vobis mea sentio. Itaque duobus verbis habeto: aut statim prelo subiicias aut reddas. Quod ni feceris, iure flagitabo et per senatum vestrum caesaris literis omnia movebo. Nam quos 32 talleros Oporinianis meo nomine exsolvistis, parati a me semper erunt vobisque erga me iniquioribus restituentur per Wechelianos.[2047] Quare cum Aubrio haerede Wechelii pactis mihi convenit, ut aut socios, qui formas suas Graecas elegantissimas offerent, admittes et ilico rem aggrediamini, aut eidem numeratis vestris 32 talleris ipsi tradatis. Caeteroqui iure et litiose, si opus erit, mea reposcam vel molestia vestra aliqua. Quis enim aequo animo tantam moram, tam iniquam, quae nec ipsa munus velit nec cum aliis communicare tulerit? Haec me serio interminari intelligas, non enim tantum laborem ad arbitrium solum vestrum et imperium, sed publicis usibus expediundos quamprimum suscepi. Omnes mendacii quasi me arguunt, nec haerere in tanto

---

[2046] Concerning Sambucus's edition of Aristotle, see the Index under "Sambucus." Also see Gerstinger, "Die Briefe," 287-289.

[2047] On the history of Sambucus's debt of 35 (!) thalers to Oporinus, which ended up with Episcopius, see letter 262, note 1495.

opere tamque utili moram hanc vestram posse censent. Quare alterutrum statim feceritis, aut edite aut reddite et, quid consilio foveatis, mihi rescribite. Vale. Kalendis Novembris. Vienna. 1582. De Trapezuntii codice idem cupio.[2048]

Address: Domino Eusebio Episcopio, typographo insigni, amico observando. Basel.

359.
Sambucus to Theodor Zwinger
9 November 1582, Vienna

The original is kept in Basel, Universitätsbibliothek, Frey Mscr II 26, no. 229. Published in Gerstinger, "Die Briefe," 269-270.

Sambucus is very much sorry about the death of Pietro Perna. He wrote to Perna's heirs, asking them to return his edition of Horace's Ars poetica, *sent to Perna nine years before, together with some fragments of famous poets, as he wants to publish it after some re-examination. He wrote to Episcopius angrily and asks Zwinger to persuade him to have his edition of Aristotle published with Wechel's most elegant types. He has got back his copy of Paulus Aegineta. He agreed with the Wechel press that they can freely proceed with Episcopius in his name. He is also writing to Samuel Grynaeus and the Oporinus firm to complain about Wolfgang Lazius's work on the Republic of Rome, sent to them eight years before, corrected and augmented by the author and checked by himself. He will claim it back in order to get it published by the Wechel press. Zwinger should scold them and if they do not appreciate the work or lack the capital, they should give it over to Jean Aubry, the son-in-law of André Wechel. He will take care of a preface afterwards. He saw Zwinger's* Methodus apodemica, *but the bookseller has not given him any copy of it. He asks Zwinger to tell Johannes Löwenklau to send the lexicon of Zonaras to the Wechels, who will forward it to Vienna or perhaps keep it for Friedrich Sylburg's work on a new lexicon. Sambucus would like to know soon what Zwinger has achieved.*

Salutem.

Doleo vehementer obitum Pernae, sed quid agamus?[2049] Haec nobis communiter via est denique voranda et reliqua vitiorum hoc modo deponenda. Scripsi ad haeredes, ut Horatii *Poeticam* meam una cum illustrium vatum fragmentis ante 9 annos ad Pernam missam remittant, ne pereant, nam recognoscam nonnulla et ita fortassis edam.[2050] Scripsi ad Episcopium vehementer, expostulando de mora editionis Aristotelis.[2051] Ac mihi rectissime facturus videris, si persuaseris, cum Wechelianis uti editionem communicent, qui se typos suos elegantissimos ex societate accommodaturos sunt polliciti, nil optatius fecerimus multis bonis ac eruditis, qui in desiderio sunt editionis.[2052] Aeginetam accepi. Conveni cum Wechelianis per me eos quidvis cum Episcopio transigere posse etc. Ad Gryneum quoque et Oporinianos scribo et conqueror de Lazii volumine

---
[2048] Concerning Sambucus's Trapezuntius-manuscript cf. the Index.
[2049] Zwinger's marginal note: "1582. Obitus Petri Pernae typographi." Perna died on 16 August 1582.
[2050] Zwinger's marginal note: "Horatius cum poetarum fragmentis." See Sambucus, *Ars poetica Horatii.* Cf. letter 261.
[2051] Zwinger's marginal note: "Mora Aristotelis."
[2052] See the preceding letter.

misso ipsis a me *De republica Romana*, qui, cum ab omnibus expetatur ante annos 8 correctum ab ipso auctore et auctum aque me revisum recensitumque ad illos gratis miseram, quod sese statim typis vulgaturos pollicebantur. Quare reposco volumen, ut Wechelianis tradatur aut quam primum extrudatur.[2053] Quod enim beneficium a me sine praemio et mercede acceperunt, cur ita premunt? Valde abs te peto, uti eorum cessationem corripias, quod si non intelligunt rem aut sumptibus non sufficiunt, dent negotium Aubrio, genero Wechelii. Ego praefationem post curabo. Tua *Apodemica* vidi, sed bibliopola nullum mihi dedit exemplum.[2054] Vale, vir doctissime et amice vetus. Si forte in D. Leonclavium incideris, aut facultas ad eum scribendi et occasio fuerit, promove preces meas, ut *Lexicon* Zonarae a me concreditum Francfortum ad Wechelianos mittat,[2055] qui Viennam ad me transmittent ac forte usibus officinae suae ad lexici novi Silburgiani confectionem aliquamdiu detinebunt.[2056] Harum mearum precum, oro, officiose et amanter citra tuum incommodum memento. Vale, raptim 9. Novembris 82. Tui studiosissimus Sambucus. Aveo brevi intelligere, quid effeceris.[2057]

Address: Clarissimo et doctissimo philosopho et medico, domino D. Theodoro Zwingero etc., amico meo observandissimo. Basell, Hern Doctor Zwinger Zu händen.

360.
Sambucus to Piero Vettori
22 November 1582, Vienna

The original is kept in Munich, BSB, Clm 735, f. 164. Published in Bandini, *Clarorum Italorum et Germanorum*, 2:154-155; Gerstinger, "Die Briefe," 271-272.

It was very important for Sambucus to learn from the Florentine legate the day before that Vettori was in good health, as he heard some contrary news. He wishes him a long and fruitful life, and to avoid what happened to André Wechel, who died. His two sons-in-law (his heirs, who are

---

[2053] The book eventually appeared in the Wechel press in 1598, including Lazius's additions, but without any mention of Sambucus's name. See letter 233, note 1354.

[2054] Zwinger's marinal note: "D. Theod. Zwingeri." Zwingerus, *Methodus apodemica*. See letter 295, note 1724.

[2055] Zwinger's marinal note: "Zonarae lexicon Graecum per Wechelianos excudendum." The lexicon attributed to Zonaras was given to Löwenklau in 1576. See letter 271, note 1552, and letter 298.

[2056] Zwinger's marinal note: "Friderici Silburgii lexicon." The "lexicon" in question might be Sylburg's *Etymologicum Magnum*, which appeared in Heidelberg in 1594. Friedrich Sylburg (1536–1596) was among the best Greek philologists of the sixteenth century and many of his editions were reprinted in the eighteenth and even in the nineteenth century. As a son of a peasant, he was able to study at German universities thanks to the support of his teachers and the bursary of Stift Wetter. In 1559 he got to know Henri Estienne and took part in the edition of the *Thesaurus Graecae linguae*. Later he taught at Latin schools but rejected university professorships, and joined the Wechel press in the early 1580s. In 1591 he moved to the Bibliotheca Palatina in Heidelberg. Many of his publishing projects show affinity with Sambucus's interests. In fact, Sylburg had a high opinion of Sambucus and confirmed after his death that "for many years nothing happened to the whole of the respublica litteraria more bitter than his premature death" (Almási, *The Uses of Humanism*, 82). In 1586 he sent a letter to Zwinger, wondering, among others, about Sambucus's work on Aristotle. See Johann Georg Jung, *Vita Friderici Sylburgii, Wetterani Hassi, polyhistoris quondam magni* (Berleburgi: apud Iohannem Iacobum Haugium 1745); Karl Preisendanz, "Aus Friedrich Sylburgs Heidelberger Zeit," *Neue Heidelberger Jahrbücher* N.F. (1937), 56-77; Antonio Rigo, "Saracenica di Friedrich Sylburg (1595): una raccolta di opere bizantine contro l'Islâm," in *I Padri sotto il torchio: le edizioni dell'antichità cristiana nei secoli 15.–16.*, ed. Mariarosa Cortesi (Florence: SISMEL, 2002), 289-310.

[2057] See Zwinger's response in letter 366.

461

Sambucus's good relations), persuaded by Sambucus, say they are ready to print Vettori's Variae lectiones *with their nice types. Sambucus sent them the second volume, which they were missing, and promised to write a preface about Vettori's merits, pointing out the differences between Vettori's work and other analogous books. Sambucus believes, they will finish it for the coming Easter. If Vettori wants to add something, he should urgently send it; they will be certainly able to insert it at least as an attachment. He would like to have Vettori's age written on (the edition).*

Salutem.

Qui a secretis est oratori vestro heri significavit de te mihi quaerenti superesse ac optime ista exacta aetate te valere, quod mihi gratissimum accidit. Nam quiddam subaudieram nuper, quod me turbarat. Precor itaque Deum optimum maximum, ut vel senio hoc annis gravi et molesto viribus tamen diuturnum esse velit, quo exquisitis tuis monimentis atque ex officina prodeuntibus frui nobis liceat. Caeterum quod te praecipue hisce nunc volo, est: Wechelus, insignis atque in caeteris typographis Galliae et Germaniae diligentia separata, mortuus nuper est.[2058] Successerunt laboribus et caeptis conatibus generi duo eruditi,[2059] mihi familiarissimi, qui sese libros tuos *Variarum lectionum* elegantissimis suis formis, si ita suaderem, impressuros nunciabant.[2060] Ego vero ilico alterum tomum, quo destituebantur, suppeditavi, institutum eorum praeclarum consilio meo confirmavi ac, ne quid eos a lucro deterreret, praefari etiam de tuis virtutibus et aliorum in hoc genere scriptionis claris, sed quantum a tuis divisi sint, indicare volui. Finietur credo ad proximum pascha. Quod si forte quid additum aut recognitum velis, statim mitte, nam si seriem typorum et formarum inire nequibunt, tamen in extremo commode ponentur et cum auctoritatis tuae commendatione. Haec breviter ac subito nacta occasione te nescire nolui. Vale atque Sambucum tuarum lucubrationum ac virtutum admiratorem aliquando etiam praeconem esse tibi persuadeas etc. Viennae 22. Septembris 82. Tuus deditissimus Ioannes Sambucus. Annos aetatis adscriptos tuis cupio.

Address: Petro Victorio etc. Florentino, viro clarissimo, domino amico praecipuo. Florentiae.

361.
Sambucus to Joachim Camerarius Jr.
25 December 1582, [Vienna]

The original is kept in Munich, BSB, Clm 10367, Nr. 185.

Clusius has brought Camerarius's letter with the message that Sambucus should write at once if he wants anything, as the courier is going back tomorrow. If Camerarius does not receive anything concerning the reform of the apothecaries, the blame lies with the courier, as all shops and bookshops are closed. If Simon Grynaeus has died, Sambucus would be very sorry, and he asks Camerarius to find out for certain from Zwinger and others. Three years ago, he sent a manuscript of Antonio

---

[2058] André Wechel died on 31 October 1581.
[2059] Claude de Marne and Jean Aubry.
[2060] Vettori's *Variae lectiones* appeared in several editions from 1553 (see, for example, letter 116, note 685). A new edition had just come out with Giunta in Florence in 1582. This may also be the reason why the heirs of Wechel dropped the idea of publication.

de Albertis's complete translation of Euclid to Grynaeus with many added demonstrations, to which he had added rare annotations by Psellos and others. Camerarius should endeavour to have it returned to Sambucus. Dasypodius is a hopeless case, neither does he print Sambucus's Euclid and many other works on mechanics and tactics, nor does he return the codices. Sambucus will be more cautious when he entrusts something in future. He will keep silent about Vulcanius, until some other good friend stirs his fire and heats up his workshop. Jean Aubry has contacted him concerning the letters of Camerarius Sr. Whatever others felt about this great man, he always had the highest thoughts in his heart. Aubry has not yet answered Veit Winsheim, but Sambucus expects that he will. God may spare them all from his ire. He extends his greetings to Julius Geuder and his New Year's wishes to Christ Herdesianus.

Salutem.

Ipso hoc natali Christi tuas mihi Clusius missit, cum nuncio: si quid te velim, hodie facerem, cras tabellarium recessurum. Ea re, si de reformatione pharmacopolarum modo nil accipis, causam in subitum ac importunum discessum tabellarii transferas, quod omnes urbanae officinae ac bibliopolia clausa teneantur. De morte Grynaei si quid tale doctissimo viro accidisset, valde, uti debeam, dolerem ac te diligenter oro, per Zvingerum et alios uti aliquid certum habeas.[2061] Nam miseram ante triennium efflagitanti Euclidem totum Albertini Florentini illius ante 80 annos mortui versionem[2062] et additas plurimas ἀποδείξεις[2063] novas et mirabiles praesentes [?] in 10 libris, cui adiunxeram Pselli et aliorum in priores eiusdem ἀποσημειώσεις[2064] raras inventum et cetera, da operam ut rehabeat Bibliothecula nostra. De Dasypodio omnis spes evanuit, qui Euclidea[2065] mea et Heronis et Constantini plurima bellica et mechanica[2066] premit, nec codices reddit, quod ipsum Henricus quoque Stephanus inique facit et alii. Cautior posthac talia committam. De Vulcanio cohibebo silentium, dum Achates[2067] alius ignem excusserit illi et officinam calefaciat. De epistolis clarissimi tui parentis Aubrius his mihi significavit et specimen simile ostendit. Quicumque sensus aliorum fuerint de tanti viri mente, sensibus, doctrina, nil nisi certa, sancta, ὀφέλιμα, ψυχαγωγικά[2068] in tacto gratoque animo cogitabit [!]. Vinshemio[2069] ille nondum respondit, sed exspecto diem. Deus optimus maximus nos respiciat, iramque, quam praefert peste, turbationibus religionis et

---

[2061] Simon Grynaeus (1539–1582), a professor of arts and medicine in Heidelberg and Basel, died on 4 September.
[2062] During his stay in Bologna in 1562, Sambucus bought four manuscripts containing the autographs of Antonio de Albertis's translations from Greek from the scribe Michele Gelmi (cf. Sambucus's note in Vienna, ÖNB, Cod. 1071, f. a.ii^r): Manuel Bryennius's *De Musica* (Cod. 10437), Alexander of Aphrodisias's commentary in the first book of *De Anima* (incomplete, Cod. 10487), the works of Archimedes (Cod. 10701) and this manuscript by Euclid, which is now lost. On Antonio de Albertis see *Catalogus translationum et commentariorum*, eds. Paul Oskar Kristeller and F. Edward Cranz (Washington: Catholic University of America Press, 1971), 2:414-415.
[2063] demonstrations
[2064] annotations
[2065] See letter 89, note 564.
[2066] See letter 247, note 1431.
[2067] A proverbial term for an especially close friend. Achates is Aeneas's best friend in Vergil's *Aeneid*.
[2068] useful, persuasive
[2069] Veit Winsheim (Vitus Ortelius Vinshemius Jr. 1521–1608) was a professor of law in Wittenberg and an editor of some posthumously published works of his famous philologist father. See Andreas Gößner, "Windsheim - Wittenberg - Warnsath: Familie und Nachkommen von Veit Örtel d. Ä. im 16. und 17. Jahrhundert," in *Veit Örtel d. Ä. aus Windsheim (1501–1570), Wittenberger Humanist, Schüler und Vertrauter Melanchthons*, ed. Andreas Gößner (Nuremberg: Verein für Bayerische Kirchengeschichte, 2022), 375-433.

tot divertiis κενοδόξων[2070] mitigat. Ἀμήν. Vale ipso natali die Christi 82. Tui additissimus I. Sambucus.

Clarissimo et magnifico domino Gaydero salutem, item Herdessiano[2071] vestro, viro doctissimo ac viro amico, mille Kalendas Ianuarii.

Address: Clarissimo viro, medico et physico reipublicae Noribergensis, domino Ioachimo Camerario, amico observandissimo. Noribergam.
Camerarius's note: 83 7. Ianuarii.

362.
Sambucus to Henricus Porsius
1583, Vienna

Published in Henricus Porsius, *Historia belli Persici, gesti inter Murathem III. Turcarum et Mehemetem Hodabende, Persarum regem, breviter ac vere conscripta ab Henrico Porsio iurisconsulto sacratissimae caesareae maiestatis ab epistolis in camera aulica et poeseos professore publico in archigymnasio Viennensi. Eiusdem Itineris Byzantini Libri III. Carminum Lib. II. Epigrammatum II. Poeta* (Frankfurt: Iohannes Wechelus, 1583), [unnumbered pages following Porsius's preface].

At Porsius's request, Sambucus ran through Porsius's narration of the history of two powerful barbarian kings, which has no certain outcome yet. He likes truth, especially when it comes from the accounts of people around us. Porsius did well to add short explanations of some foreign words, a practice sadly ignored by many modern authors. Only if he had personally participated in these events could he have written more and more precisely. Who would deny that Porsius has a good literary vein? If only these two enemies fatally destroyed each other! He is sending his greetings to their mutual patron Joachim Sintzendorf who served well with his exquisite observations as Rudolf II's legate at Constantinople.

Ioannes Sambucus Porsio[2072] suo salutem.

Narratiunculas tuas de duum potentissimorum regum barbarorum nullo dum certis exitu rebus aut conversionibus uti voluisti, percurri. Amo veritatem, quae cum proprie se circumsistentibus

---

[2070] vainglorious people
[2071] Christoph Herdesianus (1523–1585) was a jurist and theologian active in Nuremberg. He played a significant role in dogmatic disputes among the Protestant theologians. See Irene Dingel, *Concordia controversa. Die öffentlichen Diskussionen um das lutherische Konkordienwerk am Ende des 16. Jahrhunderts* (Gütersloh: Gütersloher Verlagshaus, 1996), 207-279.
[2072] Henricus Porsius (Heinrich Porsch) (1556–1610) was born in Friedberg in der Wetterau, studied in Marburg and Wittenberg, then visited Italy and came to Vienna. In 1579 he travelled to Constantinople, accompanying the imperial envoy Baron Wolf von Eizing, where he met also Joachim Sintzendorf (see note 2077 below). Upon his return, he became professor of poetry at the University of Vienna, but soon left this position for an office at the imperial court, passing also time in Prague. Later, he found employment at the Hungarian Chamber. His only known but neglected publication is the present one, which gave not only a good account of the recent (unfinished) Ottoman-Persian war (from 1578), but also included an epic poem on Porsius's travel to Constantinople, combining personal with historical narration, and a good number of his poems, partly about Ottoman subjects. On Porsius, see Johann Peter Lotichius, *Bibliotheca poetica*, pars 4 (Francofurti: sumptibus Lucae Jennisii, 1628), 120-122.

nititur, facile assensum impetrat. Recte aliquot peregrinis vocibus suas expositiunculas adhibuisti, quam diligentiam, seu melius industriam hodie iure in multis desideramus. Caeterum si te πρηκτῆρα τούτων τῶν πραγμάτων, ἢ μάρτυρ᾽ αὐτοπτον[2073] esse contigisset, nae tu pleraque aliter atque copiosius, εἰλικρινέστερον[2074] duntaxat pronunciasses. Nam egregiam pertexendi facultatem, qui ad utrunque styli genus expeditum et numerosum excellis, quis tibi non libenter tribuat? Legentur tamen haec affecta, ut quaeque ordine annotasti. Utinam vero aliquando barbarae illae acies ita infeste corruant et, ut cum veteri comico verbum permutem, arma armis ferruminent admodum,[2075] ut mutuis vulneribus depositi confectique iaceant, nobisque speculam nuper domestica rabie ostensam excidio proprio afferant pleniorem. Ἀλλὰ μὲν τοῦτο ἐν γούνασι θεῶν,[2076] ut caetera. Vale, ac magnifico communi nostro patrono domino Ioachimo a Sintzendorf[2077] etc. de rebus Christianorum pro Rudolpho II. suis Byzantinis internunciis et exquisitis observationibus optime merito salutem. Viennae.

363.
Sambucus to Johannes Crato
4 February 1583, Vienna

Published in Gerstinger, "Die Briefe," 272-274.

Sambucus is glad that Crato is finally free of work and enjoys his merited leisure. If only he could enjoy it for a long time and finish the works he intended to publish. Presently, it is very cold in Austria. Rudolf II has decided to convene a diet in Pressburg on 1 March, the Ottomans have left Hungary this winter in peace. There is various news from Byzantium: about a victory of the Persians and about Sinan deprived of his office. The day before, Belgian couriers brought news of a French plot discovered in Antwerp which aimed at the destruction of the town and which ended with the French being driven out. 800 of them were killed, including an unusual number of noblemen, while the Prince of Orange, who had no idea of the danger, was hiding in Antwerp. The agitation in Cologne is growing, preparations are made for war. The apostolic nuncio left Vienna on the last day of January to be joined by the cardinal (of Trento) in Innsbruck and proceed with him to Cologne in order to take control of the situation. Sambucus recommends Crato a student named Laurentius from Carniola, who studied together with his son and now wants to move to Wrocław to further his studies and advancement. He is said to have good morals and to serve others with diligence. If Crato writes to Henri Estienne, he should warn him of his duties and Dioscorides.

Salutem.

Te tandem exactis tot laboribus occupationibusque semotis ocio digno frui laetor.[2078] Utinam

---

[2073] a participant in these things or an eyewitness
[2074] more distinctly
[2075] Cf. a textual variant in Plautus, *Miles gloriosus*, 1335: "Labra labellis ferruminauit admodum."
[2076] But this lies in the power of gods. Cf. *Illias* 17.514; *Odyssea* 1.267; *Odyssea* 16.129.
[2077] Joachim Sintzendorf (1544–1594) imperial councillor. From 1578 he spent three years in Constantinople as a diplomat. See *Biographisches Lexikon des Kaiserthums Österreich* 35 (1877), 19.
[2078] Crato left imperial service in Prague on 29 September 1581 and moved first to his estates in Rückerts (Silesia) then a year later to Wrocław. See Gillet, *Crato von Krafftheim*, 2:254-255.

id ita sis complexus, ut tuo commodo quam diutissime fruare et, quae instituisti scripta, polias cunctisque legenda edas. Nos in Austria mediocri aere utimur, frigoribus modo intensissimis conflictamur. Caesar ad Kalendas Martias Posonium comitia imperavit.[2079] A Thurca nil hac hyeme in Ungariae confiniis infestius admissum. Byzantio varia prodeunt cum de Persarum thriumphis, tum Sinanno dignitatibus exuto, adempto equo etc.[2080] Heri cursores Belgici advolarunt, qui certis scriptis nunciant detectas esse insidias Antverpiae Gallicas, quae in universam necem urbisque excidium parabantur, eiectos Gallos, fugatos, ad 800 caesa [?], numero nobilium insolenti desiderato, Auraniae principe Antverpiae nullius conscio mali latitante.[2081] Colonienses motus crescunt, apparatus fiunt magni.[2082] Hinc nuntius pontificis[2083] Oenipontum pridie Kalendas Martii [i.e. Februarii][2084] ad cardinalem[2085] discessit, ut eo sibi itineris et legationis Coloniam adsumpto, si fieri potest, tumultus compescat, religionem scilicet importat, ne quid liberius in Coloniae fines moliantur.[2086] Laurentium hunc studiosum literarum in Carnis natum tuae excellentiae commendo, qui spe sibi alicunde data melioris conditionis istinc consequendi suaque studia et progressus urgendi ad vos proficiscitur.[2087] Fuit aliquando cum filio meo. Moribus est, ut audio, probatis, obsequendi et diligenter serviendi animo laudato. Si qua in re commodo tuo etc. illi satisfacere poteris, oro, ne miserum negligas. Vale. Vienna. 4. Februarii 83. Tuae excellentiae totus Ioannes Sambucus.

Si quando ad Henricum Stephanum scripseris, rogo, officii eum sui et Dioscoridis moneas serio.[2088] Miror hominis consilia et ingenium.

Address: Magnifico et clarissimo viro domino Ioanni Cratoni ab Craffthaim, medico et consiliario sacratissimae caesareae maiestatis, domino amico observando. Wresla.

364.
Sambucus to Emperor Rudolf II
20 February 1583, Vienna

The original is kept in Vienna, Österreichisches Staatsarchiv, Allgemeines Verwaltungs-, Finanz- und Hofkammerarchiv, Hoffinanz Ungarn 44, f. 5.

[2079] The invitations to the diet were sent out on 28 December 1582 and the diet eventually opened on 6 April 1583. See *Magyar országgyűlési emlékek, 7 (1582–1587)*, ed. Vilmos Fraknói (Budapest: Akadémia, 1881), 119-120.
[2080] Koca Sinan Pasha (1506–1596) was deprived of his office as Grand Vizier on 6 December 1582 because of the defeat of his lieutenant by the Persians at Gori.
[2081] During the "French Fury" (17 January 1583), led by Francis, Duke of Anjou and Alençon, which was discovered and thwarted, c. 1500 French soldiers were killed. See A *Generall Historie of the Netherlands*, 810-817.
[2082] The Cologne War (1583–1588) broke out when Archbishop Gebhard Truchsess, Prince-Elector of Cologne converted to Protestantism, got married (two days before Sambucus wrote his letter), and attempted to turn the ecclesiastical principality into a secular, dynastic duchy. The war was fought with international allies at both sides.
[2083] Giovanni Francesco Bonomi (1536–1587), bishop of Vercelli.
[2084] Gerstinger did not notice this chronological problem.
[2085] Andreas von Österreich (1558–1600), the son of Archduke Ferdinand II of Tirol.
[2086] See more in *Nuntiaturberichte aus Deutschland. Abtheilung 3, Band 1: Der Kampf um Köln 1576–1584*, ed. Joseph Hansen (Berlin: Bath, 1892), lvii-lviii; Gerstinger, "Die Briefe," 274.
[2087] We have no further information on this person.
[2088] On the planned Dioscorides-edition see letter 155, notes 920-921 and the Index.

Sambucus affirms that a real unicorn of this length costs at least 3,000 ducats but is worth double or triple the price in princely treasuries. He asks Rudolf to decide about it. Next, he also asks Rudolf to give him a special honorarium of 3,000 thalers in recognition of his 28 years of service, which may also be paid from the customs collected from the traffic in oxen in Mosonmagyaróvár. Otherwise, if Rudolf prefers, he can also give him and his heirs 300 thalers as a yearly pension from the incomes of (the estates) by Eisenstadt or elsewhere. On the cover, Sambucus asks Rudolf to read at least a few lines of his letter.

Potentissime Imperator, domine, domine mihi semper clementissime.

Unicornu veri et ista longitudine rari pretium est minimum et summum 3 milia ducatorum.[2089] Valet duplum, ne triplum dicam, in principum thesauris. Supplicant, quorum interest, una mecum, vestra maiestas clementissime de eo se resolvat atque benignissime expediat.

Caeterum mea separata est supplicatio ad vestram clementissimam maiestatem humillima eaque toties repetita, sed nondum recitata, vestra maiestas dignetur fidelium meorum et a 28 annis servitiorum laborumque meminisse singulari subsidii clementia, hoc est, ut me augeat iam prope fessum tribus milibus tallerorum praesentibus aut ad hanc summam evadente libero boum actu per Altenburgum etc. Aut si vestrae maiestati placet, pensionem annuam mihi meisque in posterum semper trecenti tallerorum imponet, in officiis et proventibus Eysnstatt,[2090] vel ubicumque vestrae maiestati gratiosissime videbitur. Quod beneficium perpetua sedulitate et memoria penes me, meos ac posteros constabit. Me vestrae maiestati meosque humillime commendo. Vestrae sacratissimae maiestatis humillimus subditus ac cliens Ioannes Sambucus manu propria.

Verso (Sambucus's hand): Ioanni Sambuci humillima supplicatio et memoriale. 20. Februarii vestram sacratissimam maiestatem oro, legat aliquot lineas.
Her guet [...] möct [?] [...] disse sahen ansprechen.
(Secretary's hand): Doctor Johannes Sambucus per gnade und Provision. 15. Martii 83.

365.
Sambucus to Joachim Camerarius Jr.
3 March 1583, [Vienna]

The original is kept in Munich, BSB, Clm 10367, f. 316ᵛ. Published in Gerstinger, "Die Briefe," 274-275.

Sambucus believes Jacobus Monavius has already written about the alchemical authors; they are waiting for an answer. The codex has a nice script. When a person who thinks himself to be an expert in gold-making examined the codex, he cried out that he would grab it as if it were a divine testimony. He has heard nothing of Vulcan's anvil (i.e. Bonaventura Vulcanius). Hastily written because of the courier.

[2089] See letters 333 and 336.
[2090] The estates of Eisenstadt were put in pledge to the Habsburgs in the fifteenth century. From 1571 they were administered by the Lower Austrian Chamber and used for subsidizing the archdukes.

Salutem.

Credo Monavium de scriptoribus χρυσοποιίας[2091] scripsisse, responsum expectamus.[2092] Codex facilibus ad usum characteribus exaratus. Quidam, qui sapere se aliquid in hoc studio aureo putat, eo vel inspecto exclamabat: ego ut μαρτύρια οὐράνια[2093] codicem arripiam. De Vulcani incude nil audio. Haec raptim tabellario. 3. Martii. 83. Tibi deditus Sambucus.

Address: Clarissimo viro domino Ioachimo Cammerario, medico reipublicae Noribergensis, domino amico observando. Nurnberg.
Camerarius's hand: 83. 23. Mart.

366.
Theodor Zwinger to Sambucus
12 March 1583, Basel

The original is kept in Vienna, ÖNB, Cod. 9736, f. 15ʳ. Published in Gerstinger, "Die Briefe," 271.

Zwinger had a serious talk with Eusebius Episcopius. He was quite convinced by Sambucus's letter, and since Jean Aubry drags his feet and despite his promises does not show himself, he made a contract with Jean de Sponde about the Greek-Latin edition of Aristotle. He will publish the Greek from Sambucus's codex, collate the corrections with the recent Latin edition by Argyropylus, and add notes and summaries to the text and the chapters and explanations of unclear places in the margins. He would have entered into partnership with Henri Estienne if the latter had been ready to send his types to Basel, where it could have been printed for much less money. He says he cannot contract with the Wechel press, as he is still held by the old partnership he had with Perna. The Oporinus press excuses itself with regard to difficult times, especially now that Perna's heirs are publishing Johannes Rosinus's great book on Roman antiquities, arranged according to loci communes. They fear this will massively hurt the sales of Lazius. So fare the procrastinators. He has again urged Episcopius to write an answer to Sambucus. Zwinger has not seen Johannes Löwenklau for two years, nevertheless, he will remind him of (Zonaras's) Lexicon. Sambucus will receive his Methodus apodemica *through Episcopius. The plague in Basel has now receded.*

Salutem.

Cum Episcopio egi serio.[2094] Neque vero ille parum literis tuis convictus videtur, ita ut cessante Auberio et praeter pollicitationes non comparente cum Ioanne Spondano Gallo,[2095]

[2091] goldmaking
[2092] This concerns the alchemical manuscript mentioned first in letter 354, see esp. note 2025.
[2093] heavenly testimony
[2094] This is a response to letter 359.
[2095] Jean de Sponde (1557–1595) was a French humanist, who moved to Basel in 1580, studied at the university and practiced alchemy in the environment of François Hotman. In 1582 he was working on an Aristotle-edition of Zwinger and Episcopius (see letter 307, note 1796). In 1583 he returned to France, found temporary employment at the chancellery of Henry III, king of Navarre and got married. In 1593 he converted to Catholicism. See Alan Boase, *Vie de Jean de Sponde* (Geneva: Droz, 1977).

viro doctissimo, contraxerit de Aristotelis editione Graecolatina,[2096] ita quidem ut textus Graecus ex tuo codice emendetur, cum Latina Argyropoli recentiore doctissimae correctiones conferantur, textus et capita annotentur, argumentis illustrentur, loca obscuriora breviter ad marginem explicentur. Cum H. Stephano societatem initurus fuerat, si ille characteres suos Basilaeam mittere voluisset, uti minore multo cum impendio quam Genevae excudi potuisset. Cum Wechelianis societatem inire se posse negat, cum a vetere illa Pernae nondum sit liber. Oporiani excusant se temporum difficultate, nunc vero multo maxime, quia Ioannes Rosinus antiquitatum Romanarum opus amplissimum et methodικώτατον [!][2097] per locos communes distinctum Pernae haeredibus excudendum dederit,[2098] quem Lazii distractioni plurimum verentur incommodaturum.[2099] Sic scilicet πᾶς ἀμβολίεργος ἀνὴρ ἄταισι παλαίει.[2100] Iteratus sum ut tibi rescriberet. Leonclavium intra biennium non vidi. Monebo tamen illum de *Lexico*.[2101] *Apodemica* per Episcopium accipies.[2102] Pestilentia non obscure apud nos remisit. Deus porro nostri miseratur. Tibi ego, mi Sambuce, vitam et incolumitatem ex animo opto. Basilea, XII. Martii XXCIII. Tuus ex animo Zwinger.

Address: Clarissimo viro D. Ioanni Sambuco historico caesareo amico colendo. Viennam.
Sampt einer *Methodo Apodemica*.
Sambucus's note: Ioannis Rosini antiquitatum Hist. Germ. ver. [?]

367.
Franciscus Modius to Sambucus
[Probably around 23 March 1583, Würzburg][2103]

Published in Franciscus Modius, *Novantiquae lectiones, tributae in epistolas centum* (Frankfurt: Heredes Andreae Wecheli, 1584), 80-81.

Sambucus is about to receive a fruit of his generosity. He had generously gifted to Johannes Posthius a parchment manuscript of Propertius, which was then used by Jan Meller Palmier, who recently died well before his time. Now Modius sends his additional notes from this manuscript. They may not amount to much, but, as Propertius is one of the best poets, nothing concerning him is so unimportant, that it is not worth one's while. When he considers the feeble production of modern authors, he thinks that his time is better invested in these emendations, even if they are somewhat lightweight, than in imposing some fantasies on the reader and making him waste his time. He knows that Sambucus thinks the same.

[2096] For Sambucus's plan to publish Aristotle, cf. the Index.
[2097] the most systematic
[2098] Ioannes Rosinus, *Romanarum antiquitatum libri decem* (Basileae: ex Officina haeredum Petri Pernae, 1583).
[2099] See letter 359, note 2053.
[2100] every procrastinator wrestles with regret. Cf. Hesiod, *Erga* 413.
[2101] See letter 359, note 2055.
[2102] See letter 295, note 1724.
[2103] The dating is based on the fact that Modius sent his observations on Propertius from Posthius's manuscript also to Lipsius in a letter dated 23 March 1583. Cf. Lipsius, *Epistolae*, 420-421.

Franciscus Modius[2104] Ioanni Sambuco viro clarissimo et caesareae maiestatis consiliario salutem. Viennam.

Ut hic quoque tibi liberalitatis tuae fructus constet, clarissime Sambuce, qua amicissimum mihi Ioannem Posthium[2105] archiatrum Wirzeburgicum membranaceo manu exarato Propertii exemplari munificentissime donatum voluisti,[2106] ex quo pridem multa in hoc poeta carissimus olim utrique nostrum Ianus Mellerus Palmerius,[2107] nuper inmatura morte nobis studiisque ereptus emendarat, mito nunc ecce ex eodem haec quoque post illum notata, non magni quidem illa momenti, fateor, sed tamen talia, ut de iis silendum hic mihi non putaverim, ut enim vel tenuissima sint, ut sunt certe, quid in Propertio, sui generis extra controversiam poetarum principe, adeo exiguum est, quod cura nostra indignum videri aut debeat, aut possit? Mihi sane consideranti interdum scriptorum nostri saeculi, atque in primis poetarum infelicem proventum, satius videtur in his quamlibet leviusculis tempus terere, quam miseris chartis temere quaelibet somnia illinere lectorique obtrudere, ut habeat, in quo bonas horas male perdat. Qua in re quia existimo, imo certe scio, tuas, Sambuce, rationes cum meis congruere, hoc agam potius.[2108]

368.
Christophe Plantin to Sambucus
18 May 1583, Leiden

The original is kept in Vienna, ÖNB, Cod. 9736, f. 16. Published in *Supplément à la Correspondance de Christophe Plantin*, 203-204; Gerstinger, "Ein gelehrter Briefwechsel," 13. *Plantin is happy that Sambucus liked his little gift. He is surprised that his letter did not reach Sambucus, in which he wrote that after the death of Wilhelm Canter his "sacred letters" got into the hands of Laevinus Livineius, the nephew of Laevinus Torrentius, who just returned from Italy and promised to translate them. As far as he can, Plantin will urge him in letters (it is not always safe to write from Leiden to Liege) to send (the manuscript) at least to a friend in Cologne, from whom his agent can pick it up on his way to the next book fair. Times have deteriorated so much that Plantin hardly dares publish anything with his own money that is not very well-known; the notable and rare works are neglected. Therefore Plantin left his press in the care of Franciscus Raphelengius and his bookshop in that of Jan Moretus, his son-in-law, and moved to Leiden in order to run one press there for his own pleasure and publish folio books of antique historians, encouraged, helped and (partly) financed by Justus Lipsius. He asks Sambucus to help Lipsius, or rather him and the scholarly world in this endeavour. He met Bonaventura Vulcanius, Greek professor and secretary of the University of Leiden, who promises to send back Sambucus's manuscripts and Joachim Camerarius's letters, which he thinks should not be published together*

[2104] Franciscus Modius (Frans de Maulde, 1556-1597), philologist and poet. He was born in Bruges in a noble and rich family, studied law in Douai, Leuven and Leiden, but lost his fortune in the wars and henceforth led an unstable life, relying on friends and patrons. See Paul Lehmann, *Franciscus Modius als Handschriftenforscher* (München: Beck, 1908).
[2105] On Posthius see letter 249, note 1433.
[2106] The manuscript in question is now in Groningen, Rijksuniversiteitsbibliotheek, hs. 159.
[2107] Palmier made use of the same manuscript for his *Spicilegiorum Iani Melleri Palmerii commentarius primus* (Frankfurt: Apud Georgium Corvinum impensis Sigismundi Feyrabendii, 1580), 169.
[2108] There follow fourteen emendations to Propertius on pages 81-86, which we omit here.

with those of Manuel Chrysoloras because they are different in topics and style. Plantin could not publish Sambucus's enlarged Emblemata *because of the lack of woodcutters, but as soon as the illustrations for Carolus Clusius's "Pannonian observations" are ready, he will entrust the* Emblemata *to the same woodcutter, and then they will be printed.*

Salutem plurimam.

Munuscula nostra tibi non ingrata gaudeo. Miror autem meas tibi non redditas fuisse quibus non semel scripsi volumen illud tuum sacrarum epistolarum[2109] post mortem G. Canteri pervenisse me inscio ad manus Laevini Livinaei,[2110] Laevini Torrentii[2111] nepotis qui earum versionem pollicebatur. Is autem non ita pridem ex Italia rediit et se tibi satisfacturum promisit. Urgebo, quantum licebit, per litteras (non etenim semper tutum est hinc Leodium scribere) ut saltem mittat Coloniam ad amicum, qui illud servet, donec institor meus ad nundinas proficiscens illac faciat iter. Eo siquidem calamitatis devenimus, ut nostris sumptibus vix quicquam audeamus imprimendum suscipere, nisi admodum vulgare sit, ita iam quae sunt insignia et rara negliguntur. Hinc factum ut relicta cura nostrae typographiae Francisco Raphelengio et tabernae nostrae librariae Iohanni Moreto generis meis Leidam me contulerim, ubi unum praelum animi gratia exercere statui in antiquis historiographis in folio excudendis non sine consilio et opera opeque nostri Lipsii, quem ut in hac re iuves, imo nos remque publicam, obsecro.[2112]

Vulcanium hic professorem Graecum et huius Academiae secretarium conveni. Promisit se remissurum, quae habet abs te vel a Camerario, cum quo censet Chrysoloram non imprimendum propter dissimilitudinem argumenti et styli.[2113] Laboramus penuria hominum peritorum in ligno incidendi, ea est causa, quare necdum *Emblemata* tua cum auctario recudere potuimus.[2114] Absolutis vero iconibus ad *Observationes Pannonicas* Clusii dabimus eidem incisori tuas excundendas idque, ubi factum erit, illico subiiciemus praelo.[2115] Bene vale et, si quid possumus, nomine tuo impera. Leidae, 18. Maii 1583. Tibi merito addictissimus Ch. Plantinus.

Address: Nobilitate et eruditione viro illustri D. Iohanni Sambuco, caesareae maiestatis historiographo. Viennae Austriae.
Other hand: 19 Iulii.[2116]

[2109] On Sambucus's collection of Greek letters, see letter 351, note 1998.
[2110] Laevinus Livineius (Lievens), brother of the more famous Jan Livineius (Lievens), Belgian philologist who was Plantin's collaborator.
[2111] Laevinus Torrentius (Lieven van der Beke) (1525–1595), was bishop of Antwerp from 1587. He was a learned book collector and published also Horace and Suetonius. His *Correspondance* (1583–1595) was published in three volumes by Marie Delcourt and Jean Hoyoux (Paris: Les belles Lettres, 1950–1954).
[2112] Franciscus Raphelengius (1537–1597) was a polyglot printer and bookseller in Antwerp and Leiden, later professor of Hebrew in Leiden. See Johann Braun's article in *ADB* 27 (1888), 281-283. Jan Moretus (1543–1610) had been working for Plantin from 1557 and after Plantin's death became the owner of the printing company. See Dirk Imhof, *Jan Moretus and the Continuation of the Plantin Press*, 2 vols (Leiden: Brill, 2014).
[2113] See letter 351, note 1999.
[2114] After Sambucus's death, the idea to enlarge the *Emblemata* was dropped, and Plantin republished the 1576 edition in 1584.
[2115] Carolus Clusius, *Rariorum aliquot stirpium per Pannoniam, Austriam, et vicinas quasdam provincias observatarum historia* (Antverpiae: Plantin, 1583).
[2116] Gerstinger claims it refers to the date of Sambucus's answer. Gerstinger, "Ein gelehrter Briefwechsel," 13.

369.
Sambucus to Giovanni Michiel / Baccio Valori[2117]
1 July 1583, [Vienna]

Published in Riccobonus, *De consolatione edita*, 7-8 (addressed to Giovanni Michiel).[2118] A corrupted manuscript copy (addressed to Baccio Valori) by an Italian hand is kept in Florence, Biblioteca Nazionale Centrale, Ms. Rin. 27/II inserto 6, f. 487^{r-v}.[2119] This latter has been published in Gerstinger, "Die Briefe," 264-266, note 11.

Sambucus avidly read the book on Consolation, *which is regrettably attributed to Cicero. Its author is more an industrious than a talented imitator of Cicero. The words are nicely selected but not their order and the usual circumlocutions, much less the sentence closings. The periods are too dense and frequent, with unsuitable endings, the transposition of words and verbs is strange, the structure of the work is generally weak, not to mention the few ungrammatical places. Yet, the content is philosophical and the work is suitable for imitation by the youth. Sambucus thinks the author lived in a time when Cicero's works were still not so widely available to the public and wanted to make a work closely resembling those of Cicero. His attempt merits praise. The corrupted parts should be seen in view of the original (works of Cicero) and (such) imitational practices should have a place in the schools. He agrees with the opinion of that great man (Antonio Riccoboni), who knows Cicero's works well and won fame with his style. Sambucus wishes that he used not only conjectures and comparisons of parallel places but also underlined the methodical (differences). He is sending Sadoleto's writing about the same argument, which he seems to have written as a young man in order to strengthen his style by imitating Cicero, which he also regards as a counterfeit.*

Illustrissimo viro Ioanni Mihaeli, divi Marci procuratori et patrono suo omni observantia colendo, Ioannes Sambucus S. D.

[2117] Sambucus must have known Giovanni Michiel (1516–1596) personally, who stayed several times in Vienna as Venetian ambassador (most recently in 1582, which was followed by his sojourn in Prague till 1585). Michiel was a greatly appreciated, talented and hard-working Venetian ambassador, who obtained his diplomatic experience not only in Vienna but also in Paris and London. He had moderate religious views. See the article by Gino Benzoni in *DBI* 74 (2010), 315-319. Baccio Valori (1535–1606) was a learned patrician of Florence. He was librarian of the Medici library (Biblioteca Medicea Laurenziana) and president of the Accademia del Disegno. See Henk van Veen, "Princes and Patriotism: The Self-Representation of Florentine Patricians in the Late Renaissance," in *Princes and Princely Culture 1450–1650*, eds. by Martin Grosman et al. (Leiden: Brill, 2005), 2:63-78 at 74-75.

[2118] Antonio Riccoboni, the publisher of the letter, printed a copy of the original made by Bartolomeo Silvatico and sent to his son, who was Riccoboni's student in Padua. The original must have ended up in one of Michiel's reports sent from Prague to Venice. See Riccoboni's introduction to Sambucus's letter: "Eius autem consolationem [i.e. of Jacopo Sadoleto, see below], ut verum fatear, nondum vidi. Sed commemoratam animadverti in epistola quadam, quam Iohannes Sambucus, is quem Paullus Manutius litteris suis valde exornavit, summi imperatoris historicus clarissimus, hac de re dedit ad Ioannem Michaelem, amplissimum divi Marci procuratorem, apud eius maiestatem pro serenissimo Venetiarum prencipe legatum illustrissimum, quamque ego a Bartholomaeo Sylvatico Patavino, illustrissimi senatus Veneti iurisconsulto celeberrimo ad Aloysium filium, egregiis animi bonis iuvenem ornatissimum auditorem meum [Riccoboni was teaching at the University of Padova] missam et mihi traditam, totam recitabo." Riccobonus, *De consolatione edita*, 7.

[2119] It is not very probable that Sambucus sent the same letter also to Baccio Valori, as he does not seem to have preserved drafts of his letters. Indicating Valori as the addressee of the letter, which apparently circulated more widely, might have been the error of a later scribe. In fact, as McCuaig writes, "anyone who set pen to paper in this affair had to reckon that he was writing a more or less public document, such was the general zeal for showing, copying, even printing private correspondence about the *Consolatio*." McCuaig, *Carlo Sigonio*, 306-307.

Percurri nulla fere anima recepta *De consolatione* libellum[2120] Ciceronis maiestati parum feliciter adscriptum,[2121] ex quo auctoris ingenium solutum, ad Ciceronis exemplum labore, atque exercitatione magis, quam natura, et indolis affinitate comparatum perspexi.[2122] Verba singula, et coniuncta pura, latina, exquisita, consecutiones non item et ambitus usitatos, minusque clausulas aptas comperi. Numerum sententiarum nimis conglobatum ac frequentem, epilogis haud loco idoneis munitum, hyperbata, traiectiones verborum insolentes, universam structurae rationem neglectam animadverti. Addam a vulgatis grammaticorum regulis interdum scriptorem discessisse. Philosophica sunt atque testata, quae ponit oratio, genusque dicendi atque aemulatio ad exemplum iuventutis atque styli formandi commendationem accommodata. Credo ego huius immitatorem superiori <proxima>[2123] aetate vixisse et, cum Tullii tot libri nondum vulgo comparuissent, tentare ipsum ingeniumque similitudine Ciceronis periclitari voluisse. Laudandus conatus, quae vitiosa videntur, redigenda ad fontes, studiique similitudo non excludenda a scholis. Iudicium illius magni viri probo.[2124] Ciceronis ille volumina versavit et, ut observo, ita sequitur subegitque, ut laudem scribendo consecutus sit praeclaram, sed cuperem non coniecturis modo et collatione fragmentorum, similiumque locorum comportatione, verum artificii notatione interim apertius ageret. Mitto [a me][2125] Sadoleti repertum scriptum eiusdem argumenti,[2126] quod ille admodum iuvenis stylo roborando et ex Cicerone formando exarasse videtur, quod non minus, quam adulterinum aestimo, meque illustrissimae magnificentiae tuae commendo. Ipsis Calendis Quinctilibus 1583.[2127]

[2120] The beginning of the letter seems to suggest that Michiel or Valori had previously sent a copy of the book in question, asking for Sambucus's opinion. The *Consolatio* was published originally in Venice (without the editor's name), then reprinted in Bologna and elsewhere. Cicero [i.e. pseudo-Cicero], *Consolatio. Liber quo se ipsum de filiae morte consolatus est nunc primum repertus et in lucem editus* (Venetiis: apud Hieronymum Polum, 1583). The copy used by Sambucus was the Bologna edition (see the next note).

[2121] Since reports and fragments of Cicero's lost *Consolatio* (written after the death of Cicero's daughter in 45 BC) were known to the erudite public, the "discovery" of the lost original created enormous excitement and called for public and private debates. There were probably several hundreds of letters written on the subject (see notes 2119 and 2122). Still in 1583, after a few reprints of the work, a new edition appeared (the one that apparently reached Sambucus), which already contained a refutation concerning the work's authenticity, written by Antonio Riccoboni and a defence of the work from the part of Carlo Sigonio. *M. Tullii Ciceronis Consolatio, vel De luctu minuendo. Fragmenta eius a Carolo Sigonio et Andrea Patritio exposita. Antonii Riccoboni iudicium, quo illam Ciceronis non esse ostendit. Caroli Sigonii pro eadem orationes II* (Bononiae: apud Ioannem Rossium, 1583). This edition was soon followed by Riccoboni's second invective, which already included Sambucus's supportive letter (see above). Riccoboni commented that Sambucus agreed with him, but reading his work he was missing more argument: "Est Sambucus eiusdem opinionis, cuius ego sum, fictam esse consolationem, sed pauca me scripsisse putat ad ea, quae contra ipsum afferri potuissent." (Riccobonus, *De consolatione edita*, 8.) The fact that Riccoboni quoted Sambucus's letter in full, and placed as the first among his supporters, preceding men like Johannes Crato, Guglielmo Sirleto, Marcus Antonius Muretus and Piero Vettori, is a testimony of the respect Sambucus enjoyed amon the Italians in the questions of Ciceronianism (cf. the quotation in note 2118).

[2122] On the debate over the fake oration see McCuaig, *Carlo Sigonio*, 303-346. Also see *Piero Vettori et Carlo Sigonio. Correspondance avec Fulvio Orsini*, ed. Pierre de Nolhac (Rome: Imprimerie du Vatican, 1889), 62-63. Generally, scholars have always denied the genuinity of the work and attributed it to Carlo Sigonio. Some, however, sustained that the work was an earlier forgery. Bernard Augustin Schultz argued in his dissertation (*De Ciceronis Consolatione*, Greifswald, 1860) that the author had been Gasparino Barzizza. See also Richard Forsyth et al., "Cicero, Sigonio, and Burrows: Investigating the Authenticity of the Consolatio," *Literary and Linguistic Computing* 14 (1999), 375-400.

[2123] This seems to be an addition by Riccoboni, cf. the manuscript quoted in note 2127.

[2124] i.e. Antonio Riccoboni

[2125] This is ignored by Riccoboni, cf. the manuscript quoted in note 2127.

[2126] Sadoletus, *Philosophicae consolationes*. See letters 221 and 223.

[2127] We quote the manuscript copy published in Gerstinger ("Die Briefe," 264-266) in its entirety because of the many

370.
Carlo Sigonio to Sambucus
28 September 1583, Bologna

The original is kept in Vienna, ÖNB, Cod. 9736, f. 19ʳ.

Sigonio cannot decide to whom he should be more grateful, to Sambucus, who wrote a gentle letter in relation to his State of the Jews, *which makes Sigonio feel extremely honoured, or to Friedrich Sylburg, who was the cause of this letter and the editor of the book. If Sambucus noticed the newness or roughness of some of its words, he should not be surprised; it is decreed by the laws of the Council of Trento (which is much respected in Italy) that only the expressions used in the Vulgate can be applied. Sigonio, however, did not always respect this rule, since the Vulgate translation did not always allow for the right interpretation, so he used Greek words instead. He asks for Sambucus's friendship and puts himself at his disposal.*

Carolus Sigonius Ioanni Sambuco salutem.

Nondum satis exploratum habeo, maiores ne tibi, an Sylburgio nostro gratias habeam: tibi, qui litteras ad me humanissimas cum libris meis *De republica Hebraeorum* coniunctas scripseris; illi, qui caussam eius tibi scriptionis attulerit.[2128] Neque enim aut honorificentius mihi quidquam accidere potuit, quam me a Sambuco homine nobilissimo atque ingenii et doctrinae gloria florentissimo ultro litteris appellari, neque gratius aliquid, quam meas vigilias pulcherrimis typis expressas Sylburgii viri eruditissimi consilio intueri. Quod vero tu verborum quorundam aut novitatem, aut asperitatem in illo commentario animadvertisti, noli mirari. Neque enim secus facere potui, lege concilii Tridentini, quam nostri servandam diligentissime curant, interdicente, ne quis a vulgata, quae dicitur, bibliorum tralatione discedat.[2129] Quod tamen

---

variant places. Note that we consider neither of the copies more authentic than the other. Riccoboni probably made some modifications in order to improve Sambucus's Latin and also made some arbitrary changes, see, for example, notes 2123 and 2125. "Illustris et magnifice domine! Percurri nulla fere anima recepta *De consolatione* libellum Ciceronis maiestati infeliciter adscriptum et quo autoris ingenium solitum ad Ciceronis exemplum labore atque exercitatione magis, quam natura et indolis affinitate comparatum deprehendi. Verba singula et coniuncta plura Latina exquisita, consecutiones non item et ambitus usitatos, minus clausulas aptas video, numerum sententiarum nimis conglobatum ac frequentem, epilogis haud loco idoneis munitum, hyperbata, traiectiones verborum insolentes, universa strocturae [universae structurae] rationem neglectam; ne addam a vulgatis gram[m]aticorum regulis interdum scriptorem di[s]cessisse. Philosophi tamen sunt, que ponit. Oratio genusque dicendi atque emulatio ad exemplum iuventutis atque styli formandi consuetudinem accom[m]odatum. Credo ego huius immitatorem superiore etate vississe [vixisse] et, cum nondum Tullii tot libri vulgo comparuissent, tentare ipsum ingeniumque similitudine Ciceronis periclitari voluisse laudandi conatus. Quae vitiosa videntur, redigenda ad fontes studioque similitudo non excludenda a sc[h]olis. Iudicium illis [illius] magni viri probo, Ciceronis ille volumina versavit et, ut observo, ita sequitur subegitque, ut laudem scribendam consecutus sit praeclaram, sed cuperem non cognecturis [coniecturis] modo et collatione fracmentorum [fragmentorum] similiumque locorum comportationem, verum artificii notatione interim apercius [apertius] ageret. Mitto a me Sadoloti [Sadoleti] repertum scriptum eiusdem argumenti, quod ille admodum iuvenis stylo roborando et Ciceronis formando exarasse videtur, quod non minus, quam adulterium actruo [arguo] neque[meque] ves[t]rae illustri magnificentiae commendo. Ipsis Calendis Quintilibus 83. Vestrae illustri magnificentiae Ioannes Sambuco [Sambucus]."

[2128] After its first edition, Sigonio's *De republica Hebraeorum libri VII* (Bononiae: Rossius, 1582) appeared also in Frankfurt (Wechel, 1583), prepared for print by Sylburg.

[2129] Sigonio had serious problems with censorship when publishing this book. See Fausto Parente, "Il 'De republica hebraeorum' di Carlo Sigonio," *Rivista di Storia della Filosofia* 65 (2010), 423-459 (identifying the censor in Antonio Possevino).

ego non perpetuo custodivi, quia non semper plenum aut commodum ex ea sensum elicui, ita ut nisi interdum ad Graecae auxilium confugissem, nunquam illius tractationis argumentum explicuissem. Cupio, mi Sambuce, me a te amari. Quod si feceris, mutuam in eo tibi polliceor voluntatem. Quamobrem si posthac mea omnia ad tua patere commoda tibi persuaseris, non fallam opinionem tuam. Vale. Bononiae IV. Kalendas Octobris MDLXXXIII.

Address: Illustri ac doctissimo viro Ioanni Sambuco. Vienna.
Other hand: Carolus Sigonius vir doctissimus.
Sambucus's hand: 10 Octobris 83. Sigonius.

371.
Sambucus to Michael Neander
1 November, 1583, Vienna

Published in Michael Neander, *Chronicon sive synopsis historiarum* (Lipsiae: Lamberg, 1590), 11-13.

Sambucus is happy and thankful that Neander considers him worthy of friendship. He is only too happy to reciprocate it. Neander's school and his pupils are blessed, as they have been enjoying his hard work for years. Neander has produced so many books for the public and hardly needs any encouragement to reach the pinnacle of virtue and praise. He will receive the unperishable reward from God, the renown with posterity. If Neander needs help in anything, Sambucus will not fail to provide it, even if it were difficult. His Aristotle, Dioscorides and other publications are delayed by the greed of the Basel and Geneva printers, but they will see the light of day if the printers have not completely abandoned humanity and honesty. He is working on a thick book of Hungarian history, but it will take longer to put the finishing touches on it.

Salutem.

Ego vero, mi optime Neander, etiam laetor gratiasque habeo, quod me nescio qua doctrinae opinione prolixius hausta ad tuam agregandam amicitiam putaris. Cur enim te tot egregiis ac exquisitis lucubrationibus florentissimum, quem iam pridem imis sensibus comprehendi, in animo oculisque fero, non complectar, non diligam modo, sed ἐμφατερικώτερον,[2130] ut fatear, amem colamve? Equidem dabo operam, ne in officiis et amore reddendo concedam, vel melius, profecto honorificam mentionem constanter emetiar. Felix collegium Ilfeldense, cuius procurationi tua industria proposita est! Beatos, qui audiunt et morem gerendo tibi operam dant! Tu vero iam abunde et luculente per tot annorum curriculum eam navaris. De tua officina tot clara exempla in publicos usus expedieris, nec minus de Ilfeldensibus, quam Cicero *Pro Flacco* de Massiliensibus pronunciarit.[2131] Haud est igitur cur te εἰς τὸ ἄκρον[2132] virutum totque laudum praemium cohorter, qui te conscientia decursae aetatis vigiliarumve in omnium admiratione posueris, qui aeternitatem intuendo a Deo optimo maximo aliquando

---
[2130] more insistently
[2131] Cf. Cicero, *Pro Flacco* 62.
[2132] to the summit

nullo temporum intervallo praemiis coruptibilius ornamentum sis accepturus, posteritatem in praeconiis retenturus.

Valde tibi persuadeas, si quid tibi aut tuis nostra opella efficere poterit, vel cum molestia, nil neglecturus.

Meus Aristoteles, tot horis ac noctibus a me correctus, item Dioscorides et alia typographorum avaritia Basileae et Genevae premuntur, sed videbunt aliquando lucem et, nisi prorsus humanitatem et fidem deseruerint, emergent. Iterum vale, Viennae Austriae Calendis Novembris anni 83. Tuus totus Ioannes Sambucus.

Historiae Pannoniae spissum quidem opus urgeo, sed dum attexo, polio: πολλὰ μεταξὺ κύλικος.[2133]

Address: Reverendo et clarissimo viro, domino Michaeli Neandro praeposito coenobio Ilfeldensi, amico mihi observando.

372.
Sambucus to Theodor Zwinger
7 November 1583, Vienna

The original is kept in Basel, Universitätsbibliothek, Frey Mscr II 26, no. 230. Published in Gerstinger, "Die Briefe," 275-277.

The letter of Jean de Sponde gave much hope to Sambucus, as he promised to publish Aristotle in the most correct form as soon as possible, but he was almost broken by the news from Jean Aubry (who had taken over Wechel's press), saying that he would not take part in the enterprise because of financial reasons, which Sambucus explains as avarice. Meanwhile, Zwinger should keep Sponde's enthusiasm alive, whose Homer he greatly appreciates. He should also greet the heirs of Perna, whose name Sambucus does not know, and assure them of Sambucus's affection. A certain Venetian bookseller in Vienna also owes them money. If they entrust that contract to Jean Aubry, Sambucus will make sure they do not fall victim to Italian trickery. Zwinger should entreat them to look after his corrections to Horatian Ars poetica, which include many fragments of modern poets, and make sure they send these back to "his office." He sent to the mathematics professor at Heidelberg Simon a new translation of Euclid with additional demonstrations which contains the notes of Antonio de Albertis to which he added Michael Psellos's commentary in the first six books of Euclid in the hope of it getting printed in the near future. But death thwarted this. Sambucus asks Zwinger to approach Simon Grynaeus's heirs and search for the manuscripts supplied with his seal and send them to him at his expense, together with the manuscripts kept by Perna's heirs. He is sending his greetings to Sponde, who should continue with the work he began on Aristotle.

Sambucus salutem.

Magnam mihi spem attulerant litterae clarissimi viri Spondani, qui se ad editionem Aristotelis comparatum totumque fore, ut emendatissime quam primum extrudatur, affirmabat.[2134]

[2133] there is a lot between the cup. An abbreviation of the Greek proverb πολλὰ μεταξὺ πέλει κύλικος καὶ χείλεος ἄκρου (there is a lot between the cup and the edge of the lip), transmitted in Gellius 13.18. Cf. the next letter.

[2134] See letters 366 and 376.

Sed me pene adflixit, non modo turbavit nuncius nostri bibliopolae Aubrii,[2135] qui officinam Wecheli soceri sibi adiunxit, qui de tabula manum avaricia et nescio qua ambitionis contentione sublatam retulit. Hoc certe est, quod ille dixit: πολλά μεταξὺ πέλει κύλικος καὶ χείλεος ἄκρου.[2136] Φεῦ ταλαιπωρίας τῶν ἀγαθῶν καὶ ζητήσεως τῆς ἀληθείας.[2137] Tu vero, optime mi Zvingere, nullo modo cohortationibus tuis admitte, ut Aristotelis impressio refrigescat, tantus Spondani ardor evanescat, cuius in Homero recognoscendo industriam magni facio, καὶ ὀρθὸν ὄμμα[2138] laudo.[2139] Quod ad Pernae haeredes, quia nomina ignoro, item salutabis eos exquisita meae propensionis pristinae insinuatione. Debet eisdem quidam hinc Venetus bibliopola. Si Aubrio nostro Gallo syngrapham commiserint, faxo omnibus viis, ne ipsos fraus Italica circumscribat. Atque exorabis simul, ne meae correctiones in Horatii *Artem* cum multis nostrae aetatis vatum fragmentis pereant aut corrumpantur,[2140] sed ut remittant officinae meae, si bene mihi mutuo velint. Adhuc est, quod te velim. Mathematum professori Gryneo Heydlpergam ei ita anxie exposcenti communicaveram Euclidis versionem novam demonstrationibus raris et multis auctam,[2141] magni olim de Albertis Florentini lucubrationibus illustrem,[2142] quibus Pselli ἀποδείξεις[2143] in 6 libros priores addideram.[2144] Spes certa typis repraesentatum ea brevi iri. Sed morte videtur praeventus.[2145] Haeredes igitur hisce accede, repete, oro, nominis signum mei ubique adhibitum γνησίου[2146] ergo apparebit. Eos codices comoditate tabellarii vestri huc mittito meis impensis et quod habent Pernae, nil gratius mihi praestiteris. Dominum Spondanum mea gratia milies saluta et ad incohatum opus Aristotelis urge, ad quem pluribus prima occasione. Vale, mi carissime et amantissime amice, totque obstrictum tuis officiis me memorem esse, ac dum supereo, fore constanter, tibi persuadeto ac respondeto. Vienna, 7. Novembris 83. raptim.

373.
Sambucus to Fulvio Orsini
15 November 1583, Vienna

The original is kept in Rome, BAV, Vat. lat. 4104, f. 113[r]. Published in Gerstinger, "Die Briefe," 277-279; partially published in Nolhac, *La bibliothèque de Fulvio Orsini*, 442.

Sambucus received Orsini's response and wrote to Friedrich Sylburg. Since Sylburg stays with his patron Jean Aubry, the heir of André Wechel, Sambucus wrote (also) to them about Orsini's offer. He agreed with Aubry that Orsini should send his readings into Dionysius of Halicarnassus, which he will immediately print on nice paper, together with his lives of Isaeus and Dinarchus. He has

---

[2135] Zwinger's marginal note: "Avarus Auberus Aristotelis editionem impedit."
[2136] There are many things between the cup and the tip of the lip. Cf. Erasmus, *Adagia* 401.
[2137] alas for the thoroughness of the good people and for the search for the truth. Cf. Thucydides 1.20.
[2138] keen eye
[2139] Zwinger's marginal note: "Spondani Homerum probat," referring to *Homeri quae extant omnia Graece et latine, cum commentariis Ioannis Spondani* (Basileae: Episcopius, 1583).
[2140] Zwinger's marginal note: "Sambuci correctiones in Horatii artem." See letter 359.
[2141] Zwinger's marginal note: "Euclidis nova versio repetitur."
[2142] On this manuscript see letter 361, note 2062.
[2143] demonstrations
[2144] See letter 286.
[2145] Simon Grynaeus died in 1582.
[2146] genuine

already sent a copy of Pausanias to Venice, from where Orsini can get it through the bookseller Pietro Longo. Sambucus accepts Orsini's offer of sending him the book or codex about antique doctors. As soon as he receives it, he will send a parcel of books or other things in compensation; Orsini should trust him. Orsini should send it to him quickly, together with his corrections in Halicarnassus. He has some unpublished manuscripts by Josephus Flavius and a more ample version of Georgius Cedrenus's History. He sent Orsini's Polybius-edition to some gentlemen in Poland. His Aristotle and Dioscorides are buried in Basel and Geneva. That learned man, Henri Estienne is surprised that his printing press is abandoned, while he only takes delight in his own genius. He printed Vergil in his usual way, if Orsini wants, Sambucus can send a copy. Sambucus asks Orsini to send him his notes on Plutarch's Moralia, in which he also made many additions and corrections, and also the edition by Wilhelm Xylander. Sambucus sometimes contemplates some very rare coins for a few hours. He wants to know what Orsini's conclusions were concerning those copper plates. If Orsini wants, he can give his response to Cesare dell'Arena, secretary of the apostolic nuncio to the emperor.

Molto Magnifico Signor mio osservandissimo. Salutem.

La risposta di Vostra Signoria hebbi, scrissi al Sylburgio et alhora essendo quivi suo patrone Giovanni Aubri, haerede del Wechelio, li contai fidelmente l'vostre liberale offerte etc. con il qual ho transacto, che Vostra Signoria manda le lectione sue del Halycarnasseo in qua, che lui subito à porte [?] con quella vita d'Isaeo et Dinarcho accommodata e con prefatione di Vestra Signoria in bella carta.[2147] La mandato gia per Vinezzia un exemplaro del Pausania et con prefatione d'Amaseo preposta. Vostra Signoria riceverà di Vineggia per lo libraro Pietro Longo chiamato.[2148] Quanto alli antichi Medici à me promessi peravanti, accetto la liberalità, con obligo per le presente, che come li ho ricepuro e so qui siano, che rimandero alla Vostra Signoria il parellio in libro o altro; fidasi Vostra Signoria di me. Et mandi quanto prima con le correttione del Halycarnasseo. Io tengo certi libri di Joseppo,[2149] nondum stampati, et Cedreni *Historias* locupletiores.[2150] Il Polybio di Vostra Signoria ho mandato fu [su] in Polonia à gratificar ad alchuni dotti gentilhuomoni.[2151] Il mio Aristotele et Dioscoride sono sepulti in Basilea et Geneva.[2152] Quel huomo doctissimo H[enricus] S[tephanus] meraviglia quod deserta fore typographia, suo se genio solo iam oblectat. La fatto stampar Vergilio à

[2147] Dionysius Halicarnasseus, Διονυσίου Ἁλικαρνασσέως τὰ εὑρισκόμενα, ἱστορικὰ καὶ ῥητορικὰ συγγράμματα. *Dionysii Halicarnassei scripta quae exstant omnia ... Opera et studio Friderici Sylburgii Veterensis*, 2 vols. (Francofurti: apud haeredes Andreae Wecheli, 1586). In the letter to the reader (after the dedication) Sylburg makes special mention of Orsini's important help, whom "he" contacted in Rome, asking him to check certain dubious places in the codices available in Rome. Among the works attached we also find "Commentarium ad Ammaeum de vetustis oratoribus: Lysia, Isaeo, Dinarcho."

[2148] The book in question appears to be *Pausanias, Decem regionum veteris Graeciae description, totidem libris comprehensa, Romulo Amasaeo interprete* (Leiden: apud haeredes Iacobi Juntae, 1558). A new corrected edition appeared by Wilhelm Xylander and Friedrich Sylburg in 1583 with Wechel, containing Amaseo's translation as an attachment. Pietro Longo, himself a Protestant, was trafficking with books from the North, among others from Perna and Wechel. He was put to death by the Holy Office because of his faith and because of smuggling prohibited books. See Paul F. Grendler, *The Roman Inquisition and the Venetian Press, 1540–1605* (Princeton: Princeton University Press, 2015), 186-189.

[2149] See letter 119 on Sambucus's views on Greek Josephus.

[2150] Today, we can only find a single manuscript by Cedrenus in the ÖNB, which was originally owned by Augerius Busbequius (Cod. Hist. gr. 69). Sambucus might have referred to this codex. His historical work had already been printed in Basel in 1566.

[2151] Ἐκ τῶν Πολυβίου τοῦ Μεγαλοπολίτου ἐκλογαί (as in letter 352, note 2000).

[2152] On Aristotle see the preceding letter, on the planned Dioscorides-edition see notes 920-921 to letter 155.

suo modo, si Vestra Signoria voglie, li mandaro uno.²¹⁵³ Si Vostra Signoria havessi qualche osservatione in *Moralia* del Plutarcho, sperarai [?] con le miei far [?] assai, havendo oltra la editione del Xylandro, infiniti luogi suppleti et emendati.²¹⁵⁴ Io si sono ben, è sufficiente à servili et sui amigi, Vostra Signoria comandi. Qualche horete me metto in meditationi di alchune rarissime medaglie et medaglione. In questi luogi, non vi è, si se diletti. Pacienziam. Ma [Mi] ricomando: è che habbia fatto intorno le tavole di rame, vorrià intender;²¹⁵⁵ alli 15. di Novembre 1583. Di Vostra Signoria Servitore etc. J. Sambucus.

Si piagge à Vostra Signoria potra usar la cortesia del Signor Seggretario Dottor Caesare Arena del Nuncius per [...] di sua Maiestate.²¹⁵⁶

374.
Sambucus to Joachim Camerarius Jr.
8 April 1584, Vienna

The original is kept in Munich, BSB, Clm 10367, f. 317ʳ. Published in Gerstinger, "Die Briefe," 279-280.

Sambucus had much talk recently with Carolus Clusius about Camerarius's plans concerning gathering botanical works and also the edition of Gulielmus Rovilius in Lyon. Camerarius should not be dissuaded by anyone's work in progress. He himself collated Dioscorides with others in a schematic form. He told his friends why he did not publish it. He still has a new sort of useful index to Dioscorides, which he will copy in the following days and ask for Clusius's opinion. If he will like it, Sambucus will print it or send it to Camerarius asking for his judgement. Dasypodius keeps back some of his codices and does not keep his word. He will need to take a redhibitory action unless the loaned books are not returned to the library. Camerarius should forward him a letter. He is sending his greetings to Paulus Melissus. In the postscript he complains that neither Henri Estienne publishes his edition of Dioscorides nor Eusebius Episcopius his Aristotle.

Salutem.

Multa cum Clusio nostro hisce diebus de tuis consiliis in comportandis plantarum historiis et in eas notis, multa item de Lugdunensi Rovilliana voluminis editione.²¹⁵⁷ Tu vero nullis

---

²¹⁵³ Sambucus refers to Estienne's new edition of Vergil, already published in 1576: *Publii Virgilii Maronis Poemata, novis scholiis illustrata* ([Genevae]: [Henricus Stephanus], 1583).
²¹⁵⁴ Πλουτάρχου..., *Plutarchi Chaeronensis philosophorum et historicorum principis varia scripta, quae Moralia vulgo dicuntur ... a Guilelmo Xylandro Augustano* (Basileae: Episcopius, 1574).
²¹⁵⁵ See letter 352.
²¹⁵⁶ The apostolic nuncio had been Orazio Malaspina. On the secretary (from 1578) Cesare dell'Arena, who also sent his own reports from Vienna and Pressburg after Malaspina's death in 1582, see *Nuntiaturberichte aus Deutschland. 3. Abt., Band 10. Nuntiaturen des Orazio Malaspina und des Ottavio Santacroce. Interim des Cesare dell'Arena*, ed. Alexander Koller (Berlin: De Gruyter, 2013).
²¹⁵⁷ [Jacques Daléchamps], *Historia generalis plantarum*, 2 vols. (Lugduni: apud Gulielmum Rouillium, 1586). Gulielmus Rovilius (Guillaume Rouillé) (c. 1518–1589) was a humanist publisher who started his career in Venice and became famous for his editions of Alciato and Giovio. The French botanist Jacques Daléchamps (1518–1588) had been working on a history of plants for already some years, taking it over from the physician and botanist Jean Moulins who died before. By March 1584 nine volumes had already been printed, but Daléchamps could not tell Camerarius when the work would be ready (in fact, he died before all the volumes

te aliorum molitionibus, non totis plaustris ab instituto demoveri patiare, qui et intellectum habes, et iudicio vales, quae probiora sunt, exigendi. Ego ante annos aliquot contuleram cum Dioscoride alios schematum apertorum forma. Editionem cur cohibuerim, amicis aperui. Reliquus mihi index in Dioscoridem nova arte, fructu non vulgari, quem his diebus describam et, si Clusio, quod puto, probabitur, prelo dicabo aut tecum communicabo, ut, quod voles, statuas. Dasypodius temere aliquot codices meos creditos detinet, nec fide interposita satisfaciet. Redhibitorie agendum erit, nisi mutuum certumque, quod toties petii, repraesentarit, bibliothecae steterit. Has ad ipsum, oro, mittito. Melisso salutem.[2158] Ad VI. Idus Aprilis 84. Vienna, subito. Totus tuus Sambucus.
Meus Dioscorides ab Henrico, Aristoteles ab Episcopio eisdem adhuc suffocati tenebris latent, modo ne pereant.[2159] Quae ista horum perversa et importuna avaricia?

Address: Clarissimo viro domino Ioachimo Camerario, archiatro reipublicae Norimbergensis etc., amico observando. Nurnberg. Hern Doctor Camerario.
Camerarius's hand: 84. 12 Septembris [?][2160] ultima epistula ad me scripta.

375.
Sambucus to Nicodemus Frischlin[2161]
18 April 1584, Vienna

Published in Nicodemus Frischlinus, *Strigilis grammatica, denuo ab auctore recognita et aucta. Eiusdem dialogi tres adversus Martinum quondam Crusium, professorem Tubinganum* ([Oberursel]: [Heinrich], 1587), f. β1ʳ-β2ʳ.[2162]

---

appeared). See Daléchamps's letter to Camerarius of 7 March 1584 in Universitätsbibliothek Erlangen-Nürnberg, Sammlung Trew. See also the article by Charles B. Schmitt and James J. Bono, "The correspondence of Jacques Daléchamps (1513–88) An unknown letter of Jacques Daléchamps: Local Autonomy versus Centralized Government," *Bulletin of the History of Medicine* 53 (1979), 100-127.

[2158] Paulus Melissus (Paul Schede) (1539–1602) studied in Zwickau, Erfurt, Jena, then in 1561–1564 in Vienna (with Wolfgang Lazius), where he was crowned poet laureate, and also provided some diplomatic services to the Habsburgs. He later lived in many cities and took also part in a battle in Hungary. From 1586 he was librarian of the Bibliotheca Palatina in Heidelberg. See Eckart Schäfer, "Paulus Melissus Schedius (1539–1602). Leben in Versen," in *Humanismus im deutschen Südwesten. Biographische Profile*, ed. Paul Gerhard Schmidt (Sigmaringen: Thorbecke, 2000), 239-263.

[2159] On Aristotle and Dioscorides cf. the Index under "Sambucus."

[2160] It seems very strange that this letter got to Camerarius so late, long after Sambucus's death.

[2161] Nicodemus Frischlin (1547–1590) was the son of a Lutheran minister. He was educated in Tübingen with the support of the Tübinger Stift and was a student of Martin Crusius. Thanks to his extraordinary poetic and philological talents he was given the chair of poetry and history in 1568 at the University of Tübingen and was crowned later poet laureate by Rudolf II in 1576, but his further advance was blocked by colleagues at the university. Frischlin criticised almost all of them and especially Martin Crusius. Crusius eventually managed to use one of Frischlin's orations against him (Frischlin was attacking the nobility in it), and force him to leave the city and look for teaching positions elsewhere. Yet the quarrel between former teacher and student continued on many levels, one of its products was Frischlin's criticism of Crusius's grammatical works, in which he included Sambucus's present letter. See Wilhelm Kühlmann, "Nicodemus Frischlin (1547–1590). Der unbequeme Dichter," in *Humanismus im deutschen Südwesten. Biographische Profile*, ed. Paul Gerhard Schmidt (Sigmaringen: Thorbecke, 2000), 265-288; Patrick Hadley, *Athens in Rome, Rome in Germany: Nicodemus Frischlin and the Rehabilitation of Aristophanes in the 16ᵗʰ Century* (Tübingen: Narr, 2015); Magnus Ulrich Ferber, "Colluctatio Fröschlini et Onocrusii. Die absichtlich missglückte Kommunikationsstruktur im Vorfeld des Tübinger Grammatik-Streits," in *Humanisten über ihre Kollegen. Eulogien, Klatsch und Rufmord*, eds. Karl Enenkel and Christian Peters (Münster: LIT, 2018), 145-176.

[2162] Frischlin included this letter (as the first among several other supportive letters written to him right after the preface

Sambucus praises Frischlin's grammatical writings but would have preferred if he had avoided some half-barbarian terms, using the grammars of Quintilian, Julius Caesar Scaliger and Georgius Trapezuntius. He wrote well but not enough on orthography and the grammatical and rhetorical features of orations. A speech and a sentence may be harmonious but not necessarily grammatical. A graduate student heading directly to Frischlin gave occasion to send this letter. Sambucus encourages Frischlin to use his talent for the good of the public and not despair if he is not adequately compensated by patrons, he will be acknowledged by posterity.

Ioannes Sambucus Nicodemo Frischlino S. D.

Nae tu oportune grammaticorum nugas strigili tua detegis novamque illam et vetustam disciplinam observationibus novis utiliter patefacis. Sed, mi optime Nicodeme, dum suis meritis eos tractas, maluissem voces ipsis usitatas καὶ μιξοβαρβάρους[2163] omisses. Multa, cum sponte et ingenio tuo, tum vero quos duces tibi et autores huius scriptionis fuisse video, ex Quintiliani, Scaligero, Trapezontii grammaticis Latinis meliora reddere potuisses.[2164]

Nam quid casus, declinatio, coniugatio, constructio, et infinita alia velint, nescio. Sed consilio fecisti credo, uti et sua illi recognoscerent et aptiora sequerentur. De orthographia, distinctionibus orationis, grammaticis illis et oratoriis recte monuisti, sed plenius idem praestabis, ubi liber recudetur. Oratio enim et sententia congrua esse potest, non tamen grammatica, et grammatica periodus, quae ab oratore non reciperetur. Verum haec obiter, occasionem subito ad te exarandi adferente erudito isto artium magistro, qui ad te recta profecturum aiebat. Tu vero ingenio et exquisito iudicio ad usus communes, ad tui nominis amplitudinem, quod facis, utere; si praemia modo, uti exaruit liberalitas Mecoenatum, minus respondebunt, erunt, qui agnoscent cunctis annis in posterum consecuturi, quorum memoria cum tuo nomine perennis erit. Ἔρρωσο.[2165] 14 Calendis Maii. 84. Viennae.

376.
Sambucus to Theodor Zwinger
[21 June?] 1584, Vienna

The original is kept in Basel, Universitätsbibliothek, Frey Mscr II 26, no. 231. Published in Gerstinger, "Die Briefe," 281-283.

Sambucus received Zwinger's letter with delay, which informed him about the astonishing news that Eusebius Episcopius and Jean de Sponde had abandoned the project of editing Aristotle. He had entrusted Episcopius with the manuscript on condition that he publish it as soon as possible. Zwinger would not believe how avidly Jean Aubry, Henri Estienne and others would demand the work, and strive to be at least partners of the edition. Sambucus angrily asked Episcopius to return the manuscript. If he finds it unworthy for his press, there will be others who will print

---

addressed to the rector of the University of Wittenberg) only in the second edition of his book (the first contained no supportive letters yet). His contact with Sambucus probably served to bolster his position at the imperial court.

[2163] half barbarian, half Greek

[2164] Sambucus refers to Quintilian's *Institutio oratoria* (c. 95), Julius Caesar Scaliger's *De causis linguae Latinae* (1540) and Georgius Trapezuntius's *De partibus orationis ex Prisciano compendium* (1430s).

[2165] farewell

it. He will immediately pay back Episcopius the 35 thalers, which in the name of the Oporinian bequest is available to him, as soon as he gets back the codex in good order, provided nothing is taken from "Sambucus's honey production." He is happy that there may be a substitute for Jean de Sponde, someone who lived in Paris whose name Sambucus does not remember as he does not have Zwinger's letter on hand. He asks Zwinger to press Episcopius or those who direct his typesetting. If he does not carry on or give back the manuscript, he will sue him in front of the Basel magistrate and use his patrons' power. He is sending his greetings to the heirs of Perna and asks Zwinger to urge them to publish Horace and other things. He asks Zwinger to send back Apollonius's Syntax and (the Chronicle) of Manasses to Joachim Camerarius Jr. in Nuremberg or to André Wechel's heirs, Jean Aubry and company in Frankfurt. Johann von Kittlitz came to see him during the day; he sent him to Count Julius Salm who is said to have great knowledge of that mystical art. He is sending his greetings to Jean de Sponde. If Thomas Erastus would like to take over the translation of very rare Greek alchemical books, which are a mixture of almost everything written on the subject in antiquity, Sambucus would send the codex to Zwinger. This is a book full of secrets and figures, probably the fullest and rarest in its field.

[Sambucus salutem.]

Accepi, licet serius, tuas, quibus sublatam de tabula Aristotelea manum typographi et Spondani significas. Vehementer miror, quid Episcopio in mentem et avaritiam venerit, qui ut κύων ἐν φάτνῃ[2166] nec ipse facit nec alios proficere vult. Ea conditione exemplar et vigilias tot horarum ei credideram, ut quam primum ederet, sed video hominem aut non curare amplius talia, aut non eo loco forsan habere, quo alii meum duxere. Non credis, quam Aubrius, quam Henricus et alii, quam prolixis pollicitis et gratia a me efflagitent opus, imo, si vel socii esse possint editionis, petant. Scripsi serio et vehementius etiam ad Episcopium, ne mea premat; reddat, si indigna suis prelis putat, non defore alios aeque typorum regios magistros. Triginta quinque talleri ex nomine Oporiniano reliquo mihi laxati fuere. Hos ego, modo exemplar sartum, illibatum restituat, ilico numerandos curabo, sed ita, ne quid mellificationi Sambuci dereptum sit.[2167]

Laetor clarissimum virum, de quo scribis et qui substitui Spondano, [...] si is recusarit, commode possit, qui Lutetiae aliquando vixit, sed nominis oblitus sum, quod tuas ad manus non habebam. Obtestor te, urge Episcopium et qui praelis tractandis emendandisque praesunt. Quod si diutius Episcopius cessarit ac reddere nolet, sciat me iure ipsum querelis ad magistratum suum vel sociis autoritatibus magnorum nostrorum patronorum aggressurum. Pernianis salutem, utque Horatium et alia reddant, mone.[2168] Apollonii *Syntaxin* cum Manasse, si Norimbergam ad dominum Camerarium miseris aut Francfortum ad Aubrianos seu haeredes Wechelii item tuto feceris.[2169] Vale. Kitlichius hodie me convenit,[2170] ablegavi

---

[2166] like a dog in the manger. Zwinger's interlinear note: "canis in praesepi." Cf. Erasmus, *Adagia* 913.
[2167] I.e. Sambucus will not incur expenses himself. On the messy history of this amount of money see letter 262, note 1464.
[2168] See letter 359, note 2050.
[2169] On Apollonius's *Syntax* see letter 115, note 673 and cf. the Index under "Sambucus." See also Gerstinger, "Zusammenfassung," 285-286. On Manasses's *Chronicle* see "Manasses-edition" under "Sambucus" in the Index. See also Gerstinger, "Zusammenfassung," 309-310.
[2170] Baron Johann (von) Kittlitz (Kitlic) from Lusatia. He was the dedicatee of Johannes Löwenklau's edition of Glycas's *Annales* in 1572. According to a document in HHStA, in 1566 he left for a study tour to Italy and France. On the different members of the Kittlitz family see Luděk Březina, *Der Landvogt der Niederlausitz zwischen Königsmacht und Ständen (1490–1620); ein Diener zweier Herren?* (Berlin: Berliner Wissenschafts-Verlag, 2017).

eum ad comitem Iulium Salmensem, qui artis mysteria omnium optime nosse ac tractare dicitur.[2171] XI. Kalendas Quinctilis 1584.[2172] Viennae. Tuus totus Ioannes Sambucus. Spondano, viro clarissimo, salutem meo nomine et ἅπαντα φιλικά.[2173]

Address: Praestanti ac doctissimo viro domino doctori Theodoro Zuingero Basiliensi, domino amico observando. Basell.
Postscript below the address on the back: Si doctissimus Erastus interpretationem libri chymici rarissimi Graeci, qui farrago omnium fere veterum, qui hac de arte conscripserunt, velit, mitterem ad vos;[2174] opus pienum sacrorum arcanorum, plenum figurarum et iconum θαυμαστῶν.[2175] Non puto in ea professione fumosa quidquam rarius aut absolutius, ut quidam affirmant, proditum.

377.
Franciscus Modius to Sambucus
[Unknown date, 1581 at the earliest]

Published in Franciscus Modius, *Novantiquae lectiones, tributae in epistolas centum* (Frankfurt: Heredes Andreae Wecheli, 1584), 207-209.

As no one is more familiar with Cicero than Sambucus, Modius asks his opinion on five emendations he proposes to the text of Pro Milone.

Franciscus Modius Ioanni Sambuco viro clarissimo salutem. Viennam Austriae.

Quaero ex te, clarissime et eruditissime Sambuce, cui adeo familiaris est Cicero, ut iam nemini familiarior esse possit, quid de isto eius e *Miloniana* loco censeas: *Qui* (Clodius) *cum ab equite Romano splendidissimo et forti viro T. Paconio non impetrasset, ut insulam in lacu pretio venderet, repente lintribus in eam insulam materiam, calcem caementa atque arma convexit* et cetera.[2176] Quid censeam, inquies. Nihil esse in eo dificultatis fateor, sambuce si cum vulgatis exemplaribus manuscripti libri consentirent, sed scire debes, eos ad unum omnes, teste etiam Dionysio Lambino,[2177] pro *ut insulam in lacu pretio venderet* aut *ut insulam in lacu perelio venderet* habere, aut certe *ut insulam in lacu prelio venderet*. Hoc igitur est, de quo de consulendum mihi existimavi, putesne fuisse lacum aliquem hoc aut simili nomine. Sed

---

[2171] Julius von Salm's interests in Paracelsian medicine and alchemy is documented among others by Martin Ruland's dedication of his *Curationum empiricarum et historicarum* to Salm (Basel: ex officina Henricpetrina, 1593) and by a manuscript in Hamburg (SUB, Cod. alchim 192) "Für die fallend sucht welches Theophrastus König Ferdinand mit gethailt unnd hiernach König Maximilian, Graff Julio von Salm."
[2172] Concerning the mistaken date see Gerstinger's note ("Die Briefe," 283).
[2173] all the friendship
[2174] It concerns the alchemical manuscript mentioned in letter 354 (see note 2025).
[2175] of astonishing things
[2176] Cicero, *Pro Milone* 27.
[2177] Dionysius Lambinus or Denis Lambin (1520–1572) was a philologist and professor at the Collège de France. He earned his reputation with the editions of classics, among them the complete edition of Cicero's works. Modius used the edition of 1572, which beside the notes also provides the variant readings for *Pro Milone* in the margin: *Orationum M. T. Ciceronis a Dionysio Lambino emendatarum volumen III* (Parisiis: Ioannes Bene, 1572), 2405-2443 and 2779-2794.

quando semel tibi esse molesti coepimus, sustinebimus etiam de sequentibus iudicium tuum flagitare. Ait Cicero: *Omitto socios, exteras nationes, reges, tetrarchas (vota enim feceratis, ut in eos se potius mitteret, quam in vestras possessiones, vestra tecta, vestras pecunias) a liberis, dico, a liberis, medius fidius, et a coniugibus vestris nunquam ille effrenatas suas libidines cohibuisset.*[2178] Hic ego puto considerata nostrorum et Lambini manuscriptorum codicum scriptura, legi oportere: *Omitto socios, exteras nationes, reges, tetrarchas (vota enim faceretis, ut in eos se potius immitteret, quam in vestras possessiones) a vestris tectis, vestris pecuniis, vestra tecta, vestras pecunias dico? A liberis, medius fidius, et a coniugibus vestris nunquam ille effrenatas suas libidines cohibuisset.* Et restituit ante me ita pleraque Lambinus, nisi quod illud non vidit, plane hic *faceretis*, non *feceratis* legendum esse. Quod ego sane miratus sum, cum videam illum hic adeo exercitum fuisse et illud *feceratis* contra mentem sit Ciceronis, qui non hoc dicit populum Romanum vota fecisse ut Clodius in exteros potius grassaretur, quam in se (quod ridiculum est et a vero alienum) sed facturos ea talia fuisse, si imperium is nancisci ullo modo potuisset. Praecessit iam: *Cui* (Pompeio) *se nunquam profecto tradidisset* (Milo), *nisi caussae suae confideret, praesertim omnia audienti, magna metuenti, multa suspicanti, non nulla credenti.*[2179] Vide, Sambuce, an scripserit Cicero *magna intuenti*. Quo pacto et mei manuscripti habent, et Ursinus in veteri libro se reperisse testatur,[2180] metus sane in Milonem eum, quem hic Cicero nobis depinxit suis coloribus, cadere non potest. Sequitur longo quidem intervallo, sed tamen sequitur: *Vestrae tum arae, vestrae religiones viguerunt, vestra vis valuit, quam ille omni scelere polluerat.*[2181] Sed malim: *Vestrae tum religiones viguerunt, vestra vis valuit* et cetera, omissis reliquis, quod iam ante ad ipsas aras sermonem Cicero converterit dicendo: *Vos enim iam Albani tumuli atque luci, vos, inquam, imploro atque obtestor vosque, Albanorum obrutae arae, sacrorum populi Romani sociae et etera.*[2182] Statim: *Tuque ex tuo edito monte Latialis sancte Iuppiter, cuius ille lacus, nemora*[2183] et cetera. Monet Lambinus legendum *Latiaris sancte Iuppiter*, etsi, ut ait, in nullis omnino libris ita legitur. At ego, ne quis hic Lambino propter consensum librorum dubitet credere, plane ita in Coloniensibus membranis me hunc locum perscriptum invenisse profiteor. Testatur etiam eruditissimus Franciscus Iuretus in doctissimis illis suis ad Symmachi epistolas notis apud eundem Symmachum *latiare concilium, latiaris lingua, latiaris facundia*,[2184] ut et apud Pruudentium *latiare munus*[2185] et Lactantium, quod magis huc facit, *latiaris Iuppiter*[2186] constanter in membranis legi, nihil ut iam amplius hic dubitandum videatur.

[2178] Cicero, *Pro Milone* 76.
[2179] Cicero, *Pro Milone* 61.
[2180] Fulvius Ursinus, *In omnia opera Ciceronis notae* (Antverpiae: Plantin 1581), 262.
[2181] Cicero, *Pro Milone* 85.
[2182] Cicero, *Pro Milone* 85.
[2183] Cicero, *Pro Milone* 85.
[2184] Q. Aurelii Symmachi ... epistolarum ad diversos libri decem. Cura et studio Francisci Jureti, cuius etiam notae adjectae sunt (Parisiis: Nicolaus Chesneau, 1580), 9. Franciscus Iuretus (François Juret) (1553–1626), a canon of Langres, edited and commented Symmachus, Seneca, Ivo of Chartres and other authors.
[2185] Prudentius, *Contra Symmachum* 1.395.
[2186] Lactantius, *Divinae institutiones* 1.21.3.

ABBREVIATIONS

ADB	*Allgemeine deutsche Biographie.* Vols. 1-56. Berlin, 1875–1902, repr. Berlin, 1967–1971.
BAV	Biblioteca Apostolica Vaticana
BBKL	*Biographisch-Bibliographisches Kirchenlexikon.* Vols. 1-41, eds Friedrich Wilhelm Bautz and Traugott Bautz. Nordhausen: Verlag Traugott Bautz, 1975–2013.
D.	dominus / doctor
DBI	*Dizionario Biografico degli Italiani.* Vols. 1-100. Roma: Enciclopedia Italiana, 1960-2023.
FHKA	Finanz- und Hofkammerarchiv
HHStA	Haus-, Hof- und Staatsarchiv (in Vienna, Österreichische Staatsarchiv)
MOL	Magyar Országos Levéltár
NDB	*Neue deutsche Biographie.* Vols. 1-18. Berlin, Duncker & Humblot, 1953–1997.
ÖNB	Österreichische Nationalbibliothek
ÖStA	Österreichisches Staatsarchiv
OSZK	Országos Széchényi Könyvtár (National Library of Budapest)
RE	*Paulys Real-Encyklopädie der klassischen Altertumswissenschaft.* Ed. August Pauly et al. Stuttgart: Metzler, 1894–1980.
SAT	Štátny archív v Trnave
S.	sanctus
S. D.	salutem dicit / salutem dico
S. P. D.	salutem plurimam dicit

BIBLIOGRAPHY

Abrahami Ortelii et virorum eruditorum ad eundem et ad Iacobum Colium Ortelianum epistulae. Ed. Jan Hendrik Hessels. Cantabrigiae: Typis Academiae Sumptibus Ecclesiae Londino-Batavae, 1887.

Adam, Melchior. *Vitae Germanorum philosophorum*. Haidelbergae: impensis Jonae Rosae, 1615.

___. *Vitae Germanorum iureconsultorum et politicorum, qui superiori seculo et quod excurrit floruerunt*. Francofurti: Heredes Ionae Rosae, 1620.

Almási, Gábor. *The Uses of Humanism. Andreas Dudith (1533–1589), Johannes Sambucus (1531–1584), and the East Central European Republic of Letters*. Brill: Leiden, 2009.

___. "Variációk az értelmiségi útkeresés témájára a 16. században: Forgách Ferenc és társai" [Variations on the theme of intellectual careers in the sixteenth century: Ferenc Forgách and his associates]. *Századok* 140,6 (2006), 1405-1440.

___ and Paola Molino. "Nikodemismus und Konfessionalisierung am Hof Maximilians II." *Frühneuzeit-Info* 22 (2011), 112-128.

"A magyar történet folytatója" Tanulmányok Istvánffy Miklósról [The person who continued the "Hungarian history." Studies on N. Istvánffy]. Ed. Pál Ács and Gergely Tóth. Budapest: MTA-BTK, 2018.

Aristaenetus. Ἐπιστολαὶ ἐρωτικαί. Τινὰ τῶν παλαιῶν Ἡρώων Ἐπιτάφια. *E Bibliotheca clari viri Ioannis Sambuci*. Antverpiae: Plantin, 1566.

Bach, Endre. *Un humaniste hongrois en France. Jean Sambucus et ses relations littéraires (1551–1584)*. Szeged: [Prometheus], 1932.

Bakonyi, Zsuzsanna. "Nagyszombat város követei az 1567-es pozsonyi országgyűlésen" [The legates of Trnava in the diet of 1567 of Pressburg], *Fons* 22 (2015), 429-447.

___. *Magyar nyelvű írásbeliség a 16. századi Nagyszombatban* [Hungarian vernacularism in 16th-century Nagyszombat]. Ph.D. Dissertation, Eger, 2017.

Barberi, Francesco. *Paolo Manuzio e la stamperia del popolo romano (1561–1570): con documenti inediti*. Roma: Gela, 1985.

Becker, Moritz Alois. "Die letzten Tage und der Tod Maximilians II." *Blätter des Vereines für Landeskunde von Niederösterreich* 11 (1877), 308-343.

Benzing, Josef. *Die Buchdrucker des 16. und 17. Jahrhunderts im deutschen Sprachgebiet*. Wiesbaden: Harrassowitz, 1963.

___. *Buchdruckerlexikon des 16. Jahrhunderts*. Frankfurt am Main: Klostermann, 1952.

Between Scylla and Charybdis. Learned Letter Writers Navigating the Reefs of Religious and Political Controversy in Early Modern Europe, Ed. Jeanine De Landtsheer and Henk Nellen. Leiden: Brill, 2010, 303-350.

Bibl, Viktor. "Erzherzog Ernst und die Gegenreformation in Niederösterreich, 1576–90." *Mitteilungen des Instituts für Österreichische Geschichtsforschung, Ergänzungsband* 6 (1901), 575-596.

___. *Maximilian II.: der rätselhafte Kaiser. Ein Zeitbild*. Hellerau bei Dresden: Avalun-Verl., 1929.

___, ed. *Die Korrespondenz Maximillians II. Band 1: Familienkorrespondenz 1564 Juli 26–1566 August 11*. Vienna: Holzhausen, 1916; *Band 2. Familienkorrespondenz. 1566 August 9 – 1567 Dezember 27*. Vienna: Veröffentlichungen der Kommission für neuere Geschichte Österreichs, 1921.

Birnbaum, Marianna D. *Humanists in a Shattered World. Croatian and Hungarian Latinity in the Sixteenth Century*. Ohio: Slavica, 1986.

Bonfinius, Antonius. *Rerum Ungaricarum decades quatuor, cum dimidia. Quarum tres priores, ante annos XX, Martini Brenneri Bistriciensis industria editae iamque diversorum aliquot codicum manuscriptorum collatione multis in locis emendatiores. Quarta vero decas, cum quinta dimidia, nunquam antea excusae, Ioanni Sambuci Tirnaviensis caesareae maiestatis historici etc. opera ac studio nunc demum in lucem proferuntur. Una cum rerum ad nostra usque tempora gestarum appendicibus aliquot, quorum seriem versa pagina indicabit. Accessit etiam locuples rerum et verborum toto opere memorabilium index*. Basileae: Oporinus, 1568.

___. *Symposion trimeron sive Antonii Bonfinii de pudicitia coniugali et virginitate dialogi III. Nunc primum ex bibliotheca Ioannis Sambuci viri clarissimi in lucem prolati. Libellum hunc, tam ob facetiarum et historiarum varietatem iucundissimum, quam ob multiplicem eruditionem utilissimum, emisse et legisse neminem poenitebit*. Basileae: Officina Oporiniana, 1572.

Camerarius, Joachim Sr. *Epistolarum libri quinque posteriores. Nunc primum a filiis (Ioachimo et Philippo Camerariis) in hoc secundo volumine studiose collectae et ad utilitatem publicam editae*. Francofurti: Palthen, 1595.

Cassander, Georgius. *Opera quae reperiri potuerunt omnia*. Parisiis: Drovart, 1616.

Chmel, Josef. *Die Handschriften der K. K. Hofbibliothek in Wien*. 2 vols. Vienna: C. Gerold, 1840.

Clarorum Italorum et Germanorum epistolae ad Petrum Victorium Florentinum. Ed. Angelo Maria Bandini, 2 vols. Florentiae: [n.d.], 1758–1760.

Companion to Central and Eastern European Humanism: Hungary, ed. Farkas Gábor Kiss. Berlin: De Gruyter, 2024 [forthcoming].

Correspondance de Christophe Plantin, ed. by Maurice van Durme, Jean Denucé, Max Rooses, 9 vols. Antwerp: J. E. Buschmann, 1883-1918; reprint: Nendeln: Kraus, 1968.

Costil, Pierre. *André Dudith humaniste Hongrois (1533–1589). Sa vie, son oeuvre et ses manuscrits grecs*. Paris: Les Belles-Lettres, 1935.

Crato, Johannes. *Oratio funebris de divo Maximiliano imperatore caesare augusto II*. Francofurti: Wechelus, 1577.

Dekker, Alfred M. M. "Ein unbekannter Brief des Johannes Sambucus über die Dulius-Inschrift." In *Actus. Studies in Honour of H. L. W. Nelson*. Ed. J. den Boeft and A. D. M. Kessekls. Utrecht: Instituut vor Klassieke Talen, 1982, pp. 89-108.

Deneire, Tom and Jeanine De Landtsheer. "Lipsiana in the Waller Manuscript Collection: In Particular an Unknown Letter from Johannes Sambucus (1582) and a Letter to Janus Dousa (1583) reconsidered." *Humanistica Lovaniensia* 57 (2008), 209-226.

Diogenes, Laertius . *De vita et moribus philosophorum libri X. Plus quam mille in locis restituti, et emendati ex fide dignis vetustis exemplaribus Graecis, ut inde Graecum exemplum etiam possit restitui. Opera Ioannis Sambuci Tirnaviensis Pannonii. Cum indice locupletissimo*. Antverpiae: Plantin, 1566.

Dudithius, Andreas. *Epistulae*, 7 vols.. Ed. Lech Szczucki, Tibor Szepessy, et al. Budapest: Akadémia, Argumentum, Reciti, 1992-2019.

Eunapius Sardianus. Βίοι φιλοσόφων καὶ σοφιστῶν. *E bibliotheca Ioannis Sambuci Pannonii Tirnaviensis. De vitis philosophorum et sophistarum: nunc primum Graece et Latine editus interprete Hadriano Iunio Hornano*. Antverpiae: Plantin, 1568.

Fichtner, Paula Sutter. *Emperor Maximilian II*. New Haven–London: Yale University Press, 2002.

Flood, John. *Poets Laureate in the Holy Roman Empire: A Bio-bibliographical Handbook*. Berlin: De Gruyter, 2006.

Generall Historie of the Netherlands. Ed. Edward Grimeston. London: A. Islip and G. Eld, 1608.

Gerstinger, Hans, ed. "Aus dem Tagebuch des kaiserlichen Hofhistoriographen Johannes Sambucus (1531–1584)." *Österreichische Akademie der Wissenschaften. Philologische-Historische Klasse. Sitzungsberichte* 248 (1965), 1-53.

___. "Die Briefe des Johannes Sambucus (Zsámboky) 1554-1584." *Österreichische Akademie der Wissenschaften. Philologische-Historische Klasse. Sitzungsberichte* 255 (1968), 7-356.

___. "Ein gelehrter Briefwechsel zwischen Wien und den Niederlanden aus den Zeitalter des Humanismus." *Deutsches Vaterland* 6-7 (1922), 8-14.

___. "Johannes Sambucus als Handschriftensammler." In *Festschrift der Nationalbibliothek in Wien zur Feier des 200jährigen Bestehens des Gebäudes* [Ed. Österreichische Nationalbibliothek]. Vienna: Österreichischen Staatsdruckerei, 1926, 251-400.

___. "Zusammenfassung." In Gerstinger, "Die Briefe," 285-318.

Gillet, J. F. U. *Crato von Crafftheim und seine Freunde. Ein Beitrag zur Kirchengeschichte*. Frankfurt/Main: Brönner, 1860.

Gilly, Carlos. "Zwischen Erfahrung und Spekulation. Theodor Zwinger und die religiöse und kulturelle Krise seiner Zeit (Teil 1 und 2)." *Basler Zeitschrift für Geschichte und Altertumskunde* 77 (1977), 57-137 and 79 (1979), 125-223.

Glycas, Michael. *Annales Michaeli Glycae Siculi, qui lectori praeter alia cognitu iucunda et utilia Byzantinam historiam universam exhibent: nunc primum latinam in linguam transscripti et editi per Ioannem Lewenclaium. Ex Ioanni Sambuci viri clarissimi bibliotheca. Accessit index geminus locupletissimus*. Basileae: Eusebius Episcopius, 1572.

Goetz, Helmut. "Die Geheimen Ratgeber Ferdinands I. (1503-1564)." *Quellen und Forschungen aus italienischen Archiven und Bibliotheken* 42-43 (1963), 452-494.

Goltzius, Hubertus. *C. Iulius Caesar sive historiae imperatorum caesarumque Romanorum ex antiquis numismatibus restitutae. Liber primus*. Brugis: Goltzius, 1563.

Gulyás, Pál. *Sámboky János könyvtára. Bibliotheca Ioannis Sambuci*. Budapest: Author's edition, 1941. Republished by István Monok as *A Zsámboky-könyvtár katalógusa (1587) Gulyás Pál olvasatában*. Szeged: Scriptum, 1992.

Heuser, Peter Arnold. *Jean Matal: humanistischer Jurist und europäischer Friedensdenker (um 1517-1597)*. Cologne: Böhlau, 2003.

___. "The correspondence and casual poetry of Jean Matal (c.1517–1597): a preliminary inventory." *LIAS. Sources and Documents Relating to the Early Modern History of Ideas* 30/2 (2003), 213-298.

Hippocrates, *Hippocratis Coi Asclepiadeae gentis sacrae coryphaei viginti duo commentarii tabulis illustrati: Graecus contextus ex doctissimorum virorum clarorum codicibus emendatus. Latina versio Jani Cornarii innumeris locis correcta. Sententiae insignes per locos communes methodice digestae. Theod. Zvingeri Basiliensis studio et conatu.* Basileae: Perna, 1579.

Holtzmann, Robert. *Kaiser Maximilian bis zu seiner Thronbesteigung (1527–1564).* Berlin: Schwetschke und Sohn, 1903.

Humanista történetírás és neolatin irodalom a 15–18. századi Magyarországon [Humanist historiography and Neo-Latin literature in 15th to 18th-century Hungary]. Eds. Enikő Békés, Péter Kasza and Réka Lengyel. Budapest: BTK TTI, 2015.

Humanistes du bassin des Carpates II. Johannes Sambucus. Ed. Gábor Almási and Gábor Farkas Kiss. Turnhout: Brepols, 2014.

Hunger, Friedrich W. T. *Charles de l'Escluse. Nederlandsch Kruidkundige 1526–1609.* The Hague: Nijhoff, 1942.

Illésy, János. "Zsámboky János történetíróról" [On the historian J. Sambucus]. *Századok* 34 (1899), 524-532.

Illustrium et clarorum virorum epistolae selectiores superiore seculo scriptae vel a Belgis vel ad Belgas. Ed. Petrus Bertius. Lugduni Batavorum: Ludovicus Elzevir, 1617.

Isthvanfius, Nicolaus. *Historiarum de rebus Ungaricis libri xxxiv. Editio novissima.* Viennae–Pragae–Tergesti: I. T. Trattner, 1758.

Johannes Sambucus / János Zsámboki / Ján Sambucus (1531–1584): Philologe, Sammler und Historiograph am Habsburgerhof. Eds. Gastgeber, Christian and Elisabeth Klecker. *Singularia Vindobonensia* VI. Vienna: Praesens Verlag, 2018.

Junius, Hadrianus. *Emblemata ... eiusdem aenigmatum libellus.* Antverpiae: Plantin, 1565.

___. *Epistolae, quibus accedit ejusdem vita et oratio de artium liberalium dignitate.* Ed. Junius Petrus. Dordrechti: Caimax, 1652.

___. *Epistolae selectae nunc primum editae.* Ed. Petrus Scheltema. Amstelodami: M.H. Schonekat, 1839.

___. *Nomenclator, omnium rerum propria nomina variis lingvis explicata indicans.* Antverpiae: Plantin, 1567.

The Kaleidoscopic Scholarship of Hadrianus Junius (1511–1575). Northern Humanism at the Dawn of the Dutch Golden Age. Ed. Dirk van Miert (Leiden: Brill, 2011).

Kaufmann, Thomas DaCosta. "Astronomy, Technology, Humanism and Art at the Entry of Rudolf II into Vienna, 1577." *Jahrbuch der Kunsthistorischen Sammlungen in Wien* 85-86 (1989–1990), 105-118.

Kóssa, Gyula. "Adatok Sámboky János életéhez" [Data regarding the life of Sambucus]. *Irodalomtörténeti Közlemények* 18 (1908), 370-377.

La Biblia Políglota de Amberes en la correspondencia de Arias Montano (MS. Estoc. A 902). Ed. Baldomero Macías Rosendo. Huelva: Universidad de Huelva, 1998.

Liebl, Hans. "Der Heiratskontrakt des Johannes Sambucus." *Unsere Heimat* 6 (1946–1948), 179-190.

Lipsius, Justus. *Epistolae. Pars 1: 1564–1583.* Eds. Aloïs Gerlo, M. A. Nauwelaerts and Hendrik D. L. Vervliet. Brussel: Paleis der Academien, 1978.

LX librorum Βασιλικῶν, id est, Universi iuris Romani, auctoritate principum Romanorum Graecam in linguam traducti [...] per Ioannem Leunclaium. Ex Ioanis Sambuci viri clarissimi bibliotheca. Basileae: Episcopius 1575.

MacCuaig, William. *Carlo Sigonio: The Changing World of the Late Renaissance*. Princeton: Princeton University Press, 1989.

Magyar országgyűlési emlékek 5 (Monumenta Comitialia regni Hungariae 5) (1564–1572). Ed. Vilmos Fraknói. Budapest: M. Tud. Akadémia Könyvkiadó-hivatala, 1879.

Magyar országgyűlési emlékek 6 (Monumenta Comitialia regni Hungariae 6) (1573–1581). Ed. Vilmos Fraknói. Budapest: M. Tud. Akadémia Könyvkiadó-hivatala, 1879.

Manasses, Constantinus. *Annales. Nunc primum in lucem prolati et de Graecis Latini facti per Ioannem Lewenclaium. Ex Ioanni Sambuci V. C. bibliotheca*. Basileae: Episcopius, 1573.

Matschinegg, Ingrid. *Österreicher als Universitätsbesucher in Italien (1500-1630). Regionale und soziale Herkunft – Karrieren – Prosopographie*. University of Graz, Ph.D. diss., 1999.

Menčík, Ferdinand (ed). "A Páduában tanuló Blotz Hugó levelezése erdélyi és magyarországi barátaival (1571–1574)." *Erdélyi Múzeum*, 5 (1910), 22-48.

Molino, Paola. *L'impero di carta. Storia di una biblioteca e di un bibliotecario (Vienna, 1575–1608)*. Rome: Viella, 2017.

Nicollier-De Weck, Béatrice. *Hubert Languet: 1518–1581: un réseau politique international de Melanchthon à Guillaume d'Orange*. Geneva: Droz, 1995.

Nonius Marcellus. *De proprietate sermonum, iam demum innumeris locis restitutus, multis locupletatus, ope vetustissimorum codicum et industria Hadriani Iunii medici ad D. Maximilianum imperatorem*. Antverpiae: Platin, 1565.

Nonnus Panopolitanus, Νόννου Πανοπολίτου Διονυσιακά. *Nonni Panopolitae Dionysiaca, nunc primum in lucem edita, ex Bibliotheca Ioannis Sambuci Pannonii. Cum lectionibus et coniecturis Gerarti Falkenburgii Noviomagi et indice copioso*. Antverpiae, Plantin, 1569.

Ortelius, Abraham. *Abrahami Ortelii (geographi Antverpiensis) et virorum eruditorum ad eundem ... epistulae*. Ed. John Hendrik Hessels. Cantabrigiae: Ecclesia Londino-Batava, 1887.

Palaeologus, Mauel II. *Imperatoris Manuelis Palaeologi augusti Praecepta educationis regiae ad Ioannem filium, ex Ioannis Sambuci bibliotheca, Ioanne Leonclaio interprete. His adiecimus Belisarii Neritinorum ducis eiusdem argumenti librum, cum aliis ad principum studia pertinentibus, nec umquam hactenus editis. Ad Franciscum Mediceum, magnum Thusciae ducem*. Basileae: Perna, 1578.

Pastorello, Ester. *L'epistolario manuziano. Inventario cronologico-analitico 1483–1597*. Florence: Olschki, 1957.

Philologicarum epistolarum centuria una, diversorum ... doctissimorum virorum ... insuper Richardi de Buri ... Philobiblion et Bessarionis Patriarchae Constantinopolitani ... Epistola ad senatum Venetum. Ed. Melchior H. Goldast. Francofurti: Egenolph Emmelius, 1610.

Plautus, Titus Maccius. *Comoediae viginti olim a Ioachimo Camerario emendatae, nunc vero plus quam CC versibus, qui passim desiderabantur, ex vetustissimis codicibus additis, suo quodammodo nitori restitutae, opera et diligentia Ioannis Sambuci Tirnaviensis Pannonii...* Antverpiae: Plantin, 1566.

Plotini Platonicorum facile coryphai operum philosophicorum omnium libri LIV in sex Enneades distributi (Basileae: Ad Perneam Lecythum, 1580).

Pölnitz, Götz von and Hermann Kellenbenz. *Anton Fugger, 1555–1560.* Tübingen: Mohr, 1986.

[Pseudo-]Albumasar [Abu Ma'Shar]. *Apomasaris Apotelesmata, sive de significatis et eventis insomniorum ex Indorum, Persarum Aegyptiorumque disciplinis. Depromptus ex Ioannis Sambuci V. C. bibliotheca liber, Ioanne Leunclaio interprete.* Francofurti: Andreas Wechel, 1577.

[Pseudo-]Hesychius Milesius. *Ἡσύχιου Μιλησίου Ἰλλούστριου περὶ τῶν ἐν παιδείᾳ διαλαμψάντων σοφῶν. Ex bibliotheca Ioannis Sambuci Pannonii Tirnaviensis.* Antverpiae: Plantin, 1572.

Praemissae sunt Henrici Stephani ad Iohannem Cratonem a Craftheim epistolae ex autographis nunc primum editae. Ed. Franz Passow. Vratislaviae: [s.n.], 1830.

Ransanus, Petrus. *Epitome rerum Ungaricarum velut per indices descripta, autore Petro Ranzano apud Mathiam Regem olim triennium legato. Nunc primum edita, una cum appendice quadam, opera Ioannis Sambuci. Adiecta est Rerum ad agriam gestarum anno 1552. brevis eiusdem Sambuci narratio.* Viennae: Hofhalter, 1558.

Régi Magyar nyelvemlékek, vol. 3, Tatrosi másolat és Vegyes tárgyú régi Magyar iratok. Ed. Gábor Döbrentei and Pál Jászay. Buda: Egyet. Ny., 1842.

Reineccius, Reinerus. *Methodus legendi cognoscendique historiam tam sacram quam profanam. Accessit oratio de historiae dignitate ... Additus ad Reinerum Reineccium liber epistolarum historicarum, seu de editionibus eius historicis per annos XVI. scriptarum.* Helmaestadii: Iacobus Lucius Transylvanus, 1583.ein gee

Riccobonus, Antonius. *De consolatione edita sub nomine Ciceronis, iudicium secundum, quattuor disceptationibus explicatum. Quibus se a duabus a Caroli Sigonii orationibus defendit.* Vicetiae: apud Perinum bibliopolam et Georgium Graecum, 1584.

Sadoletus, Jacobus. *Philosophicae consolationes et meditationes in adversis, Iacobo Sadoleto et Ioachimo Camerario Pabepergensi, Authoribus. Accessere et eiusdem argumenti Ioannis Sambuci, medici et historici caesarei, et Ioachimi, Ioachimi filii Camerarii epistolae et carmina.* Francofurti: Wechel, 1577.

Sambucus, Johannes. *Arcus aliquot triumphales et monumenta victoriae classicae in honorem ... Iani Austriae.* Antwerp: Plantin, 1572.

———. *Ars poetica Horatii, et in eam paraphrasis et παρεκβολα, sive commentariolum.* Antverpiae: Plantin, 1564.

———. *Catalogus librorum quos Ioannes Sambucus vel suos typis edidit, vel bibliothecae aliena pignora prodidit, vel praecipue adhuc divulganda prae manibus habet.* Vienna: n.d., 1583. (Reprinted and analysed in Gedeon Borsa and James Walsh, "Eine gedruckte Selbstbibliographie von Johannes Sambucus." *Magyar Könyvszemle* 85 (1965), 127-133.

———. *De imitatione ciceroniana dialogi tres, autore Ioanne Sambuco, Tirnavense Pannonio. Eiusdem duae orationes funebres, cum doctissimorum aetatis nostrae virorum epistolis aliquot eiusdem argumenti et epigrammatis Graecis et Latinis.* Parisiis: Aegidius Gorbinus, 1561. Second edition: *De imitatione a Cicerone petanda dialogi tres, nunc recogniti et aucti. Eiusdem Somnium Scipionis lucuenta paraphrasi et scholiis breviter commodeque illustratum.* Antverpiae: Libertus Malcotius, 1563.

———. Δημηγορίαι, *hoc est conciones aliquot ex libris Xenophontis de Paedia Cyri, breviores et selectiores, versae pro tyronibus Graecae linguae a Ioanne Sambuco Tirnaviensi Pannone. Additae sunt duae orationes contrariae, Critiae et Theramenis, ex libro secundo de Rebus gestis Graecorum. Ad haec, oratio, quod oratores ante poetas a pueris cognoscendi sint, eodem Ioanne Sambuco autore. Adiectis quoque eiusdem poematiis aliquot, aliorum propediem edendorum velut primitiis*. Basileae: Iohannes Oporinus, 1552.

———. *De rebus gestis a Francisco Ximenio Cisnerio, archiepiscopo Toletano, libri octo, authore Aluaro Gomecio: qui sunt rerum Hispanicarum. Tomus 3. Nunc primum in Germania recusi: quibus inscriptiones aliquot Tarraconenses ex historia Hispanica Ludovici Pontis adiunctae sunt. Omnia studio Ioannis Sambuci Pannonii, Caes. Maiest. consiliarii et historici. Adiectus est in fine rerum memorabilium Index*. Francofurti: A. Wechel, 1582.

———. *Emblemata, cum aliquot nummis antiqui operis*. Antverpiae: Plantin, 1564, 1566.

———. *Icones veterum aliquot ac recentium medicorum philosophorumque, elogiolis suis*. Antverpiae: Plantin, 1574.

———. *Orationes duae funebres Ioannis Sambuci Tyrnaviensis Pannonii. Cum doctistimorum aetatis nostrae virorum epistolis eiusdem argumenti, atque epigrammatis Graecis et Latinis*. Parisiis, Gilles Gourbin, 1561. (As an attachment to *De imitatione ciceroniana*.)

———. *Oratio in obitum generosi ac magnifici adoloscentis Georgii Bona Transylvani, domini in Landseehr et Laknpach etc. Qui mortus est VI Septembris anni 1559. Addita sunt in fine doctissimum aliquot virorum epitaphiae Graeca et Latina*. Patavii: Gratiosus Perchacinus, 1560.

———. *Poemata quaedam Ioannis Sambuci Tirnaviensis, Pannonii, Patavii conscripta*. Patavii: Gratiosus Perchacinus, 1555.

Siraisi, Nancy G. *History, Medicine, and the Traditions of Renaissance Learning*. Ann Arbor: University of Michigan Press, 2007.

Steinmann, Marc. "Der Libellus gnomologicus des Joachim Camerarius (1569) Bemerkungen zur Entstehungs- und Textgeschichte sowie zur pädagogischen Intention." In *Camerarius Polyhistor*, 95-123.

Supplémant à la Correspondance de Christophe Plantin, ed. Maurice van Durme. Antwerp: De Nederlandsche Boekhandel, 1955.

Sylloges epistolarum a viris illustribus scriptarum. 5 vols. Ed. Pieter Burman. Leidae: S. Luchtmans, 1727.

Pighius, Stephanus Vinandus. *Epistolarium*. Ed. Henry de Vocht. Louvain: Librairie universitaire, 1959.

Stolte, Bernard. "Joannes Leunclavius (1541–1594), Civilian and Byzantinist?" In *Reassassing Legal Humanism and its Claims*. Ed. Paul J. du Plessis and John W. Cairns. Edinburgh: University Press, 2015, 194-210.

Tardy, Lajos and Éva Moskovszky. "Zur Entdeckung des Monumentum Ancyranum (1555)." *Acta Antiqua Academiae Scientiarum Hungaricae* 21 (1973), 375-395.

Téglásy, Imre. "Conrad Gesner és magyar barátai" [Conrad Gesner and his Hungarian friends]. *Orvostörténeti Közlemények* 112 (1985), 195-209.

———. *A nyelv- és irodalomelmélet kezdetei Magyarországon (Sylvester Jánostól Zsámboky Jánosig)* [The beginning of linguistic an literary theory in Hungary (From János Sylvester to Johanne Sambucus)]. Budapest: Akadémia, 1988.

Theophylacti Bulgariae archiepiscopi explicationes in Acta Apostolorum ... Laurentio Sifano interprete. Coloniae: Haeredes Birckmanni, 1567.

Ulloa, Alfonso. *Vita del potentissimo e Christianissimo imperatore Ferdinando I; idem, Vita dell'invittissimo e sacratissimo imperator Carlo V.* Venice: V. Valgrisio, 1566.

Van Miert, Dirk. "Epilogue." In *The Kaleidoscopic Scholarship of Hadrianus Junius*, 290-305.

Vantuch, Anton. "Die Sambucusbriefe im Kreisarchiv von Trnava." *Österreichische Akademie der Wissenschaften. Philologische-Historische Klasse. Sitzungsberichte* 255 (1968), 325-356.

Várady, István. "Relazioni di Giovanni Zsámboky col'umanesimo italiano." *Corvina* 15 (1935), 3-54.

Vegetius, Publius. *Mulomedicina. Ex tribus vetustissimus codicibus varietate adiecta, unde infiniti loci addi et expurgari a quovis poterunt, usu magno public. Opera Ioannis Sambuci Pannonii*. Basileae: Perna, 1574.

Vida, Mária. "A reneszánsz orvostörténeti munkája, a 'Medicorum Philosophorumque Icones'" [Sambucus's Renaissance history of medicine]. *Orvostörténeti Közlemények* 112 (1985), 181-193.

Viskolcz, Noémi. "The fate of Johannes Sambucus's library." *Hungarian Studies* 30 (2016), 155-166.

Visser, Arnoud. *Joannes Sambucus and the Learned Image. The Use of the Emblem in Late-Renaissance Humanism*. Leiden: Brill, 2005.

Von Martels, Zweder. "The discovery of the inscription of the Res Gestae Divi Augusti." *Respublica litterarum* 14 (1991), 147-156.

Werbewcz, Stephanus de [István Werbőczy]. *Tripartitum opus iuris consuetudinarii inclyti regni Hungariae. Per spectabilem et magnificum dominum Stephanum De Werbewcz, personalis praesentiae regiae maiestatis olim locum tenentem accuratissime editum. Quarta editio, cum praefatione et indice Ioannis Sambuci etc*. Viennae: Blasius Eber, 1572.

Zon, Stephen. *Petrus Lotichius Secundus. Neo-Latin Poet*. Bern: Lang, 1983.

Zonta, Claudia. *Schlesische Studenten an italienischen Universitäten. Eine prosopographische Studie zur frühneuzeitlichen Bildungsgeschichte*. Stuttgart: Böhlau, 2004.

INDEX

Abbate, Giulio Camillo dell' 61
Abbate, Niccolò dell' 61
Abondio, Antonio 210, *211**, 219-220, 222, 225-226, 286
Adam, Melchior 322
Aegineta, Paulus 318
Aelian 90, 296
Aemilius, Paulus 249-250
Aeschylus 81, 98, 158-159, 182-183, 312
Aesculapius 334
Aesop 237, 362
Agathias 337-338
Agricola, Gnaeus Julius 306
Agustín y Albanell, Antonio 231
Aichholz, Johann 199
Alaghy family 222, 291
Albert V, Duke of Bavaria 354, 358
Alberti, Antonio de 462
Alberti, Leon Battista 476
Albrecht VII, Archduke of Austria 8, 161
Albumasar (Abu Ma'shar) 341-342
Albumasar (Pseudo-) 340, *341*, 371-372, 383-384, 388-389
Alciato, Andrea 92, 236, 303, *304*, 478
Alessandrini, Giulio 223, *224*, 343-344, 354-356, 359
Alexander Sophista 55
Alexander the Great 32-33, 113, 406
Alfonso XI of Castile 114
Allegri, Johannes 378-379
Amarantus Grammaticus 171
Amaseo, Pompilio 136-137
Amaseo, Romolo 137, 477
Ambrose of Milan 207

Amerbach, Basilius 41
Amerbach, Bonifacius 41
Amerbach, Veit 16, 28, 207
Ammaeus 477
Ammianus Marcellinus 155
Ammonius Grammaticus 121-122
Anaximander 89
Andreae, Jacobus 432
Andreas von Österreich, Cardinal 464-465
Andromachus the Elder 396
Andronicus I Comnenus, Byzantine Emperor 174
Andronicus II Comnenus, Byzantine Emperor 174
Andronicus Comnenus Ducas Palaiologus 174
Angielini, Nicolò 260-261
Anicia Juliana 318
Anna of Austria, Duchess of Bavaria 354, 358
Anne of Bohemia and Hungary 267
Anne of Foix-Candale, Queen of Hungary and Bohemia 267-268
Antenoreo, Ludovico 167-168, 170, 308
Antinous 406
Antiphon 177
Antoninus Pius, Roman Emperor 237
António, Prior of Crato
Antonius II Cauleas, Patriarch 55
Apelles 86
Aphrodisias, Alexander of 462
Aphthonius 138-139, 197
Apianus, Petrus 16, 30, 91
Apianus, Philipp *30*, 91-92

---

* Footnotes with biographical data and references are provided on the pages indicated in italics.

Apianus, Theodor 30
Apianus, Timotheus 30
Apollodorus Damascenus 326
Apollodorus of Damascus (Pseudo-) 326
Apollonius of Rhodes 81
Apollonius Dyscolus *166*, 172, 211-212, 231-232, 340-341, 481
Apostolius, Michael 55
Aratus 170, 174
Archimedes 462
Arcimboldo, Giuseppe 255
Arena, Cesare dell' 477-478
Aretaeus 435
Aretino, Pietro 236
Argyropylus, Joannes 467-468
Aristaenetus 18, 110, 117, 119-120, 138-139
Aristophanes 159, 256
Aristotle 35, 37, 50, 55, 125-126, 140-141, 171, 201, 227-229, 230, 249, 271-275, 281-282, 288-289, 298-299, 301-303, 309-310, 312, 316-318, 322-323, 326, 336, 338-340, 346, 351-352, 362-363, 373, 375-376, 383-385, 387, 390, 392-393, 400-401, 407-409, 413, 418, 420-422, 435, 437-438, 444, 447, 458-460, 467-468, 474-481
Arragos, Guillaume 320, *321*, 373
Arrian 374
Arslan, Pasha of Buda 130-131
Artaxerxes II, King of Persia 112
Asclepius 371-372
Asconius Pedianus, Quintus 171
Athanasius 171
Athenaeus 394
Attila 40
Aubery, Claude 18, *229*, 244-245, 340-341, 346-347, 349, 413, 447
Aubry, Jean 335, 346-347, 374, *375*, 387-388, 397-398, 407-408, 420-421, 442-443, 452, 458-462, 467, 475-477, 480-481

Augustín, Antonio 68, *70*, 229, 231, 450
Augustine of Hippo 95-96, 338
Augustus, Elector of Saxony 297, 315-316, 322, 432
Augustus, Roman Emperor 237, 250-251, 293, 307
Ausonius, Decimus Magnus 34, 81
Autolycus of Pitane 242-243, 392-393

Balassa, Bálint 379
Bálint, scribe 184-185
Bánchay, Georgius *184*, 198-200
Bánchay, Mathias 200
Bánffy family 136
Banno, Johann 310
Barlaam of Seminara 242-243
Bartolini, Riccardo 156-158
Bartolus, of Sassoferrato 208
Barzizza, Gasparino 472
Bassiano, Alessandro *270*, 271, 276
Bassus, Aufidius 73
Báthory, Stephen, Prince of Transylvania, King of Poland 230, 250, 338, 365-366, 378-379, 418
Batthyány, Boldizsár 13, 374, *420*, 452-456
Bauhin, Caspar 163
Baumius (Baum), Theodor 156, *157*, 164, 166, 189
Bebek, Ferenc 321-322
Bebek, György 321-322
Bechyně, Petr (von Lažany) 189
Beck, Hieronymus 164
Belsius, Johannes 55, 307
Bembo, Pietro 298, 305-306
Benavides, Marco Mantova 9, *236*, 237, 248-249, 253-254, 271, 277
Berchem, Hieronymus 424-425
Berzeviczy, Márton 229, *230*, 238-239, 248-249
Bessarion, Cardinal 55, 171, 242-243, 336, 341-342, 449
Beza, Theodore 229, 299

Biglia, Melchior 255
Birckmann, Arnold 76
Birckmann, Arnold Jr. 77, 93, 96, 103, 221
Birckmann, Johann 75-77, 103, 117, 119, 157
Bizzarri, Pietro 117
Blotius, Hugo 37, 40, 45-46, 105, 229, *230*, 231, 237-239, 248-249, 252-254, 259-260, 263, 269-271, 276-277, 296, 311, 324-325, 328-330, 333, 360, 366, 405, 410, 456-457
Bona, Georgius 16, 38, *39*, 40, 48-52, 59-60, 62, 71
Bonfini, Antonio 18, 113, 121, 143, 145, 156-157, 159-160, 163-164, 166, 172, 189, 211-212, 224, 231-232, 245, 252, 261-262, 303-304, 309-310, 339-341, 349, 351, 361, 432
Bonomi, Giovanni Francesco 464-465
Borcht, Pieter van der (the Elder) 286
Bornemissza, Péter 134, 366
Brendel, Daniel 355, 358
Breuner, Friedrich II 312
Bruni, Leonardo 338
Bruto, Giovanni Michele 249, *250*, 273-274, 281, 418-419
Bryennius, Manuel 462
Buccella, Niccolò 366
Bucer, Martin 165
Buonaccorsi, Filippo (Philippus Callimachus Experiens) 223-224
Busbequius, Augerius (Ogier Ghislain de Busbecq) 41, 221, 250, *291*, 292-293, 307, 309, 318, 360, 438, 477
Busleyden, Hieronymus van 251-252

Caesar 32-33, 72, 75, 77-79, 82, 450
Callimachus 81
Calvin, John 40, 392
Camerarius, Anna 181
Camerarius, Joachim Jr. 138, *139*, 141-145, 219-220, 298, 301, 325-327, 334, 338, 347-348, 361-362, 368, 377, 379-381, 386-387, 391-392, 394, 401, 407-408, 416-418, 425-427, 429-432, 436, 439, 449, 453-454, 461-463, 466-467, 478-479, 481
Camerarius, Joachim Sr. 41-43, 48, *138*, 139, 141, 143-145, 162, 168-169, 172-175, 177, 180-181, 198-201, 205-206, 209, 219-220, 225-226, 243, 293, 295, 297-298, 300-301, 323-324, 326, 334, 347-348, 368, 377-380, 395, 425, 429, 432, 448-449, 462, 469-470
Camerarius, Ludwig 138, 180, *181*, 300-301, 326, 368
Camerarius, Philipp 138
Campanus of Novara 467
Canter, Daniel 141-142
Canterus, Gulielmus (Willem Canter) 18, 275, 312, 321, *322*, 327, 330, 448, 469-470
Cantiuncula, Hilarius 42, 45
Capponi, Orazio 397-398, 400
Caracalla (Marcus Aurelius Antoninus), Roman Emperor 32-33, 237
Casaubon, Isaac 99, 449
Caselius, Johannes 200-201, 213, 398, 425
Casimir IV Jagiellon 268
Cassander, Georg 92-93, 95-96, 103-104, 113-115, 387
Cassiodorus 72-73
Cassius Dio 299
Castellio, Sebastian 223-224
Castelvetro, Lodovico 282
Castor of Rhodes (Pseudo-) 63-65
Cato, Marcus Porcius 50
Catullus 182, 256, 332, 425
Cavino, Giovanni da 253, 269-271
Cedrenus, Georgius 477
Cellotius, Ludovicus (Louis Cellot) 115
Celtis, Conrad 19
Centhar, magister 303

Chalcondyles (Chalkokondyles), Laonicus 156-158
Charles II, 7th count of Egmont 425
Charles V, Holy Roman Emperor 32, 91, 116, 127, 238, 268-269, 427-428
Charles IX, King of France 61
Chaudière, Guillaume 157
Choul, Guillaume du 360
Chrysoloras, Manuel *168*, 169, 297, 298, 300, 326, 347-348, 377-380, 395, 401, 425, 429-430, 432, 436, 439, 448-449, 470
Chytraeus, David 180, 420
Ciacconius, Petrus Toletanus (Pedro Chacón) 293
Cicero 66, 69, 98, 109, 112, 171, 182, 186, 192, 216, 228, 240-241, 251, 256, 258-259, 261-262, 265, 292, 297-298, 342-343, 366-367, 425, 438, 450, 471-474, 482-483, 490
Cicero (Pseudo-) 472
Clement I, Pope 400
Clement of Alexandria 79-80, 90, 97, 348
Clusius, Carolus (Charles de l'Écluse) 43, 79, 92, 179, 199, 307, *309*, 310, 365, 374, 386, 389-390, 416, 454, 462, 470, 478-479
Cobelius, Arnoldus 94
Collinus, Matthaeus 165
Concini, Bartolomeo 168
Concini, Giovan Battista 308
Constantine the Great, Roman Emperor 95-96, 233-234, 316
Constantine V Copronymus 54
Constantine VII Porphyrogenitus, Byzantine Emperor 326, 449
Conti, Primo 255
Corvinus, Elias (Raab) 371-372
Crapidel, Petrus Johannes 404
Crasso, Celso 436
Crasso, Giulio Paolo 407, 435-436
Crassus, Lucius Licinius 66, 208

Crateuas 317-318, 336, 396
Crato, Johannes von Krafftheim 21, 79, 105, *123*, 124, 130-131, 134-135, 138-140, 144-145, 156, 158, 168-169, 172-173, 200-201, 205-206, 209-211, 213-216, 218-222, 225-226, 228, 239, 242-246, 249, 251, 255-256, 263, 271, 275, 281, 291, 292-296, 304-305, 311, 313-324, 328-331, 335, 337-339, 346-347, 350-351, 353-355, 357-359, 361-366, 368-379, 381-385, 389-390, 398-399, 403-404, 407-408, 411, 414-415, 417-420, 422, 425, 438, 447, 464-465, 472
Crato, Philipp 425-426
Criegher, Giovanni 117
Critolaus of Phaselis 81
Crnka, Fran 117
Crusius, Martin 21, *440*, 441, 479
Csütörtök, Lukács 423
Cujas, Jacques 266, 281-282
Cyrus II, King of Persia 208
Cythraeus, David 425
Cythraeus, Nathan 425
Czobantzius Czaus, Ottoman legate 375

Daléchamps, Jacques 478-479
Darius III, King of Persia 112
Darmarios, Andreas 229, 231, 326, 449
Darmarios, Joannes 229, 231
Dasypodius, Conrad 142, *165*, 219-220, 242-244, 338-339, 341, 350-352, 376, 379-380, 387, 390-394, 401, 413, 437-438, 462, 478-479
Dasypodius, Petrus 165
Deák, Márton Nagy 149
Decebalus, Dacian King 176
Delfino, Zaccaria, Cardinal *100*, 101, 259-260, 299-300, 335-336
Delicasius, Johannes 35-36
Demetrius of Phaleron 33
Demetrius of Phaleron (Pseudo-) 19, 140

Demetrius Triclinius 171, 182, *183*, 312
Democritus 84, 186-187, 444
Demosthenes 171, 258
Dernschwam, Hans 55, 307
Dietrichstein, Adam 354, *355*, 357, 359, 363-364, 369, 375, 402-403, 453-454
Dietrichstein, Anna Maria 366
Dinarchus 183, 444, 476-477
Diodorus Siculus 32-33, 358
Diogenes Laertius 18, 110, 112-113, 117, 119-121, 127, 136-137, 141-142, 316
Dionysius of Halicarnassus 171, 182-183, 384-385, 444, 476-477
Dionysius Thrax 81
Diophantus of Alexandria 242-243
Dioscorides, Pedanius 18, 68, 89-90, 201, 213, 218-222, 225-227, 231-232, 239-241, 244-245, 255-256, 272-273, 313-314, 317-318, 321-322, 326, 330-332, 334-336, 339-341, 347-348, 361-362, 367-368, 375-376, 380, 383, 391, 395-396, 401, 407-409, 435, 437-438, 464-465, 474-475, 477-479
Diotelevi, Francesco 406
Diotimus Adramyttenus 173-174
Dobó, István 38
Dobos, Gergely 294
Dobos, György 237, 294
Dodonaeus (Dodoens), Rembertus 78, *79*, 353, 355-356, 359, 363-365, 368, 411
Domitian, Roman Emperor 176, 237
Don John of Austria 238
Dorat, Jean 60-61, 69, 223-225
Dornberg, Veit von 453-454
Dousa, Janus 424
Dousa, Janus Sr. 179
Doxopatres, Johannes 56, 390
Draskovich, Georgius, Cardinal 47
Duaren, François 303

Dudith, Andreas *44*, 48, 57, 68-69, 103-104, 120-121, 181, 223-224, 242-243, 389, 437-439, 447-448, 451
Duilius, Gaius 264-265, 292-293
Dürer, Albrecht 86
Dürer, Albrecht Sr. 86
Duret, Louis 178

Egerer, Cristinna 17, 140, *148*, 253, 287, 333, 391
Egerer, Jakob 410
Egerer, Koloman *148*, 150, 177-178, 180-181, 197, 199-200, 333, 391
Egerer, Koloman Jr. 140
Egmont, Filips van 363, 365
Eiseler, Andreas *253*, 254, 259-260, 270
Eiseler, Sebastian Jr. *253*, 254, 259-260, 270
Eiseler, Sebastian Sr. 253-254
Eizing, Wolf 463
Elisabeth of Austria, Queen of France 61
Elizabeth I, Queen of England 102, 154, 437, 439
Ellebodius, Nicasius 105, 229, *230*, 277-279, 300, 333, 343-344, 348,-350, 378-379, 436
Ennius 261, 262
Eparchos, Antonios 347-348
Episcopius, Eusebius 14, 142, *166*, 178-181, 189, 232, 245, 266, 271-272, 281-282, 298-299, 303, 310, 316, 321-323, 326, 339-342, 346, 349, 351-352, 375-376, 380, 387, 390, 392, 407-408, 420, 422, 435, 447, 458, 459, 467-468, 478-481
Episcopius, Nicolaus *166*, 272, 281-282, 303
Erasmus of Rotterdam 19, 40, 42-43, 76, 87-88, 93, 97-98, 106-107, 224, 305, 342, 382, 406, 456
Erastus, Thomas 426, 453-454, 481-482
Ernst, Archduke of Austria 18, 49, 279-280, 286, *350*, 357, 365-366, 399, 410-411, 413-414, 453-455

Erythraeus, Valentin 324-325, 390
Este, Ippolito d', Cardinal 69
Estienne *see* Stephanus
Euclid 141-142, 165, 171, 242-243, 299, 338-342, 351-352, 376, 379-380, 387, 390, 392-394, 462, 475-476
Eudoxus 170
Eunapius 18, 80, 94-95, 101-102, 107, 112-113, 117, 119-122, 134-137, 143, 155-156, 158-159
Euripides 41, 81, 159, 209, 217, 240-241, 348, 362, 425
Eustathius 171
Eutyches 171

Fabri (Faber), Johann 212
Fabritius (Schmid), Paulus 199, 371
Fajardo y Córdoba, Pedro 305
Falkenburgius, Gerartus 18, 61, 164, *179*, 225, 270, 387
Farnese, Alessandro, Cardinal 332, 337
Farnese, Ottavio, Duke of Parma 426, 453, 455
Farnese, Ranuccio, Cardinal 91-92
Faseolo, Giovanni 48, 50
Fekete, Ferenc 302
Ferdinand I, Holy Roman Emperor 16-17, 32, 34, 38-40, 47, 50, 52, 55, 72-77, 93, 95, 99-100, 104, 114-117, 123, 127, 131, 162, 207, 221, 250, 268-269, 280, 290-291, 361, 364, 397, 405, 418, 428, 482
Ferdinand II, Archduke of Further Austria 353, 356, 465
Fernando Álvarez de Toledo, Duke of Alba 223, 225
Ferrerio, Giovanni 68
Festus *see* Sextus Rufus
Feyerabend, Johann 303-304
Feyerabend, Sigmund 303-304
Ficino, Marsilio 371-373, 387-388, 407-408
Filips van Egmont, Count 425

Firmicus (Julius Firmicus Maternus) 182
Flacchen (Flacchius), Philipp 369
Flaccus, Lucius Valerius 474
Flamand, Jean-Marie 22
Floderiopa (Vlodrop), Ursula 225
Fonteo, Giovanni Battista 255, 272-273, 332, 336
Forgách, Ferenc *139*, 230, 250
Francis, Duke of Anjou and Alençon 426, 453, 455, 465
Franck, Bartholomäus 160
Frangepán, Anna (Szluni) 48, 412
Frangipani, Michele 255
Frederick II, King of Denmark 94, 101-102
Freigius, Johannes Thomas *249*, 265-266, 271-274, 321
Freymon, Johann Wolfgang 190
Friedrich I Barbarossa, Holy Roman Emperor 157
Friedrich IV von Wied, Archbishop-Elector of Cologne 95, 104, 115
Frischlin, Nicodemus 14, 479-480
Froben, Johann 223
Fugger family 49, 60, 62, 68, 75-76, 93, 99, 287, 293, 296, 320-323, 432, 449-450
Fugger, Anton *49*, 56-57, 93, 323
Fugger, Hans 49, 93
Fugger, Jakob 17, *48*, 49, 54, 56-57, 323
Fugger, Marx (Markus) 49, 93, 322-323
Fugger, Ulrich 97-99

Gadaldino, Agostino 299-300
Galassus, Vince 246-247
Galen 300-302, 435
Galignani, Simone *191*, 193, 238-239, 252-254, 259-260, 269-271, 276
Galilei, Galileo 168
Galle, Philip 86, 309, 313
Gárdonyi, Géza 38
Gattermayr (Gattermaier), Egidius 374, 390
Gávay, István (Balaskó) 132-133

Gaza (Gazes), Theodorus 55
Geizkofler, Michael 48-49
Gellius, Aulus 251-252, 336, 362-363, 475
Gelmi, Michele 462
Geminus 438
Gemusaeus, Hieronymus 309-310, *311*, 339-341, 346
Gemusaeus, Polykarp 309-310, *311*, 339-341, 346
Gennep, Agnès 76
Gentile, Francesco 66
Gerlach, Stephan 441
Gerstinger, Hans 21-23, 61, 74, 120, 166, 176-177, 211, 226, 228, 231, 265, 313, 321-322, 331, 335, 337, 362, 390, 399, 402, 404, 465
Gerstman, Martin 291-293
Gesner, Conrad 53, *54*, 55, 63, 67-68, 296, 396
Geuder, Julius *386*, 391, 395, 401, 416, 425-426, 429-432, 463
Ghisleri, Antonio *see* Pius V
Gifanus *see* Sifanus
Gillus (Gyllis), Wolf Georg 456
Giovio, Paolo 116, *117*, 400, 478
Giphanius, Obertus (Hubert van Giffen) 18, *105*, 362-363
Giselinus, Victor 251-252
Giunta, Bernardo 168, 461
Glaucus of Alexandria 421
Glycas, Michael 157-160, 164, 227, 244, 261-262, 276-277, 402, 481
Godefridus (?) 123
Goldast, Melchior 407
Goltzius, Hubertus 72-73, *74*, 75-79, 82, 289-290, 333
Gomecius, Alvarus (Álvar Gómez de Castro) 427
Gorgias 279
Graecus (Görög), Matthias 195
Granvelle, Antoine Perrenot de, Cardinal 230, 292

Gregoras, Nicephorus 157
Gregory the Great, Pope 95, *96*, 114-115
Gregory XIII, Pope 369
Gregory of Nazianzus 81, 161-162, 277, *278*, 391
Gregory of Nyssa 18, 55, 93, 277, *278*, 436-437
Grolier, Jean 62, 64, *65*, 83
Gruter, Lambertus 354-355, 358
Grynaeus, Samuel 265, *266*, 271-274, 459
Grynaeus, Simon (the Elder) 266, 426
Grynaeus, Simon (the Younger) 376, 426-427, *439*, 462, 475-476
Guazzo, Marco 116-117
Guérin, Thomas 249-250
Guett, Hilfreich *359*, 360, 375, 423, 431
Guicciardini, Francesco 116-117
Guicciardini, Ludovico 442-443
Gulielmus, Janus 424-425
Gunther of Pairis 157

Hadrian, Roman Emperor 83, 237, 374, 406
Hagecius, Thaddaeus (Tadeáš Hájek) 437-438
Haller, Peter 46-47
Hallerin, Maria 386
Han, Balthasar 310
Harmenopoulos, Constantine 270, 391
Harrach, Leonhard IV 414
Harrach, Leonhard V 414
Hassan, Bey of Fülek 371-372
Häusenstein (Heusenstein), Hans 370-372
Heinrich, Viennese goldsmith 333
Heliodorus of Prusa *65*, 384-385
Henricpetri, Sixtus 250
Henry III, King of France 104, 314
Henry III, King of Navarre 467
Hephaestion *64*, 138, 144-145, 162
Heraclides, Jacobus 164, 314
Heraclitus 84, 88
Herberstein, Caspar 125, 129
Herberstein, Siegmund 124, *125*, 126, 128, 130

Herdesianus, Christoph 463
Hermogenes 56, 65, 196-197, 228, 384-385, 390
Herodianus 435
Herodotus 63-65, 324
Hero of Alexandria 242-243, 326, 390, 392, 394
Herwagen, Johann 166, 231-232
Herwart, Johann Heinrich 10, 296, 320-321
Herwart, Paulus 320-321
Hesiod 98, 124, 186, 468
Hesychius 112-113, 143
Hesychius (Pseudo-) 112-113, 120-122, 134-137, 143, 155-156, 218-220, 241, 250, 255-256, 261-262, 277
Hieron 394
Hieronymus *see* Jerome
Hierutius, Horatius 449-450
Hierutius, Johannes Paulus 449-450
Hincmar, Archbishop of Reims 114-115
Hincmar, Bishop of Laon 114-115
Hipparchus 170
Hippocrates 68, 134-135, 140, 156, 158, 171-173, 219-220, 281, 317, 346-349, 355, 359, 413, 420-422, 435-438, 451
Hippolytus of Thebes 45
Hipponax 424
Hipponicus 89-90
Hirschvogel, Augustin 260-261
Hoffmann, Ferdinand *45*, 253
Hoffmann, Hans Friedrich 45
Hoffmann, Johann Friedrich *45*, 253
Homer 32-33, 81, 127, 177, 296, 406, 475-476
Horace 18, 120-121, 171, 297, 332, 339-340, 459, 470, 475-476, 481
Horváth, Markó 133-134
Hosszutóthy, György 131
Hosszutóthy, István 343-344
Hotman, François 166, 299, 467
Hubertus, Conradus *165*, 166, 178-179, 320

Huszár, Péter 455
Huttich, Johann 31-34, 37, 45
Ilsung von Tratzberg, Georg 354, 356-357
Iovius *see* Giovio
Isaak Argyros (Isaacus Monachus) 63-65, 392-393
Isaeus 183, 444, 476-477
Isidore of Seville 114-115
Isingren, Michael 303
Isocrates 171
Istvánffy, Nicolaus 17, 38, *39*, 48, 439, 455
Iuretus, Franciscus 483
Ivan the Terrible, Tsar of Russia 123-124, 432

Jagicius 166
Jagiellon, Anna, Queen of Poland 123-124
Jakab, scribe 184-185, 188
Janus Pannonius 18-19, 47, 139, 181, 453-454
Jerome 114-115
Jerome (Pseudo-) 114-115
Jiménez (Ximenius) de Cisneros, Francisco, Cardinal 286-287, 427, *428*
Jiménez (Ximenius), Rodrigo de Rada 114
Joanna of Austria, Archduchess of Austria 397-398, 400
Joanna of Castile 267
Jociscus, Andreas 56
Jo, Georg 133-134, 146-147, 149
Johannes of Alexandria 436
Johannes Chrysostomus 277-278
Johann Günther I, Count of Schwarzburg 354, 357
Johann VI von der Leyen, Archbishop-Elector of Trier 95
John VIII Palaeologus, Byzantine Emperor 351-352
Joó, János 260
Jordanes 337
Jordan, Thomas 177, *178*, 199-200, 219-220, 389

Joseph, friend 161
Josephus, Flavius 477
Joubert, Laurent 178
Julian, Roman Emperor 98
Julius of Brunswick-Lüneburg 432, 451-452
Junius, Hadrianus 18, *78*, 79-82, 84-85, 87-90, 94-99, 101-102, 105-107, 111-113, 117, 119, 155, 330-331
Juret *see* Iuretus
Justinian I, Byzantine Emperor 65, 178-179, 257-258, 388

Kádas, Fülöp (Philep) 145-146, *149*, 150, 190, 193-194
Kalmár, Imre 132, *133*, 134, 146-147, 263-264, 282-283, 285, 287-288
Kálmar, Imre 148
Kamariotes, Matthaeus 65
Karl Friedrich of Jülich-Cleves-Berg 292, 307-309
Karl II Franz, Archduke of Austria 92, *99*, 100, 110, 124, 154-155, 161, 235, 350, 361, 402-403
Keller, Johannes 75-76
Khlee, Hanns 410, 423
Kielmann, Andreas 135-136, *154*, 371-372
Kis, Mihály 152
Kiss, Farkas Gábor 22
Kittlitz, Johann 481
Klose, Samuel Benjamin 21, 313, 372, 378
Koca Sinan Pasha 464-465
Kochanowski, Jan 223-224
Komornik, Mihály 154-155, 193-195
Köpfel, Wolfgang 34
Kraus, Sebald 391
Kremer, Gabriel 31
Kremer, Georg 31, 41
Kremer, Wolfgang 31, 41
Kremer, Wolfgang Sr. 31
Krenzheim, Leonhard 414-415
Kurtz, Jakob 190

Laertius, Diogenes *see* Diogenes Laertius
Lakner, bookseller 210, 335
Lambinus, Dionysius (Denis Lambin) 227, 482
Lang, Georg 114-115
Languet, Hubert *297*, 300-301, 315, 353, 368, 380
Łaski, Olbracht (Albert) 313-314
Laurentius of Carniola, student 464-465
Laurinus, Guido 289-290
Laurinus, Marcus 73-74, *75*, 76, 82, 85, 105, 289-290, 333
Lazius, Wolfgang 116, 160, 219, 310, 340-342, 346, 351-352, 373, 421-422, 456-457, 459, 460, 467-468, 479
Lehmann, Zacharias 199-200
Leo I, Pope 95-96
Leo, Hieronymus (Girolamo Leone) 270, 276-277
Leocrates 130-131
Lessenprandt, Sebestyén (Sebastian) 294
Leunclavius (Löwenklau), Johannes 18, 159-160, *163*, 164, 172, 179, 189, 227, 244-245, 252, 266, 307, 310-311, 321, 337-338, 340-341, 346, 348-352, 370-373, 375, 380, 387-388, 390-391, 413, 421-422, 435, 441-442, 459-460, 467-468, 481
Leżeński, Marian 5, 47
Libanius (Pseudo-) 19
Liechtenstein, Hartmann II von 412
Lindanus, Wilhelm 78-79, 87
Lipsius, Justus 92, 179, *245*, 250-251, 306-307, 330-331, 366, 445-448, 468-470
Listarchos, Michael Hermodoros 348
Listhius, Johannes Jr. 231, 237-239, 253-254, 259-260, 270-271, 276-277
Listhius, Johannes Sr. *103*, 181, 229-230, 237, 239, 248-249, 253-254, 259-260, 276-277, 328, 330, 333, 343-345, 365-366, 371-372
Livineius, Jan 470

Livineius, Laevinus 448, 469-470
Livy 72-73, 109, 250-251, 308, 450
Longinus, Cassius 107, 197
Longo, Pietro 477
Lorcher, Johann Karl 325
Losonczy, Anna 379
Lotichius, Petrus Secundus 30, 39, 42, *43*, 306
Lucceius, Lucius 216
Lucian 16, 30
Lucilius 106
Lucius Verus, Roman Emperor 316, 406
Lucretius 18, 105, 274
Luther, Martin 123
Lycophron 81
Lycosthenes, Conradus (Conrad Wolffhart) 54
Lycurgus 130-131
Lysias 477
Lysippus 86

Maecenas, Gaius Cilnius 80
Maffei, Raphael (Maffeus Volaterranus) 156-157
Maillard, Jean-Françoise 22
Malaspina, Orazio 477-478
Malcotius, Libertus 75-76
Manasses, Constantine *54*, 56, 159-160, 163-164, 166, 172, 189, 227, 244, 276-277, 481
Maniquet, Jacobus 48
Manlius (Titus Manlius Imperiosus Torquatus) 251-252
Manuel II Palaeologus, Byzantine Emperor 274, 351, *352*, 371-372
Manuzio, Aldo 81, 118, 120, 122, 225
Manuzio, Aldo Jr. *43*, 44, 70-71, 120-121, 131, 229-230, 240, 292, 301-302, 305-306, 342
Manuzio, Girolamo 58
Manuzio, Ottavio 57-58

Manuzio, Paolo *43*, 44, 48, 57-59, 68-70, 120, 225-226, 239-241, 264-265, 272-273, 301-302, 305-306, 342, 348, 471
Marbach, Johannes 165
Marcus Aurelius, Roman Emperor 237, 316, 406
Margaret of Austria, Duchess of Savoy 79
Mark Antony 406
Marne, Claude de 460-461
Martial 89, 94, 97, 99
Marullus, Michael 273-274, 306
Mary, Queen of Hungary 40
Mary of Burgundy 268
Matal, Jean *92*, 93, 95-96, 103-104, 113-114, 225, 387
Matthias Corvinus, King of Hungary 18
Matthias, Holy Roman Emperor 8, 161, 279-280, 372, 403, 414, 427-428, 453, 455
Mattioli, Pietro Andrea 88, *89*, 90, 221, 232
Mauricius, Byzantine Emperor 54
Maximilian I, Holy Roman Emperor 157, 267-268
Maximilian II, Holy Roman Emperor 17-18, 31-32, 34, 37-38, 40, 42, 45-47, 49, 53, 55, 57-58, 71-72, 76, 79, 92-93, 95, 97-98, 100-106, 113-117, 123-127, 130-131, 136, 145-146, 148, 150-151, 154-155, 157-158, 161, 215, 221, 233-235, 237, 248, 250, 257, 267-269, 276, 285, 290-291, 299, 309, 316, 319-322, 327, 338, 347, 350, 353, 355-364, 369-372, 375, 378, 381-384, 387-389, 399, 405, 427-428, 437, 439, 482
Maximilian III, Archduke of Austria 161, 279-280, 427-428, 453, 455
Maximus Tyrius 112
Mazzuola, Antonio 240
Medici, Catherine 104
Medici, Cosimo 389

Medici, Francesco 397, 400
Medina, Pedro de 427-428
Melanchthon, Philipp 16, 28, 40-41, 43,
    123, 138-139, 147, 178, 201, 297
Melissus, Paulus (Paul Schede) 478-479
Menander 168-169
Mercator, Gerardus 365
Mercurialis, Hieronymus (Girolamo
    Mercuriale) *299*, 300, 302, 317-318,
    436
Mesmes, Henri de *62*, 63-65, 84
Michiel, Giovanni 14, 471-472
Micyllus, Jakob 34
Mielecki, Mikołaj 365-366
Mithradates VI, King of Pontus 318
Mitis, Thomas 165
Modius, Franciscus 424-425, 468, *469*
Mogor (Mager), Peter 132-133
Mohammad Khodabanda, King of Persia
    463
Mohr, J., captain 146-147
Moibanus, Johannes 396
Monavius (Monau), Jacobus 365, 366,
    370-372, 375, 381-382, 438, 447,
    451-452, 456-457, 466-467
Monavius (Monau), Petrus 366, *447*
Monemvasia, Arsenio di 197
Monok, István 22
Montano, Benito Arias 75, *202*, 204, 217-
    218, 309, 365
Monte, Philippe de 277-278
More, Thomas 76
Moretus, Jan 469-470
Mossóczi, László 152-153
Mossóczi, Zakariás 153
Moulins, Jean 478
Murad III, Sultan of the Ottoman Empire
    314-315, 463
Muretus, Marcus Antonius 68, *69*, 255, 472
Murmuris, Kornelios 454
Mylius, Johannes 295

Nádasdy, Ferenc *419*, 420, 453-454
Naevius, Gnaeus 98
Neander, Michael 295, 441, *442*, 474-475
Nero, Roman Emperor 251
Nervius, Bartholomaeus 103-104
Nestorius 171
Neuenahr, Hermann 225
Neuenahr, Hermann Jr. 387
Neuhaus, Joachim von 125, 127, 205, 207
Neuser, Adam 426
Neville, Henry 437, 439
Nicander Colophonius 81
Nicephorus I of Constantinople, Patriarch
    54-55
Nicephorus II Phocas 326
Nidbruck, Caspar *40*, 41-42, 114-115
Nidecki, Andreas Patricius (Andrzej
    Patrycy) *449*, 450, 472
Nifo, Agostino 366, 390
Nifo, Fabio 366, 374, 389-390
Nilus Cabasilas 40
Nizolio, Mario 228
Nonius Marcellus 82-85, 87-90, 94, 97, 99,
    101-102, 105-107, 112-113, 119,
    155
Nonnus of Panopolis 60-61, 81, 94-95, 159,
    160, 164, 166, 168-170, 179-181,
    183, 223, 225
Numa Pompilius, Roman King 33
Numenius of Apamea 371-372
Nyilas, István 133, *134*, 145-146, 149-150,
    153-154, 184-185, 188, 190, 193-
    195, 197-198, 282-283, 287, 294

Occhiali *see* Uluj Ali
Oecolampadius, Johannes 165
Oláhcsászár, Miklós 48, 412
Olahus, Nicolaus 16, *39*, 40, 48, 50-53,
    59-60, 100-101, 103, 131, 162, 195,
    230, 343
Oporinus, Johannes 41, 55, *56*, 57, 60, 88,
    140, 156-160, 162-166, 172-173,

189, 211-212, 223-226, 231-232, 303, 309-310, 339, 351-352, 421-422, 458-459, 467-468, 481
Oppianus 81
Origen of Alexandria 278
Orpheus 81
Orsini, Fulvio 70, *91*, 92, 239-240, 265, 272-273, 307, 332, 335-337, 382, 405-406, 449-450, 476-477
Orsini, Gerolama, Duchess of Parma 426
Országh, Kristóf 136
Országh, László 136, 153
Ortelius, Abraham *75*, 76-77, 85-86, 219, 260, 284, 286-287, 289, 296, 365-366, 416, 434, 442-443
Ortenburg-Salamanca, Anna 414
Otho, Roman Emperor 83
Otrer, Johannes 186, 195-196
Otrer, Michael 8, 185-186, 195-196
Otto, David 68-69
Otto Henry, Elector Palatine 454
Ovid 34, 182, 367, 381

Pajzsgyártó, Elek 149
Pajzsgyártó, Mátyás 149
Paleocappa, Konstantin 65
Palladius 67, 134, *135*, 172, 317-318, 407, 435-436
Palmier, Jan Meller 424, 469
Panaretos, Matthew Angelos 54
Panithy, Anna 194, 195
Panithy, János (Johannes) 131, *132*, 133, 146-147, 153-155, 185, 193-195
Panithy, Sophia 132-134, 153-154, 190, 193
Panithy, Zsóka (Sophia) 133, 154, 191, 194-195
Pannonius *see* Janus Pannonius
Panvinio, Onofrio 126, 265
Pappenheim, Georg Marschalk 5, 35
Paracelsus (Theophrastus von Hohenheim) 55-56, 321, 356, 454, 482

Passienus Crispus, Gaius Sallustius 251
Paulus Aegineta 134-135, 140, 156, 158, 172-173, 301-302, 317-318, 459
Pausanias 477
Pechy, Veronika 145-150
Pekry, Anna 136
Pericles 125, 129
Perna, Pietro 55, 212-213, 271, *272*, 281-282, 306, 339-340, 349, 351, 371-373, 380, 387-388, 407, 413, 417-420, 422, 435, 458-459, 467-468, 475-477, 481
Pernumia, Giovanni Paolo 191-193
Pescennius Niger, Roman Emperor 83
Petavius, Dionysius (Denis Pétau) 54
Petranský, Ivan Horváth 16
Petronius Arbiter 18, 103, 120-121
Philemon 107
Philip I of Castile (Philip the Fair) 267-269
Philip II, King of Spain 79, 202-204, 217, 238, 268, 453, 455
Philip William, Prince of Orange 464
Philo Mechanicus 326
Philo of Alexandria 117, 119-120
Philostratus Junior 79
Phocylides 81
Photius I, Patriarch 229, 231, 240, 312-313, 336, 339-341, 351-352, 383-384
Pighius, Stephanus Vinandus *292*, 293, 307-309, 311, 332
Pindar 171, 389
Pinelli, Gian Vincenzo 230, 243, 277-278, 348
Pirckheimer, Willibald 86, 386
Pisides, Georgios 81
Pithou, Pierre 227
Pius IV, Pope 69, 120, 427-428
Pius V, Pope 120-122
Plantin, Christophe 17, 61, 75, *82*, 84-85, 94, 97, 101-102, 105-106, 110, 112-113, 117-121, 162, 164, 166, 183, 202-204, 217-218, 223, 225, 232-

233, 245, 251, 275, 277-278, 286-287, 309, 311-313, 321-322, 331, 338, 362-363, 395, 434, 436, 439, 442-443, 446, 448-449, 469-470
Planudes, Maximus 54-55, 326, 449
Plato 33, 39-40, 47, 107, 112, 129, 156-157, 186-187, 192, 228, 271, 273-274, 309-310, 312, 315, 317-318, 320-324, 326, 336, 339-340, 400-401, 407-409, 417, 422
Plautus 110, 118, 120-121, 331, 425, 464
Plethon, Georgios Gemistos 55, 157, 166, 181, 183, 197, 241, 275, 289, 315, 321-323, 327, 329-330, 363
Pliny the Elder 50-51, 182, 264-265, 296, 338
Plotinus 278, 371-373, 380, 387-388, 417-422
Plutarch 143, 171, 299, 477-478
Poelmann (Pulmannus), Theodor 105-106
Polemon of Laodicea 168-169
Polybius 36, 136-137, 278, 390-391, 449, 477
Polycletus 89-90
Pompey 446
Pons d'Icart, Lluís 427-428
Pontano, Giovanni 305-306
Pope *see* Clement, Gregory, Leo, Pius
Porphyrius 81, 112-113
Porsius, Henricus 14, 463
Porto, Francesco 196, *197*, 340-341
Possevino, Antonio 473
Posthius 327
Praetorius, Balthasar 237
Praetorius, Johannes 439
Praxiteles 86
Prinzenstein, Franz 354, 357
Priscian 480
Procopius of Caesarea 337
Propertius 469
Proxenus of Thebes 32-33
Psellos, Michael 376, 462, *475*, 476

Pseudepigrapha *see* Albumasar, Apollodorus, Castor of Rhodes, Cicero, Hesychius, Jerome
Ptolemy of Ascalon 121-122
Ptolemy, Claudius 125, 128, 181-182
Puchler, Leonhard 127
Purkircher, Georg 147, *148*, 149
Pythagoras 81, 89-90, 97

Quadrigarius, Quintus Claudius 251-252
Queck, Paul 160
Quintilian 156-158, 196-197, 264-265, 292, 301-302, 309-310, 432, 480
Quintus of Smyrna 81

Rabelais, François 308
Radclyffe, Thomas 154
Radéczy, István 230, 343-345, 349, 374
Ramus, Petrus 249
Rantzau, Heinrich 451
Ranzano, Pietro 38, 45, 71
Raphelengius, Franciscus 469-470
Rapp (Rappius), pharmacist 325
Ravisius, Johannes Textor (Jean Tixier de Ravisi) 79-80
Rechnitz, Daniel *66*, 68, 337
Rechnitz, Veit 66, 337
Regius, Joachim 394
Rehdiger, Thomas 179, 263, 365
Reineccius, Reinerus 310, *451*, 452, 456-457
Reusner, Nicolaus *295*, 314, 408-409, 414-415
Révay, Ferenc 31, 41
Révay, János 31, 41
Révay, Lőrinc 31, 41
Révay, Mihály 41
Réwai *see* Révay
Richter, Sigmund 334
Riccardi, Riccardo 443-444
Riccobonus, Antonius 471-473, 490
Rihel, Josias 219-220, 232
Rithaymer, Georg 16, 199

Ritoók-Szalai, Ágnes 21
Robortello, Francesco 48, 52
Rondeletius, Gulielmus (Guillaume
    Rondelet) 42, 178
Ronsard, Pierre 61
Rosinus, Johannes 467-468
Rovilius, Gulielmus (Guillaume Rouillé) 478
Rubigallus, Paulus *109*, 342
Rubigallus, Paulus Jr. 342
Rüdinger, Esrom 180, *181*, 198-200
Rudolf II, Holy Roman Emperor 18, 49,
    79, 123, 133, 148, 250, 253, 256-
    262, 291, 317, 321-322, 350, 354-
    355, 357-358, 360-364, 369, 373,
    375, 381-382, 384, 399, 402-405,
    407, 410-411, 414, 419-420, 429,
    432, 438, 456, 463-466, 479
Rueber, Hans 363, *364*, 365-366, 374
Ruel, Jean 221, 395, *396*, 407-408, 435
Rufus of Ephesus 435
Ruland, Martin (the Elder) 482
Rumpf, Wolfgang 399, 414-415

Sabinus (Schuler), Georg 34, 42
Sadoleto, Jacopo 296-297, *298*, 300-301,
    305-306, 323-324, 326, 347-348,
    377-381, 386, 400, 471-473
Sagstetter, Urban 100-101
Saint-Gelais, Louis de Lusignan de 104
Sallust 97, 249-250, 425, 450
Salm, Eck zu 320
Salm, Julius I *365*, 366, 381-382, 481-482
Salm, Niklas I 366
Salutati, Coluccio 169
Sambucus, Albertus (Viennensis) 131, *132*,
    193-195
Sambucus, Johannes
  Albumasar-edition 341, 371-372, 383-
    384, 388-389
  Apollonius Dyscolus-edition (planned)
    166, 172, 211-212, 231-232, 340-
    341, 481

Arcus aliquot triumphales 238, 240-241,
    247-248, 255-256, 259-262, 276-
    277
Aristaenetus-edition 18, 110, 117, 119,
    138-139
Aristotle-edition (planned) 271, 273,
    281, 303, 373, 375-376, 383,
    390, 407-409, 413, 420-422, 435,
    437-438, 447, 458-459, 467-468,
    474-481
Basilica-edition 180-183, 189, 261-262,
    265-266, 270-274, 282, 288-289,
    303, 310-312, 321, 340-341
Bonfini-edition 18, 113, 121-122, 143,
    145, 156-157, 159-160, 163-164,
    172, 212, 224, 231-232, 303-304,
    310, 351, 361, 432
Bonfini Symposion-edition 166, 172,
    189, 211-212, 231-232, 245, 252,
    261-262, 339-341, 351
Catalogus librorum 18, 122, 219, 270,
    306, 340, 352, 362, 391, 449, 454
De corona Rudolphi 257, 260-262, 277,
    432
Decretorum seu articulorum aliquot 432
De Giulae et Zygethi exitu 304, 432
De imitatione Ciceroniana 17-18, 39-40,
    48-49, 66, 70, 75-76, 78-79, 91-92,
    117, 119, 385
Demetrius Phalereus-edition 140
De obitu Marci Singhmoseri 196
De obitu Sigismundi ab Herberstain 124
De rebus ad Agriam gestis 38, 157
De Thurcis 157
Diogenes Laertius-edition 18, 110, 117,
    119-121, 127, 136-137, 141-142
Dioscorides-edition (planned) 18,
    201, 220-222, 225-227, 231-232,
    239-241, 244, 255-256, 272-273,
    313-314, 317-318, 321-322, 330-
    331, 335-336, 340-341, 348, 362,
    367-368, 375-376, 380, 383, 391,

395, 407-409, 435, 437-438, 465, 474-475, 477-479
Elegia de angelis 185, 195
Emblemata 15, 17, 41, 43-44, 49, 54, 60-62, 66, 76, 78, 82-83, 87-88, 91-92, 97, 103, 105, 118, 120-121, 132, 142, 167, 250, 295, 323, 348, 366, 434, 442-443, 470
Epistulae duae 205, 213
Eunapius-edition 18, 80, 95, 107, 113, 119-122, 134-137, 143, 155-156, 158-159
Expugnatio arcis Tokay 113, 157
Glycas-edition 164, 227, 244, 261-262, 276-277, 481
Greek epithets-edition (planned) 39-40, 144-145, 162, 297-298
Greek figures-edition (planned) 121-122
Gregorius Nazianzenus-edition 161-162
Gregorius Nyssenus-edition 18
Harmenopoulos-edition (planned) 270
Hermogenes-edition (planned) 196-197
Hesychius-edition 120-122, 134-137, 143, 155-156, 219-220, 241, 250, 255-256, 261-262, 277
Hippocrates-edition (planned) 134-135, 156, 158, 172, 219-220, 437-438
Hippolytus-edition 45
Horace-edition 18, 66, 91-92, 120-121, 339-340, 459, 475-476, 481
Huttich-edition 31, 37, 45-46
Icones 78, 211-212, 220, 222, 225-226, 286, 289, 295-296
In Christi natalem 35-36
In moerore funeris Maximiliani II. 360, 362-364, 368-372, 375-376, 378, 383-384, 432
In obitum Ferdinandi 99-100
In obitum Jacobi à Stubenberg 49, 365
Libelli dialogorum (planned) 362
Lotichius-edition 42
Lotichius Secundus-edition 42

Lucian-edition 16, 30
Lucretius-edition 18, 105
Manasses-edition 54, 163-164, 166, 172, 189, 227, 244, 276-277, 481
Manuel Palaeologus-edition 274, 351-352, 371-372
Nilus Cabasilas-edition 40
Nonnus-edition 61, 164, 166, 168-170, 179, 181-183, 225
Obsidio Zigethiensis 157
Oratio in obitum Georgii Bona 39, 48, 50, 52, 62
Orationes duae funebres 48, 50-52, 59
Pannonius-edition 18, 47, 181, 454
Paulus Aegineta-edition (planned) 134-135, 156, 158, 172, 301-302
Petronius-edition 18, 103, 120-121
Plato-edition 39-40, 47
Plautus-edition 110, 118, 120-121, 134
Plotinus-edition (planned) 371-373, 380, 388, 418-422
Poemata 38-39, 60, 132-133, 138, 142
Quintilian-edition (planned) 156-157, 196-197, 301-302
Ranzano-edition 38, 45, 56, 71
Reges Ungariae 139
Somnium Scipionis 66
Stobaeus-edition 18, 166, 180-183, 196-197, 241, 274-275, 289, 312-313, 321, 327, 329-330, 362-363
Tabellae dialecticae 18
Theodorus Ducas Lascaris-edition 18, 229, 261-262
Theophylactus-edition 18, 56, 117, 119, 151
Tripartitum-edition 153, 256, 277
Tumuli heroici (planned) 339-340, 362
Ungariae descriptio 218-219, 232
Ungariae loca praecipua 219
Vegetius-edition 212, 231-232, 272, 281, 289, 299, 303
Ximenes-edition 287, 427, 432

Zosimus-edition 337, 346-347, 349, 383, 387, 434-435
Δημηγορίαι 18, 30, 61, 136-137, 166
Περὶ παναυθεντείας 233
Sambucus *see also* Zsámboky
Sannazaro, Jacopo 305-306
Sansovino, Francesco 236
Sappho 111
Saracenus *see* Sarasin
Sarasin, Jean-Antoine 221, 391, *392*, 395-396, 407-408, 435-436
Sarasin, Philibert 392
Sauli, Stefano 68-69
Savile, Henry 437-439
Scaliger, Julius Caesar 69, 480
Scharf, Friedrich 372
Scharf, Gottfried 372
Scharf, Johann 372
Scharf, Maria 372
Schegk, Jakob 417
Schiller, bookseller 172
Schnierle, Georg 431
Schorger, Andreas 430-431
Schottus, Andreas 307
Schwanbach, Johann Andrea 124, *125*, 126, 178-179
Schwendi, Johann Wilhelm 237, 311
Schwendi, Lazarus 113, *123*, 124, 164, 180, 303-304, 311, 364, 381-382, 418-419
Schwor, Michael (Mihály) *190*, 197-198
Scipio Aemilianus 32-33, 66
Scoda, Martin 288
Scottus, Johannes (Johann Schott) 156-157
Secervitius, Johannes 307-308
Seld, Georg Sigismund 28, 125, *127*, 205-207, 209, 214-216
Selim II, Sultan of the Ottoman Empire 130, *131*, 226, 312, 314
Senarega, Matteo 68-69
Serranus, Johannes (Jean de Serres) 400
Servius 182
Sextus Iulius Africanus 326

Sextus Rufus (Festus) 34, 264-265, 292
Sibrik (Sybryk), Georgius 145-150
Sidney, Philip 437-438
Sidney, Robert 438
Sifanus, Laurentius 18, *93*, 103, 151, 278
Sigismund, courier 369
Sigismund II Augustus, King of Poland 123-124, 276
Sigonio, Carlo 136-137, 450, 472-474, 490
Silius Italicus 264-265
Silvatico, Bartolomeo 471
Simler, Josias 54
Singkmoser, Mark 126, 159, *160*, 172, 185-187, 190, 196, 205, 207, 291
Sintzendorf, Joachim 463-464
Sirleto, Guglielmo, Cardinal 107, *108*, 121-122, 157, 272-273, 336, 382, 406-407, 449-450, 472
Sittard, Matthias 114-115
Socrates 33, 122, 185, 187
Sofianos, Michele 48, 230, *347*, 348
Solon 187
Sommer, Johann (Hans) *147*, 149-150, 198, 263-264, 282-283, 287-288, 294, 302-303
Soncinus, Hieronymus 156-157
Sophianos, Nikolaos 443
Sophocles 35, 81, 112, 348, 392
Speroni, Sperone 236
Spondanus, Johannes (Jean de Sponde) 401, 467, *475*, 476, 480-482
Sporischius, Johannes 440
Stainhofer, Kaspar 124
Statius 251-252
Statius, Achilles 170, 332, 336, 449-450
Stephanus of Alexandria 454
Stephanus of Athens 435
Stephanus of Byzantium 174
Stephanus, Henricus (Henri Estienne) 97, *99*, 120, 221, 232, 298-300, 309-310, 313-315, 317-318, 320-324, 331-332, 334-336, 338-341, 347-348, 351-352,

362-363, 366-368, 370, 374-376,
380, 390-391, 394-395, 400-401,
407-408, 434-436, 460, 464-465,
467-468, 477, 478-481
Stephanus, Robertus (Robert Estienne) 99,
117, 119, 299
Stesichorus 98
Stiebar, Daniel 42-43
Stiebar, Heinrich 5, 42
Stiebar, Paulus 42
Stobaeus 18, 166, 180-183, 196-197, 241,
273-275, 289, 312-313, 321-322,
327, 330, 362-363
Stotzingen, Ruprecht 13, 127, *427*
Strabo 35, 299
Streicher, Agatha 354, 356, *357*, 359
Strein, Reichard 320, *321*, 360
Strozzi, Filippo 455
Stubenberg, Jakob 49, 365
Stubenberg, Sophia 365
Stubenberg, Wolfgang 365
Stuff, Ladislaus 210-211
Sturm, Johannes 16, 30, 42, *142*, 143, 165,
384-385, 390
Suda (Suidas) 87-88, 97-98
Suetonius (Gaius Suetonius Tranquillus)
251, 307, 332, 470
Suffenus 182
Suleiman I, Sultan of the Ottoman Empire
130-131
Sulpicius Rufus, Severus 257-258
Suma, Petrus 355, 358
Sylburgius, Fridericus 341, 448, 459, *460*,
473, 476-477
Synesius 112, 130-131, 279
Szabó, Márton 193-195, 288
Szápolyai *see* Zapolya
Szegedi, Pál 265
Szegedi, Pál, Bishop of Csanád 263
Szegedi, Pál, courier 261, *263*, 264-265,
276-277, 289, 400-401
Szegedi, Pál, lector in Sárospatak 263

Szeghedy, Ferenc 146-147
Szűcs, Mihály 197-198

Tacitus 306, 330-331, 414, 438, 446-448
Tanner, Georg *41*, 42, 159-160, 166, 172,
242, 244
Tasso, Torquato 398
Telegdi, Miklós 133, 153
Tengnagel, Sebastian 454
Terence 79
Textor, Benedictus 396
Theocritus 81-82, 171
Theodore of Amasea 55
Theodore of Smyrna 55
Theodoret of Cyrus 68-69, 117, *118*
Theodorus II Ducas Lascaris, Byzantine
Emperor 18, 229, 261-262
Theodosius of Bithynia 242, *243*, 392-393
Theognis 144
Theon 171
Theophilus 178-179, 388, 435
Theophrastus 229
Theophylactus 18, 56, 93, 117, 119, 151
Thilo, Valentin 447
Thomas Magister 312
Thucydides 125, 129, 367, 476
Thurzó, Erzsébet 366
Tiberius, Roman Emperor 237, 251, 406
Tinódi, Lantos Sebestyén 38
Tiro, Cicero's freedman 67
Titus, Roman Emperor 237
Tomitano, Bernardino 236
Tonner, Johannes 48, *49*, 56-57
Torda, Ferenc 345
Torda, Miklós 345
Torda, Sigismundus Gelous (Gyalui) 31, *41*,
42, 124, 345-346
Torèlli, Francesco 389
Torèlli, Lelio 388-389
Torrentius, Laevinus 469-470
Trajan, Roman Emperor 237

Trapezuntius, Georgius *271*, 272, 299-302, 317-318, 384-385, 447, 458-459, 480
Trautson, Johann 155, 215, 363, *364*
Triclinius *see* Demetrius Triclinius
Truchsess, Gebhard, Archbishop-Elector of Cologne 465
Tucher, Paul IV *333*, 337
Tucher, Ursula 386
Tunner, Hieronymus 369
Turisan, Bernard 63
Turnèbe, Adrien 48, 68, *69*, 119, 251
Tzetzes, Joannes 171

Ulloa, Alfonso 116-117
Uluj Ali (Occhiali), Ottoman admiral 247
Ungnad, Anna 379
Ungnad, Christoph 378-379
Ungnad, David 441
Ungnad, Hans 379
Ursinus Velius, Casparus 34, 239
Ursinus, Georgius 229-230, 238
Utenhove, Karel Sr. 223
Utenhovius, Carolus *60*, 61-62, 164, 223-225

Valens, Nicolaus 397
Valerius Maximus 309, 311
Valerius (Wouters), Cornelius 92-93
Valori, Baccio 471-472
Vantuch, Anton 21
Varro 109, 261-262
Vasaeus, Johannes 114-115
Vegetius 212, 231-232, 271-272, *281*, 289, 299-300, 303
Velleius Paterculus, Marcus 449-450
Verantius, Antonius, Cardinal 55, 117, *162*, 163, 236, 246-247, 252, 260, 275, 279, 307, 343
Verantius, Faustus 260, 307
Vergil 462
Verlanius, Albertus 85
Vespasian (Titus Flavius Vespasianus), Roman Emperor 237

Vettori, Piero 22, 48, *51*, 167-170, 176-177, 180-183, 196-197, 200-201, 213, 218-222, 225-227, 241-242, 255-256, 261-265, 274, 276-277, 282, 288-289, 312-313, 383-385, 388-389, 397-398, 400, 401, 416-417, 443-444, 460-461, 472
Victorius of Aquitaine 73
Victorius, Petrus *see* Vettori Piero
Vieheuser, Siegmund 363, *364*, 368, 375-376, 399
Vigilius of Thapsus 171
Vinta, Belisario 167, *168*, 170, 288
Virgil 80, 171, 181-182, 477-478
Viskelety (Vizkelety), horse owner 154
Vitus, adolescent 337
Vives, Juan Luis 19, 76
Vladislaus II, King of Bohemia, Hungary, and Croatia 257-258, 268
Vonones I, Parthian King 292-293
Vulcanius, Bonaventura 179, 379, *380*, 425-426, 429-430, 432, 434, 436, 439, 448-450, 462, 466-467, 469-470

Was, Jakab 345-346
Weber, Johann Baptist *190*, 266-267, 329, 330-331, 363-364, 368, 370, 375-376, 399
Wechel, André 341, 374, 379, *380*, 388-389, 395, 397, 400-401, 427-428, 432, 458-461, 467-468, 475-477, 481
Weis, Leonard 143
Wenzeslaus, Archduke of Austria 161
Werbőczy, István (Stephanus de Werbewcz) 153, 256-258, 277
Wesenbeck, Matthias *398*, 399, 404, 414-415, 418-419
Willer, Georg 159, *160*, 166, 373
William I the Silent, Prince of Orange 102, 403, 465
Winneberg, Philipp von 110

Winsheim, Veit 462
Winter, Robert 223
Wolf, Hieronymus 56, *60*, 61-62, 85, 172, 223-224, 426-427
Wyler *see* Willer

Xenophon 18, 32-33, 113, 136-137, 166, 171-172, 208, 407, 434-435
Ximénez *see* Jiménez
Ximenius, Petrus (Pedro Ximénez) 92, 95-96, 103, 225
Xylander, Wilhelm 296, 298, *299*, 322-323, 331, 346, 351-352, 380, 477, 478

Zápolya, John Sigismund, King of Hungary, Prince of Transylvania 113, 123-124, 130-131, 139, 250, 279-280
Zasius, Johann Ulrich 28, 151, 172, 205-206, *207*, 208-211, 213-216
Zasius, Ulrich 207
Zay, Ferenc 55
Zelking, Karl Ludwig 372
Zenodotus 171
Žerotín, Karel 164
Zimmermann, Michael 199-200
Zippringer, Georg 410
Zonaras, Joannes 56, 196, *197*, 219-220, 351-352, 390-391, 459-460, 467
Zoppelius, magister 381
Zosimus 337-338, 346-347, 349, 383, 387, 407, 434-435
Zrinski, Juraj IV (György IV Zrinyi) *320*, 365, 371-372, 374, 420
Zrinski, Nikola (Miklós Zrinyi) 320
Zsámboky, Anna (Nyilas) 134
Zsámboky, Katalin 132
Zsámboky, Magdalena (Gávay) 132-133
Zsámboky, Péter (Szabó) 16, 120-121, 132-133, 146, 190, 196
Zsámboky, Sophia 132-133
Zwinger, Theodor 54-57, 134, 140-141, 156-157, 166-167, 172-173, 179, 189, 211-212, 219-220, 227, 231-233, 244-245, 249, 271-274, 281-282, 298-300, 303-304, 309-311, 317, 321, 339-340, 341-342, 346-349, 351-352, 362, 368, 373, 376, 387-388, 390-391, 393, 401, 412-413, 420-422, 435, 446-447, 454, 458-460, 462, 467-468, 475-476, 480-482
Zygomalas, Ioannes 441